PERSPECTIVES IN BUSINESS ETHICS
Second Edition

Laura P. Hartman
DePaul University

McGraw-Hill
Irwin

Boston   Burr Ridge, IL   Dubuque, IA   Madison, WI   New York
San Francisco   St. Louis   Bangkok   Bogotá   Caracas   Kuala Lumpur
Lisbon   London   Madrid   Mexico City   Milan   Montreal   New Delhi
Santiago   Seoul   Singapore   Sydney   Taipei   Toronto

McGraw-Hill Higher Education ⚛

A Division of The **McGraw-Hill** *Companies*

PERSPECTIVES IN BUSINESS ETHICS
Published by McGraw-Hill/Irwin, an imprint of The McGraw-Hill Companies, Inc. 1221 Avenue of the
Americas, New York, NY, 10020. Copyright © 2002, XXXX, by The McGraw-Hill Companies, Inc. All rights
reserved. No part of this publication may be reproduced or distributed in any form or by any means, or stored in
a data base or retrieval system, writhout the prior written consent of The McGraw-Hill Companies, Inc.,
including, but not limited to, in any network or other electronic storage or transmission, or broadcast for
distance learning. Some ancillaries, including electronic and print components, may not be available to
customers outside the United States.

This book is printed on acid-free paper.

2 3 4 5 6 7 8 9 0 FGR/FGR 0 9 8 7 6 5 4 3 2 1

ISBN 0072314052

Publisher: *John Biernat*
Sponsoring editor: *Andy Winston*
Editorial coordinator: *Sara E. Strand*
Marketing manager: *Lisa Nicks*
Project manager: *Anna M. Chan*
Production supervisor: *Debra R. Sylvester*
Designer: *Damian Moshak*
Supplement coordinator: *Joyce J. Chappetto*
Compositor: *Carlisle Communications, Inc.*
Typeface: *10/12 Times Roman*
Printer: *Quebecor World Fairfield Inc.*

Library of Congress Cataloging-in-Publication Data
Hartman, Laura Pincus.
    Perspectives in business ethics / Laura P. Hartman.—2nd ed.
      p. cm
    Includes bibliographical references and index.
    ISBN 0-07-231405-2 (alk. paper)
    1. Business ethics. I. Title.
HF5387.H37442002
174'.4—dc21
                              2001030195

For David, my compass, with more love than I seem to find the words to embrace.

✳✳✳

"Aim above morality. Be not simply good; be good for something."
Henry David Thoreau

"A person can't go out the way he or she came in.
Ben, a person has to add up to something."
Willy Loman in Arthur Miller, *Death of a Salesman* (Penguin Books, 1949), p. 125.
[Changed for gender neutrality.]

"If a *person* lacks integrity, nothing else matters."
Stephen Carter, *Integrity*

"Where there are no men, be thou a man."
Rabbi Hillel
[Please excuse the gender limitation; this is as it was in the original and there does not
appear to be an easy, more inclusive translation.]

Note to the Reader

This is a textbook that came to exist because I needed it. It's as simple as that. This approach may seem selfish (see Chapter 1), but I have found in my experience that when professors write texts because they themselves have a strong need, the most effective text is usually produced.

The study of ethics includes an analysis of the interests of all of the individuals who hold a stake in the outcome of any dilemma or decision ("stakeholder analysis"). In teaching business ethics at both a graduate and undergraduate level, I found myself walking into the classroom with armloads of articles, cases, and other handouts that I used to present the perspectives of each stakeholder involved in a decision. This text seeks to provide perspectives on ethical issues in a variety of different formats—similar to my efforts involving handouts for class.

The text explores traditional ethics issues by providing multiple perspectives on the same issue. For instance, in dealing with the question of cost-benefit analysis, the text presents not only a standard case discussion of the *Challenger* disaster, but also presents the different perspectives of those involved in the incident and of those who later investigated the explosion. Or, in providing an introduction to critical analysis, the text provides a reading on recent problems at Dow Corning and "where the ethicists went wrong" in their original glowing assessment of Dow Corning.

The materials in this book include:

1. Traditional textual explanations/definitions/discussion of new topics or ideas from a historical and foundational perspective.
2. Reprints of articles, whether seminal (older, traditional), or from present day analysis.
3. Short cases for brief explanatory questions and discussion in class.
4. Full-length cases for analysis with sufficient background information and guiding questions. These cases would also be supplemented either in the text or teachers' manual with projects and exercises.
5. Additional nontraditional materials such as song lyrics, excerpts from classical literature, short stories, and so on.

The varying formats not only present different perspectives, but also provide information and opinions in a manner most accessible by the students. As we all know, many of the more academic-focused articles we have read are difficult, even for seasoned ethicists. The material presented in this text is sophisticated, yet relevant and accessible.

The focus of this approach is to encourage readers to open their minds to the variety of opinions on any given issue. The result of this approach is not to persuade readers that there is no right answer to these issues, but instead to ensure that all stakeholders' perspectives are considered. The readings for each section have been chosen with this representative interest in mind.

As you read, please also consider what opinions or perspectives are not represented in this text. I appreciate any and all suggestions/additions/modifications.

ACKNOWLEDGEMENTS

This text is, in truth, the work of a host of scholars and business practitioners who offered their opinions as reviewers early on in the project or who have allowed me to compile their work in order to present a more realistic and multiperspectival approach to the study of ethics in business decision making. I am deeply indebted to these individuals, for without their work and consideration, this text would not have come to pass. In addition, I would like to thank my research assistants, David Thies (on the first edition) and Amy McCann (on the second edition), for their tireless energy and exceptional research abilities in locating some of the more exceptional materials in the text, with a special thank you for their work on the thankless task of acquiring all of the permissions for the book. Finally, I thank Andy Winston and Sara Strand at McGraw-Hill/Irwin for their support of this innovative project.

Laura P. Hartman
LHartman@wppost.depaul.edu
DePaul University, Executive Offices
1 E. Jackson Blvd.
Chicago, IL 60604
312/362-6569 FAX 312/896-7440

Contents

Part One

ETHICAL THEORIES AND APPROACHES

The purpose of this text is not to teach ethics, but instead to offer a foundation in ethical thought, followed by a variety of perspectives on difficult ethical dilemmas. The reader is encouraged to critically evaluate each perspective using her or his personal ethical theory base. Using ethics to analyze business issues is merely one form of decision making, similar to profit maximization, legal compliance, or religious beliefs. The difference, however, between ethics and these other bases for decisions is that ethics can serve as the foundation for each of the other methods. Therefore, in reaching decisions, the individual may use ethics as a guide in legal or religious compliance, and even in accomplishing profit maximization.

In fact, we already use ethics as a basis for decision making. Assume your grandmother is on her deathbed. She looks up to you and asks, as her last dying wish, that you follow her and your religion in a devout manner after she passes on. Assume, as well, that you do not plan to do this. Do you tell her that you will abide by her wishes, so that she might die a more peaceful death? Or are you honest with her and admit that you will not follow her wishes? Whichever your answer, consider *why* you feel the way you do. There is no law that requires one answer or another, not even a rule. You might believe that you should act one way or another because it is the "right" thing to do. This is your personal ethic.

Consider the response of the grandfather of Sir Adrian Cadbury, the owner of the second largest chocolate company in Britain, when the Queen sought to purchase tins of chocolates to send to each soldier serving in the Anglo-Boer War in South Africa. Cadbury was opposed to the war and was uncomfortable reaping a profit from such a transaction. On the other hand, he was striving to move forward with the company and this would mean additional work for

1

the firm. He decided to accept the order, but to do so only at cost with no additional amount for profit. The firm benefited from the work, but he did not reap a financial gain at the expense of the war.[1] Was this ethical? Would it have been unethical to deny the Queen's contract simply because he didn't approve of the purpose for which she intended to use the chocolate?

On the other hand, consider the $68 million Bausch & Lomb (B&L) recently agreed to pay to settle a consumer class action lawsuit. The plaintiffs complained that B&L had been selling three identical contact lenses under three different brand names for significantly different prices. B&L had attempted to market the lenses in different ways to different consumer groups at varying prices. Is this "wrong," "unethical?"

Volumes of literature are devoted in general terms to the question of defining ethics. Ethics involves judgments as to good and bad, right and wrong, and what ought to be. As defined by the philosopher Epicurus, ethics "deals with things to be sought and things to be avoided, with ways of life and with the *telos.*"[2] (*Telos* is the chief aim or end in life.) Ethics can be distinguished from "morals," which are rules or duties that govern our behavior as persons to persons (such as "do not tell lies" or "do not hurt another person"), and from "values," which are ends or goals sought by individuals (such as health or happiness).[3]

An ethical dilemma exists where two or more values are in conflict, and we seek from ethics a resolution to this conflict. Business ethics refers to the measurement of business behavior based on standards of right and wrong, rather than relying entirely on principles of accounting and management. For purposes of this discussion, morals are one's personal guiding principles; ethics are the ways that those morals are applied to decisions.

Finding and following the moral course is not always easy for any of us, but the difficulty may be particularly acute for the businessperson. The bottom line is necessarily unforgiving. Hence, the pressure to produce is intense and the temptation to cheat may be great. Although the law provides useful guideposts for minimum behavior, no clear moral guidelines have emerged. Therefore, when a businessperson is faced with a difficult decision, a common tactic is simply to do what he or she takes to be correct at any given moment. Indeed, in one survey of ethical views in business, 50 percent of the respondents indicated that the word *ethical* meant "what my feelings tell me is right."

Philosophers have provided powerful intellectual support for that approach. *Existentialists,* led by the famed Jean-Paul Sartre, believe standards of conduct cannot be rationally justified and no actions are inherently right or wrong. Thus, each person may reach her or his own choice about ethical principles. This view finds its roots in the notion that humans are only what we will ourselves to be. If God does not exist, there can be no human nature, because there is no one to conceive that nature.

In Sartre's famous interpretation, existence precedes essence. First humans exist, then we individually define what we are—our essence. Therefore, each of us is free, with no rules to turn to for guidance. Just as we all choose our own natures, so must we choose our

---

[1]Sir Adrian Cadbury, "Ethical Managers Make Their Own Rules," *Harvard Business Review,* September/October 1987.

[2]Diogenes Laertius, *Lives of Eminent Philosophers* (Cambridge: Harvard University Press 1925), book 10, chap. 30.

[3]This discussion of definitions is based on Lisa Newton's Vocabulary of Ethics in "Doing Good and Avoiding Evil, Part I.2," *http://www.rit.edu/~692awww/manuals/newton/dgae1p2.html.*

own ethical precepts. Moral responsibility belongs to each of us individually, and in our own ways.

But, as we have seen countless times through history, what one woman or man believes is "right" or just, many others may believe is "wrong" or evil. Consider, for instance, Germany under Nazi rule. Adolph Hitler believed he was right in his brutal acts and decisions *as strongly as* the rest of the world believed he was wrong. Existentialists would say, perhaps, that there is no right answer in this situation, while others would argue for some universal principles of right and wrong. *Relativists* contend that the ethical answer depends on the situation (that ethics is relative). They may argue that those who followed Hitler were not necessarily unethical because of the circumstances of the situation. What is right in one situation may be wrong in another. The theories discussed here offer guidance in this area, though they are by no means the only routes to decisions. ■

Chapter 1

TRADITIONAL THEORIES

Until philosophers are kings, or the kings and princes of this world have the spirit and power of philosophy, and political greatness and wisdom meet in one, and those commoner natures who pursue either to the exclusion of the other are compelled to stand aside, cities will never have rest from their evils—no, nor the human race.

—PLATO, *REPUBLIC*

Ethical theories may be divided into two categories: teleological and deontological. The distinction between the two is that teleological theories determine the ethics of an act by looking to the consequences of the decision (the ends), while deontological theories determine the ethics of an act by looking to the process of the decision (the means).

A. TELEOLOGICAL ETHICAL SYSTEMS

The teleological morality of a decision is determined by measuring the probable outcome or consequences. The theory most representative of this approach is *utilitarianism,* which seeks as its end the greatest "good" (or "utility") for the greatest number. Jeremy Bentham (1748–1832) and John Stuart Mill (1806–1873) were the chief intellectual forces in the development of utilitarianism. The most basic form of utilitarian analysis is cost-benefit analysis, where one tallies the costs and benefits of a given decision and follows the decision that provides for the greatest overall gain.

While this approach is superficially easy to apply (majority rule, profit/loss statements), there remain complexities. For instance, does one consider the impact on animals as well as humans in adding up the benefits and costs? Or, how does one weigh the good? If an action would render one person exquisitely happy and three people moderately unhappy, does the happiness of that one outweigh the unhappiness of the three? How do we measure happiness?

Utilitarianism is viewed as a strong theory because it is liberal (it appeals to no authority in resolving differences of opinion), and because it is able to describe much of the process of human decision making. On the other hand, its weakness is that there is a possibility of injustice regarding the distribution of goods. In other words, the rights of any one person are not taken into account; no rights have any greater weight than others. Consequently, certain individuals may suffer great harm, while others receive only modest benefits.

Distributive justice is another teleological approach to ethical decision making and one that is based on a concept of fairness. Devised by contemporary Harvard philosopher John Rawls, distributive justice holds that ethical acts or decisions are those that lead to an equitable distribution of goods and services. Therefore, it is critical to determine a fair method for distributing goods and services. Rawls suggests that we consider how we would distribute goods and services if we were under a "*veil of ignorance*" that prevented us from knowing our status in society (i.e., our intelligence, wealth, appearance). He asks that we consider what rules we would impose on this society if we had no idea whether we would be princes or paupers. Would we devise a system of high taxes and expensive welfare projects that, presumably, would benefit the impoverished but prove costly to the wealthy? Or would we advocate a pure market-based system that demanded each of us to be responsible for our own needs and desires?

Rawls argues that we would build a cooperative system in which benefits (e.g., income) would be distributed unequally only where doing so would be to the benefit of all, particularly the least advantaged. All those behind the veil would agree to that standard because they could not know whether they would be among the advantaged or the disadvantaged. From this system of distributive economic justice, it follows that ethical justice is measured by the capacity of the act in question to enhance cooperation among members of society. That which is determined from behind the veil of ignorance is deemed ethical through its fairness.

One way to understand the implications of distributive justice is to consider a difficult ethical dilemma. Imagine that you do not know what position you hold in connection with the outcome—you don't know whether you are going to be impacted in a beneficial way or a detrimental way by the decision. Now, without that knowledge (under the "veil of ignorance"), what decision would you make? Rawls argues that you will make the most just decision under this framework.

B. DEONTOLOGICAL ETHICAL SYSTEMS

A deontological system is based on rules or principles that govern decisions. The German philosopher Immanuel Kant (1724–1804) developed perhaps the most persuasive and fully articulated vision of ethics as measured by the rightness of rules, rather than by consequences. In this formalistic view of ethics, the rightness of an act depends little (or, in Kant's view, not at all) on the results of the act. Kant believed in the key moral concept of goodwill. The moral person is one of goodwill, and that person renders ethical decisions based on what is right, regardless of the consequences of the decision. Moral worth springs from one's decision to discharge one's duty. Thus, the student who refuses to cheat on exams is morally worthy if her or his decision springs from duty, but morally unworthy if the decision is merely one born of self-interest, such as fear of being caught.

But how does the person of goodwill know what is right? Here, Kant propounded the *categorical imperative,* the notion that every person should act on only those principles that she or he, as a rational person, would prescribe as *universal laws* to be applied to the whole of mankind. (Therefore, this approach has also been called universalism.) Put into action, the rule asks whether you would feel all right if this rule applied in every situation, to every action. (This concept is similar to a parent's asking a child, "How would you feel if everyone stole candy from their friends?")

The moral rule is categorical rather than hypothetical in that its prescriptive force is independent of its consequences—the rule guides us independently of the ends we seek. For instance, the rule does not say "Do not steal from others *if* you don't want to go to jail"; it merely states "Do not steal." The rule prescribes a rule for the means without concern for the end it produces. Kant believed that every rational creature can act according to his or her categorical imperative, because all such persons have "autonomous, self-legislating wills" that permit them to formulate and act on their own systems of rules. To Kant, what is right for one is right for all, and each of us can discover that "right" by exercising our rational faculties.

Kantian rules recognize universal rights such as freedom of speech, freedom of consent, the right to privacy, or freedom of conscience. Problems exist, however, when an individual does not know which rules to follow. For instance, you might be faced with a dilemma that pits freedom of speech against the right to privacy. Which rule wins?

Kant was not the only one to prescribe a moral system based on rules and rights. The Chinese scholar Confucius born in 551 BCE, maintained an enormous set of rules by which he suggested one should live. These rules, or maxims, do not appear to us today to be complicated; instead, they seem not to be commonplace and pedestrian. They include the following:

What you do not wish done to yourself, do not do to others.

Do not wish for quick results, nor look for small advantages. If you see quick results, you will not attain the ultimate goal. If you are led astray by small advantages, you will never accomplish great things.

When you see someone of worth, think of how you may emulate. When you see someone unworthy, examine your own character.

Wealth and rank are what people desire, but unless they be obtained in the right way they may not be possessed.

Feel kindly toward everyone, but be intimate only with the virtuous.[4]

Another deontological approach is from the perspective of religion. No theory or approach to the evaluation of actions is more rule based than religion. After all, the Ten Commandments are viewed by some as the most basic principles of behavior. Additional rules, such as "Do unto others as you would have them do unto you," also spring directly from religious thought or writings, rather than from reason or logic. The religious point of view is not so different from Kant's perspective, except that the universal principles come directly from religious beliefs. Whether one is of Christian, Jewish, Moslem, Buddhist, or other faith, the deity's laws are viewed as absolutes that must shape the whole of one's life, including work. Faith, rather than reason, intuition, or secular knowledge, provides the foundation for a moral life built on religion.

Finally, some philosophers have argued in recent years for *virtue ethics,* claiming that the key to good ethics lies not in rules, rights, and responsibilities, but in the classic notion of character. As Plato and Aristotle contended, our attention should be given to strategies for encouraging desirable character traits such as honesty, fairness, compassion, and generosity. The primary question in virtue ethics is not, "What actions are universally right?" but, "What is the best sort of life for human beings to live?" Virtue ethics applauds the person who is motivated to do the right thing and who cultivates that motivation in daily conduct. One would know the right thing by exercising judgment, rather than by applying a universal set of rules.

ARISTOTELIAN MORAL VIRTUES

Courage
Self-Control
Generosity
Magnificence
High-Mindedness
Gentleness
Friendliness
Truthfulness
Wittiness
Modesty[5]

---

[4]Confucius, *The Analects,* cited in Huston Smith, *The World's Religions* (San Francisco: HarperSanFrancisco 1991) p. 159.

[5]Steven Mintz, "Aristotelian Virtue and Business Ethics Education," *Journal of Business Ethics* 15, no. 8 (Aug. 1996), pp. 827–38, 830.

St. Thomas Aquinas, too, believed in the quest for the right thing or the good life. Aquinas, however, took the study of virtue one step beyond Aristotle when he divided virtue into the religious or theological virtues of faith, hope, and charity, and the intellectual virtues of prudence (wisdom), justice, temperance, and fortitude.[6] Both Aristotle and Aquinas believed that any individual had the potential for virtue, as virtue was learned or acquired, rather than innate. Could a modern corporation realistically aspire to be virtuous, according to Aquinas or Aristotle?

Virtue ethics might seem to be closely linked with universalism, where a set of principles is in the place of virtue ethics' set of traits. However, a part of the virtue ethics argument is that such persons are more morally reliable than those who simply follow the rules but fail to inspect, strengthen, and preserve their own personal virtues.

C. HYBRID THEORIES

A king had some empty glasses. He said, "If I pour hot water into them they will crack. If I pour ice-cold water into them they will also crack." What did the king do? He mixed the hot and the cold water together and poured it into them and they did not crack. Even so did the Holy One, blessed be He, say, "If I create the world on the basis of the attribute of mercy alone, the world's sins will greatly multiply? If I create the world on the basis of the attribute of justice alone, how could the world endure? I will therefore create it with both the attributes of mercy and justice, and may it endure!"[7]

Certain theories do not fit cleanly into one approach or another. *Personal libertarianism,* conceived by contemporary philosopher Robert Nozick, holds that morality springs from the maximization of personal freedom and that individuals should be free from the interference of others. Justice and fairness, right and wrong are measured not by equality of results (e.g., wealth) for all, but from ensuring equal opportunity for all to engage in informed choices about their own welfare. Hence, Nozick takes essentially a free market stance toward ethics. One might, at first, say that this is a deontological theory since the primary concern is protecting the right to individual freedom, whatever the consequences. On the other hand, the theory also looks to the results of an act in determining whether freedom has been restricted as a result of the decision. The primary value is liberty and the ultimate gain is gain for one's self. However, Nozick does not contend that, as an individual, one seeks only enjoyable experiences; he believes that one also seeks to be the kind of person who is loved, who has friends, respect, and so on.

Closely related to libertarianism is the concept of *ethical egoism.* The primary concern under ethical egoism is the maximization of the individual's self-interest, according to that individual. What is right is that which is right for the individual. This view minimizes the impact of the individual's choices on the rights of others. Ethical egoism identifies a means for decision making (do what you want), while also identifying the greatest good as that

---

[6]Caryn Beck-Dudley, "No More Quandaries: A Look at Virtue through The Eyes of Robert Solomon," *American Business Law Journal* 34/1 (Fall 1996), p. 119.
[7]Aba Hillel Silver, *Where Judaism Differed* (Northvale, NJ: Jason Aronson, 1987). Cited in Huston Smith, *The World's Religions* (San Francisco: HarperSanFrancisco 1991), p. 292.

which is the greatest good for the decision maker, hence a hybrid. Self-interest may be wealth, but it can also be fame, a happy family, a great job, or anything else considered important to the decision maker.

Enlightened ethical egoism (also known as *enlightened self-interest*) considers the long-range perspective of others or of humanity as a whole. One might explain this by saying that it is important to the individual that the world is a "good" world; therefore, the individual may have a *self*-interest in curbing pollution or in community projects, even though she or he may not individually and personally benefit from the decision.

In the readings that follow, consider the authors' contentions about what is "right" and "wrong." Do you agree with one of these approaches more strongly than another? In some readings, the approaches may seem more clearly in line with the theories discussed above than those in others. Can you align the others with the traditional theories, or are they more likely hybrids of those discussed? Consider, for instance, the closing argument in the Leopold and Loeb case. Darrow contends that these boys were "bad" simply because they were "made" that way. Does this argument make sense to you or would you feel that the boys were less liable for killing a young child because "they couldn't help it"?

LEVIATHAN

THOMAS HOBBES

Thomas Hobbes (1588–1679) was viewed as a materialist and as a highly pessimistic philosopher. The Leviathan presents a bleak picture of the innate qualities of human beings in the "state of nature"; without governing rules or laws, a war of all against all is certain to ensue. Hobbes contends that fear of violent death is the primary motive that causes people to create a political state by contracting to surrender their natural rights and to submit to the absolute authority of a sovereign.

Hobbes lived in a time of extreme violence. He was born around the time when Mary, Queen of Scots, was executed by Elizabeth, Queen of England. During his life, the Spanish Armada attacked England and was defeated, and piracy and buccaneering were rampant on the oceans. There was an English Civil war in the 1640s that included the execution of Charles I. London was hit repeatedly with fire and plagues. Women and men were accused of witchcraft and burned at the stake. No wonder he had a dismal view of human nature!

The Hobbesian concept of the social contract led to investigations by other political theorists (Locke, Spinoza, Rousseau) who formulated their own radically different theories of the social contract.

[13] To this war of every man against every man, this also is consequent: that nothing can be unjust. The notions of right and wrong, justice and injustice, have there no place. Where there is no common power, there is no law; where no law, no injustice. Force and fraud are in war the two cardinal virtues. Justice and injustice are none of the faculties neither of the body, nor mind. If they were, they might be in a man that were alone in the world, as well as his senses and passions. They are qualities that relate to men in society, not in solitude. It is consequent also to the same condition that there be no propriety, no dominion, no *mine* and *thine* distinct, but only that to be every man's that he can get, and for so long as he can keep it. And thus much for the ill condition which man by mere nature is actually placed in, though with a possibility to come out of it, consisting partly in the passions, partly in his reason.

***

Thomas Hobbes, *Leviathan*, pt. I, ch. 13, para. 13; 14, para. 3, 15, para. 10.

[3] But because covenants of mutual trust where there is a fear of not performance on either part (as hath been said in the former chapter) are invalid, though the original of justice be the making of covenants, yet injustice actually there can be none till the cause of such fear be taken away, which, while men are in the natural condition of war, cannot be done. Therefore, before the names of just and unjust can have place, there must be some coercive power to compel men equally to the performance of their covenants, by the terror of some punishment greater than the benefit they expect by the breach of their covenant, and to make good that propriety which by mutual contract men acquire, in recompense of the universal right they abandon; and such power there is none before the erection of a commonwealth. And this is also to be gathered out of the ordinary definition of justice in the Schools; for they say the *justice is the constant will of giving to every man his own.* And therefore where there is no *own,* that is, no propriety, there is no injustice; and where there is no coercive power erected, that is, where there is no commonwealth, there is no propriety, all men having right to all things; therefore where there is no commonwealth, there nothing is unjust. So that the nature of justice consisteth in keeping of valid covenants; but the validity of covenants begins not but with the constitution of a civil power sufficient to compel men to keep them; and then it is also that propriety begins.

***

[10] The names of just and unjust, when they are attributed to men, signify one thing; and when they are attributed to actions, another. When they are attributed to men, they signify conformity or inconformity of manners to reason. But when they are attributed to actions, they signify the conformity or inconformity to reason, not of manners or manner of life, but of particular actions. A just man, therefore, is he that taketh all the care he can that his actions may be all just; and an unjust man is he that neglecteth it. And such men are more often in our language styled by the names of righteous and unrighteous, than just and unjust, though the meaning be the same. Therefore a righteous man does not lose that title by one or a few unjust actions that proceed from sudden passion or mistake of things or persons; nor does an unrighteous man lose his character for such actions as he does or forbears to do for fear, because his will is not framed by the justice, but by the apparent benefit of what he is to do. That which gives to human actions the relish of justice is a certain nobleness or gallantness of courage (rarely found) by which a man scorns to be beholden for the contentment of his life to fraud or breach of promise. This justice of the manners is that which is meant where justice is called a virtue, and injustice a vice.

OF THE STATE OF NATURE

John Locke

John Locke (1632–1704) is considered the father of British empiricism. He was born to a puritan household and it is actually unknown whether Locke ever attended a formal school in his childhood, but he did attend Oxford later in his life. Empiricism is a philosophical doctrine holding that all knowledge is derived from experience, whether of the mind or the senses. Empiricists oppose the rationalist belief in the existence of innate ideas. A doctrine basic to the scientific method, it is associated with the rise of experimental science after the 17th century. It has been dominant in British philosophy, in the works of Hume and Berkeley. Most empiricists acknowledge certain a priori truths (e.g., principles of mathematics and logic), but John Stuart Mill and others have treated even these as generalizations deduced from experience.

Using what he called a "historical, plain method," Locke inquired into the origin, certainty, and extent of human knowledge, together with the grounds and degrees of belief, assent, and opinion. "Our business is not to know all things, but those which concern our conduct."

His Two Treatises on Government *represents the first time that the monarchy had been questioned. The whole concept of human rights and individual freedom had been heard, but Locke was the first to question whether the monarchy had a right to exist, to rule. He supported a popular government answerable to the people with liberty as the overriding value, rather than government by absolute monarchy.*

4. To understand political power aright, and derive it from its original, we must consider what estate all men are naturally in, and that is, a state of perfect freedom to order their actions, and dispose of their possessions and persons as they think fit, within the bounds of the law of Nature, without asking leave or depending upon the will of any other man.

A state also of equality, wherein all the power and jurisdiction is reciprocal, no one having more than another, there being nothing more evident than that creatures of the same species and rank, promiscuously born to all the same advantages of Nature, and the use of the same faculties, should also be equal one amongst another, without subordination or subjection, unless the lord and master of them all should, by any manifest declaration of his

---

John Locke, *Second Treatise on Government*, Ch. II, Of the State of Nature, pars. 4, 6–8, 13–14.

will, set one above another, and confer on him, by an evident and clear appointment, an undoubted right to dominion and sovereignty. . . .

6. The state of Nature has a law of Nature to govern it, which obliges every one, and reason, which is that law, teaches all mankind who will but consult it, that being all equal and independent, no one ought to harm another in his life, health, liberty or possessions; for men being all the workmanship of one omnipotent and infinitely wise Maker; all the servants of one sovereign Master, sent into the world by His order and about His business; they are His property, whose workmanship they are made to last during His, not one another's pleasure. And, being furnished with like faculties, sharing all in one community of Nature, there cannot be supposed any such subordination among us that may authorize us to destroy one another, as if we were made for one another's uses, as the inferior ranks of creatures are for ours. Every one as he is bound to preserve himself, and not to quit his station wilfully, so by the like reason, when his own preservation comes not in competition, ought he as much as he can to preserve the rest of mankind, and not unless it be to do justice on an offender, take away or impair the life, or what tends to the preservation of life, the liberty, health, limb, or goods of another.

7. And that all men may be restrained from invading others' rights, and from doing hurt to one another, and the law of Nature be observed, which willeth the peace and preservation of all mankind, the execution of the law of Nature is in that state put into every man's hands, whereby every one has a right to punish the transgressors of that law to such a degree as may hinder its violation. For the law of Nature would, as all other laws that concern men in this world, be in vain if there were nobody that in the state of Nature had a power to execute that law, and thereby preserve the innocent and restrain offenders; and if any one in the state of Nature may punish another for any evil he has done, every one may do so. For in that state of perfect equality, where naturally there is no superiority or jurisdiction of one over another, what any may do in prosecution of that law, every one must needs have a right to do.

8. And thus, in the state of Nature, one man comes by a power over another, but yet no absolute or arbitrary power to use a criminal, when he has got him in his hands, according to the passionate heats or boundless extravagancy of his own will, but only to retribute to him so far as calm reason and conscience dictate, what is proportionate to his transgression, which is so much as may serve for reparation and restraint. For these two are the only reasons why one man may lawfully do harm to another, which is that we call punishment. In transgressing the law of Nature, the offender declares himself to live by another rule than that of reason and common equity, which is that measure God has set to the actions of men for their mutual security, and so he becomes dangerous to mankind; the tie which is to secure them from injury and violence being slighted and broken by him, which being a trespass against the whole species, and the peace and safety of it, provided for by the law of Nature, every man upon this score, by the right he hath to preserve mankind in general, may restrain, or where it is necessary, destroy things noxious to them, and so may bring such evil on any one who hath transgressed that law, as may make him repent the doing of it, and thereby deter him, and, by his example, others from doing the like mischief. And in this case, and upon this ground, every man hath a right to punish the offender, and be executioner of the law of Nature. . . .

13. To this strange doctrine—*viz.,* That in the state of Nature every one has the executive power of the law of Nature—I doubt not but it will be objected that it is unreasonable for men to be judges in their own cases, that self-love will make men partial to themselves and their friends; and, on the other side, ill-nature, passion, and revenge will carry them too far in punishing others, and hence nothing but confusion and disorder will follow, and that therefore God hath certainly appointed government to restrain the partiality and violence of men. I easily grant that civil government is the proper remedy for the inconveniences of the state of Nature, which must certainly be great where men may be judges in their own case, since it is easy to be imagined that he who was so unjust as to do his brother an injury will scarce be so just as to condemn himself for it. But I shall desire those who make this objection to remember that absolute monarchs are but men; and if government is to be the remedy of those evils which necessarily follow from men being judges in their own cases, and the state of Nature is therefore not to be endured, I desire to know what kind of government that is, and how much better it is than the state of Nature, where one man commanding a multitude has the liberty to be judge in his own case, and may do to all his subjects whatever he pleases without the least question or control of those who execute his pleasure? and in whatsoever he doth, whether led by reason, mistake, or passion, must be submitted to? which men in the state of Nature are not bound to do one to another? And if he that judges, judges amiss in his own or any other case, he is answerable for it to the rest of mankind.

14. It is often asked as a mighty objection, where are, or ever were, there any men in such a state of Nature? To which it may suffice as an answer at present, that since all princes and rulers of "independent" governments all through the world are in a state of Nature, it is plain the world never was, nor never will be, without numbers of men in that state. I have named all governors of "independent" communities, whether they are, or are not, in league with others; for it is not every compact that puts an end to the state of Nature between men, but only this one of agreeing together mutually to enter into one community, and make one body politic; other promises and compacts men may make one with another, and yet still be in the state of Nature. The promises and bargains for truck, etc., between the two men in Soldania, in or between a Swiss and an Indian, in the woods of America, are binding to them, though they are perfectly in a state of Nature in reference to one another for truth, and keeping of faith belongs to men as men, and not as members of society.

GROUNDING FOR THE METAPHYSICS OF MORALS

IMMANUEL KANT

Immanuel Kant (1724–1804) was intrigued by the bases of human knowledge and understanding. In considering the origin of morals and morality, he concluded that reason is the final authority for morality. Only those actions that are undertaken from a sense of duty dictated by reason are moral; those acts that are dictated only by law or custom cannot be moral. In the following excerpt, Kant explains the categorical imperative, his basis for morality. Consider its close link to what we know as the Golden Rule.

It is clear from the foregoing that all moral concepts have their seat and origin completely a priori in reason, and indeed in the most ordinary human reason just as much as in the most highly speculative. They cannot be abstracted from any empirical, and hence merely contingent, cognition. In this purity of their origin lies their very worthiness to serve us as supreme practical principles; and to the extent that something empirical is added to them, just so much is taken away from their genuine influence and from the absolute worth of the corresponding actions. Moreover, it is not only a requirement of the greatest necessity from a theoretical point of view, when it is a question of speculation, but also of the greatest practical importance, to draw these concepts and laws from pure reason, to present them pure and unmixed, and indeed to determine the extent of this entire practical and pure rational cognition, i.e., to determine the whole faculty of pure practical reason. The principles should not be made to depend on the particular nature of human reason, as speculative philosophy may permit and even sometimes finds necessary; but, rather, the principles should be derived from the universal concept of a rational being in general, since moral laws should hold for every rational being as such. In this way all morals, which require anthropology in order to be applied to humans, must be entirely expounded at first independently of anthropology as pure philosophy, i.e., as metaphysics (which can easily be done in such distinct kinds of knowledge). One knows quite well that unless one is in possession of such a metaphysics, then the attempt is futile, I shall not say to determine exactly for speculative judgment the moral element of duty in all that accords with duty, but that the attempt is impossible, even in ordinary and practical usage, especially in that of moral instruction, to ground morals on their genuine principles and thereby to produce pure moral dispositions and engraft them on men's minds for the promotion of the highest good in the world.

***

Everything in nature works according to laws. Only a rational being has the power to act according to his conception of laws, i.e., according to principles, and thereby has he a will. Since the derivation of actions from laws requires reason, the will is nothing but practical reason. If reason infallibly determines the will, then in the case of such a being actions which are recognized to be objectively necessary are also subjectively necessary, i.e., the will is a faculty of choosing only that which reason, independently of inclination, recognizes as being practically necessary, i.e., as good. But if reason of itself does not sufficiently determine the will, and if the will submits also to subjective conditions (certain incentives) which do not always agree with objective conditions; in a word, if the will does not in itself completely accord with reason (as is actually the case with men), then actions which are recognized as objectively necessary are subjectively contingent, and the determination of such a will according to objective laws is necessitation. That is to say that the relation of objective laws to a will not thoroughly good is represented as the determination of the will of a rational being by principles of reason which the will does not necessarily follow because of its own nature. . . .

[I]n the case of this categorical imperative, or law of morality, the reason for the difficulty (of discerning its possibility) is quite serious. The categorical imperative is an a priori synthetic practical proposition, and since discerning the possibility of propositions of this sort involves so much difficulty in theoretic knowledge, there may readily be gathered that there will be no less difficulty in practical knowledge.

In solving this problem, we want first to inquire whether perhaps the mere concept of a categorical imperative may not also supply us with the formula containing the proposition that can alone be a categorical imperative. For even when we know the purport of such an absolute command, the question as to how it is possible will still require a special and difficult effort, which we postpone to the last section.

If I think of a hypothetical imperative in general, I do not know beforehand what it will contain until its condition is given. But if I think of a categorical imperative, I know immediately what it contains. For since, besides the law, the imperative contains only the necessity that the maxim should accord with this law, while the law contains no condition to restrict it, there remains nothing but the universality of a law as such with which the maxim of the action should conform. This conformity alone is properly what is represented as necessary by the imperative.

Hence there is only one categorical imperative and it is this: Act only according to that maxim whereby you can at the same time will that it should become a universal law.

Now if all imperatives of duty can be derived from this one imperative as their principle, then there can at least be shown what is understood by the concept of duty and what it means, even though there is left undecided whether what is called duty may not be an empty concept.

The universality of law according to which effects are produced constitutes what is properly called nature in the most general sense (as to form), i.e., the existence of things as far as determined by universal laws. Accordingly, the universal imperative of duty may be expressed thus: Act as if the maxim of your action were to become through your will a universal law of nature.

We shall now enumerate some duties, following the usual division of them into duties to ourselves and to others and into perfect and imperfect duties.

1. A man reduced to despair by a series of misfortunes feels sick of life but is still so far in possession of his reason that he can ask himself whether taking his own life would not be contrary to his duty to himself. Now he asks whether the maxim of his action could become a universal law of nature. But his maxim is this: from self-love I make as my principle to shorten my life when its continued duration threatens more evil than it promises satisfaction. There only remains the question as to whether this principle of self-love become a universal law of nature. One sees at once a contradiction in a system of nature whose law would destroy life by means of the very same feeling that acts so as to stimulate the furtherance of life, and hence there could be no existence as a system of nature. Therefore, such a maxim cannot possibly hold as a universal law of nature and is, consequently, wholly opposed to the supreme principle of all duty.

2. Another man in need finds himself forced to borrow money. He knows well that he won't be able to repay it, but he sees also that he will not get any loan unless he firmly promises to repay it within a fixed time. He wants to make such a promise, but he still has conscience enough to ask himself whether it is not permissible and is contrary to duty to get out of difficulty in this way. Suppose, however, that he decides to do so. The maxim of his action would then be expressed as follows: when I believe myself to be in need of money, I will borrow money and promise to pay it back, although I know that I can never do so. Now this principle of self-love or personal advantage may perhaps be quite compatible with one's entire future welfare, but the question is now whether it is right. I then transform the requirement of self-love into a universal law and put the question thus: how would things stand if my maxim were to become a universal law? He then sees at once that such a maxim could never hold as a universal law of nature and be consistent with itself, but must necessarily be self-contradictory. For the universality of law which says that anyone believing himself to be in difficulty could promise whatever he pleases with the intention of not keeping it would make promising itself and the end to be attained thereby quite impossible, inasmuch as no one would believe what was promised him but would merely laugh at all such utterances as being vain pretenses.

3. A third finds in himself a talent whose cultivation could make him a man useful in many respects. But he finds himself in comfortable circumstances and prefers to indulge in pleasure rather than to bother himself about broadening and improving his fortunate natural aptitudes. But he asks himself further whether his maxim of neglecting his natural gifts, besides agreeing of itself with his propensity to indulgence, might agree also with what is called duty. He then sees that a system of nature could indeed always subsist according to such a universal law, even though every man (like South Sea Islanders) should let his talents rust and resolve to devote his life entirely to idleness, indulgence, propagation, and, in a word, to enjoyment. But he cannot possibly will that this should become a universal law of nature or be implanted in us as such a law by a natural instinct. For as a rational being he

necessarily wills that all his faculties should be developed, inasmuch as they are given him for all sorts of possible purposes.

4. A fourth man finds things going well for himself but sees others (whom he could help) struggling with great hardships; and he thinks: what does it matter to me? Let everybody be as happy as Heaven will or as he can make himself; I shall take nothing from him nor even envy him; but I have no desire to contribute anything to his well-being or to his assistance when in need. If such a way of thinking were to become a universal law of nature, the human race admittedly could very well subsist and doubtless could subsist even better than when everyone prates about sympathy and benevolence and even on occasion exerts himself to practice them but, on the other hand, also cheats when he can, betrays the rights of man, or otherwise violates them. But even though it is possible that a universal law of nature could subsist in accordance with that maxim, still it is impossible to will that such a principle should hold everywhere as a law of nature. For a will which resolved in this way would contradict itself, inasmuch as cases might often arise in which one would have need of the love and sympathy of others and in which he would deprive himself, by such a law of nature springing from his own will, of all hope of the aid he wants for himself.

These are some of the many actual duties, or at least what are taken to be such, whose derivation from the single principle cited above is clear. We must be able to will that a maxim of our action become a universal law; this is the canon for morally estimating any of our actions. Some actions are so constituted that their maxims cannot without contradiction even be thought as a universal law of nature, much less be willed as what should become one. In the case of others this internal impossibility is indeed not found, but there is still no possibility of willing that their maxim should be raised to the universality of a law of nature, because such a will would contradict itself. There is no difficulty in seeing that the former kind of action conflicts with strict or narrow [perfect] (irremissible) duty, while the second kind conflicts only with broad [imperfect] (meritorious) duty. By means of these examples there has thus been fully set forth how all duties depend as regards the kind of obligation (not the object of their action) upon the one principle.

If we now attend to ourselves in any transgression of a duty, we find that we actually do not will that our maxim should become a universal law—because this is impossible for us—but rather that the opposite of this maxim should remain a law universally. We only take the liberty of making an exception to the law for ourselves (or just for this one time) to the advantage of our inclination. Consequently, if we weighed up everything from one and the same standpoint, namely, that of reason, we would find a contradiction in our own will, viz., that a certain principle be objectively necessary as a universal law and yet subjectively not hold universally but should admit of exceptions. But since we at one moment regard our action from the standpoint of a will wholly in accord with reason and then at another moment regard the very same action from the standpoint of a will affected by inclination, there is really no contradiction here. Rather, there is an opposition (*antagonismus*) of inclination to the precept of reason, whereby the universality (*universalitas*) of the principle is changed into a mere generality (*generalitas*) so that the practical principal of reason may meet the maxim halfway. Although this procedure cannot be justified in our own impartial judgment, yet it does show that we actually acknowledge the validity of the categorical imperative and (with all respect for it) merely allow ourselves a few exceptions which, as they seem to us, are unimportant and forced upon us.

We have thus at least shown that if duty is a concept which is to have significance and real legislative authority for our actions, then such duty can be expressed only in categorical imperatives but not at all in hypothetical ones. We have also—and this is already a great deal—exhibited clearly and definitely for every application what is the content of the categorical imperative, which must contain the principle of all duty (if there is such a thing at all). But we have not yet advanced far enough to prove a priori that there actually is an imperative of this kind, that there is a practical law which of itself commands absolutely and without any incentives, and that following this law is duty. . . .

If then there is to be a supreme practical principle and, as far as the human will is concerned, a categorical imperative, then it must be such that from the conception of what is necessarily an end for everyone because this end is an end in itself it constitutes an objective principle of the will and can hence serve as a practical law. The ground of such a principle is this: rational nature exists as an end in itself. In this way man necessarily thinks of his own existence; thus far is it a subjective principle of human actions. But in this way also does every other rational being think of his existence on the same rational ground that holds also for me; hence it is at the same time an objective principle, from which, as a supreme practical ground, all laws of the will must be able to be derived. The practical imperative will therefore be the following: Act in such a way that you treat humanity, whether in your own person or in the person of another, always at the same time as an end and never simply as a means. We now want to see whether this can be carried out in practice.

Let us keep to our previous examples.

First, as regards the concept of necessary duty to oneself, the man who contemplates suicide will ask himself whether his action can be consistent with the idea of humanity as an end in itself. If he destroys himself in order to escape from a difficult situation, then he is making use of his person merely as a means so as to maintain a tolerable condition till the end of his life. Man, however, is not a thing and hence is not something to be used merely as a means; he must in all his actions always be regarded as an end in himself. Therefore, I cannot dispose of man in my own person by mutilating, damaging, or killing him. (A more exact determination of this principle so as to avoid all misunderstanding, e.g., regarding the amputation of limbs in order to save oneself, or the exposure of one's life to danger in order to save it, and so on, must here be omitted; such questions belong to morals proper.)

Second, as concerns necessary or strict duty to others, the man who intends to make a false promise will immediately see that he intends to make use of another man merely as a means to an end which the latter does not likewise hold. For the man whom I want to use for my own purposes by such a promise cannot possibly concur with my way of acting toward him and hence cannot himself hold the end of this action. This conflict with the principle of duty to others becomes even clearer when instances of attacks on the freedom and property of others are considered. For then it becomes clear that a transgressor of the rights of men intends to make use of the persons of others merely as a means, without taking into consideration that, as rational beings, they should always be esteemed at the same time as ends, i.e., be esteemed only as beings who must themselves be able to hold the very same action as an end.

Third, with regard to contingent (meritorious) duty to oneself, it is not enough that the action does not conflict with humanity in our own person as an end in itself; the action must also harmonize with this end. Now there are in humanity capacities for greater perfection which belong to the end that nature has in view as regards humanity in our own person. To neglect these capacities might perhaps be consistent with the maintenance of humanity as an end in itself, but would not be consistent with the advancement of this end.

Fourth, concerning meritorious duty to others, the natural end that all men have is their own happiness. Now humanity might indeed subsist if nobody contributed anything to the happiness of others, provided he did not intentionally impair their happiness. But this, after all, would harmonize only negatively and not positively with humanity as an end in itself, if everyone does not also strive, as much as he can, to further the ends of others. For the ends of any subject who is an end in himself must as far as possible be my ends also, if that conception of an end in itself is to have its full effect in me.

THE TEN COMMANDMENTS

As discussed earlier, one of the earliest recorded codes of conduct is found in the Bible: the Ten Commandments. If you were given the opportunity to write 10, and only 10, commandments today, do you think that these would be the ones that you would choose? Are these sufficient? Are they realistic? In your opinion, is a good person one who follows these commandments?

1 Then God delivered all these commandments:

2 "I, the LORD, am your God, who brought you out of the land of Egypt, that place of slavery. 3 You shall not have other gods besides me. 4 You shall not carve idols for yourselves in the shape of anything in the sky above or on the earth below or in the waters beneath the earth; 5 you shall not bow down before them or worship them. For I, the LORD, your God, am a jealous God, inflicting punishment for their fathers' wickedness on the children of those who hate me, down to the third and fourth generation; 6 but bestowing mercy down to the thousandth generation, on the children of those who love me and keep my commandments.

7 "You shall not take the name of the LORD, your God, in vain. For the LORD will not leave unpunished him who takes his name in vain.

8 "Remember to keep holy the sabbath day. 9 Six days you may labor and do all your work, 10 but the seventh day is the sabbath of the LORD, your God. No work may be done then either by you, or your son or daughter, or your male or female slave, or your beast, or by the alien who lives with you. 11 In six days the LORD made the heavens and the earth, the sea and all that is in them; but on the seventh day he rested. That is why the LORD has blessed the sabbath day and made it holy.

12 "Honor your father and your mother, that you may have a long life in the land which the LORD, your God, is giving you.

13 "You shall not kill.

14 "You shall not commit adultery.

15 "You shall not steal.

16 "You shall not bear false witness against your neighbor.

17 "You shall not covet your neighbor's house. You shall not covet your neighbor's wife, nor his male or female slave, nor his ox or ass, nor anything else that belongs to him."

The Ten Commandments, Exodus 20: 1–17. The Bible.

WHEN JUSTICE
REPLACES AFFECTION
The Need for Rights
JEREMY WALDRON

If we didn't have laws, how would we act? Do you believe that our natural affection for other humans would prevail and we would all treat each other in respectful and considerate ways? What might prevent this? In the following piece, Waldron discusses philosophers Kant and Hegel as he considers rights as parameters for natural acts. He uses marriage as his primary example, investigating what happens when affection fades, but when there exist legalistic rights and duties the partners know they can fall back on.

I.

Why do individuals need rights? In a world crying out for a greater emphasis on fraternity and communal responsibility in social life, what is the point of an institution that legitimates the making of querulous and adversarial claims by individuals against their fellows? If human relations can be founded on affection, why is so much made in modern jurisprudence of formal and impersonal rights as a starting point for the evaluation of laws and institutions? In answering these questions, I take as my starting point a disagreement between the philosophers Kant and Hegel regarding the role of rights in marriage.

In his work on the philosophy of law, Immanuel Kant likened marriage to a contract between two people for "life-long reciprocal possession of their sexual faculties."[1] He was quick to add that, though it is a contract, it is "not on that account a matter of arbitrary will"; rather, it is a matter of necessity for anyone who wants to enjoy another person sexually. In sexual relations, Kant says, one party is used as an object by the other, and that *prima facie* is incompatible with the basic "Law of Humanity" prohibiting the use of any human agent as a mere means to the satisfaction of one's desires. That situation can be rectified "only . . . under the one condition that as the one Person is acquired by the other as a *res,* that same Person equally acquires the other reciprocally, and thus regains and re-establishes the rational Personality."[2] Kant went on to say that the reciprocity of rights that this solution presupposes leads to a requirement of monogamy, because in a polygamous regime, one of the partners may be giving more to the other than

Jeremy Waldron, "When Justice Replaces Affection: The Need for Rights." *Harvard Journal of Law and Public Policy 2,* no. (Summer 1988), pp. 625–31, 635–37, 640–42. Reprinted by permission.

[1] I. Kant, *The Philosophy of Law: An Exposition of the Fundamental Principles of Jurisprudence as the Science of Right* 110 (W. Hastie trans. 1887).

[2] *Id.* at 110–11.

the other is to her.[3] The contract has got to be a matter of *equal* right in order to satisfy the fundamental test of respect for persons.

Sometimes it seems that Kant was not content with this contractualist characterization of marriage. In one place, he went further and argued that the rights involved are like rights of property:

> *The Personal Right thus acquired is at the same time, real in kind. This characteristic of it is established by the fact that if one of the married Persons runs away or enters into the possession of another, the other is entitled, at any time, and incontestably, to bring such a one back to the former relation, as if that Person were a Thing.[4]*

Many have thought that such ideas are perhaps better ignored in the overall assessment of Kant's philosophy of morals.

The Kantian view of marriage as a purely contractual arrangement was adamantly repudiated by Hegel—"shameful," he said, "is the only word for it."[5] Hegel conceded that marriage originates in a contract between two people and that therefore, in its dependence on their say-so to get it underway, it has some of the contingency and "arbitrariness" that are normally associated with contractual relations.[6] But, according to Hegel, rights and contract are far from telling us the complete story about the institution. For one thing, the public character of the marriage celebration (whether the ceremony is religious or civil)—the procedures of notification, licensing, witnessing, solemnization, registration, and so on— attest to a significance that goes far beyond a mere meeting of the wills or "the mutual caprice" of the prospective partners.[7] For another thing, the parties celebrate their marriage not merely as a *quid pro quo* but in order to attain a union of desire, affection, interest, and identity that goes far beyond anything that could possibly be specified in even the fine print of a contract. There is a world of difference, on this view, between the Kantian "contract for reciprocal use" and the "love, trust, and common sharing of their existence as individuals" which is what married partners commit themselves to.[8] As Hegel puts it, if marriage begins in an agreement, "it is precisely a contract to transcend the standpoint of contract," that is, to transcend the standpoint of "individual self-subsistent units" making claims against one another, which is how contracting parties are normally understood.[9]

There are two distinct aspects to this critique. On the one hand, Hegel is attacking Kant's specific use of *contract* to characterize the marriage bond; the suggestion is that *this* legal concept is inappropriate in the particular context (though I imagine he would take even greater exception to Kant's use of the terminology of property!). On the other hand, he is also attacking the much broader target of Kant's pervasive legalism: the temptation, to which Kantians so often succumb, to reduce social institutions of all kinds to some formal array of legalistic rights and duties. Here it is not so much the idea of *contract,* but the more

---

[3]*Id.* at 111–12.

[4]*Id.* at 111.

[5]G. W. F. Hegel, *Philosophy of Right* 58, at ¶ 75 (T. Knox trans. 1967).

[6]*Id.* at 111–12, at ¶ 162.

[7]*Id.* at 113–14, at ¶ 164; *id.* at 262, at ¶ 161[A].

[8]*Id.* at 112, at ¶ 163.

[9]*Id.*

general idea of a *right,* that is out of place. This is the aspect of Hegel's critique that I will focus on, because I think it raises interesting and far-reaching issues about liberal rights-based approaches to social and communal relations.

Few of us would disagree with Hegel's basic point: Claims of right should have little part to play in the context of a normal loving marriage. If we hear one partner complaining to the other about a denial or withdrawal of conjugal *rights,* we know that something has already gone wrong with the interplay of desire and affection between the partners. The same would be true if people started talking about their *right* to a partner's fidelity, their *right* to be freed from child-care or domestic chores once in a while, their equal *right* to pursue a career, their *right* to draw equally on the family income, and so on. In each case, the substance of the claim may be indispensable for a happy and loving marriage in the modern world. But it is its presentation *as a claim*—that is, as an entitlement that one party presses peremptorily, querulously, and adversarially against the other—that would lead to our misgivings. We would certainly look for all these things in a marriage, but we would hope to see them upheld and conceded, not as matters of right, but as the natural outcome of the most intimate mutual concern and respect brought to bear by the partners on the common problems that they face. Even if rights like these were acknowledged as the ground-rules of the relationship in some sort of formal agreement drawn up by the partners, there would still be something unpleasant about their *asserting* them as rights or, as the phrase goes, *"standing on their rights"* in the normal functioning of the relationship. Such behavior would be seen as a way of blocking and preventing warmth and intimacy, replacing relatively unbounded and immediate care and sensitivity with rigid and abstract formulas of justice.

The point can be generalized: To stand on one's rights is to distance oneself from those to whom the claim is made; it is to announce, so to speak, an opening of hostilities; and it is to acknowledge that other warmer bonds of kinship, affection, and intimacy can no longer hold. To do this in a context where adversarial hostility is inappropriate is serious moral failing.[10] As Hegel put it in an Addition to the *Philosophy of Right:* "To have no interest except in one's formal right may be pure obstinacy, often a fitting accompaniment of a cold heart and restricted sympathies. It is uncultured people who insist most on their rights, while noble minds look on other aspects of the thing."[11]

II.

Is there not anything, then, to be said for the Kantian position? I think there is this. Though marriage is certainly more than a matter of rights and correlative duties, and though one will not expect to hear claims of right in a happily functioning marriage, nevertheless the

---

[10]*See, e.g.,* Young, *Dispensing with Moral Rights,* 6 *Political Theory* 63, 68(1978):

[O]ften not only is such an appeal to rights otiose, but it is morally jarring (rather than dignified) to insist on one's due. . . . This means of protecting what are conceived to be legitimate interests is, even if understandable, not morally desirable since it does nothing to mend the ruptured relations.

See also Louden, *Rights Infatuation and the Impoverishment of Theory,* 17 *J. Value Inquiry* 87, 99 (1983) ("In extreme cases [of rights infatuation], a severe form of moral inertia takes over, at which point it becomes difficult to get the rights infatuationist to do anything but claim his rights.")

[11]Hegel, *supra* note 5, at 235, at ¶ 37[A].

strength and security of the marriage commitment in the modern world depends in part on there being an array of legalistic rights and duties that the partners know they can fall back on, if ever their mutual affection fades. That is the idea I will consider in this paper.

I want to explore this idea against the background of some criticisms that have been made of rights-based liberalism. In recent years, liberal theories have come under attack from socialists and communitarians for their implausible suggestion that the bonds of social life should be thought of as constituted primarily by the rights and rights-based relations of initially atomistic individuals.[12] I will consider how much of that attack would be mitigated or refuted if liberals were to concede that the structure of rights is not constitutive of social life, but instead to be understood as a position of fall-back and security in case other constituent elements of social relations ever come apart. To go back to the marriage example, I will suggest that there is a need for an array of formal and legalistic rights and duties, not to constitute the affective bond, but to provide each person with secure knowledge of what she can count on in the unhappy event that there turns out to be no other basis for her dealings with her erstwhile partner in the relationship. The importance of rights ought to be much easier to defend from this somewhat less inflated position.

But the argument is not merely a strategic retreat for liberals. Liberals are entitled to ask their communitarian critics how this important function of security is to be performed in a community that repudiates rights and legalism, and under the auspices of a theory that gives individual rights no part to play at all. Is it to be supposed that the intimate and affective relations that characterize various forms of community will never come apart, that affections will never change, and that people will never feel the urge to exit from some relationships and initiate others? If so, communitarianism in the modern world presents itself as naive or desperately dangerous, and probably both. Or is it supposed that a society will be pervaded by such a strong background sense of affection and responsibility, that we will be able to afford to allow people to change their intimate relations as they please without any attempt to articulate formally the terms on which they are to do so? That, for example, in the marriage case, we can somehow count on goodwill to provide for the continued care of person's partner or children if they need it? Again, if this is the view that communitarians rely on, they are dangerously underestimating both the possibility for things to go wrong between human beings, and the human need for some sort of background guarantee, on which, in the last resort, one can rely in the face of that possibility.

Before continuing it may be worth saying a word or two about *communitarianism*. The new communitarianism is by no means a rigidly defined body of thought; the term refers rather to a trend in modern critiques of liberal political philosophy. In the work of writers like Roberto Unger, Michael Sandel, Alasdair Macintyre, and Charles Taylor, liberal theories of rights have been attacked for their individualism, for the way they parade the desires and interests of the human individual as the be-all and end-all of politics, at the expense of

---

[12]*See, e.g., Liberalism and Its Critics* (M. Sandel ed. 1984) (hereinafter *Liberalism*); M. Sandel, *Liberalism and the Limits of Justice* (1982); A. Macintyre, *After Virtue: A Study in Moral Theory* (1981); Taylor, *Atomism,* in *Powers, Possessions and Freedom: Essays in Honour of C. B. MacPherson* (A. Kontos ed. 1979); R. Unger, *Knowledge and Politics* (1976).

notions like community, fraternity and a shared social good.[13] It is not that liberals ignore those values altogether; but it is alleged that they give them only an instrumental significance or treat them merely as particular moral causes which individuals may or may not espouse. Partly it is a matter of perspective on society. For liberal theories of rights, the point of reference is the "unencumbered" individual, who is free to shrug off his communal and other allegiances whenever he chooses. The relatively unaffectionate and formalistic language of rights and contract theory is said to be an expression of his essential detachability from affective commitments; its formalism expresses the facts deemed most important about his moral status, without reference to any content or community. Communitarians, on the other hand, take as their point of reference the shared lives of people who regard themselves as, in Sandel's words, "defined to some extent by the community of which they are a part"[14]—people who cannot imagine a standpoint of political judgment over and above their particular communal identity.

It is important to stress that community here is not an *abstract* idea; one's communal identity depends on the particularity of one's past. As Macintyre puts it, "I am someone's son or daughter, someone else's cousin or uncle; I am a citizen of this or that city, a member of this or that guild or profession."[15] Apart from the particularity of these attachments, there is said to be no standpoint for abstract political thought, communal or individual. The discourse of this communitarian politics, then, will be informal and engaged rather than impersonal and abstract. Political thought will be a matter of the discovery and recognition of the particular social selves we are, rather than the deliberate choice and articulation of abstract principles of right. There are also other strands in the communitarian literature—notably a strand of civic republicanism that is by no means so clearly incompatible with the traditional liberal point of view—but these are the ones I deal with in this article.[16]

***

IV.

I have used the marriage example to illustrate these points, but I do not want to give the impression that marriage is my sole concern. There are other areas of law and politics that can be used to make related points about the indispensability of individual rights.

One is the area of welfare rights. It is common to hear laments about the loss of face-to-face charity and caring, whether by individuals or in family groups, and its replacement in modern society by more impersonal systems of welfare agencies and formalized welfare entitlements. Certainly, there is a very important debate to be had about the nature and extent of our provision for need in society—one that I cannot go into here. But it may be worth

---

[13]There is a good general discussion of the communitarian critique in Gutman, *Communitarian Critics of Liberalism,* 14 PHIL. & PUB. AFF. 308 (1985).

[14]*See* Sandel, *Introduction, Liberalism, supra* note 12, at 5.

[15]A. Macintyre, *supra* note 12, 204–05, *See also* M. Sandel, *supra* note 12, at 179.

[16]For a discussion of civic republicanism, *see* H. Arendt, *On Revolution* (1973), B. Smith, *Politics and Remembrance: Republican Themes in Machiavelli, Burke, and Tocqueville* (1985), and *Civic Republicanism and Its Critics,* 14 *Political Theory* 423 (1986) (symposium).

pointing out why the replacement of face-to-face caring by more impersonal structures is not altogether the disaster that some people make it out to be.

Consider care for the elderly. Age brings with it a certain amount of dependence: As one gets older, one's capacity to secure an income diminishes while one's needs increase. There have been societies, perhaps ours in an earlier age, or China, both now and in the past, where the old have been able to count on the support of their adult children as their needs increase and their capacities diminish. That mode of caring strikes us as an attractive one, for it is based on ties of kinship, affection, and love, and it reciprocates in an almost symmetrical way the care that the parent once lavished on her children.

Moreover, it has the advantage of being personal: The care is between this particular old person and her children (who can be sensitive to the detail of her needs), rather than between old people and young people in general. Still, there are good reasons in the modern world why many old people feel less than confident about relying on their children's support. One problem is demographic: Even in kin-oriented societies such as China, there are proportionately fewer working adults to support an increasing population of the aged. But other problems go deeper into modern life. People's lives and careers are complex, shifting, and often risky and demanding. They cannot always guarantee a secure base for themselves, let alone provide an assurance of security for their parents. And people are torn by other motives in modern life which, though not intrinsically hostile to the provision of this care, make it somewhat less certain that this will be something they necessarily want to do.

To insist, then, in a communitarian spirit, that care for the aged should remain the responsibility of the family, we would have to accept either or maybe both of two costs. We would have to place limits on the *other* demands that adult children would be permitted to respond to, the risks they could run, and the mobility they could seek. (I suspect, by the way, that in the present state of things, this would involve limiting once again the capacity of *women* to move and flourish outside the home. A great many of the concerns about communitarianism articulated in this paper are above all *feminist* concerns.) Or, if we were not prepared to do that (and maybe even if we were), we would have to accept the cost of exposing the elderly to a certain amount of insecurity and uncertainty in addition to the other burdens of their age. Neither in this country nor in Europe have people been willing to accept those costs. Instead, we have opted for less personal, less affective modes of care. People are encouraged to purchase an income for their old age in the marketplace, so they can rely on a pension check from a finance house even if they cannot rely on the warm support of their children. And, as a fall-back position, the impersonal agencies of the state guarantee an income, either to all the elderly, or to those who have not made or have not been able to make impersonal provision for themselves. Thus, although we may not care for them on a face-to-face basis, we both provide impersonal structures to enable them to care for themselves, and respond collectively and impersonally as a society to the rights that they have to our support. Our choice of this impersonality is well described in an English context by Michael Ignatieff in his book, *The Needs of Strangers:*

> *As we stand together in line at the post office, while they cash their pension cheques, some tiny portion of my income is transferred into their pockets through the numberless capillaries of the state. The mediated quality of our relationship seems necessary to both of us. They are dependent on the state, not upon me, and we are both glad of it. . . . My responsibilities towards them are mediated through a vast division of labour. In my name a social*

worker climbs the stairs to their rooms and makes sure they are as warm and as clean as they can be persuaded to be. When they get too old to go out, a volunteer will bring them a hot meal, make up their beds, and if the volunteer is a compassionate person, listen to their whispering streams of memory. When they can't go on, an ambulance will take them to the hospital, and when they die, a nurse will be there to listen to the ebbing of their breath. It is this solidarity among strangers, this transformation through the division of labour of needs into rights and rights into care that gives us whatever fragile basis we have for saying that we live in a moral community.[17]

It is not that a system of rights is the only imaginable way in which needs could be dealt with in a caring society. We could set things up in a way that encouraged old people to rely on the warm and loving support of their families. But even if we did that, I think we would still want to set up a system of rights as a fall-back—as a basis on which some *assurance* of support could be given, without risking the insecurity, resentment and indignity of leaving the elderly completely at "the uncertain mercy of their sons and daughters. . . ."[18]

---

[17]M. Ignatieff, *The Needs of Strangers* 9–10 (1984).
[18]*Id.* at 17.

UTILITARIANISM

JOHN STUART MILL

John Stuart Mill (1806–1873) is most often linked with philosophical empiricism and utilitarianism. As a member of Parliament, he was a staunch defender of individual liberties and argued against state interference. In fact, he was one of the first advocates of women's equality. Mill's concept of utilitarianism was a modification of Jeremy Bentham's version in that Mill enriched the concept of pleasure. While Bentham believed that all pleasures, physical and intellectual, were of equal value, Mill considered the "higher" pleasures of the mind as superior. What are the implications of this belief on decision making?

WHAT UTILITARIANISM IS

***

The creed which accepts as the foundation of morals "utility" or the "greatest happiness principle" holds that actions are right in proportion as they tend to promote happiness; wrong as they tend to produce the reverse of happiness. By happiness is intended pleasure and the absence of pain: by unhappiness, pain and the privation of pleasure. To give a clear view of the moral standard set up by the theory, much more requires to be said; in particular, what things it includes in the ideas of pain and pleasure, and to what extent this is left an open question. But these supplementary explanations do not affect the theory of life on which this theory of morality is grounded—namely, that pleasure and freedom from pain are the only things desirable as ends; and that all desirable things (which are as numerous in the utilitarian as in any other scheme) are desirable either for pleasure inherent in themselves or as means to the promotion of pleasure and the prevention of pain.

Now such a theory of life excites in many minds, and among them in some of the most estimable in feeling and purpose, inveterate dislike. To suppose that life has (as they express it) no higher end than pleasure—no better and nobler object of desire and pursuit—they designate as utterly mean and groveling, as a doctrine worthy only of swine, to whom the followers of Epicurus were, at a very early period, contemptuously likened; and modern holders of the doctrine are occasionally made the subject of equally polite comparisons by its German, French, and English assailants.

John Stuart Mill, *Utilitarianism,* chaps, II and V.

When thus attacked, the Epicureans have always answered that it is not they, but their accusers, who represent human nature in a degrading light, since the accusation supposes human beings to be capable of no pleasures except those of which swine are capable. If this supposition were true, the charge could not be gainsaid, but would then be no longer an imputation; for if the sources of pleasure were precisely the same to human beings and to swine, the rule of life which is good enough for the one would be good enough for the other. The comparison of the Epicurean life to that of beasts is felt as degrading, precisely because a beast's pleasures do not satisfy a human being's conceptions of happiness. Human beings have faculties more elevated than the animal appetites and, when once made conscious of them, do not regard anything as happiness which does not include their gratification. I do not, indeed, consider the Epicureans to have been by any means faultless in drawing out their scheme of consequences from the utilitarian principle. To do this in any sufficient manner, many Stoic, as well as Christian, elements require to be included. But there is no known Epicurean theory of life which does not assign to the pleasures of the intellect, of the feelings and imagination, and of the moral sentiments a much higher value as pleasures than to those of mere sensation. It must be admitted, however, that utilitarian writers in general have placed the superiority of mental over bodily pleasures chiefly in the greater permanency, safety, uncostliness, etc., of the former—that is, in their circumstantial advantages rather than in their intrinsic nature. And on all these points utilitarians have fully proved their case; but they might have taken the other and, as it may be called, higher ground with entire consistency. It is quite compatible with the principle of utility to recognize the fact that some kinds of pleasure are more desirable and more valuable than others. It would be absurd that, while in estimating all other things quality is considered as well as quantity, the estimation of pleasure should be supposed to depend on quantity alone.

If I am asked what I mean by difference of quality in pleasures, or what makes one pleasure more valuable than another, merely as a pleasure, except its being greater in amount, there is but one possible answer. Of two pleasures, if there be one to which all or almost all who have experience of both give a decided preference, irrespective of any feeling of moral obligation to prefer it, that is the more desirable pleasure. If one of the two is, by those who are competently acquainted with both, placed so far above the other that they prefer it, even though knowing it to be attended with a greater amount of discontent, and would not resign it for any quantity of the other pleasure which their nature is capable of, we are justified in ascribing to the preferred enjoyment a superiority in quality so far outweighing quantity as to render it, in comparison, of small account.

Now it is an unquestionable fact that those who are equally acquainted with and equally capable of appreciating and enjoying both do give a most marked preference to the manner of existence which employs their higher faculties. Few human creatures would consent to be changed into any of the lower animals for a promise of the fullest allowance of a beast's pleasures; no intelligent human being would consent to be a fool, no instructed person would be an ignoramus, no person of feeling and conscience would be selfish and base, even though they should be persuaded that the fool, the dunce, or the rascal is better satisfied with his lot than they are with theirs. They would not resign what they possess more than he for the most complete satisfaction of all the desires which they have in common with him. If they ever fancy they would, it is only in cases of unhappiness so extreme that to escape from it they would exchange their lot for almost any other, however undesirable in their own eyes. A being of higher faculties requires more to make him happy, is capable probably of more acute suffering, and certainly accessible to it at more points than one of the inferior type; but in spite of these liabilities, he can never really wish to sink into what he feels to be a lower grade of existence. We may give what explanation we please of this unwillingness; we may attribute it to pride, a name which is given indiscriminately to some of the most and to some of the least estimable feelings of which mankind are capable; we may refer it to the love of liberty and personal independence, an appeal to which was with the Stoics one of the most effective means for the inculcation of it; to the love of power or to the love of excitement, both of which do really enter into and contribute to it; but its most appropriate appellation is a sense of dignity, which all human beings possess in one form or other, and in some, though by no means in exact, proportion to their higher faculties, and which is so essential a part of the happiness of those in whom it is strong that nothing which conflicts with it could be otherwise than momentarily an object of desire to them. Whoever supposes that this preference takes place at a sacrifice of happiness—that the superior being, in anything like equal circumstances, is not happier than the inferior—confounds the two very different ideas of happiness and content. It is indisputable that the being whose capacities of enjoyment are low has the greatest chance of having them fully satisfied; and a highly endowed being will always feel that any happiness which he can look for, as the world is constituted, is imperfect. But he can learn to bear its imperfections, if they are at all bearable; and they will not make him envy the being who is indeed unconscious of the imperfections, but only because he feels not at all the good which those imperfections qualify. It is better to be a human being dissatisfied than a pig satisfied; better to be Socrates dissatisfied than a fool satisfied. And if the fool, or the pig, are of a different opinion, it is because they only know their own side of the question. The other party to the comparison knows both sides.

It may be objected that many who are capable of the higher pleasures occasionally, under the influence of temptation, postpone them to the lower. But this is quite compatible with a full appreciation of the intrinsic superiority of the higher. Men often, from infirmity of character, make their election for the nearer good, though they know it to be the less valuable; and this no less when the choice is between two bodily pleasures than when it is between bodily and mental. They pursue sensual indulgences to the injury of health, though perfectly aware that health is the greater good. It may be further objected that many who begin with youthful enthusiasm for everything noble, as they advance in years, sink into indolence and selfishness. But I do not believe that those who undergo this very common change voluntarily choose the lower description of pleasures in preference to the higher. I believe that, before they devote themselves exclusively to the one, they have already become incapable of the other. Capacity for the nobler feelings is in most natures a very tender plant, easily killed, not only by hostile influences, but by mere want of sustenance; and in the majority of young persons it speedily dies away if the occupations to which their position in life has devoted them, and the society into which it has thrown them, are not favorable to keeping that higher capacity in exercise. Men lose their high aspirations as they lose their intellectual tastes, because they have not time or opportunity for indulging them; and they addict themselves to inferior pleasures, not because they deliberately prefer them, but because they are either the only ones to which they have access or the only ones which they are any longer capable of enjoying. It may be questioned whether anyone who has remained equally susceptible to both classes of pleasures ever knowingly and calmly preferred the lower, though many, in all ages, have broken down in an ineffectual attempt to combine both.

From this verdict of the only competent judges, I apprehend there can be no appeal. On a question which is the best worth having of two pleasures, or which of two modes of existence is the most grateful to the feelings, apart from its moral attributes and from its consequences, the judgment of these who are qualified by knowledge of both, or, if they differ, that of the majority among them, must be admitted as final. And there needs be the less hesitation to accept this judgment respecting the quality of pleasures, since there is no other tribunal to be referred to even on the question of quantity. What means are there of determining which is the acutest of two pains, or the intensest of two pleasurable sensations, except the general suffrage of those who are familiar with both? Neither pains nor pleasures are homogeneous, and pain is always heterogeneous with pleasure. What is there to decide whether a particular pleasure is worth purchasing at the cost of a particular pain, except the feelings and judgment of the experienced? When, therefore, those feelings and judgment declare the pleasures derived from the higher faculties to be preferable *in kind,* apart from the question of intensity, to those of which the animal nature, disjoined from the higher faculties, is susceptible, they are entitled on this subject to the same regard.

I have dwelt on this point as being part of a perfectly just conception of utility or happiness considered as the directive rule of human conduct. But it is by no means an indispensable condition to the acceptance of the utilitarian standard; for that standard is not the agent's own greatest happiness, but the greatest amount of happiness altogether; and if it may possibly be doubted whether a noble character is always the happier for its nobleness, there can be no doubt that it makes other people happier, and that the world in general is immensely a gainer by it. Utilitarianism, therefore, could only attain its end by the general cultivation of nobleness of character, even if each individual were only benefited by the nobleness of others, and his own, so far as happiness is concerned, were a sheer deduction from the benefit. But the bare enunciation of such an absurdity as this last renders refutation superfluous.

According to the greatest happiness principle, as above explained, the ultimate end, with reference to and for the sake of which all other things are desirable—whether we are considering our own good or that of other people—is an existence exempt as far as possible from pain, and as rich as possible in enjoyments, both in point of quantity and quality; the test of quality and the rule for measuring it against quantity being the preference felt by those who, in their opportunities to experience, to which must be added their habits of self-consciousness and self-observation, are best furnished with the means of comparison. This, being according to the utilitarian opinion the end of human action, is necessarily also the standard of morality, which may accordingly be defined "the rules and precepts for human conduct" by the observance of which an existence such as has been described might be, to the greatest extent possible, secured to all mankind; and not to them only, but, so far as the nature of things admits, to the whole sentient creation.

***

ON THE CONNECTION BETWEEN JUSTICE AND UTILITY

In all ages of speculation one of the strongest obstacles to the reception of the doctrine that utility or happiness is the criterion of right and wrong has been drawn from the idea of justice. The powerful sentiment and apparently clear perception which that word recalls with a rapidity and certainty resembling an instinct have seemed to the majority of thinkers to point to an inherent quality in things; to show that the just must have an existence in nature as something absolute, generically distinct from every variety of the expedient and, in idea, opposed to it, though (as is commonly acknowledged) never, in the long run, disjoined from it in fact.

***

. . . The idea of justice supposes two things—a rule of conduct and a sentiment which sanctions the rule. The first must be supposed common to all mankind and intended for their good. The other (the sentiment) is a desire that punishment may be suffered by those who infringe the rule. There is involved, in addition, the conception of some definite person who suffers by the infringement, whose rights (to use the expression appropriated to the case) are violated by it. And the sentiment of justice appears to me to be the animal desire to repel or retaliate a hurt or damage to oneself or to those with whom one sympathizes, widened so as to include all persons, by the human capacity of enlarged sympathy and the human conception of intelligent self-interest. From the latter elements the feeling derives its morality; from the former, its peculiar impressiveness and energy of self-assertion.

I have, throughout, treated the idea of a *right* residing in the injured person and violated by the injury, not as a separate element in the composition of the idea and sentiment, but as one of the forms in which the other two elements clothe themselves. These elements are a hurt to some assignable person or persons, on the one hand, and a demand for punishment, on the other. An examination of our own minds, I think, will show that these two things include all that we mean when we speak of violation of a right. When we call anything a person's right, we mean that he has a valid claim on society to protect him in the possession of it, either by the force of law or by that of education and opinion. If he has what we consider a sufficient claim, on whatever account, to have something guaranteed to him by society, we say that he has a right to it. If we desire to prove that anything does not belong to him by right, we think this done as soon as it is admitted that society ought not to take measures for securing it to him, but should leave him to chance or to his own exertions. Thus a person is said to have a right to what he can earn in fair professional competition, because society ought not to allow any other person to hinder him from endeavoring to earn in that manner as much as he can. But he has not a right to three hundred a year, though he may happen to be earning it; because society is not called on to provide that he shall earn that sum. On the contrary, if he owns ten thousand pounds three per cent stock, he *has* a right to three hundred a year because society has come under an obligation to provide him with an income of that amount.

To have a right, then, is, I conceive, to have something which society ought to defend me in the possession of. If the objective goes on to ask why it ought, I can give him no other reason than general utility. If that expression does not seem to convey a sufficient feeling of the strength of the obligation, nor to account for the peculiar energy of the feeling, it is because there goes to the composition of the sentiment, not a rational only but also an animal element—the thirst for retaliation; and this thirst derives its intensity, as well as its moral justification, from the extraordinarily important and impressive kind of utility which is concerned. The interest involved is that of security, to everyone's feelings the most vital of all interests. All other earthly benefits are needed by one person, not needed by another; and many of them can, if necessary, be cheerfully forgone or replaced by something else; but security no human being can possibly do without; on it we depend for all our immunity from evil and for the whole value of all and every good, beyond the passing moment, since nothing but the gratification of the instant could be of any worth to us if we could be deprived of everything the next instant by whoever was momentarily stronger than ourselves. Now this most indispensable of all necessaries, after physical nutriment, cannot be had unless the machinery for providing it is kept unintermittedly in active play. Our notion, therefore, of the claim we have on our fellow creatures to join in making safe for us the very groundwork of our existence gathers feelings around it so much more intense than those concerned in any of the more common cases of utility that the difference in degree (as is often the case in psychology) becomes a real difference in kind. The claim assumes that character of absoluteness, that apparent infinity and incommensurability with all other considerations which constitute the distinction between the feeling of right and wrong and that of ordinary expediency and inexpediency. The feelings concerned are so powerful, and we count so positively on finding a responsive feeling in others (all being alike interested) that *ought* and *should* grow into *must,* and recognized indispensability becomes a moral necessity, analogous to physical, and often not inferior to it in binding force.

If the preceding analysis, or something resembling it, be not the correct account of the notion of justice—if justice be totally independent of utility, and be a standard *per se,* which the mind can recognize by simple introspection of itself—it is hard to understand why that internal oracle is so ambiguous, and why so many things appear either just or unjust, according to the light in which they are regarded.

***

It appears from what has been said that justice is a name for certain moral requirements which, regarded collectively, stand higher in the scale of social utility, and are therefore of more paramount obligation, than any others, though particular cases may occur in which some other social duty is so important as to overrule any one of the general maxims of justice. Thus, to save a life, it may not only be allowable, but a duty, to steal or take by force the necessary food or medicine, or to kidnap and compel to officiate the only qualified medical practitioner. In such cases, as we do not call anything justice which is not a virtue, we usually say, not that justice must give way to some other moral principle, but that what is just in ordinary cases is, by reason of that other principle, not just in the particular case. By this useful accommodation of language, the character of indefeasibility attributed to justice is kept up, and we are saved from the necessity of maintaining that there can be laudable injustice.

The considerations which have now been adduced resolve, I conceive, the only real difficulty in the utilitarian theory of morals. It has always been evident that all cases of justice are also cases of expediency; the difference is in the peculiar sentiment which attaches to the former, as contradistinguished from the latter. If this characteristic sentiment has been sufficiently accounted for; if there is no necessity to assume for it any peculiarity of origin;

if it is simply the natural feeling of resentment, moralized by being made coextensive with the demands of social good; and if this feeling not only does but ought to exist in all the classes of cases to which the idea of justice corresponds—that idea no longer presents itself as a stumbling block to the utilitarian ethics. Justice remains the appropriate name for certain social utilities which are vastly more important, and therefore more absolute and imperative, than any others are as a class (though not more so than others may be in particular cases); and which, therefore, ought to be, as well as naturally are, guarded by a sentiment, not only different in degree, but also in kind; distinguished from the milder feeling which attaches to the mere idea of promoting human pleasure or convenience at once by the more definite nature of its commands and by the sterner character of its sanctions.

SOME PROBLEMS OF UTILITARIANISM

RICHARD A. POSNER

Utilitarianism is not without its detractors. Seventh Circuit Judge Richard Posner, who is well known for his staunch support of cost-benefit analysis in resolving legal disputes, explores several of these in this excerpt from The Economics of Justice.

Two features of utilitarian theory require clarification at the outset.[1] First, it is a theory of both personal morality and social justice. A good man is one who strives to maximize the sum total of happiness (his own plus others'), and the good society is one that seeks to maximize that sum total. Second, the maximand, as most utilitarians view it, is not a particular psychological state—ecstasy or euphoria or whatever—but is the broadest possible concept of satisfaction. Happiness, or utility, is maximized when people (or creatures) are able to satisfy their preferences, whatever those preferences may be, to the greatest possible extent. But this formulation does not exclude the possibility that A may know B's true preferences better than B does—the possibility, that is, of paternalism.

One of the principal criticisms of utilitarianism is that its domain is uncertain. Whose happiness is to count in designing policies to maximize the greatest happiness? Does the happiness of animals count? This issue has been addressed by J. J. C. Smart:

> *Perhaps strictly in itself and at a particular moment, a contented sheep is as good as a contented philosopher. However it is hard to agree to this. If we did we should have to agree that the human population ought ideally to be reduced by contraceptive methods and the sheep population more than correspondingly increased. Perhaps just so many humans should be left as could keep innumerable millions of placid sheep in contented idleness and immunity from depredations by ferocious animals. Indeed if a contented idiot is as good as a contented philosopher, and if a contented sheep is as good as a contented idiot, then a contented fish is as good as a contented sheep, and a contented beetle is as good as a contented fish. Where shall we stop?[2]*

Reprinted from *The Economics of Justice,* with permission of the author.

[1] For some recent expositions of utilitarianism see John Plamenatz, *The English Utilitarians* (1958); J. J. C. Smart, "An Outline of a System of Utilitarian Ethics," in Smart & Williams, *supra* note 2, at 3; Rolf E. Sartorius, *Individual Conduct and Social Norms: A Utilitarian Account of Social Union and the Rule of Law* (1975). Among the classical expositions see in particular Jeremy Bentham, *Introduction to the Principles of Morals and Legislation* (1789); Leslie Stephen, *The English Utilitarians* (1900). As noted earlier, I decline to empty the term utilitarianism of much of its distinctive meaning by defining it as the class of ethical doctrines in which the morality of a course of action is judged by its social consequences.

[2] Smart, *supra* note 1, at 16.

Smart does not answer his last question. Although he finds it "hard to agree" to equating the contented sheep with the contented philosopher, he can find no basis in utilitarian theory for distinguishing them and is left in the end to remark rather lamely that "the question of whether the general happiness would be increased by replacing most of the human population by a bigger population of contented sheep and pigs is not one which by any stretch of the imagination could become a live issue."[3]

Since utility in its broad sense is something possessed by many animals, the theory seems to require including sheep and pigs in the population whose happiness is to be maximized. Smart suggests as much. But there is something amiss in a philosophical system that cannot distinguish between people and sheep. In utilitarian morality, a driver who swerved to avoid two sheep and deliberately killed a child could not be considered a bad man, because his action may have increased the amount of happiness in the world.

We could say, with Frank Knight, that people don't *want* happiness or any other version of satisfaction that might embrace what animals want: "The chief thing which the common-sense individual actually wants is not satisfactions for the wants which he has, but more, and *better* wants."[4] But this is just a version of the old utilitarian game, which leads nowhere, of dividing preferences into "higher" and "lower" on inevitably shifting and subjective grounds.

Another boundary problem of utilitarianism concerns foreigners. Should American policy be to maximize the happiness of Americans, with foreigners' happiness given a zero weight? Or is a more ecumenical perspective required? And how about the unborn? To include them in the population whose happiness is to be maximized may yield policies on abortions, adoptions, homosexuality, savings, and other issues different from those indicated if only the currently living are counted in the happiness census. Whether to include foreigners or the unborn is not an issue that utilitarianism can resolve directly, yet again it seems that if maximizing utility is to be taken seriously, the broadest possible conception of the relevant population must be used.

The problem of foreigners and the unborn is related to the old dispute over whether the utilitarian goal should be to maximize average or total happiness. If the poorer half of the population of Bangladesh were killed, the standard of living—and, for all one knows, the subjective happiness as well— of the remaining half would rise because of the higher ratio of people to land and other natural resources. However, the *total* happiness might be less. Similarly, a high birth rate may cause a reduction in the standard of living of a crowded country and, along with it, in the average happiness of the country, but this loss may be more than offset by the satisfactions, even if somewhat meager, of the added population. There is no clear basis in utilitarian theory for choosing between average and total happiness, but the latter is more consistent with a simple insistence on utility as the maximand.

In summary, the logic of utilitarianism seems to favor setting as the ethical goal the maximization of the total amount of happiness in the universe. Since this goal seems attainable only by making lots of people miserable (those of us who would have to make room for all the foreigners, sheep, or whatever), utilitarians are constantly seeking ways to contract the boundary. But to do so they must go outside of utilitarianism.

---

[3]*Id.* at 24–25.
[4]Frank Hyneman Knight, *The Ethics of Competition, and Other Essays* 22 (1935); see also *id.* at 32.

Another problem is the lack of a method for calculating the effect of a decision or policy on the total happiness of the relevant population.[5] Even within just the human population, there is no reliable technique for measuring a change in the level of satisfaction of one individual relative to a change in the level of satisfaction of another.

The Pareto approach may seem to offer a solution to the problem of measuring satisfaction. A change is said to be Pareto superior if it makes at least one person better off and no one worse off. Such a change by definition increases the total amount of (human) happiness in the world. The advantage of the Pareto approach is that it requires information only about marginal and not about total utilities. And there seems ready at hand an operational device for achieving Pareto superiority, the voluntary transaction, which by definition makes both parties better off than they were before. However, the condition that no one else be affected by a "voluntary" transaction can only rarely be fulfilled. Moreover, the voluntary-transaction or free-market solution to the problem of measuring utility begs two critical questions: whether the goods exchanged were initially distributed so as to maximize happiness (were the people with money those who derive the most happiness from the things money can buy?) and whether a system of free markets creates more happiness than alternative systems of resource allocation would.

Difficulty in deriving specific policies from ethical premises is not, however, unique to utilitarianism; it seems characteristic of ethical discussion generally. Among contemporary Kantian legal rights theorists,[6] one has only to compare Charles Fried and Richard Epstein, who, starting from seemingly identical premises regarding human respect and autonomy, derive sharply different policy implications.[7]

However, the fact that utilitarianism is no more indefinite than competing theories of moral obligation may not reconcile one to utilitarianism, especially if one favors limited government. Suppose, for example, that Bentham was correct in his belief that, lacking any real knowledge of the responsiveness to income of different individuals' happiness, we should assume that every one is pretty much alike in that respect. Then we need make only one additional, and as it happens plausible, assumption—that of the diminishing marginal utility of money income—to obtain a utilitarian basis for a goal of equalizing incomes. For on these assumptions it is easily shown that an equal distribution of income and wealth will produce more happiness than any other distribution[8] unless the costs of achieving and maintaining such a distribution equal or exceed the benefits. The qualification is critical, but it places the burden of proof on the opponent of income equalization in an area where proof is notoriously difficult to come by. This example illustrates a point made in the preceding chapter: if the

---

[5]As Hayek puts it, the practice of utilitarianism presupposes omniscience. 2. F. A. Hayek, *Law, Legislation, and Liberty* 17–23 (1976).

[6]I follow Bruce A. Ackerman, *Private Property and the Constitution* 71–72 (1977), in using the term "Kantian" to refer to a family of related ethical theories that subordinate social welfare to notions of human autonomy and self-respect as criteria of ethical conduct. Such theories need not, and usually do not, resemble closely the thought of Immanuel Kant, on which see Bruce Aune, *Kant's Theory of Morals* (1979).

[7]Among many other differences, Fried rejects Epstein's position that, *prima facie,* tort liability should be strict liability. *See* Charles Fried, *Right and Wrong* 107 (1978); and his *An Anatomy of Values: Problems of Personal and Social Choice* 187–189 (1970).

[8]*See* Jeremy Bentham, "The Philosophy of Economic Science," in 1 *Jeremy Bentham's Economic Writings* 81, 115–116 (W. Stark ed. 1952); Abba P. Lerner, *The Economics of Control: Principles of Welfare Economics* 35–36 (1944); Sartorius, *supra* note 16, at 131.

impracticality of the felicific calculus is taken to justify the utilitarian's use of guesswork, the possibilities for plausible public intervention in private activities are unlimited.

The problem of indefiniteness blends into a related objection to utilitarian thought: what one might term the perils of instrumentalism. If happiness is maximized by allowing people to own property, marry as they choose, change jobs, and so on, then the utilitarian will grant them the rights to these things, but if happiness can be increased by treating people more like sheep, then rights are out the window. People do not seem to be happier in totalitarian than in democratic states, but if they were, the consistent utilitarian would have to support totalitarianism. Utilitarianism thus seems to base rights of great importance on no firmer ground than an empirical hunch that they promote "happiness." That hunch cannot be verified by any tools we have or are likely to acquire—though some people will find one bit of evidence or another (for example, the Berlin wall) persuasive. Even within the framework of the liberal state, utilitarians who are not shy about making bold empirical guesses concerning the distribution of happiness can produce rather monstrous policy recommendations.[9]

"Moral monstrousness" is indeed a major problem of utilitarianism. Two types of monstrousness should be distinguished. One stems from the utilitarian's refusal to make moral distinctions among types of pleasure. Suppose that A spends his leisure time pulling wings off flies, while B spends his feeding pigeons, and because A has a greater capacity for pleasure than B, he derives more happiness from his leisure time. Putting aside the unhappiness of the fly, and the happiness of the pigeons, the consistent utilitarian would have to judge A a better man than B, because A's activity adds more to the sum of happiness than B's.

The other type of moral monstrousness arises from the utilitarian's readiness to sacrifice the innocent individual on the altar of social need. Alan Donagan gives the following example:

> *It might well be the case that more good and less evil would result from your painlessly and undetectedly murdering your malicious, old and unhappy grandfather than from your forebearing to do so: he would be freed from his wretched existence; his children would be rejoiced by their inheritances and would no longer suffer from his mischief; and you might anticipate the reward promised to those who do good in secret. Nobody seriously doubts that a position with such a consequence is monstrous.*[10]

Donagan seems correct in arguing that a consistent utilitarian would have to judge the murderer a good man. The utilitarian could, of course, point out that a *practice* of murdering obnoxious grandfathers would probably reduce happiness. Knowledge of the practice would make grandfathers very unhappy and in the long run would probably not benefit the heirs, because the practice would deter people from accumulating estates. But any utilitarian objections to creating an exception to the murder laws for killers of obnoxious grandfathers have no force at the level of personal morality once it is stipulated that the murder will go undetected. Yet to call the murderer in Donagan's example a "good man" does unacceptable violence to conventional moral notions.

---

[9]It should be mentioned, in fairness to the utilitarians, that Bentham is the principal, and inexhaustible, source of bizarre policy deductions from utilitarian premises. Nonetheless, utilitarians are frequently interventionist. *See, e.g.,* 3 Stephen, *supra* note 1, at 228–229, on J. S. Mill's interventionist proposals.

[10]Alan Donagan, "Is There a Credible Form of Utilitarianism?" In *Contemporary Utilitarianism* 187, 188 (Michael D. Bayles ed. 1968).

Monstrousness is a less serious problem of utilitarianism at the level of social than of personal choice. It is one thing to pick an innocent person at random and kill him to achieve some social end and another to establish an institutional structure—criminal punishment, for example—which makes it inevitable that some innocent people will suffer. No punishment system could be devised that reduced the probability of erroneous conviction to zero. Yet even at the level of social choice, utilitarianism can lead to monstrous results. Were there a group of people at once so few relative to the rest of the society, so miserable, and so hated that their extermination would increase the total happiness of the society, the consistent utilitarian would find it hard to denounce their extermination, although he would be entitled to note the anxiety costs that might be imposed on people who feared they might be exterminated next.

If monstrousness is a peril of utilitarianism, moral squeamishness, or fanaticism, is a peril of Kantian theorists. Bernard Williams poses the case of Jim, the guest of an officer in a backward country who is about to have a group of political prisoners shot.[11] The officer tells Jim that if Jim will shoot one of the prisoners, he will release the others. Williams argues that Jim has no obligation to shoot a prisoner because there is a difference between doing evil and failing to prevent evil. But the difference is hard to see in the example. If Jim declines the officer's invitation, all the prisoners will die; if he accepts it, all but one will be saved. There is no trade-off. No one will be better off if Jim declines the invitation; all but one will be worse off.

Most Kantians try to avoid fanaticism by carving exceptions to the categorical duties they impose.[12] They will say that torture is wrong even if it could be shown (as Bentham believed) to maximize happiness on balance, but will then admit that if torturing one person were necessary to save the human race it would not be wrong to torture him. Once this much is conceded, however, there is no logical stopping point. What if two innocents must be killed to save 200 million Americans—ten to save three million Chicagoans—twenty to save 60,000 residents of one Chicago neighborhood?

The tendency of Kantianism to merge into utilitarianism is illustrated by the moral philosophy of John Rawls. Although his premises are Kantian and he rejects utilitarianism because it does not take seriously the distinction between persons,[13] he defines justice as the outcome of collective choice by individuals in the "original position," that is, stripped of all their individual characteristics. He assumes that these shades choose principles of justice that will maximize their own utility, and because they are also assumed to be highly risk averse, they choose a principle that trades away much individual economic liberty for social insurance. Rawls's principle of social justice resembles Bentham's principle of maximizing income equality subject to the constraint of preserving the individual's incentive to engage in productive activity. In both cases, the optimal degree of equality depends on empirical hunches regarding the size and shape of individuals' marginal-utility schedules and the disincentive effects of egalitarian policies. The necessity of making such hunches imparts to Rawls's theory the same indefiniteness that plagues Bentham's. Rawls's concept of the "veil of ignorance" resembles the method by which the economist Abba Lerner deduced a norm of income equality from the greatest-happiness principle.[14] Lerner said that given

---

[11]*See* Bernard Williams, "A Critique of Utilitarianism," in Smart & Williams, 77, 98–99.
[12]For an example of this approach *see* Fried, *supra* note 7, at 10.
[12]For an example of this approach *see* Fried, *supra* note 7, at 10.
[13]John Rawls, *A Theory of Justice* 27 (1971).
[14]I am indebted to Gary Becker for this point.

our ignorance of the height of people's marginal-utility functions, the best assumption was that they are uncorrelated with income.[15] It is not surprising that another welfare economist, John Harsanyi, anticipated the core of Rawls's principle of justice (rational choice by people in the original position) by many years.[16]

To summarize, utilitarianism has serious shortcomings whether viewed as a system of personal morality or as a guide to social decision making; but Kantianism, the usual alternative, has its own serious defects; one of these is its resemblance to utilitarianism. . . .

---

[15]*See* Lerner, *supra* note 8.

[16]*See* John C. Harsanyi, "Cardinal Utility in Welfare Economics and in the Theory of Risk-Taking," 61 *J. Pol. Econ.* 434 (1953). Rawls acknowledges Harsanyi's contribution. *See* Rawls, *supra* note 13, at 137 n.11, 162 n.21. Harsanyi remains a sophisticated exponent of utilitarianism. *See* his "Morality and the Theory of Rational Behavior," 44 *Soc. Res.* 623 (1977).

THE ONES WHO WALK AWAY FROM OMELAS

Ursula K. Le Guin

One of the concerns with utilitarian theory is that numbers do not always tell the full story. Le Guin illustrates this problem in the following story where one person's intense suffering is insufficient to outweigh the happiness of many. The story begins with a description of Omelas, one of the happiest cities you can imagine, full of festivals, music, and joy for its inhabitants. This excerpt begins following Le Guin's description of that happiness. Consider how you would modify utilitarian theory to account for problems such as those described in this story.

. . . In a basement under one of the beautiful public buildings of Omelas, or perhaps in the cellar of one of its spacious private homes, there is a room. It has one locked door, and no window. A little light seeps in dustily between cracks in the boards, secondhand from a cobwebbed window somewhere across the cellar. In one corner of the little room a couple of mops, with stiff, clotted, foul-smelling heads, stand near a rusty bucket. The floor is dirt, a little damp to the touch, as cellar dust usually is. The room is about three paces long and two wide: a mere broom closet or disused tool room. In the room a child is sitting. It could be a boy or a girl. It looks about six, but actually is nearly ten. It is feeble-minded. Perhaps it was born defective, or perhaps it has become imbecile through fear, malnutrition, and neglect. It picks its nose and occasionally fumbles vaguely with its toes or genitals, as it sits hunched in the corner farthest from the bucket and the two mops. It is afraid of the mops. It finds them horrible. It shuts its eyes, but it knows the mops are still standing there; and the door is locked; and nobody will come. The door is always locked; and nobody ever comes, except that sometimes—the child has no understanding of time or interval—sometimes the door rattles terribly and opens, and a person, or several people, are there. One of them may come in and kick the child to make it stand up. The others never come close, but peer in at it with frightened, disgusted eyes. The food bowl and the water jug are hastily filled, the door is locked, the eyes disappear. The people at the door never say anything, but the child, who has not always lived in the tool room, and can remember sunlight and its mother's voice, sometimes speaks. "I will be good," it says. "Please let me out. I will be good!" They never answer. The child used to scream for help at night, and cry a good deal, but now it only makes a kind of whining, "eh-haa, eh-haa," and it speaks less and less often. It is so thin there are no calves to its legs; its belly protrudes; it lives on a half-bowl of corn meal and grease a day. It is naked. Its buttocks and thighs are a mass of festered sores, as it sits in its own excrement continually.

They all know it is there, all the people of Omelas. Some of them have come to see it, others are content merely to know it is there. They all know that it has to be there. Some of them understand why, and some do not, but they all understand that their happiness, the beauty of their city, the tenderness of their friendships, the health of their children, the wisdom of their scholars, the skill of their makers, even the abundance of their harvest and the kindly weathers of their skies, depend wholly on this child's abominable misery.

This is usually explained to children when they are between eight and twelve, whenever they seem capable of understanding; and most of those who come to see the child are young people, though often enough an adult comes, or comes back, to see the child. No matter how well the matter has been explained to them, these young spectators are always shocked and sickened at the sight. They feel disgust, which they had thought themselves superior to. They feel anger, outrage, impotence, despite all the explanations. They would like to do something for the child. But there is nothing they can do. If the child were brought up into the sunlight out of the vile place, if it were cleaned and fed and comforted, that would be a good thing, indeed; but if it were done, in that day and hour all the prosperity and beauty and delight of Omelas would wither and be destroyed. Those are the terms. To exchange all the goodness and grace of every life in Omelas for that single, small improvement: to throw away the happiness of thousands for the chance of the happiness of one: that would be to let guilt within the walls indeed.

The terms are strict and absolute; there may not even be a kind word spoken to the child.

Often the young people go home in tears, or in a tearless rage, when they have seen the child and faced this terrible paradox. They may brood over it for weeks or years. But as time goes on they begin to realize that even if the child could be released, it would not get much good of its freedom: a little vague pleasure of warmth and food, no doubt, but little more. It is too degraded and imbecile to know any real joy. It has been afraid too long ever to be free of fear. Its habits are too uncouth for it to respond to humane treatment. Indeed, after so long it would probably be wretched without walls about it to protect it, and darkness for its eyes, and its own excrement to sit in. Their tears at the bitter injustice dry when they begin to perceive the terrible justice of reality, and to accept it. Yet it is their tears and anger, the trying of their generosity and the acceptance of their helplessness, which are perhaps the true source of the splendor of their lives. Theirs is no vapid, irresponsible happiness. They know that they, like the child, are not free. They know compassion. It is the existence of the child, and their knowledge of its existence, that makes possible the nobility of their architecture, the poignancy of their music, the profundity of their science. It is because of the child that they are so gentle with children. They know that if the wretched one were not there snivelling in the dark, the other one, the flute-player, could make no joyful music as the young riders line up in their beauty for the race in the sunlight of the first morning of summer.

Now do you believe in them? Are they not more credible? But there is one more thing to tell, and this is quite incredible.

At times one of the adolescent girls or boys who go to see the child does not go home to weep or rage, does not, in fact, go home at all. Sometimes also a man or woman much older falls silent for a day or two, and then leaves home. These people go out into the street, and walk down the street alone. They keep walking, and walk straight out of the city of Omelas, through the beautiful gates. They keep walking across the farmlands of Omelas. Each one goes alone, youth or girl, man or woman. Night falls; the traveler must pass down village streets, between the houses with yellow-lit windows, and on out into the darkness of the fields. Each alone, they go west or north, towards the mountains. They go on. They leave Omelas, they walk ahead into the darkness, and they do not come back. The place they go towards is a place even less imaginable to most of us than the city of happiness. I cannot describe it at all. It is possible that it does not exist. But they seem to know where they are going, the ones who walk away from Omelas.

ARISTOTELIAN ETHICS

CAMILLE ATKINSON AND CANDICE FREDRICK

In the following excerpt, philosophers Atkinson and Fredrick challenge many of Aristotle's key definitions and processes. Such critical analysis is essential when applying theories from centuries ago to modern day issues. For instance, when Aristotle claims that one must receive a "proper upbringing in moral conduct," Atkinson and Fredrick appropriately question the implications of this statement. Consider the nature of a proper upbringing in Aristotle's time as compared with today's version of "moral conduct."

Before turning to this concept, Aristotle makes some important preliminary points about the study of ethics. First, ethical inquiry is not the kind of investigation in which the primary objective is abstract knowledge of the good (as it was for Plato before him); rather, the aim is to become a good person or develop a moral character (an objective similar to Kant's). Knowledge, therefore, has practical consequences, and it is only this kind of knowledge that ethics should be concerned with. "Will not the knowledge of this good, consequently, be very important to our lives? Would it not better equip us, like archers who have a target to aim at, to hit the proper mark? If so, we must try to comprehend in outline at least what this good is.

Aristotle is something of a pragmatist or realist in two respects: he does not regard knowledge as separate from action (i.e., theory is intimately connected to practice); and "the good" is something that can only be roughly or provisionally given (i.e., comprehended "in outline"). Ethics is not an exact science, nor is it conducive to mathematical formulation and/or demonstration. And, to expect it to be so would be a gross misunderstanding of what it entails. "For precision cannot be expected in the treatment of all subjects alike [and] a well-schooled man is one who searches for that degree of precision in each kind of study which the nature of the subject at hand admits."

A second claim Aristotle makes early on lends a degree of irony or paradox to the study of ethics. He asserts that before one can even begin to inquire into the nature of the good "one must first have received a proper upbringing in moral conduct." What does this mean? Is it an indication of Aristotle's elitism, as some would assert? It would appear that in order to become good, it is necessary to be good already. Or, that in order to learn what goodness consists of, one must have already been taught what it is. Doesn't this render any study of ethics superfluous at best, pointless at worst? For if one already possesses knowledge of the good, then there is no need for inquiring further. Or is there?

First, we must remember that an account of the good can only be given "in outline," so any investigation into it can never be complete or exhaustive. We will always need to fill in the blanks, so to speak; thus, our understanding of it will forever be merely provisional. Moreover, Aristotle is really making a much deeper point here: specifically, that the kind of practical wisdom necessary for moral action is not ultimately teachable. It is not simply a matter of learning some basic principles or formulas (like the axioms of geometry) and then applying them consistently in particular cases. If that were true, then why do we not have child prodigies, or geniuses of any age for that matter, in the field of ethics as we do in mathematics, music, or chess? Far from being the mechanical application of universal principles (as Kant, or even Mill, would have us believe), ethical inquiry requires a certain disposition—a desire, tendency, or willingness to do good—as well as a sufficient amount of life "experience" to draw from. This disposition is something that can only be nurtured over time, preferably from childhood on up.

In this sense, Aristotle seems to be validating one of our contemporary assumptions about human psychology; namely, that individuals are affected by their environment and are especially impressionable when they are young. What constitutes a "good upbringing" is certainly a matter of heated debate, and we do not assume that there is only one paradigm for such. But, the idea that it is necessary to instill some moral sensibility and sensitivity in children at an early age and to reinforce this throughout adolescence is rarely a matter of contention. Further, it should be equally clear that if someone has no basic desire to act rightly or avoid wrongdoing, if one does not care to discover what constitutes ethical or unethical action, then no amount of education will ever be sufficient to ensure moral behavior or check immoral behavior. So, what we find in this study of ethics is a blurring of the distinction between feeling and reasoning. Specifically, without the assumption that one cares about morality, we cannot even begin to inquire as to get to what might constitute moral action. Thus, Aristotle's ethics is written for those who at least *want* to know what goodness entails, and this is not something that can be taught in the strict sense.

What about Aristotle's second requirement, [that] of "experience"? What does this mean? Aristotle claims that practical wisdom itself is a form of "perception"—that is, the ability to "see" what kind of action is called for under particular circumstances or to discern what the good would consist of when faced with an actual situation in which a choice must be made. "Practical wisdom is concerned with particulars, as well [as with universals], and knowledge of particulars comes from experience. But a young man has no experience, for experience is the product of a long time." And, once more, this kind of experience cannot be gotten secondhandedly: in other words, it cannot be taught or learned in a formal or academic manner. However, it appears again as if we are stuck in a circle—to be wise requires experience, yet one first needs to be wise in order to reflect upon and understand one's various experiences, making sense of them in such a way that these experiences can provide material for moral deliberation.

Is this an instance of circular reasoning, which one must seek to avoid? Or, is it simply a fundamental and inescapable paradox of human existence? Aristotle suggests the latter, and we would concur. It is one of the essential tragedies of life and, at the same time, one of its cosmic jokes that when we need wisdom the most (when we are young), we are the least likely to have it, although we may think otherwise. When we do seem to have wisdom, we no longer need it as desperately, and can also recognize how elusive it really is. This seems to be life's ultimate paradox—the more we know, the more we know that we know so very little; and the less we know of life, the more certain we are. (Perhaps this is why those who are "experienced" so often try to give their wisdom away by dispensing it to others—again, ironically, to those who need it most but are also the least likely to want or appreciate it!) In sum, practical wisdom is concerned both with "universals" (general principles regarding the good that can only be given roughly or in outline) as well as with "particulars" (those unique and irreducible features of a concrete situation). . . . Martha Nussbaum makes some brilliant observations on this point in the *The Fragility of Goodness*.

NUSSBAUM ON ARISTOTLE

In Chapter 10 of her book, Nussbaum says that we need to ask "what Aristotelian general rules and accounts are and are not, and how the person of practical wisdom uses them." In the very next paragraph, she states that "[o]ne possibility is that the rules and universal principles are guidelines or rules of thumb: summaries of particular decisions, useful for purposes of economy and aids in identifying the salient features of the particular case." Of course, this is an interpretation that remains faithful to Aristotle's admonition that any general account of the good can only be given in outline and that practical wisdom must ultimately take its cue from, and respond to, the particulars of the case at hand. Aristotle criticizes general rules "both for lack of concreteness and for lack of flexibility." Is this not the heart of the criticism of Kant and Mill?—that their theories left both too much room for interpretation and too little room for responding to specific needs or demands. Thus, good deliberation can accommodate the intricacies and messiness of the concrete while simultaneously seeking the universal in the particular—that is, it does not assume that a rule "rules" the particulars; but rather, it allows them "to govern themselves and to be normative for correctness of rule." As Nussbaum states: "[g]ood deliberation accommodates itself to what it finds, responsively and with respect for complexity."

Another way of putting this is that means (the *how* of moral action) and ends (the objective or aim of morality) are codetermined, that "the end itself is only concretely specified in deliberating about the means appropriate to a particular situation." What this entails is that a general rule for action can only be deemed correct retrospectively, as we cannot know beforehand what will follow from the choices that we make. This does leave us vulnerable to some extent to what Nussbaum calls "moral luck," and we really can't expect much more given the complexities of human actions and relations. For instance, let us say that one is faced with a difficult choice between two jobs. While one may involve a substantial salary increase, it will also require moving her family to another state or city and taking on greater responsibility. The other job by contrast may provide greater security, more pleasant work, and working relationships. How can she say ahead of time with any degree of assurance which will be the right choice? What she cannot do is not choose, for even that is ultimately a passive sort of choice. It may turn out that, after taking one of the positions, new information is revealed that confirms or validates the correctness of the choice made. But, how much of this is merely due to "good" luck? And, if the reverse were to occur—she regrets her decision after having acted upon it—could one really claim that the source of error was simply bad deliberation? How can we make sense of this element of moral luck?

Nussbaum distinguishes three features of choice that show why we will always remain vulnerable to these contingencies to some extent, or why it is the case that practical wisdom or moral deliberation can never be systematic. "First, there is the *mutability* or lack of fixity of the practical." As much as we may desire and seek the kind of security and stability provided by universal laws, we live in a world of change that is inherently insecure. Thus, practical wisdom must remain responsive, perhaps even creative, in order to meet the demands of a world that is always in process. Second, there is the *indeterminacy* of the practical. To illustrate this point, Nussbaum calls on an example taken from Aristotle himself where he shows that there can be no comprehensive definition of good joke telling. Just as it is clear that there is no science of humor, as it is closer to an art or creative skill, and that what constitutes a good sense of humor is both culturally and personally variable, so too should we regard ethical deliberation in this light. A good comedian, for example, must be responsive to his or her audience in the same manner in which the practically wise person must be capable of responding to the different demands of a particular situation. In a recent *Time* magazine article this point was made with regard to the debate surrounding artificial intelligence: specifically, that "the hardest thing for computers is the 'simple' stuff. Sure they can play great chess, a game of mechanical rules and finite options. But making small talk is another matter. So, too, with recognizing a face or recognizing a joke." In other words, the article claims, "the biggest challenge is giving machines common sense." This "common sense," whether it means the capacity to make or respond to a joke, perceive the tone in which something is said, or recognize which words or actions would be appropriate in a particular situation, is not something mechanical or scientifically objective. Lastly for Nussbaum, there is the feature of *non-repeatability*—namely, that we must recognize the existence of *ultimate* particulars. "This is in part a function of the complexity and variety already mentioned: the occurrence of properties that are, taken singly, repeatable in an endless variety of combinations make the complex whole situation a non-repeatable particular."

There may be many salient or relevant circumstances that must be taken into consideration in any good deliberation. Again, her health and that of the child, her employment history, as well as the original agreement and interests of the company are all relevant features which, taken as a whole, are non-repeatable. Thus, her employer cannot apply general rules in a mechanical fashion—imposing them upon concrete cases without first "seeing" what the relevant issues are or determining whether or not they fit.

In sum, we cannot expect the kind of comfort afforded by the universal application of basic principles when confronted with ethical choices. Rules have only a limited usefulness: they must be regarded as guiding rather than as binding. They point the way, perhaps with a wave of the hand towards some general direction, but cannot function as definitive markers that point directly at something. Nussbaum refers to them as "tentative guides" or "summaries" that enable us "to be flexible, ready for surprise, prepared to see, resourceful at improvisation." For example, one may say that corporate downsizing is generally wrong, but this does not mean that it is so in all cases. As with lying, there may be good reasons for generally refraining from doing so. However, in some particular instances, there may be even more compelling reasons for not telling the truth or taking steps to reduce a company's overhead costs by eliminating jobs. This should then make clear why Aristotle insists that the person of practical wisdom must have a wealth of experience to draw from. People cannot be good at moral deliberation unless they have been able to cultivate their responsiveness, and maintain their composure under the stress of such decision making. It is this life and work history that allows the wise person to "see" what the universal is which is disclosed or revealed in a particular case. Though it is true that, in one sense, the case is non-repeatable, in another sense, such would be "unintelligible without the guiding and sorting power of the universal."

We now need to turn to the role of this "universal," as thus far the "particular" has taken precedence. For ultimately, Nussbaum asserts that the relationship goes both ways with each illuminating the other. What then is this universal, and how does it act as a guide? And, how do particulars and universals codetermine each other?

It is the experienced person of practical wisdom who acts as the standard of good deliberation and judgment, according to Aristotle. This is the "thoroughly human being" who "does not attempt to take up a stand outside of the conditions of human life, but bases his or her judgment on long and broad experience of these conditions." Moreover, this is not an individual who seeks to escape from or suppress desires and passions (as Kant would have it), but one who has cultivated, and continues to cultivate, these important sources of motivation. However, what the practically wise person desires most of all is to act ethically, and this person will cultivate what is conducive to that. "He or she will be concerned about friendship, justice, courage, moderation, generosity; his desires will be formed in accordance with these concerns; and he will derive from this internalized conception of value many ongoing guidelines for action, pointers as to what to look for in a particular situation." For Aristotle, desires and inclinations are not merely animal impulses indicative of our bestial and amoral nature, as Kant would have us believe. Instead, they are "responsive intentional elements, capable of flexible ethical development." As choice is defined by Aristotle as "deliberate desire," thus placing it in between appetite and reason, it is only through moral choices that values can be made manifest in the world of human relations. And, just as our intellectual faculties can be developed or cultivated, so too can the affective side of our characters be molded along ethical lines or distorted in various ways. This underscores again Aristotle's concern with bringing up children in such a way that they are sensitized to moral issues as soon as possible, since "it is no small matter whether one habit or another is inculcated in us from early childhood; on the contrary, it makes a considerable difference, or, rather, all the difference."

But, who is this person of practical wisdom that brings the universal element to, or makes it manifest in, the particular situation? Is he or she merely an empty ideal or a real possibility? If the latter, then what can we do to encourage such character development?

Nussbaum speaks of this individual as one who is rooted in a community and is committed to a conception of the good life, which is expressed in and includes the values mentioned above. But, most specifically, this is a character who seeks moderation in everything. We could say that this is Aristotle's universal principle. However, it is one that is malleable, and its goodness is dependent upon who is interpreting or applying it. "Proper virtuous choice requires, if it is to be virtue, the combination of correct selection with correct passional response." And, presumably, it is the practically wise person who will have developed this harmonious relation between her passions and reason, which will allow her to make appropriate choices, or to "see" what the appropriate response would be, in any situation. Is this an unrealistic ideal? Perhaps, if we expect such a person to always and forever respond correctly and leave no room for human frailty, fallibility, or luck. However, what is also problematic in Aristotle is the reliance upon the traditional values of the community. For this is a reliance that seems to preclude the possibility of criticism, which would allow one to determine whether these values had become outmoded, stagnant, or even destructive. And, even if we accept some loose conception of friendship and justice, for example, as moral ideals, isn't it possible that the hardest ethical choice a person might be faced with would be one in which these two values conflict? In other words, to what principle do we appeal when the choice is between benefiting a friend or acting justly? Or, put more generally, what do we do when we must choose between two universal goods? Is Aristotle's concept of moderation at all helpful, or even relevant, here?

DISTRIBUTIVE JUSTICE

John Rawls

Contemporary Harvard philosopher John Rawls is known as the father of an ethical theory called distributive justice, which holds that ethical acts or decisions are those that lead to an equitable distribution of goods and services. His description of this approach follows below.

We may think of a human society as a more or less self-sufficient association regulated by a common conception of justice and aimed at advancing the good of its members.[1] As a co-operative venture for mutual advantage, it is characterized by a conflict as well as an identity of interests. There is an identity of interests since social co-operation makes possible a better life for all than any would have if everyone were to try to live by his own efforts; yet at the same time men are not indifferent as to how the greater benefits produced by their joint labors are distributed, for in order to further their own aims each prefers a larger to a lesser share. A conception of justice is a set of principles for choosing between the social arrangements which determine this division and for underwriting a consensus as to the proper distributive shares.

Now at first sight the most rational conception of justice would seem to be utilitarian. For consider: each man in realizing his own good can certainly balance his own losses against his own gains. We can impose a sacrifice on ourselves now for the sake of a greater advantage later. A man quite properly acts, as long as others are not affected, to achieve his own greatest good, to advance his ends as far as possible. Now, why should not a society act on precisely the same principle? Why is not that which is rational in the case of one man right in the case of a group of men? Surely the simplest and most direct conception of the right, and so of justice, is that of maximizing the good. This assumes a prior understanding of what is good, but we can think of the good as already given by the interests of rational individuals. Thus just as the principle of individual choice is to achieve one's greatest good, to advance so far as possible one's own system of rational desires, so the principle of social choice is to realize the greatest good (similarly defined) summed over all the members of society. We arrive at the principle of utility in a natural way: by this principle a society is rightly ordered, and hence just, when its institutions are arranged so as to realize the greatest sum of satisfactions.

The striking feature of the principle of utility is that it does not matter, except indirectly, how this sum of satisfactions is distributed among individuals, any more than it matters, except indirectly, how one man distributes his satisfactions over time. Since certain ways of distributing things affect the total sum of satisfactions, this fact must be taken into account in arranging social institutions; but according to this principle the explanation of common-sense precepts of justice and their seemingly stringent character is that they are those rules which experience shows must be strictly respected and departed from only under exceptional circumstances if the sum of advantages is to be maximized. The precepts of justice are derivative from the one end of attaining the greatest net balance of satisfactions. There is no reason in principle why the greater gains of some should not compensate for the lesser losses of others; or why the violation of the liberty of a few might not be made right by a greater good shared by many. It simply happens, at least under most conditions, that the greatest sum of advantages is not generally achieved in this way. From the standpoint of utility the strictness of common-sense notions of justice has a certain usefulness, but as a philosophical doctrine it is irrational.

If, then, we believe that as a matter of principle each member of society has an inviolability founded on justice which even the welfare of everyone else cannot override, and that a loss of freedom for some is not made right by a greater sum of satisfaction enjoyed by many, we shall have to look for another account of the principles of justice. The principle of utility is incapable of explaining the fact that in a just society the liberties of equal citizenship are taken for granted, and the rights secured by justice are not subject to political bargaining nor to the calculus of social interests. Now, the most natural alternative to the principle of utility is its traditional rival, the theory of the social contract. The aim of the contract doctrine is precisely to account for the strictness of justice by supposing that its principles arise from an agreement among free and independent persons in an original position of equality and hence reflect the integrity and equal sovereignty of the rational persons who are the contractees. Instead of supposing that a conception of right, and so a conception of justice, is simply an extension of the principle of choice for one man to society as a whole, the contract doctrine assumes that the rational individuals who belong to society must choose together, in one joint act, what is to count among them as just and unjust. They are to decide among themselves once and for all what is to be their conception of justice. This decision is thought of as being made in a suitably defined initial situation one of the significant features of which is that no one knows his position in society, nor even his place in the distribution of natural talents and abilities. The principles of justice to which all are forever bound are chosen in the absence of this sort of specific information. A veil of ignorance prevents anyone from being advantaged or disadvantaged by the contingencies of social class and fortune; and hence the bargaining problems which arise in everyday life from the possession of this knowledge do not affect the choice of principles. On the contract doctrine, then, the theory of justice, and indeed ethics itself, is part of the general theory of rational choice, a fact perfectly clear in its Kantian formulation.

Once justice is thought of as arising from an original agreement of this kind, it is evident that the principle of utility is problematical. For why should rational individuals who have a system of ends they wish to advance agree to a violation of their liberty for the sake of a greater balance of satisfactions enjoyed by others? It seems more plausible to suppose that, when situated in an original position of equal right, they would insist upon institutions which returned compensating advantages for any sacrifices required. A rational man would not accept an institution merely because it maximized the sum of advantages irrespective of its effect on his own interests. It appears, then, that the principle of utility would be rejected as a principle of justice, although we shall not try to argue this important question here. Rather, our aim is to give a brief sketch of the conception of distributive shares implicit in the principles of justice which, it seems would be chosen in the original position. The philosophical appeal of utilitarianism is that it seems to offer a single principle on the basis of which a consistent and complete conception of right can be developed. The problem is to work out a contractarian alternative in such a way that it has comparable if not all the same virtues.

In our discussion we shall make no attempt to derive the two principles of justice which we shall examine; that is, we shall not try to show that they would be chosen in the original position.[2] It must suffice that it is plausible that they would be, at least in preference to the standard forms of traditional theories. Instead we shall be mainly concerned with three questions: first, how to interpret these principles so that they define a consistent and complete conception of justice; second, whether it is possible to arrange the institutions of a constitutional democracy so that these principles are satisfied, at least approximately; and third, whether the conception of distributive shares which they define is compatible with common-sense notions of justice. The significance of these principles is that they allow for the strictness of the claims of justice; and if they can be understood so as to yield a consistent and complete conception, the contractarian alternative would seem all the more attractive.

The two principles of justice which we shall discuss may be formulated as follows: first, each person engaged in an institution or affected by it has an equal right to the most extensive liberty compatible with a like liberty for all; and second, inequalities as defined by the institutional structure or fostered by it are arbitrary unless it is reasonable to expect that they will work out to everyone's advantage and provided that the positions and offices to which they attach or from which they may be gained are open to all. These principles regulate the distributive aspects of institutions by controlling the assignment of rights and duties throughout the whole social structure, beginning with the adoption of a political constitution in accordance with which they are then to be applied to legislation. It is upon a correct choice of a basic structure of society, its fundamental system of rights and duties, that the justice of distributive shares depends.

The two principles of justice apply in the first instance to this basic structure, that is, to the main institutions of the social system and their arrangement, how they are combined together. Thus, this structure includes the political constitution and the principal economic and social institutions which together define a person's liberties and rights and affect his life-prospects, what he may expect to be and how well he may expect to fare. The intuitive idea here is that those born into the social system at different positions, say, in different social classes, have varying life-prospects determined, in part, by the system of political liberties and personal rights, and by the economic and social opportunities which are made available to these positions. In this way the basic structure of society favors certain men over others, and these are the basic inequalities, the ones which affect their whole life-prospects. It is inequalities of this kind, presumably inevitable in any society, with which the two principles of justice are primarily designed to deal.

Now the second principle holds that an inequality is allowed only if there is reason to believe that the institution with the inequality, or permitting it, will work out for the advantage of every person engaged in it. In the case of the basic structure this means that all inequalities which affect life-prospects, say, the inequalities of income and wealth which exist between social classes, must be to the advantage of everyone. Since the principle applies to institutions, we interpret this to mean that inequalities must be to the advantage of the representative man for each relevant social position; they should improve each such man's expectation. Here we assume that it is possible to attach to each position an expectation, and that this expectation is a function of the whole institutional structure: it can be raised and lowered by reassigning rights and duties throughout the system. Thus the expectation of any position depends upon the expectations of the others, and these in turn depend upon the pattern of rights and duties established by the basic structure. But it is not clear what is meant by saying that inequalities must be to the advantage of every representative man. . . . [One] . . . interpretation [of what is meant by saying that inequalities must be to the advantage of every representative man] . . . is to choose some social position by reference to which the pattern of expectations as a whole is to be judged, and then to maximize with respect to the expectations of this representative man consistent with the demands of equal liberty and equality of opportunity. Now, the one obvious candidate is the representative man of those who are least favored by the system of institutional inequalities. Thus we arrive at the following idea: the basic structure of the social system affects the life-prospects of typical individuals according to their initial places in society, say, the various income classes into which they are born, or depending upon certain natural attributes, as when institutions make discriminations between men and women or allow certain advantages to be gained by those with greater natural abilities. The fundamental problem of distributive justice concerns the differences in life-prospects which come about in this way. We interpret the second principle to hold that these differences are just if and only if the greater expectations of the more advantaged, when playing a part in the working of the whole social system, improve the expectations of the least advantaged. The basic structure is just throughout when the advantages of the more fortunate promote the well-being of the least fortunate, that is, when a decrease in their advantages would make the least fortunate even worse off than they are. The basic structure is perfectly just when the prospects of the least fortunate are as great as they can be.

In interpreting the second principle (or rather the first part of it which we may, for obvious reasons, refer to as the difference principle), we assume that the first principle requires a basic equal liberty for all, and that the resulting political system, when circumstances permit, is that of a constitutional democracy in some form. There must be liberty of the person and political equality as well as liberty of conscience and freedom of thought. There is one class of equal citizens which defines a common status for all. We also assume that there is equality of opportunity and a fair competition for the available positions on the basis of reasonable qualifications. Now, given this background, the differences to be justified are the various economic and social inequalities in the basic structure which must inevitably arise in such a scheme. These are the inequalities in the distribution of income and wealth and the distinctions in social prestige and status which attach to the various positions and classes. The difference principle says that these inequalities are just if and only if they are part of a larger system in which they work out to the advantage of the most unfortunate representative man. The just distributive shares determined by the basic structure are those specified by this constrained maximum principle.

Thus, consider the chief problem of distributive justice, that concerning the distribution of wealth as it affects the life-prospects of those starting out in the various income groups. These income classes define the relevant representative men from which the social system is to be judged. Now, a son of a member of the entrepreneurial class (in a capitalist society) has a better prospect than that of the son of an unskilled laborer. This will be true, it seems, even when the social injustices which presently exist are removed and the two men are of equal talent and ability; the inequality cannot be done away with as long as something like the family is maintained. What, then, can justify this inequality in life-prospects? According to the second principle it is justified only if it is to the advantage of the representative man who is worse off, in this case the representative unskilled laborer. The inequality is permissible because lowering it would, let's suppose, make the working man even worse off than he is. Presumably, given the principle of open offices (the second part of the second principle), the greater expectations allowed to entrepreneurs has the effect in the longer run of raising the life-prospects of the laboring class. The inequality in expectation provides an incentive so that the economy is more efficient, industrial advance proceeds at a quicker pace, and so on, the end result of which is that greater material and other benefits are distributed throughout the system. Of course, all of this is familiar, and whether true or not in particular cases, it is the sort of thing which must be argued if the inequality in income and wealth is to be acceptable by the difference principle.

We should now verify that this interpretation of the second principle gives a natural sense in which everyone may be said to be made better off. Let us suppose that inequalities are chain-connected: that is, if an inequality raises the expectations of the lowest position, it raises the expectations of all positions in between. For example, if the greater expectations of the representative entrepreneur raises that of the unskilled laborer, it also raises that of the semi-skilled. Let us further assume that inequalities are close-knit: that is, it is impossible to raise (or lower) the expectation of any representative man without raising (or lowering) the expectations of every other representative man, and in particular, without affecting one way or the other that of the least fortunate. There is no loose-jointedness, so to speak, in the way in which expectations depend upon one another. Now with these assumptions, everyone does benefit from an inequality which satisfies the difference principle, and the second principle as we have formulated it reads correctly. For the representative man who is better off in any pair-wise comparison gains by being allowed to have his advantage, and the man who is worse off benefits from the contribution which all inequalities make to each position below. Of course, chain-connection and close-knitness may not obtain; but in this case those who are better off should not have a veto over the advantages available for the least advantaged. The stricter interpretation of the difference principle should be followed, and all inequalities should be arranged for the advantage of the most unfortunate even if some inequalities are not to the advantage of those in middle positions. Should these conditions fail, then, the second principle would have to be stated in another way.

It may be observed that the difference principle represents, in effect, an original agreement to share in the benefits of the distribution of natural talents and abilities, whatever this distribution turns out to be, in order to alleviate as far as possible the arbitrary handicaps resulting from our initial starting places in society. Those who have been favored by nature, whoever they are, may gain from their good fortune only on terms that improve the well-being of those who have lost out. The naturally advantaged are not to gain simply because they are more gifted, but only to cover the costs of training and cultivating their endowments and for putting them to use in a way which improved the position of the less fortunate. We are led to the difference principle if we wish to arrange the basic social structure so that no one gains (or loses) from his luck in the natural lottery of talent and ability, or from his initial place in society, without giving (or receiving) compensating advantages in return. (The parties in the original position are not said to be attracted by this idea and so agree to it; rather, given the symmetries of their situation, and particularly their lack of knowledge, and so on, they will find it to their interest to agree to a principle which can be understood in this way.) And we should note also that when the difference principle is perfectly satisfied, the basic structure is optimal by the efficiency principle. There is no way to make anyone better off without making someone worse off, namely, the least fortunate representative man. Thus the two principles of justice define distributive shares in a way compatible with efficiency, at least as long as we move on this highly abstract level. If we want to say (as we do, although it cannot be argued here) that the demands of justice have an absolute weight with respect to efficiency, this claim may seem less paradoxical when it is kept in mind that perfectly just institutions are also efficient.

Our second question is whether it is possible to arrange the institutions of a constitutional democracy so that the two principles of justice are satisfied, at least approximately. We shall try to show that this can be done provided the government regulates a free economy in a certain way. More fully, if law and government act effectively to keep markets competitive, resources fully employed, property and wealth widely distributed over time, and to maintain the appropriate social minimum, then if there is equality of opportunity underwritten by education for all, the resulting distribution will be just. Of course, all of these arrangements and policies are familiar. The only novelty in the following remarks, if there is any novelty at all, is that this framework of institutions can be made to satisfy the difference principle. To argue this, we must sketch the relations of these institutions and how they work together.

First of all, we assume that the basic social structure is controlled by a just constitution which secures the various liberties of equal citizenship. Thus the legal order is administered in accordance with the principle of legality, and liberty of conscience and freedom of thought are taken for granted. The political process is conducted, so far as possible, as a just procedure for choosing between governments and for enacting just legislation. From the standpoint of distributive justice, it is also essential that there be equality of opportunity in several senses. Thus, we suppose that, in addition to maintaining the usual social overhead capital, government provides for equal educational opportunities for all either by subsidizing private schools or by operating a public school system. It also enforces and underwrites equality of opportunity in commercial ventures and in the free choice of occupation. This result is achieved by policing business behavior and by preventing the establishment of barriers and restriction to the desirable positions and markets. Lastly, there is a guarantee of a social minimum which the government meets by family allowances and special payments in times of unemployment, or by a negative income tax.

In maintaining this system of institutions the government may be thought of as divided into four branches. Each branch is represented by various agencies (or activities thereof) charged with preserving certain social and economic conditions. These branches do not necessarily overlap with the usual organization of government, but should be understood as purely conceptual. Thus the allocation branch is to keep the economy feasibly competitive, that is, to prevent the formation of unreasonable market power. Markets are competitive in this sense when they cannot be made more so consistent with the requirements of efficiency and the acceptance of the facts of consumer preferences and geography. The allocation branch is also charged with identifying and correcting, say, by suitable taxes and subsidies wherever possible, the more obvious departures from efficiency caused by the failure of prices to measure accurately social benefits and costs. The stabilization branch strives to maintain reasonably full employment so that there is no waste through failure to use resources and the free choice of occupation and the deployment of finance is supported by strong effective demand. These two branches together are to preserve the efficiency of the market economy generally.

The social minimum is established through the operations of the transfer branch. Later on we shall consider at what level this minimum should be set, since this is a crucial matter; but for the moment, a few general remarks will suffice. The main idea is that the workings of the transfer branch take into account the precept of need and assign it an appropriate weight with respect to the other common-sense precepts of justice. A market economy ignores the claims of need altogether. Hence there is a division of labor between the parts of the social system as different institutions answer to different common-sense precepts. Competitive markets (properly supplemented by government operations) handle the problem of the efficient allocation of labor and resources and set a weight to the conventional precepts associated with wages and earnings (the precepts of each according to his work and experience, or responsibility and the hazards of the job, and so on), whereas the transfer branch guarantees a certain level of well-being and meets the claims of need. Thus it is obvious that the justice of distributive shares depends upon the whole social system and how it distributes total income, wages plus transfers. There is with reason strong objection to the competitive determination of total income, since this would leave out of account the claims of need and of a decent standard of life. From the standpoint of the original position it is clearly rational to insure oneself against these contingencies. But now, if the appropriate minimum is provided by transfers, it may be perfectly fair that the other part of total income is competitively determined. Moreover, this way of dealing with the claims of need is doubtless more efficient, at least from a theoretical point of view, than trying to regulate prices by minimum wage standards and so on. It is preferable to handle these claims by a separate branch which supports a social minimum. Henceforth, in considering whether the second principle of justice is satisfied, the answer turns on whether the total income of the least advantaged, that is, wages plus transfers, is such as to maximize their long-term expectations consistent with the demands of liberty.

Finally, the distribution branch is to preserve an approximately just distribution of income and wealth over time by affecting the background conditions of the market from period to period. Two aspects of this branch may be distinguished. First of all, it operates a system of inheritance and gift taxes. The aim of these levies is not to raise revenue, but gradually and continually to correct the distribution of wealth and to prevent the concentrations of power to the detriment of liberty and equality of opportunity. It is perfectly true, as some have said,[3] that unequal inheritance of wealth is no more inherently unjust than unequal inheritance of intelligence; as far as possible the inequalities founded on either should satisfy the difference principle. Thus, the inheritance of greater wealth is just as long as it is to the advantage of the worst off and consistent with liberty, including equality of opportunity. Now by the latter we do not mean, of course, the equality of expectations between classes, since differences in life-prospects arising from the basic structure are inevitable, and it is precisely the aim of the second principle to say when these differences are just. Indeed, equality of opportunity is a certain set of institutions which assures equally good education and chances of culture for all and which keeps open the competition for positions on the basis of qualities reasonably related to performance, and so on. It is these institutions which are put in jeopardy when inequalities and concentrations of wealth reach a certain limit; and the taxes imposed by the distribution branch are to prevent this limit from being exceeded. Naturally enough where this limit lies is a matter for political judgment guided by theory, practical experience, and plain hunch; on this question the theory of justice has nothing to say.

The second part of the distribution branch is a scheme of taxation for raising revenue to cover the costs of public goods, to make transfer payments, and the like. This scheme belongs to the distribution branch since the burden of taxation must be justly shared. Although we cannot examine the legal and economic complications involved, there are several points in favor of proportional expenditure taxes as part of an ideally just arrangement. For one thing, they are preferable to income taxes at the level of common-sense precepts of justice, since they impose a levy according to how much a man takes out of the common store of goods and not according to how much he contributes (assuming that income is fairly earned in return for productive efforts). On the other hand, proportional taxes that treat everyone in a clearly defined uniform way (again assuming that income is fairly earned) and hence it is preferable to use progressive rates only when they are necessary to preserve the justice of the system as a whole, that is, to prevent large fortunes hazardous to liberty and equality of opportunity, and the like. If proportional expenditure taxes should also prove more efficient, say, because they interfere less with incentives, or whatever, this would make the case for them decisive provided a feasible scheme could be worked out.[4] Yet these are questions of political judgment which are not our concern; and, in any case, a proportional expenditure tax is part of an idealized scheme which we are describing. It does not follow that even steeply progressive income taxes, given the injustice of existing systems, do not improve justice and efficiency all things considered. In practice we must usually choose between unjust arrangements and then it is a matter of finding the lesser injustice.

Whatever form the distribution branch assumes, the argument for it is to be based on justice: we must hold that, once it is accepted, the social system as a whole—the competitive economy surrounded by a just constitutional legal framework—can be made to satisfy the principles of justice with the smallest loss in efficiency. The long-term expectations of the least advantaged are raised to the highest level consistent with the demands of equal liberty. In discussing the choice of a distribution scheme we have made no reference to the traditional criteria of taxation according to ability to pay or benefits received; nor have we mentioned any of the variants of the sacrifice principle. These standards are subordinate to the two principles of justice; once the problem is seen as that of designing a whole social system, they assume the status of secondary precepts with no more independent force than the precepts of common sense in regards to wages. To suppose otherwise is not to take a sufficiently comprehensive point of view. In setting up a just distribution branch these precepts may or may not have a place depending upon the demands of the two principles of justice when applied to the entire system.

***

The sketch of the system of institutions satisfying the two principles of justice is now complete.

***

In order . . . to establish just distributive shares a just total system of institutions must be set up and impartially administered. Given a just constitution and the smooth working of the four branches of government, and so on, there exists a procedure such that the actual distribution of wealth, whatever it turns out to be, is just. It will have come about as a consequence of a just system of institutions satisfying the principles to which everyone would agree and against which no one can complain. The situation is one of pure procedural justice, since there is no independent criterion by which the outcome can be judged. Nor can we say that a particular distribution of wealth is just because it is one which could have resulted from just institutions although it has not, as this would be to allow too much. Clearly there are many distributions which may be reached by just institutions, and this is true whether we count patterns of distributions among social classes or whether we count distributions of particular goods and services among particular individuals. There are definitely many outcomes and what makes one of these just is that it has been achieved by actually carrying out a just scheme of co-operation as it is publicly understood. It is the result which has arisen when everyone receives that to which he is entitled given his and others' actions guided by their legitimate expectations and their obligations to one another. We can no more arrive at a just distribution of wealth except by working together within the framework of a just system of institutions than we can win or lose fairly without actually betting.

This account of distributive shares is simply an elaboration of the familiar idea that economic rewards will be just once a perfectly competitive price system is organized as a fair game. But in order to do this we have to begin with the choice of a social system as a whole, for the basic structure of the entire arrangement must be just. The economy must be surrounded with the appropriate framework of institutions, since even a perfectly efficient price system has no tendency to determine just distributive shares when left to itself. Not only must economic activity be regulated by a just constitution and controlled by the four branches of government, but a just saving-function must be adopted to estimate the provision to be made for future generations. . . .

NOTES

1. In this essay I try to work out some of the implications of the two principles of justice discussed in "Justice as Fairness," which first appeared in the *Philosophical Review,* 1958, and which is reprinted in *Philosophy, Politics and Society,* Series II, pp. 132–57.

2. This question is discussed very briefly in "Justice as Fairness," *see* pp. 138–41. The intuitive idea is as follows. Given the circumstances of the original position, it is rational for a man to choose as if he were designing a society in which his enemy is to assign him his place. Thus, in particular, given the complete lack of knowledge (which makes the choice one of uncertainty), the fact that the decision involves one's life-prospects as a whole and is constrained by obligations to third parties (e.g., one's descendants) and duties to certain values (e.g., to religious truth), it is rational to be conservative and so to choose in accordance with an analogue of the maximum principle. Viewing the situation in this way, the interpretation given to the principles of justice earlier is perhaps natural enough. Moreover, it seems clear how the principle of utility can be interpreted; it is the analogue of the Laplacean principle for choice uncertainty. (For a discussion of these choice criteria, *see* R. D. Luce and H. Raiffa, *Games and Decisions* [1957], pp. 275–98.)

3. Example F. von Hayek, *The Constitution of Liberty* (1960), p. 90.

4. *See* N. Kaldor, *An Expenditure Tax* (1955).

THE ENTITLEMENT THEORY

ROBERT NOZICK

Nozick's theory is basically ethics according to contract rights. His primary thesis is that liberty upsets patterns. You may have a basic distribution of resources, but given free exchanges, that pattern of distribution will be upset. As long as exchanges are freely entered into, they must (by the definition of free) be ethical. Can you conceive of situations where this might not be so or where it might cause a conflict?

Robert Nozick (b. 1938) believes that everyone is entitled to contractual freedom, and that interfering with that freedom would be unethical. Freedom grants individuals the right to self-development and self-fulfillment. Liberty is a greater societal value than justice. Contrast Nozick's concept of freedom and free exchange with Rawl's patterned distribution.

The minimal state is the most extensive state that can be justified. Any state more extensive violates people's rights. Yet many persons have put forth reasons purporting to justify a more extensive state. It is impossible within the compass of this book to examine all the reasons that have been put forth. Therefore, I shall focus upon those generally acknowledged to be most weighty and influential, to see precisely wherein they fail. In this chapter we consider the claim that a more extensive state is justified, because it is necessary (or it is the best instrument) to achieve distributive justice.

The term "distributive justice" is not a neutral one. Hearing the term "distribution," most people presume that some thing or mechanism uses some principle or criterion to give out a supply of things. Into this process of distributing shares some error may have crept. So it is an open question, at least, whether *re*distribution should take place; whether we should do again what has already been done once, though poorly. However, we are not in the position of children who have been given portions of pie by someone who now makes last-minute adjustments to rectify careless cutting. There is no *central* distribution, no person or group entitled to control all the resources, jointly deciding how they are to be doled out. What each person gets, he gets from others who give to him in exchange for something, or as a gift. In a free society, diverse persons control different resources, and new holdings arise out of the voluntary exchanges and actions of persons. There is no more a distributing or distribution of shares than there is a distributing of mates in a society in which persons choose whom they shall marry. The total result is the product of many individual decisions which the different individuals involved are entitled to make. Some uses of the term "distribution," it is true, do not imply a previous distributing appropriately judged by some criterion (for example, "probability distribution"); nevertheless, despite the title of this chapter, it would be best to use a terminology that clearly is neutral. We shall speak of people's holdings; a principle of justice in holdings describes (part of) what justice tells us (requires) about holdings. I shall state first what I take to be the correct view about justice in holdings, and then turn to the distribution of alternate views.

THE ENTITLEMENT THEORY

The subject of justice in holdings consists of three major topics. The first is the *original acquisition of holdings,* the appropriation of unheld things. This includes the issues of how unheld things may come to be held, the process, or processes, by which unheld things may come to be held, the things that may come to be held by these processes, the extent of what comes to be held by a particular process, and so on. We shall refer to the complicated truth about this topic, which we shall not formulate here, as the principle of justice in acquisition. The second topic concerns the *transfer of holdings* from one person to another. By what processes may a person transfer holdings to another? How may a person acquire a holding from another who holds it? Under this topic come general descriptions of voluntary exchange, and gift and (on the other hand) fraud, as well as reference to particular conventional details fixed upon in a given society. The complicated truth about this subject (with placeholders for conventional details) we shall call the principle of justice in transfer. (And we shall suppose it also includes principles governing how a person may divest himself of a holding, passing it into an unheld state.)

If the world were wholly just, the following inductive definition would exhaustively cover the subject of justice in holdings.

1. A person who acquires a holding in accordance with the principle of justice acquisition is entitled to that holding.
2. A person who acquires a holding in accordance with the principle of justice in transfer, from someone else entitled to the holding, is entitled to the holding.
3. No one is entitled to a holding except by (repeated) applications of 1 and 2.

The complete principle of distributive justice would say simply that a distribution is just if everyone is entitled to the holdings they possess under the distribution.

A distribution is just if it arises from another just distribution by legitimate means. The legitimate means of moving from one distribution to another are specified by the principle of justice in transfer. The legitimate first "moves" are specified by the principle of justice in acquisition.[1] Whatever arises from a just situation by just steps is itself just. The means of change specified by the principle of justice in transfer preserve justice. As correct rules of inference are truth-preserving, and any conclusion deduced via repeated application of such rules from only true premises is itself true, so the means of transition from one situation to another specified by the principle of justice in transfer are justice-preserving, and any situation actually arising from repeated transitions in accordance with the principle from a just situation is itself just. The parallel between justice-preserving transformations and truth-preserving transformations illuminates where it fails as well as where it holds. That a conclusion could have been deduced by truth-preserving means from premises that are true suffices to show its truth. That from a just situation a situation *could* have arisen via justice-preserving means does *not* suffice to show its justice. The fact that a thief's victims voluntarily *could* have presented him with gifts does not entitle the thief to his ill-gotten gains. Justice in holdings is historical; it depends upon what actually has happened. We shall return to this point later.

Not all actual situations are generated in accordance with the two principles of justice in holdings: the principle of justice in acquisition and the principle of justice in transfer. Some people steal from others, or defraud them, or enslave them, seizing their product and preventing them from living as they choose, or forcibly exclude others from competing in exchanges. None of these are permissible modes of transition from one situation to another. And some persons acquire holdings by means not sanctioned by the principle of justice in acquisition. The existence of past injustice (previous violations of the first two principles of justice in holdings) raises the third major topic under justice in holdings: the rectification of injustice in holdings. If past injustice has shaped present holdings in various ways, some identifiable and some not, what now, if anything, ought to be done to rectify these injustices? What obligations do the performers of injustice have toward those whose position is worse than it would have been had the injustice not been done? Or, than it would have been had compensation been paid promptly? How, if at all, do things change if the beneficiaries and those made worse off are not the direct parties in the act of injustice, but, for example, their descendants? Is an injustice done to someone whose holding was itself based upon an unrectified injustice? How far back must one go in wiping clean the historical slate of injustices? What may victims of injustice permissibly do in order to rectify the injustices being done to them, including the many injustices done by persons acting through their government? I do not know of a thorough or theoretically sophisticated treatment of such issues. Idealizing greatly, let us suppose theoretical investigation will produce a principle of rectification. This principle uses historical information about previous situations and injustices done in them (as defined by the first two principles of justice and rights against interference), and information about the actual course of events that flowed from these injustices, until the present, and it yields a description (or descriptions) of holdings in the society. The principle of rectification presumably will make use of its best estimate of subjunctive information about what would have occurred (or a probability distribution over what might have occurred, using the expected value) if the injustice had not taken place. If the actual description of holdings turns out not to be one of the descriptions yielded by the principle, then one of the descriptions yielded must be realized.

The general outlines of the theory of justice in holdings are that the holdings of a person are just if he is entitled to them by the principles of justice in acquisition and transfer, or by the principle of rectification of injustice (as specified by the first two principles). If each person's holdings are just, then the total set (distribution) of holdings is just. To turn these general outlines into a specific theory we would have to specify the details of each of the three principles of justice in holdings: the principle of acquisition of holdings, the principle of transfer of holdings, and the principle of rectification of violations of the first two principles. I shall not attempt that task here. (Locke's principle of justice in acquisition is discussed below.) . . .

HOW LIBERTY UPSETS PATTERNS

It is not clear how those holding alternative conceptions of distributive justice can reject the entitlement conception of justice in holdings. For suppose a distribution favored by one of these nonentitlement conceptions is realized. Let us suppose it is your favorite one and let us call this distribution D_1; perhaps everyone has an equal share, perhaps shares vary in accordance with some dimension you treasure. Now suppose that Wilt Chamberlain is greatly in demand by basketball teams, being a great gate attraction. (Also suppose contracts run only for a year, with players being free agents.) He signs the following sort of contract with a team: In each home game, twenty-five cents from the price of each ticket of admission goes to him. (We ignore the question of whether he is "gouging" the owners, letting them look out for themselves.) The season starts, and people cheerfully attend his team's games; they buy their tickets, each time dropping a separate twenty-five cents of their admission price into a special box with Chamberlain's name on it. They are excited about seeing him play; it is worth the total admission price to them. Let us suppose that in one season one million persons attend his home games, and Wilt Chamberlain winds up with $250,000, a much larger sum than the average income and larger even than anyone else has. Is he entitled to this income? Is this new distribution, D_2, unjust? If so, why? There is *no* question about whether each of the people was entitled to the control over the resources they held in D_1; because that was the distribution (your favorite) that (for the purposes of argument) we assumed was acceptable. Each of these persons *chose* to give twenty-five cents of their money to Chamberlain. They could have spent it on going to the movies, or on candy bars, or on copies of *Dissent* magazine, or of *Monthly Review.* But they all, at least one million of them, converged on giving it to Wilt Chamberlain in exchange for watching him play basketball. If D_1 was a just distribution, and people voluntarily moved from it to D_2, transferring parts of their shares they were given under D_1 (what was it for if not to do something with?), isn't D_2 also just? If the people were entitled to dispose of the resources to which they were entitled (under D_1), didn't this include their being entitled to give it to, or exchange with, Wilt Chamberlain? Can anyone else complain on grounds of justice? Each other person already has his legitimate share under D_1. Under D_1, there is nothing that anyone has that anyone else has a claim of justice against. After someone transfers something to Wilt Chamberlain, third parties *still* have their legitimate shares; *their* shares are not changed. By what process could such a transfer among two persons give rise to a legitimate claim of distributive justice on a portion of what was transferred, by a third party who had no claim of justice on any holding of the others *before* the transfer? To cut off objections irrelevant here, we might imagine the exchanges occurring in a socialist society, after hours. After playing whatever basketball he does in his daily work, or doing whatever other daily work he does, Wilt Chamberlain decides to put in *overtime* to earn additional money. (First his work quota is set; he works time over that.) Or imagine it is a skilled juggler people like to see, who puts on shows after hours.

Why might someone work overtime in a society in which it is assumed their needs are satisfied? Perhaps because they care about things other than needs. I like to write in books that I read, and to have easy access to books for browsing at odd hours. It would be very pleasant and convenient to have the resources of Widener Library in my back yard. No society, I assume, will provide such resources close to each person who would like them as part of his regular allotment (under D_1). Thus, persons either must do without some extra things that they want, or be allowed to do something extra to get some of these things. On what basis could the inequalities that would eventuate be forbidden? Notice also that small factories would spring up in a socialist society, unless forbidden. I melt down some of my personal possessions (under D_1) and build a machine out of the material. I offer you, and others, a philosophy lecture once a week in exchange for your cranking the handle on my machine, whose products I exchange for yet other things, and so on. (The raw materials used by the machine are given to me by others who possess them under D_1, in exchange for hearing lectures.) Each person might participate to gain things over and above their allotment under D_1. Some persons even might want to leave their job in socialist industry and work full time in this private sector. . . . Here I wish merely to note how private property even in means of production would occur in a socialist society that did not forbid people to use as they wished some of the resources they are given under the socialist distribution D_1. The socialist society would have to forbid capitalist acts between consenting adults.

The general point illustrated by the Wilt Chamberlain example and the example of the entrepreneur in a socialist society is that no end-state principle or distributional patterned principle of justice can be continuously realized without continuous interference with people's lives. Any favored pattern would be transformed into one unfavored by the principle, by people choosing to act in various ways; for example, by people exchanging goods and services with other people, or giving things to other people, things the transferrers are entitled to under the favored distributional pattern. To maintain a pattern one must either continually interfere to stop people from transferring resources as they wish to, or continually (or periodically) interfere to take from some persons resources that others for some reason chose to transfer to them. (But if some time limit is to be set on how long people may keep resources others voluntarily transfer to them, why let them keep these resources for *any* period of time? Why not have immediate confiscation?) It might be objected that all persons voluntarily will choose to refrain from actions which would upset the pattern. This presupposes unrealistically (1) that all will most want to maintain the pattern (are those who don't, to be "reeducated" or forced to undergo "self-criticism"?), (2) that each can gather enough information about his own actions and the ongoing activities of others to discover which of his actions will upset the pattern, and (3) that diverse and far-flung persons can coordinate their actions to dove-tail into the pattern. Compare the manner in which the market is neutral among persons' desires, as it reflects and transmits widely scattered information via prices, and coordinates persons' activities.

It puts things perhaps a bit too strongly to say that every patterned (or end-state) principle is liable to be thwarted by the voluntary actions of the individual parties transferring some of their shares they receive under the principle. For perhaps some *very* weak patterns are not so thwarted. Any distributional pattern with any egalitarian component is overturnable by the voluntary actions of individual persons over time; as is every patterned condition with sufficient content so as actually to have been proposed as presenting the central core of distributive justice. Still, given the possibility that some weak conditions or patterns may not be unstable in this way, it would be better to formulate an explicit description of the kind of interesting and contentful patterns under discussion, and to prove a theorem about their instability. Since the weaker the patterning, the more likely it is that the entitlement system itself satisfies it, a plausible conjecture is that any patterning either is unstable or is satisfied by the entitlement system.

NOTE

1. Applications of the principle of justice in acquisition may also occur as part of the move from one distribution to another. You may find an unheld thing now and appropriate it. Acquisitions also are to be understood as included when, to simplify, I speak only of transitions by transfers.

CLOSING ARGUMENT IN LEOPOLD AND LOEB CASE

CLARENCE DARROW

Clarence Darrow (1857–1938) was considered one of the most effective orators of his time. He is perhaps best known for his role as defense attorney during the famous Scopes trial in 1925 during which he defended the right to teach Charles Darwin's theory of evolution. The excerpt that follows is taken from Darrow's oral argument to the court in the appeal for the lives of Richard Loeb and Nathan Leopold, two affluent young men who were convicted of kidnapping and murdering Robert Franks, age 14. Darrow's job was not to reverse the conviction but to persuade the court not to impose the death penalty as a sentence. In doing so (and winning), Darrow discussed the concept of evil as human nature.

It is interesting to also consider Leopold's thoughts after the murder about his motive and about how he felt at the time:[1]

> *My motive, so far as I can be said to have had one, was to please Dick. Just that—incredible as it sounds. I thought so much of the guy that I was willing to do anything—even commit murder—if he wanted it bad enough. And he wanted to do this—very badly indeed. For the commission of the crime itself, I had no enthusiasm. Instead, I had a feeling of deep repugnance.... It was just an experiment. It is as easy for us to justify as an entomologist in impaling a beetle on a pin.*

> ***

> *'Well,' I said to myself, 'it's over. There's no turning back now. How on earth could I ever have got involved in this thing? It was horrible—more horrible even than I figured it was going to be. But that's behind me now. Somehow I never believed that it would happen—that we'd actually go through with it. But it's done. And now, at least, there aren't any decisions to make. I'll be able to put all my thought on not making any slips—on staying one jump ahead of the police. But that's nonsense! Nobody's ever going to suspect me. I wish it weren't over with—that there were still time to change my*

Attorney for the Damned, Arthur Weinberg, ed., pp. 42–44, 49–50, 86–88. Copyright 1957, 1989 by Arthur Weinberg. Reprinted with permission of Lila Weinberg.

[1]This and following quotes were taken from The Leopold and Loeb Trial web page, maintained by Prof. Douglas Linder, *http://www.law.umkc.edu/faculty/projects/ftrials/leoploeb/LEO_LEOW.HTM.*

mind. But what's the use of wishing things that are impossible? The thing I've got to do now is be careful to do all the ordinary, normal things just as I've always done them. I'll stop at a drugstore and call Connie to confirm our date for tomorrow night.'

When asked what he felt about the possibility of the death penalty in the form of a hanging, Leopold responded:

It had been my own personal preference at the outset to make no attempt to avoid the extreme penalty. I had desired to plead not guilty and, by refraining from offering any defense whatsoever, positively to court execution. My reasons for this view were twofold: first, I believed, and evidently Judge Caverly agreed, that speedy execution of the death penalty would be much easier for us defendants than the slow, day-by-day torture of spending the rest of our lives in prison. Second, I felt that the pain to our families and the humiliation and shame they must suffer would, in the long run, be less if we were hanged than if we were sentenced to life imprisonment. The shock and the grief were enormous in either event, but I hoped that with Dick and me removed from the scene the wound might begin slowly to heal and the memory to become gradually less vivid and painful. So long as we were alive and in prison I feared that we should be a festering sore, that we should be subjected to periodic bursts of publicity in the newspapers, and that the anguish we had caused our families would never be allowed to abate. I might say that in the thirty-three years that have elapsed I have found no reason to change my mind.

Looking back from the vantage point of today, I cannot understand how my mind worked then. For I can recall no feeling then of remorse. Remorse did not come until later, much later. It did not begin to develop until I had been in prison for several years; it did not reach its full flood for perhaps ten years. Since then, for the past quarter century, remorse has been my constant companion. It is never out of my mind. Sometimes it overwhelms me completely, to the extent that I cannot think of anything else.

. . . What do they want? Tell me, is a lifetime for the young boys spent behind prison bars—is that not enough for this mad act? And is there any reason why this great public should be regaled by a hanging?

I cannot understand it, Your Honor. It would be past belief, excepting that to the four corners of the earth the news of this weird act has been carried and men have been stirred, and the primitive has come back, and the intellect has been stifled, and men have been controlled by feelings and passions and hatred which should have died centuries ago.

My friend Savage pictured to you the putting of this dead boy in this culvert. Well, no one can minutely describe any killing and not make it shocking. It is shocking. It is shocking because we love life and because we instinctively draw back from death. It is shocking wherever it is and however it is, and perhaps all death is almost equally shocking.

But here is the picture of a dead boy, past pain, when no harm can come to him, put in a culvert, after taking off his clothes so that the evidence would be destroyed; and that is pictured to this court as a reason for hanging. Well, Your Honor, that does not appeal to me as strongly as the hitting over the head of little Robert Franks with a chisel. The boy was dead.

I could say something about the death penalty that, for some mysterious reason, the State wants in this case. Why do they want it? To vindicate the law? Oh, no. The law can be vindicated without killing anyone else. It might shock the fine sensibilities of the state's counsel that this boy was put into a culvert and left after he was dead, but, Your Honor, I can think of a scene that makes this pale into insignificance. I can think, and only think, Your Honor, of taking two boys, one eighteen and the other nineteen, irresponsible, weak, diseased, penning them in a cell, checking off the days and the hours and the minutes until they will be taken out and hanged. Wouldn't it be a glorious day for Chicago? Wouldn't it be a glorious triumph for the state's attorney? Wouldn't it be a glorious triumph of justice in this land? Wouldn't it be a glorious illustration of Christianity and kindness and charity? I can picture them, wakened in the gray light and morning, furnished a suit of clothes by the State, led to the scaffold, their feet tied, black caps drawn over their heads, stood on a trap door, the hangman pressing a spring so that it gives way under them; I can see them fall through space—and—stopped by the rope around their necks.

This would surely expiate placing Bobby Franks in the culvert after he was dead. This would doubtless bring immense satisfaction to some people. It would bring a greater satisfaction because it would be done in the name of justice. I am always suspicious of righteous indignation. Nothing is more cruel than righteous indignation. To hear young men talk glibly of justice. Well, it would make me smile if it did not make me sad. Who knows what it is? Does Mr. Savage know? Does Mr. Crowe know? Do I know? Does Your Honor know? Is there any human machinery for finding it out? Is there any man who can weigh me and say what I deserve? Can Your Honor? Let us be honest. Can Your Honor appraise yourself, and say what you deserve? Can Your Honor appraise these two young men and say what they deserve? Justice must take account of infinite circumstances which a human being cannot understand.

If there is such a thing as justice it could only be administered by one who knew the inmost thoughts of the man to whom he was meting it out. Aye, who knew the father and mother and the grandparents and the infinite number of people back of him. Who knew the origin of every cell that went into the body, who could understand the structure and how it acted. Who could tell how the emotions that sway the human being affected that particular frail piece of clay. It means more than that. It means that you must appraise every influence that moves men, the civilization where they live, and all society which enters into the making of the child or the man! If Your Honor can do it—if you can do it you are wise, and with wisdom goes mercy.

No one with wisdom and with understanding, no one who is honest with himself and with his own life, whoever he may be, no one who has seen himself the prey and the sport and the plaything of the infinite forces that move man, no one who has tried and who has failed—and we have all tried and we have all failed—no one can tell what justice is for someone else or for himself; and the more he tries and the more responsibility he takes, the more he clings to mercy as being the one thing which he is sure should control his judgment of men.

It is not so much mercy either, Your Honor. I can hardly understand myself pleading to a court to visit mercy on two boys by shutting them into a prison for life.

For life! Where is the human heart that would not be satisfied with that?

Where is the man or woman who understands his own life and who has a particle of feeling that could ask for more? Any cry for more roots back to the hyena; it roots back to the hissing serpent; it roots back to the beast and the jungle. It is not a part of man. It is not a part of that feeling which, let us hope, is growing, though scenes like this sometimes make me doubt that it is growing. It is not a part of that feeling of mercy and pity and understanding of each other which we believe has been slowly raising man from his low estate. It is not a part of the finer instincts which are slow to develop; of the wider knowledge which is slow to come, and slow to move us when it comes. It is not a part of all that makes the best there is in man. It is not a part of all that promises any hope for the future and any justice for the present. And must I ask that these boys get mercy by spending the rest of their lives in prison, year following year, month following month, and day following day, with nothing to look forward to but hostile guards and stone walls? It ought not to be hard to get that much mercy in any court in the year 1924.

These boys left this body down in the culvert, and they came back and telephoned home that they would be too late for supper. Here, surely, was an act of consideration on the part of Leopold, telephoning home that he would be late for supper. Dr. Krohn says he must be able to think and act because he could do this. But the boy who, through habit, would telephone his home that he would be late for supper had not a tremor or a thought or a shudder at taking the life of little Bobby Franks for nothing, and he has not had one yet. He was in the habit of doing what he did when he telephoned—that was all; but in the presence of life and death, and a cruel death, he had no tremor and no thought. . . .

. . . You know it has been done too many times. And here for the first time, under these circumstances, this court is told that you must make an example. . . .

Can you administer law without consideration? Can you administer what approaches justice without it? Can this court or any court administer justice by consciously turning his heart to stone and being deaf to all the finer instincts which move men? Without those instincts I wonder what would happen to the human race?

If a man could judge a fellow in coldness without taking account of his own life, without taking account of what he knows of human life, without some understanding—how long would we be a race of real human beings? It has taken the world a long time for man to get to even where he is today. If the law was administered without any feeling of sympathy or humanity or kindliness, we would begin our long, slow journey back to the jungle that was formerly our home.

How many times has assault with intent to rob or kill been changed in these courts to assault and battery? How many times has felony been waived in assault with a deadly weapon and a man or boy given a chance? And we are asking a chance to be shut up in stone walls for life. For life. It is hard for me to think of it, but that is the mercy we are asking from this court, which we ought not to be required to ask, and which we should have as a matter of right in this court and which I have faith to believe we will have as a matter of right.

Is this new? Why, I undertake to say that even the state's attorney's office—and if he denies it I would like to see him bring in the records—I will undertake to say that in three cases out of four of all kinds and all degrees, clemency has been shown.

Three hundred and forty murder cases in ten years with a plea of Guilty in this county. All the young who pleaded guilty, every one of them—three hundred and forty in ten years with one hanging on a plea of Guilty, and that a man forty years of age. And yet they say we come here with a preposterous plea for mercy. When did any plea for mercy become preposterous in any tribunal in all the universe?

We are satisfied with justice, if the court knows what justice is, or if any human being can tell what justice is. If anybody can look into the minds and hearts and the lives and the origin of these two youths and tell what justice is, we would be content. But nobody can do it without imagination, without sympathy, without kindliness, without understanding, and I have faith that this Court will take this case, with his conscience, and his judgment and his courage and save these boys' lives.

Now, Your Honor, let me go a little further with this. I have gone over some of the high spots in this tragedy. This tragedy has not claimed all the attention it has had on account of its atrocity. There is nothing to that.

What is it?

There are two reasons, and only two that I can see. First is the reputed extreme wealth of these families; not only the Loeb and Leopold families, but the Franks family, and of course it is unusual. And next is the fact it is weird and uncanny and motiveless. That is what attracted the attention of the world.

Many may say now that they want to hang these boys; but I know that giving the people blood is something like giving them their dinner. When they get it they go to sleep. They may for the time being have an emotion, but they will bitterly regret it. And I undertake to say that if these two boys are sentenced to death and are hanged, on that day a pall will settle over the people of this land that will be dark and deep, and at least cover every humane and intelligent person with its gloom. I wonder if it will do good. I wonder if it will help the children—and there is an infinite number like these. I marveled when I heard Mr. Savage talk. I do not criticize him. He is young and enthusiastic. But has he ever read anything? Has he ever thought? Was there ever any man who had studied science, who has read anything of criminology or philosophy—was there ever any man who knew himself who could speak with the assurance with which he speaks? . . .

Your Honor stands between the past and the future. You may hang these boys; you may hang them by the neck until they are dead. But in doing it you will turn your face toward the past. In doing it you are making it harder for every other boy who, in ignorance and darkness, must grope his way through the mazes which only childhood knows. In doing it you will make it harder for unborn children. You may save them and make it easier for every child that sometime may stand where these boys stand. You will make it easier for every human being with an aspiration and a vision and a hope and a fate.

I am pleading for the future; I am pleading for a time when hatred and cruelty will not control the hearts of men, when we can learn by reason and judgment and understanding and faith that all life is worth saving, and that mercy is the highest attribute of man.

I feel that I should apologize for the length of time I have taken. This case may not be as important as I think it is, and I am sure I do not need to tell this court, or to tell my friends that I would fight just as hard for the poor as for the rich. If I should succeed in saving these boys' lives and do nothing for the progress of the law, I should feel sad, indeed. If I can succeed, my greatest reward and my greatest hope will be that I have done something for the tens of thousands of other boys, for the countless unfortunates who must tread the same road in blind childhood that these poor boys have trod; that I have done something to help human understanding, to temper justice with mercy, to overcome hate with love.

I was reading last night of the aspiration of the old Persian poet, Omar Khayyam. It appealed to me as the highest that I can vision. I wish it was in my heart, and I wish it was in the hearts of all.

> So I be written in the Book of Love,
>
> I do not care about that Book above;
>
> Erase my name or write it as you will,
>
> So I be written in the Book of Love.

Tears were streaming down the judge's face as Darrow finished his plea. A newspaper reported, "The stuffed courtroom was like a black hole. Hardly a breath of air moved in it. Yet the crowd that was massed around Darrow sat motionless in attention as the weary old man gathered up all the threads of his argument for the final restatement."

Another newspaper said the lines in Darrow's face were "deeper, the eyes haggard. But there was no sign of physical weariness in the speech, only a spiritual weariness with the cruelties of the world."

Chicago newspapers and many others throughout the country printed Darrow's more-than-twelve-hour plea in full or in part.

A newspaper reporter said, "There was scarcely any telling where his voice had finished and where silence had begun. His own eyes were not the only ones that held tears."

State's Attorney Crowe summed up the case for the State. He talked for two days. Court adjourned.

On September 10, 1924, the Chief Justice of the Criminal Court of Cook County sentenced the defendants to imprisonment for life on the murder indictment and 99 years on the kidnapping charge.

Editorialized the *New York Morning Telegram* the following day: "Law, the bastard daughter of justice, handed her mother a frightful beating in Chicago yesterday."

The *New York Times* said: "Had the youthful murderers been poor and friendless, they would have escaped capital punishment precisely as Leopold and Loeb have escaped it."

The boys were taken to Joliet penitentiary.

There, twelve years later, Loeb was killed in a prison fight. Leopold, who is still in the penitentiary, has made several unsuccessful pleas for his freedom.

Since this excerpt was written, Leopold was released from prison and died from natural causes.

WHENEVER I NEED TO DO SOME SERIOUS THINKING . . .

WATTERSON

"Whenever I need to do some serious thinking. . . ," "Calvin & Hobbes" cartoon by Watterson. Reprinted with permission of Universal Press Syndicate.

Chapter 2

APPLICATION OF TRADITIONAL THEORIES TO MODERN BUSINESS DECISION MAKING

Give each man thy ear, but few thy voice.
Take each man's censure but reserve thy judgment.

—POLONIUS'S ADVICE TO
HIS DEPARTING SON,
LAERTES, IN *HAMLET,*
ACT 1, SCENE 3

The person who is trustworthy in very small matters is also trustworthy in great ones; and the person who is dishonest in very small matters is also dishonest in great ones.

—LUKE 16:10

A. MORAL REASONING AND MODELS

In answering the question in the text introduction to Chapter 1 about your grandmother's request at her deathbed, you resorted to *some form* of decision making. Perhaps you might call it gut instinct. Moral reasoning is a more intentional form of decision making where the actor considers the basis for and implications of the decision before acting. The decision maker considers evidence and reaches conclusions, or judgments, about the right and wrong way to act. Moral reasoning can suffer from being too absolute (where one believes that the same rule applies, no matter the circumstances) or from being too relativistic (where the answer always seems to depend entirely on the circumstances).

In order to avoid these two extremes, one might look to a model of reasoning such as the traditional *stakeholder* model of decision making. Stakeholders include all of the groups and/or individuals affected by a decision, policy, or operation of a firm or individual. Stakeholder theory suggests that, in reaching ethical decisions, we respond to the following inquiries:

A. What is the moral dimension? What is the ethical issue?
B. Who are the interested parties? Who is impacted? What are their relationships?
C. What values are involved?
D. What alternatives do you have in your decision?
E. What is the weight of the benefits and the burdens of each alternative on each impacted party?
F. Are there any analogous cases?
G. Can I discuss the case with relevant others? Can I gather additional opinions or perspectives?
H. Is the decision in line with legal and organizational rules?
I. Am I *comfortable* with the decision? Can I live with it?[1]

Other approaches may prove just as useful. Philosophers/ethicists often ask the decision maker to consider whether she or he would feel all right if *The New York Times* (or whatever is your relevant daily newspaper) printed this decision as a front page article, or whether it could be explained to a 10-year-old child so that the child thinks it is the right decision, or whether it will stand the test of time through generations in the firm.

Philosopher Laura Nash suggests asking oneself 12 questions prior to reaching a decision in an ethical dilemma:

---

[1] Adapted from Chris MacDonald, University of British Columbia Centre for Applied Ethics, "A Guide to Moral Decision Making," http://www.ethics.ubc.ca/~chrismac.

1. Have your defined the problem accurately?
2. How would you define the problem if you stood on the other side of the fence?
3. How did the situation occur in the first place?
4. Who was involved in the situation in the first place?
5. What is your intention in making this decision?
6. How does this intention compare with likely results?
7. Who could your decision or action injure?
8. Can you engage the affected parties in a discussion of the problem before you make your decision?
9. Are you confident that your decision will be as valid over a long period as it seems now?
10. Could you disclose without qualms your decision or action to your boss, your CEO, the board of directors, your family, or society as a whole?
11. What is the symbolic potential of your action if understood?
12. Under what conditions would you allow exceptions to your stand?[2]

A simple, two-step approach seems to consolidate many of the issues and questions raised by the elaborate processes discussed above. In evaluating any decision, consider two elements: your *integrity and accountability.* Integrity, meaning consistency in values, would require that the decision maker define her or his values, as well as create a prioritization of those values. Then, when faced with a dilemma or conflict between two or more of these values, the decision maker will have internal guidance regarding the direction her or his decision should take. Second, no matter which direction is taken, the decision maker must be accountable to all stakeholders who are impacted by this decision. That would require a consideration of the alternatives available and the impact of each alternative on each stakeholder.

For instance, assume that times are very tough at your firm and that your superior has informed you that you must cut 10 percent of your present 50-person workforce in order to help the firm avoid a possible bankruptcy filing. You will consider the values at stake and reach some decision about whom to terminate. However, in terminating employees, you offer the employees as much notice as possible, you do not walk them out under armed guard, you offer outplacement counseling to help them to continue their lives, and so on. You accept responsibility for the impact of your decision on those affected.

Integrity (*gives guidance as to what to do in a conflict*):
- Discern what is right and wrong (personal values).
- Act on what you have discerned (your values).
- Say openly that you are acting on what you have discerned.

Accountability:
- Identify possible courses of action in line with values.
- Identify impact of decision on others and their impact on you.
- *Balance that impact with personal interests.*
- Be accountable to others when you choose to impact them.

---

[2]Laura Nash, "Ethics Without the Sermon," *Harvard Business Review* 56, no. 6 (1981), pp. 80–81.

B. MORAL DECISION MAKING IN BUSINESS: INDIVIDUAL PROCESSES

No one teaches or takes a course in business ethics without hearing the all-too-familiar refrain, "Hey, isn't business ethics an oxymoron?" On the other hand, some argue that ethics is a natural market consequence of business. Scholars George and John Steiner have identified six primary sources of ethics in the American business arena.

1. *Genetic inheritance.* Although the view remains theoretical, sociobiologists have in recent years amassed persuasive evidence and arguments suggesting that the evolutionary forces of natural selection influence the development of traits such as cooperation and altruism that lie at the core of our ethical systems. Those qualities of goodness often associated with ethical conduct may, in some measure, be a product of genetic traits strengthened over time by the evolutionary process.

2. *Religion.* Via a rule exemplified by the Golden Rule (or its variations in many religions) and the Ten Commandments, religious morality is clearly a primary force in shaping our societal ethics. The question here concerns the applicability of religious ethics to the business community. The question is all the more relevant since the Golden Rule is not limited to Western thought. Consider these words of Confucius:

> *There are four things in the Way of the profound person, none of which I have been able to do. To serve my father as I would expect my son to serve me. To serve my ruler as I would expect my ministers to serve me. To serve my elder brother as I would expect my younger brothers to serve me. To be the first to treat friends as I would expect them to treat me. These I have not been able to do.[3]*

Could the Golden Rule serve as a universal, practical, helpful standard for the business person's conduct?

3. *Philosophical systems.* To the Epicureans, the quality of pleasure to be derived from an act was the essential measure of its goodness. The Stoics, like the Puritans and many contemporary Americans, advocated a disciplined, hardworking, thrifty lifestyle. These philosophies and others, like those cited earlier, have been instrumental in our society's moral development.

4. *Cultural experience.* Here, the Steiners refer to the rules, customs, and standards transmitted from generation to generation as guidelines for appropriate conduct. Individual values are shaped in large measure by the norms of the society.

5. *The legal system.* Laws represent a rough approximation of society's ethical standards. Thus, the law serves to educate us about the ethical course in life. The law does not and, most would agree, should not be treated as a vehicle for expressing all of society's ethical preferences. Rather, the law is an ever-changing approximation of current perceptions of right and wrong.

6. *Codes of conduct.* Steiner and Steiner identify three primary categories of such codes. Company codes, ordinarily brief and highly generalized, express broad expectations about fit conduct. Second, company operating policies often contain an ethical dimension.

---

[3]Confucius, *The Doctrine of The Mean*, ch. 13; *The Analects*, XIV: 28.

Express policies as to gifts, customer complaints, hiring, and other decisions serve as a guide to conduct and as a shield by which the employee can protect against unethical advances from those outside the firm. Third, many professional and industry associations have developed codes of ethics, such as the Affirmative Ethical Principles of the American Institute of Certified Public Accountants. (Codes of conduct are further discussed in Chapter 7.) In sum, codes of conduct seem to be a growing expression of the business community's sincere concern about ethics. However, the utility of such codes remains unsettled.

What forces determine which companies or businesspersons end up ethical and which do not? Psychologist Lawrence Kohlberg believes that some individuals are simply better prepared to make ethical judgments than are others. He built a comprehensive theory of moral development in which he claimed that moral judgment evolves and improves primarily as a function of age and education.

Kohlberg, via interviews with children as they aged, was able to identify moral development as movement through distinct stages, with the later stages being viewed as more advanced than the earlier ones. Kohlberg identified six universal stages grouped into three levels:

Preconventional level (Level 1):

Stage 1:   Obey rules to avoid punishment.

Stage 2:   Follow rules only if it is in own interest, but let others do the same. Conform to secure rewards.

Conventional level (Level 2):

Stage 3:   Conform to meet the expectations of others. Please others. Adhere to stereotypical images.

Stage 4:   Doing right is one's duty. Obey the law. Uphold the social contract and order.

Postconventional, or principled, level (Level 3):

Stage 5:   Current laws and values are relative. Laws and duty are obeyed on rational calculations to serve the greatest number.

Stage 6:   Follow self-chosen universal ethical principles. In the event of conflicts, principles override laws.[4]

At the postconventional level, the individual is able to reach independent moral judgments that may or may not be in conformity with conventional societal wisdom. Thus, the Level 2 manager might refrain from sexual harassment because it constitutes a violation of company policy and the law. A manager at Level 3 might reach the same conclusion, but her or his decision would have been based on independently defined, universal principles of justice.

---

[4]For an elaboration of Kohlberg's stages, see, e.g., W. D. Boyce and L. C. Jensen, *Moral Reasoning* (Lincoln, NE: Univ. of Nebraska Press, 1978), pp. 98–109.

Kohlberg found that many adults never pass beyond Level 2. Consequently, if Kohlberg is correct, many managers may behave unethically simply because they have not reached the upper stages of moral maturity.

Kohlberg's model is based on very extensive longitudinal and cross-cultural studies over a period of more than three decades. For example, one set of the Chicago-area boys was interviewed at 3-year intervals for a period of 20 years. Thus the stages of moral growth exhibit "definite empirical characteristics" such that Kohlberg was able to claim that his model had been scientifically validated. While many critics remain, the evidence, in sum, is supportive of Kohlberg's general proposition.

Carol Gilligan offers a conception of moral development that runs contrary to Kohlberg's analysis. Instead of finding that individuals grow toward more autonomous, global decision making, Gilligan finds that individuals grow toward more complex webs of "caring" relationships. Gilligan's ethics of care was based on her findings that there exists a way of thinking about moral issues at variance with Kohlberg's sixth stage, and that this alternative was more common among women based on their different life experiences.

Gilligan found the following:

In a series of studies designed to investigate the relationship between conceptions of self and morality, and to test their association with gender and age, two moral voices could reliably be distinguished in the way people framed and resolved moral problems and in their evaluations of choices they made. One voice speaks of connection, not hurting, care, and response; and one speaks of equality, reciprocity, justice and rights. . . . The pattern of predominance, although not gender specific, was gender related.[5]

Gilligan, therefore, had a different conception of moral development:

First focus:	Caring for self and ensuring survival.
Transition stage:	Self focus as unacceptably selfish.
Second focus:	Responsibility and material care for dependent others, self-sacrifice.
Transition stage:	Questions illogic of inequality between needs of others and self.
Third focus:	Dynamic relationship between self and others.[6]

---

[5]Carol Gilligan, "Remapping the Moral Domain: New Images of Self in Relationship," in C. Gilligan, J. Ward, and J. McClean Taylor (eds.), *Mapping the Moral Domain* (Cambridge: Center for the Study of Gender, Education and Human Development and Harvard Univ. Press, 1988).

[6]Carol Gilligan, *In a Different Voice* (Cambridge: Harvard Univ. Press, 1982).

Consider the similarities and differences between Gilligan's and Kohlberg's analyses. In evaluating the actions of others, is it more helpful to consider their position along Kohlberg's scale or Gilligan's? Which seems more realistic as you apply it to others? Gilligan is often criticized for her general conclusion that women and men (as a result of life experiences) reason differently. Do you agree or disagree with that proposition?

C. MORAL DECISION MAKING IN BUSINESS: CORPORATE PROCESSES

A corporation, through its individual decision makers, might be viewed as having reached one of Kohlberg's levels. But is a corporation the same as a "moral person"? Of course, the corporation has long been treated as a person of sorts in the eyes of the law. We can legitimately hold the corporation legally blameworthy for employee wrongs. But can we attribute moral responsibility to the corporation? Ordinarily, we consider an individual morally responsible for act or event x only (1) if the person did x or caused x to occur and (2) if the person's conduct was intentional. Does a corporation ever do or cause any event? And even if a corporation could act, could it do so with intent? In a sense, can a corporation even think?

Philosopher Peter French posits that a corporation can be considered an "actor" since it has an organizational system of decision making (the organizational chart) and a set of policies and procedures for actions. Thus, the judgments and actions of individuals within the corporation are actually governed by the corporation itself, that is, the will of the corporation. Critics of this approach argue that, while a corporation may be similar to an individual in some ways, it is certainly distinct in others. For instance, the corporation does not have the same rights as individuals, such as the right to life.

Even if we are persuaded that the corporation could be treated as a moral actor, do we want to do so? We might answer yes because, in the event of wrongdoing, we could avoid the nearly impossible task of finding the guilty party within the corporate maze. Why not simply place the blame (or at least part of it) on the organization? But if we were to do so, would we somehow depreciate perhaps the central moral precept in our society—the notion that each of us must accept responsibility for our actions?

D. BUSINESS ETHICS IN PRACTICE

When questioned regarding the forces that contribute to unethical decision making in working life, managers point to the behavior of their superiors and the nature of company policy regarding wrongdoing. Hence, we assume that an organization committed to ethical quality can institute some structures and procedures to encourage decency. Codes of conduct are a common corporate ethics tool (discussed in further detail in Chapter 7). But the question remains: can we somehow encourage ethical behavior on the part of managerial decision makers?

As mentioned earlier, ethics is but one mode of decision making in the corporate environment. Is it possible to persuade corporate managers that ethics *should* be the basis of their decisions? Of course, if ethical behavior *always* led to higher profits as well as higher quality products or services, the market would take care of everything. The ethical business person would be more likely to succeed than the unethical business person. However, while higher ethics may lead to higher profits (see Chapter 5), they do not *always* do so. We have all heard tales of those who successfully avoided responsibility for their unethical acts, while reaping millions in the meantime, or of those that actually go to jail for wrongful conduct, only to have their millions restored to them upon their release. As long as there is some perceived benefit to unethical behavior, some decision makers may be persuaded to leave their ethics at the door.

Modern theories of economics and ethics may prove useful in understanding and encouraging ethical behavior in business. Consider the implications of a lawless system, where we relied solely on market forces to encourage behavior. Would companies be unleashed to act in unethical ways, or would there be any reason to believe that companies would refrain from wrongful conduct (or conduct we considered wrongful, since no law would be broken)? Does the market ensure fairness? Justice? Some scholars believe that the marketplace does, indeed, foster ethical and honest behavior. It is argued that there is some market value to honesty and ethics—that consumers reward firms that are straight with them, firms in which they can place their trust. Consider drugstore giant Walgreen's adage "The Pharmacy America Trusts" or Johnson & Johnson's "Trust in Tampax." Truth might be the best policy, as the Roman philosopher Seneca noted that "time discovers truth."[7]

Economists Dwight Lee and Richard McKenzie support this contention. They explain that a business person may act honestly because of the high costs of dishonesty.[8] This is not to say that a business person cannot profit through dishonesty, but simply that the risks/potential costs of dishonesty are higher than those of honesty.

> *[I]n addition to being a virtue from a strictly moral perspective, honesty is also important for quite instrumental reasons. An economy in which people deal with each other honestly produces more wealth than one in which people are chronically dishonest because more exchanges occur directing resources into their most productive employments.[9]*

An earlier perspective is offered by St. Augustine in his treatise "On Lying," where he explains that "when regard for truth has been broken down or even slightly weakened, all things will remain doubtful."[10]

On the other hand, should *all* behavior be regulated, in every situation? Should fairness and justice be completely legislated? Recently, states have enacted laws prohibiting drivers licenses to individuals who failed to pay their family support. This was considered a crossover of law and behavioral justice. Paying family support really has nothing to do with whether one should be able to drive in that state; however, the state is using its muscle to persuade behavior it considers right. In addition, in an effort to prevent even the appearance of impropriety, states have enacted conflict-of-interest statutes in connection with public workers. These statutes prohibit activities that might *lead* to or give the appearance of wrongful conduct, even where none exists.

---

[7]F. Richard Ciccone, "Truth and The American Way," *Chicago Tribune,* May 12, 1996, sec. 2, p. 8.

[8]Dwight Lee and Richard McKenzie, "How the Marketplace Fosters Business Honesty," *Business & Society Review* (Winter 1995), pp. 5–9.

[9]*Id.* at 5.

[10]St. Augustine, "On Lying," cited in Sissela Bok, "Lying: Moral Choice in Public & Private Life" (Vintage Books, 1999)

LEGISLATING ETHICAL BEHAVIOR, TEXAS-STYLE?

Standards of Conduct and Conflict of Interest
Sec. 572.001. Policy; Legislative Intent
(a) It is the policy of this state that a state officer or state employee may not have a direct or indirect interest, including financial and other interests, or engage in a business transaction or professional activity, or incur any obligation of any nature that is in substantial conflict with the proper discharge of the officer's or employee's duties in the public interest.

(b) To implement this policy and to strengthen the faith and confidence of the people of this state in state government, this chapter provides standards of conduct and disclosure requirements to be observed by persons owing a responsibility to the people and government of this state in the performance of their official duties.

(c) It is the intent of the legislature that this chapter serve not only as a guide for official conduct of those persons but also as a basis for discipline of those who refuse to abide by its terms.

***

Sec. 572.051. Standards of Conduct
A state officer or employee should not:
(1) accept or solicit any gift, favor, or service that might reasonably tend to influence the officer or employee in the discharge of official duties or that the officer or employee knows or should know is being offered with the intent to influence the officer's or employee's official conduct;

(2) accept other employment or engage in a business or professional activity that the officer or employee might reasonably expect would require or induce the officer or employee to disclose confidential information acquired by reason of the official position;

(3) accept other employment or compensation that could reasonably be expected to impair the officer's or employee's independence of judgment in the performance of the officer's or employee's official duties;

(4) make personal investments that could reasonably be expected to create a substantial conflict between the officer's or employee's private interest and the public interest; or

(5) intentionally or knowingly solicit, accept, or agree to accept any benefit for having exercised the officer's or employee's official powers or performed the officer's or employee's official duties in favor of another.[11]

---

[11]Chapter 572, §001, §051, Texas Government Code (1991); http://gold.utsystem.edu/Ethics/standcon.htm.

SHORT HYPOTHETICAL CASE

Your company's marketing department has placed a classified ad seeking applicants for a job that doesn't exist. The company is not named in the ad. Your company wants to accomplish two things. First, the firm wants to know which of its employees is out looking for a new position. Second, it wants to entice competitors' employees in for an interview, hoping to gain valuable information about the competition. You have been assigned to field calls and to interview the competition. What do you do?

Hypotheticals were written by Catherine Haselden and are included in her manuscript, "The Ethics Game." 704/337-2395, 803/286-1951.

IT SEEMS RIGHT IN THEORY BUT DOES IT WORK IN PRACTICE?

NORM BOWIE

Can these theories work? Can theories guide business decision makers toward more ethical decisions? Often students and others who explore concepts of business ethics in connection with their application to the "real world" contend that these values work only in theory and not at all in practice. Consider Bowie's defense of the discipline.

I have frequently used these arguments with executives who may find them theoretically persuasive, but who, nonetheless, think their practical implication is limited. They point out that in the real world in which business actually operates not everyone breaks contracts and not everyone freeloads. Some do but not all. Knowing that, isn't it to the strategic advantage of the firm to be the one who does break contracts or otherwise freeloads? After all, in terms of pure self-interest, the best world for a person or firm is one where everyone else plays by the rules except you, isn't it?

In asking that question I point out that one is no longer asking a question of ethics (the executives are already convinced that theoretically such activity is wrong), but rather a prudential question of strategy. Although Kant would feel no need to answer it, Kantian-type arguments can be brought to bear on the prudential question. The common approach of these arguments is to show that the self-defeating nature of actions based on maxims that cannot be universalized cut in long before complete universalization would take place. That was the point with my Georgetown student example. The fact that Georgetown students bounced more checks than the rest of the population did not bring about the collapse of payment by check. But it did for Georgetown students who did business in the proximity of Georgetown University.

What is significant but often overlooked by philosophers is that Kant's universalizability formulation of the categorical imperative is subject to empirical support. In some ways that should not be surprising. If someone tries to create a round square we can predict that no one will succeed. Similarly, if stealing or cheating when universalized is conceptually incoherent, then we would expect the collapse of certain institutions and practices if stealing or cheating became universal in our society, or at the very least those institutions would not be available for a subset of society. Now we do not have a case of universalized cheating any more than we have a case of absolute zero or a perfect vacuum. But we do have close approximations. We can empirically observe that Kantian-type effects take place when actions whose maxims cannot be universalized reach a certain threshold. We began the chapter by providing examples of what happens to credit when people do not pay their bills. A Kantian could predict that if enough checks of seafood customers bounce, the seafood store will stop taking checks. She could also predict that if people do not repay loans, the banks will fail.

There are positive stories that illustrate Kant's point as well. That is, there are stories showing that when a threshold of morality is reached, certain institutions become possible and, when economically feasible, will develop. Russia is in the process of starting a stock exchange. The difficulties in doing so, however, have been great, in part because company spokespersons would not provide accurate financial information about their companies. As a Kantian would expect, investors will not be forthcoming if they believe that the members of the exchange lie about their companies. Gradually, a few companies including Irkutsk Energo, Bratsky LPK, and Rostelecom were able to establish a reputation as truthtellers. These companies were then able to attract investors and have done well. *The Wall Street Journal* put it this way:

> *When the chief engineer of Irkutsk Energo addressed a gathering of 250 Western fund managers last March, he gave a straightforward presentation of the Russian utility's assets, liabilities and investment policy. This was anything but typical in Russia where enterprises usually withhold even basic information from investors. . . . This winter (1995) a few mavericks proved the value of corporate glasnost. As these companies drew foreign interest, others followed. Of the 50 most actively traded Russian companies, 10 are ardently wooing foreign investors. Last year there were two. . . . "There is a clear differentiation in the market between those companies that get it and those that don't," says Nancy Curtin head of the Emerging Europe funds for Baring Asset Management.*

In trying to establish a stock market, the Russians faced the problem that lying about the finances of the firm was perceived to be nearly universal. As a Kantian would expect, so long as the perception was held, Russian society could not have a stock market that reflected the rational values of the firms. Since investors knew that the information about the firms was false, there was no alternative way for them to get a reasonable figure about a firm's value. (Thus, the Securities and Exchange Commission provides a genuine contribution in the USA because it forces firms to be more truthful.) However, once a sufficient number of firms were perceived as being truthful about their finances, the stock prices of those firms rose rapidly to reflect rational expectations of the firms' worth.

And the success of these honest firms has led other firms to be more honest, to the point where the Russian stock market is thriving. The March 24, 1997, *Business Week* carried a story entitled "The Rush to Russia." In 1996 the Russian stock market was up 127 percent and it had already gained 65 percent in 1997. Of course, more honesty on the part of Russian companies is not the explanation for the rise in the stock market. Rather, sufficient honesty is a necessary condition for there to be a stock market at all.

As an aside, business ethicists are often asked how a business that wishes to be ethical should behave when other businesses are clearly behaving unethically. These executives would like to be ethical but believe they would be at a competitive disadvantage if they were ethical. And sometimes they would be. But, as our example of the Russian stock market shows, sometimes a firm has a clear competitive advantage if it is ethical when most other firms are not. Nearly all of us have horror stories to tell about auto-repair shops. Suffice it to say that the industry does not have a good reputation. Think of how successful an auto-repair shop would be if it had a reputation for honesty. This point is not merely theoretical. In Bloomington, Minnesota I dealt with a devout Christian who left the repair facility of a major dealer to open his own repair facility. I was one of his first customers. I could call in the morning and get my car fixed that day. Within a year, I might have to wait nearly a week because he was so busy. In relating these positive examples, I am not arguing that one ought to be honest because it pays. I am pointing out that sometimes as a matter of fact it does. More remarkably in some cases it pays the most when most other competitors are not honest. Sometimes, contrary to popular opinion, the best competitive position for you is when all (or a large number of) your competitors are perceived to be (or are) dishonest and you are and are perceived to be honest. My car repairman in Minnesota occupies just that world.

The force of failure to follow the categorical imperative can be found in business practices themselves. Both the strategy literature and the popular business press extol the virtues of strategic alliances. In an era where companies are urged to focus on their core competencies (those things which they do most effectively), strategic alliances have become a crucial part of doing business. The Kantian moral philosopher would urge her firm to avoid alliances with firms that are not moral in Kant's sense, i.e., they constantly practice business according to maxims that are not universalizable, e.g., they lie or cheat. Why would a firm want to partner with another firm that lies and cheats, especially when all members of a partnership are jointly and severally liable for the product they jointly produce?

Supplier problems are not unique to the economies emerging from communism. Failure to heed Kant's dictum that a self-contradictory maxim cannot be universalized has created tremendous problems for General Motors and Volkswagen. General Motors promoted Jose Ignacio Lopez de Arroirtua (Lopez) on the basis of his success in lowering the cost of supplier products. His success in this area arose primarily through his practice of continually reopening negotiations with suppliers and providing the proprietary information of one supplier to other suppliers so that these suppliers could provide the product more cheaply. A morally sensitive person would characterize these activities as lying and stealing respectively. As we have shown, the maxims that permit lying and stealing cannot be universalized. Thus, what Lopez did was wrong.

And General Motors made an imprudent decision in promoting him. Is it any surprise that Lopez left GM for the German company Volkswagen, allegedly taking with him several associates and many cartons of GM's proprietary purchasing data? Furthermore, is it any surprise that, in a recent survey, the suppliers of auto parts rated GM worst of all the automakers? How will GM fare as it enters what *Fortune* calls the new economy where cars cost less because the auto industry relies more on cheaper high-quality suppliers? The strategic advice is that manufacturers should partner with their suppliers. But why would a supplier want to partner with a manufacturer that has promoted someone who lied and stole from them?

To strengthen this point, the November 25, 1996, issue of *Business Week* indicates that Lopez's former dealings with suppliers of GM have brought similar problems to Volkswagen. Lopez is expected to be charged by German prosecutors with the theft of trade secrets. Meanwhile in the USA, GM began legal action against Volkswagen CEO Ferdinand Piech and other company executives for up to $4 billion in damages. On November 29, 1996, the Volkswagen Board accepted Lopez's "resignation." Shortly thereafter GM and Volkswagen reached a settlement, but Lopez's problems in both the USA and Germany remain.

In arguing that sound ethical business practices can support a positive bottom line, I am not arguing that this is always the case. Sometimes ethics does not pay but costs. In those cases Kantian morality requires that a business firm do what is ethically required even if it does not pay. However, I hope I have shown that doing what is morally required is not always unprofitable. Sometimes being moral enhances the bottom line rather than reduces it.

In summary, I have tried to show how Kant's universalizability formulation of the categorical imperative can be used to test the moral legitimacy of contemplated actions in business. In using that test we have an argument as to why certain actions like the breaking of contracts, stealing, and competing unfairly are morally wrong. We have also seen that if immoral actions such as those cited cross a critical threshold, the business institutions that presuppose norms of truthfulness and fairness will become unstable and in extreme circumstances even cease to exist. Furthermore, through the use of numerous examples I have tried to show that Kant's arguments are of more than theoretical interest. They have predictable real-world applications.

THE ART OF WAR
SUN TZU

Is business just another form of war? Can business practitioners learn from the strategic analysis utilized in combat? Consider the application of the following statements by Master Sun Tzu and his disciples to traditional business decision making and strategic planning.

1: STRATEGIC ASSESSMENTS

***

MEI YAOCHEN

Whether you live or die depends on the configuration of the battleground; whether you survive or perish depends on the way of battle.

MASTER SUN

Therefore measure in terms of five things, use these assessments to make comparisons, and thus find out what the conditions are. The five things are the way, the weather, the terrain, the leadership, and discipline.

DU MU

Five things are to be assessed—the way, the weather, the lay of the land, the leadership, and discipline. These are to be assessed at headquarters—first assess yourself and your opponent in terms of these five things, deciding who is superior. Then you can determine who is likely to prevail. Having determined this, only then should you mobilize your forces.

***

MASTER SUN

The Way means inducing the people to have the same aim as the leadership, so that they will share death and share life, without fear of danger.

CAO CAO

This means guiding them by instruction and direction. Danger means distrust.

Zhang Yu

If the people are treated with benevolence, faithfulness, and justice, then they will be of one mind, and will be glad to serve. The *I Ching* says, "Joyful in difficulty, the people forget about their death."

***

Du Mu

Also, if a general lacks the planning ability to assess the officers and place them in positions where they can use the best of their abilities, instead assigning them automatically and thus not making full use of their talents, then the army will become hesitant.

Huang Shigong said, "Those who are good at delegating responsibility employ the intelligent, the brave, the greedy, and the foolish. The intelligent are glad to establish their merit, the brave like to act out their ambitions, the greedy welcome an opportunity to pursue profit, and the foolish do not care if they die."

If your own army is hesitant and confused, you bring trouble on yourself, as if you were to bring enemies in to overcome you.

***

Master Sun

So only a brilliant ruler or a wise general who can use the highly intelligent for espionage is sure of great success. This is essential for military operations, and the armies depend on this in their actions.

Du Mu

It will not do for the army to act without knowing the opponent's condition, and to know the opponent's condition is impossible without espionage.

SOME THOUGHTS ON THE MEANING OF BUSINESS ETHICS

BARBARA LEY TOFFLER

Toffler is the director of Ethics and Responsible Business Practices Consulting at Arthur Andersen LLP, New York. This area of Arthur Andersen's practice helps businesses to address issues related to ethics. The following article is included in the firm's marketing materials.

I. RESPONSIBLE VERSUS COMPLIANT OR ETHICAL

The 1990s have seen an explosion of programs focused on good behavior in both public and private sector institutions. Most of these activities are called either compliance programs or ethics programs. Compliance programs generally deal with adherence to laws, regulations, policies and procedures, while ethics programs include compliance issues, but tend to focus on ethical reasoning and analysis (e.g., rights analysis, which asks who has rights in a particular situation). Most of the compliance programs are reasonably effective in informing employees of the laws, regulations, etc., and in telling them about the consequences of noncompliance; and many of the ethics programs do raise ethical awareness. Few of either, however, are successful at weaving those ideas into the fabric of employees' daily work.

Compliance programs usually resemble law enforcement: Participants are potential offenders who are told by corporate law enforcement officials—lawyers, internal auditors, internal affairs officers—what they must do and what will happen to them if they disobey. Although usually unintended, the tone is often punitive or paternalistic, neither of which makes employees feel respected and capable.

Ethics programs, on the other hand, often fall into the Sunday school or sermonizing category. Often delivered by human resources or a corporate social policy group, the focus of an ethics program is frequently on being a good person and doing the right thing, but without attention to institutional realities, the effect of those realities on employee behavior, and how employees can learn to manage the realities—all of which are essential to behaving ethically. (An example is a business ethics book co-authored by Kenneth Blanchard and Norman Vincent Peale referred to by many as The One-Minute Manager Meets the Power of Positive Thinking—in which, if the manager does the right thing, everything will turn out fine. Real life usually requires more complex management.)

The word *responsible,* however, encompasses both compliant and ethical, but includes much more. A program that focuses on responsible employee behavior begins with an assumption that employees want to do the right thing, but recognizes that they may face impediments to doing so effectively. It then (1) instructs them in the laws, regulations, policies, and procedures they must know and follow, (2) assists them in understanding the kinds of dilemmas they may face in their jobs and the role their institution plays in those dilemmic situations, (3) guides them in applying the laws, regulations, etc., to their work, and (4) helps them develop skills to resolve their dilemmas. A key message of a responsible business practices program is that the institution respects the employees and their capabilities, and expects them to be responsible and accountable for the actions they take. In other words, the program says they are part of the team.

II. HELPING PEOPLE DO THE RIGHT THING MEANS UNDERSTANDING WHY THEY DO WRONG

Most compliance and ethics programs begin with the assumption that if individuals want to do the right thing, they will do it. But that is not always the case. Let's look at an example:

In 1987, the Internal Revenue Service of the United States discovered that employees in three of its offices—Fresno, Philadelphia, and Andover, Massachusetts—were flushing tax returns and/or related documents down the toilets. Stories appeared in the national media, the Service was embarrassed, and of course, the guilty individuals were terminated. Generally, the focus was on the people who had done wrong and the concern that the IRS had not properly instructed its employees in correct behavior.

But, in reality, why did this unfortunate series of events occur?

The Service needed, and was authorized by Congress, to purchase a new computer system to meet its expanding needs. A system made by a foreign manufacturer was found to best meet the specifications. However, Congress felt it was important that the U.S. government buy American, so the IRS found a U.S. source that claimed the capability of meeting the specs. However, it turned out that not only did the system not have the necessary capacity (it did not meet the specs), it also was of inferior quality—it kept breaking down. Between capacity and quality problems, down-time increased and processing of returns was delayed. When processors came in on weekends to catch up on backlogged work, they often found the system under repair.

At the same time, the evaluation system for these processors measured backlog—what was still piled up on their desks. Since the computer system could not handle the work and supervisors were pressuring processors to get the work off their desks or suffer bad evaluations, processors did get the paper work off their desks—by throwing them into the toilets!

The reason for recounting this story is not to exonerate the return processors. What they did was wrong and they were appropriately disciplined. However, it is critical to note that they did not destroy documents because they did not want to do the right thing, or that they did not know that what they were doing was wrong. Processors destroyed documents because they knew no way to legitimately raise their concerns and be part of finding a solution to the problems, and their supervisors had not been encouraged to be available to subordinates to hear concerns and support problem resolution. Neither processors nor supervisors felt part of a team effort, and all felt that to raise a problem meant that you would be seen as part of the problem (the kill-the-messenger syndrome). Further, the IRS had never stopped to consider the impact of new technology on its employees (which would be significant even with a well-running new system), and to provide avenues for assistance.

There is another example, this one in the private sector, that is worth recalling here:

The public was appropriately horrified when it was discovered that the breast implants made by Dow Corning were leaking silicone into womens bodies. Many said that somebody should have reported the problem when it was seen in the lab, and that here was more evidence of the need for ethics programs. The fact is that Dow Corning had a model ethics program, celebrated in a Harvard Business School case. One element of the program included groups of 35 employees meeting with the CEO, who asked them to tell him of any concerns they had. No one ever raised leaking implants at one of these sessions. Why? In this case, we do not have information on what really happened. But we all must assume that some gap existed in the elegant ethics program—a gap between helping people analyze what was right and wrong in a situation, and helping them do something about it.

III. WHY DO PEOPLE DO WRONG?

There are several reasons why people do wrong:

1.   Character Reasons: There are those who do wrong because they do not know right from wrong, they do not care if they do right, they are out for self-gain, or they resent authority. No program will reach such people. An institution hopes to find them and remove them.

2.   Information-related Reasons: In these cases, people want to do right, but (1) do not have the information they need (laws, policies, etc.), or (2) have the information they need, but do not understand it, or (3) have the information they need, understand it, but do not know how to apply it, and (4) they do not know where to go for help, or fear that if they ask for help they will be seen as incompetent. Most newcomers to an organization find themselves in this situation. So a good program must provide information in a clear, user-friendly way, with the message: This is what you need to know; this is where you can go to learn what you need to know. Now you are being held accountable.

3.   Expectation-related Reasons: In these situations, people know what is right and wrong, and know the laws and policies. But they think one of two things: (*a*) They believe their supervisor or the company expects them to ignore the problem and just get on with the job. This often happens when the problem is relatively small and the cost in time or money is significant. Or (*b*) they experience the Move-it effect, where they feel they are being pressured by superiors to Move it . . . Don't give me an argument, just get it done. In these cases, individuals often believe that if they raise legitimate concerns, they will put themselves at job or career risk.

4.   Judgment-related Reasons: In these kinds of cases, people face true dilemmas where there is no clear right answer. Often they are trying to meet two conflicting good values. One company had two statements in its Standards of Conduct: One supported affirmatively hiring and promoting women and minorities and the other stated there must be no discriminatory behavior. Many felt it was hard to know what was right when hiring. Often dilemmas concern two conflicting regulations. A utility company manager had a hard time deciding how to remove asbestos from scrubbers. To remove asbestos, the scrubbers had to be shut down for longer than EPA allows. To not remove the asbestos would violate EPA regulations. The manager knew the regulations, wanted to do the right thing, and still faced a problem. (The resolution involved working with senior management to approach the regulatory agency for a variance.)

A successful program, a Responsible Business Practices program, must be based on an understanding of why people do wrong things. It must include (1) instruction for all employees—both individual contributors and those with supervisory/managerial responsibilities—in the laws, policies, etc., they must uphold, and (2) skill building, guidance and resources to address the causes of wrongdoing. As well, the company must provide mechanisms to give employees the support and guidance they need, and to enable them to ask for help without feeling foolish or incompetent.

The able employee of the 21st century must be committed to doing right, must have the information necessary to do right, and must have the resources and support essential to solve problems and resolve dilemmas.

AMERICA'S PERSECUTED MINORITY
Big Business
Ayn Rand

As will also be discussed in Chapter 3, Ayn Rand is best known for her economic theory, objectivism. Objectivism is a form of ethical egoism which suggests that we accept the fact that we all act in our own self-interest. We should be free to do so, as long as we do not infringe on anyone else's right to act in her or his own self-interest. The following lecture reflects her concern that business is constantly subject to a tolerated persecution, always blamed for the sins, errors, or failures of other groups. It was given at the Ford Hall Forum in Boston, Massachusetts, on December 17, 1961, and at Columbia University in 1962.

If a small group of men were always regarded as guilty, in any clash with any other group, regardless of the issues or circumstances involved, would you call it persecution? If this group were always made to pay for the sins, errors, or failures of any other group, would you call *that* persecution? If this group had to live under a silent reign of terror, under special laws, from which all other people were immune, laws which the accused could not grasp or define in advance and which the accuser could interpret in any way he pleased—would you call *that* persecution? If this group were penalized, not for its faults, but for its virtues, not for its incompetence, but for its ability, not for its failures, but for its achievements, and the greater the achievement, the greater the penalty—would you call *that* persecution?

If your answer is "yes"—then ask yourself what sort of monstrous injustice you are condoning, supporting, or perpetrating. That group is the American businessmen.

The defense of minority rights is acclaimed today, virtually by everyone, as a moral principle of a high order. But this principle, which forbids discrimination, is applied by most of the "liberal" intellectuals in a *discriminatory* manner: it is applied only to racial or religious minorities. It is not applied to that small, exploited, denounced, defenseless minority which consists of businessmen.

Yet every ugly, brutal aspect of injustice toward racial or religious minorities is being practiced toward businessmen. For instance, consider the evil of condemning some men and

"America's Persecuted Minority: Big Business," lecture given by Ayn Rand at The Ford Hall Forum, Boston, MA, 12/17/61 and Columbia University. Reprinted by permission of the Estate of Ayn Rand.

absolving others, without a hearing, regardless of the facts. Today's "liberals" consider a businessman guilty in any conflict with a labor union, regardless of the facts of issues involved, and boast that they will not cross a picket line "right or wrong." Consider the evil of judging people by a double standard and of denying to some the rights granted to others. Today's "liberals" recognize the workers' (the majority's) right to their livelihood (their wages), but deny the businessmen's (the minority's) right to *their* livelihood (their profits). If workers struggle for higher wages, this is hailed as "social gains"; if businessmen struggle for higher profits, this is damned as "selfish greed." If the workers' standard of living is low, the "liberals" blame it on the businessmen; but if the businessmen attempt to improve their economic efficacy, to expand their markets, and to enlarge the financial returns of their enterprises, thus making higher wages and lower prices possible, the same "liberals" denounce it as "commercialism." If a non-commercial foundation—*i.e.,* a group which did not have to *earn* its funds—sponsors a television show, advocating its particular views, the "liberals" hail it as "enlightenment," "education," "art," and "public service"; if a businessman sponsors a television show and wants it to reflect *his* views, the "liberals" scream, calling it "censorship," "pressure," and "dictatorial rule." When three locals of the International Brotherhood of Teamsters deprived New York City of its milk supply for fifteen days—no moral indignation or condemnation was heard from the "liberal" quarters; but just imagine what would happen if *businessmen* stopped that milk supply for one hour—and how swiftly they would be struck down by that legalized lynching or pogrom known as "trust-busting."

Whenever, in any era, culture, or society, you encounter the phenomenon of prejudice, injustice, persecution, and blind, unreasoning hatred directed at some minority group—look for the gang that has something to gain from that persecution, look for those who have a vested interest in the destruction of these particular sacrificial victims. Invariably, you will find that the persecuted minority serves as a scapegoat for some movement that does not want the nature of its own goals to be known. Every movement that seeks to enslave a country, every dictatorship or potential dictatorship, needs some minority group as a scapegoat which it can blame for the nation's troubles and use as a justification of its own demands for dictatorial powers. In Soviet Russia, the scapegoat was the bourgeoisie; in Nazi Germany, it was the Jewish people; in America, it is the businessmen.

America has not yet reached the stage of a dictatorship. But, paving the way to it, for many decades past, the businessmen have served as the scapegoat for *statist* movements of all kinds: communist, fascist, or welfare. For whose sins and evils did the businessmen take the blame? For the sins and evils of the bureaucrats.

A disastrous intellectual package-deal, put over on us by the theoreticians of statism, is the equation of *economic* power with *political* power. You have heard it expressed in such bromides as: "A hungry man is not free," or "It makes no difference to a worker whether he takes orders from a businessman or from a bureaucrat." Most people accept these equivocations—and yet they know that the poorest laborer in America is freer and more secure than the richest commissar in Soviet Russia. What is the basic, the essential, the crucial principle that differentiates freedom from slavery? It is the principle of voluntary action *versus* physical coercion or compulsion.

The difference between political power and any other kind of social "power," between a government and any private organization, is the fact that *a government holds a legal monopoly on the use of physical force.* This distinction is so important and so seldom recognized today that I must urge you to keep it in mind. Let me repeat it: *a government holds a legal monopoly on the use of physical force.*

No individual or private group or private organization has the legal power to initiate the use of physical force against other individuals or groups and to compel them to act against their own voluntary choice. Only a government holds that power. The nature of governmental action is: *coercive* action. The nature of political power is: the power to force obedience under threat of physical injury—the threat of property expropriation, imprisonment, or death.

Foggy metaphors, sloppy images, unfocused poetry, and equivocations—such as "A hungry man is not free"—do not alter the fact that *only* political power is the power of physical coercion and that freedom, in a political context, has only one meaning: *The absence of physical coercion.*

The only proper function of the government of a free country is to act as an agency which protects the individual's rights, i.e., which protects the individual from physical violence. Such a government does not have the right to *initiate* the use of physical force against anyone—a right which the individual does not possess and, therefore, cannot delegate to any agency. But the individual does possess the right of self-defense and *that* is the right which he delegates to the government, for the purpose of an orderly, legally defined enforcement. A proper government has the right to use physical force *only* in retaliation and *only* against those who initiate its use. The proper functions of a government are: the police, to protect men from criminals; the military forces, to protect men from foreign invaders; and the law courts, to protect men's property and contracts from breach by force or fraud, and to settle disputes among men according to objectively defined laws.

These, implicitly, were the political principles on which the Constitution of the United States was based; implicitly, but not explicitly. There were contradictions in the Constitution, which allowed the statists to gain an entering wedge, to enlarge the breach, and, gradually, to wreck the structure.

***

A system of pure, unregulated laissez-faire capitalism has never yet existed anywhere. What did exist were only so-called mixed economies, which means: a mixture, in varying degrees, of freedom and controls, of voluntary choice and government coercion, of capitalism and statism. America was the freest country on earth, but elements of statism were present in her economy from the start. These elements kept growing, under the influence of her intellectuals who were predominantly committed to the philosophy of statism. The intellectuals—the ideologists, the interpreters, the assessors of public events—were tempted by the opportunity to seize political power, relinquished by all other social groups, and to establish their own versions of a "good" society at the point of a gun, i.e., by means of legalized physical coercion. They denounced the free businessmen as exponents of "selfish greed" and glorified the bureaucrats as "public servants." In evaluating social problems, they kept damning "economic power" and exonerating political power, thus switching the burden of guilt from the politicians to the businessmen.

All the evils, abuses, and iniquities, popularly ascribed to businessmen and to capitalism, were not caused by an unregulated economy or by a free market, but by government intervention into the economy. The giants of American industry—such as James Jerome Hill or Commodore Vanderbilt or Andrew Carnegie or J. P. Morgan—were self-made men who earned their fortunes by personal ability, by free trade on a free market. But there existed another kind of businessmen, the products of a mixed economy, the men with political pull, who made fortunes by means of special privileges granted to them by the government, such men as the Big Four of the Central Pacific Railroad. It was the political power behind their activities—the power of forced, unearned, economically unjustified privileges—that caused dislocations in the country's economy, hardships, depressions, and mounting public protests. But it was the free market and the free businessmen that took the blame. Every calamitous consequence of government controls was used as a justification for the extension of the controls and of the government's power over the economy.

***

What should we do about it? We should demand a reexamination and revision of the entire issue of antitrust. We should challenge its philosophical, political, economic, and *moral* base. We should have a Civil Liberties Union—for businessmen. The repeal of the antitrust laws should be our ultimate goal; it will require a long intellectual and political struggle; but in the meantime and as a first step, we should demand that the jail-penalty provisions of these laws be abolished. It is bad enough if men have to suffer financial penalties, such as fines, under laws which everyone concedes to be non-objective, contradictory, and undefinable, since no two jurists can agree on their meaning and application; it is obscene to impose prison sentences under laws of so controversial a nature. We should put an end to the outrage of sending men to jail for breaking unintelligible laws which they cannot avoid breaking.

Businessmen are the one group that distinguishes capitalism and the American way of life from the totalitarian statism that is swallowing the rest of the world. All the other social groups—workers, farmers, professional men, scientists, soldiers—exist under dictatorships, even though they exist in chains, in terror, in misery, and in progressive self-destruction. *But there is no such group as businessmen under a dictatorship.* Their place is taken by armed thugs: by bureaucrats and commissars. Businessmen are the symbol of a free society—the symbol of America. If and when they perish, civilization will perish. But if you wish to fight for freedom, you must begin by fighting for its unrewarded, unrecognized, unacknowledged, yet best representatives—the American businessmen.

THE ONE-MINUTE MORALIST

ROBERT SOLOMON

Solomon posits a question that will be asked again and again by authors throughout this text: Does ethics in business lead to profits? Is good ethics good for business?

Once there was a bright young businessman who was looking for an ethical manager.

He wanted to work for one. He wanted to become one.

His search had taken him over many years to the far corners of the business world.

He visited small businesses and large corporations.

He spoke with used-car dealers, chief executive officers of Fortune 500 companies, management-science professors, vice presidents for strategic planning, and one-minute managers.

He visited every kind of office, big and small, carpeted and tiled, some with breathtaking views, some without any view at all.

He heard a full spectrum of ethical views.

But he wasn't pleased with what he heard.

On the one hand, virtually everyone he met seemed frank, friendly, and courteous, adamant about honesty even to the point of moral indignation. People were respectful of one another, concerned about their employees, and loyal to their own superiors. They paid their debts and resented the lawsuits in which they considered themselves the innocent party, victims of misunderstanding and antibusiness sentiment. They complained about regulation and the implied distrust of their integrity. They proudly asserted that they were producing quality products or services that truly did satisfy consumer demand, making the world a better—even if only a very slightly better—place in which to live.

Their superiors were proud of their trustworthiness.

Their subordinates were confident of their fairness.

But, on the other hand, when they were asked for their views about ethics and business, what all of these people had to say was startling, to say the least.

The answers varied only slightly.

"You have to understand that it's a jungle out there!"

"Listen, I'm a survivor."

"If I don't do it, the other guy will."

"You've got to be realistic in this business."

"Profits—that's what it's all about. You do whatever you have to."

"The One-Minute Moralist," from *The New World of Business.* Reprinted by permission of Rowman & Littlefield Publishers.

And when our bright young businessman brought up the topic of business ethics, he invariably heard:

"There aren't any ethics in business"; or . . .

"*Business Ethics*—the shortest book in the world."

The latter usually with a grin.

At the same time, however, many executives shook their heads sadly and expressed the private wish that it were otherwise.

He met a few unscrupulous businessmen who admitted cutting corners, who had made a profit and were proud of it.

He met others who had cut corners and were caught. "This is a cutthroat world," they insisted, often contradicting this immediately by complaining about the injustice of being singled out themselves.

He met several self-proclaimed "ethical managers" who insisted that everyone who worked for them—and of course they themselves—had to be Perfectly Virtuous, to the letter of the Moral Law.

These managers' subordinates generally despised them, and their departments were rife with resentment. More than one employee complained about autocratic management and dogmatic ineffectiveness; a philosophical assistant manager pointed out the difference between morality and moralizing. Almost everyone pointed out that the principles that were so precisely printed out in both memos and plaques above their desks were usually impossible to apply to any real ethical issues. Their primary effect was rather to cast a gray shadow of suspected hypocrisy over everyday business life.

Our bright young businessman was discouraged. He could not understand why the conscientious, sociable, civilized, thoroughly ethical flesh-and-blood managers he met in the office talked in their off moments like the most cynical prophets of corporate Darwinism.

The flesh-and-blood managers complained that the public did not appreciate them.

The cynical prophets joked, "There are no ethics in business," and then wondered why people didn't trust them.

Our bright young businessman was perplexed: Could there be ethics in the real business world? he wondered. Were compromises and cut corners inevitable? he asked. Did the untrammeled pursuit of virtue have to be either hypocrisy or damaging to the bottom line, as he now feared?

And then he met the One-Minute Moralist.

The bright young businessman presented the One-Minute Moralist with his dilemma. The One-Minute Moralist answered him without hesitation.

"You don't understand ethics," he said. "And you don't understand business either.

"You set up an absurd dichotomy between ethical absolutism and the so-called real world, and then you wonder how ethics can possibly be at home in business, and whether business can function without cutting corners and making uneasy compromises. But cutting corners presumes that there are sharply delineated corners. And talking so uneasily of compromise (that is, compromising one's moral principles rather than compromising with other people) seems to assume that ethics consists of engraved principles rather than relations between people who (more or less) share values and interests.

"But ethics isn't a set of absolute principles, divorced from and imposed on everyday life. Ethics is a way of life, a seemingly delicate but in fact very strong tissue of endless adjustments and compromises. It is the awareness that one is an intrinsic part of a social order, in which the interests of others and one's own interests are inevitably intertwined. And what is business, you should ask, if not precisely that awareness of what other people want and need, and how you yourself can prosper by providing it? Businesses great and small prosper because they respond to people, and fail when they do not respond. To talk about being 'totally ethical' and about 'uneasy compromises' is to misunderstand ethics. Ethics is the art of mutually agreeable tentative compromise. Insisting on absolute principles is, if I may be ironic, unethical.

"Business, on the other hand, has nothing to do with jungles, survivalism, and Darwin, whatever the mechanisms of the market may be. The 'profit motive' is an offensive fabrication by people who were out to attack business, which has curiously—and self-destructively—been adopted by business people themselves. Business isn't a single-minded pursuit of profits; it is an *ethos,* a way of life. It is a way of life that is at its very foundation ethical. What is more central to business—any kind of business—than taking contracts seriously, paying one's debts, and coming to mutual agreements about what is a fair exchange? Ethics isn't superimposed on business. Business is itself an ethics, defined by ethics, made possible by ethics. Two hundred years ago, Benjamin Franklin insisted that business is the pursuit of virtue. If you find yourself wondering or doubting whether virtue is possible in business, I suggest you reexamine your ideas about business.

"If you want to talk about hypocrisy, by the way, it is not just to be found in such bloated phrases as 'the untrammeled pursuit of virtue.' There is just as much hypocrisy in the macho, mock-heroic insistence that business is a tough-minded, amoral struggle for survival and profits rather than a staid and established ethical enterprise.

"Now you've had your Minute. When you think about business and ethics, don't worry about whether one is possible along with the other. In America, at least, nothing is more ethical than good business."

IS BUSINESS BLUFFING
ETHICAL?

ALBERT Z. CARR

*One of the most often discussed articles in many introductory busi-
ness ethics courses, Carr's article deftly asserts that bluffing in business may be ethical. Carr explains how bluffing (deceiving) in certain
situations may be more acceptable than in others. On the other hand,
there is a true benefit from a reputation for honesty in business, as
well. Do you believe the distinctions Carr makes in his discussion are
clear or arbitrary?*

A respected businessman with whom I discussed the theme of this article remarked with
some heat, "You mean to say you're going to encourage men to bluff? Why, bluffing is nothing more than a form of lying! You're advising them to lie!"

I agreed that the basis of private morality is a respect for truth and that the closer a businessman comes to the truth, the more he deserves respect. At the same time, I suggested
that most bluffing in business might be regarded simply as game strategy—much like bluffing in poker, which does not reflect on the morality of the bluffer.

I quoted Henry Taylor, the British statesman who pointed out that "falsehood ceases to
be falsehood when it is understood on all sides that the truth is not expected to be spoken"—
an exact description of bluffing in poker, diplomacy, and business. I cited the analogy of the
criminal court, where the criminal is not expected to tell the truth when he pleads "not
guilty." Everyone from the judge down takes it for granted that the job of the defendant's
attorney is to get his client off, not to reveal the truth; and this is considered ethical practice. I mentioned Representative Omar Burleson, the Democrat from Texas, who was
quoted as saying, in regard to the ethics of Congress, "Ethics is a barrel of worms."[1]—a pun-
gent summing up of the problem of deciding who is ethical in politics.

I reminded my friend that millions of businessmen feel constrained every day to say
yes to their bosses when they secretly believe *no* and that this is generally accepted as permissible strategy when the alternative might be the loss of a job. The essential point, I said,
is that the ethics of business are game ethics, different from the ethics of religion.

He remained unconvinced. Referring to the company of which he is president, he declared: "Maybe that's good enough for some businessmen, but I can tell you that we pride
ourselves on our ethics. In 30 years not one customer has ever questioned my word or asked
to check our figures. We're loyal to our customers and fair to our suppliers. I regard my
handshake on a deal as a contract. I've never entered into price fixing schemes with my

"Is Business Bluffing Ethical?" by Albert Z. Carr. Reprinted with permission of Harvard Business School
Publishing.

competitors. I've never allowed my salesmen to spread injurious rumors about other companies. Our union contract is the best in our industry. And, if I do say so myself, our ethical standards are of the highest!''

He really was saying, without realizing it, that he was living up to the ethical standards of the business game—which are a far cry from those of private life. Like a gentlemanly poker player, he did not play in cahoots with others at the table, try to smear their reputations, or hold back chips he owed them.

But this same fine man, at that very time, was allowing one of his products to be advertised in a way that made it sound a great deal better than it actually was. Another item in his product line was notorious among dealers for its "built-in obsolescence." He was holding back from the market a much-improved product because he did not want it to interfere with sales of the inferior item it would have replaced. He had joined with certain of his competitors in hiring a lobbyist to push a state legislature, by methods that he preferred not to know too much about, into amending a bill then being enacted.

In his view these things had nothing to do with ethics; they were merely normal business practice. He himself undoubtedly avoided outright falsehoods—never lied in so many words. But the entire organization that he ruled was deeply involved in numerous strategies of deception.

***

THE POKER ANALOGY

We can learn a good deal about the nature of business by comparing it with poker. While both have a large element of chance, in the long run the winner is the man who plays with steady skill. In both games ultimate victory requires intimate knowledge of the rules, insight into the psychology of the other players, a bold front, a considerable amount of self-discipline, and the ability to respond swiftly and effectively to opportunities provided by chance.

No one expects poker to be played on the ethical principles preached in churches. In poker it is right and proper to bluff a friend out of the rewards of being dealt a good hand. A player feels no more than a slight twinge of sympathy, if that, when—with nothing better than a single ace in his hand—he strips a heavy loser, who holds a pair, of the rest of his chips. It was up to the other fellow to protect himself. In the words of an excellent poker player, former President Harry Truman, "If you can't stand the heat, stay out of the kitchen." If one shows mercy to a loser in poker, it is a personal gesture, divorced from the rules of the game.

Poker has its special ethics, and here I am not referring to rules against cheating. The man who keeps an ace up his sleeve or who marks the cards is more than unethical; he is a crook, and can be punished as such—kicked out of the game or,—in the Old West, shot.

In contrast to the cheat, the unethical poker player is one who, while abiding by the letter of the rules, finds ways to put the other players at an unfair disadvantage. Perhaps he unnerves them with loud talk. Or he tries to get them drunk. Or he plays in cahoots with someone else at the table. Ethical poker players frown on such tactics.

Poker's own brand of ethics is different from the ethical ideals of civilized human relationships. The game calls for distrust of the other fellow. It ignores the claim of friendship.

Cunning deception and concealment of one's strength and intentions, not kindness and openheartedness, are vital in poker. No one thinks any the worse of poker on that account. And no one should think any the worse of the game of business because its standards of right and wrong differ from the prevailing traditions of morality in our society.

DISCARD THE GOLDEN RULE

This view of business is especially worrisome to people without much business experience. A minister of my acquaintance once protested that business cannot possibly function in our society unless it is based on the Judeo-Christian system of ethics. He told me:

> *I know some businessmen have supplied call girls to customers, but there are always a few rotten apples in every barrel. That doesn't mean the rest of the fruit isn't sound. Surely the vast majority of businessmen are ethical. I myself am acquainted with many who adhere to strict codes of ethics based fundamentally on religious teachings. They contribute to good causes. They participate in community activities. They cooperate with other companies to improve working conditions in their industries. Certainly they are not indifferent to ethics.*

That most businessmen are not indifferent to ethics in their private lives, everyone will agree. My point is that in their office lives they cease to be private citizens; they become game players who must be guided by a somewhat different set of ethical standards.

The point was forcefully made to me by a Midwestern executive who has given a good deal of thought to the question:

> *So long as a businessman complies with the laws of the land and avoids telling malicious lies, he's ethical. If the law as written gives a man a wide-open chance to make a killing, he'd be a fool not to take advantage of it. If he doesn't, somebody else will. There's no obligation on him to stop and consider who is going to get hurt. If the law says he can do it, that's all the justification he needs. There's nothing unethical about that. It's just plain business sense.*

This executive (call him Robbins) took the stand that even industrial espionage, which is frowned on by some businessmen, ought not to be considered unethical. He recalled a recent meeting of the National Industrial Conference Board where an authority on marketing made a speech in which he deplored the employment of spies by business organizations. More and more companies, he pointed out, find it cheaper to penetrate the secrets of competitors with concealed cameras and microphones or by bribing employees than to set up costly research and design departments of their own. A whole branch of the electronics industry has grown up with this trend, he continued, providing equipment to make industrial espionage easier.

Disturbing? The marketing expert found it so. But when it came to a remedy, he could only appeal to "respect for the golden rule." Robbins thought this a confession of defeat, believing that the golden rule, for all its value as an ideal for society, is simply not feasible as a guide for business. A good part of the time the businessman is trying to do unto others as he hopes others will not do unto him.[2] Robbins continued:

Espionage of one kind or another has become so common in business that it's like taking a drink during Prohibition—it's not considered sinful. And we don't even have Prohibition where espionage is concerned; the law is very tolerant in this area. There's no more shame for a business that uses secret agents than there is for a nation. Bear in mind that there already is at least one large corporation—you can buy its stock over the counter—that makes millions by providing counterespionage service to industrial firms. Espionage in business is not an ethical problem; it's an established technique of business competition.

"We Don't Make the Laws"

Wherever we turn in business, we can perceive the sharp distinction between its ethical standards and those of the churches. Newspapers abound with sensational stories growing out of this distinction:

> We read one day that Senator Philip A. Hart of Michigan has attacked food processors for deceptive packaging of numerous products.[3]

> The next day there is a congressional to-do over Ralph Nader's book, *Unsafe At Any Speed,* which demonstrates that automobile companies for years have neglected the safety of car-owning families.[4]

> Then another Senator, Lee Metcalf of Montana, and journalist Vic Reinemer show in their book, *Overcharge,* the methods by which utility companies elude regulating government bodies to extract unduly large payments from users of electricity.[5]

These are merely dramatic instances of a prevailing condition; there is hardly a major industry at which a similar attack could not be aimed. Critics of business regard such behavior as unethical, but the companies concerned know that they are merely playing the business game.

Among the most respected of our business institutions are the insurance companies. A group of insurance executives meeting recently in New England was startled when their guest speaker, social critic Daniel Patrick Moynihan, roundly berated them for "unethical" practices. They had been guilty, Moynihan alleged, of using outdated actuarial tables to obtain unfairly high premiums. They habitually delayed the hearings of lawsuits against them in order to tire out the plaintiffs and win cheap settlements. In their employment policies they used ingenious devices to discriminate against certain minority groups.[6]

It was difficult for the audience to deny the validity of these charges. But these men were business game players. Their reaction to Moynihan's attack was much the same as that of the automobile manufacturers to Nader, of the utilities to Senator Metcalf, and of the food processors to Senator Hart. If the laws governing their businesses change, or if public opinion becomes clamorous, they will make the necessary adjustments. But morally they have in their view done nothing wrong. As long as they comply with the letter of the law, they are within their rights to operate their businesses as they see fit.

The small business is in the same position as the great corporation in this respect. For example:

> In 1967 a key manufacturer was accused of providing master keys for automobiles to mail-order customers, although it was obvious that some of the purchasers might be automobile thieves. His defense was plain and straightforward. If there was nothing in the law to prevent him from selling his keys to anyone who ordered them, it was not up to him to inquire who ordered them, it was not up to him to inquire as

to his customers' motives. Why was it any worse, he insisted, for him to sell car keys by mail, than for mail-order houses to sell guns that might be used for murder? Until the law was changed, the key manufacturer could regard himself as being just as ethical as any other businessman by the rules of the business game.[7]

Violations of the ethical ideals of society are common in business, but they are not necessarily violations of business principles. Each year the Federal Trade Commission orders hundreds of companies, many of them of the first magnitude, to "cease and desist" from practices which, judged by ordinary standards, are of questionable morality but which are stoutly defended by the companies concerned.

In one case, a firm manufacturing a well-known mouthwash was accused of using a cheap form of alcohol possibly deleterious to health. The company's chief executive, after testifying in Washington, made this comment privately:

> *We broke no law. We're in a highly competitive industry. If we're going to stay in business, we have to look for profit wherever the law permits. We don't make the laws. We obey them. Then why do we have to put up with this "holier than thou" talk about ethics? It's sheer hypocrisy. We're not in business to promote ethics. Look at the cigarette companies, for God's sake! If the ethics aren't embodied in the laws by the men who made them, you can't expect businessmen to fill the lack. Why, a sudden submission to Christian ethics by businessmen would bring about the greatest economic upheaval in history!*

It may be noted that the government failed to prove its case against him.

***

THE INDIVIDUAL & THE GAME

An individual within a company often finds it difficult to adjust to the requirements of the business game. He tries to preserve his private ethical standards in situations that call for game strategy. When he is obliged to carry out company policies that challenge his conception of himself as an ethical man, he suffers.

It disturbs him when he is ordered, for instance, to deny a raise to a man who deserves it, to fire an employee of long standing, to prepare advertising that he believes to be misleading, to conceal facts that he feels customers are entitled to know, to cheapen the quality of materials used in the manufacture of an established product, to sell as new a product that he knows to be rebuilt, to exaggerate the curative powers of a medicinal preparation, or to coerce dealers.

There are some fortunate executives who, by the nature of their work and circumstances, never have to face problems of this kind. But in one form or another the ethical dilemma is felt sooner or later by most businessmen. Possibly the dilemma is most painful not when the company forces the action on the executive but when he originates it himself—that is, when he has taken or is contemplating a step which is in his own interest but which runs counter to his early moral conditioning. To illustrate:

> The manager of an export department, eager to show rising sales, is pressed by a big customer to provide invoices which, while containing no overt falsehood that would violate a U.S. law, are so worded that the customer may be able to evade certain taxes in his homeland.

A company president finds that an aging executive, within a few years of retirement and his pension, is not as productive as formerly. Should he be kept on?

The produce manager of a supermarket debates with himself whether to get rid of a lot of half-rotten tomatoes by including one, with its good side exposed, in every tomato six-pack.

An accountant discovers that he has taken an improper deduction on his company's tax return and fears the consequences if he calls the matter to the president's attention, though he himself has done nothing illegal. Perhaps if he says nothing, no one will notice the error.

A chief executive officer is asked by his directors to comment on a rumor that he owns stock in another company with which he has placed large orders. He could deny it, for the stock is in the name of his son-in-law and he has earlier formally instructed his son-in-law to sell the holding.

Temptations of this kind constantly arise in business. If an executive allows himself to be torn between a decision based on business considerations and one based on his private ethical code, he exposes himself to a grave psychological strain.

This is not to say that sound business strategy necessarily runs counter to ethical ideals. They may frequently coincide; and when they do, everyone is gratified. But the major tests of every move in business, as in all games of strategy, are legality and profit. A man who intends to be a winner in the business game must have a game player's attitude.

The business strategist's decisions must be as impersonal as those of a surgeon performing an operation—concentrating on objective and technique, and subordinating personal feelings. If the chief executive admits that his son-in-law owns the stock, it is because he stands to lose more if the fact comes out later than if he states it boldly and at once. If the supermarket manager orders the rotten tomatoes to be discarded, he does so to avoid an increase in consumer complaints and a loss of goodwill. The company president decides not to fire the elderly executive in the belief that the negative reaction of other employees would in the long run cost the company more than it would lose in keeping him and paying his pension.

All sensible businessmen prefer to be truthful, but they seldom feel inclined to tell the *whole* truth. In the business game truth-telling usually has to be kept within narrow limits if trouble is to be avoided. The point was neatly made a long time ago (in 1888) by one of John D. Rockefeller's associates, Paul Babcock, to Standard Oil Company executives who were about to testify before a government investigating committee: "Parry every question with answers which, while perfectly truthful, are evasive of *bottom* facts."[8] This was, is, and probably always will be regarded as wise and permissible business strategy.

For Office Use Only

An executive's family life can easily be dislocated if he fails to make a sharp distinction between the ethical systems of the home and the office—or if his wife does not grasp that distinction. Many a businessman who has remarked to his wife, "I had to let Jones go today" or "I had to admit to the boss that Jim has been goofing off lately," has been met with an indignant protest. "How could you do a thing like that? You know Jones is over 50 and will have a lot of trouble getting another job." Or, "You did that to Jim? With his wife ill and all the worry she's been having with the kids?"

If the executive insists that he had no choice because the profits of the company and his own security were involved, he may see a certain cool and ominous reappraisal in his wife's eyes. Many wives are not prepared to accept the fact that business operates with a special code of ethics. An illuminating illustration of this comes from a Southern sales executive who related a conversation he had had with his wife at a time when a hotly contested political campaign was being waged in their state:

> I made the mistake of telling her that I had had lunch with Colby, who gives me about half my business. Colby mentioned that his company had a stake in the election. Then he said, "By the way, I'm treasurer of the citizens' committee for Lang. I'm collecting contributions. Can I count on you for a hundred dollars?"
>
> Well, there I was. I was opposed to Lang, but I knew Colby. If he withdrew his business I could be in a bad spot. So I just smiled and wrote out a check then and there. He thanked me, and we started to talk about his next order. Maybe he thought I shared his political views. If so, I wasn't going to lose any sleep over it.
>
> I should have had sense enough not to tell Mary about it. She hit the ceiling. She said she was disappointed in me. She said I hadn't acted like a man, that I should have stood up to Colby.
>
> I said, "Look, it was an either-or situation. I had to do it or risk losing the business."
>
> She came back at me with, "I don't believe it. You could have been honest with him. You could have said that you didn't feel you ought to contribute to a campaign for a man you weren't going to vote for. I'm sure he would have understood."
>
> I said, "Mary, you're a wonderful woman, but you're way off the track. Do you know what would have happened if I had said that? Colby would have smiled and said, 'Oh, I didn't realize. Forget it.' But in his eyes from that moment I would be an oddball, maybe a bit of a radical. He would have listened to me talk about his order and would have promised to give it consideration. After that I wouldn't hear from him for a week. Then I would telephone and learn from his secretary that he wasn't yet ready to place the order. And in about a month I would hear through the grapevine that he was giving his business to another company. A month after that I'd be out of a job."
>
> She was silent for a while. Then she said, "Tom, something is wrong with business when a man is forced to choose between his family's security and his moral obligation to himself. It's easy for me to say you should have stood up to him—but if you had, you might have felt you were betraying me and the kids. I'm sorry that you did it, Tom, but I can't blame you. Something is wrong with business!"

This wife saw the problem in terms of moral obligation as conceived in private life; her husband saw it as a matter of game strategy. As a player in a weak position, he felt that he could not afford to indulge an ethical sentiment that might have cost him his seat at the table.

Playing to Win

Some men might challenge the Colbys of business—might accept serious setbacks to their business careers rather than risk a feeling of moral cowardice. They merit our respect—but as private individuals, not businessmen. When the skillful player of the business game is compelled to submit to unfair pressure, he does not castigate himself for moral weakness.

Instead, he strives to put himself into a strong position where he can defend himself against such pressures in the future without loss.

If a man plans to take a seat in the business game, he owes it to himself to master the principles by which the game is played, including its special ethical outlook. He can then hardly fail to recognize that an occasional bluff may well be justified in terms of the game's ethics and warranted in terms of economic necessity. Once he clears his mind on this point, he is in a good position to match his strategy against that of the other players. He can then determine objectively whether a bluff in a given situation has a good chance of succeeding and can decide when and how to bluff, without a feeling of ethical transgression.

To be a winner, a man must play to win. This does not mean that he must be ruthless, cruel, harsh, or treacherous. On the contrary, the better his reputation for integrity, honesty, and decency, the better his chances of victory will be in the long run. But from time to time every businessman, like every poker player, is offered a choice between certain loss or bluffing within the legal rules of the game. If he is not resigned to losing, if he wants to rise in his company and industry, then in such a crisis he will bluff—and bluff hard.

Every now and then one meets a successful businessman who has conveniently forgotten the small or large deceptions that he practiced on his way to fortune. "God gave me my money," old John D. Rockefeller once piously told a Sunday school class. It would be a rare tycoon in our time who would risk the horse laugh with which such a remark would be greeted.

In the last third of the twentieth century even children are aware that if a man has become prosperous in business, he has sometimes departed from the strict truth in order to overcome obstacles or has practiced the more subtle deceptions of the half-truth or the misleading omission. Whatever the form of the bluff, it is an integral part of the game, and the executive who does not master its techniques is not likely to accumulate much money or power.

NOTES

1. *The New York Times,* March 9, 1967.
2. *See* Bruce D. Henderson, "Brinkmanship in Business," HBR March–April 1967, p. 49.
3. *The New York Times,* November 21, 1966.
4. New York, Grossman Publishers, Inc., 1965.
5. New York, David McKay Company, Inc., 1967.
6. *The New York Times,* January 17, 1967.
7. Cited by Ralph Nader in "Business Crime," *The New Republic,* July 1, 1967, p. 7.
8. Babcock in a memorandum to Rockefeller (Rockefeller Archives).

PROFIT
Some Moral Reflections
PAUL F. CAMENISCH

The issues of profit, its moral meaning, justification, and role, need careful examination. Mistakes to be avoided in making moral sense of profit include the assumption that profitability establishes a company's moral rectitude. Profit is too complex a phenomenon to establish any such thing. Steps toward clarifying these issues include distinguishing profit as the goal of the corporation from the larger goals of the economy itself, and clarifying what we mean by "profit." 'Profit' often includes the moral or value consideration of having been rightly or fairly earned. This provides one starting point internal to business for formulating standards for business ethics.

Profit is only rarely the central focus of business ethics discussions. In fact, when profit *as such* becomes the focus, we are no longer doing business ethics in the usual sense but are rather raising the question of the moral legitimacy of the business system itself. This is quite a different enterprise.

Nevertheless, it would be a mistake to conclude that profit does not play a significant role in business ethics. In fact, it appears to be one of the most important and persistent background elements in such discussions. After all, business ethics currently focuses almost exclusively on for-profit corporations, even though they share many characteristics and problems with not-for-profit enterprises. Apparently profit is widely thought to be a significant, even a *morally* significant distinguishing factor.

In fairness to business ethicists who are often accused of raising the profit issue, it should be noted that the focus on this subject is sometimes sharpened by business people themselves. Aided and abetted by academics such as Peter Drucker (1981), some business people are convinced that the major motivation of business ethicists is an antibusiness animus, which presumably translates very easily into a morally based rejection of profits as such. Such persons often concentrate on exposing and discrediting such a bias, or on showing how most measures recommended by ethically concerned critics will threaten profits and thus endanger the corporation itself. At this point the conversation either focuses on profit or comes to an end.

"Profit: Some Moral Reflections," by Paul Camenisch, from *Journal of Business Ethics* 6 (1987), pp. 225–31. Reprinted by permission of Kluwer Academic Publishers.

WHY PROFIT ALWAYS HOVERS AND SOMETIMES DOMINATES

If we are to get beyond this problem with profits, we must ask why it frequently looms so large, perhaps even larger in popular response to business than in academic discussions. Surveys consistently show that the average citizen greatly overestimates corporate profit. This results in part from the consumer's assumption that any shortfall between the price of goods or services and the perceived value received is the result of corporate profit. Anytime an increasingly demanding and educated buying public feels shortchanged in the market-place, the conviction will grow that profits are soaring beyond all reason. Of course such shortfall actually represents the costs of poor management, inefficient production and marketing, etc. But it is the consumer's perception rather than the reality itself that determines the direction and tone of the discussion.

Profit sometimes becomes an easy target for the critic because of the way it is defined. If profit is what is left of gross receipts after all expenses have been paid, then the critic's obvious question is, "What justifies profit, what is profit repayment for?" Wages and benefits for workers, payment for raw materials, taxes, advertising and other marketing costs, return on needed capital are all generally seen by consumers as costs legitimately passed on as part of the product's price. But if *all* these have been taken care of, and only then is the remainder treated as profit, business is hard pressed to say what profit is payment for, how it is earned, why deserved. The usual move at this point is to define profit as what is left after all *tangible,* or all *specifiable* and *quantifiable* costs have been paid. Thus profit becomes payment or reward for certain intangibles crucial to production and marketing. Risk, entrepreneurial creativity and initiative, uncertainty, deferring use of one's resources to make them available as capital, are some of the possibilities here. While this definition provides a bit more justification for profit, it is still quite an intangible one. Furthermore, the impossibility of measuring such intangible elements makes it difficult if not impossible to answer the almost inevitable next question, "How *much* profit is appropriate?"

Finally, profit is always a potential focus because the solutions to many business ethics problems threaten to eat into profits. Appropriate responses to problems such as pollution, adequate wages and benefits, safe, even pleasant working conditions, non-discriminatory personnel policies backed by appropriate recruitment, training and even retraining programs, careful husbanding of non-renewable resources, honest, informative advertising, production of safe, durable products—all of these frequently involve the expenditure of additional funds which can only come from what was previously treated as profits. Thus, for example, the pollution debate is not between business which favors pollution, and citizens who oppose it. It is between two sides which agree that pollution is undesirable but who will not always agree on what is a tolerable cost for reducing it. Thus while corporations do not pursue profit only (Adam, 1973; Lennox, 1984), that may seem to be the case when other morally indicated goals are resisted in order to protect profits.

Furthermore, business will often be at a significant disadvantage when profits are in this way set in tension with the needs or wants of other constituencies because the intangible elements which might justify profits do not, in the eyes of many persons, stand up well against the more immediate, basic and tangible needs of other claimants, such as more adequate wages and benefits for workers, clean air and water for all, or employee and consumer safety.

MISTAKES TO BE AVOIDED

Premature Defensiveness

There are several pitfalls awaiting persons wishing to make good moral and human sense out of profits in response to the above questions. First, it should be noted that according to the above analysis, profit can end up on the defensive not just because of ill-will, antibusiness animus or massive ignorance about economics and the capitalist system. On occasion these factors may contribute to profit's problems. But many problems arise from the response of ordinary persons who predictably identify more easily with those basic interests and needs which often seem to be ranged against profit than they do with profit itself. Thus for business instinctively to charge forth to do battle with ill will and antibusiness sentiments when profit is raised as an issue is usually premature, off-target and counterproductive.

Excessive Generalizing

Two other mistakes to be avoided are more conceptual in nature but are still important beyond academic circles. The first is the tack taken by H. B. Acton (1980) and others who argue that the pursuit of profits is simply one manifestation of the desire of everyone—whether investor, wage earner, supplier, or consumer—to possess more than one has. Such a generalizing of the meaning of profit and of profit seeking aims at answering critics of profit in two ways. The first depends on the belief that if a drive can be shown to be universal in humans and therefore apparently innate, it is beyond ethical examination and moral criticism. But this ignores the obvious fact that we are often held responsible for the way we permit even innate and universal traits or drives to shape our conduct. This approach also suggests that even if profit and profit seeking are morally objectionable, it ill behooves any of us to say so since none of our hands are clean in this matter.

But the price paid for any gains in this defense of profit is too high. Such expansion robs the idea of profit of all specificity, and any moral analysis of the central phenomenon in view—the conscious, systematic, and sustained pursuit of increased wealth through investment in capitalistic undertakings—is obstructed in two distinct ways. On the one hand, we find ourselves with traditionally accepted and intuitively persuasive moral distinctions which we can no longer make because this broadened definition reduces these phenomena to a single thing. Thus Rockefeller's (or was it Carnegie's) probably apocryphal response to the question of how much money is enough—"Just a little bit more"—becomes morally indistinguishable from the starving child's plea for his third breadcrust in a week. Both are 'profit' seekers, desiring to increase their share of the available material resources. That equation is not only conceptually unhelpful, it is morally intolerable. On the other hand, this greatly enlarged definition of profit, by tempting us to reduce our defense or profit to the minimalist insistence that everyone does it, removes the motivation for seeking the positive moral points that can be made on behalf of profit in a capitalist or mixed economy.

Profit as Moral Justifier

The second unhelpful move is for business too facilely to appeal to profits as a proof of its integrity and morality so that making a profit serves as a moral vindication—"How could we be doing so well if we weren't doing good?" Such an appeal makes most sense on the assumption that the amount of profit is determined by the workings of some objective laws of nature or of economics which in proper proportion reward some contribution made or some characteristics possessed by the profit maker. Several brief cases show not only why such an appeal is not persuasive, but demonstrate that the very concept of profit itself is becoming problematic. For example, *Crain's Chicago Business* reported that United Airlines "earned only $15.1 million in the first six months despite tax benefits of $148 million" (Merrion, 1983). The obvious question is why we call that a $15.1 million 'earnings' rather than a $132.9 million loss to, or at least subsidy by U.S. taxpayers. Similarly, on February 1, 1984, a *Wall Street Journal* editorial noted that "Federal handouts to agriculture exceeded net farm income in 1983" (Bovard, 1984). Again one might well ask what "net income" means here, or "Whose profit and how earned, and whose loss are we dealing with?"

On September 12, 1983, under a headline reading "Low-income project turns a profit," *Crain's Chicago Business* reported that on a low income housing rehabilitation project in which it had invested $940,000 in risk capital, and had provided other financing through letters of credit, Indiana Standard estimated its pre-tax profit at $600,000 to $800,000 (Wagner, 1983). The article reports that this project also involved the following elements: the Illinois Housing Development Authority provided a $13.8 million tax-exempt loan; federal subsidies guaranteed that 70 percent of each unit's rent would be paid for up to 30 years; the city of Chicago loaned the partnership $3.3 million at 1.5 percent interest; the congressionally chartered for-profit National Housing Partnership purchased 99 percent of the partnership owned by Rescorp and Indiana Standard and sold 95 percent to investors seeking tax shelters; residents of the development will pay only 30 percent of the rent. By the end of all this, the head of the uninitiated spins as he wonders what it cost the taxpayers to generate that 'profit' for Indiana Standard. No iron laws of economics here! In fact, one can be forgiven for suspecting that to call that money 'profit' is little more than a polite convention.

And finally, financial analysis of some recent corporate earnings statements shows that earnings or profit can be as much an accountant's creation or enhancement of reality as a corporation's reward for performance. For example, according to one analysis, Polaroid's claimed 21 cents a share earnings for the first quarter of 1984 drops to 2 cents a share when one eliminates gains over the previous year from certain non-operating and quite possibly non-repeating items (lower tax rate—5 cents a share; currency gains—7 cents; lower interest expenses—5 cents; lower depreciation for plant and equipment—2 cents) (Dorfman, 1984). To what extent then does this 'profit' increase over the year-ago earnings of 7 cents per share accurately inform us about corporate performance in its distinctive task of producing and marketing goods and services, and the appropriate reward for such performance in the competitive market place?

Perhaps these are not typical cases. But at the very least they show that the terms 'profit', 'earnings', and 'net income' are used quite casually. At most, they show that these ideas have been severed from the simple definitions of profit most of us begin with, definitions which underlie most versions of the position that profit is morally justified and morally justifying. Here it becomes clear that profit, at least for major actors in our current economy, is the result of complex interactions among a variety of economic, political and other forces, most of which are beyond the control or even the direct influence of the business, which nevertheless claims the resulting profit as its just reward. Thus, for example, it is virtually impossible in the end to say what the $600,000–$800,000 represents except the amount Indiana Standard is permitted to claim at the end of an extremely complex series of interactions. Whether and why this is an appropriate profit (i.e., whether proportional to any other factor involved or to any actual contribution Standard made) is impossible to establish.

Nor is it only governmental decisions which alter supposedly simple and autonomous economic dynamics to determine profit. The action last year of U.S. auto makers granting their top managers millions of dollars in bonuses shows that certain elements within corporations can simply decree whether certain portions of company assets will be treated as profit or as resources available for meeting other 'expenses' such as executive bonuses. Thus to appeal to profits as a moral vindication of the company and its operations is in at least some cases to pull the rabbit out of the hat only after one—with the help of several allies, both witting and unwitting—has first carefully placed the rabbit there.

HELPFUL WAYS FORWARD

Distinguishing Corporate Goals from the Economy's Goals

How then do we begin to bring greater clarity to the discussion of profit and its moral dimensions? I offer a few modest suggestions. First, it will be helpful to distinguish between the goals or purposes of a corporation and those of business as such, or to make the point clearer still, between those of a corporation and those of the economic system as such. Business leaders, sincerely and with the best of intentions, sometimes state that the primary purpose of a corporation is not to make a profit, but to meet human needs, to serve the consumer, etc. While this may be true of some corporations, and while on some level it may be true of all corporations, the public in general finds such statements unpersuasive, even hypocritical, and many stockholders may possibly see them as indicative of managerial mis- or malfeasance.

However, business persons making such statements are trying to say something which is both true and important. But it is said more clearly and persuasively if the distinction just suggested is observed. It may well help clear the air if corporations would simply acknowledge that their primary purpose is to make a profit and then stood ready to show why and how that is a defensible, a necessary, even a good thing in the present system. But at the same time they should acknowledge—and this would seem to be what executives trying to cast an altruistic light on corporations are trying to say—that the purpose of business, or of the economic system of which the corporation is a part, is not to make profit making possible, but to fulfill human needs or to provide goods and services which sustain and enhance life (Camenisch, 1981). This identifies profit's proper place within the corporation while acknowledging its subordination to larger societal purposes beyond the corporation.

This distinction between the corporation's internal and external purposes, or perhaps better, between the purpose of the part (the corporation) and that of the whole (the total society and its economic system) may initially seem to raise conceptual as well as practical problems. But in fact we constantly live with this distinction. The purpose or motive of the person who weekly loads my trash onto the sanitation department truck most likely does not coincide either with the department's goal or with the purpose of the city in establishing such a department. But *as long as the individual's goals do not interfere with those of the larger entity,* this need not concern us and we can honestly say that the individual is simultaneously serving both purposes. And this can be said without denying that the individual legitimately has his own distinctive purposes, such as making a living, supporting his family, etc.

We should have no more uneasiness in making parallel statements about the corporation's goal of profit making in relation to the goals of the larger society. The corporation whose pursuit of profit is consistent with, or even is a means to helping society fulfill its economic tasks pursues two different but compatible and entirely honorable sets of goals. This way of seeing things avoids testing the public's credulity by telling it that the primary goal of for-profit corporations is not profit. It would also put corporations and their goals in the appropriate perspective of their relation to the larger society and its needs. Thus profit making as such might cease to be a moral issue and would raise problems only when it began to jeopardize the larger societal goals to which it is to be subordinated.

Clarifying the Meaning of Profit

The second and more substantive move would be to open the discussion not on whether profit is morally defensible or legitimate, but on what we mean by it. Conceptually it is not always easy to distinguish profit from apparently similar phenomena. How, for example, do 'profits' differ, from lottery winnings, from $10,000 I find on the street, from an inheritance, from income from juice loans, from taking money under false pretenses, from simple theft? After all, all of these frequently leave one with a 'profit'. For the moment let us grant that their illegality eliminates theft, juice loans and taking money under false pretenses as serious comparisons. And yet the recent E. F. Hutton check rigging case cautions us against too facile a dismissal of these comparisons. Thinking now as morally concerned citizens and not simply as accountants, should the gains realized by Hutton in that practice have been considered profits? Were they profits until the scheme was uncovered, at which point they became "ill-gotten gains"? If, after paying the fine, court costs, and refunds to banks, Hutton still comes out ahead—which does not seem unlikely given the length, size, and complexity of the practice—what should their 'profit' be called? Does simply considering it profit in any way taint those profits which were legitimately gained and with which it is now lumped as gross income? Just what are the limits to what can be considered profit.

To return to our list of comparisons, perhaps the element of sheer chance eliminates the $10,000 found on the street from being considered profit. But what about the lottery winnings or the inheritance? No law was broken. I did make some investment and do certain things to attain the goal (I knew aging and wealthy Aunt Gertrude was lonely and enjoyed Sunday drives in the country.) And I profited. Ah, but gains are properly called 'profits' only if they result from 'business activity'. So why then is buying a lottery ticket not 'business', while investing in a highly speculative stock is?

This question of what constitutes 'business activity' is an important one, but more interesting here is another element which is almost invariably introduced to distinguish profit, properly speaking, from some of these other gains, especially the more questionable ones. This is the idea that profit must be *earned,* must even be fairly and justly earned, that it must be a 'reasonable' profit. If we had difficulty defining 'profit' and 'business activity', we can surely expect no fewer problems with such notoriously elusive terms as 'fairly', 'justly', and 'reasonable'.

PROFIT AND MORAL JUSTIFICATION

This idea of profit as earned, justified and proportionate is almost certainly behind the invoking of profitability as a moral legitimation of the corporation and its activity that was dismissed above as misleading given the diverse factors now influencing business outcomes. However, it is now time to acknowledge that this group of interconnected ideas does have some role in our understanding of profit and its place in the assessment—moral as well as economic—of corporate performance.

Challenged to explain, even to justify their profit, corporate leaders seem to have four kinds of responses available. The first, which most critical consumers may suspect is descriptively the most accurate one is that the amount of profit is determined by whatever the market will bear. Few business people publicly state this answer since it sounds so much like, "grab all you can and run." But where Adam Smith's "invisible hand" is still thought to function, this answer will be seen not as a license to exploit, but as a realistic recognition of ordinary, even automatic market limitations on over-charging. Nevertheless, because Smith's analysis is unknown to many, and is rejected by many others, and because our economic experience is so different from that represented by Smith's simple model of the market, this answer is usually, and probably wisely avoided by business persons as appearing to legitimate virtually unlimited profit taking without claiming any moral justification for it.

A second answer to the challenge to explain and justify profits, already met above, but mentioned here for the sake of completeness, can be a species of the first. But rather than seeming to remove the limits to profit making, it explicitly invokes such limits in the form of some automatic and impersonal laws of economics which will set limits to what can be charged through the interplay of various market forces. In addition to what was said above about the current inadequacies of this approach, we will here simply note the widely recognized ways such controlling market mechanisms are impeded, obstructed, even defeated by monopoly, oligopoly, various forms of governmental interventions, including subsidy of business, and the difficulty of new producers entering extremely complex and highly technical markets.

A third answer to the questions of justifying profits and their amount is for business to appeal to the public to trust business's own conscience to keep it within appropriate limits specified in part by business's various contributions which ought to be rewarded, and by what business needs to survive. While some persons may find this answer acceptable and while some corporations do deserve to be so trusted, carefully examined this answer finally fails because of its paternalism. Paternalism, which in the present context means the need for some to rely on the voluntary good will and intentions of others, is increasingly out of fashion in this society for a number of good reasons. Thus, at a time when the law, traditional professions, and other agencies in the society are being criticized for their paternalism, it is unlikely that business will be permitted to answer the question of the appropriate limits on profits by appeal to its own internal controls to be exercised on behalf of, but without examination or control by the public.

The fourth answer to our question tries to justify profits in the most direct and usual sense of that term. Here the business person claims that profit and its amount are justified by some contribution of business and/or its owners, for which the profit is an appropriate repayment or reward. For this response to be persuasive, two conditions will have to be met.

First and most obviously, that 'contribution' will have to be specifically identified. Otherwise we are back to a paternalism in which we simply take the corporation's own word concerning its virtue, its trustworthiness, or its profit-deserving contribution. The second condition to be met is that the contribution so specified not be so abstract and intangible that it is able to justify virtually any amount of profit, and so leaves unanswered the question of proportionate or appropriate profit.

The frequency with which business persons resort to this last response raises the question of whether "being justified" is helpfully treated as a part of the definition of profit, or whether this element is extraneous to profit so that business gains are properly considered 'profit' even when they cannot be justified in any of the usual ways. This is in part a linguistic or definitional question of how we use the term 'profits'. (Even at this level, however, we ought not to forget that language reflects and perpetuates our moral conceptions and commitments, and thus should be chosen carefully.)

But this is also more than a linguistic issue, for if, according to wide usage, profit is only truly profitable when it is deserved according to some publicly specifiable and generally accepted criteria, then one can begin to argue that at least some of the moral standards applying to business need not be imported from outside business by "business ethicists," but that they are inherent in the very basic concepts, such as 'profit' by which we understand and structure our economic system. I can think of no development which would portend better for progress in business ethics than such a discovery *within* business of some of its governing moral norms. Carefully attended to, the idea of profit as it is frequently used offers an excellent starting point for identifying just such internal moral norms for business. On the other hand, insulated from any such moral considerations and limitations, profit will indeed be difficult for business to defend and, whether explicitly articulated or not, will continue to be a potential obstacle to productive dialogue in business ethics.

REFERENCES

1. Acton, H. B.: 1980, "The Profit Motive," in M. Missner (ed.), *Ethics of the Business System* (Sherman Oaks, CA: Alfred Publishing Co., Inc.), pp. 21–39.
2. Adam, J., Jr.: 1973, "Put Profit in Its Place," *The Harvard Business Review* **51,** 150–158.
3. Bovard, J.: February 1, 1984, "Soaring Succor for Select Business," *Wall Street Journal* **23,** 9.
4. Camenisch, P. F.: 1981, "Business Ethics: On Getting to the Heart of the Matter," *Business and Professional Ethics Journal* **1,** 59–69.
5. Dorfman, D.: July 28, 1984, "3 Well-known Stocks with Earnings of Dubious Quality," *Chicago Tribune,* Section 2, pp. 1 and 11.
6. Drucker, P.: 1981, "What Is Business Ethics?" *The Public Interest* **63,** 18–36.
7. Lennox, D.: April 3, 1984, "Ethical Companies Weigh More than Profits," *Crain's Chicago Business* **7,** no. 18, pp. 11–12.
8. Merrion, P.: October 10, 1983, "UAL Sticks to Its Game Plan," *Crain's Chicago Business* **6,** no. 41, pp. 3 and 56.
9. Wagner, L. M.: Sept. 12, 1983, "Low-Income Project Turns a Profit," *Crain's Chicago Business* **6,** no. 37, p. 22.

THE IDEAS OF AYN RAND

RONALD MERRILL

Ayn Rand promulgated an economic theory called objectivism and is known for her work incorporating objectivism into novels such as The Fountainhead *and* Atlas Shrugged. *Merrill describes objectivism and compares it to various other theories. Objectivism is really a version of ethical egoism that focuses on self-interested acts because, as Rand contends, all of us always and only act in our own self-interest. Contrary to popular belief, however, Rand sees nothing wrong with selfishness; instead, she berates those who are too selfless, calling them* second-handers. *(See text introduction to this chapter.) Consider for yourself when this has not been the case. (Note that she would claim that even an anonymous donation is selfishly motivated since you would be satisfying some need of your own to help others.)*

THE OBJECTIVIST ETHICS

Rand's most substantial contribution to philosophical thought lies in the field of ethics. It was Ayn Rand who, after 2,000 years of failed attempts, finally proposed a viable solution to the fundamental problem of ethics: deriving normative from factual statements, or, less formally, deriving 'ought' from 'is'. Philosophers have long recognized this as a major problem. Indeed, in the twentieth century most philosophers have despaired of the prospect of developing any sort of logically justifiable ethics. Arguably Ayn Rand's most important accomplishment was producing a solution to this problem. In response, her opponents have concentrated their fire primarily on her ethical reasoning.

I hope, therefore, the reader will forgive me for devoting a great deal of space to this subject. The following discussion will not only present Rand's reasoning, but analyze it in some depth. I will suggest that the Objectivist ethics can be made more rigorous if certain arguments are reformulated. Then I will compare Rand's approach to Aristotle's and show how she can deal with the moral skepticism of Hume. The various arguments of Rand's critics will be surveyed. Finally, I want to look at the implications of the Objectivist ethics and consider some ways in which it may be extended.

Every human society has had ethical precepts, claims that one 'ought' to do, or not do, certain things. How can such claims be justified? The historic justifications have been such as: 'You ought to, because I say so'. Or: 'You ought to because God, speaking through me,

Excerpts from *The Ideas of Ayn Rand*, by Ronald Merrill. Reprinted by permission of Open Court.

says so'. Or: 'You ought to because all the rest of us took a vote and the majority says so'. Or: 'You ought to because if you don't we'll burn you at the stake'.

At least in modern times we would not accept any of these modes of argument to settle a factual question such as, say, whether the earth revolves around the sun. Why should we accept them in determining moral questions? But if we don't, just how should we determine the truth of a moral dilemma?

Rand attacks the problem of ethics by going to the root, to a question of 'meta-ethics'. Instead of asking, 'Which morality is correct?' she asks, 'Just what *is* a "morality," anyway?' There are many possible moralities which might be correct: Christian ethics, the Ten Commandments, 'Seek the greatest good of the greatest number', 'Do what thou wilt is the whole of the law', and many others have been asserted. But what do they all have in common? What is a morality?

A morality—any morality—is a set of rules to guide the actions of an individual human being. This—and only this—is what all possible moralities have in common. This is the definition of a morality. (Rand puts it: "A code of values to guide man's choices and actions.")

Well, given this, asks Rand, why should there be any morality at all? This is of course a normative question, so let's rephrase it in factual terms: What would happen to a man who practiced no morality?

A man who practiced no morality would be a man whose behavior was guided by no rules at all. Even Alistair Crowley's morality has a rule ('Do what thou wilt') but our hypothetical literally amoral man could not follow even his whims consistently. He would have to behave as if his brain were connected to a random number generator. What would happen to him? He would of course quickly die.

This suggests that the connection between factual and normative statements is man's life. Man needs morality to live. Man ought to do certain things, because they are necessary in order for him to be. He 'is' because he does what he 'ought'.

Now the skeptic might say, 'You are assuming that I ought to choose life—what if I don't?' It is tempting to reply (as, in effect, John Galt does), 'Fine. If you prefer death, shut up and die.' But this is inadequate; it refutes the arguer, perhaps, but not the argument. It is not enough merely to demonstrate that altruism is a morality based on a premise of death. We need to make a positive argument to show that morality must be based on the standard of human life. To my mind Rand's argument for this position is insufficiently rigorous. However, I will assert that her line of reasoning is basically sound and that it can be put on a very strong footing.

***

ENDS AND ENDS IN THEMSELVES

The classical philosophical tradition in ethics, tracing back to the Greeks, seeks an 'ultimate end' of human action. The argument typically runs as follows:

Consider a goal, alpha. This goal actually is a means to an end, another goal, beta. But beta is itself a means to another goal, gamma, and so on. Can we find some ultimate goal, call it omega, which is an end in itself, not a means to any other end? If we can, and if we can show that every goal is ultimately a means to omega, then we have a basis for ethics.

Suppose, for instance, that we could establish that every human action is aimed at the individual's happiness. We are compelled to assume this proposition in strong form: A person does nothing, and can do nothing, purposeful unless the purpose is to serve his happiness. Even if he thinks he is doing something for other reasons, his real objective is and must be his own happiness. Then ethics reduces to a matter of engineering, so to speak; one need merely determine the most efficient way to serve one's happiness.

The proposed ethical 'end-in-itself' has been variously identified as justice, love, equality, the greater glory of God, and many other things. But in the end nobody has been able to satisfactorily establish that all goals are means to some end-in-itself.

Has Rand found the answer? It looks problematic at first glance. *Is* life an end-in-itself? Do humans *never* regard life as a means to an end? . . . And is life the *only* end-in-itself? Do humans *never* seek any other value for its own sake? Critics have seen this premise as the crucial weak point of the Randian argument.

Rand's chain of reasoning will not hold unless she can show that, as a matter of metaphysical fact, there is no 'end in itself' other than life. What if there are other ultimate ends, unrelated to, and perhaps even incompatible with, life or survival? Then it will *not* follow that all values must serve to sustain life. So Rand in adopting this argument requires herself to prove a negative.

At best this is going to be difficult, and probably it will be impossible. Take just one prospective counterexample: reproduction. Even with modern medicine a woman faces a noticeable risk of death in having a child. Taking into account economic and other costs, one can scarcely argue that reproduction makes a net contribution to the survival of the parents. It certainly seems plausible to assert that people value their offspring as ends in themselves, and not just as means to the survival of the parents.

Before we can deal with the problem we have identified, we must recognize that Rand is not using the term 'end in itself' in its traditional sense:

> *Metaphysically,* life *is the only phenomenon that is an end in itself: a value gained and kept by a constant process of action.*

Clearly this is not the usual conception of an 'end in itself'. But just what does it mean, then? Here is a paraphrase by Harry Binswanger: ". . . only life is an action directed toward the perpetuation of itself." And illuminating this in more detail:

> *A common misconception is that of thinking of 'survival' as if it were some single vital action that occurs after all the other actions [necessary to life] have been completed. 'Survival', however, means the continuation of the organism's life, and the organism's life is an integrated sum composed of all those specific actions which contribute to maintaining the organism in existence. In this sense in living action the parts are for the sake of the whole: the specific goal-directed actions are for the sake of the organism's capacity to repeat those actions in the future.*
>
> *An ultimate goal, if it is truly ultimate, must be an 'end in itself'. An 'end in itself' gives the appearance of a vicious circle: it is something sought for the sake of itself. This circulatory vanishes when we regard* life *as an end in itself: actions at a given time benefit survival, which means they make possible the organism's repetition of those actions in the future, being then again directed toward survival, which means their repetition, and so on.*

What Rand and Binswanger seem to be saying is that life is an 'end in itself' in an unusual and very special meaning: Life is an ordered collection of activities, which are means to achieving an end, which is—simply those activities. Every action taken to sustain life is simultaneously a means (because it supports life) and an end (because life is by definition simply the collective of such actions).

This conception of life is not only accurate and perceptive, but enormously fruitful for ethics. What's more, it offers a way to escape from the need to prove a negative in the argument for the Objectivist ethics.

THE MEANS TEST

At this point I want to suggest that we can reformulate Rand's argument in a way that leads to the same conclusions, without encountering the difficulty that we discovered above. All we need do is recognize that Rand's idea of 'life' as a sort of self-contained vortex of values which are simultaneously ends and means allows us to reverse the traditional program, as follows.

Consider a goal, Z. Attaining this goal is dependent on another goal, Y, which is a means to Z. Y in turn is dependent on another means, X, and so on. Is there some ultimate *means*, A, which is a means for all other goals? There is indeed: Life is a prerequisite for pursuing any other goal.

We are now in a position to ignore the problem of competing 'ends in themselves'. Let us argue as follows: Man must choose what values to pursue. But can something be a value if its attainment would be such as to eliminate or reduce one's ability to pursue values? To seek an end while rejecting an essential means to that end, is to act (means) to gain and/or keep a value (end) while not so acting—which is a contradiction. So whatever ultimate ends there may be, one can seek them only if, and to the extent that, one values that which serves one's own life. Whether or not life is the *only* ultimate end, it is an end which is a necessary means to any and all other ends.

The Aristotelian flavor of this approach becomes evident if we phrase the argument this way:

> *This goal is a means for all other goals, and not for some special genus apart from others. And all men value it, because it underlies all values. For a value which everyone must hold, who values anything at all, is not arbitrary. Evidently then such a value is the most certain of all; which value this is, let us proceed to say. It is the life of man* qua *man.*

To my mind this line of argument offers the prospect of putting the Objectivist ethics on a truly solid logical footing.

***

ROBERT NOZICK VERSUS THE COUNT OF MONTE CRISTO

No philosophical disputation would be complete without an example of the classic meaning-switch cheapo, and in the debate over Objectivist ethics Robert Nozick has provided the most ingenious application of this traditional technique.

Nozick asserts that one cannot derive an ethics from the fact that life is a prerequisite for all other values and cites a counter-example: Being cured of cancer is obviously a value. But having cancer is a prerequisite for being cured of cancer. Does this mean that having cancer is a value?

Well, let us take this sophomore stumper in the spirit in which it is intended and have some fun with it. A dedicated dialectician could dance a pleasant polka with Nozick by taking the affirmative of the question. For instance: Who has not on some occasion abstained from eating before a special meal, in order that hunger may sharpen the appetite and the enjoyment? Perhaps we should go all the way with the Count of Monte Cristo. He asserted that nobody could know true joy who had not experienced the ultimate depths of suffering, and went so far as to let a friend think his fiancée had died so he would be really happy when he learned she hadn't. A professional philosopher no doubt could convince us that it really does make sense to beat your head against a brick wall in order to enjoy the sensation when you stop.

But we must be moving on. Let's point out that Nozick has dropped the context that gives meaning to the value he is invoking. 'Being cured of cancer' is a value only to someone who has cancer. Modern cancer cures range from unpleasant to devastatingly painful; nobody would consider the cure a value in itself.

In short, there is an obvious distinction, which Nozick is fogging, between the circumstances which make something a value, and the means used to attain that value. When we say that Philosophy 101 is a prerequisite for Philosophy 102, we mean that the student will need the information, concepts, and skills taught in the first course in order to profit from the second. We may also say that a certain amount of ignorance of philosophy is a 'prerequisite' for Philosophy 102, in the sense that if the student already knows the material he won't benefit from taking the course—but now we are using 'prerequisite' in an entirely different meaning of the term.

***

THE DIVINE RIGHT OF CAPITAL

Is Maximizing Returns to Shareholders a Legitimate Mandate?

MARJORIE KELLY

In response to what she sees as the problems of capitalism—bloated CEO pay, sweatshops, speculative excess to stagnant wages, corporate welfare, and environmental indifference—Kelly explores the question of whether maximizing shareholder wealth is an appropriate mandate for business. This mandate, she contends, arises from the unconscious belief that property owners (wealth holders, shareholders) matter more than others resulting in an economic aristocracy.

Where does wealth come from? More precisely, where does the wealth of major public corporations come from? Who creates it?

To judge by the current arrangement in corporate America, one might suppose capital creates wealth—which is odd, because a pile of capital sitting there creates nothing. Yet capital-providers (stockholders) lay claim to most wealth that public corporations generate. They also claim the more fundamental right to have corporations managed on their behalf. Corporations are believed to exist for one purpose alone: to maximize returns to shareholders. This principle is reinforced by CEOs, *The Wall Street Journal,* business schools, and the courts. It is the law of the land—much as the divine right of kings was once the law of the land. Indeed, "maximizing returns to shareholders" is universally accepted as a kind of divine, unchallengeable mandate.

It is not in the least controversial. Though it should be.

What do shareholders contribute, to justify the extraordinary allegiance they receive? They take risk, we're told. They put their money on the line, so corporations might grow and prosper. Let's test the truth of this with a little quiz:

Stockholders fund major public corporations—True or False?

False. Or, actually, a tiny bit true—but for the most part, massively false. What's intriguing is that we speak as though it were entirely true: "I have invested in AT&T," we say—imagining AT&T as a steward of our money, with a fiduciary responsibility to take care of it. In fact, "investing" dollars don't go to AT&T but to other speculators. Equity "investments" reach a public corporation only when new common stock is sold—which for major corporations is a rare

---

event. Among the Dow Jones Industrials, only a handful have sold any new common stock in 30 years. Many have sold none in 50 years.

The stock market works like a used car market, as accounting professor Ralph Estes observes in *Tyranny of the Bottom Line.* When you buy a 1989 Ford Escort, the money doesn't go to Ford. It goes to the previous owner. Ford gets the buyer's money only when it sells a new car. Similarly, companies get stockholders' money only when they sell new common stock—which mature companies rarely do. According to figures from the Federal Reserve and the Securities and Exchange Commission, about 99 percent of the stock out there is "used stock." That is, 99 out of 100 "invested" dollars are trading in the purely speculative market, and never reach corporations.

Public corporations do have the ability to sell new stock. And they do need capital (funds beyond revenue) to operate—for inventory, expansion, and so forth. But they get very little of this capital from stockholders. In 1993, for example, corporations needed $555 billion in capital. According to the Federal Reserve, sales of common stock contributed 4 percent of that. I used this fact in a pull-quote for a magazine article once, and the designer changed it to 40 percent, assuming it was a typo. It's not. Of all capital public corporations needed in 1993, stockholders provided 4 percent.

Well, yes, critics will say—that's recently. But stockholders did fund corporations in the past.

Again, only a tiny bit true. Take the steel industry. An accounting study by Eldon Hendriksen examined capital expenditures in that industry from 1900 to 1953, and found that issues of common stock provided only 5 percent of capital. That was over the *entire first half of the 20th century,* when industry was growing by leaps and bounds.

So, what *do* stockholders contribute, to justify the extraordinary allegiance they receive? Very little. And that's my point.

Equity capital is provided by stockholders when a company goes public, and in occasional secondary offerings later. But in the life of most major companies today, issuance of common stock represents a distant, long-ago source of funds, and a minor one at that. What's odd is that it entitles holders to extract most of the corporation's wealth, forever. Equity investors essentially install a pipeline, and dictate that the corporation's sole purpose is to funnel wealth into it. The pipeline is never to be tampered with—and no one else is to be granted significant access (except executives, whose function is to keep it flowing).

The truth is, the commotion on Wall Street is not about funding corporations. It's about extracting from them.

The productive risk in building businesses is borne by entrepreneurs and their initial venture investors, who do contribute real investing dollars, to create real wealth. Those who buy stock at sixth or seventh hand, or 1,000th hand, also take a risk—but it is a risk speculators take among themselves, trying to outwit one another like gamblers. It has little to do with corporations, except this: Public companies are required to provide new chips for the gaming table, into infinity.

It's odd. And it's connected to a second oddity—that we believe stockholders *are* the corporation. When we say, "A corporation did well," we mean its shareholders did well. The company's local community might be devastated by plant closings, its groundwater contaminated with pollutants. Employees might be shouldering a crushing workload, doing without raises for years on end. Still we will say, "The corporation did well."

One does not see rising employee income as a measure of corporate success. Indeed, gains to employees are losses to the corporation. And this betrays an unconscious bias: that employees are not really part of the corporation. They have no claim on wealth they create, no say in governance, and no vote for the board of directors. They're not citizens of corporate society, but subjects.

Investors, on the other hand, may never set foot inside "their" companies, may not know where they're located or what they produce. Yet corporations exist to enrich investors alone. In the corporate society, only those who own stock can vote—like America until the mid-1800s, when only those who owned land could vote. Employees are disenfranchised.

We think of this as the natural law of the free market. It's more accurately the result of the corporate governance structure, which violates free-market principles. In a free market, everyone scrambles to get what they can, and they keep what they earn. In the construct of the corporation, one group gets what another earns.

The oddity of it all is veiled by the incantation of a single, magical word: "ownership." Because we say stockholders "own" corporations, they are permitted to contribute very little, and take quite a lot.

What an extraordinary word. One is tempted to recall Lycophron's comment, during an early Athenian slave uprising against the aristocracy. "The splendour of noble birth is imaginary," he said, "and its prerogatives are based upon a mere word."

PSYCHOETHICS
A Discipline Applying Psychology
to Business Ethics
Terri Kaye Needle　　Martin J. Lecker

The following overviews of four case studies demonstrate the rela-
tionship between psychological theory and ethical and moral devel-
opment. The opinions of these four individuals are those of the
authors and are based on research conducted by the authors.

ANITA RODDICK

. . . Anita Roddick's firm philosophy of life is that you can be a business person, make money and use that money to initiate social change. She has become the embodiment of free enterprise, social consciousness, and success. She has become the most outspoken activist businesswoman of the decade.

This once unemployed mother went on to become Businesswoman of the Year, Communicator of the Year, Retailer of the Year, and recipient of the United Nations Environmentalist Award to the Amazon, where she has started cottage industries to help save the rain forest. Profiled by *Time, Newsweek,* and a host of women's magazines, Anita Roddick has become the voice of business in the 90's, an era hungry for principles and change. She took her natural products and $7,000 in borrowed money, built a chain of more than 600 shops, created a franchising system and eventually a public company.

Anita Roddick opened the first Body Shop in Brighton, England, in 1976. She believed in herself from the time she was 18 years old and found out from her mother that her stepfather was really her father. It gave her confidence in her gut feelings because she felt so close to him and not to the other man in her life who was supposed to be her father (Gilligan, Chart I).

Her young-adult life as a hippie, backpacking through Europe, Israel, Greece, Africa, Tahiti, and Australia in the 1960's was unconventional. Although she worked as a teacher, it was only to earn enough money to travel. She met and married a fellow traveler and free spirit, Gordon Roddick, and they had two daughters together. In 1976, Gordon was embarking on a year's journey horsebackriding through South America, and Anita needed to support herself and her two children (Maslow, Chart II).

CHART 1

Kohlberg		Gilligan
Decision Based on Justice/Rights		**Decision Based on Care/Relationships**

Stage 1

Obedience and Punishment
—Decision based on fear and avoidance of punishment.
—Obedience to authority.
—Everyone for himself.
—"I" statements.

—Concern is for self.
—Survival is based on strength, rather than caring.
—"I gotta be tough. I gotta look out for me."

Stage 2

Individualism and Reciprocity
—No thoughts of anyone else except as they serve you.
—Satisfying one's own needs.
—Does not share another's perspective.
—"What's in it for me?"
—"What do I have to give up?"

PRECONVENTIONAL
SELF-FOCUSED

TRANSITION—self-interest is thought of as selfish; starts to be concerned for others.

Stage 3

Interpersonal Conformity
—Takes interpersonal relationships into account.
—Has good intentions.
—Wants to gain approval.
—"Good" and "nice" behavior.
—"How can I do this so most people will like me?"

—Good is equated with caring for others according to conventions of feminine self-sacrifice.
—"Always care more for others than for me, no matter what the expense."

Stage 4

CONVENTIONAL
GROUP-FOCUSED

TRANSITION—word "selfish" reappears when "self-sacrifice" is rejected as unequal.
—"Hey what about me? I'm entitled."

Law and Order
—Obeying the law.
—Inflexible.
—"It's always wrong to break the law.

Stage 5

Social Contract
Reasoning, regardless of society.
—Gets away from stage 4 rigidity.
—Protection of individual rights with impartiality.
—Concerned with needs of human beings.
—Rules and laws can be changed.

—Moral to CARE is obligation extended to oneself on an equal basis with others.
—"How can I resolve this so that everyone is cared for equally?"
—Everyone can't be cared for equally!

Stage 6

POST CONVENTIONAL
UNIVERSAL-FOCUSED

Universal Ethical Principles
—Solution is worked out to be just for everyone.
—High principle of preserving life.

CHART II

ABRAHAM MASLOW—HIERARCHY OF NEEDS

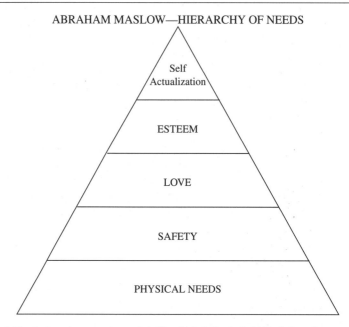

1. Physical needs are most essential. They include food, clothing, shelter, sleep, activity, water, and biological needs.

2. Safety needs include freedom from fear, pain, failure, punishment, and threats.

3. Love needs involve both giving and receiving love. People need to have a feeling of belonging.

4. Esteem and self-worth needs are related to self-image, confidence, independence, and the need to achieve and feel adequate. Esteem needs also relate to how others see and respect you.

5. Self-actualization needs refer to the desire for self-fulfillment, a desire to become everything one is capable of becoming.

She opened the Body Shop and immediately began to sell the truth about cosmetics, an unheard of practice at that time, that would propel her into the limelight. She gave unconventional people a chance (Gilligan, Chart I). In early 1977, Anita got a call from an herbalist on a pay phone asking if she could market his shampoo. He had trouble selling it because it looked and smelled awful. He was just starting his career and was living in the woods alone—like a hippie, mixing herbs in his kitchen. She gave Mark Constantine his first break (Gilligan, Chart I). She took a chance and he came through. Building on Carol Gilligan's Theory of Care and Response to Need, Anita and her employee, Katie, responded to the needs of the London marathon runners. They stood along the route and handed out samples of peppermint foot lotion, created by Mark Constantine and one of the top selling items in the Body Shop. It not only softened the skin, it also helped with foot odor.

Using Carl Jung's theory of the collective unconscious, Anita and Gordon Roddick were able to team their company, in 1985, with the Greenpeace Mission. They paid for hundreds of posters showing the Greenpeace slogan that said, "You can join Greenpeace at the Body Shop." The socially conscious involvement continues today with involvements in: Save the Whale Campaign, Friends of the Earth, and Amnesty International. A new dimension has been added to the Roddicks' life together. A spiritual dimension has emerged, using their success for promoting social concerns. Anita Roddick said, "You don't have to lose your soul to succeed in business."

BEN COHEN

In 1978, with a $12,000 investment, Ben Cohen and Jerry Greenfield opened a small ice cream parlour. Today, it is a multi-million-dollar, publicly held corporation and is internationally recognized as a benchmark for being socially responsible. Ben Cohen developed the social mission statement, "A business has a responsibility to give back to the community." For this reason, Ben Cohen's psychological background will be analyzed for this research.

As a child, Cohen was highly intelligent, who as the valedictorian of his sixth grade class was voted "most likely to succeed." Placed in an advanced junior high school program, Cohen had to learn things his own way, refused to do his homework, and was perceived by his teachers as being rebellious. Yet, he was extremely creative and excelled in any project that he found interesting. Upon meeting Jerry Greenfield in high school, both were found to possess many common characteristics, including high intelligence, creativity, and a nontraditional work ethic of, "If it's not fun, why do it?" This philosophy would guide Cohen to a multitude of careers, including learning how to produce homemade ice cream via a correspondence course, jointly taken with Greenfield.

Cohen's friendship with Jerry enabled him to feel connected, or as psychologist Carol Gilligan termed it, "an attachment." It was because of this attachment to Greenfield, and Cohen's further perception that he connected (or felt attached) to his customer, that Cohen was able to progress to another ethical level, that psychologist Lawrence Kohlberg called "the sixth stage of universal ethical principles." This sixth stage is part of a justice principle, based upon an agent who makes ethical decisions for himself and everyone else to live by as well. This was exemplified by Cohen's philosophy of putting the community ahead of its stockholders, in what was termed "a linked prosperity."

To further support his socially responsible philosophy, a Ben and Jerry's foundation was developed. Cohen gave the foundation fifty thousand shares of his stock as an initial endowment. Furthermore, Cohen announced that Ben and Jerry's would donate seven and a half percent of its pretax profits to the foundation that in turn would give away the money for projects to nonprofit organizations that were models for social change. All of these social contributions exemplify Kohlberg's sixth stage.

LEONA HELMSLEY

Leona Helmsley was convicted on 33 felony counts, divided into four groups of offenses including: conspiracy, tax evasion, filing false tax returns, and mail fraud. She was sentenced to four years in prison on each group of offenses. This was a total of 16 years, but the sentences would run concurrently and this amounted to 4 years in federal prison.

Her childhood is clouded in obscurity—she changed both her name and the facts of her early life. Lena Rosenthal was one of four children born in 1919. She had two older sisters whom she didn't get along with. Friction between them was so deep that she didn't speak to either of them, and refused to even attend their respective funerals in the early 1980's and mid 1980's (Gilligan/Kohlberg Chart I). Leona didn't relate to either of the two moral objectives in her life: **to treat others fairly** and **not to turn away from those in need.** She married Leo Panzirer, a lawyer, in 1938, who was 12 years her senior. She gave birth to her only child, a son, in 1940. The marriage ended by 1949. She was alone, dependent on minimal child support and alimony. Her family refused to help her. (Maslow, Levels 1, 3, 4). She married and divorced the same man twice, Joseph Lubin, so by 1962 she was on her own again. She was now in her 40's. She got a job in real estate, and she was a natural. Leona began as a receptionist at Pease and Elliman, a prestigious residential brokerage firm. She had no intention of sitting behind the front desk while others were earning commissions selling and renting apartments. Leona was not a team player. She got promoted to showing apartments herself, part-time. She steered clients away from other brokers behind their backs. Leona was out for Leona! (Kohlberg, Chart I, stage 2). She kept moving up. She pressured and bullied tenants to buy apartments in buildings her company owned that were going co-op or condominium in such a harsh and brutal way, that she almost lost her real estate license (Gilligan, Chart I). Some people loved her attention to detail and would work with no one else. Others despised her tactics. After only 10 years in the business she became Vice-President of Pease & Elliman, earning a salary and commission in the six figures. She had made it! Soon after she was introduced to Harry Helmsley who offered her a job as Senior Vice President at a salary of one half of a million dollars. She had come a long way since she started as a low-paid receptionist in a real estate office. She was past 50 when she accepted Harry Helmsley's offer.

MICHAEL MILKEN

In April 1990, Michael Milken pleaded guilty to six felonies—including conspiracy, securities fraud, mail fraud, and filing false tax forms—and agreed to pay $600 million in penalties in return for federal prosecutors' agreement to drop the remaining 92 charges originally brought against him by the federal government in 1989. Seven months later, Federal District Judge Kimba Wood sentenced him to 10 years in prison, three additional years of probation, and 5,400 hours of community service.

Michael Milken's father, Bernard, was an accountant who would be willing to help his wealthy clients locate creative tax solutions to their problems. However, on a personal basis, Bernard Milken was far more risk-averse. Many times, Bernard would reject business opportunities because they appeared too risky. Yet, at home, Michael was taught to share, to help others, but not to receive recognition for his efforts. This covert trait became useful later on, since Milken never personally took credit for any one of his profitable dealings. Nonetheless, he would try to help others and share his own successes with them.

One example of his sharing values was that when he took his college fraternity's funds and invested them, he guaranteed that he would keep 50 percent of the fraternity profits invested, but also pay back 100 percent of any losses. Ironically, this is what he did while at Drexel Burnham Lambert as a junk-bond chief trader. In some instances, Milken would personally guarantee, to a select number of clients that he would pay back 100 percent of any losses when they invested in high-risk junk bonds. However, he refused to file the forms that were legally required of traders who personally guaranteed their clients against un-foreseen losses.

However, according to his probation officer, Milken was a product of a deep insecurity. He needed to be needed. As a result, Milken saw himself as the "Candy Man." In a dysfunctional world, he would make everything right for everybody. In essence, two psychological theories may explain his unethical decisions: Maslow's third level of belonginess and Gilligan's theory of attachment. In both theories, Milken displays a proclivity towards pleasing others for purposes of acceptance. Furthermore, a third theory, Kohlberg's stage three, the interpersonal conformity stage, may be used. In this stage a person makes moral decisions because he wants to be a member of the team, and what is right will be determined by what is expected of you by people close to you. Therefore, Kohlberg's third stage personifies the psychological motivation that led to Milken's unethical actions and eventually to his demise.

PONDERING
PROMETHEUS

KIREN DOSANJH

As many of us have heard repeated throughout our education, one finds lessons in the oddest places. While one might more appropriately expect to read excerpts from mythology in a classics course or maybe in a literature course, one would not usually expect to find it in a business ethics course. Yet, that is where, perhaps, it is most appropriate. As one might recall, myths have all of the necessary elements for ethical dilemmas, and then for their resolution. Characters in myth are often faced with challenging dilemmas; because of his or her human flaws, the decision maker is tested to make the right decision; in the end, the lesson prevails. Professor Dosanjh uses myth in her ethics courses to allow us to view situations from fresh and novel perspectives. Consider the application to business ethics of the following precis of Prometheus. Can you think of other examples of common-day representations of this archetype?

After the Gods created the world, it was time for the appearance of mankind. The task was delegated to Prometheus, the Titan who had helped Zeus in the war with the Titans. Prometheus, whose name means "forethought," was very wise, while his brother Epimetheus, whose name means "afterthought," was scatterbrained and impulsive. Before creating men, Epimetheus decided to give animals the gifts of strength, swiftness, courage, cunning, fur, wings, shells, etc. After realizing that nothing good was left for men, he turned to his brother for help.

Prometheus took over the task and thought of a way to make man superior to animals. He made men upright like the gods, and then gave them a gift that offered a better protection than the gifts that his brother had bestowed on animals. He went to the sun, where he lit a torch and brought down fire.

Zeus, furious at Prometheus for giving the gift of fire to men, which gave god-like powers for creation to these mortals, quickly forgot the debt he owed Prometheus for his role in conquering the Titans. He had his servants, Force and Violence, seize Prometheus and chain him to "a high-piercing headlong rock," as they told him "that this was the "fruit you reap for your man-loving ways," for not dreading "God's anger" and for giving "to mortals honor not their due."

Reprinted with permission of the author. Adapted from Edith Hamilton's *Mythology*.

Mere vengeance was not the only motive behind Zeus's punishment of Prometheus. Zeus wanted to force him to disclose a very important secret. Zeus knew that fate had decreed that one day he would be dethroned by a son not yet born, but only Prometheus knew who would be the mother of this Son. Zeus sent his messenger, Hermes, to the rock-bound Prometheus, to ask him to disclose the secret. Prometheus protested: "Go and persuade the sea wave not to break. You will persuade me no more easily." Hermes warned him that worse suffering awaited him, such as being eaten alive by an eagle for eternity.

Generations later, Prometheus was released. Zeus was apparently willing to allow Hercules to slay the eagle and deliver Prometheus from his chains. While we do not know whether Prometheus revealed his secret when he was freed, one thing is certain: Prometheus did not yield under the tremendous pressure exerted by Zeus.

THE EXAMINATION OF PROMETHEUS AS INSPIRATION FOR ETHICAL BEHAVIOR

Universal Themes Reflected in the Myth

* Rebelling against injustice at the hands of those in power.

* Humanism.

* Progress.

* Withstanding suffering in defense of one's beliefs.

Relevance to Business Ethics and Ethical Behavior   Prometheus shows that, through the use of reason, we can maintain our autonomy in the face of tremendous pressure. His reason allowed him to act freely in concert with his beliefs. As Marvin Kohl wrote in his article, "The Nature of Promethean Ethics," (*The Humanist,* January/February, 1996), Prometheus stands for the "will to aspire to the power of the gods and to stand against unnecessary suffering and the evils of the status quo." The use of rationality in creating rules for moral behavior may have been pioneered by Prometheus, not Immanuel Kant.

Kohl further observes that Prometheus seems to have been motivated by his overriding love of humanity. In giving fire to mankind, he bestowed upon them the ability not only to protect themselves, but to make scientific advances which would allow them to be self-sufficient and powerful. Prometheus also demonstrates that we should not sacrifice progress for the sake of convenience.

His refusal to reveal a secret that would surely lead to the destruction of another, at great personal cost, makes Prometheus the archetypal protector of confidentiality. An interesting footnote to this analysis is that the son who would dethrone Zeus, was also destined to be the rescuer of Prometheus. Thus, Prometheus may have acted as a utilitarian, suffering in the present for an overall benefit for others that would ultimately include him.

Prometheus's courage in maintaining confidential information in the face of extortion, his defiance of malevolent authority in giving power to the weak, and his protective concern for humanity can serve as an inspiration for ethical behavior in modern business.

The Modern-Day Prometheus   Jan Carlzon, CEO of Scandinavian Airlines, turned the corporate structure upside-down by giving power to the "lower ranks" of the organization. He has shown a Promethean concern for those without power, and a bold, innovative spirit. Those who maintain confidences in the face of extortion, or despite short-term benefits, are descendants of Prometheus's heroic defense of autonomy and principle.

VENTURING BEYOND COMPLIANCE

LYNN SHARP PAINE

Paine identifies two strategems to encourage and support an ethical corporate culture: legal compliance and organizational integrity. Consider which might be more effective from a long-term perspective? Which would be easier to implement? Which do you think is more prevalent in the business environment?

How can managers insure that individuals in their companies conduct business in a way that is responsible and ethically sound? This challenge involves organizational design and a number of specific managerial tasks.

WHY THE ETHICS FOCUS?

In the past decade, a number of factors have brought ethical matters into sharper focus.

Globalization   Global expansion has brought about greater involvement with different cultures and socioeconomic systems. With this development, ethical considerations—such as the different assumptions about the responsibilities of business, about acceptable business practices, and about the values needed to build a cohesive, successful organization—become more important.

Technology   The added capabilities of technology have created a new level of transparency and immediacy to business communication. Now the conduct of businesses around the globe is more exposed than it ever was before.

Competition   Rising competition brings with it added pressure to cut corners. Simultaneously, leaders are looking for new ways to differentiate their companies and move them to a new level of excellence. Some believe that a proactive ethical stance can have a positive impact on the bottom line.

Public Perception and the Law   There is a perceived decline in social ethics that yields uncertainty. Managers are no longer comfortable assuming that employees joining their companies possess the desired ethical values. And public expectations, too, have changed: That which was once deemed acceptable is now more readily scrutinized. New

Lynn Sharp Paine, "Venturing beyond Compliance," *The Evolving Role of Ethics in Business,* report no. 1141–96-ch, pp. 13–16 (The Conference Board, Inc.: New York, NY 1996). Email: *info@conference-board.org* laws and stepped-up enforcement efforts have increased the risk of personal and organizational liability.

TWO STRATEGIES EMERGE

Most managers are choosing either a *legal compliance* strategy or an *organizational integrity* strategy to support ethics in their companies. These strategies differ markedly in their conception of ethics, human behavior, and management responsibility. While the organizational integrity strategy fully acknowledges the importance of compliance with the law, its aim is to achieve right conduct in general. Thus, it is more comprehensive and broader than the legal compliance strategy. Companies that adopt an organizational integrity strategy are concerned with their identity—who they are and what they stand for—and with how they conduct internal and external affairs. These matters are less clear-cut (and hence, more demanding) than those handled by a legal compliance approach.

These strategies differ in several fundamental ways:

Ethos   The legal compliance strategy regards ethics as a set of limits, boundaries over which we must not cross. The compliance approach is externally driven. Here, ethics is viewed as something that *has* to be done.

The organizational integrity strategy defines ethics as a set of principles to guide the choices we make. Companies that adopt this approach choose their own standards for conducting business on an individual and company-wide basis.

Objectives   The compliance approach is geared toward preventing unlawful conduct and criminal misconduct in particular. The integrity approach, by comparison, has a more lofty goal: to achieve responsible conduct across-the-board, even if not required by law.

Leadership   While companies with a compliance approach place lawyers at the helm, the integrity approach is captained by company managers. To insure that their efforts are thorough and effective, these managers are assisted by lawyers, human resources specialists, and other experts.

Methods   The compliance focus emphasizes the rules people must not violate. It uses increased oversight and stepped-up penalties to enforce these rules. An integrity approach acknowledges the need for a brake on people's behavior from time to time, but treats ethics as a steering mechanism rather than the brake itself. Here, ethics infuses the organization's leadership, its core systems, and its decision-making processes.

Behavioral Assumptions   Finally, the two approaches rest on very different philosophies of human nature. The compliance strategy's ideas are rooted in deterrence theory—how to prevent people from doing bad things by manipulating the costs of misconduct. The integrity strategy views people as having a fuller, richer set of needs and motivations. While it acknowledges that people are guided by material self-interest and the threat of penalties, it also identifies the other drivers of human nature—individual values, ideals, and the influence of peers.

LIMITATIONS OF A COMPLIANCE-BASED APPROACH

Why go beyond compliance? While legal compliance is a must, a legal compliance approach to company ethics has several specific limitations:

- Compliance is not terribly responsive to many of the day-to-day concerns that managers and employees face. It follows the law, which is generally backward looking. For a company on the cutting edge of technology, of new financing mechanisms, of new practices, the law is not very helpful as a guide.

- The majority of hot-line calls are not about unlawful or criminal misconduct. They deal with gray areas and with issues of supervisory practice and fair treatment. A legal compliance approach does not provide answers to these types of questions. Therefore, it does not adequately address employees' real concerns and needs.

- The typical legal compliance program runs directly counter to the philosophy of empowerment. Empowerment gives employees discretion, resources, and authority, and then trusts them to make good decisions. Compliance programs, though, reduce discretion, increase oversight, and tighten controls. If a company tries to put forth an empowerment effort and a compliance-driven ethics program at the same time, the two will cancel each other out. This will result in a lot of employee cynicism.

- A legal compliance program is just not very exciting. Compliance is important, but the law was not designed to inspire human excellence so much as to set a floor for acceptable behavior. Since the law has to apply to everyone, its standards are not as demanding as we might choose for ourselves and for our companies.

CHALLENGES TO AN INTEGRITY-BASED APPROACH

If you are really interested in organizational effectiveness and organizational development rather than just avoiding liability, an integrity-driven approach is far more promising. But four challenges must be met before an organizational integrity approach can work:

1. *Developing an ethical framework.* Organizational integrity requires a much more robust concept of organizational identity and responsibility than does compliance.
2. *Aligning practice with principles.* This can be very problematic, especially in organizations whose structure, systems, and decision processes run counter to the values and principles espoused by senior management.
3. *Overcoming cynicism.* In *The Cynical Americans,* Donald L. Kanter and Phillip H. Mervis' study of cynicism in the United States (San Francisco, Josey-Bass Publishers, 1989, p. 1), it was revealed that almost 43 percent of Americans fit the profile of the cynic; that is, one who regards selfishness, dishonesty, and fakery as at the core of human behavior. People often adopt cynicism as a self-defense mechanism. This frame of reference often prevents people from seeing reality, and can act as a barrier to instilling ethical values.
4. *Resolving ethical conflicts.* We all have conflicting responsibilities from time to time. If we are very creative, we may be able to solve potential conflicts before they unfold. Sometimes, though, hard trade-offs—between right and right, between two "goods"—must be made.

NAVIGATING WITH THE ETHICAL COMPASS

How do you begin to create an ethical compass or a framework for integrity? A useful starting point is to begin by answering some questions related to the four fundamental sources of responsibility.

- Purpose—What is the organization's fundamental reason for being—its ultimate aims?

- People—Who are the constituencies to whom the company is accountable and on whom it depends for success? What are their legitimate claims and interests?

- Power—What is the organization's authority and ability to act?

- Principles—What are the organization's obligations or duties, as well as its guiding aspirations and ideals?

If used as a set of reference points, these questions can help develop a framework against which to benchmark progress on ethical matters (see Exhibit 1).

EXHIBIT 1

The Four Points of an Ethical Compass

How can managers develop a framework for integrity?

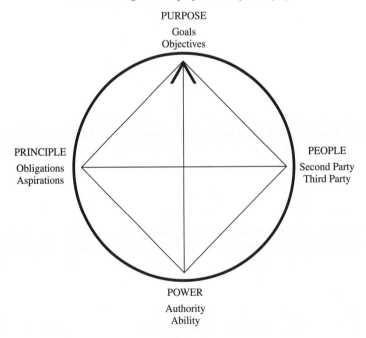

© Lynn Sharp Paine, 1995

The framework of ideas is only a start. Putting it into practice is the difficult part. People often wonder why a gap exists between the espoused values and everyday behavior, when in fact, a gap *should* exist to some degree. If you are fully satisfying your ideals and aspirations, most likely your standards are not high enough. If the gap between principle and practice becomes a chasm, though, it becomes hypocrisy, which is even worse.

MANAGEMENT: PUTTING IT TOGETHER

Integrity-based ethics management efforts have contributed to organizational effectiveness in several fundamental ways. Companies that have adopted such programs report fewer and less serious problems of misconduct. Often this is because problems are caught earlier and are dealt with at the onset. In some cases, an integrity approach can yield strengthened competitiveness: it facilitates the delivery of quality products in an honest, reliable way. This approach can enhance work life by making the workplace more fun and challenging. It can improve relationships with constituencies and can instill a more positive mindset that fosters creativity and innovation. And while an organizational integrity approach cannot guarantee bottom-line performance improvements, it is important to understand that ethics is a very practical matter. The purpose of ethics is to enhance our lives and our relationships both inside and outside of the organization.

Clearly, achieving and maintaining integrity requires intense commitment and involvement from managers company-wide. This goes beyond the so-called "tone" set by senior management. It involves specific leadership tasks and behaviors, starting with the development of the integrity framework. Managers must insure that company systems support responsible behavior. Then they must personally model responsible decision making. These leadership tasks are all essential to building the high-integrity organization.

THE CONSTITUTION AND SERVICEMASTER'S FIRST COMPANY OBJECTIVE

THE SERVICEMASTER COMPANY

The ServiceMaster Company was founded in 1929 as a moth-proofing company by Marion Wade, a former minor league baseball player. Now it is one of America's largest service companies, serving more than 6 million customers through companies such as Trugreen Chemlawn, Terminix, Merry Maids, and American Home Shield. Service-Master's objectives include four areas of focus: "To honor God in all we do, to help people develop, to pursue excellence, and to grow profitably." The first objective has an impact on every aspect of the firm's business. "We believe that every person—regardless of personal beliefs or differences—has been created in the image and likeness of God. We seek to recognize the dignity, worth and potential of each individual and believe that everyone from service worker to company president has intrinsic worth and value."

Integrating God into the workplace, however, has the potential to conflict with a person's First Amendment right to the free exercise of religion. ServiceMaster addresses this concern in the following material.

INTRODUCTION

The ServiceMaster Enterprise exists, first and foremost, for the purpose of our four Company objectives. The philosophy of our Company demands that we have absolute standards for determining what is right and good in the way we treat our employees, our customers, and our vendors. We believe strongly that our objectives and standards do not waver or change depending on the exigencies of a particular issue or the day to day pressure to meet customer expectations and to reach short term financial goals. Rather, our business depends on seeing the truth through the distractions of an aggressive service business. We are deeply committed to the vision of ServiceMaster and the fact that our business is in reality "training and developing people" to make them the best that they can be.

We are not afraid to state our first Company objective in terms of "God." We believe strongly in the right of companies and individuals to express their religious beliefs freely as mandated by our Constitution. The following represents ServiceMaster's analysis of the interplay between our first Company objective and the Constitution.

Pursuant to the Constitution, all individuals, as well as companies, have a right to religious freedom. This principle is encompassed in our vision of our first Company objective.

TO HONOR GOD IN ALL WE DO

What It Means

It means that employees, partners, and representatives must conduct themselves in the marketplace according to the highest moral and ethical standards. It also means that employees, partners, and representatives must treat fellow employees, customers, and vendors, really anyone we deal with, with respect and dignity. There are absolutes, right and wrong, and we commit ourselves to doing business the "right" way.

What It Does Not Mean

It does not mean that employees, partners, and representatives have to believe in God or any particular God. It does not mean that anyone is forced to choose between their religion and their job. It is the outward manifestation of the objective in terms of conduct and treatment of others that cannot be compromised, not the personal beliefs of any particular employee.

Why We Articulate It in Terms of God

Our founders believed, and our current leadership continue to believe, that a "reference point" of God that is unwavering is the best way to set the course for our business. Contrary to current societal trends we do not believe it is necessary to secularize everything. Indeed, we strongly believe in the provisions of the Constitution that grant us all religious freedom. In fact, in stating our first Company objective as we do we recognize, respect, and promote everyone's right to religious freedom.

Chapter 3

INDIVIDUAL DECISION MAKING

Lessons Learned from the Foundations

"Careful Decision Making"	"CALVIN & HOBBES" CARTOON
"Quiz Yourself on Business Ethics"	DAWN-MARIE DRISCOLL, W. MICHAEL HOFFMAN, EDWARD PETRY
"Morality: The Basic Rules"	ROBERT SOLOMON
"The Real Life of a Student: Term Papers for Sale"	SCHOOL SUCKS WEBSITE
"The Good Samaritan"	LUKE 10:30–37, THE BIBLE
"Should Ethics Be Taught in College?"	DAVID THIES
Obedience to Authority	STANLEY MILGRAM
"The day has come . . . to take an accounting of my life"	

This above all: to thine own self be true, and it must follow, as the night the day, Thou canst not then be false to any man.

—SHAKESPEARE

Jordan Baker: I thought you were rather an honest, straight-forward person. I thought it was your secret pride.
Nick Carraway: I'm thirty. I'm five years too old to lie to myself and call it honor.

—F. SCOTT FITZGERALD

To be nothing but yourself, in a world which is doing its best to make you everybody else, means to fight the hardest battle which any human being can fight, and never stop fighting.

—E. E. CUMMINGS

Inez (a lesbian woman who drove her lover's husband to his death):
One always dies too soon—or too late. And yet one's whole life is
complete at that moment, with a line drawn neatly under it, ready for
the summing up. You are—your life, and nothing else.

—JEAN-PAUL SARTRE

Consider Inez's statement in the Sartre quote above: "You are—your life, and nothing else." Consider how you feel about your accomplishments, your challenges, your actions and decisions. If one were to look at this life from the outside, would that person find it to be worthwhile, good, right, or any other positive judgment? You might believe that a part of our soul is left with each decision we make, and our lasting impact on this earth is evidenced by the "indentations" we make on the lives of others and our environment. If so, then you might also believe that we will all be judged on the basis of these indentations that we leave behind.

Do you consider that you act only in your own self-interest at all times, or would you contend that you ignore your personal interests in order to act in the interests of others at times? When you make a choice that is for your own good but against someone else's are you accountable to that other individual for the impact of your decision. Some theorists argue that we act *only* in our own self-interest, that even something like an anonymous donation satisfies your personal need to do that act. Controversial author and philosopher Ayn Rand goes one step further and contends that those who do concern themselves with the interests of others do so to their own detriment or for purely selfish reasons. In discussing this "selflessness," the protagonist of Rand's novel, *The Fountainhead,* Howard Roark, states as follows:

> *And isn't that the root of every despicable action? Not selfishness, but precisely the absence of a self. Look at them. The man who cheats and lies but preserves a respectable front. He knows himself to be dishonest, but others think he's honest and he derives his self respect from that, second-hand. . . . The frustrated wretch who professes love for the inferior and clings to those less endowed, in order to establish his own superiority by comparison. The man whose sole aim is to make money. Now I don't see anything evil in a desire to make money. But money is only a means to an end. If a man wants it for a personal purpose—to invest in his industry, to create, to study, to travel, to enjoy luxury—he's completely moral. But the men who place money first go much beyond that. Personal luxury is a limited endeavor. What they want is ostentation: to show, to stun, to entertain, to impress others. They're second-handers.[1]*

Would you consider yourself someone Rand derides, a "second-hander?" Do you agree with her judgment, her derision of these types of individuals, or would you instead stand up for the second-hander? How would Rand respond to the biblical case of Solomon and the two mothers? Two women came to King Solomon, both claiming to be the mother of a young child. The king said that he would cut the child in half and give each purported mother her half of the child. As he prepared to do this, one mother told him to stop and agreed to give the (entire) child to the other woman. King Solomon then determined that this must be the true mother of the child since she was prepared to give up her child in order to save him. Did the true mother act in her own best interests or the interests of another and how would Rand explain this decision?

---

[1] Ayn Rand, *The Fountainhead* (New York: Signet Books 1971) pp. 606–7.

As discussed in the introduction to Chapter 1, ethics demands the integrity to act according to your personal values as well as accountability for each decision that we make in our lives according to those values. ("Great minds don't think alike; they think for themselves!") If someone were asked to choose between allowing a loved one to die by following the law, or breaking the law in order to allow him or her to live, many would be willing to break the law. Their justification might be, "I had no choice—I had to do it to save my loved one." The truth is that we all have choices. If you are asked to choose between terminating a subordinate or losing your job, you might fire the worker, claiming, "I have no choice but to do this. Sorry." In fact, you would have a choice—terminate the subordinate or lose your job. You may not like the alternatives offered, but it is a choice nonetheless.

As a student or as an employee or employer, you are faced with a variety of alternatives. It will be up to you to determine the course of your actions. In a well-publicized case involving the Electrical Manufacturers firm, recent college graduates were found guilty of conspiring to fix prices and otherwise violate the antitrust statutes. In response to questions about their guilt, the young employees claimed, "I got out of school and this was how it was done." Does that explain the behavior to you? Consider how you would feel if you were (or had been) asked to do something with which you were uncomfortable during your first year of work. Do you think you would refuse? Would you quit? Of course, your response probably depends on the nature of the request, but questioning accepted business practice is difficult, no matter the cost.

Similarly, in her rather infamous short story "The Lottery," author Shirley Jackson describes a small town where every citizen draws lots to see who will be subject to a stoning. Yet, as repulsive as it may seem, as you read the story, you realize that the one whose name is drawn in the lottery is stoned to death by the rest of the villagers. Why do these individuals participate in such an arcane annual ritual? Perhaps particularly because it is a ritual, an accepted manner of practice in that town's culture and those who do not participate may suffer greater woes. Of course, we would all like to believe that we would never participate in such an event, but consider all of the rituals in which you do participate, although perhaps you would not if you considered them more deeply.

In a 1991 study, researchers determined that business undergraduate students are the most likely to have cheated on a test, when compared to pre-law students and the general population.[2] In response to a statement claiming that *not* cheating is the best way to get ahead in the long run, business students claimed, "This is the Nineties. You snooze, you lose."[3] Does this mean that, perhaps, there is a failure in ethics in the business arena because the people who go into business already cheat? Or is it that business students are aware that the business arena demands this type of unethical conduct, so they prepare themselves for it from the start? Competitiveness might make the border between ethical and unethical become blurred. Either way, as our parents once told us, simply because an environment is replete with a certain type of behavior does not mean that we must follow suit, nor does it

---

[2]Rick Tetzeli, "Business Students Cheat Most," *Fortune,* July 1, 1991, p. 14. See also research of James Stearns and Shaheen Borna that found that MBA students were more likely to cheat than convicted felons, in "A Comparison of the Ethics of Convicted Felons and Graduate Business Students: Implications for Business Practice and Business Ethics Education," *Teaching Business Ethics* 2 (1998), pp. 175–95.

[3]*Id.* at 18.

relieve us of our responsibility for actions in that environment ("If Janie jumps off a bridge, are you going to follow," they would say).

It may be telling regarding your future decision-making choices whether you believe that you will be held accountable for your actions, whether you believe that you will be caught, or more esoterically, whether you believe "The world is out to get you," "You should do whatever you can to get ahead," "Everyone cheats," "Honest people lose in the end," or other cynical doctrines. Are these the type of people with whom you work, or for whom you work? Are these types of individuals more or less likely to act unethically? To be accountable for their actions?

In the readings that follow, a variety of perspectives are offered in connection with this concept of free choice and accountability, beginning with an audit of your own ethical perspective.

Short Hypothetical Case

A mining company plans to open a gold mine in the area. You are hired by the company to acquire the land. Your commissions and bonuses on this multi-million-dollar deal will be substantial. A large tract of land in the center of the proposed mine is owned by an uneducated farmer who has lived on this land all of his life. He has no knowledge of the plans for the mine. A smaller tract, near the site, but not part of the proposed land purchase, is owned by an influential member of the county council. He knows about the coming development. You know you can acquire the farmer's land for a fraction of its value. The council member has already started raising objections to the mine. What do you do?

Hypotheticals were written by Catherine Haselden and are included in her manuscript "The Ethics Game."

Win as Much as you Can would work here!

"Calvin & Hobbes" cartoon by Watterson. Reprinted with permission of Universal Press Syndicate.

QUIZ YOURSELF ON BUSINESS ETHICS

DAWN-MARIE DRISCOLL, W. MICHAEL HOFFMAN, EDWARD PETRY

The following quiz was developed to help you to identify your own ethical awareness and to give you a greater understanding of your personal perspective.

. . . For questions 1 and 2, circle the answers you think are correct. More than one may qualify.

1. **Ethics is _____**
   a. A branch of philosophy that deals with values as they relate to human conduct.
   b. The study of what is good and right for people. It asks the question: How should I act, especially when my actions directly or indirectly affect others?
   c. A fad, a topic that is kept alive by the media on days when there is no hard news to report.

2. **Business ethics is _____**
   a. The application of ethical principles and methods of analysis to business.
   b. A topic of study that is now required at all business schools accredited by the American Assembly of Collegiate Schools of Business.
   c. An oxymoron.

In recent years there have been many tales of moral crises faced by organizations. How many of the following do you recognize? Again, more than one answer may be correct.

3. **Fraud and abuse was so common at NORTEL, Ltd., a giant Canadian telecommunications corporation, that:**
   a. It was estimated that one indictable offense occurred each and every working day.
   b. One manager defrauded the company for more than $6 million and then used the company's facilities to engage in widespread wiretapping, all the while amassing a private stockpile of arms.
   c. The company has since established a remarkably effective fraud prevention program and is emerging as a leader in the Canadian business ethics movement.

---

4. **For 15 minutes, executives at the Maine shipbuilder Bath Iron Works gave in to the temptation to cheat. Their ethical lapse:**
   a. Nearly destroyed the company's 100-year-old reputation for integrity.
   b. Put 8,000 jobs in peril.
   c. Ended the gubernatorial aspirations of the company's widely admired leader.
   d. Pushed the company to establish safeguards at the board and officer levels to increase ethical oversight at the top.

5. **A former president of the United Way was:**
   a. An entrepreneur and business genius who created the "greatest health and human services delivery system in history."
   b. A flawed leader who misused United Way funds to support a long-distance romance with a young woman just out of high school.
   c. Both of the above; in fact his successes helped shape an organization that all but made his failures inevitable.

What do business leaders think about the ethics of business? Deloitte & Touche surveyed more than a thousand officers and directors of corporations together with other business leaders. Are your views on the topic in sync with theirs? Circle the answers to questions 6 through 8 that you think are correct.

6. **Is the American business community troubled by ethical problems?**
   a. Yes
   b. No

7. **Has the issue of business ethics become overblown?**
   a. Yes
   b. No

8. **How do high ethical standards affect a company's competitive position?**
   a. Strengthen
   b. Weaken
   c. No effect

Has the increased acceptance of the concept of business ethics translated into actual changes in the workplace? In the years 1985, 1990, and 1992, the Center for Business Ethics surveyed the Fortune 1000 to find out what changes—if any—were being made to build ethics into corporate policies and programs. Circle the answers you think are correct for questions 9 through 13.

9. **What percentage of the Fortune 1000 are planning to expand efforts to incorporate ethics into their daily operations?**
   a. More than 90 percent
   b. About 50 percent
   c. Less than 25 percent

10. **The most common motive(s) given for implementing ethics initiatives is (are) to:**
    a. Improve profits
    b. Provide guidelines for conduct
    c. Improve public image
    d. Be socially responsible

11. What percentage of the Fortune 1000 have written ethics policies?
   a. More than 90 percent
   b. About 50 percent
   c. Less than 25 percent

12. What percentage of the Fortune 1000 have employee ethics training?
   a. More than 90 percent
   b. About 50 percent
   c. Less than 25 percent

13. Since 1987, the number of large corporations with ethics officers (whose primary function is to create or maintain the company's ethics program) has:
   a. Stayed about the same
   b. Increased slightly
   c. More than doubled

While there has been a decade of steady growth in the number of corporations implementing corporate ethics policies and programs, the new Federal Sentencing Guidelines for Organizations has certainly piqued the business community's interest and led to a sharp increase in its efforts. Circle the answers you think are correct for questions 14 through 16. More than one answer may be correct.

14. The Guidelines apply only to large corporations.
   a. True
   b. False

15. Under the Guidelines organizations may be required to pay restitution and may be placed on probation for up to five years. The Guidelines also cite specific aggravating factors that can increase the organization's fine up to:
   a. 400 percent
   b. 100 percent
   c. 50 percent

16. The Guidelines call on organizations to create "effective programs to prevent and detect violations of law." These programs must include:
   a. Established compliance standards.
   b. Specific individual(s) assigned to oversee compliance.
   c. Due care in delegating discretionary authority.
   d. Steps to communicate standards and procedures, e.g., training programs and publications.
   e. Steps to achieve compliance, e.g., monitoring, auditing, and reporting systems.
   f. A record of consistent enforcement of standards.
   g. Procedures to review and modify the program after an offense.

Hopefully your company is one of those making a serious effort to build ethics into its daily operations. When an ethics dilemma arises, it's unfortunately often the case that, at least initially, you're still facing it alone. What should you do? Circle the answers you think are correct for questions 17 through 19. More than one may be correct.

17. Possible scenarios: (1) You are an employee at a public utility and discover that rate payers' money is being used illegally to finance political campaigns. (2) You

are an employee at a phone company that holds "pervert conventions" every year to "entertain" suppliers. (3) You have a choice of blowing the whistle to your company's officers and possibly facing retaliation or of going outside the company and blowing the whistle to the government and collecting a multi-million-dollar bonus.

When faced with such ethical dilemmas, which of the following questions should you ask yourself?

a.   Have I looked at the problem from the perspective of all the affected parties? Whose interests have priority?

b.   Who will be harmed and who will be helped? Is there an alternative course of action that will minimize harm?

c.   If I act unethically, can I get away with it?

d.   Am I confident that my decision will seem as reasonable over a long period of time as it does now?

e.   Would I be willing to disclose my decision to my boss, the board, the general public, my family?

18. If the dilemma is still unresolved, you should:

a.   Consult your company's written ethics policies.

b.   Use your company's hotline or helpline.

c.   Talk to your company's ethics officer or ombudsman.

d.   Call your mother.

19. What companies have faced moral crises, learned their lessons, and now serve as models for how to integrate ethics into their organizations?

THE BUSINESS ETHICS QUIZ—ANSWERS
Question 1

The study of ethics is at least five thousand years old, and ethics was first explicitly applied to business in the Code of Hammurabi around 2100 BC. If it's a fad, it's the longest one ever. . . . A and B are correct.

Question 2

A and B are correct. If you answered C, you're out of date. Businesses that ignore ethics are businesses at risk.

Questions 3–5

For each, all of the answers are correct.

Questions 6–8

According to the Deloitte & Touche Survey, 94 percent of the business leaders thought the American business community was troubled by ethical problems, only 32 percent thought the issue was overblown, and 63 percent thought high ethical standards strengthened competitiveness.

Questions 9–13

According to the Center for Business Ethics 1990 survey, more than 90 percent of the Fortune 1000 are planning to increase their business ethics efforts. Their principal motives were to provide guidelines for employee conduct and to be socially responsible (about 95 percent each). Only 43 percent said they were doing so to improve public image, and only 30 percent said they were motivated by profit. More than 90 percent of the Fortune 1000 have written ethics policies, and about 50 percent offer ethics training to employees. According to the Center for Business Ethics' Ethics Officer Survey of the Fortune 1000, the number of large corporations with ethics officers has more than doubled since 1987.

Questions 14–16

The Guidelines apply to business organizations of all sizes including those as small as 10 employees. They also apply to unions, governments and political subdivisions, and non-profit organizations. If there is high-level complicity, a prior record of the same offense and obstruction of the investigation, the organization's fine could increase 400 percent above the stipulated base fine. The Guidelines call for an "effective program" that includes all of the listed components. Having such a program can reduce an organization's fine by up to 60 percent.

Question 17

If you answered C, go to jail, go directly to jail, do not pass Go, and take this book with you!

Question 18

All four answers are correct. Answers A through C are the standard steps under any "effective program." Answer D is not required under the Guidelines, but it wouldn't hurt to call your mother more often, would it?

Question 19

A hint: They include one of the "baby bells" [and] a giant in the defense industry. . .

MORALITY
The Basic Rules
ROBERT SOLOMON

Solomon discusses the importance of moral rules and whether there may be a list of rules to govern behavior and proposes a definition of morality—three of the more difficult tasks in ethical theory!

I don't like violence. I'm a businessman. Blood is a big expense.
MARIO PUZO, *THE GODFATHER*

Ethics is a matter of *ethos,* participation in a community, a practice, a way of life. Business ethics is a function of the business ethos. Within itself, the mentality of business may be a game mentality, but not all of business ethics is defined by this gamelike business *ethos* or by the business community. The nature of business is circumscribed by society, which tends to encourage or discourage particular aspects of business on the basis of its own ideals and well-being. But there is also a more general set of basic rules that are not part of or partial to any particular society, community, or practice. These rules apply everywhere and determine the legitimacy of every practice. These are the rules of *morality.*

Morality is not the same as moralizing, and being moral does not mean being righteous. It means only *doing right.* Most of the time being moral is no big deal. One doesn't praise an accountant for not cheating on the corporation's tax return, and one doesn't praise an employee for not stealing from the company. Morality is most noticeable in its absence, except, perhaps, when a person succeeds in remaining moral under enormous pressure to be otherwise. But morality in general is not heroism; it is simply not doing what no one should think of doing in the first place. In practical business contexts, morality is rarely an issue, not because the possibility of immoral but lucrative behavior does not exist at every turn but because it is assumed—it *must* be assumed—that no amount of gain will justify a breach of morality. Morality and business are mentioned together when a business venture is *immoral,* and there is never a question of which—business or morality—will win that competition. Moral rules are the trump cards of every business transaction.

Given the importance of moral rules, one might like a list of them, but such an exercise is probably a waste of time. Anyone who doesn't know them already isn't going to learn anything. (It's not like learning a new computer language.) But, for starters, how about

Thou shalt not kill

Thou shalt not steal

Robert Solomon, "Morality: The Basic Rules," from *The New World of Business.* Reprinted by permission of Rowman & Littlefield, Publishers.

Thou shalt not commit adultery

Thou shalt not bear false witness

Thou shalt not cheat on thy taxes

Thou shalt not knowingly do harm

Don't be cruel

Etc.

We could go on. There are moral rules that are in dispute, such as the morality of pre-marital sex and the morality of children's advertising. There are moral rules that conflict—especially in times of extreme stress, in wartime or the corporate equivalent thereof. But of morality itself there is surprisingly little to say (until we get to a highly theoretical level, which is not appropriate here). Moral laws are unambiguous and not open to debate. They simply say,

DON'T DO IT!

Against breaches of morality there are no good arguments, whatever a person's status, however powerful the company, however great the profits. In fact, considerable damage may be done by a company spokesman trying to argue against a moral rule, perhaps more damage than the original transgression itself. In this context, we should recall once again the Lockheed spokesman's heedless complaint, defending himself against a morally ambiguous charge: "When a company wants its products to be bought at all costs, [can it] realistically decline the request [for payoffs] on the grounds that it is not a good thing from the ethical point of view?"

The answer to that question is, simply, "Yes."

The practical problem with moral rules is never whether or not to accept them; it is rather how to apply them. Granted that one must accept the principle "Thou shalt not kill," does that include the lives of animals? Does it prohibit any risky industrial activity like mining coal, in which some employees will lose their lives? Does it prohibit the manufacture of any product, like guns or knives, that *might,* if abused, cause fatal injuries? Granted that one accepts the principle that one should not steal—that is, take someone else's property without paying a fair and agreed-upon price for it—does that mean that one should not take advantage of a company in trouble by buying up inventory or perhaps the company itself? Should a business person take advantage of the stupidity or negligence of a supplier or a customer—for example, if the first forgets to send a bill or the second overpays one? Granted that one should tell the truth and ought not to cheat on taxes, does that preclude such common business practices as tax deferrals and shelters?

What is morality, given that it occupies such an unchallengeable place in our (and every) society? Simply stated, morality consists of those rules that circumscribe legitimate activity for every citizen (or visitor). Such rules are the boundaries of a tolerable social life and guarantee the security of those things a society values most—individual life and well-being, obviously, but, in our society at least, extraordinary freedom, private property, personal and social relationships, freedom from terror, and the "pursuit of happiness." But beyond this essential function, the nature of morality is a matter of violent dispute. There are those who insist that morality is inextricably tied to religion—or to a particular religion—and impossible without. There are those who insist on a strict interpretation of an exact set of moral rules, with no room for other interpretations and no exceptions based on current social facts and needs. And there are those who believe that morality is nothing but a set of local social restrictions that (with some risk) can be flouted or bypassed at will. (One sometimes finds people in business who defend the ultrastrict view of morality in their personal lives but are virtually amoral in professional life, thus provoking the most vehement critics of business.) But whatever else it may be, morality is at least the following:

1. MORALITY IS A LIVING PHENOMENON, no matter how ancient its codes and principles. Our primary moral precept is the autonomy of each individual and every generation to rethink and decide for themselves what is right and what is wrong.
2. MORALITY IS WHAT ONE DOES, not what one says or how loudly and publicly one regrets doing wrong afterward—a recent fashion. Apologizing on the national news after being convicted of a crime is not necessarily a mark of morality.
3. MORALITY IS A SHARED SENSE OF VALUES. It is possible that only one person in the company is right and everyone else is wrong, but how do we recognize when that lone voice is indeed correct? Only because that lone voice finds a much larger audience outside the company, and agreement on the moral principles with which the company itself will be condemned.
4. MORALITY ISN'T ACCIDENTAL. It is not what one does that counts but what one does *knowingly.* Promoting the right person by mistake isn't being moral. Giving money to a charity by mistake isn't charity.
5. MORALITY REQUIRES COMPASSION. Cold-blooded obedience of the rules isn't enough.
6. MORALITY IS A WAY OF LIFE, a state of character. It's not a matter of forcing oneself to comply. The self-satisfaction of being a "good person" is motive enough.
7. MORALITY IS NOT A SUBSTITUTE FOR LIFE. We are a "cryptomoral" society that delights in clever criminals and charming con men, and not only in the movies. We are a law-abiding society, but we are also attracted to people who break the rules. No one who knows our society should ever expect a morally perfect business world. But such characters and their stories provide the spice of business life, not its substance. To be moral is an unquestioned good. To be a moralizing bore, a dogmatic stick-in-the-mud in the name of morality, is not good. In the words of Tom Peters, "The line between ethical purity and arrogant egocentrism is a fine one."

THE REAL LIFE OF A STUDENT
Term Papers for Sale
—SCHOOL SUCKS WEBSITE

The following Internet website, www.schoolsucks.com, was created by Kenneth Sahr, a 24-year-old Miami college student. School Sucks is a World Wide Web site for term papers and exams. The site solicits papers and exams from college students who submit them electronically. Sahr collected much of this material by e-mailing fraternities and requesting copies of old term papers, traditionally stockpiled by frats. They are then available to other students who wish to use them. As you might imagine, this site is not favored by academics, who view it as encouraging plagiarism. However, don't judge the site before reviewing some of the materials included below. The administrators of the site believe that it will not lead to plagiarism but instead will force professors to constantly update their courses and exams.

Following the School Sucks information are two e-mail transmissions from professors to an academic listserver discussing the difficult issues raised by a site such as this. What do you think? Is it ethical to coordinate a site such as this? Recall the words of Confucius from The Analects: *"Those who are born with knowledge are the highest. Next come those who attain knowledge through study. Next again come those who turn to study after having been vexed by difficulties. The common people, in so far as they make no effort to study even after having been vexed by difficulties, are the lowest" (chap. XVI, par. 9).*

ELECTRONIC LETTER TO PROFESSORS FROM SCHOOL SUCKS*

Welcome to School Sucks!

I'm sure you've heard lots about School Sucks. It is my pleasure to take this opportunity to clarify a few matters for you.

Here are a few points:

1. This page, unlike the termpaper mills, does not charge students. Therefore both students and professors have full access to School Sucks. Students

---

The Real Life of a Student: Term Papers for Sale.
*www.schoolsucks.com material. Reprinted with permission from Kenny Sahr, creator and publisher of School Sucks.

know you are fully aware of this site and therefore should not be turning in papers from this site.

2. Were this a library of thesis (i.e. graduate level) papers, would there be a problem?

3. The academic world is based on tenure. This is important as it ensures continuity in education. It also poses a great risk—it insulates professors from the "rat race" that their students will soon be joining.

Basic Darwinism tells us that without a struggle there is no progress. No checks and balances. You may or may not be aware of this, but your students feel that many of you are mediocre in your profession.

How much time have you spent on acquiring new teaching methods in the past few years? Compare that to how much time you have spent trying to get your book published.

Granted, not every professor fits in this category—to be fair, this is a minority.

But School Sucks is forcing you to re-evaluate your role as educators. School Sucks is forcing mediocre professors assigning mediocre assignments to wake up. It was you who notified the media of the existence of this site, yet it is you who will benefit the most from the existence of such a popular site.

4. Many of you are reminding School Sucks of the perhaps less than satisfactory level of some of the papers featured. School Sucks couldn't agree more—and we point out that the papers featured here are a cross reference of the level of students across the globe. Please do not pass the buck on this one.

I personally believe that the Pandora's box which is now open will further education, not impede it. Did this site make you rethink the roles of many in education? I believe so.

HOW TO USE THE RESOURCES ON SCHOOL SUCKS (AND ELSEWHERE) TO WRITE PAPERS AND NOT GET INTO TROUBLE.

The purpose of this page is to inform you about plagiarism. In her book *A Writer's Reference,* Diana Hacker defines three acts which are considered plagiarism:

(1) failing to cite quotations and borrowed ideas, (2) failing to enclose borrowed language in quotation marks, and (3) failing to put summaries and paraphrases in your own words. (261)

When done intentionally, plagiarism is a dishonest act; an act of cheating. Dishonesty sucks; plagiarism sucks because it

> cheats the person who plagiarizes because that person does not learn to put ideas into his/her own words which improves thinking and writing skills; cheats other students who took the time and effort to do their own work; cheats the person who did the original work by not giving that person credit for it;

> is not worth the risk of getting caught and getting a zero on the paper, or failing the class, or other disciplinary action. Professors and TA's can find SCHOOL SUCKS as easy as you.

Nobody likes someone who cheats in a game of pickup basketball, or in a game of tennis, or a chess match. And it doesn't feel very good when you have to compete against someone who has gained an unfair advantage over you by cheating. Let the same sense of honor apply when writing a paper.

And don't let flimsy excuses get in the way, either. You know them.

"I will only do it once," "A few sentences won't hurt," or "It's me against the system."

If you are under a lot of *stress* or having problems, ask for help rather than turning to a dishonest act.

Plagiarism can also happen unintentionally when one doesn't know the rules for citation. When this happens, a person can still be held responsible. *Ouch.* Hopefully, this paper will provide you with practical information to understand what plagiarism is and how to avoid it so that you can use the resources on School Sucks (and elsewhere) properly. If you have questions, ask the instructor before you act.

Based on Diana Hacker's definition of plagiarism given above, there are three rules to follow to avoid plagiarism.

> Rule #1:
> Thou shalt not copy someone else's writing, word for word, and claim it as one's own. These words are not yours. When used in a paper, someone else's exact words must have quotation marks and a citation.

> Rule #2:
> Thou shalt cite the source (including page number(s)) of all quotations **as well as** any borrowed ideas in the paper.

> Rule #3:
> If thou summarizes someone else's ideas in a paper, the information has to be put in one's own words in addition to being properly cited. This means you cannot copy some of the author's sentences and add a few of your own to make it sound different, and you cannot use synonyms with the same basic sentence structure as the original work and then claim the work as your own.

FEEDBACK STUDENTS PROFESSORS ADVERTISE SUBMIT
EXAMS   CLASSIFIED ADS   CALENDAR

SCHOOL SUCKS
BUSINESS

- Essay on the Soda Wars
- Economic Analysis of Hawaii
- Coca-Cola and Its Evolution
- Comparison of Mail Communications
- Waterford Crystal: a Case Analysis
- Corporate Development during the Industrial Revolution
- Postal Service as a Monopoly
- TQM in Foodservice
- Agrarian Discontent in the Late 1800's
- Growth of New York's Business between 1825 and 1860
- The Fed and Interest Rates
- Ethics in Business
- Tobacco Advertising and Its Dangerous Effects on Young People
- In Search of Excellence
- Productivity Growth Hypothesis

History Law Science
Arts Business English

From:	Kent Schenkel*
To:	Multiple recipients of list ALSBTALK
Date:	7/19/96 7:21 am
Subject:	Re: plagiarism and cheating (fwd)

Information from the mail header

Sender:	"Academy of Legal Studies in Business (ALSB) Talk"
Poster:	Kent Schenkel
Subject:	Re: plagiarism and cheating (fwd)

I tell my students that while the law can combat, mitigate, and even practically eradicate many social ills, there are limits to what it can do. High profile examples include the S&L bailout—private civil suits were perceived to be inadequate to correct the problem.

As for the age-old problem of cheating and fraud, resources are always available for those who wish to use them. To cite an example within the scope of the current issue—I remember a guy when I was an undergrad (some 17 years ago) who bought a term paper from a mail-order company, and he got an A on it.

A thought on the issue from a positive perspective: These students are going to be out in the business world where an abundance of opportunities exist for cheating, fraud, etc. To the extent that the same temptations exist in the college environment they get a chance to learn how they would handle them.

And now is our chance to have some influence.

We can (and do) teach ethical approaches to problem-solving and dispute resolution. I, for one, think most students would not buy "canned" term papers.

And for those who would, rules exist to punish those who get caught. But those rules will never be a substitute for an inner sense of right and wrong.

Kent Schenkel
UNC-Wilmington

From:	Kenneth Schneyer*
To:	Multiple recipients of list ALSBTALK
Date:	7/18/96 8:27 pm
Subject:	Re: plagiarism and cheating (fwd)

Information from the mail header

Sender:	"Academy of Legal Studies in Business (ALSB) Talk"
Poster:	Kenneth Schneyer
Subject:	Re: plagiarism and cheating (fwd)

Joan's message led me to explore the site she described, and also to do a Web search for similar sites. There seem to be a number of sites devoted to either selling or writing term papers at costs ranging from $6 to $10 per page.

---

*Responses by Kent Schenkel and Ken Schneyer are reprinted with permission of the authors.

Here are the addresses of some additional sites I found:

http://www.termpaperwarehouse.com/tpw/
http://www.execpc.com/~hppapers/
http://wahoo.netrunner.net/~dolphin/pprs.htm
http://www.termpapersonline.com/

Some of these contain clear, repeated disclaimers indicating that the papers are not intended to be handed in as the student's own work, that the owner will refuse to deliver papers to students if the owner believes that the student will turn it in as his/her own work, that there is no promise that the paper will satisfy the student's course if it is turned in as the students own work, and/or that turning the paper in as the student's own work may violate honor codes etc. (One such site, however, which contained such disclaimers, also contained an offer to provide papers on disks "to avoid time-consuming retyping!" Why would you need to retype a paper that is being used for research purposes only?)

However, the site Joan pointed out, www.schoolsucks.com, contains such a disclaimer only if the student specifically clicks for it. In other words, it is possible for the student to download a paper without seeing the disclaimer. Further, the site contains indications (through words like "cheaters", "scam", and so forth) that it *is* intended to be used for that purpose. This particular site, I think, might be engaged in wire fraud. I have sent an e-mail message to the Justice Department outlining the bare facts and asking whether they will investigate.

In the case of the sites with the repeated disclaimers, it's hard to tell what recourse we have. A site that loudly tells students not to turn papers in as their own work, but to use them as research guides only, probably can't be accused of conspiracy to do anything unless there is some indication that the reader is supposed to know the warning is insincere.

I think, therefore, that this may be a pretty serious situation. You can't get access to the papers on file without paying for them, in most situations, and of course the newly written papers are completely inaccessible. What to do?

Ken Schneyer

THE GOOD SAMARITAN

—LUKE

The Bible offers us parables in order to teach lessons. The following story is related by Jesus in the Gospel according to Luke. Many people do not even know that the "good samaritan" has its origins in the Bible. Instead, they look at a good samaritan as someone who, for better or worse, helps another out of civic compassion. Do you know people who act like this? Would the world be a better place if everyone acted as the good samaritan? Why doesn't everyone (or every organization) act like the good samaritan? What is there to lose?

30 Jesus replied: "There was a man going down from Jerusalem to Jericho who fell prey to robbers. They stripped him, beat him, and then went off leaving him half-dead. 31 A priest happened to be going down the same road; he saw him but continued on. 32 Likewise there was a Levite who came the same way; he saw him and went on. 33 But a Samaritan who was journeying along came on him and was moved to pity at the sight. 34 He approached him and dressed his wounds, pouring in oil and wine. He then hoisted him on his own beast and brought him to an inn, where he cared for him. 35 The next day he took out two silver pieces and gave them to the innkeeper with the request: 'Look after him, and if there is any further expense I will repay you on my way back.'

36 "Which of these three, in your opinion, was neighbor to the man who fell in with the robbers?" 37 The answer came, "The one who treated him with compassion." Jesus said to him, "Then go and do the same."

The Good Samaritan, Luke 10: 30–37. The Bible

SHOULD ETHICS BE TAUGHT IN COLLEGE?

—David Thies

David Thies, a college senior on his way to law school in a few months, evaluates the role of ethics instruction at the college level. By that time, has students' ethical style or "competency" already been formed, such that a course in ethics will have no bearing? Can ethics be taught at any age? If you were put in charge of a group of 18-year-olds, how would you go about teaching them ethics or ethical behavior? Do you agree with Thies's conclusions?

One enters college with a moral and ethical code developed as a result of the influence of environmental factors such as one's parents, friends, community, and education. But, is ethical development complete by the time one enters college? I believe the answer is a no. Until college, many of us have moral codes developed based upon the consequences of our acts. We looked to teachers, parents, peers, and religious leaders for guidance. Oftentimes, unethical acts were avoided due to the possible consequences imposed by these "guides," similar to the early stages of Kohlberg's moral development scheme. I believe that ethics goes far beyond this fear of retribution or punishment. One's understanding of ethics is complex; situations on the surface may seem to lack a need for ethical evaluation, while careful analysis reveals an underlying dilemma. Ethics, and the critical thinking skills necessary to tackle these difficult moral problems, should be an integral part of every college culture.

Educational institutions should accept their responsibility as educators as well as character developers. An atmosphere of ethics, via a strong code of conduct and an emphasis on ethical development in the classroom and beyond, creates a cultural norm. Those members who may have a less than adequate ethical foundation often conform to this ethical norm in order to be accepted. Engaging students' minds in ethical issues is a powerful way to build an ethical character, and there is no place more appropriate for this challenge than in the universities. Students reflect and become actively aware of the ethical nature of decision making. They often break down and redevelop their own moral code. Maybe they learn that it is no longer acceptable to bend the rules in order to succeed. The creation of this ethical culture will produce graduates with higher ethical standards as they enter public or private professions.

When facing an ethical dilemma in the workplace, these dilemmas are extremely complicated and require split-second decision making. It is because of these circumstances that a strong ethical base must be developed *prior* to entering the workplace. Informed decision

---

Source: David Thies, "Should Ethics Be Taught in College?" Reprinted by permission of the author.

making at all levels should be the goal of educational institutions. This ability can only be acquired through an ethics course plus the integration of ethics conversations into other courses. The presentation of ethical theories, case studies, and different perspectives on ethics in the classroom environment develops critical thinking skills, moral foundations, and ethical frameworks.

As I leave college, I truly believe my own personal ethic has developed throughout my experiences as a student. When faced with tough moral choices, I now bring to my decision tools I did not have before I started college. I also feel that if I had written this opinion on the teaching of ethics on my first day as a college freshman, it would have been much different. I challenge readers to write down their opinions and to continually readdress this question throughout their academic and professional careers.

OBEDIENCE TO AUTHORITY

—STANLEY MILGRAM

Milgram believed that obedience "is as basic an element in the struc-
ture of human life as one can point to." He believed that communal life
was not possible without some system of authority. "It is only the man
dwelling in isolation who is not forced to respond, through defiance or
submission, to the commands of others." Milgram conducted the ex-
periment discussed below in response to his concerns about obedience
to Nazi commands during World War II. "These inhumane policies
may have originated in the mind of a single person, but they could only
have been carried out on a massive scale if a very large number of
people obeyed orders." Subsequent to his experiment, Milgram ex-
plained that something far more dangerous than hatred was revealed
by his work, "the capacity for man to abandon his humanity—indeed,
the inevitability that he does so—as he merges his unique personality
into larger institutional structures." Imagine the implications for the
impact of corporate cultures!

Consider, as you read the description of the experiment and the
responses of the subjects, what you believe your response might have
been. Are we as free thinking as we usually believe?

. . . The Nazi extermination of European Jews is the most extreme instance of abhorrent immoral acts carried out by thousands of people in the name of obedience. Yet in lesser degree this type of thing is constantly recurring: ordinary citizens are ordered to destroy other people, and they do so because they consider it their duty to obey orders. Thus, obedience to authority, long praised as a virtue, takes on a new aspect when it serves a malevolent cause; far from appearing as a virtue, it is transformed into a heinous sin. Or is it?

The moral question of whether one should obey when commands conflict with conscience was argued by Plato, dramatized in *Antigone,* and treated to philosophic analysis in every historical epoch. Conservative philosophers argue that the very fabric of society is threatened by disobedience, and even when the act prescribed by an authority is an evil one, it is better to carry out the act than to wrench at the structure of authority. Hobbes stated further that an act so executed is in no sense the responsibility of the person who carries it out but only of the authority that orders it. But humanists argue for the primacy of individual conscience in such matters, insisting that the moral judgments of the individual must override authority when the two are in conflict.

***

In order to take a close look at the act of obeying, I set up a simple experiment at Yale University. Eventually, the experiment was to involve more than a thousand participants and would be repeated at several universities, but at the beginning, the conception was simple. A person comes to a psychological laboratory and is told to carry out a series of acts that come increasingly into conflict with conscience. The main question is how far the participant will comply with the experimenter's instructions before refusing to carry out the actions required of him.

But the reader needs to know a little more detail about the experiment. Two people come to a psychology laboratory to take part in a study of memory and learning. One of them is designated as a "teacher" and the other a "learner." The experimenter explains that the study is concerned with the effects of punishment on learning. The learner is conducted into a room, seated in a chair, his arms strapped to prevent excessive movement, and an electrode attached to his wrist. He is told that he is to learn a list of word pairs; whenever he makes an error, he will receive electric shocks of increasing intensity.

The real focus of the experiment is the teacher. After watching the learner being strapped into place, he is taken into the main experimental room and seated before an impressive shock generator. Its main feature is a horizontal line of thirty switches, ranging from 15 volts to 450 volts, in 15-volt increments. There are also verbal designations which range from SLIGHT SHOCK TO DANGER—SEVERE SHOCK. The teacher is told that he is to administer the learning test to the man in the other room. When the learner responds correctly, the teacher moves on to the next item; when the other man gives an incorrect answer, the teacher is to give him an electric shock. He is to start at the lowest shock level (15 volts) and to increase the level each time the man makes an error, going through 30 volts, 45 volts, and so on.

The "teacher" is a genuinely naïve subject who has come to the laboratory to participate in an experiment. The learner, or victim, is an actor who actually receives no shock at all. The point of the experiment is to see how far a person will proceed in a concrete and measurable situation in which he is ordered to inflict increasing pain on a protesting victim. At what point will the subject refuse to obey the experimenter?

Conflict arises when the man receiving the shock begins to indicate that he is experiencing discomfort. At 75 volts, the "learner" grunts. At 120 volts he complains verbally; at 150 he demands to be released from the experiment. His protests continue as the shocks escalate, growing increasingly vehement and emotional. At 285 volts his response can only be described as an agonized scream.

Observers of the experiment agree that its gripping quality is somewhat obscured in print. For the subject, the situation is not a game; conflict is intense and obvious. On one hand, the manifest suffering of the learner presses him to quit. On the other, the experimenter, a legitimate authority to whom the subject feels some commitment, enjoins him to continue. Each time the subject hesitates to administer shock, the experimenter orders him to continue. To extricate himself from the situation, the subject must make a clear break with authority. The aim of this investigation was to find when and how people would defy authority in the face of a clear moral imperative.

There are, of course, enormous differences between carrying out the orders of a commanding officer during times of war and carrying out the orders of an experimenter. Yet the essence of certain relationships remains, for one may ask in a general way: How does a man behave when he is told by a legitimate authority to act against a third individual? If anything, we may expect the experimenter's power to be considerably less than that of the general, since he has no power to enforce his imperatives, and participation in a psychological experiment scarcely evokes the sense of urgency and dedication engendered by participation in war. Despite these limitations, I thought it worthwhile to start careful observation of obedience even in this modest situation, in the hope that it would stimulate insights and yield general propositions applicable to a variety of circumstances.

***

A commonly offered explanation is that those who shocked the victim at the most severe level were monsters, the sadistic fringe of society. But if one considers that almost two-thirds of the participants fall into the category of "obedient" subjects, and that they represented ordinary people drawn from working, managerial, and professional classes, the argument becomes very shaky. Indeed, it is highly reminiscent of the issue that arose in connection with Hannah Arendt's 1963 book, *Eichmann in Jerusalem.* Arendt contended that the prosecution's effort to depict Eichmann as a sadistic monster was fundamentally wrong, that he came closer to being an uninspired bureaucrat who simply sat at his desk and did his job. For asserting these views, Arendt became the object of considerable scorn, even calumny. Somehow, it was felt that the monstrous deeds carried out by Eichmann required a brutal, twisted, and sadistic personality, evil incarnate. After witnessing hundreds of ordinary people submit to the authority in our own experiments, I must conclude that Arendt's conception of the *banality of evil* comes closer to the truth than one might dare imagine. The ordinary person who shocked the victim did so out of a sense of obligation—a conception of his duties as a subject—and not from any peculiarly aggressive tendencies.

That is, perhaps, the most fundamental lesson of our study: ordinary people, simply doing their jobs, and without any particular hostility on their part, can become agents in a terrible destructive process. Moreover, even when the destructive effects of their work become patently clear, and they are asked to carry out actions incompatible with fundamental standards of morality, relatively few people have the resources needed to resist authority. A variety of inhibitions against disobeying authority come into play and successfully keep the person in his place.

Sitting back in one's armchair, it is easy to condemn the actions of the obedient subjects. But those who condemn the subjects measure them against the standard of their own ability to formulate high-minded moral prescriptions. That is hardly a fair standard. Many of the subjects, at the level of stated opinion, feel quite as strongly as any of us about the moral requirement of refraining from action against a helpless victim. They, too, in general terms know what ought to be done and can state their values when the occasion arises. This has little, if anything, to do with their actual behavior under the pressure of circumstances.

If people are asked to render a moral judgment on what constitutes appropriate behavior in this situation, they unfailingly see disobedience as proper. But values are not the only forces at work in an actual, ongoing situation. They are but one narrow band of causes in the total spectrum of forces impinging on a person. Many people were unable to realize their values in action and found themselves continuing in the experiment even though they disagreed with what they were doing.

***

George Orwell caught the essence of the situation when he wrote:

As I write, highly civilized human beings are flying overhead, trying to kill me. They do not feel any enmity against me as an individual, nor I against them. They are only "doing their duty," as the saying goes. Most of them, I have no doubt, are kind-hearted law abiding men who would never dream of committing murder in private life. On the other hand, if one of them succeeds in blowing me to pieces with a well-placed bomb, he will never sleep any the worse for it.

From each person in the experiment we derive one essential fact: whether he has obeyed or disobeyed. But it is foolish to see the subject only in this way. For he brings to the laboratory a full range of emotions, attitudes, and individual styles. Indeed, so varied in temperament and manner are the people passing through the laboratory that it sometimes seems a miracle that we emerge with any regularities at all. One subject may be an inarticulate bricklayer, diffident and awkwardly humble in the presence of a scientist. He is followed by a self-assured businessman, who thrusts his cigar at the experimenter to underscore his assertions.

We need to focus on the individuals who took part in the study not only because this provides a personal dimension to the experiment but also because the quality of each person's experience gives us clues to the nature of the process of obedience.

***

JAN RENSALEER, INDUSTRIAL ENGINEER (IN EXPERIMENT 2)

The subject is a thirty-two-year-old industrial engineer, sporting blond hair and a mustache. He is self-contained and speaks with a trace of a foreign accent. He is neatly dressed. In the interview he tells us that he emigrated from Holland after the Second World War and that he is a member of the Dutch Reformed Church. He is mild-mannered and intelligent.

When the victim complains at the 150-volt level, the subject turns to the experimenter and asks, "What do I do now?"

The experimenter tells him to continue.

The engineer presses his hand to his head and proceeds with the test. He glances more and more often at the experimenter. At 255 volts, he pushes the chair away from the shock generator and turns to the experimenter:

MR. RENSALEER: Oh, I can't continue this way; it's a voluntary program, if the man doesn't want to go on with it.

EXPERIMENTER: Please continue.

(A long pause.)

MR. RENSALEER: No, I can't continue. I'm sorry.

EXPERIMENTER: The experiment requires that you go on.

MR. RENSALEER: The man, he seems to be getting hurt.

EXPERIMENTER: There is no permanent tissue damage.

MR. RENSALEER: Yes, but I know what shocks do to you, I'm an electrical engineer, and I have had shocks . . . And you get real shook up by them—especially if you know the next one is coming. I'm sorry.

EXPERIMENTER: It is absolutely essential that you continue.

MR. RENSALEER: Well, I won't—not with the man screaming to get out.

EXPERIMENTER: You have no other choice.

MR. RENSALEER: I *do* have a choice. (*Incredulous and indignant:*) Why don't I have a choice? I came here on my own free will. I thought I could help on a research project. But if I have to hurt somebody to do that, or if I was in his place, too, I wouldn't stay there. I can't continue. I'm very sorry. I think I've gone too far already, probably.

When asked who was responsible for shocking the learner against his will, he said, "I would put it on myself entirely."

He refused to assign any responsibility to the learner or the experimenter.

"I should have stopped the first time he complained. I did want to stop at that time. I turned around and looked at you. I guess it's a matter of . . . authority, if you want to call it that: my being impressed by the thing, and going on although I didn't want to. Say, if you're serving in the army, and you have to do something you don't like to do, but your superior tells you to do it. That sort of thing, you know what I mean?"

"One of the things I think is very cowardly is to try to shove the responsibility onto someone else. See, if I now turned around and said, 'It's your fault . . . it's not mine,' I would call that cowardly."

Although this subject defied the experimenter at 255 volts, he still feels responsible for administering any shocks beyond the victim's first protests. He is hard on himself and does not allow the structure of authority in which he is functioning to absolve him of any responsibility.

Mr. Rensaleer expressed surprise at the underestimation of obedience by the psychiatrists. He said that on the basis of his experience in Nazi-occupied Europe, he would predict a high level of compliance to orders. He suggests, "It would be interesting to conduct the same tests in Germany and other countries."

The experiment made a deep impression on the subject, so much so that a few days after his participation he wrote a long, careful letter to the staff, asking if he could work with us.

"Although I am . . . employed in engineering, I have become convinced that the social sciences and especially psychology, are much more important in today's world. . . ."

THE DAY HAS COME
... TO TAKE AN
ACCOUNTING
OF MY LIFE

The following poem, of unknown though traditional origins, is reprinted from a prayerbook used by the Makom Shalom congregation in Chicago, Illinois. The prayerbook is meant to be used during the Jewish New Year services for Rosh Hoshanah and Yom Kippur, in early Autumn. During these holidays, called the "high holidays," Jews are asked to review their year and to contemplate those reasons for joy and for atonement, as the poem articulates.

Have I dreamed of late; Of the person I want to be,
Of the changes I would make; in my daily habits,
In the way I am with others; In the friendship I show compassions,
Woman friends, man friends, my partner,
In the regard I show my father and mother; Who brought me out of childhood?

I have remained enchained too often to less than what I am.
But the day has come to take an accounting of my life.

Have I renewed of late; My vision of the world I want to live in,
Of the changes I would make; In the way my friends are with each other,
The way we find out whom we love; The way we grow to educated people,
The way in which the many kinds of needy people; Grope their way to Justice?

I, who am my own kind of needy person, have been afraid of visions.
But the day has come to take an accounting of my life.

Have I faced up of late; To the needs I really have—
Not for the comforts which shelter my unsureness,
Not for the honors which paper over my self,
Not for the handsome beauty in which my weakness masquarades,
Not for the unattractiveness in which my strengths hide out—

I need to be loved. Do I deserve to be?
I need to love another. Can I commit my love?
Perhaps its object will be less than my visions.
Perhaps I am not brave enough; To find a new vision
Through a real and breathing person.

"The Day Has Come to Take an Accounting of My Life," in *Gates: A Machzor* (Chicago: Makom Shalom/The Community, 1994). Reprinted with permission of Rabbi Allen Secher.

I need to come in touch with my own power,
Not with titles; Not with possessions, money, high praise,
But with the power that is mine; As a child of the Power that is the universe
To be a comfort, a source of honor,
Handsome and beautiful from the moment I awoke this morning
So strong . . . That I can risk the love of someone else
So sure . . . That I can risk to change the world
And know that even if it all comes crashing down
I shall survive it all—
Saddened a bit, shaken perhaps; Not unvisited by tears,
But my dreams shall not crash down. My visions not go glimmering.
So long as I have breath, I know I have the strength, to transform what I can be
To what I am.

The day has come . . . to take an accounting of my life.

Chapter 4

CRITICAL ETHICAL ANALYSIS BASED ON AN UNDERSTANDING OF PERCEPTUAL DIFFERENCES AND VARYING PERSPECTIVES:
A Decision-Making Model

From here that looks like a bucket of water, but from an ant's point of view, it's a vast ocean; from an elephant's point of view, it's just a cool drink; and to a fish, of course, it's home.

—NORTON JUSTER,
THE PHANTOM TOLL BOOTH

Throughout this text, you are asked to reach your own conclusions and judgments in connection with ethical issues and dilemmas. In earlier sections, we have discussed a variety of models for decision making that may prove fruitful in this effort. In this section, there are several readings that more specifically explain and/or highlight the multiperspectival approach that will be taken throughout the text.

The text presents you with a variety of perspectives in connection with each topic area of business ethics. The basis for this approach is the theory, first propounded by philosopher Ed Freeman, called stakeholder analysis. Stakeholder theory asks a decision maker to consider, in reaching a decision, the interests of each individual or entity that holds a stake in that decision or that will be affected by the decision. The model of this approach was discussed earlier in the section on moral reasoning.

In order to consider the stakeholders of a decision, it is critical to be able to understand the interests of each party, to be able to empathetically evaluate what the potential impact on that stakeholder will be and what the stakeholder's perspective on the decision is likely to be. This is not as easy as it may first appear. For instance, one might not necessarily understand all of the parties who might be impacted, or one might not completely understand the nature of each party's interest, or even the effect the decision will have in the end.

> *It is often difficult for those who look on the tradition of the Red Man from the outside or through the "educated" mind to understand that no object is what it appears to be, but it is simply the pale shadow of a Reality. It is for this reason that every created object is* wakan, *holy, and has a power according to the loftiness of the spiritual reality it reflects. The Indian humbles himself before the whole of creation because all visible things were created before him and, being older than he, deserve respect.*[1]

Several readings included in this section offer a practical application of stakeholder theory. For instance, the seminal business ethics case "The Parable of the Sadhu" offers a specific analysis of the interests and motivations of each decision maker in the parable. Similarly, in "A Jury of Her Peers," Glaspell demonstrates how different individuals may see different implications when viewing the same scene. Werhane's "Rashomon Complex" offers a similar demonstration in connection with the Ford Pinto case, a classic business ethics dilemma. Finally, several interpretations of Dow Corning's experience with silicone implants are included in an effort to illustrate how ethicists have viewed potentially unethical behavior. In reading later segments of this text, try to contemplate the variety of perspectives that may be offered on the same topic and consider your response only after evaluating the anticipated perspectives of each stakeholder in connection with the issue.

---

[1]From a letter written by Joseph Epes Brown, quoted in Schuon, *The Feathered Sun,* 47, cited in Huston Smith, *The World's Religions* (San Francisco, CA: HarperSanFrancisco, 1991), p. 379.

A STAKEHOLDER THEORY OF THE MODERN CORPORATION

R. EDWARD FREEMAN

Freeman delineates the basics of stakeholder theory and challenges the primacy of the shareholder in corporate decisions.

INTRODUCTION

Corporations have ceased to be merely legal devices through which the private business transactions of individuals may be carried on. Though still much used for this purpose, the corporate form has acquired a larger significance. The corporation has, in fact, become both a method of property tenure and a means of organizing economic life. Grown to tremendous proportions, there may be said to have evolved a "corporate system"—which has attracted to itself a combination of attributes and powers, and has attained a degree of prominence entitling it to be dealt with as a major social institution.[1]

Despite these prophetic words of Berle and Means (1932), scholars and managers alike continue to hold sacred the view that managers bear a special relationship to the stockholders in the firm. Since stockholders own shares in the firm, they have certain rights and privileges, which must be granted to them by management, as well as by others. Sanctions, in the form of "the law of corporations," and other protective mechanisms in the form of social custom, accepted management practice, myth, and ritual, are thought to reinforce the assumption of the primacy of the stockholder.

The purpose of this paper is to pose several challenges to this assumption, from within the framework of managerial capitalism, and to suggest the bare bones of an alternative theory, *a stakeholder theory of the modern corporation*. I do not seek the demise of the modern corporation, either intellectually or in fact. Rather, I seek its transformation. In the words of Neurath, we shall attempt to "rebuild the ship, plank by plank, while it remains afloat."[2]

My thesis is that I can revitalize the concept of managerial capitalism by replacing the notion that managers have a duty to stockholders with the concept that managers bear a fiduciary relationship to stakeholders. Stakeholders are those groups who have a stake in or claim on the firm. Specifically I include suppliers, customers, employees, stockholders, and the local community, as well as management in its role as agent for these groups. I argue that the legal, economic, political, and moral challenges to the currently received theory of

---

the firm, as a nexus of contracts among the owners of the factors of production and customers, require us to revise this concept. That is, each of these stakeholder groups has a right not to be treated as a means to some end, and therefore must participate in determining the future direction of the firm in which they have a stake.

The crux of my argument is that we must reconceptualize the firm around the following question: For whose benefit and at whose expense should the firm be managed? I shall set forth such a reconceptualization in the form of a *stakeholder theory of the firm.* I shall then critically examine the stakeholder view and its implications for the future of the capitalist system.

THE ATTACK ON MANAGERIAL CAPITALISM

The Legal Argument

The basic idea of managerial capitalism is that in return for controlling the firm, management vigorously pursues the interests of stockholders. Central to the managerial view of the firm is the idea that management can pursue market transactions with suppliers and customers in an unconstrained manner.

The law of corporations gives a less clearcut answer to the question: In whose interest and for whose benefit should the modern corporation be governed? While it says that the corporations should be run primarily in the interests of the stockholders in the firm, it says further that the corporation exists "in contemplation of the law" and has personality as a "legal person," limited liability for its actions, and immortality, since its existence transcends that of its members. Therefore, directors and other officers of the firm have a fiduciary obligation to stockholders in the sense that the "affairs of the corporation" must be conducted in the interest of the stockholders. And stockholders can theoretically bring suit against those directors and managers for doing otherwise. But since the corporation is a legal person, existing in contemplation of the law, managers of the corporation are constrained by law.

Until recently, this was no constraint at all. In this century, however, the law has evolved to effectively constrain the pursuit of stockholder interests at the expense of other claimants on the firm. It has, in effect, required that the claims of customers, suppliers, local communities, and employees be taken into consideration, though in general they are subordinated to the claims of stockholders.

For instance, the doctrine of "privity of contract," as articulated in *Winterbottom v. Wright* in 1842, has been eroded by recent developments in products liability law. Indeed, *Greenman v. Yuba Power* gives the manufacturer strict liability for damage caused by its products, even though the seller has exercised all possible care in the preparation and sale of the product and the consumer has not bought the product from nor entered into any contractual arrangement with the manufacturer. Caveat emptor has been replaced, in large part, with caveat venditor.[3] The Consumer Product Safety Commission has the power to enact product recalls, and in 1980 one U.S. automobile company recalled more cars than it built. Some industries are required to provide information to customers about a product's ingredients, whether or not the customers want and are willing to pay for this information.[4]

The same argument is applicable to management's dealings with employees. The National Labor Relations Act gave employees the right to unionize and to bargain in good faith. It set up the National Labor Relations Board to enforce these rights with management.

The Equal Pay Act of 1963 and Title VII of the Civil Rights Act of 1964 constrain management from discrimination in hiring practices; these have been followed with the Age Discrimination in Employment Act of 1967.[5] The emergence of a body of administrative case law arising from labor-management disputes and the historic settling of discrimination claims with large employers such as AT&T have caused the emergence of a body of practice in the corporation that is consistent with the legal guarantee of the rights of the employees. The law has protected the due process rights of those employees who enter into collective bargaining agreements with management. As of the present, however, only 30 percent of the labor force are participating in such agreements; this has prompted one labor law scholar to propose a statutory law prohibiting dismissals of the 70 percent of the workforce not protected.[6]

The law has also protected the interests of local communities. The Clean Air Act and Clean Water Act have constrained management from "spoiling the commons." In an historic case, *Marsh v. Alabama,* the Supreme Court ruled that a company-owned town was subject to the provisions of the U.S. Constitution, thereby guaranteeing the rights of local citizens and negating the "property rights" of the firm. Some states and municipalities have gone further and passed laws preventing firms from moving plants or limiting when and how plants can be closed. In sum, there is much current legal activity in this area to constrain management's pursuit of stockholders' interests at the expense of the local communities in which the firm operates.

I have argued that the result of such changes in the legal system can be viewed as giving some rights to those groups that have a claim on the firm, for example, customers, suppliers, employees, local communities, stockholders, and management. It raises the question, at the core of a theory of the firm: In whose interest and for whose benefit should the firm be managed? The answer proposed by managerial capitalism is clearly "the stockholders," but I have argued that the law has been progressively circumscribing this answer.

The Economic Argument

In its pure ideological form managerial capitalism seeks to maximize the interests of stockholders. In its perennial criticism of government regulation, management espouses the "invisible hand" doctrine. It contends that it creates the greatest good for the greatest number, and therefore government need not intervene. However, we know that externalities, moral hazards, and monopoly power exist in fact, whether or not they exist in theory. Further, some of the legal apparatus mentioned above has evolved to deal with just these issues.

The problem of the "tragedy of the commons" or the free-rider problem pervades the concept of public goods such as water and air. No one has an incentive to incur the cost of cleanup or the cost of nonpollution, since the marginal gain of one firm's action is small. Every firm reasons this way, and the result is pollution of water and air. Since the industrial revolution, firms have sought to internalize the benefits and externalize the costs of their actions. The cost must be borne by all, through taxation and regulation; hence we have the emergence of the environmental regulations of the 1970s.

Similarly, moral hazards arise when the purchaser of a good or service can pass along the cost of that good. There is no incentive to economize, on the part of either the producer or the consumer, and there is excessive use of the resources involved. The institutionalized practice of third-party payment in health care is a prime example.

Finally, we see the avoidance of competitive behavior on the part of firms, each seeking to monopolize a small portion of the market and not compete with one another. In a number of industries, oligopolies have emerged, and while there is questionable evidence that oligopolies are not the most efficient corporate form in some industries, suffice it to say that the potential for abuse of market power has again led to regulation of managerial activity. In the classic case, AT&T, arguably one of the great technological and managerial achievements of the century, was broken up into eight separate companies to prevent its abuse of monopoly power.

Externalities, moral hazards, and monopoly power have led to more external control on managerial capitalism. There are de facto constraints, due to these economic facts of life, on the ability of management to act in the interests of stockholders.

A STAKEHOLDER THEORY OF THE FIRM

The Stakeholder Concept

Corporations have stakeholders, that is, groups and individuals who benefit from or are harmed by, and whose rights are violated or respected by, corporate actions. The concept of stakeholders is a generalization of the notion of stockholders, who themselves have some special claim on the firm. Just as stockholders have a right to demand certain actions by management, so do other stakeholders have a right to make claims. The exact nature of these claims is a difficult question that I shall address, but the logic is identical to that of the stockholder theory. Stakes require action of a certain sort, and conflicting stakes require methods of resolution.

Freeman and Reed (1983)[7] distinguish two senses of *stakeholder*. The "narrow definition" includes those groups who are vital to the survival and success of the corporation. The "wide-definition" includes any group or individual who can affect or is affected by the corporation. I shall begin with a modest aim, to articulate a stakeholder theory using the narrow definition.

Stakeholders in the Modern Corporation

Figure 1 depicts the stakeholders in a typical large corporation. The stakes of each are reciprocal, since each can affect the other in terms of harms and benefits as well as rights and duties. The stakes of each are not univocal and would vary by particular corporation. I merely set forth some general notions that seem to be common to many large firms.

Owners have financial stake in the corporation in the form of stocks, bonds, and so on, and they expect some kind of financial return from them. Either they have given money directly to the firm, or they have some historical claim made through a series of morally justified exchanges. The firm affects their livelihood or, if a substantial portion of their retirement income is in stocks or bonds, their ability to care for themselves when they can no longer work. Of course, the stakes of owners will differ by type of owner, preferences for money, moral preferences, and so on, as well as by type of firm. The owners of AT&T are quite different from the owners of Ford Motor Company, with stock of the former company being widely dispersed among 3 million stockholders and that of the latter being held by a small family group as well as by a large group of public stockholders.

FIGURE 1

A Stakeholder Model of the Corporation.

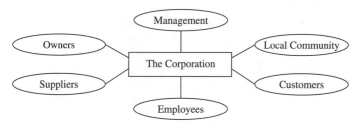

Employees have their jobs and usually their livelihood at stake; they often have specialized skills for which there is usually no perfectly elastic market. In return for their labor, they expect security, wages, benefits, and meaningful work. In return for their loyalty, the corporation is expected to provide for them and carry them through difficult times. Employees are expected to follow the instructions of management most of the time, to speak favorably about the company, and to be responsible citizens in the local communities in which the company operates. Where they are used as means to an end, they must participate in decisions affecting such use. The evidence that such policies and values as described here lead to productive company-employee relationships is compelling. It is equally compelling to realize that the opportunities for "bad faith" on the part of both management and employees are enormous. "Mock participation" in quality circles, singing the company song, and wearing the company uniform solely to please management all lead to distrust and unproductive work.

Suppliers, interpreted in a stakeholder sense, are vital to the success of the firm, for raw materials will determine the final product's quality and price. In turn the firm is a customer of the supplier and is therefore vital to the success and survival of the supplier. When the firm treats the supplier as a valued member of the stakeholder network, rather than simply as a source of materials, the supplier will respond when the firm is in need. Chrysler traditionally had very close ties to its suppliers, even to the extent that led some to suspect the transfer of illegal payments. And when Chrysler was on the brink of disaster, the suppliers responded with price cuts, accepting late payments, financing, and so on. Supplier and company can rise and fall together. Of course, again, the particular supplier relationships will depend on a number of variables such as the number of suppliers and whether the supplies are finished goods or raw materials.

Customers exchange resources for the products of the firm and in return receive the benefits of the products. Customers provide the lifeblood of the firm in the form of revenue. Given the level of reinvestment of earnings in large corporations, customers indirectly pay for the development of new products and services. Peters and Waterman (1982)[8] have argued that being close to the customer leads to success with other stakeholders and that a distinguishing characteristic of some companies that have performed well is their emphasis on the customer. By paying attention to customers' needs, management automatically addresses the needs of suppliers and owners. Moreover, it seems that the ethic of customer service carries over to the community. Almost without fail the "excellent companies" in Peters and Waterman's study have good reputations in the community. I would argue that Peters and Waterman have found multiple applications of Kant's dictum, "Treat persons as ends unto themselves," and it should come as no surprise that persons respond to such respectful treatment, be they customers, suppliers, owners, employees, or members of the local community. The real surprise is the novelty of the application of Kant's rule in a theory of good management practice.

The local community grants the firm the right to build facilities and, in turn, it benefits from the tax base and economic and social contributions of the firm. In return for the provision of local services, the firm is expected to be a good citizen, as is any person, either "natural or artificial." The firm cannot expose the community to unreasonable hazards in the form of pollution, toxic waste, and so on. If for some reason the firm must leave a community, it is expected to work with local leaders to make the transition as smoothly as possible. Of course, the firm does not have perfect knowledge, but when it discovers some danger or runs afoul of new competition, it is expected to inform the local community and to work with the community to overcome any problem. When the firm mismanages its relationship with the local community, it is in the same position as a citizen who commits a crime. It has violated the implicit social contract with the community and should expect to be distrusted and ostracized. It should not be surprised when punitive measures are invoked.

I have not included "competitors" as stakeholders in the narrow sense, since strictly speaking they are not necessary for the survival and success of the firm; the stakeholder theory works equally well in monopoly contexts. However, competitors and government would be the first to be included in an extension of this basic theory. It is simply not true that the interests of competitors in an industry are always in conflict. There is no reason why trade associations and other multiorganizational groups cannot band together to solve common problems that have little to do with how to restrain trade. Implementation of stakeholder management principles, in the long run, mitigates the need for industrial policy and an increasing role for government intervention and regulation.

The Role of Management

Management plays a special role, for it too has a stake in the modern corporation. On the one hand, management's stake is like that of employees, with some kind of explicit or implicit employment contract. But, on the other hand, management has a duty of safeguarding the welfare of the abstract entity that is the corporation. In short, management, especially top management, must look after the health of the corporation, and this involves balancing the multiple claims of conflicting stakeholders. Owners want higher financial returns, while customers want more money spent on research and development. Employees want higher wages and better benefits, while the local community wants better parks and day-care facilities.

The task of management in today's corporation is akin to that of King Solomon. The stakeholder theory does not give primacy to one stakeholder group over another, though there will surely be times when one group will benefit at the expense of others. In general, however, management must keep the relationships among stakeholders in balance. When these relationships become imbalanced, the survival of the firm is in jeopardy.

When wages are too high and product quality is too low, customers leave, suppliers suffer, and owners sell their stocks and bonds, depressing the stock price and making it difficult to raise new capital at favorable rates. Note, however, that the reason for paying returns to owners is not that they "own" the firms, but that their support is necessary for the survival of the firm, and that they have a legitimate claim on the firm. Similar reasoning applies in turn to each stakeholder group.

A stakeholder theory of the firm must redefine the purpose of the firm. The stockholder theory claims that the purpose of the firm is to maximize the welfare of the stockholders, perhaps subject to some moral or social constraints, either because such maximization leads to the greatest good or because of property rights. The purpose of the firm is quite different in my view.

"The stakeholder theory" can be unpacked into a number of stakeholder theories, each of which has a "normative core," inextricably linked to the way that corporations should be governed and the way that managers should act. So, attempts to more fully define, or more carefully define, a stakeholder theory are misguided. Following Donaldson and Preston, I want to insist that the normative, descriptive, instrumental, and metaphorical (my addition to their framework) uses of "stakeholder" are tied together in particular political constructions to yield a number of possible "stakeholder theories." "Stakeholder theory" is thus a genre of stories about how we could live. Let me be more specific.

A "normative core" of a theory is a set of sentences that includes among others, sentences like:

(1) Corporations ought to be governed . . .
(2) Managers ought to act to . . .

where we need arguments or further narratives which include business and moral terms to fill in the blanks. This normative core is not always reducible to a fundamental ground like the theory of property, but certain normative cores are consistent with modern understandings of property. Certain elaborations of the theory of private property plus the other institutions of political liberalism give rise to particular normative cores. But there are other institutions, other political conceptions of how society ought to be structured, so that there are different possible normative cores.

So, one normative core of a stakeholder theory might be a feminist standpoint, one rethinking how we would restructure "value-creating activity" along principles of caring and connection.[9] Another would be an ecological (or several ecological) normative cores. Mark Starik has argued that the very idea of a stakeholder theory of the *firm* ignores certain ecological necessities.[10] Exhibit 1 is suggestive of how these theories could be developed.

In the next section I shall sketch the normative core based on pragmatic liberalism. But, any normative core must address the questions in columns A or B, or explain why these questions may be irrelevant, as in the ecological view. In addition, each "theory," and I use the word hesitantly, must place the normative core within a more full-fledged account of how we could understand value-creating activity differently (column C). The only way to get on with this task is to see the stakeholder idea as a metaphor. The attempt to prescribe one and only one "normative core" and construct "a stakeholder theory" is at best a disguised attempt to smuggle a normative core past the unsophisticated noses of other unsuspecting academics who are just happy to see the end of the stockholder orthodoxy.

EXHIBIT 1

A Reasonable Pluralism

	A. **Corporations ought to be governed . . .**	**B.** **Managers ought to act . . .**	**C.** **The background disciplines of "value creation" are . . .**
Doctrine of Fair Contracts	. . . in accordance with the six principles.	. . . in the interests of stakeholders.	—business theories —theories that explain stakeholder behavior
Feminist Standpoint Theory	. . . in accordance with the principles of caring/connection and relationships.	. . . to maintain and care for relationships and networks of stakeholders.	—business theories —feminist theory —social science understanding of networks
Ecological Principles	. . . in accordance with the principle of caring for the earth.	. . . to care for the earth.	—business theories —ecology —other

If we begin with the view that we can understand value-creation activity as a contractual process among those parties affected, and if for simplicity's sake we initially designate those parties as financiers, customers, suppliers, employees, and communities, then we can construct a normative core that reflects the liberal notions of autonomy, solidarity, and fairness as articulated by John Rawls, Richard Rorty, and others.[11] Notice that building these moral notions into the foundations of how we understand value creation and contracting requires that we eschew separating the "business" part of the process from the "ethical" part, and that we start with the presumption of equality among the contractors, rather than the presumption in favor of financier rights.

The normative core for this redesigned contractual theory will capture the liberal idea of fairness if it ensures a basic equality among stakeholders in terms of their moral rights as these are realized in the firm, and if it recognizes that inequalities among stakeholders are justified if they raise the level of the least well-off stakeholder. The liberal ideal of autonomy is captured by the realization that each stakeholder must be free to enter agreements that create value for themselves, and solidarity is realized by the recognition of the mutuality of stakeholder interests.

One way to understand fairness in this context is to claim *a la* Rawls that a contract is fair if parties to the contract would agree to it in ignorance of their actual stakes. Thus, a contract is like a fair bet, if each party is willing to turn the tables and accept the other side. What would a fair contract among corporate stakeholders look like? If we can articulate this ideal, a sort of corporate constitution, we could then ask whether actual corporations measure up to this standard, and we also begin to design corporate structures which are consistent with this Doctrine of Fair Contracts.

Imagine if you will, representative stakeholders trying to decide on "the rules of the game." Each is rational in a straightforward sense, looking out for its own self-interest. At least *ex ante,* stakeholders are the relevant parties since they will be materially affected. Stakeholders know how economic activity is organized and could be organized. They know general facts about the way the corporate world works. They know that in the real world there are or could be transaction costs, externalities, and positive costs of contracting. Suppose they are uncertain about what other social institutions exist, but they know the range of those institutions. They do not know if government exists to pick up the tab for any externalities, or if they will exist in the nightwatchman state of libertarian theory. They know success and failure stories of businesses around the world. In short, they are behind a Rawls-like veil of ignorance, and they do not know what stake each will have when the veil is lifted. What ground rules would they choose to guide them?

The first ground rule is "The Principle of Entry and Exit." In any contract that is negotiated, the corporation must have clearly defined entry, exit, and renegotiation conditions, or at least it must have methods or processes for so defining these conditions. The logic is straightforward: each stakeholder must be able to determine when an agreement exists and has a chance of fulfillment. This is not to imply that contracts cannot contain contingent claims or other methods for resolving uncertainty, but rather that it must contain methods for determining whether or not it is valid.

The second ground rule I shall call "The Principle of Governance," and it says that the procedure for changing the rules of the game must be agreed upon by unanimous consent. Think about the consequences of a majority of stakeholders systematically "selling out" a minority. Each stakeholder, in ignorance of its actual role, would seek to avoid such a situation. In reality this principle translates into each stakeholder never giving up its right to participate in the governance of the corporation, or perhaps into the existence of stakeholder governing boards.

The third ground rule I shall call "The Principle of Externalities," and it says that if a contract between A and B imposes a cost on C, then C has the option to become a party to the contract, and the terms are renegotiated. Once again the rationality of this condition is clear. Each stakeholder will want insurance that it does not become C.

The fourth ground rule is "The Principle of Contracting Costs," and it says that all parties to the contract must share in the cost of contracting. Once again the logic is straightforward. Any one stakeholder can get stuck.

A fifth ground rule is "The Agency Principle" that says that any agent must serve the interests of all stakeholders. It must adjudicate conflicts within the bounds of the other principals. Once again the logic is clear. Agents for any one group would have a privileged place.

A sixth and final ground rule we might call "The Principle of Limited Immortality." The corporation shall be managed as if it can continue to serve the interests of stakeholders through time. Stakeholders are uncertain about the future but, subject to exit conditions, they realize that the continued existence of the corporation is in their interest. Therefore, it would be rational to hire managers who are fiduciaries to their interest and the interest of the collective. If it turns out the "collective interest" is the empty set, then this principle simply collapses into the Agency Principle.

Thus, the Doctrine of Fair Contracts consists of these six ground rules, or principles:

(1) The Principle of Entry and Exit
(2) The Principle of Governance
(3) The Principle of Externalities
(4) The Principle of Contracting Costs
(5) The Agency Principle
(6) The Principle of Limited Immortality

Think of these ground rules as a doctrine which would guide actual stakeholders in devising a corporate constitution or charter. Think of management as having the duty to act in accordance with some specific constitution or charter.

Obviously, if the Doctrine of Fair Contracts and its accompanying background narratives are to effect real change, there must be requisite changes in the enabling laws of the land. I propose the following three principles to serve as constitutive elements of attempts to reform the law of corporations.

The Stakeholder Enabling Principle

Corporations shall be managed in the interests of its stakeholders, defined as employees, financiers, customers, employees, and communities.

The Principle of Director Responsibility

Directors of the corporation shall have a duty of care to use reasonable judgment to define and direct the affairs of the corporation in accordance with the Stakeholder Enabling Principle.

The Principle of Stakeholder Recourse

Stakeholders may bring an action against the directors for failure to perform the required duty of care.

Obviously, there is more work to be done to spell out these principles in terms of model legislation. As they stand, they try to capture the intuitions that drive the liberal ideals. It is equally plain that corporate constitutions which meet a test like the doctrine of fair contracts are meant to enable directors and executives to manage the corporation in conjunction with these same liberal ideals.

NOTES

1. Cf.A. Berle and G. Means, *The Modern Corporation and Private Property* (New York: Commerce Clearing House, 1932), 1. For a reassessment of Berle and Means' argument after 50 years, see *Journal of Law and Economics* 26 (June 1983), especially G. Stigler and C. Friedland, "The Literature of Economics: The Case of Berle and Means," 237–68; D. North, "Comment on Stigler and Friedland," 269–72; and G. Means, "Corporate Power in the Marketplace," 467–85.

2. The metaphor of rebuilding the ship while afloat is attributed to Neurath by W. Quine, *Word and Object* (Cambridge: Harvard University Press, 1960), and W. Quine and J. Ullian, *The Web of Belief* (New York: Random House, 1978). The point is that to keep the ship afloat during repairs we must replace a plank with one that will do a better job. Our argument is that stakeholder capitalism can so replace the current version of managerial capitalism.

3. *See* R. Charan and F. Freeman, "Planning for the Business Environment of the 1980s," *The Journal of Business Strategy* 1 (1980): 9–19, especially p. 15 for a brief account of the major developments in products liability law.

4. *See* S. Breyer, *Regulation and Its Reform* (Cambridge: Harvard University Press, 1983), 133, for an analysis of food additives.

5. *See* I. Millstein and S. Katsh, *The Limits of Corporate Power* (New York: Macmillan, 1981), Chapter 4.

6. Cf.C. Summers, "Protecting All Employees Against Unjust Dismissal," *Harvard Business Review* 58 (1980): 136, for a careful statement of the argument.

7. *See* E. Freeman and D. Reed, "Stockholders and Stakeholders: A New Perspective on Corporate Governance," in C. Huizinga, ed., *Corporate Governance: A Definitive Exploration of the Issues* (Los Angeles: UCLA Extension Press, 1983).

8. *See* T. Peters and R. Waterman, *In Search of Excellence* (New York: Harper and Row, 1982).

9. *See,* for instance, A. Wicks, D. Gilbert, and E. Freeman, "A Feminist Reinterpretation of the Stakeholder Concept," *Business Ethics Quarterly,* Vol. 4, No. 4, October 1994; and E. Freeman and J. Liedtka, "Corporate Social Responsibility: A Critical Approach," *Business Horizons,* Vol. 34, No. 4, July–August 1991, pp. 92–98.

10. At the Toronto workshop Mark Starik sketched how a theory would look if we took the environment to be a stakeholder. This fruitful line of work is one example of my main point about pluralism.

11. J. Rawls, *Political Liberalism* (New York: Columbia University Press, 1993); and R. Rorty, "The Priority of Democracy to Philosophy" in *Reading Rorty: Critical Responses to Philosophy and the Mirror of Nature (and Beyond),* ed. Alan R. Malachowski (Cambridge, MA: Blackwell, 1990).

THE PARABLE OF THE SADHU

BOWEN H. MCCOY

This parable is based on the true experience of the author, Bowen Mc-Coy, a senior executive from Morgan Stanley, who decided that he needed a sabbatical from the hectic life he had created. His answer was an extended trek through the Himalayas. The goal of this trek was to reach Muklinath, an ancient holy village on the other side of an 18,000-foot ice-covered pass. The parable offers McCoy's reflections upon his return from the experience.

Last year, as the first participant in the new six-month sabbatical program that Morgan Stanley has adopted, I enjoyed a rare opportunity to collect my thoughts as well as do some traveling. I spent the first three months in Nepal, walking 600 miles through 200 villages in the Himalayas and climbing some 120,000 vertical feet. On the trip my sole Western companion was an anthropologist who shed light on the cultural patterns of the villages we passed through.

During the Nepal hike, something occurred that has had a powerful impact on my thinking about corporate ethics. Although some might argue that the experience has no relevance to business, it was a situation in which a basic ethical dilemma suddenly intruded into the lives of a group of individuals. How the group responded I think holds a lesson for all organizations no matter how defined.

THE SADHU

The Nepal experience was more rugged and adventuresome than I had anticipated. Most commercial treks last two or three weeks and cover a quarter of the distance we traveled.

My friend Stephen, the anthropologist, and I were halfway through the 60-day Himalayan part of the trip when we reached the high point, an 18,000-foot pass over a crest that we'd have to traverse to reach the village of Muklinath, an ancient holy place for pilgrims.

Six years earlier I had suffered pulmonary edema, an acute form of altitude sickness, at 16,500 feet in the vicinity of Everest base camp, so we were understandably concerned about what would happen at 18,000 feet. Moreover, the Himalayas were having their wettest spring in 20 years; hip-deep powder and ice had already driven us off one ridge. If we failed to cross the pass, I feared that the last half of our "once in a lifetime" trip would be ruined.

The night before we would try the pass, we camped at a hut at 14,500 feet. In the photos taken at that camp, my face appears wan. The last village we'd passed through was a sturdy two-day walk below us, and I was tired.

During the late afternoon, four backpackers from New Zealand joined us, and we spent most of the night awake, anticipating the climb. Below we could see the fires of two other parties, which turned out to be two Swiss couples and a Japanese hiking club.

To get over the steep part of the climb before the sun melted the steps cut in the ice, we departed at 3:30 A.M. The New Zealanders left first, followed by Stephen and myself, our porters and Sherpas, and then the Swiss. The Japanese lingered in their camp. The sky was clear, and we were confident that no spring storm would erupt that day to close the pass.

At 15,500 feet, it looked to me as if Stephen were shuffling and staggering a bit, which are symptoms of altitude sickness. (The initial stage of altitude sickness brings a headache and nausea. As the condition worsens, a climber may encounter difficult breathing, disorientation, aphasia, and paralysis.) I felt strong, my adrenaline was flowing, but I was very concerned about my ultimate ability to get across. A couple of our porters were also suffering from the height, and Pasang, our Sherpa sirdar (leader), was worried.

Just after daybreak, while we rested at 15,500 feet, one of the New Zealanders, who had gone ahead, came staggering down toward us with a body slung across his shoulders. He dumped the almost naked, barefoot body of an Indian holy man—a sadhu—at my feet. He had found the pilgrim lying on the ice, shivering and suffering from hypothermia. I cradled the sadhu's head and laid him out on the rocks. The New Zealander was angry. He wanted to get across the pass before the bright sun melted the snow. He said, "Look, I've done what I can. You have porters and Sherpa guides. You care for him. We're going on!" He turned and went back up the mountain to join his friends.

I took a carotid pulse and found that the sadhu was still alive. We figured he had probably visited the holy shrines at Muklinath and was on his way home. It was fruitless to question why he had chosen this desperately high route instead of the safe, heavily traveled caravan route through the Kali Gandaki gorge. Or why he was almost naked and with no shoes, or how long he had been lying in the pass. The answers weren't going to solve our problem.

Stephen and the four Swiss began stripping off outer clothing and opening their packs. The sadhu was soon clothed from head to foot. He was not able to walk, but he was very much alive. I looked down the mountain and spotted below the Japanese climbers marching up with a horse.

Without a great deal of thought, I told Stephen and Pasang that I was concerned about withstanding the heights to come and wanted to get over the pass. I took off after several of our porters who had gone ahead.

On the steep part of the ascent where, if the ice steps had given way, I would have slid down about 3,000 feet, I felt vertigo. I stopped for a breather, allowing the Swiss to catch up with me. I inquired about the sadhu and Stephen. They said that the sadhu was fine and that Stephen was just behind. I set off again for the summit.

Stephen arrived at the summit an hour after I did. Still exhilarated by victory, I ran down the snow slope to congratulate him. He was suffering from altitude sickness, walking 15 steps, then stopping, walking 15 steps, then stopping, Pasang accompanied him all the way up. When I reached them, Stephen glared at me and said: "How do you feel about contributing to the death of a fellow man?"

I did not fully comprehend what he meant.

"Is the sadhu dead?" I inquired.

"No," replied Stephen, "but he surely will be!"

After I had gone, and the Swiss had departed not long after, Stephen had remained with the sadhu. When the Japanese had arrived, Stephen had asked to use their horse to transport the sadhu down to the hut. They had refused. He had then asked Pasang to have a group of our porters carry the sadhu. Pasang had resisted the idea, saying that the porters would have to exert all their energy to get themselves over the pass. He had thought they could not carry a man down 1,000 feet to the hut, reclimb the slope, and get across safely before the snow melted. Pasang had pressed Stephen not to delay any longer.

The Sherpas had carried the sadhu down to a rock in the sun at about 15,000 feet and had pointed out the hut another 500 feet below. The Japanese had given him food and drink. When they had last seen him he was listlessly throwing rocks at the Japanese party's dog, which had frightened him.

We do not know if the sadhu lived or died.

For many of the following days and evenings Stephen and I discussed and debated our behavior toward the sadhu. Stephen is a committed Quaker with deep moral vision. He said, "I feel that what happened with the sadhu is a good example of the breakdown between the individual ethic and the corporate ethic. No one person was willing to assume ultimate responsibility for the sadhu. Each was willing to do his bit just so long as it was not too inconvenient. When it got to be a bother, everyone just passed the buck to someone else and took off. Jesus was relevant to a more individualistic stage of society, but how do we interpret his teaching today in a world filled with large, impersonal organizations and groups?"

I defended the larger group, saying, "Look, we all cared. We all stopped and gave aid and comfort. Everyone did his bit. The New Zealander carried him down below the snow line. I took his pulse and suggested we treat him for hypothermia. You and the Swiss gave him clothing and got him warmed up. The Japanese gave him food and water. The Sherpas carried him down to the sun and pointed out the easy trail toward the hut. He was well enough to throw rocks at a dog. What more could we do?"

"You have just described the typical affluent Westerner's response to a problem. Throwing money—in this case food and sweaters—at it, but not solving the fundamentals!" Stephen retorted.

"What would satisfy you?" I said. "Here we are, a group of New Zealanders, Swiss, Americans, and Japanese who have never met before and who are at the apex of one of the most powerful experiences of our lives. Some years the pass is so bad no one gets over it. What right does an almost naked pilgrim who chooses the wrong trail have to disrupt our lives? Even the Sherpas had no interest in risking the trip to help him beyond a certain point."

Stephen calmly rebutted, "I wonder what the Sherpas would have done if the sadhu had been a well-dressed Nepali, or what the Japanese would have done if the sadhu had been a well-dressed Asian, or what you would have done, Buzz, if the sadhu had been a well-dressed Western woman?"

"Where, in your opinion," I asked instead, "is the limit of our responsibility in a situation like this? We had our own well-being to worry about. Our Sherpa guides were unwilling to jeopardize us or the porters for the sadhu. No one else on the mountain was willing to commit himself beyond certain self-imposed limits."

Stephen said, "As individual Christians or people with a Western ethical tradition, we can fulfill our obligations in such a situation only if (1) the sadhu dies in our care, (2) the sadhu demonstrates to us that he could undertake the two-day walk down to the village, or (3) we carry the sadhu for two days down to the village and convince someone there to care for him."

"Leaving the sadhu in the sun with food and clothing, while he demonstrated hand-eye coordination by throwing a rock at a dog, comes close to fulfilling items one and two," I answered. "And it wouldn't have made sense to take him to the village where the people appeared to be far less caring than the Sherpas, so the third condition is impractical. Are you really saying that, no matter what the implications, we should, at the drop of a hat, have changed our entire plan?"

THE INDIVIDUAL VS. THE GROUP ETHIC

Despite my arguments, I felt and continue to feel guilt about the sadhu. I had literally walked through a classic moral dilemma without fully thinking through the consequences. My excuses for my actions include a high adrenaline flow, a superordinate goal, and a once-in-a-lifetime opportunity—factors in the usual corporate situation, especially when one is under stress.

Real moral dilemmas are ambiguous, and many of us hike right through them, unaware that they exist. When, usually after the fact, someone makes an issue of them, we tend to resent his or her bringing it up. Often, when the full import of what we have done (or not done) falls on us, we dig into a defensive position from which it is very difficult to emerge. In rare circumstances we may contemplate what we have done from inside a prison.

Had we mountaineers been free of physical and mental stress caused by the effort and the high altitude, we might have treated the sadhu differently. Yet isn't stress the real test of personal and corporate values? The instant decisions executives make under pressure reveal the most about personal and corporate character.

Among the many questions that occur to me when pondering my experience are: What are the practical limits of moral imagination and vision? Is there a collective or institutional ethic beyond the ethics of the individual? At what level of effort or commitment can one discharge one's ethical responsibilities?

Not every ethical dilemma has a right solution. Reasonable people often disagree; otherwise there would be no dilemma. In a business context, however, it is essential that managers agree on a process for dealing with dilemmas.

The sadhu experience offers an interesting parallel to business situations. An immediate response was mandatory. Failure to act was a decision in itself. Up on the mountain we could not resign and submit our résumés to a headhunter. In contrast to philosophy, business involves action and implementation—getting things done. Managers must come up with answers to problems based on what they see and what they allow to influence their decision-making processes. On the mountain, none of us but Stephen realized the true dimensions of the situation we were facing.

One of our problems was that as a group we had no process for developing a consensus. We had no sense of purpose or plan. The difficulties of dealing with the sadhu were so complex that no one person could handle it. Because it did not have a set of preconditions that could guide its action to an acceptable resolution, the group reacted instinctively as individuals. The cross-cultural nature of the group added a further layer of complexity. We had no leader with whom we could all identify and in whose purpose we believed. Only Stephen was willing to take charge, but he could not gain adequate support to care for the sadhu.

Some organizations do have a value system that transcends the personal values of the managers. Such values, which go beyond profitability, are usually revealed when the organization is under stress. People throughout the organization generally accept its values, which, because they are not presented as a rigid list of commandments, may be somewhat ambiguous. The stories people tell, rather than printed materials, transmit these conceptions of what is proper behavior.

For 20 years I have been exposed at senior levels to a variety of corporations and organizations. It is amazing how quickly an outsider can sense the tone and style of an organization and the degree of tolerated openness and freedom to challenge management.

Organizations that do not have a heritage of mutually accepted, shared values tend to become unhinged during stress, with each individual bailing out for himself. In the great takeover battles we have witnessed during past years, companies that had strong cultures drew the wagons around them and fought it out, while other companies saw executives, supported by their golden parachutes, bail out of the struggles.

Because corporations and their members are interdependent, for the corporation to be strong the members need to share a preconceived notion of what is correct behavior, a "business ethic," and think of it as a positive force, not a constraint.

As an investment banker I am continually warned by well-meaning lawyers, clients, and associates to be wary of conflicts of interest. Yet if I were to run away from every difficult situation, I wouldn't be an effective investment banker. I have to feel my way through conflicts. An effective manager can't run from risk either; he or she has to confront and deal with risk. To feel "safe" in doing this, managers need the guidelines of an agreed-on process and set of values within the organization.

After my three months in Nepal, I spent three months as an executive-in-residence at both Stanford Business School and the Center for Ethics and Social Policy at the Graduate Theological Union at Berkeley. These six months away from my job gave me time to assimilate 20 years of business experience. My thoughts turned often to the meaning of the leadership role in any large organization. Students at the seminary thought of themselves as antibusiness. But when I questioned them they agreed that they distrusted all large organizations, including the church. They perceived all large organizations as impersonal and opposed to individual values and needs. Yet we all know of organizations where peoples' values and beliefs are respected and their expressions encouraged. What makes the difference? Can we identify the difference and, as a result, manage more effectively?

The word "ethics" turns off many and confuses more. Yet the notions of shared values and an agreed-on process for dealing with adversity and change—what many people mean when they talk about corporate culture—seem to be at the heart of the ethical issue. People who are in touch with their own core beliefs and the beliefs of others and are sustained by them can be more comfortable living on the cutting edge. At times, taking a tough line or decisive stand in a muddle of ambiguity is the only ethical thing to do. If a manager is indecisive and spends time trying to figure out the "good" thing to do, the enterprise may be lost.

Business ethics, then, has to do with the authenticity and integrity of the enterprise. To be ethical is to follow the business as well as the cultural goals of the corporation, its owners, its employees, and its customers. Those who cannot serve the corporate vision are not authentic business people and, therefore, are not ethical in the business sense.

At this stage of my own business experience I have a strong interest in organizational behavior. Sociologists are keenly studying what they call corporate stories, legends, and heroes as a way organizations have of transmitting the value system. Corporations such as Arco have even hired consultants to perform an audit of their corporate culture. In a company, the leader is the person who understands, interprets, and manages the corporate value system. Effective managers are then action-oriented people who resolve conflict, are tolerant of ambiguity, stress, and change, and have a strong sense of purpose for themselves and their organizations.

If all this is true, I wonder about the role of the professional manager who moves from company to company. How can he or she quickly absorb the values and culture of different organizations? Or is there, indeed, an art of management that is totally transportable? Assuming such fungible managers do exist, is it proper for them to manipulate the values of others?

What would have happened had Stephen and I carried the sadhu for two days back to the village and become involved with the villagers in his care? In four trips to Nepal my most interesting experiences occurred in 1975 when I lived in a Sherpa home in the Khumbu for five days recovering from altitude sickness. The high point of Stephen's trip was an invitation to participate in a family funeral ceremony in Manang. Neither experience had to do with climbing the high passes of the Himalayas. Why were we so reluctant to try the lower path, the ambiguous trail? Perhaps because we did not have a leader who could reveal the greater purpose of the trip to us.

Why didn't Stephen with his moral vision opt to take the sadhu under his personal care? The answer is because, in part, Stephen was hard-stressed physically himself, and because, in part, without some support system that involved our involuntary and episodic community on the mountain, it was beyond his individual capacity to do so.

I see the current interest in corporate culture and corporate value systems as a positive response to Stephen's pessimism about the decline of the role in the individual in large organizations. Individuals who operate from a thoughtful set of personal values provide the foundation for a corporate culture. A corporate tradition that encourages freedom of inquiry, supports personal values, and reinforces a focused sense of direction can fulfill the need for individuality along with the prosperity and success of the group. Without such corporate support, the individual is lost.

That is the lesson of the sadhu. In a complex corporate situation, the individual requires and deserves the support of the group. If people cannot find such support from their organization, they don't know how to act. If such support is forthcoming, a person has a stake in the success of the group, and can add much to the process of establishing and maintaining a corporate culture. It is management's challenge to be sensitive to individual needs, to shape them, and to direct and focus them for the benefit of the group as a whole.

For each of us the sadhu lives. Should we stop what we are doing and comfort him; or should we keep trudging up toward the high pass? Should I pause to help the derelict I pass on the street each night as I walk to the Yale Club en route to Grand Central Station? Am I his brother? What is the nature of our responsibility if we consider ourselves to be ethical persons? Perhaps it is to change the values of the group so that it can, with all its resources, take the other road.

THE RASHOMON EFFECT

PATRICIA WERHANE

The abstract of this article offers background to the piece. Consider how perspective alters judgment. Can you think of times when your perspective may have altered your judgment? What does this say of our justice system? What does it say of our information system as a whole? Do you obtain most of your news from (and therefore base your judgments on) television news shows? the newspaper? How might you ensure that your judgment is based on the most broad and unbiased perspectives?

The Academy Award winning 1960s Japanese movie Rashomon *depicts an incident involving an outlaw, a rape or seduction of a woman, and a murder or suicide of her husband told from four different perspectives; that of the outlaw, the woman, the husband, and a passerby. The four narratives agree that the outlaw came upon the woman and her husband, the outlaw tied up the husband, sex took place between the woman and the outlaw in front of the bound husband, and the husband was found dead. How these events occurred and who killed the husband (or whether he killed himself) differs with each narrative.*

Applied ethics uses case stories to illustrate ethical issues, and it evaluates the stories or cases through moral theories and moral reasoning. The way we present cases or stories or describe the "facts," that is, the narratives we employ and the mental models that frame these narratives, affect the content of the story, the moral analysis, and subsequent evaluation of events. Indeed, we cannot present a case or tell a story except through the frame of a particular narrative or mental model. When one narrative becomes dominant, we appeal to that story for the "facts," taking it as representing what actually happened. Yet we seldom look at the narrative we use nor are we often aware of the "frame" or mental model at work. If my thesis is not mistaken, then, it is just as important, morally important, to examine different narratives about the cases we use as it is to carry out the ethical analysis.

To demonstrate what I am talking about, I am going to recount narratives of a well-worn case, the Ford Pinto. I shall illustrate how different commentators present what one of them has called "independently supportable facts" (Schmitt and May, 1979, p. 1022). In each instance I cite, the commentator claims that he is presenting facts, not assumptions, commentary, or conjecture. Yet, for some reason, these "facts" seem to differ from each other. The accounts of the case I shall use are Mark Dowie's "Pinto Madness" from September/ October 1977 *Mother Jones,* later revised and printed in *Business and Society;* "Beyond Products Liability" by Michael Schmitt and William W. May from the *University of Detroit*

Journal of Urban Law, Summer 1979; Manuel Velasquez's treatment of Pinto in his book *Business Ethics* (second ed.); Dekkers L. Davidson and Kenneth Goodpaster's Harvard Business School case, "Managing Product Safety: The Ford Pinto"; Ford Motor Company's statements from their law suit, *State of Indiana* v. *Ford Motor Company;* and Michael Hoffman's case/essay "The Ford Pinto," printed in *Taking Sides.* It will become evident that one narrative, Mark Dowie's, one of the earliest accounts of the case, becomes the dominant one.

> *There is one indisputable set of data upon which all commentators agree. On May 28, 1972, Mrs. Lily Gray was driving a six-month old Pinto on Interstate 15 near San Bernardino, California. In the car with her was Richard Grimshaw, a thirteen-year-old boy. . . . Mrs. Gray stopped in San Bernardino for gasoline, got back onto the freeway (Interstate 15) and proceeded toward her destination at sixty to sixty-five miles per hour. As she approached Route 30 off-ramp, . . . the Pinto suddenly stalled and coasted to a halt in the middle lane . . . the driver of a 1962 Ford Galaxie was unable to avoid colliding with the Pinto. Before impact the Galaxie had been braked to a speed of from twenty-eight to thirty-seven miles per hour.*
>
> *At the moment of impact, the Pinto caught fire and its interior burst into flames. The crash had driven the Pinto's gas tank forward and punctured it against the flange on the differential housing. . . . Mrs. Gray died a few days later. . . . Grimshaw managed to survive with severe burns over 90 percent of his body. (Velasquez, 199, p. 122; Grimshaw v. Ford Motor Co., p. 359).*

In 1978 a jury awarded Grimshaw at least 125 million dollars in punitive damages. *Auto News* printed a headline "Ford Fights Pinto Case: Jury Gives 128 Million" on February 13, 1978. The number $125 million is commonly cited and is in the court records as the sum of the initial punitive award. This award was later reduced on appeal to $3.5 million, a fact that is seldom cited.

What is the background for the development of the Pinto? According to public statements made by Lee Iacocca, then CEO of Ford, to meet Japanese competition Ford decided to design a subcompact car that would not weigh over 2,000 pounds nor cost over $2,000 (Davidson/Goodpaster, 1983). According to Davidson/Goodpaster, Ford began planning the Pinto in June 1967, ending with production beginning in September 1970, a 38-month turnaround time as opposed to the industry average of 43 months for engineering and developing a new automobile (Davidson/Goodpaster, 1983, p. 4). Mark Dowie claims that the development was "rushed" into 25 months (Dowie, p. 20); Velasquez says it occurred in "under two years" (Velasquez, p. 120); Hoffman claims that Ford "rushed the Pinto into production in much less than the usual time" (Hoffman, p. 133). While the actual time of development may seem unimportant, critics of the Pinto design argue that *because* it was "rushed into production" Pinto was not as carefully designed nor checked for safety as a model created over a 43-month time span (Dowie, Velasquez).

The Pinto was designed so that the gas tank was placed behind the rear axle. According to Davidson/Goodpaster, "At that time almost every American-made car had the fuel tank located in the same place" (p. 4). Dowie wonders why Ford did not place the gas tank over the rear axle, Ford's patented design for their Capri models. This placement is confirmed by Dowie, Velasquez and some Ford engineers to be the "safest place." Yet, according to Davidson/Goodpaster other studies at Ford showed that the Capri placement actually increased the likelihood of ignition inside the automobile (p. 4). Moreover, such placement reduces storage space and precludes a hatchback design. Velasquez argues that "[b]ecause the Pinto was a rush project, styling preceded engineering" (p. 120), thus accounting for the gas tank placement. This fact may have been derived from Dowie's quote, allegedly from a "Ford engineer who doesn't want his name used," that "this company is run by salesmen, not engineers; so the priority is styling, not safety" (p. 23).

Dowie argues that in addition to rushing the Pinto into production, "Ford engineers discovered in pre-production crash tests that rear-end collisions would rupture the Pinto's fuel system extremely easily" (p. 18). According to Dowie, Ford crash-tested the Pinto in a secret location and in every test made at over 25 mph the fuel tank ruptured. But according to Ford, while Pinto's gas tank did explode during many of its tests, this was because, following government guidelines, Ford had to test the car using a fixed barrier standard wherein the vehicle is towed backwards into a fixed barrier at the speed specified in the test. Ford argued that Pinto behaved well under a less stringent moving-barrier standard, which, Ford contended, is a more realistic test (Davidson/Goodpaster; *State of Indiana* v. *Ford*).

Ford and the commentators on this case agree that in 1971, before launching the automobile, an internal study was conducted that showed that a rubber bladder inner tank would improve the reliability of Pinto during tests. The bladder would cost $5.08 (Dowie, p. 29; Schmitt and May, 1979, p. 1023), $5.80 (Davidson/Goodpaster) or $11 (Velasquez, p. 120). The $11 figure probably refers to a design adjustment that Ford would have had to make to meet a later new government rollover standard (see below). However, the idea of this installation was discarded, according to Ford because of the unreliability of the rubber at cold temperatures, a conjecture no one else mentions. Dowie also contends that Ford could have reduced the dangers from rear-end collisions by installing a $1 plastic baffle between the gas tank and the differential housing to reduce the likelihood of gas tank perforation. I can find no other verification of this fact.

All commentators claim that Ford did a cost/benefit analysis to determine whether it would be more costly to change the Pinto design or assume the damages for burn victims, and memos to that effect were evidence at the Grimshaw trial (*Grimshaw* v. *Ford Motor Co.,* 570). However, according to Davidson/Goodpaster and Schmitt/May, this estimate was done in 1973, the year *after* the Grimshaw accident, in response to evaluating a proposed new government rollover standard. To meet that requirement would cost $11 per auto, Ford calculated. Ford used government data for the cost of a life ($200,000 per person), and projected an estimate of 180 burn deaths from rollovers. The study was not applicable to rear-end collisions as commentators, following Dowie's story, claimed.

There are also innuendoes in many write-ups of this case that the $200,000 figure was Ford's price of a human life. Dowie says, for example, "Ever wonder what your life is worth in dollars? Perhaps $10 million? Ford has a better idea: $200,000." In fact, it was the U.S. government's 1973 figure.

How many people have died as a result of a rear-end collision in a Pinto? "By conservative estimates Pinto crashes have caused 500 burn deaths to people who would not have been seriously injured if the car had not burst into flames. The figure could be as high as 900," Dowie claimed in 1977 (p. 18). Hoffman, in 1984, repeats those figures word for word (p. 133). Velasquez, more cautious, claims that by 1978 at least 53 people had died and "many more had been severely burnt" (p. 122), and Schmitt and May, quoting a 1977 article in *Business and Society Review,* estimate the number at "at least 32" (p. 1024; May, p. 102 at 16). Davidson/Goodpaster claim that by 1978 NHTSA estimated there were 38 cases which involved 27 fatalities.

There was a second famous Pinto accident that led the State of Indiana to charge Ford with criminal liability. The facts in that case upon which all agree are reported by Hoffman as follows:

> *On August 10, 1978, a tragic automobile accident occurred on U.S. Highway 33 near Goshen, Indiana. Sisters Judy and Lynn Ulrich (ages 18 and 16, respectively) and their cousin Donna Ulrich (age 18) were struck from the rear in their 1973 Ford Pinto by a van. The gas tank of the Pinto ruptured, the car burst into flames, and the three teenagers were burned to death. (p. 132)*

There are two points of interest in this case, points that helped to exonerate Ford in the eyes of the jury in the Indiana trial. First, in June of 1978 Ford recalled 1.5 million of its Pintos to modify the fuel tank. There is some evidence that the Ulrich auto had not participated in the recall (*State of Indiana* v. *Ford Motor Company*). Secondly, Ulrich's Pinto was hit from behind at 50 miles an hour by a van driven by a Mr. Duggar. Mr. Duggar, who was not killed, later testified that he looked down for a "smoke" when he then hit the car, although the Ulrichs had their safety blinkers on. Found in Duggar's van were at least two empty beer bottles and an undisclosed amount of marijuana. Yet this evidence, cited in the *State of Indiana* v. *Ford Motor Co.* case, are seldom mentioned in the context of the Ulrich tragedy, nor was Duggar ever indicted.

The point of all this is not to exonerate Ford nor to argue for bringing back the Pinto. Rather, it is to point out a simple phenomenon—that a narrative—a story—can be taken as fact even when other alleged equally verifiable facts contradict that story. Moreover, one narrative can become dominating such that what it says is taken as fact. Dowie's interesting tale of the Pinto became the prototype for Pinto cases without many of the authors going back to see if Dowie's data was correct or to question why some of his data contradicts Ford's and government claims. Moreover, Dowie's reporting of Grimshaw becomes a prototype for the narrative of Ulrich case as well, so that questions concerning the recall of the Ulrich auto and Mr. Duggar's performance were virtually ignored. Such omissions not only make Ford look better. They also bring into question these reports and cases.

Let me mention another set of stories, those revolving around the more recent Dow Corning silicone breast implant controversy. From the volumes of reports there are a few facts upon which everyone agrees. Dow Corning has developed and manufactured silicone breast implants since 1962. It is one of a number of manufacturers that include Bristol Myers Squibb, Baxter, and 3M. In 1975 it changed the design of the implant to a thinner shell that, according to the company, was more "natural," thus less likely to harden over time. Out of the almost 2 million women who have had implants, at least 440,000 have joined class action suits or brought individual law suits claiming to have experienced a variety of illnesses, including autoimmune diseases such as lupus and rheumatoid arthritis, connective tissues diseases, scleroderma, cancer, and various other malaises such as pain, fatigue, insomnia, memory loss, and/or headaches (*New York Times,* 1995, p.C6; Angell, p. 18).

Since this is an evolving case not all the positions and narratives have sufficiently solidified to make exhaustive comparisons. But let me focus on three points. First, there is a very simple question, Do silicone breast implants cause cancer and other diseases, in particular, connective tissue or autoimmune diseases? Second, did the industry, and Dow Corning in particular, cover up or not inform physicians or women patients of the risks of implantation? Third, did Dow Corning fail "to acknowledge and promptly investigate signs of trouble?" (See bibliography for citations.)

The first question is the most simple and the most puzzling. A seldom cited fact in the case is that pacemakers and a number of other implants are made from silicone, because silicone is thought to be the most inert of all possible implant substances. Yet pacemaker wearers have not sued for illnesses that allegedly result from that implant. According to pathologist Nir Kossovsky, however, silicone breast implants can affect the immune system and cause a variety of harms to the system. This is particularly acute when an implant ruptures (Taubes, 1995). Yet in numerous independent epidemiological studies investigators have been unable to establish any but the weakest correlation between breast implants and cancer, connective tissue disease, or autoimmune diseases (Sánchez-Guerrero et al., 1995; Giltay et al., 1994; McLaughlin and Fraumeni, 1994). The most extensive of these is a longitudinal study by Brigham and Women's Hospital of 87,318 women nurses from the ages of 30 to 55 covering their medical records over a 14-year span. This study, partly funded by the NIH, is the basis for what will be a larger study of 450,000 women. (It should also be noted that silicone breast implants were withdrawn from the market by the FDA, not because they were proven to be harmful but because the FDA concluded that the evidence was not strong enough to show they were not harmful.) Despite what an overwhelming number of scientists consider to be overwhelming evidence, a number of lawsuits have been won by claimants who argue they became ill because of implants.

The second question—Did Dow Corning cover up evidence?—is also equally puzzling. Dow Corning claims, of course, that they did not. This is partly because they instigated their own studies that found no conclusive link between implants and disease, and partly because from the very beginning they did in fact inform *physicians* about risks of implants, including possibility of rupture or hardening in some patients. It is only recently, since 1985, that Dow Corning has developed brochures to be distributed to candidates for implantation.

The third question seems to become moot if implants do not cause disease. Yet more is at stake here. Dow Corning and other silicone breast implant manufacturers depended on the narratives of science. They imagined that scientific evidence and only scientific evidence would count as evidence in the courts, that the media would not print a story to the contrary when such scientific evidence was conclusive, and that the emotional fact that women with implants became ill would become a dominant factor in what appeared to be a matter of science. We have here a number of narratives: the scientific evidence reports, Dow Corning's defense of their consent procedures, and lawsuits that focus on the illnesses. There is also a set of media narratives that focus on the emotional reactions of ill women (not all media narratives do this), the dominating examples of which are the *Business Week* article "Informed Consent" (Byrne, 1995) and John Byrne's book, which was produced from this reporting. This article focuses on the emotional trauma of Colleen Swanson, the wife of a Dow Corning manager, John Swanson, who recently resigned from Dow Corning after 27 years of employment. Colleen Swanson had had implants 17 years ago and has been suffering from a variety of illnesses almost since the end of the operation. While Byrne focuses on Colleen's emotional suffering he cites the epidemiological evidence but puts that evidence in doubt by stating:

Recent studies from Harvard Medical School and the Mayo Clinic, among others, have case doubt on the link between implants and disease. But critics have attacked these studies on numerous grounds—among them that they look only for recognized diseases such as lupus, rather than the complex of ailments many recipients complain of. (Byrne, 1996, p. 116)

Again I am not trying to whitewash this case. But it is interesting how the fact of illnesses in women with implants has been conflated with the causal claim of "illnesses caused by silicone breast implants." Perhaps it is the notion of causality that should be brought into question. The dominating emotional narratives have simply overshadowed the scientific ones. It is no wonder that Dow Corning cannot figure out what happened since they focused primarily on the scientific narratives. Moreover they seemed to assume that physicians performing implant surgery were all reasonable professionals who would inform their patients uniformly and thoroughly about the risks of implantation. (One cannot even with good conscience construct a narrative that claims that scientists are male-dominated and thus biased in their data analysis, because these studies have been conducted by men and women of a variety of scientific and medical backgrounds and nationalities.)

What can we say about the role of narratives? As I have argued elsewhere (Werhane, 1991, 1992) human beings do not simply perceive the data of their experiences unedited, so to speak. Each of us orders, selects, structures, and even censors our experiences. These shaping mechanisms are mental models or schema through which we experience the world. The selection processes or schema are culturally and socially learned and changed, and almost no perspective or model is permanent or unalterable. But we never see the world except through a point of view, a model, or framing mechanism. Indeed, narratives that shape our experiences and influence how we think about the world are essential to the facts of our experience. At the same time, these mental models or schema and these narratives are not merely subjective. They represent points of view that others share or can share, and they are, or can be, what Amartya Sen calls "positionally objective." Sen writes:

What we can observe depends on our position vis-a-vis the objects of observation. . . . Positionally dependent observations, beliefs, and actions are central to our knowledge and practical reason. The nature of objectivity in epistemology, decision theory, and ethics has to take adequate note of the parametric dependence of observation and inference on the position of the observer.

Position-dependency defines the way in which the object appears "from a delineated somewhere." This "delineated somewhere," however, is positionally objective. That is, any person in that position will make similar observations, according to Sen. I would add that the parameters of positionality are not merely spatial but could involve a shared schema. For example, managers at Ford had access to a lot of the same data about the Pinto. Ford's decision not to recall the Pinto despite a number of terrible accidents could be defended as a positionally objective belief based on the ways in which managers at Ford processed information on automobile crashes. (Gioia, 1991) Similarly, Dow Corning's reluctance to stop manufacturing silicone implants could be construed as positionally objective from their focus on scientific evidence and reliance on responsible surgeons. Colleen Swanson and other ill recipients of implants also adopt a positionally objective view, from their perspective as very ill people with implants.

However, a positionally objective point of view could be mistaken in case it did not take into account all available information. Thus, as Sen points out, in most cases one need not unconditionally accept a positionally objective view. Because of the variety of schema with which one can shape a position, almost any position has alternatives, almost every position has its critics. I would qualify that further. Even allegedly positionally objective phenomena are still phenomena that have been filtered through the social sieve of a shared mental model or schema.

As I have just demonstrated, some narratives are more closely based on actual experiences; others are taken from the narratives of others which we have accepted "as true"; still others are in the form of stories. For example, the movie *Wall Street* tells a story about Wall Street that reshapes our perception of investment banking. These perspectives are necessarily incomplete, they can be biased, or they can be constituted by someone else's framing of experience. So, for example, as E. H. Gombrich the art historian relates, following Albrecht Durer's famous etching of a rhinoceros, for a very long time naturalists as well as artists portrayed rhinos with "armored" layers of skin, when in fact, a simple look at a rhino belies that conclusion (Gombrich). Similarly, Dowie's portrayal of the Pinto case became the prototype for other case descriptions. Byrne's *Business Week* article and his subsequent book on the Dow-Corning breast implant controversy appear to be becoming the prototype factual bases for analyzing that case. What happens in these instances is that "life imitates art," or the "grammar," the alleged data of the narrative creates the essence of the story.

Does this mean that one can never arrive at facts or truths? The short answer is "yes" or "no." The longer answer is more complicated. The thesis that experience is always framed by a perspective or point of view is closely related to another thesis, Wittgenstein's claim that "*[e]ssence* is expressed by grammar" (Wittgenstein, 1953, § 371), that is, in short, that all our experiences are framed, organized, and made meaningful only through the language we employ to conceive, frame, think, describe, and evaluate our experiences. Whether or not all experiences are linguistically constituted is a topic for another essay. What is important is what Wittgenstein does not say, that "essence is *created* by grammar" (Anscombe, 1976, p. 188). Nor did he hold that view, as I have argued in detail elsewhere (Werhane, 1992). To put the point in more Kantian terms, there is data or "stuff" of our experience that is not created or made up (although sometimes we can and do make up the content of our experiences when we envelop ourselves in fantasy) and, indeed, the distinction between "reality" and "fantasy" may be just that—that we do not make up the content of our experience. Nevertheless, that data or content or "stuff" is never pure—it is always constituted and contaminated by our perspective, point of view, or mental model.

At the same time, we are able to engage in "trans-positional" assessments or what Sen has called a "constructed 'view from nowhere.' " A trans-positional view from nowhere is a constructed critique of a particular conceptual scheme, and no positionally objective view is merely relative nor immune from challenge. This sort of assessment involves comparing various positionally objective points of view to see whether one can make coherent sense of them and develop some general theories about what is being observed. These trans-positional assessments are *constructed* views, because they too depend on the conceptual scheme of the assessors. From a trans-positional point of view conceptual schemes themselves can be questioned on the basis of their coherence and/or their explanatory scope. Although that challenge could only be conducted from another conceptual scheme, that assessment could take into account a variety of points of view. Still, revisions of the scheme in question might produce another conceptual scheme that more adequately or more comprehensively explained or took into account a range of phenomena or incidents. Together, studying sets of perspectives can get at how certain events are experienced and reported, and even, what mental models, schemes, or narratives are at work in shaping the narratives about these experiences. While one can never get at those from a pure *tabula rasa,* nevertheless one can achieve a limited, dispassionate view from somewhere.

Near the end of *Rashomon* the narrator of the tale, who is also the bystander, decries the lack of trust in society engendered from the impossibility of ascertaining the truth. The cases we develop must be done with care. In using others' cases and narratives one should study not just the facts as presented in the case narratives. Rather, we need to examine the ways in which the facts are constituted to make a story or a case, and one should become aware of how some of those cases can become prototypical narratives that we imitate. The so-called "classics" like Pinto need to be revisited or they will become cliched prototypes. And we need to be wary of assumptions generated by these prototypes such as the assumption that Dow Corning caused egregious harms, perhaps even deliberately, to the over 2 million women who have their breast implants. While we cannot arrive at The Truth we can at least approximate it more fully. Only then will we who teach and write in applied ethics become, in the words of Henry James, "finely aware and richly responsible" (Nussbaum, 1990).

BIBLIOGRAPHY

Angell, Marcia. 1995. "Are Breast Implants Actually OK?" *The New Republic,* September 11, 17–21.

_____. 1996. *Science on Trial.* New York: W. W. Norton & Co.

Anscombe, G. E. M. 1976. "The Question of Linguistic Idealism." *Essays on Wittgenstein in Honour of G. H. Von Wright.* Acta Philosophica Fennica, Vol. 28. ed. Jaakko Hintikka. Amsterdam: North Holland Publishing Co., 181–215.

Byrne, John A. 1995. "Informed Consent." *Business Week,* October 2, 104–116.

_____. 1996. *Informed Consent: A Story of Personal Tragedy and Corporate Betrayal.* New York, McGraw-Hill Companies.

Davidson, Dekkers, and Kenneth E. Goodpaster.1983. "Managing Product Safety: The Ford Pinto." Harvard University Graduate School of Business Administration Case #9–383–129. Boston: Harvard Business School Press.

Dowie, Mark. 1977a. "Pinto Madness." *Mother Jones,* September/October, 18–32.

_____. 1977b. "How Ford Put Two Million Firetraps on Wheels." *Business and Society Review,* 23: 46–55.

"Ford Fights Pinto Case: Jury Gives 128 Million." 1978. *Auto News,* February 13, 1.

Gabriel, S. E., et al. 1994. "Risk of Connective-Tissue Diseases and Other Disorders after Breast Implantation." *New England Journal of Medicine,* 330: 1697–1702.

Giltay, Erik J., et al. 1994. "Silicone Breast Protheses and Rheumatic Symptoms: A Retrospective Follow Up Study." *Annals of Rheumatic Diseases,* 53: 194–196.

Gioia, Dennis. 1991. "Pinto Fires and Personal Ethics: A Script Analysis of Missed Opportunities." *Journal of Business Ethics,* 11: 379–389.

Gombrich, E. H. 1961. *Art and Illusion.* Princeton: Princeton University Press.

Grimshaw v. *Ford Motor Co.* 1978. No. 197761. Super CT. Orange County, CA, February 6.

Hoffman, Michael. 1984. "The Ford Pinto." Rpt. in *Taking Sides.* Ed. Lisa H. Newton and Maureen M. Ford. Dushkin Publishing Group, 132–137.

Kolata, Gina. 1995. "Proof of a Breast Implant Peril Is Lacking, Rheumatologists Say." *New York Times,* October 25.

McLaughlin, Joseph K., and Joseph F. Fraumeni Jr. 1994. "Correspondence Re: Breast Implants, Cancer, and Systemic Sclerosis." *Journal of the National Cancer Institute,* 86: 1424.

Nussbaum, Martha. 1990. *Love's Knowledge.* New York: Oxford University Press.

Sanchez-Guerrero, Jorge, et al. 1995. "Silicone Breast Implants and the Risk of Connective-Tissue Diseases and Symptoms." *New England Journal of Medicine,* 332: 1666–1670.

Schmitt, Michael A., and William W. May, 1979. "Beyond Products Liability: The Legal, Social, and Ethical Problems Facing the Automobile Industry in Producing Safe Products." *University of Detroit Journal of Urban Law,* 56: 1021–1050.

Sen, Amartya. 1993. "Positional Objectivity." *Philosophy and Public Affairs.*

State of Indiana v. *Ford Motor Co.* (179), No. 11-431, Cir. Ct. Pulaski, IN.

Taubes, Gary. 1995. "Silicone in the System." *Discover,* December, 65–75.

Velasquez, Manuel. 1988. *Business Ethics,* 2d ed. Englewood Cliffs: Prentice-Hall, Inc.

Werhane, Patricia H. 1991. "Engineers and Management: The Challenge of the Challenger Incident." *Journal of Business Ethics,* 10: 605–616.

_____, _____. 1992. *Skepticism, Rules, and Private Languages.* Atlantic Highlands, NJ: Humanities Press.

_____. 1998. "Moral Imagination and Management Decision-Making." *New Avenues of Research in Business Ethics.* Edited by R. Edward Freeman. New York: Oxford University Press.

Wittgenstein, Ludwig. 1953. *Philosophical Investigations.* Trans. G. E. M. Anscombe. New York: Macmillan and Co.

A JURY OF HER PEERS

Susan Glaspell

In the following short story, Martha Hale and her husband are taken by the sheriff and his wife to the Wrights' home, where Mrs. Hale had found Mr. Wright strangled to death the previous morning. Mrs. Wright, pleading ignorance, was arrested and is awaiting charges. The women were at the house to gather Mrs. Wright's clothes and to see to her preserves. The men mocked the women's "trifles" and teased them about not missing any "clues" while they were to go about their more serious business of finding a motive. In a basket of patches waiting to be quilted, the women find a canary, strangled. The following excerpt discusses why they decide to conceal this evidence that might incriminate her.

Consider why the women notice some of these clues, but the men ignore the same evidence. Is it relevant that this story was written before women were allowed to sit on juries? Is justice blind, or gender-specific? Should it matter in our system who is the judge and who is the judged?

"Mrs. Peters!"

"Yes, Mrs. Hale?"

"Do you think she—did it?"

A frightened look blurred the other things in Mrs. Peters' eyes.

"Oh, I don't know," she said, in a voice that seemed to shrink away from the subject.

"Well, I don't think she did," affirmed Mrs. Hale stoutly. "Asking for an apron, and her little shawl. Worryin' about her fruit."

"Mr. Peters says—" Footsteps were heard in the room above; she stopped, looked up, then went on in a lowered voice: "Mr. Peters says—it looks bad for her. Mr. Henderson is awful sarcastic in a speech, and he's going to make fun of her saying she didn't—wake up."

For a moment Mrs. Hale had no answer. Then, "Well, I guess John Wright didn't wake up—when they was slippin' that rope under his neck," she muttered.

"No, it's *strange*," breathed Mrs. Peters. "They think it was such a—funny way to kill a man."

She began to laugh; at sound of the laugh, abruptly stopped.

"That's just what Mr. Hale said," said Mrs. Hale, in a resolutely natural voice. "There was a gun in the house. He says that's what he can't understand."

"Mr. Henderson said, coming out, that what was needed for the case was a motive. Something to show anger—or sudden feeling."

"Well, I don't see any signs of anger around here," said Mrs. Hale. "I don't—"

She stopped. It was as if her mind tripped on something. Her eye was caught by a dish towel in the middle of the kitchen table. Slowly she moved toward the table. One half of it was wiped clean, the other half messy. Her eyes made a slow, almost unwilling turn to the bucket of sugar and the half empty bag beside it. Things begun—and not finished.

After a moment she stepped back, and said, in that manner of releasing herself:

"Wonder how they're finding things upstairs? I hope she had it a little more red-up up there. You know,"—she paused, and feeling gathered,—"it seems kind of *sneaking;* locking her up in town and coming out here to get her own house to turn against her!"

"But, Mrs. Hale," said the sheriff's wife, "the law is the law."

"I s'pose 'tis," answered Mrs. Hale shortly.

She turned to the stove, saying something about that fire not being much to brag of. She worked with it a minute, and when she straightened up she said aggressively:

"The law is the law—and a bad stove is a bad stove. How'd you like to cook on this?"— pointing with the poker to the broken lining. She opened the oven door and started to express her opinion of the oven; but she was swept into her own thoughts, thinking of what it would mean, year after year, to have that stove to wrestle with. The thought of Minnie Foster trying to bake in that oven—and the thought of her never going over to see Minnie Foster—.

She was startled by hearing Mrs. Peters say: "A person gets discouraged—and loses heart."

The sheriff's wife had looked from the stove to the sink—to the pail of water which had been carried in from outside. The two women stood there silent, above them the footsteps of the men who were looking for evidence against the woman who had worked in that kitchen. That look of seeing into things, of seeing through a thing to something else, was in the eyes of the sheriff's wife now. When Mrs. Hale next spoke to her, it was gently:

"Better loosen up your things, Mrs. Peters. We'll not feel them when we go out."

Mrs. Peters went to the back of the room to hang up the fur tippet she was wearing. A moment later she exclaimed, "Why, she was piecing a quilt," and held up a large sewing basket piled high with quilt pieces.

Mrs. Hale spread some of the blocks on the table.

"It's log-cabin pattern," she said, putting several of them together. "Pretty, isn't it?"

They were so engaged with the quilt that they did not hear the footsteps on the stairs. Just as the stair door opened Mrs. Hale was saying:

"Do you suppose she was going to quilt it or just knot it?"

The sheriff threw up his hands.

"They wonder whether she was going to quilt it or just knot it!"

There was a laugh for the ways of women, a warming of hands over the stove, and then the county attorney said briskly:

"Well, let's go right out to the barn and get that cleared up."

"I don't see as there's anything so strange," Mrs. Hale said resentfully, after the outside door had closed on the three men—"our taking up our time with little things while we're waiting for them to get the evidence. I don't see as it's anything to laugh about."

"Of course they've got awful important things on their minds," said the sheriff's wife apologetically.

They returned to an inspection of the blocks for the quilt. Mrs. Hale was looking at the fine, even sewing, and preoccupied with thoughts of the woman who had done that sewing, when she heard the sheriff's wife say, in a queer tone:

"Why, look at this one."

She turned to take the block held out to her.

"The sewing," said Mrs. Peters, in a troubled way. "All the rest of them have been so nice and even—but—this one. Why, it looks as if she didn't know what she was about!"

Their eyes met—something flashed to life, passed between them; then, as if with an effort, they seemed to pull away from each other. A moment Mrs. Hale sat there, her hands folded over that sewing which was so unlike all the rest of the sewing. Then she had pulled a knot and drawn the threads.

"Oh, what are you doing, Mrs. Hale?" asked the sheriff's wife, startled.

"Just pulling out a stitch or two that's not sewed very good," said Mrs. Hale mildly.

"I don't think we ought to touch things," Mrs. Peters said, a little helplessly.

"I'd just finish up this end," answered Mrs. Hale, still in that mild, matter-of-fact fashion.

She threaded a needle and started to replace bad sewing with good. For a little while she sewed in silence. Then, in that thin, timid voice, she heard:

"Mrs. Hale!"

"Yes, Mrs. Peters?"

"What do you suppose she was so—nervous about?"

"Oh, *I* don't know," said Mrs. Hale, as if dismissing a thing not important enough to spend much time on. "I don't know as she was—nervous. I sew awful queer sometimes when I'm just tired."

She cut a thread, and out of the corner of her eye looked up at Mrs. Peters. The small, lean face of the sheriff's wife seemed to have tightened up. Her eyes had that look of peering into something. But the next moment she moved, and said in her thin, indecisive way:

"Well, I must get those clothes wrapped. They may be through sooner than we think. I wonder where I could find a piece of paper—and string."

"In that cupboard, maybe," suggested Mrs. Hale, after a glance around.

One piece of the crazy sewing remained unripped. Mrs. Peters' back turned, Martha Hale now scrutinized that piece, compared it with the dainty, accurate sewing of the other blocks. The difference was startling. Holding this block made her feel queer, as if the distracted thoughts of the woman who had perhaps turned to it to try and quiet herself were communicating themselves to her.

Mrs. Peters' voice roused her.

"Here's a birdcage," she said. "Did she have a bird, Mrs. Hale?"

"Why, I don't know whether she did or not." She turned to look at the cage Mrs. Peters was holding up. "I've not been here in so long." She sighed. "There was a man round last year selling canaries cheap—but I don't know as she took one. Maybe she did. She used to sing real pretty herself."

Mrs. Peters looked around the kitchen.

"Seems kind of funny to think of a bird here." She half laughed—an attempt to put up a barrier. "But she must have had one—or why would she have a cage? I wonder what happened to it."

"I suppose maybe the cat got it," suggested Mrs. Hale, resuming her sewing.

"No; she didn't have a cat. She's got that feeling some people have about cats—being afraid of them. When they brought her to our house yesterday, my cat got in the room, and she was real upset and asked me to take it out."

"My sister Bessie was like that," laughed Mrs. Hale.

The sheriff's wife did not reply. The silence made Mrs. Hale turn round. Mrs. Peters was examining the birdcage.

"Look at this door," she said slowly. "It's broke. One hinge has been pulled apart."

Mrs. Hale came nearer.

"Looks as if someone must have been—rough with it."

Again their eyes met—startled, questioning, apprehensive. For a moment neither spoke nor stirred. Then Mrs. Hale, turning away, said brusquely:

"If they're going to find any evidence, I wish they'd be about it. I don't like this place."

"But I'm awful glad you came with me, Mrs. Hale." Mrs. Peters put the birdcage on the table and sat down. "It would be lonesome for me—sitting here alone."

"Yes, it would, wouldn't it?" agreed Mrs. Hale, a certain determined naturalness in her voice. She picked up the sewing, but now it dropped in her lap, and she murmured in a different voice: "But I tell you what I *do* wish, Mrs. Peters. I wish I had come over sometimes when she was here. I wish—I had."

"But of course you were awful busy, Mrs. Hale. Your house—and your children."

"I could've come," retorted Mrs. Hale shortly. "I stayed away because it weren't cheerful—and that's why I ought to have come. I"—she looked around—"I've never liked this place. Maybe because it's down in a hollow and you don't see the road. I don't know what it is, but it's a lonesome place, and always was. I wish I had come over to see Minnie Foster sometimes. I can see now—" She did not put it into words.

"Well, you mustn't reproach yourself," counseled Mrs. Peters. "Somehow, we just don't see how it is with other folks till—something comes up."

"Not having children makes less work," mused Mrs. Hale, after a silence, "but it makes a quiet house—and Wright out to work all day—and no company when he did come in. Did you know John Wright, Mrs. Peters?"

"Not to know him. I've seen him in town. They say he was a good man."

"Yes—good," conceded John Wright's neighbor grimly. "He didn't drink, and kept his word as well as most, I guess, and paid his debts. But he was a hard man, Mrs. Peters. Just to pass the time of day with him—." She stopped, shivered a little. "Like a raw wind that gets to the bone." Her eye fell upon the cage on the table before her, and she added, almost bitterly: "I should think she would've wanted a bird!"

Suddenly she leaned forward, looking intently at the cage. "But what do you s'pose went wrong with it?"

"I don't know," returned Mrs. Peters; "unless it got sick and died."

But after she said it she reached over and swung the broken door. Both women watched it as if somehow held by it.

"You didn't know—her?" Mrs. Hale asked, a gentler note in her voice.

"Not till they brought her yesterday," said the sheriff's wife.

"She—come to think of it, she was kind of like a bird herself. Real sweet and pretty, but kind of timid and—fluttery. How—she—did—change."

That held her for a long time. Finally, as if struck with a happy thought and relieved to get back to everyday things, she exclaimed:

"Tell you what, Mrs. Peters, why don't you take the quilt in with you? It might take up her mind."

"Why, I think that's a real nice idea, Mrs. Hale," agreed the sheriff's wife, as if she too were glad to come into the atmosphere of a simple kindness. "There couldn't possibly be any objection to that, could there? Now, just what will I take? I wonder if her patches are in here—and her things."

They turned to the sewing basket.

"Here's some red," said Mrs. Hale, bringing out a roll of cloth. Underneath that was a box. "Here, maybe her scissors are in here—and her things." She held it up. "What a pretty box! I'll warrant that was something she had a long time ago—when she was a girl."

She held it in her hand a moment; then, with a little sigh, opened it.

Instantly her hand went to her nose.

"Why—!"

Mrs. Peters drew nearer—then turned away.

"There's something wrapped up in this piece of silk," faltered Mrs. Hale.

"This isn't her scissors," said Mrs. Peters in a shrinking voice.

Her hand not steady, Mrs. Hale raised the piece of silk. "Oh, Mrs. Peters!" she cried. "It's—"

Mrs. Peters bent closer.

"It's the bird," she whispered.

"But, Mrs. Peters!" cried Mrs. Hale. "*Look* at it! Its neck—look at its neck! It's all—other side *to.*"

She held the box away from her.

The sheriff's wife again bent closer.

"Somebody wrung its neck," said she, in a voice that was slow and deep.

And then again the eyes of the two women met—this time clung together in a look of dawning comprehension, of growing horror. Mrs. Peters looked from the dead bird to the broken door of the cage. Again their eyes met. And just then there was a sound at the outside door.

Mrs. Hale slipped the box under the quilt pieces in the basket, and sank into the chair before it. Mrs. Peters stood holding to the table. The county attorney and the sheriff came in from outside.

"Well, ladies," said the county attorney, as one turning from serious things to little pleasantries, "have you decided whether she was going to quilt it or knot it?"

"We think," began the sheriff's wife in a flurried voice, "that she was going to—knot it."

He was too preoccupied to notice the change that came in her voice on that last.

"Well, that's very interesting, I'm sure," he said tolerantly. He caught sight of the birdcage. "Has the bird flown?"

"We think the cat got it," said Mrs. Hale in a voice curiously even.

He was walking up and down, as if thinking something out.

"Is there a cat?" he asked absently.

Mrs. Hale shot a look up at the sheriff's wife.

"Well, not *now*," said Mrs. Peters. "They're superstitious, you know; they leave."

She sank into her chair.

The county attorney did not heed her. "No sign at all of anyone having come in from the outside," he said to Peters, in the manner of continuing an interrupted conversation.

"Their own rope. Now let's go upstairs again and go over it, piece by piece. It would have to have been someone who knew just the—"

The stair door closed behind them and their voices were lost.

The two women sat motionless, not looking at each other, but as if peering into something and at the same time holding back. When they spoke now it was as if they were afraid of what they were saying, but as if they could not help saying it.

"She liked the bird," said Martha Hale, low and slowly. "She was going to bury it in that pretty box."

"When I was a girl," said Mrs. Peters, under her breath, "my kitten—there was a boy took a hatchet, and before my eyes—before I could get there—" She covered her face an instant. "If they hadn't held me back I would have"—she caught herself, looked upstairs where footsteps were heard, and finished weakly—"hurt him."

Then they sat without speaking or moving.

"I wonder how it would seem," Mrs. Hale at last began, as if feeling her way over strange ground—"never to have had any children around?" Her eyes made a slow sweep of the kitchen, as if seeing what that kitchen had meant through all the years. "No, Wright wouldn't like the bird," she said after that—"a thing that sang. She used to sing. He killed that too." Her voice tightened.

Mrs. Peters moved uneasily.

"Of course we don't know who killed the bird."

"I knew John Wright," was Mrs. Hale's answer.

"It was an awful thing was done in this house that night, Mrs. Hale," said the sheriff's wife. "Killing a man while he slept—slipping a thing round his neck that choked the life out of him."

Mrs. Hale's hand went out to the birdcage.

"His neck. Choked the life out of him."

"We don't *know* who killed him," whispered Mrs. Peters wildly. "We don't *know*."

Mrs. Hale had not moved. "If there had been years and years of—nothing, then a bird to sing to you, it would be awful—still—after the bird was still."

It was as if something within her not herself had spoken, and it found in Mrs. Peters something she did not know as herself.

"I know what stillness is," she said, in a queer, monotonous voice. "When we homesteaded in Dakota, and my first baby died—after he was two years old—and me with no other then—"

Mrs. Hale stirred.

"How soon do you suppose they'll be through looking for evidence?"

"I know what stillness is," repeated Mrs. Peters, in just that same way. Then she too pulled back. "The law has got to punish crime, Mrs. Hale," she said in her tight little way.

"I wish you'd seen Minnie Foster," was the answer, "when she wore a white dress with blue ribbons, and stood up there in the choir and sang."

The picture of that girl, the fact that she had lived neighbor to that girl for twenty years, and had let her die for lack of life, was suddenly more than she could bear.

"Oh, I *wish* I'd come over here once in a while!" she cried. "That was a crime! That was a crime! Who's going to punish that?"

"We mustn't take on," said Mrs. Peters, with a frightened look toward the stairs.

"I might 'a' *known* she needed help! I tell you, it's *queer,* Mrs. Peters. We live close together, and we live far apart. We all go through the same things—it's all just a different kind of the same thing! If it weren't—why do you and I *understand?* Why do we *know*—what we know this minute?"

She dashed her hand across her eyes. Then, seeing the jar of fruit on the table, she reached for it and choked out:

"If I was you I wouldn't *tell* her her fruit was gone! Tell her it *ain't.* Tell her it's all right—all of it. Here—take this in to prove it to her! She—she may never know whether it was broke or not."

She turned away.

Mrs. Peters reached out for the bottle of fruit as if she were glad to take it—as if touching a familiar thing, having something to do, could keep her from something else. She got up, looked about for something to wrap the fruit in, took a petticoat from the pile of clothes she had brought from the front room, and nervously started winding that round the bottle.

"My!" she began, in a high, false voice, "it's a good thing the men couldn't hear us! Getting all stirred up over a little thing like a—dead canary." She hurried over that. "As if that could have anything to do with—with—My, wouldn't they *laugh?*"

Footsteps were heard on the stairs.

"Maybe they would," muttered Mrs. Hale—"maybe they wouldn't."

"No, Peters," said the county attorney incisively; "it's all perfectly clear, except the reason for doing it. But you know juries when it comes to women. If there was some definite thing—something to show. Something to make a story about. A thing that would connect up with this clumsy way of doing it."

In a covert way Mrs. Hale looked at Mrs. Peters. Mrs. Peters was looking at her. Quickly they looked away from each other. The outer door opened and Mr. Hale came in.

"I've got the team round now," he said. "Pretty cold out there."

"I'm going to stay here awhile by myself," the county attorney suddenly announced. "You can send Frank out for me, can't you?" he asked the sheriff. "I want to go over everything. I'm not satisfied we can't do better."

Again, for one brief moment, the two women's eyes found one another.

The sheriff came up to the table.

"Did you want to see what Mrs. Peters was going to take in?"

The county attorney picked up the apron. He laughed.

"Oh, I guess they're not very dangerous things the ladies have picked out."

Mrs. Hale's hand was on the sewing basket in which the box was concealed. She felt that she ought to take her hand off the basket. She did not seem able to. He picked up one of the quilt blocks which she had piled on to cover the box. Her eyes felt like fire. She had a feeling that if he took up the basket she would snatch it from him.

But he did not take it up. With another little laugh, he turned away, saying:

"No; Mrs. Peters doesn't need supervising. For that matter, a sheriff's wife is married to the law. Ever think of it that way, Mrs. Peters?"

Mrs. Peters was standing beside the table. Mrs. Hale shot a look up at her; but she could not see her face. Mrs. Peters had turned away. When she spoke, her voice was muffled.

"Not—just that way," she said.

"Married to the law!" chuckled Mrs. Peters' husband. He moved toward the door into the front room, and said to the county attorney:

"I just want you to come in here a minute, George. We ought to take a look at these windows."

"Oh—windows," said the county attorney scoffingly.

"We'll be right out, Mr. Hale," said the sheriff to the farmer, who was still waiting by the door.

Hale went to look after the horses. The sheriff followed the county attorney into the other room. Again—for one moment—the two women were alone in that kitchen.

Martha Hale sprang up, her hands tight together, looking at that other woman, with whom it rested. At first she could not see her eyes, for the sheriff's wife had not turned back, since she turned away at that suggestion of being married to the law. But now Mrs. Hale made her turn back. Her eyes made her turn back. Slowly, unwillingly, Mrs. Peters turned her head until her eyes met the eyes of the other woman. There was a moment when they held each other in a steady, burning look in which there was no evasion nor flinching. Then Martha Hale's eyes pointed the way to the basket in which was hidden the thing that would make certain the conviction of the other woman—that woman who was not there and yet who had been there with them all through the hour.

For a moment Mrs. Peters did not move. And then she did it. With a rush forward, she threw back the quilt pieces, got the box, tried to put it in her handbag. It was too big. Desperately she opened it, started to take the bird out. But there she broke—she could not touch the bird. She stood helpless, foolish.

There was the sound of a knob turning in the inner door. Martha Hale snatched the box from the sheriff's wife, and got it in the pocket of her big coat just as the sheriff and the county attorney came back into the kitchen.

"Well, Henry," said the county attorney facetiously, "at least we found out that she was not going to quilt it. She was going to—what is it you call it, ladies?"

Mrs. Hale's hand was against the pocket of her coat.

"We call it—knot it, Mr. Henderson."

WHERE AND WHY DID BUSINESS ETHICISTS GO WRONG? THE CASE OF DOW CORNING CORPORATION

DARYL KOEHN

Dow Corning is a contradiction in itself: it was one of the first firms to institute a senior level code of conduct committee and received accolades from ethicists for forging ahead in this area, while it also declared bankruptcy after some claimed it ignored numerous complaints of serious medical problems in connection with its products: silicone breast implants. Later, it was alleged that Dow even destroyed a survey that disclosed the medical issues customers had with the implants. John Byrne was an engineer who expressed concern early on for the lack of safety testing.

Update to Dow Corning: In 1993, Dow Corning unveiled a $4.25 billion plan—the largest mass injury settlement ever—to settle all silicone breast implant claims (Thomas Burton, "Adding Insult to Injury," Progressive, *July, 1994, p. 8). Individual women would receive between $200,000 and $2 million each. Many criticized the plan as being extravagantly generous to certain claimants and "stingy" to others. By 1995, 440,000 women had joined in the settlement. However, 15,000 women decided to try their luck filing individual suits against Dow and opted out of the settlement (Michael Hoffman et al.,* The Ethical Edge, *p. 134). Dow filed for bankruptcy in 1995, effectively freezing all claims and delaying payment to claimants for years. Four months after Dow's filing, a federal judge declared the original settlement dead.*

In the following analysis, Koehn describes the history of the Dow Corning case and discusses why ethicists may originally have been misled regarding the ethical culture at Dow.

In the early 1980's, it seemed Dow Corning Corporation (DCC) could do no wrong. It hit the billion dollar sales mark in 1986. What is more, it maintained its competitiveness while

---

acting in a fashion many judged ethically exemplary. In fact, a highly complimentary case study was done in 1984 by a Harvard business ethicist lauding various of the company's ethical initiatives. Yet by 1989, the company was in the midst of a public relations fiasco over its manufacture and marketing of silicone breast implants or "mammaries." The company had been found guilty of fraud for suppressing internal memos suggesting that these implants were less safe than the company's marketing literature represented them to be. Juries had awarded several multimillion dollar awards to women who claimed to have been seriously harmed by their implants. A criminal investigation had been launched into DCC's business practices. Although this investigation was subsequently dropped for lack of evidence, fifteen members of Congress urged (in July 1995) Janet Reno, the U.S. Attorney General, to examine whether a senior manager of DCC had perjured himself when testifying before Congress several years earlier. In 1995, DCC filed for bankruptcy, claiming it did not have the funds necessary to fund the $4.23 billion settlement that had been reached for paying women who had been part of class action lawsuits against the company.

Whether or not silicone implants are safe is a highly contested matter. Some of DCC's own studies suggest they may not be safe. In particular, leaked silicone may harm the immune system. Later DCC studies seem to indicate that silicone is inert within the human body. Studies by researchers at University of Michigan and Mayo Clinic have been interpreted as showing that there is no link between silicone breast implants and autoimmune disease. However, critics have charged that these studies are suspect because the samples used were too small to be statistically significant and because the research was funded in part by DCC and the plastic surgeons who have a financial interest in showing that these implants are safe. While many women with implants firmly believe these implants to be the cause of their problems, their symptoms are diverse. Removal of the implants has not always improved their condition. Although the United States declared a moratorium on cosmetic surgeons implanting this product, the British government chose to leave them on the market after deciding women with implants were at no greater risk of contracting autoimmune disease than those without the implants.

This paper does not aim at resolving the scientific controversy regarding the safety of the implants. Nor does it try to build a case that DCC's production and manufacture of these implants were unethical. While I would question the goodness of many of DCC's reported actions, I am less interested in passing judgment on this company than in discovering what we can learn from its difficulties. To this end, I want to consider, first, why DCC won praise for its ethics initiatives; and second, what factors and forces, if any, business ethicists failed to consider when assessing the ethical goodness of DCC. I am interested in what mistakes business ethicists made in thinking about DCC's ethics and in learning what we can from these errors.

PART 1: THE ETHICS PROGRAM AT DCC

DCC sponsored many ethics initiatives. The company wrote and published a corporate code of ethics as early as 1977. While many codes emphasize matters of etiquette or remaining within the law, DCC's code was noteworthy for stressing integrity and respect. The 1977 code read: "The watchword of Dow Corning worldwide activities is integrity . . . We believe that business is best conducted and society best served within each country when business practice is based on the universal principles of honesty and integrity." The code goes on to say that "We recognize that our social responsibilities must be maintained at the high standards which lead to respect and trust by society. A clear definition of our social responsibilities should be an integral part of our corporate objectives and be clearly communicated to every employee."

Furthermore, the code was widely disseminated and was hung in the corridors of the corporation. The then CEO of the company, Jack Ludington, sent a letter to every employee urging him or her to read the code and to contact Ludington if they had any questions. Ludington and other managers of DCC consistently referred to the code of ethics in their speeches. Since various areas faced different ethical challenges, the areas were allowed to devise their own separate codes, although these codes still needed to be consistent with DCC's corporate code. Efforts were made to solicit employee feedback concerning the code and to keep the code current by revising it every two years. As John Swanson, the manager–business communications specialist who was the only permanent member of the Business Conduct Committee, put it, "The code of conduct is a 'living' statement, one that can change as accepted business practices change."

In addition, DCC instituted annual audits beginning in 1977 both to communicate the code and to solicit feedback as well as to monitor compliance. The audits were conducted by a newly created committee at DCC—the Business Conduct Committee. Up to 40 audits per year were conducted at the area level (e.g., in Mexico City, Toronto, Brussels, Hong Kong). Since different areas had different concerns (e.g., requests for bribes were more prevalent in Asia than in some other areas), the audits were tailored to the area being evaluated. Every effort was made to include regional personnel who were actually dealing with problems in the day to day business operation of the company. The results of the audit were documented and kept on file at headquarters, but the intent was not punitive. Rather the audits were an attempt to educate employees concerning the code and to highlight potential problems or ambiguities with the code itself. Some of the audit sessions were videotaped. These tapes were then shared with area personnel to educate them concerning the audit process.

Finally, the BCC developed corporate training modules on the code and a semi-annual opinion survey. The survey attempted to measure whether employees knew about the code and whether DCC's ethics initiatives were making a real difference in the life of the corporation.

Business ethicists praised DCC for its meaningful code and for its serious commitment to making ethics a regular part of business practice. It certainly looked as though management was serious about these various initiatives. Rising executives were regularly assigned to do a stint on the rotating Business Conduct Committee and were expected to spend up to 15% of their time per week on ethical issues. However, initiatives by themselves do not make a company ethical. In the next section, I explore several important dimensions of corporate life that were completely ignored by the *Harvard Business Review* study, dimensions that played a pivotal role in how DCC handled the growing public concern regarding the safety of silicone breast implants manufactured by the company.

PART 2: WHAT BUSINESS ETHICISTS FORGOT TO CONSIDER

Factor 1: Managerial Hubris

Although the CEO of DCC supported the ethics initiative, he met with some resistance from senior area personnel who believed that DCC was already a thoroughly ethical company. For example, Phil Brooks, a senior employee in Hong Kong, wrote a memo to Ludington arguing that DCC had no problem "and that our house doesn't need putting in order. Therefore we need to agree on the purpose of any Code and that purpose must arise from some need. What is the need if we already believe (as I do) that we are morally, legally, and ethically correct in all aspects of our business conduct?"

The certainty implicit in this claim is remarkable. Given that DCC had just begun ethics audits to uncover what various managers' actual practices were, it seems odd to claim that one already knows that DCC is behaving completely correctly—legally, ethically, and morally. The certainty that DCC was an entirely ethical company is doubly striking because it seems to have been widely held. As the controversy surrounding silicone breast implants deepened, another senior manager, Silas Braney, would proclaim, "I can say, without any qualification, that never in my 30 years at Dow Corning did I ever know of anyone doing anything illegal, unethical, or immoral." His sentiments echo those of CEO Ludington who, in the late 1970's, claimed that his corporate managers "would not intentionally do anything questionable and would even blow the whistle if they learned of any actual wrongdoing within the company." Again, the certainty seems rather misplaced, given that the company experienced a good deal of resistance to some parts of the code from some of its managers who believed that the code was making DCC uncompetitive. It is doubtful whether Ludington was warranted in asserting that DCC's employees would definitely blow the whistle on unethical practices by corporate employees if these employees in many cases (see Brooks quote above) did not accept that some of their past practices were in fact unethical.

More generally, such certainty on the part of management evinces an attitude that is antithetical to ethical reasoning. As Aristotle puts it, the "stuff" of ethical discourse is controversy because practical matters do not admit of the same degree of certainty as mathematical or scientific subjects. To reason ethically, therefore, consists at least in part in being willing to submit one's beliefs to the scrutiny and challenges of others. If agents begin with the position that they and their company have done no wrong, this very process of discussion is short-circuited. This shutting off of the possibility of discussion may itself be an ethical wrong, yet this possibility cannot get raised in this atmosphere of certainty.

All of the processes in the world will make little difference if people are fundamentally committed to the proposition that neither they nor their colleagues have done any wrong. One sees the consequences of this certainty quite clearly in the book on the breast implant controversy to which DCC insider John Swanson contributed. Key players at DCC are certain that the breast implants they helped to design and manufacture are absolutely safe. Indeed, they are so certain of their moral rectitude that they dismiss as "crazy" all of the women who think they have been harmed by their implants. Even after the Federal Drug Administration ordered companies manufacturing breast implants to prove that they were safe, some senior managers at DCC insisted that there was no ethical issue connected with the marketing of silicone breast implants. While the implants may turn out not to be the cause of these women's health problems, such demonizing of these women hardly seems consistent with DCC's professed commitment to respect the dignity of employees and of customers and to treat them fairly. It is, however, consistent with a certain hubris that appeared as early as 1977 in DCC's managers' view of the company's ethics initiatives. To the extent business ethicists quoted these hubristic claims but ignored the arrogance implicit in them, they were misled in their judgment of the company.

Factor 2: Corporate History

Another striking feature of HBR's analysis of DCC's ethics was the total disregard of the company's history. The case study looked at DCC at just one point in time—the late 1970's. While the case study was updated in the 1980's it still made no mention of the company's history. This oversight is striking because Dow Corning is a subsidiary of Dow Chemical. Managers moved between the two companies. Indeed, Keith McKennon, the manager brought in as the new CEO to provide decisive leadership at DCC as the lawsuits and bad publicity began to mount, was formerly an executive vice-president at Dow Chemical. Dow Chemical, in turn, had invented and marketed napalm, Agent Orange and, along with Merill-Dow, Benedictin, a morning sickness pill suspected of causing birth defects. These products all proved tremendously controversial in the late 1960's and 1970's. I do not here want to argue the morality of Dow Chemical's decision to produce these products nor the way in which the company responded to criticism of these products. It may be that any company in the chemical and pharmaceuticals business runs certain risks by producing powerful compounds whose long-term effects may not be immediately obvious. However, I do want to insist that this history and the behavior of the players in these earlier controversies is relevant to judging the ethics of Dow Corning because some of these same people were responsible for deciding how to respond to the press, whether to voluntarily pull the implants, how aggressively to respond to lawsuits, etc. In fact, CEO McKennon was apparently appointed to head DCC because he was internally regarded as the consummate "fireman" who successfully put out the Agent Orange controversy when it threatened to flame out of control.

A corporation is like a living organism. It has a history, and how it behaves in the present is a function of its past experiences, acquired habits and attitudes and the stories it tells itself concerning the past. To ignore such matters and to merely focus on the present behavior of corporate employees can and likely will lead both the business ethicist and the company astray. For if a company's management behaved questionably in the past, and if the company showed no willingness to engage in any soul-searching regarding these past actions, what reason is there to think that management will suddenly mend its ways and its habits just because a company institutes a code of conduct and sets up some ethics training sessions?

This tendency to ignore corporate history is endemic in the business ethics literature. We philosophers report some event or action. We raise a number of questions about behavior in this event, yet we rarely situate this event in the company's history or relate it to the company's past deeds. While this isolation of an action may give the illusion of analytic clarity, it seriously falsifies the actual process of choice. Choices are always made by human beings who have acquired certain habits of choice by dint of dealing with past crises and problems. To describe ethics processes such as DCC's "ethics audits" in isolation from the people doing and undergoing the audit will tell us little about the real value of these processes.

Factor 3: Corporate Culture

A third factor is the company's internal culture. By "culture," I mean both the totality of factors (history, environment, sanctions, etc.) that lead employees to embrace certain characteristic ways of viewing the world and this worldview itself, since, as it develops, it, too, becomes a controlling factor. The HBR case study attempts to characterize this culture. We read that "DCC's culture was open, informal, and relaxed; little emphasis was placed on official status or a traditional organizational chart with clear-cut reporting relationships." As far as it goes, this judgment appears sound. DCC was known for being a highly matrixed company with many dotted line reporting relations. Employees routinely met in the halls to informally share information and to make decisions. The problem with this assessment of culture is not so much that it was wrong but that it was very incomplete. The HBR article assessed culture entirely in light of the company's reporting structure. However, we can also get a feel for culture by examining where people spend most of their time and energy, what behaviors are rewarded, and who the heroes of the company are. When these are considered, we get a rather different view of DCC's culture.

At the time the HBR article was written, one out of every ten employees of DCC was involved in new product development. This number is relatively high and suggests that there was a great deal of interest in not merely developing but also probably a good bit of pressure to successfully market new products to the consumer. Such pressure can result in a company rushing products to market before the product's safety has been adequately established. Swanson tells the story of how he had been sent to publicly announce a new silicon handwash; however, at the last minute he received a panicked call cancelling the product rollout because the product adversely affected monkeys. The rollout of breast implants may also have been premature. It appears, for example, that DCC provided implants to surgeons who placed them in women while the company was still doing initial safety testing on animals.

DCC was also distinguished by a tendency to lionize its scientists. The company's "hall of fame" featured pictures of the chemists who had made new discoveries concerning silicone or who had invented silicone-based products. There was a widespread perception among employees that to advance one had to be a scientist. The non-scientists within the company seemed to take the scientists' word as gospel. John Swanson relates how psychologically difficult it was for him to even consider the possibility that silicone might not be inert because he and his colleagues had been told for years by scientists that the material did not react with the body in any way. In short, the culture at DCC was one that prided itself on being scientifically expert.

On the one hand, a culture of people who pride themselves on their expertise may be driven by professional self-esteem to produce products that can be trusted not to harm the end-users. On the other hand, expertise may feed arrogance and lead employees to feel contempt for those who are not experts like them. At one point, DCC refused to take any questions from reporters on the ground that such people lacked scientific credentials. There is also a danger that expertise will lead those who view themselves as professionals to over-look the client's needs entirely. Thus we have doctors speaking of curing AIDs or the virus rather than the patient. A similar displacement seems to have occurred at DCC where both the surgeons and apparently the company itself restrictively defined a "failed implant" as one damaged in manufacture. The patient might experience pain or discomfort or require surgery to implant a new device, but these cases were not counted as failed implants. It was not until several years into the controversy over the implants that a CEO at DCC finally would say that the company's overriding responsibility was to women who had the im-plants. Although DCC's own code of corporate ethics gives priority to treating the customer fairly and with respect, the code proved no match for the corporate culture of expertise.

It might be objected that it is unfair to criticize business ethicists for failing to fully comprehend a corporation's culture. Persons who write case studies and consultants rarely have access to the corporate memos and jokes that often prove so revealing of a company's culture. Nor are they around long enough to get much of a feel for how the company oper-ates. There is some truth in this objection but it does not completely exonerate business ethi-cists. These facts suggest that we business ethicists need to be extremely circumspect when praising a company as ethically good. We need to be aware of our limitations and do the most we can to widen our focus to include other features of the culture, features of the sort described above.

Factor 4: The Wider Culture

The culture of a particular corporation is not freestanding. It is always embedded in the larger national culture (and global one, too, to the extent that it makes sense to speak of a global culture). Whether a corporation will act ethically depends at least in part on what pressures and expectations the wider culture brings to bear on the corporation and the way in which the corporation responds to them. In some cases, refusing to meet these expecta-tions may be the most ethical response, especially if these expectations are ill-formed, un-realistic, or the product of suspect motivations. Business ethicists need to consider, therefore, whether the company in question has shown itself willing to sometimes say "no" to people.

In the case of DCC, the company faced pressure from plastic surgeons to develop a host of products they could use. In some cases, the silicone products were clearly of use in pro-moting people's health (e.g., a shunt used to drain fluid from the brain). However, breast implants did not unambiguously fall into this category. Although they could be, and were, used to rebuild the breasts of women who had mastectomies, most implants were used for purely cosmetic reasons. The plastic surgeons knew there was a huge market for these mam-maries and that there was big money to be made because a surgeon could do up to six im-plants per day at a charge of $1000/implant (1970's dollar value). Furthermore, the plastic surgeons had the money and connections to increase this market. They lobbied hard to have small breasts defined as a disease so that insurance companies would pay for the breast en-largements the plastic surgeons were promoting.

From almost the moment DCC entered the implant market, it was involved with a prod-uct that was of questionable value and that was being promoted by doctors who had a vested interest in having women come to see themselves as defective. Although some women with small breasts may very well have low self-esteem, this condition hardly qualifies as a "disease" in the normal sense of the term. Many women with small breasts do not lack self-esteem so the symptomology is questionable. Furthermore, the condition generally is not debilitating in the way cancer or polio is. Even if some small-breasted women were to have difficulty functioning because of a lack of self-confidence, the "cure" arguably lies not in encouraging them to have surgery (with its attendant possible complications) but in fighting the propaganda that would have such women view themselves as inferior. It could be argued that this "disease" was manufactured to play on the fears of vulnerable parties who perhaps are already short on self-esteem. If this logic is sound, then DCC was in the business of not just manufacturing breast implants but of manipulating vulnerable people as well. DCC failed to ask itself early on: Why are we in this business anyway? The business ethicists who evaluated the ethics program at DCC also failed because they did not examine whether DCC product rollout process was thoughtful. Instead, they focused largely on the existence of a code of conduct and audits, neither of which directly speaks to the question of how DCC was dealing with external pressures and expectations.

Factor 5: Good Time Ethics

As I noted earlier, the HBR case study focused on processes of ethical review at DCC but did not consider in any detail exactly what cases were coming up for review. From the code, it was clear that DCC thought that it was most exposed in the area of bribery, kickbacks or political contributions in its foreign operations. Swanson characterized the cases he dealt with as ranging from instances of alleged sexual harassment to cases where an employee was arrested for brawling in a barroom. What is most striking about this list is that many of the charges were one-time violations by a single employee. The cases did not involve systemic wrongdoing nor did they threaten any of the company's core business lines. After he left the company, Swanson himself characterized the company as having a "good time" ethics program—i.e., a program that functioned well only as long as the sums of money involved were not very large.

Philosophers surely need to be sensitive to the likelihood that acting well may be appealing to a company and its employees only as long as doing the right thing is not an expensive proposition. Before praising a corporation as ethical, business ethicists need to examine whether the company has faced any hard tests. Johnson & Johnson showed it was truly concerned about the customer when it recalled all of its Tylenol product is after a customer had died from ingesting some of this product. One could argue that DCC's decision not to stop selling the silicone implants was of a different order. Both Johnson & Johnson and the police knew that the death was the result of some Tylenol having been tampered with, while the evidence linking the implants to many of the reported conditions was ambiguous. Given that there were risks as well in having the implants removed, DCC might have caused more harm by unduly alarming women and frightening them into "ex-plants." Still, the basic point remains: When evaluating a company's behavior, it is necessary to consider the extent to which the company has faced significant temptations not to do the right thing.

Factor 6: Character and Commitment

This last comment brings me to the sixth and final factor that business ethicists have tended to overlook in their case study—the issue of character and commitment. Paper codes and conduct committees are virtually worthless if people within the firm are not committed to avoiding wrongdoing. In fact, without such a commitment, a structure such as a business conduct committee may wind up being pernicious. Members may use the committee to avoid having to assume personal responsibility for their acts. Some literature suggests that people are less likely to do the right thing when they are a member of a group and take their cues from the collective than when they are confronting a crisis alone. This is not to say that, for people who are genuinely committed to acting well, the committee may provide a valuable sounding board for thinking through choices. But much will depend on the character and motivations of those on the board.

The problem thus becomes one of assessing the commitment of employees and management to acting well. All of the factors mentioned above need to be considered in arriving at a thoughtful judgment of this commitment. The DCC case suggests several other considerations especially relevant to the question of commitment. It is interesting that DCC was originally driven to adopt its ethical initiative only after Congress passed the Foreign Corrupt Practices Act in 1977. This act imposed fines on corporations and up to $10,000 in fines or five years in prison on individuals convicted of violating the act. The prospect of prison time no doubt proved sobering to many CEOs who were criminally liable if they "knew or had reason to know that their agents used the payments received from the U.S. concern to pay a foreign official for a prohibited purpose." The original impulse behind a move to develop an ethics initiative does not necessarily taint the entire resulting ethics initiative. Swanson, for example, apparently initially thought of the Business Conduct Committee as so much window dressing but over the years the committee and the rest of DCC's ethics program came to symbolize for him a genuine commitment to do the right thing. Nevertheless, if senior management understands its ethics program merely or largely as a strategy for avoiding getting into legal trouble, the company is not likely to do the right thing in those cases where it thinks it either will not be caught or can use the legal system to its advantage.

The corporate compensation system should be considered as well. At DCC, people were told, on the one hand, that they should avoid paying bribes to officials in order to get business; but, on the other hand, they believed they would be evaluated entirely on their contribution to the bottom line. The employees received a dual signal. Under such circumstances, employees may justifiably wonder about the sincerity of the company's commitment to doing the right thing.

Third, business ethicists should look to the possible effects of ownership structure (public vs. private) on a company's ethics. No doubt there are decent family-owned businesses. Clearly public ownership is neither a necessary nor a sufficient condition for encouraging ethically good behavior. Nevertheless, it may be that a company like DCC, which was accountable only to Dow Chemical and Corning Inc., will be less responsive to concerns about its actions than it would be if it were forced to confront and report to shareholders directly. Corporate structure does have ethical implications and should not be ignored.

Finally, it may prove insightful to ask employees who is responsible for ethics within their company. The right answer surely is: "I am." Every person who performs a deed places himself or herself within the ethical realm and becomes accountable for the actions he or she voluntarily initiates. Yet, at DCC, one man—Swanson—was viewed as "Mr. Ethics" and the "guardian of the company's ethics." The fact that Swanson apparently accepted these titles and the fact that they were given to him in the first place should have been a sign that something was seriously awry. No single person can know what others are doing around the world. Nor can he justly be held responsible for actions beyond his control that others initiate. Business ethicists seem to have been so impressed by Swanson's integrity that they forgot that one person does not a corporation make.

CONCLUSION

Although I have been critical of business ethicists' praise of Dow Corning, I am aware that I, too, might have spoken of the company's code and ethics program in glowing terms had I been the one writing a case study of the company back in 1977. However, the issue is not whether business ethicists sometimes err in their judgments but whether they show themselves willing to learn from their past errors. Like companies, we are judged by our histories and by our character and commitments. While it is the human condition to err, it is also part of our condition to be able to identify our mistakes as such and to learn from them. The above analysis represents one answer to the question of where and why we philosophers erred in our judgment of one company. The errors are generic in the sense that they are the sort we might make when evaluating any company and its actions. The good news is that, since these errors are generic, we can take the lesson learned from DCC to heart and do better the next time.

JUST BECAUSE IT'S LEGAL, IS IT ETHICAL?

JEFFREY SEGLIN

Often business decision makers seek answers to ethical dilemmas from the law. However, as scholar and journalist Jeffrey Seglin discusses in the following article, the law is not always the appropriate oracle.

It's very possible for an owner or manager of a company to make a perfectly legal decision without ever exploring the ethical aspects of the decision. That's not to suggest that making a decision that is legal is inherently unethical. It's just that sometimes the law gives us an excuse to ignore whether the action we are taking is right or wrong.

The bankruptcy laws in the United States are a perfect example. In theory, they're a wonderful tool that give troubled business owners the opportunity to turn their businesses around rather than go under. When a company files for protection under chapter 11 of the bankruptcy code, it can keep its creditors at bay while it tries to work out a plan to reorganize itself so it can overcome its financial troubles. In theory, this is a good thing, because if the business emerges from chapter 11 protection rather than liquidating its assets in a chapter 7 bankruptcy filing, the chances are that creditors will ultimately be paid and the company itself will continue to contribute to the economy by creating jobs, paying taxes, and engaging in commerce.

There "are many reasons why a business gets sick, but they don't necessarily mean it should be destroyed," observes Judge James A. Goodman, the chief bankruptcy judge for the district of Maine. Hundreds of thousands of businesses that at one time or another had financial difficulties survive today as the result of chapter 11 proceedings. They continue to contribute to employment, tax revenues, and overall growth. It's counterproductive to destroy the business value of an asset by liquidating it and paying it out in a chapter 7 if that company shows signs of being able to recover in a reorganization. As for creditors, one of the provisions of the bankruptcy code is that in order for a reorganization to be confirmed, the creditor must get not less than he or she would have gotten in a chapter 7 liquidation. So why not go through with the reorganization?"[1]

Judge Goodman argues that in spite of the fact that 80 percent of businesses that file chapter 11 protection never make it out of bankruptcy, the fact that 20 percent do makes the bankruptcy laws all the more worthwhile.

"If a doctor had a 20 percent success rate with terminal cancer cases, you'd say, 'That's incredible!' Well, that's what we've got—companies that are terminal. We take the nearly dead and show them how to operate better, and one-fifth survive. What's wrong with that?" the judge asks.

The fact that there are roughly 1.4 million bankruptcy filings a year hasn't helped calm the perception that bankruptcy is being used as a shield to keep those who owe from paying back those who are owed. But the reality is that, of those 1.4 million filings, the vast majority are personal filings rather than business filings.

According to the American Bankruptcy Institute, while the number of bankruptcies filed from October 1, 1997, to September 30, 1998, was up 5.1 percent over the previous year and hit a record number of 1,436,964, the vast majority of those—96.7 percent—were personal filings. Business bankruptcy filings actually decreased by 15.1 percent from the previous year to 47,125.[2]

Regardless of the numbers, the perception remains that the number of businesses hiding behind bankruptcy laws rather than repaying their debts is epidemic. Those who are involved closely in such cases, like Judge Goodman, argue that this perception is not accurate.

"Of course there are abuses," says Judge Goodman, "but in my opinion having been on the bench as a judge for 17 years and having practiced bankruptcy law for 20 years before that, the percentage of abuses is minimal. It's almost nil."[3]

But when a company fails, does the owner of that business have an ethical responsibility beyond the laws to make good on all of his debts, even if it means paying back creditors after the business has ceased operations? After all, after a company owner liquidates the assets of his business under chapter 7 bankruptcy protection and uses whatever proceeds are raised to pay off debtors, he can turn around and start a new company without ever paying off the people or businesses he owed money to when the prior company went bust.

Or are the bankruptcy laws, which forgive the business owner from the responsibility of paying back all that is owed, enough punishment? While it's perfectly legal to go out and start a new business without regard for past debts owed, some owners have made the decision that that's not enough, that they have a responsibility to make good on their past debts. And sometimes, the whole question gets mucked up in what side of the owing fence you're on.

ARE LAWS ABSOLUTION FROM HAVING TO THINK?

Forget whether or not you should have the responsibility to pay back your debts for a moment. The whole area of bankruptcy protection raises a far more interesting issue. And that's that it's a prime example of how laws and regulations, however well-intentioned, have resulted in a nation of business owners who are forgiven from having to think through the implications of their actions. If the law allows such and such behavior, the argument goes, then that's what I'm obligated to do—no more, no less.

Well, fine. But somewhere along the line, were business owners absolved from having to do some hard thinking on what their actions might mean? What they might say to the business community? What they might say about us and how we want to be perceived? Remember, this business community is likely one in which, post-dead company, you're going to be operating for a long, long time.

Now, don't get me wrong. I'm not suggesting that the laws are wrong or that after thinking through the meaning of your actions you might not decide to do precisely the same thing as you would have done had you just blindly followed the letter of the law.

When did we become a nation of people like Ilsa in the movie *Casablanca,* who looks longingly into Rick's eyes and sighs, "You'll have to do the thinking for both of us." Please. Just because the law makes it so doesn't mean we shouldn't have to think long and hard about our actions, just as we'd do in any other aspect of our business.

Be real, I can hear you saying it. (Or thinking it silently to yourself as you roll your eyes.) Who wants to sit around and participate in self-flagellation sessions where you go over in painful detail everything you owe to everybody you've disappointed—your customers, your vendors, your employees, your creditors, and not least, yourself? Especially when you're in the midst of something as painful as losing your business and everything you built? I can think of few takers for the role. It's only when you're on the other side of the fence—when you're one of the ones being stiffed—that you spend time wondering loudly why the bankrupt business owner doesn't think about doing the right thing.

That's pretty much what happened to Daniel J. Driscoll, the owner of Darlyn Development Corp., a $4 million general contracting company in Marlboro, Massachusetts, when he found himself looking at the cover of the November 1995 issue of *Inc.* magazine. There, staring out from the cover with a plate of roasted chicken with all the fixings was George Naddaff, the entrepreneur who discovered Boston Chicken, at the time a fast-growing restaurant franchise success story that in 1993 had become one of the hottest public offerings on record.[4]

Mr. Driscoll was incensed. So he took pen to paper and wrote the magazine a letter. In part, he wrote: "While I find it wonderfully motivating that one business can flourish because of the ideas and actions of Mr. George Naddaff, I also find it infuriating that the same man could flaunt to the business world that he had $14 million to invest in a new venture, when he has not paid small businessmen like myself for his business ventures that failed." When asked about that failed venture in that November 1995 article, Naddaff told *Inc.* senior editor, Joshua Hyatt: "I'd like to forget about it."[5]

"Why should a man who has all the money he did be able to walk away from a million-dollar debt?" Driscoll asked. "They should make it illegal. If you have the funds to pay your debt, then you shouldn't be able to walk away. . . . When he realized that his concept wasn't going to be the next Boston Chicken, he pulled the plug on it and fucked everybody."[6]

Naddaff and his partners at Olde World Bakeries, the corporation which owned Coffee by George, had invested roughly $5 million in the drive-through coffee kiosk concept before they realized it wasn't going to work. They decided to liquidate the business and arrived at an agreement to pay their creditors roughly 30 cents of every dollar that was owed. Driscoll was one of the creditors who had agreed to the payout.

Driscoll may have agreed to the payout, but he was none too pleased that it ever came to having to make this choice. What bothered Driscoll had nothing to do with whether Naddaff followed the law. Driscoll doesn't doubt that he did. But in spite of the fact that what Naddaff did was legal, Driscoll thinks he shouldn't have gotten off as easily as he did. Since Naddaff had the resources from his personal wealth or his other business dealings to make good on his debts, Driscoll believes that he should have been made to pay back his creditors in whole.

GOING BEYOND WHAT THE LAW REQUIRES

Regardless of the fact that the laws about how much of your personal assets are protected when a company goes out of business vary from state to state, some business owners who have been in the same position as Naddaff say that they believe the right thing to do in such circumstances is to go beyond what's required by the law to make good on your debts.

In 1985, Hawkeye Pipe Services Inc., a manufacturer of pipes for oil rigs, went out of business. Its founder, Bill Bartmann, owed more than $1 million to creditors. But Bartmann says he decided not to reach a liquidation agreement as Naddaff had with creditors. Nor did he file for bankruptcy. Instead, he decided that he would pay back all the money he owed, no matter how long it took him to do so.

"I was born and raised in Iowa, and back in the Calvinistic Puritan Protestant work ethic kind of environment, you were supposed to pay your bills," says Bartmann, who went on to found Commercial Financial Services Inc. (CFS), which in 1998, was a roughly $1 billion debt-collection company based in Tulsa, Oklahoma. "It just seemed inherently wrong to try to escape by using a law—granted, it was a valid law, and I am a lawyer—as an escape hatch or excuse. It just didn't seem the proper thing to do."

After he closed the doors on Hawkeye Pipe Services, Bartmann says it took him two and a half years to pay everyone back in full. But he says he did.

"You know the American capitalistic system is the neatest on the globe," says Bartmann. "It's a wonderful environment to allow people to go out and assume the risks and rewards of life. Now, people understand the reward side very easily. I don't think they understand the reciprocal side is that they should be obligated to pay the piper if indeed there are any assets with which to do that. The question is do they have a responsibility beyond the legal requirements?"

In October 1998, an anonymous letter was written to CFS's bond ratings agencies which questioned CFS's collection rates. Bond ratings were pulled and CFS was cut off from that source of revenues. Bartmann resigned as CEO in late October 1998 and on December 11, the company filed for bankruptcy protection. Bartmann continued going into the office every day as a consultant for the company for the fee of $1 per year. But by late January, according to local press reports, he sent an e-mail to CFS employees saying that his daily presence at the company "had the potential of creating a conflict in how the company is run." In late June, it was reported that employees were notified by e-mail that the company was closing its doors. It remains to be seen if Bartmann has any intention to make sure that all of the debtors owed money by CFS are paid back in full should the company not reemerge from bankruptcy protection.[7]

Chris Graff is another company founder who thinks company owners have a responsibility that goes beyond what the law requires. Or, at least he believed he did. Graff, is the president of Marque Inc., a successful ambulance manufacturer based in Goshen, Ind. But in a previous business, Graff didn't have such good fortune.

His furniture-making business, Geste Corp., went out of business in 1989. Graff auctioned off the company's assets, but, he says "After the auction, I didn't have everybody paid off. I was about 10 grand short. So I went to work and paid it back out of my income." Graff says it took him roughly four months to pay back the money that was still owed.

"I guess it's just a moral or ethical issue for me," he says. "When we make a decision to do something, we should be able to explain that decision in the same way to anybody who asks, be it our spouse, our business partner, an employee, a creditor, or a customer. I have to sleep at night."

Beyond their take on whether it was moral or not, Bartmann and Graff were oblivious to the fact that their efforts to pay back their creditors all the money owed could have very practical aspects to it. "I understand how people view bankruptcy," said Bartmann. "I guess I rationalized it pretty quickly that although I was eligible to take the easy cure, to do so would forever taint me with that stigma."

As a result of going through the difficult chore of paying back all the money he owed his creditors, when Bartmann was trying to secure working capital for CFS, he used his earlier act as reassurance that "lending me money now again is the safest risk you're ever going to take."

REFERENCES

1. Robert A. Mamis, "Why Bankruptcy Works," *Inc.,* October 1996: 39.
2. "Bankruptcies Break Another Record During 12-Month Period Ending Sept.," November 23, 1998. Posted on American Bankruptcy web site at www.abiworld.org.
3. Interview by the author with Judge James A. Goodman, January 1998.
4. In what seems to be a classic example of what goes around comes around, Boston Chicken filed for chapter 11 bankruptcy protection in October 1998. By the time of the filing, George Naddaff was not with the management team running the company. *See* Mike Hofman, "Boston Chicken Files Ch. 11 as Troubles Come Home to Roost," *Inc.* Online, October 7, 1998.
5. Joshua Hyatt, "The Next Big Thing," *Inc.,* November 1995: 62.
6. Jeffrey L. Seglin, "Brother, Can You Spare 30 Cents on the Dollar?" *Inc.,* April 1998. The case study told here was originally told in a different form in this article in *Inc.* magazine. Unless noted otherwise, while the telling of the story is new, the quotes from the subjects in this case are drawn from this article.
7. Shaun Schafer, "CFS still looks for buyers." *Tulsa World,* January 27, 1999; and Julie Bryant, "Founder of CFS won't be in office," January 22, 1999. Also: Clytie Bunyan and Andy Parsons, "You've Got No Job, E-Mail Says," *The Daily Oklahoman,* June 24, 1999.

Chapter 5

ETHICS AND CORPORATE SOCIAL RESPONSIBILITY
One and the Same?

"The Social Responsibility of Business Is to Increase Its Profits"	MILTON FRIEDMAN
"Arguments for and against Corporate Social Responsibility"	N. CRAIG SMITH
The Wealth of Nations	ADAM SMITH
"Maximizing Ethics and Profits"	PATRICK PRIMEAUX, S.M.
"Smith and Friedman on the Pursuit of Self-Interest and Profit"	HARVEY JAMES, FARHAD RASSEKH
Dodge v. *Ford Motor Co.*	HON. J. OSTRANDER
"How Business Can Be Good"	JEFFREY SEGLIN
"A Hanging"	GEORGE ORWELL
"Reputation Quotient: Surveys Find Many Consumers Hold Companies Responsible for Their Actions"	PRICEWATERHOUSE-COOPERS
"Transformation at Shell: Commerce and Citizenship"	PHILLIP MIRVIS

Business has to take account of its responsibilities to society in coming to its decision, but society has to accept its responsibilities for setting the standards against which those decisions are made.

—SIR ADRIAN CADBURY[1]

---

[1]"Ethical Managers Make Their Own Rules," *Harvard Business Review,* September/October 1987.

By "social responsibility," we mean the intelligent and objective concern for the welfare of society that restrains individual and corporate behavior from ultimately destructive activities, no matter how immediately profitable, and leads in the direction of positive contributions to human betterment, variously as the latter may be defined.[2]   —KENNETH R. ANDREWS

> Fill your bowl to the brim
> and it will spill.
> Keep sharpening your knife
> and it will be blunt.
> Chase after money and security
> and your heart will never unclench.
> Care about people's approval
> and you will be their prisoner.
> Do your work, then step back.
> The only path to serenity.
> —Tao Te Ching

Is there a social responsibility of business? This question has been asked numerous times in a variety of ways, with just as many answers. Central to this question is perhaps the underlying determination of what responsibility business has at all. Do you ask yourself whether your friends, colleagues, parents, or others have a social responsibility? Probably, at some point. You might see your colleague drop some trash on the floor and walk on. You may feel that this person should stop and pick it up instead of continuing. Your belief about the responsibility of business may be no more than this—a firm should clean up after itself, so to speak. On the other hand, there are some theorists who believe that firms owe something back to the society that supports it, and that this debt is greater than the debt of the individual members of society.

The article by Milton Friedman in this section is perhaps the best known argument for a purely *profit-based* social responsibility of business (though Adam Smith was probably among the first to articulate this concept). Friedman is not ignoring ethical responsibility in his analysis; he is merely suggesting that decision makers are acting ethically if they follow their firm's self-interest. Primeaux expands on Friedman's analysis in order to find a corporate social responsibility within a profit-maximizing framework. Consider the qualities of a successful firm—it meets the needs of its market. If the market demands socially responsible behavior, a firm may be successful only by demonstrating this behavior. On the other hand, if the market places no value at all on socially responsible behavior, it is unlikely that a firm would be encouraged by profit to exhibit this behavior. Professor James Wilson explains that, "while free markets will ruthlessly eliminate inefficient firms, the moral sentiments of man will only gradually and uncertainly penalize immoral ones. But, while the quick destruction of inefficient corporations

---

[2]Kenneth R. Andrews, *The Concept of Corporate Strategy* (Burr Ridge, IL: Irwin Co. 1971) p. 120.

threatens only individual firms, the slow anger at immoral ones threatens capitalism, and thus freedom itself."[3]

The general public seems to disagree with Friedman's underlying presumption. A *BusinessWeek*/Harris poll of over 1,000 Americans found that 95 percent reject the notion that a corporation's role is limited to profit maximization.[4] Further, there may be other arguments for a socially responsible firm. Employees who are well treated in their work environments may prove more loyal, and more effective and productive in their work. Liz Bankowshi, director of Social Missions at Ben & Jerry's Homemade Ice Cream Company, claims that 80 to 90 percent of their employees work at Ben & Jerry's because "they feel they are part of a greater good."[5] The impact on the bottom line, therefore, stems not only from customer preference but also from employee preference. The problem with a focus on preference, however, is that social responsibility becomes merely social marketing. That is, a firm may use an image of social responsibility to garner customer support or employee loyalty while the facts do not evidence a true commitment. Are motivations relevant? Paul Hawken, cofounder of Smith & Hawken gardening stores and an advocate of business social responsibility, reminds us:

> You see tobacco companies subsidizing the arts, then later you find out that there are internal memos showing that they wanted to specifically target the minorities in the arts because they want to get minorities to smoke. That's not socially responsible. It's using social perception as a way to aggrandize or further one's own interests exclusively.[6]

What about the perspective of the *receiving* organization? Should an organization simply accept funding from any possible source? Consider the dilemma an organization faces, for instance, when a donor offers funds that would further the organization's objectives but the donor's image is completely contrary to those of the organization? Does the organization have the right or responsibility to question the motives of its benefactor? Since a major contribution often amounts to a type of partnership arrangement, should organizations be concerned about linking their images to that of their donors?[7] The answers to these questions may, in fact, lie more in the intention of the recipient than in that of the donor.

On the other hand, if the market does not encourage responsibility for social causes, should a firm engage in this behavior? And, indeed, is this a responsibility only of firms, or are we responsible for supporting firms that fail to exhibit socially responsible behavior? If we stand by and allow irresponsible actions to take place using profits garnered by our purchases, do we bear any responsibility? Consider this dilemma as you read George Orwell's "A Hanging."

---

[3]James Wilson, quoted by Elmer W. Johnson at the Hansen-Wessner Memorial Lecture, "Corporate Soulcraft in The Age of Brutal Markets," Northwestern University, May 2, 1996.

[4]*Business Ethics* (November/December 1996), p. 6.

[5]Joel Makower, *Beyond The Bottom Line* (New York: Simon & Schuster, 1994), p. 68.

[6]*Ibid.,* p. 15.

[7]I appreciate the assistance of Jennifer Wiggins in regard to social responsibility and the arts. These questions derived from her work on this topic.

There exist disagreements even among scholars who advocate a social responsibility. For instance, to whom does the firm owe this responsibility? To the employees? The community? The consumers? All stakeholders? As we have seen in previous sections, it may not be possible to satisfy the needs of each and every stakeholder in a situation. Therefore, what is the prioritization of this social responsibility? Consider the case of the spotted owl and the loggers in the Pacific Northwest, discussed later in connection with ethics and the environment. Logging poses a danger of extinction to the spotted owl, but discontinuing logging activities poses a hardship on the logging communities and those connected with them. Animal rights activists consider the interests of society in preserving the spotted owl to be predominant, while others consider the interests of the loggers and their communities to be predominant. Whether you are persuaded by the fact that this is a conflict between humans and animals or by the fact that a specie might be endangered, the answer is found only in your personal prioritization scheme.

Finally, what is the nature of this responsibility? In the case study found later in this section, involving Shell Oil Company, you are asked to consider a firm's responsibility to a community where it conducts operations. Is profit for the firm the only guiding principle, or should the impact of its decision on others be considered, even where the law allows the decision? Shell's rehabilitative actions subsequent to NGO pressure seem not to have been motivated by a legal duty to act. However, interestingly enough, a recent appellate court decision held that a lawsuit against Shell for allegedly aiding and abetting in the torture and murder of Nigerian activists who opposed drilling on their lands was allowed to proceed (in a decision dated September 14, 2000).[8]

Perhaps the answer to the quandary of the nature of social responsibility lies somewhere in the middle of all of these arguments. Philosopher Ayn Rand contends that our one and only social responsibility is to ourselves, but that this concern does not act as a barrier to helping others:

> *The moral purpose of one's life is the achievement of happiness. This does not mean that he is indifferent to all men, that human life is of no value to him, and that he has no reason to help others in an emergency—but it does mean that he does not subordinate his life to the welfare of others, that he does not sacrifice himself to their needs, that the relief of their suffering is not his primary concern, that any help he gives is an act of generosity, not of moral duty.*[9]

In the end, does good ethics mean good business? Does corporate social responsibility translate into fiscal responsibility? A landmark study by Professors Stephen Erfle and Michael Frantantuono found that firms that were ranked highest in terms of their records on a variety of social issues (including charitable contributions, community outreach programs, environmental performance, advancement of women, and promotion of minorities) had greater financial performance as well. Financial performance was better in terms of operating income growth, sales-to-assets ratio, sales growth, return on equity, earnings-to-asset growth, return on investment, return on assets, and asset growth.[10]

---

[8]*Wiwa* v. *Royal Dutch Petroleum Co.,* Docket No. 99-7223 (2d Cir. Ct. App., 2000).
[9]Ayn Rand, *The Virtue of Selfishness,* p. 49.
[10]Joel Makower, *Beyond the Bottom Line* (New York: Simon & Schuster, 1994), pp. 70–71.

Previous studies had found both supporting and conflicting results (though supporting results seem to outweigh conflicting). Professor Ullman summarizes the results of previous empirical studies on the relationship between social and financial performance as follows:

- Seven showed a positive relationship between social and financial performance.

- Three showed a negative relationship between social and financial performance.

- One showed a positive relationship between the promotion of women and financial performance and a negative relationship between charitable contributions and financial performance.

- One showed a U-shaped relationship, meaning that extreme social performance (good or bad) was negatively related to financial performance.

- Two found no effect.[11]

Take a look at the Reputation Quotient and consider whether a better reputation should be the guiding motivation for these types of activities. Does Johnson & Johnson reap a financial benefit from being ranked as the most reputable company in America by ResponsibilityInc? The jury remains out on a concrete linkage between social performance and financial performance.

*Look at a well-run company and you will see the needs of its stock-
holders, its employees, and the community at large being served simultaneously.*   —ARNOLD HIATT, FORMER CEO, STRIDE RITE CORP.

---

[11]A. Ullman, "Data in Search of a Theory: A Critical Examination of the Relationships among Social Performance, Social Disclosure, and Economic Performance of U.S. Firms," *Academy of Management Review* (July 1985), pp. 545–57.

THE SOCIAL RESPONSIBILITY OF BUSINESS IS TO INCREASE ITS PROFITS

Milton Friedman

In perhaps the seminal article in the challenge to corporate social responsibility, Nobel Prize–winning economist Milton Friedman articulates his objections to the presumption that business owes something extra to our social environment. Consider the recent influx of "socially conscious" firms (or at least those that appear socially conscious) in the marketplace: Ben & Jerry's, The Body Shop, Working Assets Long Distance, and others. Is this the direction of the future? **Should** *this be the direction of the future?*

When I hear businessmen speak eloquently about the "social responsibilities of business in a free-enterprise system," I am reminded of the wonderful line about the Frenchman who discovered at the age of 70 that he had been speaking prose all his life. The businessmen believe that they are defending free enterprise when they declaim that business is not concerned "merely" with profit but also with promoting desirable "social" ends; that business has a "social conscience" and takes seriously its responsibilities for providing employment, eliminating discrimination, avoiding pollution, and whatever else may be the catchwords of the contemporary crop of reformers. In fact they are—or would be if they or anyone else took them seriously—preaching pure and unadulterated socialism. Businessmen who talk this way are unwitting puppets of the intellectual forces that have been undermining the basis of a free society these past decades.

The discussions of the "social responsibilities of business" are notable for their analytical looseness and lack of rigor. What does it mean to say that "business" has responsibilities? Only people can have responsibilities. A corporation is an artificial person and in this sense may have artificial responsibilities, but "business" as a whole cannot be said to have responsibilities, even in this vague sense. The first step toward clarity in examining the doctrine of the social responsibility of business is to ask precisely what it implies for whom.

Presumably, the individuals who are to be responsible are businessmen, which means individual proprietors or corporate executives. Most of the discussion of social responsibility is directed at corporations, so in what follows I shall mostly neglect the individual proprietors and speak of corporate executives.

Milton Friedman, "The Social Responsibility of Business Is to Increase Its Profits." Reprinted by permission of *The New York Times*.

In a free-enterprise, private-property system, a corporate executive is an employee of the owners of the business. He has direct responsibility to his employers. That responsibility is to conduct the business in accordance with their desires, which generally will be to make as much money as possible while conforming to the basic rules of the society, both those embodied in law and those embodied in ethical custom. Of course, in some cases his employers may have a different objective. A group of persons might establish a corporation for an eleemosynary purpose—for example, a hospital or a school. The manager of such a corporation will not have money profit as his objectives but the rendering of certain services.

In either case, the key point is that, in his capacity as a corporate executive, the manager is the agent of the individuals who own the corporation or establish the eleemosynary institution, and his primary responsibility is to them.

Needless to say, this does not mean that it is easy to judge how well he is performing his task. But at least the criterion of performance is straightforward, and the persons among whom a voluntary contractual arrangement exists are clearly defined.

Of course, the corporate executive is also a person in his own right. As a person, he may have many other responsibilities that he recognizes or assumes voluntarily—to his family, his conscience, his feelings of charity, his church, his clubs, his city, his country. He may feel impelled by these responsibilities to devote part of his income to causes he regards as worthy, to refuse to work for particular corporations, even to leave his job, for example, to join his country's armed forces. If we wish, we may refer to some of these responsibilities as "social responsibilities." But in these respects he is acting as a principal, not as an agent; he is spending his own money or time or energy, not the money of his employers or the time or energy he has contracted to devote to their purposes. If these are "social responsibilities," they are the social responsibilities of individuals, not of business.

What does it mean to say that the corporate executive has a "social responsibility" in his capacity as businessman? If this statement is not pure rhetoric, it must mean that he is to act in some way that is not in the interest of his employers. For example, that he is to refrain from increasing the price of the product in order to contribute to the social objective of preventing inflation, even though a price increase would be in the best interests of the corporation. Or that he is to make expenditures on reducing pollution beyond the amount that is in the best interests of the corporation or that is required by law in order to contribute to the social objective of improving the environment. Or that, at the expense of corporate profits, he is to hire "hard-core" unemployed instead of better qualified available workmen to contribute to the social objective of reducing poverty.

In each of these cases, the corporate executive would be spending someone else's money for a general social interest. Insofar as his actions in accord with his "social responsibility" reduce returns to stockholders, he is spending their money. Insofar as his actions raise the price to customers, he is spending the customers' money. Insofar as his actions lower the wages of some employees, he is spending their money.

The stockholders or the customers or the employees could separately spend their own money on the particular action if they wished to do so. The executive is exercising a distinct "social responsibility," rather than serving as an agent of the stockholders or the customers or the employees, only if he spends the money in a different way than they would have spent it.

But if he does this, he is in effect imposing taxes, on the one hand, and deciding how the tax proceeds shall be spent, on the other.

This process raises political questions on two levels: principle and consequences. On the level of political principle, the imposition of taxes and the expenditure of tax proceeds are governmental functions. We have established elaborate constitutional, parliamentary, and judicial provisions to control these functions, to assure that taxes are imposed so far as possible in accordance with the preferences and desires of the public—after all, "taxation without representation" was one of the battle cries of the American Revolution. We have a system of checks and balances to separate the legislative function of imposing taxes and enacting expenditures from the executive function of collecting taxes and administering expenditure programs and from the judicial function of mediating disputes and interpreting the law.

Here the businessman—self-selected or appointed directly or indirectly by stockholders—is to be simultaneously legislator, executive, and jurist. He is to decide whom to tax by how much and for what purpose, and he is to spend the proceeds—all this guided only by general exhortations from on high to restrain inflation, improve the environment, fight poverty, and so on and on.

The whole justification for permitting the corporate executive to be selected by the stockholders is that the executive is an agent serving the interests of his principal. This justification disappears when the corporate executive imposes taxes and spends the proceeds for "social" purposes. He becomes in effect a public employee, a civil servant, even though he remains in name an employee of a private enterprise. On grounds of political principle, it is intolerable that such civil servants—insofar as their actions in the name of social responsibility are real and not just window-dressing—should be selected as they are now. If they are to be civil servants, then they must be elected through a political process. If they are to impose taxes and make expenditures to foster "social" objectives, then political machinery must be set up to make the assessment of taxes and to determine through a political process the objectives to be served.

This is the basic reason why the doctrine of "social responsibility" involves the acceptance of the socialist view that political mechanisms, not market mechanisms, are the appropriate way to determine the allocation of scarce resources to alternative uses.

On the grounds of consequences, can the corporate executive in fact discharge his alleged "social responsibilities"? On the other hand, suppose he could get away with spending the stockholders' or customers' or employees' money. How is he to know how to spend it? He is told that he must contribute to fighting inflation. How is he to know what action of his will contribute to that end? He is presumably an expert in running his company—in producing a product or selling it or financing it. But nothing about his selection makes him an expert on inflation. Will his holding down the price of his product reduce inflationary pressure? Or, by leaving more spending power in the hands of his customers, simply divert it elsewhere? Or, by forcing him to produce less because of the lower price, will it simply contribute to shortages? Even if he could answer these questions, how much cost is he justified in imposing on his stockholders, customers and employees for this social purpose? What is his appropriate share and what is the appropriate share of others?

And, whether he wants to or not, can he get away with spending his stockholders', customers', or employees' money? Will not the stockholders fire him? (Either the present ones or those who take over when his actions in the name of social responsibility have reduced the corporation's profits and the price of its stock.) His customers and his employees can desert him for other producers and employers less scrupulous in exercising their social responsibilities.

This facet of "social responsibility" doctrine is brought into sharp relief when the doctrine is used to justify wage restraint by trade unions. The conflict of interest is naked and clear when union officials are asked to subordinate the interest of their members to some more general purpose. If the union officials try to enforce wage restraint, the consequence is likely to be wildcat strikes, rank-and-file revolts, and the emergence of strong competitors for their jobs. We thus have the ironic phenomenon that union leaders—at least in the U.S.—have objected to Government interference with the market far more consistently and courageously than have business leaders.

The difficulty of exercising "social responsibility" illustrates, of course, the great virtue of private competitive enterprise—it forces people to be responsible for their own actions and makes it difficult for them to "exploit" other people for either selfish or unselfish purposes. They can do good—but only at their own expense.

Many a reader who has followed the argument this far may be tempted to remonstrate that it is all well and good to speak of Government's having the responsibility to impose taxes and determine expenditures for such "social" purposes as controlling pollution or training the hard-core unemployed, but that the problems are too urgent to wait on the slow course of political processes, that the exercise of social responsibility by businessmen is a quicker and surer way to solve pressing current problems.

Aside from the question of fact—I share Adam Smith's skepticism about the benefits that can be expected from "those who affected to trade for the public good"—this argument must be rejected on grounds of principle. What it amounts to is an assertion that those who favor the taxes and expenditures in question have failed to persuade a majority of their fellow citizens to be of like mind and that they are seeking to attain by undemocratic procedures what they cannot attain by democratic procedures. In a free society, it is hard for "good" people to do "good," but that is a small price to pay for making it hard for "evil" people to do "evil," especially since one man's good is another's evil.

I have, for simplicity, concentrated on the special case of the corporate executive, except only for the brief digression on trade unions. But precisely the same argument applies to the newer phenomenon of calling upon stockholders to require corporations to exercise social responsibility (the recent G.M. crusade for example). In most of these cases, what is in effect involved is some stockholders trying to get other stockholders (or customers or employees) to contribute against their will to "social" causes favored by the activists. Insofar as they succeed, they are again imposing taxes and spending the proceeds.

The situation of the individual proprietor is somewhat different. If he acts to reduce the returns of his enterprise in order to exercise his "social responsibility," he is spending his own money, not someone else's. If he wishes to spend his money on such purposes, that is his right, and I cannot see that there is any objection to his doing so. In the process, he, too, may impose costs on employees and customers. However, because he is far less likely than a large corporation or union to have monopolistic power, any such side effects will tend to be minor.

Of course, in practice the doctrine of social responsibility is frequently a cloak for actions that are justified on other grounds rather than a reason for those actions.

To illustrate, it may well be in the long-run interest of a corporation that is a major employer in a small community to devote resources to providing amenities to that community or to improving its government. That may make it easier to attract desirable employees, it may reduce the wage bill or lessen losses from pilferage and sabotage or have other worthwhile effects. Or it may be that, given the laws about the deductibility of corporate charitable contributions, the stockholders can contribute more to charities they favor by having the corporation make the gift than by doing it themselves, since they can in that way contribute an amount that would otherwise have been paid as corporate taxes.

In each of these—and many similar—cases, there is a strong temptation to rationalize these actions as an exercise of "social responsibility." In the present climate of opinion, with its widespread aversion to "capitalism," "profits," the "soulless corporation," and so on, this is one way for a corporation to generate goodwill as a by-product of expenditures that are entirely justified in its own self-interest.

It would be inconsistent of me to call on corporate executives to refrain from this hypocritical window-dressing because it harms the foundations of a free society. That would be to call on them to exercise a "social responsibility"! If our institutions, and the attitudes of the public make it in their self-interest to cloak their actions in this way, I cannot summon much indignation to denounce them. At the same time, I can express admiration for those individual proprietors or owners of closely held corporations or stockholders of more broadly held corporations who disdain such tactics as approaching fraud.

Whether blameworthy or not, the use of the cloak of social responsibility, and the nonsense spoken in its name by influential and prestigious businessmen, does clearly harm the foundations of a free society. I have been impressed time and again by the schizophrenic character of many businessmen. They are capable of being extremely farsighted and clearheaded in matters that are internal to their businesses. They are incredibly short-sighted and muddle-headed in matters that are outside their businesses but affect the possible survival of business in general. This short-sightedness is strikingly exemplified in the calls from many businessmen for wage and price guidelines or controls or income policies. There is nothing that could do more in a brief period to destroy a market system and replace it by a centrally controlled system than effective governmental control of prices and wages.

The short-sightedness is also exemplified in speeches by businessmen or social responsibility. This may gain them kudos in the short run. But it helps to strengthen the already too prevalent view that the pursuit of profits is wicked and immoral and must be curbed and controlled by external forces. Once this view is adopted, the external forces that curb the market will not be the social consciences, however highly developed, of the pontificating executives; it will be the iron fist of government bureaucrats. Here, as with price and wage controls, businessmen seem to me to reveal a suicidal impulse.

The political principle that underlies the market mechanism is unanimity. In an ideal free market resting on private property, no individual can coerce any other, all cooperation is voluntary, all parties to such cooperation benefit or they need not participate. There are no values, no "social" responsibilities in any sense other than the shared values and responsibilities of individuals. Society is a collection of individuals and of the various groups they voluntarily form.

The political principle that underlies the political mechanism is conformity. The individual must serve a more general social interest—whether that be determined by a church or a dictator or a majority. The individual may have a vote and say in what is to be done, but if he is overruled, he must conform. It is appropriate for some to require others to contribute to a general social purpose whether they wish to or not.

Unfortunately, unanimity is not always feasible. There are some respects in which conformity appears unavoidable, so I do not see how one can avoid the use of the political mechanism altogether.

But the doctrine of "social responsibility" taken seriously would extend the scope of the political mechanism to every human activity. It does not differ in philosophy from the most explicitly collectivist doctrine. It differs only by professing to believe that collectivist ends can be attained without collectivist means. That is why, in my book "Capitalism and Freedom," I have called it a "fundamentally subversive doctrine" in a free society, and have said that in such a society, "there is one and only one social responsibility of business—to use its resources and engage in activities designed to increase its profits so long as it stays within the rules of the game, which is to say, engages in open and free competition without deception or fraud."

ARGUMENTS FOR AND AGAINST CORPORATE SOCIAL RESPONSIBILITY

N. CRAIG SMITH

Smith responds to Friedman's contentions in the following excerpt.

There are five principal arguments against corporate social responsibility: the problem of competing claims (the role of profit), competitive disadvantage, competence, fairness, and legitimacy. Each will be considered in turn.

COMPETING CLAIMS—THE ROLE OF PROFIT

Friedman argues that the notion of social responsibility in business 'shows a fundamental misconception of the character and nature of a free economy'. Business's function is economic, not social. Accordingly, it should be guided and judged by economic criteria alone. Action dictated by anything other than profit maximisation, within the rules of the game, impairs economic efficiency and represents a taxation on those bearing the costs of such inefficiency, most notably the stockholders. The role of the corporation is to make a profit and maximise social welfare through the efficiency which that entails, and as Simon *et al.* put it, 'Consideration of any factors other than profit-maximising ones either results in a deliberate sacrifice of profits or muddies the process of corporate decision-making so as to impair profitability'. So, to quote Silk and Vogel, 'In short, the corporation will best fulfill its obligation to society by fulfilling its obligation to itself'. However, this argument falls down in a number of ways. Simon *et al.* identify four reasons. First, it emphasises the profits of the individual firm as opposed to the corporate sector, which may not mean the highest efficiency from society's point of view. Second, there is the distinction between the short term and the long term. Social goals may be profitable in the long term, for the reasons . . . of enlightened self-interest. Third, there are other indicators of well-being besides profitability. Because of the uncertainty about what will be profitable, corporate goals in practice place profitability second, seeking an assurance of a required minimum profit. Fourth, and finally, there is the concern for the efficient use of national resources. Because of social costs, profitability is not necessarily the best measure of effectiveness. Indeed, they argue, 'the argument for efficient allocation of resources would appear to require the corporation to locate and regulate the social consequences of its own conduct'.

N. Craig Smith, "Arguments for and against Corporate Social Responsibility," excerpted from *Morality and The Market* (New York: Routledge, 1990), pp. 69–76.

Furthermore, Simon *et al.* suggest that if these arguments are not accepted, the negative injunction against social injury would, at least, have to be respected. In other words, Friedman ignores the moral minimum: 'Most of the debate on corporate responsibility, by rather carelessly focusing on what we have termed affirmative duties . . . has obscured what seems to be the fundamental point: that economic activity . . . can have unwanted and injurious side-effects, and that the correction of these indirect consequences require self-regulation'. (There are some similarities here with Heilbroner's point that pure profit-maximisation could amount to social irresponsibility. . . . Essentially, the main criticism of this argument against corporate social responsibility—the need for profit maximisation—is its basis in an inappropriate economic model, the competitive model of capitalism; particularly because of social costs and the question of who the profits are for. Noting the argument about the separation of ownership and control and the consequent limited influence of shareholders over the conduct of professional managers, Ackerman quotes a statement by the chairman of Xerox which pointedly illustrates the inapplicability of the notion of profit-maximisation for shareholders: 'If we ran this business Wall Street's way, we'd run it into the ground . . . We're in this business for a hell of a long time and we're not going to try to maximise earnings over the short run'.

COMPETITIVE DISADVANTAGE

The competitive disadvantage argument against corporate social responsibility suggests that because social action will have a price for the firm it also entails a competitive disadvantage. So, either such works should be carried out by government or, at least, legislated for so that all corporations or industries will be subject to the same requirements. Mintz and Cohen show that such a consideration was paramount in Alfred Sloan's 1929 decision not to fit safety glass to Chevrolets, 'one of the single most important protections ever devised against avoidable automotive death, disfigurement and injury'. Sloan was concerned about public anxiety over automobile safety and did not wish to publicise hazards. In his correspondence with Lammont du Pont over the possible supply of safety glass he observes that despite General Motors' La Salles and Cadillacs being equipped with safety glass, sales by Packard, one of their competitors, had not been materially affected. So Sloan wrote, 'I do not think that from the stockholder's standpoint the move on Cadillac's part has been justified'. Sloan was still reluctant even when he recognized that such a feature would come in the end, he did not want to hurry it along: 'The net result would be that both competition and ourselves would have reduced the return on our capital'. Even when Du Pont noted that Ford had started to fit safety glass in the windshields of all their cars, Sloan observed: 'It is not my responsibility to sell safety glass'.

Green notes that Sloan's rejection of safety glass because it would add slightly to price and because his competitors lacked the 'lifesaving technology' should not be possible today because companies could go to the government to urge minimum standards and thereby avoid placing the firm at a competitive disadvantage. And as Simon *et al.* observe, the competitive disadvantage argument against social responsibility is difficult to accept when the social injury is caused by one firm but not its industry peers—as in Sloan's refusal to fit safety glass even after it was fitted to the windshields of all Ford cars. But if the social injury is not unique to one firm then 'the individual corporation can at least be expected to work for industrywide self-regulation within the limits of anti-trust laws; or the individual firm can work for government regulation'. What this ignores, however, is that many industries are ultimately in competition with other industries and there may then be a competitive disadvantage for the industry as a whole in relation to substitution goods. This issue of inter-industry competition aside, the criticism of the competitive disadvantage argument is essentially sound. In approbation of his position, Friedman quotes Adam Smith's comment: 'I have never known much good done by those who affected to trade for the public good.' While healthy skepticism might be desirable, the oligopolistic form of most markets and increased consumer knowledge and awareness makes such a position inappropriate. There are other reasons besides. Ackerman's observations on the advantages and disadvantages of early corporate response to social demands suggest that an early response, while it may seem unnecessary, does provide flexibility. Perhaps more significant, though, is his recognition that the area of discretion within which managers act is quite broad and as competition is conducted on many fronts there is scope for an early response, particularly when the potential benefits are also considered.

COMPETENCE

Friedman asks, 'If businessmen do have a social responsibility other than making maximum profits for stockholders, how are they to know what it is?' This implies the competence argument against corporate social responsibility. Simon *et al.* identify three ways in which, it may be claimed, a firm is not competent to deal with social issues. First, there is the claim that corporations do not have the technical skills to deal with social issues. This, they suggest, will vary from case to case and, given the notion of last resort in the Kew Gardens Principle . . . can only be valid if some other party can do the job better. Second, there is the claim that corporations do not know what is good for society and some other institution, such as government, knows better. But, they observe, 'a corporation's alleged lack of insight into the nature of the good is not a reason for objecting to its social activities unless they are deliberately coercive'. Third, there is the claim that incompetent attempts to resolve social issues waste shareholders' money. But, suggest Simon *et al.,* this is only true if management needs to be made more accountable to the shareholder. Alternatively, such a claim could be countered by pointing to the separation of ownership and control and the role of the professional manager. These factors notwithstanding, the argument of competence can only be applicable to affirmative actions; there is still, as Simon *et al.* note, the moral minimum of the negative injunction against social injury, for which competence cannot be an issue.

Bradshaw, a practitioner writing in this area (as President of Atlantic Richfield Company), does point out that 'corporations cannot cure all social ills, and, indeed, in many areas should not even try . . . This nation is richly endowed with many and varied institutions. Social change is, I believe, accomplished through these many institutions and not through any one'. He goes on to argue that business people should stick to their competencies, but, bearing in mind his observation that the rules of the game are changing, work 'within those competencies [and] become a prime mover for change at the rule-making level, whether it is in national government, regional areas or states'. Similarly, Silk and Vogel report the comments of the executives at the Conference Board meetings who contended that if they try to operate outside their special area of competence they will invariably get into trouble: 'We shouldn't accept responsibility for what we don't know about'. Elsewhere, Vogel observes that many social issues do not present much scope for solution by business. Moreover, it is not realistic to expect the business community to assume a leading role in balancing social needs with economic imperatives, because it would be inconsistent with the political views of business: 'The social reforms whose enactment have so dramatically improved the lot of the average American over the last 75 years mostly were adopted in spite of business lobbying, not because of it . . . if business is to perform as well as it can, it requires pressure from those outside it'.

So on the competency argument one must conclude that while there is the moral minimum, social actions beyond this are constrained by what business is able, competent, and willing to do. As Rockefeller notes: 'No one sector of our society is competent to deal with these problems . . . The only answer is that all sections must become involved, each in its own distinctive way, but in full and collaborative relationship with the others'.

FAIRNESS—DOMINATION BY BUSINESS

Friedman asks, 'Is it tolerable that these public functions of taxation, expenditure, and control be exercised by the people who happen at the moment to be in charge of particular enterprises, chosen for those posts by strictly private groups?' This is the fairness argument against corporate social responsibility. Heilbroner's concern about corporations playing God has already been noted. In a similar vein, Davis and Blomstrom observe, 'combining social activities with the established economic activities of business would give business an excessive concentration of power . . . [which] would threaten the pluralistic division of powers which we now have among institutions, probably reducing the viability of our free society'. As Levitt notes, 'The corporation would eventually invest itself with all-embracing duties, obligations, and finally powers—ministering to the whole man and molding him and society in the image of the corporation's narrow ambitions and its essentially unsocial needs'. Big business acting in accord with notions of social responsibility gives managers more discretionary power over the lives of others in three ways, as Simon *et al.* observe: by political action (lobbying), the creation of private government (within the organisation), and by a smothering effect—domination by business values.

However, they counter, if business does have this power then the problem is to control it, not think it presents a problem only in the social policy context. One must also consider what is worse: a lack of self-regulation may be more arbitrary in its effects:

> We grant that even corporate self-regulation may have some spill-over effect—that the attempt to avoid or correct a self-caused social injury may have some influence on the freedom of action of others. Such effects will, we think, be relatively insignificant when compared to the benefits of self-correction.

Moreover, they ask that even if affirmative modes of corporate social responsibility involve manipulation, should one fault genuine efforts to help? Besides which, the distinction between leadership and manipulation is a fine one. They conclude on this issue: 'We are convinced that the type of corporate self-regulation we have proposed will help to limit the arbitrary and oppressive impact of corporate activity, rather than the opposite, and therefore does not present a fairness problem'.

LEGITIMACY—THE ROLE OF GOVERNMENT

The final principal argument against corporate social responsibility is legitimacy: social issues are the concern of government. Or, as one executive commented at the Conference Board meetings: 'We pay the government well. It should do its job and leave us alone to do ours.' As Silk and Vogel comment, the business person feels 'non business' contributions should be voluntary and government has legitimate social concerns which business supports in the payment of taxes. Simon *et al.* identify three positions in this argument. First, unless business acts then government will act, with all the attendant disadvantages of government intervention cited by critics of government encroachment of private spheres. Moreover, corporate social problem-solving may be preferable because it is pluralistic and is therefore likely to be preferred by the people. This position seeks to minimise the role of government. Second, as Levitt and Friedman suggest, corporate involvement in social problems is likely to be bungled, which in itself will lead to government intervention. This has the disadvantages of both government and business interference in the private sphere: again, a position which can be employed to support business action to minimise government's role. The third position claims that only government can deal with market imperfections. This is because some encroachment is viewed as necessary (the mixed market position) and there needs to be an orderly division of labour. They counter that again these positions against corporate social responsibility reflect only on the affirmative duty and not on the negative injunction against social injury. In any event, there is still a case for self-regulation because the duplication of effort cannot in itself be harmful, federal agencies tend to represent industry interests anyway, and much corporate activity is overseas and outside government jurisdiction.

Simon *et al.* conclude on these five principal arguments against corporate social responsibility:

> *These points do carry weight with respect to some affirmative modes of corporate social action, but we find these objections unpersuasive in application to self-regulating activity. Whatever debate there may be over more expansive notions of corporate responsibility, a self-policing attempt to take into account the social consequences of business activity and at least an attempt to avoid or correct social injury represents a basic obligation.*

The problem of competing claims, competitive disadvantage, competency, fairness, and legitimacy are the principal arguments against corporate social responsibility. Other arguments include: the public being misled about who bears the cost of corporate social action, believing it to be free; the problem of determining benefits, costs, and priorities; the weakened international balance of payments—reduced efficiency raises costs and may put companies at a competitive disadvantage internationally; and the lack of a broad base of support among all groups in society. Also, as Beesley and Evans observe, Friedman's argument must be seen within the context in which it is presented, as 'part of an argument holding that property rights, as for instance manifest in company shareholdings, and, more fundamentally, the right to engage freely in economic activity, are necessary (but admittedly not sufficient) conditions for the maintenance of Western-style political freedom'. . . . Essentially this argument, the others briefly mentioned, and the principal arguments have been answered and found to be lacking. This is due mainly to their dependence on an inappropriate socioeconomic model of contemporary society, and their failure to account for social costs and the moral minimum of the negative injunction against social injury.

The arguments for corporate social responsibility are implied above. They emphasise changes in public expectations of business; enlightened self-interest; the avoidance of government intervention; the extent of corporate power and the need to balance this with responsibility in self-regulation; and business resources. It is worth concluding this chapter by quoting Steiner and Steiner's summary in review of the arguments for and against corporate social responsibility:

> *Business decision making today is a mixture of altruism, self-interest, and good citizenship. Managers do take actions that are in the social interest even though there is a cost involved and the connection with long-range profits is quite remote. These actions traditionally were considered to be in the category of 'good deeds'. The issue today is that some people expect—and some managers wonder whether they should respond to the expectation—that business should assume a central role in resolving major social problems of the day in the name of social responsibility . . . Business cannot do this, nor should it try. Larger corporations, however, clearly feel that the old-fashioned single-minded lust for profits tempered with a few 'good deeds' must be modified in favour of a new social concern. Society also expects its business leaders to be concerned. The issue is not whether business has social responsibilities. It has them. The fundamental issue is to identify them for business in general and for the individual company.*

The identification of these responsibilities and ensuring they are met—as well as the continuing problem of corporate power ignored by Steiner and Steiner—demand social control of business. . . .

THE WEALTH OF NATIONS

Adam Smith

Adam Smith (1723–1790) is perhaps best known as the father of modern capitalism and the market approach to decision making through his seminal text, A Wealth of Nations. *Less known is his work on values entitled* A Theory of Moral Sentiments *where he provides a value base for his market. Justice and fairness serve as the bases of Smith's theories and he believes that society could exist without any mutual love or affection. However, in* Moral Sentiments, *Smith articulates his belief that humankind has a fundamental concern for others and beneficence, without which the market could not operate.*

> *How selfish soever man may be supposed, there are evidently some principles in his nature, which interest him in the fortune of others, and render their happiness necessary to him, though he derives nothing from it, except the pleasure of seeing it. (*Theory of Moral Sentiments, *p. 9)*

Smith introduced a concept of the "impartial spectator," a type of conscience that functions as an inner disinterested judge, encouraging empathy within the decision maker. In other words, the decision maker, in reaching a decision, would consider the perspective of the impartial spectator and evaluate the impact of her or his possible decision on others (compare the impartial spectator to its later incarnation as stakeholder theory and Rawls's distributive justice). Smith also introduced the idea of the "invisible hand," a force that guides our decisions to a market-based end in the public interest. In fact, Smith contends that we are more likely to act in the public interest unintentionally guided by the invisible hand than if we intended it in the first place! Consider this oft-cited quote from Smith's Wealth of Nations:

> *Every individual . . . neither intends to promote the public interest, nor knows how much he is promoting it. . . . [B]y directing [his] industry in such a manner as its produce may be of the greatest value, he intends only his own gain, and he is in this, as he is in many other cases, led by an invisible hand to promote an end which was no part of his intention. Nor is it always the worse for society that it was no part of it. By pursuing his own interest he frequently promotes that of society more effectually than when he really intends to promote*

Adam Smith, *The Wealth of Nations,* vol. 1, book I, ch. 1, "Of the Division of Labor," ch. 2, "Of the Principle Which Gives Occasion to the Division of Labor.

*it. I have never known much good done by those who affected to trade for the public good. It is an affectation, indeed, not very common among merchants, and very few words need to be employed in dissuading them from it. (*An Inquiry into the Nature and Causes of the Wealth of Nations, *edited by R. Campbell, A. Skinner, W. Todd (Oxford: Clarendon Press, 1976), book IV, chap. ii, para. 9)*

According to Smith, capitalism (as we now call his market-based system) is not without its flaws. Smith admitted that a division of labor where individuals do those tasks for which they are best "suited" might cause atrophy in the minds of those confined to simple, repetitive tasks. Relevant to our purposes here, he also admitted that the privileges afforded the rich and famous might make them less prone to virtue. Smith's answer to these and other concerns was public education. Education could provide breadth to an otherwise regimented mind. How could this concept be applied to our present corporate society?

BOOK I

OF THE CAUSES OF IMPROVEMENT IN THE PRODUCTIVE POWERS OF LABOR AND OF THE ORDER ACCORDING TO WHICH ITS PRODUCE IS NATURALLY DISTRIBUTED AMONG THE DIFFERENT RANKS OF THE PEOPLE

Chapter I Of the Division of Labor

The greatest improvement in the productive powers of labor, and the greatest part of the skill, dexterity, and judgment with which it is anywhere directed, or applied, seem to have been the effects of the division of labor. . . .

To take an example, therefore, from a very trifling manufacture; but one in which the division of labor has been very often taken notice of, the trade of the pin-maker; a workman not educated to this business (which the division of labor has rendered a distinct trade), nor acquainted with the use of the machinery employed in it (to the invention of which the same division of labor has probably given occasion), could scarce, perhaps, with his utmost industry, make one pin in a day, and certainly could not make twenty. But in the way in which this business is now carried on, not only the whole work is a peculiar trade, but it is divided into a number of branches, of which the greater part are likewise peculiar trades. One man draws out the wire, another straightens it, a third cuts it, a fourth points it, a fifth grinds it at the top for receiving the head; to make the head requires two or three distinct operations; to put it on is a peculiar business, to whiten the pins is another; it is even a trade by itself to put them into the paper; and the important business of making a pin is, in this manner, divided into about eighteen distinct operations, which in some manufactories, are all performed by distinct hands, though in others the same man will sometimes perform two or three of them. I have seen a small manufactory of this kind where ten men only were employed, and where some of them consequently performed two or three distinct operations.

But though they were very poor, and therefore but indifferently accommodated with the necessary machinery, they could, when they exerted themselves, make among them about twelve pounds of pins a day. There are in a pound upwards of four thousand pins of a middling size. Those ten persons, therefore, could make among them upwards of forty-eight thousand pins in a day. Each person, therefore, making a tenth part of forty-eight thousand pins, might be considered as making four thousand eight hundred pins in a day. But if they had all wrought separately and independently, and without any of them having been educated to this peculiar business, they certainly could not each of them have made twenty, perhaps not one pin in a day; that is, certainly, not the two hundred and fortieth, perhaps not the four thousand eight hundredth part, of what they are at present capable of performing in consequence of a proper division and combination of their different operations.

In every other art and manufacture, the effects of the division of labor are similar to what they are in this very trifling one; though in many of them, the labor can neither be so much subdivided, nor reduced to so great a simplicity of operation. The division of labor, however, so far as it can be introduced, occasions, in every art, a proportionate increase of the productive powers of labor. . . .

This great increase of the quantity of work, which in consequence of the division of labor, the same number of people are capable of performing, is owing to three different circumstances: first, to the increase of dexterity in every particular workman; secondly, to the saving of the time which is commonly lost in passing from one species of work to another; and lastly, to the invention of a great number of machines which facilitate and abridge labor, and enable one man to do the work of many.

First, the improvement of the dexterity of the workman necessarily increases the quantity of the work he can perform; and the division of labor, by reducing every man's business to some one simple operation and by making this operation the sole employment of his life, necessarily increases very much the dexterity of the workman. A common smith, who, though accustomed to handle the hammer, has never been used to make nails, if upon some particular occasion he is obliged to attempt it, will scarce, I am assured, be able to make about two or three hundred nails in a day, and those too very bad ones. A smith who has been accustomed to make nails, but whose sole or principal business has not been that of a nailer, can seldom with his utmost diligence make more than eight hundred or a thousand nails in a day. I have seen several boys under twenty years of age who had never exercised any other trade but that of making nails, and who, when they exerted themselves, could make, each of them, upwards of two thousand three hundred nails in a day. The making of a nail, however, is by no means one of the simplest operations. The same person blows the bellows, stirs or mends the fire as there is occasion, heats the iron, and forges every part of the nail: In forging the head too he is obliged to change his tools. The different operations into which the making of a pin or of a metal button is subdivided, are all of them much more simple; and the dexterity of the person, of whose life it has been the sole business to perform them, is usually much greater. The rapidity with which some of the operations of those manufacturers are performed exceeds what the human hand could, by those who had never seen them, be supposed capable of acquiring.

Secondly, the advantage which is gained by saving the time commonly lost in passing from one sort of work to another is much greater than we should at first view be apt to imagine it. It is impossible to pass very quickly from one kind of work to another, that is carried on in a different place, and with quite different tools. A country weaver who cultivates a small farm must lose a good deal of time in passing from his loom to the field, and from the field to his loom. When the two trades can be carried on in the same workhouse, the loss of time is no doubt much less. It is even in this case, however, very considerable. . . .

Thirdly, and lastly, every body must be sensible how much labor is facilitated and abridged by the application of proper machinery. . . .

. . . A great part of the machines made use of in those manufactures in which labor is most subdivided were originally the inventions of common workmen, who, being each of them employed in some very simple operation, naturally turned their thoughts toward finding out easier and readier methods of performing it. Whoever has been much accustomed to visit such manufacturers must frequently have been shown very pretty machines which were inventions of such workmen in order to facilitate and quicken their own particular part of the work. In the first fire-engines, a boy was constantly employed to open and shut alternately the communication between the boiler and the cylinder, according as the piston either ascended or descended. One of those boys, who loved to play with his companions, observed that, by tying a string from the handle of the valve which opened this communication to another part of the machine, the valve would open and shut without his assistance, and leave him at liberty to divert himself with his play-fellows. One of the greatest improvements that has been made upon this machine, since it was first invented, was in this manner the discovery of a boy who wanted to save his own labor. . . .

It is the great multiplication of the productions of all the different arts, in consequence of the division of labor, which occasions, in a well-governed society, that universal opulence which extends itself to the lowest ranks of the people. Every workman has a great quantity of his own work to dispose of beyond what he himself has occasion for; and every other workman being exactly in the same situation, he is enabled to exchange a great quantity of his own goods for a great quantity, or, what comes to the same thing, for the price of a great quantity of theirs. He supplies them abundantly with what they have occasion for, and they accommodate him as amply with what he has occasion for, and a general plenty diffuses itself through all the different ranks of the society. . . .

Chapter II Of the Principle Which Gives
Occasion to the Division of Labor

This division of labor, from which so many advantages are derived, is not originally the effect of any human wisdom which foresees and intends that general opulence to which it gives occasion. It is the necessary, though very slow and gradual, consequence of a certain propensity in human nature which has in view no such extensive utility: the propensity to truck, barter, and exchange one thing for another.

. . . In almost every other race of animals each individual, when it is grown up to maturity, is entirely independent, and in its natural state has occasion for the assistance of no other living creature. But man has almost constant occasion for the help of his brethren, and it is in vain for him to expect it from their benevolence only. He will be more likely to prevail if he can interest their self-love in his favor, and show them that it is for their own advantage to do for him what he requires of them. Whoever offers to another a bargain of any kind, proposes to do this. Give me that which I want, and you shall have this which you want, is the meaning of every such offer; and it is in the manner that we obtain from one another the far greater part of those good offices which we stand in need of. It is not from the benevolence of the butcher, the brewer, or the baker, that we expect our dinner, but from their regard to their own interest. We address ourselves, not to their humanity but to their self-love, and never talk to them of our own necessities but of their advantages. Nobody but a beggar chooses to depend chiefly upon the benevolence of his fellow-citizens. Even a beggar does not depend upon it entirely. The charity of well-disposed people, indeed, supplies him with the whole fund of his subsistence. But though this principle ultimately provides him with all the necessaries of life which he has occasion for, it neither does nor can provide him with them as he has occasion for them. The greater part of his occasional wants are supplied in the same manner as those of other people, by treaty, by barter, and by purchase. With the money which one man gives him he purchases food. The old clothes which another bestows upon him he exchanges for other old clothes which suit him better, or for lodging, or for food, or for money, with which he can buy either food, clothes, or lodging, as he has occasion.

As it is by treaty, by barter, and by purchase that we obtain from one another the greater part of those mutual good offices which we stand in need of, so it is this same trucking disposition in which originally gives occasion to the division of labor. In a tribe of hunters or shepherds a particular person makes bows and arrows, for example, with more readiness and dexterity than any other. He frequently exchanges them for cattle or for venison with his companions; and he finds at last that he can in this manner get more cattle and venison than if he himself went to the field to catch them. From a regard to his own interest, therefore, the making of bows and arrows grows to be his chief business, and he becomes a sort of armorer. Another excels in making the frames and covers of their little huts or moveable houses. He is accustomed to be of use in this way to his neighbors, who reward him in the same manner with cattle and with venison till at last he finds it his interest to dedicate himself entirely to this employment, and to become a sort of house carpenter. In the same manner a third becomes a smith or a brazier; a fourth a tanner or dresser of hides or skins, the principal part of the clothing of savages. And thus the certainty of being able to exchange all that surplus part of the produce of his own labor, which is over and above his own consumption, for such parts of the produce of other men's labor as he may have occasion for, encourages every man to apply himself to a particular occupation, and to cultivate and bring to perfection whatever talent or genius he may possess for that particular species of business.

The difference of natural talents in different men is, in reality, much less than we are aware of; and the very different genius which appears to distinguish men of different professions, when grown up to maturity, is not upon many occasions so much the cause as the effect of the division of labor. The difference between the most dissimilar characters, between a philosopher and a common street porter, for example, seems to arise not so much from nature as from habit, custom, and education. When they came into the world, and for the first six or eight years of their existence, they were, perhaps, very much alike, and neither their parents nor play-fellows could perceive any remarkable difference. About that age, or soon after, they come to be employed in very different occupations. The difference of talents comes then to be taken notice of, and widens by degrees, till at last the vanity of the philosopher is willing to acknowledge scarce any resemblance. But without the disposition to truck, barter, and exchange, every man must have procured to himself every necessary and convenience of life which he wanted. All must have had the same duties to perform, and the same work to do, and there could have been no such difference of employment as could alone give occasion to any great difference of talents. . . .

MAXIMIZING ETHICS AND PROFITS

PATRICK PRIMEAUX, S.M.

Primeaux offers a practical rejoinder to critics of Friedman, arguing for the possibility of a balance between money and ethics that is based on a theory of profit maximization.

Business is the highest level of human activity and the highest level of social good. Some of the greatest pieces of art the world has ever known are a good meal, a Boeing 747, a BMW, a PC, a CAT scanner, a refrigerator. By any measure, the kind of behavior needed to produce these works of art constitutes the highest level of human activity and the highest level of social good. After all, it is people engaged in business who deliver all the goods and services the community wants—better health care, schools for our children, food for our tables, and shelter for our families.

Business demands excellence and creativity. Men and women in business are artists and scientists. The activities in which they engage are like those required to produce a great symphony, a well-written play, a fine painting, a vintage wine, or a new scientific discovery. These activities demand excellence and require an abundance of creativity.

These words appear in the opening chapter of a book John Stieber and I wrote about business ethics.[1] Stieber and I want to reflect a positive and optimistic evaluation of business and of the men and women in business. However, when we read newspapers, watch television, or listen to business people conversing, we know that this positive evaluation of business is not universally accepted. Everyone knows that men and women in business are interested in one thing: money. And, as everyone also knows, men and women in business will do anything that has to be done to make money. That's the name of the game. That's what business is really all about.

If that's the case, why bother talking about ethics? When Milton Friedman claims that the ethical mandate of business is to increase shareholder profit, he's talking about money and he's talking about ethics. Connecting the two, he probably did more than any other theorist to advance business ethics. Now we hear executives of major corporations giving commencement speeches about ethics. "What will it look like on the front page of the *New York Times?*" and "Think of yourself as running for mayor" they propose as guiding principles for ethics in business. What they are advising is business as usual. Do what you have to do to maximize profits, but make it look good to the public and to the Securities and Exchange Commission. We might commend them for their practicality, but why not ask them

Patrick Primeaux, S.M., "Maximizing Ethics and Profits." Reprinted by permission of the author.

[1]For a fuller examination of the theory and implications of the argument reflected in this essay, see Patrick Primeaux and John Stieber, *Profit Maximization: The Ethical Mandate of Business* (San Francisco: Austin & Winfield, 1995) and an article of the same title in the *Journal of Business Ethics* 13, no. 4 (1994), pp. 287–94.

to become even more practical? Why don't they recommend, as Charles E. Quinn does, that everyone simply invest in a personal paper shredder?

The problem for business and for business ethics is the equation of business with money, specifically bottom-line accounting profits, and the pressure to increase those profits quarterly or annually. That motivating objective is itself reflective of an ethical code. It consists of an ethical principle, and demands a certain kind of behavior consistent with that principle. The organization is structured, people are hired, jobs are described, managers are held accountable, raw materials are acquired, and technology engaged to increase that bottom line. Everything and everybody within the company is directed by that profit-maximizing principle and expected to conform to its demands.

Stieber and I want to create another ethical code for business, one which still takes money seriously. We also want to provide a framework or blueprint for business and for people in business to be able to appreciate the ethics of business, and to regulate themselves rather than waiting for political, legal, and religious demands to be imposed on them from the outside. In other words, we want to tie business ethics to profit maximization, but to a broader understanding of profit maximization than that usually ascribed to rational, numerical bottom-line accounting profits.

When numbers become more important than anything else, everything and everyone in the company becomes valued in those same mathematical and numerical terms. When people or things are valued for their contribution to increased profit margins, they are identified numerically and treated as such. They are themselves valued simply with respect to their contribution to profits. The philosopher would say that they are objectified for utility. They are treated as objects and valued simply for their contribution to production. It is when this happens that business and men and women in business leave themselves wide open to criticism and to regulation from the law, from philosophy, or from religion.

That's the problem with Friedman's ethical imperative. It is too myopic, too focused on bottom-line accounting profits alone and, because of that, values the factors of production only insofar as they are useful for production and for rationally-and-numerically determined profits. It also reflects Friedman's values, what is important to him, how he views people and the world, especially the world of nature which provides the raw resources which go into productivity. It is evident that the values he wants to encourage are focused exclusively on utility, on usefulness to production. Is there not another value system which appreciates people and things for their own positive existence, their own presence in the world, rather than how they can be useful to us? Asking that question raises questions about ourselves.

What are our values? What do we value? Who do we value? How do we value ourselves? The subject and objects of each of these questions, as well as the contexts of the questions themselves, suggest that we are presuming different meanings of the word *value*. In the first case, we're asking about morals or ethics, about behavior. In the second question, we're inquiring about objects. In the third, the focus is on people other than ourselves. The fourth question is about ourselves, about self-identity. However, although used in different ways to ask different questions, the contextual nuances suggest a commonality and continuity of behavior, possessions, others, and ourselves. How can all of these be connected?

They are connected by value, and value suggests relationship. To ask questions about value is to ask questions about relationship, about how we perceive ourselves, others—

perhaps God—and the objects we possess. Value not only suggests relationships, but similarity and continuity within our perceptions and considerations of the things we have, the people we meet, and the persons we are becoming. Today, in our world, that bonding is primarily economic.

The first meaning of the word *value* in *Webster's* is "a fair return or equivalent in goods, services, or money for something exchanged," and the second is "the monetary worth of something: marketable price."[2] The third meaning is "relative worth, utility, or importance," and the fourth is "a numerical quantity assigned or computed." These definitions not only provide answers to our questions, but lead us to conclude that who and what we value, as well as our values, are defined primarily in economic terms: money, utility, numerical quantity. Not only is money an object, it is an object that can be quantified numerically. Its utility, its usefulness, is also quantified numerically.

But, let's not focus on money alone. Surely what we value, as well as our values, cannot be determined by money alone. They can also be determined by what money can buy and what money can provide. Even then, that focus on money is too myopic, as would be any appreciation for economics that would concentrate on money alone, or even on what money can buy. It is that understanding of economics which is misleading, for it subjects economics to numbers and accounting principles.

Profit maximization is not, however, only an accounting notion. There is also an economic definition of profit maximization which is much broader in scope and reference than any accounting formulation. Actually, the two are almost identical, defining profits as total revenues minus total costs (TR − TC). The real difference surfaces within total costs. The accountant would define total costs with respect to fixed costs and variable costs (TC = FC + VC). The economist would widen that definition to include opportunity costs so that total costs involves fixed costs, variable costs, and opportunity costs (TC = FC + VC + OC).

So what? The inclusion of opportunity costs within decision-making opens the doors to a broader perspective. That broader perspective goes beyond money and numbers. It moves beyond the bottom line to question a whole list of concerns which go into, and contribute to, that bottom-line maximization of profits. In other words, economic profit maximization is not content to focus on the numbers. Economic profit maximization wants to know how those profits are realized.

What are opportunity costs? Opportunity costs are usually defined as the forgone goods and services that could have been produced from a given set of scarce resources that was used to produce some other goods and services. There are two key phrases in this definition of opportunity costs that should help us understand their role in business decision making. The two phrases are "the forgone goods and services" and "from a given set of resources."

Assume that a business has a fixed amount of money from the earnings it has retained to invest for its owners. Further, suppose it decides to start a used car lot in an Amish town. Once these resources ("a given set of resources") are committed to the project, they can never be used to produce any other goods and services for the community such as health care, education, or housing ("forgone goods and services").

---

[2]Henry Bosley Woolf, ed., *Webster's New Collegiate Dictionary* (Springfield, MA: G. & C. Merriam Company, 1981).

Besides the usual kinds of business considerations associated with this decision (location, lease, hiring, taxes, etc.), there is a serious ethical consideration to be addressed. The Amish do not drive cars. Were the decision makers insensitive to this ethical behavior, the project would fail and the resources would be lost.

If the project were to fail because the management of this company was insensitive to the ethics of the situation, the opportunity costs for the community would be that of a whole set of scarce resources used to produce something consumers did not want, i.e., did not value. These wasted resources can never be used to produce anything else. The opportunity cost for the firm is the loss of money from a set of scarce resources that could have been used for another project.

From a more philosophical perspective there are some implications of opportunity costs we can apply to ourselves as men and women in business as well as to the business itself. First, opportunity costs imply that in every decision, in every choice, there is a negation, a rejection. This means that statements like "it's OK as long as no one gets hurts" become downright silly. Someone or something is always hurt, negated, or rejected in any choice to pursue one opportunity rather than another. Second, opportunity costs remind us that we can't have or do everything because resources are scarce. In other words, opportunity cost decision making serves to make the obvious even more so. Anything and everything is a scarce resource. Third, opportunity costs suggest that every decision about anything is an ethical decision. To choose one thing over another, or one course of action in preference to another, implies values. It also implies good and bad, right and wrong. This is especially the case when decisions are made about scarce resources. The very appreciation of scarcity suggests that any abuse or misuse of any resource is wrong. Fourth, opportunity-cost decision making opens wide the horizons of consideration. It moves beyond any immediate and short-term concerns to refer to implications and considerations for the widest possible scope of reference. It moves beyond numbers to encompass the whole of human experience, the whole of the world's ecology. That is, it encourages us to consider anything and everything that could possibly affect profits—both within and without the company. The establishment of a used-car lot in an Amish community fails precisely because the religious traditions of the people of that community were ignored. In opportunity-cost decision making, nothing can be ignored. To do so would incur opportunity costs, waste scarce resources, and would, for that reason, provide the grounding for unethical behavior.

How do we know whether a company is being ethical or not? To do so we would have to investigate its use of scarce resources. Within economics, we have a framework of reference within which to pursue that investigation. We can isolate the factors of production, and examine the costs associated with those factors. The factors of production are, of course, the scarce resources that enter into production.

The factors of production are usually described as four: land, labor-time, creativity/entrepreneurship, and capital. The costs associated with land are paid as rent, to labor-time as wages, to creativity-entrepreneurship as profit, to capital as interest. Tying the costs of production to the factors of production implies an ethical imperative based in efficiency. To use these resources inefficiently leads to waste, abuse, and misuse. That inefficiency translates into unnecessary costs, and reflects not only inefficiency, but waste of scarce resources.

Since the time of Adam's and Eve's eviction from the Garden of Eden, everything and anything has become a scarce resource. While in the Garden, they had everything they wanted. Why? They had an infinite number of resources available to them. Outside the Garden, they found that resources were limited. Moreover, they quickly discovered that to acquire the things they wanted, these scarce resources had to be used efficiently.

They also quickly discovered that once an animal was slaughtered for food and clothing, that animal would never be able to provide additional food and clothing. There would be other animals, though, and for a time it might have seemed that these existed in limitless, infinite numbers. As time progressed, and as the earth became more and more populated, the number of animals available for food and clothing became more and more scarce. In today's world, we can easily argue from casual observation and ordinary experience, that anything and everything is a scarce resource; that once used for one purpose, the resource no longer exists for any other purpose.

In economics, that realization of the scarcity of resources is translated into the principle of opportunity costs. Actually, the monetary value we attach to human labor and time, as well as to personal creativity, land, and even money, is itself an indication of scarcity. Once any of these resources is brought into production, any opportunity for an alternative use is forgone. Measuring its actual use with respect to its potential use, provides an indication of the value of a given resource, i.e., a measure of whether or not the person or thing is employed towards its maximum value or potential. To do otherwise would prove inefficient, for it would involve waste, abuse, or misuse of a valuable and scarce resource. It would also be inefficient, for it would result in unwarranted costs.

The principle of opportunity costs can be assessed personally as well as corporately. Given the many choices we have in life, the college student can choose between preparing for an exam the following day or socializing with friends. As opportunity-cost decision making implies both choice and negation, to choose to spend time and expend energy poring over class notes and text books necessitates the rejection of the company of one's friends. The costs of studying are weighed with the costs of socializing for the scarce resources of time and energy require a choice. To choose one requires the negation of the other. The question to ask is, which will be more efficient? Another question to ask is, which will cost more in the long run?

We need to ask the same question when choosing between two desirable alternatives in business. A really intelligent, responsible, and productive secretary who is paid a salary commensurate with market standards, even though contributing more than required or expected of that standard, provides a practical and common example. The decision hinges on capital and the most efficient use of that capital. Should he receive a higher salary, or should that same money—a scarce resource—be used to increase bottom-line accounting profits? Choosing to direct the money towards profits could mean the secretary leaving the firm for higher-salaried employment by another firm. The costs of hiring and training a replacement, perhaps one contributing less than the former secretary, could exceed the costs of a salary raise. In that case, the scarce resource of the original secretary, as well as the scarce resource of capital, would be wasted and misused, especially in the long run. Directly pertaining to ethics, no one would consider the decision bearing on this case to be a good one. With respect to costs, no one would judge this use of the person as well as of capital to be good and efficient.

Perhaps the most abused of the factors of production is that of creativity/entrepreneurship. Although afforded a market-level salary, our exceptionally efficient secretary is not rewarded. Only senior managers and directors are considered worthy of pay for the creativity of their decisions, especially those of bringing creative people into the firm. A creative and entrepreneurial spirit can, however, be found at every level of the organizational structure and also rewarded in a manner proportionate to contribution to profit. Our exemplary secretary should be compensated for her creativity. So also should the janitor who saves the company money by using cleaning supplies sparingly while, at the same time, complying with the dictates of her job description.

Opportunity-cost decision making leads to profit-maximization insofar as it recognizes the scarcity of all of its resources, and uses those resources as efficiently as possible. To evaluate whether a company is profit-maximizing, then, one needs to look beyond bottom-line accounting profits to identify what those profits represent. To do that, one would have to study the costs incurred by each of the factors of production, to assess those costs in terms of opportunity costs, and to evaluate those opportunity costs from a long-term perspective. This kind of assessment would answer the most important question of practical and ethical concern: Are all of the factors of production being used as efficiently as possible?

This perspective commends itself for good business and good business ethics because it originates directly within business theory and practice. It also commends itself because it encourages business to move beyond bottom-line accounting profits to consider people and things not only as valuable for production, but also as valuable in themselves—as scarce resources having value and dignity. It also commends itself because we could then equate good business and good business ethics.

SMITH AND FRIEDMAN ON THE PURSUIT OF SELF-INTEREST AND PROFIT

HARVEY S. JAMES, JR.,
FARHAD RASSEKH

The purpose in the following essay is to delineate Adam Smith's doctrine and Milton Friedman's thesis as they relate to business ethics. The authors analyze the economics of the pursuit of self-interest and profit as well as the moral constraints that Smith and Friedman impose on business conduct. A careful reading of both economists reveals that Smith's doctrine and Friedman's thesis embody ethical and other-regarding considerations, which have important implications for business activity. The authors describe these implications and provide examples and applications of the moral constraints Smith and Friedman advocate.

I. INTRODUCTION

The modern market system owes its intellectual roots to the writings of the Scottish moral philosopher and political economist Adam Smith. Smith designed a social system in which markets, where people ostensibly pursue their self-interest, assume a central role. Smith used the metaphor "invisible hand" to show how the pursuit of self-interest unintentionally and unknowingly promotes the public interest. The invisible hand doctrine is one of the most influential ideas in history.

A major theme in the field of business ethics concerns the "social responsibility of corporations," which has attracted considerable attention in recent years. In this regard, the economist and Nobel laureate Milton Friedman has argued that the only social responsibility of business is to maximize its profit. Friedman's thesis, which is an extension of Smith's doctrine, represents one of the most controversial arguments in business ethics.

II. THE ECONOMICS AND ETHICS OF SELF-INTEREST

Adam Smith (1723–1790), a leading figure of the Enlightenment, set out to discover the rules and laws that govern a civil and prosperous society. He began his inquiry with his first book, *The Theory of Moral Sentiments* (TMS), in 1759 in which he analyzed, among other

"Smith and Friedman on the Pursuit of Self-Interest and Profit," by Harvey James and Farhad Rassekh. Reprinted with permission of the authors.

things, the motives behind moral behavior. As a part of his social design, Smith in 1776 published his treatise on political economy, *An Inquiry into the Nature and Causes of the Wealth of Nations* (WN). Although it is in the latter book that Smith focused on the requisites for a viable and prosperous economy, to understand the moral constraints Smith places on economic behavior completely and accurately one must study both books.[1]

Smith predicates his system on the observation that we are naturally endowed with a powerful "desire of bettering our condition, a desire which . . . comes with us from the womb, and never leaves us till we go into grave" (WN, p. 709). Smith also observes "a certain propensity in human nature . . . the propensity to truck, barter, and exchange one thing for another" (WN, p. 25). These natural impulses lead to division of labor because specializing in production and trading in the marketplace improve our living standards.

Further, Smith delves into the motivation behind market exchanges. Here the choice is between self-interest and benevolence. Although Smith believes benevolence is a praiseworthy virtue, he does not think humans are capable of being benevolent all the time. In this regard, he notes:

> *Benevolence may, perhaps, be the sole principle of action in the Deity, and there are several, not improbable, arguments which tend to persuade us that it is so. It is not easy to conceive what other motive an independent and all-perfect Being, who stands in need of nothing external, and whose happiness is complete in himself, can act from. But whatever may be the case with the Deity, so imperfect a creature as man, the support of whose existence requires so many things external to him, must often act from many other motives.* (TMS, p. 305)

If human beings are too imperfect and too weak to act out of benevolence, then self-interest is the inevitable choice when an exchange occurs within the market. Moreover, as the economic historian Jacob Viner observed, Smith maintains that virtues such as sympathy and benevolence rule non-market and familial relationships. But since market exchanges are anonymous and mechanical, sympathy and benevolence are "insufficiently strong as a disciplinary force" and thus self-interest "would be the dominant psychological force" in the market.[2] In the following passage, Smith explains why markets operate on self-interest:

> *Man has almost constant occasion for the help of his brethren, and* it is in vain for him to expect it from their benevolence only. *He will be more likely to prevail if he can interest their self-love in his favour, and shew them that it is for their own advantage to do for him what he requires of them . . . and it is this manner that we obtain from one another the far greater part of those good offices which we stand in need of. It is not from benevolence of the butcher, the brewer, or the baker, that we expect our dinner, but from their regard to their own interest, we address ourselves, not to their humanity but to their self-love, and never talk to them of our own necessities but of their advantages.* Nobody but a begger chuses (sic) to depend chiefly upon the benevolence of his fellow-citizens. (WN, pp. 26–27, emphasis added)

---

[1]Adam Smith's books are *The Theory of Moral Sentiments* (Indianapolis: Liberty Classics, 1984), and *An Inquiry into the Nature and Causes of the Wealth Nations* (Indianapolis: Liberty Classics, 1981).

[2]Jacob Viner, "The 'Economic Man,' or the Place of Self-Interest in a 'Good society,'" reprinted in Douglas Irwin (ed.), *Jacob Viner, Essays on the Intellectual History of Economics* (Princeton: Princeton University Press, 1991), p. 74 (originally published in 1959).

The last sentence of Smith's remarks suggests that it would be undignified for human beings to appeal to the benevolence of others for their needs. Far more importantly, though, Smith argues that the unintended consequences of self-interested actions frequently benefit society. This analysis leads to the invisible hand doctrine. Here are Smith's remarks:

> *As every individual, therefore, endeavors as much as he can to employ his capital in the support of domestick industry, and so to direct that industry that its produce may be of the greatest value; every individual necessarily labours to render the annual revenue of the society as great as he can. He generally, indeed, neither intends to promote the publick interest, nor knows how much he is promoting it. By preferring the support of domestick to that of foreign industry, he intends only his own security; and by directing that industry in such a manner as its produce may be of the greatest value, he intends only his own gain, and he is in this, as in many other cases, led by an invisible hand to promote an end which was no part of his intention. Nor is it always the worse for the society that it was no part of it. By pursuing his own interest he frequently promotes that of the society more effectually than when he really intends to promote it.* (WN, p. 456)

How does the pursuit of individual self-interest promote that of the society? Consider the following chain of events in the computer industry: The proliferation of computers in the early 1970s increased demand for computer operators, programmers, and engineers. College students quickly realized the promising opportunities in the computer industry and in large numbers majored in computer-related fields. Thus, students' pursuit of their own interests (i.e., majoring in computers because of job opportunities) met the needs of the computer industry, which in turn met the needs of the society. The evolution of the computer industry, of course, has continued over the years because businesses and individuals benefit enormously from computers. Our demand for computers (i.e., our pursuit of self-interest) continues to attract investment and talents into this industry. The people who enter the computer business also pursue their own interests. *The Wall Street Journal* reports that the U.S. computer industry attracts people from all over the world. For example, it reports, "nearly one third of start-up companies in Silicon Valley are headed by an Indian or Chinese immigrant."[3]

The operation of the invisible hand (i.e., promoting the common good while pursuing self-interest), Smith observes however, is bound by ethical constraints. First and foremost, he distinguishes between self-interest and selfishness. In the introduction to TMS, two noted scholars of Smith point out that "Smith recognizes a variety of motives, not only for actions in general but also for virtuous action. These motives include self-interest or, to use the eighteenth-century term, self-love. It is this, not 'selfishness,' that comes to the fore in WN. Smith distinguished the two expressions, using 'selfishness' in the pejorative sense for such self-love as issues in harm or neglect of other people."[4] The depth of Smith's disapproval of selfish behavior can be discerned from the following passage:

> *that to feel much for others and little for ourselves, that to restrain our selfish, and to indulge our benevolent affections, constitutes the perfection of human nature; and can alone*

[3] Stephen Gotz-Richter and Daniel Bachman, "Welcome More Immigrants," *Wall Street Journal,* July 22, 1999, p. A26.

[4] D. D. Raphael and A. L. Macfie, "Introduction," in Smith, *The Theory of Moral Sentiments,* Indianapolis: Liberty Classics, 1984, p. 22.

produce among mankind that harmony of sentiments and passions in which consists their whole grace and propriety. (TMS, p. 25)

In fact, Smith sets the parameters within which one may pursue self-interest and compete with others. To distinguish right from wrong, Smith introduces an imaginary figure, a moral judge, which he calls the "impartial spectator." Consider the following passage:

There can be no proper motive for hurting our neighbor. . . . To disturb his happiness merely because it stands in the way of our own, to take from him what is of real use to him merely because it may be of equal or of more use to us, is what no impartial spectator can go along with. . . . In the race for wealth, honors, and preferments, he may run as hard as he can, and strain every nerve and every muscle, in order to outstrip all his competitors. But if he should justle, or throw down any of them, the indulgence of the spectators is entirely at an end. It is a violation of fair play, which they cannot admit of. (TMS, pp. 82–83, emphasis added)

Therefore, one may work hard to outcompete others, but one ought not to justle to get ahead. In business, "justling," or selfish behavior, includes fraud, deception, lack of concern for public welfare, mistreatment of employees, etc. Although these actions may be illegal, there are legal actions that are ethically questionable. For example, suppose some firms in the computer industry lobby the government for restrictions on immigration because they wish to limit the number of competitors. Such action amounts to justling and throwing down potential competitors, rather than straining every nerve to improve quality and productivity. A restriction on immigration would benefit the existing firms at the expense of consumers and potential entrepreneurs. Smith would consider such policy to be unjust because, in his words, "to hurt in any degree the interest of one order of citizens for no other purpose but to promote that of some other, is evidently contrary to that justice and equality of treatment which the sovereign owes to all different orders of his subjects" (WN, p. 654).

For self-interested actions not to turn selfish, Smith believes that justice must rule business conduct. He notes:

All systems either of preferences or restraint, therefore, being thus completely taken away, the obvious and simple system of natural liberty establishes itself of its own accord. Every man, as long as he does not violate the laws of justice, is left perfectly free to pursue his own interest his own way, *and to bring both his industry and capital into competition with those of any man, or order of men.* (WN, p. 687, emphasis added)

In an analysis of the Smithian system, Viner remarks that to Smith "justice is a negative virtue; it consists of refraining from injury to another person and from taking or withholding from another what belongs to him. . . . Smith considered justice, so understood, to be the necessary foundation of a viable society."[5]

In summary, a careful reading of Smith makes it clear that while he condones the pursuit of self-interest in the marketplace, he argues that we ought to refrain from injuring others. In particular, Smith believes that self-interest should be moderated by a sense of justice toward others in the marketplace. The application of Smith's philosophy to business conduct may be

---

[5]Jacob Viner, "Adam Smith," reprinted in Irwin (ed.), *Jacob Viner, Essays on the Intellectual History of Economics,* p. 262.

explained as the distinction between self-interest and selfishness as well as the observation and administration of justice in the sense of avoiding harm to others.

III. THE ECONOMICS AND ETHICS OF PROFIT

Although Friedman was awarded the Nobel Prize for his work on economic stabilization policy and monetary history, his most influential and controversial writings concern the philosophical subjects of freedom, corporate responsibility, and the role of government in society.[6] Here we focus on his thesis that the only social responsibility of corporations is to maximize profit. To understand Friedman's thesis, one must study carefully his philosophy of economic activity, particularly his books *Capitalism and Freedom* (CF) and *Free to Choose* (FC), and his article "The Social Responsibility of Business is to Increase its Profits" (SRB).[7]

One of Friedman's principal objectives in these writings is to delineate the proper roles of government and individual responsibility in society. Specifically, he seeks to demonstrate what he calls the "fecundity of freedom" (FC, p. 3)—that is, the overriding significance of individual freedom in both the political and economic realms. Friedman takes the "freedom of the individual, or perhaps the family, as [the] ultimate goal in judging social arrangements" (CF, p. 12). For him, freedom is the fundamental criterion by which one should judge individual actions. Thus, social processes that increase individual freedom should be encouraged while those that are restrictive or coercive should be avoided.

Because Friedman values individual freedom so highly, he strongly advocates market mechanisms characterized by voluntary exchanges between individuals. For this reason, he draws heavily on the philosophy and analysis of Adam Smith in the *Wealth of Nations*. According to Friedman:

> *Adam Smith's key insight was that both parties to an exchange can benefit and that,* so long as cooperation is strictly voluntary, *no exchange will take place unless both parties do benefit. No external force, no coercion, no violation of freedom is necessary to produce cooperation among individuals all of whom can benefit.* (FC, pp. 1–2; emphasis in original)

Indeed, Friedman's thesis that corporations should maximize profit is derived from Smith's account of the benefits to society of individuals and corporations freely trading in the marketplace. In fact, Friedman advances a number of teleological arguments in support of his thesis. For instance, one advantage to a society characterized by economic freedom (i.e., voluntary exchange) in the pursuit of profit is that it "provides an offset to whatever concentration of political power may arise" (FC, p. 3). According to Friedman, competitive, profit-driven capitalism is a means of ensuring that political freedom endures. Another

---

[6]It is remarkable that Milton Friedman won the Nobel Prize in Economics in 1976, the bicentennial anniversary of the signing of the Declaration of Independence in the United States as well as the publication of Smith's *Wealth of Nations.*

[7]Milton Friedman's books are *Capitalism and Freedom* (Chicago: University of Chicago Press, 1962) (republished in 1982), and *Free to Choose: A Personal Statement* (New York: Harcourt, Brace, and Jovanovich, 1980), published with his wife, Rose Friedman. The article is "The Social Responsibility of Business is to Increase its Profits," *New York Times Magazine,* September 13, 1970, pp. 32–33, 122–26.

benefit is economic prosperity, not just to society but also to groups that otherwise are disadvantaged due to racial or other prejudices. In this regard, Friedman states that it is a

> *striking historical fact that the development of capitalism has been accompanied by a major reduction in the extent to which particular religious, racial, or social groups have operated under special handicaps in respect of their economic activities; have, as the saying goes, been discriminated against. . . . [A] free market separates economic efficiency from irrelevant characteristics. . . . [T]he purchaser of bread does not know whether it was made from wheat grown by a white man or a Negro, by a Christian or a Jew. In consequence, the producer of wheat is in a position to use resources as effectively as he can, regardless of what the attitudes of the community may be toward the color, the religion, or other characteristics of the people he hires.* (CF, pp. 108, 109)

When individuals and corporations maximize profits, resources are used most effectively because the pursuit of profit requires the minimization of all (social) costs of engaging in economic activity. The social cost of producing, say A, is the forgone benefit to society of the next best alternative, say B, that the same amount of resources could produce. Firms, in attempting to maximize profit while producing A, end up minimizing what society has to sacrifice (i.e., B), an important benefit to a society faced with limited resources. The concept and the process here are akin to Smith's invisible hand. By maximizing profits (i.e., pursuing self-interest) business owners and managers minimize the social cost without knowing or intending it.

Furthermore, Friedman argues that corporate executives who pursue any goal other than profit maximization, such as advancing social causes, may not know what constitutes society's best interest, and they may do it at the expense of some other people. "Can self-selected private individuals decide what the social interest is? Can they decide how great a burden they are justified in placing on themselves or their stockholders to serve that social interest?" (CF, pp. 133–34). Hence, Friedman is skeptical of the *net* social benefits of business executives trying to act in the social (rather than corporate) interest. As an illustration, Friedman observes that "during the 1930s, German businessmen used some corporate money to support Hitler and the Nazis. Was that a proper exercise of social responsibility?"[8]

Friedman also advances deontological arguments in support of his thesis. For example, he asserts that corporate executives who pursue any goal other than profit maximization (and thus necessarily reduce profit) violate their specific responsibilities and duties. He states:

> *In a free-enterprise, private-property system, a corporate executive is an employee of the owners of the business. He has a direct responsibility to his employers. That responsibility is to conduct the business in accordance with their desires, which generally will be to make as much money as possible.* (SRB, p. 33)

A corporate executive who forgoes maximum profit by spending corporate money on social causes is "imposing taxes" on the stockholders and is "deciding how the tax proceeds shall be spent" (SRB, pp. 33, 122). When this occurs, Friedman reasons, the executive

---

[8]Milton Friedman, "Milton Friedman Responds: A Business and Society Review Interview," *Business and Society Review* 1, 1972, p. 6.

ceases to be an employee of a private enterprise and instead becomes a "self-selected" public employee or civil servant (SRB, p. 122), who seeks "to attain by undemocratic procedures what [he] cannot attain by democratic procedures" (SRB, p. 124). Moreover, even if the actions can be justified as serving the corporate interest because they promote the company's product, Friedman rejects such actions as "hypocritical window-dressing" and considers them to be "approaching fraud" (SRB, 124).

Although business executives and managers have an obligation to the corporation, in SRB Friedman clearly states that the pursuit of profit must be constrained by both legal and ethical considerations. Business executives should maximize profits "while conforming to the basic rules of the society, both those embodied in law and those embodied in ethical custom" (SRB, p. 33). For example, Friedman believes that the pursuit of profit should *not* be interpreted narrowly to mean that one might do *whatever* action will result in greater economic returns (even if it is technically legal). In this respect Friedman is consistent with Smith's view that there is a distinction between self-interest and selfishness. According to Friedman, there is a

> *broad meaning that must be attached to the concept of "self-interest." Narrow preoccupation with the economic market has led to a narrow interpretation of self-interest as myopic selfishness, as exclusive concern with immediate material rewards. Economics has been berated for allegedly drawing far-reaching conclusions from a wholly unrealistic "economic man" who is little more than a calculating machine, responding only to monetary stimuli. That is a great mistake.* Self-interest is not myopic selfishness. *It is whatever it is that interests the participants, whatever they value, whatever goals they pursue.* (FC, p. 27, emphasis added)

Furthermore, individuals have a profound obligation "to wrestle with" the ethical implications of the choices they make, as expressed in this passage by Friedman:

> *[In] a society freedom has nothing to say about what an individual does with his freedom; it is not an all-embracing ethic. Indeed, a major aim . . . is to leave the ethical problem for the individual to wrestle with. The "really" important ethical problems are those that face an individual in a free society—what he should do with his freedom. There are thus two sets of values . . . the values that are relevant to relations among people, which is the context in which he assigns first priority to freedom; and the values that are relevant to the individual in the exercise of his freedom, which is the realm of individual ethics and philosophy.* (CF, p. 12)

In addition to these ethical considerations, Friedman places two other important restrictions on the pursuit of profit: Business people must commit no deception or fraud, and they must maintain open and free competition (see CF, p. 133).[9] These restrictions mean that individuals are free to pursue their interests (such as making a profit) as long as they do not interfere with the economic (and political) freedom of others. Such interference occurs when individuals in business, for instance, breach contracts, cheat customers, misrepresent the efficacy of their products, withhold important information on product safety, sabotage a competitor's operations, or monopolize markets by political means, such as lobbying the government for protection against imports.

---

[9]Friedman repeats these two restrictions at the end of his SRB article.

For an illustration of Friedman's thesis, consider the following example. Suppose a company president learns that the firm's manufacturing operations, and those of competitors, discharge a harmful pollutant, and suppose the pollutant is not subject to the country's environmental regulations (i.e., continuing to pollute is not illegal). Should the company president conceal that information and continue manufacturing the product? Certainly, keeping the knowledge secret would increase company profits, at least in the short run. But, Friedman would argue the company president ought to inform the public and accept the consequences of the environmental problem because failing to do so would be tantamount to deception. And, if the pollutant causes harm to others, then it violates the important principle of freedom because others are involuntarily affected by the action of the company president. That is, costs, or "negative externalities," are imposed on others.

Friedman recognizes that "[a]lmost everything we do has some third-party [negative] effects, however small and however remote" (FC, p. 31). Hence, he distinguishes between two types of harms: Harm as a consequence of decisions individuals make when they freely enter into risky transactions, and harm caused by such "external" effects as deception and illegal and unethical actions. Friedman accepts harm of the first type as a necessary by-product of a free society; but he maintains that individuals, in pursuit of profits (or any other reward from one's activities), should not cause harm of the second type. The pursuit of profit ought to be constrained—not by the desire to exercise social responsibility (i.e., to do good), but rather by respect for the rights of others to enter into mutually profitable transactions. The principal constraints Friedman advocates, which Michael Novak describes as "no small moral agenda,"[10] are that executives should obey the law, observe society's ethical customs, commit no deception and fraud, and maintain an open and competitive environment.

VI. APPLICATIONS

Cases in business ethics can be analyzed by applying the criteria that Smith and Friedman have proposed and we reviewed above. Here we analyze two well-known cases.[11] The first case involves the selling of fire-retardant but cancer-causing children pajamas in the third world countries. In the mid-1970s, millions of pairs of children pajamas containing a new flame-retardant chemical were manufactured and sold in the U.S. Then, in 1977, the Consumer Product Safety Commission banned the sale of the pajamas in the U.S. because the fire-retardant fabric had been linked to kidney cancer in children. Prohibited from selling in the U.S. the pajamas already produced, manufacturers sold millions of pairs to exporters, who resold them in Third World countries where the sale of the product had not been banned.

Should the manufacturers sell the pajamas to exporters in order to minimize their losses (or even turn a profit), knowing they are banned in the U.S. for health reasons? Should the exporters market the pajamas in the Third World? A superficial reading of Smith and Friedman might suggest that they would condone the marketing of the pajamas in the Third World countries because they believe in the pursuit of self-interest and profit. However, as

---

[10]Michael Novak, *Business as a Calling* (New York: Free Press, 1996), p. 141.

[11]The source of both cases is William Shaw and Vincent Barry, *Moral Issues in Business* (Belmont, CA: Wadsworth, 1998), pp. 25–27, 211–13.

we saw in the analysis of the Smithian system, the manufacturers and exporters must carefully distinguish between self-interest and selfishness. That is, they must ask if they are causing harm to others for personal gain. If the manufacturers and exporters acted selfishly and unjustly, Smith would condemn the action as unethical.

Friedman would state that the manufacturers and exporters are free to take actions that minimize losses or that produce profits for the firms so long as the actions are legal, do not involve deception or fraud, and do not interfere with the competitive processes of the market. According to Friedman's moral constraints on profit maximization, the manufacturers must ensure that the exporters and potential customers are fully informed of the possible carcinogenic effects of the pajamas. If the producers (and exporters) failed to inform the Third World countries that the product had been banned in the U.S., Friedman would denounce the sale as unethical.

The second case involves the action of Raybestos-Manhattan and Johns-Manville towards their employees who were infected with asbestosis, a lung disease. During the early 1930s, executives at the two companies became aware of the hazards their employees faced from inhaling asbestos dust. Here we may ask: Should the companies inform their workers of the health-related effects of inhaling asbestos dust, even though workers who contracted the disease were still able to work? Dr. K. Smith, the medical director of a Johns-Manville facility, testified that "as long as the man is not disabled, it is felt that he should not be told of his condition so that he can live and work in peace and the Company can benefit by his many years of experience."[12] Of course, the companies may find it in their own interest (i.e., profit maximizing) to keep their workers in the dark. In fact, Dr. Smith explained, "the corporation is in business to make products, to provide jobs for people and to make money for stockholders . . . and if the application of a caution label identifying a product as hazardous would cut out sales, there would be serious financial implications." However, it should be quite clear that both Smith and Friedman would argue that the companies acted unethically because they allowed harm to come upon their employees. Furthermore, Friedman would stress that the companies have an ethical obligation to disclose the information to their workers and to the public, since to do otherwise would constitute deception.

---

[12]Shaw and Barry, p. 212.

DODGE V. FORD MOTOR CO.

HON. J. OSTRANDER

Henry Ford believed that there should be a Ford in every garage; in other words, that Ford cars should be made for and be affordable by everyone. At the time of this case, that meant a reduction in the price of a Ford automobile from $440 to $360 and a refusal to pay stock dividends. John and Horace Dodge were shareholders in Ford's company and believed that Ford's primary responsibility was to make a profit for his shareholders. Dodge sued (and eventually opened his own firm producing Dodge automobiles!). Do you agree with the majority or with the concurrence (or with neither)?

. . . The plan, as affecting the profits of the business for the year beginning August 1, 1916, and thereafter, calls for a reduction in the selling price of the cars. It is true that this price might be at any time increased, but the plan called for the reduction in price of $80 a car. The capacity of the plant, without the additions thereto voted to be made (without a part of them at least), would produce more than 600,000 cars annually. This number, and more, could have been sold for $440 instead of $360, a difference in the return for capital, labor and materials employed of at least $48,000,000. In short, the plan does not call for and is not intended to produce immediately a more profitable business but a less profitable one; not only less profitable than formerly but less profitable than it is admitted it might be made. The apparent immediate effect will be to diminish the value of shares and the returns to shareholders.

It is the contention of plaintiffs that the apparent effect of the plan is intended to be the continued and continuing effect of it and that it is deliberately proposed, not of record and not by official corporate declaration, but nevertheless proposed, to continue the corporation henceforth as a semi-eleemosynary institution and not as a business institution. In support of this contention they point to the attitude and to the expressions of Mr. Henry Ford.

Mr. Henry Ford is the dominant force in the business of the Ford Motor Company. No plan of operations could be adopted unless he consented, and no board of directors can be elected whom he does not favor. One of the directors of the company has no stock. One share was assigned to him to qualify him for the position, but it is not claimed that he owns it. A business, one of the largest in the world, and one of the most profitable, has been built up. It employs many men, at good pay.

"My ambition," said Mr. Ford, "is to employ still more men, to spread the benefits of this industrial system to the greatest possible number, to help them build up their lives and their homes. To do this we are putting the greatest share of our profits back in the business."

Dodge v. Ford Motor Co., 204 Mich. 459; 170 N.W. 668 (1919), excerpt.

"With regard to dividends, the company paid sixty per cent on its capitalization of two million dollars, or $1,200,000, leaving $58,000,000 to reinvest for the growth of the company. This is Mr. Ford's policy at present, and it is understood that the other stockholders cheerfully accede to this plan."

He had made up his mind in the summer of 1916 that no dividends other than the regular dividends should be paid, "for the present."

QUESTION: For how long? Had you fixed in your mind any time in the future, when you were going to pay—

ANSWER: No.

QUESTION: That was indefinite in the future?

ANSWER: That was indefinite, yes, sir.

The record, and especially the testimony of Mr. Ford, convinces that he has to some extent the attitude towards shareholders of one who has dispensed and distributed to them large gains and that they should be content to take what he chooses to give. His testimony creates the impression, also, that he thinks the Ford Motor Company has made too much money, has had too large profits, and that although large profits might be still earned, a sharing of them with the public, by reducing the price of the output of the company, ought to be undertaken. We have no doubt that certain sentiments, philanthropic and altruistic, creditable to Mr. Ford, had large influence in determining the policy to be pursued by the Ford Motor Company—the policy which has been herein referred to.

It is said by his counsel that—

"Although a manufacturing corporation cannot engage in humanitarian works as its principal business, the fact that it is organized for profit does not prevent the existence of implied powers to carry on with humanitarian motives such charitable works as are incidental to the main business of the corporation."

And again:

"As the expenditures complained of are being made in an expansion of the business which the company is organized to carry on, and for purposes within the powers of the corporation as hereinbefore shown, the question is as to whether such expenditures are rendered illegal because influenced to some extent by humanitarian motives and purposes on the part of the members of the board of directors."

In discussing this proposition, counsel have referred to decisions such as Hawes v. Oakland . . .; Taunton v. Royal Ins. Co. . . .; Henderson v. Bank of Australasia . . .; Steinway v. Steinway & Sons . . .; People, ex rel. Metropolitan Life Ins. Co., v. Hotchkiss. . . . These cases, after all, like all others in which the subject is treated, turn finally upon the point, the question, whether it appears that the directors were not acting for the best interests of the corporation. We do not draw in question, nor do counsel for the plaintiffs do so, the validity of the general propositions stated by counsel nor the soundness of the opinions delivered in the cases cited. The case presented here is not like any of them. The difference between an incidental humanitarian expenditure of corporate funds for the benefit of the employees, like the building of a hospital for their use and the employment of agencies for the betterment of their condition, and a general purpose and plan to benefit mankind at the expense of others, is obvious. There should be no confusion (of which there is evidence) of the duties which Mr. Ford conceives that he and the stockholders owe to the general public and the duties which in law he and his codirectors owe to protesting, minority stockholders. A business corporation is organized and carried on primarily for the profit of the stockholders. The powers of the directors are to be employed for that end. The discretion of directors is to be exercised in the choice of means to attain that end and does not extend to a change in the end itself, to the reduction of profits or to the nondistribution of profits among stockholders in order to devote them to other purposes.

There is committed to the discretion of directors, a discretion to be exercised in good faith, the infinite details of business, including the wages which shall be paid to employees, the number of hours they shall work, the conditions under which labor shall be carried on, and the prices for which products shall be offered to the public. It is said by appellants that the motives of the board members are not material and will not be inquired into by the court so long as their acts are within their lawful powers. As we have pointed out, and the proposition does not require argument to sustain it, it is not within the lawful powers of a board of directors to shape and conduct the affairs of a corporation for the merely incidental benefit of shareholders and for the primary purpose of benefiting others, and no one will contend that if the avowed purpose of the defendant directors was to sacrifice the interests of shareholders it would not be the duty of the courts to interfere.

We are not, however, persuaded that we should interfere with the proposed expansion of the business of the Ford Motor Company. In view of the fact that the selling price of products may be increased at any time, the ultimate results of the larger business cannot be certainly estimated. The judges are not business experts. It is recognized that plans must often be made for a long future, for expected competition, for a continuing as well as an immediately profitable venture. The experience of the Ford Motor Company is evidence of capable management of its affairs. It may be noticed, incidentally, that it took from the public the money required for the execution of its plan and that the very considerable salaries paid to Mr. Ford and to certain executive officers and employees were not diminished. We are not satisfied that the alleged motives of the directors, in so far as they are reflected in the conduct of the business, menace the interests of shareholders. It is enough to say, perhaps, that the court of equity is at all times open to complaining shareholders having a just grievance. . . .

The decree of the court below fixing and determining the specific amount to be distributed to stockholders is affirmed. In other respects, except as to the allowance of costs, the said decree is reversed. Plaintiffs will recover interest at five per cent per annum upon their proportional share of said dividend from the date of the decree of the lower court. Appellants will tax the costs of their appeal, the two-thirds of the amount thereof will be paid by plaintiffs. No other costs are allowed.

STEERE, FELLOWS, BROOKE, and STONE, J. J., concurred with OSTRANDER, J.

CONCUR: MOORE, J. (concurring). I agree with what is said by Justice OSTRANDER upon the subject of capitalization. I agree with what he says as to the smelting enterprise on the River Rouge. I do not agree with all that is said by him in his discussion of the question of dividends. I do agree with him in his conclusion that the accumulation of so large a surplus establishes the fact that there has been an arbitrary refusal to distribute funds that ought to have been distributed to the stockholders as dividends. I therefore agree with the conclusion reached by him upon that phase of the case.

BIRD, C. J., and KUHN, J., concurred with MOORE, J.

HOW BUSINESS CAN BE GOOD (AND WHY BEING GOOD IS GOOD FOR BUSINESS)

JEFFREY L. SEGLIN

Scholar and Columnist Seglin comments on the interesting lack of moral outrage at the excesses of the 90s versus the excesses of the 80s and its "decade of greed." Perhaps, he suggests, the acceptance and support of our young entrepreneurs in the 90s and today reflect an actual change of direction in the moral compasses of those wealthy few, rather than a change in society's perceptions. Is "ethics" the difference?

In a recent front-page article in *The Wall Street Journal,* Jacob Schlesinger wondered: "Why have the '90s so far eluded the 'Decade of Greed' label that hung over the '80s?" The news was certainly full of stories of young millionaires bursting forth in record numbers due to the boom in technology stock prices. And you couldn't turn a page without seeing any number of CEO compensation packages tip in at millions of dollars in salaries and perks.

There were no cries of moral outrage, Schlesinger suggests, because in this new economy everybody's income is rising. Not only those at the top are sharing in the spoils of business, whether in the form of better returns on a 401(k) plan invested in aggressive mutual funds, or just more cash in each paycheck. But the point that people are missing, he wrote, is that even when almost everyone's income is rising, a "growing disparity in affluence can hurt the less-well off." If a middle class family in San Francisco earns 33% more than the national average because young Silicon Valley millionaires have bid up the prices of homes, it's only a matter of time before someone cries foul.

I was taken aback not so much by the article's sentiment as by its source. Here was *The Wall Street Journal*—the archconservative voice of capitalism—drawing attention to the problems endemic to outrageous income disparities at a time when that particular cause hadn't the news cachet it held during the greed-drenched '80s.

"Business ethics," a topic that for years has been relegated to the deep interior of business publications or the fringes of business school curriculum, suddenly has status. Where the word "ethics" might once have been anathema to any corporate devotee, discussion of it is increasingly seen as not only important but also as critical to a company's success.

A SHIFT IN THINKING

The standard argument made among business people used to be that a business's responsibility was first and foremost to its shareholders. Economists Milton Friedman and Alfred Carr were chief among those propagating that once-prevailing wisdom.

In a 1970 *New York Times Magazine* article, Friedman wrote his now well-known argument that a business's social responsibility is to its stockholders; therefore, the main objective is to increase profits. In 1967, Carr argued that business is a game in which there are certain rules. He held that a person would set aside personal ethics and values in order to meet the needs of the corporation.

However, proponents of "virtue ethics" believe that it's wrong-headed to think that we can, or ever could, park our personal beliefs at the door when we enter the corporate world. John Morse, in the *Journal of Applied Philosophy,* observed that "the virtue theorist insists that any ethical decision we make is based on a set of dispositions we have acquired throughout our life. When someone acts unethically in a business transaction, this is bound to break down the good character habit that he or she has developed up to this point. The virtue theorist denies that there is an ability to separate the 'business' self from the 'private' self, because the actions in each realm form dispositions which apply to a person's general manner of acting."

Morse concludes that "Friedman and Carr are wrong, for they try to separate the moral ramifications of actions within a business environment from their effects on the individuals with whom business comes into contact. Business has to be seen as a moral entity which is an integral part of the community, and it must therefore be concerned about the welfare of the community within which it is situated, as well as the welfare of the individuals whom it influences."

WHAT'S ETHICAL BEHAVIOR?

Johnson & Johnson is often heralded as a company whose ethical behavior is exemplary. Looking at how this company's core beliefs affects the way it handles critical ethical decisions can help demonstrate how a clear commitment to ethical behavior in business can define how a business operates, both inside and outside its walls.

The company clearly prioritizes its responsibilities in its corporate credo: first to its customers, second to its employees, third to its management, fourth to the communities in which it operates, and fifth to its stockholders. "Business must make a sound profit," reads the credo in describing this fifth responsibility, but at Johnson & Johnson that concern comes after the rest.

In 1982 the company decided to recall 31 million bottles of Tylenol from store shelves after eight people died from cyanide-laced capsules. That recall cost Johnson & Johnson $240 million and cut its profit on $5 billion in revenues that year by almost 50 percent. The tampering was not the company's fault, but it decided to act even before it had complete information on what had happened. The product containers were redesigned and new tamper-proof packaging was introduced. Johnson & Johnson's immediate response saved the Tylenol brand and won the company rave reviews. Ironically, the move turned out to be a huge marketing coup that resulted in significant goodwill from customers.

When a class of business students was asked to comment on the ethics of the case, more than one student responded by saying that the case wasn't an example of ethical decision-making at all: The company benefited from the whole affair. Since it turned out to be a great marketing move, where was the ethical problem?

What the students failed to recognize was that we all make ethical decisions on a daily basis. Sometimes it's as simple as deciding whether or not to credit a coworker with an idea of hers that you bring up in a meeting. Other times it may be deciding just how much information you disclose to colleagues about an office rumor making the rounds.

The results of such decisions rarely have the magnitude of a Tylenol case, but they are ethical decisions nonetheless. Based on what you know of the acceptable behavior of the group you belong to, you're trying to decide on the right thing to do.

Ethics. The word "ethics" derives from the Greek term ethos; one of the modern definitions of ethos is "accustomed place." In the New Testament, ethos was used in the more or less classic sense of a "home place"—the place of safety, where humans and animals alike could gather at the end of the day and be protected. By extension, it came to be used as a description of the norms of behavior that provided a comparable protection to the coherence of a society.

So ethical decisions can be said to be decisions that ensure the safety of a society's sense of order and justice. But trying to determine what falls into that sense of order and justice can be difficult. The range between right and wrong can be vast. We generally recognize—or at least we hope we do—when we're operating at the margins. We can tell when we're going well beyond what's expected in the way of right behavior. And we also know when something falls squarely into the category of questionable or wrong behavior.

What we struggle with every day is operating between the extremes. How completely right do we really need to be in our behavior?

In business, the pressures are magnified, because business owners and managers are faced with competing demands to keep a company going. Does the need to make a profit outweigh the need to reward our employees fairly? Does making payroll count more than paying vendors? Do we cut corners on manufacturing processes to keep costs down when our shortcuts might result in unsafe or polluting outcomes? Does our commitment to an employee in trouble outweigh the financial burden he places on the company?

A story told by the CEO of a $14 million computer consulting company points out how grueling and complex such decisions can be. A high-level employee failed to show up at a client's location one morning for a software installation. The employee was an alcoholic who apparently had had a relapse. In the end it cost his company half of its $200,000 fee.

The CEO received conflicting recommendations about whether to fire the employee. Some suggested giving the employee another chance and enrolling him in a rehabilitation program. Others said the only way the employee would get help would be if he were allowed to hit rock bottom. After much agonizing, the CEO decided to offer the rehabilitation program.

Everything seemed fine for about eight months after the employee finished the program. Then he failed to show up for work again. This time he cost the company about $5,000. Again, the CEO had to decide what to do. Advice he received skewed toward letting the employee go, but—after some agonizing—the CEO decided to help him again.

While the CEO may have been prolonging the alcoholic's resistance to getting sober, his decision brings to life how good people in business try to do good by the people in their world, in this case a troubled employee. "Business is easy compared to life," the CEO said when retelling the story. "We're just laymen with good hearts and crossed fingers."

Invariably people who run or manage businesses find themselves facing decisions that will clearly affect their employees' lives. Navigating through these relentless dilemmas is a day-to-day, moment-to-moment process.

FIRST, THE LAWYERS

When we talk about ethical behavior in business, too frequently we're really talking about the kind of behavior people need to avoid litigation. We put behavior policies in place so we don't get sued for sexual harassment, penalizing minority workers, or slandering poor-performing employees.

With workplace litigation exploding over the past several years—more than 24,000 wrongful termination suits were filed in 1997 alone, up from 10,000 in 1990—the actions of business people too often are driven by what will keep a cap on legal costs rather than by what we really believe is right.

When this happens, we relegate many ethical decisions to the human resources or legal departments and stop thinking about it for ourselves.

The fear of discrimination suits may be legitimate. A 1997 survey by the Society for Human Resource Management found that of 616 personnel executives who responded, 53 percent said their organizations had been sued at least once by former employees in the last five years; nearly half the 611 suits they reported involved claims of discrimination.

Fears of litigation make even the most self-enlightened manager question his or her own judgment about employees, how to manage them, and how to be fair in the workplace. The solution is to go back to making decisions based on the merit of a candidate rather than the fear of what might happen should this candidate not work out or not like the way we manage. It may seem perilous to take such a stand, but it's the only way to break free of the management gridlock that has overtaken so many businesses.

FINDING A PLACE

The deeper challenge is not merely to get businesses or corporations to change, but to get the people who are making decisions within these organizations to change the way they think—to realize that the same care they take to behave ethically in their personal lives should drive the decisions they make in their professional lives. One of the good things about the blurring lines between our personal and professional lives is that it makes who we are and how we behave seem more connected to our beliefs and the way we interact with other people and the community at large—whether we're at work or not.

The whole concept of "business ethics" is brought more sharply into focus when we recognize that such a notion is inextricably tied to the individuals who make up that business. It is ridiculous to think that we can fob off onto others ethical decisions that must be made without having to take responsibility for our own inaction.

"Ethics is how we behave when we decide we belong together," writes Margaret Wheatley and Myron Kellner-Rogers in their book, *A Simpler Way.* "Daily we see this interplay of ethics and belonging in our own lives. We want to be part of an organization. We observe what is accepted or rewarded and we adapt. But these ethics are not always good. We may agree to behaviors that go against personal or societal values. Months or years later, we dislike the person we have become. Did we sacrifice some essential aspect of ourselves in order to stay with an organization? What was the price of belonging?"

At the end of the day, that's the true question: In our effort to belong, have we become the people we swore we never wanted to be?

A HANGING

George Orwell

Do we feel a responsibility for that which occurs in front of us, though not as a result of us? This story discusses the response to that question. Does it matter more to you that something happens to someone you know, rather than to a complete stranger? Or that the person impacted by an event will know if it was your responsibility, rather than some stranger's? In "The Hanging," do you wonder about the nature of the prisoner's offense? Should it matter or do you take the state's decision as to his guilt as sufficient justification? If you were called to serve on a jury and, prior to hearing the case or the nature of the alleged offense, were asked if you would be willing to impose the death penalty under certain circumstances, what would be your response?

"The Hanging" is relevant to our ethics inquiry for its perspective on accountability. If you disagree with an event, how far will you go (if at all) to stop that event from occurring?

It was in Burma, a sodden morning of the rains. A sickly light, like yellow tinfoil, was slanting over the high walls into the jail yard. We were waiting outside the condemned cells, a row of sheds fronted with double bars, like small animal cages. Each cell measured about ten feet by ten and was quite bare within except for a plank bed and a pot of drinking water. In some of them brown silent men were squatting at the inner bars, with their blankets draped round them. These were the condemned men, due to be hanged within the next week or two.

One prisoner had been brought out of his cell. He was a Hindu, a puny wisp of a man, with a shaven head and vague liquid eyes. He had a thick, sprouting moustache, absurdly too big for his body, rather like the moustache of a comic man on the films. Six tall Indian warders were guarding him and getting him ready for the gallows. Two of them stood by with rifles and fixed bayonets, while the others handcuffed him, passed a chain through his handcuffs and fixed it to their belts, and lashed his arms tight to his sides. They crowded very close about him, with their hands always on him in a careful, caressing grip, as though all the while feeling him to make sure he was there. It was like men handling a fish which is still alive and may jump back into the water. But he stood quite unresisting, yielding his arms limply to the ropes, as though he hardly noticed what was happening.

Eight o'clock struck and a bugle call, desolately thin in the wet air, floated from the distant barracks. The superintendent of the jail, who was standing apart from the rest of us, moodily prodding the gravel with his stick, raised his head at the sound. He was an army doctor, with a grey toothbrush moustache and a gruff voice. "For God's sake hurry up, Francis," he said irritably. "The man ought to have been dead by this time. Aren't you ready yet?"

Francis, the head jailer, a fat Dravidian in a white drill suit and gold spectacles, waved his black hand. "Yes sir, yes sir," he bubbled. "All iss satisfactorily prepared. The hangman iss waiting. We shall proceed."

"Well, quick march, then. The prisoners can't get their breakfast till this job's over."

We set out for the gallows. Two warders marched on either side of the prisoner, with their rifles at the slope; two others marched close against him, gripping him by arm and shoulder, as though at once pushing and supporting him. The rest of us, magistrates and the like, followed behind. Suddenly, when we had gone ten yards, the procession stopped short without any order or warning. A dreadful thing had happened—a dog, come goodness knows whence, had appeared in the yard. It came bounding among us with a loud volley of barks, and leapt round us wagging its whole body, wild with glee at finding so many human beings together. It was a large woolly dog, half Airedale, half pariah. For a moment it pranced round us, and then, before anyone could stop it, it had made a dash for the prisoner, and jumping up tried to lick his face. Everyone stood aghast, too taken aback even to grab at the dog.

"Who let that bloody brute in here?" said the superintendent angrily. "Catch it, someone!"

A warder, detached from the escort, charged clumsily after the dog, but it danced and gambolled just out of his reach, taking everything as part of the game. A young Eurasian jailer picked up a handful of gravel and tried to stone the dog away, but it dodged the stones and came after us again. Its yaps echoed from the jail walls. The prisoner, in the grasp of the two warders, looked on incuriously, as though this was another formality of the hanging. It was several minutes before someone managed to catch the dog. Then we put my handkerchief through its collar and moved off once more, with the dog still straining and whimpering.

It was about forty yards to the gallows. I watched the bare brown back of the prisoner marching in front of me. He walked clumsily with his bound arms, but quite steadily, with that bobbing gait of the Indian who never straightens his knees. At each step his muscles slid neatly into place, the lock of hair on his scalp danced up and down, his feet printed themselves on the wet gravel. And once, in spite of the men who gripped him by each shoulder, he stepped slightly aside to avoid a puddle on the path.

It is curious, but till that moment I had never realized what it means to destroy a healthy, conscious man. When I saw the prisoner step aside to avoid the puddle, I saw the mystery, the unspeakable wrongness, of cutting a life short when it is in full tide. This man was not dying, he was alive just as we were alive. All the organs of his body were working—bowels digesting food, skin renewing itself, nails growing, tissues forming—all toiling away in solemn foolery. His nails would still be growing when he stood on the drop, when he was falling through the air with a tenth of a second to live. His eyes saw the yellow gravel and the grey walls, and his brain still remembered, foresaw, reasoned—reasoned even about puddles. He and we were a party of men walking together, seeing, hearing, feeling, understanding the same world; and in two minutes, with a sudden snap, one of us would be gone—one mind less, one world less.

The gallows stood in a small yard, separate from the main grounds of the prison, and overgrown with tall prickly weeds. It was a brick erection like three sides of a shed, with planking on top, and above that two beams and a crossbar with the rope dangling. The hangman, a grey-haired convict in the white uniform of the prison, was waiting beside his machine. He greeted us with a servile crouch as we entered. At a word from Francis the two warders, gripping the prisoner more closely than ever, half led, half pushed him to the gallows and helped him clumsily up the ladder. Then the hangman climbed up and fixed the rope round the prisoner's neck.

We stood waiting, five yards away. The warders had formed in a rough circle round the gallows. And then, when the noose was fixed, the prisoner began crying out to his god. It was a high, reiterated cry of "Ram! Ram! Ram! Ram!" not urgent and fearful like a prayer or a cry for help, but steady, rhythmical, almost like the tolling of a bell. The dog answered the sound with a whine. The hangman, still standing on the gallows, produced a small cotton bag like a flour bag and drew it down over the prisoner's face. But the sound, muffled by the cloth, still persisted, over and over again: "Ram! Ram! Ram! Ram! Ram!"

The hangman climbed down and stood ready, holding the lever. Minutes seemed to pass. The steady, muffled cry from the prisoner went on and on, "Ram! Ram! Ram!" never faltering for an instant. The superintendent, his head on his chest, was slowly poking the ground with his stick; perhaps he was counting the cries, allowing the prisoner a fixed number—fifty, perhaps, or a hundred. Everyone had changed color. The Indians had gone grey like bad coffee, and one or two of the bayonets were wavering. We looked at the lashed, hooded man on the drop, and listened to his cries—each cry another second of life; the same thought was in all our minds; oh, kill him quickly, get it over, stop that abominable noise!

Suddenly the superintendent made up his mind. Throwing up his head he made a swift motion with his stick. "Chalo!" he shouted almost fiercely.

There was a clanking noise, and then dead silence. The prisoner had vanished, and the rope was twisting on itself. I let go of the dog, and it galloped immediately to the back of the gallows; but when it got there it stopped short, barked, and then retreated into a corner of the yard, where it stood among the weeds, looking timorously out at us. We went round the gallows to inspect the prisoner's body. He was dangling with his toes pointed straight downwards, very slowly revolving, as dead as a stone.

The superintendent reached out with his stick and poked the bare body; it oscillated, slightly. "*He's* all right," said the superintendent. He backed out from under the gallows, and blew out a deep breath. The moody look had gone out of his face quite suddenly. He glanced at his wrist-watch. "Eight minutes past eight. Well, that's all for this morning, thank God."

The warders unfixed bayonets and marched away. The dog, sobered and conscious of having misbehaved itself, slipped after them. We walked out of the gallows yard, past the condemned cells with their waiting prisoners, into the big central yard of the prison. The convicts, under the command of warders armed with lathis, were already receiving their breakfast. They squatted in long rows, each man holding a tin pannikin, while two warders with buckets marched round ladling out rice; it seemed quite a homely, jolly scene, after the hanging. An enormous relief had come upon us now that the job was done. One felt an impulse to sing, to break into a run, to snigger. All at once everyone began chattering gaily.

The Eurasian boy walking beside me nodded towards the way we had come, with a knowing smile: "Do you know, sir, our friend (he meant the dead man), when he heard his appeal had been dismissed, he pissed on the floor of his cell. From fright.—Kindly take one of my cigarettes, sir. Do you not admire my new silver case, sir? From the boxwallah, two rupees eight annas. Classy European style."

Several people laughed—at what, nobody seemed certain.

Francis was walking by the superintendent, talking garrulously: "Well, sir, all hass passed off with the utmost satisfactoriness. It wass all finished—flick! like that. It iss not always so—oah, no! I have known cases where the doctor wass obliged to go beneath the gallows and pull the prisoner's legs to ensure decease. Most disagreeable!"

"Wriggling about, eh? That's bad," said the superintendent.

"Ach, sir, it iss worse when they become refractory! One man, I recall, clung to the bars of hiss cage when we went to take him out. You will scarcely credit, sir, that it took six warders to dislodge him, three pulling at each leg. We reasoned with him. 'My dear fellow,' we said, 'think of all the pain and trouble you are causing to us!' But no, he would not listen! Ach, he wass very troublesome!"

I found that I was laughing quite loudly. Everyone was laughing. Even the superintendent grinned in a tolerant way. "You'd better all come out and have a drink," he said quite genially. "I've got a bottle of whisky in the car. We could do with it."

We went through the big double gates of the prison, into the road. "Pulling at his legs!" exclaimed a Burmese magistrate suddenly, and burst into a loud chuckling. We all began laughing again. At that moment Francis's anecdote seemed extraordinarily funny. We all had a drink together, native and European alike, quite amicably. The dead man was a hundred yards away.

SURVEYS FIND MANY CONSUMERS HOLD COMPANIES RESPONSIBLE FOR THEIR ACTIONS

PRICEWATERHOUSECOOPERS
CHARLES FOMBRUN
THE REPUTATION INSTITUTE

In the first global survey of its kind, 40 percent of 22,000 consumers around the world reported that during the past year they have responded negatively to actions by a company perceived as not socially responsible. Half of this number, or one in five worldwide, reported avoiding a company's product or speaking out against it to others. These results are consistent with a U.S. survey sponsored by PricewaterhouseCoopers and The Reputation Institute, conducted online last month, which found that a surprising number of consumers said they act on their feelings about companies at the cash register. In fact, a quarter of the 10,830 Reputation Institute survey respondents said that during the past year they had boycotted a company's products or urged others to do so when they didn't agree with its policies and actions.

WE KNOW YOUR RQ. DO YOU?

Want to know what stakeholders really think of your company? Wish you could find out how they rate you compared with the competition?

The Harris-Fombrun Reputation Quotient[SM] (RQ) is designed to help identify the relative placement of your company's reputation among competitors in the marketplace. It also reveals the areas that might be weakening your position. Developed jointly by Harris Interactive and Professor Charles Fombrun of New York University's Stern School of Business and Executive Director of the Reputation Institute (*www.reputations.org*), RQ is a syndicated study that draws on Harris Interactive's global database of more than 6.2 million cooperative respondents.

WHAT DOES RQ MEASURE?

We know what drives your company's reputation, and who you have to please. The Reputation Quotient study uncovers what key stakeholder groups—the General Public, Customers, Corporate Employees, General Investors, and Consumer Boycotters—think about your company. It tells you how they feel about the six dimensions that are the key components of every company's reputation, as well as the *20 attributes* that make up those dimensions. The study can help you identify ways you can leverage this information to your reputation's advantage.

- Emotional Appeal: How much the company is liked, admired, and respected.

- Products & Services: Perceptions of the quality, innovation, value, and reliability of the company's products and services.

- Financial Performance: Perceptions of the company's competitiveness, profitability, growth prospects, and risk.

- Vision & Leadership: How much the company demonstrates a clear vision, strong leadership, and an ability to recognize and capitalize on market opportunities.

- Workplace Environment: Perceptions of how well the company is managed, what it's like to work there, and the quality of its employees.

- Social Responsibility: Perceptions of the company as having high standards in its dealings with people, good causes, and the environment.

Data from the RQ study are carefully weighted to ensure that the sample is representative of the specified population. The RQ can also be administered by telephone, by mail, or in person when online interviews are not possible.

THE 20 ATTRIBUTES OF REPUTATION

The Harris-Fombrun Reputation Quotient develops a company's rating among competitors based on 20 attributes comprising the six dimensions of reputation.

- **Emotional Appeal**
  Have a good feeling about the company.
  Admire and respect the company.
  Trust the company a great deal.

- **Products & Services**
  Stands behind its products and services.
  Develops innovative products and services.
  Offers high quality products and services.
  Offers products and services that are a good value for the money.

- **Financial Performance**
  Has a strong record of profitability.
  Looks like a low-risk investment.
  Looks like a company with strong prospects for future growth.
  Tends to outperform its competitors.

- **Vision & Leadership**
  Has excellent leadership.
  Has a clear vision for its future.
  Recognizes and takes advantage of market opportunities.

- **Workplace Environment**
  Is well-managed.
  Looks like a good company to work for.
  Looks like a company that would have good employees.

- **Social Responsibility**
  Supports good causes.
  Is an environmentally responsible company.
  Maintains high standards in the way it treats people.

PURPOSE OF THE STUDY

To identify the *companies* that a representative sample of Americans hold in highest regard, and to rate those companies based on the six dimensions of reputation using the Harris-Fombrun Reputation Quotient[SM] (RQ). *The Wall Street Journal* published these results on the front page of its Marketplace section on September 23, 1999.

HOW WAS THE STUDY CONDUCTED?

The study was carried out in two phases during July 1999 and August 1999. In Phase 1, Harris Interactive conducted online and telephone interviews with 4,500 respondents throughout the U.S. Respondents were asked to nominate the companies they believed to have the best and worst reputations. The nomination process utilized both open-ended questions (i.e., unprompted), as well as close-ended questions using a prompted list of 60 companies developed by an expert panel. In Phase 2, another 10,830 respondents provided detailed ratings of the 30 best-regarded companies and a control group of 10 other companies.

The 40 companies selected to be rated (i.e., the 30 RQ Gold companies and the Comparison 10) were based on the number of nominations received in Phase 1. It is important to note that a company did not have to have been included in the prompt list in Phase 1 (the Nomination Phase) in order to be included in Phase 2 (the RQ Rating Phase). In fact, 12 of the 30 companies that make up the RQ Gold had not appeared on the prompt list for the nomination phase.

Final results were weighted to be representative of the U.S. adult population. Weighting variables included both demographic and other, non-demographic variables.

RQ scores were then calculated for each company based on respondents' ratings (using 7-point scales) on the 20 individual attributes. Each company's RQ was calculated by summing the ratings on the 20 attributes as a percentage of the total possible score (i.e., 7 $\times$ 20). Each of the 40 rated companies was evaluated by an average of 445 respondents.

Each RQ rating has an "estimated sampling tolerance" of $+/-$ 1.5. In comparing any two RQ scores, a difference of 1.96 would be considered significantly different at the 90% confidence level.

THE 30 BEST-REGARDED COMPANIES IN AMERICA

1. Johnson & Johnson
2. Coca-Cola
3. Hewlett-Packard
4. Intel
5. Ben & Jerry's
6. Wal-Mart
7. Xerox
8. Home Depot
9. Gateway
10. Disney
11. Dell
12. General Electric
13. Lucent
14. Anheuser-Busch
15. Microsoft
16. Amazon.com
17. IBM
18. Sony
19. Yahoo!
20. AT&T
21. FedEx
22. Procter & Gamble
23. Nike
24. McDonald's
25. Southwest Airlines
26. AOL
27. Daimler-Chrysler
28. Toyota
29. Sears
30. Boeing

TRANSFORMATION AT SHELL

Commerce and Citizenship

Philip H. Mirvis

What follows illustrates how Shell sought a balance between interests and tried to integrate sometimes competing principles over what was to be a complex, energizing, and surely fractious five-year stretch. It shows how linking the themes of citizenship with commerce helped to awaken the need for and animate the Group's transformation in the first half of this period. Over the second half, in turn, these two themes would be more or less aligned to the point that Shell would measure and report on its social and environmental record alongside its financial performance, and engage the global public in a "two-way conversation" over profits and principles.

April 1995 Following a daring helicopter raid, environmental activists from Greenpeace occupied an oil storage platform of the Royal Dutch/Shell Group scheduled to be sunk in the seas of the North Atlantic. After fighting their way aboard through water cannons, the protesters threatened to chain themselves to the 40-story-tall Brent Spar unless Shell changed its plan to dump what they called a "toxic timebomb." Through a steady stream of faxed updates, televised interviews, and sensational videos issued from its floating press center, Greenpeace rallied public opinion around the world behind its cause. Sympathizers firebombed two gas stations in Germany and John Majors and Helmut Kohl, then leading respectively the governments of Britain and Germany, were in public conflict over what Shell should do. In response to the tumult, the oil giant issued a detailed accounting of the financial costs and environmental, health, and safety hazards that it said favored the deep-water disposal of the rig versus hauling it back to shore.

October 1995 At that same year's annual meeting of shareholders, underneath a giant banner scolding "MURDERERS," protestors demanded that Shell's leaders be held accountable for despoiling the Ogoni people's homeland in southeastern Nigeria and for provoking the government to arrest tribal leader Ken Saro-Wiwa. Following what many saw as a show trial, Saro-Wiwa was sentenced to death for involvement in ecoterrorism. Editorials throughout Europe and the U.S. joined in condemnation of the Nigerian government and Shell's complicity, as did NGOs all over the world. In this instance, the oil giant owned up

Excerpted from Philip Mirvis, "Transformation at Shell: Commerce *and* Citizenship," *Business & Society Review* 105, no. 1 (2000), pp. 63–84.

to environmental problems and worked behind the scenes on Saro-Wiwa's behalf with business and political figures in Africa and the West. However, citing its longstanding principle of "noninterference" in the politics of a host country, Shell did not participate in economic and political sanctions against Nigeria's rulers who proceeded with the execution.

September 1998   Glowing editorials and affirmations from formerly adversarial interests followed publication of Shell's report "Profit and Principles—does there have to be a choice?" The document rated the Group's performance against each of its business principles, which had been updated as a result of the Spar and Nigeria incidents to affirm support for human rights and sustainable development of natural resources. Its publication was a milestone in Shell's efforts to improve its social and environmental record through self-scrutiny, two-way dialogue with relevant stakeholders, and open disclosure of its performance in these regards. Widely praised for candor, humility, and evenhanded review of dilemmas facing the company, it marked Shell's turn over some three-and-a-half years from a comparative pariah to a leader in global corporate citizenship.

What is behind this dramatic shift in Shell's outlook? What accounts for the depth and breadth of its socially responsible turnaround? At first glance this might be cast as a *textbook* example of a corporation taking a crisis to heart, learning lessons, and then responding vigorously—with an eye to correcting wrongs, doing things right, and restoring public favor. But what this explanation misses is that Shell's advances in social and environmental performance were integrated with, and very much guided by, a more comprehensive effort aimed at changing business performance and the Group's culture. Indeed, what came to be the *transformation* of the Group was launched in mid-1994 by a commercial need when neither the Brent Spar nor Nigerian crises could be foreseen.

This paper describes phases of this transformation, beginning with its focus on business performance in 1994 through to its emphasis on sustainable development—encompassing both commerce *and* citizenship—as the millennium dawns (see Table 1). The idea of being a good corporate citizen, defined variously in terms of the proper role of business in society, as allegiance to high-minded principles, and as a set of responsible practices, takes on added dimensions when juxtaposed against commercial drivers. At once, this puts firms at the intersection of societal interests, commonly referred to as stakeholders, and stresses the need to balance these interests when making decisions and taking action. It also calls on the firms to integrate principles—economic, social, and environmental—when doing business, a notion that Shell embraced under the theme of sustainable development.

***

SHELL'S TRANSFORMATION

In my experience, it is rare for a company to take a *wholistic* approach to changing the ways it does business.[1] For instance, firms that face performance pressures typically focus on fixing their business portfolio, cost structure, market position, staff quality, and such well before attending to matters of citizenship—if they do so at all. In turn, crisis-driven changes, whether stimulated by operational, political, or environmental upsets, most often involve "fire fighting," engage only a few relevant work units, and seldom have any carryover once the fire is put out. At Shell, by contrast, simultaneous attention was to "hard" and "soft" aspects of performance and nearly every part of the enterprise would be touched by change.

TABLE 1

Shell Transformation, 1994–1999

	1994/1995	1996	1997	1998	1999
OUTSIDE IN		Customer Survey Employee Survey Expectations Study	Shell.com Tell Shell campaign		
MEASUREMENT & DISCLOSURE		Financials published; comparative data. Benchmarking	Healthy, Safety & Environment Report	Shell Report I	Shell Report II
PROGRAMS		Business Framework Implementation BFI (community service)	BFI cont. Core Purpose Workshops	BFI cont.	BFI cont.
VISION & STATEMENTS		FIRST CHOICE Strategic Business Framework	WORLD'S MOST ADMIRED CO. Revised General Bus. Principles	Social Investment	SUSTAINABLE DEVELOPMENT Profits vs. Principles Media Campaign Business Week cont. Renewables program
TRANSFORMATION ACTIVITIES	Corporate Review Transformation Top 50 Leadership Meetings I & II	Lines of Business To 50 Meet III Olympic Targets	WoMAC Study	Top 500 Meeting: Business Week	
EXTERNAL AFFAIRS		Brent Spar Website Spar Dialogues Nigerian Visit w/ Journalists	Spar proposals Nigeria Website	Spar recycled	
EXTERNAL EVENTS	Brent Spar Seizure Nigerian Protests	British Petroleum Transformation	Shareholder Petition Kyoto Standards		Oil Industry Mergers

275

To appreciate the magnitude of Shell's undertakings, it may help to distinguish between the very focused, programmatic, incremental change efforts underway in many organizations nowadays and the transformative type of change. Scholars typically do so based on the degree of discontinuity in the firm's environment, the breadth and depth of changes undertaken, and the predictability of change processes and results.[2] Shell's efforts started out in a rather circumscribed frame when, in early 1994, then the chairman of the firm's committee of managing directors (CMD), Cor Herkströter, launched a review of the corporate center's relationship to operating companies around the globe. A study of staff and structure, by McKinsey and Co., recommended that Shell form global lines of business. This restructuring would yield some cost savings and focus line management attention and accountability away from geographic regions and toward the business lines of exploration, refining and retail, chemicals, and coal and gas. It was uncertain, however, whether national operating companies would support these proposals (which reduced country CEOs' scope and responsibilities); and it was unclear what additional changes would be required to make this structure work. Thus Herkströter called Noel Tichy, a management professor from the University of Michigan, who had worked with CEO Jack Welch at General Electric, for advice and assistance.

Tichy assembled a consulting team of change agents and subject matter experts (including this author) to assist in change management. Our initial work with the CMD, beginning in spring 1995, concerned Shell's "case for change." Cor's prime goal was to improve significantly the financial results of the Group. With pressure mounting from the capital markets and the shareholder rights movement gaining momentum in Europe, the need to increase annual returns was acknowledged, somewhat grudgingly, by the rest of the CMD. What were the opportunities and threats? A close look at market trends and growth rates revealed that hypercompetition from supermarkets and convenience stores (already significant in the US) was spreading through Europe and into Asia. In addition, traditional competitors and new entrants were seizing profitable portions of the exploration-production-consumption value chain.[3] These developments in the firm's competitive and investment environment threatened to make Shell's business model obsolete. To progress, Shell would need to revamp its retail strategy, redo non-fuel offerings, and reconsider its role in coal, natural gas, and power generation. Then came the occupation of and outcry over the Brent Spar and upheaval in Nigeria.

One stimulant to transformation is discontinuity—to the point that past knowledge and practice in an enterprise no longer seem to apply to a new situation. Certainly the Spar and Nigerian situations were perceived as discontinuous because, in addition to creating an immediate crisis for the firm, they portended a hard-to-understand and surely consequential upheaval in Shell's social and political environment. And this was only the beginning: throughout 1995, and over the next three years, the world's largest company would face media probes and political pressures akin to those encountered by Union Carbide, after the Bhopal chemical plant explosion, and Exxon, after the Valdez oil spill. Interestingly, the Group's future scenarios about likely business and social trends, fabled for having successfully prepared managers for oil price shocks during the embargoes of the 1970s, were of little help this year.[4] Indeed, the 1995 scenarios did not anticipate any sociopolitical or environmental upheavals. Thus Shell leaders were neither intellectually nor emotionally prepared to deal with a seismic shift in their environment. Consider: on the commercial side, they had to contend with hungrier investors, savvier competitors, and a faster-changing customer base than ever before, while, on the social front, they were dealing with menacing protestors, anxious politicians, and an increasingly cynical public.

As the CMD considered these matters, they also diagnosed the strengths and weaknesses of the Group. Certainly Shell's global reach, wealth, and longstanding relationships would be strengths to build on as would a high level of technical acumen. On the downside, one director doubted the commercial know-how of current executives and their appetite for competition. Another worried that layers of bureaucracy were stifling initiative and turning talent away. Then Mark Moody-Stuart, a CMD member who would figure prominently in Shell's turnaround as a corporate citizen, asked whether the prevailing 'rational-technical' mindset of staff, an acknowledged strength, might also be a weakness. He speculated that it had led management to misread the emotional upset and misinterpret opponents' contrary views in the case of the Spar and Nigeria. And, by extension, might that mindset also deafen Shell to new and unfamiliar customer segments around the globe; and to the challenging points of view of environmentalists and human right's activists?

At Cor's urging, the CMD "held up the mirror" and examined the Shell Group's culture in toto. In so doing, they highlighted a tendency toward insularity and an attitude of arrogance in dealings with, on the one hand, investors and customers and, on the other, with NGOs and the public. The CMD concurred that they and Shell overall gave primacy in decisions to analysis and hard facts rather than to dialogue and empathy. And they lamented the inability of people both inside and outside the company to talk openly and fully about problems and concerns.

A second defining characteristic of transformation concerns the breadth and depth of needed change. Plainly, reorganization would not address the range of threats and weaknesses facing the Group in 1995; nor would it capitalize on some of Shell's strengths and the opportunities at hand. Efforts to improve would have to simultaneously speak to financial, commercial, social, and environmental matters. Furthermore, a host of cultural factors, having to do with Shell's communication climate, inside and outside, and styles of leadership and decision making, were implicated in the need for change. Recognition dawned that the old Shell would have to die and a new culture be birthed.

This death/rebirth theme is an important indicator of the depth of transformation. On an emotional level, it asks for disengagement from the past, a difficult matter in any instance but even more so given the centennial history of Shell and its legacy of superior performance. On the practical side, it would mean that besides having to rev up Shell's business engine, the CMD would also have to reshape its image, refashion its identity, and reenergize its people.

In late 1995, they would take their case to Shell's top 50 leaders to mobilize them for action—to where remained to be determined.

THE AWAKENING

Change efforts typically begin with a phase of "unfreezing" or what Tichy terms an "awakening."[5] This broadens the base of participation in diagnoses, often stimulates internal conflict and debate, and evokes widespread resistance to change. To this point, although operating companies had expressed reservations about proposed changes, some understanding had been reached over their roles in the to-be-formed businesses, and the CMD had signaled that every area would be implicated in Group-wide change. To make the "business case" for this broader-based transformation, detailed analyses of Shell's financial performance were discussed at a meeting of the top leaders in October 1995. In principle, these findings about Shell's lagging financial and retail results were indisputable and constituted an inarguable case for action. But, in Shell, as in so many companies, some discredited the data and downplayed the urgency of action.

To counteract this, Larry Selden, a finance professor from Columbia University, presented data on Shell's results relative to top performers within and outside of the oil industry. These latter data raised the visibility of the Group's comparatively anemic rate of growth. On the retail front, in turn, Shell's shop performance was found wanting when matched against that of 7-Eleven, Tescos, and other convenience stores with fuel on offer.

This diagnosis of "current reality" served as a proverbial "wake up call" that the Group, while still hugely profitable, was not a top-performer in financial returns. The money message, cool and factual, aimed to shatter self-perceptions of superiority. Just as important, these comparative statistics challenged Shell's tendency toward insularity and arrogance—cultural characteristics deemed undesirable by the CMD.

At this point, the CMD also began to address cultural characteristics in Shell's handling of the Brent Spar. By way of background, protestors were removed from the Spar in May, 1995 and Greenpeace called for a boycott of Shell in Europe—a move that evoked righteous indignation given the "scientific" case in favor of sinking the rig. One month later Herkströter announced that the Group was abandoning its original plan and any other variations of deepwater disposal. As the press published its final features on Greenpeace's "David vs. Goliath" victory, Shell published its own version of the story. A team of project engineers and public affairs specialists put historical and technical data about the Spar along with correspondence with government officials on to a CD-ROM, and sent it to subject-matter experts and relevant opinion leaders, both supporters and critics. In turn, an independent technical group from Norway was hired to audit the Spar's contents and investigate allegations of toxicity. The result of these efforts would be a modest and somewhat Pyrrhic victory: UK television executives admitted to their "lack of objectivity" in covering the story and later Greenpeace would apologize to Shell for "inaccuracies" in its charges.

***

Collecting themselves, CMD members began to speak about their inefficacy in relation to the Spar and Nigeria and criticized themselves for being too inward-looking, defensive, and uncommunicative with one another and the outside world. At the same time, they pointed to the insularity and arrogance of the Group. The message was plain: just as the CMD would have to change so also would the Shell culture. In theory, this sort of self-criticism encourages people to "disidentify" with undesired elements of their culture.[6] However, at the end of 1995, there was no consensus among Shell's top fifty that a seismic shift in culture was desirable— or feasible. Steps had been taken: the CMD was asserting leadership and out in front of proposed changes in the business structure and culture of the Group. And, as a matter of symbol and substance, Shell's top fifty had submitted letters of resignation from the "old" Shell and submitted written letters of applications to the "new" firm. Still, there was lingering resentment over the CMD's criticism of Shell and, as yet, no shared image of the new.

TOWARD THE 'NEW SHELL'

The next phase of transformation involves the definition of the new—often described as a "vision" of the future in recognition of its aspirational character and emotional appeal. At a third offsite meeting, in March 1996, several business heads and operating company CEOs worked together with the CMD to put their aspirations for the Group into words. One vision was to become the "top performer of 'first choice.' " These words were judged meaningful in every language spoken in Shell and the prefix of "first choice" could be completed with reference to investors, customers, and employees, as well as to the public.

To put substance to this slogan, Shell's top fifty were challenged to set Olympic-level targets for financial performance. Could Shell, a carbon-era company, grow its business like silicon-based firms? Many questioned this proposition and pointed out that Shell's massive size worked against high rates of growth. Yet, others countered, General Electric was not a high tech company and earned double digit growth through the 1990s. Thus emboldened, targets were set in Shell for double-digit revenue growth. This points to another distinguishing characteristic of transformation: the lack of a model or, more colloquially, a roadmap for reaching the desired end point. In this instance, there were no foreseeable exploration opportunities, product plans, and market openings that would lead Shell to breakthrough growth. Undaunted, the top fifty proclaimed that Shell would thus have to achieve "breakthrough" performance to reach this goal.

Absent specific plans to reach its targets, the CMD issued what it termed the "Shell Business Framework." This detailed a series of desired culture changes that were deemed essential to breakthrough performance. As an example, cognizant of stifling bureaucracy, Cor called for a new mindset in the Group that aimed to "unleash talent." Other desired changes in culture included a shift from insularity, arrogance, secrecy, and diffuse accountability to: 1) an active external focus or management from the "outside-in," 2) open communication inside and outside the Group, 3) transparency of information and operations, and 4) single point accountability.

To personalize these themes, each member of the CMD prepared their own storyline about the need for change, aspirations for the future, and the culture that Shell would need to get there.[7] In turn, each of Shell's top fifty leaders scripted their own stories and presented them to staff in a cascade down the hierarchy of the company. Literally hundreds of meetings were held in early 1996 to wake people up down the line and mobilize them for transformation.

To this point, Shell's case for change and business framework had a decidedly commercial emphasis. Significantly, Herkströter had committed Shell to redraft its "Statement of General Business Principles" in light of Brent Spar and Nigeria. And the top fifty had called for more disclosure of data on Shell's environmental and social record and agreed that the Group's involvement in the developing world needed single point CMD oversight. But there were no Olympic-level social targets and neither a common understanding of nor commitment to transformation as a corporate citizen in early 1996. These would come when Shell began remaking itself.

REMAKING SHELL—1996 & 1997

The third generic phase of organizational transformation involves a remaking of the organization. The aim, in the language of change agentry, is to reduce the "gap" between the current reality and future vision through a variety of innovations in the organization. Often, development of these innovations requires more discrete diagnoses, goal setting, and the like. In early 1996, Shell launched at least three major fact-finding efforts to guide its remaking. One was a survey of staff that asked about their current work conditions, and aspirations for themselves and the company. It confirmed declining levels of motivation due to red tape, a lack of financial incentives, and limiting career paths. At the same time, it highlighted strong desires for more freedom, a voice in decisions, and a financial stake in performance. A survey of retail customers, in turn, showed continuing brand loyalty overall but disaffection among segments over the Spar and Nigeria and a perception that Shell was "old fashioned." Finally, there was a massive study of "Changing Societal Expectations." In this, over one hundred opinion leaders in business, government, and NGOs, representing over fifty countries, participated in either interviews or roundtable discussions about the role of global companies in society.

Furthermore, the practice of benchmarking began to spread throughout the Group. On the financial side, for example, Shell's performance was contrasted with that of both industry competitors and top corporate performers overall in presentations to staff as well as to analysts. In the areas of exploration, refining, and retail, graphs and charts began to stress Shell's position relative to competitors. And, on the social front, Shell launched a study in mid-1996 of the influence of "stakeholders" on other large companies around the world. Over four hundred senior executives from thirty firms rated the influence of various internal and external interests on their companies and talked about how they handled them. Plainly, the CMD's calls for Shell to "listen" to its stakeholders, to face fully the external world, and to manage from the outside in were being heard in the Group.

Rebuilding the Business   The creation of lines of business at the beginning of 1996 was the most visible part of Shell's transformation. Each of these businesses, in turn, developed their own agenda for driving change through their organization. For example, the retail business launched its Business Framework Implementation (BFI) workshop series. Beginning in late 1996 (and continuing through 1999), work teams from over seventy operating companies, along with marketing and research-and-development teams, went through BFI programs.[8]

Each team would begin the six-month program with a diagnosis of their current performance and culture and set aspirational performance targets. To fill in the gap, the teams would take a close look at work flows and time management, benchmark work improvement best practices inside and outside of the Group, and then implement new activities designed to promote growth and increase returns. To ensure that this process was brought into the mainstream management of the business, country teams engaged in business reviews with the CMD member head of oil products, Steve Miller, and senior oil products executives. In these reviews, business results and work methods were openly and fully discussed with other teams and relevant parties offering comments and advice. These "new" Shell reviews emphasized transparency in operations and communication between and among all those having an interest in the business. To instill accountability and reward success, performance results were tracked to individuals and incentive pay was pegged to performance.

Redefining Reputation   Even as new activities embodying the new Shell culture moved down into the businesses, efforts began to spread change horizontally across lines of business. In mid-1996, a number of "value creation" teams, composed of younger managers and professionals from around Shell, and sponsored by a CMD member, were formed to study and make recommendations about broad business problems. The first teams addressed cost leadership, brand value, the use of best practices, and corporate reputation, an effort known by the acronym WoMAC. This team set its sights on turning Shell into the "World's Most Admired Company."

The WoMAC team built on then emerging Shell transformation themes. With the help of Charles Fombrun, a business professor at NYU, the team constructed a model of the "causes and consequences" of changes in a company's reputation.[9] Among other things, this showed how social and environmental issues, such as the Spar and Nigerian situations, would affect perceptions of Shell by customers, investors, employees, and recruits. As to vision, whereas line managers asked what would make Shell the "first choice" of investors, customers, and suppliers, the WoMAC team asked about first choice among the public. For benchmarking purposes, Shell was compared against top firms using various reputation rankings and social investor's scorecards. The case for action was generalized: Shell was not in the top quartile in financial performance; neither was its corporate reputation so highly ranked.

To spread these findings, and build awareness of reputation throughout the Group, the WoMAC team recommended that Shell attend to its "core purpose." Accordingly, managers and employees in the corporate centers and nearly fifty countries participated in what were called core purpose workshops. Here they would discuss the raison d'être of, say, Hewlett Packard, Disney, and Coca-Cola, and then consider "what (Shell) stands for." After sifting through the results of the workshops, Shell claimed its core purpose to be "Helping People to Build a Better World."

Managing Social Performance   One unit thoroughly transformed in 1996 and 1997 addressed external affairs. Prior to the creation of lines of business, the external affairs of Shell were handled by corporate staff and otherwise decentralized. National operating companies managed their own governmental affairs, dealings with "local" stakeholders, and many aspects of corporate citizenship. Two factors turned this around. First, external affairs became a "service" company after the restructuring and thus had to compete on the open market with social and environmental consultancies. To do so required upgrading its talent and sophistication. Second, extreme decentralization was blamed for miscommunications and, to some extent, for mistakes made in dealings with governments and NGOs in the case of the Spar and Nigeria. In the "new" Shell, external affairs would be more centralized and the "reformed" unit would have to educate the group on best practice.

Shortly after taking charge of the unit, Karen de Segundo beefed up its "issue management" capability and hired in new managers from other firms and NGOs. In keeping with the new cultural themes, she rebuilt media relations to be more open and disclosive in dealing with the public and developed an in-house magazine to disseminate heretofore confidential findings on various stakeholder surveys, the study on reputation, and social and environmental innovations in the Group. External affairs also began to conduct workshops in operating companies around the globe on topical issues, and prepared "fast track" information kits on how to monitor issues, dialogue with stakeholders, and deal with consultants.

This enhanced capability was very much in evidence in Shell's follow-up to the Spar and Nigerian situations—which was led by external affairs. For instance, in the spring of 1996, Shell moved from one-way to two-way communication when it opened a Brent Spar website where visitors could get background information and updates on the Spar and register their views. In the fall, representatives from environmental groups, engineering firms, universities, trade unions, churches, and the like met in London to review developments in a dialogue facilitated by an independent third party, the Environmental Council. Interestingly, Shell and Greenpeace joined together in a seminar about media coverage of the Spar, and technical experts of the two organizations met periodically to review proposals on its disposal.

Then Shell solicited proposals for the on-shore disposal of the Spar. Two hundred proposals were reviewed and winnowed down to a "short list" of six. These were then reviewed by independent evaluators and discussed in several dialogue sessions with interested parties in 1997. In January 1998, Shell announced that the Spar would be "re-used" in Norway as a ferry quay. News coverage of its recycling was almost universally positive.

The way forward in Nigeria was not as refined or restorative but did have many of the same components. As for communications, Shell conducted and published a review of its environmental record in Nigeria and held an in-house workshop to brief executives and provide them with a communication package. Throughout 1996, it hosted more than twenty European journalists in Nigeria and gave them full access to Shell facilities and people. Articles about the situation, many pro-Shell in tone, appeared in the world press. Furthermore, as it had done with the Spar, Shell created a "Shell in Nigeria" website to tell its story and get feedback. And it met with select NGOs throughout 1997 including the World Council of Churches, a strong voice for justice in Africa, to enhance its role among the Ogoni.

New Business Principles   Early on, self-criticism by the CMD of its handling of the Spar and Nigeria was limited to staff within the company. In 1997, however, Cor went public with a critique of Shell's global citizenship. One article summed it up neatly: "Shellman says sorry." He and the CMD faced a challenge in fall, 1997 when an investment group tabled a resolution for UK shareholders calling on Shell to name the executive accountable for environmental and corporate responsibility issues. It also demanded that Shell adopt global standards and issue a Group-wide report on its performance in these areas. The Board rejected this resolution and it was defeated by shareholders. Nevertheless, by the time of the meeting, many of the resolution's aims had been met:

- CMD Chairman Cor Herkströter was assigned responsibility for all ethical and environmental matters;

- Shell issued an updated Statement of General Business Principles that made explicit its commitment to human rights and clarified its stance on 'political interference'; and

- Shell pledged itself to environmental and social reporting on a Group-wide basis.

INSTITUTIONALIZING CHANGE—1998 & 1999

Group-wide innovations that bespoke the new Shell would continue through 1998 and 1999. For instance, the Group would stage its first "Business Week" where over five hundred managers and professionals came together to review the business, dialogue with analysts, industry watchers, and various outside experts, share best practices, and engage in good fellowship. Note how the leadership corps had increased from fifty in 1995 to five hundred three years later. This furthered open communication and broadened participation in governance—consistent with the desire to "unleash talent." The outreach continued with the dawn of Shell Business Television, a program on business trends and developments broadcast throughout the Group, and expanded use of a Shell intranet and the World Wide Web. No longer insular, Shell reached out to staff and opened itself to the world.

Institutionalization is that last phase of transformation where new ideas, practices, and cultural changes become part of the fabric of the organization. In this phase at Shell, new practices were evident in all aspects of running the business. For example, the lines of business had begun to manage *outside-in* by dialoguing with investors, surveying their customers, and benchmarking themselves against the best of the best. Similarly, external affairs continued to garner input from stakeholders and scour reputation rankings. The results were favorable.[10] In a poll conducted by the *Financial Times* in early 1997, Shell ranked 11th of Europe's "most respected companies."[11] Several months later, *Fortune* ranked Shell as Britain's "most admired company" and among the top five in Europe.[12]

Shell's ongoing efforts at *open communication* about business results, both inside and outside the company, were amplified in various information campaigns, stakeholder dialogues, and in the innovative use of the World Wide Web for disclosure of data and two-way communication. Visitors to the website could not only "tell Shell" their views, but also link to the web pages of Greenpeace and like-minded NGOs, industry watchers, and even Shell's competitors.[13]

Accounting for Profits and Principles   Shell made good on its pledge to account for its social and environmental performance in 1998. Interestingly, one theme that had emerged loud and clear from its studies of changing expectations was that many people do not trust what companies *say;* rather they pay attention to what they *do.* The crisp conclusion was that the public had little tolerance for "tell me" communications and instead had a "show me" attitude. This would necessitate *transparency* in operations and much more *disclosure* of results. Thus, a social accountability team was formed to "show" whether or not Shell was living up to its business principles. The team issued its first report in 1998, "Profits and Principles—does there have to be a choice?" It detailed Shell's performance against its eight revised business principles and highlighted a set of issues and dilemmas on which to dialogue with recipients. Acclaimed for issuing the most comprehensive corporate social report in existence, the Shell team established social accounting principles and gained independent verification of some key statistics.

To add accountability to this scheme, Shell began to have its operating company chief executives prepare and "sign off" letters affirming that their company had 1) operated within applicable laws and in accord with ethical guidelines, 2) followed health, safety, and environmental policies, and 3) conformed to Shell's Business Principles. To give this process some teeth, external auditors verified some of the statistics cited in these letters. And Shell subsequently dismissed some senior executives who did not follow or enforce the Business Principles.

A second report, "People, Planet & Profits—an act of commitment," issued in 1999, reflected maturity in these regards. Under the mantle of sustainable development, it presented a clear, cogent, and concise accounting of Shell's interfaces with society, measured in terms of economic, social, and environmental performance. Compared to the prior one, the new report had more data and was more disclosive. Interestingly, it combined data from

Shell's annual financial report and health, safety, and environment audit with newly collected social data to present a comprehensive picture of the Group. This report is available electronically on the Group's website.

Community Service   During this same period, each of Shell's business lines and operating companies has taken steps to introduce new business and social practices. One example of social innovation is the use of community service in BFI programs.[14] Shell's top fifty leaders got a taste of this in their first leadership meeting in late 1995 when they worked with recovering addicts in a clinic in London. Steve Miller, head of oil products, moved it down the ranks such that country teams have built playgrounds in a low-income housing area, refurbished schools, and spent time with society's least advantaged—even as they introduced changes to improve sales and returns to shareholders.

Miller offered several reasons in favor of Shell's involvement in the community. For instance, market research showed that customers have strong feelings about Shell—pro and con—based on their identification with the company. Interestingly, these surveys found that customers were not nearly so identified with the other oil majors. In Miller's eyes, visible community service was a way to "show" customers that Shell cared about their community. In addition, he expressed a strong personal belief that service to the community simply makes people feel better about themselves.

Social Investment   More broadly, the Group has adopted a new philosophy about its role in communities. It no longer speaks in philanthropic terms about its "contributions," rather it now makes "social investments." An annual report, "Sharing a Vision—Shell's Investment in Society," tracks and reports on its social investments in every operating company. This continues a trend away from localness and toward globalness in the business and social arenas. The most recent report says that Shell has increased its investments 15 percent annually the past few years.

Nowhere is this more evident than in Nigeria. Some $36 million was devoted to vocational training for 1700 Ogoni youth, funding college scholarships, immunizing 100,000 children, and supporting local agriculture. Shell partnered with a UK NGO, Living Earth, to profile other community needs and prepare a response to them. This involved interviews with 700 men and women in the Niger Delta and an assessment of current programs. That said, there remain many critics of Shell's environmental and social performance in the Niger Delta.

***

WILL IT ENDURE?

The jury is still out on the results of Shell's business transformation. Certainly the Group has not recorded financial breakthroughs on a pace with GE's turnaround, but neither did it reduce staff significantly or sell off substantial chunks of its portfolio as has been commonplace in U.S.-company restructurings. Interestingly, trimming the portfolio is on Shell's agenda in 2000 as is aggressive reliance on its own internal capital market to fund projects. Overall, I would argue that Shell has been somewhat "Americanized" in its heightened attention to shareholders and analysts and in its adoption of new cultural values. Still, in performance and in culture change, it lags the best of the best of U.S. companies and, perhaps, British Petroleum in its own industry.[15]

At the same time, Shell is a leader in citizenship and is introducing a new corporate model. Certainly in its social and environmental reporting, involvement in multi-sector forums, and interest in eco-commerce, Shell may embody a new kind of European company that relates multiple stakeholders and responds to green sensibilities. To the extent that the tone is set at the top, the words of Mark Moody-Stuart speak to the heart of transformed Shell's business:

> *In the next century, sustainable business will have to be responsible and sensitive to the needs of everyone involved. It will be guided by more than one parameter. The demands of economics, of the environment and of contributing to a just society are all important for a global commercial enterprise to flourish. To neglect any one of them is to threaten the whole.[16]*

NOTES

1. To see this wholistic approach in a business from its start up, see Philip H. Mirvis, "Environmentalism in Progressive Businesses," *Journal of Organizational Change Management* 7:4, 1994, 82–100.
2. On how scholars differentiate between "routine" and "transformational," see Philip H. Mirvis, "Organization development: Part II—A revolutionary perspective," in *Research in Organizational Change and Development v4,* eds. Richard W. Woodman and William A. Pasmore (Greenwich, CT: JAI Press, 1990).
3. See T. Bleakley, D. S. Gee, and R. Hulme, "The Atomization of Big Oil," *The McKinsey Quarterly 2* (1997), 123–142.
4. On Shell scenarios, see Arie de Geus, *The Living Company* (London: Nicholas Brealy, 1997).
5. See Noel M. Tichy and Stratford Sherman, *Control Your Destiny Or Someone Else Will* (New York: Doubleday/Currency, 1993).
6. See Noel M. Tichy and Mary Anne Devanna, *The Transformational Leader* (New York: John Wiley and Sons, 1986); and Donald N. Michael and Philip H. Mirvis, "Changing, Erring, and Learning," in *Failures in Organizational Development and Change,* eds. Philip H. Mirvis and David N. Berg (New York: Wiley Interscience, 1977).
7. On storytelling, see Howard Gardner, *Leading Minds: An Anatomy of Leadership* (New York: Basic Books, 1995); Noel M. Tichy and Eli Cohen, *The Leadership Engine* (New York: Harper Business, 1997).
8. See Janet Guyon, "Why Is the World's Most Profitable Company Turning Itself Inside Out" *Fortune* (4 August 1997), 52–57; and Richard Pascale, "Change How You Define Leadership and You Change How You Run a Company," *Fast Company* (April/May 1998), 113–119.
9. See Charles J. Fombrun, *Reputation: Realizing Value from Corporate Image* (Boston, MA: Harvard Business School Press, 1996). Fombrun, Gardberg and Barnett's article in this volume extends Fombrun's reputation work further.
10. Media analysis of Europe in 1997 found favorable coverage of Shell's handling of the Brent Spar outweighing unfavorable coverage by two-to-one. And polls on Shell's image in Germany, where demonstrations against the company continued through 1996, showed a substantial uptick in 1997. Some 56% felt that Shell cared about the environment (versus only 5% right after the Spar).
11. PriceWaterhouse/*Financial Times* survey on Europe's most respected companies, April 1997.
12. *Fortune,* July 1997.
13. *www.shell.com.*
14. On community service, see Noel M. Tichy, Andy R. McGill, and Linda St. Clair, *Global Corporate Citizenship: Doing Business in the Public Eye* (San Francisco: The New Lexington Press, 1997).
15. See Steven E. Prokesch, "Unleashing the Power of Learning: An interview with British Petroleum's John Browne," *Harvard Business Review* (September/October 1997), 147–168. Chris Marsden, formerly of BP, offers another analysis of BP's citizenship status and change efforts in his article in this volume.
16. Mark Moody-Stuart, *The Values of Sustainable Business in the Next Century* (London: Address at St. Paul's Cathedral, 12 July 1999).

Chapter 6

CORPORATE STRATEGY AND DECISION MAKING
Accountability

The trouble with the rat race is that, even if you win, you're still a rat.   LILY TOMLIN

When we speak, we are afraid our words will not be heard, nor
welcomed; but when we are silent, we are still afraid.
So it is better to speak,
Remembering that we were never meant to survive all.   —AUDRE LORDE

Take care to guard against all greed, for though one may be rich,
one's life does not consist of possessions.   LUKE 12:15

Good ethics is good business. Have you heard that before? Did you believe it? Theorists argue about whether ethical decisions lead to higher profits than unethical decisions. While we are all familiar with examples of unethical decisions leading to high profits, there is general agreement that, in the long run, ethics pays off. But the question of what is an ethical decision remains. Lao Tzu in the *Tao Te Ching* contends that there is no crime greater than having too many desires and no misfortune greater than being covetous.[1] How would Taoism view the acts and intentions of a profit-maximizing firm in today's market?

Consider the demise of small bookstores all over the country. In the past several years, large, multipurpose bookstores such as Crown Books and Barnes & Noble have seemed to take over the literary consumption landscape. Chicago, alone, has seen the collapse of a number of old standbys, bookstores that had been in the city for years serving a specific, sometimes idiosyncratic, population rather than the entire book-purchasing community. These stores (Krochs and Brentanos, Stuart Brent, Guild Books, and others) could not survive next to chain superstores that provide a greater selection of low priced alternatives.

Stuart Brent, a longtime bookseller on prestigious Michigan Avenue in Chicago, recently was forced out of business by competition from Borders and other chain bookstores opening right down the street from him. Brent's store was one where the salespeople could remember your name, where there were large, comfy chairs in which to peruse the books, where there were experts available on literary issues, and where they knew just the right book for your Uncle Gordy. Brent's sales went down 30 percent with the opening of Borders Bookstore three blocks away. "Supermarkets," he snorts, "Philistines. My father used to speak of 'men you'd have to stand on tiptoes to talk to.' Where are those men today?" Even Mayor Richard Daley mourned the loss in a telegram sent to Brent on closing day, "Michigan Avenue will miss you, as much as it was enhanced by your fine store and elegant presence."[2] A traditional tale of David and Goliath?

The chain superstores argue that it is not. Instead, these stores contend that they are merely serving the needs of their customers in a more effective, efficient manner, and therefore deserve a larger share of the market. "It's no longer simply the big, stupid best-seller

---

[1]Lao Tzu, *Tao Te Ching,* Book 2, XLVI: 105.
[2]Jeff Lyon, " For Starters," *Chicago Tribune, Sunday Magazine,* January 14, 1996, p. 6.

stores and the small, elegant, literary bookstores," says shopper and Northwestern University Professor Joseph Epstien. "Places like Barnes & Noble and Borders stock the good books, too. I doubt that Stuart Brent had anything these stores don't, except in his specialty of psychoanalytic books."[3] Perhaps these larger bookstores aren't so much predators as they are simply players—answering the needs of the public.

Is there any responsibility of a large chain store entering a small community market? Consider as well the tales of Walgreens stores entering small towns where there is one established pharmacy equipped with a pharmacist who has been serving that public for many years. The pharmacist cannot compete with the economies of scale available to a large firm like Walgreens, so she closes her doors. Is Walgreens to blame? Perhaps. But is it at *fault?* It is using its size to a competitive advantage to reap greater profits for its owners.

Consider what ethical and unethical steps might be taken in the name of profits. Is offering a larger selection, lower prices, and a different ambience unethical? Is an act ethical because it results in higher profit or in spite of it? Consider the examples suggested by Jason Lunday and opinion expressed in Al Gini's article. Accountability is directly addressed in the discussion of the Federal Sentencing Guidelines—some ask, what better way to encourage ethical behavior than to financially reward those who engage in it and financially punish those who do not? On the issue of accountability, one might also want to check out the perspectives of various consumer and advocacy groups in connection with well-known businesses at any of the following websites:

- *www.bankofamericafraud.org*

- *www.boycottameritech.com*

- *www.cokespotlight.org*

- *www.ihatestarbucks.com*

- *www.noamazon.com*

- *www.starbucked.com*

- *www.walmartsurvivor.com*

The question of gathering competitive intelligence has been raised to a critical level with the advent of new technology that allows for more invasive information-gathering techniques. As long as you're not breaking any laws in gathering information, does that make it ethical? How did you feel about the technology-based firm, Oracle, when you learned that it was paying janitorial staff to send to Oracle all of the trash of a political action group affiliated with Microsoft? Technically, this firm had thrown away the materials, but does that mean it is all right for Oracle to sift through it? How should you decide? The questions in this area are difficult to categorize, yet there is usually something that simply doesn't seem appropriate in many situations.

Later articles in this chapter ask you to consider your accountability in connection with the safety of airline travel. How much more might you be willing to pay to travel in safer

---

[3]John Blades, "Staying Alive," *Chicago Tribune,* March 20, 1996, sec. 5, pp. 1, 4.

aircrafts? Anything at all? If you say no amount more than that which you already pay, are you silently or passively allowing the standard of risk that currently exists?

Finally, there are several readings relating to the space Shuttle Challenger explosion. Consider why the decision makers made the decision to launch in the first place. Was it really that the industry had a culture of "no guts, no glory?" Perhaps it was the risk inherent in space travel that defined the culture. Do you believe they would change their minds now or not? In the end, what can we learn from this experience? How could the discussion or negotiation have been better structured to have arrived at a different result? Are you convinced by Gladwell's thesis that no one should be blamed for disasters like the Challenger explosion? Do we consistently seek a party to blame when unfortunate consequences result from human action or inaction? Is blame always appropriate, or are there times when bad things happen, but nothing could have been done in advance to have prevented it? Where should the accountability lie here?

SHORT HYPOTHETICAL CASE

You are a project manager for a recliner manufacturer. A young child died after his head was caught in the leg rest on a recliner of the same design as yours. You learn that several children have died in this manner; you did not manufacture any of the recliners involved. A federal regulatory agency has studied the problem and has determined that a safeguard would cost $0.25 per chair. However, the agency estimates that lawsuits for all anticipated deaths and injuries will cost only $0.11 per chair. The agency therefore will not require the safeguards to be installed. Your major competitors have decided it is not cost-effective to install the safeguard. What will you do?

Hypotheticals were written by Catherine Haselden and are included in her manuscript "The Ethics Game."

PROFITABLE ETHICAL PROGRAMS

JASON LUNDAY

*In response to a previous e-mail to a listserver on teaching business
ethics, Lunday identifies some apparently successful ethical business
practices from the annals of business history.*

. . . Some apparently successful ethical business practices:

(In some cases, the companies claim a very direct bottom-line effect to certain ethical practices. Others claim that their ethical practices contribute to an overall corporate climate which cuts waste, encourages efficiency, promotes community/marketplace goodwill, allowing the company a healthy bottom line.)

1. 3M—through its Pollution Prevention Program (3P), initiated in the mid-1970s, the corporation claims to have decreased its production and emission of air, solid, and water pollutants by billions of lbs. AND saved the company over $500 million during its first 15 years. It did so by using its expertise in innovation to find new ways of manufacturing which led to fewer pollutants. To qualify for the 3P program, ideas had to meet three of four measures, only one of which was cost savings. [See Alfred Marcus, *Business and Society: Strategy, Ethics, and the Global Economy,* Irwin, Chicago, 1996.]

While 3M was considered the first, I understand that a large number of companies have successfully accomplished similar environmental initiatives, reducing pollutants and saving money. Contact the Management Institute for Environment and Business, Washington, DC, for examples.

2. Levi Strauss—with a strong history of employee goodwill, LSCO has worked for numerous years to insure that its employee policies demonstrate respect for workers and their lives. It has consistently paid workers at the top of the industry and granted benefits uncommon among its competitors (like year-round employment). Further, it has encouraged strong employee communication and idea-sharing. It has expected that such treatment would create mutual respect. This apparently came true when a South American operation effectively communicated one of its new product launches to headquarters during a time of overall lagging sales. The idea, Dockers, became the biggest product introduction in U.S. history and reinvigorated the company. [See Jeffrey Edwards and Jason Lunday, *Levi Strauss & Co.: The South Zarzamora Street Plant,* Darden Graduate Business School Case Bibliography.]

There are other stories of how factory employees have taken pay cuts, done without raises, and accepted other risks at certain times because of the company's fair treatment and with an expectation that such a well-managed company will overcome periodic difficulties.

3. South Shore Bank—the company came up with the great idea to help its local community, a depressed area of Chicago, where few could get bank loans. In finding ways to

grant credit where other banks would not, South Shore not only helped a community pick itself back up, it increased bank earnings.

[Sorry, don't have a reference handy. South Shore has won Business Ethics Magazine's annual award in recent years, so a past edition of the magazine will overview the company's story.]

4.   Johnson & Johnson—need we say more on this one? For a treatment of this, see *Managing Corporate Ethics,* Francis Aguilar, Oxford University Press, New York, 1994.

5.   Delta Air Lines—Delta also has a strong history of employee relations, to the extent that, for years, it was the only non-unionized airline. This allowed the carrier flexibility during recessions to move workers around in order to maximize manpower in key areas. It also traditionally allows the airline to have employees perform multiple tasks so that it does not have to hire additional workers. The airline had, for many years, consistently been at the top of the Dept. of Transportation's lowest complaint list. It generally is still there, occasionally being beat out by Southwest. Employee goodwill because of the company's treatment also helps the company keep a very low employee/seat miles ratio. Some years back, because of exceptional treatment, the employees chipped in and bought the company a passenger jet. Delta has also ended up as one of the country's most admired companies for many years. [Personal unpublished research—if you want article references, just ask. I've got a lot.]

6.   Lincoln Electric—arc welding. Company claims that strong employee orientation has allowed it to earn exceptional profits. [See *Managing Corporate Ethics,* Francis Aguilar, Oxford University Press, New York, 1994.]

7.   Honda—attention to customer quality allowed it strong entrance into U.S. market. [*Business and Society,* Alfred Marcus, Irwin, Chicago, 1996.]

8.   BFI—effort to help New York rid itself of corruption in the trash hauling business gave the company early entry into a lucrative market. [See recent *Fortune* cover story.]

9.   Socially responsible companies Body Shop, Ben & Jerry's, Tom's of Maine, etc.: each claims that their orientation to meeting stakeholder needs—in a variety of forms—allowed them to become large players in their respective markets. [See *Body and Soul,* Anita Roddick, *The Soul of a Business,* Tom Chappell, don't know Ben & Jerry's book.]

10.   Merck—another company at the very top of Fortune's Most Admired Companies. The company ended up paying millions of dollars to formulate, manufacture, and distribute a drug which cures river blindness, which is generally found in poor regions of lesser developed countries. The goodwill alone from this has apparently, like J&J and Tylenol, given it many consumers' trust. Granted, it would be difficult to quantify how much that is worth, but I doubt that Vagelos or the current chairman would deny it has been worth a lot.

11.   Sears, Roebuck—when questions arose about possible inappropriate sales practices of product warranties, which, by the way, were making BIG money for the retailer, they retrained their associates to ensure that the warranties were not being pushed on customers or otherwise sold unethically. Expecting a drop in warranty sales, they instead were hit with a sizeable increase. [See *Ethikos* back issue, can't remember the date. Also, personal consulting experience with them.]

Business ethics books are generally filled with cases of companies which have gotten into trouble. We don't see enough of the good stories since, I suppose, we simply expect this. However, the positive examples can go a long way in encouraging prosocial behavior, which, like deterrence theory, is another aspect of business ethics.

MORAL LEADERSHIP
AND BUSINESS ETHICS

Al Gini

How do you judge the ethics of a leader? What makes one leader ethical and another unethical? Does it depend on the impact of that leader on her or his followers? Gini identifies the parameters within which we might appropriately judge a leader and the structural restraints imposed upon corporate leadership. Consider the impact of these restraints on the decisions and actions of leaders. Do they justify any (or all) leadership decisions?

. . . How do we judge the ethics of a leader? Clearly, no leader can be expected to be perfect in every decision and action made. As John Gardner has pointed out, particular consequences are never a reliable assessment of leadership.[1] The quality and worth of leadership can only be measured in terms of what a leader intends, values, believes in or stands for—in other words, character. In *Character: America's Search for Leadership,* Gail Sheehy argued, as did Aristotle before her, that character is the most crucial and most elusive element of leadership. The root of the word "character" comes from the Greek word for engraving. As applied to human beings, it refers to the enduring marks or etched-in factors in our personality, which include our in-born talents as well as the learned and acquired traits imposed upon us by life and experience. These engravings define us, set us apart and motivate behavior.

In regard to leadership, said Sheehy, character is fundamental and prophetic. The "issues (of leadership) are those of today and will change in time. Character is what was yesterday and will be tomorrow."[2] For Sheehy, character establishes both our day-to-day demeanor and our destiny. Therefore, it is only useful but essential to examine the character of those who desire to lead us. As a journalist and longtime observer of the political scene, Sheehy contends that the Watergate affair of the early 1970s serves as a perfect example of the links between character and leadership. As Richard Nixon demonstrated so well, said Sheehy: "The Presidency is not the place to work out one's personal pathology."[3] Leaders rule us, run things, wield power. Therefore, said Sheehy, we must be careful whom we choose as leaders. Because whom we choose, is what we shall be. If, as Heraclitus wrote, "character is fate," the fate our leaders reap will also be our own.

Putting aside the particular players and the politics of the episode, Watergate has come to symbolize the failings and failures of people in high places. Watergate now serves as a

---

Al Gini, "Moral Leadership and Business Ethics." Reprinted by permission. Al Gini is an associate professor of philosophy at Loyola University of Chicago and managing editor of *Business Ethics Quarterly.*

[1] John W. Gardner, *On Leadership* (New York: The Free Press, 1990), p. 8.
[2] Gail Sheehy, *Character: America's Search for Leadership* (New York: Bantam Books, 1990), p. 311.
[3] *Ibid.,* p. 66.

watershed, a turning point, in our nation's concern for integrity, honesty and fair play from all kinds of leaders. It is not a mere coincidence that the birth of business ethics as an independent, academic discipline can be dated from the Watergate affair and the trials that came out of it. No matter what our failings as individuals, Watergate sensitized us to the importance of ethical standards and conduct from those who direct the course of our political and public lives. What society is now demanding, and what business ethics is advocating, is that our business leaders and public servants should be held accountable to an even higher standard of behavior than we might demand and expect of ourselves.

Mutual Purposes and Goals   The character, goals and aspirations of a leader are not developed in a vacuum. Leadership, even in the hands of a strong, confident, charismatic leader remains, at bottom, relational. Leaders, good or bad, great or small, arise out of the needs and opportunities of a specific time and place. Leaders require causes, issues and, most importantly, a hungry and willing constituency. Leaders may devise plans, establish an agenda, bring new and often radical ideas to the table, but all of them are a response to the milieu and membership of which they are a part. If leadership is an active and ongoing relationship between leaders and followers, then a central requirement of the leadership process is for leaders to evoke and elicit consensus in their constituencies, and conversely for followers to inform and influence their leaders. This is done in at least two ways, through the use of power and education.

The term "power" comes from the Latin *posse:* to do, to be able, to change, to influence or effect. To have power is to possess the capacity to control or direct change. All forms of leadership must make use of power. The central issue of power in leadership is not, "Will it be used?" but, rather, "Will it be used wisely and well?" According to James MacGregor Burns, leadership is not just about directed results; it is also about offering followers a choice among real alternatives. Hence, leadership assumes competition, conflict and debate whereas brute power denies it.[4] "Leadership mobilizes," said Burns, "naked power coerces."[5] But power need not be dictatorial or punitive to be effective. Power can also be used in a noncoercive manner to orchestrate, direct and guide members of an organization in the pursuit of a goal or series of objectives. Leaders must engage followers, not merely direct them. Leaders must serve as models and mentors, not martinets. "Power without morality," said novelist James Baldwin, "is no longer power."

For Peter Senge teaching is one of the primary jobs of leadership.[6] The "task of leader as teacher" is to empower people with information, offer insights, new knowledge, alternative perspectives on reality. The "leader as teacher" said Senge, is not just about "teaching" people how "to achieve their vision" but, rather, is about fostering learning, offering choices and building consensus.[7] Effective leadership recognizes that in order to build and achieve community, followers must become reciprocally coresponsible in the pursuit of a common enterprise. Through their conduct and teaching, leaders must try to make their fellow constituents aware that they are all stakeholders in a conjoint activity that cannot

---

[4]James MacGregor Burns, *Leadership* (New York: Harper Torchbooks, 1979), p. 36.
[5]*Ibid.,* p. 439.
[6]For Senge the three primary tasks of leadership include: leader as designer; leader as steward; leader as teacher.
[7]Peter M. Senge, *The Fifth Discipline* (New York: Double/Currency Books, 1990), p. 353.

succeed without their involvement and commitment. Successful leadership believes in and communicates some version of the now famous Hewlett Packard motto: "The achievements of an organization are the results of the combined efforts of each individual."

In the end, says Abraham Zaleznick, "leadership is based on a compact that binds those who lead with those who follow into the same moral, intellectual and emotional commitment."[8] However, as both Burns and Rost warned us, the nature of this "compact" is inherently unequal because the influence patterns existing between leaders and followers are not equal. Responsive and responsible leadership requires, as a minimum, that democratic mechanisms be put in place which recognize the right of followers to have adequate knowledge of alternative options, goals and programs, as well as the capacity to choose between them. "In leadership writ large, mutually agreed upon purposes help people achieve consensus, assume responsibility, work for the common good and build community."[9]

STRUCTURAL RESTRAINTS

There is, unfortunately, a dark side to the theory of the "witness of others." Howard S. Schwartz in his radical, but underappreciated, managerial text *Narcissistic Process and Corporate Decay*,[10] argued that corporations are not bastions of benign, other-directed ethical reasoning. Nor can corporations, because of the demands and requirements of business, be models and exemplars of moral behavior. The rule of business, said Schwartz, remains the "law of the jungle," "the survival of the fittest," and the goal of survival engenders a combative "us against them mentality" which condones the moral imperative of getting ahead by any means necessary. Schwartz calls this phenomenon "organizational totalitarianism": Organizations and the people who manage them create for themselves a self-contained, self-serving world view, which rationalizes anything done on their behalf and which does not require justification on any grounds outside of themselves.[11] The psychodynamics of this narcissistic perspective, said Schwartz, impose Draconian requirements on all participants in organizational life: do your work; achieve organizational goals; obey and exhibit loyalty to your superiors; disregard personal values and beliefs; obey the law when necessary, obfuscate it whenever possible; and, deny internal or external discrepant information at odds with the stated organizational worldview. Within such a "totalitarian logic," neither leaders nor followers, rank nor file, operate as independent agents. To "maintain their place," to "get ahead," all must conform. The agenda of "organizational totalitarianism," said Schwartz, is always the preservation of the *status quo*. Within such a logic, like begets like, and change is rarely possible. Except for extreme situations in which "systemic ineffectiveness" begins to breed "organization decay," transformation is never an option.

In *Moral Mazes* Robert Jackall, from a sociological rather than a psychological perspective, parallels much of Schwartz's analysis of organizational behavior. According to critic and commentator Thomas W. Norton, both Jackall and Schwartz seek to understand

---

[8]Abraham Zaleznik, "The Leadership Gap," *Academy of Management Executive* (1990), V.4, N.1, p. 12.

[9]Joseph C. Rost, *Leadership for the Twenty-First Century*, p. 124.

[10]Howard S. Schwartz, *Narcissistic Process and Corporate Decay* (New York: New York University Press, 1990).

[11]Howard S. Schwartz, "Narcissism Project and Corporate Decay: The Case of General Motors," *Business Ethics Quarterly*, V.1, N.3, p. 250.

why and how organizational ethics and behavior are so often reduced to either dumb loyalty or the simple adulation and mimicry of one's superiors. While Schwartz argued that individuals are captives of the impersonal structural logic of "organizational totalitarianism," Jackall contends that "organizational actors become personally loyal to their superiors, always seeking their approval, and are committed to them as persons rather than as representatives of the abstractions of organizational authority." But in either case, both authors maintain that organizational operatives are prisoners of the systems they serve.[12]

According to Jackall, all organizations (to be exact, he is specially referring to American business organizations) are examples of "patrimonial bureaucracies" wherein "fealty relations of personal loyalty" are the rule and the glue of organizational life. Jackall argued that all corporations are like fiefdoms of the middle ages, wherein the Lord of the Manor (CEO, President) offers protection, prestige and status to his vassals (managers) and serfs (workers) in return for homage (commitment) and service (work). In such a system, said Jackall, advancement and promotion are predicated on loyalty, trust, politics and personality as much as, if not more than, on experience, education, ability and actual accomplishments. The central concern of the worker/minion is to be known as a "can-do-guy," a "team player," being at the right place at the right time and master of all the social rules. That's why in the corporate world, says Jackall, 1,000 "atta-boys" are wiped away with one "oh, shit!"

As in the model of a feudal system, Jackall maintains that employees of a corporation are expected to become functionaries of the system and supporters of the *status quo*. Their loyalty is to the powers that be; their duty is to perpetuate performance and profit; and their values can be none other than those sanctioned by the organization. Jackall contends that the logic of every organization (place of business) and the collective personality of the workplace conspire to override the wants, desires and aspirations of the individual worker. No matter what a person believes off the job, said Jackall, on the job all of us to a greater or lesser extent are required to suspend, bracket or only selectively manifest our personal convictions.

> *What is right in the corporation is not what is right in a man's home or his church. What is right in the corporation is what the guy above you wants from you.*[13]

For Jackall the primary imperative of every organization is to succeed. This logic of performance, what he refers to as "institutional logic," leads to the creation of a private moral universe. A moral universe that, by definition, is totalitarian (self-sustained), solipsistic (self-defined) and narcissistic (self-centered). Within such a milieu truth is socially defined and moral behavior is determined solely by organizational needs. The key virtues, for all alike, become the virtues of the organization: goal-preoccupation, problem solving, survival/success and, most importantly, playing by the "house rules." In time, said Jackall, those initiated and invested in the system come to believe that they live in a self-contained worldview which is above and independent of outside critique and evaluation.

---

[12]Thomas W. Norton, "The Narcissism and Moral Mazes of Corporate Life: A Commentary on the Writings of H. Schwartz and R. Jackall," *Business Ethics Quarterly*, V.2, N.1, p. 76.
[13]Robert Jackall, *Moral Mazes* (New York: Oxford University Press, 1988), p. 6.

For both Schwartz and Jackall, the logic of organizational life is rigid and unchanging. Corporations perpetuate themselves, both in their strengths and weakness, because corporate cultures clone their own. Even given the scenario of a benign organizational structure which produces positive behavior and beneficial results, the etiology of the problem, and the opportunity for abuse that it offers, represents the negative possibilities and inherent dangers of the "witness of others" as applied to leadership theory. Within the scope of Schwartz's and Jackall's allied analysis, "normative" moral leadership may not be possible. The model offered is both absolute and inflexible, and only "regular company guys" make it to the top. The maverick, the radical, the reformer are not long tolerated. The "institutional logic" of the system does not permit disruption, deviance or default. . . .

The term moral leadership often conjures up images of sternly robed priests, waspishly severe nuns, carelessly bearded philosophers, forbiddingly strict parents and something ambiguously labeled the "moral majority." These people are seen as confining and dictatorial. They make us do what we should do, not what we want to do. They encourage following the "superego" and not the "id." A moral leader is someone who supposedly tells people the difference between right and wrong from on high. But there is much more to moral leadership than merely telling others what to do.

The vision and values of leadership must have their origins and resolutions in the community of followers, of whom they are a part, and whom they wish to serve. Leaders can drive, lead, orchestrate and cajole, but they cannot force, dictate or demand. Leaders can be the catalyst for morally sound behavior, but they are not, by themselves, a sufficient condition. Leaders by means of their demeanor and message must be able to convince, not just tell others, that collaboration serves the conjoint interest and well-being of all involved. Leaders may offer a vision, but followers must buy into it. Leaders may organize a plan, but followers must decide to take it on. Leaders may demonstrate conviction and willpower, but followers, in the new paradigm of leadership, should not allow the leader's will to replace their own.[14] To reiterate the words of Abraham Zaleznick: "Leadership is based on a compact that binds those that lead with those who follow into the same moral, intellectual and emotional commitment."

Joseph C. Rost has argued, both publicly and privately, that the ethical aspects of leadership remain thorny. How, exactly, do leaders and collaborators in an influence relationship make a collective decision about the ethics of a change that they want to implement in an organization or society? Some will say, "Option A is ethical," while others will say, "Option B is ethical." How are leaders and followers to decide? As I have suggested, ethics is what "ought to be done" as the preferred mode of action in a "right-vs.-right," "values-vs.-values" confrontation. Ethics is an evaluative enterprise. Judgments must be made in regard to competing points of view. Even in the absence of a belief in the existence of a single universal, absolute set of ethical rules, basic questions can still be asked: How does it impact on self and others? What are the consequences involved? Is it harmful? Is it fair? Is it equitable? Perhaps the best, but by no means definitive, method suited to the general needs of the ethical enterprise is a modified version of the scientific method: A) *Observation,* the recognition of a problem or conflict; B) *Inquiry,* a critical consideration of facts and issues

---

[14]Garry Wills, *Certain Trumpets,* p. 13.

involved; C) *Hypothesis,* the formulation of a decision or plan of action consistent with the known facts; D) *Experimentation and Evaluation,* the implementation of the decision or plan in order to see if it leads to the resolution of the problem. There are, of course, no perfect answers in ethics or life. The quality of our ethical choices cannot be measured solely in terms of achievements. Ultimately and ethically, intention, commitment and concerted effort are as important as outcome: What/why did leader/followers try to do? How did they try to do it?

Leadership is hard to define, and moral leadership is even harder. Perhaps, like pornography, we only recognize moral leadership when we see it. The problem is, we so rarely see it. Nevertheless, I am convinced that without the "witness" of moral leadership, standards of ethics in business and organizational life will not occur or be sustained. Leadership, even when defined as a collaborative experience, is still about the influence of individual character and the impact of personal mentoring. Behavior does not always beget like behavior on a one-to-one ratio, but it does establish tone, set the stage and offer options. Although it is mandatory that an organization as a whole—from top to bottom—make a commitment to ethical behavior to actually achieve it, the model for that commitment has to originate from the top.[15] Labor Secretary Robert Reich recently stated: "The most eloquent moral appeal (argument) will be no match for the dispassionate edict of the market."[16] Perhaps, the "witness" of moral leadership can prove to be more effective.

---

[15]Dolecheck, *"Ethics: Take It From the Top,"* p. 14.
[16]William Pfaff, "It's Time for a Change in Corporate Values," *Chicago Tribune,* Jan. 16, 1996, p. 17.

TOPIC STUDY: FEDERAL SENTENCING GUIDELINES

If the profit argument is insufficient to encourage ethical decision making, consider the impact of the federal sentencing guidelines. The guidelines, enacted in 1991 to assist federal judges in sentencing convicted individuals and organizations, require judges to consider "aggravating and mitigating" circumstances in determining sentences and fines. Many companies claim that they were generally law abiding, that one "bad apple" created the problem. The United States Sentencing Commission (USSC) allows these firms to show that, in effect, they tend the rest of their orchard well.

These guidelines apply both to large corporations and to small organizations that might not have initiated an ethics program. Between 1991 and 1995, 56 percent of all sentenced organizations had fewer than 20 employees (Linda Farrell and O.C. Ferrell, "Ethics Training: Its Time Has Come," Forum *80, no. 9 [October 1996], p.8).*

The fine range for corporate unethical and illegal behavior is based on the seriousness of the offense (a base fine) multiplied by some figure representing the culpability of the organization. For instance, a score is modified based on the level of authority and size of the organization (one to five points), the prior history (one or two points), any violation of an order (one or two points), obstruction of justice (three points), whether there exists an effective program to prevent and detect violations (deduction of three points), and whether there is self-reporting, cooperation, and acceptance of responsibility (deduction of five points, two points, or one point). Where a firm has a culpability score of 10 or more, the fine will range from $20 million to $40 million. Where a firm has a culpability score of zero or less, the fine will range from $500,000 to $2 million. (All data are taken from USSC, "Corporate Crime in America: Strengthening the Good Citizen Corporation," Proceedings of the Second Symposium on Crime and Punishment in the United States, *Sept. 7–8, 1995 [Washington, DC]. See also USSG, sec. 8C2.7; chap. 8, introductory comment.)*

In addition, the guidelines suggest a seven-step plan toward due diligence in preventing and detecting criminal conduct by a firm's employees and agents (see three-point reduction of culpability above). In this section, you will read several discussions, both pro and con, relating to the guidelines and their anticipated impact.

UNITED STATES SENTENCING COMMISSION DATA

Organizational Defendants Sentenced Prior to the Guidelines
(January 1, 1984, through June 30, 1990)

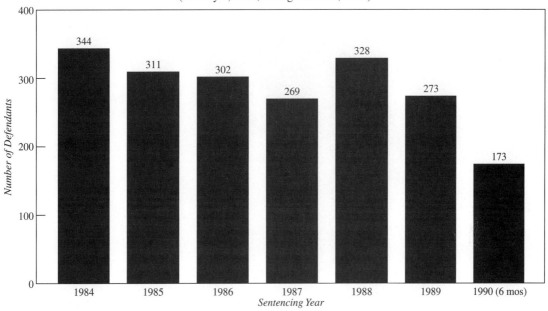

SOURCE: United States Sentencing Commission.

Organizational Defendants Sentenced Pursuant to the Guidelines
(November 1, 1987, through June 30, 1995)

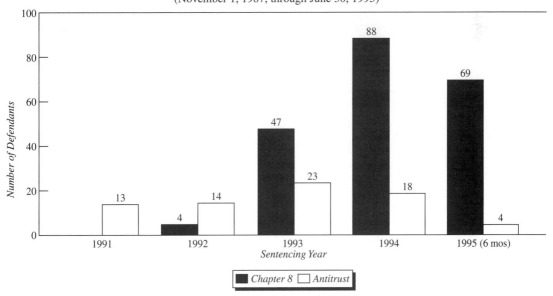

SOURCE: United States Sentencing Commission.

Number of Employees for Organizations Sentenced Pursuant to the Guidelines
(November 1, 1987, through June 30, 1995)

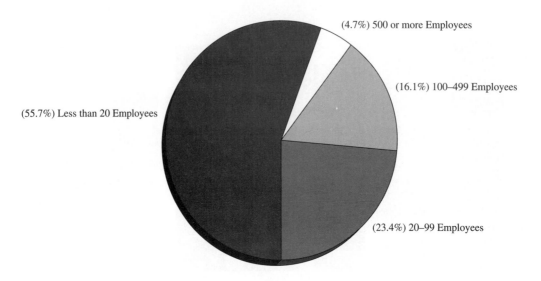

(4.7%) 500 or more Employees

(16.1%) 100–499 Employees

(55.7%) Less than 20 Employees

(23.4%) 20–99 Employees

"Organizational Defendants Sentenced Prior to the Guidelines," "Organizational Defendants Sentenced Pursuant to the Guidelines," "Number of Employees for Organizations Sentenced Pursuant to the Guidelines." Reprinted from "Corporate Crime in America: Strengthening the 'Good Citizen' Corporation," *Proceedings of the Second Symposium on Crime and Punishment in the United States,* United States Sentencing Commission, September 7–8, 1995 (Washington, DC) pp. 247–48.

HOFFMAN-LAROCHE CASE

A Sentencing Guidelines Milestone

JEFFREY M. KAPLAN

When the corporate sentencing guidelines went into effect in November 1991, prosecutors, compliance officers and others noted that fines under the new law could reach as high as $290 million or even greater. After the Daiwa Bank prosecution in 1996—which resulted in a $340 million criminal fine—punishment beyond the $290 million figure was no longer just a theoretical possibility. Later that year, a Delaware court, in the Caremark decision, raised the prospect of individual liability for a fine under the corporate sentencing guidelines, by permitting shareholders to sue directors personally for losses arising from failure to ensure that their company had put in place "an effective program to prevent and detect violations of law," which is the guidelines' articulation of a meaningful compliance program.

Now, another sentencing guidelines milestone has been reached. In May 1999, F. Hoffman-LaRoche, Ltd.—a large Swiss pharmaceutical company—was convicted of an antitrust conspiracy and fined $500 million. This is the largest criminal fine in the history of American law.

According to documents filed in court and other accounts, Hoffman-LaRoche, BASF AG (a German firm), and Rhone Poulenc SA (of France), engaged in a conspiracy from 1990 to 1999 to control the price and sales volume of a wide range of vitamins used as nutritional supplements or to enrich human food and animal feeds (including vitamins A, B2, B5, C, E and beta carotene). The conspiracy involved annual meetings to plan production, divide the market and fix prices, with follow-up sessions to enforce compliance. One member of the cartel referred to it as "Vitamins, Inc."

U.S. Assistant Attorney General for Antitrust, Joel Klein, said that "[t]his conspiracy has affected more than $5 billion of commerce in products found in every American household." According to some estimates, prices of vitamins were pushed up by 15–40 percent.

In addition to the record fine against Hoffman-LaRoche, BASF AG will pay a fine of $225 million, which is also one of the largest financial penalties ever imposed in a criminal

Jeffrey M. Kaplan, "Hoffman-LaRoche Case: A Sentencing Guidelines Milestone," *Ethikos and Corporate Conduct Quarterly* 13, no. 1 (July/August 1999), pp. 1–11. Reprinted with permission of *Ethikos and Corporate Conduct Quarterly.*

case. Rhone Poulenc, on the other hand, was not prosecuted at all. Because it brought evidence of the conspiracy to the government's attention, it was a beneficiary of the Antitrust Division's amnesty program. According to Gary Spratling, Deputy Assistant Attorney General, Rhone Poulenc's cooperation "led directly to the charges and the decision of the defendants" to plead guilty.

The fines will likely not be the only costs to the companies for their offenses. They also face class action lawsuits from businesses that bought vitamins. Hoffman-LaRoche and BASF have announced that they will attempt to settle the cases, but doing so may be costly in light of the admission of liability. Additionally, Karel Van Miert, the EU Competition Commissioner, declared after the U.S. prosecutions were announced, "This kind of cartel needs to be fined very heavily. It needs to be punished." Indeed, authorities in Canada, Europe and Australia have begun their own investigations into the matter.

In addition, the former head of Roche's global marketing division, Dr. Kumo Sommer, was charged with participating in the conspiracy and with lying to government investigators. He agreed to plead guilty, serve 4 months in prison, and pay a $100,000 fine. (The extent of *individual* financial liability under the sentencing guidelines is often underappreciated. In one recent antitrust case, an executive was fined $10 million.)

Hoffman-LaRoche is clearly an important prosecution. But looking beyond the headlines, what are the implications of this case for those engaged in business ethics and compliance work?

LESSON 1: THE NEED FOR STRONG ANTITRUST COMPLIANCE

Many of the largest fines under the corporate sentencing guidelines have involved antitrust violations. In addition to the penalties against Hoffman-LaRoche and BASF, at least three other companies have been fined $100 million or more in the past few years. Indeed, there are apparently about 35 federal grand juries investigating price-fixing in a variety of industries. The number of *state* investigations is harder to ascertain but could also be large, given the increasing emphasis on antitrust enforcement at the state level (as evidenced, among other ways, by the participation of many state attorneys general in the *Microsoft* case).

Despite this, many companies—particularly those that are moving from purely regulated into more entrepreneurial endeavors—have not adopted meaningful antitrust compliance measures. The risk of such inaction is great, given that the Antitrust Division has been on record for several years in setting forth the types of steps it expects to see in compliance programs. These include, according to Deputy Assistant Attorney General Spratling, "both regular and unannounced audits of price changes, discount practices and bid sheets, conducted by those familiar with the firm's past and present business practices and trained in recognizing questionable divergence, [and] [b]oth regular (scheduled) and unannounced audits of front-line pricing and bidding personnel to test their level of understanding of the antitrust laws and their degree of compliance with a program's requirements and standards relating to prevention and detection, backed up by disciplinary mechanisms and potential penalties for failures."

Spratling has also emphasized that "the elements of a compliance program, particularly the audit elements, should be 'customized'—that is, designed and targeted to the firm's specific organization, operation, personnel, and business practices."

In the face of this clear guidance and the dramatically escalating penalties for non-compliance, any company's failure to take meaningful antitrust compliance measures will likely be inexplicable to the government, shareholders and others.

LESSON 2: THE VALUE OF SELF-REPORTING

The importance of *timely* self-reporting could not be more starkly apparent than from the results of the vitamin price-fixing conspiracy. Two firms—Hoffman-LaRoche and BASF—will pay fines totaling $725 million. Yet the third conspirator—Rhone Poulenc—avoided prosecution altogether, because it was the first to report the crime to the government.

While the value of such cooperation may be most dramatically evident in the antitrust area (given the amnesty program), the same general principle applies to virtually every other risk areas as well. Indeed, the *Daiwa Bank* case, involving a $340 million fine under the corporate sentencing guidelines, was premised largely on the defendant's *late* reporting of a crime by one of its employees.

Yet self-reporting requires more than good intentions (or, in the case of some companies, a formal self-reporting policy). Unless companies have the means to *uncover* internal wrongdoing it is unlikely that they will receive the type of early warning that is often the key to prompt self-reporting. For this and other reasons, compliance auditing—emphasized in Spratling's recommendations—should not be limited to the antitrust area.

***

LESSON 5: THE WORST IS LIKELY YET TO COME

Assistant Attorney General Klein announced that with the Hoffman-LaRoche and BASF pleas, the Antitrust Division had "already secured more than $900 million in criminal fines in this fiscal year," which, he said, is "more than three times our previous annual record; in fact, more than the total amount of fines in the entire history of U.S. antitrust enforcement."

But records are clearly made to be broken, and it is likely that some prosecutors are already looking for a way to top the $500 million mark. Indeed, as great as the penalties were against Hoffman-LaRoche, they actually could have been worse. Spratling noted that the sentencing guidelines would have permitted a fine of as high as $1.3 billion.

Which company will make history with the first *billion* dollar fine? It will likely be one whose executives fail to heed the lessons of *Hoffman-LaRoche*. ❏

THE PRINCE

NICCOLÒ MACHIAVELLI

Niccolò Machiavelli (1469–1527) was born to a Florentine family distinguished by its history of political prominence. Unfortunately for Niccolò, his father (an unsuccessful lawyer) and his immediate family were beset by chronic financial woes. Machiavelli held significant positions in the government of Florence. As an ambassador, he was able to gather information about the chaotic world of international and Italian politics. He was also a military technician responsible for overseeing the city's military preparedness. As the defense minister, he was known for substituting a citizen's militia for the mercenary system. His power and influence ended in 1512, when the Spanish, in league with the pope, attacked Florence.

Machiavelli's writings were shocking and highly controversial. The Prince was banned by the pope; some critics contend that he led to modern totalitarianism. But Machiavelli saw The Prince as a realistic account of the qualities necessary for political success. He believed that although some common virtues (e.g., moderation, clemency, chastity, gentleness, generosity, vigor, religion, and devotion) might be praiseworthy, they were not what the real world required. A person with these virtues would be good—but too good for this world, and a disastrous leader. Instead, a leader would need qualities like energy, boldness, and shrewdness.

Compare this philosophy to that of Lao Tzu, who wrote in Tao Te Ching:

A leader is best
When people barely know that he exists.
Of a good leader, who talks little,
When his work is done, his aim fulfilled,
They will say, "We did this ourselves." (Chapter 17)

Machiavelli believed in divorcing ethics from politics, contending that "a weak Christian makes a better president than a strong one. . . . [A president] needs to be unscrupulous, without strong standards and beliefs." Since public acts often have unforeseen consequences, Machiavelli believed that a political agent may be excused for performing certain acts that would be ethically indefensible in private life.

. . . Going further down our list of qualities, I recognize every ruler should want to be thought of as compassionate and not cruel. Nevertheless, I have to warn you to be careful about being compassionate. Cesare Borgia was thought of as cruel; but this supposed cruelty of his restored order to the Romagna, united it, rendered it peaceful and law-abiding. If you think about it, you will realize he was, in fact, much more compassionate than the people of Florence, who, in order to avoid being thought cruel, allowed Pistoia to tear itself apart.[1] So a ruler ought not to mind the disgrace of being called cruel, if he keeps his subjects peaceful and law-abiding, for it is more compassionate to impose harsh punishments on a few than, out of excessive compassion, to allow disorder to spread, which leads to murders or looting. The whole community suffers if there are riots, while to maintain order the ruler only has to execute one or two individuals. Of all rulers, he who is new to power cannot escape a reputation for cruelty, for he is surrounded by dangers. Virgil has Dido say:

> Harsh necessity, and the fact my kingdom is new, oblige me to do these things,
> And to mass my armies on the frontiers.[2]

Nevertheless, you should be careful how you assess the situation and should think twice before you act. Do not be afraid of your own shadow. Employ policies that are moderated by prudence and sympathy. Avoid excessive self-confidence, which leads to carelessness, and avoid excessive timidity, which will make you insupportable.

This leads us to a question that is in dispute: Is it better to be loved than feared, or vice versa.[3] My reply is one ought to be both loved and feared; but, since it is difficult to accomplish both at the same time, I maintain it is much safer to be feared than loved, if you have to do without one of the two. For of men one can, in general, say this: They are ungrateful, fickle, deceptive and deceiving, avoiders of danger, eager to gain. As long as you serve their interests, they are devoted to you. They promise you their blood, their possessions, their lives, and their children, as I said before, so long as you seem to have no need of them. But as soon as you need help, they turn against you. Any ruler who relies simply on their promises and makes no other preparations, will be destroyed. For you will find that those whose support you buy, who do not rally to you because they admire your strength of character and nobility of soul, these are people you pay for, but they are never yours, and in the end you cannot get the benefit of your investment. Men are less nervous of offending someone who makes himself lovable, than someone who makes himself frightening. For love attaches men by ties of obligation, which, since men are wicked, they break whenever their interests are at stake. But fear restrains men because they are afraid of punishment, and this fear never leaves them. Still, a ruler should make himself feared in such a way that, if he does not inspire love, at least he does not provoke hatred. For it is perfectly possible to be feared and not hated. You will only be hated if you seize the property or the women of your subjects and citizens. Whenever you have to kill someone, make sure you have a suitable excuse and an obvious reason; but, above all else, keep your hands off other people's property; for men are quicker to forget the death of their father than the loss of their inheritance. Moreover, there

---

[1] In 1501.

[2] Virgil, *Aeneid,* I, 563–4.

[3] Cicero, *De officiis,* bk. 2, ch. 7, § 23–24.

are always reasons why you might want to seize people's property; and he who begins to live by plundering others will always find an excuse for seizing other people's possessions; but there are fewer reasons for killing people, and one killing need not lead to another.

When a ruler is at the head of his army and has a vast number of soldiers under his command, then it is absolutely essential to be prepared to be thought cruel; for it is impossible to keep an army united and ready for action without acquiring a reputation for cruelty. Among the extraordinary accomplishments of Hannibal, we may note one in particular: He commanded a vast army, made up of men of many different nations, who were fighting far from home, yet they never mutinied and they never fell out with one another, either when things were going badly, or when things were going well.[4] The only possible explanation for this is that he was known to be harsh and cruel. This, together with his numerous virtues [*virtù*], meant his soldiers always regarded him with admiration and fear. Without cruelty, his other virtues [*virtù*] would not have done the job. Those who write about Hannibal without thinking things through both admire the loyalty of his troops and criticize the cruelty that was its principal cause. If you doubt my claim that his other virtues [*virtù*] would have been insufficient, take the case of Scipio.[5] He was not only unique in his own day, but history does not record anyone his equal. But his army rebelled against him in Spain.[6] The sole cause of this was his excessive leniency, which meant his soldiers had more freedom than is compatible with good military discipline. Fabius Maximus criticized him for this in the senate and accused him of corrupting the Roman armies. When Locri was destroyed by one of his commanders,[7] he did not avenge the deaths of the inhabitants, and he did not punish his officer's insubordination. He was too easygoing. This was so apparent that one of his supporters in the senate was obliged to excuse him by saying he was no different from many other men, who were better at doing their own jobs than at making other people do theirs. In course of time, had he remained in command without learning from his mistakes, this aspect of Scipio's character would have destroyed his glorious reputation. But, because his authority was subordinate to that of the senate, not only were the consequences of this defect mitigated, but it even enhanced his reputation.

I conclude, then, that, as far as being feared and loved is concerned, since men decide for themselves whom they love, and rulers decide whom they fear, a wise ruler should rely on the emotion he can control, not on the one he cannot. But he must take care to avoid being hated, as I have said.

---

[4]Hannibal (ca. 247–183 B.C.) campaigned in Italy from 218 to 203 B.C. Machiavelli's source is Polybius, bk. 11, ch. 19.

[5]Scipio (ca. 236–183 B.C.) defeated Hannibal at Zama in North Africa (202 B.C.).

[6]In 206 B.C. Livy, bk. 28, chs. 24–29.

[7]In 205 B.C.

ETHICAL DILEMMAS REGARDING COMPETITIVE INTELLIGENCE

Thomas Furtado

How far should a company go in seeking sensitive information about competitors? What are the parameters for ethical competition? The following case asks you to consider these and other issues surrounding the nature of free market competition. Do you do something simply because you can? Imagine you are in a competitor's office and you see confidential information related to your industry sitting on her desk. She leaves the room for a moment to speak with someone. Do you take a look? What factors would enter into your decision? Does it matter whether "anyone else would do it"?

PART A

Gathering and Using Competitor Information

Transformations in the technology of generating and storing information, and the increasing reliance on "knowledge workers" in business and commerce, mean that timely information and creative ideas are often the key differentiators in competitive industries like high-tech engineering and manufacturing, computers, financial services, and industrial and commercial electronics. In an age when clones can appear overnight, companies must take all possible precautions to protect their information from competitors for as long as possible. Likewise, successful businesses will vigorously seek to learn as much as possible about competitors' products and plans.

What are appropriate principles to follow in gathering and using competitive information? Is anything acceptable as long as it is not illegal? Does it matter in what industry and/or in what region of the world we do business?

What Is Competitive Information?

One major U.S. corporation with worldwide business activities defines competitive information as follows: It "includes anything related to the competitive environment or to a competitor—for example, information related to products, markets, pricing, or business

---

plans. This information could be drawn from published sources or could otherwise be widely available to the public. Some of this information will be oriented to a specific competitor ('competitor information') and some competitor information would be considered 'proprietary,' 'business confidential,' or 'trade secret' which a business would attempt to hold closely."

As this definition suggests, much competitive information exists in public channels and can be obtained legitimately. For instance, traditional techniques for protecting information have been patents, copyrights and trademarks. While these provide legal protection, the information is in the public domain. By following the patent applications of a firm's employees, a competitor could quickly get a picture of their research. In fact, many companies openly discuss competitive intelligence and some have departments well known in the industry which are dedicated to gathering such information.

Legal gathering of information readily available in the public domain, then, does not raise any ethical concerns. Just as clearly, on the other side, obviously illegal activities such as break-ins, computer hacking, and wiretaps are not ethically ambiguous. Even the people who commit such actions are fully aware they are breaking the law. The tough ethical questions arise when information is gathered in ways that do not fit neatly into either of these categories.

Sources of Competitive Information

One of the most frequent sources of competitive information, especially proprietary information, is a company's own employees. Despite intellectual property agreements intended to establish company ownership of creative efforts funded by the firm, employees still sometimes turn over proprietary information to a competitor. Bitter, disillusioned employees, who have perhaps been by-passed for promotions and other opportunities, see giving confidential data to a competitor as rectifying past wrongs done to them.

Company employees may also be negligent. Extremely sensitive data are left exposed on a desk while the employee goes elsewhere. Folders are left on someone else's desk while attending a meeting. Sales reps leave their briefcases in a customer's office while they go out for lunch. Phone conversations that can be overheard in a public place are often the source of confidential data for someone who happens to be at the right place at the right time.

Customers can also be a source of competitive information. In many cases they are as negligent with the supplier's data as they sometimes are with their own. In other cases, the customer may deliberately give one supplier's proprietary information to another during a bidding process. Some customers choose instead to give all the information from all bidders to the others in an effort to make the process more competitive. They may do so even when the data were furnished to them by the suppliers with "proprietary" and "secret" markings.

Another source of competitive information is technical seminars and conferences. Often attendees target speakers at breaks and attempt to learn critical information. They are most successful at this when they misrepresent themselves, either with a fake name badge or no badge at all, letting the target person think they are merely curious participants and certainly not a competitor.

What Actions Are Ethically Appropriate?

As these examples illustrate, managers in highly competitive industries are faced with numerous opportunities both to actively gather competitive information and to use information that may have been given to them. Consider the following example:

You are the engineering director of a large international firm working on a new compact disk that will be able to produce high-quality video on the same size surface as an audio disk. You have two formidable competitors and the stakes are enormous. Not only must this small disk be capable of playing movies of up to three hours duration, but to capture the video market from cassette tape, the equipment must have recording capability. All three of you have solved the first challenge, but no one seems to be breaking through on the recording issue. Your own engineers have had little success in this regard.

While attending a technical seminar on the subject whose participants also include representatives from your competitors, you listen to a presentation by an engineer from one of the competitors. The presentation touches on the recording problem in a way that makes you think they may have solved the problem.

PART B

Protecting Competitive Information: The Lopez Case

Part A of this case focused generally on how competitor information is gathered, received and used. But when a firm seeks to protect its own information, complications can sometimes arise when the "giver" and the "receiver" disagree over the facts and over the extent and limits of what can be protected. A case in point is the incident concerning Mr. José Ignacio Lopez de Arriortua, the head of global purchasing at General Motors who left to join Volkswagen in a similar position in March 1993.

Within a month, GM claimed that Mr. Lopez had taken with him highly secret information about their Opel division in Germany. Shortly thereafter, GM filed a complaint with the German courts alleging industrial spying and theft. In subsequent months, General Motors went to court to prevent Mr. Lopez from working for Volkswagen, and also attempted to prevent seven other GM employees who had left with him from working for VW. At the time of this writing, many of the issues are still in the courts awaiting decisions. The German courts ruled, however, that Mr. Lopez and his team could begin work at Volkswagen.

Although the details are not entirely clear and the situation may be resolved through legal remedies or an out-of-court settlement by mid-year 1995, the following general account based on published reports provides a springboard for considering important ethical issues in cases like this.

Background at General Motors

General Motors has been the largest auto manufacturer in the world for several decades. In the 1980s, however, GM began to lose market share to Japanese and German auto makers, and by the early 1990s, it was also dealing with a strong resurgence of Ford and Chrysler. In particular, GM had been slow to change its manufacturing processes, and consequently found itself competing with higher cost structures than many of its competitors.

One bright spot in the GM story was the performance of its German company, Adam Opel AG, which had slashed costs considerably through a very aggressive approach to its suppliers. The architect of this initiative was José Ignacio Lopez, Opel's head of purchasing. Through what some called heavy-handed tactics, Mr. Lopez had successfully renegotiated many supplier contracts to provide much lower costs, and he was given much of the credit for the turnaround of GM in Europe. By 1993, General Motors was a very close second to Volkswagen in auto production in Europe.

In the meantime, GM had brought Mr. Lopez to Detroit in May 1992 to replicate his achievements as the head of global purchasing for the entire organization. Using the same aggressive approach, he soon began to make a difference in the company and was named the auto industry's "Man of the Year" for 1992 by a major trade publication in Detroit. Ironically, only a few months later, he was the center of a major confrontation between General Motors and Volkswagen.

Lopez Moves to Volkswagen

Volkswagen, the largest auto producer in Europe, had fallen on hard times in the early 1990s. Like GM, it was having a difficult time keeping its costs in line and staying competitive. Over the past several years, it had seen General Motors and its Opel company cut into its market share. Obviously, VW was well aware of the role Mr. Lopez had played in the GM resurgence.

Some time in early 1993, Volkswagen and Mr. Lopez began to talk. Mr. Lopez had reportedly become disenchanted with his employer over what he saw as a broken promise. Apparently feeling betrayed, he decided to leave GM.

General Motors Reaction

Once Mr. Lopez told GM Chief Executive John Smith that he was leaving, events moved swiftly. A week later, on March 16, 1993, Mr. Lopez was appointed head of purchasing and production for Volkswagen, and within another week, seven of his colleagues, who had followed him from Opel to Detroit, resigned from General Motors to join him at VW. On April 7, Mr. Smith made the first serious allegation that Mr. Lopez may have stolen secret documents and plans about future GM and Opel products and strategies, a charge Mr. Lopez denies. Six weeks later, GM went to court in Germany alleging that Lopez and others had stolen secret competitive information.

In the two years since, charges and countercharges have been made by individuals and the companies concerned. Boxes of documents were found and seized by the courts. Volkswagen denied the material was secret and went so far as to suggest the documents were planted by Opel security forces. Opel and GM attempted to ban Lopez and the other seven from working for VW, but they lost this case in the German Labor Law court in Wolfsburg in September 1994. At this point, Mr. Lopez had been on the job for over a year and was receiving full support over the incident from the Volkswagen head, Ferdinand Piëch.

AIRLINE TRAVEL
Safety at What Price?
KENNETH K. BOYER

You want a low-price ticket to your favorite destination, but how low? How do you think airlines lower their prices? The following article cautions that sometimes the lowest price to the consumer is not the best option.

Many people take the convenience and ease of air travel for granted. . . . The growth of air travel is largely based on two factors: low prices and excellent safety. Greater competition among airlines has generated low fares which benefit the consumer, allowing passengers to travel long distances quickly and cheaply. In fact, low prices can be viewed as one of the major factors fueling the boom in air travel. Yet, while low prices may lure passengers away from other modes of travel (train, automobile, boat), safety remains a critical qualifier. Without a good safety record, airlines would not be able to attract customers at any price. In fact, commercial airline travel is one of the safest modes of travel: according to the National Safety Council the fatality rate for people traveling by automobile was 37 times greater than that for people traveling on U.S. airlines during the period from 1980 to 1992.

Several discount airlines such as Southwest, Valujet and America West have prospered by offering very low prices for air travel, while at the same time larger airlines such as United, American and Delta have been forced to lower their prices to remain competitive. How have these airlines managed to cut costs in order to fund reductions in prices? Several techniques have been used, including outsourcing of maintenance activities, labor savings through new contracts with airline personnel, and increasing the lifetime of airplanes.

The issue of airline safety has recently become a hotly debated topic following a spate of recent crashes, including TWA flight 800 (230 passengers killed) off Long Island and Valujet flight 592 (110 passengers killed) in the Everglades. The Federal Aviation Administration (FAA) thoroughly investigates every accident and incident in order to identify causes, and prevent future accidents. The FAA also regulates U.S. airports, commercial airlines, pilots, etc., in an attempt to ensure safe airline travel. The ultimate goal is to achieve a 100% safety record, yet the reality is that some accidents are likely to occur despite the best efforts of every agency associated with airline travel. Greater regulation and attention to safety should result in improved safety, yet may also result in increased costs. There is an inherent trade-off between low cost and safety. How should a balance be struck between the two objectives? The following discussion examines two factors that affect both cost and safety.

MAINTENANCE OF AIRCRAFT

Airplane maintenance accounts for 15% to 20% of an airline's direct operating costs. For instance, American Airlines spends approximately $1.5 billion per year on maintenance. Because maintenance represents such a large cost, reducing these costs has become a primary means for airlines to decrease their operating costs. Larger airlines often enjoy certain economies of scale based on the ability to build dedicated maintenance facilities and spread the huge costs incurred over a large fleet of planes. Many smaller airlines such as Valujet have opted to outsource much of their maintenance in an effort to reduce costs. This practice can lead to saving between 20% and 30% on maintenance costs, but at what price in terms of safety?

A major trade-off associated with outsourcing maintenance is that the airline no longer directly controls this critical safety element. The risk of mistakes or poor quality repairs increases as the number of companies involved grows. Outsourcing also adds an additional layer of communication, forcing airlines to expend additional energy monitoring not only their own personnel, but also the work performed by an external organization. For many smaller airlines this additional coordination may simply be too great a challenge. In fact, several airlines have experienced close calls due to poor maintenance. For example, in June 1996 an engine on a Valujet flight at Atlanta exploded. The engine had been overhauled and sold to Valujet by a repair station in Turkey that lacked FAA approval.

The safety concerns associated with outsourcing are compounded by the increasing use of counterfeit, or bogus, parts. Numerous FAA inspectors say the problem of substandard parts has grown dramatically over the past five years. This growth is in part because the nation's aging airline fleet needs more parts. Cash-strapped small and start-up airlines are more likely to be hit with bogus parts because their extensive outsourcing of maintenance makes quality assurance much more difficult. Bogus parts played a role in at least 166 U.S.-based aircraft accidents or less serious mishaps from 1973 to 1993 according to *Business Week*. Yet, the actual number may have been far greater since it is impossible to determine the cause of a crash in many cases.

WHY ARE BOGUS PARTS A GROWTH BUSINESS?

A single Boeing 747 has approximately 6 million parts. Many of these parts will have been replaced five times or more by the time the plane is ten years old. Airlines, which lose between $20,000 and $100,000 in revenue for each day a plane is grounded, must depend on a mostly unregulated network of 5,000 dealers to keep spare parts in stock. Opportunities for unscrupulous dealers to cut corners or blatantly falsify records abound in this system. For example, a broker can buy scrap compressor blades for jet engines for as little as $1 each. Once smoothed and coated, these blades can then be sold for $1200. One repair station rewelded worn-out turbine blades. The blades then broke off, damaging the engine on a commuter aircraft.

The potential profit from supplying bogus parts is so large that Detective Luis Vergera, a bogus parts specialist in Miami's Dade County Police Department, says, "I know of people who quit running drugs and switched to aircraft parts because it was more profitable." So, what can be done to stem the tide of bogus parts? Requiring every part to be traced back to an approved manufacturer would be prohibitively expensive and "we'd all go out of business tomorrow," according to Michael Rioux, vice-president of engineering and maintenance at the Air Transport Association, an industry group representing 21 major airlines. While the FAA says it recognizes "the need for additional guidance dealing with the issue of documentation of parts," it has failed to act decisively in moving toward new standards.

The question of how to deal with the problem of bogus parts highlights a fundamental conflict within the FAA. In essence FAA has a dual mission to both promote the business of aviation and ensure public safety. Critics contend that the FAA has historically erred on the side of commerce.

While airline safety overall is very good, there certainly are some problems and risks associated with air travel. There are several questions which the FAA must grapple with: What approach should be used to monitor and ensure safety when airlines outsource their maintenance and to prevent the use of bogus parts? How much effort would be allocated to safety—in other words, what is the break-even point between cost and safety? How should a balance be struck between low-cost travel and greater safety? After all, while perfect safety is in theory attainable, it may come at a prohibitive cost.

REFERENCES

1. Zimba, S., "Preventive Maintenance Keeps Planes Airworthy," *Chicago Tribune,* September 15, 1996, sect. 5, pp. 1, 4.
2. Dahl, J., and Miller, L., "Which Is the Safest Airline? It All Depends . . . ," *The Wall Street Journal,* July 24, 1996, p. B1.
3. Stern, W., "Warning! Bogus Parts Have Turned Up in Commercial Jets. Where's the FAA," *Business Week,* June 10, 1996, pp. 84–92.
4. Condom, P., "Is Outsourcing a Winning Solution," *Interavia Business and Technology,* May 1994, p. 34.

TOPIC STUDY: SPACE SHUTTLE
CHALLENGER DISASTER

SPACE SHUTTLE
CHALLENGER
Mission 51-L Launch Decision
KURT HOOVER AND WALLACE T. FOWLER

In the following materials published on the website of the University of Texas, Hoover and Fowler describe the events that led to the space shuttle Challenger *disaster in 1986. Consider whether there are any similarities between this case and the Ford Pinto case. What would you have hoped that decision makers had learned from the Pinto case that may have helped in this case?*

On January 28, 1986, the Space Shuttle Challenger was launched for the last time. The decision to launch the Challenger was not simple. Certainly no one dreamed that the Shuttle would explode less than two minutes after lift-off. Much has been said and written about the decision to launch. Was the decision to launch correct? How was the decision made? Could anyone have foreseen the subsequent explosion? Should the decision-making procedure have been modified? These questions are examined in this case study.

BACKGROUND

The Space Shuttle

The Space Shuttle is the most complicated vehicle ever constructed. Its complexity dwarfs any previous project ever attempted, including the Apollo project. The Apollo project possessed a very specific goal—to send men to the moon—whereas the Space Shuttle program has a wide variety of goals, some of which conflict. The attempt to satisfy conflicting goals is one of the chief roots of difficulty with the design of the Space Shuttle. Originally, the design was to be only a part of NASA's overall manned space transportation system, but because of politics and budget cuts, it was transformed from an integral component of a system to the sole component of the manned space program.

Kurt Hoover and Wallace T. Fowler, "Space Shuttle Challenger: Mission 51-L Launch Decision." http://www.ac.utexas.edu/~lehman/ethics/challeng.htm#back. Reprinted by permission of the authors.

The Space Shuttle was the first attempt to produce a truly reusable spacecraft. All previous spacecraft were designed to fly only a single mission. In the late 1960's, NASA envisioned a vehicle which could be used repeatedly, thus reducing both the engineering cost and hardware costs. However, the resulting vehicle was not as envisioned. It had severe design flaws, one of which caused the loss of the Challenger.

NASA Planning and Politics

NASA's post-Apollo plans for the continued manned exploration of space rested on a three-legged triad. The first leg was a reusable space-transportation system, the Space Shuttle, which could transport men and cargo to low earth orbit (LEO) and then land back on Earth to prepare for another mission. The second leg was a manned orbiting space station that would be resupplied by the Shuttle and would serve as both a transfer point for activities further from Earth and as a scientific and manufacturing platform. The final leg was the exploration of Mars, which would start from the Space Station. Unfortunately the politics and inflation of the early 70's forced NASA to retreat from its ambitious program. Both the Space Station and the Journey to Mars were delayed indefinitely, and the United States manned space program was left standing on one leg—the Space Shuttle. Even worse, the Shuttle was constantly under attack by a Democratic Congress and poorly defended by a Republican president.

To retain Shuttle funding, NASA was forced to make a series of major concessions. First, facing a highly constrained budget, NASA sacrificed the research and development necessary to produce a truly reusable shuttle and instead accepted a design that was only partially reusable, eliminating one of the features that made the shuttle attractive in the first place. Solid rocket boosters (SRBs) were used instead of safer liquid fueled boosters because they required a much smaller research-and-development effort. Numerous other design changes were made to reduce the level of research and development required.

Second, to increase its political clout and to guarantee a steady customer base, NASA enlisted the support of the United States Air Force. The Air Force could provide the considerable political clout of the Defense Department and had many satellites which required launching. However, Air Force support did not come without a price. The Shuttle payload bay was required to meet Air Force size and shape requirements, which placed key constraints on the ultimate design. Even more important was the Air Force requirement that the Shuttle be able to launch from Vandenburg Air Force Base in California. This constraint required a larger cross range than the Florida site, which in turn decreased the total allowable vehicle weight. The weight reduction required the elimination of the design's air-breathing engines, resulting in a single-pass unpowered landing that greatly limited the safety and landing versatility of the vehicle.

FACTORS AFFECTING THE LAUNCH DECISION

Pressures to Fly

As the year 1986 began, there was extreme pressure on NASA to "Fly out the Manifest." From its inception the Space Shuttle program had been plagued by exaggerated expectations, funding inconsistencies, and political pressures. The ultimate design was shaped almost as much by politics as physics. President Kennedy's declaration that the United States would land a man on the moon before the end of the decade had provided NASA's Apollo program with high visibility, a clear direction, and powerful political backing. The Space Shuttle program was not as fortunate; it had neither a clear direction nor consistent political backing.

System Status and Competition

In spite of all its early difficulties, the Shuttle program looked quite good in 1985. A total of 19 flights had been launched and recovered, and although many had experienced minor problems, all but one of the flights could rightfully be categorized as successful. However, delays in the program as a whole had led the Air Force to request funds to develop an expendable launch vehicle. Worse still, the French launch organization Arianespace had developed an independent capability to place satellites into orbit at prices the Shuttle could not hope to match without greatly increased federal subsidization (which was not likely to occur as Congress was becoming increasingly dissatisfied with the program). The Shuttle was soon going to have to begin showing that it could pay for itself. There was only one way this could be done—increase the number of flights.

For the Shuttle program, 1986 was to be the year of truth. NASA had to prove that it could launch a large number of flights on time to continue to attract customers and retain Congressional support. Unfortunately, 1986 did not start out well for the Shuttle program. Columbia, Flight 61-C, had experienced a record four on-pad aborts and had three other schedule slips. Finally, on Mission 61-C, Columbia was forced to land at Edwards Air Force Base rather than at Kennedy Space Center as planned. The delays in Columbia's launch and touchdown threatened to upset the launch schedule for the rest of the year.

Not only did Columbia's landing at Edwards require it to be ferried back to the Cape, but several key shuttle parts had to be carried back by T-38 for use on the other vehicles. These parts included a temperature sensor for the propulsion system, the nose-wheel steering box, an air sensor for the crew cabin, and one of the five general-purpose computers. At the time of the Challenger explosion, NASA supposedly had four complete shuttles. In reality there were only enough parts for two complete shuttles. Parts were passed around and reinstalled in the orbiters with the earliest launch dates. Each time a part was removed or inserted, the shuttles were exposed to a whole host of possible servicing-induced problems.

In addition to problems caused by the Flight 61-C of Columbia, the next Columbia flight, 61-E, scheduled for March, also put pressure on NASA to launch the Challenger on schedule. The March flight of Columbia was to carry the ASTRO spacecraft, which had a very tight launch window because NASA wanted it to reach Halley's Comet before a Russian probe arrived at the comet. In order to launch Columbia 61-E on time, Challenger had to carry out its mission and return to Kennedy by January 31.

Politics

NASA had much to gain from a successful Flight 51-L. The "Teacher in Space" mission had generated much more press interest than other recent shuttle flights. Publicity was and continues to be extremely important to the agency. It is a very important tool that NASA uses to help ensure its funding. The recent success of the Space Shuttle program had left NASA in a Catch-22 situation. Successful Shuttle flights were no longer news because they were almost ordinary. However, launch aborts and delayed landings were more newsworthy because they were much less common.

In addition to general publicity gained from flight 51-L, NASA undoubtedly was aware that a successful mission would play well in the White House. President Reagan shared NASA's love of publicity and was about to give a State of the Union speech. The value of an elementary teacher giving a lecture from orbit was obvious and was lost neither on NASA nor on President Reagan.

SEQUENCE OF EVENTS

Monday, January 27

On Monday NASA had attempted to place Challenger in orbit, only to be stymied by a stripped bolt and high winds. All preliminary procedures had been completed and the crew had just boarded when the first problem struck. A microsensor on the hatch indicated that it was not shut securely; it turned out that the hatch had been shut securely and that the sensor was malfunctioning, but valuable time was used determining that the sensor was the problem.

After the hatch was closed, the external hatch handle could not be removed. The threads on the connecting bolt were stripped, and instead of cleanly disengaging when turned, the handle simply spun around. Attempts to use a portable drill to remove the handle failed. Technicians on the scene asked Mission Control for permission to saw the bolt off. Fearing some form of structural stress to the hatch, engineers made numerous time-consuming calculations before giving the go-ahead to cut off the bolt. The entire process consumed almost two hours before the countdown was resumed.

Misfortunes continued. During the attempts to verify the integrity of the hatch and remove the handle, the wind had been steadily rising. Chief Astronaut John Young flew a series of approaches in the Shuttle training aircraft and confirmed the worst fears of Mission Control. The crosswinds at the Cape were in excess of the level allowed for the abort contingency. The opportunity had been missed and the flight would have to wait until the next possible launch window, the following morning. Everyone was quite discouraged, especially since extremely cold weather was forecast for Tuesday, which could further postpone the launch.

Tuesday, January 28

After the canceled launch on Monday morning there was a great deal of concern about the possible effects of weather. The predicted low for Tuesday morning was 23° F, far below the nominal operating temperature for many of the Challenger's subsystems. Undoubtedly, as the sun came up and the launch time approached, both air temperature and vehicle would warm up, but there was still concern. Would the ambient temperature become high enough to meet launch requirements? NASA's Launch Commit Criteria stated that no launch should occur at temperatures below 31° F. There was also concern over any permanent effects on the Shuttle due to the cold overnight temperatures.

All NASA centers and subcontractors involved with the Shuttle were asked to determine the possible effects of cold weather and present any concerns. In the meantime Kennedy Space Center went ahead with its freeze-protection plan. This plan included the use of using anti-freeze in the huge acoustic damping ponds and allowing warm water to bleed through pipes, showers, and hoses to prevent freezing.

The weather for Tuesday morning was to be clear and cold. Because the overnight low was forecast at 23° F, there was doubt that Challenger would be much above freezing at launch time. The Launch Commit Criteria included very specific temperature limits for most systems on the shuttle. A special wavier would be required to launch if any of these criteria were not met. Although these criteria were supposedly legally binding, Marshall Space Flight Center administrator Larry Mulloy had been routinely writing waivers to cover the problems with the SRBs on the recent Shuttle flights.

Engineers at Morton Thiokol, the SRB manufacturer in Utah, were very concerned about the possible effects of the cold weather. The problems with the SRBs had been long known to engineers Roger Boisjoly and Allan McDonald, but both felt that their concerns were being ignored. They felt that the request by NASA to provide comment on the launch conditions was a golden opportunity to present their concerns. They were sure that Challenger should not be launched in such conditions as those expected for Tuesday morning. Using weather data provided by the Air Force, they calculated that at the 9:00 A.M. launch time the temperature of the O-rings would be only 29° F. Even by 2:00 P.M., the O-rings would have warmed only to 38° F.

The design validation tests originally done by Thiokol covered only a very narrow temperature range. The temperature data base did not include any temperatures below 53° F. The O-rings from Flight 51-C, which had been launched under cold conditions the previous year, showed very significant erosion. This was the only data available on the effects of cold, but all the Thiokol engineers agreed that the cold weather would decrease the elasticity of the synthetic rubber O-rings, which in turn might cause them to seal slowly and allow hot combustion gas to surge through the joint.

Based on these results, the engineers at Thiokol recommended to NASA Marshall that Challenger not be launched until the O-rings reached a temperature of 53° F. The management of Marshall was flabbergasted, and demanded that Thiokol prove that launching was unsafe. Such a response was a complete reversal of normal procedure. Normally, NASA required its subcontractors to prove that something was safe. Now they were requiring their subcontractors to prove that something was unsafe. Faced with this extreme pressure, Thiokol management asked its engineers to reconsider their position. When the engineers stuck to their original recommendations not to fly, Thiokol management overruled them and gave NASA its approval to launch.

Rockwell, the company that manufactured the Orbiter, also had concerns about launching in cold and icy conditions. Their major concern was the possibility of ice from either the Shuttle or the launch structure striking and damaging the vehicle. Like Thiokol, they recommended against the launch, and they too were pressed to explain their reasoning. Instead of sticking with their original strong recommendation against launch, the Rockwell team carefully worded their statement to say that they could not fully guarantee the safety of the Shuttle.

In its desire to fly out its manifest, NASA was willing to accept Rockwell's statement as a recommendation. The final decision to launch, however, belonged to Jesse Moore. He was informed of Rockwell's concerns, but was also told that they had approved the launch. The engineers and management from NASA Marshall chose not to even mention the original concerns of Thiokol. Somehow, the warnings and concerns were diminished as they were communicated up each step of the ladder of responsibility.

Late Monday night the decision to push onward with the launch was made. Despite the very real concerns of some of the engineers familiar with the actual vehicle subsystems, the launch was approved. No one at NASA wanted to be responsible for further delaying an already delayed launch. Everyone was aware of the pressure on the agency to fly out the manifest, yet no one would have consciously risked the lives of the seven astronauts. The potential rewards had come to outweigh the potential risks. Clearly, there were many reasons for launching Challenger on that cold Tuesday morning, and a great deal of frustration from the previous launch attempt remained.

PRE-LAUNCH EVENTS

Although the decision to launch on Tuesday had been made late on Monday night, it was still possible that something might force NASA to postpone the launch. However, the decision to launch had been made, and nothing was going to stand in the way; the "press on" mentality was firmly established, and even if all of Florida froze over, Challenger would launch.

The pre-launch inspection of Challenger and the launch pad by the ice-team was unusual to say the least. The ice-team's responsibility was to remove any frost or ice on the vehicle or launch structure. What they found during their inspection looked like something out of a science-fiction movie. The freeze protection plan implemented by Kennedy personnel had gone very wrong. Hundreds of icicles, some up to 16 in. long, clung to the launch structure. The handrails and walkways near the shuttle entrance were covered in ice, making them extremely dangerous if the crew had to make an emergency evacuation. One solid sheet of ice stretched from the 195-ft. level to the 235-ft. level on the gantry. However, NASA continued to cling to its calculations that there would be no damage due to flying ice shaken loose during the launch.

THE LAUNCH

As the SRBs ignited, the cold conditions did not allow the O-rings to properly seal. Within the first 300 milliseconds of ignition, both the primary and secondary O-rings on the lowest section of the right SRB were vaporized across 70° of arc by the hot combustion gases. Puffs of smoke with the same frequency as the vibrating booster are clearly present in pictures of the launch. However, soon after the Challenger cleared the tower, a temporary seal of glassy aluminum-oxides from the propellant formed in place of the burned O-rings and Challenger continued skyward.

Unfortunately, at the time of greatest dynamic pressure, the shuttle encountered wind shear. As the Challenger's guidance control lurched the Shuttle to compensate for the wind shear, the fragile aluminum-oxide seal shattered. Flame arched out of the joint, struck the external tank and quickly burned through the insulation and the aluminum structure. Liquid hydrogen fuel streamed out and was ignited. The Challenger exploded.

When the remains of the cabin were recovered, it became apparent that most of the crew survived the explosion and separation of the Shuttle from the rest of the vehicle. During the 2-min.-45-sec. fall to the ocean, at least four of the personal egress packs were activated and at least three were functioning when the Challenger struck the water. The high-speed impact with the water produced a force of 200g and was undoubtedly the cause of death for all the crew.

Post-Crash Events

Since the crash of Challenger, NASA and external investigators have taken a look at both the shuttle and the sequence of events that allowed it to be launched. The SRBs have gone through significant redesign and now include a capture feature on the field joint. The three Marshall administrators most responsible for allowing the SRB problems to go uncorrected have all left NASA. Following the recommendations of the Rogers commission, NASA has attempted to streamline and clean up its communication lines. A system for reporting suspected problems anonymously now exists within NASA. In addition, the astronauts themselves are now much more active in many decision-making aspects of the program. The former NASA Administrator, Admiral Richard Truly, is a former shuttle astronaut.

SAFETY AND ETHICS ISSUES

There are many questions involving safety and/or ethics that are raised when we examine the decision to launch the Challenger. Obviously, the situation was unsafe. The ethics questions are more complex. If high standards of ethical conduct are to be maintained, then each person must differentiate between right and wrong and must follow the course that is determined to be the right, or ethical, course. Frequently, the determination of right or wrong is not simple, and good arguments can be made on both sides of the question. Some of the issues raised by the Challenger launch decision are listed below.

1. Are solid rocket boosters inherently too dangerous to use on manned spacecraft? If so, why are they a part of the design?
2. Was safety traded for political acceptability in the design of the Space Shuttle?
3. Did the pressure to succeed cause too many things to be promised to too many people during the design of the Space Shuttle?
4. Did the need to maintain the launch schedule force decision makers to compromise safety in the launch decision?
5. Were responsibilities being ignored in the writing of routine launch waivers for the Space Shuttle?
6. Were managers at Rockwell and Morton Thiokol wise (or justified) in ignoring the recommendations of their engineers?
7. Did the engineers at Rockwell and Morton Thiokol do all that they could to convince their own management and NASA of the dangers of launch?
8. When NASA pressed its contractors to launch, did it violate its responsibility to ensure crew safety?
9. When NASA discounted the effects of the weather, did it violate its responsibility to ensure crew safety?

REFERENCES

1. "Actions to Implement the Recommendations of the Presidential Commission of the Space Shuttle Challenger Accident," National Aeronautics and Space Administration, Washington, DC, July 14, 1986.
2. *Challenger: A Major Malfunction.* Malcolm McConnell. Doubleday & Company, Inc. Garden City, NY. 1987.
3. *Prescription for Disaster.* Joseph J. Trento. Crown Publishers Inc. New York, NY. 1987.
4. "Report of the Presidential Commission of the Space Shuttle Challenger Accident," The Presidential Commission of the Space Shuttle Challenger Accident, Washington, DC, June 6, 1986.

ROGER BOISJOLY
ON THE SPACE
SHUTTLE DISASTER

ROGER BOISJOLY

The following information regarding Roger Boisjoly introduces his materials on the World Wide Web:

Roger Boisjoly had over a quarter century's experience in the aerospace industry in 1985 when he became involved in an improvement effort on the O-rings which connect segments of Morton Thiokol's Solid Rocket Booster, used to bring the Space Shuttle into orbit. Boisjoly has spent his entire career making well-informed decisions based on his understanding and belief in a professional engineer's rights and responsibilities. For his honesty and integrity leading up to and directly following the shuttle disaster Roger Boisjoly was awarded the Prize for Scientific Freedom and Responsibility from the American Association for the Advancement of Science.

It is interesting to note Roger Boisjoly's concerns regarding the Hoover and Fowler materials that precede these. Boisjoly, in a telephone conversation with me, expressed his concern over Hoover and Fowler's characterization of the Challenger events in the beginning of their materials. After reading their statement that "no one dreamed that the Shuttle would explode less than two minutes after lift-off," Boisjoly asked me, "What am I, a hologram?" He also indicated that the claim that NASA had Launch Commit Criteria of 31° F or higher was merely heresay and that he didn't believe that this standard ever existed. Instead, he said that there was an actual performance criterion for the booster of 40° F, which certainly would not have been met.

In the following materials, Boisjoly explains the nature of his involvement in the O-ring decision and his reaction to NASA's handling of this issue. In addition, you will find interoffice Morton-Thiokol memoranda discussing the "potential failure criticality" of the O-ring problem and encouraging postponement of the shuttle mission.

III. BEING ASKED TO SOFTEN THE URGENCY OF THE O-RING PROBLEM

My notebook entry on August 15, 1985, reads as follows: "An attempt to form the team (referring to the Solid Rocket Motor seal erosion team) was made on 19 July 1985. This attempt virtually failed and resulted in my writing memo 2870:FY86:073. This memo finally got some response and a team was formed officially. The first meeting was held on August 15, 1985, at 2:30 P.M." The memo referred to is the one I read to the Presidential Commission on February 25, 1986, which was written to the vice president of engineering at Morton Thiokol on July 31, 1985. The memo ended by saying, "It is my honest and very real fear that if we do not take immediate action to dedicate a team to solve the problem, with the field joint having the number one priority, then we stand in jeopardy of losing a flight along with all the launch pad facilities."

During this July period, NASA headquarters in Washington, D.C., asked Morton Thiokol to prepare a presentation on the problems with all the booster seals. The presentation was prepared on August 19, 1985, with Morton Thiokol personnel in attendance.

Morton Thiokol was then asked in September to send a representative to a conference in October to discuss the seals and solicit help from the experts. I prepared and presented a six page overview of the joints and the seal configuration to approximately 130 technical experts on October 7, 1985. However, I was given strict instructions, which came from NASA, not to express the critical urgency of fixing the joint but only to emphasize the joint improvement aspect during my presentation.

VI. A MANAGEMENT DECISION OVERRIDES A RECOMMENDATION NOT TO LAUNCH

The major activity that day focused upon the predicted 18 degrees Fahrenheit overnight temperature and meeting with engineering management to persuade them not to launch. The day concluded with the hurried preparation of fourteen viewgraphs which detailed our concerns about launching at such a low temperature. The teleconference started with a history of O-ring damage in field joints. Data was presented showing a major concern with seal resiliency and the change to the sealing timing function and the criticality of this on the ability to seal. I was asked several times during my portion of the presentation to quantify my concerns, but I said I could not since the only data I had was what I had presented and that I had been trying to get more data since last October. At this comment, the general manager of Morton Thiokol gave me a scolding look as if to say, "Why are you telling that to them?" The presentation ended with the recommendation not to launch below 53 degrees. This was not well received by NASA. The Vice President of Space Booster Programs, Joe Kilminster, was then asked by NASA for his launch decision. He said he did not recommend launching based upon the engineering position just presented. Then Larry Mulloy of NASA asked George Hardy of NASA for his launch decision. George responded that he was appalled at Thiokol's recommendation but said he would not launch over the contractor's objection. Then Larry Mulloy spent some time giving his interpretation of the data with his conclusion that the data presented was inconclusive.

Just as he finished his conclusion, Joe Kilminster asked for a five-minute off-line caucus to re-evaluate the data and as soon as the mute button was pushed our general manager,

Jerry Mason, said in a soft voice, "We have to make a management decision." I became furious when I heard this because I knew that an attempt would be made by management to reverse our recommendation not to launch.

Some discussion had started between the managers when Arnie Thompson moved from his position down the table to a position in front of the managers and once again tried to explain our position by sketching the joint and discussing the problem with the seals at low temperature. Arnie stopped when he saw the unfriendly look in Mason's eyes and also realized that no one was listening to him. I then grabbed the photographic evidence showing the hot gas blow-by and placed it on the table and, somewhat angered, admonished them to look and not ignore what the photos were telling us, namely, that low temperature indeed caused more hot gas blow-by in the joints. I too received the same cold stares as Arnie with looks as if to say, "Go away and don't bother us with the facts." At that moment I felt totally helpless and that further argument was fruitless, so I, too, stopped pressing my case.

What followed made me both sad and angry. The managers were struggling to make a pro-launch list of supporting data. . . . During the closed managers' discussion, Jerry Mason asked in a low voice if he was the only one who wanted to fly. The discussion continued, then Mason turned to Bob Lund, the vice-president of engineering, and told him to take off his engineering hat and put on his management hat. The decision to launch resulted from the yes vote of only the four senior executives since the rest of us were excluded from both the final decision and the vote poll. The telecon resumed, and Joe Kilminster read the launch support rationale from a handwritten list and recommended that the launch proceed. NASA promptly accepted the recommendation to launch without any probing discussion and asked Joe to send a signed copy of the chart.

The change in decision so upset me that I do not remember Stanley Reinhartz of NASA asking if anyone had anything else to say over the telecon. The telecon was then disconnected so I immediately left the room feeling badly defeated.

MEMO ON O-RING EROSION

Interoffice Memo

31 July 1985

TO: R. K. Lund
                     Vice President, Engineering

CC: B. C. Brinton, A. J. McDonald,
                     L. H. Sayer, J. R. Kapp

FROM: R. M. Boisjoly
                     Applied Mechanics—Ext. 3525

SUBJECT: SRM O-Ring Erosion/Potential Failure Criticality

This letter is written to insure that management is fully aware of the serious-ness of the current O-ring erosion problem in the SRM joints from an engineering standpoint.

The mistakenly accepted position on the joint problem was to fly without fear of failure and to run a series of design evaluations which would ultimately lead to a solution or at least a significant reduction of the erosion problem. This position is now drastically changed as a result of the SRM 16A nozzle joint erosion which eroded a secondary O-ring with the primary O-ring never sealing.

If the same scenario should occur in a field joint (and it could), then it is a jump ball as to the success or failure of the joint because the secondary O-ring cannot respond to the clevis opening rate and may not be capable of pressurization. The result would be a catastrophe of the highest order—loss of human life.

An unofficial team [a memo defining the team and its purpose was never pub-lished] with leader was formed on 19 July 1985 and was tasked with solving the problem for both the short and long term. This unofficial team is essen-tially nonexistent at this time. In my opinion, the team must be officially given the responsibility and the authority to execute the work that needs to be done on a non-interference basis (full time assignment until completed.)

It is my honest and very real fear that if we do not take immediate action to dedicate a team to solve the problem with the field joint having the number one priority, then we stand in jeopardy of losing a flight along with all the launch pad facilities.

R. M. Boisjoly

Concurred by:
J. R. Kapp, Manager
Applied Mechanics

MEMO FROM A. R. THOMPSON ON THE FLIGHT SEAL

Interoffice Memo

2871:Fy86:141
22 August 1985

TO: S. R. Stein
                       Project Engineer

CC: J. R. Kapp, K. M. Sperry, B. G. Russell, R. V. Ebeling,
                       H. H. McIntosh, R. M. Salita, D. M. Ketner

FROM: A. R. Thompson, Supervisor
                       Structures Design

SUBJECT: SRM Flight Seal Recommendation

The O-ring seal problem has lately become acute. Solutions, both long and short term are being sought, in the mean time flights are continuing. It is my recommendation that a near term solution be incorporated for flights following STS-27 which is currently scheduled for 24 August 1985. The near term solution uses maximum possible shim thickness and a .292 +. 005/−.003 inch dia O-ring. . . . A great deal of effort will be required to incorporate these changes. However, . . . the O-ring squeeze is nearly doubled for the example (STS-27A). A best effort should be made to include a max shim kit and the .292 dia O-ring as soon as it is practical. Much of the initial blow-by during O-ring sealing is controlled by O-ring squeeze. Also more sacrificial O-ring material is available to protect the sealed portion of the O-ring. The added cross-sectional area of the .292 dia O-ring will help the resilience response by added pressure from the groove side wall.

Several long term solutions look good; but, several years are required to incorporate some of them. The simple short term measures should be taken to reduce flight risks.

A. R. Thompson

ART/jh

REPORT OF THE PRESIDENTIAL COMMISSION ON THE SPACE SHUTTLE CHALLENGER ACCIDENT

These materials are located at the World Wide Web site for the official Presidential Commission report on the Challenger *accident.*

CHAPTER 8: PRESSURES ON THE SYSTEM

With the 1982 completion of the orbital flight test series, NASA began a planned acceleration of the Space Shuttle launch schedule. One early plan contemplated an eventual rate of a mission a week, but realism forced several downward revisions. In 1985, NASA published a projection calling for an annual rate of 24 flights by 1990. Long before the Challenger accident, however, it was becoming obvious that even the modified goal of two flights a month was overambitious.

In establishing the schedule, NASA had not provided adequate resources for its attainment. As a result, the capabilities of the system were strained by the modest nine-mission rate of 1985, and the evidence suggests that NASA would not have been able to accomplish the 14 flights scheduled for 1986. These are the major conclusions of a Commission examination of the pressures and problems attendant upon the accelerated launch schedule.

FINDINGS

1. The capabilities of the system were stretched to the limit to support the flight rate in winter 1985/1986. Projections into the spring and summer of 1986 showed a clear trend; the system, as it existed, would have been unable to deliver crew training software for scheduled flights by the designated dates. The result would have been an unacceptable compression of the time available for the crews to accomplish their required training.

2. Spare parts are in critically short supply. The Shuttle program made a conscious decision to postpone spare parts procurements in favor of budget items of per-

---

"Pressures on the System," "Recommendations of the Presidential Commission," from the *Report of the Presidential Commission on the Space Shuttle Challenger Accident.* http://www.ksc.nasa.gov/shuttle/missions/51-1/docs/rogers-commission/table-of-contents.html.

ceived higher priority. Lack of spare parts would likely have limited flight operations in 1986.

3. Stated manifesting policies are not enforced. Numerous late manifest changes (after the cargo integration review) have been made to both major payloads and minor payloads throughout the Shuttle program.

Late changes to major payloads or program requirements can require extensive resources (money, manpower, facilities) to implement.

If many late changes to "minor" payloads occur, resources are quickly absorbed.

Payload specialists frequently were added to a flight well after announced deadlines.

Late changes to a mission adversely affect the training and development of procedures for subsequent missions.

4. The scheduled flight rate did not accurately reflect the capabilities and resources.

The flight rate was not reduced to accommodate periods of adjustment in the capacity of the work force. There was no margin in the system to accommodate unforeseen hardware problems.

Resources were primarily directed toward supporting the flights and thus not enough were available to improve and expand facilities needed to support a higher flight rate.

5. Training simulators may be the limiting factor on the flight rate: the two current simulators cannot train crews for more than 12–15 flights per year.

6. When flights come in rapid succession, current requirements do not ensure that critical anomalies occurring during one flight are identified and addressed appropriately before the next flight.

RECOMMENDATIONS OF THE PRESIDENTIAL COMMISSION

The Commission has conducted an extensive investigation of the Challenger accident to determine the probable cause and necessary corrective actions. Based on the findings and determinations of its investigation, the Commission has unanimously adopted recommendations to help assure the return to safe flight.

The Commission urges that the Administrator of NASA submit, one year from now, a report to the President on the progress that NASA has made in effecting the Commission's recommendations set forth below:

I. DESIGN

The faulty Solid Rocket Motor joint and seal must be changed. This could be a new design eliminating the joint or a redesign of the current joint and seal. No design options should be prematurely precluded because of schedule, cost or reliance on existing hardware. All Solid Rocket Motor joints should satisfy the following requirements:

The joints should be fully understood, tested and verified.

The integrity of the structure and of the seals of all joints should be no less than that of the case walls throughout the design envelope.

The integrity of the joints should be insensitive to:

Dimensional tolerances.
Transportation and handling.
Assembly procedures.
Inspection and test procedures.
Environmental effects.
Internal case operating pressure.
Recovery and reuse effects.
Flight and water impact loads.

The certification of the new design should include:

Tests which duplicate the actual launch configuration as closely as possible.
Tests over the full range of operating conditions, including temperature.

Full consideration should be given to conducting static firings of the exact flight configuration in a vertical attitude.

Independent Oversight

The Administrator of NASA should request the National Research Council to form an independent Solid Rocket Motor design oversight committee to implement the Commission's design recommendations and oversee the design effort. This committee should:

Review and evaluate certification requirements.
Provide technical oversight of the design, test program and certification.
Report to the Administrator of NASA on the adequacy of the design and make appropriate recommendations.

II. SHUTTLE MANAGEMENT STRUCTURE

The Shuttle Program Structure should be reviewed. The project managers for the various elements of the Shuttle program felt more accountable to their center management than to the Shuttle program organization. Shuttle element funding, work package definition, and vital program information frequently bypass the National STS (Shuttle) Program Manager.

A redefinition of the Program Manager's responsibility is essential. This redefinition should give the Program Manager the requisite authority for all ongoing STS operations. Program funding and all Shuttle Program work at the centers should be placed clearly under the Program Manager's authority.

Astronauts in Management

The Commission observes that there appears to be a departure from the philosophy of the 1960s and 1970s relating to the use of astronauts in management positions. These individuals brought to their positions flight experience and a keen appreciation of operations and flight safety.

NASA should encourage the transition of qualified astronauts into agency management positions.

The function of the Flight Crew Operations director should be elevated in the NASA organization structure.

Shuttle Safety Panel

NASA should establish an STS Safety Advisory Panel reporting to the STS Program Manager. The Charter of this panel should include Shuttle operational issues, launch commit criteria, flight rules, flight readiness and risk management. The panel should include representation from the safety organization, mission operations, and the astronaut office.

III. CRITICALITY REVIEW AND HAZARD ANALYSIS

NASA and the primary Shuttle contractors should review all Criticality 1, 1R, 2, and 2R items and hazard analyses. This review should identify those items that must be improved prior to flight to ensure mission safety. An Audit Panel, appointed by the National Research Council, should verify the adequacy of the effort and report directly to the Administrator of NASA.

IV. SAFETY ORGANIZATION

NASA should establish an Office of Safety, Reliability and Quality Assurance to be headed by an Associate administrator, reporting directly to the NASA Administrator. It would have direct authority for safety, reliability, and quality assurance throughout the agency. The office should be assigned the work force to ensure adequate oversight of its functions and should be independent of other NASA functional and program responsibilities.

The responsibilities of this office should include:

The safety, reliability and quality assurance functions as they relate to all NASA activities and programs.

Direction of reporting and documentation of problems, problem resolution and trends associated with flight safety.

V. IMPROVED COMMUNICATIONS

The Commission found that Marshall Space Flight Center project managers, because of a tendency at Marshall to management isolation, failed to provide full and timely information bearing on the safety of flight 51-L to other vital elements of Shuttle program management.

NASA should take energetic steps to eliminate this tendency at Marshall Space Flight Center, whether by changes of personnel, organization, indoctrination or all three.

A policy should be developed which governs the imposition and removal of Shuttle launch constraints.

Flight Readiness Reviews and Mission Management Team meetings should be recorded.

The flight crew commander, or a designated representative, should attend the Flight Readiness Review, participate in acceptance of the vehicle for flight, and certify that the crew is properly prepared for flight.

VI. LANDING SAFETY

NASA must take actions to improve landing safety.

The tire, brake and nosewheel steering systems must be improved. These systems do not have sufficient safety margin, particularly at abort landing sites.

The specific conditions under which planned landings at Kennedy would be acceptable should be determined. Criteria must be established for tires, brakes and nosewheel steering. Until the systems meet those criteria in high fidelity testing that is verified at Edwards, landing at Kennedy should not be planned.

Committing to a specific landing site requires that landing area weather be forecast more than an hour in advance. During unpredictable weather periods at Kennedy, program officials should plan on Edwards landings. Increased landings at Edwards may necessitate a dual ferry capability.

VII. LAUNCH ABORT AND CREW ESCAPE

The Shuttle program management considered first-stage abort options and crew escape options several times during the history of the program, but because of limited utility, technical infeasibility, or program cost and schedule, no systems were implemented. The Commission recommends that NASA:

Make all efforts to provide a crew escape system for use during controlled gliding flight.

Make every effort to increase the range of flight conditions under which an emergency runway landing can be successfully conducted in the event that two or three main engines fail early in ascent.

VIII. FLIGHT RATE

The nation's reliance on the Shuttle as its principal space launch capability created a relentless pressure on NASA to increase the flight rate. Such reliance on a single launch capability should be avoided in the future.

NASA must establish a flight rate that is consistent with its resources. A firm payload assignment policy should be established. The policy should include rigorous controls on cargo manifest changes to limit the pressures such changes exert on schedules and crew training.

IX. MAINTENANCE SAFEGUARDS

Installation, test, and maintenance procedures must be especially rigorous for Space Shuttle items designated Criticality 1. NASA should establish a system of analyzing and reporting performance trends of such items.

Maintenance procedures for such items should be specified in the Critical Items List, especially for those such as the liquid-fueled main engines, which require unstinting maintenance and overhaul.

With regard to the Orbiters, NASA should:

Develop and execute a comprehensive maintenance inspection plan.

Perform periodic structural inspections when scheduled and not permit them to be waived.

Restore and support the maintenance and spare parts programs, and stop the practice of removing parts from one Orbiter to supply another.

CONCLUDING THOUGHT

The Commission urges that NASA continue to receive the support of the Administration and the nation. The agency constitutes a national resource that plays a critical role in space exploration and development. It also provides a symbol of national pride and technological leadership.

The Commission applauds NASA's spectacular achievements of the past and anticipates impressive achievements to come. The findings and recommendations presented in this report are intended to contribute to the future NASA successes that the nation both expects and requires as the 21st century approaches.

DEPARTMENT OF DISPUTATION
Blowup
MALCOLM GLADWELL

According to new risk theorists, no one should be blamed for disasters like the Challenger *explosion. We consistently seek a party to blame when unfortunate consequences result from human action or inaction. Is blame always appropriate, or are there times when bad things happen, but we cannot be angry at anyone?*

In the technological age, there is a ritual to disaster. When planes crash or chemical plants explode, each piece of physical evidence—of twisted metal or fractured concrete—becomes a kind of fetish object, painstakingly located, mapped, tagged, and analyzed, with findings submitted to boards of inquiry that then probe and interview and soberly draw conclusions. It is a ritual of reassurance, based on the principle that what we learn from one accident can help us prevent another, and a measure of its effectiveness is that Americans did not shut down the nuclear industry after Three Mile Island and do not abandon the skies after each new plane crash. But the rituals of disaster have rarely been played out so dramatically as they were in the case of the Challenger space shuttle, which blew up over southern Florida on January 28th ten years ago.

Fifty-five minutes after the explosion, when the last of the debris had fallen into the ocean, recovery ships were on the scene. They remained there for the next three months, as part of what turned into the largest maritime salvage operation in history, combing a hundred and fifty thousand square nautical miles for floating debris, while the ocean floor surrounding the crash site was inspected by submarines. In mid-April of 1986, the salvage team found several chunks of charred metal that confirmed what had previously been only suspected: the explosion was caused by a faulty seal in one of the shuttle's rocket boosters, which had allowed a stream of flame to escape and ignite an external fuel tank.

Armed with this confirmation, a special Presidential investigative commission concluded the following June that the deficient seal reflected shoddy engineering and lax management at NASA and its prime contractor, Morton Thiokol. Properly chastised, NASA returned to the drawing board, to emerge thirty-two months later with a new shuttle—Discovery—redesigned according to the lessons learned from the disaster. During that first post-Challenger flight, as America watched breathlessly, the crew of the Discovery held a short commemorative service. "Dear friends," the mission commander, Captain Frederick H. Hauck, said, addressing the seven dead Challenger astronauts, "your loss has meant that we could confidently begin anew." The ritual was complete. NASA was back.

But what if the assumptions that underlie our disaster rituals aren't true? What if these public postmortems don't help us avoid future accidents? Over the past few years, a group of scholars has begun making the unsettling argument that the rituals that follow things like plane crashes or the Three Mile Island crisis are as much exercises in self-deception as they are genuine opportunities for reassurance. For these revisionists, high-technology accidents may not have clear causes at all. They may be inherent in the complexity of the technological systems we have created.

This month, on the tenth anniversary of the Challenger disaster, such revisionism has been extended to the space shuttle with the publication, by the Boston College sociologist Diane Vaughan, of *The Challenger Launch Decision* (Chicago), which is the first truly definitive analysis of the events leading up to January 28, 1986. The conventional view is that the Challenger accident was an anomaly, that it happened because people at NASA had not done their job. But the study's conclusion is the opposite: it says that the accident happened because people at NASA had done exactly what they were supposed to do. "No fundamental decision was made at NASA to do evil," Vaughan writes. "Rather, a series of seemingly harmless decisions were made that incrementally moved the space agency toward a catastrophic outcome."

No doubt Vaughan's analysis will be hotly disputed in the coming months, but even if she is only partly right the implications of this kind of argument are enormous. We have surrounded ourselves in the modern age with things like power plants and nuclear-weapons systems and airports that handle hundreds of planes an hour, on the understanding that the risks they represent are, at the very least, manageable. But if the potential for catastrophe is actually found in the normal functioning of complex systems, this assumption is false. Risks are not easily manageable, accidents are not easily preventable, and the rituals of disaster have no meaning. The first time around, the story of the Challenger was tragic. In its retelling, a decade later, it is merely banal.

2.

Perhaps the best way to understand the argument over the Challenger explosion is to start with an accident that preceded it—the near-disaster at the Three Mile Island (T.M.I.) nuclear-power plant in March of 1979. The conclusion of the President's commission that investigated the T.M.I. accident was that it was the result of human error, particularly on the part of the plant's operators. But the truth of what happened there, the revisionists maintain, is a good deal more complicated than that, and their arguments are worth examining in detail.

The trouble at T.M.I. started with a blockage in what is called the plant's polisher—a kind of giant water filter. Polisher problems were not unusual at T.M.I., or particularly serious. But in this case the blockage caused moisture to leak into the plant's air system, inadvertently tripping two valves and shutting down the flow of cold water into the plant's steam generator.

As it happens, T.M.I. had a backup cooling system for precisely this situation. But on that particular day, for reasons that no one really knows, the valves for the backup system weren't open. They had been closed, and an indicator in the control room showing they were closed was blocked by a repair tag hanging from a switch above it. That left the reactor dependent on another backup system, a special sort of relief valve. But, as luck would have it, the relief valve wasn't working properly that day, either. It stuck open when it was supposed to close, and, to make matters even worse, a gauge in the control room which should have told the operators that the relief valve wasn't working was itself not working. By the time T.M.I.'s engineers realized what was happening, the reactor had come dangerously close to a meltdown.

Here, in other words, was a major accident caused by five discrete events. There is no way the engineers in the control room could have known about any of them. No glaring errors or spectacularly bad decisions were made that exacerbated those events. And all the malfunctions—the blocked polisher, the shut valves, the obscured indicator, the faulty relief valve, and the broken gauge—were in themselves so trivial that individually they would have created no more than a nuisance. What caused the accident was the way minor events unexpectedly interacted to create a major problem.

This kind of disaster is what the Yale University sociologist Charles Perrow has famously called a "normal accident." By "normal" Perrow does not mean that it is frequent; he means that it is the kind of accident one can expect in the normal functioning of a technologically complex operation. Modern systems, Perrow argues, are made up of thousands of parts, all of which interrelate in ways that are impossible to anticipate. Given that complexity, he says, it is almost inevitable that some combinations of minor failures will eventually amount to something catastrophic. In a classic 1984 treatise on accidents, Perrow takes examples of well-known plane crashes, oil spills, chemical-plant explosions, and nuclear-weapons mishaps and shows how many of them are best understood as "normal." If you saw last year's hit movie "Apollo 13," in fact, you have seen a perfect illustration of one of the most famous of all normal accidents: the Apollo flight went awry because of the interaction of failures of the spacecraft's oxygen and hydrogen tanks, and an indicator light that diverted the astronauts' attention from the real problem.

Had this been a "real" accident—if the mission had run into trouble because of one massive or venal error—the story would have made for a much inferior movie. In real accidents, people rant and rave and hunt down the culprit. They do, in short, what people in Hollywood thrillers always do. But what made Apollo 13 unusual was that the dominant emotion was not anger but bafflement—bafflement that so much could go wrong for so little apparent reason. There was no one to blame, no dark secret to unearth, no recourse but to re-create an entire system in place of one that had inexplicably failed. In the end, the normal accident was the more terrifying one.

***

4.

There is another way to look at this problem, and that is from the standpoint of how human beings handle risk. One of the assumptions behind the modern disaster ritual is that when a risk can be identified and eliminated a system can be made safer. The new booster joints on the shuttle, for example, are so much better than the old ones that the overall chances of a Challenger-style accident's ever happening again must be lower—right? This is such a straightforward idea that questioning it seems almost impossible. But that is just what another group of scholars has done, under what is called the theory of "risk home-ostasis." It should be said that within the academic community there are huge debates over how widely the theory of risk homeostasis can and should be applied. But the basic idea, which has been laid out brilliantly by the Canadian psychologist Gerald Wilde in his book *Target Risk,* is quite simple: under certain circumstances, changes that appear to make a system or an organization safer in fact don't. Why? Because human beings have a seem-ingly fundamental tendency to compensate for lower risks in one area by taking greater risks in another.

Consider, for example, the results of a famous experiment conducted several years ago in Germany. Part of a fleet of taxicabs in Munich was equipped with antilock brake systems (A.B.S.), the recent technological innovation that vastly improves braking, particularly on slippery surfaces. The rest of the fleet was left alone, and the two groups—which were oth-erwise perfectly matched—were placed under careful and secret observation for three years. You would expect the better brakes to make for safer driving. But that is exactly the opposite of what happened. Giving some drivers A.B.S. made no difference at all in their accident rate; in fact, it turned them into markedly inferior drivers. They drove faster. They made sharper turns. They showed poorer lane discipline. They braked harder. They were more likely to tailgate. They didn't merge as well, and they were involved in more near-misses. In other words, the A.B.S. systems were not used to reduce accidents; instead, the drivers used the additional element of safety to enable them to drive faster and more reck-lessly without increasing their risk of getting into an accident. As economists would say, they "consumed" the risk reduction, they didn't save it.

Risk homeostasis doesn't happen all the time. Often—as in the case of seat belts, say—compensatory behavior only partly offsets the risk-reduction of a safety measure. But it happens often enough that it must be given serious consideration. Why are more pedestri-ans killed crossing the street at marked crosswalks than at unmarked crosswalks? Because they compensate for the "safe" environment of a marked crossing by being less vigilant about oncoming traffic. Why did the introduction of childproof lids on medicine bottles lead, according to one study, to a substantial increase in fatal child poisonings? Because adults became less careful in keeping pill bottles out of the reach of children.

Risk homeostasis also works in the opposite direction. In the late nineteen-sixties, Sweden changed over from driving on the left-hand side of the road to driving on the right, a switch that one would think would create an epidemic of accidents. But, in fact, the op-posite was true. People compensated for their unfamiliarity with the new traffic patterns by driving more carefully. During the next twelve months, traffic fatalities dropped seventeen percent—before returning slowly to their previous levels. As Wilde only half-facetiously argues, countries truly interested in making their streets and highways safer should think about switching over from one side of the road to the other on a regular basis.

It doesn't take much imagination to see how risk homeostasis applies to NASA and the space shuttle. In one frequently quoted phrase, Richard Feynman, the Nobel Prize–winning physicist who served on the Challenger commission, said that at NASA decision-making was "a kind of Russian roulette." When the O-rings began to have problems and nothing happened, the agency began to believe that "the risk is no longer so high for the next flights," Feynman said, and that "we can lower our standards a little bit because we got away with it last time." But fixing the O-rings doesn't mean that this kind of risk-taking stops.

There are six whole volumes of shuttle components that are deemed by NASA to be as risky as O-rings. It is entirely possible that better O-rings just give NASA the confidence to play Russian roulette with something else.

This is a depressing conclusion, but it shouldn't come as a surprise. The truth is that our stated commitment to safety, our faithful enactment of the rituals of disaster, has always masked a certain hypocrisy. We don't really want the safest of all possible worlds. The national fifty-five-mile-per-hour speed limit probably saved more lives than any other single government intervention of the past twenty-five years. But the fact that Congress lifted it last month with a minimum of argument proves that we would rather consume the recent safety advances of things like seat belts and air bags than save them. The same is true of the dramatic improvements that have been made in recent years in the design of aircraft and flight-navigation systems. Presumably, these innovations could be used to bring down the airline-accident rate as low as possible. But that is not what consumers want. They want air travel to be cheaper, more reliable, or more convenient, and so those safety advances have been at least partly consumed by flying and landing planes in worse weather and heavier traffic conditions.

What accidents like the Challenger should teach us is that we have constructed a world in which the potential for high-tech catastrophe is embedded in the fabric of day-to-day life. At some point in the future—for the most mundane of reasons, and with the very best of intentions—a NASA spacecraft will again go down in flames. We should at least admit this to ourselves now. And if we cannot—if the possibility is too much to bear—then our only option is to start thinking about getting rid of things like space shuttles altogether.

Chapter 7

CORPORATE STRATEGY AND DECISION MAKING
Corporate Culture and Reputation Management

I am not afraid of storms, for I am learning to build my ship.   —LOUISA MAY ALCOTT

The readings in this chapter consider the corporate response to public demands for ethical behavior and the concern for the "appearance of propriety": the corporate reputation. As you review the readings in this section, ponder the following (facetious and sarcastic) recommendations for leadership offered by Gen. Colin Powell as a result of the frustration he experienced during the mishandling of the Iranian hostage crisis:

1. Release facts slowly, behind the pace at which they are already leaking to the public.
2. Don't tell the whole story until forced to do so.
3. Emphasize what went well and euphemize what went wrong.
4. Become indignant at any suggestion of poor judgment or mistakes.
5. Disparage any facts other than your own.
6. Accuse critics of Monday-morning generalship.
7. Accept general responsibility at the top, thus clearing everybody at fault below.[1]

Why do firms engage in ethical behavior? Earlier chapters have suggested profit motives; but, as was also discussed, an ethical decision does not always lead to the highest profits possible. Perhaps the firm engages in ethical decision making because "it's the right thing to do," as Sears Roebuck and Co. says in its ethics materials. Perhaps, however, as some of the readings in this section suggest, engaging in ethical behavior, implementing ethics programs, or instituting codes of conduct all contribute both to the internal culture of the firm as well as to the external stakeholders' perceptions of the firm. Is there anything wrong with paying attention to these external perceptions?

---

[1]Colin Powell and Joseph Persico, *My American Journey* (New York: Random House, 1995), p. 250.

MANAGING ETHICS AND LEGAL COMPLIANCE
What Works and What Hurts

LINDA KLEBE TREVINO, GARY R. WEAVER, DAVID G. GIBSON,
AND BARBARA LEY TOFFLER

Some ethics programs work and others do not. What are the differences between the two groups?

A survey of employees at six large American companies asked the question: "What works and what hurts in corporate ethics/compliance management?" The study found that a values-based cultural approach to ethics/compliance management works best. Critical ingredients of this approach include leaders' commitment to ethics, fair treatment of employees, rewards for ethical conduct, concern for external stakeholders, and consistency between policies and actions. What hurts effectiveness most are an ethics/compliance program that employees believe exists only to protect top management from blame and an ethical culture that focuses on unquestioning obedience to authority and employee self-interest. The results of effective ethics/compliance management are impressive. They include reduced unethical/illegal behavior in the organization, increased awareness of ethical issues, more ethical advice seeking within the firms, greater willingness to deliver bad news or report ethical/legal violations to management, better decision making because of the ethics/compliance program, and increased employee commitment.

Ten years ago, a Business Roundtable report titled *Corporate Ethics: A Prime Business Asset* suggested that "there are no precise ways to measure the end results of the widespread and intensive efforts to develop effective corporate ethics programs. Despite this difficulty in measuring their accomplishments, corporate ethics and legal compliance programs have become even more widespread over the last decade. Companies are investing millions of dollars on ethics and compliance management. A recent survey of Fortune 1000 firms found that 98% of responding firms address ethics or conduct issues in formal documents. Of those firms, 78% have a separate code of ethics, and most distribute these policies widely within the organization. Many employees also receive ethics training and have access to a telephone line for reporting problems or seeking advice. Much of this activity has been attributed to the 1991 U.S. Sentencing Commission's Guidelines for organizational defendants. The Guidelines prescribe more lenient sentences and fines to companies that have taken measures to prevent employee misconduct.

What do these ethics and legal compliance programs actually accomplish? A firm's approach to ethics and legal compliance management has an enormous impact on employees' attitudes and behaviors. In this study, we found that specific characteristics of the formal ethics or compliance program matter less than broader perceptions of the program's orientation toward values and ethical aspirations. What helps the most are consistency between policies and actions as well as dimensions of the organization's ethical culture such as ethical leadership, fair treatment of employees, and open discussion of ethics in the organization. On the other hand, what hurts the most is an ethical culture that emphasizes self-interest and unquestioning obedience to authority, and the perception that the ethics or compliance program exists only to protect top management from blame.

In order to investigate what works and what hurts in ethics and compliance management, we administered a survey to over 10,000 randomly selected employees at all levels in six large American companies from a variety of industries. The companies varied in their ethics/compliance program approaches. Because we were relying on employees' perceptions, we had to be concerned about socially desirable responses—having employees tell us what they thought we wanted to hear rather than the truth. We took a number of steps to guard against such biased responding. Surveys were completely anonymous, they were sent to employees' homes, and they were returned directly to the researchers for analysis.

***

WHAT INFLUENCES ETHICS/COMPLIANCE PROGRAM EFFECTIVENESS?

There are several key organizational and program design factors that are associated with ethics/compliance management effectiveness. . . .

1. Program Orientation

Ethics/compliance programs can be designed with very different goals and orientations. Previous research has referred to two types of approaches, a compliance-based approach and an integrity or values-based approach. According to [L. S.] Paine ["Managing for Organizational Integrity," *Harvard Business Review,* March/April 1994, pp. 106–17], a compliance approach focuses primarily on preventing, detecting, and punishing violations of the law, while a values-based approach aims to define organizational values and encourage employee commitment to ethical aspirations. She asserts that the values-based approach should be more effective than a compliance-based approach because a values-based approach is rooted in personal self-governance and is more likely to motivate employees to behave in accordance with shared values. She argues that compliance approaches can be counterproductive because they emphasize avoiding punishment instead of self-governance.

They define ethics in terms of legal compliance rather than ethical aspirations, and they implicitly endorse a "code of moral mediocrity."

A recent study of Fortune 1000 firms was conducted in part to determine the orientations of their ethics/compliance management efforts. The survey found that the compliance and values-based approaches are not mutually exclusive. Rather, most firms' approaches to ethics/compliance management combine these orientations in some way. Nevertheless, the compliance approach predominated over the values-based approach in over half of the firms. The U.S. Sentencing Guidelines (implemented in late 1991) contribute to the development of compliance approaches because fines and sanctions for companies convicted of crimes vary dramatically depending upon management's cooperation and whether the firm has a legal compliance program in place.

Given that a compliance-based approach predominates in most firms, our study needed to test the contention that a values-based approach is "better" (achieves more positive outcomes) than a compliance-based approach. Also, many companies hope to maintain or improve their public image and relationships with external stakeholders by adopting an ethics/compliance program. Therefore, we identified an orientation toward satisfying external stakeholders (customers, the community, suppliers) as a third approach in our study. Alternatively, employees sometimes suspect that an ethics/compliance program is introduced in part to protect top management from blame for ethical failures or legal problems. In fact, Paine associated this suspicion with a compliance-based program, suggesting that skeptical employees may see a compliance-oriented program as "nothing more than liability insurance for senior management." Another of Badaracco and Webb's interviewees put it this way: "I'm cynical. To me, corporate codes of conduct exist to cover the potential problems companies may have. It provides deniability. It gives the employers an excuse. . . . The top officers can say, 'These employees messed up. They violated our way of doing business' " [L. Badaracco and A. P. Webb, "Business Ethics: A View from the Trenches," Winter 1995, pp. 8–28]. Therefore, we also assessed the impact of a "protect top management from blame" orientation.

2. A Values Orientation Is the Most Effective Single Orientation

Across the six firms in this study, employees perceived the presence of each of the four orientations (compliance-based, values-based, external stakeholder, and protect top management) to varying degrees, and all of them were important in influencing outcomes. However, it is clearly most important to have a program that employees perceive to be values-based. In these six companies, if employees perceived a values-based program, each of the seven outcomes studied was significantly more positive and the relationships were quite strong. Unethical/illegal behavior was lower, awareness of ethical/legal issues was higher, and employees were more likely to look for advice within the firm, to be willing to deliver bad news to management, and to report ethical violations. They also were more committed to the organization and more likely to believe that decision making was better because of the ethics/compliance program.

3. Compliance and External Orientations Are Also Helpful

Outcomes were also more positive if employees perceived a compliance or an external stakeholder orientation. Contrary to Paine's argument, if employees perceived a compliance-based program, all of the outcomes were significantly more positive. However, the relationships were not as strong as with the values orientation. If employees perceived an external stakeholder orientation, once again the same outcomes were significantly more positive. However, the relationships were even weaker than those for compliance orientation.

4. Combining These Orientations May Be Effective

The data also supported the idea that these orientations are not mutually exclusive. For example, values orientation is highly correlated with compliance orientation (correlation = .60) and with external stakeholder orientation (correlation = .53). So, it is clearly possible to design a program that combines these different orientations, while also emphasizing a values-based approach. A values orientation can be backed up with accountability systems and discipline for violators. Values can include a concern for customers, suppliers, and the community as well as shareholders and internal stakeholders such as employees. The ideal mix of orientations likely depends on specific organizational circumstances, such as the organization's culture, product, and industry.

5. "Protect Top Management" Is Clearly a Harmful Approach

Not surprisingly, where employees perceived that the ethics/compliance program was oriented toward protecting top management from blame, all of the important outcomes were significantly more negative. These relationships were particularly strong and negative for commitment to the organization, for the perception that it's okay to deliver bad news to management, and that employees would report ethical/legal violations to management. In addition, unethical/illegal behavior was higher, employees were less aware of ethical issues, and they were less likely to seek advice about ethical concerns. Furthermore, they did not believe that decision making was better because of the ethics/compliance program.

SUMMARY OF PROGRAM ORIENTATION FINDINGS

A key finding of this study is the importance of designing an ethics program that is perceived by employees to be first and foremost about shared organizational values and about guiding employees to act on their ethical aspirations. Such programs motivate employees to be aware of ethical or legal issues, report bad news to management, report ethical or legal violations, and refrain from engaging in unethical or illegal conduct. In addition, unethical/illegal behavior is reduced, employee commitment is higher, and employees believe that decision making in the organization is better because of the ethics program.

This values-based approach can be supplemented with an orientation toward legal compliance and satisfying external stakeholders. Valuing external stakeholders such as customers and the community has a positive impact on all outcomes, as does holding employees accountable for their behavior through monitoring and disciplinary systems. Discipline for rule violators serves an important symbolic role in organizations—it reinforces standards, upholds the value of conformity to shared norms, and maintains the perception that the organization is a just place where wrongdoers are held accountable for their actions.

Finally, a program must avoid conveying the message to employees that it exists to protect top management from blame. Having a program that is perceived in this way by employees may be worse than having no program at all. Recall Paine's proposal that employees were likely to associate a compliance approach with this "protect top management from blame" orientation. Our data did not support this contention. There was little association between employees' perceptions of the program as compliance-oriented and their perceptions of the program as being oriented toward protecting top management from blame. However, this protect-top-management orientation was even less likely to be associated with a program that employees perceived to be values-based. Perhaps the most important message to executives is that this protect-top-management perception is real. Employees judge top management's motives in implementing an ethics/compliance program. Also, it is important that they perceive it to be a sincere attempt to have all employees do what's right rather than just an attempt to create legal "cover" for executives in case of a legal mishap.

FORMAL AND INFORMAL ETHICS/COMPLIANCE PROGRAM CHARACTERISTICS

With regard to specific ethics/compliance program and organizational characteristics, we asked employees about formal characteristics including the official policies, procedures, offices, and supporting structures (e.g., telephone hotline). We also asked for employees' perceptions of the more informal ways ethics and compliance concerns are handled every day (e.g., how well the company "follows through" on its policies).

FORMAL PROGRAM CHARACTERISTICS ARE RELATIVELY UNIMPORTANT

All six companies in the study had the "basics" of a comprehensive ethics/compliance program: an ethics/compliance office and officer, a formal code of conduct, and a telephone hotline. Despite the existence of these formal program characteristics, employees may be more or less aware of them and more or less likely to use them. Therefore, we asked employees how familiar they were with the code's contents and how frequently they referred to the code for guidance. Interestingly, these factors had little impact on the outcomes, especially unethical conduct. It simply did not matter much whether employees were familiar with or referred frequently to the company's code of conduct. We also asked employees whether their company has a formal mechanism for raising ethical and legal compliance issues and concerns and whether ethics is a formal part of performance evaluation in the company. Both of these program characteristics are dynamic, requiring some kind of ongoing attention from the organization; whereas a code can be drafted, distributed, and forgotten. To the extent that employees perceived the company to have a formal mechanism for raising concerns and to make ethics a formal part of performance appraisal, all of the outcomes were significantly more positive.

PROGRAM FOLLOW-THROUGH IS ESSENTIAL

With regard to program follow-through, we asked employees whether the company works hard to detect violators, whether the company follows up on ethical concerns raised by employees, and whether there is consistency between ethics/compliance policies and actual organizational practices. Follow-through tells employees that a focus on ethics and legal compliance represents a sincere commitment on the part of management.

The more that employees in our study perceived the organization to be following through, the more positive were all of the outcomes. Further, employees' perceptions of follow- through were much more important than their perceptions of the formal characteristics. Employees' perception that the company's actions are consistent with its policies were particularly important. Employees need to perceive that policies are not just "window dressing" and that the company follows words with actions. Therefore, an approach that goes beyond the mere establishment of formal programs is necessary if employees are to be convinced that the organization really means what it says.

ETHICAL CULTURE IN THE ORGANIZATION

Managing ethics in organizations is not just about managing formal ethics/compliance programs. Researchers have suggested that the broader ethical context in an organization—referred to as the ethical climate or culture—is particularly important, perhaps more important than specific ethics/compliance program goals or characteristics. The elements of ethical culture that guide employee thought and action include leadership, reward systems, perceived fairness, ethics as a topic of conversation in the organization, employee authority structures, and an organizational focus that communicates care for employees and the community.

EXECUTIVE AND SUPERVISORY LEADERSHIP

A decade ago, the Business Roundtable report *Corporate Ethics: A Prime Business Asset* referred to the crucial role of top management. "To achieve results, the Chief Executive Officer and those around the CEO need to be openly and strongly committed to ethical conduct, and give constant leadership in tending and renewing the values of the organization."

We were interested in the role of executive leadership because executives play a crucial role in creating, maintaining, and changing ethical culture. We also wanted to investigate the role of supervisory leadership. Leaders at every level serve as role models, and employees have more daily contact with their supervisors than they do with executive leaders. Supervisors are responsible for rewards and punishments and they carry the message of how things are really done in the organization. Therefore, in separate sets of questions we asked employees for their perceptions of executive and supervisory ethical leadership.

Perceptions of these two groups were highly related (correlation = .78), suggesting that employees don't think differently about supervisors and executive leaders with regard to their attention to ethics and legal compliance. Essentially, if executive leaders value and pay attention to ethics, so do supervisory leaders.

Leadership was a key ethical culture factor—one of the most important factors in the study. Where employees perceived that supervisors and executives regularly pay attention to ethics, take ethics seriously, and care about ethics and values as much as the bottom line, all of the outcomes were significantly more positive. Employees paint all leaders with the same broad ethical brush. When it comes to ethics, leaders are leaders, and the level (supervisory or executive) doesn't seem to matter much to employees.

FAIR TREATMENT OF EMPLOYEES

We also explored a less obvious aspect of ethical culture—employees' perceptions of general fair treatment in the organization. Why should general fair treatment of employees be related to ethics-related outcomes? First, the word *ethics* can mean different things to different people or groups. Kent Druyvesteyn, former ethics officer at General Dynamics, said that when managers say "ethics," employees hear "fairness." To most employees, ethics means how the organization treats them and their coworkers. This helps to explain why so many calls to ethics hotlines concern human resources issues of fair treatment in hiring, layoffs, performance appraisals, and promotions. Also, recent research has highlighted the importance of fair treatment for ethics-related outcomes such as employee theft. When employees feel that they are treated unfairly, they may try to "balance the scales of justice" by engaging in unethical behaviors such as stealing from the organization. Some companies have acknowledged this connection between fair treatment and ethics management. For example, we know of a company that sees the elimination of executive dining rooms and other perks as important to making their ethics programs work. Employees see that rules apply to everyone because every employee, up to the CEO, has to have expense reports signed. "That sends a good message [to employees]. . . . Nobody is above the rules and code of conduct. . . . A high level person could get dismissed if they violated [a rule] as much as another person." Another company pegged executive pay to employee pay because of similar concerns about the implications of fair and consistent employee treatment for ethics management.

It is important to note that the survey questions concerning fair treatment had nothing to do with the ethics/compliance program. Rather, they were general questions that asked whether employees think of the company as fair in terms of rewards and punishments (do employees get the rewards and punishments they deserve), whether employees are treated fairly in general, and whether supervisors treat employees with courtesy, dignity, and respect. Employees' perception of fair treatment was strongly related to all outcomes and was one of the most important factors in the study. It had the strongest correlation with employee commitment and with the perception that it's acceptable to deliver bad news to management.

Companies demonstrate their good ethics to employees primarily through fair treatment. If a company passes the "fair treatment test," employees are more likely to be open to ethics and legal compliance initiatives and to cooperate in making them successful.

ETHICS IN DISCUSSIONS AND DECISIONS

We also asked employees whether people in the company talk openly about ethics and values and whether ethics and values are integrated into decisions. One of the ways ethics and values get "baked into" the corporate culture is to make these sorts of discussions the norm. Our previous experience with one company provides an example of how this should not be done. An oil company employee asked if he could bring an ethical problem to a meeting of divisional presidents. Their immediate response was, "If he wants to talk ethics, let him talk to a priest or a psychiatrist. The office is no place for it." Imagine what employees would think of a formal ethics/compliance program in such an environment.

In our study, perceptions that ethics is talked about and integrated into decision making were important for all outcomes. Open discussion of ethics and values in the company was particularly important for employee commitment, the perception that it's acceptable to deliver bad news, the belief that employees would report an ethics violation, and that decision making is better because of the ethics/compliance program.

REWARD SYSTEMS THAT SUPPORT ETHICAL CONDUCT

Good managers know that people do what's rewarded and avoid doing what's punished. Therefore, an ethical culture should include a reward system that supports ethical conduct. We asked employees whether ethical behavior is rewarded and unethical behavior is punished in their organizations. Perceptions of both of these dimensions were important for all outcomes. However, employee perceptions that ethical behavior is rewarded were more important than were perceptions that unethical behavior is punished. The belief that ethical behavior is rewarded was particularly important for employees' commitment and their perceptions that it's okay to deliver bad news to management and that employees would be likely to report ethical violations.

UNQUESTIONING OBEDIENCE TO AUTHORITY

An ethical organizational culture must emphasize each individual's accountability and responsibility for his or her own actions and an obligation to question authority when something seems wrong. An unethical culture is more likely to require unquestioning obedience to authority—"Just do as I say and don't ask any questions." In this study, we found that where employees perceived a structure that expects unquestioning obedience to authority, all outcomes were significantly more negative. Most affected were employee commitment to the organization, willingness to report an ethical or legal violation, and willingness to deliver bad news to management.

ORGANIZATIONAL FOCUS

Research on ethical climate has found that employees' perceptions of the organization's focus are associated with both unethical behavior and employee commitment. In this study, we considered three types of focus: employee focus (where employees perceive an organizational focus on what's best for them and their coworkers); community focus (where employees perceive an organizational focus on what's best for customers and the public); and self-interest focus (where employees perceive that everyone in the organization is simply out for himself or herself).

Where employees perceived the organization to be focused on what's best for employees (employee focus) or for customers and the public (community focus), all of the outcomes were significantly more positive. However, where employees perceived that people in the organization were mostly out for themselves (self-interest focus), all outcomes were significantly more negative.

SUMMARY OF ETHICAL CULTURE FINDINGS

As a set, the ethical culture factors emerged as the most important influential factors. Of these factors, leadership, fairness perceptions, the perception that ethics is discussed in the organization, and the perception that ethical behavior is rewarded were the most significant factors in the study. As to "what hurts" in ethics/compliance management, two culture factors were quite harmful. Outcomes were more negative where employees perceived an expectation of unquestioning obedience to authority, and where they perceived a focus on self-interest rather than concern for employees and/or the community.

WHAT WORKS AND WHAT HURTS IN ETHICS/COMPLIANCE MANAGEMENT: PRESCRIPTIONS FOR ACTION

What should firms be doing if they want to achieve the most positive outcomes from their ethics/compliance management efforts? What should they avoid doing?

1. Tap the Trenches—Employee Perceptions Matter

Badaracco and Webb recently presented "a view from the trenches" in a report that summarized the results of in-depth interviews with recent graduates of the Harvard MBA program. These young managers reported pressures to be unethical, insufficient help from formal ethics programs, and executives who were "out-of-touch" on ethical issues. The authors recommended in-depth interviews with lower-level employees to learn more about employee perceptions. While few companies have the resources to conduct in-depth interviews with a large number of employees, they can conduct surveys and focus groups to learn what their employees are thinking. Employees can tell a company a great deal about what's going on in its trenches. Our survey suggests that they are willing to report both the positive and the negative, such as the extent to which they perceive strong ethical leadership, employee fair treatment, and consistency between words and actions, or the extent to which they perceive a focus on self-interest and unquestioning obedience to authority. Obviously, asking these questions may make ethical issues more salient to employees. Therefore, asking the questions assumes that you want to know the answers and that you are willing to take corrective action.

2. Build A Solid Ethical Culture

The ethics officer in a Fortune 500 company once stated, "I have a hard time when people [ask] me, 'Tell me about your company's ethics plan.' I want to tell them about everything we do. Because in my mind, everything we do is part of it." This quote demonstrates that ethics/compliance management is first and foremost a cultural phenomenon. As noted, ethical culture factors were among the most powerful factors in this study. It is not enough to have formal policies and programs. To achieve desired outcomes, concerns for ethics and legal compliance must be baked into the culture of the organization. Therefore, attention to the ethical culture should come first in any corporate ethics/compliance effort. Executive leaders and supervisors must regularly show they care about ethics and shared values (including demonstrating that values are as important as the bottom line), and they must show that they care through words and consistent actions. Consider employees' reactions when the CEO of a major bank who preached responsible use of corporate resources sent a corporate plane to

California to pick up a pair of shoes for his wife. This CEO didn't understand that his actions spoke louder than his words.

3. Create a Values-Based Program that Incorporates Accountability and Care for Stakeholders

When it comes to creating a formal ethics/compliance program, managers need not choose between values-based and compliance-based approaches. Rather, these approaches are complementary. They are further complemented by an approach that is concerned about external stakeholders. However, to be most effective, formal efforts to manage ethics and legal compliance should be oriented primarily toward values. A values approach can include valuing customers and the community, as well as employee accountability for ethical conduct.

4. Focus on Formal Program Follow-Through

Some companies approach ethics/compliance management with the idea that all they need to do is check off the U.S. Sentencing Commission's seven requirements for due diligence by appointing an ethics officer, writing and distributing a formal code of conduct, communicating standards via codes and training programs, and setting up hotlines and investigative procedures. The results of this study suggest that simply putting formal staff, structures, and procedures into place does little to influence important outcomes. More important were employees' perceptions that the company follows through on its formal codes, policies, and procedures by working hard to detect violators and by following up on ethical concerns raised by employees. Most important was the perception that actual practice is consistent with formal policies. Again, actions speak louder than words.

***

CONCLUSION

Contrary to the Business Roundtable's decade old statement, our study found that there are ways to measure the end results of corporate ethics and compliance programs. There are a number of important outcomes that can be measured reliably via employee surveys and that can be linked to key program and organizational influences.

A values-based cultural approach to ethics/compliance management works best. This approach requires the sincere commitment of leadership at all levels, including ongoing attention to key issues such as fair treatment of employees, rewards for ethical conduct, concern for external stakeholders, and consistency between words and actions. The ethics/compliance program itself should be values-based, motivating employees to aspire to ethical conduct, encouraging them to question authority when ethics are at stake, and holding them accountable for rule violations. The results of such an approach are impressive. They produce highly committed employees who are aware of ethics and compliance issues, who seek advice within the organization, and who are willing to deliver bad news to their managers or report ethical/legal violations. Results also include less unethical/illegal behavior in the organization and better decision making because of the organization's ethics/compliance efforts.

CORPORATE CODES, OMBUDSPERSONS AND ASSOCIATIONS

In order to act with integrity, as discussed earlier, a firm must first articulate its values, its priorities. The most prevalent form of values articulation and communication is a corporate mission, code of conduct, or code of ethics. Once the firm has defined its individual value structure, individual decision makers within the firm have guidance in connection with difficult dilemmas. Codes may refer to general areas of business conduct or may apply to a specific area of the firm's business. Reebok, for example, has Human Rights Production Standards that assist it in ensuring that the factories it uses have humane working conditions.

Other strategies exist to communicate corporate values as well as to continually update corporate programs and make them more effective. Some firms have used corporate ombudspersons. An ombudsperson is someone who is neither an advocate for the firm nor for the employee; instead, she or he often administers a general reporting structure that holds fairness to all parties as its most important goal. A firm may also serve as part of an association such as the Ethics Officers Association, which allows representatives to continually explore developing issues that face the firm.

CORPORATE CODES AND ETHICS PROGRAMS
MICHAEL C. DECK

In the following selection, Michael Deck explains research conducted to gather and to analyze 200 codes of conduct. The researcher found that while many firms have codes, they are not always communicated to stakeholders, nor are they always adhered to. Consider whether any firm you have worked for has had a code and whether you felt it was completely integrated into the decision-making functions of the firm.

Michael C. Deck, "Corporate Codes and Ethics Programs," www.kpmg.ca/ethics/eth_clks.htm First presented at "Business Practices under NAFTA: Developing Common Standards for Global Business," University of Colorado-Denver, December 8–10, 1994. Reprinted by permission of the author.

STAKEHOLDER THEORY

Our research program has examined more than seventy Canadian corporations over the last ten years. As we studied the data, it became clear that the managers of successful companies no longer regard shareholders as the sole and necessarily most important stakeholders in the corporation. The concept of shareholders endowed with a right to the maximization of profits is being replaced by the concept of stakeholders, of which shareholders comprise only one group. The shareholder is no longer the preeminent stakeholder, to be rewarded at the expense of other stakeholders. . . .

What this research shows is that when management or the board of a company favour one group of stakeholders at the expense of other primary stakeholder groups, difficulties always develop. When shareholders are favoured unfairly, when maximizing the bottom line takes full priority, customers or employees or suppliers invariably will be short-changed. . . .

MANAGING ETHICS IN THE WORKPLACE

If we agree that values, ethics, and moral principles are essential to sound decision making, how does a manager go about managing that aspect of the organization?

In looking for an answer to that question, we thought it would make sense to begin looking for the values, ethics, and moral principles of an organization in its Code of Ethics. Beginning three years ago, our Centre undertook to gather and to analyse 200 corporate codes. We learned that while corporations do indeed have values, ethics, and moral principles, these are not always communicated in a code of ethics and may in fact be quite different from what the code might lead one to believe.

While it would be ingenuous to think that ethical behavior within an organization can be changed simply by posting a list of high sounding principles, it is equally naive to imagine that the ethics of an organization "just happens and there's nothing to be done about it."

Every organization, as Steven Brenner points out, has an ethics program, whether it knows it or not.[1] The ethics program is that set of factors both explicit and implicit which communicate corporate values, define parameters of decision making, and establish the ground rules for behaviour. This is similar to what Robert Jackall has described as "institutional logic." An effective ethics program encourages behaviour consistent with corporate principles.

Explicit elements of a corporate ethics program include the things which an organization says it believes in, and the efforts made to communicate those principles directly. The centerpiece of the explicit components is the corporate code. In order to evaluate the effectiveness of a corporate code, the purpose of the code must be considered. Corporate codes can serve a variety of purposes: from "image enhancing" to "due diligence defense," from guidance for employees who want to "do the right thing" to helping an employee resist pressure from a superior. The corporate code and its implementation can raise issues of ethics to a conscious level and legitimate discussion.[2]

Our research on about 200 corporate codes revealed some interesting details about their nature and purpose.[3] Using the Stakeholder Model, we sorted out the statements made in these codes according to which stakeholder's interests were being addressed. One observation is that most of the text in these codes is concerned with the duty and responsibility of the employee to the company. Put more strongly, it seems that the most common purpose of a corporate code is to protect the firm from its employees. This is borne out by the observation that the most frequently cited "reason why" for ethical behaviour is that violations will hurt the company. The problem with this approach is that if the possibility of getting caught (and incurring the penalty) is apparently small, then the reason for ethical behaviour evaporates. . . .

The analysis of these codes also looked at the "approach" used for each statement, categorizing each as Guiding Principle, Act & Disclose, Seek Advice, or Rule. These categories lie along a scale which we describe as "Source of Control."

. . . This analysis [made it] clear that there were really three basic types of codes, differentiated by the source of control.

The terms *"Code of Ethics," "Code of Conduct,"* and *"Code of Practice"* are often used interchangeably. It is useful, however, to distinguish among these terms in order to establish a basic typology. Each basic code type has a different intent and purpose.

Codes of Ethics are statements of values and principles which define the purpose of the company. These codes seek to clarify the ethics of the corporation and to define its responsibilities to different groups of stakeholders as well as defining the responsibilities of its employees. These codes are expressed in terms of credos or guiding principles. Such a code says: "This is who we are and this is what we stand for," with the word "we" including the company and all its employees, whose behaviour and actions are expected to conform to the ethics and principles stated in the code.

Codes of Practice are interpretations and illustrations of corporate values and principles, and they are addressed to the employee as individual decision maker. In effect they say: "This is how we do things around here." Such a code seeks to shape the expression of the corporation's stated values through the practices of its employees. Codes of practice tend to rely on guidelines for decision making, using such rules of thumb as "act and disclose" or "seek advice." This approach takes a view of ethics as "what we do because it is our character."

Codes of Conduct are statements of rules: "This is what you must (or must not) do," as distinct from the code of ethics, which is stating: "This is how we expect you to behave." Codes of Conduct typically are comprised of a list of rules, stated either affirmatively or as prohibitions. Penalties for transgressions may be identified and systems of compliance and appeal defined. Potential conflicts of interest are often described, with appropriate rules for guidance. This approach takes a view of ethics as what is not to be done (or seen not to be done) in view of the consequences.

In practice, corporate codes tend to include elements of all three types, but for analytical purposes it is helpful to consider these three basic types as benchmarks. Each of the three types is useful and each can be appropriate or necessary in particular business and organizational settings. For example, in a divisionalised corporation, it would be appropriate to draft a Code of Ethics in order to enunciate the company's overall purpose and the guiding principles and ethics that govern its actions and behavior. At the divisional and functional area levels, different and divisionalised Codes of Conduct and Practice are appropriate, so long as the rules, examples, and guidelines are not in conflict with the statement of the corporation's guiding principles and ethics. . . .

HAVE ETHICS PROGRAMS FAILED?

It is interesting to note at this point that recent research has found no significant correlation between corporations having a code of ethics and a reduction in ethical violations.[4] Is the problem that the code was badly written? Probably not. Is there a problem with implementation? A more likely suspect, since, of the 90% of companies that have codes, only 28% do any training. There is, however, another factor which, I would suggest, accounts for these findings. I referred earlier to the implicit components of an ethics program. It may well be that the failure of the explicit components to produce results is the result of their having to fight an uphill battle against the implicit components.

If the goal is to produce behaviour which is in line with the explicit values, principles, and ethics of the organization, then congruency between the explicit and implicit components of the ethics program is essential.

To evaluate the potential effectiveness of an ethics program we propose several criteria which can be applied to the explicit components, beginning with the published code of ethics/practice/conduct. Assuming that the corporate code is satisfactory, the next step is to evaluate implementation efforts. Ultimately, the success and effectiveness of the program will depend on the next step, which is an honest and objective audit of the "implicit" components.

One danger of using a phrase such as "ethics program" is that it might suggest a requirement for a large scale, disruptive, and expensive process. Just the opposite is true. As I said at the beginning of this section, every corporation already has an ethics program. What is proposed here is a framework for looking at the effectiveness of what is already in place and for identifying what, if any, aspects need strengthening or modification. The ethical ground rules, values, and practices of an organization develop incrementally over time and will require time to change.

NOTES

1. Brenner, S. N., "Ethics Programs and Their Dimensions," *Journal of Business Ethics,* Vol. 11: 391, 399, 1992.
2. Metzger, M., D. R. Dalton, and J. W. Hill, "The Organization of Ethics and the Ethics of Organizations: The Case for Expanded Organizational Ethics Audits," *Business Ethics Quarterly,* Vol. 3, Issue 1, 1993, pp. 27–43.
3. The details of this research are expanded in M. B. E. Clarkson and M. C. Deck, "Applying the Stakeholder Management Model to the Analysis and Evaluation of Corporate Codes," in *Business and Society in a Changing World Order,* pp. 55–76 (Best Papers volume of the 1992 Conference of the International Association for Business and Society), Dean C. Ludwig, Editor. Edwin Mellen Press, New York. 1993.
4. Rich, A. J., C. S. Smith, and P. H. Mihalek: 1990, "Are Corporate Codes of Conduct Effective?" *Management Accounting* (September), pp. 34–35.

MOTOROLA AS OVID
Using Myth to Inspire Ethical Behavior in Business
Kiren Dosanjh

This article explores how the use of classical mythology in business ethics training can foster employees' ethical behavior, and suggests how the corporate culture could benefit from the creation of its own myths. After addressing the mechanistic approach to business ethics training, this article discusses the relevance of myth in constructing and promoting a moral order. In explaining this relevance, the article explores the psychological significance of myth. The classical myths of Prometheus, Narcissus, and the Judgment of Paris are summarized and analyzed for their ethical themes and their analogies found in modern ethical dilemmas in business. Through its analyses of these myths, this article hopes to serve as a model for the use of myth in business ethics training, and as a call for the creation of new myths in the business environment.

INTRODUCTION

In a sincere effort to promote ethical behavior, companies have created codes of conduct that pronounce what is and is not acceptable behavior for their employees while they are engaged in the course of business. These codes may be promulgated at obligatory ethics training sessions, which might incorporate case studies selected to emphasize the importance the company assigns to compliance. This mechanistic approach to the problem of unethical business practices assumes that ethical behavior will result from mere knowledge of prescribed ethical standards. Corporate codes of conduct and accompanying training sessions certainly fulfill an educational function in teaching the organization's definition of ethical behavior. Yet more may be required to truly promote ethical behavior.

In order for the communication of a company's values to translate into actual business practices, the sources of ethical dilemmas should be identified and explored. The external sources of ethical dilemmas are readily determined: it is the firm requiring a minimum number of billable hours, the client demanding a particular outcome, or the supplier expecting certain benefits to result from a contract. How and why one perceives ethical conflict in these situations is ultimately determined by one's own beliefs and intentions. The contrasting complexities of hope and despair, courage and weakness, virtue and desire all conspire to create moral ambiguities in our minds. These sources of conflict exert great force in the face of external pressures, and will exert still a greater force if left untouched and unspoken. In Jungian terms, the tension between conscious intention and an unacknowledged "shadow self" can result in counterproductive and ultimately self-destructive acts (Harris and Platzner, 1995). To reduce this tension and inspire ethical behavior will require an imaginative stretch beyond the realm of that which can be readily defined and known.

Myths are vehicles by which we can make this journey into the internal sources of ethical conflict. As Bill Moyers posits in his introduction to *The Power of Myth* (Campbell, 1988), "All these Greek Gods and stuff are not irrelevant, but line the walls of our interior system of belief." More than simple stories or mere antiquated explanations of natural phenomena, myths offer expressions of universal experience, translations of ethical dilemmas, and illumination of the Jungian "shadow." As Jung identified them, mythic characters can be viewed as archetypes, models or patterns that "spring from the collective unconscious of the entire human race" (Harris and Platzner, 1995). More meaningful than a credo, more effective than case studies, myths can inspire ethical behavior in business by connecting the imagination to shared experience.

The use of myth in corporate ethics training may meet with resistance. "Myth" has come to be known in the vernacular as a synonym for a falsehood. The current mechanistic approach taken to business ethics training would support this definition of myth. A defense to the use of myth as a guide to exploring the larger questions of morality can be found in Thomas Mann's definition of myth as "eternal truth, in contrast to empirical truth" (May 1991). An endorsement to the incorporation of myth in ethics training would come from Plato, who suggested that the future citizens of the ideal republic begin their literary education with the telling of myths, rather than mere facts, as the foundation to learning of virtue and courage (May 1991).

THE NEED FOR MODERN MYTH

Through a creative use of myth, corporations could help to fill a vacancy in the cultural landscape. Myths express beliefs and moral goals. The lack of myths is a loss of language even to begin to communicate meaningfully on such issues (May 1991). Living in a mythical vacuum leads to ethical rootlessness, for there is no structure through which society's beliefs may be heard and felt. Greek philosopher Lucretius observed in the Third Century A.D. that the breakdown in mythological belief had left "aching hearts in every home" (May 1991). Modern authority Joseph Campbell echoed this observation in asserting that modern industrial societies face so many social problems because they fail to embrace a powerful mythology that informs individuals of their place in and connection to society (Campbell, 1988).

Campbell further urged that modern societies should form myths in terms of current circumstances, to help the "aching hearts" truly make sense of their internal and external worlds (Campbell, 1988). The microcosm of modern society, the business community, offers a potent source of new myths that can help form moral awareness in the corporate culture in particular, and aid in the creation of contemporary mythology for society at large.

For these new corporate myths to form and take hold, the use of myth should not be confined to ethics training sessions. To create a corporate culture embracing its own mythology will require an ongoing search for the heroes and goddesses who at this moment could be closing a merger, advising a client, or completing a billing statement. This search does not look for the next case study, but rather is seeking reminders that the struggles and dilemmas we face are not isolated inconveniences, but universal in nature and import. An analysis of classical mythology can inform this search, and serve as a basis for understanding the universal themes exhibited in the new myths.

PROMETHEUS: PROTECTOR OF CONFIDENTIALITY, PROMULGATOR OF JUSTICE

The myth of Prometheus contains several important themes of moral relevance. Considered at once to be the archetypal rebel against injustice dealt by those in power and the ultimate humanist, Prometheus can teach much about ethical behavior in the face of conflicts of interest, extortion, and malevolent authority. Prometheus could also be the ultimate consultant on constructing an organizational structure that promotes ethical behavior.

The Myth of Prometheus

After the Gods created the world, it was time for the appearance of mankind. The task was delegated to Prometheus, the Titan who had helped Zeus in the war with the Titans, and his brother, Epimetheus. Prometheus, whose name means "forethought," was very wise, while his brother, whose name means "afterthought," was scatterbrained and impulsive. Before creating men, Epimetheus decided to give animals the gifts of strength, swiftness, courage, cunning, fur, wings, and shells. After realizing that nothing good was left for men, he turned to his brother for help.

Prometheus took over the task and thought of a way to make man superior to animals. He made men upright like the gods, and then gave them a gift that offered a better protection than those bestowed on animals. He went to the sun, where he lit a torch and brought down fire.

Zeus, furious at Prometheus for giving the gift of fire to men, which gave god-like powers for creation to these mortals, quickly forgot the debt he owed to Prometheus for his role in conquering the Titans. He had his servants, Force and Violence, seize Prometheus and chain him to a "high-piercing headlong rock," as they told him "that this was the fruit you reap for your man-loving ways," for not dreading "God's anger" and for giving "to mortals honor not their due."

Mere vengeance was not the only motive behind Zeus' punishment of Prometheus. Zeus wanted to force him to disclose a very important secret. Zeus knew that fate had decreed that one day he would be dethroned by a son not yet born, but only Prometheus knew who would be the mother of this son. Zeus sent his messenger, Hermes, to the rock-bound Prometheus, to ask him to disclose the secret. Prometheus protested: "Go and persuade the sea wave not to break. You will persuade me no more easily." Hermes warned him that worse suffering awaited him, such as being eaten alive by an eagle for eternity.

Generations later, Prometheus was released. Zeus was apparently willing to allow Heracles to slay the eagle and deliver Prometheus from his chains. While we do not know whether Prometheus revealed his secret when he was freed, one thing is certain: Prometheus did not yield under the tremendous pressure exerted by Zeus (Hamilton, 1969).

Prometheus and Rational Autonomy

While Prometheus is a Titan, he finds himself in a human struggle between a choice of doing good for others at great cost or being indifferent to maintain personal safety. Prometheus shows that through the use of reason, humans can maintain their moral freedom in deciding which course of action to take in the face of tremendous pressure. His reason allowed him to act freely in concert with his beliefs. As Marvin Kohl wrote, Prometheus stands for the "will to aspire to the power of the gods and to stand against unnecessary suffering and the evils of the status quo" (Kohl, 1996). Prometheus submits to intolerable pain because he has a free mind and a consciousness of the distinction between absolutes of good and evil (Harris and Platzner, 1995).

Prometheus represents the power of rational autonomy to change outcomes intended by those who are bestowed with seemingly ultimate control over events. Through a rational choice, Prometheus goes to the territory of the gods and usurps an element of their domain over which they wanted exclusive control. If Prometheus had maintained deference to a malevolent authority, he would have stifled his higher impulses and his rational understanding of morality. The use of rationality in creating moral rules for behavior may have been pioneered by Prometheus, not Immanuel Kant. The intellectual honesty and fidelity to reason exhibited by Prometheus are virtues in themselves (Harris and Platzner, 1995).

Prometheus and Humanity

Zeus had planned to allow the human race to attempt survival in darkness, but Prometheus took pity on the mortals and gave them the means by which they could reach their potential (Harris and Platzner, 1995). Prometheus was motivated by his overriding love of humanity in giving fire to mankind (Kohl, 1996). Thus, humans had bestowed upon them the ability not only to protect themselves, but to make scientific advances which would allow them to be self-sufficient and powerful. All this was given at great personal cost to Prometheus.

Prometheus and Confidentiality

His refusal to reveal a secret that would surely lead to the destruction of another, at great personal cost, makes Prometheus the archetypal protector of confidentiality. Given the number of mothers to his many children, Zeus was at a loss regarding the identity of the woman who would bear him a son who was destined to usurp his power. Zeus used horrifying extremes of torture to extort this information from Prometheus, with no luck. One interpretation of his motivation is that Prometheus understood that to conform to the demands of Zeus would be to extinguish the light that he had brought to earth (Harris and Platzner, 1995). In order to protect the fruits of his higher motivation, Prometheus had to safeguard his secret.

Prometheus the Arrogant Troublemaker

The role of Prometheus as protector of mortals and rebel against injustice is clear. However, another perspective may see Prometheus as an arrogant lawbreaker. In the play by Aeschylus, *Prometheus Bound,* the chorus reacts to his obstinance by charging that Prometheus is foolishly defying wise self-interest. His extreme pursuit of his own concept of good not only jeopardizes his well-being, but the maintenance of public order as well. Some commentators suggest that the myth of Prometheus represents two opposing but equally plausible versions of what is right (Harris and Platzner, 1995). Prometheus serves as an archetype of individuals faced with the choice of following their own values or silently allowing the social order to define its own justice.

Prometheus Today

Perhaps the most important lesson Prometheus offers modern business is the benefits gained from an equitable distribution of power. When those of all ranks influence decision-making, the tension between an individual's values and the actions of the organization is lessened. The preservation of the general order is upheld through the reduction of individual, internal ethical conflict that may result in rebellion against authority.

Jan Carlzon, CEO of Scandinavian Airlines, turned the corporate structure "upside-down" by giving power to the "lower ranks" of the organization. He recognized that the real "moments of truth" were created at the traditionally lower levels of the organizational structure, and wanted to promote their occurrence and visibility in the company (Autry, 1991). If Zeus had bestowed the gift of fire on humans to promote their creativity, he would have avoided the rebellion of Prometheus. Further, he would have reaped the benefits of being the one viewed as the benefactor of human power. As it stands, Carlzon's bold innovation bespeaks not of Zeus-like authority, but of Promethean concern for those without power and appreciation for the creative potential that lies within them.

NARCISSUS: EGOMANIAC OR MYOPIC MINION?

The myth of Narcissus as told by the Roman poet Ovid illustrates the role of myth as a source of personal identity and as an expression of common experience. The story speaks of the lonely individualism that results from the disease called "narcissism" in modern times. Curing narcissism may lead to the ethical resolution of moral dilemmas faced in business, and the cure lies in understanding the roots of the pain of Narcissus.

The Story of Narcissus

Narcissus was a beautiful youth who greeted all advances of young maidens with his usual coldness. He would pass by the loveliest women without a glance, no matter how hard they tried to make him look at them, their broken hearts meaning nothing to him.

One of those wounded by Narcissus' scorn prayed that "he who loves not others love himself." The goddess Nemesis, whose name means righteous anger, answered that prayer. As Narcissus bent over a clear pool to take a drink, he saw his own reflection. He was mesmerized, feeling the love others had suffered for him. He cried for his inability to reach the one he loved, for when he tried to touch his own reflection, the image vanished. He felt compelled to stay and watch his own reflection, oblivious to all else. He was so transfixed that he could not move. He pined away perpetually over the pool until he died (Hamilton, 1969).

Narcissus and Narcissism

Narcissus could not see beyond the surface to the truth, and did not accept his connection to the world around him. The "narcissistic" personality lacks the capacity to fully understand his relation to others, or to recognize that meaning is found beyond appearances.

Thus, narcissists exist in an ethical vacuum, for they are never made aware of their values. Unless values can be tested through conflict, they will never be fully developed. If the narcissist is not fully connected to the world around him, then his ethical development will be stunted from lack of conflict.

Narcissus and Manipulation

An often overlooked element to the myth of Narcissus is the role played by the goddess Nemesis. She compels Narcissus to remain transfixed by his own appearance. Surely, Narcissus was vulnerable to such spells due to his own vanity that caused hurt to others. Nevertheless, Narcissus can be viewed as a victim of manipulation. The goddess who acts with "righteous anger" may be too quick to fulfill prayers made in haste.

Narcissus Today

The modern-day Narcissus could be staring at a billing sheet, preparing to complete it with false claims. He or she may be thinking only of his or her own appearance and advancement, and not seeing the impact false claims may have on the firm or its clients. Perhaps this myopia finds its roots in the narcissist's own ambition, making him or her vulnerable to the commands of an authority figure.

If those in authority act to complete short-term goals of generating a certain number of billable hours, then they might place pressure on those in the narcissist's position with their "bottom-line" emphasis. This pressure is perhaps emblematic of a business with no vision of the future, and no appreciation for the effects it has on society. Such pressure, and such a short-term, myopic vision of success in business, create a fertile environment for unethical conduct. Without awareness of or appreciation for the long-term consequences of the actions he or she contemplates, the modern-day Narcissus becomes merely a reflection of mediocre aspirations with no lasting, meaningful contribution, and the thoughtless tool for harm. In order to avoid narcissism, those in authority should understand the "side effects" of their short-sightedness, and expand their own vision to include positive, long-term social contribution.

JUDGMENT OF PARIS: THE LURE AND FOLLY OF BRIBERY

A bribe offered and taken is the reason why the Trojan War was fought, as told in this myth.

The Tale of the Judgment of Paris

The evil goddess of Discord, Eris, was often not invited to social events on Mount Olympus. The wedding of Peleus, a mortal, and the sea nymph Thetis, which was arranged by Zeus, was no exception. Eris appeared uninvited and threw into the banquet hall a golden apple marked "for the fairest." Of course all the goddesses in attendance wanted it, but the choir was narrowed down to three finalists: Aphrodite, Hera, and Pallas Athena. Zeus declined to be the judge, and told the goddesses to seek out Paris, the young son of King Priam of Troy, to make the decision.

When the three goddesses arrived at the prince's home, where he tended sheep and lived with a beautiful nymph, they immediately offered him bribes. He was not asked to judge them on their beauty, but only to consider their offered bribes. Hera promised to make him Lord of Europe and Asia; Athena said that she would make him the victorious leader of the Trojans against the Greeks; and Aphrodite offered that the fairest woman in all the world would be his. Paris, knowing that one day he would inherit his father's power, and certain that he possessed all the wisdom he needs, gave Aphrodite the golden apple.

The fairest woman in the world was Helen, wife of Menelaus, whom Helen's father had made King of Sparta. Aphrodite led Paris to Sparta, where he followed without a thought to his live-in nymph. When Menelaus left for Crete, Paris immediately undertook to break that vow, and took Helen back to Troy. Despite official protests, Paris refused to return Helen. King Priam felt honor-bound to defend his son, although this would surely lead to war with Menelaus.

Those who had vied for Helen's hand before her father chose his son-in-law had taken a vow: If any harm fell to the man who would marry Helen, the others would champion his cause. Thus, Menelaus was able to raise an impressive army with which to wage war against Troy (Hamilton, 1969).

Judgment of Paris and Moral Responsibility

This myth represents the freedom of choice offered to humans, and its accompanying burden. There is no guidance offered to Paris to inform his decision. His values are tested with no forethought, and he chooses beauty or love over power and wisdom. Did Paris make the correct choice? Accompanying freedom of choice is moral responsibility (Harris and Platzner, 1995). Without proper guidance, Paris was left to make a choice based on his perception of his immediate desires and needs.

Judgment of Paris and the Folly of Bribery

Paris is instructed by the goddesses to not judge them on their merits, but to select the winner based solely on the value of her bribe. He is not given the express choice to ignore the bribes and resort to a dispassionate judgment. Paris is also not told of the grave long-term consequences of taking Aphrodite's bribe. When faced with bribery, one's values are put to a harsh test. Without any guidance as to the immorality of bribery or the adverse affects of taking a bribe, one may be vulnerable to the lure of the short-term benefits offered by the bribe.

Judgment of Paris Today

A modern myth maker for the international business environment is Motorola. Around 1950, a senior executive was negotiating with officials of a foreign government for a lucrative deal. The executive chose to end the negotiations before the deal was completed because the officials had asked for one million dollars in "fees." Not only was the executive supported by CEO Robert Galvin, he achieved mythic status in the retelling of this story through the decades at Motorola (Donaldson, 1996). Informed undoubtedly by a strong personal ethic which was supported by a corporate ethos against bribery, the executive withstood the pressure of the luring bribe offered to him.

CONCLUSION

Through a study of classical myths, the internal sources of ethical conflict are revealed. The use of myth can add a deeper dimension to business ethics training as a guide for the exploration of the drives that may compel an individual to behave unethically. Such an approach to training offers an opportunity to meaningfully discuss the underlying issues to ethical conflict. Further, certain interpretations of myths offer dramatic lessons in the ill effects of unethical business practices.

Organizational behavior can also be informed by the study of myth. By applying the wisdom contained in the myths to managerial decisions, ethical behavior in business may be promoted by creating an environment in which the tension between individual values and organizational methods is lessened. Finally, corporations should strive to create their own myths through which ethical behavior may be inspired through example of the ethical resolution of recognizable dilemmas. In this way, corporations can create not only an ethical corporate culture, but promote social awareness and development of ethics as well.

REFERENCES

Harris, S. L., and G. Platzner: 1995, *Classical Mythology: Images and Insights* (Mayfield Publishing Co., Mountain View, CA), pp. 37–38, 232–236, 425–427.

Campbell, J.: 1988. *The Power of Myth* (Doubleday, New York, NY), pp. xii, 160.

May, R.: 1991, *The Cry for Myth* (Dell Publishing, New York, NY), pp. 16, 22, 27.

Hamilton, E.: 1969, *Mythology: Timeless Tales of Gods and Heroes* (Mentor Publishing Co., New York, NY), pp. 78–81, 91–92, 186–188.

Kohl, M.: 1996, "The Nature of Promethean Ethics," *The Humanist,* January/February 1996, 45–46.

Autry, J. A.: 1991, *Love and Profit: The Art of Caring Leadership* (Avon, New York, NY), p. 161.

Donaldson, T.: 1996, "Values in Tension: Ethics Away from Home," *Harvard Business Review,* September/October 1996, 60.

STONYFIELD FARM'S MISSION STATEMENT

As mentioned in the chapter introduction, a mission statement may serve several different purposes and may be designed to serve the interests of various stakeholders. The following statement is consistently referred to as laudatory because of their commitment to a multi-stakeholder approach.

Welcome!

A Barn's Eye View of Stonyfield Farm

Company Profile / Our Mission

Our Main "Moovers"

In the "Moos"

"Moos" Release

Yogurt Works Tour & Visitors' Center

Welcome to Stonyfield Farm. We're 150 people in Londonderry, NH committed to producing the best-tasting, healthiest, "udderly" natural refrigerated yogurts, frozen yogurts and ice cream possible, and trying to do some good in the world while we're at it.

[About Stonyfield Farm] [Our Products] [Happenings] [Earth Action]
[Kids Stuff] [Healthwise] [Recipes & Yogurt Tips] [Store Locator]
[Contact Us] [Frequently Asked Questions]

Stonyfield Farm's Mission Statement. Reprinted with permission of Stonyfield Farms.

Sign up for "Moos"   Recipes   Contact Us   Frequently Asked Questions   Store Locator

A Barn's Eye View of Stonyfield Farm

Company Profile / Our Mission

Our Main "Moovers"

In the "Moos"

"Moos" Release

Visitors' Center

Company Profile

Stonyfield Farm isn't your average yogurt and Stonyfield Farm isn't your average company. We don't make yogurt with artificial ingredients or advertise with glitzy TV commercials. We're 150 people in a small New Hampshire town who are committed to producing the best-tasting, healthiest yogurts, frozen yogurts and ice cream possible, and trying to do some good in the world while we're at it.

Stonyfield Farm began in 1983 as an organic farming school with a few Jersey cows (the ones that make the sweetest milk), and a great-tasting yogurt recipe. Today our products include all natural Certified Organic refrigerated yogurts, soft serve frozen yogurt and Certified Organic ice cream and frozen yogurt, all sold across the U.S.

Our Mission

- To produce the very highest quality all natural and Certified Organic products that taste incredible.

- To educate consumers and producers about the value of protecting the environment and of supporting family farmers and sustainable farming methods.

- To serve as a model that environmentally and socially responsible businesses can also be profitable.

- To provide a healthful, productive and enjoyable work place for all employees, with opportunities to gain new skills and advance personal career goals.

- To recognize our obligations to stockholders and lenders by providing an excellent return on their investment.

[About Stonyfield Farm] [Our Products] [Happenings] [Earth Action]
[Kids' Stuff] [Healthwise] [Recipes & Yogurt Tips] [Store Locator]
[Contact Us] [Frequently Asked Questions] [Sign Our Guest Book]

DO CODES OF CONDUCT DELIVER THE GOODS?

Maureen Quigley

Mission statements are constantly and consistently developed by firms, though there is only some conclusive evidence of their impact. Quigley asks the questions that many corporations therefore would like answered!

Companies adopt a range of ways and means to tackle ethical problems found within their supply chains, such as abuse of safety standards in factories in developing countries. Each approach has inherent strengths and pitfalls, yet each represents a step in a process of improving conditions. Companies most commonly start by adopting codes of conduct and internal monitoring systems. But are such steps enough? Experiences of the Pentland Group suggest that companies facing the difficult and complex demands of ethical trading will need more than formulaic codes or monitoring.

A code can be an essential first step. It defines key principles and aspirations, and companies can often use their purchasing power to urge suppliers' compliance with it. Yet such leverage is limited in scope because:

- it hinges on a buyer committed to taking a large percentage of a supplier's production

- it offers no advantage to smaller companies that lack significant purchasing power

- it could be used unfairly to discriminate against small to medium-sized enterprises

- it is piecemeal, tackling issues on factory-by-factory basis rather than addressing larger root causes

- it may be used cosmetically to guard corporate reputations rather than improve conditions.

A second, more progressive phase is where a company implements a code of conduct, either by imposing it on suppliers or by more collaborative means, then works to integrate the principals of the code into its own supply chain management and other management systems. The blending together of principals and actions is essential to sustainable ethical trading.

Nonetheless, the roots of the problems and dilemmas found in manufacturing are too complex to be sorted out on a factory-by-factory basis. Tackling problems found in worker health and safety involves looking at external forces and conditions, such as the capacity of

---

civic institutions to regulate, enforce and provide essential services to businesses and workers. The route to lasting improvement is to overcome contextual barriers, inefficiencies and inequalities commonly associated with underdevelopment, that impede sustainable change. Companies that seek to be a positive force for change need to take a developmental approach that is characterised by (although not limited to):

- local ownership of issues

- collaborative relationships with suppliers

- multi-sectoral partnerships

- capacity building of institutions.

These values define a long-term strategy that fuses integrated management systems with partnership development. Traces of this method have been found traditionally within extractive industries. However, it is an option and an opportunity for companies of varying size and in all sectors. Strategic partnerships enable small companies to overcome vast resource requirements of a developmental approach by complementing partners' expertise and material contributions. Partnerships cannot be limited to suppliers and workers, but must include competitors, local and foreign governmental institutions and NGOs if they are to build a comprehensive strategy for change.

Debate within ethical trading circles remains steeped in issues of how best to monitor and to evaluate company codes. As more companies develop codes, it is clear that codes represent only part of a process. Given the vast effort expended on monitoring, one must question whether resources might be better applied to treating the root causes of problems rather than to monitoring symptoms. Advocates for ethical trading must be aware of the risk of failing to see the forest for the trees. The challenge for corporations, nongovernmental organisations, unions, and governments is to develop viable, collaborative programs to root out the causes of human rights abuses and unsatisfactory working conditions.

THE PRINCE

NICCOLÒ MACHIAVELLI

This excerpt from Machiavelli's The Prince *discusses how a prince (or person with governing power, generally) gains his (or her) reputation. Machiavelli concludes that dignity is the most important quality. Based on this, do you think that Machiavelli would be impressed by our business and government leaders today? Do you agree with his contentions? If not, why not?*

CHAPTER TWENTY-ONE: WHAT A RULER SHOULD DO IN ORDER TO ACQUIRE A REPUTATION

Nothing does more to give a ruler a reputation than embarking on great undertakings and doing remarkable things. In our own day, there is Ferdinand of Aragon, the present King of Spain. He may be called, more or less, a new ruler, because having started out as a weak ruler he has become the most famous and most glorious of all the kings of Christendom. If you think about his deeds, you will find them all noble, and some of them extraordinary. At the beginning of his reign he attacked Granada, and this undertaking was the basis of his increased power.[1] In the first place, he undertook the reconquest when he had no other problems to face, so he could concentrate upon it. He used it to channel the ambitions of his Castilian barons, who, because they were thinking of the war, were no threat to him at home. Meanwhile, he acquired influence and authority over them without their even being aware of it. He was able to raise money from the church and from his subjects to build up his armies. Thus, this lengthy war enabled him to build up his military strength, which has paid off since. Next, in order to be able to engage in more ambitious undertakings, still exploiting religion, he practiced a pious cruelty, expropriating and expelling from his kingdom the Marranos:[2] an act without parallel and truly despicable. He used religion once more as an excuse to justify an attack on Africa.[3] He then attacked Italy and has recently[4] invaded France. He is always plotting and carrying out great enterprises, which have always kept his subjects bewildered and astonished, waiting to see what their outcome would be.

---

[1]The Muslim state of Granada was conquered between 1480 and 1492.

[2]The Marranos were Jews who had been forced to convert to Catholicism. On misinterpretatons of this term, see Edward Andrew, "The Foxy Prophet: Machiavelli Versus Machiavelli on Ferdinand the Catholic," *History of Political Thought* 11 (1990), 409–22.

[3]In 1509.

[4]In 1512.

And his deeds have followed one another so closely that he has never left space between one and the next for people to plot uninterruptedly against him.

It is also of considerable help to a ruler if he does remarkable things when it comes to domestic policy, such as those that are reported of Mr. Bernabò of Milan.[5] It is a good idea to be widely talked about, as he was, because, whenever anyone happened to do anything extraordinary, whether good or bad, in civil life, he found an imaginative way to reward or to punish them. Above all a ruler should make every effort to ensure that whatever he does it gains him a reputation as a great man, a person who excels.

Rulers are also admired when they know how to be true allies and genuine enemies: That is, when, without any reservations, they demonstrate themselves to be loyal supporters or opponents of others. Such a policy is always better than one of neutrality. For if two rulers who are your neighbors are at war with each other, they are either so powerful that, if one of them wins, you will have to fear the victor, or they are not. Either way, it will be better for you to take sides and fight a good fight; for, if they are powerful, and you do not take sides, you will still be preyed on by the victor, much to the pleasure and satisfaction of his defeated opponent. You will have no excuse, no defense, no refuge. For whoever wins will not want allies who are unreliable and who do not stand by him in adversity; while he who loses will not offer you refuge, since you were not willing, sword in hand, to share his fate.

The Aetolians invited Antiochus to Greece to drive out the Romans.[6] Antiochus sent an ambassador to the Achaeans, who were allies of the Romans, to encourage them to remain neutral, while the Romans urged them to fight on their side. The ruling council of the Achaeans met to decide what to do, and Antiochus's ambassador spoke in favor of neutrality. The Roman ambassador replied: "As for what they say to you, that it would be sensible to keep out of the war, there is nothing further from your true interests. If you are without credit, without dignity, the victor will claim you as his prize."

It will always happen that he who is not your ally will urge neutrality upon you, while he who is your ally will urge you to take sides. Rulers who are unsure what to do, but want to avoid immediate dangers, generally end up staying neutral and usually destroy themselves by doing so. But when a ruler boldly takes sides, if your ally wins, even if he is powerful, and has the ability to overpower you, he is in your debt and fond of you. Nobody is so shameless as to turn on you in so ungrateful a fashion. Moreover, victories are never so overwhelming that the victor can act without any constraint: Above all, victors still need to appear just. But if, on the other hand, your ally is defeated, he will offer you refuge, will help you as long as he is able, and will share your ill-fortune, in the hope of one day sharing good fortune with you. In the second case, when those at war with each other are insufficiently powerful to give you grounds to fear the outcome, there is all the more reason to take sides, for you will be able to destroy one of them with the help of the other, when, if they were wise, they would be helping each other. The one who wins is at your mercy; and victory is certain for him whom you support.

Here it is worth noting a ruler should never take the side of someone who is more powerful than himself against other rulers, unless necessity compels him to, as I have already implied. For if you win, you are your ally's prisoner; and rulers should do everything they

---

[5] Bernabò Visconti ruled Milan from 1354 to 1385.
[6] 192 B.C. The source is Livy, bk. 35, chs. 48, 49.

can to avoid being at the mercy of others. The Venetians allied with the King of France against the Duke of Milan, when they could have avoided taking sides; they brought about their own destruction.[7] But when you cannot help but take sides (which is the situation the Florentines found themselves in when the pope and the King of Spain were advancing with their armies to attack Lombardy)[8] then you should take sides decisively, as I have explained. Do not for a moment think any state can always take safe decisions, but rather think every decision you take involves risks, for it is in the nature of things that you cannot take precautions against one danger without opening yourself to another. Prudence consists in knowing how to assess risks and in accepting the lesser evil as a good.

A ruler should also show himself to be an admirer of skill [*virtù*] and should honor those who are excellent in any type of work. He should encourage his citizens by making it possible for them to pursue their occupations peacefully, whether they are businessmen, farmers, or are engaged in any other activity, making sure they do not hesitate to improve what they own for fear it may be confiscated from them, and they are not discouraged from investing in business for fear of losing their profits in taxes; instead, he should ensure that those who improve and invest are rewarded, as should be anyone whose actions will benefit his city or his government. He should, in addition, at appropriate times of the year, amuse the populace with festivals and public spectacles. Since every city is divided into guilds or neighborhoods, he ought to take account of these collectivities, meeting with them on occasion, showing himself to be generous and understanding in his dealings with them, but at the same time always retaining his authority and dignity, for this he should never let slip in any circumstances.

---

[7]In 1499.
[8]In 1512.

Part Two

ETHICS IN THE BUSINESS DISCIPLINES

Chapter 8

ETHICS AND HUMAN RESOURCES MANAGEMENT:
Values of the Employment Relationship

TOPIC STUDY: DRUG TESTING

"Issues in Drug Testing for the Private Sector"	GEORGE GRAY DARREL BROWN
"Is Employee Drug Testing the Answer?"	THOMAS GALLOT MARK COHEN ERIC FILLMAN
"ACS Herbal Tea Company Materials"	

TOPIC STUDY: COMPENSATION—COMPARABLE WORTH

"The Question of Wages"	RUTH ROSENBAUM
American Nurses Association v. *State of Illinois*	U.S. APPELLATE COURT FOR THE SEVENTH CIRCUIT
"Is Pay Equity Equitable?"	LAURA B. PINCUS NICK MATHYS
"A Free Market Approach to Comparable Worth"	LAURA B. PINCUS

TOPIC STUDY: EMPLOYEE LOYALTY: WHISTLEBLOWING

"Whistleblowing and Trust: Some Lessons from the ADM Scandal"	DARYL KOEHN
"The Case of George and the Military Aircraft"	M. C. MCFARLAND

TOPIC STUDY: DISCRIMINATION AND AFFIRMATIVE ACTION—LEGISLATED ETHICS?

"I'm Not Supposed to Laugh at the Way People Look"	PETE MUELLER
"Some Issues in Employment Discrimination on Grounds of Race, Sex, and Age"	RICHARD POSNER
"In Defense of Non-Diversity"	T. J. RODGERS
"Diversity Management: A New Organizational Paradigm"	JACQUELIN GILBERT BETTE ANN STEAD JON M. IVANCEVICH
"Business Sues 'Discrimination Testers' Posing as Job Applicants"	TAMMY WEBBER
"Affirming Affirmative Action"	JESSE L. JACKSON

We can invest all the money on Wall Street in new technologies, but we can't realize the benefits of improved productivity until companies rediscover the value of human loyalty.

—FREDERICK REICHHELD,
DIRECTOR, BAIN & CO.

In 1960, about one-third of the American workforce was represented by unions. Today, that figure is about 11 percent. Collective bargaining, established to protect the interests of workers, has proven inadequate to the task. Not surprisingly, federal and state regulations governing work practices has exploded. The variety of protections is prodigious: antidiscrimination laws, wage and hour laws, worker safety laws, unemployment compensation, workers' compensation, and social security, to name a few.

The purpose of this section is to present ethical dilemmas that face the worker, whether she or he is an employee on an assembly line, the manager of a restaurant, or the CEO of a large corporation. While the perspectives change, similar conflicts (and stakeholders) present themselves. The predominant theme is that at some point in each person's life, she or he will be an employee or an employer, and it is critical to recognize the stakes each player may have in any given dilemma. The section will provide a textual background relating to the employment relationship, its origins, and its regulation, as well as readings relevant to this topic. Articles are also included that address the issue of the balance of power within the employment relationship, downsizing, employee loyalty, discrimination, and compensation issues.

Drug Testing   Whether an employer tests its employees for drug usage requires a delicate balance between the right of the employer to protect its interests and the right of the employee to be free from wrongful intrusions into her or his personal affairs. Since the employer is often responsible for legal violations of its employees committed in the course of their job, the employer's interest in retaining control over every aspect of the work environment increases. On the other hand, employees may argue that their drug usage is only relevant if it impacts their job performance. Until it does, the employer should have no basis for testing.

Country singer Tom T. Hall would likely advocate drug testing as he croons, "If you hang all the people, you'll get all the guilty." However, consider the possibilities of incorrect presumptions in connection with drug testing. For instance, in his book, *Drug Abuse in the Workplace: An Employer's Guide for Prevention,* Mark de Bernardo suggests that crudely wrapped cigarettes, razor blades or eye droppers, frequent trips to the bathroom, or dressing inappropriately for the season may be warning signs of drug use.[1] On the other hand, it does not take a great deal of imagination to come up with other, more innocuous alternative possibilities. Yet, an employer may decide to test based on these "signs."

In a study examining the attitudes of college students to drug testing programs, researchers found that "virtually all aspects of drug testing programs are strongly accepted by some individuals and strongly rejected by others."[2] The only variable that the researchers found indicative of a student's attitude was whether the student had ever used drugs in the past. Where a student had never used drugs, she or he was more likely to find drug testing programs acceptable.[3] In general, the following factors contribute to greater acceptance and approval by workers: programs that use a task force made up of employees and their supervisors, a completely random program, effective communication of procedures, programs that offer treatment other than termination for first-time offenders, and programs with no distinction between supervisory and other workers.

---

[1]Mark A. de Bernardo, *Drug Abuse in the Workplace: An Employer's Guide for Prevention,* available from the U.S. Chamber of Commerce, 1615 H Street, NW, Washington, DC 20062.
[2]Kevin Murphy, George Thornton, and Douglas Reynolds, "College Students' Attitudes toward Employee Drug Testing Programs," *Personnel Psychology* 43 (1990), p. 615.
[3]Id.

Compensation   One of the most heated issues in any discussion of human resource management is salary. Often workers believe that they are underpaid for their work, that employers might not always treat them fairly, or that they are not appreciated. One of the most sensitive areas in connection with salary and fairness is gender discrimination. Title VII of the 1964 Civil Rights Act places race, color, and national origin among those "protected classes" against which discrimination is forbidden. The act was directed primarily to improving the employment opportunities of blacks, but it applies to all races and colors (including whites and Native Americans). The national origin provision forbids discrimination based on one's nation of birth, ancestry, or heritage. Therefore, an employment office sign reading "Mexicans need not apply" would clearly be unlawful. In addition, the Equal Pay Act of 1963 specifically provides that men and women must be paid equal pay for equal work. Accordingly, failure to fairly compensate workers may constitute both a legal and an ethical breach.

The fact is, when any employment decision is made, discrimination exists. Does that surprise you? Isn't it appropriate for an employer to discriminate based on actual qualifications such as education and experience (for some jobs)? In fact, employers can, should, and do discriminate based on perfectly acceptable grounds. You wouldn't find it strange or wrong for a business to require a human resources degree for applicants to a position as vice president of human resources. American law merely forbids discrimination on a *few, specific, non–job related* factors (such as religion and race), as you will see below.

An employer seeking to avoid a violation of Title VII or the Equal Pay Act can adjust its wage structure by raising the pay of the disfavored sex. Lowering the pay of the favored sex violates the act. Paying women and men the same amount for the same work is simple enough in principle, but the legal issues have proved slippery, indeed. For example:

1. Is travel reimbursement a "wage?" Maternity payments? (According to the federal government, no.)
2. Must the plaintiff establish a *pattern* of sex-based wage discrimination? (According to the federal government, no.)
3. Are jobs unequal in effort and thus "unequal work" when a part of one job includes tasks that females are physically unable to perform? (No, if those tasks do not constitute a substantial part of the job.)

In the leading case of *Corning Glass Works* v. *Brennan,* the U.S. Supreme Court was faced with the question of whether different shifts constituted differing "working conditions." Women had been engaged in glass inspection on the day shift. Corning added a night shift of inspectors, which, due to state "protective" laws, was composed entirely of males. The night shift demanded and received higher wages than the female day inspectors. The Supreme Court held that the time of day in and of itself is not a *working condition.* That term, the Court said, refers to "surroundings" and "hazards." However, shift differentials could lawfully constitute a "factor other than sex" if established by the employer.

Comparable Worth   Equal pay for equal work is hardly a radical notion, but equal pay for work of comparable value would, if fully realized, dramatically alter the nature of the American labor market. *Comparable worth* calls for determining the compensation to be paid for a position based on the job's intrinsic value in comparison to wages being paid for other jobs requiring comparable skills, effort, and responsibility and having comparable worth to the organization.

The argument is that the dollar value assigned to jobs held predominantly by men is higher than the value assigned to jobs held predominantly by women. To proponents of comparable worth, such disparities cannot be explained by market forces. They argue that women are the continuing victims of sex discrimination in violation of Title VII of the Civil Rights Act of 1964.

A variety of studies have contrasted pay scales in traditionally female jobs with those in traditionally male jobs where the jobs are judged to be of comparable worth. For example, licensed practical nurses in Illinois in 1983 earned an average of $1,298 per month, while electricians earned an average of $2,826. A 1987 Child Welfare League study fixed the median salary of garbage collectors at $14,872 annually, as compared with $12,800 for child care workers. The same study found social workers with master's degrees earned about $21,800 per year, while auto salespeople averaged $22,048.

There may be market explanations for the inequality between wages in occupations which are traditionally male-dominated as opposed to those jobs which are traditionally female-dominated. Economist and jurist Judge Richard Posner explains:

> *[While] irrational or exploitive discrimination is one possibility[,] another is that male wages include a compensatory wage premium for the dirty, disagreeable and often strenuous jobs that men dominate presumably because their aversion to such work is less than women's. Another (these are not mutually exclusive of course) is differences in investments in market-related human capital (earning capacity). If a woman allocates a substantial part of her working life to household production, including child care, she will obtain a substantially lower return on her market human capital than a man planning to devote much less time to household production. [Consequently, the woman] will therefore invest less in that human capital. Since earnings are in part a return on one's human capital investments (including education), women's earnings will be lower than men's. In part this will show up in the choice of occupations: Women will be attracted to occupations that don't require much human capital. Of course the amount of time women are devoting to household production is declining, so we can expect the wage gap to shrink if the economic model is correct.*[4]

Posner concludes by qualifying his comments by stipulating "if the economic model is correct." Why might you believe that this model would not be correct or that the wage gap may not shrink completely? If actual prejudice (i.e., pre-judging) exists, that is, if women are *believed* to be less valuable as workers than men, regardless of their *actual* abilities, then employers may continue to hire men at higher wages. In other words, even though women are actually spending less time at home and the household and child care duties are more likely to be split, employers may still *believe* that women will get pregnant and quit. Given this prejudice, employers will not pay women commensurate with men, notwithstanding market influences. Do you agree?

A number of companies, state governments, and several foreign countries practice some form of comparable worth, but most continue to rely on the market as the best measure of

---

[4]Richard Posner, *Economic Analysis of Law* (Boston: Little Brown & Co., 1986), pp. 313–14.

worth. The U.S. Supreme Court has yet to directly explore the substance of the comparable worth debate. In the *Gunther* case, the Court held, in effect, that Title VII does not forbid the comparable worth theory. However, the federal appeals court decisions to date have rejected the comparable worth theory in the context of Title VII sex discrimination.

Can the Market "Fix" Discrimination?   If the market were left to its own devices, wouldn't you expect firms that discriminate to fall by the wayside? That is, if a firm hires its employees based on prejudices and discriminatory views (such as women can't do a certain job), then it is limiting its pool of possible employees. Another firm that does not discriminate can choose from the larger pool and is more likely to obtain the *most* qualified individual for the job. Judge Richard Posner explains the economic impact of this theory in terms of race discrimination as follows:

> *In a market of many sellers, the intensity of the prejudice against blacks will vary considerably. Some sellers will have only a mild prejudice against them. These sellers will not forgo as many advantageous transactions with blacks as their more prejudiced competitors (unless the law interferes). Their costs will therefore be lower, and this will enable them to increase their share of the market. The least prejudiced sellers will come to dominate the market in much the same way as people who are least afraid of heights come to dominate occupations that require working at heights: they demand a smaller premium.*[5]

Under what circumstances would Posner's argument fail? Consider the implications if the discriminating firm held a monopoly on its good or service. What is the effect of regulation such as Title VII on Posner's argument? Consider his approach above as you read the excerpt from his text later in this section.

Discrimination and Affirmative Action   Efforts toward the elimination of discrimination in employment over the past 30 years have, indeed, resulted in a more diverse workforce. Diversity refers to the presence of differing cultures, languages, ethnicities, races, affinity orientations, genders, religious sects, abilities, social classes, ages, and national origins of the individuals in a firm. This diversity has brought with it countless benefits to the workplace, but has also created conflicts that were not previously present. Where individuals from different backgrounds are brought together for the first time, *and* where negative stereotypes previously ruled interactions between these two groups, sensitivity to the potential for conflict is necessary. Efforts at multiculturalism, defined as the acknowledgement and promotion of diversity through celebration and appreciation of various cultures in the workplace, is one response.

Other problems exist that one might not necessarily consider. For example, reflect on a report by the U.S. Commission on Civil Rights that addresses the unique predicament of Asian Americans. The report documents widespread discrimination against Asian Americans, who have long been considered to have escaped the national origin barriers that face other cultures. The report contends that the typical Asian stereotype of being hardworking,

---

[5]*Ibid.*, p. 616.

intelligent, and successful is actually a detriment to Asian Americans. This stereotype results in the problems of poor Asians being overlooked, in preventing successful Asian Americans from becoming more successful, in placing undue pressure on young Asian Americans to succeed in school, and in discrediting other minorities by arguing that "if Asian Americans can succeed, so can other minorities."[6] In an article highlighting the report, *Fortune* magazine intuits that the problem is really that the commission is "being driven crazy by the fact that Asian Americans have been succeeding essentially *without the benefit of affirmative action.* The ultimate problem is not that they may make other minorities look bad—it is that they are making the civil rights bureaucracy look irrelevant."[7] Some theorists argue that formal affirmative action measures have often served to create a greater divide rather than to draw people closer.

The establishment of civil rights in the workplace sometimes cannot be achieved, in the short run, simply by avoiding discriminatory practices. Obviously, obeying the law is expected of all. However, as a matter of social policy, we have decided that mere compliance with the civil rights laws, guaranteeing equal opportunity in the workplace, is not always adequate to correct the wrongs of discrimination. Among other problems, a great deal of time ordinarily would need to pass before the lingering effects of past discrimination would no longer be felt if we were to do nothing more than not practice discrimination. Therefore, we have decided as a society to implement the policy that we label affirmative action as a means of remedying past wrongs and preventing the same in the future. In following an affirmative action plan, employers consciously take positive steps to seek out minorities and women for hiring and promotion opportunities, and they often employ goals and timetables to measure progress toward a workforce that is representative of the qualified labor pool.

Affirmative action efforts arise in two ways: (1) courts may order implementation of affirmative action after a finding of wrongful discrimination, and (2) employers may voluntarily adopt affirmative action plans. Some do so because they believe it is a wise management strategy or because they approve of affirmative action as a matter of social policy, or both. Others may adopt affirmative action because they wish to do business with the federal government. All government contractors must meet the affirmative action standards of the Office of Federal Contract Compliance Programs. As discussed above, those standards consist essentially of established goals and timetables for strengthening the representation of "underutilized" minorities and women.

Good Policy?   Affirmative action is one of the most hotly disputed social issues in contemporary life. Minorities and women have been the victims of discrimination. Should white males "pay" for those wrongs? Critics decry affirmative action as "reverse discrimination." They argue that affirmative action is paternalistic and encourages the view that minorities and women can progress only with the aid of white males. Studies confirm that affirmative action plans stigmatize minorities and women in the minds of coworkers. Minorities and women are often assumed to have achieved their positions via "quotas" and not as the result of their efforts and abilities.

---

[6]"Up from Inscrutable," *Fortune,* April 6, 1992, p. 20.
[7]Id.

Now, many white males feel that they are surrounded and under siege by the forces of affirmative action and multiculturalism. Even if so, *Newsweek* argues that being a white man is still a very comfortable role in contemporary America:

> *But is the white male truly an endangered species, or is he just being a jerk? It's still a statistical piece of cake being a white man, at least in comparison with being anything else. White males make up just 39.2 percent of the population, yet they account for 82.5 percent of the Forbes 400 (folks worth at least $265 million), 77 percent of Congress, 92 percent of state governors, 70 percent of tenured college faculty, almost 90 percent of daily-newspaper editors, 77 percent of TV news directors. They dominate just about everything but NOW and the NAACP.*

Affirmative Action in Practice   *United Steelworkers of America v. Weber* is perhaps the clearest Supreme Court statement to date about the permissible boundaries of affirmative action. Weber, a white male, challenged the legality of an affirmative action plan that set aside for black employees 50 percent of the openings in a training program until the percentage of black craft workers in the plant equaled the percentage of blacks in the local labor market. Weber was denied entry to the training program. The federal district court and the federal court of appeals held for Weber, but the U.S. Supreme Court reversed. Therefore, under *Weber,* race-conscious affirmative action remedies *can* be permissible. Several qualities of the Steelworkers' plan were instrumental in the Court's favorable ruling:

1. The affirmative action was part of a plan.
2. The plan was designed to "open employment opportunities for Negroes in occupations which have been traditionally closed to them."
3. The plan was temporary.
4. The plan did not unnecessarily harm the rights of white employees. That is—
   a. The plan did not require the discharge of white employees.
   b. The plan did not create an absolute bar to the advancement of white employees.

Therefore, affirmative action in situations like that in *Weber* does not constitute unlawful reverse discrimination. The Supreme Court clarified the law's affirmative action commands a bit further in the *Burdine* case, in which the Court asserted that Title VII does not require the employer to hire a minority or female applicant whenever that person's objective qualifications were equal to those of a white male applicant. Therefore, "the employer has discretion to choose among equally qualified candidates, provided the decision is not based upon unlawful criteria."

Sexual Harassment   One additional area of recent concern, especially in connection with the balance of power in the workplace, is sexual harassment. Sexual harassment evolved through a traditional application of Title VII: treating someone differently because of her or his gender is unlawful under Title VII. There are two types of sexual harassment that fit within this broad prohibition: quid pro quo and hostile environment. Quid pro quo exists where a supervisor offers an employment benefit in exchange for sexual activity or where a supervisor refuses to give an employee-deserved benefit unless she or he engages in sexual activity. Hostile environment sexual harassment is not so easily defined. The Supreme

Court, through a host of cases, explains that a hostile environment exists where a work environment is severely or pervasively altered such that a reasonable person would find it offensive or abusive.

The definition of a hostile environment is thus rather complicated and amorphous. The court has defined it in such a way as to make it a hybrid of a subjective and objective test. First, the plaintiff must show that the environment would be considered offensive to a reasonable person (objective analysis); then the plaintiff must *also* show that she or he, individually, was offended by the situation (subjective analysis). For this reason, it is difficult to state conclusively whether any given circumstance might be considered to be sexual harassment. On the other hand, we are given some parameters. The facts that give rise to the claim must be severe or pervasive. A one-time event would not constitute sexual harassment unless it is severe; and a relatively benign event might become sexual harassment where it is pervasive. In order to shed more light on this characterization, *Harris v. Forklift* is included in the readings that follow, as well as several readings related to EEOC recommendations in this area.

SHORT HYPOTHETICAL CASES

a. Four of the original owners of a metal fabricating company are selling out to the fifth owner. The company has been successful and, after 25 years, employs 250 people in the plant and 150 in the office. In evaluating the company, the new sole owner sees much duplication: 5 accountants could do the job that 20 now handle. In every office department, the company has overhired. Cutting back would dramatically improve the company's profits. But the company is a small, close-knit community and the employees have long service records and are extremely loyal. As the new sole owner, what do you do?

b. You recently started working in the personnel department of a large company. The personnel manager has asked you to tell any black applicants that the company is not hiring; if the person fills out an application, you are to tell the personnel manager that the applicant is black. What do you do?

c. Your department manager has asked you to be her confidant and to relay to her any complaints or problems you overhear from your coworkers. She assures you that the information will be kept highly confidential. She says that she is doing this in an effort to improve her effectiveness and to address the issues that workers may not be willing to bring to her attention. The department's performance in the past has been poor. If she can turn it around, she'll be in line for a promotion, you would be in line for her job, and no cutbacks in staff would need to be made. What do you do?

Hypotheticals were written by Catherine Haselden and are included in her manuscript "The Ethics Game."

THE ETHICS OF EMPLOYMENT LAW
Whose Power is it Anyway?
ROGER J. JOHNS, JR.

INTRODUCTION

In this essay, the system of state and federal employment discrimination laws in the United States is subjected to analysis under the Utilitarian theory of ethics, in order to develop some insight into modeling the ethicality of the exercise of governmental authority to alter the balance of power between the owners of the firm and its employees. The author does not, however, intend a criticism of the philosophical motive of this system of laws, since it is the writer's belief that the principle of equal opportunity is essential to the vitality of society.

A fundamental premise of this analysis is that this alteration of the balance of power between the employer and the employee is actually a transfer, to some degree, of ownership of the firm from the owner-employer to the employee. Ownership, as that term is used in a strict legal sense, is the "[c]ollection of rights to use and enjoy property . . . the exclusive right of possession, enjoyment, and disposal; involving as an essential attribute the right to control, handle, and dispose."[1] To the extent the balance of power is altered in favor of the employee, there is a transfer of control, and to the extent there is a transfer of control, there is, by definition, a transfer of some part of ownership. The idea that property ownership can be transferred simply by a regulatory deprivation of a significant measure of control, has a long history in the Due Process jurisprudence under the United States Constitution.[2] While it is beyond the scope of this writing to subject particular anti-discrimination laws to scrutiny under the Due Process Clause, in order to determine whether there has been a taking sufficient to warrant a payment of compensation, the idea of a regulatory taking is raised here to provide a foundation in law for the premise that transfers of control, by operation of law, can constitute transfers of ownership.

The system of employment discrimination law in this country consists of a collection of state and federal statutes, and regulations, and the administrative and court cases decided thereunder, as well as local ordinances. Together, these laws prohibit discrimination in the workplace on the basis of a variety of traits like race, color, religion, national origin, sex,[3]

"The Ethics of Employment Law: Whose Power Is It Anyway?" by Roger Johns. Reprinted by permission of the author.

[1] *Black's Law Dictionary* 712 (5th ed., 1979).

[2] *See, e.g., Pennsylvania Coal* v. *Mahon Co.,* 260 U.S. 393 (1922).

[3] *See,* 42 U.S.C. § 2000e–2 (Title VII of the Civil Rights Act of 1964) for the prohibition against using race, color, religion, sex, or national origin in employment decisions.

age,[4] disability,[5] sexual orientation, medical condition, marital status,[6] and others—traits considered by the enactors of these rules to be irrelevant to decisions by the employer regarding various aspects of the employer-employee relationship such as whom to hire, fire, promote, demote, train, compensate, interview, discipline, or lay off. . . .

The desired effect of all of these various forms of anti-discrimination law is to eliminate workplace discrimination on the basis of the traits specified in the law. In order to accomplish this purpose, anti-discrimination laws use two general techniques: (1) the law deprives the employer of the power to make decisions about individuals on the basis of the traits specified in the law free of legal consequences, and (2) the law provides the employee some legal or regulatory mechanism for enforcing the law against employers that the employee believes have violated it. Without debating, for the moment, the propriety or necessity of the deprivation, it is important to focus on the fact that the deprivation and the enforcement mechanism exist. And, it is important to focus on the fact that, absent the law, the employer would retain the legal authority to make employment decisions on the basis of any trait of an employee or applicant, regardless of the relevance of the trait to the job held or applied for, or the employment benefit involved, and without fear of legal consequences. Again, without, at this point, debating the propriety or necessity of using these techniques, it is important to recognize that these techniques accomplish a transfer of control over, and, therefore, ownership of some aspect of the firm from the owner-employer to the employee.

ETHICAL THEORIES

Typically, theories of ethics are divided into two broad categories: teleological and deontological. Teleological theories measure the ethics or correctness of an act by the amount of good it produces. Deontological theories, on the other hand, are unconcerned with the consequences of an act, and judge its ethicality, instead, on the basis of the duty or obligation out of which the impulse to act arises. The ethicality of the system of employment laws described above, and the premise that the enactment and implementation of these laws constitute a transfer of ownership of the firm from the owner-employer to the employee, will be assessed under the teleological theory known as utilitarianism.

UTILITARIANISM AND THE LAW OF EMPLOYMENT DISCRIMINATION

. . . The first element of the analysis of any action under the theory of utilitarianism must be a precise identification of the action under consideration. In a field as complex as law creation and implementation, this would be difficult at best since the process involves hundreds

---

[4]*See,* 29 U.S.C. § 623 (Age Discrimination in Employment Act).

[5]*See,* 29 U.S.C. § 791, 793, and 794 (Rehabilitation Act of 1973), and 42 U.S.C. § 12112 (Americans with Disabilities Act of 1990).

[6]Although there are no federal statutes prohibiting workplace discrimination on the basis of these traits, there are state and local laws, in some places which prohibit workplace discrimination on the basis of these, and other traits. *See, e.g.,* 28 N.M. Stat. Ann. § 28-1-7, and the regulations promulgated thereunder.

of discrete component acts. So, for present purposes, it will be necessary to confine the analysis to a distillation of the component acts, represented by an expression of the common character of the acts. To this end, the thesis stated above, of the transfer of power and ownership from the employer-owner to the employee, will serve as a proxy for all of the component acts in the process of creating and implementing employment discrimination laws. Proceeding from this point, the next logical step in the calculus of utilitarianism is to identify the elements of pleasure and the elements of pain generated by this transfer of power and attempt to quantitatively compare them. In order to do this in an orderly fashion, it will be necessary to first identify the members of the population under consideration, and then to identify the explicit pluses and minuses that accrue to each member or to various groups of members.

The entirety of the population under consideration here is the entire population of the country. To simplify the analysis, the population can be categorized into two fairly distinct subgroups and one *in globo* group, on the ground that each group has, to some degree, different interests, and would seem to experience qualitatively distinct, but sometimes overlapping consequences of the ownership transfer. The *in globo* group is the entire population of the country (Society) and the subgroups are (1) Employers, and (2) Employees. Beginning with the group containing the most direct beneficiaries, Employees, we can develop a list of at least some of the pleasures (or goods) and the painful consequences that they derive from the transfer of ownership.

Employee Goods

Freedom from discrimination by employers on the basis of traits irrelevant to ability.

The ability to access a government operated system of administrative investigation, and conciliation of claims of discrimination, at no cost to the employee.

Participation in a workplace in which overt discrimination is more likely to be held in check.

Employer Goods

Presence of a clearly stated public policy.

The presence of legal forces in the market place tending to ensure the most qualified workforce.

The financial and other rewards of operating with the most qualified workforce.

Employee Pain

Fear of retaliation in the wake of the assertion of a claim.

In cases where affirmative action played a part, uncertainty over whether one's status is a result of one's abilities.

Possibility of ostracism by other employees, in the wake of the assertion of a claim.

Employer Pain

Fear of the assertion of false claims.

The expenditure of monetary, human, and temporal resources in order to ensure compliance.

The expenditure of monetary, human, and temporal resources in responding to claims.

Resentment at having to expend resources on compliance or defense.

Societal Goods

The presence of legal forces in the market place tending to ensure the most qualified workforce.

The presence of legal forces in the market place tending to promote tolerance and a sense of community and the attendant benefits thereof.

Resentment over feeling forced to comply.

Societal Pain

The expenditure of monetary, human, and temporal resources in order to ensure compliance.

The presence of legal forces in the market place tending to promote resentment among those groups whose members feel victimized by law.

For purposes of comparison of the relative goods and pain, three paired groupings are useful: (I) Employer-Employee, (II) Employer-Society, and (III) Employee-Society. While comparisons and evaluations of the specific goods and pain experience by each group are important, and will be taken up eventually, some conceptual analysis must be done first.

Beginning with Pair I, one will immediately recognize that the number of employees will be vastly greater than the number of employers, and, consequently, there will be a greater number of beneficiaries over which to spread any net good or pain. Keeping the *greatest good for the greatest number* idea in mind, we can simplify our analysis by positing certain generic situations, which can be expressed mathematically. For instance, note that in the situation described by the equations below, the mere fact that Employees constitute a numerically larger group than Employers, means that, with respect to pair I, the ethicality of the employment discrimination is somewhat ambiguous.

Assume that:

1. Employer Goods − Employer Pain = A
2. Employee Goods − Employee Pain = B

If $A - B = 0$ (i.e., $A = B$), and N_E and N_R are the number of Employees and Employers, respectively, then $B/N_E < A/N_R$. But the interpretation of this will be at best, inconclusive because one is now faced with choosing which of two situations is ethically preferable. With respect to the Employer group, a given amount of good will be distributed over a smaller population resulting in a greater amount of good per person. With respect to the Employee group, the same amount of good that was available to the Employers will be distributed over a much larger group, resulting in a much lower amount of good per person, but at least some good accruing to each member of the much larger group. Thus, one must decide whether the ethical ideal is achieved where there is a great amount of good for a small group or a lesser amount of good for a larger group. Since this is a personal preference, on the part of each observer, the analysis herein will proceed, for the present, on the assumption that the potential of a situation to achieve the ideal of the greatest good for the greatest number is the ethically preferable situation.

Assume, now, that the difference between A and B is such that the good available to the Employee group is the greater. In this situation, the greater amount of good, distributed over the larger population will result in the greatest good for the greatest number, only if the magnitude of the good per person ratio is great enough to overcome the dilution of the larger group. Thus, even when the difference between A and B is such that the amount of good available to the Employee group is greater, achievement of the greatest good for the greatest number occurs only when the difference between A and B is huge. In other words, when we require satisfaction of both the *greatest good* and the *greatest number* elements of the analysis, the ethical ideal is achieved only when the difference between A and B is great enough that $B/N_E > A/N_R$. This occurs only when the amount of good accruing to the Employee group is greater than $(B)(N_R)$.

When the difference between A and B is such that the good accruing to the Employer group is greater, the greatest good per person is most readily achieved, because of the numerical inferiority of the group, but this same numerical inferiority precludes satisfaction of the *greatest number* aspect of the analysis.

At first blush, it seems that if achieving the greatest good for the greatest number is the ideal, then systems which result in $A/N_R > B/N_E$, which can never have the potential to bring about the ideal, should not be the goal. But this is true only when the calculation is made over an infinitely short time horizon. Once the time factor is taken into account, interpretations of the calculations change. For instance, if, at every given moment, the system of employment discrimination law results in $B/N_R > A/N_E$ (i.e., the greater good accrues to the Employee group), the *greatest good for the greatest number* ideal will remain constantly satisfied, but only so long as the Employee group constitutes the larger group and the difference between A and B is great enough so that $B/N_E > A/N_R$. Over time, however, the extent to which the Employee group is consistently favored with the greater good will be positively related to the extent to which the Employer group is discouraged from creating new employment opportunities. If, over time, this sufficiently reduces the business formation impulse, the size of the Employee group, or the degree to which A exceeds B, then the potential for $B/N_E > A/N_R$ to produce the greatest good for the greatest number declines. The somewhat paradoxical result is that in the short run $A/N_R > B/N_E$ can never result in the ideal, but it can, in the long run, foster the ability of $B/N_E > A/N_R$ to achieve the ideal, and while $B/N_E > A/N_R$ will always produce the ideal in the short run, it will defeat itself in the long run. Obviously, what is called for is an exquisite balance. Given the vagaries of human nature, it is not likely that any sort of static balance could be hoped for, but a dynamic balance, over time, in which both $B/N_E > A/N_R$ and $A/N_R > B/N_E$ are adequately nurtured by the system probably could be approached.

It is interesting to note, that, at least conceptually, analysis using Employer-Society and Employee-Society pairs arrive at the same point. While it may be analytically useful to describe and treat the Employee and Employer groups as distinct in all interests and goals, the reality is obviously very different. As an observer of the twists and turns in the relationships between the different immigrant and ethnic groups in the United States recently stated, "We may not have all come over on the same ship, but we're all in the same boat now." The point of relating this observation here is that while the Employee and Employer groups may have different characteristics, interests, and goals, in the long run, the success of each will be dependent upon the success of the other.

By definition, the size of the combined groups will always constitute the largest group, a state of affairs that presents, again by definition, the greatest potential to satisfy the *great-*

est number aspect of the analysis. The remaining aspect, *greatest good,* then becomes likelier as A + B increases. The sum A + B will increase even if one of the terms tends toward or becomes zero, so long as the other term grows in value. However, as the analysis of the Employer-Employee pair revealed, there can come a point beyond which the growth in B, to the exclusion of A, can result, in the long run, in a diminution of B, and vice versa. Thus, without a great deal of analysis, it seems fairly reasonable to conclude that the ethical ideal is achieved by pursuing the same balance across every grouping.

COMPARING SPECIFIC GOODS AND PAIN

In order to arrive at any sort of practical understanding of the effect of the system of employment discrimination laws, the goods and pain listed above will need to be quantified and plugged into the variables A and B, in order to determine whether $B/N_E > A/N_R$, $A/N_R > B/N_E$, or $A/N_R = B/N_E$. Some of these factors will obviously confound any attempt at meaningful quantification. The fear factors and resentment fall into this category. Some factors, however, such as expenditure of monetary, human, and temporal resources, will yield, at least to some degree, to a quantitative approach. In any event, it is important to recognize from the outset that with respect to the monetary, human and temporal factors, virtually all of the resource movements resulting from the operation of the law will be away from the employer in the form of tax dollars, defense costs, record keeping costs, payments of judgments and settlements, employee and management time that could have been spent on revenue-producing activities, and the like. Once the claim process is initiated by the employee, the best outcome the employer can hope for is that no liability will be found. The employer will, nevertheless, have expended some resources in pursuit of this result. There are no scenarios in which the immediate net resource position of the employer will be greater after the conclusion of a claim, regardless of the outcome. For the employee, on the other hand, there are many scenarios in which the net resource position of the employee could be enhanced as a result of the claim/litigation/settlement process. From the employer's perspective, then, the best that can be hoped for under the current system is that the process will be efficient and will produce some form of benefit in excess of the other resources it consumes.

With respect to the efficiency of the process, it is surprisingly good. For the six years 1989 to 1994, the EEOC received 824,201 charges to process, and, during the same period, it resolved 741,688, or 89% of its inventory. During the same period, its budget appropriations totalled $1,230,839,000 and it recovered $973,300,369 in monetary benefits for individuals who had filed claims, 31% of which was recovered through litigation, and all of which was paid by employers or their insurers. Overall, the EEOC spent $1.27 in tax dollars for each dollar it recovered for individuals who filed claims. Stated differently, the EEOC produced a 79% return on investment, which by probably any standard, is amazingly high, and amazingly costly to employers.

The benefits that employers might expect to enjoy from this efficiency, would be the increased revenues and profits resulting from the enhanced productivity of the most efficient workforce that non-discrimination could produce. But, even if the only monetary expenditures on the part of employers were the payment of judgments and settlements (which is obviously not the case), the enhancements to productivity would need to be about $162,000,000 per year. Factoring in the cost to employers of dollars spent on legal fees and costs, or on preventive training, or record keeping, or time spent responding to or taking preventive measures to avoid claims, would require the enhancements to produce considerably more than $162 million. This may be possible, but to the extent it is, such benefits would accrue to employers as a group. It would not be the case that each employer would receive enhancements in an amount equal to the resources expended. Thus, many individual employers will suffer. And, maybe they should. From a deontological[7] perspective such considerations as cost are irrelevant, so long as justice is produced.

Looked at from a more cold-eyed perspective, the benefits to individual employees, recovered through the EEOC claim process, constitute transfers of money from the capital-creating employer to the employee. Individual employees benefit directly, and society benefits in some intangible, and probably unmeasurable, ways, but the productive capacity of employers is impaired. In a healthy economy, though, the productive capacity can probably withstand a great deal of this sort of stress before its viability is visibly compromised. Ultimately, the ethicality of the system of employment discrimination laws, at least from a utilitarian point of view, will come down to how it affects the country's competitive advantage in the global marketplace, and solutions will, as they inevitably do, arise out of necessity. Perhaps the focus will be shifted from the workplace to the early classroom. Perhaps disincentives for frivolous claims should be built into the system. Perhaps empirical study will show that there are already sufficient increases in societal goods, in the form of increases in productivity, greater social harmony, and other benefits, to justify the current system. Perhaps a body of wisdom that flourished here in times past can provide guidance.

A VOICE FROM THE PAST

As occasionally occurs, the profundity of some past thinker's observations about the age in which he or she writes can be gauged by the relevance of those thoughts to the present day. An example of such a thinker particularly appropriate for discussion here is the nineteenth century economist Frederic Bastiat. In Bastiat's short book, *The Law,*[8] the idea of legal plunder is articulated to describe the actions of a government gone completely awry. He begins by defining the purpose of government as a mechanism, ordained by the governed through a limited surrender of individual liberty and authority, and set up for the sole purpose of interposing the pooled protective powers of all citizens between the innocent and the predatory. He proceeds from this minimalist premise to a justification of the idea that, in practice, government should exercise this function only in response to an affirmative act of plunder committed by one citizen or group against another, with plunder being defined as the taking by force, of the life, liberty or property of another. Any other use of governmental power, he argued, goes beyond the government's authority, and constitutes what he terms legal plunder—the taking, by the government, of that which belongs to one, and giving it to another. He expressed much chagrin at the double standard, at work in France at the time of his writing, of criminalizing the act of an individual taking that which does not belong to him from

---

[7]Under deontological theories of ethics the rightness of actions is judged on the basis of the worthiness of the duty or motive behind the act, regardless of the consequence.

[8]Citation to the book, generally.

its rightful owner, while clothing the same act in legality when accomplished by legislation, to serve the interests of a politically favored segment of the population.

The obvious difficulty with Bastiat's approach is that there is no way to limit which rights or things fit within the definitions of liberty and property, without injecting the bias of the definer. For instance, one could, with little effort, argue persuasively that the right to a job is a legitimate property right of every member of society, the protection of which is within the sphere of what Bastiat considered to be government's appropriate domain. This is, of course, a giant loophole through which the spirit of Bastiat's philosophy could be subverted by the mores of whoever exerts sufficient control over the machinery of government. Nevertheless, conceding the inherent limitation imposed by the Theorem of Incompleteness,[9] regarding the ability of any system to yield only intended results, it would seem that Bastiat's philosophical and moral stance of strictly limited governmental action provides some useful guidance in achieving balance in the system of employment discrimination laws. The most practical reason that comes to mind for adopting such a stance is unreliability of the political winds. A fair wind today could sweep one onto the rocks tomorrow.

CONCLUSIONS AND PROGNOSTICATIONS

Of late, two competing phenomena indicate a shift from the typical scenario of the past where the majority of the skirmishes along legislatively drawn employment discrimination lines were carried out mostly by individual plaintiff's pursuing individual actions against individual employers. One of these phenomena is the concerted action by large voter-blocs to roll back the heretofore seemingly endlessly advancing frontier of employee rights. Proposition 209, passed by the voters of California in 1996, essentially outlawed affirmative action in the state. The premise underlying this assault on affirmative action by the California voters, and others, is based largely on affirmative action's somewhat contradictory nature: it permits,[10] and in some cases mandates[11] that discrimination be practiced for the purpose of ending discrimination. More precisely, it is argued by opponents of affirmative action that affirmative action employs politically-favored discrimination as a weapon to combat politically-disfavored discrimination. In nature, when two antithetical phenomena encounter each other, such as matter and antimatter, there is a violent reaction resulting in the annihilation of both. Within the human sphere, however, all we have gotten so far is the violent reaction, in the form of heated rhetoric and the phenomenon of so-called reverse-discrimination litigation, with each side of the issue insisting that the tactics of the other are unfair. Instead of annihilating discrimination, it appears that affirmative action, and, for that matter, other antidiscrimination measures, have, if the increasing frequency of litigation is any indication, simply exposed the extent to which employment discrimination is occurring

---

[9]Kurt Gödel, developed the Theorem of Incompleteness, which, in a very non-technical formulation, holds that no system of rules can be devised in which even a correct application of the rules to the field over which the rules were designed to operate will invariably yield a result within the intended domain. In other words, paradoxical results are an inherent inevitability in the operation of every system. *See generally,* Hofstadter, Douglas R., *Gödel, Escher, Bach: An Eternal Golden Braid,* Basic Books, New York, 1979.

[10]*See,* 42 U.S.C. 2000e-5(g)(1).

[11]*See* 29 U.S.C. § 793 and, Exec. Order 11,246, 30 F.R. 12319, September 28, 1965.

or is believed to be occurring. Another, high-profile example of concerted voter action occurred when, in 1993, the voters of Colorado amended the state's constitution to make it illegal to protect individuals from employment discrimination based upon their sexual orientation.

The other of these phenomena is concerted action by plaintiffs in employment discrimination lawsuits in the form of the relatively recent proliferation of class-action employment discrimination lawsuits arising in the wake of the Civil Rights Act of 1991. The Mitsubishi and Texaco class-action suits are just two of the more prominent examples of this. While individual action under the antidiscrimination laws, will never become atypical, the phenomena cited above can certainly be viewed as an indictment by both those who stand to gain (i.e., the individual beneficiaries of these legislative power transfers) and those who are at some risk of losing out (i.e., defendant-employers, potential defendants, and those adversely affected by affirmative action) of the ineffectiveness of individual action.

Both phenomena are costly reactions to the current system. Neither phenomenon portends harmony. Both involve manipulations of government-created processes from a reactive posture, and it seems likely that the propagation of both will lead to more resentment and mistrust. It is ironic that in Bastiat's exposition on the miscast role of the French government of his times, he cites, with great envy, the fledgling government of the United States as the acme of a properly confined system. Perhaps these phenomena are the indicators that the societal experience necessary to an understanding of the need for balance is accumulating.

TOPIC STUDY: DOWNSIZING

Right before Christmas in 1995, AT&T announced that it would lay off 40,000 workers in an effort to cut costs and to boost revenues. At that time, its stock was trading at around $65 per share. By September 1996, when, hopefully, AT&T expected to show some positive results of this massive action, its stock was trading at just above $50 per share—a loss of 23 percent in less than a year ("Watch Out, Widows," *Newsweek,* October 7, 1996, p. 59). If downsizing is presumably detrimental to those who lose their jobs, one would expect there to be large gains somewhere to justify the cuts. Unfortunately (for both terminated employees as well as shareholders), the connection between downsizing and increased profits is not so clear.

To present downsizing in a more positive light, companies are continually creating new ways to refer to the practice, for example: release of resources, career-change opportunities, reshaping, schedule adjustments, involuntary separation from payroll, and elimination of employment security policy (see William Lutz, *The New Doublespeak* [New York: HarperCollins, 1996]).

METAPHOR OF THE SURVIVING CHILDREN
DAVID DOER

In order to better understand the emotional and other effects of downsizing, David Doer offers the following metaphor. Take a moment to consider its implications. Do you believe that it is a fitting metaphor? What parts of it work and what parts do not ring true? What can we learn from this type of exercise? Do you think that it helps us to be a bit more compassionate when we are asked to actually "feel" something in this way?

Imagine a family: a father, a mother, and four children. The family has been together for a long time, living in a loving, nurturing, trusting environment. The parents take care of the children, who reciprocate by being good.

Every morning the family sits down to breakfast together, a ritual that functions as a bonding experience, somewhat akin to an organizational staff meeting. One morning, the children sense that something is wrong. The parents exchange furtive glances, appear nervous, and after a painful silence, the mother speaks. "Father and I have reviewed the family budget," she says, looking down at her plate, avoiding eye contact, "and we just don't have enough money to make ends meet!" She forces herself to look around the table and continues, "As much as we would like to, we just can't afford to feed and clothe all four of you. After another silence she points a finger. "You two must go!"

"It's nothing personal," explains the father as he passes out a sheet of paper to each of the children. "As you can see by the numbers in front of you, it's simply an economic decision—we really have no choice." He continues, forcing a smile, "We have arranged for your aunt and uncle to help you get settled, to aid in your transition."

The next morning, the two remaining children are greeted by a table on which only four places have been set. Two chairs have been removed. All physical evidence of the other two children has vanished. The emotional evidence is suppressed and ignored. No one talks about the two who have disappeared. The parents emphasize to the two remaining children, the survivors, that they should be grateful, "since, after all, you've been allowed to remain in the family." To show their gratitude, the remaining children will be expected to work harder on the family chores. The father explains that "the workload remains the same even though there are two less of you." The mother reassures them that "this will make us a closer family!"

"Eat your breakfast, children," entreats the father. "After all, food costs money!"

. . . [Now, consider the following questions:]

1. *What were the children who left feeling?* Most managers say, "anger," "hurt," "fear," "guilt," and "sadness."
2. *What were the children who remained feeling?* Most managers soon conclude that the children who remain have the same feelings as those who left. The managers also often report that the remaining children experience these feelings with more intensity than those who left.
3. *What were the parents feeling?* Although the managers sometimes struggle with this question, most of them discover that the parents feel the same emotions as the surviving children.
4. *How different are these feelings from those of survivors in your organization?* After honest reflection, many managers admit that there are striking and alarming similarities.
5. *How productive is a workforce with these survivor feelings?* Most managers conclude that such feelings are indeed a barrier to productivity. Some groups move into discussions about effects of survivor feelings on the quality of work life and share personal reflections.

THE WORKERS IN THE VINEYARD

MATTHEW

In the following parable, the early workers who toiled the whole day long in the brutal heat are paid what they originally agreed to, while workers who did not work as long also received this full day's wage. Is this fair? Does that matter? To whom? What would be the impact of this practice if it were to become universal? Why might a manager practice a wage plan such as this? Is there any such thing as a fair daily wage or is it determined merely by market forces?

1 "The kingdom of heaven is like a landowner who went out at dawn to hire laborers for his vineyard. **2** After agreeing with them for the usual daily wage, he sent them into his vineyard. **3** Going out about nine o'clock, he saw others standing idle in the marketplace, **4** and he said to them, 'You too go into my vineyard, and I will give you what is just.' **5** So they went off. [And] he went out again around noon, and around three o'clock, and did likewise. **6** Going out about five o'clock, he found others standing around, and said to them, 'Why do you stand here idle all day?' **7** They answered, 'Because no one has hired us.' He said to them, 'You too go into my vineyard.' **8** When it was evening the owner of the vineyard said to his foreman, 'Summon the laborers and give them their pay, beginning with the last and ending with the first.' **9** When those who had started about five o'clock came, each received the usual daily wage. **10** So when the first came, they thought that they would receive more, but each of them also got the usual wage. **11** And on receiving it they grumbled against the landowner, **12** saying, 'These last ones worked only one hour, and you have made them equal to us, who bore the day's burden and the heat.' **13** He said to one of them in reply, 'My friend, I am not cheating you. Did you not agree with me for the usual daily wage? **14** Take what is yours and go. What if I wish to give this last one the same as you? **15** [Or] am I not free to do as I wish with my own money? Are you envious because I am generous?' **16** Thus, the last will be first, and the first will be last."

"The Workers in the Vineyard," Matthew 20: 1–16, *The Bible*.

THE ETHICS OF DOWNSIZING

FRANK NAVRAN

Navran addresses some of the primary concerns about downsizing practices.

IS DOWNSIZING EVER ETHICAL?

Organizations in every segment of business, industry, government and education are downsizing. The very act of forcing people to leave their employment is rife with ethics-related questions. In this article, we will consider one of the most fundamental questions: *Is downsizing ever ethical?*

The truth is that unless an organization was designed expressly and overtly for the purpose, it is not in business to provide employment. Jobs are the by-product of successful organizational endeavors, not their intended output.

Furthermore, downsizing is not necessarily a desperate move on the part of failing organizations. It can be, and probably should be, a strategic choice designed to serve the best interests of an organization. We should not be constrained by the false belief that current organizational effectiveness or financial success is a de facto argument against doing what is necessary to ensure continuing success. A healthy profit picture and downsizing are not mutually exclusive.

But this is only a partial answer to the question. We have merely said that organizational downsizing is not intrinsically unethical. To answer more fully, we have to look at a number of issues. First, some definitions:

> *Values*—this term refers to a set of beliefs. Values are how one defines what is right, fair and good. This definition applies whether we consider individual values, organizational values or societal values.

> *Ethics*—here we mean choices and the observable, behavioral manifestation of values-based decisions.

> *Ethical dilemma*—this is a situation where every viable option requires the decision maker to choose between conflicting values. Under these conditions, any decision under consideration will violate one or more values even as it honors others.

> *Ethical congruence*—a situation where one's decision is consistent with, aligns with, the applicable set(s) of values. Under these circumstances, a choice to take some action will harmonize with the decision maker's values.

"The Ethics of Downsizing," by Frank Navran, http://www.navran.com/. . . . /95-04/04-95a.html. Reprinted by permission of the author.

Bearing these definitions in mind, we find that determining whether the decision to downsize is ethical means determining whether that choice is congruent with the values of at least two different constituencies:

Those who must leave the organization against their will.

Those who remain after the downsizing.

To frame the ethical issues faced by these two constituencies, we must first agree on a set of values to use as a reference point. For this discussion, we will employ four values suggested by Kenneth W. Johnson, JD. He uses the acronym EPIC to define the values set:

E = Empathy: Caring about the consequences of one's choices as they affect others. Being concerned with the effect one's decisions have on those who have no say in the decision itself.

P = Patience: Taking time to consider and deliberate the long-term consequences of a choice before making that choice and acting upon it.

I = Integrity: Making choices that are consistent with each other and with the stated and operative values one espouses. Striving for ethical congruence in one's decisions.

C = Courage: Choosing to do what one believes is right even if the result will not be to everyone's liking or may lead to personal loss.

THOSE WHO MUST LEAVE

Being forced to leave a job, irrespective of separation allowances, pension enhancements or any of the other tools used by organizations to soften the blow, feels wrong. It feels like it must violate some values, and typically it does.

Empathy—the act of dismissal can be unempathetic, since it negatively affects those who are forced to give up their chosen path, no matter what future success may await them and since they typically feel as though they had no voice in the decision.

Patience—if the decision to downsize is perceived to be a faddish response to competitive pressures it will appear impatient or premature to those who must leave. If it is perceived as anything less than a well-developed, strategic response to demands on the organization, then it fails the patience criterion.

Integrity—where there was either an implied or spoken promise of continuing employment as the repayment for employee loyalty and/or the successful completion of assigned work, the decision—and hence the organization and its leaders—may be thought to lack integrity.

Courage—downsizing can sometimes be seen to be about creating victims and displacing blame rather than accepting responsibility and choosing the more difficult, moral high ground.

THOSE WHO REMAIN

Surviving a downsizing has its own ethical issues. Surviving employees will often share perceptions about the ethics of this decision with those who are being forced to leave. They also experience their own emotional reactions—anger, guilt, fear and depression—when asked to take up the slack by doing more work, learning new tasks, and all for the same or less money than before the downsizing occurred.

Empathy—asking people to do more with less and for less can seem unfair. Downsizing organizations put terrible pressures on their surviving employees, and that often affects their families as well. This can seem to show a lack of caring on the part of decision makers, an insensitivity to the reality that employees are people with full lives and responsibilities outside of work.

Patience—organizations which downsize often have a sense of urgency about realizing the promised benefits of doing more with less. If this rush to a new order is seen to be without a basis in fact, and if the decision makers are viewed as being unaware of what is needed to get the job done, then the decision can be seen to violate the patience ethic.

Integrity—in organizations where downsizing is imposed at the same time that executive and/or stockholders are receiving substantial bonuses, there can be the perception of a double standard. When the organization's stated values include an assertion that "we value our employees," downsizing can be seen to violate the integrity value.

Courage—if executives blame their superiors (CEO's, boards of directors, special interests or stockholders) for the necessity to downsize, and speak or act as though they had no choice, the message can be that they lacked the courage to do what is right, to stand up for those who have served them loyally, no matter the personal risk. This is viewed as cowardice.

CONCLUSION

As with most complex organizational issues, the question of whether downsizing is ethical has no easy answer. Perhaps the best that can be hoped for is that the decision makers apply the EPIC test to their choice:

That they demonstrate empathy for all of those affected by their decision: the employees who leave and those who remain behind. That they display patience, avoiding a premature knee-jerk reaction. That the decision be based on a critical understanding of its stimuli and its consequences. That they show integrity as they strive to live according to their word and match their actions to their professions of belief. And finally that they have the courage to do the right thing, even when the right thing may be the more difficult thing to do.

GENERAL MOTORS CORPORATION AND THE ART OF TRUTH-TELLING[1]

JASON DRUCKER

Michael Moore's popular documentary, Roger and Me, exposes the impact of the General Motors downsizing plan on Flint, Michigan, a midwestern town that relied in great part on GM's presence in its town for employment and community support. Drucker discusses the issue of trust and truth-telling as it is reflected in GM's actions.

I.

The exchange of sentiments is the guiding factor in social intercourse, and truth must be the guiding principle herein. Without truth social intercourse and conversation becomes valueless. We can only know what a man thinks if he tells us his thoughts, and when he undertakes to express them he must really do so, or else there can be no society of men.[2]

No doubt, the imperative to "tell the truth" is a commonplace platitude and for the most part such an injunction pervades the moral atmosphere. As little children we are urged to tell the truth about naughty things we have done. As young adults we are told that we have to tell the truth about evenings that have extended hours beyond curfews. And, as adults we are confronted by friends, colleagues, and lovers who expect, even demand, the truth from us—the truth of our feelings and opinions, perhaps our misdeeds. Yet, as much as we think the truth *should* be told, what exactly does it mean to tell it—the whole truth and nothing but the truth? Businessmen and other professionals, it would seem, are not exempt from the obligation of truth-telling. Or are they? This lack of truth-telling seems to be one of the many themes of "Roger & Me,"[3] Michael Moore's sensational 1989 hit-movie depicting the situation in Flint, Michigan, when General Motors Corporation laid off thousands of workers in the late 1980s.[4] It's not only what General Motors *does say* about the layoffs that

---

"General Motors and the Art of Truth-Telling," by Jason Drucker. Reprinted by permission of the author.

[1]Thanks to Daryl Koehn for her helpful comments on an earlier draft of this manuscript.

[2]Immanuel Kant, "Ethical Duties Towards Others: Truthfulness," in *Lectures on Ethics,* trans. Louis Infield (New York: Harper & Row, 1963), 224.

[3]Produced, directed, and written by Michael Moore. Distributor: Warner Brothers. Video distributor: Warner Home Video. A Dog-Eat-Dog Film Production.

[4]See Ronald Edsforth, "Review of 'Roger & Me' " *American Historical Review* 96 (October 1991): 1145–1147. "Michael Moore's subject is the decline of his hometown, Flint, Michigan, the birthplace and largest production center of the General Motors Corporation. From the mid-1970s to the late 1980s, Flint was rocked by corporate decisions that closed several major factories and moved other important GM product lines out of the city. Together, General Motors' plant closings and modernization programs reduced its Flint-area work force from a peak of 79,000 in the early 1970s to just 49,000 in 1989" (1145).

seems to be particularly troubling for the film-maker—in other words, the "official story" of the General Motors pullout—but also, what the corporation *failed to say* or *said in an unsatisfactory way.*

But before we get there, we might want to ask: why should we pay attention to what a corporation says? After all, don't people speak, not corporations? Actually, representatives of corporations, in the form of lobbyists and public relations specialists, are paid to speak on behalf of the interests of the corporation; they are charged with making statements that reinforce the image of the corporation, or rather, the image that a company would like to project. Advertisements also speak in the sense that they make claim to what we—the consumers—can expect from a product or a service. The law itself recognizes advertising as an act of speech and requires that advertisers not intentionally misrepresent their products. According to the Advertising Code of American Business, "advertising shall tell the truth, and shall reveal significant facts, the concealment of which would mislead the public."[5] But here, once again, the notion of truth seems fairly flexible and less than comprehensive, especially if it is to be taken as a regulative ideal or model form of speech conduct. After all, how many products are there that claim to be "the best"?

Perhaps the truth is never expected to be told in the course of normal business transactions and all claims should be measured with a healthy degree of skepticism.[6] We seldom feel empathy for the person who is misled by the everyday slogans of an advertisement or the routine pitches of a salesperson. How, then, do we determine the ethical parameters of a speech-act if we normally expect everything to be less than the full truth? What kind of provisional understanding can we have of a legitimate speech-act? For instance, if a lobbyist knows that he needs to promote the interests of a corporation, but also recognizes that it is self-interested to speak both persuasively and truthfully, he still has a great degree of latitude in positioning his remarks. How, then, are we to know what counts as an appropriate way for him to speak?

Tom Kay, a lobbyist for General Motors, appears to be remarkably forthright throughout the movie. He tells Michael Moore that:

> *[GM] is a corporation that is in business to make a profit and it does what it has to do to make a profit. That is the nature of corporations or companies. It's why people take their own money and invest it in a business so they can make money. It isn't to honor their hometown.*

However, while the lobbyist does provide us with a fairly honest bottom-line, his truth-telling quickly spirals into empty rhetoric. He continues to tell us:

> *I'm sure that Roger Smith [the CEO of General Motors] has a social conscience as strong as anybody else in the country. . . . Because a guy is an automobile executive does not make him inhuman. . . . He has as much concern about these people as you do. . . . Nobody likes to see anybody laid off or put in a hardship situation.*

---

[5]See "The Advertising Code Case," in *Ethical Theory and Business,* eds. Tom L. Beauchamp and Norman E. Bowie (Englewood Cliffs, NJ: Prentice Hall, 1988), 186.

[6]See Albert Z. Carr, "Is Business Bluffing Ethical?" in *Ethical Theory and Business,* eds. Tom L. Beauchamp and Normal E. Bowie (Englewood Cliffs, NJ: Prentice Hall, 1988), 438–442.

The viewers are, or course, fairly dubious about Roger Smith's intense concern for the workers of Flint. In fact, Michael Moore attempts to validate this skepticism by interviewing Smith, but the CEO is less than amenable to this prospect and successfully manages to avoid the filmmaker throughout the movie. From Moore's perspective, perhaps no one likes to see hardship, but as long as one doesn't have to serve as a witness to inhumanity, he may remain morally exempt.

Now, what exactly do we expect to hear from the lobbyist or representative of a corporation, and more importantly, what *should* we expect? As Immanual Kant has indicated, truth-telling may be the most legitimate form of conduct in speech, but the idea that we should "tell the truth" begs the question about what constitutes the truth that is to be told. As most people know, we regularly distort, alter, manipulate information in order to better tailor it to our circumstances. And this applies not only to *what* we say, but to *how* we say it. For instance, how would a woman narrate to a police officer that she just ran a red-light and how would she tell the same story to her friend? What elements in the story would she emphasize, and then de-emphasize, based on who she was talking to? How would we tell a child that her dog was hit by a car? What aspects of the story would be omitted altogether and where would we most significantly alter details in our enterprise of "truth-telling"? We may understand the imperative to "tell the truth" but the presentation of truth is a little more tricky and takes a bit of practice. Indeed, if there was only one way to be truthful, we wouldn't need public relations specialists, advertising firms, or lobbyists.

Kant believes that we typically "arrange our conduct either to conceal our faults or to appear other than we are. We possess the art of simulation."[7] And Michael Moore seems to concur with this estimation, especially in the case of General Motors. For instance, how would we evaluate the following statement, made by what appears to be another bureaucratic flunky:

> *I think most of you are aware that this is the first major plant closing to take place in Flint. Let me rephrase that: this is not a plant closing, it's the loss of one product line.*

For all ostensible purposes, though, it certainly appears that plants are shutting down. After all, we do get to see Michael Moore inside a plant as the last car is being sent down the assembly line and we do witness a spokeswoman for General Motors tell Moore that this last day at the plant is a very private time for the laid-off workers. If these plants aren't being closed down, why are people not coming to work the following morning? Why are people upset? Why are plants being demolished or boarded up? Why are people moving out of Flint? Perhaps he is self-deluded and really believes that General Motors is simply eliminating a product, but I suspect that this is not the case. Especially when he continues in his muddled way to say that "I'm trying to impress upon the employees that are being laid off that there is nothing out there for them to depend upon for the future."

Clearly there is more going on here than the closing of a product line and this latter comment is more to the point. When a product line is abolished customers are restricted from purchasing a product that was once available for consumption. When a plant closes, people lose jobs. The shift in speech intends to ultimately evade responsibility for the shutting down of the plants. But the extent of General Motors' responsibility to keep the plants

---

[7]Kant, "Truthfulness," 224.

viable is one of the tacit questions being asked in this movie. What the transition in speech appears to do is to actively disclaim the lived experiences of the workers, the stories of which Michael Moore has attempted to recover. The workers who are laid off from General Motors do not experience the "closing of a product line," and [they do experience] the harsh reality of the plant's being shut down. Notice how the language itself skirts the issue that is central to the workers' concerns. From the perspective of the workers, and that is what I contend "Roger & Me" tries to represent, such language attempts to minimize the extent to which a potential offense is perpetuated against them. That effacement in the language manages to perpetuate the affront or, as one might say, add insult to injury.

An analysis of corporate rhetoric appears to be particularly needed here. What has occurred in Flint is certainly the "closing of a product line," *but is that really the truth?* Michael Moore's footage here is particularly revealing since he catches the manager restating the frame for the event, drawing the viewer into the inconsistencies of the corporate narrative. What is characterized first as a "plant closing" has been strategically restated to be the "closing of the product line." Do both descriptions adequately reflect the fundamental reality here at the plant? Is one proposition more truthful than the other, or do they both say something about different people's perspectives of the truth itself?

One might similarly analyze the word "downsize," another "happier-sounding phrase" that is meant to sugarcoat a less than desirable state of affairs: being fired.[8] At least from the perspective of the workers, the truth is apparent, and the words are meant to shield General Motors' management who may have the less than fulfilling job of delivering termination notices to their soon-to-be-ex-colleagues and staff. On the other hand, Deputy Sheriff Fred Ross, given the responsibility of evicting delinquent tenants from their homes in Flint, makes no attempt to poeticize the harshness that words are sometimes used to cover over. There is no cloaking of the truth here since the deputy has no public relations man to speak for him, and even if he did have this mediator, the soon-to-be-evicted tenants would ultimately understand the message delivered at their doorstep when he knocks: "Get out."

Michael Moore effectively presents a number of instances in which the exercise of truth-telling becomes foregrounded. While the examples he presents suggest a certain degree of humor in comparison to the general indictment against General Motors, they make a singular and consistent point: that the way one frames an issue or event can be fundamentally misleading, but it can also be plainly offensive. It may even make some acts like firing tens of thousands of workers appear morally permissible. Bob Eubanks, the star-host of the Newlywed game and one of the most well-known ex-residents of Flint, implicitly understands these conventions of normal and proper discourse, and this is the reason, no doubt, that Moore includes footage of his appearance at the local country fair into the final version of the film. Consider the following exchange about what constitutes an acceptable question:

> *Michael Moore: What about questions like: How heavy are your breasts?*
> *Bob Eubanks: I never ask that question. I will say: How much does your wife's chest weigh?*
> *But there's a lot of difference in that question you just asked. A hell of a lot of difference. . . .*
> *I wouldn't ask that question for anything in the world. I wouldn't even say breast.*

---

[8]See William Safire, "Downsized," *New York Times Magazine,* May 26, 1996: 12.

At least Bob Eubanks would like us to think he has high standards. He knows how far he can go in order to communicate a meaning without saying what he shouldn't, and that's why the game-show host is able to get a rise out of his audience.

Is there a correct way to frame a certain issue? Does language naturally conform to certain situations so that we can deem language an appropriate description of a state of affairs? If corporate language is part of the problem, it doesn't strike me as an incidental fact that Moore records these disparate moments when speech itself seems to break down or when an event's characterization in language seems particularly apt, or conversely, wholly inappropriate. Take the case of the "bunny lady" (as my students call her), a resident of Flint who is currently unemployed, on welfare, and clearly struggling to make ends meet. In order to supplement her already meager income, she breeds rabbits and sells them to anyone who is willing to provide her with some additional money. What is so revealing about Moore's analysis is that the rabbits themselves don't come unmediated to their new owners. Rather, the rabbits themselves are available as either "pets" or "meat"—two very different and perhaps contradictory ways of framing the rabbit in language. What does it mean for a rabbit to be a "pet" as opposed to "meat"? I think that the analogy is very transparent, and while it may be heavy-handed, it shows the extreme options we have when we choose our language to describe our situations, or in this case, the rabbit's predicament. As the bunny lady states so eloquently: "If you don't sell them as pets, you've got to get rid of them as meat." I guess it should come as no surprise that the cages the rabbits are kept in look a lot like the General Motors' plants.

Is there a legitimate and illegitimate form of speech, then? If only our situation was as simple as the Scrabble player who comes to the now defunct Hyatt hotel in Flint and finds that her word, "partier," is not considered acceptable since the "official" Scrabble dictionary does not list it. We, on the other hand, have no manual or guidebook that will tell us what kind of language is off-limits. As she tells us, "parties" and "partied" are her best alternatives, but "partier" will not cut it. She does not seem particularly distraught at her situation even though she seems convinced that "partier" is, in fact, a word in the English language (I couldn't find it in the dictionary either). Then again, why should she be upset? Remember: Scrabble is just a game.

A philosopher like Immanuel Kant is less than helpful in telling us how a corporation or corporate representative should speak since he argues for the absoluteness of his dictum to tell the truth,[9] even though he is quick to tell us that the smart man, and especially the good conversationalist, will never find himself in this position. Rather than lying, he will "invent on the spur of the moment something noncommittal."[10] He thus avoids having to be deceptive. On the other hand, Kant does admit that we can be deceptive by not saying anything, for instance, in the case of packing a bag in order to give people the impression that I am going on vacation.[11] The point is clear: not every untruth counts as a lie, and it is only

---

[9]For Kant, lying or false promising is only possible because of the assumption that normal discourse will be truthful. See *The Moral Law: Kant's Groundwork of the Metaphysics of Morals,* trans. H. J. Paton (New York: Barnes and Noble, Inc., 1948).

[10]Kant, "Truthfulness," 226.

[11]Kant says that it "is possible to deceive without making any statement whatever." See "Truthfulness," 226.

those active deceptions that we intend to communicate to another that are particularly problematic. Kant states as much when he writes that:

> *Not every untruth is a lie; it is a lie only if I have expressly given the other to understand that I am willing to acquaint him with my thought. Every lie is objectionable and contemptible in that we purposely let people think that we are telling them our thoughts and do not do so. We have broken our pact and violated the right of mankind.*[12]

But if we can avoid difficult questions—in other words, if we refuse to answer the questions that are put to us—are we in the clear? If we can avoid situations that oblige us to tell the truth are we exempt from ethical considerations? Does self-insulation serve as a moral cure-all?

Perhaps Roger Smith has done the most appropriate thing by keeping his mouth shut, and not letting his language compound the damage his actions have done in the public eye. And, by Kant's estimation, this is the best idea: "If a man tries to exhort the truth from us and we cannot tell it to him and at the same time do not wish to lie, we are justified in resorting to equivocation in order to reduce him to silence and to put a stop to his questionings. If he is wise, he will leave it at that."[13] Roger Smith appears to understand the prudence of Kant's remarks since he refuses to engage with Moore during a stockholder's meeting and turns off Moore's microphone so he can avoid being asked difficult questions.

While Michael Moore, no doubt, has exaggerated certain elements of the General Motors "story" in order to more effectively package his own message—paradoxically, what he criticizes General Motors for doing—his insights are still significant, even if they've only been thematized (as opposed to documented) in "Roger & Me." If these attempts to ask Roger Smith honest questions about the shutdown of the plants are indeed staged, as I am persuaded they must be, these various instances are not meant to serve as examples of when Roger has been evasive. Michael Moore is making his point a bit more indirectly and allegorically: there are no forthcoming questions because corporate bureaucrats effectively hide themselves from watching the very misery that they wreak on others' lives in the pursuit of profit. There is, in fact, no need to tell the truth because Roger Smith, for instance, has insulated himself from being asked questions to which he would know how to respond. As Ronald Edsforth says, while these various encounters to speak with Roger Smith are indeed staged, "they also effectively disclose the way that corporate decision makers . . . who have the power to make or break a community, insulate themselves from the injuries, the pain, and the anger their policies may create."[14] And, if he is asked, Kant has indicated to us his likely ignorance or non-response.

But, as we know, remaining silent itself sends a certain kind of message; sometimes it is ambiguous, but in many cases, words are not needed. One ex-worker at a General Motors plant, when asked what he has to say to Roger Smith, proclaims, "I can't mention it on TV." Unquestionably we can fill in the bleeps for him. Similarly, Moore portrays a typical, understanding Flint resident who has quite a few things that she *could* say about the "fat cats" at General Motors, but chooses not to. She proclaims herself a "lady" because she will

---

[12]Kant, "Truthfulness," 228.
[13]Kant, "Truthfulness," 229.
[14]Ronald Edsforth, "Review of 'Roger & Me'," 1146.

not sink so low as to demean herself and say what she thinks. The implication is clear: she has no intention to deceive and would prefer to maintain her composure in the face of immoral conduct:

> *[Roger Smith can] get off his big bucks and start giving some of it back to [his] workers. I'm sick and tired of these damn fat cats. I could say a few choice words, but I'm a lady and I was raised a lady so I won't say what I really feel but I could use some very unsavory language as far as fat cats.*

Whereas General Motors, on the other hand, has remained noticeably silent about the plant closings—and in this case, silence is an admission of certain guilt. As Kant tells us, the silent individual is usually considered to be "suspect."[15]

The same is true of the spokeswoman for General Motors, who, as an appointed "voice" of the corporation, refuses to speak to Michael Moore because, in her estimation, he doesn't represent anyone. Silence, then, is a powerful weapon. As Kant reminds us, "We are, for instance, not naturally tempted to speak about and to betray our own misdemeanors."[16] From the perspective of the workers which Moore wants to represent, the spokeswoman can hardly avoid hanging her own neck if she talks. Consider the following exchange:

> *Michael Moore: Why can't we talk to you if you're the spokesperson?*
> *Spokesperson: You can talk to me . . .*
> *MM: We will go down there if you'll come down and talk to us.*
> *S: No, I don't think I'll talk to you.*
> *MM: You're the spokesperson and you will not speak to us about why the plant is closing?*
> *S: You don't represent anybody and you're a private interest and no I won't speak to you.*
> *MM: We happen to be citizens of this community here; it's not a private interest.*

This silencing takes place on a number of levels . . . throughout the narrative. One African-American woman who raises vocal objections to her imminent eviction is temporarily allowed to stay in her home because Michael Moore's camera has captured the despair of her voice. Once out of the camera lights, though, her eviction is reinstated, and so the viewer learns that without a forum to capture her voice, life proceeds along its self-interested way. Without a microphone or a camera that can record her story for an audience comprised of people who can hold others accountable, she too, then, is effectively silenced and by all accounts, mute.

II.

One of the most remarkable features of "Roger & Me" is Moore's capacity to produce a film that is mediated through the perspective of the workers who are not normally given the channels in order to address their concerns, especially to the impersonal corporation. The film is an opportunity for viewers to witness truth-telling from the perspective of the poor and disenfranchised and not solely from the vantage points of the wealthy and powerful.

---

[15]Kant, "Truthfulness," 226.
[16]Kant, "Truthfulness," 225.

Humbly asking what the working-man would want to know, Michael Moore asks the questions that have strategically not been answered:

> *Maybe I got this wrong but I thought companies lay off people when they've hit hard times. GM was the richest company in the world and it was closing factories when it was making profits in the billions.*

And by asking questions and giving some preliminary responses, Moore is able to begin a dialogue that never got started. As he puts it in his own words, what is so successful about this movie is that "[t]he working person [finally] gets to give a Bronx cheer to management. I think people left 'Roger & Me' with that sense of 'Yeah! Finally, one for our side.' "[17]

Is the movie, though, just a trophy for the working class that narrates without regard for what is true? Has Michael Moore himself been co-opted by his own desire to stick it to General Motors? Throughout the film, Michael Moore seemed to suggest the ethical obligation to speak properly about what we describe, that legitimacy in speech requires a willingness to accurately narrate or express a state of affairs. While the imperative to tell the truth seems by all standards to be logically and necessarily ethical, it also has a double requirement: to respond with words that encourage such a reciprocal "exchange of sentiments." But too often we return a falsehood with a falsehood. We're more likely to respond to an abuse with another abuse, and with what seems to be good reason since anger generally provokes strong emotions. "Why shouldn't I be angry," Moore said in another context. "Why can't we look at these corporations who in the eighties and nineties have got filthy rich at the expense of millions of people losing their jobs? Why shouldn't I use every device I can to go after them?"[18] But if this is the case, hasn't Michael Moore gone against his own criticisms of General Motors? And if Moore is going to use any device to satisfy his anger against General Motors, how reliable are we to take his indictment of the company? Does using every device mean that he can also be deceptive in his practices, just like he has accused General Motors of doing? And if Moore, too, is being deceptive in his presentation of the case against General Motors, is he excused because, as one critic put it, Moore is "openly one-sided"[19] whereas General Motors is just plain manipulative?

I might be inclined to argue that Michael Moore symptomatically reproduces some of the ills of which he criticizes General Motors, and in the end, it is the "official story" of General Motors, "Roger & Me," and the stories of Flint residents seen in tandem with each other that provides for a more dynamic version of the truth. Perhaps what the narrative poses for the viewer is the question about how much truth one person could ever possibly reveal. In other words, we must wonder how anyone could ever tell the truth on his own. For instance, take the case where a young child in tears runs up to his parent and declares, "Johnny hit me." On face value, the statement itself explains fairly little about the events that have just transpired, but based on a parent's love for a child, a mother may judge that the action was done with malice. What the parent may not know is that the child solicited the abuse or that it was, in fact, an accident. Only by rounding out the statement, through a series of questions and exchanges with other parties directly concerned with the event, does

---

[17]Jolie Solomon, " 'Roger & Me' Redux," *Newsweek,* October 5, 1992: 79.

[18]"Success," *The New Yorker* 68 (October 12, 1992): 45.

[19]Annette Insdorf, "Who Made 'Roger & Me'?" *American Film* 15 (November 1989): 14.

the truth itself begin to emerge. While the statement itself—Johnny hit me—may be true and quite accurately reflect what has occurred, the proposition is what I might characterize as "impoverished" since it doesn't sufficiently reveal the "whole story." It may turn out that everyone has been convinced by their own impoverished versions of the truth. And isn't this exactly the problem: that everyone has been hijacked by their own true stories?

In the case of the upwardly-mobile residents of Flint who seem untouched by the ills of the city, truth-telling probably means something very different for them than for the laid-off workers. In one instance, a socialite at a Great Gatsby party tries to argue that Flint is a great place to live. Michael Moore's film shows us that this is probably true, but only for her and her friends. Similarly, an older woman relaxing on a golf course thinks that many of the laid-off workers are just lazy and "some of them . . . just want to take the easy way out." After all, she tells us, "we have such a good welfare system." And, from her perspective, that is probably true. At the end of "Roger & Me," Moore catches up with Roger Smith at a General Motors' Christmas party. When asked if he will come to Flint to meet with former General Motors' workers, many of whom have been evicted from their homes, Smith's response is that General Motors did not evict them. Indeed, we would have to agree with Smith's statement. But to claim an utterly disinterested, and ultimately disingenuous pose of non-responsibility, is similarly illegitimate. Perhaps we have caught Roger Smith at a bad moment, perhaps there are a number of logical explanations for the erosion of Flint, but, inevitably, Smith takes Kant's advice: if you know that you are going to be forced to lie, try to avoid the interlocutor! It is not surprising, then, that we watch Smith scurry off after pleading his ignorance and providing his own impoverished form of the truth. In Moore's estimation, it isn't that the truth hasn't been told, but not everyone's version of the truth has been given adequate expression nor are the ideas of the workers regularly given an opportunity for airing.

If "Roger & Me" is a heavy-handed, one-sided account of the General Motors' situation, then maybe this is exactly the point. As Miles Orvell has suggested, we expect the truth from documentary but not from satire, and "Roger & Me" is more like the latter than the former, maybe even a combination of the two.[20] But the notion of documentary is certainly relevant here, since "Roger & Me" is no doubt consistent with *the truth claims of the workers* who have every reason to justifiably believe that they are getting screwed over by management. While the full picture may in fact be impoverished, "Roger & Me" is a true account of the Flint workers' self-perception of their predicament.

I have tried to argue that we have an imperative to try our language and engage in dialogue with other individuals in order to best express the reality of a situation. There may be no explicit legitimacy assigned to the actual content of our speech, but we may be obliged to "manage" our speech with the self-consciousness that our words may be disrespectful to others and perhaps not adequately or sufficiently conform to the reality our words purport to describe. It is only by essaying or assessing the statements of a number of parties or stakeholders that this truth-telling might take its place. While it would be difficult to weigh these various responsibilities without further investigation of the purported offenses, it seems to

---

[20]Miles Orvello, "Documentary Film and the Power of Interrogation: American Dream & Roger and Me," *Film Quarterly* 48 (Winter 1994): 10–18.

me worthwhile to consider the speech-acts of various parties and consider the extent to which they may be considered justifiably offensive.

Certainly "Roger & Me" prompts a number of interesting questions about the legitimacy of GM's actions: Did the company treat its employees appropriately? Did General Motors encourage the Flint community to have a false sense of reliance upon the company for endlessly meeting its needs? Or, was Flint short-sighted in not considering a future without General Motors? In my estimation, no one party can successfully illuminate these issues. Rather, as Kant says, it is "[f]reedom of investigation [that] is the best means to consolidate the truth."[21] The truth itself needs to be negotiated by all these various perspectives, and without the viewpoints of the workers, the fuller picture may never have been told. In this sense, Moore's willingness to narrate another side of the story provides us with a rounder, more balanced sense of the Flint, Michigan, layoffs. In the end, this may only show that truth and discourse can never seamlessly coincide.

---

[21]Kant, "Truthfulness," 235.

PINNACLE BRANDS
A Strike Puts Employees Up to Bat
GILLIAN FLYNN

When baseball struck out in 1994, Pinnacle Brands Inc. a trading card company—could have followed others' leads with layoffs. Instead, it tossed the ball to employees, challenging them to save their jobs with money making ideas.

Downsizing in general and even single terminations present some of the greatest challenges to management in terms of emotional struggles. Companies, however, often mistakenly believe that these terminations are their only options for survival. Pinnacle thought otherwise and, in its creativity, salvaged positions and employees slated for termination. Would this work in other firms?

Are you American? Then you must love baseball. And you probably still wince a bit at the debacle of 1994, when those on-field heroes, the boys of summer, packed up their gear and headed home. The strike hit us hard. Most Americans were beyond bitter—we felt robbed, cheated out of our national pastime. There was no joy in Mudville, nor any other baseball-loving town.

If you think the average Joe was upset, consider the organizations linked to baseball because it's not just a national pastime, it's a national business. Take, for instance, trading card companies. When baseball shut down, so did a huge chunk of their sales. Smaller card companies literally went bankrupt. Larger ones survived, but only after huge headcount slashes.

Of the top five trading card manufacturers, only one got through the strike with no layoffs: Pinnacle Brands Inc. It did so by issuing an intriguing challenge to its employees: If they could devise new ways to replace the $40 million of lost trading card revenue, they would keep their jobs. Pinnacle's workforce emerged from the strike victorious with a sales jump of 80% in two years. In a season without heroes on the baseball field, these employees became heroes on the business field.

One Strike Can Mean You're Out (of Business)

It was a tense spring at Pinnacle Brands. Each day the murmurs of a 1994 strike grew stronger, so did employees' fears. At that time, baseball cards represented 65% of Pinnacle's business. "Here we were getting ready for what could be a no-baseball season," remembers

"Pinnacle Brands: A Strike Puts Employees Up to Bat," by Gillian Flynn. Reprinted with permission of Workforce Online, www.workforceonline.com.

Carlo Frappolli, vice president of HR. "When the stars aren't hitting home runs and aren't pitching no-hitters, people don't want to buy their cards. Everyone was nervous."

Frappolli and Chairman & CEO Jerry Meyer began discussing what-ifs. A strike would all but nullify the company's need for 190 full-time employees. However, both Meyer and Frappolli strongly believed workers should be viewed as revenue producers, not expense items. Unlike executives at many companies, their first reaction wasn't to lay people off. Pinnacle's regard for its workforce is reflected in the company's operating philosophies, four of which directly address the employer-employee relationship:

- Treat all employees with dignity and respect

- Deliver good news with grace

- Deliver bad news quickly and with brutal honesty

- Reward for results, not efforts.

In the first week of July, the strike ceased to be a rumor. Soon, the season was canceled. There was no good news to deliver, but the remaining three operating principles were about to come into play. Upon the official declaration of the season as null and void, Meyer convoked employees for a meeting. He delivered two messages. First, he quickly and honestly explained to employees that the company had just hit a dangerously rough patch. It was sink-or-swim time. Second and most important, he delivered the game plan: "He told the folks, 'I'm not going to save your jobs. You're going to save your jobs. You know what you can change and what you can do differently,'" says Frappolli.

Carolyn Corbin, founder of the Center for the 21st Century in Dallas, a think tank on future socioeconomic issues, believes Pinnacle's approach should serve as a role model for companies going through similar crises. "Very few companies take that risk," she says. "But in a way, it's not a risk at all because it puts the responsibility on the people to 'pay for themselves.' There isn't cash flow anymore, it's people flow: People will have to be generating, directly or indirectly, revenue for their keep or they can't stay."

The majority of Pinnacle employees remained wary at first, particularly the production people, who'd been subjected to continual cyclical layoffs under the company's former owner. Carol Anderson, an executive assistant in the finance division, recalls the workforce jitters: "Everybody sort of said, 'Uh-oh, what does this mean to us?' I think everybody went home that night a little nervous. But I thought we should give it a shot. At least it was we'd all sink or swim together, not just lay off people."

Meyer and Frappolli provided encouragement by setting up opportunities for employees to gather in informal teams and discuss ideas. Teams were deliberately cross-departmental. For instance, if employees had a new-product idea, a team would include someone from the creative end, a person from photography, people from marketing and finance. This gave employees insight into each step of a process so they didn't get blindsided halfway into a plan because they lacked the necessary perspective. It wasn't long before some amazing ideas started floating past supervisors' desks.

Pinnacle Has a Winning Season

One of the very first bright ideas came not from the COO or CFO, but someone just as in tune with the company's operations: Pinnacle's custodian. She came to Frappolli with a simple observation: The company spent approximately $50,000 a year on refrigerated sodas and bottled waters for every conference room and most executive offices, as well as personalized cups to boot. "So we stopped that," says Frappolli. "If executives feel they need to have sodas, they should go out and buy them themselves. That idea came from someone who sweeps the floors."

As soon as an employee's suggestion proved useful, Pinnacle immediately recognized him or her by printing out a big colorful poster with the person's name on it and many thanks. Some employees were spotted for a dinner with a spouse or friend at any Dallas restaurant of their choice. Others got round-trip airfare to visit nearby cities. "We tried to personalize it," says Frappolli. "Maybe we'd get them a signed football if they were a player's big fan. We tried to give things that mean something to that person."

Another simple but effective idea came in response to a newly developing area. Pinnacle had begun making pogs for Frito-Lay's division in Mexico; a 3-D pog went into every bag of chips. To understate it, the item was popular. The introduction of pogs spurred sales from 40 million bags of chips a week to 80 million and there's only 50 million people in all of Mexico. Problem was, the orders were growing so exponentially, Pinnacle couldn't keep up. In danger of losing the contract, a manufacturing supervisor set his carpentry—yes, carpentry—skills to work. On his own time, he made a "shaker table." The homemade contraption literally shakes the pogs as they come onto a ramp so they shoot down different avenues, allowing more workers to pack them. It increased Pinnacle's production capacity by tenfold—the company shipped over a billion pogs that summer. "If you looked at this table, you'd think your 10-year-old could have made it," says Frappolli. "But it's a good idea and no one had thought of it. It let us hit the order."

Employees were encouraged not just to concentrate on their own areas, but also to think outside the box. A public relations manager, for instance, was looking at the 1996 Olympics with dollar bills in his eyes. He'd been to previous Olympics and had seen how well pins had sold. He contacted one of the few companies licensed to sell Olympic pins in Atlanta, a company that lacked the distribution channels Pinnacle had established. Now that company makes the pins and Pinnacle distributes them. The venture brought in almost $20 million in revenue.

Throughout the process, Pinnacle struggled against formalizing it too much. Employees would contact either Frappolli or their supervisors with ideas. "I found from my days at large companies that programs can bog you down," says Frappolli. "With us it's if you've got a good idea that will work, let's do it. Let's quantify savings so we know it works and then reward that employee." How did the company know if an idea would work? It grabbed all the stakeholders and asked them if it was worth trying. The company tried to emphasize the positive. Maybe the first idea wasn't a home run, but if employees remained encouraged, they might hit the next one out of the ballpark.

One of the employees who scored big was Anderson. As an employee in the finance department, she was privy to the exorbitant costs of trademark searches. Every time the company came up with a new name for a trading card, it had to pay a trademark attorney to do a search to make sure it hadn't been trademarked. Anderson decided to create a database for Pinnacle, to track what trademarks it owned and which ones it had searched in the past. Although she had no training in legal or intellectual-property issues, she wasn't afraid to ask a lot of questions. Anderson worked to set up the system—at home and on weekends, even on lunch breaks—for almost three months before it was up and running. It has saved more than $100,000.

Toward the close of '94, there still hadn't been even a peep about layoffs. Employees were revitalized. "Each day and each week and each month they saw we weren't laying people off and our competition was—some were laying off half their workforces, shutting entire plants down," says Frappolli. "They saw we weren't doing any of that and it really built some steam."

Pinnacle was lucky it had a tough and energized workforce, because it wasn't in the clear until fall 1995. Baseball sales are strong this spring, however, and the company is breathing a collective sigh of relief. But the message remains clear—just because we're bouncing back doesn't mean we should relax. Keep the ideas coming. Says Corbin: "What Pinnacle has done is to tell employees, 'Keep justifying your job. Earn your keep if you want to stay here.' Rather than the organization choosing who stays and who goes, the people themselves choose through their actions. What Pinnacle is doing is the most honest, empowering thing it can do."

Anderson says employees are still at it—she herself is exploring a new database. She gives much of the credit to the Pinnacle culture. "It's an atmosphere in which you can take on as much responsibility as you want," Anderson says. "If you were to leave Pinnacle—and I have no intention of doing so—you could honestly look your employer in the face and say, 'I can do anything you throw at me.' "

Truly mutual admirers, Frappolli says a lot of the credit goes to the Pinnacle workforce—a uniquely excellent group of people. "I think it would be dangerous to say that this is a template that could work across America," he says. "You need special kinds of people who believe in themselves and understand that they control their own destiny. These employees know that if they deliver results they're going to have a job and if they don't they might not. They prefer to bet on themselves rather than having a company take care of them."

Pinnacle's mission statement is "to provide unexpected delight in everything we do." In its rally against layoffs, the company certainly provided unexpected delight to a business community jaded by "unavoidable" downsizings. When the crowds cheer to the crack of the bat this week, we should reserve a portion of the adulation for the heroes off the field.

WHEN FEAR OF FIRING
DETERS HIRING

JEFFREY L. SEGLIN

If a firm believes that a termination is more likely to be challenged on discriminatory grounds by a woman or minority, is that firm less likely to hire those individuals in the first place? This is the concern expressed by some in this article. How can we prevent this counter-intuitive result?

Over the last few years, several people have spoken to me about their reluctance to hire people whose race, color, creed or national origin—or age, disability or sex—put them in protected classes under anti-discrimination law.

The reasoning goes this way: You have to be absolutely sure that someone in a protected class is the best possible candidate, because people in these categories can make your life miserable with litigation if you ever have to dismiss them.

"It's a dirty little secret" that people are thinking this way, said Tama Starr, president of Artkraft Strauss, a sign-making company in New York, and one of the few business people who has spoken out on the subject. Those who subscribe to these ideas "have to choose between different protected classes and weigh the risk of hiring them," she said, adding, "This is a very obnoxious way to think."

Managers tread on swampy ethical terrain when they allow fear of possible problems to deter them from hiring apparently capable minority applicants—or to hesitate so long over a decision that a candidate loses interest or gives up in frustration.

The fear of discrimination suits is not wholly groundless. A 1997 survey conducted by the Society for Human Resource Management found that of 616 personnel executives who responded, 53 percent said their organizations had been sued at least once by former employees in the last five years; nearly half the 611 suits they reported involved claims of discrimination.

But Martha R. A. Fields, chief executive of Fields Associates, a management consulting firm in Cambridge, Mass., says the risk of a suit is often an excuse that masks a deeper motive for not hiring people in protected classes. It is more likely, Ms. Fields said, that managers really just feel safer hiring people like themselves.

Some people, she said, find it easy to think to themselves: "If I know people who are like me, I know the good, bad, and the ugly about them. If I don't know them and I see images of them in the media, I'm, like, 'Oh man, those black people, they might be welfare-dependent, or criminals, or crime victims. I don't know if I really want to bring that into my organization.'"

Increasingly, such bias is economically irrational as well as unethical. "The demographics of this country are shifting in major ways," Ms. Fields noted, as minority groups, especially Hispanic people, account for a rapidly growing share of the population and its purchasing power. "Consumers want to see people like themselves in organizations," Ms. Fields said.

Another underlying problem is managers who are poor at managing. Some who speak these fears are simply afraid to fire anyone—not just someone in a protected class—and shy away from situations they perceive as requiring them to take a chance.

To avoid hiring problem employees from any group, managers just "need to do a good job of checking resumes, identifying the time gaps and verifying simple facts," said Mary C. Dollarhide, an employment lawyer with Paul, Hastings, Janofsky & Walker in Stamford, Conn. For $200 to $300, a manager can also get a criminal background check on a candidate and a docket search to see if he or she often files lawsuits. "If you do your due diligence, you're going to stand a much better chance of not bringing in the gripers, complainers, bad actors and poor performers," Ms. Dollarhide said.

But a thorough screening does not absolve managers of having to manage. "If you get somebody in your midst whom you fail to discipline because you're afraid you're going to get slammed for having reprimanded someone in a protected class, well, guess what: The failure to do that is going to land you in exactly the same spot," Ms. Dollarhide said. "If the employee is terminated, he can sue and you're left with no records to support your case."

Much sound management translates into ethical behavior. Employees who are treated fairly, honestly and directly are both less likely to require dismissal and less likely to sue over it later.

That frees everyone to concentrate on the business they enjoy. "I still believe that people are good and honest and they want to do a nice job," said Ms. Starr of Artkraft. "Having to fight through more stupidity just hampers everybody's humanity."

TOPIC STUDY: THE BALANCE OF POWER

MASCULINE VERSUS FEMININE STYLES

Camille Atkinson

Candice Fredrick

Do men and women lead differently? Should men and women be led differently? These are some of the challenging questions addressed in the authors' discussion of leadership styles. This excerpt is included in this volume because treating people differently or having different expectations on whatever bases may give rise to ethical dilemmas. Should women act "naturally" in the workplace or "like men" in order to fit in? Should we treat women differently because of these differences? Is this unfair, or is it instead unfair not to take the differences into account?

Nearly all of the available literature discusses a distinction between "masculine" and "feminine" styles of leadership. And, in order to clarify this difference, two pairs of metaphors are nearly always appealed to. For instance, when describing an organization and its leaders in "traditional" or masculine terms, the two analogies that are almost universally invoked are team sports (like football with its coach, quarterback, and specialized players) or the military (with its ranking of officers, chain of command, and special units). However, there are two contrasting metaphors for a feminine conception of power and authority that are as prevalent as the masculine ones—namely, a "web," or network of relations, with a center or locus that resonates outward into various branches and subdivisions, or the family insofar as it is understood as an integrated whole involving interpersonal relations and intimate connections. Presumably, the masculine models evoke images of a rigid hierarchy emphasizing order and individual role identification and construe success as "winning" in the short-term according to what is measurable or quantifiable; while the feminine paradigms are designed to accentuate an essentially fluid structure with greater emphasis on relationships in which individuals play different roles and share power and in which success is more long-term oriented and includes intangibles like personal satisfaction or happiness. In war as in sports, individuals are said to thrive on "competition" with each aiming to achieve his personal "best"; while in a family or network, the whole is said to be "greater

"Balance of Power"—"Masculine vs. Feminine Styles," in *Women, Ethics and the Workplace* by Camille Atkinson and Candice Fredrick. Reprinted with permission of the authors.

than the sum of its parts," "cooperation" is fostered and everyone shares credit as well as responsibility. But, one might ask, is this an accurate portrait of team sports or military activities? Isn't it instead true that both the feminine and masculine paradigms are dependent upon the cooperation, or personal sacrifices, of each and every member? Don't officers or coaches even go so far as to claim that one should regard his team or squad as he would his own family? Another problem with claiming that the sports and military metaphors are strictly masculine is the implication that women do not belong in these arenas—that is, that they are somehow inherently unsuited for the rigors of athletic competition or a soldier's life. This itself is a hotly debated ethical question that is far from being resolved.

Nonetheless, many women in the Catalyst survey said that they felt compelled to adopt a "masculine" attitude in order to succeed at higher levels of management, despite feeling that it threatened their own sense of personal identity. This included such things as demonstrating company loyalty, keeping their personal lives out of the office, and "not rocking the boat." But what makes these traits particularly "masculine"? The presumption here is that a woman's sense of identity somehow depends upon *rocking* the boat, *bringing* her personal problems into the workplace, and *not* being loyal to the company or her coworkers. What is more remarkable is that it was the women themselves who made these claims. This indicates how deep certain sexist assumptions run and how so many men and women, regardless of educational background, still march to them, however unconsciously. Psychological researchers only add to this further and validate such presuppositions when they maintain that "[w]omen's traits, behaviors, attitudes, and socialization are said to make them inappropriate or deficient as managers because of such factors as fear of success or their unwillingness to take risks."[1] Yet, claims such as these do not square with empirical evidence. For what could be more risky than bearing and raising children? What other endeavor is so fraught with uncertainty and has so unpredictable an outcome? On the other hand, there were also women who claimed that simply "being themselves" contributed to their success. This entailed leading by "recognition and encouragement" and seeking to "empower" others rather than commanding or controlling. So, the camp appears to be split between women who find it necessary to emulate a paradigm of leadership that is not their own and those who follow a model of their own making that fits their unique sense of self. In addition, while some corporations are actively adopting a more "female" approach to management, others remain resistant to any changes or innovations in the workplace.

Still, nearly all of the women quoted acknowledged having to "prove" themselves to their male coworkers, conceding that they were not afforded any benefit of doubt, as would have been the case if they were men. Whether they adapted to the masculine style of leadership, or maintained one with which they personally were more comfortable, the burden of proof remained on them to demonstrate that they, in fact, could be effective managers. This constitutes an incredible waste of time and energy that could surely be spent more productively—and may provide us with a hint as to why some women don't even want to get into "the corporate game" to begin with. But if women do break these barriers somehow, then what? What do women do once they have reached the upper rungs of the corporate ladder? And, is there one particular style of leadership which is favored above others?

Other studies have been done that asked women these questions—namely, what is their preferred style of management now that they are in a position to choose one for themselves? Again, according to these anecdotal accounts, a uniquely feminine approach emerged in contrast to a traditional or distinctly masculine style. What these studies concluded is that the feminine model is more "open" and flexible, reflecting a willingness to embrace ambiguity in situations where decisions are called for, whereas men look for a more rule-oriented, secure system that will enable them to make effective choices and ensure the best results.

This hearkens back to Carol Gilligan's distinction between an ethic of care and a justice orientation, which, in turn, presupposes a Kantian account of moral choice. . . . For Gilligan claims that women manifest a greater capacity for, or are better attuned to, evaluating matters that are ambiguous or unquantifiable and require some "reading between the lines." Moreover, if emphasis is placed primarily on relationships, which is what she claims women do, then clearly those are the kinds of connections that cannot possibly be measured or determined with mathematical precision (in either personal or professional contexts). Again, this is where an implicit appeal to a family metaphor comes in, for women who are wives and mothers must remain flexible and responsive to the individualized needs of different family members; there can be no single approach to dealing with all of the surprises and circumstances that may arise. These claims also bring us back to Nancy Hartsock, who insisted that a different notion of power and community is operative in the private realm of the household than in the public realm or marketplace. However, she believes, that justice and equality are more likely to be achieved if we bring some of these private values into the marketplace, just as Gilligan believes that men and women each have something to learn from the different emphases and attitudes of the other. So, what specifically are these "feminine" values that are manifested in a female conception of leadership? And, in what ways are they distinct from a "masculine" attitude or approach?

MASCULINE VS. FEMININE VALUES

The way in which most writers on leadership have distinguished between men's and women's styles is by appealing to a basic distinction in what each values. Where men are said to value individuality and the rewards of a competitive work environment, women, it is claimed, value cooperative enterprises that preserve or enhance relationships. As noted above, in the Catalyst survey, some female executives struggled to fit into the corporate structure and, at the same time, maintain their own unique sense of personal identity. Apparently, these women embodied the kind of care ethic described by Gilligan and felt uncomfortable having to suppress it, along with the values that it entails, in order to fit into a corporate structure. They believed that who they were in their private lives (mothers, wives, friends, lovers) was inappropriate for office relations or their professional circumstances if they wanted to succeed in this "alien" culture. This separation of the personal and the professional was something they resented, but could not avoid if they wished to advance. However, upon reaching a top managerial position, it appeared that many of these women were able to develop a style with which they were comfortable, one that included a more personal or personable approach to doing business. In other words, they attempted to overcome this separation of their private and public lives by integrating the former into the latter.

In order to defend a specifically "feminine" style of leadership, most authors draw upon the work of Carol Gilligan. What Gilligan did with moral development in contradistinction to Lawrence Kohlberg, Sally Helgesen does with leadership contra Henry Mintzberg. However, where Gilligan recorded responses from both male and female adolescents, Mintzberg limited his studies to five male managers and Helgesen, to four female executives or entrepreneurs. At this point, one might already suspect that the results of such studies would be similarly skewed, given the small number of participants and the fact that Mintzberg as well as Helgesen limited their studies to only one sex. Nonetheless, both researchers make claims that resonate with findings of many other surveys, studies, and psychological theories; so it might be worthwhile to consider what each has to say and assess their positions.

In 1968, Mintzberg studied the requirements for successful management successfully by observing what it was that top managers actually did in their daily activities. All of his subjects were men, and a basic pattern emerged: First, they worked at a very fast pace and took little time out for reflection and activities not directly related to the immediate tasks at hand. Secondly, the workday was characterized by discontinuity and fragmentation due to interruptions in the scheduled routine and/or unanticipated problems. Lastly, they had difficulty sharing information, delegating duties, and tended to tie their sense of personal identity to the position they held in the company—all of which reflects an inability to detach *who* they are as individuals from *what* they do as managers. In general, the portrait that was exhibited through this study was of a manager who focused on ends over means, had a "goal orientation" rather than a "process orientation," and thrived on the pressures endemic to competition and rapid decision making. When Hegelsen did her study on management, however, a different picture emerged.

While Mintzberg concentrated on five men, Helgesen interviewed and observed four women and discovered a style that stood in stark contrast from the one described above. First, the women she studied worked at a slower, steadier pace and took time for breaks and activities that were not necessarily work-related. Secondly, they maintained a sense of wholeness or "flow" by weaving surprises or interruptions into the work-day, indicating a more flexible sense of time and scheduling. And lastly, they saw themselves as playing many roles, sharing information, delegating tasks and, in general, being a part of a network of relation-ships. In sum, women appeared to be as concerned with means—*how* the job gets done or the process itself—as with the fact *that* it gets done or the ends and objectives. Again, we see how women are characterized as prone to creating a cooperative work environment where each employee is valued as an important part of a whole web of relations, whereas it is claimed that men thrive on the personal satisfaction that results from "winning" a competitive edge.

These two distinct styles are discussed in other literature as well, and the portraits are remarkably similar. For instance, Aburdene and Naisbitt provide us with a list of different attributes—one belonging to "traditional management," the other to "women's leadership." The traditional style is characterized as hierarchical, controlling, and dependent upon a system of rank and order-giving. It seeks to limit and define individuals' roles within the corporate structure, demanding respect for certain positions but not others. And it is fundamentally mechanistic, taking an impersonal view towards the worker, who is simply a cog in the machinery designed to perform one specialized job. On the other hand, the feminine style supposedly relies upon strategies of empowering others, establishing and maintaining personal connections, and asking questions rather than disseminating "answers" or giving orders. In this way, it is claimed that consideration for all is facilitated, and workers are seen as persons whose creativity is encouraged by allowing them greater flexibility and latitude in the variety of tasks they might perform. For Aburdene and Naisbitt, this feminine approach is preferred and represents the trend in leadership style. According to their prognostications, it is women who now have the advantage and who will transform the corporate environment, as they "encourage participation, share power and information, enhance other people's self-worth, and get others excited about their work."

Thus, discipline and order is "out" and innovation and diversity is "in," making women the "natural" leaders of the future. But, one might ask, is this type of behavior really "natural" to women? And, whether it is or not, should it be encouraged as good for business or the best approach for women? What also strikes us as odd is the manner in which typical capitalist assumptions and values are being denigrated as not suited to the interior realm of the corporate structure, but are not questioned at all when it comes to the fundamental economic structure of our society. That is, "cooperation," among coworkers at least, is now being encouraged over and against "competition"; yet the socioeconomic system in which we live, and the basic paradigm for relations between corporations, is a competitive one. At this point, it would seem that certain critical questions must be raised. Before we do so in detail, however, there is one last text to consider that reflects on traditional approaches to conflict management and the ways in which masculine styles of leadership value reason. . . .

HARRIS V. FORKLIFT SYSTEMS, INC.

One of the areas most discussed in employee training these days is sexual harassment, which was relatively unheard of prior to the Anita Hill—Clarence Thomas incident several years ago. Subjects of sexual harassment are now filing suits against their employers in record numbers. Defining what constitutes sexual harassment or what is a "hostile environment" is difficult and circumstantial. The following case exemplifies some of these challenging issues.

. . . JUSTICE O'CONNOR delivered the opinion of the Court.

In this case we consider the definition of a discriminatorily "abusive work environment" (also known as a "hostile work environment") under Title VII of the Civil Rights Act of 1964.

I

Teresa Harris worked as a manager at Forklift Systems, Inc., an equipment rental company, from April 1985 until October 1987. Charles Hardy was Forklift's president.

The Magistrate found that, throughout Harris' time at Forklift, Hardy often insulted her because of her gender and often made her the target of unwanted sexual innuendos. Hardy told Harris on several occasions, in the presence of other employees, "You're a woman, what do you know" and "We need a man as the rental manager"; at least once, he told her she was "a dumb ass woman." Again in front of others, he suggested that the two of them "go to the Holiday Inn to negotiate [Harris'] raise." Hardy occasionally asked Harris and other female employees to get coins from his front pants pocket. He threw objects on the ground in front of Harris and other women, and asked them to pick the objects up. He made sexual innuendos about Harris' and other women's clothing.

In mid-August 1987, Harris complained to Hardy about his conduct. Hardy said he was surprised that Harris was offended, claimed he was only joking, and apologized. He also promised he would stop, and based on this assurance Harris stayed on the job. But in early September, Hardy began anew: While Harris was arranging a deal with one of Forklift's customers, he asked her, again in front of other employees, "What did you do, promise the guy . . . some [sex] Saturday night?" On October 1, Harris collected her paycheck and quit.

Harris then sued Forklift, claiming that Hardy's conduct had created an abusive work environment for her because of her gender. The United States District Court for the Middle District of Tennessee, adopting the report and recommendation of the Magistrate, found this to be "a close case," but held that Hardy's conduct did not create an abusive environment.

Sexual Harassment: *Harris v. Forklift Systems, Inc.,* 510 U.S. 17 (1993).

The court found that some of Hardy's comments "offended [Harris], and would offend the reasonable woman," but that they were not

> *so severe as to be expected to seriously affect [Harris'] psychological well-being. A reasonable woman manager under like circumstances would have been offended by Hardy, but his conduct would not have risen to the level of interfering with that person's work performance.*
>
> *Neither do I believe that [Harris] was subjectively so offended that she suffered injury.... Although Hardy may at times have genuinely offended [Harris], I do not believe that he created a working environment so poisoned as to be intimidating or abusive to [Harris].*

In focusing on the employee's psychological well-being, the District Court was following Circuit precedent. The United States Court of appeals for the Sixth Circuit affirmed in a brief unpublished decision.

We granted certiorari to resolve a conflict among the Circuits on whether conduct, to be actionable as "abusive work environment" harassment (no quid pro quo harassment issue is present here), must "seriously affect [an employee's] psychological well-being" or lead the plaintiff to suffer injury....

II

Title VII of the Civil Rights Act of 1964 makes it "an unlawful employment practice for an employer . . . to discriminate against any individual with respect to his compensation, terms, conditions, or privileges of employment, because of such individual's race, color, religion, sex, or national origin." As we made clear in Meritor Savings Bank v. Vinson, this language "is not limited to 'economic' or 'tangible' discrimination. The phrase 'terms, conditions, or privileges of employment' evinces a congressional intent 'to strike at the entire spectrum of disparate treatment of men and women' in employment," which includes requiring people to work in a discriminatorily hostile or abusive environment. When the workplace is permeated with "discriminatory intimidation, ridicule, and insult" that is "sufficiently severe or pervasive to alter the conditions of the victim's employment and create an abusive working environment," Title VII is violated.

This standard, which we reaffirm today, takes a middle path between making actionable any conduct that is merely offensive and requiring the conduct to cause a tangible psychological injury. As we pointed out in Meritor, "mere utterance of an . . . epithet which engenders offensive feelings in an employee" does not sufficiently affect the conditions of employment to implicate Title VII. Conduct that is not severe or pervasive enough to create an objectively hostile or abusive work environment—an environment that a reasonable person would find hostile or abusive—is beyond Title VII's purview. Likewise, if the victim does not subjectively perceive the environment to be abusive, the conduct has not actually altered the conditions of the victim's employment, and there is no Title VII violation.

But Title VII comes into play before the harassing conduct leads to a nervous breakdown. A discriminatorily abusive work environment, even one that does not seriously affect employees' psychological well-being, can and often will detract from employees' job performance, discourage employees from remaining on the job, or keep them from advancing in their careers. Moreover, even without regard to these tangible effects, the very fact that the discriminatory conduct was so severe or pervasive that it created a work environment abusive to employees because of their race, gender, religion, or national origin offends Title VII's broad rule of workplace equality. The appalling conduct alleged in Meritor, and the reference in that case to environments " 'so heavily polluted with discrimination as to destroy completely the emotional and psychological stability of minority group workers' " merely present some especially egregious examples of harassment. They do not mark the boundary of what is actionable.

We therefore believe the District Court erred in relying on whether the conduct "seriously affected plaintiff's psychological well-being" or led her to "suffer injury." Such an inquiry may needlessly focus the factfinder's attention on concrete psychological harm, an element Title VII does not require. Certainly Title VII bars conduct that would seriously affect a reasonable person's psychological well-being, but the statute is not limited to such conduct. So long as the environment would reasonably be perceived, and is perceived, as hostile or abusive, there is no need for it also to be psychologically injurious.

This is not, and by its nature cannot be, a mathematically precise test. We need not answer today all the potential questions it raises, nor specifically address the EEOC's new regulations on this subject. But we can say that whether an environment is "hostile" or "abusive" can be determined only by looking at all the circumstances. These may include the frequency of the discriminatory conduct; its severity; whether it is physically threatening or humiliating, or a mere offensive utterance; and whether it unreasonably interferes with an employee's work performance. The effect on the employee's psychological well-being is, of course, relevant to determining whether the plaintiff actually found the environment abusive. But while psychological harm, like any other relevant factor, may be taken into account, no single factor is required.

III

Forklift, while conceding that a requirement that the conduct seriously affect psychological well-being is unfounded, argues that the District Court nonetheless correctly applied the Meritor standard. We disagree. Though the District Court did conclude that the work environment was not "intimidating or abusive to [Harris]," it did so only after finding that the conduct was not "so severe as to be expected to seriously affect plaintiff's psychological well-being," and that Harris was not "subjectively so offended that she suffered injury." The District Court's application of these incorrect standards may well have influenced its ultimate conclusion, especially given that the court found this to be a "close case."

We therefore reverse the judgment of the Court of Appeals, and remand the case for further proceedings consistent with this opinion.

So ordered. . . .

FARAGHER V. CITY OF BOCA RATON

At the end of June 1998, the United States Supreme Court issued two opinions on the same day that served to further articulate the standards by which a firm might be held liable for the sexual harassment of an employee by one of its supervisory employees. Prior to these decisions, this issue had blossomed into one of the more tremendously unclear areas of employer liability. Firms had little legal guidance as to whether they would be held liable for harassment within their walls, even when they had no knowledge of the activities. The following case clearly explains those circumstances under which employers might have a legal defense to liability for sexual harassment.

I

Between 1985 and 1990, while attending college, petitioner Beth Ann Faragher worked part time and during the summers as an ocean lifeguard for the Marine Safety Section of the Parks and Recreation Department of respondent, the City of Boca Raton, Florida (City). During this period, Faragher's immediate supervisors were Bill Terry, David Silverman, and Robert Gordon. In June 1990, Faragher resigned.

In 1992, Faragher brought an action against Terry, Silverman, and the City, asserting claims under Title VII, 42 U.S.C. § 1983, and Florida law. So far as it concerns the Title VII claim, the complaint alleged that Terry and Silverman created a "sexually hostile atmosphere" at the beach by repeatedly subjecting Faragher and other female lifeguards to "uninvited and offensive touching," by making lewd remarks, and by speaking of women in offensive terms. The complaint contained specific allegations that Terry once said that he would never promote a woman to the rank of lieutenant, and that Silverman had said to Faragher, "Date me or clean the toilets for a year." Asserting that [*781] Terry and Silverman were agents of the City, and that their conduct amounted to discrimination in the "terms, conditions, and privileges" of her employment, 42 U.S.C. § 2000e-2(a)(1), Faragher sought a judgment against the City for nominal damages, costs, and attorney's fees.

In February 1986, the City adopted a sexual harassment policy, which it stated in a memorandum from the City Manager addressed to all employees. . . . In May 1990, the City revised the policy and reissued a statement of it. Although the City may actually have circulated the memos and statements to some employees, it completely failed to disseminate its policy among employees of the Marine Safety Section, with the result that Terry, Silverman, Gordon, and many lifeguards were unaware of it. . . .

Faragher v. City of Boca Raton, 524 U.S. 775 (1998).

From time to time over the course of Faragher's tenure at the Marine Safety Section, between 4 and 6 of the 40 to 50 lifeguards were women. . . . During that 5-year period, Terry repeatedly touched the bodies of female employees without invitation, would put his arm around Faragher, with his hand on her buttocks, . . . and once made contact with another female lifeguard in a motion of sexual simulation. . . . He made crudely demeaning references to women generally . . . , and once commented disparagingly on Faragher's shape. . . . During a job interview with a woman he hired as a lifeguard, Terry said that the female lifeguards had sex with their male counterparts and asked whether she would do the same. . . .

Silverman behaved in similar ways. He once tackled Faragher and remarked that, but for a physical characteristic he found unattractive, he would readily have had sexual relations with her. . . . Another time, he pantomimed an act of oral sex. . . . Within earshot of the female lifeguards, Silverman made frequent, vulgar references to women and sexual matters, commented on the bodies of female lifeguards and beachgoers, and at least twice told female lifeguards that he would like to engage in sex with them. . . .

Faragher did not complain to higher management about Terry or Silverman. Although she spoke of their behavior to Gordon, she did not regard these discussions as formal complaints to a supervisor but as conversations with a person she held in high esteem. . . . Other female lifeguards had similarly informal talks with Gordon, but because Gordon did not feel that it was his place to do so, he did not report these complaints to Terry, his own supervisor, or to any other city official. . . . Gordon responded to the complaints of one lifeguard by saying that "the City just [doesn't] care.". . .

In April 1990, however, two months before Faragher's resignation, Nancy Ewanchew, a former lifeguard, wrote to Richard Bender, the City's Personnel Director, complaining that Terry and Silverman had harassed her and other female lifeguards. . . . Following investigation of this complaint, the City found that Terry and Silverman had behaved improperly, reprimanded them, and required them to choose between a suspension without pay or the forfeiture of annual leave. . . .

***

While indicating the substantive contours of the hostile environments forbidden by Title VII, our cases have established few definite rules for determining when an employer will be liable for a discriminatory environment that is otherwise actionably abusive. Given the circumstances of many of the litigated cases, including some that have come to us, it is not surprising that in many of them, the issue has been joined over the sufficiency of the abusive conditions, not the standards for determining an employer's liability for them. There have, for example, been myriad cases in which District Courts and Courts of Appeals have held employers liable on account of actual knowledge by the employer, or high-echelon officials of an employer organization, of sufficiently harassing action by subordinates, which the employer or its informed officers have done nothing to stop. . . . In such instances, the combined knowledge and inaction may be seen as demonstrable negligence, or as the employer's adoption of the offending conduct and its results, quite as if they had been authorized affirmatively as the employer's policy. . . .

***

We therefore agree with Faragher that in implementing Title VII it makes sense to hold an employer vicariously liable for some tortious conduct of a supervisor made possible by abuse of his supervisory authority, and that the aided-by-agency-relation principle . . . provides an appropriate starting point for determining liability for the kind of harassment presented here. Several courts, indeed, have noted what Faragher has argued, that there is a sense in which a harassing supervisor is always assisted in his misconduct by the supervisory relationship. . . . The agency relationship affords contact with an employee subjected to a supervisor's sexual harassment, and the victim may well be reluctant to accept the risks of blowing the whistle on a superior. When a person with supervisory authority discriminates in the terms and conditions of subordinates' employment, his actions necessarily draw upon his superior position over the people who report to him, or those under them, whereas an employee generally cannot check a supervisor's abusive conduct the same way that she might deal with abuse from a co-worker. When a fellow employee harasses, the victim can walk away or tell the offender where to go, but it may be difficult to offer such responses to a supervisor, whose "power to supervise—[which may be] to hire and fire, and to set work schedules and pay rates—does not disappear . . . when he chooses to harass through insults and offensive gestures rather than directly with threats of firing or promises of promotion. . . . Recognition of employer liability when discriminatory misuse of supervisory authority alters the terms and conditions of a victim's employment is underscored by the fact that the employer has a greater opportunity to guard against misconduct by supervisors than by common workers; employers have greater opportunity and incentive to screen them, train them, and monitor their performance.

***

In order to accommodate the principle of vicarious liability for harm caused by misuse of supervisory authority, as well as Title VII's equally basic policies of encouraging forethought by employers and saving action by objecting employees, we adopt the following holding in this case. . . . An employer is subject to vicarious liability to a victimized employee for an actionable hostile environment created by a supervisor with immediate (or successively higher) authority over the employee. When no tangible employment action is taken, a defending employer may raise an affirmative defense to liability or damages, subject to proof by a preponderance of the evidence. . . . The defense comprises two necessary elements: (a) that the employer exercised reasonable care to prevent and correct promptly any sexually harassing behavior, and (b) that the plaintiff employee unreasonably failed to take advantage of any preventive or corrective opportunities provided by the employer or to avoid harm otherwise. While proof that an employer had promulgated an antiharassment policy with complaint procedure is not necessary in every instance as a matter of law, the need for a stated policy suitable to the employment circumstances may appropriately be addressed in any case when litigating the first element of the defense. And while proof that an employee failed to fulfill the corresponding obligation of reasonable care to avoid harm is not limited to showing an unreasonable failure to use any complaint procedure provided by the employer, a demonstration of such failure will normally suffice to satisfy the employer's burden under the second element of the defense. No affirmative defense is available, however, when the supervisor's harassment culminates in a tangible employment action, such as discharge, demotion, or undesirable reassignment. . . .

Applying these rules here, we believe that the judgment of the Court of Appeals must be reversed. The District Court found that the degree of hostility in the work environment rose to the actionable level and was attributable to Silverman and Terry. It is undisputed that these supervisors "were granted virtually unchecked authority" over their subordinates, "directly controlling and supervising all aspects of [Faragher's] day-to-day activities." . . . It is also clear that Faragher and her colleagues were "completely isolated from the City's higher management. . . . The City did not seek review of these findings.

While the City would have an opportunity to raise an affirmative defense if there were any serious prospect of its presenting one, it appears from the record that any such avenue is closed. The District Court found that the City had entirely failed to disseminate its policy against sexual harassment among the beach employees and that its officials made no attempt to keep track of the conduct of supervisors like Terry and Silverman. The record also makes clear that the City's policy did not include any assurance that the harassing supervisors could be bypassed in registering complaints. . . . Under such circumstances, we hold as a matter of law that the City could not be found to have exercised reasonable care to prevent the supervisors' harassing conduct. Unlike the employer of a small workforce, who might expect that sufficient care to prevent tortious behavior could be exercised informally, those responsible for city operations could not reasonably have thought that precautions against hostile environments in any one of many departments in far-flung locations could be effective without communicating some formal policy against harassment, with a sensible complaint procedure.

III

The judgment of the Court of Appeals for the Eleventh Circuit is reversed, and the case is remanded for reinstatement of the judgment of the District Court.

It is so ordered. . . .

THE FARAGHER AFFIRMATIVE DEFENSE
An Overview and Checklist
KIREN DOSANJH

Given the complexities of the legal precedents set by the courts in the preceding cases, Professor Dosanjh has developed a decision tree framework for employers to use in determining whether the affirmative defense is available to them.

Anti-discrimination statutes such as Title VII of the Civil Rights Act of 1964 offer remedies for the harm caused by employment discrimination. However, their primary goal is to promote fair employment practices through the recognition of employers' liability for discriminatory treatment of employees. In two 1998 decisions, *Burlington Industries, Inc. v. Ellerth,* and *Faragher v. City of Boca Raton,* the United States Supreme Court made clear that employers face vicarious liability under Title VII for unlawful harassment by supervisors. Further, and perhaps more significantly, the *Faragher/Ellerth* decisions offer employers strong incentive to use reasonable care in preventing and promptly addressing harassing behavior.

Under the *Faragher/Ellerth* decisions, an employer may be able to avoid liability or limit damages by establishing an affirmative defense recognized by the Supreme Court. This affirmative defense is based on two premises: (1) employers must take reasonable measures to prevent and promptly correct any harassing behavior, and (2) employees have a responsibility to take advantage of any preventive or corrective opportunities provided by the employer.

However, this affirmative defense is not always available. If the supervisory harassment resulted in a tangible job detriment, such as demotion or termination, the employer will be vicariously liable for harm caused by the supervisor. Additionally, an employer who merely included an anti-harassment policy in its employment manual, but did not provide sufficient training or an adequate complaint procedure for employees, will not be able to raise a successful affirmative defense. The need for anti-harassment training and a "user-friendly" complaint procedure is essential to effective prevention and correction of harassing conduct.

While the *Faragher/Ellerth* decisions addressed sexual harassment, the standard of liability and the affirmative defense applies to harassing behavior regarding other protected bases, such as race and religion. Therefore, in taking reasonable measures to prevent and correct sexually harassing behavior in the workplace, employers should address other forms of unlawful harassment.

Is the Affirmative Defense Available?

A. Is the alleged harasser a "supervisor"?
Does the alleged harasser have immediate or successively higher authority over the employee?

> **If "no"** → **affirmative defense is not available**
> **If "yes"** → **then continue . . .**

B. Did the harassment culminate in a "tangible employment action"?
  1. Did the employee suffer a "significant change in employment status"? Consider:
    a. Did the supervisor take official action against the employee? e.g.:
      • Was there an official act of the enterprise taken against the employee?
      • Was action taken against the employee that was documented in official company records?
      • Was action taken against the employee that was subject to review by higher level supervisors?
      • Was action taken against the employee that required formal approval of the enterprise?
    b. Did the supervisor's actions against the employee inflict direct economic harm?
    c. Examples of "tangible job action" include:
      • Hiring and firing
      • Failure to promote
      • Demotion
      • Undesirable reassignment
      • Decision causing significant change in benefits

> **If "yes"** → **affirmative defense is not available**
> **If "no"** → **affirmative defense is available**

C. First Prong of the Affirmative Defense: Did the employer exercise reasonable care to prevent and promptly correct harassment?
  1. Did the employer establish, publicize, and enforce an effective anti-harassment policy and complaint procedure?
    a. Did the policy clearly explain what conduct would be prohibited?
    b. Did the policy state that the employer would address harassment before it rises to the level of a violation of federal law?
    c. Did the policy make clear that employees are protected against retaliation in reporting or providing information related to harassment complaints?
    d. Did the policy outline an effective complaint process? Consider:
      1) Did the procedure provide accessible points of contact for the initial complaint, rather than requiring employees to complain first to their supervisors?
      2) Did the procedure designate at least one official outside an employee's chain of command to take complaints of harassment?

3) Did the policy contain information about the time frames for filing charges of unlawful harassment with the EEOC or state fair employment practice agencies?

e. Did the policy clearly state that the employer will protect the confidentiality of harassment allegations to the extent possible?

f. Did the employer create an effective investigative process? Consider:

1) Will the employer promptly determine whether a detailed fact-finding investigation is necessary?

2) If necessary, will the fact-finding investigation be launched immediately?

3) If necessary, will the employer undertake intermediate measures before completing the investigation to ensure that further harassment does not occur?

4) Will the employer ensure that the individual who conducts the investigation will objectively gather and consider the relevant facts?

g. Did the policy assure that immediate and appropriate corrective action would be taken? In determining appropriate remedial measures:

1) Balance competing concerns by taking disciplinary action that is proportional to the seriousness of the offense

2) Do not penalize the complainant (e.g., transferring complainant against his or her will)

3) Take steps that are designed to stop the harassment, such as:
    a) Oral or written warning or reprimand
    b) Transfer or reassignment of harasser
    c) Demotion
    d) Reduction of wages
    e) Suspension
    f) Discharge
    g) Training or counseling of harasser
    h) Monitoring of harasser to ensure that harassment does not recur

4) Take steps to correct the effects of harassment on the employee, such as
    a) Restoration of leave taken because of the harassment
    b) Expungement of negative evaluations in employee's personnel file that arose from the harassment
    c) Reinstatement
    d) Apology from harasser
    e) Monitoring treatment of employee

h. If feasible, did the employer provide training to all employees to ensure their understanding of their rights and responsibilities?

2. Did the employer take other preventive and corrective measures?

a. Did the employer provide training to supervisors and managers to ensure that they understand their responsibilities under the employer's anti-harassment policy and complaint procedure?

b. Did the employer correct harassment regardless of whether an employee filed an internal complaint? (e.g., eliminating graffiti, addressing observed unwelcome conduct in violation of anti-harassment policy)

    c. Did the employer keep track of supervisory conduct to ensure compliance with the anti-harassment policy and complaint procedure?

    d. Did the employer keep records of all complaints of harassment?

> **If "no"**   →   **affirmative defense is not available**
>
> **If "yes"**   →   **then continue . . .**

D. Second prong of affirmative defense: Did the employee exercise reasonable care?

  1. Did the employee file a complaint?

> **If "yes"**   →   **did the employee:**

    a. Fail to provide information to support his or her allegation?

    b. Give untruthful information?

    c. Otherwise fail to cooperate in the investigation?

> **If yes**   →   **affirmative defense is not defeated by the complaint**

    d. Did the employee unreasonably delay in making a complaint?

> **If "yes"**   →   **employer may use affirmative defense to reduce damages**
>
> **If "no"**   →   **was the employee's failure to complain unreasonable?**

If the employer can carry its burden to prove that the employee's failure to complain was unreasonable, the affirmative defense will be successful.

Consider:

    a. Did the employee un*reasonably* fear retaliation?

    b. Did the employee *unreasonably* perceive obstacles to complaints, such as undue expense, inaccessible points of contact for making complaints, etc.?

    c. Did the employee un*reasonably* believe that the complaint process was ineffective?

QUESTIONS AND ANSWERS FOR SMALL EMPLOYERS ON EMPLOYER LIABILITY FOR HARASSMENT BY SUPERVISORS

THE U.S. EQUAL EMPLOYMENT OPPORTUNITY COMMISSION

In addition to Prof. Dosanjh, The EEOC also found it useful to articulate specific guidelines for employers. These guidelines for employers and suggested questions for complainants and alleged harassers codify the safe harbor exceptions outlined in the cases.

Title VII of the Civil Rights Act (Title VII) prohibits harassment of an employee based on race, color, sex, religion, or national origin. The Age Discrimination in Employment Act (ADEA) prohibits harassment of employees who are 40 or older on the basis of age, and the Americans with Disabilities Act (ADA) prohibits harassment based on disability. All of the anti-discrimination statutes enforced by the EEOC prohibit *retaliation* for complaining of discrimination or participating in complaint proceedings.

The Supreme Court issued two major decisions in June of 1998 that explained when employers will be held legally responsible for unlawful harassment by supervisors. The EEOC's *Guidance on Employer Liability for Harassment by Supervisors* examines those decisions and provides practical guidance regarding the duty of employers to prevent and correct harassment and the duty of employees to avoid harassment by using their employers' complaint procedures.

1. When does harassment violate federal law?

- Harassment violates federal law if it involves discriminatory treatment based on race, color, sex (with or without sexual conduct), religion, national origin, age, disability, or because the employee opposed job discrimination or participated in an investigation or complaint proceeding under the EEO statutes. Federal law does not prohibit simple teasing, offhand comments, or isolated incidents that are not extremely serious. The conduct must be sufficiently frequent or severe to create a hostile work environment or result in a "tangible employment action," such as hiring, firing, promotion, or demotion.

"Questions and Answers for Small Employers on Employer Liability for Harassment by Supervisors," by the U.S. Equal Employment Opportunity Commission (2000).

2.   Does the guidance apply *only to sexual harassment?*

• No, it applies to *all* types of unlawful harassment.

3.   When is an employer legally responsible for harassment by a supervisor?

• An employer is always responsible for harassment by a supervisor that culminated in a tangible employment action. If the harassment did not lead to a tangible employment action, the employer is liable unless it proves that: 1) it exercised reasonable care to prevent and promptly correct any harassment; *and* 2) the employee unreasonably failed to complain to management or to avoid harm otherwise.

4.   Who qualifies as a "supervisor" for purposes of employer liability?

• An individual qualifies as an employee's supervisor if the individual has the authority to recommend tangible employment decisions affecting the employee *or* if the individual has the authority to direct the employee's daily work activities.

5.   What is a "tangible employment action"?

• A "tangible employment action" means a significant change in employment status. Examples include hiring, firing, promotion, demotion, undesirable reassignment, a decision causing a significant change in benefits, compensation decisions, and work assignment.

6.   How might harassment culminate in a tangible employment action?

• This might occur if a supervisor fires or demotes a subordinate because she rejects his sexual demands, or promotes her because she submits to his sexual demands.

7.   What should employers do to *prevent and correct harassment?*

• Employers should establish, distribute to all employees, and enforce a policy prohibiting harassment and setting out a procedure for making complaints. In most cases, the policy and procedure should be in writing.

• Small businesses may be able to discharge their responsibility to prevent and correct harassment through less formal means. For example, if a business is sufficiently small that the owner maintains regular contact with all employees, the owner can tell the employees at staff meetings that harassment is prohibited, that employees should report such conduct promptly, and that a complaint can be brought "straight to the top." If the business conducts a prompt, thorough, and impartial investigation of any complaint that arises and undertakes swift and appropriate corrective action, it will have fulfilled its responsibility to "effectively prevent and correct harassment."

8.   What should an anti-harassment *policy* say?

• An employer's anti-harassment policy should make clear that the employer will not tolerate harassment based on race, sex, religion, national origin, age, or disability, or harassment based on opposition to discrimination or participation in complaint proceedings. The policy should also state that the employer will not tolerate retaliation against anyone who complains of harassment or who participates in an investigation.

9. What are important *elements of a complaint procedure?*

- The employer should encourage employees to report harassment to management before it becomes severe or pervasive.

- The employer should designate more than one individual to take complaints, and should ensure that these individuals are in accessible locations. The employer also should instruct all of its supervisors to report complaints of harassment to appropriate officials.

- The employer should assure employees that it will protect the confidentiality of harassment complaints to the extent possible.

10. Is a complaint procedure adequate if employees are instructed to report harassment to their immediate supervisors?

- No, because the supervisor may be the one committing harassment or may not be impartial. It is advisable for an employer to designate at least one official outside an employee's chain of command to take complaints, to assure that the complaint will be handled impartially.

11. How should an employer *investigate* a harassment complaint?

- An employer should conduct a prompt, thorough, and impartial investigation. The alleged harasser should not have any direct or indirect control over the investigation.

- The investigator should interview the employee who complained of harassment, the alleged harasser, and others who could reasonably be expected to have relevant information. The *Guidance* provides examples of specific questions that may be appropriate to ask.

- Before completing the investigation, the employer should take steps to make sure that harassment does not continue. If the parties have to be separated, then the separation should not burden the employee who has complained of harassment. An involuntary transfer of the complainant could constitute unlawful retaliation. Other examples of interim measures are making scheduling changes to avoid contact between the parties or placing the alleged harasser on non-disciplinary leave with pay pending the conclusion of the investigation.

12. How should an employer *correct harassment?*

- If an employer determines that harassment occurred, it should take immediate measures to stop the harassment and ensure that it does not recur. Disciplinary measures should be proportional to the seriousness of the offense. The employer also should correct the effects of the harassment by, for example, restoring leave taken because of the harassment and expunging negative evaluations in the employee's personnel file that arose from the harassment.

13. Are there *other measures* that employers should take to prevent and correct harassment?

- An employer should correct harassment that is clearly unwelcome regardless of whether a complaint is filed. For example, if there is graffiti in the workplace containing racial or sexual epithets, management should not wait for a complaint before erasing it.

- An employer should ensure that its supervisors and managers understand their responsibilities under the organization's anti-harassment policy and complaint procedures.

- An employer should screen applicants for supervisory jobs to see if they have a history of engaging in harassment. If so, and the employer hires such a candidate, it must take steps to monitor actions taken by that individual in order to prevent harassment.

- An employer should keep records of harassment complaints and check those records when a complaint of harassment is made to reveal any patterns of harassment by the same individuals.

14. Does an employee who is harassed by his or her supervisor have any *responsibilities?*

- Yes. The employee must take reasonable steps to avoid harm from the harassment. Usually, the employee will exercise this responsibility by using the employer's complaint procedure.

15. Is an employer legally responsible for its supervisor's harassment if the *employee failed to use* the employer's complaint procedure?

- No, unless the harassment resulted in a tangible employment action or unless it was reasonable for the employee not to complain to management. An employee's failure to complain would be reasonable, for example, if he or she had a legitimate fear of retaliation. The employer must prove that the employee acted unreasonably.

16. If an employee complains to management about harassment, should he or she wait for management to complete the investigation before *filing a charge* with EEOC?

- It may make sense to wait to see if management corrects the harassment before filing a charge. However, if management does not act promptly to investigate the complaint and undertake corrective action, then it may be appropriate to file a charge. The deadline for filing an EEOC charge is either 180 or 300 days after the last date of alleged harassment, depending on the state in which the allegation arises. *This deadline is not extended because of an employer's internal investigation of the complaint.*

***

SECTION I. QUESTIONS TO ASK PARTIES AND WITNESSES

When detailed fact-finding is necessary, the investigator should interview the complainant, the alleged harasser, and third parties who could reasonably be expected to have relevant information. Information relating to the personal lives of the parties outside the workplace would be relevant only in unusual circumstances. When interviewing the parties and witnesses, the investigator should refrain from offering his or her opinion.

The following are examples of questions that may be appropriate to ask the parties and potential witnesses. Any actual investigation must be tailored to the particular facts.

Questions to Ask the Complainant

- Who, what, when, where, and how: Who committed the alleged harassment? What exactly occurred or was said? When did it occur and is it still ongoing? Where did it occur? How often did it occur? How did it affect you?

- How did you react? What response did you make when the incident(s) occurred or afterwards?

- How did the harassment affect you? Has your job been affected in any way?

- Are there any persons who have relevant information? Was anyone present when the alleged harassment occurred? Did you tell anyone about it? Did anyone see you immediately after episodes of alleged harassment?

- Did the person who harassed you harass anyone else? Do you know whether anyone complained about harassment by that person?

- Are there any notes, physical evidence, or other documentation regarding the incident(s)?

- How would you like to see the situation resolved?

- Do you know of any other relevant information?

Questions to Ask the Alleged Harasser

- What is your response to the allegations?

- If the harasser claims that the allegations are false, ask why the complainant might lie.

- Are there any persons who have relevant information?

- Are there any notes, physical evidence, or other documentation regarding the incident(s)?

- Do you know of any other relevant information?

Questions to Ask Third Parties

- What did you see or hear? When did this occur? Describe the alleged harasser's behavior toward the complainant and toward others in the workplace.

- What did the complainant tell you? When did s/he tell you this?

- Do you know of any other relevant information?

- Are there other persons who have relevant information?

SECTION II. CREDIBILITY DETERMINATIONS

If there are conflicting versions of relevant events, the employer will have to weigh each party's credibility. Credibility assessments can be critical in determining whether the alleged harassment in fact occurred. Factors to consider include:

- Inherent plausibility: Is the testimony believable on its face? Does it make sense?

- Demeanor: Did the person seem to be telling the truth or lying?

- Motive to falsify: Did the person have a reason to lie?

- Corroboration: Is there witness testimony (such as testimony by eye-witnesses, people who saw the person soon after the alleged incidents, or people who discussed the incidents with him or her at or around the time that they occurred) or physical evidence (such as written documentation) that corroborates the party's testimony?

- Past record: Did the alleged harasser have a history of similar behavior in the past?

None of the above factors are determinative as to credibility. For example, the fact that there are no eye-witnesses to the alleged harassment by no means necessarily defeats the complainant's credibility, since harassment often occurs behind closed doors. Furthermore, the fact that the alleged harasser engaged in similar behavior in the past does not necessarily mean that he or she did so again.

TOPIC STUDY: DRUG TESTING

ISSUES IN DRUG TESTING FOR THE PRIVATE SECTOR

GEORGE R. GRAY AND DARREL R. BROWN

Gray identifies some of the key issues related to drug testing for the private sector.

A recent survey of Fortune 500 companies on the use of workplace drug testing indicates that illegal drug use among employees remains a serious concern for employers.

Eighty-eight percent of the responding companies currently conduct drug testing of applicants as part of the preemployment physical examination. Of the companies that did not conduct drug tests, 80 percent indicated that they have plans to begin applicant testing.

Virtually all employers conducting applicant testing indicated that the tests were administered during the final stages of processing. When questioned on what actions the company took when an applicant tested positive, all employers responded that they did not hire the individual, although many volunteered that they would consider the applicant after a period ranging from 30 days to one year. Only one company mentioned that they would retest at the applicant's expense. No companies suggested the options of conducting a second test or using a more accurate type of test.

The survey found that 60 percent of companies test current employees, and a majority of those firms (75 percent) conduct those tests for cases of suspected abuse. Twenty-one percent said they conduct routine, periodic tests of all employees in sensitive positions, and 8 percent test randomly among workers in sensitive positions. Another 8 percent of employers said they conduct routine, periodic tests for all employees.

When a current employee tests positive, the most frequent course of action taken by companies involves referral to an employee assistance program. Retesting, testing after rehabilitation, termination and other disciplinary actions were mentioned less frequently. The practice, however, clearly varies with the sensitivity of the position in relation to security and the safety of other individuals.

ISSUES OF CONCERN

Right to privacy: Despite the fact that the constitutional right to privacy does not apply to private-sector employment, many people feel strongly that drug testing is too "invasive" and violates an important right. This is probably the primary impetus behind local and state legislative efforts to ban drug testing among current employees. San Francisco, for example, has barred employers from ordering urinalysis and other tests on current employees unless "clear evidence" exists that the worker's drug use endangers others. Some observers have predicted that other cities—even some states—could restrict or prohibit random testing of current employees, except when safety is the issue.

Although such proposals have been introduced in several states, these legislatures have not yet adopted them as laws. Employers convinced of the need for testing should consider taking a more active role in their area when such legislation is proposed. This could include employee education, public awareness campaigns and testimony before legislative bodies.

Testing error: Much has been written about the validity and reliability of tests, the debate over broad-spectrum versus narrow-spectrum tests and incompetent testing laboratories.

Drug-testing laboratories, however, may be the weakest link in the system since these companies operate in an unregulated environment. The proliferation of new firms, many lacking in expertise and often overloaded by the increase in corporate drug testing, add to the problem. A Centers for Disease Control study of 13 laboratories, for example, reported in 1988 that error rates up to 66 percent were found. The report concluded that none of the labs studied were reliable. It is in every employer's interest to work for testing standards, to insist that certain quality standards be adhered to by laboratories working for them, and to make sure those standards are met.

Testing costs: The most commonly used screening tests are relatively inexpensive, reportedly on the order of $5 per sample. High error rates, however, have led toxicologists to recommend confirmatory testing for all positive samples. Such tests are more sophisticated to ensure greater accuracy and, in turn, can cost about $90. For a large corporation with a lot of testing activity, this becomes truly expensive. For small employers, such testing may seem prohibitive.

Employee morale: Testing current employees seems to promote a statement that employers do not trust their workers to behave responsibly regarding drug use. Although such perceptions cannot be avoided totally, careful education efforts about the need for testing can help prepare workers for a new program. A program directed toward sensitive positions or departments, tailored to a company's specific problems, and carefully designed to avoid communicating a feeling of mistrust among all employees appears to be a company's best approach in drug testing.

IS EMPLOYEE DRUG TESTING THE ANSWER?

THOMAS GOLLOT, MARK COHEN, AND ERIC FILLMAN

Gollot, Cohen, and Fillman debate the appropriateness of drug testing in the workplace.

POINT
BY THOMAS A. GOLLOT

Everyone seems to be in agreement that we have a drug problem in America and we need to do something about it. But people disagree on solutions for this national crisis. Some are choosing to confront the problem through drug testing.

Drug testing is a means of identifying the user and scaring the naive experimenter into staying straight. Drug testing is not a solution to the drug problem, but it does give the nation a better handle on it.

Those opposed to drug testing have voiced four primary objections: inaccuracy of the tests, inconvenience and possible violations of privacy, fear of job loss on detection and the overall cost.

Two things are important concerning these arguments: the integrity of the laboratory and the employer. Laboratory integrity is easier to monitor than employers' integrity but there are proper procedures for checking both. The percentage of misdiagnoses caused by human error is minimal compared to the benefits of drug testing. Most employers are ethical. They care about their employees and want to prevent drug addiction. In addition, training new labor costs the company more money than rehabilitation.

It is an inconvenience to submit to a drug test. Nobody likes to give urine specimens. It's aggravating. My employees at Gollot and Sons Transfer and Storage Co. must submit to drug testing if they want to work for my company—or any other trucking company. Starting Dec. 21, drug testing will be required by the U.S. Department of Transportation for the trucking industry, regardless of the size of the carrier. It's too bad that people have to be inconvenienced like this.

It's also too bad that more than 80 percent of the people serving time in state prisons are there because of drug-related crimes. Maybe if they had been inconvenienced by a drug test, they wouldn't be where they are now.

As far as invasion of privacy is concerned, it's a weak excuse. Urine samples can be collected and validated without direct observation. An inexpensive dye can be used to confirm that the sample is genuine, temperature checks can be made of urine samples and "specific gravity" analysis and other methods can ensure validity while maintaining privacy. The

---

fear of observation or undignified positioning while urinating should not be given as a reason to avoid drug testing.

Testing can be a legitimate concern for people who abuse illegal drugs. Their fears of detection and job loss are what deter drug use. But states also must mandate rehabilitation programs for drug-addicted workers. Drug users are not going to submit to treatment unless it's mandatory.

The initial drug screening of an employee costs about $20. A more detailed identification of drug substance costs more. For example, the Gas Chromatography and Mass Spectrophotometry tests cost more than $70 a person. The Baumgartner chronological hair sampling test costs about $30 per substance identified.

Yes, testing costs money. But we can afford the cost. What we can't afford is the continued drain and waste of the nation's talent and the weakening and corruption of people.

I have introduced legislation in the Mississippi Senate that would require all elected and appointed state officials to submit to a drug test. Government leaders need to show leadership. We represent the public's trust and we have a responsibility that goes with that trust.

We don't want government officials who might be abusing drugs making policy decisions, just as we do not want to be on an airplane with a pilot tampering with drugs. The Federal Aviation Agency has mandated regular random drug checks for all commercial pilots. State governments should follow the FAA's lead.

In addition, the U.S. Air Force requires random drug testing for all military personnel. The FBI also requires that all agents be routinely tested for drug use. As one agent said, "I wouldn't want my life to depend on an agent on drugs."

We need to make drug testing mandatory for public officials, not only to set an example, but because it makes sense.

COUNTERPOINT
BY MARK B. COHEN AND ERIC S. FILLMAN

Drug use is a great threat to the health of millions of Americans, and the crime that drug use generates is a threat to millions more.

That is why in our battle against drugs we must not subject innocent lives to further risks. The danger with drug testing is that, without appropriate safeguards, it can become a means of harassment and a series of booby traps for non-drug-using workers.

If it leads to the firing, instead of the rehabilitation, of an occasional drug user, it can push that person deeper into the drug culture.

Legislators should examine not only the goals behind drug testing, but how these programs actually function.

This topic was studied in-depth by the Pennsylvania House Labor Relations Committee before legislation was introduced requiring companies using drug testing to offer employee assistance programs, more rigorous confirmation tests and opportunities for workers to reform themselves.

At one public hearing, James Moran, executive director for the Philadelphia Project on Occupational Safety and Health, graphically depicted the scene of a worker in a bathroom stall and the physical, undignified stance she had to position herself in to give a urine sample while being observed for security reasons. "Suppose this was your mother," Moran asked.

Attempting to verify drug use by way of blind, random, arbitrary testing of individuals without some standard of probable or just cause can damage the fabric of workplace dignity and morale. A constructive alternative lies in testing only under circumstances where there is a reasonably articulable suspicion of intoxication causing impaired ability to perform normal duties.

Testing in this manner will help ensure that the innocent worker is not unjustly forced through the indignity of drug testing at the whim of a supervisor.

Employee assistance programs designed to meet the unique needs of specific businesses and employees must serve as functional, integrated parts of the workplace. If employers intend to test for drug use, they should be adequately prepared for the results of such tests and use such results in a socially responsible manner.

Failing their initiative to do so, legislatures have a responsibility to regulate this practice to guarantee the proper use of such testing and the availability of counseling and treatment programs for those who need them.

We all must remember that drug abuse is a health and social problem, not just a police problem. Employers genuinely interested in combating the drug problems of the workplace have the responsibility to make a sincere effort to help troubled employees.

The continued success and proliferation of employee assistance programs in recent years suggest that such programs respond to the true needs of employers and chemically dependent persons alike.

Training new employees is costly. Employers should not pursue the wasteful approach of discharging employees in their efforts to combat drug abuse in the workplace. Health professionals have long recognized that job security is positively related to treatment of chemically dependent persons.

The ultimate goal of employers should be to prevent further drug use, not to reinforce its abuse by adding reasons for an employee to turn to drugs, such as the loss of a job.

Firing otherwise productive workers on the basis of drug tests is not a satisfactory answer to the problem of drug abuse in the workplace.

As far as legal remedies are concerned, constitutional attacks on drug testing speak only to public employers, not private employers. But privacy is compromised with involuntary testing, regardless of the nature of employment.

Urine samples contain a vast amount of personal information to which an individual has a legitimate expectation of privacy. In addition to detecting drugs, urine can identify an employee's medical history, including such conditions as venereal disease, epilepsy and schizophrenia, as well as an employee's susceptibility to diseases such as heart attacks and sickle cell anemia.

The implications of obtaining such information from a urine bottle are staggering. Employers possess a great, unchecked potential to weed out employees unjustly on the basis of health risks completely dissociated with job responsibilities. Again, proper regulation will ensure that injustices like this do not occur on the basis of the limited technology used by employers.

The limited technology of today does not do what employers need it to do: establish or verify worker impairment.

ACS HERBAL TEA COMPANY MATERIALS

The following material is taken from the World Wide Web site of ACS Herbal Tea Company and is designed to assist individuals in avoiding detection of drugs during standard drug tests. The first question for readers is truly whether it is appropriate to even include this material in this volume. Perhaps it is unethical to broadcast this information, even when it is readily available on the Internet. On the other hand, if you believe that testing employees for drug use is not ethical, then is avoiding detection justified?

With all the pressures of society to drug test everyone, we offer a complete line of products designed to detoxify you from all the bad pollutants and toxins in today's world (he he he).

We also offer information about passing drug tests and ways to solve the problem of drug testing in today's workplace. Guaranteed negative results or we'll refund your money. Getting you clean and helping you pass drug tests is our main business.

We are committed to providing our Customer's with the Highest Quality Drug Testing Detox Products available. Each of our drug testing products are designed for a specific purpose or for specific time constraints. Each does its job with great reliability, each is over 99.9% effective!

WHEN EVERYTHING IS RIDING ON THIS TEST, ONLY USE THE BEST!

Herbal Cleansing Shampoo

This Product is used for the Hair Follicle Drug Test. About 9% of all drug testing is done by examining the hair shaft. BioCleanse shampoo will completely eliminate the toxins from the inner part of the hair shaft or cutical area. When doing this product you will experience a warm tingling sensation. When this happens the product is penetrating deep into the hair shaft and dissolving the toxins, to be rinsed away. Two 30 minute treatments the day before and two 30 minute treatments the day of and your hair is truly "clean."

ACS Herbal Tea Co.'s Herbal Cleansing Shampoo! BioCleanse is a remarkable Product! Only $29.95

***

ACS Herbal Tea Company materials reprinted with permission of ACS Herbal Tea Company, *www.123zip.com.*

Randomizer

Our Randomizer completely Eliminates or Destroys all toxins in a urine sample. Just pour contents of the vial in your specimen cup and then add urine to sample. All Toxins will be eliminated in 10–15 seconds, even THC metabolites. Frequent smokers may need to use 2 bottles. 99.9% Effective

Our competitors' products of this kind are made in crystal form, which is very difficult to mix. Our product is a Liquid, which mixes immediately. No Waiting, No mixing.

Only $24.95 per bottle

***

Testimonials from Some of Our Customers

From: G & C
subject: This stuff works!!!!!!!!!!!!!

Just wanted to thank you for your product. This stuff WORKS! I just tested negative and four days ago I was positive. The product WORKS, the home tests WORK!!!! I would recommend it to anyone. I can't tell you how HAPPY I am with these results.
Follow the directions and you will see the results. I highly recommend the home test, it is the best peace of mind you will ever experience! Thank you again!!!!!!!

***

from: elmo
subject: you can use my name

hey that Maxout is ruff . . . but it did what you said it would do. If it can clean me out it will work for anyone. 2 of my friends are using it now . . . we will see how it works on them.

Bud Bradley

TOPIC STUDY: COMPENSATION— COMPARABLE WORTH

THE QUESTION OF WAGES

Ruth Rosenbaum, TC, Ph.D.

In discussing employee compensation, the question of wage levels often goes beyond the "going rate" to a concern for whether the "going rate" is where it should be. Is this the ethical wage to be paying a worker? Rosenbaum provides some definitional context for the discussion below.

In the United States at this time many city governments are considering a requirement that companies that do business with the government pay a "living wage." The federal government and some state governments have recently enacted legislation to raise the "minimum wage." Union leaders call for "just wages." Persons who have moved from receiving federal or state assistance into low-paying jobs sometimes talk about "slave wages." Middle and upper-level management personnel who have been laid off face big "reductions" in their salaries, or wages. The media carries reports of scandalous conditions of sweatshops worldwide. Truly, work and the financial remuneration for that work are central to people's lives and are in the forefront of the difficulties of the world's globalized economy.

In addressing this issue, the Center for Reflection, Education and Action (CREA) uses a set of working definitions of wage levels that describes the purchasing power that workers are able to earn. Awareness of these levels can assist in discussions and decisions about wages. While many higher wage levels exist, CREA has found that the following terminology and definitions are the most helpful in discussions.

Level 1: Marginal Survival Wage. This wage level does not provide for adequate nutritional needs. Starvation is prevented, but malnutrition, illnesses, and early deaths are the result.

Level 2: Basic Survival Wage. This wage level allows for meeting immediate survival needs, including basic food, used clothing, minimal shelter, and fuel for cooking.

Level 3: Short Range Planning Wage. This level meets basic survival needs, and in addition provides the possibility of a small amount of discretionary income.

Such income allows for minimal planning beyond living from paycheck to paycheck. It allows for occasional purchase of needed item(s) as small amounts can be set aside after meeting basic survival needs.

Level 4: Sustainable Living Wage. This wage level meets basic needs including food, clothing, housing, energy, transportation, healthcare and education. It provides sufficient money to enable participation in culturally required activities (including celebrations of births, weddings, funerals, and related activities.)

Level 5: Sustainable Community Wage. This level provides enough discretionary income to allow the workers to support the development of small businesses in a local community, including the support of cultural and civic needs of that community, and preservation of the environment for future generations.

CREA has used another construct set in systemic analysis study groups, and found them to be helpful in considering wages. This set involves looking at wages from the perspective of whether they are legal, ethical, moral, and just.

1. Legal: Legal minimum wage means no more than what companies can pay without violating the law of the country or state. Legal minimum wages are not predicated on nutritional needs, or any other needs workers have on an on-going basis. Often, they are predicated or based on a country's or a region's perceived need to attract businesses. When this happens, workers' wages become a competitive advantage or disadvantage, depending upon one's viewpoint. Corporations seek production sites where wages are kept as low as possible by the legal standards, so that the corporation itself may become more "profitable." We see this reflected in the numerous codes of conduct which individual corporations and industries are producing. These corporate standards assert that what the company is doing is legal, that the company adheres to the minimum wage laws of the countries in which it operates. These corporate standards, communicated to the public as both legal and acceptable, then become normative, despite their negative effects on workers.

2. Ethical: Leaving aside philosophical discussion of the meaning of ethics, it is important to recognize that business ethics, medical ethics, etc., have become colloquially understood as behavior which is acceptable within a particular group. Therefore, business ethics or the ethics within a particular business segment can be understood as industry's self-defined and self-accepted standard of practice. In other words, what the industry says about itself as acceptable practice becomes the accepted public standard. Again, we see this reflected in industry codes of conduct. The ethical standard for workers' wages has become that which keeps the corporation competitive. At the opposite poles of corporate organization, we see CEO salaries increasing at incredible rates while workers at the bottom of the corporate structure are often forced by the system to compete in a race to the bottom. The expression that is used for this industry standard of wages is "the prevailing industry wage/salary."

3. Moral: When we raise moral questions about wages, we are immediately forced to raise the question as to the purpose of wages. From a moral standard, the wages of the workers should reflect the contributions they make to the corporations in which they are employed. Likewise, workers should be able to meet their own needs and the needs of their dependents. It is important in this context to define need not as "bare minimum" but as those

needs which allow the worker and his/her family to be productive, contributing members of their communities.

From a religious perspective, the moral standards regarding wages proceed from the belief that each and all human beings are made in the image and likeness of a divine Creator. Human beings are not to be seen as machines, which need a minimum of fuel and maintenance in order to produce. To be a human being means to be both an individual person and a person in relationship, and therefore the wages earned for the work a person does should reflect the requirements of those relationships. These include significant time to spend with one's family, the need for a workday short enough for people to develop relationships and to serve their communities, wage levels sufficient to allow for the sustainable growth of their communities.

4.   Just: Justice deals with the distribution of the benefits from Earth's resources, or the benefits resulting from the production and sale of products and services by any corporation or business. Justice requires that we raise the issue of the ongoing concentration of wealth throughout the world in the hands of the few within each country, and in the hands of some countries more than others. The unequal concentration of wealth in the hands of a few deprives the vast majority of persons the benefit of those resources.

In both our private and our public conversations about wages, we need to be very careful to use terminology that accurately reflects what we are trying to say and to accomplish. Are we talking about wages that are legal, ethical, moral or just? How does it make a difference? Within faith communities, is not part of our role to raise questions/initiate conversation regarding corporate responsibility and wages that moves from standards of legality and corporate ethics to the standards of moral and just wages?

Considering these various levels and constructs helps us to identify our own experiences of money and wages, and to examine more critically the wage levels that exist in our own and in other parts of the world. We are led to ask: Who determines these wage levels? How? On what authority? Why? What is the source of the mind-set that it is acceptable for some groups of people to be given wages for their work that keeps them and their families at the lowest levels, even when their work is the groundwork for an enterprise? What cultural and societal values and standards are operative? Who sets and enforces these standards? On what authority? How? Why?

Examining questions such as these helps us to look deeper into the underlying systemic causes of the injustices in our economic system and opens us up to creative ways of acting for a more just world. Indeed, they force us to examine our own attitudes, values, and standards, and to try to understand where they came from, and to name them in honesty and humility. CREA has found that it is the persons on the bottom, those far from the sources of power, who can raise the most perceptive questions, and provoke the sharpest analysis. Listening to their experiences and their analysis may not be comfortable, but it will help fill in our own gaps of knowledge, bring us closer to truth, and our world closer to justice.

AMERICAN NURSES ASSOCIATION V. STATE OF ILLINOIS

The following Seventh Circuit decision is one of the few written court decisions to specifically address comparable worth. In this case, a nurses association brought a claim for discrimination in the wages of its members, claiming that they were underpaid because they were in traditionally female-dominated positions. Judge Posner (a University of Chicago professor and free market advocate) held that no cause of action exists on a comparable worth theory. Posner refuses to apply comparable worth theory because he says that "it is not the sort that judges are well equipped to resolve intelligently." Do you agree? Who would be better equipped than a judge who can sit and hear all of the facts? Are you persuaded by comparable worth theory?

. . . POSNER, Circuit Judge.

This class action charges the State of Illinois with sex discrimination in employment, in violation of Title VII of the Civil Rights Act of 1964, and the equal protection clause of the Fourteenth Amendment. The named plaintiffs are two associations of nurses plus 21 individuals, mostly but not entirely female who work for the state in jobs such as nursing and typing that are filled primarily by women. The suit is on behalf of all state employees in these job classifications. . . . [T]he [plaintiffs] charge that the state pays workers in predominantly male job classifications a higher wage not justified by any difference in the relative worth of the predominantly male and the predominantly female jobs in the state's roster. . . .

Comparable worth is not a legal concept, but a shorthand expression for the movement to raise the ratio of wages in traditionally women's jobs to wages in traditionally men's jobs. Its premises are both historical and cognitive. The historical premise is that a society politically and culturally dominated by men steered women into certain jobs and kept the wages in those jobs below what the jobs were worth, precisely because most of the holders were women. The cognitive premise is that analytical techniques exist for determining the relative worth of jobs that involve different levels of skill, effort, risk, responsibility, etc. These premises are vigorously disputed on both theoretical and empirical grounds. Economists point out that unless employers forbid women to compete for the higher-paying, traditionally men's jobs—which would violate federal law—women will switch into those jobs until the only difference in wages between traditionally women's jobs and traditionally men's jobs will be that necessary to equate the supply of workers in each type of job to the demand. Economists have conducted studies which show that virtually the entire difference

American Nurses Association v. State of Illinois, 783 F.2d 716 (7th Cir. 1986).

in the average hourly wage of men and women, including that due to the fact that men and women tend to be concentrated in different types of job, can be explained by the fact that most women take considerable time out of the labor force in order to take care of their children. As a result they tend to invest less in their "human capital" (earning capacity); and since part of any wage is a return on human capital, they tend therefore to be found in jobs that pay less. Consistently with this hypothesis, the studies find that women who have never married earn as much as men who have never married. To all this the advocates of comparable worth reply that although there are no longer explicit barriers to women's entering traditionally men's jobs, cultural and psychological barriers remain as a result of which many though not all women internalize men's expectations regarding jobs appropriate for women and therefore invest less in their human capital.

On the cognitive question economists point out that the ratio of wages in different jobs is determined by the market rather than by any a priori conception of relative merit, in just the same way that the ratio of the price of caviar to the price of cabbage is determined by relative scarcity rather than relative importance to human welfare. Upsetting the market equilibrium by imposing such a conception would have costly consequences, some of which might undercut the ultimate goals of the comparable worth movement. If the movement should cause wages in traditionally men's jobs to be depressed below their market level and wages in traditionally women's jobs to be jacked above their market level, women will have less incentive to enter traditionally men's fields and more to enter traditionally women's fields. Analysis cannot stop there, because the change in relative wages will send men in the same direction: fewer men will enter the traditionally men's jobs, more the traditionally women's jobs. As a result there will be more room for women in traditionally men's jobs and at the same time fewer opportunities for women in traditionally women's jobs—especially since the number of those jobs will shrink as employers are induced by the higher wage to substitute capital for labor inputs (e.g., more word processors, fewer secretaries). Labor will be allocated less efficiently; men and women alike may be made worse off.

Against this the advocates of comparable worth urge that collective bargaining, public regulation of wages and hours, and the lack of information and mobility of some workers make the market model an inaccurate description of how relative wages are determined and how they influence the choice of jobs. The point has particular force when applied to a public employer such as the State of Illinois, which does not have the same incentives that a private firm would have to use labor efficiently.

[1] It should be clear from this brief summary that the issue of comparable worth . . . is not of the sort that judges are well equipped to resolve intelligently or that we should lightly assume has been given to us to resolve by Title VII or the Constitution. An employer (private or public) that simply pays the going wage in each of the different types of job in its establishment, and makes no effort to discourage women from applying for particular jobs or to steer them toward particular jobs, would be justifiably surprised to discover that it may be violating federal law because each wage rate and therefore the ratio between them have been found to be determined by cultural or psychological factors attributable to the history of male domination of society; that it has to hire a consultant to find out how it must, regardless of market conditions, change the wages it pays, in order to achieve equity between traditionally male and traditionally female jobs; and that it must pay backpay, to boot. We need not tarry over the question of law presented by this example because as we un-

derstand the plaintiffs' position it is not that a mere failure to rectify traditional wage disparities between predominantly male and predominantly female jobs violates federal law. The circuits that have considered this contention have rejected it; see the *AFSCME* case discussed below; we shall see shortly that this rejection may be compelled by the Supreme Court's decisions in the *Davis* and *Feeney* cases.

The next question is whether a failure to achieve comparable worth—granted that it would not itself be a violation of law—might permit an inference of deliberate and therefore unlawful discrimination, as distinct from passive acceptance of a market-determined disparity in wages. The starting point for analyzing this question must be *County of Washington v. Gunther.* Women employed to guard female prisoners were paid less than men employed to guard male prisoners. Since male prison inmates are more dangerous than female ones and since each male guard on average guarded ten times as many prisoners as each female guard, the jobs were not the same. Therefore, paying the male guards more could not violate the Equal Pay Act of 1963, which requires equal pay only for equal work. The issue was whether it could violate Title VII, and the Court held that it could. A comparable worth study figured in this conclusion. The plaintiffs had alleged (and the allegation had to be taken as true for purposes of appeal, because the complaint had been dismissed, as in this case, for failure to state a claim) that the county had conducted a comparable worth study and had determined that female guards should be paid 95 percent of what male guards were paid; that it had then decided to pay them only 70 percent; "and that the failure of the county to pay [the plaintiffs] the full evaluated worth of their jobs can be proved to be attributable to intentional sex discrimination. Thus, [the plaintiffs'] suit does not require a court to make its own subjective assessment of the value of the male and female guard jobs, or to attempt by statistical technique or other method to quantify the effects of sex discrimination on the wage rates." . . .

The *AFSCME* case resembles our hypothetical case of the firm accused of sex discrimination merely because it pays market wages. *AFSCME* shows that such a case is not actionable under Title VII even if the employer is made aware that its pattern of wages departs from the principle of comparable worth to the disadvantage of women (plus the occasional male occupant of a traditionally woman's job) and even if the employer is not so much a prisoner of the market that it cannot alter its wages in the direction of comparable worth, as eventually the State of Washington did. The critical thing lacking in *AFSCME* was evidence that the state decided not to raise the wages of particular workers *because* most of those workers were female. Without such evidence, to infer a violation of Title VII from the fact that the state had conducted a comparable worth study would, again, just discourage such studies.

. . . The plaintiffs can get no mileage out of casting a comparable worth case as an equal protection case. . . . [T]he equal protection clause is violated only by intentional discrimination; the fact that a law or official practice adopted for a lawful purpose has a racially differential impact is not enough.

IS PAY EQUITY
EQUITABLE?

LAURA B. PINCUS AND NICHOLAS J. MATHYS

In the following article, Mathys and I argue that a simplistic evalua-tion of pay equity does not consider the intrinsic rewards offered by some positions. These rewards might include greater autonomy, flex-ibility, different work tasks, or others. When these intrinsic rewards are coupled with the salary paid in those positions, perhaps the com-pensation is similar to a higher-paying job with fewer intrinsic re-wards.

. . . Much has been written about the disparity in wages between men and women. The fa-miliar phrase, "70 cents on the dollar" has been repeated as the basic comparison between the value of women in employment to that of men.[1] However, though allegedly slightly higher today than at the time of its first calculation, it is the contention of these authors that this figure overstates the compensation disparity which exists between male and female workers. Furthermore, the extent of that disparity has been greatly exaggerated by prior re-search and writing that has failed to recognize all of the variables that must be considered in the determination of "compensation." Instead, prior research has focused on the *specific* disparity between the dollar amount of the wages paid to women and the wages paid to men in similar positions. It has failed to adequately answer the question: "Why are people paid what they are paid?" As one researcher states: "whereas women may feel underpaid, they may not feel undercompensated."[2] For instance, as women are more likely to be the indi-viduals who care for children, women may place a higher value on positions which offer flexible hours, work at home possibilities, or day care centers at the workplace.

The Equal Pay Act as it was originally envisioned applied only to workers performing the *same* job. As the comparable worth movement developed, the Act took on a broader ap-plication; equal pay was now arguably warranted for "similar" jobs. The definition of "sim-ilar" was expanded to include not only equal positions but also jobs that had equal worth as defined by job evaluation analyses. The authors are in entire agreement with the original, narrow application of the Equal Pay Act, requiring that individuals in the same position should be paid equal compensation, regardless of their gender. It is the determination of what constitutes equal compensation that begs the question.

"Is Pay Equity Equitable?" by Laura Pincus, Nick Mathys. Reprinted by permission of the authors.

[1]Kleiman, "Women's Lower Pay Adds Up to Lower Pensions," *Chicago Tribune* (November 18, 1991). B. C. Nor-ris, "Comparable Worth, Disparate Impact; and The Market Rate Salary Problem: A Legal Analysis and Statisti-cal Application," *California Law Review,* 71, 730 (1983). G. Meng, "All the Parts of Comparable Worth," *Personnel Journal,* 99 (November 1990). J. Hollenbeck, D. Ilgen, C. Ostroff, J. Vancouver, "Sex Differences in Occupational Choice, Pay and Worth: A Supply-Side Approach to Understanding the Male-Female Wage Gap," *Personnel Psychology,* 40, 715 (1987).

[2]Hollenbeck et al., pp. 715, 717.

The issue which serves as the focal point in this paper is not whether the jobs are similar, but whether the areas in which the positions are dissimilar constitute, in themselves, a difference in compensation. In other words, the functional responsibilities of a male-dominated position and a female-dominated position may be similar (as determined by job evaluation techniques), but the female may receive greater intrinsic compensation (as explained below) and less remunerative compensation than the male. Therefore, the employer's defense under the Equal Pay Act is not that the male and female employee are performing different jobs, but instead that the compensation received is actually of equal value though not in equal ratios of monetary gain and other benefits. . . .

WHAT CONSTITUTES COMPENSATION?

Compensation, at least in theory, represents the reward to an individual for contributions made to the organization—first for job-related contributions and second (at least for some jobs) for performance contributions. *Equity theory* holds that there is a large number of potential contributions and benefits that are recognized and considered relevant to both parties in the employment exchange. It is the sum total of all these contributions made by the individual employee and rewards (financial and otherwise) offered by the organization that goes into the determination of equity (see Figure 1). It is our contention that the proponents of pay equity focus almost exclusively on pay to determine whether people are being

FIGURE 1

Equity Model for Employment Exchange

Contributions Being Brought to Organization by Individual	Rewards (Benefits) Being Offered to Individual by Organization

Balance Needed

Skills/Abilities	A. *Extrinsic*
Education	—Pay
Experience	—Fringe Benefits
"Potential"	—Job Security
Performance	—Promotion Opportunities
Personality Traits	—Social Relations
Energy Level	—Closeness to Home
Values	—Organization Culture
Flexibility	—Organization Working Relationships
	B. *Intrinsic*
	—Challenge
	—Variety
	—Autonomy
	—Significance of Task
	—Sense of Achievement

"treated equitably," when it is obvious that pay (or compensation) is only one motivation (albeit a major one) why people accept a position or desire a particular career.

Let's expand on this. The variety of rewards offered in the employment exchange is large. However, they fall into two general categories: those that are *intrinsic* (provided by the job itself) and those that are *extrinsic* (provided by factors outside the job). Examples of extrinsic rewards include pay, fringe benefits, job security, social satisfaction, and recognition by one's supervisor. Examples of intrinsic rewards include a sense of accomplishment attained from the job, its challenge, variety, and degree of autonomy.

In determining the variants of pay equity, organizations and unions (along with economists) have tended to focus their attention on the economic basis of the employment exchange. On the other hand, psychologists and other behavioral scientists have taken a broader view by identifying a sizable number (over 100) of nonfinancial rewards in studies on job satisfaction.[3] Following are some examples of nonfinancial rewards desired by individuals.

To some employee groups, job security and safety issues may be important. The pleasant, sanitized working conditions in many office settings attract more job candidates than do more hazardous, less-skilled jobs resulting in lower pay being offered to those candidates. Also, many positions in governmental agencies are viewed as more secure against layoffs than "equivalent" private sector positions. Greater job security along with better fringe benefits usually offered by the public sector can explain much of the seeming disparity between the pay of jobs in the public and private sector.

Other people look for friendships and sociability from their job. For these people, jobs that allow for social interaction will be viewed more favorably than those that require individual work.

Some workers desire scheduling flexibility as an important nonfinancial reward and may trade this for (be satisfied with) less pay. Students, spouses with small children, and individuals holding two or more jobs, among others, are often found in this group.

Another nonfinancial reward factor is job status. Many financial institutions have many layers of "vice-presidents" who are not paid at the levels suggested by the title. The title can be viewed as "psychic" pay.

Finally, to some the job may be seen as a "cause" or "calling." The sense of achievement and satisfaction of fulfilling a desired purpose in life or the emotional significance of the task may "compensate" for lower than normal financial rewards. Examples of some occupational groups affected are artists, many jobs dealing with social issues and causes, and educators.

The conclusion drawn from the above is that comparable worth exponents ignore the differences in intrinsic and nonfinancial rewards offered by jobs of "comparable worth" even in the same organization. These differences need much further study rather than assuming away all things but pay, and calling it equity.

Worse yet, comparable worth proponents constantly use misleading comparisons such as "women are paid approximately 70¢ per $1 paid to men."[4] These differences are the re-

---

[3]E. E. Lawler, *Pay and Organizational Effectiveness: A Psychological View* (New York: McGraw-Hill, 1971). F. Herzberg, *Work and The Nature of Man* (Cleveland: World Books, 1966).

[4]U.S. Bureau of the Census, *Current Population Reports,* Series P-60, No. 174 (Washington, D.C.: U.S. Printing Office, 1992), pp. 112–118.

sult of so many factors (such as type/level of jobs, experience differences, industry differences, personal characteristics, etc.) that one cannot assume the "unexplained" difference is proof of discrimination.

FACTORS AFFECTING PAY DIFFERENCES

Even if only pay is looked at, we believe pay equity proponents drastically overstate the extent of pay differences between men and women. In order to determine the extent of pay differences in similar jobs, one needs to hold constant the effects of factors such as the following.

Type of industry and company: Studies suggest that employees in some jobs can receive as much as a 20 percent increase simply by switching industries in the same geographic area while performing basically similar jobs.[5] Also, firms and industries that have a greater ability to pay their employees should not be compared with those that are less profitable.[6] For example, in Chrysler's efforts to stave off bankruptcy, the company requested and obtained pay concessions from UAW workers.

Size of organization: Research indicates that small companies usually pay less than large organizations.[7] Other research suggests that women "like" smaller companies.[8] Pay differences between genders may result, but are women less satisfied?

Marital status: Macro economic data shows that the economic effects of marriage and parenthood are significant and often directly opposite in their effects on men and women. For instance, marriage increases a man's participation rate in the labor force compared to single men and reduces a woman's labor force participation rate compared to single women.[9] Also, a married man's hours worked annually increase with the number of children, while a married woman's hours tend to decrease with more children.[10] Thus married men with children work more and earn more than single men, while the reverse is true for women. In fact, women who remain single earn over 93 percent of the income of single men (18 years old and over).[11] In the end, the major difference is *not* between men and women but between married women and everyone else.

Age group: Research indicates that the gender wage gap is larger for older than younger workers. At age 20–24 the gap is 89 percent and widens to 65 percent for those 55–64 years

---

[5]E. Groshen, "Sources of Wage Dispersion: How Much Do Employers Matter?" Working paper, Harvard University Department of Economics (1985).

[6]G. Bahar, M. Jensen, K. Murphy, "Compensation and Incentives: Practice vs. Theory," *Journal of Finance,* 593–616. B. Gerhardt, G. Milkovich, "Organizational Differences in Managerial Compensation and Financial Performance," F. Foulkes, Ed., *Executive Compensation in 1990s* (Boston: Harvard Business School Press, 1990).

[7]W. Mellow, "Employer Size and Wages," *Review of Economics and Statistics,* 495–501 (1982). D. Evans, L. Leighton, "Why Do Smaller Firms Pay Less?" *Journal of Human Resources, 26* 3, 562–580 (1989). A. Weiss, H. Landau, "Wages, Hiring Standards and Firm Size," *Journal of Labor Economics, 2,* 4, 477–479 (1984).

[8]W. Oi, "Neglected Women and Other Implications of Comparable Worth," *Contemporary Policy Issues,* 4, 2, 21–32 (1986).

[9]W. Bowen, T. Finegan, *The Economics of Labor Force Participation* (Princeton: Princeton University Press, 1969).

[10]S. Smith, "Estimating Annual Hours of Labor Force Activity," *Monthly Labor Review* (February 1983), p. 19.

[11]U.S. Bureau of The Census, pp. 124–127.

of age. Factors accounting for this gap could include a greater career orientation of the post-Civil Rights age group and the fact that women bear the brunt of child care responsibility, resulting in pay erosion over time because of being placed on the "mommy track."[12]

Experience: We have already noted that, on the average, men work more hours per week than women (roughly 6 percent more). Although the gap is narrowed over time, this results in the fact that after 16 years out of school, women still average half as much labor market experience as men.[13] Since women still lag behind men in the total workforce experience (especially in older age groups), it is important that age cohort studies take this into account. This can be done by comparing younger age groups (20–30 years old) to reduce the effect or by comparing men and women with the same years of experience. Research shows that the male/female pay differential is reduced by about half when years of experience rather than age cohorts are used.

Education: Currently men and women are graduating from college in nearly equal numbers. The careers women are entering are changing and so too are the college majors chosen by women. This is significant, since a college major is the strongest factor affecting income of college graduates. A major in engineering or accounting brings the highest income for both men and women while a major in education brings the lowest.[14] In 1964, nearly half (42.5 percent) of all bachelors degrees earned by women were in education. By 1981 it declined to 18 percent. Today the fields attracting women are those that were traditionally male-dominated, especially in the professional areas. In 1964, women earned fewer than 5 percent of medical, law, and MBA degrees. In 1984, one-fourth of medical degrees, one-third of law degrees and one-fourth of MBAs were earned by women.

These facts are significant, since research shows clearly that it is *type* of education not *years* of education that matters. Common sense suggests that a degree in the humanities is not equivalent to a degree in electrical engineering. Research studies that use years of education as proxies for all the differences in an individual's skills, abilities, and quality of education received are doomed to reach erroneous conclusions. . . .

DIRECTION FOR FURTHER RESEARCH

The failure of researchers to properly identify the extent of disparity and to recognize the degree of equality actually evidenced in the area of gender compensation results in negative consequences. Through increased awareness, continued education and greater opportunities for women, the magnitude of gender-based employment discrimination is being reduced.

First, the continued use of statistics such as "women are paid 70 cents on the dollar compared to men" fosters an atmosphere of distrust in the workplace. When added to the normal secrecy of most organizational compensation systems, the chance for heightened barriers between men and women is increased. It is time for responsible people to discuss the gender-based pay issue on grounds that take into account all relevant reward factors and

---

[12]E. Erlich, "The Mommy Track," *Business Week* (March 20, 1989), 123–128.

[13]V. Fuchs, "Women's Quest for Economic Equality," *Journal of Human Resources, 26,* 3562–80 (1991).

[14]J. Estelle, N. Abraham, J. Conaty, D. To, "College Quality and Future Earnings," Working Paper, SUNY-Stonybrook Department of Economics (1989).

sound statistical bases. Lacking an understanding of statistics, many women are led to believe that they are underpaid compared to men doing the same job.

Second, researchers need to undertake studies that hold constant factors known to affect compensation besides gender. These factors were discussed above and include types of industries and companies, size of organization, and a variety of personal work-related characteristics such as age, years of work experience, type and extent of education, and marital status. In addition, the effect that intrinsic reward factors have on market forces that may affect pay should be considered and evaluated.

Third, requiring employers to increase the amounts they pay to women will critically reduce the opportunities available to women who are marginal performers.[15] If an employer is compelled to raise the wages of any of its employees, that employer may not be able to afford the same number of employees. The added cost is likely to force the employer to reduce the number of people employed. In determining which employees to discharge, the employer likely will retain the best performers and terminate those whose performance is marginally adequate. Unfortunately, among this group will be women who are most in need of protection against discrimination. In addition, this solution reduces the flexibility of other benefit options. These options include flexible hours and day care programs, which may be valued as compensatory benefits, but employers will lose the incentive to provide women and others benefits which they actually value greatly.

REDUCING GENDER-BASED WAGE DIFFERENCES

In lieu of a pay equity analysis, there are a number of solutions that would help to reduce any actual disparities which remain between the compensation of men and women. First, the education of women in the United States must begin to emphasize career opportunities for women in non-traditional occupations at an early age.[16] Our conventional pigeonholing of women in certain career paths and men in others must be removed in favor of a more balanced approach based on skill and potential rather than preconceived, traditional expectations. Women should receive similar educational preparation and counseling for any occupation and be equally equipped to obtain similar positions as men, allowing them to more effectively exert their market power. Ironically, many of the counselors giving advice in our primary and secondary schools are themselves women.

Second, there is a need to emphasize the societal need as well as the economic benefit to the employer to provide day care, parental leave, flexible hours/shifts, and other non-monetary compensation which allow women to remain in employment positions instead of following the "mommy track" and retreating from their positions at the onset of children. If one accepts the reality that women are equally qualified for almost every position as men, then the inability to retain women upon the birth of their children must be seen as the loss to the workforce of valuable resources. As women (and their spouses) advance to higher decision-making levels in organizations, these benefits are more often being implemented. If employers were to provide support for working mothers, these individuals would not suffer the economic and social pressure felt by many to leave the workforce,

---

[15]L. Fischel, "Comparable Worth and Discrimination in Labor Markets," *U. Chi. L. Rev.,* 53, 891.
[16]Hollenbeck et al., 1987, pp. 715, 718.

and employers would benefit from the increased pool of potential employees. In addition, research has shown that firms which provide this support report strengthened employee loyalty, decreased absenteeism and increased productivity.[17]

Third, women must be increasingly aware of the value of their market power. In the long run, pay equity and comparable worth will not assist the greatest population of female workers, individuals who have merely adequate abilities. Firms may be less willing to take a chance with a potential employee if employers believe that they will have difficulty terminating them because of potential liability. For instance, suppose an employer has the option of hiring a female applicant or a male applicant, both of whose applications evidence adequate abilities. The employer may hesitate in hiring the female applicant because, if she does not work out and is terminated, there is a greater risk of a discrimination action. In addition, the employer could hire the male applicant at a lower wage than his other employees until such time as that individual proves himself, even though he would generally hire all workers at the same wage. On the other hand, the employer does not have this flexibility in hiring the female applicant because the law requires the employer to pay to her the same wage as a male in the position for which he is hiring her.

Wages are determined by the market, not by any *ex ante* determination of relative merit. As stated earlier, if women act rationally as a group, they would be able to create a supply and demand ratio that would force the wages for women up to meet that lack of supply. Women are forced to make decisions with which, perhaps, men have not traditionally been faced. What must be understood is that, in the past, women were willing to accept low paying positions because, as a general rule, they had husbands who would support them. The ones that did not were forced to take positions solely based on the salaries offered, and may have forgone portions that they truly would have preferred. Now, more women do not have that marital support and may be forced into certain positions due to the salaries offered.

The answer to this market imperfection, therefore, is not only to require employers to provide women wages equal to those men receive (as this would lead to a supply and demand curve that is superficially supported), but also to encourage women to identify and exercise their market power, as do other underrepresented classes.

[17]W. List, "Employers Find Rewards in Employment Equity," *Canadian Business Review,* 35 (Spring 1989).

A FREE MARKET
APPROACH TO
COMPARABLE WORTH

LAURA B. PINCUS

The following article supports Posner's criticisms of comparable worth theory. I argue that the market should be able to correct any discrepancy between male and female wages and that, if it does not correct this difference, there are other means by which women (using market power) may be able to argue for increased wages.

The issue of comparable worth exemplifies the imperfection of market effects. The argument made by proponents of comparable worth is that women earn between 59% to 65% of men's earnings because they are systematically segregated into jobs that are traditionally held by women and traditionally underpaid. Champions of comparable worth argue that each job has an inherent value irrespective of the market, that the market thus is imperfect in its valuation of females in these positions, and that the law should create a hierarchy of job positions that are comparable in worth and set wages accordingly. They refuse to accept that an employee's economic worth is determined by his or her salary. Due to this flawed approach, they fail to recognize that incomparable wages derive not from faulty wage-value scales but from the supply and demand curves that are formed.

Proponents argue instead that the supply curve for female employees is skewed in certain positions due to discrimination in the marketplace. Assume that nursing and auto maintenance require approximately the same skill level (I am making no realistic comment, this is only an example). Next assume that female nurses comprise 90% of the nurses in this country and that male auto mechanics comprise 90% of the mechanics in this country. Proponents of a comparable worth system would contend that these percentages (or similar ones) exist due to two related reasons: Women are forced into nursing because this is accepted as a job which "should" be staffed by women, and they are forced out of other positions that are predominantly male because of similar discriminatory employment barriers. As the employers know that the women have no bargaining power because they have no other jobs to go to that will pay more, they do not have to pay women as much as they would have to pay men to lure them to the same positions.

The purpose of this paper is to address the arguments proposed by proponents of a comparable worth system using the analytical approach defined as "objectivism" and to explain why regulation of employment decisions is best left to market forces. Objectivism is a political and social philosophy first developed and cultivated by author and philosopher Ayn Rand. The essence of objectivism is the recognition that Woman or Man is an end in herself or himself. One applies this concept through the utilization of an "objective absolute," which regards reality as set by the Reason of Nature. Facts are recognized as independent of one's emotions or influences [i.e., wishing it will happen does not make is so]. No one person decides what is right or wrong, nature does not decide; Man and Woman merely observe and attempt to act in furtherance of what is right. While some may identify this conclusion as moral realism, this is incorrect as morality is subjective while "right" and "wrong," according to Rand, are objective.

As there is one set of absolutes by which all are governed, the distinctions among individuals exist by virtue of characteristics unique to each individual. Objectivism thus encourages every individual to realize his or her own independence, a right derived from his or her nature as a rational being. This does not mean, as most critics believe, that one naturally has the right to do as he or she pleases, no matter the cost to others or to society. What it does mean is that individuals have the right to exist for their own sakes, neither sacrificing their selves to others nor requiring the sacrifice of others to themselves. The individual recognizes all others' right to the same freedom and may not restrict that right.

The most volatile topic of objectivism, and of Rand's writings, is her concept of "egoism" or "rational selfishness." Rand explains that an "egoist" is one who does not sacrifice others but instead stands above the need of using others in any manner.[1] She contends that this is the only form of close association and mutual respect possible between individuals.[2] "Rational selfishness" is a concept that does not embrace a moral evaluation of good or evil but merely acknowledges that selfishness, by definition, is a concern with one's own interests. As long as one is a rational being, he or she will act at all times in his or her own best interest, within the confines of his or her power. This concept is best defined by examining the difference between one's interest in creation and one's interest, instead, in theft. The distinction between the two lies in the object of the pursuit, the object each actor values and each actor's conception of his or her own self-interest. Rand argues that, as there is a set of absolute rules, a rational person motivated by self-interest will view creation of the object as a proper goal, as opposed to theft of the object.

Critics view such support of selfishness as detrimental to our fundamental social structure as there will be no charity, no giving of one's self for the benefit of others. However, the critics incorrectly assume that one cannot gain from the activities mentioned, that pure altruism exists and that such altruism is good (in its meaning as "opposed to evil"). These assumptions are not logical conclusions. First, one gives to charity or helps one in need because he or she has a desire to do so. Failure to act upon the desire precludes self-satisfaction. The impetus behind charitable acts is therefore satisfaction of the actor through satisfaction of the desires of the recipient. There is personal gain to the actor. Second, due to the fact that one's motivation for all that he or she does during his or her lifetime is self-interest, altruism, in its most strict sense of selflessness, cannot possibly exist. Third, altruism in this traditional sense is insulting to rational minds as it permits no concept of humans except as "sacrificed animals and profiteers-on-sacrifice, as victims and parasites" as opposed to a more genuine and realistic portrayal of men and women as self-supporting and self-respecting individuals.[3]

---

[1] Ayn Rand, *For The New Intellectual* (Random House: New York, 1961), p. 94.
[2] Ibid.
[3] Ayn Rand, *The Virtue of Selfishness* (New American Library: New York, 1964), p. xii.

The moral obligation owed by one human being to another is only the obligation of rationality one owes to himself or herself. This rationality comes only through thought. The egoist is the creator, and the selfless man is the one who does not think but instead learns from the thoughts of others. Man and Woman have the power to be independent thinkers, individuals and free, self-interested actors in their lives. Any denial of these freedoms will also deny our society of the whole of its parts.

Society, accordingly, can benefit from the exercise of self-interest on the part of all of its members. The American governmental system encourages self-interested behavior through its political-economic system: laissez-faire capitalism. The American system is one which prescribes that individuals do not act as victims and slayers but instead as equal traders, by free, voluntary exchanges for their mutual benefit.[4] The role of the capitalist government is merely to protect individual rights, requiring a complete separation of the government and the country's economics. This has not, and potentially may not, be accomplished in the United States. Yet, this is the ideal system in which to protect one's rights.

As can be inferred from objectivist theory, it is not the duty of the government to exercise an individual's rights, it is the duty of each individual to assert those rights, and the government only will intervene in situations where one's rights infringe upon another's. In a perfect capitalist society, the market controls all that is produced, the price at which it is produced, and the manner in which it is produced. There should be no outside influences that dictate some conclusion other than that reached by clear market demands. Critics argue that the market may lead to unfair consequences; yet, it is the concept of "unfair" that is the issue, not the market. An actor will act in such a way that he or she will influence the market to some extent; yet, due to the fact that he or she is behaving rationally, these influences must be fair by definition. That which is rational and logical must be fair. Without this certainty, there could be no objective determination of "equity." Therefore, the imperfections of market effects occur solely due to irrational decisions made by players in that market.

In connection with the concept of comparable worth, and applying the fundamental theories of objectivism, the argument that all women are trapped in "female occupational ghettos" appears insupportable. First, there are positions open to women in areas which may be dominated by men. If women cannot obtain those positions, there is already a legal remedy against that type of discrimination through enforcement of Title VII of the Civil Rights Act.

Second, it is not a valid argument that women have been in certain positions for many years and thus should not have to change their jobs merely to obtain a higher paying job. This is the nature of the market. If women act rationally as a group, they might be able to create a supply and demand ratio that would force the wages for nurses up to meet that lack of supply. What these women are contending, however, is that they would like to stay in their present positions and also make the amount of money they feel that they deserve. The employers obviously do not feel threatened that these women will leave if they pay them a low salary, NOT because they know that the women have nowhere else to go, but because this has been their experience.

What must be realized under such a scenario is that, in the past, women were willing to accept low paying positions because, as a general rule, they had husbands who would

---

[4]"Introducing Objectivism," *The Objectivist Newsletter* (Aug. 1962), p. 35.

support them. The ones that did not were forced to take positions solely based on the salaries offered, and may have forgone positions that they truly would have preferred. Now, more women do not have that marital support and may be forced into certain positions due to the salaries offered. Men must do this also; it is naive to believe that this is not the case.

The answer to this market imperfection, therefore, is not to provide women with higher wages in certain positions which they claim are undervalued. This would lead to a supply and demand curve that is superficially supported, forcing resources into areas where the demand is slight and leaving other areas which are objectively valued by participants in the market without sustenance. Without voluntary exchange by independent judgment there could be no trade, save for that which was dictated. An actor acts in her or his own self interest and is therefore attracted by the full scope of rewards of a particular activity or job. If there is an intrinsic value to each position in employment, given to it my market definition of priority of resource allocation, is there not also an intrinsic value to other things? And therefore, prices, too, must be set. Why are women's shoes more expensive than men's? Women's clothes? Women's soap? If we intend to retain a free market economy, the question of value of services or of goods must be left for the market.

Objectivism does not oppose the reality that women are as valuable as are men in the perfect employment market. While there are irrational actors who play in this market, they will not prevail. The rational profit seekers, acting in their self interest, will realize the potential of women. Females continue to be viewed by some remnants of the historical discriminators as less able to participate. To force a specific treatment of these new entrants without allowing the market to respond on its own will do nothing more than prove to these traditionalists that the problem of discrimination cannot be handled on a rational level of reason. "To deal with men [women] by force is as impractical as to deal with nature by persuasion."[5] All that is necessary to some demonstration of the value of the female worker, of which there has been much, in order to force a market response. I refuse to demean women to the extent that I feel do these critics. Women are capable of asserting their independence and in doing so, they will vie for positions that are traditionally male-dominated, and if refused they will use the law to prevent their discrimination. Their sense of self must be exalted, not the value that they feel our male-dominated society should place on them. There are examples of this everywhere one looks, yet many simply claim that this is not enough and that more should be done to pave their way to independence. Until they begin to act in their own self-interest, and use the market that exists to further their position in this society, they will continue to be treated as if they are not independent, and as if they have no selves.

---

[5]Ayn Rand, *Philosophy: Who Needs It?* (New American Library: New York), p. 32.

TOPIC STUDY: EMPLOYEE LOYALTY—WHISTLEBLOWING

Do you feel that you have a right to take a pen or two home from work because you give so much to your boss that goes unrewarded? Of 1,423 individuals surveyed, About Work found that 49 percent felt that it was acceptable to take home staplers from work, 14 percent felt that pens were appropriate, and 13 percent felt that it was all right to take home computer disks for personal use (http://www.aboutwork.com/bon/poll_ad.cgi.). Does your firm owe you anything in exchange for your performance, devotion, and loyalty? That is, does your firm owe you anything in addition to your salary? Do you feel a loyalty to the firm? What might serve to increase or decrease the amount of loyalty you feel?

WHISTLEBLOWING AND TRUST
Some Lessons from the ADM Scandal
DARYL KOEHN

"Whistleblowing" occurs when an employee informs the public of inappropriate activities going on inside the organization. More limited definitions of the term include the requirement that the whistleblowing relate to an activity requested of the whistleblower, such as when an individual is asked to lie on federal reporting documents to protect the firm. Philosopher Norman Bowie contends that whistleblowing is not justified unless the following characteristics are present:

1. *It is done based on an appropriate moral motive.*
2. *The individual has exhausted all internal channels for dissent.*
3. *The individual's belief regarding the inappropriate conduct is based on evidence that would persuade a reasonable person.*
4. *The individual has carefully analyzed the situation to determine the serious nature of the violation, the immediacy of the violation, and the specificity of the violation.*
5. *The individual's action is commensurate with responsibility for avoiding and/or exposing moral violations.*

"Whistleblowing and Trust: Some Lessons from the ADM Scandal," by Daryl Koehn. Reprinted by permission of the author. (http://condor.depaul.edu/ethics/beat.html)

6. *The individual's action has some chance of success, exposing and/or avoiding the moral violation (Norman Bowie, Business Ethics [Englewood Cliffs, NJ: Prentice Hall, 1982], pp.142–43).*

"No servant can serve two masters. He will either hate one and love the other, or be devoted to one and despise the other (Luke 16: 13). Koehn evaluates the concept of trust as it applies to the Archer Daniels Midland whistleblowing case. In doing so, she highlights the responsibilities of both the whistleblower and the firm. Interestingly enough, she concludes that there are times when whistleblowing is not ethically correct. Do you agree with her conclusion? Is she persuasive?

The 1980's witnessed a flurry of articles regarding the ethics of whistleblowing. These articles tended to focus on three issues: (1) the definition of whistleblowing; (2) whether and when it was permissible to violate one's obligations of loyalty to colleagues or one's profession/corporation; and (3) whether a threat to the public interest actually obligates someone with knowledge of this threat to make this knowledge public.[1] These same issues have surfaced in recent discussions of the act of whistleblowing by Mark Whitacre at Archer Daniels Midland. While I do not think these three issues are morally irrelevant to a discussion of whistleblowing, I am troubled by the fact that the entire discussion to date has focused on the issue of duty. In this commentary, I want to focus less on the question of duty and more on the question of personal, corporate, and public trust: Does whistleblowing foster or destroy moral trust? What makes whistleblowers and the companies for whom they work worthy of employee and public trust?

I shall use the alleged events at ADM to explore these questions. The reader should keep in mind that I am not writing a case history of whistleblowing at ADM. At the time of this writing, we have yet to hear much of the company's side of the story nor do we know exactly what evidence Whitacre has to support his allegation that the company engaged in price-fixing with their competitors. What matters for my purposes here is not that these events did occur but that they could have occurred and they raise serious and interesting questions for corporate, individual and public behavior.

PART ONE: WHISTLEBLOWING AND ITS EFFECTS ON TRUST

It will be helpful to begin with a working definition of a whistleblower. Following Sissela Bok, I shall define whistleblowers as persons who "sound an alarm from within the very organization in which they work, aiming to spotlight neglect or abuses that threaten the public interest."[2] Several features of this definition are relevant to thinking about trust. First, the whistleblower claims to be acting in the public interest. He or she tries to occupy the moral highground by calling attention to some matter the whistleblower thinks the public will be, or should be, concerned about. I say "concerned about" rather than simply "interested in" because the whistleblower claims to be more than a mere tattler. If I were to disclose the religious preferences of my boss, we would not think such disclosure constituted whistleblowing because it is hard to see what public interest is involved. Given the very real risks of being fired, demoted, ostracized, or attacked by those the whistleblower is accusing of negligence or abuse, the whistleblowers generally must think of themselves as on something akin to a mission. They try to portray themselves as acting on behalf of an interest higher than their own—the public interest.

I dwell on this point to emphasize that the whistleblower has made some assumptions as to what constitutes the public interest. He may have erred in his assessment of the nature of the public interest. Or he may have misevaluated his "facts." The facts may be unsound, or they may be sound yet irrelevant to the public interest. If we take trust as the trustor's belief that he or she is the recipient of the good will of the trusted party, the whistleblower can be thought of as portraying himself as a trustworthy person who has acted in good will toward the public and who merits the public's trust. Mark Whitacre, for example, portrayed himself as the white knight of the consumer, a consumer whom ADM had allegedly declared to be the enemy.[3] However, if Whitacre's accusations result in the demise of ADM and the loss of a major supplier of consumer goods, we may well wonder whether Whitacre has acted in fact in the public's interest. Moreover, Whitacre himself arguably has something of a skewed view of public interest since he seems perfectly willing to engage in predatory, monopolistic pricing.[4] According to his own account, he balked at his company's pricing policy only when his colleagues tried to engage in price-fixing.[5] Given that the customer is hurt by monopolistic pricing as well as price-fixing, his whistleblowing at this late date may be less an attempt to aid the customer and the public than to save his own skin. More generally, if and when a whistleblower's motives are mixed, we have some reason to wonder, on the one hand, whether he is trustworthy and, on the other hand, to perhaps be more sympathetic to a company who charges that the whistleblower has betrayed it and the public as well.

Second, the whistleblower believes that there is a substantial audience who will attend to her disclosures. If an employee calls up the press and discloses that the CEO wears blue shirts to work every day, his announcement is likely to be greeted by the reporter with a stifled yawn, if not a burst of profanity. To say that the whistleblower's disclosure is in the public interest just is to say that it has the makings of a good story. The tale, therefore, will likely attract the press and maybe the regulatory authorities as well. It can quickly become sensationalized as people begin to speculate on the extent and magnitude of the alleged corporate misconduct. Furthermore, the regulatory authorities may begin an elaborate investigation on the theory that any abuse known by one individual may just be the tip of the iceberg. The Federal authorities, for example, are not merely subpoenaing many of ADM's records; they have also asked for the records of many of ADM's competitors.[6] There is a very real danger of a witchhunt, for as Bok reminds us, secret police almost always rely on informers and have a history of widening the charges against those accused.[7] Such reflections suggest that it is incumbent upon a whistleblower who truly wants to merit the public's trust to try to explore issues internally before going public with her accusations.

There are, of course, difficulties associated with going public internally. I shall say more about these shortly. My point here is that whistleblowing may harm public trust in our institutions, rather than restore it, if whistleblowing creates a whirlwind of suspicion and the impression that corruption is everywhere. Fellow employees of whistleblowers may be justifiably irritated at a colleague who makes accusations to the press without ever running these same charges by them or without seeking their interpretation of actions and events within the corporation. It may be unfair for the corporation to try to dismiss a whistleblower as a troublemaker with few social skills. On the other hand, the whistleblower may very well be someone who is overly suspicious or inclined to make wild accusations without verifying her facts. Moreover, if the whistleblower does not try to work internally first to try to resolve what she perceives as a problem, it is difficult to see how she can claim to be trying to right the problem. It is striking that Whitacre, by his own account, had heard allegations of price-fixing for many years and had simply ignored them,[8] treating them as though they were someone else's problem. But if he really cared for the company and for the public interest, why did he not investigate these charges when he first heard them? Given that he was in line to be president of ADM, he surely should have worried about this problem and taken steps to address a problem that he was bound to inherit. Conversely, one wonders why he would have wanted to be president of a company that was in his judgment engaged in dastardly deeds. At a minimum, it seems as though he should have interested himself many years ago in the question of whether and why ADM had a history of tolerating price-fixing.

Another way of putting the point is as follows: Whistleblowers are part and parcel of the corporate culture on which they blow the whistle. They are often rather senior because it is those issuing orders who usually have the most control over and the most knowledge about what is occurring within the corporation. At the point of public disclosure, the whistleblower assigns responsibility for the abuse to someone else and thereby distances himself from any responsibility. But matters are rarely so clean. If one has worked many years for a company, taken a salary from them, followed their policies, then one is arguably complicitous in the practices of that corporation. The traditional discussion of whistleblowing pits the individual's loyalty to the company against his loyalty to himself. But this formulation presupposes that that self is a private self, totally independent of the company. I am saying that the self is a company self as well. And while it may be convenient for the whistleblower to talk as though it is him against the big bad company, such talk is suspect to the extent that the whistleblower has supported that company. Blowing the whistle may not increase public trust to the extent the public is rightly suspicious of the whistleblower's own history within the corporation.

Third, the whistleblower is levelling an accusation of neglect or abuse at particular persons within the corporation. These accusations are not pleasant for the accused whose lives may be permanently disrupted by what may turn out to be false charges. At a minimum, the lives of the accused will be unsettled for a substantial amount of time as the press picks up the story and as investigations run their course. While no one should be above the law, we also should not be insensitive to the need for due process. We should also remember that passions almost always run high around whistleblowers' accusations because the whistleblower's charge applies to present activities of a corporation or profession.[9] No one blows the whistle or shows much interest in past abuses with few present effects or in remote, unlikely future events. The alleged danger is present and the person's emotions are engaged, which is all the more reason for exercising extreme caution in making charges and in evaluating them.

The above observations suggest that corporate employees and leaders rightly are concerned about the effect of whistleblowing not merely on corporate morale but on the ability of employees to work together in relative harmony. This harmony becomes close to impossible when the atmosphere is a highly charged one of mutual suspicion. Note that I am not saying that an employee has an overriding loyalty of duty to the group for which he works. It may well be, as Ronald Duska has argued, that the corporation is not the kind of group to which one can be loyal.[10] In any case, there is no prima facie duty to be loyal to any group. A profession such as medicine is worth serving not because it is a group but because its end—the health of individuals—is a genuine good. The end, not the group per se, commands group members' loyalty. We do not, for example, say that agents have a prima facie duty to the Ku Klux Klan or the mafia. The person who leaves such a group does not override a prima facie duty. Rather, there never was a duty to be a part of a group engaged in unethical behavior.

My point then is not that the employee acts wrongly because whistleblowing is disloyal. The wrongness in the whistleblowing consists instead in acting to destroy the workplace atmosphere if and when this destruction could have been avoided by adopting a less accusatory stance or by working within the corporation. Whistleblowing may destroy trust. And trust within a corporation is good when the trust is a reasoned trust, born of open and probing discussions with one's peers regarding matters of joint concern. Whistleblowing should be evaluated in light of its consequences for this reasoned trust, not in light of its effects on irrational loyalty or its relation to a non-existent prima facie duty of group loyalty.

PART TWO: RESPONSIBILITIES OF BOTH WHISTLEBLOWER AND CORPORATION

This last comment raises what I take to be the central moral issue connected with whistleblowing: What can both whistleblower and corporation do to foster reasoned trust and to avoid a situation in which employees feel they have to go outside the company to get their concerns addressed?

Given the very real dangers associated with whistleblowing and the all-too-human propensities toward self-righteousness and misinterpretation, it is clear that the would-be whistleblower and corporation alike should make every effort to discuss perceived abuses and negligence before it gets to the point where the whistleblower thinks a public accusation must be made. The corporation thus has a responsibility to provide a regular forum for free and open discussion of possible abuses. Participants should have equal and reciprocal rights to question one another, to bring evidence, etc. They should not be penalized in any way for participation in this forum. It is striking that ADM had no such forum. In fact, communication was so bad within the company that the CEO's own son apparently did not know until after the fact that the father had called in the FBI to help investigate whether production at ADM was being sabotaged.[11]

Conversely, the whistleblower must be willing to come forward and be identified. It is close to impossible for the accused to mount a defense or even seek clarification when the accuser is anonymous. This requirement to publicly participate increases the odds that the would-be whistleblower will doublecheck her facts before going public. Discussion will also tend to dispel employees' perception that corruption is everywhere. In fact, regular discussion should deflate a good deal of the anger and anxiety regarding corporate problems. Employees will come to see that, yes, their corporation has problems and oversights but, yes, their corporation is routinely and professionally addressing these difficulties. Participation in such a forum will require a good deal of courage on the part of employees and a good bit of restraint on the part of a corporate hierarchy tempted to retaliate against any and all perceived threats.

Second, it is incumbent on corporate leadership to examine the tasks they impose on their employees. An employee can only be morally required to do that which is possible. If the employee is placed in an untenable position, then he will feel anxious, trapped, and may be driven to try to escape from this position by taking his predicament public in an effort to gain public sympathy and support. Whitacre, for example, apparently was expected to do cut-rate pricing with a view to grabbing a large market share while at the same time showing either minimal losses or a profit.[12] Price-fixing becomes a temptation in a corporate environment with these unreasonable expectations, and reasoned trust is not given much of a chance to flourish. For their part, the employees must critically examine the position they are being asked to assume. It is curious that Whitacre professed unease about recruiting competitors for their expertise when he himself seems to have been recruited from a German competitor precisely for his expertise![13] Uncritical naivete on the part of employees becomes morally culpable to the extent that they fail to raise objections that would promote in-house discussion of possible unethical practices.

Third, a company that desires the reasoned trust of its employees must grant the employees access to information about the company's practices. When a whistleblower accuses a company of malpractice, all employees of the corporation feel slightly tainted and anxious. They may feel betrayed not just by the whistleblower but also by the company whom they perceive as having hid relevant information from them. Secrecy encourages corporate paranoia. One of the best ways to combat it is to run as open a corporation as possible. The more access employees have, the more the corporation can legitimately hold them accountable for their actions and the more responsibility the employees will feel for actions they have known about and have had a chance to discuss. If there is genuine access to information about corporate practices, employees have a responsibility to seek out and to consider the implications of this information. It becomes less legitimate for them to bury their heads in the sand and then at some late date cry "Foul!" And this is how it should be in corporations where all parties are genuinely committed to acting well.

Fourth, and finally, all members of the corporation have a responsibility to critically examine their actions, even if they have been taught to perform these acts and been rewarded for doing so. A recent study comparing Japanese and American managers' attitudes towards ethics showed that the American managers were far more focussed on marketing than their foreign competitors and tended to think of immorality as occurring largely within marketing. This focus is problematic in several ways. It encourages managers to overlook ways in which they are treating their employees badly (e.g., by imposing unreasonable job requirements upon them). Furthermore, to the extent that American managers see only particular marketing practices as immoral, they fail to consider whether marketing itself may not be in some ways immoral. For example, does the idea of "targeting" specific groups of people for specific products wind up instrumentalizing the customer? If this customer is little more than a means to selling this product, it is not much of a leap to begin to think (as ADM allegedly did) of the customer as an enemy whose demand for low prices is keeping the company from attaining maximal profit.[14] More thought needs to be given to the nature of the core practices of business and less attention devoted to the bribery, price-fixing, etc., which may merely be symptoms of a sick practice. Unless and until these practices are well-scrutinized by the people who are engaged in them and who have the most knowledge about them, we should expect to continue to have a series of nasty abuses springing up and surprising us.

The corporate atmosphere also should be scrutinized. ADM's anti-bureaucratic rhetoric is a case in point. Whitacre mentions it several times and indicates that ADM has historically prided itself on its ability to get things done.[15] However, what gets dismissed as bureaucracy is often the system of checks and balances within the firm. Anti-bureaucratic rhetoric may encourage, at worst, an attitude of lawlessness and at best, a "can-do" approach which may, as in the case of Whitacre, breed enthusiasm but not do much for thoughtfulness.

CONCLUSION

While whistleblowing sometimes may be the only way to call attention to serious abuses by professions or corporations, whistleblowing is not unambiguously ethically good. It is perhaps best seen as an option of last recourse. Rather than concentrating on when whistleblowing is moral, our time would be better spent thinking about how to improve corporate and professional environments so that employees and clients will not be driven to adopt this strategy.

NOTES

1. Ronald Duska, "Whistleblowing and Employee Loyalty," in Tom L. Beauchamp and Norman E. Bowie, *Ethical Theory and Business* (Englewood Cliffs, NJ: Prentice Hall, 1993), pp. 312–316.
2. Sissela Bok, "Whistleblowing and Professional Responsibility," in Beauchamp, op.cit.
3. Mark Whitacre as told to Ronald Henkoff, "My Life as a Corporate Mole for the FBI," in *Fortune,* Sept. 4, 1995, pp. 56–62.
4. Ibid.
5. Ibid. Ronald Henkoff comments that Whitacre's preferred approach to pricing "sounds a lot like predatory pricing," in Henkoff, "So Who Is This Mark Whitacre, and Why Is He Saying These Bad Things about ADM," in *Fortune,* Sept. 4, 1995, pp. 64–67.
6. See "Suicide Hurts Government's ADM Case," Monday, August 14, 1995, at clari.news.crime.murders on the Worldwide Web.
7. Bok, op.cit.
8. Whitacre. op.cit.
9. Bok also discusses the fact that the charges apply to present wrongdoing. Bok, op.cit.
10. Duska, op.cit.
11. Whitacre, op.cit.
12. Ibid.
13. Ibid.
14. Ibid.
15. Ibid.

THE CASE OF GEORGE AND THE MILITARY AIRCRAFT

M. C. McFarland

George knows that a plane that passed all of its tests might still be defective; his employer plans to go forward with flight-testing. George struggles between his conflicting duties—he feels obligated to his employer but he also feels a duty to protect public safety. How would you resolve this dilemma?

The past several months, George, an electrical engineer working for an aerospace contractor, has been the quality control manager on a project to develop a computerized control system for a new military aircraft. Early simulations of the software for the control system showed that, under certain conditions, instabilities would arise that would cause the plane to crash. The software was subsequently patched to eliminate the specific problems uncovered by the tests. After the repairs were made, the system passed all of the required simulation tests.

George is convinced, however, that those problems were symptomatic of a fundamental design flaw that could only be eliminated by an extensive redesign of the system. Yet, when he brought his concern to his superiors, they assured him that the problems had been resolved, as shown by the tests. Anyway, to reevaluate and possibly redesign the system would introduce delays that would cause the company to miss the delivery date specified in the contract, and that would be very costly.

Now, there's a great deal of pressure on George to sign off on the system and allow it to be flight-tested. It has even been hinted that, if he persists in delaying release of the system, the responsibility will be taken away from him and given to someone who is more compliant.

What makes the situation so difficult for George is that he must choose between conflicting duties: loyalty to self, family, employer, and superiors versus the obligation to tell the truth and protect others from harm.

"The Case of George and the Military Aircraft" in "Urgency of ethical standards intensifies in computer community," by M.C. McFarland. Portions reprinted, with permission, from *IEEE Computer*, volume 23, pp. 77–81 (1990).

TOPIC STUDY: DISCRIMINATION AND AFFIRMATIVE ACTION— LEGISLATED ETHICS?

I'M NOT SUPPOSED TO LAUGH AT THE WAY PEOPLE LOOK

PETE MUELLER

Some people argue that we have gone too far as a society in terms of what is "P. C.," or politically correct. Cartoonist Pete Mueller offers his opinion of the situation in this drawing.

SOME ISSUES IN EMPLOYMENT DISCRIMINATION ON GROUNDS OF RACE, SEX, AND AGE

RICHARD POSNER

Seventh Circuit Court Judge and lecturer at the University of Chicago Richard Posner offers his market theory as applied to discrimination. Posner addresses three issues: why unions have long refused to admit black workers, comparable worth, and mandatory retirement. Posner is known for his logical, well-reasoned analyses, though they are not always in line with society's preferred result. Are you persuaded by the judge's arguments? If you were asked to debate him on these issues, what would be your arguments or criticisms of his reasoning?

. . . Racial discrimination in employment is a part of a larger issue—that of the causes and cures of racial discrimination. . . . Here we shall discuss one specialized topic in racial discrimination and also employment discrimination against women and the aged.

Many unions long refused to admit black workers. Why? Economics suggests an answer. As we have seen, unions seek to raise the wage rate above the competitive level; and to the extent they succeed, an excess demand for union jobs is created. There are various ways in which this excess demand could be eliminated. One would be by auctioning off union membership. The successful bidders would be those willing to pay an entrance fee equal to the present value of the difference between the union wage scale and the wages in their next best employment. This would be the method of rationing used if unions were simply firms enjoying monopoly power over labor—firms that bought labor at the competitive wage and resold it to employers at a monopoly wage. But unions are not firms; they are representatives (however imperfect) of the workers, and they will not adopt a rationing method that would deny the union membership any net wage gains from membership. The problem with nonmonetary rationing methods, however, is that they induce applicants to expend real resources. If admission to the union is based on work skills, for example, applicants will incur real costs to obtain the requisite skills, and the competition in obtaining skills may result in eliminating the expected monopoly profits of union membership . . . What makes criteria involving race or some other relatively immutable status (such as being the son of a union member) attractive is that they do not invite heavy expenditures on qualifying; the costs of changing one's race or parents are prohibitive.

The central economic question relating to employment discrimination against women is explaining the persistently higher average wage of men compared to women (women's wages per hour are on average about 60 percent of men's wages).[1] Irrational or exploitive discrimination is one possibility. Another is that male wages include a compensatory wage premium for the dirty, disagreeable, and strenuous jobs that men dominate presumably because their aversion to such work is less than women's. Another (these are not mutually exclusive possibilities, of course) is differences in investments in market-related human capital (earning capacity). If a woman allocates a substantial part of her working life to household production, including child care, she will obtain a substantially lower return on her market human capital than a man planning to devote much less time to household production, and she will therefore invest less in that human capital. Since earnings are in part a return on one's human capital investments (including education), women's earnings will be lower than men's.[2] In part this will show up in the choice of occupations: Women will be attracted to occupations that don't require much human capital. Of course the amount of time women are devoting to household production is declining, so we can expect the wage gap to shrink if the economic model is correct.

Comparable worth refers to the movement, now being pressed in courts and legislatures, for raising the wage level of job classifications filled primarily by women (e.g., secretarial work) to that of predominantly male job classifications (e.g., truck driving).[3] The proposal is to determine the actual worth of the different jobs, and if the worth is the same equalize the wages (by raising the lower wage level) regardless of the market conditions. The effort to divorce worth from market value is troubling to an economist. If a truck driver is paid more than a secretary, even though the secretary works just as long hours and has as good an education, the economist's inclination will be to assume that the market is compensating a skill that is in shorter supply, or is offsetting a disamenity, rather than making arbitrary distinctions based on fast-vanishing stereotypes. The economist would therefore assume that if measurements of comparable worth failed to pick up the different worths of the two types of job, this was because of the crudeness of the measuring devices rather than the absence of real differences.

In any event, consider what the consequences will be if comparable worth is implemented. If wages in jobs now dominated by women are raised, the number of jobs available will shrink, as employers seek to substitute other, and now cheaper, inputs (e.g., word

---

[1] With certain adjustments the real percentage is estimated for 1974 at 66 percent, in *Improvements in the Quality of Life: Estimates of Possibilities in the United States, 1974–1983,* at 194 (Nestor E. Terleckyj ed. 1975).

[2] See Jacob Mincer & Haim Ofek, "Interrupted Work Careers: Depreciation and Restoration of Human Capital," 17 *J. Human Resources* 3 (1982); Jacob Mincer & Solomon W. Polachek, "Family Investments in Human Capital: Earnings of Women," 82 *J. Pol. Econ.* S76 (1974); "Trends in Women's Work, Education, and Family Building," 3 *J. Labor Econ.* S1 (1985).

[3] See June O'Neill, *Comparable Worth* (Urban Institute and U.S. Commn. on Civil Rights, unpublished, Jan. 29, 1985); June O'Neill & Hal Sider, *The Pay Gap and Occupational Segregation: Implications for Comparable Worth* (Urban Institute and U.S. Commn. on Civil Rights, unpublished, Dec. 29, 1984); *Comparable Worth: Issue for the 80's* (U.S. Commn. on Civil Rights, 1984); *Comparable Worth: An Analysis and Recommendations* (U.S. Commn. on Civil Rights, 1985).

processors for typists), and as customers substitute other products for those made by firms whose wage bills and hence prices have risen because of comparable worth. At the same time, men will start competing more for those jobs, lured by the higher wages. So female employment in a job classification that had been (for whatever reason) congenial to women may (why not will?) drop. Some displaced women will find new employment in the predominantly male occupations such as truck driving—perhaps replacing men who have become secretaries! But these women may not be happier in their new jobs; after all, there is nothing to stop a woman today from becoming a truck driver if that is what she wants to be. Finally, under comparable worth the incentives of women to invest in human capital usable in the traditional men's jobs will drop as the relative wages in those jobs drop, so that in the end occupational sex segregation may not be greatly affected.

Federal law forbids public or private employers to force their employees to retire before the age of 70, with the exception of a few job classifications such as airline pilot. The economist is naturally troubled by the government's intervening in the decision of a private employer to use age as a basis for terminating employment either on a retail or wholesale (mandatory retirement age) basis. The reply is that the use of age is arbitrary. Although this is true, it does not provide a good economic reason for government intervention in the employment market. The use of a single, readily determinable characteristic such as age as the basis for an employment decision economizes on the costs of information. True, there is diseconomy as well as economy: Sometimes a more competent older worker will be replaced by a less competent younger one. But that does not make the employer's use of age as a proxy for competence, crude as the proxy is, inefficient. The employer's objective is to minimize the sum of the costs of suboptimal retention decisions resulting from lack of individualized assessment of workers' abilities and the information costs of making such assessments.[4] If the sum is minimized by having a mandatory retirement age, the employer will have a mandatory retirement age; otherwise he will not. There is no externality calling for government intervention.

---

[4]This decisional problem is strikingly like that of deciding how much procedure to provide to litigants.

IN DEFENSE OF NON-DIVERSITY

T. J. RODGERS

T. J. Rodgers is the president and chief executive officer of Cypress Semiconductor. He wrote the following letter in response to a letter from Doris Gormley, OSF, the director of corporate social responsibility for the Sisters of St. Francis of Philadelphia. Sr. Doris Gormley had told him that her order would vote against the Cypress board of directors because it lacked women and minority members. The Wall Street Journal *reported that he wrote the first draft of this letter to Sr. Gormley on his way home from work the day he received it, "clamping his teeth down on the microcassette recorder when he had to change gears." The letter from Rodgers was sent not only to Sr. Gormley but also to all of Cypress's shareholders. Rodgers received hundreds of replies from shareholders, almost all positive (91 percent of 605 letters). Do you agree? Would Rodgers' letter encourage you to support him, and even to purchase Cypress stock?*

May 23, 1996

Doris Gormley, OSF
Director, Corporate Social Responsibility
The Sisters of St. Francis of Philadelphia
Our Lady of Angels Convent—Glen Riddle
Aston, PA 19014

Dear Sister Gormley:

Thank you for your letter criticizing the lack of racial and gender diversity of Cypress's Board of Directors. I received the same letter from you last year. I will reiterate the management arguments opposing your position. Then I will provide the philosophical basis behind our rejection of the operating principles espoused in your letter, which we believe to be not only unsound, but even immoral, by a definition of that term I will present.

The semiconductors business is a tough one with significant competition from the Japanese, Taiwanese, and Koreans. There have been more corporate casualties than survivors. For that reason, our Board of Directors is not a ceremonial watchdog, but a critical management function. The essential criteria for Cypress board membership are as follows:

- Experience as a CEO of an important technology company.

Letter from T. J. Rodgers to Doris Gormley, OSF. Dir., Corporate Social Responsibility, The Sisters of St. Francis of Philadelphia Our Lady of Angels Convent, May 23, 1996. Reprinted by permission of the author.

- Direct expertise in the semiconductor business based on education and management experience.

- Direct experience in the management of a company that buys from the semiconductor industry.

A search based on these criteria usually yields a male who is 50-plus years old, has a Masters degree in an engineering science, and has moved up the managerial ladder to the top spot in one or more corporations. Unfortunately, there are currently few minorities and almost no women who chose to be engineering graduate students 30 years ago. (That picture will be dramatically different in 10 years, due to the greater diversification of graduate students in the '80s.) Bluntly stated, a "woman's view" on how to run our semiconductor company does not help us, unless that woman has an advanced technical degree and experience as a CEO. I do realize there are other industries in which the last statement does not hold true. We would quickly embrace the opportunity to include any woman or minority person who could help us as a director, because we pursue talent—and we don't care in what package that talent comes.

I believe that placing arbitrary racial or gender quotas on corporate boards is fundamentally wrong. Therefore, not only does Cypress *not* meet your requirements for boardroom diversification, but we are unlikely to, because it is very difficult to find qualified directors, let alone directors that also meet investors' racial and gender preferences.

I infer that your concept of corporate "morality" contains in it the requirement to appoint a Board of Directors with, in your words, "equality of sexes, races, and ethnic groups." I am unaware of any Christian requirements for corporate boards; your views seem more accurately described as "politically correct," than "Christian."

My views aside, your requirements are—in effect—immoral. By "immoral," I mean "causing harm to people," a fundamental wrong. Here's why:

- I presume you believe your organization does good work and that the people who spend their careers in its service deserve to retire with the necessities of life assured. If your investment in Cypress is intended for that purpose, I can tell you that each of the retired Sisters of St. Francis would suffer if I were forced to run Cypress on anything but a profit-making basis. The retirement plans of thousands of other people also depend on Cypress stock—$1.2 billion worth of stock—owned directly by investors or through mutual funds, pension funds, 401(k) programs, and insurance companies. Recently, a fellow 1970 Dartmouth classmate wrote to say that his son's college fund ("Dartmouth, Class of 2014," he writes) owns Cypress stock. Any choice I would make to jeopardize retirees and other investors from achieving their lifetime goals would be fundamentally wrong.

- Consider charitable donations. When the U.S. economy shrinks, the dollars available to charity shrink faster, including those dollars earmarked for the Sisters of St. Francis. If all companies in the U.S. were forced to operate according to some arbitrary social agenda, rather than for profit, all American companies would operate at a disadvantage to their foreign competitors, all Americans would become less well off (some laid off), and charitable giving would decline precipitously. Making Americans poorer and reducing charitable giving in order to force companies to follow an arbitrary social agenda is fundamentally wrong.

- A final point with which you will undoubtedly disagree: Electing people to corporate boards based on racial preferences is demeaning to the very board members placed under such conditions, and unfair to people who are qualified. A prominent friend of mine hired a partner who is a brilliant, black Ph.D. from Berkeley. The woman is constantly insulted by being asked if she got her job because of preferences; the system that creates that institutionalized insult is fundamentally wrong.

Finally, you ought to get down from your moral high horse. Your form letter signed with a stamped signature does not allow for the possibility that a CEO could run a company morally and disagree with your position. You have voted against me and the other directors of the company, which is your right as a shareholder. But here is a synopsis of what you voted against:

- Employee ownership. Every employee of Cypress is a shareholder and every employee of Cypress—including the lowest-paid—receives new Cypress stock options every year, a policy that sets us apart even from other Silicon Valley companies.

- Excellent pay. Our employees in San Jose averaged $78,741 in salary and benefits in 1995. (That figure excludes my salary and that of Cypress's vice presidents; it's what "the workers" really get.)

- A significant boost to our economy. In 1995, our company paid out $150 million to its employees. That money did a lot of good: it bought a lot of houses, cars, movie tickets, eyeglasses, and college educations.

- A flexible health-care program. A Cypress-paid health-care budget is granted to all employees to secure the health-care options they want, Including medical, dental, and eye care, as well as different life insurance policies.

- Personal computers. Cypress pays for half of home computers (up to $1,200) for all employees.

- Employee education. We pay for our employees to go back to school, and we offer dozens of internal courses.

- Paid time off. In addition to vacation and holidays, each Cypress employee can schedule paid time off for personal reasons.

- Profit sharing. Cypress shares its profits with its employees. In 1995, profit sharing added up to $5,000 per employee, given in equal shares, regardless of rank or salary. That was a 22% bonus for an employee earning $22,932 per year, the taxable salary of our lowest-paid San Jose employee.

- Charitable work. Cypress supports Silicon Valley. We support the Second Harvest Food Bank (food for the poor), the largest food bank in the United States. I was chairman of the 1993 food drive, and Cypress has won the food-giving title three years running. (Last year, we were credited with 354,131 pounds of food, or 454 pounds per employee, a record.) We also give to the Valley Medical Center, our Santa Clara-based public hospital, which accepts all patients without a "VISA check."

Those are some of the policies of the Board of Directors you voted against. I believe you should support management teams that hold our values and have the courage to put them into practice.

So, that's my reply. Choosing a Board of Directors based on race and gender is a lousy way to run a company. Cypress will never do it. Furthermore, we will never be pressured into it, because bowing to well-meaning, special-interest groups is an immoral way to run a company, given all the people it would hurt. We simply cannot allow arbitrary rules to be forced on us by organizations that lack business expertise. I would rather be labeled as a person who is unkind to religious groups than as a coward who harms his employees and investors by mindlessly following high-sounding, but false, standards of right and wrong.

You may think this letter is too tough a response to a shareholder organization voting its conscience. But the political pressure to be what is euphemized as a "responsible corporation" today is so great that it literally threatens the well being of every American. Let me explain why.

In addition to your focus on the racial and gender equality of board representation, other investors have their pet issues; for example, whether or not a company:

- is "green," or environmentally conscious.

- does or does not do business with certain countries or groups of people.

- supplies the U.S. Armed Forces.

- is "involved in the community" in appropriate ways.

- pays its CEO too much compared with its lowest-paid employee.

- pays its CEO too much as declared by self-appointed "industry watchdogs."

- gives to certain charities.

- is willing to consider layoffs when the company is losing money.

- is willing to consider layoffs to streamline its organization (so-called downsizing).

- has a retirement plan.

- pays for all or part of a health-care plan.

- budgets a certain minimum percentage of payroll costs for employee training.

- places employees on its Board of Directors (you forgot this one).

- shares its profits with employees.

We believe Cypress has an excellent record on these issues. But that's because it's the way we *choose* to run the business for ourselves and our shareholders—not because we run the business according to the mandates of special-interest groups. Other companies, perhaps those in older industries just trying to hold on to jobs, might find the choices our company makes devastating to their businesses and, consequently, their employees. No one set of choices could be correct for all companies. Indeed, it would be impossible for any company to accede to all of the special interests, because they are often in conflict with one another. For example, Cypress won a San Jose Mayor's Environmental Award for water conservation. Our waste water from the Minnesota plant is so clean we are permitted to put it directly into a lake teeming with wildlife. (A game warden station is the next door neighbor to that plant.) Those facts might qualify us as a "green" company, but some investors would claim the opposite because we adamantly oppose wasteful, government-mandated, ride-sharing programs and believe that car-pool lanes waste the time of the finest minds in Silicon Valley by creating government-inflicted traffic jams—while increasing pollution, not decreasing it, as claimed by some self-declared "environmentalists."

The May 13, 1996 issue of *Fortune* magazine analyzed the "ethical mutual funds" which invest with a social-issues agenda, and currently control $639 billion in investments. Those funds produced an 18.2% return in the last 12 months, while the S&P 500 returned 27.2% The investors in those funds thus lost 9% of $639 billion, or *$57.5 billion in one year,* because they invested on a social-issues basis. Furthermore, their loss was not simply someone else's gain; the money literally vanished from our economy, making every American poorer. That's a lot of houses, food, and college educations that were lost to the "higher good" of various causes. What absurd logic would contend that Americans should be harmed by "good ethics"?

Despite our disagreement on the issues, The Sisters of St. Francis, the ethical funds, and their investors are merely making free choices on how to invest. What really worries me is the current election-year frenzy in Washington to institutionalize "good ethics" by making them law—a move that would mandate widespread corporate mismanagement. The "corporate responsibility" concepts promoted by Labor Secretary Reich and Senator Kennedy make great TV sound bites, but if they were put into practice, it would be a disaster for American business that would dwarf the $57 billion lost by the inept investment strategy of the "ethical funds." And that disaster would translate into lost jobs and lost wages for all Americans, a fundamental wrong.

One Senate proposal for "responsible corporations," as outlined in the February 26 issue of *Business Week,* would grant a low federal tax rate of 11% to "responsible corporations," and saddle all other companies with an 18% rate. One seemingly innocuous requirement for a "responsible corporation," as proposed by Senators Bingaman and Daschle, would limit the pay of a "responsible" CEO to no more than 50 times the company's lowest-paid, full-time employee. To mandate that a "responsible corporation" would have to limit the pay of its CEO is the perfect, no-lose, election-year issue. The rule would be viewed as the right thing to do by voters who distrust and dislike free markets, and as a don't-care issue by the rest. But the following analysis of this proposal underscores the fact that the simplistic solutions fashioned by politicians to provide fear and anger against America's businesses often sound reasonable—while being fundamentally wrong.

Consider the folly of the CEO pay limit as it applies to Intel: the biggest semiconductor company in the world, the leader of America's return to market dominance in semiconductors, the good corporate citizen, the provider of 45,325 very-high-quality jobs, the inventor of the random-access memory, the inventor of the microprocessor, and the manufacturer of the "brains" of 80% of the world's personal computers. Suppose that Intel's lowest-paid trainee earns $15,000 per year. The 50 to 1 CEO salary rule would mandate that the salary of Intel's co-founder and CEO, Andy Grove, could be no more than $750,000. Otherwise, Intel would face a federal tax rate of 18% rather than 11%. Last year, Andy Grove earned

$2,756,700, well over that $750,000 limit, and Intel's pretax earnings were $5.6 billion. Seven percentage points on Intel's tax rate translates into a whopping $395 million tax penalty for Intel. Consequently, the practical meaning of this "responsible corporation" law to Intel would be this gun-to-the-head proposition: "Either cut the pay of your Chief Executive Officer by a factor of four from $2,756,700 to $750,000, or pay the federal government an extra $395 million in taxes."

The Bingaman-Daschle proposal would limit the pay of the CEO of the world's most important semiconductor company to less than that of a second-string quarterback in the NFL! That absurd result is not about "responsible corporations," but about two leftist senators, out of touch with reality, making political hay, causing harm, and labeling it "good." Their plan is particularly immoral in that it would cause the losses inherent in practicing their newly invented false moral standard to fall upon all investors in American companies, even though the government itself had not invested in those companies.

Meanwhile, my current salary multiple of 25 to 1 relative to our lowest-paid employee would qualify Cypress as a "responsible corporation," only because we are younger and not yet as successful as Intel—a fact reflected by my lower pay. If Cypress had created as much wealth and as many jobs as Intel, and if my compensation were higher for that reason, then, according to the amazingly perverse logic of the "responsible corporation," Cypress would be moved from the "responsible" to the "irresponsible" category for having been more successful and for having created more jobs! A final point: Why should either Intel or Cypress, both companies making 30% pre-tax profit, be offered a special tax break by the very politicians who would move on to the next press conference to complain about "corporate welfare"?

How long will it be before Senators Kennedy, Bingaman, and Daschle hold hearings on "irresponsible corporations" that pay tens of millions of dollars to professional athletes? Or are athletes a "protected group," leaving CEOs as their sole target? If not, which Senate Subcommittee will determine the "responsible" pay level for a good CEO with 30% pre-tax profit, as compared to a good pitcher with 1.05 earned run average? These questions highlight the absurdity of trying to replace free market pricing with the responsible-corporation claptrap proposed by Bingaman, Daschle, Kennedy, and Reich.

In conclusion, please consider these two points: First, Cypress is run under a set of carefully considered moral principles, which rightly include making a profit as a primary objective. Second, there is a fundamental difference between your organization's right to vote its conscience and the use of coercion by the federal government to force arbitrary "corporate responsibilities" on America's businesses and shareholders.

Cypress stands for personal and economic freedom, for free minds and free markets, a position irrevocably in opposition to the immoral attempt by coercive utopians to mandate even more government control over America's economy. With regard to our shareholders who exercise their right to vote according to a social agenda, we suggest that they reconsider whether or not their strategy will do net good—after all of the real costs are considered.

Sincerely,
T. J. Rodgers
President CEO

DIVERSITY MANAGEMENT

A New Organizational Paradigm

JACQUELINE A. GILBERT, BETTE ANN STEAD,
AND JON M. IVANCEVICH

Currently, an increasing number of organizations are attempting to enhance inclusiveness of underrepresented individuals through proactive efforts to manage their diversity. Diversity management is defined against the backdrop of its predecessor, affirmative action. Selected examples of organizations that have experienced specific positive bottom-line results from diversity management strategies are discussed. A conceptual model is provided to examine antecedents and consequences of effective diversity management. Additional research areas identified from the model and literature review result in a number of research propositions intended to enhance the exploration and understanding of diversity management.

> *To manage diversity effectively, a corporation must value diversity; it must have diversity, and it must change the organization to accommodate diversity and make it an integral part of the organization.*
>
> *—Sessa, Diversity in the Workplace*

In the past few years, a seemingly endless stream of academic literature and advertisements, as well as popular books and videotapes which tout the benefits of diversity in the workplace, have filled bookshelves and the airwaves. Increased diversity has been suggested to enhance problem solving capabilities of a group, to provide better service to a diverse customer base, and to boost organizational creativity. To harness all of these activities into a cogent plan, it has further been suggested that organizations engage in "diversity management." Diversity management is a voluntary organizational program designed to create greater inclusion of all individuals into informal social networks and formal company programs.

Voluntary organizational diversity initiatives may be particularly important in an era in which the concept of affirmative action is changing. Currently a number of states, as well as the courts, are debating the future fate of affirmative action. The end result may be the dismantling of programs which are perceived as providing advantage for any specific

---

group. Consequently, it may be necessary for organizations desiring a diverse workforce to cultivate their own unique methods for addressing diversity. While diversity management is popularized in the literature as a necessary program for organizations desiring to remain competitive, the concept of diversity management remains nebulous.

***

PERCEPTIONS OF AFFIRMATIVE ACTION

Title VII of the 1964 Civil Rights Act was an important impetus that gave minority individuals the hope of equal employment opportunity. Title VII was articulated as a mission statement. There was no specific strategy until April 2, 1972, when Executive Order 11246, which outlined affirmative action, was signed by President Lyndon B. Johnson. The goals and timetables for affirmative action were contained in a later executive order signed by President Richard M. Nixon.

Although affirmative action still receives strong support from many, inaccurate perceptions of affirmative action stem from incorrect use of the term "quota," and the omission of the word "qualified." Throughout the 70's, 80's, and 90's, examples of the word "quota" being used in association with affirmative action can be found.

Goals, unlike quotas, do not require hiring workers when there are no vacancies, or hiring unqualified workers.

Even though the intent of affirmative action is to ensure equal employment opportunity for all, negative perceptions, combined with poor implementation at the organization level, have resulted in a social policy which is considered ineffective and unjust by some. Specific negative perceptions of affirmative action are illustrated by the following:

- Affirmative action has created a spoils system in which people who actually have never experienced discrimination are reaping benefits at the expense of white males.

- Lower hiring and performance standards have been applied to minorities.

- Compensatory awards administered under affirmative action stigmatize beneficiaries through lowering of merit based admissions/hiring criterion.

- Minorities have achieved their professional goals and no longer need affirmative action. According to the Small Business Association, in 1992 minority owned firms (which make up 9% of the business population) only obtained 4.1% of federal government contracts. Although women are not a numerical minority in the population, they have retained the minority label because they comprise a small representation in the power hierarchy of organizations.

The above perceptions have contributed to affirmative action being construed by some members of both majority and minority groups as a flawed initiative.

In addition, recent studies have found that those hired under the auspices of affirmative action are perceived as less competent than majority workers and less qualified for the position they hold. Negative reactions toward affirmative action are apparent from several reverse discrimination suits—Wygnant v. Jackson Board of Education (1986), U.S. v. Paradise (1987), Johnson v. Santa Clara County (1987), Firefighters v. City of Cleveland (1986), and Adarand Constructors, Inc. v. Pena (1995). Although affirmative action was designed to redress past discrimination and injustices perpetuated by society, inaccurate perceptions persist, in part because affirmative action outcomes are presumed to violate basic tenets of social justice.

Possible reasons for negative reactions stem from the belief that affirmative action hires are recruited on the basis of irrelevant workplace characteristics. As such, affirmative action is regarded by some as a "handout" program which presumably does not take into account the capabilities of targeted groups. This phenomenon is described in the affirmative action literature as the "discounting" principle in which phenotype is the dominant screening criterion.

***

Negative perceptions may lead to the eventual downfall of affirmative action. Recently, the validity of affirmative action as a hiring technique has been questioned both by individual states as well as the federal government, leaving its continuance unsure. If the courts invalidate affirmative action, then organizations which consider diversity a competitive advantage will formulate their own programs to capitalize on an increasingly heterogenous workforce. Voluntary efforts to deal with diversity related issues have been termed diversity management.

DIVERSITY MANAGEMENT COMPARED WITH AFFIRMATIVE ACTION

Although affirmative action and its consequences are in some cases negatively portrayed, the successor of affirmative action, diversity management, has been suggested a crucial element in organizational survival. [It has been argued] that effectively managed workplace diversity can create a competitive advantage in the areas of cost, resource acquisition, marketing, creativity, problem-solving, and organizational flexibility. [It has been further suggested] that managing diversity may result in higher organizational productivity, and ultimately in higher profit. In terms of individuals, the diversity literature states that effectively managed diversity can lead to decreases in frustration and turnover for women and people of color. At the group level, effectively managed diversity has the potential to lead to increased problem solving capabilities. Empirical research supports the notion that diversity management can have a positive spillover effect in the workplace. [It was also recently] found that women hired in organizations which valued diversity were seen as more qualified for the jobs which they held. In this same study, the affirmative action label stigmatized women regardless of job type. A perception of enhanced competence should mitigate employment discrimination against minority individuals.

Creating a culture which values and appreciates differences requires major, systematic, planned change efforts, which are typically not part of affirmative action plans. Diversity management has been considered a new organizational paradigm in that it moves beyond a human resource model based solely on legal compliance to one that suggests there is inherent value in diversity.

[One author has described] an organizational continuum in terms of diversity initiative implementation, comprised of three types: monolithic, plural, and multicultural. In monolithic organizations, the extent of commitment to affirmative action is the existence of an affirmative action plan. In plural organizations, minorities may be more aggressively recruited and promoted, but are ultimately expected to assimilate into the dominant culture. Plural organizations espouse affirmative action to the exclusion of initiatives which promote true employee integration. The multicultural organization represents the ideal, a place in which differences are appreciated and used to gain competitive advantage. Multicultural organizations are suggested to promote both attitudinal and structural integration of minorities and to effectively manage corporate diversity.

ORGANIZATIONAL BENEFITS

The following arguments [have been identified] for managing cultural diversity to achieve competitive advantage.

1. cost—reducing turnover and absenteeism
2. resource acquisition—attracting the best personnel as the labor pool shrinks and changes
3. marketing—bringing insight and cultural sensitivity to the marketing effort
4. creativity—increasing creativity and innovation
5. problem solving—bringing a wider range of perspectives and more thorough critical analysis
6. system flexibility—reacting to environmental changes faster and at less cost

The results of these arguments are reflected in the experience of organizations identified in Table I.

Studies have also shown an increase in workers' average age, a shortage of skilled workers, and a more diverse consumer base in the United States. People of color in the U.S. now buy more as a group than any of our international trading partners. African Americans, Asians, and Hispanics are expected to reach 25% of the nation's consumer base and are forecasted to have annual spending power of $650B by the year 2000. Just as minorities may prefer to work for an employer who values diversity, they may also prefer to buy from such an organization. The diverse workforce's perspective serves to identify products, services, and marketing strategies appropriate for a diverse consumer base, and may result in better quality ideas for goods and services (see Figure 1).

[It has been noted] that the presentation of a solid business case increases the likelihood of obtaining leadership commitment and resources needed to successfully implement diversity initiatives.

CEO INITIATION AND CONTINUATION

Organizations featured as diversity leaders view valuing differences as a total cultural change, rather than as an isolated component of organizational policy designed to satisfy governmental mandates. CEOs of these organizations believe that diversity management makes sense both from a perspective of justice and a perspective of improving the "bottom line."

The diversity program at Xerox was initiated at the top. From the founder, Joseph Wilson, to CEO Paul Allaire, managerial attention to increased workforce diversity has been mandated. CEOs at Xerox have considered proactive attention to diversity both a social re-

TABLE I

Bottom Line Results from Effectively Managing Diversity
J. A. Gilbert et al.

Vought Aircraft Company—Increased output from 70% to 101% after several minority replacements, a minority supervisor, and some team building.

Ortho Pharmaceuticals—Calculated $500,000 savings from managing diversity due to lower turnover among minorities.

Avon Corporation—Turned formerly unprofitable inner-city markets into among the most productive U.S. markets by giving Black and Hispanic managers substantial authority over those markets.

Hoechst Celanese—Changed the polyester textile division from an 18-year money loser to posting a substantial profit after recruiting an African American director and a diverse business team.

Suquet Insurance Agency—Received Equitable's agency award for overall effectiveness and profitability with more than a dozen different nationalities represented in its sales force.

MONY Financial Services—Drew on immigrant manager's experience to hire and train a sales force that understood the concerns of the Asian-Indian community in which the office has significant sales.

Toyota Dealership (Miami)—Integrated cultural awareness through respect, targeted advertising, bilingual salespeople, and special events to break down barriers. Increased sales by 400% over six years; captured more than 50% of the Miami Hispanic market.

Volkswagen Dealership (San Francisco)—Used cultural sensitivity training to achieve a five-fold increase in overall sales per month. Understood role of Chinese family elders as ultimate decision makers for major purchases.

Inland Steel—Moved people who brought different perspectives (women, Hispanics, Blacks) into key positions at Ryerson Coil Processing. Ryerson became profitable for the first time in its history.

Rank Organization PLC—Let new mothers phase in their return to work as a way to cut recruitment and training costs. After five years, saved $1.5M by raising its retention rate for skilled women from 20% to 80%.

Dupont—African American employees recently opened up promising new makers for its agricultural products by focusing on African American farmers. The multicultural team gained about $45 million in new business world-wide by changing the way DuPont develops and markets decorating materials. The team recommended an array of new colors that appealed to overseas customers.

---

sponsibility and a sound business strategy. Xerox's approach has gone far beyond the limits of affirmative action. Xerox was one of the first organizations to use caucus groups (discussion and advocate groups representing ethnicity, sexual orientation, gender, and race) to advance the platforms of minority employees through direct communication with top management. Diversity training for managers, compensation equity, career development, and human resource strategic planning are also emphasized. Xerox is committed to achieving a balanced workforce, with the goal of parity in representation of all employees in all job categories. Through planned change efforts, the diversity of Xerox's workforce has been maintained even though downsizing has occurred.

J. C. Penney has also changed its culture because of CEO initiated change. The organization hopes to achieve a goal of 46% representation of women within most management

FIGURE 1

A model of effective diversity management.

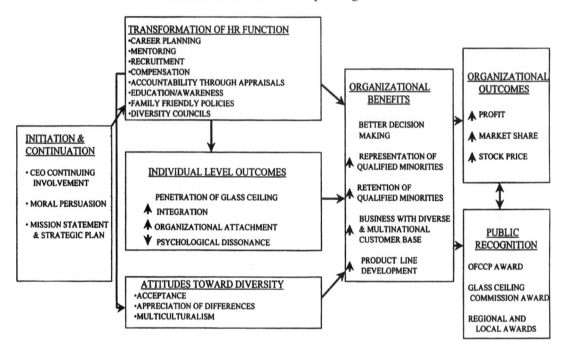

levels in the near future. In addition to diversity and sensitivity training, J. C. Penney's offers formal mentoring programs, seminars on networking skills, on-site child care, career pathing, as well as internal and external programs designed to promote gender equality.

At Xerox and J. C. Penney's, organizational commitment to diversity was initiated by the CEO. The transformational leadership skills of these CEOs acted as a catalyst to organizational change. They were able to convince their organizations that managing diversity was a business imperative and a moral obligation, and not simply a governmental mandate. CEOs at the above mentioned organizations galvanized their workforces to take diversity seriously through moral persuasion, through personally surveying change efforts, and through concerted efforts to change employees' awareness of key issues. J. C. Penney's and Xerox changed their mission statements and strategic plans to incorporate diversity related goals, and subsequently demonstrated their commitment to diversity through initiating organizational cultural change.

Other CEOs who now advocate valuing diversity as a corporate goal came to that realization as a result of legal battles. The following diversity programs were initiated after litigation: Denny's—Denny's was once an example of entrenched prejudice. To change corporate culture, Jim Adamson, CEO, devised a four-part strategy: (1) make organizational structure less hierarchical; (2) make diversity a performance criteria for all managers; (3) require all employees to attend workshops on racial sensitivity; (4) continually emphasize the importance of diversity.

Shoney's—Shoney's settled a $134M class action suit that named more than 200 current and former executives, supervisors and managers who had disparaged blacks, blocked their promotions, or fired or declined to hire them for racial reasons.

Since 1989, Shoney's has added 83 black dining-room supervisors, 2 of 24 vice presidents, 1 of 9 board members, 13 franchise owners, and has spent an estimated $17M annually to buy goods and services from minority-owned companies. Fleet Financial Group—After spending over $100M settling lawsuits for allegedly biased lending practices, CEO Terrence Murray told shareholders at the annual meeting that he and Chairman Joel Alvord "cannot change the past, but we certainly can and will reshape our future." A plan to improve employee sensitivity to diversity ties managers' bonuses to these efforts. A "diversity council" has been created and hundreds of managers have been enrolled in diversity training.

[It has been] found that legal interventions were most strongly associated with those organizations that had the lowest percentages of either females or people of color. However, lawsuits do not have to be the motivating factor for firms to act. Newly appointed CEO at Procter and Gamble John Pepper is committed to increasing organizational diversity as a means of attracting the best talent and serving diverse markets.

TRANSFORMATION OF THE HUMAN RESOURCE FUNCTION

As Figure 1 suggests, diversity as a strategic imperative will result in structural organizational changes, specifically in augmentation of the human resource function. An inclusive description of diversity management initiatives is found in Morrison's 1992 book, *The New Leaders*. Through in-depth interviews with an array of managerial personnel from 16 organizations, Morrison uncovered 52 diversity practices and 23 accountability practices used in organizations which were trying to promote a culture of valuing differences. These initiatives suggest that simply a one- or two-day diversity training program is insufficient to create the cultural change necessary for minority individuals to feel fully integrated in the workplace. Under the rubric of diversity management, entire personnel systems (e.g., compensation, performance appraisal, mentoring, career pathing) are modified to promote employee inclusion. Figure 1 presents a sampling of the more common human resource systems targeted in a diversity change effort.

***

In recent years, the U.S. Sentencing Guidelines provide a solid business reason for the development of company ethics programs by offering reduced fines to companies who come forward, state their problems and their solutions, and demonstrate an ongoing ethics (compliance) program. These guidelines have been a successful government initiative by providing companies with strong incentives. However, diversity management cannot depend solely on laws, since compliance represents only minimum acceptable standards of behavior. Ethical behavior focused on diversity management takes knowledge, commitment and work beyond the law. By the year 2000, only 15% of the workforce's net increase will be white males (Johnston, 1987). Since some believe that many managers are unsure how to motivate demographically diverse work groups in light of their cultural differences, backgrounds, values, and assumptions, the increasingly diverse workforce will likely require management styles that allow for integration into the organization. A service based economy requires employees who can successfully relate to customers in diverse markets, while an increasingly global marketplace necessitates cultural understanding on the part of vendors and customers alike. Organizations which do not make diversity a strategic objective may experience inability to sell in diverse markets, a tarnished organizational image as a result of discriminatory lawsuits, and ultimately, demise. The fact that the future labor force will be comprised primarily of minority members, combined with the fact that a future labor shortage is expected across all job categories, makes valuing employee differences an even stronger organizational mandate. Given rapidly increasing workforce diversity, it is important for researchers to provide managers with a knowledge base from which to draw inferences on managing their diverse workforces. Continued study of diversity management, including tests of the current theory and propositions, is needed to assess the impact of diversity initiatives and to aid managers in their quest for organizational improvement.

BUSINESS SUES 'DISCRIMINATION TESTERS' POSING AS JOB APPLICANTS

Tammy Webber

Review the practices described by the article that follows. Is anything wrong with posing as a job applicant to see whether recruitment and selection is conducted on appropriate bases? How else would a rejected applicant gain this information from an employer? Consider what policies you would want in place to try to protect against this type of activity or to ensure that your company doesn't suffer from the same challenge as Guardian Security.

When Lolita Pierce, a black woman, applied for a job as a receptionist at a Chicago business in 1995, she was told that selected applicants would be called later for second interviews.

A few hours later, Eve Loftman, a white woman with similar credentials, was tested, interviewed and offered the job. But the women were not looking for work.

They were employment testers, hired by the Legal Assistance Foundation of Chicago, a not-for-profit agency, to find whether businesses discriminate.

Now the strategy is being tested in court in cases that ask whether it is legal to misrepresent one's self to an employer in an effort to document discrimination.

Business Advocates Say "No"

Guardian Security Services, the target of the 1995 race-bias sting, is suing two black testers, Kyra Kyles and Pierce, and the Legal Assistance Foundation, claiming that presenting fake qualifications and feigning interest in a job amount to fraud. Guardian is suing for unspecified damages.

"State law says you cannot commit fraud and using testers is fraud," said Guardian attorney Douglas Darch, who denies that the company treated the black applicants unfairly.

The company in September won a victory when a federal judge threw out a discrimination lawsuit filed by the black testers. U.S. District Judge Suzanne Conlon said the testers cannot sue for discrimination because they did not really want the job and suffered no harm. The agency is appealing the ruling.

The federal Equal Employment Opportunity Commission earlier this year dropped plans to file its own lawsuit in a similar Chicago employment-bias case after House Speaker

"Business Sues 'Discrimination Testers' Posing as Job Applicants," by Tammy Webber. Reprinted with permission of the Associated Press.

Newt Gingrich criticized the use of testers. Gingrich promised to support a budget increase for the agency if it promised not to spend the money on programs that create new cases, and focused instead on a backlog of cases.

"Why go out seeking discrimination haphazardly when it can be said that it is sitting on your doorstep?" Gingrich said.

Civil rights advocates say testers—long used to document housing discrimination—are needed to investigate employers. Most such testing is done by private groups with financial support from government agencies.

"Nobody says, 'I'm not going to hire you because you're a woman or if you're African American,' " said Rod Boggs, director of the Washington Lawyers' Committee for Civil Rights in Washington.

The Fair Housing Act authorizes the use of discrimination testers in housing. But there is no federal law or definitive court ruling on employment testers, making the Chicago case an important test, both sides agree. Boggs said cases decided by the federal court for the District of Columbia law allow testers and agencies that use them to sue.

Boggs said he knows of no other case in which employment-bias testers were countersued by the company that they accused of discrimination.

"The law does not say anything about having to be willing to take the job if you got it," Boggs said. "A lot of people who interview don't want the job; they may be testing the market."

Most employment testing has been done in Chicago and Washington, but programs are being considered in New York and San Francisco, he said.

AFFIRMING AFFIRMATIVE ACTION

JESSE L. JACKSON

Rev. Jesse Jackson, president and founder of the Rainbow/PUSH Coalition, first became involved in the civil rights movement in the mid-1960s when he worked with Martin Luther King, Jr., and the Southern Christian Leadership Conference. Since then, he has focused his energy on advocating for minority rights and the rights of the disadvantaged. In the following press release, Jackson articulates his perspective on controversial issues surrounding affirmative action. The release is a response to arguments put forth by the Republican majority elected to Congress in 1994, which advocated abolishing affirmative action programs. He believes that critics of affirmative action have capitalized on the fears of the American public regarding the competition of the global marketplace. Do you agree with Jackson's discussion of myths versus facts? Given that you are reading this several years after Jackson's statistics were compiled, do you notice any recent changes since the material was released in 1995? Are you convinced that affirmative action is still mandated by public fears and biased attitudes, or has this country come to a place and time where such programs are no longer necessary?

There is great tension in our country today. There are economic fears and insecurities that are real and must be corrected. But there are the hostile voices of fear and demagoguery using the tactic of scapegoating, turning American against American, neighbor against neighbor.

SCAPEGOATING THE DISADVANTAGED

We have a smiling face on our economy—the stock market has hit its all-time high, Wall Street is booming, the top 20% of all Americans are doing very well. But there is beneath that face a nauseous stomach, the underbelly of our economy, that is not as fortunate. Our rank-and-file workers are feeling insecure and with good reason. For the past two years, they've been working longer and making less at less stable jobs. America once exported products; we now export jobs and plants.

Workers feel the pain of the globalization of the economy, the impact of competing with cheaper, less secure, more vulnerable workers. When you combine this with the impact of "reinventing" or reducing government, exporting jobs, downsizing corporations, ending the Cold War (there is nobody to fight), closing military bases, plants, and family

"Affirming Affirmative Action," by Jesse L. Jackson, from a press release to the National Press Club, March 1, 1995.

farms, while increasing the military budget, it is not surprising that we, as a nation, are feeling anxious.

Nike, Reebok, LA Gear, Westinghouse, Smith Corona, and many of our other manufacturing companies have moved offshore. RCA, once symbolized by the dog listening to its master's voice, is an image which no longer applies. Today, the master speaks a language the dog cannot understand.

In the face of this profound structural crisis in our national economy, we need leadership to provide a clear analysis and constructive solutions to appease our anxieties. Instead, women and people of color are being used as scapegoats and objects of vilification.

While we witness congressional attacks on Aid to Families with Dependent Children, Congress blindly embraces Aid for Dependent Corporations. There is an attack on welfare but tiptoeing around S&L thieves, buccaneer bankers, a trillion and one-half dollar military budget to defend Europe, Japan, and South Korea at a time when they are able to share the burden of their own defense.

Instead of identifying these real problems and finding real solutions, many are perpetrating falsehoods and spreading myths blaming the weakest in our society for the excesses of the few. The new Republican congressional majority is using affirmative action to divide our nation for political gain.

MYTH VERSUS FACT

Affirmative Action is under attack. The Republicans want to rip it. The President wants to review it. We must look at America before Affirmative Action and since Affirmative Action. We must look at the remaining gap in wages between men and women, whites and people of color. We must determine its necessity by data, not by anecdotes.

It is a myth that white males are being hurt and discriminated against because of Affirmative Action Programs. White males are 33% of the population, but

- 80% of Tenured Professors

- 80% of the U.S. House of Representatives

- 90% of the U.S. Senate

- 92% of the Forbes 400

- 97% of School Superintendents

- 99.9% of Professional Athletic Team Owners; and

- 100% of U.S. Presidents

Since the inception of this nation, white males were given preferential or deferential treatment—for the right to vote, the right to own land, to apply for loans and institutions of higher education. In the late 1800's white males were given a million acres of oil and soil-rich land under the Homestead Act as a bonus to go west and replace Native Americans. As current statistics show, such preferential treatment carries over to 1995.

It is a myth that Affirmative Action creates preferences for women and people of color. After 250 years of slavery, 100 years of apartheid, and 40 years of discrimination—history, of course, is unbroken continuity—we cannot burn the books, we cannot scorch the Earth.

This unbroken record of race and sex discrimination has warranted a conservative remedy—Affirmative Action. Those who have been locked out need the law to protect them from the "tyranny of the majority." That is the genius of our Constitution, with its checks and balances and balance of power. We need not be race neutral, but race inclusive. We need not be color and gender blind, but color- and gender-caring. The Good Samaritan was not blind to a damaged man of another race, another religion, and another language; he was caring.

The conservative remedy of affirmative action seeks to repair the effects of past and *present* discrimination. It creates equal opportunities for people who have been historically and currently discriminated against. Affirmative Action does not mean "quotas"—in point of fact, it is *illegal* for employers to prefer *unqualified* applicants over qualified ones. What Affirmative Action mandates is the use of goals and timetables to diversify our workforce and universities.

It is a myth that Affirmative Action has hurt people of color, women, or the nation. Affirmative Action has benefitted our entire nation. The first beneficiaries are U.S. corporations. We have the strongest, most diversified workforce in the world. We urge the President to convene corporate leaders and let them assume the burden and the obligation to make a statement sharing their experience of the advantages of having a diversified, educated workforce. Affirmative Action has benefitted white women and their families as a result of two-wage earners in their households. It has benefitted blacks, browns, Native Americans, Asians, veterans, and the disabled. It has turned tax consumers into taxpayers and revenue-generators. It has created a new middle class. It has diversified our workforce and has made us a better nation. I literally went to jail to open up building trades unions so that we might become carpenters and brickmasons and glazers and have the right to work with a skill, and earn a livable wage.

REVIEW MUST BE BASED ON DATA, NOT MYTH

As the President pursues his review it must be based on data, not myth. We urge him to convene the Chair of the EEOC [Equal Employment Opportunity Commission], a rather invisible position, the Chair of the Office of Contract Compliance, and indeed the Chair of the U.S. Civil Rights Commission. And let's have a review, not a retreat. A review to renew a commitment to fairness and to complete unfinished business.

The President is calling for a review. When he does his review, he will discover that Department of Labor statistics illustrate clear disparities in the representation of women and people of color in the American workforce as compared to white men.

In the 1994 labor market, while women represented 51.2% of the U.S. adult population, African Americans 12.4%, and Latinos 9.5%.

- 22% of all doctors were women, 4% African American, 5% Latino

- 24% of all lawyers were women, 3% African American, 3% Latino

- 42% of all professors were women, 5% African American, 2% Latino

- 16% of all architects were women, 1% African American, 3% Latino

- 31% of all scientists were women, 4% African American, 1% Latino

- 8% of all engineers were women, 4% African American, 3% Latino

In May 1994, the National Rainbow Coalition [a civil rights organization] released a study of the National Broadcast Corporation (NBC) which highlights a pattern of racial and gender discrimination in hiring practices in its New York division. ABC and CBS do not vary very much. We found:

- Out of 645 employees of the News Division, 354 were white males, 261 were white females (a total of 96%), 8 were black males, 8 black females, 7 Latino females, 1 Latino male, 3 Asian males and 3 Asian females, 0 Native Americans.

- Of the key employee positions, 142 were white males, 121 were white females, 3 black males, 2 black females, 1 Latino male, 1 Latino female, 0 Asians, and 0 Native Americans.

- Out of 386 employees in NBC's East Coast Entertainment Division, 237 were white males, 130 white females, 6 black males, 3 black females, 5 Latino males, 1 Latino female, 4 Asian males, 0 Asian females and 0 Native Americans.

Patterns of present-day discrimination—of being locked out. This is not a gene factor. This is a pattern based upon cultural, race, and sex bias.

AFFIRMATIVE ACTION IS STILL NEEDED

We cannot fall prey to the inane notion that discrimination is an evil of the past. It is today a very painful reality. As the figures above demonstrate, representation of women and people of color in the American workforce has improved, but is hardly sufficient. We still have a long way to go. When Affirmative Action was being enforced, gains were made, but during Reagan-Bush years, many of the gains were lost. One need look no further than the well-documented disparity in pay between white men, women, and people of color:

- In 1975, median income as a *percentage of white men's salaries* was 74% for African American men, 72% for Latino men, 58% for white women, 55% for African American women, and 49% for Latino women.

- At the height of the Reagan-Bush years in 1985, median income for African American men had dropped to 70%, for Latino men to 68%, rose for white women to 63%, and nominally increased to 57% for African American women and 52% for Latino women.

- In 1993, the figures reflect an increase for African American men to 74%, the rate for Latino men fell to 64%, 70% for white women, and 53% for African American women.

When the President reviews college and professional athletics, he will find great disparities in the positions of power between women, people of color, and white men:

- When the Chargers and the Super Bowl champion 49ers met on Super Bowl Sunday in 1994, there were no people of color or women in positions of power. Yet over 60% of those on the field were African Americans. But beyond the playing field, from coaches to athletic directors, to owners, the same situation is evident in NCAA [National Collegiate Athletic Association] athletic programs. We have effectively gone from picking cotton balls to picking basketballs, baseballs, and footballs. Upward mobility is severely limited.

When the President reviews institutions of higher education, he will find an attack on scholarships and, in effect, the globalization of American doctoral degrees according to a NAFEO (National Association For Equal Opportunity) report:

- Today African Americans comprise only 9.9% of the 12 million students enrollment in two- and four-year undergraduate institutions.

- In 1993, of the 6,496 doctorates awarded in physical sciences only 41 (0.6%) were awarded to African Americans, 89 (1.4%) were awarded to Latinos, and 2,818 (43.3%) were awarded to foreign students (whose countries we subsidize).

- Of all of the 39,754 doctorates awarded in 1993, African Americans received 1,106 (2.8%), Latinos received 834 (2.1%), and foreign students received 12,173 (30.6%).

Lest we forget, forms of preferences have traditionally been granted in higher education on non-racial grounds. For example, we have not yet heard the call to deny children of alumnae special consideration in the admissions process.

When the President reviews government contracting practices, he will find empirical proof that when controls are eliminated, we witness a return to pre-Affirmative Action underrepresentation in our economy. Since the *Croson* decision, minority contracting in the city of Richmond, Virginia—a city of about 70% African American—went from 35% to 1%—reverting back to its pre-Affirmative Action levels.

When the President reviews lending practices, he will find that access to capital and credit is denied to women and people of color because lending decisions are so arbitrary and subjective. Unless there is a reinvestment plan with goals, targets and timetables, the traditionally locked out will never gain access to capital. The contract is useless without the capital. Women and minorities have often had to joint venture with larger, white male firms in order to obtain the necessary capital.

A RENEWED COMMITMENT

Upon completion of his review, we urge the President to renew his commitment to Affirmative Action and enforce Affirmative Action laws as a way of expanding our economy and making us bigger and better and stronger. We hope that he will make the Equal Employment Opportunity Commission and the Office of Contract Compliance and Civil Rights Commission visible agencies and forces for good. The falsely accused need protection, and hope, and opportunity, not scapegoating, and review, and divisiveness, and undue blame.

Chapter 9

ETHICS AND MARKETING

Letter to *Business Ethics* Magazine Subscribers	GORDON RODDICK
Letter from Marjorie Kelly	MARJORIE KELLY
Materials from the Body Shop Social Statement Website	THE BODY SHOP
Social Evaluation: The Body Shop International, 1995	KIRK HANSON

Ethics in advertising? Advertising is about as ethical as the American public. . . . It has about the same moral standards as the upper socio-economic strata of society because it is created, approved and paid for by the upper echelons of modern U.S. society.

—MORRIS HITE

[A]dvertising is a non-moral force, like electricity, which not only il-luminates but electrocutes. Its worth to civilization depends upon how it is used.

—J. WALTER THOMPSON
AGENCY BUSINESS PITCH
(1925)

In a survey of 1,076 marketing professionals asking for the most difficult ethical issues they face in their work, respondents cited the following: bribery (gifts, questionable payments), fairness (conflicts of interest, manipulation), honesty (lying, misrepresentation), price issues (differential or predatory pricing), products (safety, infringement), personnel, confidentiality, advertising (puffing versus misrepresentation), manipulation of data, and purchasing (reciprocity in supplier selection).[1]

One response to many of these issues is that marketing has such a bad reputation in certain areas that consumers expect deception and prepare themselves against it. For instance, no reasonable person would believe absolutely everything we were told by a used-car salesperson. For that reason, many of the statements uttered by car salespeople are considered to be mere "puffing" rather than true misrepresentation—a reasonable person would not be misled.

Consider the following advertising techniques and whether they are unethical. Some marketing material uses vague claims such as "fights odors," "best at cleaning tough kitchen stains," "tastes good like a cigarette should." What about claims that offer no comparison, such as "more body and shine to your hair," "life is better with . . ."? Advertisers may also

---

[1]Lawrence Chonko and Shelby Hunt, "Ethics and Marketing Management: An Empirical Investigation," *Journal of Business Research* (1985) 13, pp. 339–59.

claim that a product has a quality that every product of its type contains. Is this misleading? Some products are said to contain special ingredients about which no one really knows anything. Have you ever considered what benefit a breath freshener product has if it contains a "sparkling drop of retsyn"? Would a reasonable person be misled by any of these claims, and is that the appropriate standard for the ethical content of these claims?

The issue of the "battling claims," where similarly believable sources make competing claims about products or services, is best exemplified by the materials on The Body Shop in this section. A reputable magazine first printed what was considered an expose on claims of the socially and environmentally conscious Body Shop store chain. The Body Shop responded, as did the critics. The Body Shop produced a social audit of the firm and the critics produced their own. In reading these materials, it becomes impossible to ascertain where the truth actually exists.

Marketing Tobacco   Four hundred eighty-five billion cigarettes. That means a lot of zeros. That is the number of cigarettes Americans consumed during 1994. That doesn't include the amount of tobacco used in cigars, cigarillos, pipes, self-rolled, chewing tobacco, and snuff. U.S. expenditures for tobacco products during that same year totaled $47.1 billion, paying for the salaries of almost 700,000 workers.[2] In the meantime, the United States has a $50 billion medical bill for tobacco-related illnesses, and 153,000 people died from lung cancer.[3]

Is it ethical for companies to continue to market a product which has been shown to be hazardous to one's health? Is the sale of tobacco any different from the sale of guns? Beyond any discussion of the ethics of marketing cigarettes in general lies the controversy surrounding the marketing of tobacco products to underage smokers. The federal government is seeking to further regulate the sale of tobacco products. If a manufacturer complies with regulation in this area, do you consider it ethical? Consider the lobbying efforts by tobacco companies seeking to influence the regulatory environment surrounding tobacco sales. Thomas Lauria, spokesperson for the Tobacco Institute, the industry's lobbying group, claims that the antismoking lobbyists go too far—"We are only strong because 700,000 people [are employed in the tobacco industry] and 50 million customers choose to buy these products. That's more people than voted for Bill Clinton."[4]

The Body Shop Controversy   Many readers will be familiar with The Body Shop's trademark green stores selling all sorts of bath and cosmetic items for men and women. You might not be so familiar with the controversy surrounding The Body Shop's claims of environmentally and socially friendly business tactics. After Jon Entine, a newspaper journalist, first uncovered and revealed some startling details disputing The Body Shop's claims in *Business Ethics* magazine, Gordon Roddick, chairman of the Body Shop and husband of Body Shop owner Anita Roddick, responded by sending a letter to all *Business Ethics* subscribers defending The Body Shop and chastising both the magazine and Entine for shoddy reporting. His letter is reproduced below, along with additional information from both sides.

---

[2]The Tobacco Institute, *Tobacco Industry Profile: 1995* (1995).

[3]American Cancer Society, "Cancer Facts and Figures—1994."

[4]Christina Kent, "Daunting Hurdles Ahead: Tobacco Industry Declares War on FDA Regulation," *American Medical News,* September 11, 1995, p. 1(4).

The interesting part about this controversy is that one might expect the dispute to concern facts that can be verified—does The Body Shop misrepresent its activities or not? However, in reading the audits and the contentions below, you may find yourself persuaded by one argument, only to be dissuaded by the next piece.

Notwithstanding this introduction, be wary of concern for either side. As mentioned in an informal review of this text by Kevin Gibson, an ethics professor at Marquette University:

I'm not sure if this is a personal bias, but this might not be as significant a case as it first appears. The Body Shop and Ben & Jerry's are the acknowledged paragon cases of selling social responsibility. The emperors turned out to have less fancy clothes than promised, and so the market did a reality check resulting in (somewhat) lower sales. Entine's article is marketplace information resulting in a market correction. My problem in both these cases is that they are selling luxury items to folks with disposable incomes, and so many of the problems with caveat emptor disappear. To elaborate: "buyer beware" has its problems when we are dealing with a market that has little relative power and little access to information. The Body Shop and Ben & Jerry's lied (or "spun" the truth) and this has a chilling effect on the market, but still those who were hurt are not homeless as a result. I find my students to be very cynical about marketing anyway, and most sympathetic when powerless people are ripped off. However, they have no great problem with exploiting the rich or ignorant rich.[5]

We can all agree that the generic purpose of marketing and advertising efforts is to sell more of the specific product or service discussed. The question in marketing ethics is how far one may go in her or his efforts before those efforts become unethical.

SHORT HYPOTHETICAL CASE

a. You publish a successful teen magazine. Magazines are, at best, barely profitable, and you rely on attracting and keeping major advertisers. Over the years, you have bowed to pressure from tobacco company advertisers and have not run antismoking articles in your magazines. Now, however, you are increasingly concerned that tobacco ads are targeting teens, and preteens are more likely to smoke or to use smokeless tobacco. At the same time, major tobacco companies have merged with food companies. In the past, these food and tobacco companies have accounted for a large part of your advertising sales. Do you continue to omit antitobacco articles?

[6]Hypotheticals were written by Catherine Haselden and are included in her manuscript "The Ethics Game."

---

[5]Kevin Gibson, review comments to Irwin Co., October 5, 1996, p. 3.

TOPIC STUDY:
MARKETING ETHICS

MARKETING ETHICS
Some Dimensions of the Challenge
PAUL F. CAMENISCH

Camenisch contends that marketing should enhance the information and the freedom of decision of the potential customer. Marketers suggest that the market drives out those that violate this goal, but Camenisch is unconvinced. Instead, he believes that marketers are tempted to appeal to our baser, darker side. Notwithstanding these influences, Camenisch advocates a marketing environment of self-regulation guided by a vision of advertising and business in the service of society and by the marketer's sense of personal integrity, rather than through external controls. Given the admitted tension between our integrity and our "darker" side, do you agree that this is the best solution?

The tension between the imperatives of economic survival in the competitive marketplace and ethics is a very real one for many individuals and corporations. Any such tensions can be magnified and complicated in marketing since the marketing firm must not only survive in its own market, but must, as one factor in that survival, deal with the question of what it must do, or what its clients *think* it must do, to ensure the clients' survival in their marketplaces. Practitioners must vividly portray these complex and difficult situations for academic ethicists from time to time, lest the ethical analysis and recommendations offered by the latter lose all touch with the harsh realities business people actually face.

At the same time, the integrity of the ethicists' own profession requires that they keep pressing practitioners not to relax the tension they feel by abandoning ethics and capitulating to the demands of the marketplace. Confronting practitioners with hard questions about such matters is not, or certainly need not be, the attack of hostile outsiders determined to expose the soft underbelly of business to a critical public. It can also be the challenge of the loyalist who believes that businesspersons are often sufficiently sensitive to such issues and that business can be sufficiently creative to find ways to be simultaneously successful and ethical.

Paul F. Camenisch, "Marketing Ethics: Some Dimensions of the Challenge." Reprinted by permission of Kluwer Academic Publishers from the *Journal of Business Ethics,* v. 10 (1992).

One way to press such a concern about ethics in business, and specifically in marketing is by holding up the issue of the social responsibility of business, which I understand to refer to the doing of societal good unrelated or minimally related to the business activity in view. It is in some ways a kind of "add-on" ethic for business. Following Milton Friedman many business persons dismiss such social responsibility as an inappropriate add-on for business people and organizations operating in the competitive marketplace. They often maintain not that business does no social good, but that business that does its business well is already performing a number of positive services to society and its members through the creation of jobs, the paying of taxes, and the generating of beneficial and/or desired products and services. Additional social responsibility is simply seen as excessive and inappropriate. While I think the issue of corporate social responsibility cannot be dismissed this easily, I will here focus on another dimension of the business-society relationship by raising the question of the ethics of business activity itself, the question of the ethics which is in some sense internal to that activity. In our current case, that means the ethic that is internal to marketing. Here we deal not with some add-on to business but with an element integral to business activity.

One can begin thinking about an ethic internal to a given kind of activity by asking what the goal or purpose of that activity is. By this I mean not the goals or purposes of the various parties engaged in that activity; those are almost unlimited in their variety. I mean rather the purpose or goal of the activity itself, specifically its *societal* purpose, the reason that society permits, encourages, even facilitates such activity.

The goals of marketing have been variously stated and I will not here conclusively answer the question of which is its definite goal. The goal perhaps most often assumed and supported by commonsense observation of the business enterprise is that marketing's goal is to increase the company's profits by increasing the sales of its product. Some students of business and marketing, either because they fear that a focus on profit will give too much of a toehold to the critic, or because they know a company's profits depend on many factors other than marketing, prefer to see the goal of marketing as creating a market, or creating a customer. But to this amateur observer such ideas do not really change the thrust of the first answer. They only buffer it by putting another layer between the activity and its ultimate goal. Why does a company want to create a market except to increase its sales? And why create a customer except to buy its products or services?

However put, such answers may be more or less adequate when marketing is viewed from the side of the marketer. But marketing is a societal enterprise. It occurs in society, with society's permission and support, and purportedly, in part for society's benefit. Presumably it is therefore to some extent subject to the moral regulations and expectations society and potential customers attach to it.

But what is marketing's purpose when seen from other perspectives, specifically those of the larger society and of the customer? These two perspectives are not identical. But given that all of us are customers in much of our lives, this perspective represents the larger society better than does the perspective of businesspersons who represent only a portion of the population.

To speak of the goal of marketing from this perspective we must go beyond the simple idea of moving the product or increasing sales, since these as such serve the larger society only indirectly at best. One might attempt to bring together the goals of marketing as seen by business and as seen by the customer or the larger society by suggesting that the goal of responsible marketing is to inform the customer about the product so that sales will increase. This goal of informing the potential customer can be brought one step closer to specifically moral considerations by drawing on philosopher Richard DeGeorge and others who have suggested that transactions are more likely to be morally defensible if both parties enter it freely and fully informed. Assuming that marketing and marketers want to be part of morally defensible transactions, one might then say that viewed societally, the goal of marketing should be to increase the likelihood and frequency of free and informed transactions in the marketplace. Or, to put it negatively, marketing ought not to decrease the likelihood of such free and informed market transactions.

The information requirement is easy enough to state, even if determining what constitutes being fully informed is not. Unfortunately we are also familiar with the various ways it can be compromised. Blatant untruths would seem to be relatively rare in current advertising. But partial truths, the misleading embellishing of the facts (the fixed focus camera becomes "focus free," the unsized bathrobe becomes "one-size-fits-all"), propositions intentionally implied to be true but not actually stated, still abound. Here we meet a variety of unresolved and perhaps unresolvable matters: How much hard information do customers want and deserve? How much of the relevant information are marketers obligated to provide and how much should potential customers be left to seek out on their own? In planning advertising so as not to mislead the public, are marketers to envision the average citizen, however that elusive will 'o the wisp is defined, or the especially vulnerable or gullible citizen—the child, the aged, the simple-minded? How much of the policing of advertising should be taken on by the government and how much left up to the industry.

But in spite of these and related questions, the most complex part of the problem of morally defensible transactions probably has to do with the question of freedom. Clear, honest information relevant to the goods or services being marketed is almost certain to enhance the potential customer's freedom in the transaction, or at least it will not diminish that freedom. But except for the highly technical information aimed at limited markets such as stereophiles, and price advertising of grocery specials and automobile deals, very little of marketing has to do with hard information about the product. Any student of marketing knows that much of contemporary marketing consists of techniques which can be used to "hook" the potential customer on the product in a way that potentially diminishes clear, rational decision making about the product or service being offered. These of course include enhancing the symbolic value of products by associating them with celebrities, including them in sexually provocative advertising campaigns, linking them with deeply held values and commitments, or presenting them as solutions to widely shared insecurities and fears. This is not to say that all puffery is inappropriate. But it is to say that the lines between legitimate puffery, distortion, deception and the psychological "hooking" of the potential customer are not easy to draw, and that the more the interaction is cluttered by irrelevant "information," the more likely the seller is trying to prevent a fully informed and free decision by the customer.

Of course some will dismiss this goal of marketing as the recommendation of a well-meaning but idealistic academician. But before doing that, one should consult that almost perennial final appeal of the defender of the marketplace, Adam Smith. The market he was willing to defend is one in which there is no fraud or coercion and in which all participants are adequately informed about the transaction. Of course we will not always agree on what constitutes adequate information. But here we are more interested in the principle of adequate information for the participant than we are in the details of definition or the mechanics of enforcement.

But perhaps most decisive for the argument being made here is the point made by many marketers that the marketplace is not turned into a moral reality only by moral considerations brought to it from the outside—the moral convictions of the various participants, or the societal guidelines established for its conduct. Rather, the marketplace is itself already a moral as well as an economic mechanism even prior to any externally imposed moral requirements. There are moral constraints built into the very dynamics through which marketing works. For example, contemporary marketing practitioners often argue that dishonest marketing will be unsuccessful marketing, that the market will weed out those who violate the common morality. I am not entirely convinced that that is true, at least in the short run. Products that conspicuously and almost immediately fail to perform have been rejected by the public in spite of aggressive and clever marketing campaigns. But that is a very limited category of test cases. Increasingly we deal more in very complex products and services whose performance, especially long-run performance, and potential negative impacts are not easily assessed by the layperson. Just what sort of performance level, length of service, and maintenance and repair costs are reasonable for such products as modern automobiles, or the electronic products which now flood our lives? What are the truly significant potential harms of the countless chemical products from pharmaceuticals to fertilizers we now scatter freely through our lives and our environment? These are much more complex judgments than whether the miracle knife advertised on television can slice both tin cans and ripe tomatoes in that order with equal aplomb, or whether the new copier really does produce X copies per minute with greater clarity than the old machine. The variety and complexity of products most of us now purchase in the consumer society mean that virtually no unassisted layperson can make truly informed rational decisions about such purchases. The question then is whether marketing will be an ally or an obstacle in our making such decisions. Where it is the latter it is clearly morally indefensible on the criteria suggested here. But even if marketing is merely neutral in terms of its impact on the freedom and informed character of the transaction, it is not clear how one would justify the increase it generates in the ultimate cost of the product.

There is another set of concerns which are an element in the issues raised above, but which also have a life of their own in the discussion of advertising ethics. These concerns arise in relation to advertising that critics see as appealing to our baser, darker, less admirable side—our penchant towards violence, exploitative sex, and the desire to control and manipulate other persons. The usual defense of such advertising is that marketers here are simply offering us what we want, whether in the product or service offered, or in the marketing which sells it. Such a defense is backed up by the claim that they have discovered what we want both by experience and by marketing research through surveys and focus groups. But given the more than 100 billion dollars poured annually into advertising and the shaping of the consumer's view of the world, it should hardly surprise us that advertisers find in the minds and psyches of many consumers what they have been helping put there for decades. It is no trick to pull a rabbit from a hat as long as one chooses the hat into which one has previously put the rabbit. Nor are advertisers cleared of responsibility for such advertising even if this baser side is rooted in something other than prior marketing efforts, which it no doubt is. The question still remains whether marketing and its clients should not only exploit that side of us for the sake of sales, but legitimate it and give it respectable, public standing by making it seem to be not only a natural and universal, but even the dominant dimension of the human self.

Of course if these questions are to be answered and the answers then enforced by agencies outside the marketing enterprise, we encounter the very complex and troubling issues of censorship in a free society. It is much to be preferred for everyone's sake that marketers and their clients raise these questions in a serious manner that can, where indicated, lead to self-regulation. This is most likely to happen if they look at these issues not just from the perspective of business, but as responsible citizens of a society in which they, their children, families and friends must also join with the rest of us in building and sustaining liveable, humane communities.

This raises the issue, met by many occupational and professional groups, of how we relate our work or our professional roles to our other roles in the society—our roles as responsible citizens, as members of communities responsible for the raising and moral formation of children, as members of religious communities and other voluntary associations. Do these other dimensions of our selves figure into our reflections on appropriate marketplace activity? If so, then economic survival, whether individual or corporate, cannot be the only, or even the last and decisive consideration. Or do we recommend a compartmentalization, a walling off of these various roles from each other that denies the marketer a consistency, an integrity among the various things she is and does? Little need be said here about the individual and societal pathologies that result from such an approach. The only viable alternative seems to be a proper vision of the world which subordinates marketing to business, and business to the goals and purposes of the larger society, so that the tensions among these and the other spheres of one's life are reduced to a minimum and one can fulfill one's various roles with a sense of personal integrity.

My focus has been on the possible moral problems posed by contemporary marketing. That is not because there is no positive case to be made for marketing. It rather reflects my assigned task and the fact that the interesting ethical discussions occur there rather than around the positive side of advertising, such as its alerting us to the availability of new products, the helpful information it does sometimes convey, and the possible reduction in price resulting from the larger volume of sales generated.

It would be an impossible and a pointless task to attempt a cost/benefit analysis on the basis of the above considerations to decide if advertising as a whole is morally defensible. It should be neither impossible nor pointless to do such a calculus about some specific forms of advertising for those who are prepared to acknowledge that marketing must be seen in the context of the larger society, of the sorts of human communities we are trying to build and of the sorts of persons we are trying to become.

BENEFITING SOCIETY AND THE BOTTOM LINE

PAUL BLOOM, PATTIE YU HUSSEIN, AND LISA SZYKMAN

In the past, most "social marketing" campaigns came from the non-profit or government sectors. In the last decade, these authors argue, many private corporations have moved to the forefront of promoting social causes, reaping substantial benefits. The authors sought to identify and to evaluate the success of several social marketing initiatives, with a primary focus on whether society is better off because of the program and whether corporate involvement allowed the program to perform better than if it were managed by a nonprofit or governmental agency. If the answer to both questions was yes, the researchers concluded that the program would be both efficient and effective. Examples of these effective and efficient programs follow below.

. . . A corporate social marketing program is an initiative in which marketing personnel who work for a corporation or one of its agents devote significant amounts of time and effort toward persuading people to engage in a socially beneficial behavior. . . .

FIBER CONSUMPTION

One of the most widely publicized and extensively examined corporate social marketing programs—based on our definition of such a program—is the All-Bran cereal campaign conducted by Kellogg Co. in collaboration with the National Cancer Institute. Started in the mid-1980s, this campaign encouraged the eating of a high-fiber, low-fat diet (in part by consuming Kellogg's All-Bran) as a means of reducing the risks of some types of cancer. Print ads, television spots, mailings to health professionals, and public speaking engagements all were used to deliver this basic message. The toll-free telephone number of the National Cancer Institute's Information Service was placed on the back panel of the All-Bran box.

As a first attempt to incorporate a very strong, credible, preventive health message in an ad for a commercial product, this campaign attracted considerable comment and review. Several studies looked at the campaign's impact on consumer knowledge, attitudes, and behavior.

"All of these studies confirm that the Kellogg campaign had significant impact on consumers' knowledge, attitudes, and practices regarding consumption of fiber," according to

Paul Bloom, Pattie Yu Hussein, Lisa Szykman, "Benefiting Society and the Bottom Line." Reprinted from *Marketing Management,* Winter 1995, by permission of the American Marketing Association.

communications researchers Vicki Friemuth and her colleagues. "Although it is not possible to attribute these changes to the Kellogg campaign directly, given the extensive exposure of the campaign, it seems reasonable to assume the campaign was quite influential."

"The Cancer Information Service data provide an opportunity to directly link the campaign to the consumer reaction," Friemuth et al. said in a 1988 American Journal of Public Health article. "Nearly 20,000 calls were made to the CIS in the first year after the campaign by individuals who specifically identified either the cereal box or the TV commercial as the motivation for their call."

Additionally, the business press reported that the campaign was associated with a substantial boost in All-Bran's sales as well as an increase in sales and share for all Kellogg cereals.

The results achieved by this campaign are generally recognized to be something that could not have been achieved by the National Cancer Institute or any other nonprofit group acting alone. The funding and know-how provided by Kellogg's marketing people, coupled with the credibility of the National Cancer Institute, created positive outcomes for both Kellogg and society.

BENEFITS OF WALKING

A good example of a social marketing campaign that has many direct benefits plus strong ties to the product is Rockport Co.'s campaign to educate Americans on the health benefits of walking.

In 1982, Rockport (now a division of Reebok) began the campaign to give "a corporate soul for its comparatively pedestrian walking shoe business," said Don Oldenburg in a Fall 1992 *Business and Society Review* article, "Big Companies Plug Big Causes for Big Gains."

As part of the campaign, Rockport distributed over 2 million brochures and founded the Rockport Walking Institute, dedicated to studying and promoting fitness walking.

Rockport's campaign has been credited with starting the fitness walking craze. In addition, today's sales reflect a twentyfold increase over the company's sales in 1982, and many consumers relate the Rockport brand name with walking and good health.

CHANGE YOUR BATTERY

The roots of Eveready's "Change Your Clock, Change Your Battery" campaign came from a simple yet highly compelling finding that no other group had addressed: One-third of all smoke alarms in place do not work because their batteries are worn out or missing. This situation, according to the International Association of Fire Chiefs (IAFC), is to blame for the majority of deaths, serious injuries, and property damage caused by fires every year.

Armed with this information, Eveready Battery Co., the leader in the 9-volt battery category used by most smoke detectors, launched a public education campaign in 1988 to encourage Americans to change their smoke detector barriers once a year when they change their clocks from daylight-saving time every fall.

To strengthen the programs's credibility, Eveready recruited the IAFC as a cosponsor, and fire chiefs in 37 target cities participated during the first year. A multitiered publicity campaign created exclusive exposure, including placements on TV networks and nationally syndicated talk shows at both the national and local levels. Since then, more than 4,000 fire departments across the country have adopted the program, and the number continues to grow.

The campaign has so far generated 1 billion media impressions with an advertising equivalency of $20.9 million. Coverage highlights included six national wire placements, features in *USA Today,* and reports by "Dear Abby," "The Today Show," "Good Morning America," "Larry King Live," "Regis & Kathie Lee," "CNN Headline News," "CBS Week-end News," *Parade* magazine, the Mutual Broadcasting Network, 1,772 local newspapers, more than 500 local TV stations, and 1,000 radio shows.

Now in its seventh year, the promotion boosted overall category sales by 8% during its first year alone, with Eveready garnering most of those sales. From a qualitative standpoint, "Change Your Clock, Change Your Battery" has received outstanding coverage because it's an important news story. More important, response to the program indicates that the campaign is well on its way toward institutionalizing a new home safety habit. . . .

GETTING 'INN' SHAPE

An example of a program that is not tied to product sales but does urge people to engage in behaviors that provide direct personal benefits is the "Inn Shape with Residence Inn" campaign run by Marriott's chain of extended-stay hotels. Using media stories and brochures, Residence Inns have been urging people to eat better and exercise more, at the hotel and at all times.

Working with the American Heart Association to develop recipes (for in-room cooking) and exercises (for in-room workouts), the chain has obtained considerable publicity and distribution of materials. However, we were not able to find out whether the program has motivated changes in the diets or exercise habits of the hotels' guests.

BREAST CANCER CRUSADE

Avon's Breast Cancer Crusade is an example of a social marketing campaign that is not directly tied to the company's product, but does have direct benefits to consumers. Avon initiated the five-year marketing campaign in 1993 to educate women about breast cancer and encourage them to follow the guidelines for early detection.

As part of the campaign, Avon makes extensive use of its sales representatives. They sell pink enamel breast cancer awareness ribbons (modeled after the red AIDS awareness ribbons), the proceeds of which go to fund local education programs and early-detection programs for low-income and minority women, and distribute brochures and information about the benefits of early detection. And, because many of the interactions between sales reps and customers occur on a one-to-one basis, sales representatives are trained to offer support and guidance about breast cancer.

Avon also uses its catalog and advertising to promote the crusade. For example, in a 30-second Avon commercial that aired during a one-hour ABC special on breast cancer, viewers were given a toll-free number to call for more information. In October 1993, Avon underwrote a one-hour PBS program, entitled "The Breast Cancer Test." In conjunction with the special, Avon sales reps distributed more than 15 million educational fliers discussing the 10 most-asked questions about breast cancer. . . .

TREAD LIGHTLY!

Jeep, a company that prides itself on its longstanding effort to be environmentally responsible, was a founding member of Tread Lightly! a nonprofit organization started by the U.S. Forest Service and Bureau of Land Management to protect the environment by encouraging ethical and responsible off-road practices. Tread Lightly! reminds off-roaders to consider the potential impact of their actions on the environment. The organization's pledge can be easily summarized in a few main points:

- Never venture off established trails.

- Respect the rights of hikers, skiers, and campers to enjoy their activities undisturbed.

- Educate yourself by obtaining travel maps and regulations from public agencies, comply with signs and barriers, and ask owners' permission to cross private property.

- Avoid streams, lake shores, meadows, muddy roads and trails, steep hillsides, wildlife, and livestock.

- Drive responsibly to protect the environment and preserve opportunities to enjoy your vehicle on wildlands.

Jeep reinforces the Tread Lightly! message in several different ways. First of all, in its advertising, vehicles are shown only on approved roads or trails. Second, each year the company organizes several "Jeep Jamborees," gathering together Jeep owners and experts for several days of off-road adventure and education. Finally, Jeep incorporates the Tread Lightly! message into product brochures and videos that Jeep owners receive with their vehicles. . . .

BENEFITS AND DRAWBACKS

Even though social marketing programs benefit society, corporations must weigh the societal benefits provided by a particular program against the costs of persuading people to perform socially beneficial behaviors. Some social marketing programs achieve the desired results very efficiently while others end up being too expensive for what they accomplish. Still others may never attain the level of commitment and resources needed to raise awareness, stimulate action, or encourage repeated behavior in significant ways.

In some situations, corporations might be less capable than nonprofit organizations or government agencies to change behavior or control costs. Nevertheless, many corporations have the following comparative advantages in managing social marketing programs:

- Corporate marketers often have done extensive consumer research, giving them a level of understanding of consumer behavior in a certain context or market that makes them better able to design and place persuasive messages about socially beneficial behaviors for a particular target audience. For example, companies such as Kellogg or Quaker have knowledge of consumer eating habits that might help in determining the best way to promote healthier diets.

- Corporate marketers have more experience putting together the kind of multifaceted, comprehensive marketing programs that are needed to achieve significant changes in behavior. Many nonprofit and government programs have limited resources at their disposal, restricting the number of marketing tools they can deploy for each campaign (e.g., only public service announcements or pamphlets). Increased repetition of the social message, using a variety of techniques, can probably lead to more change in behavior, thereby making the campaign more successful.

- Corporate marketers have substantial credibility on certain topics, giving them an edge on persuasion. For example, a company such as Johnson & Johnson has several highly successful and popular health care brands (e.g., Band-Aid, Tylenol, K-Y Jelly), and the company's ties with the Robert Wood Johnson Foundation, which is well-known for its philanthropic activities in health care, further enhance credibility in this arena.

- Corporate marketers don't have the same political pressures as nonprofits and government agencies. The need to answer to legislators, advisory committees, or nonprofit board members on issues such as "wasting money on marketing" can inhibit the success of social marketing programs. Additionally, corporate marketers might not have to pay as much attention to being politically correct by ensuring a campaign's relevancy to all minority segments and special interest groups. Efforts that try to be everything to everybody become diluted—and therefore ineffective. A corporate social marketing campaign can target a specific audience, define the promise, and deliver a power message.

While nonprofit organizations (including government agencies) often have limited resources, they also have their own comparative advantages:

- Society already has trust and confidence in many nonprofit organizations. Because most nonprofits exist for the sole benefit of society, and not to make money, most people do not question their motives. Therefore, when delivering messages to the public, nonprofit organizations may be viewed as more credible than their corporate counterparts.

- Nonprofits have more experience in their own causes than do corporations. This knowledge could help them tailor more effective messages to specific audiences.

- Experts in the field might be more willing to share crucial information with nonprofit organizations than with corporations. Like the general public, field experts may question the motives of the corporations, especially if the company's bottom line is directly tied to its social marketing campaign. . . .

ABOUT THE ETHICS OF BUSINESS COMPETITION

Matti Estola

The author compares competition in business to competition in sports. Is this a fair comparison? What might be the challenges to the comparison or where might we learn from this juxtaposition?

COMPETITION IN BUSINESS AND IN SPORT

. . . The competition in business and in sport is similar in many ways. We can think of the firms in one industry as teams playing in the same series. The rules of sporting games are clearly stated, and if one team does not follow them, it can be ruled out of the series or punished some other way. The rules concerning the firms' competition are presented in the laws of societies, and there also exists international laws the firms must obey. If all teams obey the rules of the game, they find out their ranking by playing against each other, and we can consider that the competition is fair.

Error-correcting and motivating coaching, as well as learning from other teams, are suitable strategies for succeeding in sporting games. If one team does not hire good players and coaches, and other teams do, this team will not manage. Similarly if one firm does not employ skillful workers, or does not raise at the leading positions the most qualified managers, that firm will not succeed. If all firms compete about customers according to the existing laws, then the most effective firms will win the competition, and we can consider that the competition is fair. The competition process is analogous in both cases, and it guarantees the development of the players' (workers') skills, playing tools (production technology) and playing strategies (organizing the production). In both cases the co-operative skills of players (workers) and coaches (managers) are an essential requirement for success.

High ethics is a general requirement in sport. The athletes competing in olympic games swear an oath about fair competition obeying the accepted rules. An athlete is considered to behave immorally, if he uses forbidden drugs or does not try to win the competition until the last moment. The last requirement allows the betting on the winner, because it rules out pre-negotiated results. Giving up in the middle of the game makes the playing meaningless, which decreases the winner's joy of winning the game. Competing in sporting spirit requires that the winner can enjoy his victory, which occurs if other players have seriously tried to win the game.

In this vein we can say that business competition meets the requirements of high morals if all firms try to succeed in the business and they use legal methods in the competition. The existing laws of societies do not, however, judge illegal all immoral behavior of firms; for instance, firms' marketing does not always meet the requirements of high morals. If the laws of societies allow firms to compete by unfair methods, it is the politicians' task to prescribe the necessary laws which prohibit this. This takes place in economies all the time in the form of prescribing new laws protecting workers, consumers, the environment, etc.

If the laws of societies do not represent high morals, it has serious effects on the fairness of the business competition. For example, the referees in NHL ice-hockey allow much more rough playing than the European referees. This makes the judging of the games between European and North American teams difficult, and it is common that the North American teams refuse to play if there are European referees. Playing with North American referees forces the European teams to play rough, which has perhaps led the game in the wrong direction. This example shows that if the rules of a game allow competition with nasty methods, every player is forced to use such methods if he wishes to remain in the game.

If we consider only the ethics of competition, morally high level teams, firms and individuals should play fair. On the other hand, there always exist individuals with low morals, and if the means of the competition are not controlled, the competition will favour these persons. If we thus want that the most effective teams, firms and individuals win the competition, we have to set strict rules for the competition and make sure that these rules are followed. These rules should represent high morals. An important element in this is that the laws (rules) are similar in every country. If, for instance, the environmental laws (doping rules) vary between countries, those countries with less stringent laws (rules) attract pollutant industries (doped athletes) because of their lower costs (better practicing conditions). The international trade of these products (international competition between athletes) then favours the pollutant firms (doped athletes), which makes the competition unfair.

CONCLUSIONS

We studied the business competition by comparing it to the competition in sports. Competition is an important means of development in all of these cases, although it can be crude and immoral. In sports and business the rules (laws) can be prescribed so that immoral competition becomes punishable. . . . With suitable rules and effective control, competition is an effective source of economic development, and it meets the requirements of high morals. . . .

HOW FAR SHOULD YOU GO TO ACT AS A CORPORATE SPY?

KIRK O. HANSON

Hanson relates an incident where an individual is faced with the classic ethical dilemma: do what you think is right and, perhaps, not end up with the best result or do what you know is bending the rules but end up in a "better" position. The following circumstances may present themselves to you, no matter what your industry. How would you react?

There are always opportunities to get ahead by cutting an ethical corner here and there. An incident related by one of my former students demonstrates this:

George, who had recently completed his degree, was hired by a small software firm to help prepare its marketing plans for a new product. George's boss asked him to find out what he could about the future product plans of the company's two competitors.

George asked two co-workers how he should go about this.

"Call them up and tell them you are a student doing a paper at State," one suggested. "They'll be a lot looser talking to a student than they would to a competitor."

"Don't you know some old friends who have gone to work at the other two companies?" the other said. "Just go have lunch with them and trade some information about our new product for some information about their future plans. You can be a star here, and they can earn some brownie points at their company, too. That is the way things work now. We all help each other out. You never know when your company is going to go under, and you will need a friend elsewhere."

George certainly wanted to impress his boss with his ability to get the information on the competitors, but he was worried about how far he should go to get it.

He is facing one of the fundamental realities of business life: There is always an easier way of getting things done, if you're willing to skirt the boundary of acceptable behavior and compromise your own integrity.

Misrepresenting yourself when talking to a competitor is simply wrong. Every firm has the obligation to protect its confidential information but can't do so if you are engaged in deception. The case is less clear if the company representative started talking without knowing who George was. Some consulting firms now require their researchers to state, "We are doing a study for a competitor in your industry" before having a conversation.

Trading confidential information is to me an even more serious issue. George would be enticing a friend to violate his or her obligation to protect proprietary information—and George himself would be violating his own obligation to protect information about his em-

---

ployer's product plans. Though company loyalty is clearly eroded today, the obligation to protect proprietary information is fundamental. George is not in a position to judge whether he is getting better information than he is giving—and certainly has not been authorized to do so.

Beyond the specific decision George is making, he is deciding at the outset of his career whether his personal style will be one of expediency or one of integrity.

We all have had bosses and co-workers who always choose the easy way out. Such a boss manipulates monthly reports to look good and blames his or her failings on subordinates. The expedient boss is obvious to those who work for him or her, if not to the more senior managers in the company.

The expedient co-worker is the one who is always looking out for No. 1. He may fudge on expense reports to "reward" himself for all his hard work. Or puff up his contribution to projects to take more of the credit than he deserves. Or dump the tough problems on co-workers. You can work with such a person, but you can never trust him completely.

What did George do in our situation above? He felt uncomfortable about "trading" confidential information with old friends, but he did call the competitors and claim to be a student doing a paper for class. The competitors were very talkative and gave him information he did not think he could have gotten any other way. But George felt queasy about what he had done.

When a similar assignment came up a couple of weeks later, he resolved to handle it without subterfuge and told his co-workers so. They kidded him that he had "lost his nerve" and was "naive." But George kept his promise to himself and today remains wary of temptations to "do it the easy way."

NESTLÉ AND THE CONTROVERSY OVER THE MARKETING OF BREAST MILK SUBSTITUTES

CHARLES McCoy, SHEILA EVERS, MEINOLF
DIERKES, AND FRED TWINING

How should a firm respond to protests against the ethics of its marketing programs? Nestlé had to face this issue in connection with the marketing of its breast milk substitutes for infants in developing countries. This controversy has raged for more than two decades and centers on Nestlé's claim that its milk substitute should be used in the early months of a baby's life. In fact, babies in developing countries often suffered from fatal diarrhea and other ailments as a result of mixing the formula with unsafe water. What, if anything, should Nestlé be doing now toward resolving this controversy? Should it take any actions in relation to its critics, governments, the World Health Organization, or the public? How could effective, independent monitoring be achieved at this point?

PART A

Once known in the United States as the Swiss company that sold coffee and chocolate, Nestlé may be better known today as the center of a 21-year-old controversy over the ethics of its infant formula marketing practices. This short case focuses on Nestlé's role, but attention should also be given to the actions of all parties in the conflict:

- other manufacturers of infant formula,

- action groups that have been critical of Nestlé,

- UNICEF and the World Health Organization.

The controversy has gone through five distinct stages as described in the following sequence of events:

Case Study: Charles McCoy, Sheila Evers, Meinolf Dierkes, Fred Twining, "Nestlé and the Controversy over the Marketing of Breast Milk Substitutes," published by the Council for Ethics in Economics (Case 6, 1995). Copyright © 1995 Council for Ethics in Economics.

1968–1976

Bottle feeding as a dangerous substitute for breast feeding in the developing world emerged as an issue. An action group in Britain published *The Baby Killers* in 1974; it was translated into German by a Swiss group as *Nestlé totet babys* (*Nestlé Kills Babies*). Nestlé sued and won in court. However, the worldwide publicity was a victory for the critics; Nestlé became the focus of the controversy.

1977–1980

An international boycott of Nestlé products was organized by INFACT (Infant Formula Action Coalition). U.S. Senate hearings, presided over by Ted Kennedy, further damaged Nestlé's reputation. In response, Nestlé begins to make policy changes. The United Methodist Church (U.S.) sets up a task force to investigate the controversy and make recommendations on appropriate action. After study, the task force reported that Nestlé is changing its policies and recommended against joining the boycott.

1981–1988

The World Health Organization adopts an International Code of Marketing of Breast-milk Substitutes (1981). New Nestlé management declares its intention to follow the WHO Code. The company's two top leaders meet with the Methodist Task Force in the U.S. In an important strategic move Nestlé forms an independent commission, chaired by former U.S. Senator Edmund Muskie, to monitor Nestlé compliance with the WHO Code. Its members were chosen to represent a broad spectrum of constituencies and technical expertise.

1988–1992

Disagreements over the integration of the WHO Code and Nestlé's compliance with it lead to a resumption of the boycott in 1988 by some action groups. The Muskie Commission sponsored an extensive study of hospitals in Mexico which discovered that health care organizations in developing countries discourage breast feeding. The Muskie Commission dissolves itself in 1991, saying that Nestlé is in compliance with the WHO Code.

1993–1995

Reports from action groups, based on surveys by their world-wide network of observers, accuse the infant formula industry of multiple violations of the WHO Code. Nestlé management investigated the charges and denied most of the findings of the action group studies. These results intensified the growing distrust between the action groups and Nestlé.

Background of the Controversy

Nestlé was founded in 1867 by Henri Nestlé, a chemist who developed a breast-milk substitute. "During the first months," Nestlé wrote, "the mother's milk will always be the most natural nutriment" but "there will never be enough woman's milk to nourish all the children that are born. We must then seek some suitable substitute. . . . I have endeavored to make a food suitable for infants, and fulfilling all the conditions sought for by physicians."[1]

Nestlé, S.A., is now a huge multinational corporation with annual sales of nearly $50 billion and more than 200,000 employees. Nestlé is the world's largest producer and distributor of infant formula, with 37% of the market in 20 developing nations and 39% of the market in five European countries in 1992. Nestlé's worldwide share of the infant formula market declined, however, from 40% in 1981 to 27% in 1992. Sales of infant formula are less than 2% of its annual total sales. Profit percentages are reported as 1% in developed nations and .5% in developing countries. The ratio of Nestlé infant formula sales to live births in developing countries is far lower than the ratio in developed nations.

Using infant formula as a substitute for breast milk in the early months of a baby's life is the center of the controversy. In 1972, the U.N. Protein Advisory Group stated: "It is clearly important to avoid actions that would accelerate the trend away from breast feeding. . . . At the same time, it is essential to make formulas, foods, and instructions for good nutrition of their infants available to those mothers who do not breast feed for various reasons."[2] Nestlé says it endorses this view. In the 1970s, action groups, concerned about the people of developing countries, charged that the marketing of infant formula led to a decline in breastfeeding and that the use of breast-milk substitutes in developing societies caused infant deaths from diarrhea and other ailments. This is because users did not understand the dangers of bottle-feeding when formula was mixed with unsafe water. Research has confirmed the danger of bottle-feeding.[3] In 1974, a pamphlet critical of the baby food industry was published in Britain with the title *The Baby Killers*. A group in Switzerland published it in German as *Nestlé totet babys (Nestlé Kills Babies.)* Nestlé leaders expressed their shock, affirmed Nestlé's support for breastfeeding, and sued the Swiss group. Though Nestlé won the case in court, the judge said that Nestlé should review its marketing practices to avoid criticism in the future. The worldwide publicity given the case was a victory for the critics and placed Nestlé at the center of the controversy.

In 1977, advocacy groups led by the Infant Formula Action Coalition (INFACT) organized a boycott of Nestlé products. In May 1978, Senator Edward M. Kennedy chaired U.S. Senate hearings on the infant formula industry, resulting in further damage to Nestlé's reputation. Many religious, educational, and labor groups joined the boycott, which was effective enough to get Nestlé's attention.

In the early 80s, the course of the controversy changed.

- *First, in 1981, the WHO Code was adopted.* This landmark action provides criteria for judging infant formula marketing practices. It did not resolve all controversy: (a) because differences of definition and interpretation remain, and (b) because adoption and enforcement is needed by WHO member nations, most of which have been slow to act.

- *Second, the United Methodist Church (U.S.) declined to join the boycott* and set up a Task Force (MTF) to investigate and recommend appropriate action. The MTF reported that Nestlé was changing its policies, recommended against the boycott, and questioned the fairness and truthfulness of the charges made by some critics.[4]

- *Third, new leadership emerged at Nestlé.* Helmut Maucher, CEO, and Dr. Carl Angst, Executive Vice President, announced their intention to follow the WHO Code and, in 1982, met directly with the MTF to discuss Nestlé's revised marketing policies and practices.

- *Fourth, Nestlé established an independent commission to monitor the company's compliance with the WHO Code,* chaired by former U.S. Senator Edmund S. Muskie. In 1984 the INFACT-led boycott was suspended.

The Activities of the Muskie Commission

Commission membership included critics of the infant food industry, religious leaders, and scholars from public health and related disciplines. The Commission investigated alleged violations of the WHO Code by Nestlé, clarified ambiguities, checked on Code infractions, sponsored studies of health and nutritional issues affecting mothers and children in the Third World, and met with Nestlé management to evaluate policy and suggest changes.

In 1991, the Muskie Commission dissolved, stating that Nestlé was in compliance with the WHO Code and had internal means to investigate and resolve complaints. Also, the International Association of Infant Food Manufacturers had appointed an ombudsman to deal with allegations against its members.

The Boycott Renewed

Though Nestlé and the industry were changing their practices toward conformity with the WHO Code, criticism continued and has been increasing. In 1988, the boycott was renewed, led by the International Boycott Committee (INBC), International Baby Food Action Network (IBFAN), Baby Milk Action (United Kingdom), and Action for Corporate Accountability (U.S.). IBFAN issues periodic reports called *Breaking the Rules,* accusing the infant food industry of multiple violations of the WHO Code. The gulf between Nestlé and its critics is shown in that, after investigation of the alleged violations, only 3 of 455 charges were found by Nestlé to be accurate and these 3 were reported as corrected.

PART B

Nestlé Corporate Culture, Ethical Values, and Strategies

The infant formula controversy has been unsettling for a Nestlé management group that takes pride in its strong corporate culture and ethics.

The current Nestlé organization is both centralized and decentralized. As a multinational, Nestlé operates with subsidiaries that have considerable freedom within firm overall policies. Company-wide management functions are located in Vevey, Switzerland: top line managers, financial control and administration, strategic business groups, research and development, purchasing and export, and the zone managers for the five operating areas around the globe. Each zone has its own decentralized operating groups, able to adapt to the diverse cultures of each zone and country. In the view of its managers, the growth and success of Nestlé is based upon its strong corporate culture and capable leadership, with high levels of mutual trust and loyalty among managers drawn from the many nations in which Nestlé conducts business. But one wonders, has the strength of its culture led to internal rigidity, an inability to learn as an organization, and an inability to adapt to changing social conditions? All the attention given the infant formula controversy by Nestlé seems to some to have been greater than is warranted by the volume of sales or profits. A few Nestlé managers would prefer to drop the product, but most say the commitment to market infant formula in developing countries, based on company tradition and values more than on profit, is too strong.

Nestlé managers believe the company is highly ethical, making many contributions to third-world communities. Senior management today regards the hostile reactions to critics in the 1970s as mistakes, fostering an atmosphere of distrust and mutual suspicion, and they believe that many marketing practices in the 1970s were wrong. Nestlé says it has supported the WHO Code from the time it was adopted and has been implementing the Code ever since. Nestlé managers regret that the infant formula issue continues to hurt the company's reputation and express willingness to work with critics to improve the health and nutrition of children and mothers around the world. They believe that the company has learned from past experience and has adopted more responsible policies toward developing nations. One executive said: "We came to the conclusion that to serve the developing countries we should . . . develop, manufacture, and sell low-cost products, including infant formula, based on local raw materials fitted to the tastes and nutritional needs of children up to age five, not just for charitable reasons. We believe it will serve the long-term interests of Nestlé. And I am very happy that at the same time we can do some good for the people of those countries."

Views of Nestlé's Critics

The scholar who conducted the most extensive study of the infant formula controversy, S. Prakash Sethi, says that Nestlé's actions in the 1970s "could not have been better designed to play into the hands of its adversaries." And further: "The company was a prisoner of its own values set and operational philosophy. Nestlé's values set revolved around conventional business values: a good product, efficiently sold, in every possible market and with flexible marketing and promotional strategies that would adapt to the needs of individual country markets, and by people who were both dedicated to the company and proud of their ability to perform successfully under various operating and competitive conditions. Nestlé's management was also insular and looked to its own traditions for guidance. The company jealously guarded its freedom to manage its far-flung world-wide operations as it saw fit as long as they were in harmony with local laws. The preservation of maximum management discretion was one of the core values of the company, reinforced by the fact that it was also in harmony with the intellectual and cultural orientation of the Swiss-based management and the personal inclinations of its then top management."[5]

In his subsequent evaluation of the company's performance in relation to the controversy until 1994, Sethi sees no substantial improvements with reference to environmental scanning for new constituencies, corporate communications dealing with external issues-related constituencies, the development of strategic assets related to the controversy, or organizational structure and decision-making processes—that is, Nestlé's organizational learning.[6]

The action groups that have led the renewed boycott see Nestlé still as placing profit above humane values. They believe that Nestlé and the entire infant formula industry could take far greater initiative in controlling the free and low-cost distribution of infant formula. The view of some critics is that infant formula should be treated as a drug that is dangerous if misused. If not entirely withdrawn from the market, it should be available only on prescription and used under controlled conditions. Any vendor of dangerous drugs must take responsibility in relation to its eventual end use.

In addition, the industry is seen by some as slippery, not to be trusted. Indeed, industry managers are seen as trying to discredit their critics and trusting neither the action groups nor UNICEF and WHO.

The action groups are especially critical of the continued giving of free and low-cost samples that they regard as blatant violations of the WHO Code. Though having far fewer resources than industry, the action groups regard as a breakthrough the network of sources in the developing world that has enabled them to publish the multiple violations cited in *Breaking the Rules.* The action groups want independent and more effective monitoring.

Health Care Practices in Developing Countries: The Mexico Study and the Baby Friendly Hospital Initiative

A major study of health care sponsored by Nestlé through the Muskie Commission investigated the hospital procedures for newborns in Mexico and how these practices influenced breast feeding by mothers while in the hospitals and later *(Infant Feeding in Mexico, 1991).* Directed by Sheldon Margen, M.D., and V. J. Melnick, M.D., the study involved 59 hospitals in three widely separated regions in Mexico and concluded that existing hospital practices discourage breast feeding and influenced mothers to adopt bottle feeding using infant formula. This study and others in Thailand and Cote d'Ivoire made it clear that health care practices must be changed if the health and nutrition of children and mothers in developing countries are to be improved.

In 1991, WHO and UNICEF launched the Baby Friendly Hospital Initiative with Ten Steps to promote health care practices that support and encourage breast feeding. The Baby Friendly Hospital Initiative is a promising approach in promoting better health and nutrition for infants and mothers. The infant food industry's role so far has been to agree to remove all free supplies of infant formula from hospitals in developing nations on a country-by-country basis.

In 1995, follow-up research by Enrique Rios, M.D., Dr.P.H., found that the Mexico Study had influenced important policy changes and practices toward promoting breastfeeding in two major health care systems in Mexico, with 234 Mexican hospitals now certified as Baby Friendly Hospitals, and had contributed to the creation of a National Breastfeeding Committee. This update suggests that cooperation among industry, critics, and academic researchers as represented in the Mexico study can produce positive changes, though much more remains to be done.[7]

Divergent Points of View

The following significant quotes have been drawn from the many interviews and sources consulted on which this case is based:

An industry executive: "Whatever our viewpoint, most can agree that our major aim ought to be improving the health and nutrition of mothers and children everywhere. That's the central problem."

An industry critic: "The baby food people are slippery. If they would stop giving free or low-cost infant formula, as they promised, we might be able to cooperate on basic problems of health care, with Baby Friendly Hospitals at the center of our efforts."

A health care expert: "Poverty, disease, bad water, inadequate education, and poor health practices are pervasive obstacles to overcoming malnutrition and bad health of children and mothers in the Third World. Our highest priority should be getting good information on problems and cooperation toward improving the situation."

A Nestlé executive: "I believe it is ethical for Nestlé to produce infant formula. But from a business perspective, there are too many problems. It would be better to drop it. That is *my* opinion. But there's no easy way Nestlé will go against its commitment."

Senator Edward M. Kennedy (1978): "Can a product that requires clean water, good sanitation, adequate family income, and literate parents to follow printed instructions be properly and safely used in areas where water is contaminated, sewage runs in the streets, poverty is severe, and illiteracy is high?"

Two involved Britons: "There must be other ways than confrontation through advocacy groups to achieve better health and nutrition for mothers and children." "The issue is multinational accountability. They are a law unto themselves and find ways to evade responsibility. The voluntary groups bring them to account."

A Nestlé manager: "There is no point in fighting or continuing to throw bricks; we have to gain some minimal level of trust. The company was overly aggressive in its marketing in the early 70s. But we began improving and, with the passage of the WHO Code, have really been *trying*. We don't, however, get much credit for it."

A woman's view: "To the extent that the boycotts succeed in their purpose of restricting access to formula, they serve to take the choice to breastfeed or not out of the hands of women . . . and have doctors and scientists in the developing countries decide if *this* bottlefeeding is 'necessary,' or if *that* woman is an 'appropriate' receiver of infant formula."

A UNICEF spokesperson: "Because of the widespread abandonment of breastfeeding, 1.3 million infant deaths occur each year. Countless more survive the fatal odds but suffer impaired growth and development because their mothers were not informed about the life-saving properties of breastfeeding."

A scholarly observer: "In the process of emphasizing extremes, a vast middle ground is lost to inflaming rhetoric with results that are neither enlightening nor conducive to reaching consensus on implementable public policy options."

WHO Executive Director, January 1994: "It is considered that the underlying principles governing relevant national measures should include clear definitions, which are communicated to and understood by all parties: transparent monitoring and reporting procedures to determine whether alleged violations contravene national measures; and a monitoring authority established under government responsibility. It is hoped that this long-standing and contentious issue can be resolved rapidly."

A management academician: "Organizational learning begins by producing different perceptions of the organization's internal and external environments. New perceptions are followed by development of a new vision, mission, and strategy and by their implementation."

ENDNOTES

1. Henri Nestlé, chemist. *Memorial on the Nutrition of Infants.* Vevey, Switzerland: Loertscher & Son, 1869: 1, 3.
2. Statement 23, Protein Advisory Group of the United Nations, 18 July, 1972.
3. See Roy E. Brown, "Breast Feeding in Modern Times," *The American Journal of Clinical Nutrition,* 26:485–6 (May 1973) and Carol Adelman, "Infant Formula, Science and Politics," *Policy Review,* Winter 1988: 107–126.
4. "Recommendations of the United Methodist Infant Formula Task Force, October, 1982," and "Fourth Report of the Infant Formula Task Force, April 28, 1982."
5. Sethi, *Multinational Corporations,* 68, 69.
6. *Ibid.,* 351–352, 371–377.
7. Enrique Rios, "A Follow-Up Study on Current Policies and Practices of Infant Feeding in Mexican Hospitals," April 1995.

TOPIC STUDY: ADVERTISING

IS IT EVER RIGHT TO LIE? (ON TRUTH IN ADVERTISING)

ROBERT SOLOMON

Ask yourself Solomon's first question: Is it ever right to lie? Do you answer that immediately, from your gut, with no? Most of us would instead offer qualifying comments, then say that (generally) we think it is a bad idea. Now, do you expect advertisers to lie? Do you answer yes immediately? Maybe. Many of us take advertisements with a grain of salt, and Solomon addresses this phenomenon.

Is it ever right to lie?

No.

Now, let's get down to business.

It may never be right to tell a lie, but nevertheless it is often prudent, preferable, and—if the way people behave is any indication at all of morals—popular as well.

Consider the familiar dilemma of HGT sales representative John G., who is asked whether his product is in fact as good as a Xerox. One curious fact is that John G. owns a Xerox himself, but another not insignificant fact is that he is employed by the HGT company to sell their line of products, not to express his personal preferences or conduct a neutral survey of product quality. What does he do? What can he do? Of course, he says, "Yes—and better besides." Is he lying? Or just doing his job? He is doing both, of course, but should we say that he is thereby doing wrong?

"Truth" and "falsehood" are evasive qualities even in an academic seminar or a scientist's laboratory; they are even more so in the real world. Is a lover lying to himself when he says that his love is the "most wonderful woman in the world"? Is a salesman lying to a customer when he praises an imperfect product? To be sure, there is such a thing as outright deception—the standard case in which a used-car salesman insists that an old convertible is in excellent mechanical condition, knowing full well that the unhappy new owner will be lucky to get the heap off the lot. But one can also argue that shopping at certain used-car lots (the kind advertised by a hand-painted sign that says,—"Honest Harry Has the Bargains") car-

Robert Solomon, "Is It Ever Right to Lie? (On Truth in Advertising)," *The New World of Business.* Reprinted by permission of Rowman & Littlefield Publishers.

ries with it the knowledge of risk on the part of the buyer, risking a trade-off for the bargain. What counts as "honest" is already put into question. Of course, there are outright lies—falsification of the odometer reading or the false claim that the engine was overhauled 3,000 miles ago, but there is a certain latitude in lying that depends on the context, the customer, and the costs. Not only lying but giving misleading information is intolerable in the health-care industry—for example, not mentioning the side effects of a new drug. Showing hyper-dramatic demonstrations of "action" toys to children or giving technical information to people who cannot possibly understand it may involve neither false nor misleading information but nevertheless may be morally dubious (given the huge proportion of the adult population that can be swayed by mere adjectives such as "scientific" or "natural"). Cost counts, too. Exaggerated claims for the cleaning powers of an inexpensive soap product or the convenience of a household gadget advertised on TV for (inevitably) $19.95 are more easily forgiven than even mildly bloated praise for the value of a new house or bulldozer. On the other hand, it is clear that it is not only self-defeating but cruel to tell a customer *everything* horrible that might befall him with his product. (Imagine the warnings that would have to accompany even such a simple household appliance as a food processor.)

Lying may always be wrong, but some lies are much more wrong than others. Truth may always be desirable, but the "whole truth and nothing but the truth" is just as likely to be a nightmare.

To say that it is never right to lie is not the same as to say that one should never lie. It is rather to say that a lie is always a later resort, a strategy that is not a first choice. If the salesman could sell his wares by saying nothing but the truth, he could, should, and would do so. But one must always excuse a lie, by showing that some greater evil would result from telling the truth or, most often, simply by showing that there is minimal harm done by lying and that, in this context, the lie is not wholly inappropriate. The one thing that a person cannot do is to think that telling a lie—*any* lie—is just as good or right as telling the truth, and so needs no special justification for doing so.

Lying has almost always been considered a sin or an immoral act. In a best-selling book, Sissela Bok has argued that lying is always wrong because, in a variety of ways, it always has bad consequences—worse, that is, than if the lie had not been told. Common experience indicates otherwise, perhaps, for the general attitude both in business and in society is that lies have a perfectly proper social place. Indeed there are clearly contexts in which it would be wrong *not* to lie. Lies can prevent family fights and quarrels among couples. They can prevent bad feelings and help avoid misunderstandings. And, often, they can help an employee keep his or her job. ("I was caught in traffic" is a transparent lie but sometimes an acceptable excuse for being late; "I hated the idea of coming to work so much that I forgot to set the alarm" is, though true, utterly unacceptable.)

We can all agree, looking only at short-term and immediate benefits, that the harm done by some lies is considerably less than the harm that would be done by telling the "unvarnished truth." An employer forced to fire a mediocre worker is certainly not to be blamed for saying that "financial exigencies" have forced him to lay off several low-seniority personnel, instead of telling the truth, which is that the fellow borders on incompetence and doesn't have either the charm or the imagination of a pocket calculator. An advertiser would be judged an idiot, not honest, if he baldly stated that this pain remedy is no more or less effective than any other on the market, though its packaging is prettier. Nevertheless, there are reasons for saying that lying is always wrong.

The first reason has to do with the enormous amount of effort involved in telling a lie—any lie. The truth—even the incomplete truth—is an enormously complex network of interlocking facts. Anyone who has found himself caught in the nervous web of fabrications involved in even such a simple lie as, "We don't know a thing about what our competitors are doing" ("Then how do you know that. . .?") knows how many seemingly disparate facts can come crashing in when a lie has torn just a small piece out of the truth. As recent national politics has so prominently displayed, the cost of a cover-up is often many times more than the damage done by the lie itself, even if the cover-up is successful.

The second reason looks beyond the short-term benefits of lying to the longer-term damage, which may be harder to see. Every lie diminishes trust. A lie discovered is guaranteed to undermine faith in the liar, but, more subtly, *telling* a lie diminishes one's trust in others. ("If I'm lying to them, they are probably lying to me as well.") Most Americans now look at television advertising as if it were nothing but a tissue of lies—ironically making the more successful ads just those that ignore substantial content and concentrate on memorable associations and effects. A businessman may make many a profit through deception—for a while—but unless one wants to keep on the road for the rest of one's life (sounds good at twenty, not so good at forty), deception almost always catches up and destroys just the business it used to ensure. As long-term investments, lies are usually a bad risk.

The third and strongest reason for thinking that it is never right to lie was suggested by Kant. He asked himself the question, "What would happen if lying were generally accepted? For example, "What would happen if it were an everyday and unexceptional feature of the business world that one person would borrow money from another with no intention whatever of repaying the loan?" His answer was that telling the truth and, in the example, borrowing money would both become impossible, so that if I were to approach you and ask for a $10,000 loan, which I would promise to repay on the first of the year, you would simply laugh in my face, since everyone by then would know that such promises were not to be taken seriously. Lying, in other words, must always be wrong, since to treat lying as acceptable undermines just that trust that makes telling the truth meaningful.

Does this mean that one should never lie? Well, no. But it does mean that it is never right to tell a lie; that telling a lie always requires extra thought and some very good reasons to show that this cardinal violation of the truth should be tolerated.

This said, perhaps we should clear up a few common misconceptions about the place of lying in business. It is sometimes suggested that advertising is always a lie, since it tells only one side of the story and that side, needless to say, in the best possible light. But now it is important to distinguish—in facing any such accusation—among the following:

1. telling less than the whole truth;
2. telling a biased truth, with one's own interests in mind;
3. idealizing one's products or services;
4. giving misleading information; that is, true statements that are intended to be misunderstood or misinterpreted;
5. stating obvious falsehoods;
6. stating vicious falsehoods.

An obvious falsehood, for example, is the displayed claim of some toothpaste manufacturers—that use of a certain gel will overnight convert Shy Sam or Plain Jane to Fabulous Fred or Super Sally, the heartthrob of the high-school prom. One might object to other aspects of such advertising, but "It isn't true" seems too silly to say.

Vicious falsehoods, on the other hand, are those that are not at all obvious and are a deliberate and possibly dangerous form of deception. Saying that a product will do such and such when it will not is vicious deception, as is intentionally withholding information—for example, the flammability of children's pajamas or the side effects of a popular over-the-counter drug. Misleading information can be as vicious as false information—indeed it is only a matter of logical nuance that allows us to distinguish between the two.

It is impossible to tell the "whole story," especially in the limited time of a fifteen-second radio or TV slot or in the small space available on a paper package. But advertising isn't supposed to be a scientific study, even if it utilizes some (more or less) scientific evidence on the product's behalf. Of course advertising expresses a bias on the behalf of the product. Of course it idealizes the product in its presentation. But neither bias nor idealization is lying, and it is surely foolish to insist that advertising, unlike almost every other aspect of social life, be restricted to the simple, boring truth—that is, that this product is not much different from its competitors and that people have lived for hundreds of thousands of years without any of them.

It is often challenged—these days with Orwellian overtones—that advertising in general and TV advertising in particular have turned the American consumer into something of a supermarket zombie, without a will of his or her own, without judgment, buying hundreds of innocuous but sometimes tasteless products that no one really needs. But the zombie image contradicts precisely what lies beneath the whole discussion of truth—namely, the confidence that we are, more or less, capable of making value judgments on our own, and that if we buy or even need to buy products that are of no particular cosmic importance, this does not signal either the end of civilization or the disintegration of the human mind. Encouraging someone to buy a product that is only a fad or a mark of status is not deception, and to call it that tends to undermine the ethical distinction that is of enormous importance—between vicious falsehoods and any number of other "varnishings" of the truth. These may be vulgar. They may encourage us to compete for some pretty silly achievements—the shiniest (and most slippery) floor, a car that can win the grand prix (to be driven in bumper-to-bumper traffic up and down the freeway), a soap that makes one speak in a phony Irish brogue. But to condemn all advertising is to make it impossible to attack vicious advertising and thus to bring about the logical conclusion imagined by Kant—an entire world in which no one believes anything, in which advertising serves at most as a source of amusement and seduction of the feeble-minded.

Let's end our discussion of lying by commenting once again on Alfred Carr's suggestion that business is like poker, that it has its own rules, which are different from ordinary ethics. One of these rules, supposedly, is the permissibility of lying. But business (like poker) forbids lying. Contrary to Carr, a generally accepted practice of lying would undermine the business world faster than any external threat that has ever faced it. Promises and contracts, if not good faith, are the presuppositions of all business. The exact nature of truth in advertising may be controversial, but advertising in general must be not only based on fact but believable and truthworthy. If it were not, the commercial world in America would be about as effective as the provocations of Hari Krishnas in America's airports—an annoyance to be ignored as we all go on with the rest of our lives.

Honesty isn't just the best policy in business; it is, in general, the only possible policy.

WHETHER EVERY LIE IS A MORTAL SIN

St. Thomas Aquinas

Aquinas addresses a question similar to that posed by Solomon. Are you persuaded by Aquina's logic?

. . . We proceed thus to the Fourth Article:—

Objection 1. It seems that every lie is a mortal sin. For it is written (Ps. vi. 7): *Thou wilt destroy all that speak a lie,* and (Wis. i. II): *The mouth that belieth killeth the soul.* Now mortal sin alone causes destruction and death of the soul. Therefore every lie is a mortal sin.

Obj. 2. Further, whatever is against a precept of the decalogue is a mortal sin. Now lying is against this precept of the decalogue: *Thou shalt not bear false witness.* Therefore every lie is a mortal sin.

Obj. 3. Further, Augustine says (*De Doctr. Christ.* i. 36): *Every liar breaks his faith in lying, since forsooth he wishes the person to whom he lies to have faith in him, and yet he does not keep faith with him, when he lies to him: and whoever breaks his faith is guilty of iniquity.* Now no one is said to break his faith or *to be guilty of iniquity,* for a venial sin. Therefore no lie is a venial sin.

Obj. 4. Further, the eternal reward is not lost save for a mortal sin. Now, for a lie the eternal reward was lost, being exchanged for a temporal meed. For Gregory says (*Moral.* xviii) that *we learn from the reward of the midwives what the sin of lying deserves: since the reward which they deserved for their kindness, and which they might have received in eternal life, dwindled into a temporal meed on account of the lie of which they were guilty.* Therefore even an officious lie, such as was that of the midwives, which seemingly is the least of lies, is a mortal sin.

Obj. 5. Further, Augustine says (*Lib. De Mend.* vxii) that *it is a precept of perfection, not only not to lie at all, but not even to wish to lie.* Now it is a mortal sin to act against a precept. Therefore every lie of the perfect is a mortal sin: and consequently so also is a lie told by anyone else, otherwise the perfect would be worse off than others.

On the contrary, Augustine says on Ps. v. 7, *Thou wilt destroy,* etc.: *There are two kinds of lie that are not grievously sinful yet are not devoid of sin, when we lie either in joking, or for the sake of our neighbor's good.* But every mortal sin is grievous. Therefore jocose and officious lies are not mortal sins.

I answer that, A mortal sin is, properly speaking, one that is contrary to charity whereby the soul lives in union with God, as stated above (**Q.** 24, **A.** 12; **Q.** 35, **A.** 3). Now a lie may be contrary to charity in three ways: first, in itself; secondly, in respect of the evil intended; thirdly, accidently.

St. Thomas Aquinas, "Whether Every Lie Is a Mortal Sin," *Summa Theologica,* 2.2, ques. 110, art. 4, cited in *Lying: Moral Choice in Public and Private Life.*

A lie may be in itself contrary to charity by reason of its false signification. For if this be about divine things, it is contrary to the charity of God, whose truth one hides or corrupts by such a lie; so that a lie of this kind is opposed not only to the virtue of charity, but also to the virtues of faith and religion; wherefore it is a most grievous and a mortal sin. If, however, the false signification be about something the knowledge of which affects a man's good, for instance if it pertain to the perfection of science or to moral conduct, a lie of this description inflicts an injury on one's neighbor, since it causes him to have a false opinion, wherefore it is contrary to charity, as regards the love of our neighbor, and consequently is a mortal sin. On the other hand, if the false opinion engendered by the lie be about some matter the knowledge of which is of no consequence, then the lie in question does no harm to one's neighbor; for instance, if a person be deceived as to some contingent particulars that do not concern him. Wherefore a lie of this kind, considered in itself, is not a mortal sin.

As regards the end in view, a lie may be contrary to charity, through being told with the purpose of injuring God, and this is always a mortal sin, for it is opposed to religion; or in order to injure one's neighbor, in his person, his possessions or his good name, and this also is a mortal sin, since it is a mortal sin to injure one's neighbor, and one sins mortally if one has merely the intention of committing a mortal sin. But if the end intended be not contrary to charity, neither will the lie, considered under this aspect, be a mortal sin, as in the case of a jocose lie, where some little pleasure is intended, or in an officious lie, where the good also of one's neighbor is intended. Accidentally a lie may be contrary to charity by reason of scandal or any other injury resulting therefrom: and thus again it will be mortal sin, for instance if a man were not deterred through scandal from lying publicly.

Reply Obj. 1. The passages quoted refer to the mischievous lie, as a gloss explains the words of Ps. v. 7, *Thou wilt destroy all that speak a lie.*

Reply Obj. 2. Since all the precepts of the decalogue are directed to the love of God and our neighbor, as stated above (**Q. 44, A.** 1, *ad* 3: **I-II, Q.** 100, **A.** 5 *ad* I), a lie is contrary to a precept of the decalogue, in so far as it is contrary to the love of God and our neighbor. Hence it is expressly forbidden to bear false witness against our neighbor.

Reply Obj. 3. Even a venial sin can be called *iniquity* in a broad sense, in so far as it is beside the equity of justice; wherefore it is written (I John iii. 4): *Every sin is iniquity.* It is in this sense that Augustine is speaking.

Reply Obj. 4. The lie of the midwives may be considered in two ways. First as regards their feeling of kindliness towards the Jews, and their reverence and fear of God, for which their virtuous disposition is commended. For this an eternal reward is due. Wherefore Jerome (in his exposition of Isa. ixv. 21, *And they shall build houses*) explains that God *built them spiritual houses.* Secondly, it may be considered with regard to the external act of lying. For thereby they could merit, not indeed eternal reward, but perhaps some temporal meed, the deserving of which was not inconsistent with the deformity of their lie, though this was inconsistent with their meriting an eternal reward. It is in this sense that we must understand the words of Gregory, and not that they merited by that lie to lose the eternal reward as though they had already merited it by their preceding kindliness, as the objection understands the words to mean.

Reply Obj. 5. Some say that for the perfect every lie is a mortal sin. But this assertion is unreasonable. For no circumstance causes a sin to be infinitely more grievous unless it transfers it to another species. Now a circumstance of person does not transfer a sin to another species, except perhaps by reason of something annexed to that person, for instance if it be against his vow: and this cannot apply to an officious or jocose lie. Wherefore an officious or a jocose lie is not a mortal sin in perfect men, except perhaps accidentally on account of scandal. We may take in this sense the saying of Augustine that *it is a precept of perfection not only not to lie at all, but not even to wish to lie:* although Augustine says this not positively but dubiously, for he begins by saying: *Unless perhaps it is a precept,* etc. Nor does it matter that they are placed in a position to safeguard the truth: because they are bound to safeguard the truth by virtue of their office in judging or teaching, and if they lie in these matters their lie will be a mortal sin: but it does not follow that they sin mortally when they lie in other matters. . . .

LYING

St. Augustine

Augustine perhaps puts an end to this quandary about whether it is right to lie by defining several different types of lies. Which of his arguments is most persuasive?

ON LYING

. . . The first type of lie is a deadly one which should be avoided and shunned from afar, namely, that which is uttered in the teaching of religion, and to the telling of which no one should be led under any condition. The second is that which injures somebody unjustly: such a lie as helps no one and harms someone. The third is that which is beneficial to one person while it harms another, although the harm does not produce physical defilement. The fourth is the lie which is told solely for the pleasure of lying and deceiving, that is, the real lie. The fifth type is that which is told from a desire to please others in smooth discourse. When these have been avoided and rejected, a sixth kind of lie follows which harms no one and benefits some person, as, for instance, when a person, knowing that another's money is to be taken away unjustly, answers the questioner untruthfully and says that he does not know where the money is. The seventh type is that which is harmful to no one and beneficial to some person, with the exception of the case where a judge is questioning, as happens when a person lies because he is unwilling to betray a man sought for capital punishment, that is, not only a just and innocent person but even a criminal, because it belongs to Christian discipline never to despair of the conversion of anybody and never to block the opportunity for repentance. Now, I have spoken at length concerning these last two types, which are wont to evoke considerable discussion, and I have presented my opinion, namely, that by the acceptance of sufferings which are borne honorably and courageously, these lies, too, may be avoided by strong, faithful, and truthful men and women. The eighth is that type of lie which is harmful to no one and beneficial to the extent that it protects someone from physical defilement, at least, from that defilement which we have mentioned above. Now, the Jews considered a defilement to eat with unwashed hands. If anyone considers that as defilement, then a lie must not be told in order to avoid it. However, we are confronted with a new problem if a lie is such that it brings injury to any person, even though it protects another person from that defilement which all men detest and abhor. Should such a lie be told if the injury resulting from it is not in the nature of the defilement of which we have been treating? The question here does not concern lying; rather, it is whether harm should be done to any person, not necessarily through a lie, so that such defilement may be warded off from another person. I am definitely inclined to oppose such license. Even though the

---

St. Augustine, "Lying," from *Treatises on Various Subjects.*

most trivial injuries are proposed, such as that one which I mentioned above in regard to the one lost measure of grain, they disturb me greatly in this problem as to whether we ought to do injury to one person if, by that wrong, another person may be defended, or protected against defilement. But, as I have said, that is another question. . . .

AGAINST LYING

You have sent me much to read, dear brother Consentius, you have sent me much to read. [. . .] I am quite delighted with your eloquence, with your memory of sacred Scripture, with your adroitness of mind, with your distress in stinging indifferent Catholics, with your zeal in raging against even latent heretics. But I am not persuaded that they should be drawn out of hiding by our lies. For, why do we try with so much care to track them and hunt them down? Is it not so that, when they have been caught and brought into the open, we may either teach them the truth themselves or else, by convicting them of error, keep them from harming others? Is it not, in short, so that their falsehood may be blotted out or guarded against and God's truth be increased? Therefore, how can I suitably proceed against lies by lying? Or should robbery be proceeded against by means of robbery, sacrilege by sacrilege, and adultery by adultery? "But if through my lie the truth of God has abounded," are we, too, going to say, "why should we not do evil that good may come from it?" You see how much the Apostle detests this. But what is it to say: "Let us lie in order to bring lying heretics to the truth, if not the same as saying, "Why should we not do evil that good may come from it?" Or is lying sometimes a good, or sometimes not an evil? Why, then, has it been written: "Thou hatest all the workers of iniquity: thou wilt destroy all that speak a lie"? He has not made exception of some or said indefinitely: "Thou wilt destroy tellers of lies," so as to allow that certain ones be understood, but not every one. But he has brought forth a universal proposition, saying: "Thou wilt destroy all that speak a lie." Or, because it has not been said: "Thou wilt destroy all that speak any lie or that speak any lie whatsoever," are we to think, therefore, that room has been made for a certain kind of lie and that God will not destroy those who tell a certain kind of lie, but only those who tell unjust lies, not any lie whatsoever, because there are found just lies, too, which ought actually to be matter for praise rather than reproach?

(2) Do you not see how much this argument supports the very ones whom we are trying to catch as great quarry by our lies? That, as you yourself have shown, is precisely the opinion of the Priscillianists. To establish this opinion they produce evidence from Scripture, urging their followers to lie as if in accordance with the example of the Patriarchs, Prophets, Apostles, and angels, not hesitating to add even Christ our Lord Himself, thinking that they cannot otherwise prove their falsehood to be true except by saying that the Truth is mendacious. They must be refuted, not imitated. We must not participate with the Priscillianists in that evil in which they are proved to be worse than all other heretics, for they alone, or at least they especially, in order to hide what they think is their truth, are found to give dogmatic sanction to lying. And this great evil they deem just, for they say that what is true must be kept in the heart, but that it is no sin to utter what is false with the tongue to strangers. They say that it has been written: "He that speaketh truth in his heart," as if that were sufficient for justice, even if one tells a lie with his tongue when a stranger and not a neighbor is listening. On this account they even think that the Apostle Paul, when he had

said: "Put away lying and speak truth," at once added: "each one with his neighbor, because we are members of one another," so that it plainly might be lawful and dutiful to tell a lie to those who are not our neighbors in the community of truth and not, as it were, our comembers.

***

(36) But, because we are men and live among men, I confess that I am not yet in the number of those who are not troubled by compensatory sins. Often, in human affairs, human sympathy overcomes me and I am unable to resist when someone says to me: "Look, here is a patient whose life is endangered by a serious illness and whose strength will not hold out any longer if he is told of the death of his dearly beloved only son. He asks you whether the boy is still alive whose life you know is ended. What will you answer when, if you say anything except 'He is dead' or 'He is alive' or 'I don't know,' the patient will believe that he is dead, because he realizes that you are afraid to say and do not want to lie? It will be the same no matter how hard you try to say nothing. Of the three convincing answers, two are false: 'He is alive' and 'I don't know,' and you cannot utter them without lying. But, if you make the one true answer, namely, that he is dead, and if the death of the anguished father follows hard upon it, people will cry that he was slain by you. And who can bear to hear them exaggerate the evil of avoiding a beneficial lie and of loving homicide as truth?" I am moved by these arguments—more powerfully than wisely! For, when I put before my mind's eye the intellectual beauty of Him from whose mouth nothing false proceeded, then, although my weakness reverberates in palpitation before the radiance of the truth shining ever more brightly, I am so inflamed by love of such great beauty that I despise all human considerations that call me back from there. It is hard for this feeling to persist so far that its effect is not lost in time of temptation. Indeed, when I am contemplating the luminous good on which there is cast no shadow of a lie, I am not moved by the fact that, when we are unwilling to lie and men die upon hearing what is true, truth is called homicide. Why, if a shameless woman expects to be defiled and then dies of her fierce love because you do not consent, will chastity also be homicide? Or, indeed, because we read: "We are the fragrance of Christ for God, alike as regards those who are saved and those who are lost; to these an odor that leads to death, but to those an odor that leads to life," shall we also pronounce the fragrance of Christ to be homicide? But, because we are men and because human sympathy generally overcomes or harasses us amid such questions and objections, therefore, he, too, added, And for such offices; who is sufficient?

(37) Besides these there is the more distressing fact that, if we grant that we ought to lie about the son's life for the sake of that patient's health, little by little and bit by bit this evil will grow and by gradual accessions will slowly increase until it becomes such a mass of wicked lies that it will be utterly impossible to find any means of resisting such a plague grown to huge proportions through small additions. Hence, it has been most providentially written: "He that contemneth small things, shall fall by little and little." What of the fact that such lovers of this life as do not hesitate to prefer it to the truth want us not only to lie but also to perjure ourselves in order that a man may not die, nay, in order that a man who must sooner or later die may die a little later? They would have us take the name of the Lord our God in vain in order that the vain health of a man may not pass away a little sooner. And

there are in these matters learned men who even make rules and set limits for when we ought and when we ought not to be perjured. O where are you, ye fountains of tears? And what shall we do? Where shall we go? Where shall we hide ourselves from the wrath of truth, if we not only disregard the avoidance of lies, but venture in addition to teach perjuries? Let the advocates and defenders of lies look to what kind or kinds of lying it pleases them to justify! Only in the worship of God may they grant that we must not lie; only from perjuries and blasphemies may they restrain themselves; only where God's name, God's testimony, God's oath is introduced, only where talk of divine religion is brought forth, may no one lie, or praise or teach or enjoin lying or say that lying is just. About other kinds of lies, let him who believes that we ought to lie choose for himself what he thinks is the mildest and most innocent kind of lying. This much I know, that even he who teaches that we ought to lie wants to appear to be teaching the truth. For, if what he teaches is false, who would want to study the false doctrine where the teacher deceives and the learner is deceived? But if, in order that he may be able to find some pupil, he declares that he is teaching the truth when he teaches that we ought to lie, how will that lie be of the truth, since John the Apostle protests that "no lie is of the truth?" Therefore, it is not true that sometimes we ought to lie. And what is not true we should never try to persuade anyone to believe.

GOT . . . BEER?!

Better than Milk, New Survey Shows!

PEOPLE FOR THE ETHICAL TREATMENT OF ANIMALS

The following publicity item was created and disseminated by People for the Ethical Treatment of Animals (PETA) as part of its publicity campaign surrounding the treatment of dairy cows. The campaign was specifically directed at college campuses and, subsequent to its inception, was severely chastised by groups included the Mothers Against Drunk Driving (MADD) as inappropriate and insensitive to the drinking problems and pressures often found on college campuses. In response to MADD's concerns, PETA pulled the "Got . . . Beer?" campaign materials from college settings, "notwithstanding the enormously positive response from college students" and redirected those interested to its "Dump Dairy" campaign, instead. Included below are materials from both campaigns. Do you believe the "Got . . . Beer?" campaign is inappropriate on college campuses? Is the "Dump Dairy" campaign as effective as "Got . . . Beer?"

"Got . . . Beer?! Better than milk, new survey shows!" Reprinted with permission of People for the Ethical Treatment of Animals (PETA).

GOT... BEER?!

People for the Ethical Treatment of Animals

is urging college students to wipe off those milk mustaches and replace them with ... foam? The largest animal rights group in the world is releasing the results of research showing that beer is actually better for you than milk. PETA is giving away bottle openers that say, "Drinking responsibly means not drinking milk–save a cow's life," to college students who visit www.MilkSucks.com.

The dairy industry spends more than $300 million every year to convince people to drink gallons of the white stuff, but PETA's sentiments are with savvy health officials who warn that dairy products have four major drawbacks. Milk and cheese: 1) are loaded with fat and cholesterol and devoid of complex carbohydrates; 2) are frequently contaminated with pesticides and drugs; 3) are linked to diabetes, heart disease, and certain cancers; and 4) may even cause osteoporosis, the very disease that the dairy industry loves to use as a selling point in its ads, because the excess protein in dairy products leaches calcium from the bones. (The Harvard Nurses' Study shows almost twice as many bone breaks among women who drink three glasses of milk a day as compared to women who drink little to no milk.)

Here's why beer is better

A nutritional comparison of beer and milk reveals that:

- Beer has zero fat; milk is loaded with it.

- Beer has zero cholesterol; milk contains 20 mg of cholesterol in every 8-oz. serving.

- Beer doesn't contain hormones or antibiotics, while milk contains an ever-increasing variety of the pesticides and antibiotics fed to cows, including rBGH, the notorious growth hormone that can give guys breasts.

- Beer has half a gram of fiber in every cup; milk has no fiber whatsoever.

- Beer has only 12 mg of sodium per 122 mg. Milk is sky-high in sodium.

- The high-animal protein content of milk actually leaches calcium from the bones. In the U.S., Norway, and Sweden–where people consume the most dairy products–women have the highest rates of osteoporosis in the world. Regions of the world where dairy products are not part of the culture, such as China and Japan, are virtually osteoporosis-free. A study published by the *Journal of Clinical Nutrition* found that by the time she is 65, the average female American dairy-drinker will have lost 35 percent of her original bone density. The average female American vegetarian will have lost only 18 percent.

- Unless you drink the stuff on your way up Mount Everest, beer won't give you a stroke. However, dairy products contribute to almost every disease except carpal tunnel syndrome, including stroke; iron-deficiency; allergies; cancers of the prostate, breast, colon, and ovaries; asthma; heart disease; and even the common cold (milk helps promote the production of mucus).

PETA's main "beef" is, of course, about the treatment of the mother cows and their calves on factory farms. Today's dairy cow is treated like nothing more than a milk machine–chained by her neck in a concrete stall for months, her udders genetically modified to produce so much extra milk that they sometimes drag on the feces and urine covered cement. She is kept pregnant by artificial insemination to keep milk production high; her male calves are traumatically taken away from her at 1 to 2 days old and chained inside cramped dark crates to be killed for veal. The milk that is meant for them ends up on our supermarket shelves. There are no retirement homes for dairy cows. When their usefulness to dairy farmers is over, they get shoved into a truck and sent off to slaughter.

PETA's College Action Campaign coordinator Morgan Leyh counsels, "Colleges have been busy banning kegs from campus. But we say, 'Ditch the dairy, not the beer!' "

United States Department of Agriculture Nutritional Data for Milk and Beer.		
	MILK (1 cup, 2% milk)	BEER (1 cup)
Fat (g)	5	0
Fiber (g)	0	.5
Sodium (mg)	122	12
Cholesterol (mg)	20	0
Calories	122	97

Of course, while all this is true, PETA recommends fresh juices, soy milk, and mineral water–even soda–over milk or beer.

March 16, 2000

Dean Wilkerson
National Executive Director
Mothers Against Drunk Driving
511 E. John Carpenter Fwy., Ste. 700
Irving, TX 75062-8187

1 page via fax:972-869-2206 (hard copy to follow)

Dear Mr. Wilkerson:

We have seriously considered MADD's concerns about PETA's "Got Beer?" parody materials, and we have decided to pull our materials that refer to drinking beer from college campuses. We will, of course, continue the anti-milk campaign, but from a different angle.

As I think you appreciate, PETA's aim was never to promote beer drinking. Our materials recommend fruit juices, soy milk, and mineral water over milk or beer. We included beer in our nutritional comparison to focus attention a bit irreverently, on the fact that milk is so awful for you that even a glass of beer—widely recognized as no health food—would be a better choice than a glass of milk.

We will now refocus our "Milk Sucks" Campaign on the terrible suffering of hyper-ovulated, artificially inseminated, worn-out mother cows and their calves who are torn from their mothers and made to suffer so that college students and others can drink the milk that nature intended for them. As a result of our campaign, over 1,500 college students have decided to get involved in the fight against dairy. They will be asked to help post up our new "Missing" ads, modeled after the "Missing" ads on milk cartons and featuring a veal calf raised for veal.

We're pleased that the spotlight on our anti-dairy campaign has been able to help MADD bring more attention to the issue of drunk driving, while also drawing attention to the cruelty and unhealthiness of dairy products. Because all of us here feel that your work is so valuable, I am enclosing $500 in individual contributions to MADD from PETA employees. We will also add a link from our "Got Beer?" Web site to MADD's Web site.

Good luck in your good work. Please wish us well in ours!

Very truly yours,

Ingrid Newkirk
President

PeTA
PEOPLE FOR THE ETHICAL
TREATMENT OF ANIMALS

501 FRONT STREET
NORFOLK, VA 23510
TEL 757-622-PETA
FAX 757-622-0457

www.peta-online.org
info@peta-online.org

AN INTERNATIONAL
ORGANIZATION DEDICATED
TO PROTECTING
THE RIGHTS OF ALL ANIMALS

Mothers Against Drunk Driving

511 E. John Carpenter Fwy. Suite 700 • Irving, Texas 75062-8187 • Telephone (214) 744-MADD • FAX (972) 864-2206/2207 • www.madd.org
NATIONAL OFFICE

March 21, 2000

Ms. Ingrid Newkirk
President
People for the Ethical Treatment of Animals
501 Front Street
Norfolk, VA 23510

VIA FAX: 757-562-0457 (hard copy to follow)

Dear Ms. Newkirk:

We received the hard copy of your faxed letter dated March 16, 2000, along with the $500.00 contribution. While we appreciate the acknowledgement of MADD's mission, we feel we must return the enclosed donations from your organization and staff members. If you truly wish to support MADD's efforts, please do the right thing and stop asking students to drink alcohol.

As our national president stated in a letter faxed March 16, we are extremely disappointed to see that the "Got Beer" campaign continues to appear on the PETA Web site. While pulling the irresponsible campaign from college campuses is an important step, you are continuing to encourage students – many under the legal drinking age of 21 – to drink beer instead of milk through your Web site. Again, we ask that you immediately remove all "Got Beer" campaign references and terminate your link to MADD's Web site. We are unable to accept your contributions or allow a link to the MADD site because of the implied association with PETA's animal rights issues – issues which are unrelated to our mission to stop drunk driving, support the victims of this violent crime and prevent underage drinking.

We received numerous phone calls and e-mails from the public and PETA supporters voicing their concerns about the "Got Beer" campaign. We hope to hear from you soon regarding our requests.

Sincerely,

Dean Wilkerson
Executive Director

cc: MADD Board of Directors

531

March 24, 2000

Mr. Dean Wilkerson
Executive Director
MADD
511 E. John Carpenter Fwy., Ste. 700
Irving, TX 75062-8187

Dear Mr. Wilkerson:

Your recent letter would have been well received if, instead of attacking us and insulting our staff and their families, you had acknowledged any of the good that has come out of the PETA campaign — for your organization, which received a greater platform at a crucial time for your issue than in any previous year, i.e. just before Spring Break, and for the issues that concern not only MADD but all decent people, namely drunken driving (which PETA has never advocated), underage drinking (which PETA has never advocated), and binge drinking (which PETA has never advocated). As someone here said, MADD got more exposure in two days than it has had in two years.

We realize that MADD used PETA as an easy target and we do not resent that. Without your drawing the media to our campaign, PETA would not have been able to let as many people as we did know that modern milk production is abusive to cows, promotes the notoriously cruel veal industry, and produces a product that eventually kills more people than drunken driving, through coronary artery disease, stroke, cancers, and other milk- (and meat-) related diseases.

Not that I would presume to know your agenda, but surely, now that the media fuss has abated, MADD should be rechanneling its energies into more productive avenues, say, for example, the fact that every sporting event of widespread interest to high school and college students is sponsored by beer and alcohol companies? That would seem more useful than niggling about our Web site. When college students or older people ask what the fuss was all about, we are not about to tell them that they're not intelligent enough to read the facts and make up their own minds. Let me also make it clear, PETA is not against beer-drinking, it is against milk-drinking, for ethical reasons. Beer-drinking is legal in this country and PETA has never suggested that any individual under the legal drinking age start drinking the stuff. When visitors to www.MilkSucks.com read our materials, they realize that.

Finally, by returning contributions from people who work at PETA, whereas you do not presumably return contributions from people who work at Budweiser or Coors, or even at the National Rifle Association or Ku Klux Klan headquarters, you have allowed your prejudices regarding our humane agenda to let you refuse money that MADD could have used to help stop problem drinking. Instead of seizing the opportunity to welcome new individual members, you have, instead, left a bad taste in their mouths. That is a shame and a missed opportunity to keep up MADD's good work.

Very truly yours,

Ingrid E. Newkirk
President

PETA

PEOPLE FOR THE ETHICAL
TREATMENT OF ANIMALS

501 FRONT STREET
NORFOLK, VA 23510
TEL 757-622-PETA
FAX 757-622-0457

www.peta-online.org
info@peta-online.org

AN INTERNATIONAL
ORGANIZATION DEDICATED
TO PROTECTING
THE RIGHTS OF ALL ANIMALS

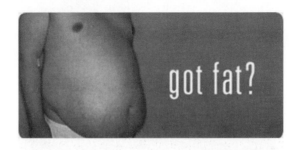

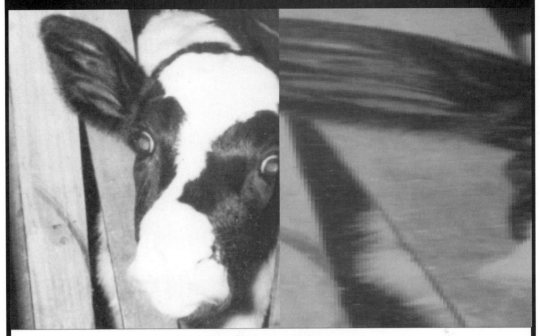
535

RECENT ISSUES IN ADVERTISING LAW AND ETHICS

Compendium

JEF I. RICHARDS

Professor Richards has amassed a compendium of examples of recent ethical challenges in advertising. Consider as you peruse the list how many of these advertisements seem familiar and, if so, whether the ethical or legal challenge occurred to you when you first experienced the advertisement. Has law and/or ethics gone too far when it asks whether there is misrepresentation when Coca Cola claims that "things go better with Coke" or when Gallo claims to "sell no wine before its time" or when Avis claims that "We try harder"?

The following certainly is *not* an exhaustive list of issues that have arisen over the past few years. Not even close. These are provided as a broad sampling of such issues, to illustrate the multitude of considerations in the area of advertising law and ethics.

1996

A Pepsi for a Fighter   John Leonard, in compliance with the terms of Pepsi's advertising offer, delivered 15 "Pepsi Points" and a check for $700,008.50 to PepsiCo to claim a new Harrier jet. The jet had been depicted in a Pepsi Stuff TV commercial, as a part of a points-for-stuff promotion. The commercial offered a variety of prizes in exchange for points, and as a joke added that for 7 million points consumers could claim the Harrier fighter jet. Pepsi refused to deliver the $70 million jet to Leonard, so he sued.[1]

Is It Any Wonder?   Perrier's "Wonderbubbles" posters in Europe raised the hackles of feminists. The posters were designed as a spoof on Playtex's Wonderbra ad campaign, but Perrier's campaign depicted bare-breasted women with bottle caps hiding their nipples. The ads were pulled by Perrier.[2]

"Recent Issues in Advertising Law and Ethics: Compendium," compiled by Jef I. Richards, University of Texas at Austin. Reprinted with permission of the author.

[1] Associated Press, "Man follows rules of Pepsi game, wants fighter jet," *Austin American-Statesman,* August 7, 1996, p. A10.

[2] "Found Art," *Advertising Age, July 29, 1996, p. 26.*

What's Beneath This?   In 1987, TV networks ended a moratorium on using live models in underwear commercials. Today, it seems that underwear ads are becoming more and more blatant in their sexual appeals. A recent Victoria's Secret commercial was rejected by all three major networks as too racy. As a result of this perceived trend, some media buyers are talking about the possibility of greater network "zoning" of time periods in which sexy commercials could appear.[3]

***

Hucksters and the CyberKids   A petition has been submitted to the Federal Trade Commission, asking that advertising on the Internet be restricted. The petition claims that advertisers are invading children's privacy and creating improper relationships between kids and commercial spokescharacters, like Tony the Tiger. One ad industry exec says, "We believe that every advertising issue has been modified to be treated as a children's protection issue."[4]

Obscene Frogs   After Ohio rejected labels for Bad Frog beer, Michigan's Liquor Control Commission decided to take a closer look at the labels, which it had previously approved. On second look, the Commission said it may stop sales of the beer unless it changes the labels. On the label, a frog is shown with an extended middle finger. (Do frogs have fingers?) The slogan on the label declares, "He's mean, green and obscene." A Michigan Assistant Attorney General agreed that the labels were "obscene."[5]

We Don't Trust Ads   A worldwide survey of consumers found that 72 percent believe marketers exaggerate health benefits of their products. And 70 percent are convinced that marketers brainwash children. Only 38 percent agreed that marketers give consumers accurate information.[6]

1995

Ads Cause Smoking   A study, conducted by a medical researcher, says that kids are twice as likely to be influenced to smoke by tobacco ads as by peer pressure. In the survey, about 60 percent of nonsmokers age 12–17 were able to name their favorite cigarette ad. The researcher claims these children are more receptive to smoking and more likely to become smokers than other nonsmokers in that age group.[7]

Mayor Says: Pull Your Pants Down   A campaign by Levi Strauss hung a pair of Dockers pants, worth about $55, under plastic shields in Manhattan bus shelters. The pants were on

---

[3]Pat Sloan, "Underwear ads caught in bind over sex appeal," *Advertising Age,* July 8, 1996, p. 27.

[4]Nora Fitzgerald, "Watching the Kids: The Internet opens a new front in the battle over children's ads," *Adweek,* May 6, 1996, p. 26.

[5]Todd Pruzan, "Bad Frog beer triggers an amphibious assault," *Advertising Age,* April 1, 1996, p. 54.

[6]"The world's view of marketers," *Ad Age International,* January 15, 1996, p. 10.

[7]"Ads lure youths to smoking, studies find," *Austin American-Statesman,* October 18, 1995.

top, and a part, of an ad for Dockers. The ad had the word "Nice" at the top and the word "Pants" at the bottom. If the pants were stolen, the following message would be revealed in their place: "Apparently they were very nice pants." The Mayor and others were upset, claiming this ad was encouraging people to vandalize the bus shelters. Gannett Outdoor, which sold the ad space, agreed to remove the ads.[8]

***

Media Buying Worth Killing For   The executive director, and anchorman, of a Russian TV network was killed after his company announced a halt on "irritating" advertising. It is believed that his death is tied to that announcement, because of the large sums of money lost by media wholesalers as a consequence of that decision.[9]

Reading, Writing, and Advertising   The Consumers Union published a report, "Captive Kids," that concludes advertising has become pervasive in the nation's schools. The report argues that schools should be ad-free zones that shelter students from commercial messages.[10]

---

[8]Lawrence Van Gelder, "Advertiser Agrees to Rescind 'Invitation' to Steal Trousers," *The New York Times,* September 27, 1995, p. A1.

[9]Steven Gutterman, "Anchorman's slaying point to ad scandal," *Advertising Age,* May 1, 1995, p. 44.

[10]Joan Beck, "Selling out: The nation's schools have thrown open their doors to the wrong kinds of advertisers," *Chicago Tribune,* April 27, 1995, Perspective Section, p. 27.

PORTRAYAL OF WOMEN IN ADVERTISING

CAMILLE ATKINSON AND CANDICE FREDRICK

The authors explain that women, and in particular young girls, experience advertising differently than men. Are you persuaded by their discussion? If so, what can be done to combat the potential for negative impact on women's self-esteem?

While all factions share similar concerns and worries regarding children's exposure to an unbridled media, young girls are a particularly vulnerable group, especially when speaking of the effects of advertising. In a sexist society where any trait labeled "feminine" tends to be devalued or exploited, young girls learn through the media how to behave and look if they want to obtain the beauty and character of the "ideal" woman.[1] Early in their lives, women have a sense that something about them isn't quite right, and appearance takes on monumental importance as the girl matures. Open a magazine, any magazine, or pass a string of billboards along a highway and you will see the image of the beautiful woman: extremely thin, large breasted, sexually available, with flawless skin. This prototypical "beauty" is seen everywhere; clothes and products are designed for her and those who aspire to be like her. This is quite a feat when we consider that 33 percent of American women wear a size sixteen or larger![2] What should one do when besieged with this paradigm if she does not measure up (speaking both literally and figuratively)? This archetypal figure represents a body type that only 5 percent of women actually possess. However, the beauty industry has come to the rescue: make-up; products to eliminate wrinkles, blemishes, cellulite or any other physical flaw; plastic surgery, exercise videos and dieting tips.

Because such products are aggressively advertised, eating disorders are all too common among young women who accept the myth of the "perfect" body. These disorders, which involve both physical and mental health issues, are on the rise in the United States; whereas thirty years ago, they were almost entirely unheard of. Today, they are being called "the socio-cultural epidemic of our time."[3] This is underscored when we consider that the revenues of the diet industry are $33 billion. Furthermore, 72 percent of women report that they will be on a diet in any given year[4]—despite the fact that 95 percent of people who look to the diet industry to lose weight gain it all (and then some) back again.[5]

Can we even imagine men following a similar path to meet such a narrowly defined ideal? Of course some men diet, but we cannot find examples of men looking like hunger posters or behaving childlike in order to be attractive to women. Nor does the average man pick at a salad or raw vegetables at dinner, instead of ordering a meal. Men are afforded the dignity of being able to age gracefully and still be considered attractive. Showing a few wrinkles and gray hair is even deemed sexy for men. Many actors are cast as a desirable leading man despite graying or the loss of hair and weathered skin. Newscasters can show evidence of their age if they are male; but we are hard-pressed to find women who can successfully look or act their age and remain employable on television or the big screen.

In her book *The Beauty Myth,* Naomi Wolf talks about how this obsession with perfection came into being.[6] In the 1950s, advertising revenues soared as manufacturers targeted the American housewife, who was often bored with the repetitive tasks of housekeeping. Household products were marketed to make her life easier and more efficient. However, with the advent of a 1960s style feminism and economic instability, many women entered the workforce. Shrewd business people recognized that they needed a new "hook" that did not pertain only to the closed environment of the home. Advertisers sought an obsession that women could take with them to work, and this is how cosmetic/toiletries promotional campaigns began. By 1989 this strategy was well entrenched with beauty products offering $650 million in advertising revenues to magazines; while soaps, cleansers, and polishes yielded only one tenth that amount.[7]

Even certain gains coming out of the women's movement of the 1960s and 1970s have been given an ironic spin by advertisers. For example, the idea that a woman could be naturally beautiful without props has been co-opted, and entire lines of products have been developed to promote the "natural look." A look, however, that could only be obtained with the help of the beauty industry. Now women can wear make-up without it being apparent that they are doing so and seem instead to be blessed with "natural beauty." Even eye color can be changed with tinted contact lenses—the general preference being blue. Moreover, this obsession has created new categories of what counts as attractive, such as the over-forty-but-forever-young look.[8] Scientific approaches to skin care, cosmetic surgery and fitness programs promise to stave off the inevitable changes of maturing, and magazine articles relating to diet increased 70 percent from 1968 to 1972. Articles on diet continued to rise steadily from 60 percent in the year 1979 to 66 percent in the month of January 1980 alone.[9] One of the models of the "fit for life," eternally attractive yet over-forty woman, is the actress and fitness guru Jane Fonda. She is also a woman with a long, sad history of eating disorders—over twenty years of eating and purging. Openly speaking of her disorder she said: "Society says we have to be thin, and while most of us don't have much control over our lives, we can control our weight, either by starving to death or by eating all we want and not showing the effect.[10] In order to "not show the effect" yet still eat heartily a pattern of binge-and-purge must be routinely followed. Fonda speaks of her bulimia as the secret device she used to maintain the physical perfection that was expected of her. Now the publicly stated approach to controlling her weight is physical fitness and "sensible eating."

It is ironic that the goal in each case is the same: control over one's body. Of course, physical fitness does not carry the health dangers of an eating disorder, but the message is no different: find a way to maintain this image of self-control and ideal beauty, regardless of whether or not this reflects a deeper truth and no matter what the cost. The unfortunate message remains that women need to find ways to reach these ideals of eternal youth and physical perfection, though perhaps through "healthier" channels. Something is amiss here, for in either case the burden falls upon women alone. That is, few people question these ideal images or ask how they originated. Perhaps men, too, should wonder why they hold onto such a narrow definition of what is beautiful, and look at the damage it may be doing to their wives, lovers, daughters, mothers, and sisters.

One criticism is that women themselves have helped to create or, at least, perpetuate this false conception of beauty that is portrayed in the media and advertising. After all, it is they who buy the magazines that typecast them into an ideal that is so hopeless and debilitating (as Andy Rooney argued in a *60 Minutes* episode). It is women who submit their bodies and themselves to diets, surgery, and whatever else it takes to remain young, attractive, and competitive. But what are they actually competing for? Is male attention the main goal or obtaining a husband? Are these reasons sufficient for explaining why a woman would risk her health and happiness? If so, how can this account for the "lipstick lesbians" who also buy into the advertising ideal? Why *do* so many women buy into a view of themselves that is virtually impossible and ultimately self-defeating? These kinds of questions are rarely asked, except by self-proclaimed feminists, and answers can only be speculative at best. However, maybe the "why" queries—or search for causes—are ultimately less important than asking, what should we do now? Or, where does one go from here if she wants to overcome these fears of being less than "perfect"? Perhaps one can begin simply by becoming more aware.

Could it be that a commitment to understanding how the professional (advertisers) affects the personal (women's lives) merely reflects a prejudice of a small group of highly educated, professional women influenced by the feminist movement? And, that most are not even interested in how deeply advertising has effected them? This is a criticism leveled by Camille Paglia, the antifeminist writer and lecturer, who basically feels the women's movement is run by East Coast, elitist intellectuals who are making "much ado about nothing." This view supposes that there is something wrong with being educated or an intellectual, and that there is something wrong with this type of woman reflecting upon the position of women in general. It takes a combination of strength, financial resources, and independence to face and overcome the traditionally prevailing model of women's worth or lack thereof. If we accept this, then it is only the educated, financially independent woman who can afford to critically examine this media image and attempt to bring this awareness to others. Women already caught up in the cycle of emotional as well as financial dependency on men lack the resources which would enable them to think, let alone act, in ways that might put their already modest standard of living in jeopardy. Many women have to channel their energies on just surviving and caring for children; they have little time left for contemplating or challenging the pros and cons of constricting gender roles but they are nonetheless hurt by them. It takes time, confidence, and security to confront the status quo.

Regardless, what is wrong with one group of women fighting the battles for those who cannot? Wouldn't seeing yourself as "your sister's keeper" be consistent with a care ethics that values relationships? If financially independent women are in a better position to raise others' consciousness and effect change, doing so should be a virtue not a fault. Moreover, there is a long respected tradition in our country in which those who are privileged speak out and help those who are less fortunate. The Kennedy family has been such an example of this *noblesse oblige*—that is, the moral obligation that goes along with power, wealth and social standing.

The image of women in advertising and other media is so ingrained in society that people don't even recognize it as damaging. Even in college classes, it is only after researching advertising in depth that students start to look critically at advertisements that have long been viewed as benign or neutral. Educating the public facilitates heightened sensitivity to the fact that advertisers work extremely hard, with the help of experts, to have anything but a "neutral" effect on the consumer.

For advertisements to be effective they have to play on fears that are based, at least partly, in reality. And, in fact, many women are afraid of losing love and domestic stability as they age and become less youthful in appearance. Moreover, almost half of all marriages end in divorce and the old story of a man leaving his middle-aged wife for a younger woman is not a myth. Advertisers find easy prey in the very real anxiety many women feel. Men do not have this same kind or degree of concern. As stated before, men can have gray hair and wrinkles and still be considered sexy. And in movies when mature men are teamed with a love interest, the woman is usually much younger and this seems quite "normal." But, more importantly, men are not financially dependent on women the way women are on men, despite social and political advancements. As Wollstonecraft indicated so many years ago: women are prized for their physical beauty and this is one of the few sources of "power" granted them. This may also explain why even some lesbians, who do not look to men for emotional or financial support, continue to aspire to the same standards of beauty. Specifically, beautiful women tend to be valued in ways that the "average" woman is not. They are seen as more powerful, competent, or, simply, as overall better human beings. Women in Hollywood complain that there are fewer and fewer scripts for them as they mature, regardless of their talent or abilities. Even with all that plastic surgery can do for those who are wealthy enough to afford it, one cannot stay young eternally, and fighting the inevitable process of aging is depressing and time-consuming. It saps women's energy to such a degree that sometimes they have little left over for more productive activities. And perhaps this is the objective: keeping women on the defensive about how they look allows them to be taken less seriously making them less threatening to men.[11] Whether or not one agrees with this, it is still clear that women have to be convinced to enter into this futile chase for eternal youth and this impossible ideal of beauty for many businesses to realize profit.

It would not be fair to blame advertising alone for how women are portrayed in media images, but there can be no doubt that business and profit play a significant role and, at the very least, exacerbate sexist assumptions regarding what is feminine and attractive. It is hoped that the next generation of women will not be blindly led by the beauty industry. For transcending cultural conditions is no easy task when a society has been so saturated. Women and men working in the field of ethics can teach students to critically examine advertisements and consider their effects on themselves. Most importantly they need to be empowered to avoid the trap of thinking that media images are innocuous or that the beauty industry, in particular, is only giving the public what they want.

NOTES

1. Jean Kilbourne, *Still Killing Us Softly* [videocassette] (Cambridge, Mass.: Cambridge Documentary Films, 1987).
2. *People Magazine,* June 3, 1996.
3. Eva Szekely, *Never Too Thin* (Toronto: The Women's Press, 1988), p. 12.
4. Jean Kilbourne, *Slim Hopes* [videocassette] (Northhampton, Mass.: Media Education Foundation, 1995).
5. Ibid.

6. Naomi Wolf in her book *The Beauty Myth,* offers a good historical explanation of how the beauty myth came into being and the ensuing beauty culture that has been built around this myth. She is an excellent source for further research on the relationship between feminism and this change of advertising focus.
7. Naomi Wolf, *The Beauty Myth* (New York: Anchor Books, 1991), p. 66.
8. For a good discussion of "over forty" beauty, see "Changing Landscapes," by Wendy Chapkis, *Women Images and Reality* (Mountain View, Calif. Mayfield Publishing Co., 1995), pp. 94–95.
9. Naomi Wolf, *The Beauty Myth,* p. 67.
10. Leo Janus, "Jane Fonda, Finding Her Golden Pond," *Cosmopolitan,* January 1985, p. 170.
11. See Susan Faludi, *Backlash* (New York: Doubleday Publishing, 1992).

TOPIC STUDY: THE BODY SHOP CONTROVERSY

BODY SHOP SCRUTINIZED

JOAN BAVARIA, ERIC BECKER, AND SIMON BILLENNESS

The following article offers a brief overview of the controversy surrounding cosmetic and body care retailer The Body Shop and its claims of social responsibility. The story unfolds as you will see from the following material, which includes a letter from Gordon Roddick of The Body Shop to the subscribers of Business Ethics *magazine after the magazine published an expose of The Body Shop's allegedly false claims.* Business Ethics *magazine publisher Marjorie Kelly's response to that letter (standing behind the facts as stated in the original article) follows. After that letter, you will find Body Shop mission and principles, as well as social audit material published by both The Body Shop and its independent auditor, Kirk Hanson. The final judgment is really up to you. What do you believe? Who is credible and how do you decide? What additional information would you need to make up your mind?*

In the past few weeks the British press has focused on The Body Shop's social record with an intensity normally reserved for the Royal Family. Since the story broke, Body Shop's stock has fallen from almost 250 pence to a low of 205 pence. Recently, the stock has recovered to 216 pence.

Two main questions emerge from this debate:

- Why did this issue reach such a boiling point?

- What is The Body Shop's social record?

HOW THE STORY STARTED . . .

In September 1991 *Franklin's Insight* profiled The Body Shop, awarding the company our highest social ratings. However, since then, we have received information that challenges

Joan Bavaria, Eric Becker, Simon Billenness, "Body Shop Scrutinized," from *Insight,* published by Franklin Research and Development. Reprinted by permission of Franklin Research and Development.

our initial assessment of the company. A German newsletter noted that The Body Shop uses non-plant derived ingredients in its products. A British animal rights organization criticized the company's animal testing policy. Early this year, investigative reporter Jon Entine provided us with considerable information about apparent contradictions between The Body Shop's image and its actual record on social issues. As we independently investigated, we verified some of Entine's claims.

As 1994 progressed, we also became concerned about the growth prospects of The Body Shop's stock. In early June, *Franklin's Insight* lowered its stock recommendation to a "hold," citing a rise in the stock's price and expansion plans by a competitor. At an early June Social Investment conference in Toronto, Jon Entine discussed the results of his research on the firm. On June 14, callers to *Franklin's Insight's* weekly hotline heard that Body Shop stock had been further downgraded from a "hold" to a "sell" recommendation. On June 17 and on June 22, Franklin Research & Development Corporation sold all 45,950 of its clients' shares in The Body Shop. The following July 15 issue of *Franklin's Insight* stated:

> *Last month we lowered Body Shop to a hold based on concerns that its major competitor [Bath & Body Works] was accelerating its growth in the U.S. and Europe. Given this concern and fears that a fairly negative upcoming magazine article may put some near-term price pressure on the stock, we are lowering our rating to a sell.*

For a while all was quiet. Then on August 19, *Financial Times* reporter Andrew Jack wrote about Franklin Research's decision to sell its Body Shop stock two months before. The London edition's headline, somewhat inaccurately read, "US ethical fund turns against Body Shop." At that point, we had simply "turned against" The Body Shop *stock.* We had still not reached a conclusion on the company's overall social performance.

Then the British Press seemed to declare open season on The Body Shop fueled in part by leaks from Entine's story. Journalists followed the gyration of the stock, probed into the background of Entine and speculated as to the contents of his forthcoming article for the U.S. magazine *Business Ethics,* which was published September 1.

The Body Shop has come to its own defense. The company has released a 32-page "Memorandum of Response to the Allegations of Jon Entine." The Body Shop later released a strong reply to the *Business Ethics* article, which it labeled "recycled rubbish." Anita Roddick was quoted calling one animal rights group which criticized The Body Shop "a bunch of babies."

As the issue has died down a bit in the mainstream media, the debate has intensified within the progressive investment and business community. We hope that our following findings help to shed some light on The Body Shop's social record and serve as another chapter in the emerging profile of the company.

LIMITATIONS

The staff of Franklin Research & Development have spent an extraordinary amount of time verifying the information used in this article. We strive to avoid using inflammatory language or assuming the motives of others. We print information that we believe to be true. But we are not chemists, lawyers or anthropologists, nor do we have the resources and contacts of an investigative news organization. It is also hard to establish the facts of an issue that is being so hotly debated. Consequently, we do not attempt to reach a definitive conclusion, but we try instead to state the facts of the issue as we have been able to ascertain them.

THE BODY SHOP: AS WE SEE IT NOW

Our view of The Body Shop's social record has undergone considerable changes since our last profile. The issue is not necessarily just whether The Body Shop has a good or bad relative record of corporate responsibility. The Body Shop has clearly set for itself high standards. However, the company has also enjoyed positive tangible benefits from those publicly espoused standards while, apparently, failing to meet many of them.

Moreover, and perhaps more importantly, the company has compounded what otherwise might be isolated and curable difficulties by repeatedly failing to provide material information to back up its claims and by repeatedly taking a combative stance with its critics. This defensive and almost secretive posture violates what we consider to be cornerstones of social responsibility: openness and accessibility at the highest level of management. We believe we should hold even the most well-intentioned company accountable to this standard. We hope that the following article fairly represents the record of The Body Shop in several key areas.

FRANCHISES

Since The Body Shop is largely a wholesaler and franchisor, the company's dealings with its franchisees are an important part of the firm's record of corporate responsibility. We have no evidence of problems between the company and its British franchisees. However, there appear to be serious disputes between The Body Shop and some overseas franchisees.

In June 1994, The Body Shop settled a breach of contract suit with its former Norwegian franchisee. In a counterclaim, The Body Shop's former Asian head franchisee is suing the company for conspiracy and breach of obligation. In March 1994, the U.S. Federal Trade Commission (FTC) began an investigation of The Body Shop. According to the U.S. General Accounting Office, in the period 1989–92, the FTC received more than 1,360 complaints but began only 78 franchise rule and business opportunity investigations. Of the 78 cases, the FTC filed 14 court cases, closed 31 cases and continued investigating 33 cases.

The FTC has issued a civil investigation demand (CID), to at least one former Body Shop franchisee. The Body Shop confirms that current franchisees have also received FTC questionnaires. FTC Franchise Rule Director Steven Toporoff told *Insight* that there is no clear distinction between an FTC inquiry and an investigation. He added that the FTC uses CID's "fairly frequently" and in instances where the FTC is unable to obtain information voluntarily. In a letter from the FTC, purported to be to a former Body Shop franchisee, it is revealed that the franchisee was concerned that providing information to the FTC would violate a provision in the contract for the resale of the franchise to the franchisor that requires the franchisee "not to write about or speak about or do or perform directly or indirectly, any act injurious or prejudicial to the good will associated with franchisors' proprietary marks or business."

Susan Kezios, president of the American Franchisee Association, told *Insight* she has received complaints from about 10 of The Body Shop's 58 franchisees. It is unclear whether the franchisees are complaining about the conduct of Body Shop employees or company head franchisees. However, some of the complaints include allegations that prospective franchisees were misled about their expected earnings when they were quoted the lower merchandise prices charged to head franchisees when, in fact, they later had to pay the higher price charged to franchisees. Both Kezios and a staff member of the House Committee on Small Business—which investigates franchising—told *Insight* that The Body Shop treats its franchisees no better than most franchisors. Kezios added that The Body Shop franchisees that contacted her insisted on anonymity and seemed "more fearful" than franchisees she had spoken to at other companies.

Body Shop investor relations manager Angela Bawtree told *Insight* of steps the company had recently taken to improve its relationship with franchisees. Over the last year, The Body Shop has set up a committee of franchisees and corporate management. In addition, in some cases, the company now provides loan guarantees for franchisees. The Body Shop has also decided in some cases to open stores in more marginal locations itself before selling them to franchisees. As a measure of franchisee satisfaction with The Body Shop, Bawtree cited the firm's low turnover of franchisees.

We hope that The Body Shop works to resolve the apparent problems with its franchisees. However, the existence of the FTC investigation and the lawsuits do force us to question The Body Shop's reputation as a responsible business partner.

PRODUCT QUALITY

There is evidence that challenges The Body Shop's claim that its products are of "high quality." Letters between The Body Shop and its franchisees dating from 1990 and 1991 mention problems with old and contaminated products. In 1993, a batch of 151 bottles of contaminated banana shampoo were sold to U.S. consumers. According to documents obtained through the Freedom of Information Act, the Food & Drug Administration (FDA) inspected The Body Shop's new headquarters in North Carolina on October 7, 8 and November 12 of 1993. The inspectors found seven irregularities including improper sampling for bacteria in bulk containers, skipped tests and failure to follow up bacteria problems with its product filling jets, missing records to document proper cleaning and sanitizing of its equipment and inconsistent handling of consumer complaints.

According to Angela Bawtree, the banana shampoo incident occurred at a time when The Body Shop was moving operations from New Jersey to North Carolina. She also notes that, while the FDA made recommendations after its inspection, it did not issue a notice of violation. According to Bawtree, over 60% of such inspections result in the issuance of a notice of violation and, in the last three years, more than 100 such notices have been issued to cosmetics firms. The Body Shop also claims that the FDA inspection was prompted by Jon Entine. We would feel much more comfortable with The Body Shop's response to the issue of product quality if the company focused more on what actions it has taken to prevent future problems and less on trying to discredit Jon Entine.

NATURAL PRODUCTS

In The Body Shop's early years, its products were described as "natural" even though they contained chemical and synthetic ingredients. Several years ago The Body Shop started to more accurately describe its products as "naturally-based." However, as recently as September 1992, Anita Roddick said in an interview with *Business Ethics* that The Body Shop "just [used] food stuffs rather than chemical formulas."

Angela Bawtree told *Insight* that the dominant ingredient in many Body Shop products is water, which is natural. However, using this standard, almost any personal care product could be labeled "naturally-based." In fact, while the company's products derive their names, if not their fragrance or color, from flowers, vegetables or fruits, one is hard pressed to find Body Shop products without synthetic ingredients. For example, the Aloe Hair Gel label reads "Water, Rosewater, SD Alcohol 40-B, Aloe Vera Gel, PVP (setting agent), Triethanolamine, PEG-75 Lanoline, Propylene Glycol, Carbomer 940, Phenoxyethanol, Polysorbate 20, Methylparaben, Benzophenone-4, Disodium EDTA, Sodium Dehydroacetate, Propylparaben, Fragrance, FD&C Yellow No. 5, FD&C Blue No. 1."

While we cannot pretend to have done any more than the most cursory research on this point, *Insight* observes that two readily available competing products, "Shampure," by Aveda and Tom's of Maine's "natural shampoo," both appear to use all natural ingredients and, unlike The Body Shop, make it clear on the product label where the ingredients were obtained.

We cannot determine if The Body Shop intentionally misrepresented the nature of its products. The question that we pose is whether The Body Shop should be held responsible for the public perception of its products if that perception diverges from the truth?

We would answer "yes" to the question even though this means holding The Body Shop to a higher standard. In today's marketplace, companies regularly employ exaggeration and allow misinterpretation as a general practice. However, Anita Roddick has clearly denounced this standard puffery and has portrayed The Body Shop as "the most honest cosmetics company in the world." Since The Body Shop has recently stated that it is "a leader in product disclosure" and since we believe that The Body Shop has benefited from subtle public misperceptions, we feel that it should, at least, join Aveda and Tom's of Maine in stating the source of each ingredient on its product packaging.

ENVIRONMENT

There has been much media coverage of three leaks of product from The Body Shop's former New Jersey warehouse. According to the records of the company and the local Hanover Sewerage Authority, at least 62 gallons of shampoo and shower gel were released. It also appears that the spills were first identified by the officials of the Hanover Sewerage authority and traced back to The Body Shop. Although the pattern of spills suggests that management at The Body Shop's facility was lax in its safeguards and tardy in its reporting, the severity of the incidences is immaterial compared to the company's overall environmental record.

The Body Shop's record of environmental auditing and disclosure is impressive. The Body Shop is a signatory of the CERES Principles, an environmental code of conduct created by environmentalists and social investors including the Franklin Research. Moreover, The Body Shop is also the only company that we know of to have set up environmental management systems and an annual environmental audit that follows the voluntary European Union Eco-Management and Audit Regulation. The Body Shop has made efforts to comply with the regulation since it was available in draft form in 1991. In its 1993/94 "Green Book" The Body Shop provides an independently verified environmental statement according to

EU regulation standards for the company's main UK Watersmead facility. The statement includes comparable information on energy efficiency, water usage and waste generation going back three years. The Green Book also contains information on product stewardship, training and some information on the environmental impact of its facilities around the world. While we question whether The Body Shop has lived up to its claims in other areas of its business, we find its stated efforts on environmental disclosure to be well founded.

TRADE NOT AID

"Trade Not Aid" (recently renamed "Direct Trading") has been a high-profile Body Shop slogan. It refers to the firm's "direct sourcing projects," which according to The Body Shop "create livelihoods for economically stressed communities. . . ." Images of Anita Roddick traveling the world and developing products using ingredients from indigenous communities have been at the heart of The Body Shop's public relations efforts. Gordon Roddick claims that "Trade Not Aid is quickly growing into a cornerstone for The Body Shop. . . . The next ten years will see a huge development in this part of our business." But Trade Not Aid has come under fire from some activists and anthropologists who feel the projects are, in fact, patronizing and exist more for the benefit of The Body Shop's image than for the communities they purport to assist. Others have criticized The Body Shop for focusing so much attention on a program which accounts for a small percentage of its business.

Fair trade initiatives are inherently complex and are easy targets for critics who feel that it is "neo-colonialism." But it is a relatively new field, especially for corporate involvement, and we would withhold judgment about the overall impact of such programs until there is further evidence that they are either constructive or destructive.

We see three issues at the heart of the debate. First, is Trade Not Aid based on a well researched understanding of economic, environmental and anthropological issues? Second, has The Body Shop worked sensitively with communities in implementing its projects? Third, has The Body Shop accurately represented its Trade Not Aid activities? While it is hard to characterize the whole program based on one or two projects, because of space and time considerations we will focus principally on The Body Shop's project with the Kayapo Indians in Brazil.

In 1991 The Body Shop began working with the Kayapo to harvest Brazil Nut oil, which is used in its bestselling Brazil Nut Hair Conditioner. The Body Shop also buys beaded wristbands made by Kayapo women. In its promotional materials The Body Shop states that the harvest of Brazil Nuts is "a viable and sustainable alternative to cutting down their forests." But according to Terence Turner, an anthropologist at the University of Chicago, the Kayapo make the bulk of their income from selling logging and mining concessions on their lands, precisely the activities that The Body Shop claims it is preventing. Turner told *Insight* that the money the Kayapo make from the Brazil Nut oil and wristbands is just supplemental income that could never match the level of income achieved by selling logging and mining rights.

But Darrell Posey, an Oxford anthropologist who has worked with both the Kayapo and The Body Shop, told *Insight* that "the forces are great and the subversion by logging companies is irresistible. It is unfair to expect that The Body Shop project could offset these forces. We all underestimated the power and ruthlessness of the logging mafia. . . . They will stop at nothing." Given the complexity of the issue, we question whether it is appropriate for The Body Shop to claim that purchases of Brazil Nut Conditioner "give [the Kayapo] an income to help protect the Amazon rainforest," as stated in Body Shop stores. But we find it difficult to fault The Body Shop merely for participating in an effort to assist indigenous peoples through trade agreements.

Turner told *Insight* that The Body Shop set up the Brazil Nut Oil project as a "commercial operation" managed by a non–Indian Brazilian, Saulo Petean, rather than as a trade arrangement between two equal parties. He says that the Kayapo make fair wages, but that they are not in control of the project, which is run in an authoritarian manner by Petean. Turner says the Kayapo have called repeatedly for his removal, to no avail.

The Body Shop responds that Petean is "an ally of indigenous peoples," and that "he has to act as the liaison and organizational instructor for the Kayapo to help them control the use of the airplane, keep the accounts, . . . appoint officers and register the businesses for export." Posey says that The Body Shop "sent a person as experienced as existed to work and live with the Kayapo and guide both sides in this project." Nevertheless, according to The Body Shop, Petean "is scheduled to turn over all aspects of the trade links in August of 1995." But the question raised is whether The Body Shop's Trade Not Aid programs "give people control over their resources, land and lives," as claimed. Posey states that "The Body Shop has done as good a job as anyone could expect." Another anthropologist told *Insight,* "If the Kayapo had run the project from day one, it probably would have failed."

Turner states that the firm's work with the Kayapo is "a public relations ploy above all" which aids The Body Shop in promoting its image while offering the Kayapo little trade in return. The Body Shop has used images of the Kayapo extensively in its stores and its "information broadsheets." According to Turner, the Kayapo have not been compensated for these images, which have furthered The Body Shop's corporate image as an environmentally and culturally sensitive company.

In response, The Body Shop claims that it pays the Kayapo well above market price for Brazil Nut oil, thereby implicitly compensating the Kayapo for the use of their images. But Turner says there is no true market price, as there is only one other producer of Brazil Nut oil worldwide. According to The Body Shop's Mark Johnston, the images have been shown to and approved by Kayapo representatives. The Body Shop also agreed to a broad covenant with the Kayapo that outlines a set of principles for any future trading arrangements, including clauses covering intellectual property rights (IPR). It aims to ensure that future commercial development of products based on Kayapo knowledge would be implemented in full and equal cooperation with the Kayapo. The covenant was not signed by either party and is not a legal document. Mark Johnston of The Body Shop told *Insight* it would be used as a template for trading contracts. To date The Body Shop has signed no formal IPR agreements with its Trade Not Aid partners, despite publicizing a May 1993 announcement that it intended to sign an IPR agreement with an indigenous group.

Despite the difficulties with these projects, all parties acknowledge that the Kayapo do not want The Body Shop to pull out. In fact, other Kayapo villages have asked The Body Shop to establish new projects. A Kayapo statement released by The Body Shop says, "The chiefs are pleased with the businesses they make with The Body Shop because it is a way for the community to earn money to buy the things they need without having to work in the city. . . . We discuss our business with The Body Shop, as equals, from company to company."

Other Trade Not Aid projects offer fewer obstacles, such as The Body Shop's purchases of organic Blue Corn flour from the Santa Ana Pueblo in New Mexico. Jerry Kinsman, the manager of the project told *Insight* the tribe has had a "very honest, straightforward relationship" with The Body Shop. But we find it misleading when The Body Shop claims that the project "indirectly" affects 3 villages and 500 Native Americans. Kinsman told *Insight* that the project employs 9 full-time equivalent Native American employees and that all profits (which are tiny) are reinvested in the project, not distributed to the community.

Richard Adams of New Consumer, a British consumer advocacy group, has criticized The Body Shop for sourcing a tiny fraction of its ingredients through Trade Not Aid, yet publicizing the projects heavily. The Body Shop admits that, "although direct sourcing from such communities is currently just a small percentage of all our trade, we intend to increase this practice wherever possible." Adams has repeatedly requested The Body Shop to disclose what percentage of its raw materials purchases are obtained through Trade Not Aid projects. While it has not responded directly to this request, The Body Shop states that its Trade Not Aid purchases from producers amounted to £1.2 million in FY1994, double that of the previous year. Based on those figures, Adams has calculated that in FY1993 just 0.165% of gross retail sales ended up in the pockets of Trade Not Aid producers.

The Body Shop states that it is increasing the number of ingredients sourced through Trade Not Aid, citing recent purchases of cocoa butter and shea butter from cooperatives. Adams has stated that he is encouraged by The Body Shop's commitment to working with alternative trade organizations and non-government organizations involved in fair trade initiatives.

As in other areas *Insight* examined, we found The Body Shop less than forthright when presenting its Trade Not Aid program in company materials. Though its flyers may be factually accurate, they leave the impression that The Body Shop ethically sources all or most of its ingredients, rather than the tiny number that are part of Trade Not Aid. For example, in a Spring 1994 publication The Body Shop offered the headline "How We Do Business: DIRECT TRADING." In much smaller print, the flyer acknowledged that direct sourcing is "just a small percentage of all our trade." We feel that the language that The Body Shop uses in its literature still requires revision if it is to truly reflect the scale of the projects it supports.

CHARITABLE GIVING

Over the past year, The Body Shop's level of charitable giving has increased dramatically, from 0.89% of pretax profits in the fiscal year ending February 1993 to nearly 3% of pretax profits in 1994. This new figure compares well to the average annual U.S. corporate giving figure of 1.9% but falls short of the level of contributions made by such socially responsible corporations as Dayton Hudson (5%), Ben & Jerry's (7.5%) and Patagonia (10%). However, it should be noted that The Body Shop's figure does not take into account its employees' voluntary activities taken on company time as well as the publicity provided by The Body Shop to organizations like Amnesty International in its company campaigns.

CORPORATE GOVERNANCE

As both investors and as a company that has taken the effort to recruit an active board made up of a majority of qualified outside directors, we are frankly not impressed by The Body

Shop's inability thus far to name a single independent board member. The Body Shop currently does not comply with the British "Code of Best Practice" recommended by the Report of the Committee on the Financial Aspects of Corporate Governance. Consequently, the company's stockholders lack such independent checks and balances as an independent audit and remuneration committee. The Body Shop has repeatedly promised that the appointment of independent directors will be forthcoming.

RESPONSE TO CRITICISM

The issue that has concerned us the most is The Body Shop's extremely combative response to criticism and its readiness to use legal action or threats of legal action. For instance, in its replies to the article in *Business Ethics,* The Body Shop repeatedly attacks the credibility of its critics, sometimes using invective, rather than just addressing the criticism.

Since our first contact with The Body Shop on this issue in March, The Body Shop has stated consistently that they first encountered Jon Entine when he was preparing a story for ABC's Primetime but that ABC decided not to run the story and Jon Entine no longer works for ABC. We feel this statement strongly implies that ABC fired Entine, a point that ABC has denied. We feel that Jon Entine's background is irrelevant.

In a recent press release, The Body Shop characterized the recent *Business Ethics* article on the company as "a poorly researched piece in a tiny newsletter." According to *Business Ethics,* the magazine received letters from The Body Shop's attorneys threatening possible legal action for libel before the article was even published. According to Angela Bawtree, The Body Shop is still reviewing its legal position in regard to the magazine. If, as it claims, *Business Ethics* checked and published the article in good faith and a lawsuit would bankrupt the magazine, we would consider a lawsuit by The Body Shop as unfair and likely to stifle further legitimate public discussion of the company.

We are also particularly concerned at the way in which The Body Shop has treated Richard Adams, Director of New Consumer, a British non-profit that publishes research on corporate responsibility issues. In our view, Adams has, since the fall of last year, made legitimate requests to The Body Shop for information that backs up the company's claims. The Body Shop has refused to provide what we would consider to be readily obtainable and non-proprietary information, such as the amount of goods bought through its Trade Not Aid programs, stating: "[Adams'] close relationship with, and support for, Entine's 'investigation' over the past year makes all his opinions highly suspect." We find this claim of "guilt-by-association" unwarranted considering the thoughtful and fair tone of Adams' writing for New Consumer and his extensive experience in the field of alternative trading relationships with developing countries.

CONCLUSION

After months of research, *Insight* has come to believe that certain recent criticism of The Body Shop is justified. In our view, the problems are quite correctable and there is evidence that the company is currently making improvements in almost all areas. Two important points remain unresolved.

The first is the gap between The Body Shop's image and its reality. We believe that any company seeking public approval must accept responsibility not only for what is said literally but also for the impression that is left. Through clever public relations, The Body Shop carefully cultivated an image which is inconsistent with the company's sometimes less than impressive performance, and we believe that the company should take measures to close the gap.

The second major problem we have with The Body Shop is its response to criticism, particularly in the press. Although there is a cultural difference between practices in Britain and practices in America where the First Amendment guarantees free speech, The Body Shop's consistent use of character assassination and its habit of assuming motives is offensive and virtually unheard of in our experience. The Body Shop's bombastic tactics have set back any legitimate attempts by the company to change and seem to be currently triggering a backlash. In our opinion, it is important that the company be much more constructive with its critics. The wounds left by the company's defensiveness will be hard to heal. But nothing is impossible.

LETTER TO BUSINESS ETHICS SUBSCRIBERS

GORDON RODDICK

Shortly after the publication of Body Shop criticism in an article in Business Ethics *magazine, Gordon Roddick sent the following letter to its subscribers, in defense of The Body Shop. How Mr. Roddick obtained the list of subscribers is still in controversy.*

22 September 1994

Dear fellow *Business Ethics* subscriber,

I sit down to write this letter with some anger and considerable sadness. It concerns the article "Shattered Image," which appeared in the September/October issue of *Business Ethics.* As you are probably aware, that article contained allegations that maligned and defamed our company, my wife and me. Although a representative of The Body Shop is quoted in the article, making it appear that we were given an opportunity to respond, in fact we were not informed of most of the charges prior to publication. Such treatment would be indefensible under any circumstances, but it is especially troubling when the right to a fair hearing is denied by a magazine with "ethics" in its title.

It has become clear that writing to you personally is the only way we can be sure you will have the chance to hear our side of the case. Hence, this letter.

Frankly, it is difficult to know where to begin rebutting an article filled with as many lies, distortions, and gross inaccuracies as this one. I suppose we have to give the author some credit for throwing together such an impressive volume of information. It is his attempt to confuse and misrepresent the reality of a company that has struggled hard for 18 years to be in the forefront of a movement seeking a different way of doing business.

Where the information comes from is another matter. Of the 22 sources named in the article, 10 are disgruntled former employees or franchisees, current competitors, or disappointed bidders for our business, all of whom obviously have personal reasons for wanting to make The Body Shop look bad. Four other sources have either strenuously denied their quotes or said their words have been used out of context in a way that entirely distorts their meaning. Yet another five sources are cited for opinions they expressed about social investment in general, opinions that have been turned around so as to make them appear to be highly critical of The Body Shop.

Letter to *Business Ethics* magazine subscribers from Gordon Roddick, chairman of The Body Shop, dated Sept. 22, 1994.

There is, in fact, almost no attempt to observe the normal standards of journalism. The article cites two people as "independent experts," for example, without mentioning that they are among our competitors. Elsewhere, a competitor's marketing newsletter is used to provide "expert analysis," again without noting the obvious conflict of interest. And another alleged "source," The Federal Trade Commission, has already issued a flat-out denial that it has commented on The Body Shop practices in any way, shape, or form. We understand from the FTC that *Business Ethics* has agreed to print a correction in the next issue.

But to see what is really going on here, it is necessary to look at some of the specific allegations in detail. Consider the opening snapshot of two former franchisees, Stacy and Larry Benes, who are portrayed as terrified, bankrupt people somehow done in by our malfeasance. The implication is that such stories are common throughout our organization. Nothing could be further from the truth.

To begin with, there is more to the Beneses' story than the author chose to report. Stacy and Larry Benes were like many other people who come to us for a franchise, whenever we begin trading in a country or a region. They bring us their hopes and dreams, which may or may not be achievable. We try to select franchisees with realistic expectations and the ability to fulfill them. It is very much in our interest as a franchisor to do so. Sometimes we make mistakes in our selection.

In the case of the Beneses, we were led to believe that Larry had a full-time job and Stacy would run the shop, which would thus have to provide income for just one person. Whatever they say now, they were clearly told at the time that a single shop in Charlottesville, Va., could not possibly do more, at least in the first few years. Whether it could do even that well depended to a great degree on what the Beneses were prepared to put into it. Sadly, they turned out to be neither good franchisees nor good retailers. They so mismanaged the business that a group of their employees came to us to complain about their behavior and their values. Meanwhile, they were taking out more than $80,000 a year for themselves in their first year of operations—somewhat more than either Anita or I were paid annually during The Body Shop's first decade. Eventually, they wound up in financial difficulty, owing the company more than $200,000 for products they had bought from us on credit and then sold. Rather than sue them for payment, we agreed to repurchase the store.

As unfortunate as such episodes are, it is ridiculous to suggest they are typical of our relationships with franchisees. Within 24 hours of this article's publication, 95% of our U.S. franchisees signed a letter repudiating the accusations in it. The fact is that we operate on a worldwide basis trading either directly or through head franchisees in more than 40 countries with more than 1,100 stores, of which 1,000 are owned by approximately 650 franchisees. There are always some disputes between franchisor and franchisees. That's the nature of business. But our disputes have actually been far milder than is common. In 18 years of operation, we have terminated the contract of only one franchisee, and that was in England. (She had fired all her employees on grounds that could only be described as lunatic. We put them on our payroll, some 50 people in all, many of whom had mortgages and other financial obligations, and we kept paying them until the dispute was resolved.) In addition, we had litigation in Norway that was settled amicably. There is presently litigation in Singapore, but we are hopeful it, too, can be settled.

Such conflicts are the daily bread of any business. The unusual part is that we have had so few of them, as *Business Ethics* would surely have discovered had it checked the facts of this article with independent franchising experts. Instead, it appears to have relied on the author's own biased sources, who naturally confirmed what they'd already said to him.

The same pattern repeats itself throughout the article. There is, for example, the assertion that we stole The Body Shop's name, concept, and products from Jane Saunders and Peggy Short, who had a natural cosmetic business of the same name based in Berkeley, Ca. The charge is pure rubbish. Jane and Peggy do not make such claims. They have stated that the company "didn't rip us off" and that there have always been "fundamental differences" between their stores and ours. (I am using their words here.) Had they thought otherwise, we would probably not have been able to develop the warm and cordial relationship we have with them and their companies, a relationship that continues to this day.

Indeed, the fundamental differences in our retail styles and appearance are instantly obvious to anyone who visits the two companies' shops. After the author of "Shattered Image" showed up at the Saunders', we heard from Jane Saunder's daughter, Ann, who wrote us saying a man named Jon Entine (the author of the *Business Ethics* article) had "barged in" on her and starting making claims about our supposed larceny. She told him she "had no knowledge of anything he was talking about." She said "his 'facts' are wrong." Entine has since alleged that there is a gag order preventing Jane Saunders, Peggy Short, and others from commenting on the relationship. In her letter, Ann wrote that she specifically told him there was no such gag order.

Another person supposedly under a gag order is Mark Constantine, who was a major supplier to us for more than a decade and whom we worked with to develop many of our early products. He wrote me after reading the opinions ascribed to him in the article. Judge his remarks about Entine for yourself:

> It would appear that he has edited, or, worse, twisted my comments. Taking a few of the points, "Roddick's first business partner, cosmetologist Mark Constantine (who is under a gag order prohibiting him from discussing it)," . . . "suggest that Anita knew about the Berkeley company."
>
> Oh how I wish I had been your business partner! . . . "cosmetologist," I am not a cosmetologist.
>
> "Under a gag order", no gag order. See the interview in last Sunday's Mirror as an example. Anyway, how can I suggest something if I'm under a gag order?
>
> He suggested that Anita knew about the Berkeley company, and I was shocked when he asked me. I didn't deny it because I did not know. I was entertained to see the examples he chose of similarities: "loofah sponges and glycerin and rosewater lotion."
>
> I take offense at the next paragraph, "The Body Shop's most basic myth." Anita was the first person to recognize that the products that I formulated had a greater amount of "naturals" than any others on the market, then or now. She gave me a much needed break at a time when no one was interested in natural ingredients as anything but label claims. I went to great pains to explain this, and the guy phoned me back and read this paragraph to me. It was rubbish then, and I told him, and it's still rubbish now.

Mark's letter reflects the frustration we have all felt in trying to deal with this article. There are sensible questions that could be raised, and we would all learn from such a discussion. I make no appeal for The Body Shop to be exempt from criticism or scrutiny. We are happy to open up our hearts, our minds, and our company to those who wish to examine us, provided they accept their responsibility to be balanced and fair.

But I am at a loss to find *anything* balanced or fair in this article. In its zeal to impugn our commitment to our principles, it goes after our Trade Not Aid program, building its attack around an utterly irrelevant statistic—the percentage of our ingredients that come from Trade Not Aid projects. What is this number supposed to reveal? It certainly tells nothing about the effectiveness of our efforts. Or the amount of time and energy we have put into nurturing these projects. Or the obstacles we have had to overcome due to the lack of infrastructure in disenfranchised, Third World communities—transport difficulties, investment problems, absence of technological capabilities, cultural issues, the need to build trust and personal relationships, and so on. One single ingredient, such as Brazil nut oil or cocoa butter, may take two years or more to source and develop. Believe me, there are much easier ways to do business than by taking on the problems of such projects. We don't do it to "save the planet." In most cases, we do it because we are asked to help by the disenfranchised communities themselves. The only significant measure of our success is the number of people who are directly and beneficially affected by our activities. That number, I am proud to say, runs into the thousands. It can best be verified by talking to the communities we have assisted—another thing *Business Ethics* neglected to do.

A letter was written to *Business Ethics* on 26th August 1994 from Jerry Kinsman, the program manager of Santa Ana Agricultural Enterprises (The Pueblo of Santa Ana is a federally recognized American Indian Tribe located in New Mexico). In this letter he says: "*I hope you will give some importance to what representatives of Body Shop's trading partners have to say about that company.*"

However, *Business Ethics* chose to ignore that request.

Kinsman writes:

> Be assured that the people of Santa Ana Pueblo are very pleased with and proud of the connection with Body Shop. Whereas the direct profit from sales to BSI [The Body Shop] has been very beneficial, it should be noted that the relationship has had an indirect multiplier effect on the Tribe's Blue Corn business. Public notice from the association, in and of itself, has brought in more public notice—and more business. Santa Ana has become the place to observe successful Native American development efforts. Has Body Shop been the singular cause of that accomplishment? Clearly not! More than any other factor, the Tribe's achievements are a function of some very savvy people knowing what they want for themselves. Has Body Shop been important? Clearly yes! . . . I must inform you that Santa Ana is not a victim of BSI. Rather, the Tribe is an ardent supporter of its approach to trade.

And let me tell you about a Trade Not Aid project that produces *no* ingredients for our products. It is called *The Big Issue,* and it is a newspaper sold by about 2,000 vendors, almost all of them homeless people, in London, Edinburgh, Glasgow, Manchester, and several other cities in our own backyard. Its average weekly circulation is 200,000. It has been going for three years now and has been financially self-sufficient on an operating basis for some time. Recently it moved into a new building with a print shop, meeting rooms, and a cafe.

I myself started this project after seeing the homeless newspaper called *Street News* being sold in New York. I persuaded an old friend of mine to be the editor. Together we launched *The Big Issue* despite a feasibility study warning against the idea. The Body Shop put in $450,000 over two years, and The Body Shop Foundation contributed another $350,000. As large as the investment was, the possibility of losing the money was not, in fact, the greatest risk we faced. Far more serious was the risk that the project might go wrong and wind up harming our reputation. That is always a danger when you work with disadvantaged people. In the case of the homeless, you are wide open to accusations of promoting drug abuse, violence, alcoholism, welfare fraud, and so on—all issues around which passions run high. The possibility of scandal is a given. You can't avoid it, especially in the early phases of a project, when you are feeling your way and haven't yet figured out the necessary controls. So far we have been lucky. We have also had an enormous amount of help—from the police authorities, commercial businesses, and non-profit foundations. We have thanked them all in the newspaper itself. Still the fact remains that the risk was, and is, ours. If scandal comes, if the project fails, The Body Shop will take the heat.

We are not looking here for credit, or recognition. I would not have brought it up at all but for this unscrupulous attack in a magazine called *Business Ethics*. I mention *The Big Issue* only because it is one of several projects that we talk little about, but that have provided some small measure of hope or work for a lot of people. Those people are the entire reason for doing these things. Yet they are the ones who get lost when high-minded organizations quibble about the percentage of ingredients produced under our Trade Not Aid policy.

I could go on and on cataloguing the error and misrepresentation in this article, but it would take a small book to answer every one of Entine's allegations. We have, in fact, prepared such a document and would be happy to send it to you if you are interested. Meanwhile, there are a couple of other matters I must address, including the charge by Entine, and the editors of *Business Ethics*, and others that we have used thuggery and legal threats to suppress legitimate criticism of The Body Shop.

Let me say straight off that Anita and I are very protective of the business we have built, and we have probably been oversensitive and overdefensive to criticism at times. But look at the history.

In 1992, representatives of a company called Fulcrum Productions approached us about a program on The Body Shop they wanted to make for Channel 4, a British television channel. They asked for our help, assuring us they would produce a fair and balanced piece. We let them film at our headquarters in England and our Soapworks factory in Glasgow. We gave them volumes of printed material as well as in-house videos, films, and stills that they wound up using in the program. They had full access to the company. We answered every question they raised. Both Anita and I made ourselves available for interviews on camera. Subsequently, the producer admitted, under oath, that we had been very cooperative.

The program Fulcrum produced was a shamefully biased piece that defamed The Body Shop, Anita, and me. In order to keep it from being sold into the 40-odd other countries where we trade, we decided after lengthy deliberation to sue Channel 4 and Fulcrum Productions.

We won the libel action after a grueling six-week trial in the British High Court. Thousands of documents, internal memos, position papers, and videos were paraded before the jury, along with every other scrap of information that might possibly be relevant. Anita and I and others in the company were cross-examined for days on end. I personally put in four days in the witness box. The intensity of the process made a social audit look like a day at the fairground.

Contrary to what you may have heard, truth *is* a defense against libel in the U.K. Had the charges in the program proved to be truthful, Fulcrum and Channel 4 would have won the case, and we would have had to pay their legal bills. Instead, we were completely vindicated. The jury found in favor of Anita, myself, and The Body Shop. The defendants had to pay damages of 276,000 pounds plus our court costs. Our total award required them to pay us in excess of one and a half (1.5) million dollars. In addition, they were served with an injunction forbidding them from repeating any of the defamatory statements they were found to have made, including those concerning our public positions on environmental, human rights, and animal testing issues.

It would be difficult to imagine a more public airing of the issues surrounding The Body Shop. It would be equally unimaginable that rational human beings would willingly subject themselves twice to the level of stress involved in such a court action.

Four weeks after the end of the trial, Jon Entine showed up at our headquarters in England, saying he was working on a piece about The Body Shop for ABC's Prime Time Live. We gave him hundreds of pages of documents and offered to provide more. Within days, however, we began hearing from suppliers, franchisees, and independent organizations about his investigation of us. His technique was literally to harass people until he got something he could use. He called one of our suppliers more than seven times in two days. Whenever he got hold of somebody, he would misrepresent what another person had said in an aggressive attempt to elicit "on-the-record" responses from the person he was talking to. These remarks he would then repeat to his next subject, distorting them as necessary. In this manner, he created a maelstrom of misinformation and fear wherever he went.

We eventually got fed up with all this and contacted people at ABC to advise them of their producer's outrageous behavior. Entine left ABC with the program unfinished. He alleges, of course, that we intimidated the network. It is hard to believe that a major news organization with a reputation for hard-nosed investigative journalism would be intimidated by the likes of The Body Shop, especially if we are as supposedly evil and as despicable as he had said on many occasions. Then again, we do not know for sure what happened at ABC. Our best source is the deputy editor of *The Sunday Times,* England's leading weekend newspaper, who wrote me a letter on October 8, 1993, after we had questioned a story the newspaper had run on the proposed Prime Time Live piece following its cancellation: In his letter he said:

> We [The Sunday Times] *have now established what we did not know then, that ABC discovered Entine had made a number of mistakes in his methodology, so serious that they had in effect fired him some 10 days before. Entine, probably unknown to ABC, was however picking up his messages from a phone on his old desk in the ABC building. We now understand from ABC sources that Entine is regarded as out of control and has been running around saying some wild things.*

So, whatever may have happened inside ABC, Entine was misrepresenting himself as part of ABC to a journalist at *The Sunday Times* after he had already left the network. Moreover, he was telling the journalist that the Prime Time Live segment would be shown when he knew it would not. As it turned out, he was playing much the same game with the Food and Drug Administration.

Unbeknownst to us, Entine, while still at ABC, had gone to the FDA with a number of untrue allegations, leading inspectors to make a surprise visit to our new headquarters in Wake Forest, N.C. They issued no citations or violation notices. Undeterred, Entine, now gone from ABC, but leaving the FDA inspector with the impression that he was still with them and headed our way with hidden cameras—got the FDA to make a second inspection.

Again, no citations. Having failed twice, Entine did not give up—he obtained a copy of the internal FDA notes of their visits and leaked them to other journalists, trying to start a story that we had problems with the FDA.

There was one problem with his strategy, however, and he was well aware of it. The internal documents made it absolutely clear that the FDA inspections were initiated *"in response to allegations made by a Prime Time news reporter."* Entine found a simple solution to his problem. By his own admission, he falsified the FDA documents to blot out his name and all references to himself as the source of the "complaints"; he circulated the FDA documents that directly misled other reporters to believe he, Jon Entine, was not at the start, middle and end of this whole episode.

Let's face it: this is not the behavior of a responsible journalist. I dare say it is not the behavior of a journalist at all. I certainly cannot imagine a real journalist launching a campaign to drive down the share price of a company he was writing about. Yet Entine did just that, even calling up Peter Lynch's office to urge him to dump Fidelity's holdings of The Body Shop stock. Entine also showed up in Toronto at a meeting of the Social Investment Forum and harangued the assembly about The Body Shop until he was told to sit down. He then proceeded to hand out copies of a grossly defamatory article he had written about us for *Vanity Fair,* which had rejected it. This same article he circulated to social activists, fair trade organizations, animal rights advocates, and others on both sides of the Atlantic. Still others he called up and harangued about *"the most evil corporation* [he had] *encountered in twenty years of reporting,"* as he described us to Jay Harris, the publisher of *Mother Jones,* a magazine that has tangled with some pretty evil corporations in its day. Entine was quoted in one newspaper saying that his impending revelations would be *"the story of the century,"* putting us right up there with the moon landing, two world wars, the Holocaust, the war in Vietnam, the end of the Soviet Union, and countless human and ecological disasters. All of which would have been worth a good laugh had he not also taken to harassing Anita in public and in private. At that point, his obsession became both unnerving and a bit frightening.

In the face of such attacks, I make no apologies for anything we have done to protect ourselves. It is not "legal thuggery" to defend your family, your employees, your friends and associates, your principles, and your reputation from someone who is hell-bent on doing as much damage to them as he can. There is a difference between criticism and character assassination. Just as there are environmental laws to stop polluters, so there are libel laws to stop irresponsible and damaging reports. We protested vigorously to *Vanity Fair* for assigning an article on The Body Shop to Jon Entine. We told the magazine we would cooperate with any responsible journalist they cared to have write about us, but we would not deal with Entine under any circumstances. *Vanity Fair* dropped the article. *Business Ethics* picked it up.

I cannot tell you how disheartening it is to find the attack on us coming now from people with whom we had always supposed we shared common commitments and common values. That Entine succeeded in driving down our share price was thanks largely to Franklin Research and Development, whose President, Joan Bavaria, wrote a column for *Business Ethics* in the same issue. Franklin sold 50,000 shares of The Body Shop stock on the strength of Entine's rejected *Vanity Fair* article. This information was relayed to the *Financial Times* in London, which ran an article about it, setting off a firestorm in the British press. Only later did Franklin even make a pretense of investigating Entine's charges. How this qualifies as "ethical investing" is beyond me.

Which brings us to *Business Ethics.* When we learned of the magazine's intention to publish a version of Entine's article, we informed the editors of our history with him and asked for an opportunity to review the piece for factual inaccuracies. The editors declined. One of our staff, Angela Bawtree, then visited the *Business Ethics* offices, but very few of the allegations contained in the article were put to her. Editor Craig Cox later refused her offer of follow-up information.

The editors have since tried to portray themselves as crusading journalists standing up to a bullying corporation. They have boasted loudly about taking out libel insurance. They have made much of their fear of publishing in Britain and their insistence that distributors sign pledges not to sell the magazine in any Commonwealth country. But, as noted above, truth is a defense against libel under British law. They face no risk if their article is factual. If we did sue them (something we have not threatened to do), they could recover all their legal expenses—assuming, that is, they could prove the accuracy of Entine's charges. So why didn't they publish in the U.K.? And what were their motives in publishing the article at all?

Perhaps the answer lies in a letter that Marjorie Kelly, publisher and editor-in-chief of *Business Ethics,* sent to her financial backers in August, just prior to publication of the Entine article.

> *"This piece will be talked about,"* she wrote. *"It will create a stir.* . . . It's the best thing we've ever done. It could put us on the map."

The emphasis, I'm afraid, is hers.

Let me reiterate in closing that we have a detailed response to every single allegation Entine makes in his article and elsewhere. We will happily provide those responses to all who care to read them, but now we wish to get back to work. We have taken a severe kicking from the press on both sides of the Atlantic and elsewhere in the world. Perhaps there is some balance in that. We have also had a lot of good press over the years, some of it excessive in its enthusiasm. I suppose we should learn to live with excessive attacks as well.

In the future, I hope there will be objective and detailed reporting on our business. Some of the conclusions would no doubt be critical, but I am also certain a fair analysis would reveal a company that has tried very hard and has much to be proud of. We chose a difficult and thorny path. With the help of many others, we will continue to tread that path with pride and vigor.

In any event, the time for anger is past. We know the world is filled with businesses concerned with "putting something back." We hope they will not sit around too long in detailed analysis and therapy as a result of the hoopla created by this attack on us.

After the Channel 4 libel case, we ourselves began the process of producing a methodology for a definitive social audit of our company, following the lead of Ben & Jerry's and other companies. It is a mammoth undertaking, aimed at analyzing our social performance against the expectations created by ourselves and others. Along with our financial and environmental reports, it should provide a complete picture of the business, available to all. We expect to have a report by mid 1995. It will come as a great relief, most of all to us, who will use it to improve on the shortcomings it will undoubtedly highlight.

And what of *Business Ethics?* To date, two prominent members of its editorial advisory board have resigned, questioning the ethics of the magazine. We wonder if Marjorie Kelly has achieved the circulation boost she was counting on. The episode has certainly provided a reminder of the potential conflict between business needs and editorial principles. Perhaps Marjorie's words at the end of her "Musings" piece in the same issue of *Business Ethics* should now be read in a new light.

> *What we may have neglected in our enthusiasm is ethics. Good, old-fashioned ethics. Also known as integrity. It's not something to shout about in our marketing packages, but if we can't live up to it, we won't have much to shout about for long.*

We agree entirely. Enthusiasm in the pursuit of greater circulation is no substitute for ethics. I can only hope that the standards Marjorie articulates will be applied to *Business Ethics* magazine in the future.

Yours truly,

Gordon Roddick
Chairman

LETTER FROM
MARJORIE KELLY

MARJORIE KELLY

January 13, 1995

From: Marjorie Kelly, Publisher and Editor-in-Chief, *Business Ethics*

"Shattered Image: Is The Body Shop Too Good to Be True?" was the cover story of the September/October 1994 issue of *Business Ethics,* the magazine of socially responsible business, read by progressive businesspeople and investors nationwide.

In my twenty years in journalism, I have never before seen a piece so *difficult to investigate and yet so* well-researched, so path-breaking, and so wide-reaching in its impact. *It is being discussed in boardrooms across the country.* It promises to change social investing, to lead to an increase in independent social audits, and in general to help business toward a greater social maturity. After The Body Shop article, I think you'll be seeing far less puffery in corporate ethics claims, and more hard facts to back up claims that are made.

You may have heard about The Body Shop article, for hundreds of reports about it have been published in the U.S., Great Britain, and as far away as Australia and Nigeria. I am honored to have published this piece, and honored to have worked with Jon Entine. I commend him to you as a truly extraordinary investigative journalist. He published this story against almost overwhelming opposition, yet he prevailed. . .

SUMMARY OF THE ARTICLE

"Shattered Image" reported on how the international franchisor and natural cosmetics maker The Body Shop—a $700 million firm known internationally as a premier socially responsible company—has for years secretly engaged in business practices that fall far short of its exaggerated social claims. Entine's evidence shows *that in area after area, The Body Shop's social reputation has been more image than reality:* its "natural" cosmetics contained numerous petrochemicals and preservatives, stories about the exotic origins of products were fabricated, environmental practices and charitable contributions fell far short of company statements. Third World sourcing of ingredients was greatly exaggerated, and franchisee relations were so troubled as to merit an FTC investigation.

Despite this dubious history, The Body Shop enjoyed worldwide prestige as a premier ethical company. *Ralph Nader called founder Anita Roddick "the most progressive business person I know. Inc. magazine featured Roddick on the cover, saying, "This Woman Has Changed Business Forever." USA Today dubbed her "The Mother Theresa of Capitalism."*

Memorandum from Marjorie Kelly, publisher and editor, *Business Ethics,* for public consumption, Jan. 13, 1995. Reprinted by permission of the author.

Whenever journalists sniffed a bit of the contrary truth and attempted to publish it, the company used heavy-handed legal threats to keep the stories under wraps. Among the publishers who backed off negative stories because of libel threats were *Vanity Fair, International Management,* the *London Daily Mail,* the *London Daily Telegraph,* and ABC. . . .

OBSTACLES OVERCOME IN THE REPORTING

Jon Entine was the first to uncover and tell this story in its entirety. It is a story no one expected and few were willing to believe. And Entine reported it against great odds—including fourteen libel threats in writing from the company, a slanderous campaign against him by the company's PR firm Hill and Knowlton, a campaign by The Body Shop to get sources to recant (several did right before press time), the imposition of gag orders on franchisees and employees, and the apparent hiring of a private investigation firm to follow Entine (as well as my staff at *Business Ethics*).

Business Ethics also received written libel threats from The Body Shop, as well as a campaign attacking us—directed at our editorial advisory board (one advisory board member quit: Ben Cohen of Ben & Jerry's, a personal friend of The Body Shop). After the story was published, the company obtained the *Business Ethics* subscriber list—by renting it under the name "Hoffman and Associates," purporting to mail a nonprofit fundraising catalogue—and used the list to mail a 10-page letter to our subscribers, accusing us of publishing lies and distortions. They conducted a similar campaign of vilification against Jon Entine, through numerous press releases and statements.

As Jon Entine went out on a limb to report this story, I put my company on the line to publish it. Facing a threat of libel, my staff and I were under fierce pressure to fact-check everything in the article. We consulted closely with a libel lawyer, and spent weeks fact-checking; we have an entire banker's box of documents from Jon Entine as evidence. Yet I know these are but a fraction of the materials he himself has. Whenever Entine's story and The Body Shop's story conflicted, we checked it out—and Entine's facts invariably were solid. Whenever we had any doubt about a fact or a source, we pulled it—and Entine always had another source, another fact, which made precisely the same point.

When we were reluctant to quote a franchisee who called The Body Shop a "Gambino crime family," Entine showed us two other sources who had used uncannily similar language. When it seemed heavy-handed to use a quote saying the company's products were like those of "Payless Drug Story" (though selling at two or three times the price), Entine showed us three other sources who had said, literally, the products were of "drug store quality." When several sources recanted at the last minute, under pressure from The Body Shop, we pulled them—and Entine had other sources at the ready, so there was no harm to the story.

The depth and quality of Entine's research was extraordinary. I've never seen anything like it.

The wealth of sources and material Entine had was staggering. Though fully half his sources were not willing to have their names used, Entine succeeded in putting together a densely factual story using *only one unnamed source.* It is a testimony to his skill as a reporter that he got so many sources on the record, using their names in print—despite The Body Shop's fiercely litigious reputation. . . .

ACTION RESULTING FROM PUBLICATION OF THE INVESTIGATION

As the editor who founded *Business Ethics* nine years ago, and a journalist who has followed the development of socially responsible business for over a decade, I can say unequivocally that Entine's article has changed the face of business ethics forever. It marks a turning point, a painful but necessary loss of naivete. Society no longer can pretend to draw a line between the "good guy" corporations like Ben & Jerry's, and "bad guy" corporations like Dow Chemical. Entine's article obliterated that line.

As Joan Bavaria, creator of the CERES Principles and president of Franklin Research (a social investing firm), wrote: "We are entering a new era in the world of socially responsible managing and investing. It is not a black world or a white world with neat and crisp lines of demarcation, and it doesn't lend itself to sound bites. It is the real world of complex systems, internal contradictions, and uneven, interrupted progress."

She called for the abandonment of "screening" in social investing, and for the invention of a system "beyond screens." This is very significant, coming from the woman who founded the Social Investment Forum—the central trade group for social investing professionals—because screening has been the central premise of social investing for thirty years. Bavaria's change of heart on this point was a direct result of Jon Entine's article.

A second major impact of Entine's article is the rising call for independent social audits. Should such a practice take root, companies could no longer garner points simply for making social claims. They would have to back them up. A call for such audits was made by Gary Hirshberg—founder of Stonyfield Yogurt, and chairman of the prestigious Social Venture Network—as a direct result of Entine's article.

As Hirshberg wrote: "The recent media frenzy regarding The Body Shop is an inevitable phase in the evolution of the corporate social responsibility concept . . . the issues are *measurement* and *disclosure,* and I believe that our businesses' chances for success as change catalysts hinge on our moving decisively toward a uniform, independent auditing methodology that accomplishes both."

Another, surprising, effect of Entine's story has been seen within The Body Shop itself: it has increased charitable giving, hired a new coordinator for Third World trade, and pledged to do a complete internal social audit and to publish the results.

Employees who had tried to tell The Body Shop the truth, over the years, had been fired. A quality control manager who spoke to the FDA was fired. Others were threatened into silence. Jon Entine broke that silence, and his words have been heard. And remarkably, the company is acknowledging the need for change.

Donald David, editor of *Drug & Cosmetic Industry,* [a] trade journal, said Entine's piece was "the best researched and lucidly written expose on any cosmetic company I have ever read in my 39 years of covering that business."

The article led to a firestorm of press coverage, including NPR coverage, articles in the *New York Times, USA Today, Financial Times* of London, *New York* magazine, and countless other media, as well as a major symposium in the *Utne Reader.*

In addition to the hundreds of articles that have been published, Entine has been invited to speak about the article to the National Conference on Ethics, the National Association for Biomedical Research, Loyola University Center for Values in Business, Bentley College, Columbia School of Journalism, and many other places.

Entine's investigation of The Body Shop is truly a watershed event in the history of socially responsible business. I believe this story will become a "business parable" for years to come—much as Johnson and Johnson and the Tylenol incident has become a business parable. It is through vivid stories like these that we learn the truth of our world. And this story would not have been told were it not for the courage and professionalism of Jon Entine.

Sincerely,

Marjorie Kelly
Publisher and Editor-in-Chief

THE BODY SHOP
SOCIAL STATEMENT
WEB SITE

Welcome to **The Values Report,** an independently verified assessment of how The Body Shop impacts on the environment and society, and on the Company's animal protection policy.

Our approach to auditing follows the sequence of THINK-ACT-CHANGE. We THINK about the issues facing our business and industry today and reflect these in our policies; we ACT by monitoring our impact on the environment and publishing details of these; and we will CHANGE and reduce our impacts in the future by setting ourselves targets and campaigning in order to achieve continuous improvement.

Also explore *our approach* to ethical auditing, *our reason for being,* 20 years of *defining moments,* a special letter for *American readers* and a *summary* of the report. You can also read a copy of an *independent social assessment of The Body Shop by Kirk Hanson,* business ethics and social responsibility professor at Stanford University Graduate School of Business, USA

MISSION STATEMENT

Our Reason for Being:

To dedicate our business to the pursuit of social and environmental change.

To Creatively balance the financial and human needs of our stakeholders: employees, customers, franchisees, suppliers and shareholders.

To Courageously ensure that our business is ecologically sustainable: meeting the needs of the present without compromising the future.

To Meaningfully contribute to local, national and international communities in which we trade, by adopting a code of conduct which ensures care, honesty, fairness and respect.

To Passionately campaign for the protection of the environment, human and civil rights, and against animal testing within the cosmetics and toiletries industry.

To Tirelessly work to narrow the gap between principle and practice, whilst making fun, passion and care part of our daily lives.

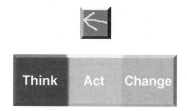

THE BODY SHOP BILL OF RIGHTS AND RESPONSIBILITIES

The Rights of the Company:

To make the final decision.

To recruit the best people for the job.

To dismiss people when justified.

To expect a high level of contribution, performance and commitment.

To expect respect for its values.

The Responsibilities of the Company:

To do its best to provide a secure environment for its employees.

To look for new ways of doing things.

To educate employees about the Company's culture and values.

To educate employees about the Company's business.

To provide adequate induction and training.

To consider existing employees first when looking at new opportunities.

To meet all relevant employment legislation.

To be honest to employees about what we are offering.

To listen, care and support.

To be fair.

To walk the talk.

To say thank you.

The Rights of the Individual:

To have a voice, to challenge.

To have equality of opportunity.

To be trained to do your job.

To be developed as an individual.

To be rewarded fairly for the work you do; to understand how your pay is determined.

To know how the business is doing.

To be told the truth about things that will affect you.

To have a piece of the action.

To have the opportunity to do your best.

The Responsibilities of the Individual:

To think.

To learn.

To be honest.

To try your hardest, to do your best.

To treat others with trust and respect.

To take responsibility for your own actions.

To acknowledge the efforts of others.

To obey the rules.

To stand against injustice.

This Mission Statement and Bill of Rights and Responsibilities is the driving force for everything we do, and is the yardstick against which the Human Resources function, and the Company Culture function, and indeed The Body Shop as a whole, can be measured in its dealing with its people.

It covers all aspects of the Human Resources function from Training and Development to Pay and Remuneration, from Recruitment to Pensions, from Induction to Appraisals, from Equal Opportunities to Administration systems. It recognises and publishes the special nature of The Body Shop's relationship with its employees, in which they are not just resources for the Company, but are people whose own needs and aspirations are recognised and taken seriously.

At its heart is the phrase "meeting each other's needs" which in four words incorporates virtually the whole of our behaviour and actions whilst working at The Body Shop.

SOCIAL STATEMENT

The publication of this Social Statement marks the first attempt by The Body Shop to systematically audit, verify and disclose the Company's performance on social matters. But it is just the beginning. It is the starting point for more effective dialogue and communication with all our stakeholders. The entire process has taken us about three years: researching, planning, and implementing. The methodology we have adopted is described in detail in an accompanying document, 'The Body Shop Approach to Ethical Auditing,' setting out all of our ethical auditing and reporting practices, but it is important to recognise here what have been our major influences. Certainly, we have taken as our philosophical starting point the belief that all stakeholders should have an effective voice in commenting upon and shaping a company's behaviour. We do not believe that a company is only in business to serve the interests of a limited number of stakeholders.

Our methodology has drawn heavily on our own research into the history of private and public sector social accounting, auditing and assessment. We have also learned a great deal from the recent experiences of organisations like the Sbn Bank in Denmark, Traidcraft in the UK and Ben and Jerry's in the U.S. In learning from these examples we have endeavoured to synthesise and develop an approach which makes sense not just for The Body Shop, but, we hope, for other organisations too.

We have systematically collected the views of key stakeholders by techniques not dissimilar to those used by market researchers: open meetings, interviews, confidential focus groups and large scale surveys. In designing survey questionnaires our Ethical Audit department has observed rigorous standards to ensure that all issues of relevance to stakeholders or raised by them, e.g., in focus groups, were included. And we took professional advice from the Institute for Employment Studies (IES) to ensure clarity in questionnaire design and analysis. All surveys were conducted anonymously and confidentially, with completed forms returned directly to IES; stakeholders were also invited to make direct contact with our audit verifiers, the New Economics Foundation (NEF).

We have also tried to report on quantitative indicators of social performance relevant to stakeholder groups. In selecting performance indicators we have been mindful of the types of information often requested by the ethical investment community and by consumer interest organisations such as the Council for Economic Priorities in the U.S. In trying to collect these data we have become aware of the limitations of some of our own internal information systems. We will endeavour to improve on our reporting of these performance standards in future years.

The purpose of our social audit was not to focus on specific criticism or issues. It was to deal broadly with only one accounting period and not the entire history of the Company. Thus we have not investigated individual allegations of wrongdoing or inefficiency, but we have provided a platform for all views, including critical and minority views.

Our audit and disclosure processes have been subject to independent verification by the New Economics Foundation (NEF). They have engaged, in turn, an Audit Review Panel, whose names are listed on the verification page of this Statement, to advise them.

Our advisers and consultants have been very influential in shaping our social audit and indeed this Statement. Our experience has been positive, but it is clear that there is still much work to be done to develop the practice of social auditing to the standards now being followed for environmental auditing. However, we now have four years' experience in implementing the EU Eco-management and Audit Regulation and three years' experience in researching, developing and applying a social audit methodology. So we are able to confirm that the two audit processes are compatible, that measurement techniques (though different) can produce useful data in both cases, and that it is possible to independently verify audit procedures and produce public statements of performance for both environmental and social issues.

EMPLOYEES

Good News:

83% of employees agreed with the founders' statement that "Our success depends on the commitment, skill, creativity, and good humour of our employees."

93% of employees either agreed or strongly agreed that The Body Shop lives up to its mission on the issues of environmental responsibility and animal testing.

79% of employees either agreed or strongly agreed that working for The Body Shop has raised their awareness of pressing global issues.

75% of employees say they are proud to tell others they are part of The Body Shop.

71% of employees enjoy their job.

Bad News:

45% of employees were quite or very dissatisfied with the way The Body Shop encourages them to obtain qualifications.

26% of employees could not recall ever having a job appraisal.

23% of employees felt the best way for them to develop their career was to change companies.

53% of employees either disagreed or strongly disagreed that the behaviour and decision-making of managers was consistent throughout the Company.

The Future:

A new strategy for learning and development (including the issue of in-service qualifications).

Reinforcement of career development.

Reinforcement of new appraisal procedures.

Improved internal communications, particularly via managers in New initiatives on equal opportunities. . . .

SHAREHOLDERS

Good News:

90% of shareholders agreed or strongly agreed that The Body Shop takes active steps to make its business more environmentally responsible.

76% of shareholders agreed or strongly agreed that the Company's business practices reflect a high standard of ethics.

78% of shareholders were satisfied with the information they receive on The Body Shop's financial performance.

75% of shareholders either agreed or strongly agreed that the Company's annual report and accounts provide a comprehensive picture of The Body Shop's overall performance.

Bad News:

29% of shareholders either disagreed or strongly disagreed that the Company enjoys the trust of the financial community.

33% of shareholders either had no opinion or disagreed that The Body Shop has a clear long-term business strategy. The Body Shop share price fell from a high of £2.63 on 11 May 1994 to a low of £1.68 on 8 February 1995, ending the financial year 1994/95 at £1.82.

The Future: While The Body Shop remains a public company it will:

Aim to maximize shareholder interests while also balancing the needs of other stakeholders.

Develop and build relationships with shareholders and prospective shareholders.

Operate a progressive dividend policy.

COMMUNITY INVOLVEMENT

Good News:

In 1994/95 The Body Shop's directly employed staff gave an estimated 19,500 hours to projects in the community.

87% of recipients of funding from The Body Shop Foundation ('The Foundation') either agreed or strongly agreed that The Body Shop takes active steps to make its business more environmentally responsible.

More than 90% of The Foundation grantees were satisfied with: i) the dedication to issues, ii) integrity and transparency and iii) clarity and competence of individuals whom they dealt with in The Body Shop Foundation.

In 1994, The Body Shop donated 2.3% of pre-tax profits to charity. This compares favourably with other UK companies, eg: 2.16% for the Co-operative Bank and 0.44% for Boots.

Bad News:

75% of The Body Shop employees do not participate actively in the community volunteering programme.

Nearly half of grantees either disagreed or strongly disagreed that it was easy to identify the right decision-makers in The Body Shop Foundation.

Nearly one-third of grantees felt The Body Shop Foundation communicates its grant making policy clearly in selected areas.

The Future:

Launch of a new six-point plan for the encouragement of community volunteering.

Formalisation of arrangements for community liaison around The Body Shop's principal operating sites.

Implementation of a ten-point plan by The Body Shop Foundation to improve effectiveness and communications.

Introduction of better performance indicators and service standards for the Foundation Campaigns (and relations with non-governmental organisations).

SOCIAL EVALUATION
The Body Shop International, 1995
KIRK O. HANSON

INTRODUCTION

This report presents the results of an independent evaluation of the social practices, performance and impact of The Body Shop International (referred to as The Body Shop in this report). The Board of The Body Shop commissioned this study late in 1994 and it was conducted between January and December 1995. This report evaluates the social performance of the company during the 1994–1995 period. Kirk O. Hanson, the author, is Senior Lecturer at the Stanford Graduate School of Business in California and has worked in the field of business responsibility for almost thirty years.

The company requested an examination of its social performance on those dimensions addressed in its Mission Statement and Trading Charter, but authorized me to include any other dimensions which I felt were critical to an assessment of its social impact and the fulfillment of its mission.

This report has limitations. At this time, there is no generally accepted methodology for a social audit or social assessment. This report draws upon the work done by many others to develop criteria and standards for social performance, but is still dependent to a significant extent upon my own experience and judgment regarding good social practice. Secondly, one cannot hope to examine all aspects of the behavior of a worldwide enterprise like The Body Shop, nor document every instance of exemplary or deficient behavior, even if given unlimited time to do so. Therefore, this evaluation rests upon the examination and tests which can be done in the 60 working days I spent on the project. While I may have issued individual acts which are significant, I believe I have captured accurately the overall social performance of the company. I hope this report will be useful to The Body Shop in its own efforts to improve its social performance and to others who wish to evaluate its behavior. I also hope this report will be useful to those who are committed to extending the methodology of social assessment and to improving the social performance of their own companies. The Body Shop encouraged me to approach this project in a way that it might advance our collective understanding of social auditing. I am grateful to them for the extra time and expense this entailed.

Overall, I believe The Body Shop demonstrates greater social responsibility and better social performance than most companies of its size. Certain dimensions of its social behavior, however, raise concerns and should be addressed promptly by the company. Other aspects of its social record are about the same as other companies and must be improved if the company seeks to distinguish itself as a leader in social responsibility. The Body Shop

Excerpts from Kirk Hanson, *Social Evaluation: The Body Shop International, 1995.* Reprinted by permission of the author.

has made mistakes in the past, but its management today has committed itself to correcting those errors. This report is part of that process. The social performance measured in this report benefits greatly from the substantial efforts already launched by the company in 1994 and 1995 to address areas of weakness.

I believe the social record of The Body Shop must be viewed with the perspective that this is by any measure a large company—with 1995 turnover (sales) of £220 million ($352 million). Retail sales totaled £500 million ($800 million) in 1210 stores in 45 countries. Company employment totalled 3300. The Body Shop has 572 independent franchisees and sub franchisees operating stores around the world and employing several thousand employees. Achieving outstanding social performance in a rapidly growing, large and global business is a very difficult task.

This evaluation can be viewed as a complement to the company's internally developed Values Report released late in January 1966. My report takes advantage of the data collected for that Values Report, but addresses a broader set of performance issues and the worldwide operations of the company. . . .

I sought to evaluate the record of The Body Shop against "comparable companies," against the company's own values and goals, against the practices of the most outstanding companies ("best practice"), and against the company's claims regarding its social performance. While detail on various of these standards is presented in the text of this report, I have chosen to present a "score" of one to five stars based on how The Body Shop compares to "comparable" companies or the "average company" in the UK and the U.S.

To present my evaluations, I have used the following five star system:

***** Performance Much Better than Comparable Companies.

**** Performance Better than Comparable Companies.

*** Performance Similar to Comparable Companies.

** Performance Worse than Comparable Companies.

* Performance Much Worse than Comparable Companies.

A three rating is therefore "average." Given the stated goal of The Body Shop to be a leader in social responsibility, there is still room for significant improvement in those dimensions rated three. Even in those areas rated four, there are usually aspects of performance which fall short of "best practice," of the company's own aspirations, and sometimes of the company's public statements about itself. . . .

After preparing drafts of this evaluation, I presented the highlights of this evaluation orally at the December 1995 meeting of the Board of Directors and written drafts subsequently to selected company officials. I listened to their reactions and feedback but, following the ground rules established at the outset of the project, made my own decisions about whether to incorporate these additional perspectives. I alone determined the content of this final report.

GENERAL SUMMARY

The Body Shop International is a company publicly committed to social values and to having a substantial and positive impact on society. Its Memorandum of Association (similar to U.S. company's articles of incorporation and by-laws), Mission Statement and Trading Charter are exemplary documents, committing the company to a vision of responsible enterprise that is uncommon among businesses, particularly larger businesses such as The Body Shop has become. The goals of the company embrace both social as well as economic objectives. The Trading Charter extends this dual commitment to the core business of the company, highlighting the pursuit of economic and environmental sustainability, economic development for the disadvantaged, and respect for the rights and human rights of all who trade with the company.

The company's social campaigns, conducted through the medium of the retail shop and shop windows, represent in effect a second "product line," one designed to leverage the shop space and customer traffic for social change. Some campaigns, such as the company's plea for Nigerian Ken Saro-Wiwa, have been fought in the public press and through high profile speeches by founder Anita Roddick and other company executives.

The company's record of social performance has been strongest in areas where it has pursued social causes independent of the traditional trading and commercial activities of the company. Over the past ten years, the company has made significant contributions to the animal welfare movement, to environmental awareness, to communities in which it operates, and to the human rights movement.

The social impact of the company's day-to-day business activities, by contrast, is mixed—outstanding in some areas and in need of significant management attention in others. Some weaknesses have their origins in the rapid growth of the company over the past ten years. Management talent, time and systems have been stretched very thinly in some key areas. This is due in part to the fact that The Body Shop has been growing into a global enterprise of almost 1400 stores in 45 countries which works through 21 head franchisees and over 500 sub franchisees, each of which is an independent business. Nonetheless, I believe that until very recently the company has given more attention to its "social campaigns" than it has to improving the social impact of its day-to-day business dealings with its shareholders, employees, franchisees, customers, local communities and suppliers.

The company has not made the relationship with its shareholders a priority concern. The combined holdings of founders Anita and Gordon Roddick and early partner Ian McGlinn, whose interest is represented on the Board of Directors by the Roddicks, total about 52% of the company's stock. On key dimensions of concern to shareholders, such as financial performance, governance structure, and maintaining the quality of management, The Body Shop has demonstrated mixed performance. Disclosure to minority shareholders and the compensation of executives has generally been acceptable.

The company's relations with its employees have also been mixed. On one hand the company has good benefits and an open and enthusiastic culture. Employees in the UK and in the U.S. report that they are proud to tell others that they work for The Body Shop. On the other hand, it has done less well in defining the jobs of employees, in helping employees plan careers, and in keeping them informed about company developments. Many basic management tasks of importance to employees have not been well executed.

The company's relations with head franchisees and sub franchisees, its most important business partners, have also been varied. Some of the same failings which affect shareholders—particularly inconsistent management—are of importance to franchisees as well. Of most concern, however, has been the day-to-day working relationships between The

Body Shop and its franchise system. Many franchisees believe they do not receive enough and timely information and believe their complaints/suggestions are not taken seriously enough by the company.

The company's relations with its customers are generally good, though some of its past promotional claims and follow-up on consumer complaints raise concerns. The company is working hard to reduce the hype and exaggeration which had crept into the company's public statements, but still has work to do. In many areas of the world, there are no effective systems for following up on consumer complaints and feedback.

Supplier relationships are generally good, though a few suppliers indicate that they have been approached by company representatives with unethical proposals, always a risk in purchasing and a cause for concern.

Relations with local communities are generally strong. Company philanthropic contributions are above average, but as yet are not as strategically planned and executed as they might be. The employee benefit by which employees can volunteer locally on company time is innovative, but has not yet been well promoted or widely used.

Relations with the public and the media are an area of substantial concern. In the past the company has not demonstrated adequate openness and transparency, accuracy in its general communications and willingness to entertain constructive criticism. This report and other corporate efforts, however, demonstrate a commitment to change this record.

As noted earlier, the company's record is most outstanding in its contributions to social change. However, even in the company's chosen areas of priority concern—environmental sustainability, animal rights and human rights—there is room for improvement.

The company has been subject to many charges of irresponsible behavior over the past two years. Many of these charges have no merit whatsoever. Others I have been unable to verify and have found still others to be accurate but greatly overblown in their significance. A few of the charges do have substance and are addressed in this report. Some have even argued that the company has cynically used claims of social concern for pure commercial advantage. I am convinced the company and its employees are genuinely committed to making The Body Shop a force for social change.

Finally, The Body Shop has been an important and powerful example to many other businesses and to consumers that it is possible to serve both social as well as economic goals. It has also pioneered many social innovations that have stimulated others to try similar efforts. The company's impact as an exemplary business, however, has at times been weakened by some of the behaviors noted in this report.

RATINGS BY DIMENSIONS OF SOCIAL PERFORMANCE

Company Values and Mission

Company Purpose *****

The company's strong commitment to both commercial success and to social betterment is exceptional among larger companies. The Memorandum of Association was amended by the company in 1994 to state clearly that the objectives of the company include supporting campaigns and educational programs for human and civil rights, establishing trading relationships with communities in need, implementing policies aimed at protecting the natural environment and supporting campaigns against animal testing in the cosmetics industry.

The Body Shop Mission Statement . . . states the company will "balance the financial and human needs of our stakeholders." It states further that The Body Shop will "passionately campaign for the protection of the environment, human and civil rights and against animal testing within the cosmetics and toiletries industry." The deliberate blend of commercial product and social campaign is unique in my experience, at least at the scale it is pursued by The Body Shop.

The Trading Charter, . . . adopted in 1994, makes more explicit the values and standards to be achieved in business and trading relationships. While other parts of this report will conclude the company does not fully achieve its aspirations, the goals and enabling documents are exceptional among any set of comparable companies.

Advocacy of Responsible Business ****

Company founder Anita Roddick is an extraordinary advocate for corporate responsibility and a vision of business as an agent of social betterment and change. Many of the company's activities and much of its communication are geared to encouraging other companies to emulate the model The Body Shop has developed. At the same time, the company and its founder are sometimes too critical of the behavior of other companies and institutions and fail to acknowledge and encourage the efforts and accomplishments of others.

The company has been in the forefront of developments regarding social auditing and the development of a definition of responsible business behavior. The company's own Values Report, published in January 1996, addresses and evaluates many dimensions of corporate behavior. This report, with its measures of social responsibility, is another demonstration of the company's commitment to promoting standards for responsible business. Ms. Roddick has, in the past year, spearheaded the development of the New Academy of Business, a seminar program to teach principles of responsible business. While all these efforts can be improved, they demonstrate a continuing advocacy of responsible business.

Relations with the Public

Accuracy of Communication **

The Body Shop's leadership has long been committed to honest and straightforward communication—in its promotional claims and all its public statements. Unfortunately, there has been a pattern of exaggeration and occasional failure to substantiate many statements made for and by The Body Shop. Some of this pattern is traceable to the company's natural ebullience and enthusiasm, some to the eagerness to "sell" the company's message and products, and some to an inaccurate assumption that ideas developed by top managers have been instantly implemented by the organization.

Some company representatives have been too quick to present every action of the company as the "first, best and most socially conscious." Some statements and publications of the company have so emphasized the use of "natural" ingredients and the indigenous origins of ingredients and accessories that many customers have assumed the products were "all natural" or "mostly sourced in the Third World." The Body Shop bears some of the responsibility for these assumptions, though a close reading of company statements indicates most claims were worded to avoid direct misrepresentation. Nonetheless, store visits demonstrated that a significant minority of shop clerks, in both company-owned and franchised stores, misrepresent the naturalness and origins of products. The problem was somewhat more pronounced in stores visited in the greater London area than in stores visited in the greater San Francisco area.

This pattern has weakened the credibility of the company and the impact of its actual accomplishments. Weeding out this pattern takes long term attention and effort. The company has initiated an "information audit" designed to preview and verify any written document or oral presentation to be made by the company. The system has not yet been completely effective.

One charge which has attracted recent comment is that the concept and products of The Body Shop were not conceived of entirely by the founders. I found no evidence to prove the founders knew of a California-based company known as The Body Shop before opening their first shop. However, it is clear, and the founders have verified, that they learned of the California company during the first year of the company's existence and used promotional and product ideas from the California company in early merchandising and catalogs. There was nothing illegal in such imitation, though statements of The Body Shop have not fully disclosed the creative inspiration provided by the California company. When The Body Shop entered the U.S. in 1988, it paid the owners of the California based company more than $3.5 million (£2.2 million) for the name "The Body Shop" in the U.S., Japan and elsewhere. It also offered to make them the head franchisee for a portion of the U.S., an offer they accepted but eventually sold back to the company. Additional royalties will be paid over a 10 year period. The total of all payments to the end of 1995 was $4.4 million (£2.75 million).

Reaction to Criticism *

The most serious concern to be raised regarding the company's record of social responsibility is its reaction to criticism. It is the one area I feel compelled to give a single star rating for the 1994–1995 period, though the publication of this Social Evaluation and the recently released "Values Report" represent a new willingness to confront criticism openly.

In the past, The Body Shop has reacted strongly and defensively to reports that it may not live entirely up to its values or claims. The record of the company's dealings with the media over the past several years clearly shows this defensiveness. It has at times been unwilling to entertain even valid concerns, and has been inclined to use legal warnings to dampen criticism of the company. While it must be stated in the company's defense that few companies have faced such determined and persistent attacks as has The Body Shop, the company has reacted poorly to criticism even from "friends," franchisees and employees.

There are differences in libel law between the UK and the U.S., and British companies are generally more aggressive in pressing for corrections in published and broadcast reports. Even by UK standards, however, the company's reactions have been stronger and more defensive than the "average" company. Company officials today suggest their attitudes were shaped by the 1993 Channel 4 libel case in the UK and subsequent attacks by an American journalist. In the Channel 4 case, the company sued the independent network and proved in court the broadcast was inaccurate and malicious. By U.S. standards, the Channel 4 broadcast was relatively mild and the inaccuracies typical of "entertainment" television. But in the UK context and for The Body Shop, the impact was traumatic.

In responding to the critical article "Shattered Image" in the U.S. magazine *Business Ethics* in September 1994, and to coverage of the article's charges as reported in the British press, the company overreacted badly. Company officials today regret some aspects of their own behavior during this intense period, though they argue they had a right to defend themselves against inaccurate charges. I do not question this right, but believe the strong language used in many company statements and other steps taken were unnecessary and overly defensive.

It is undoubtedly difficult to face criticism after being hailed uncritically for so many years as the embodiment of a new way of doing business. Part of the defensiveness results from a real concern that criticism will damage the interests of the franchisees and the social agenda being pursued by the company.

The Body Shop has, in my view, encouraged criticism from others by being excessively critical of other companies and institutions. The Body Shop executives have at times stated that others—in the investment community, in the media, in industry, and in business schools (!)—are motivated solely by baser concerns and are doing nothing of social usefulness. This has unfortunately encouraged many to look for and to welcome criticism of the company.

It is also true that any company which makes socially responsible claims a key element in its marketing will be scrutinized to a much greater extent and will be held to a higher standard than a company which does not. Under these circumstances, the company must demonstrate extraordinary transparency and a willingness to hear and act on criticism of any dimension of its behavior.

Chapter 10

ETHICS IN FINANCE AND ACCOUNTANCY

A. ETHICS IN THE FINANCE INDUSTRY

Over 17 percent of respondents to a large-scale survey of investment analysts about ethical behavior reported that they failed to use diligence and thoroughness in making investment recommendations.[1] That's almost one in five. How would you feel if one of the five recommendations you received from your investment counselor was not thoroughly researched? Should it be "buyer beware" or do you rely on the analyst in making all of your investment decisions? Fifteen percent of the analysts surveyed also admitted to communicating inside information and writing reports to support predetermined conclusions. Yet, in the same survey, these analysts rated themselves higher on an ethical scale than politicians, attorneys, corporate bankers, and corporate managers!

Obviously, trust is an integral issue for all involved in the finance industry. After all, what more can an analyst offer than her or his integrity and trustworthiness? There is no real, tangible product to sell, nor is there the ability to "try before you buy." Therefore, treating clients fairly and building a reputation for fair dealing may be the finance professional's greatest assets. Harvard Professor Greg Dees highlights some of these critical issues in his essay, "Deciding What Is Fair," where he discusses the unique finance issues that might arise in the area of entrepreneurship. The following are a few ethically challenging areas of finance.

Insider Trading   Insider trading is an area that, on the surface and from a legal perspective, seems black and white. If someone trades based on inside information, it's illegal and wrong. On the other hand, if someone has worked very hard to obtain a certain position in a firm and, by virtue of being in that position, the individual is privy to inside information, isn't it just for that person to take advantage of the information since she or he has worked so hard to obtain the position? Is it really wrong? Unethical? Consider an issue that might be closer to home. If your brother has always been successful in whatever he does in the business world, is it unethical to purchase stock in the company he just acquired. Others don't know quite how successful he has been so are you trading on inside information? Would you tell others? What about officers in one company investing in the stocks of their client companies? No legal rules exist other than traditional SEC rules on insider trading, but isn't there something about this that simply doesn't feel "right"?

In many circumstances, not only in finance but also in other areas of business, the actor believes that she is justified in her actions or that he is steering clear of the line that divides ethical and unethical behavior (i.e., staying on the *right* side of the line!). Dennis Levine, convicted for insider trading, was one of those people. Consider the discussion that follows and what might have prevented him (or would prevent others) from getting into this treacherous spot in the first place.

Ethical Investing   There is another side to ethical investing—the obligations of the individual investor. Does the investor have a duty to invest in socially responsible firms? That would seem a bit far-fetched. But isn't it a bit hypocritical for someone to complain a great deal about the lack of social responsibility in corporate America, but then to refuse to financially support

---

[1] E. Theodore Veit and Michael Murphy, "Ethics Violations: A Survey of Investment Analysts," *Journal of Business Ethics* 15 (1996), pp. 1287–97.

the firms who *are* socially responsible? Investors show their support by choosing their investments. If socially responsible firms fail in the public stock exchanges, they will have no capital with which to conduct socially responsible acts—a clear correlation. On the other hand, the complexity of markets and firm activities make it extremely difficult to make wise investment choices in this regard. From the alternate perspective, at least one study seems to evidence stockholder interest in socially responsible activities. Paine et al. report that, despite limited publicity of "good news" (such as the inclusion of a firm in *Business Ethics Magazine's* 100 "Best Corporate Citizens"), there is short-term positive impact on a firm's stock price, documenting a strong link between corporate citizenship and stock prices.[2]

Takeovers, Mergers, and Leveraged Buyouts (LBOs)   Are we a better society because we allow hostile takeovers than we would be if we did not? Companies may perform more efficiently as a result of the threat of a takeover looming at their door. On the other hand, perhaps companies perform efficiently *despite* the threat of takeovers. How well do you work when you know that someone else is after your job? Sometimes better, sometimes worse. Since the market often reflects short-term judgments of long-term decisions, hostile takeovers have been criticized as forcing short-term solutions where a more effective solution would be preferable. In addition, in order to finance the takeovers, many firms take on huge internal debts, paid off only as long as the company is doing well but left as a market loss when the company is threatened with higher costs.

When a firm is threatened with a takeover, decision makers sometimes react by attempting to take the company private through the issuance of bonds. This is often accomplished by issuing high-risk, or "junk," bonds in order to repurchase stock. Does this satisfy the directors' fiduciary duty to shareholders? The decision makers have a duty to the shareholder to increase stock price, but also a self-interest in keeping stock prices low for repurchase. Utilitarian theory may be best applied here. When the public hears of an LBO or restructuring, it is often assumed that jobs may be lost and the rich will just get richer. But, people often fail to realize that the money of the rich is not just sitting under a mattress somewhere—it is invested in the market. LBOs often trim the fat off of companies and make them more efficient (through increased productivity, lower prices, and an increase in *long-term* employment).

Another vexing market issue in connection with takeovers is *greenmail*. You decide to buy some shares of a company. After purchasing those shares, you find out some information related to this firm which, when made public, causes an extreme rise in the stock price. Have you done anything wrong by making this information public? It doesn't appear so. Greenmail is not much different. Greenmail occurs where a potential takeover agent purchases stock in a company. After the purchases have totaled 5 percent, the agent must announce its intention to take over the company, if that is its intent. The stock price goes up in anticipation of the takeover battle. The takeover agent ends up selling its shares back to the firm for this increased price (or sometimes a higher, negotiated price) when the attacked company struggles to thwart the takeover. Is this any different from the facts in the first scenario? Is this unethical?

---

[2]Whiton Paine et al., "An Event Study of One Link Between 'Good News' and Socially Responsible Investing," available from the author at *whitons@worldnet.att.net.*

Some contend that the ethics of the situation depend on the real intent of the takeover agent. If there was never any real intent to complete the takeover, but instead merely to increase the price and sell back, then the practice would be considered unethical. They argue that someone with a real intent may propose a restructuring plan and, if management adopts it, the agent would withdraw its offer. The profit received from selling the shares back to the firm would be not unethical but a "consultant's fee" for offering assistance to the firm! Are you convinced? What is the key problem with this argument? Aren't you bothered that the firm didn't have the free choice of whether to "hire" this assistance or not? It was forced on them and they were threatened to "use it or lose it." Free choice is nonexistent.

How could this type of behavior be prevented? Legislation has been proposed to thwart these attempts at greenmail, requiring for instance that proposed takeover agents have 100 percent of funding available for the takeover at the time of the announcement. Can you think of other mechanisms or would you argue that the free market should prevail without any regulation of this type? Is this evidence of a free market success or breakdown?

Evidence of something that might more arguably be justified by free market theory is *golden parachutes.* The term refers to the guarantee to the chief executives of a firm that they will be "taken care of" in the event of a takeover. This provision is often in the bylaws of the firm long before it becomes a takeover target and may actually serve to dissuade certain takeover agents because of the potential costs involved. Some theorists argue that golden parachutes preserve the integrity of the executives' fiduciary duties because they know that they will be taken care of whether the firm, or their jobs, remain in existence or not. On the other hand, should corporate funds really go to this end? Aren't executives paid awfully well in some cases precisely because they are willing to take these risks?

Financial issues may pose the greatest ethical dilemmas simply because they frequently pit money against other priorities. Perhaps the best way to solve these ethical issues in finance is to consider your personal priority scheme long before the dilemma presents itself. Money is seductive, sometimes more so than the right thing to do.

B. ETHICS IN ACCOUNTANCY

If you were to look in a standard business textbook, you might find the following definition of accounting: "the process by which any business keeps track of its financial activities by recording its debits and credits and balancing its accounts." Accounting offers us a system of rules and principles which govern the format and content of financial statements. Accounting, by its very nature, is a system of principles applied to present the financial position of a business and the results of its operations and cash flows. It is hoped that adherence to these principles will result in fair and accurate reporting of this information.

There is a distinction between an accountant who works for a company and has an obligation as an employee to that company, and an independent certified public accountant who may be hired by a company as outside counsel. In the second case, that individual comes in to perform an audit for the benefit, in truth, of the public, the shareholders, and the government, in order to maintain the public's confidence. In that regard, companies would love to be able to direct what that outside accountant says because people believe the "independent" nature of the audit. On the other hand, if accountants were merely rubber stamps for the word of the corporation, they would no longer be believed nor considered "independent."

Now, would you consider an accountant to be a watchdog or a bloodhound? Does an accountant stand guard or instead seek out problematic reporting? The answer to this question may depend on whether the accountant is employed internally by a firm or works as outside counsel.

The ethical issues surrounding accounting practices are varied. They include underreporting income, falsifying documents, allowing or taking questionable deductions, illegally evading income taxes, and otherwise engaging in fraud. In order to prevent accountants from being put in these types of conflicts, the American Institute of CPAs publishes their professional rules.

In addition, the Financial Accounting Standards Board governs accounting practices and establishes the generally accepted accounting principles (GAAP) that stipulate the methods by which accountants gather and report information. However, the International Accounting Standards Committee is in the process of developing standards (to be completed by 1998) that would allow foreign companies to sell securities in the United States as long as their accounting conforms to the international standards, even if it does not comply with the GAAP.[3]

Imagine the consternation of U.S. firms that would be required to comply with GAAP while foreign firms could merely comply with the new standards. And the difference could be great. The international standards allow firms far more discretion in the manner of reporting, permitting the accountant to choose which accounting practice to apply in a given situation. Since different accounting practices may place a firm in a better or worse light, the onus of standing up to firms who want to use the discretion to report misleading figures would be on the accountant.

Accountants are also governed by the American Institute of Certified Public Accountants (AICPA) which has a Code of Professional Conduct. The Code relies on the judgment of accounting professionals in carrying out their duties rather than stipulating a set of extremely specific rules. But can these standards keep pace with readily changing accounting activities in newly emerging firms such as the dot-coms? *Fortune* magazine devoted an entire cover story recently to the accounting sleight of hand in which dot-coms are engaging to "pull revenues out of thin air."[4]

In any case, would standards be enough? As you will see from the cases that follow, the answers to ethical dilemmas are not always so easily found within the rules and regulations governing the industry.

Short Hypothetical Finance and Accounting Cases

a. Garcia Corporation is a 20-year-old, publicly traded company that generates $50,000,000 in annual sales of commercial food prep equipment. Most of Garcia's sales growth has come from selling the same basic product line to newly opened restaurants. Consequently, Garcia has managed to modestly increase its profits over the previous year's performance and declare a higher dividend for its shareholders during most years.

---

[3]Floyd Norris, "Will U.S. Accounting Rules be Irrelevant?" *New York Times,* December 29, 1996, Business p. 1.
[4]Jeremy Kahn, "Presto Chango! Sales Are Huge!" *Fortune,* Mar. 20, 2000, *http://www.fortune.com/fortune/2000/03/20/net.html*

In the past five years, however, the restaurant industry in which most Garcia customers compete has suffered from a major shake-up. Several established restaurant chains and more than a few new start-ups have failed. As a result, the restaurant equipment market has been flooded with used goods, which sell for half the cost of new equipment. Garcia's equipment sales this year have declined while it waits for this temporary glut to disappear, and the company may post a slight loss (the company's first) as a result.

Most of Garcia's stockholders are investors who expect the company's profits, share value, and dividends to increase. Although they are sympathetic to tough economic times, the stockholders will sell off their shares and refuse to buy additional shares in the future if the company's fortunes decline. To keep its stockholders content, Garcia plans to make an accounting change in its depreciation policy on its auto fleet from double-declining-balance to straight-line. The company would show a slight profit this year and hopefully give its management time to boost the company's sales and profitability the next year.

Are these plans ethical, given the fact that the change would be disclosed and that shareholders are still getting the same information? Are the shareholders' expectations realistic? Does this matter?

b. Since 1894, ABC Steel Company has manufactured and distributed sheet metal fabricated in its mills to many American and foreign companies. Until the mid-1970s, this family-operated company had been a very healthy and profitable operation, but the company's fortunes began to change when it faced stiff quality and price competition from foreign steel manufacturers. ABC suffered a strong decline in sales and closed several plants as a result.

During the early 1980s, ABC replaced both its aging plant equipment and its aging management team. Most of the equipment ABC once used in its manufacturing process was installed during the 1950s and had been repaired, modified, and expanded, but never replaced. By closing more than half of its existing operations, ABC concentrated on its remaining facilities and purchased $50,000,000 of modern equipment that allowed it to successfully compete with foreign steelmakers.

The stockholders also replaced the family that started the company with a younger, more aggressive management team. The stockholders paid the managers competitive salaries but also realized that good managers frequently changed positions every few years. As an incentive to encourage the management's loyalty and performance, the stockholders also offered them $3,000,000 in lucrative stock options that could be exercised when the earnings per share (EPS) first exceeded $2 per share, a rather sizable increase to expect at that time.

By November 1994, the company projected annual earnings of $20,000,000 and had 11,000,000 shares outstanding and $18,000,000 in cash reserves for future investment. Since the 1980s and 1990s, the company's sales steadily grew to a respectable amount, but the manufacturing equipment once again began to show signs of its age. The management team was faced with a decision: Should it recommend that the company spend the $18,000,000 in available cash on the more modern equipment or use it to repurchase 1,500,000 shares of stock? What would be the consequences if the management team repurchased the stock? How might this decision affect the stockholders? What would you do if you were a member of the management team?

c. Maria and Sam were having lunch at the University Coffee House. "I have a problem that I'd like your advice about," said Sam. "I prepare all of the expense reports in the department. Most of the time when people travel or have business meals, they exceed the limits."

"Do you mean the university limits on amounts reimbursed per person per meal and the daily limits on hotel accommodations?" asked Maria.

"That's right," said Sam. "When people exceed the university limits, my supervisor has me add fictitious tips and taxi fares on business trips to increase the expense reimbursement. My supervisor claims that the university limits are just too low. Everyone knows that, so everyone 'pads' expense accounts.

"But I just don't feel good about this situation," Sam continued. "Normally, if I have a question about the ethics of certain practices, I would talk to my supervisor."

"That probably won't accomplish much in this case. Perhaps you could talk to your supervisor's boss," Maria suggested.

"If my supervisor found out, I'd be in big trouble," said Sam. "Besides, maybe all the higher-ups condone this practice. Maybe everyone pads the expense accounts. Maybe I have to go along with the practice to keep my job." What should Sam do?

d. Bill Merino works in the inventory control group at a company that produces stone-washed jeans. A good friend of Bill's manages the stitching department at the same company. At the end of a recent month, Bill reviewed the stitching department's production cost report and found the department had no beginning work in progress inventory, had started 27,000 pairs of jeans, and had produced only 24,000 pairs. "That leaves 3,000 pairs in ending inventory," Bill thought. "That's a lot of jeans they didn't finish."

Later, Bill visited his friend who managed the stitching department. "Why all this ending inventory?" Bill asked.

"One of the new workers set several machines wrong, and the stitching was bad on 2,400 pairs," the manager replied. "We set those aside and we'll fix them when we have some free time. The other 600 pairs are complete now and have been transferred out. Our entire operation was slower because of the machine problem."

"Company policy is to send all defective products to the rework department. They can fix the jeans. That's their job," Bill said.

"No way!" exclaimed the stitching department manager. "We'd all be in trouble if plant management found out. The worker who messed up would probably be fired. I don't want that. This is our little problem and we'll take care of it."

What should Bill do? Would your answer change if Bill learned that the stitching department had fixed the jeans and had sent them on to the next department?

From *Essentials of Managerial Accounting* by James Don Edwards, Roger Hermanson, and Michael Maher, copyright © 1994 Business One–Irwin, and from *Essentials of Financial Accounting* by James Don Edwards, Roger Hermanson, and Michael Maher, copyright © 1994 Business One–Irwin. Reprinted by Permission.

THE ETHICS OF REWARD SYSTEMS IN THE FINANCIAL SERVICES INDUSTRY

RONALD DUSKA

When one engages the services of a financial advisor or an investment management consultant, that person's salary is earned in part or wholly through commissions. Since commissions are often based on the amount of the transaction, it appears that the rewards structure may be in conflict with the interests of those the individual seeks to serve—the client. Professor Duska evaluates this tension in the following article.

A major ethical question facing the financial services industry is "To what extent do commissions (as reward systems) influence unethical behavior?" It seems intuitively clear that when a financial services professional is faced with selling one of two products of equal benefit to a client, he naturally would sell the product which brings the higher commission. After all, human beings are self-interested animals, as we were reminded by Adam Smith in the famous passage from his book *The Wealth of Nations*.

> *It is not from the benevolence of the butcher, the brewer or the baker, that we expect our dinner, but from their regard to their own interest. . . . We address ourselves not to their humanity but to their self-love, and never talk to them of our own necessities but of their advantages.*[1]

Nevertheless, while Smith recognizes that we are motivated by self-interest, he also reminds us that we are morally obliged to forgo our self-interest if its pursuit leads to an injustice.

> *Every man,* as long as he does not violate the laws of justice, *is left perfectly free to pursue his own interest his own way, and to bring both his industry and capital into competition with those of any other man, or order of man.*[2]

Clearly it violates the law of justice to sell an inferior financial product to a client in order to collect a greater commission. That would constitute pursuing one's self-interest at the expense of another, a paradigmatic instance of selfish behavior, which is wrong (Ayn Rand to the contrary notwithstanding).[3]

However, to the extent that behavior is motivated by self-interest, it would seem that commission structures have a powerful effect on what products agents sell. Poorly designed

"The Ethics of Reward Systems in the Financial Services Industry," by Ronald Duska, *Business & Society Review* 104, no. 1 (1999), p. 34. Reprinted with permission of Blackwell Publishing Co.

commission structures tempt agents to violate justice and provide incentives for unethical behavior. Keith Darcy[4] makes this point by saying, "Show me your commission structure and I'll show you your values." For Darcy, following our intuitive insight, it seems that a commission-based industry leads to a clear conflict between the agent's interest and the client's interest.

Given that human beings are subject to temptation, and that many of the financial services industries, such as the life insurance industry, have heavily front end loaded commission structures, is it any wonder that one of the chief sins (faults) in the insurance and financial services industry is churning or twisting—i.e., "excessive trading of a client's account which increases the broker's commissions, but usually leaves the client worse off or no better off than before?"[5]

To combat the churning or twisting of account holdings and unnecessary replacements of life insurance policies, as well as to curtail the sale of products unfit for clients' needs, the financial services industry lately has moved to replace current commission structures with fees for services or levelized commissions. This is expected to be especially helpful in areas such as the life insurance industry where heavily front loaded commissions encourage unnecessary replacement of policies. There is also serious reconsideration of the use of trips and vacations as bonuses for increased sales, since these are seen as creating unnecessary conflicts between the brokers or agents and their clients.

As we indicated, a reward system that adopts a fee for services method of paying brokers and agents intuitively makes good sense, for it separates the self-interest of the agent which is served by selling the product from the advice to buy the product. Human beings are unquestionably influenced by their environment and by their self-interest. Whatever controls can be put into effect to provide motivation for acting on behalf of the client instead of oneself makes eminent sense, if the goal of the company is to promote the best interest of the client.

But for those interested in maintaining the status quo, changing commission structures is problematic. "Proponents of changing commission structures need a dose of hard core reality," the defenders of commission structures would respond. Although economists continually talk of efficient markets where there is a level playing field and information is available to all, the fact is that in the real world it is to a person's personal advantage to compete with asymmetrical information. We all look for market inefficiencies (bargains) in the market to exploit. Those inefficiencies and asymmetries of information are what bargains are all about. The fact is, clients depend on the broker or agent to find them bargains which will exploit inefficiencies. For that, brokers expect to be compensated well. But since the brokers are compensated well, they are also expected to be able to overcome short-term temptations and depend on the long-term benefits they can bring to their clients for their ultimate rewards.

In a competitive world we have agents and principals, and expect agents to look out for the best interest of their principals. In many cases in an agency relationship, it is precisely because the agent has more knowledge than the principal that he or she is retained. Attempts to counteract the temptations that accompany the one-sidedness of such asymmetrical information give rise to the necessity of a professional, i.e., one who has expert knowledge in some area and a spirit of altruism toward one's client or patients. The spirit of professionalism has been appealed to in financial services to help the financial service providers avoid the temptations of self-interest.

In this vein, Larry Bear reminds us that in some cases, those where the other has less information through no fault of their own, to take advantage of asymmetrical information is unfair. It is important to consider the effect of this asymmetrical information. It doesn't have to be turned into an economic advantage. For example, we go to a doctor precisely because we recognize the asymmetrical information and are counting on it, i.e., we are counting on the doctor or the professional to have the requisite information. Those with this information, the professionals, then have a duty not to misuse the asymmetrical information. It must be used properly. Professionals are expected to overcome temptations such as commission structures.

While pointing out that compensation programs are signaling messages about values and have some conflicts and dilemmas associated with them, David Larcker[6] also points out that they are just one of the motivating pressures of one of the stakeholders in a market situation, all of whom want the benefit of the bargain. The market is the leveler of conflicting pressures.

First, employees are under pressure to sell products.

Second, shareholders are looking to take short-term profits and have returns exceed the cost of capital.

Third, customers are looking for fair compensation.

Conflicts of interest are built into the system, and commission compensation programs are not inherently bad. A good design will or can encourage ethical behavior. Still, such programs will require active monitoring by upper level management to see that they are aligned with customers and shareholder's interests. For example, some insurance companies in the 1980s were more interested in servicing their agents than their customers. Such an environment is ripe for unethical behavior.

Some companies have rid themselves of the supposedly tempting environment. Garry Parr[7] refers to the practices of Morgan Stanley. For Morgan Stanley, to be compensated on the basis of the conclusion of a transaction creates a clear conflict between client and agent self-interest. To motivate their people to give the right advice, they don't pay commissions. They do pay bonuses at the end of the year, but determine the bonus by measuring the business performance in the light of a long-term orientation. Part of the compensation is tied to restricted stock that must be held for the long term. "Our goal is to enhance the franchise, building the long-term value of Morgan Stanley," Parr said. "We try to orient people toward the long term, both in how they are developing and through compensation paid mostly in restricted stock. It ties us all to the good fortunes and risks of the business."[8]

However, the intuitive appraisal of the situation noted above bespeaks a rather crude economic determinism and an almost uncritical acceptance of a psychological egoism, which holds that everyone always pursues their own self-interest. It is intriguing to note that Smith did not believe in this sort of determinism, and that recent studies tend to support his view. In the first words of his *Theory of Moral Sentiments,* Adam Smith says:

> *Howsoever selfish man may be supposed, there are evidently some principles in his nature, which interest him in the fortune of others, and render their happiness necessary to him, though he derives nothing from it except the pleasure of seeing it . . . That we often derive sorrow from the sorrow of others, is a matter of fact too obvious to require any instances to prove it; for this sentiment, like all the other original passions of human nature, is by no means confined to the virtuous and humane, though they perhaps may feel it with the most*

exquisite sensibility. The greatest ruffian, the most hardened violator of the laws of society, is not altogether without it.

As we have no immediate experience of what other men feel, we can form no idea of the manner in which they are affected, but by conceiving what we ourselves should feel in the like situation.[9]

How much will adapting, modifying or eliminating the commission system, or other rewards systems, bring about more ethical behavior? It is impossible to say, since relatively little empirical research has been conducted about the effects of commission and reward systems on behavior.

However, an intriguing set of studies by Nancy Kurland[10] might give us a clearer picture of what motivates good people to do bad things. Kurland investigated what motivated financial services professionals to recommend and sell products.

She was concerned that bonuses such as vacations to exotic islands and commission structures which favored high-risk products over safer products might affect a broker's objectivity in recommending products to a client. Amazingly she found that *commission did not significantly predict the willingness of agents to disclose information to clients,* even when that information would have a negative effect on the agent's commission or bonus. She found that *salespeople were also motivated by moral beliefs, behavioral controls and attitudes in the firm.*

The influence of behavioral controls should not surprise us, since one of the primary behavioral controls is the law. Most companies in the financial services industry have stringent compliance codes, and the government imposes regulations such as those from the United States Securities and Exchange Commission, state insurance regulations and the pressures of the sentencing guidelines. Thus, commissions might tempt the agent to selfish behavior, but the threat of law enforcement keeps agents looking out for the best interests of clients.

However, the other, perhaps surprising, motivating factor Kurland found (unless we remember what Adam Smith said) is that people also are motivated by their moral beliefs and their moral attitudes. In this case, we can go back to common sense and trust in another of our intuitions. In spite of the cynicism of those who think everyone acts selfishly, we do believe that people can escape economic determinism and be motivated by moral beliefs. People have fellow feeling, and want to look out for the welfare of others. They value their integrity, which does not let them use another merely as a means to their own selfish ends. So we agree with Smith that there is a fellow feeling that leads to empathy and makes its consequent justice possible.

Kurland's studies seem to warrant the following claim: that all or most humans have an implicit notion of fairness, as is manifest in something like the Golden Rule, and that they are motivated by that just as they are motivated by self-interest. When we couple our built in notions of fairness with our fellow feeling or empathy, moral attitudes or beliefs are bound to (likely to) kick in, leading us to treat our fellow humans with fairness, in spite of the cost to us.

There is a final factor that Kurland mentions which promotes ethical behavior, and that is the attitude of the company. This, I take it, is what is behind the claims of those like Lynn Sharp Paine[11] and Larry Bear,[12] when they say that a compliance system without an ethics program will fail. Bear at the conference said compensation must be surrounded by supervision and controls. "The challenge is putting controls in for people above and below." What follows from this point of view is that structuring companies to take ethics into account should help improve the moral behavior of a company's agents. Agents should be motivated not simply to avoid punishment or make themselves better off by better commissions or bonuses, but by the desire simply to do the right thing by our fellow human beings.

What is finally remarkable is that the claims of Bear and Lynn Sharp Paine, that compliance is not enough and that ethics needs to be brought to bear to bring about integrity in business, which are validated by Kurland's study, have been strengthened by a recent empirical study conducted by Gary Weaver and Linda Trevino.[13] Weaver and Trevino found that ethical behavior in companies is enhanced when a companywide ethics program is added to a compliance program.

Since, as Kurland finds, moral beliefs and company attitudes motivate, Weaver and Trevino's findings which confirm that ethics programs in conjunction with compliance programs produce more ethical behavior than compliance programs in isolation can be explained by the fact that our moral attitudes drive our behavior, even when it is not in our interest.

The implications of all this are manifold. We need to realize that complex human behavior is driven by a host of factors—appeals to self-interest, behavioral controls, cultural attitudes and moral beliefs. It is perhaps the price we pay for late twentieth century cynicism that we do not recognize that our fellow human beings are as powerfully moved by the last of these, their moral beliefs which involve and demand adherence to principles of justice, as they are by fear and self interest.

Recently, at the San Diego Zoo, I observed the dominant male gorilla taking food out of the mouth of one of the younger gorillas. His aggressive brutality—his following the law of the jungle, so to speak—reminded me of the quote from Rabbi Brickner with which Tom Donaldson concluded the Zicklin meetings. "It's what people do when they are alone and no one's looking and they know they won't get caught that makes the difference between a civilization and a jungle."[14]

Before determining how to structure a company's ethics programs and before dismantling all the current reward systems, it might behoove the financial services industry to engage in more studies like those of Kurland to help determine more carefully—with less cynicism and without a priori acquiescence in a crude economic determinism—what motivates agents and brokers.

NOTES

1. Adam Smith, *The Wealth of Nations,* IV, ii, 9.
2. Adam Smith, *The Wealth of Nations,* IV, ix, 51.
3. Rand entitled one of her books *The Virtue of Selfishness*. But the title is simply perverse, given the ordinary language meaning of the word *selfishness*. *Selfishness* has a connotation of unethical behavior. We distinguish (or at least should distinguish) in English between *selfish* and *self-interested* behavior. Both behaviors are in the agent's interest. However, selfish behavior is at the expense of another where that is unjustified. Hence, by the ordinary meaning of the word, the lexical definition, selfish behavior is wrong. One can speculate that it was for the shock value that Rand systematically misused the word in her work.
4. Keith Darcy, Executive Vice President, IBJ Schroder Bank and Trust Company, remarks at the Zicklin Center Conference.
5. John Downes and Jordan Elliot Goodman, *Money's Complete Guide to Personal Finance and Investment Terms* (Woodbury, NY: Barron's Educational Service, Inc., 1985), 62.

6. Dave Larcker, Ernst and Young Professor of Accounting, The Wharton School, remarks at the Zicklin Center Conference.

7. Garry Parr, Managing Director, Morgan Stanley, remarks at the Zicklin Center Conference.

8. Garry Parr, as quoted in a draft of selected remarks from the Zicklin Center Conference.

9. Adam Smith, *The Theory of Moral Sentiments* (Oxford University Press, 1976), Part I, Section I, Chap. I, 1 and 2.

10. Nancy Kurland, Summary of remarks presented at the Zicklin Center Conference on her behalf by Thomas Dunfee. Cf. also the following: "The Ethical Implications of the Straight-Commission Compensation System—An Agency Perspective," *Journal of Business Ethics* 10 (1991), 757–766; "Ethics, Incentives, and Conflicts of Interest: A Practical Solution," *Journal of Business Ethics* 14 (1995), 465–475. "Trust, Accountability, and Sales Agents' Dueling Loyalties," *Business Ethics Quarterly* 6:3 (1996), 289–310.

11. Lynn Sharp Paine, "Managing for Organizational Integrity," *Harvard Business Review* 72 (1994), 106–117.

12. Larry Alan Bear, Stern School of Business, New York University, remarks at the Zicklin Center Conference.

13. Gary R. Weaver, University of Delaware and Linda Klebe Trevino, Pennsylvania State University, "Attitudinal and Behavioral Outcomes of Corporate Ethics Programs: An Empirical Study of the Impact of Compliance- and Values-Oriented Approaches," a presentation at the Academy of Management Annual Meeting, August 10, 1998, San Diego. This field survey investigated the relationships of the perceived values and compliance orientations of an ethics program to employee outcomes. A values-based orientation was associated with seven outcomes. A compliance-based orientation was associated with two outcomes. The interaction of the two orientations was associated with employees' willingness to report misconduct.

14. Rabbi Balfour Brickner as quoted by Tom Donaldson at the Zicklin Center Conference meeting.

TOPIC STUDY:
ETHICAL INVESTMENT

WHAT HAS "ETHICAL INVESTMENT" TO DO WITH ETHICS?

BETTER WORLD

The term "ethical investing" is largely used to correspond with investments that pass certain filters and investments only in firms that do not engage in or invest in tobacco manufacturing. Betterworld asks whether ethical investment is even possible.

WHAT IS ETHICAL INVESTMENT?

There are four main players in the ethical investment business. First are what we might call the investment institutions. Perhaps the best known of these is a bank, the Co-operative Bank—"We'll never invest in companies who carelessly pollute"—but there are many others. The Clerical Medical Evergreen Fund Ethical Policy, the Friends Provident Stewardship Fund Ethical Policy, the Scottish Equitable Ethical Trust Ethical Policy, the NPI Global Care Fund Ethical Policy, and Ethical Financial Limited and its *Guide to Socially Responsible Investment* are just a few examples of institutions, policies and literature in which we find moral terms deployed. "Care," "socially responsible" and "ethical." "Ethical" is the most frequently used.

It is largely a self-awarded title. The institutions describe themselves or their investment plans, their endowment policies, personal pension plans, life-assurance or other investments as "ethical." They may use the term in their advertising. The fact that it is self-awarded is not to say that it is arbitrary. On the contrary, the investments that are termed "ethical" are chosen according to increasingly standardized criteria. So-called ethical investments may rule out alcohol, arms or environmental damage, to name but three from an extremely long overall list.

Some of the institutions explicitly deny that they are being judgmental in this. They do so in two ways. First they point out that they are but providing a service to would-be customer investors, the second group of players, who already have established personal preferences about what they consider moral investments. The investment institution merely puts together packages which suit such preferences. Many such institutions also explain that the information they use to find out which companies and which products to invest in (this is the third group of players, the companies producing chemicals, arms or whatever) is derived from an information organization, such as EIRIS (Ethical Investment Research Service). The information organizations are the fourth and last major player. Thus NPI states: "The team works closely with the independent company EIRIS which helps in identifying companies which meet the criteria for the Global Care Unit Trust." Scottish Equitable states: "We use the independent services of EIRIS to advise on the suitability of shares for ethical investment." Friends Provident "commissions research from the independent EIRIS" and Clerical Medical "subscribes to EIRIS".

Over the years a number of criteria have come to be used to define an investment as ethical. The investment institutions appear to accept them as such, at least conventionally. They certainly use the word "ethical" to describe such investments. EIRIS, for it's part also disclaims any act of judgment. "I should add that EIRIS does not make ethical judgments on Company Groups (that is, producer companies). Our role is to assemble information on which concerned investors may base their own judgments."

The history of how these criteria emerged and who helped them to emerge is not the object of this study, though it might well repay someone's attention. Our interest is in the list as it now stands. A few passing comments might be made however. Some items appear to have a Christian, perhaps Methodist origin such as the frequent emphasis on avoiding investments in alcoholic beverages and gambling, and sometimes pornography. Did pacifism, religious or secular, lead to the standard mention of arms as to be avoided? Others would seem to have a health dimension, such as tobacco. Yet others have been prompted by the environmental movement and the animal rights movement. Yet others—about employment conditions, for example—owe something to affirmative action and Third World activism. It is sometimes said that the growth in Ethical Investment has been spectacular although admittedly from a small baseline. What has been even more spectacular is the growth in the items on the list, the number of criteria.

***

WHAT PRODUCTS AND PRACTICES ARE DEFINED AS ETHICAL?

Any analysis of the ethical character of EI (ethical investing) must start with the list of products and processes they define as ethical and unethical. There are three groups. First a heterogeneous group including, as mentioned above, arms, gambling and alcohol. Next, green and animal rights categories. Last, categories to do with conditions of employment. These are further divided into positive or negative: "does the company invest in tobacco?" If yes, then bad. "Does the company do all it can to further environmental sustainability?" If yes, then good. A further division is according to whether the matter is more or less factual. A company either does or does not produce tobacco. Whether it sustains the environment or produces pornography may require further judgment. *Thus,* the NPI policy mentioned above will avoid investment in companies which publish, print or distribute newspapers classed by EIRIS sources as pornographic. An environmental questionnaire sent by the Swiss-based Centre Info., another information group, asks, "Have you signed the Principles of the Coalition for Environmentally Responsible Economics (CERES)?" And IRRC, the Investor Responsibility Research Center, a US-based information group, asks, "Does your company endorse the goals of the South African Council of Churches Code of Corporate Conduct?" The assumptions here are, I assume, that these third parties, EIRIS, CERES and the South African Council of Churches, are sound, well informed and ethically sophisticated judges of ethical corporate conduct.

Without anticipating the discussion below, we should start by noting that the list of "ethical" concerns is long and not obviously coherent. There is certainly no one explicit organizing ethical principle or even code of ethics which accounts for the collection of products and processes on the overall list. Of course, not all the advocates and personnel of ethical investment subscribe to the entire list. But what more can we say about the list?

The key terms on an ethical list might include several of the following:

- Armaments

- Tobacco

- Gambling

- Any products, e.g., pharmaceuticals and cosmetics, using animal experimentation

- Any products, e.g., fur, involving "inhumane" animal use

- Beers, wines and spirits

- Inhumane farming

- Involvement in the nuclear industry

- Investment in countries with unethical regimes (in the past, notably South Africa)

- Failure to promote equal opportunities

- Failure to match First World employment conditions in Third World countries

- Lack of trade union rights

- Inadequate level of giving to charity

- Inadequate level of community involvement

- Political donations

- Unreadiness to disclose information to EI information groups

- Inadequate health and safety record

- Excessive greenhouse gases

- Use of tropical hardwood

- Excessive effluent discharge

- Pesticides

- Advertising complaints

- Mining

It is clear that some of these are products, e.g., alcohol. Others of them are processes or company actions such as the way it employs or the way it uses the environment. While the distinction is not entirely satisfactory, it is important. . . .

THE WAY SOME ETHICAL INVESTORS TRADE ON THE WORD "ETHICAL"

Our interest is in one question only. Many EI activists are keen to make sure industry advertising is honest and informative. Is their own self-description honest and informative? How ethical is ethical investment? "Ethical" is not just a term which has become conventional, one which could be replaced by any other such as "the neutral investments of personal preference" or the perhaps "pejorative ideological investments." "Ethical" is a crucial trading term for ethical investors. Replace it with these other descriptions and what is lost is highly significant. Thus the company Ethical Financial uses the word in its name and describes itself as founded on principles of "caring," as promoting "socially responsible investment." EI, say the EI people, is for "concerned" investors.

So the EI companies and activists, with little apparent sense of modesty, describe themselves and their products as ethical, caring, socially responsible, positive and concerned. Generously, some also suggest that their clients will be ethical, caring, socially responsible, positive and concerned. Investors who do not invest in the way described as ethical and companies which make products or engage in practices not on the approved list may sense an implication that they are *unethical.* Whether they are entitled to draw such an implication is not clear in all cases. But it is more than clear in some. Thus the Ethical Financial company not only brands its own products ethical but explicitly says that "as many as 75 per cent of the top shares may have some 'unethical' link." Some of them, it continues, abuse the world's natural resources and exploit its people and animals. And exploiting people, if not so much animals and not necessarily resources, is bad behavior in any one's book.

So there you have it. On the one hand morally good investments, on the other morally bad investments. Are those EI people, the investors and companies who do so, justified in awarding themselves this prestigious label of moral goodness and in casting investments and investors which do not follow their ideas as morally bad?

CAN PRODUCTS BE MORALLY GOOD OR EVIL?

Professor Kenneth Minogue notes that the term "ethics" is a rhetorical blockbuster referring to forms of conduct which are unambiguously good and bad: the rejection of criminality. Lying, betrayal, exploitation, and other types of behavior (whose concrete forms may be much more ambiguous than their abstract description).

> *Ethical investment seems little concerned with these things, which are in any case the forms of conduct which could not be caught in the questionnaire nets with which professional ethical investors trawl for iniquities.*

However, "ethical investment seems to be concerned with such things as smoking, drinking alcohol, trading in arms—things which are disapproved of by specific moral attitudes—Puritanism, perhaps, and pacifism, but whose moral character is controversial. Since about

35 per cent of the population smokes, one imagines they would not regard dealing in tobacco as particularly immoral.

> *In any case, the target is abstract, in the sense that making or trading in arms may be judged good or bad according to who gets the arms and how they are used. In other words, the indicators, the criteria of judging, used by the ethical investors are deficient.*

One of the major deficiencies is the reduction of complex or controversial moral issues to good/bad product lists. As mentioned above, a lot, not all, but a lot of EI depends on such product-based lists. There are ethical traditions, perhaps dominant ethical traditions, which would find this strange. For instance, a dominant Christian tradition sees products or creatures as not good or bad. The morals come in according to how man uses them. Are they used in accordance with God's wish for his people? In which case that is a right use of creatures. Or against it? In which case it is wrong. The product itself, whether natural or man-made has no moral quality. Morality depends on free will, choice, intention, and foreknowledge. Products have none of these things. Of course their makers may have such intentions. There may be products made in such a way that only one use is likely and that immoral. Pornography may be such a case. But even then it is only likely. And most other products have multiple uses, some of which are good and some bad. Moreover it is the user who decides such use, not the maker. It is the buyer, the user, who has intention, foreknowledge, and the other conditions of moral action. A producer could collude in immoral use with a user but that would have to be established in individual cases. It does not follow from immoral use of a product that the producer or the production is immoral.

***

OTHER ETHICAL TRADITIONS AND EI

So far I have been mainly concerned with that Christian ethical tradition which makes *use* of product the central ethical matter. What happens when we turn to other related traditions? One central strand in Western ethical thinking places the virtues at the defining heart of ethics. Ethical action is the cultivation of virtues. These often turn out to be a mixture of Christian, classical, (e.g., often Greco-Roman, stoical), and bourgeois virtues. They include honesty, charity, perseverance, fortitude, chastity, fidelity, courage and many others. But when we look at the characterization of both products and processes as ethical in the EI literature, what is striking is the sheer absence of such virtues. The exception again might be pornography and arguably some forms of gambling. But again, the key word is "arguably." Gambling is not obviously, clearly and always and gravely a departure from the virtues.

These two items apart, it is the sheer absence of the traditional virtues in EI literature which is striking. And that goes for processes too. Are EI activists concerned to distinguish firms which reward employee loyalty from those which do not? Companies which advantage employees of good character at the expense of those of poor character? They show little such interest. If they are interested in virtue at all it is in certain virtues which have to do with vogueish conceptions of "justice" and revolve around a very narrow obsession with allocational rights. As with all highly selective approaches to ethics, the question to ask is

"What is the principle of selection?" Why, for instance is there much concern about disparities of pay between men and women but so little concern about honesty, duty, service, fortitude, or any one of two dozen other virtues—and their rewards.

To take an instance in which two actions are both about allocational justice. Much EI literature is concerned with equal rewards for equal work. A company which pays women less than men for the same work might fall foul of some EI guidelines. But what of a company that does not discriminate when it should, which pays two persons the same wage when one has worked harder than the other; that too breaks a principle of justice that rewards should be different according to contributions made. It is difficult not to see the selection of one ethical/justicial concern and the neglect of the other about just desserts as governed by a further principle, that of socialism/egalitarianism.

Virtue ethics see ethics as rooted in the intentions of people. "Consequentialist" ethics define right and wrong actions by their consequences. Thus, in the latter, actions are good or bad according to whether they lead to good consequences. These are often but not always some variant on an increase in the sum total of human happiness. There are ethicists who would argue that happiness distribution is nothing to do with ethics in the proper sense. But even if we permit that it is, once again, whether something adds to the total of human happiness or detracts from it is, in the case of nearly all products and most processes, a matter to be calculated on the evidence concerned. Decent persons of contrasting views can and do debate whether alcohol adds to the sum of human happiness. Clearly it is associated with misery for a few people, those whose lives are ruined by alcohol-related disease or drunken-driving. It also gives pleasure to many. Is the misery of the few greater than the pleasure of the many? And what of the benefits conferred to those who receive health services or schools paid for by alcohol taxes? I do not see how such a debate can ever be finally concluded. It depends on yet further judgments and values. But at least it is a debate. What is not warranted is the *assumption* that alcohol is associated with net harm. And still less warranted is the assumption that any harm is the fault of the producer rather than that of the drunken driver or excessive drinker.

To sum up so far: it is a bizarre ethics which places at its center the idea that certain products are ethical or unethical. It is not bizarre to suggest that certain processes such as employment practices may be ethical or unethical but it is eccentric to use a highly selective list of virtues as criteria to decide whether they are ethical or unethical. It is worse than eccentric to be coy—in much of their public literature—about revealing the principles on which such selections are made. It may even be unethical.

In the few cases when it might be arguable that a product—by foreknowledge of its unethical use—makes the producer culpable, it actually has to be argued with appropriate evidence that such foreknowledge exists and that the use did indeed result in net harm or wrong. The same goes for other categories such as companies operating under oppressive regimes. It cannot be assumed. In fact to assume it without evidence and argument is itself unjust, that is, unethical.

***

CONCLUSION: ETHICAL INVESTMENT
AND THE LESSER OF EVILS

The overall objection to ethical investment codes is their aggressive simplicity. It is a simplicity which ill fits them for ethical work. Moral choices often involve balance and judgment. To be sure, that fact is often used by immoralists to justify their immoralism. But it remains true. Professor Anthony O'Hear puts the point succinctly: "Investing ethically is not a straightforward matter. The issues involved are often disputed, and almost always complex. The danger with an ethical investment movement is that it will focus on particular causes, and elevate them into absolutes, disregarding difficulties and counter-arguments."

Ethical investment as currently codified gives a heroes-and-villains picture of the economic world with some investments portrayed as ethical and others portrayed as not. As such it actually subverts moral education and the cultivation of fine moral sensibility. Instead it offers what look like slogans, and slogans which seem highly selective in their ideological provenance. That, of course, may be what those people EIRIS calls its "customers" want. And there is no reason why it and the various investment institutions should not continue to serve them and their preferences. The only objection this report makes is that they should not describe what they are doing as *ethical* investment.

If this Report is correct in its conclusions, then the proponents of "ethical" investment should cease to trade on this controversial term "ethical" and describe their favored activities more neutrally. It also means that the companies besieged with questionnaires by the "ethical" investment activists should consider themselves under no automatic *moral* obligation to reply.

IS THERE A COST TO BEING SOCIALLY RESPONSIBLE IN INVESTING?

JOHN B. GUERARD, JR.

A key concern of all investors is financial return. For investors in "socially responsible investments," should there be a lower expectation of return? If one could show that socially responsible investing led to higher returns, wouldn't people follow that pattern of investment simply because they could make more money? Based on this conclusion, one might expect that these socially responsible investments and funds would yield lower returns. Mr. Guerard challenges that hypothesis.

Should an investor expect different returns in socially-screened and unscreened universes? Should a composite model combining traditional value factors with a consensus growth variable produce different returns for socially-screened and unscreened portfolios? We find that returns in socially-screened and unscreened universes do not differ significantly. We also find that a composite model using value and growth variables produces an expected return ranking list that generates equivalent excess returns in socially-screened and unscreened portfolios. There is literature in academic and professional investment journals that suggests socially responsible investing may produce higher (but not significantly higher) risk-adjusted portfolio returns than merely using all available stocks in the equity universe. Hamilton, Jo, and Statman (1993) found that 17 socially responsible mutual funds established prior to 1985 outperformed traditional mutual funds of similar risk for the 1986–1990 period. However, the relative monthly outperformance of 7 basis points was not statistically different from zero. It is also not obvious what criteria were used to determine the socially-responsible universe in the study.

In May of 1990, Kinder, Lydenberg, Domini & Co. (KLD) developed the Domini Social Index (DSI) by eliminating S&P 500 companies that failed to pass South Africa, product, environmental, military, nuclear power, and employee relations screens and including 50 non-S&P 500 stocks with "good" records on corporate citizenship, product quality, board representation of women and minorities. Luck and Pilotte, in a Journal of Investing (1993) study found that the Domini Social Index outperformed the S&P 500 Index during the May 1990–September 1992 period, primarily due to the higher growth sensitivity of the Domini Index. Luck and Pilotte used the BARRA Performance Analysis package (PAN)

"Is There a Cost to Being Socially Responsible in Investing?" by John B. Guerard, Jr. Reprinted with permission of the Social Investment Forum.

and found that the 400 securities in the DSI produced an annualized active return of 233 basis points relative to the S&P 500. However, specific asset selection relating to eliminating non-social companies and including "good" companies comprised 199 basis points of the active return. This provided evidence of the "green effect," as the outperformance was attributable to selecting socially responsible companies. Luck and Pilotte noted that the May 1990–September 1992 period was characterized by positive growth factor and size returns (smaller stocks outperformed larger-capitalized stocks as a rule during this period). Kurtz and DiBartolomeo in a *Journal of Investing* (1996) study found 19 basis points of monthly outperformance of the DSI relative to the S&P 500 for the May 1990–September 1993 period which was attributed to the higher price volatility and higher price-to-book ratios of the DSI stocks.

The College Retirement Equities Fund (CREF) Social Choice Account, also provides a real world example of how socially responsible funds can outperform. The Social Choice Fund exceeded $1.5 billion, as of December 1996, and is a balanced account of approximately 62 percent equity and 38 percent long-term bonds (as of December 31, 1995). The Social Choice Account earned an average annual return of 12.41 percent for the five years ending December 31, 1996. CREF's Stock Account, composed of stocks representative of U.S. equities (66 percent), U.S. growth stocks (17 percent), and foreign stocks (17 percent), earned a 13.58 percent average annual return for the five-years ending December 31, 1996. The relative composition of the CREF Stock Account was given as of December 31, 1995. It is difficult to compare the equity performance of the CREF Social Choice Account with the CREF Stock Account because the various equity and asset compositions may create different risk levels; however, one does not find the substantial underperformance in the CREF Social Choice Account relative to the Stock Account. The CREF Social Choice experience lends credence to the theory that socially responsible funds can produce good performance.

J. Rothchild espoused a very different view as he labeled socially-screened investing a "dumb" idea in *Fortune,* May 1996. It is the case that 24 socially-screened mutual funds in the Morningstar universe have substantially underperformed the S&P 500 during the past five and ten years. However, the difference between the average return on socially-screened equity mutual funds and the 2034 unscreened equity mutual funds drops from −417 basis points over the past five years to −105 basis points over the past ten years, a less meaningful differential, particularly given the very small number of socially-screened equity mutual funds with long-term track records. There are only six socially-screened equity mutual funds with five-year track records in the Morningstar universe and only Dreyfus Third Century and Parnassus have ten-year records.

J. D. Diltz presented a third, more neutral, point of view in two recent studies in which he found no statistically significant difference in returns for 14 socially screened stock portfolios vs. 14 unscreened stock portfolios generated from a universe of 159 securities during the 1989–1991 period. Diltz found that only the environmental and military business screens created a statistically significant difference in returns at the 5 percent confidence level during the 1989–1991 period.

The literature on the impact of social screening on returns provides mixed conclusions. At a minimum, the studies of the DSI and the CREF Social Choice Account suggest that it does not cost investors to invest socially. Vantage Global Advisors (Vantage) subscribes to the position that a socially-screened portfolio does not produce different returns than an unscreened portfolio. Vantage's experience indicates that it is not "dumb" to be a socially conscious investor. How a manager implements the investment process impacts returns, not social screening. We will examine the returns of Vantage's 1300 stock unscreened universe and a 950 stock screened universe and determine if the returns are different at the 5 percent level of significance. In addition, we will explore how the characteristics of those universes may differ, resulting in short-term return differences. Finally, we will provide evidence suggesting an investment process that adds value using an unscreened universe is not impacted by social screening.

We find that there is no significant difference between the average monthly returns of the screened and unscreened universes during the 1987–1994 period. Indeed, from January 1987 to December 1994, there is less than a 15 basis point differential in equally-weighted annualized stock returns. The screens used in this analysis are provided by Kinder, Lydenberg, and Domini (KLD) and are as follows: Military, Nuclear Power, Product (Alcohol, Tobacco and Gambling), and Environment. The Vantage unscreened 1300 stock universe produced a 1.068 percent average monthly return during the January 1987–December 1994 period, such that a $1.00 investment grew to $2.77. A corresponding investment in the socially-screened universe would have grown to $2.74, representing a 1.057 percent average monthly return. There is no statistically significant difference in the respective return series, and more important, there is no economically meaningful difference in the return differential. The variability of the two return series is almost equal during the 1987–1994 period. One can test for statistically significant differences in the two return series using the F-test, which examines the differences in series mean (returns) relative to the standard deviations of the series. When one applies the F-test, one finds that series are not statistically different from one another.

If there is no long-term return difference, short-term variations are due to style and size biases of a screened portfolio. As an example, let us examine the financial characteristics of the stocks in Vantage's unscreened and socially-screened universes as of December 1994. The unscreened Vantage universe of 1300 stocks had BARRA growth and book-to-price sensitivities of 0.185 and 0.306, whereas the socially-screened Vantage universe had corresponding BARRA growth and book-to-price sensitivities of 0.269 and 0.279, respectively. The unscreened universe had an average market capitalization of $3.433 billion in December 1994 whereas the socially-screened universe had a mean capitalization of $2.796 billion. The average BARRA growth and book-to-price sensitivities of the excluded securities were -0.164 and 0.414, respectively, and the average market capitalization of the excluded stocks exceeded $6.1 billion.

Thus, socially-screened-out stocks had higher market capitalizations and were more value-oriented than the unscreened universe, a condition noted by Lloyd Kurtz and Dan DiBartolomeo in their *Journal of Investing* study previously mentioned. There was a statistically significant difference between the unscreened Vantage universe's lower price-to-book ratio and the higher price-to-book ratio of the Vantage screened universe. Professors Fama and French at the University of Chicago found that smaller stocks with lower price-to-book ratios tended to outperform larger stocks with higher price-to-book ratios in the very long-run. The higher price-to-book ratio of the screened universe represents a risk exposure to a socially responsible investor. The screened universe is more sensitive to BARRA growth factor return than the Vantage unscreened universe and this exposure should help relative performance for socially responsible investors when the BARRA growth factor return outperforms the BARRA value factor (as measured by the book-to-price, bp) return.

Should these differences in portfolio characteristics impact a manager's ability to add value? Although we have noted that much of the recent socially-responsible literature has been concerned with the impact of screening on BARRA growth and value exposures, in a forthcoming study in the *Journal of Investing,* we found no statistically significant differences in the expected return ranking procedure to select stocks within socially-screened and unscreened universes. Let us examine the information coefficients (ICs) for a composite model in the Vantage unscreened 1300 stock universe and its corresponding socially-screened universe. ICs measure the correlation between ranked composite scores and ranked subsequent total return. The ranked composite score is generated from a larger universe of 3000 stocks. That score is then used to forecast returns in the individual screened and unscreened universes. The composite model produces statistically significant ICs (as measured by an average t-value) in both socially-screened and unscreened universes. The most preferred stocks in the socially-screened and unscreened universe outperform the respective benchmarks. The least preferred stocks consistently underperform the benchmarks. The regression-weighted model combined value (using Compustat data) and growth (estimated using I/B/E/S data) factors. The ICs of the unscreened and socially-screened universes are shown in the chart below.

The information coefficients for both the screened and unscreened universes are statistically significant and the quintile spread, defined to be the return of the most preferred

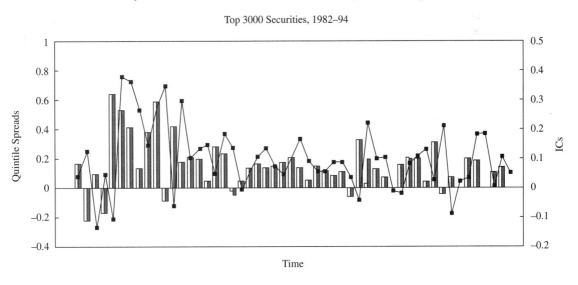

Socially-Screened and Unscreened ICs and Quintile Spreads

Top 3000 Securities, 1982–94

securities less the return of the least preferred securities using the composite model, is significantly positive. Thus, the ICs are consistently positive and the differences in the ICs between screened and unscreened universes are not statistically significant.

There has been no statistically significant difference between the average returns of a socially-screened and unscreened universe during the 1987–1994 period. One should be attentive when selecting a socially-screened mutual fund or manager. Performance can vary dramatically across managers, but should not vary due to social screening over the long term.

SELECTED REFERENCES

Diltz, J. D., 1995, "Does Social Screening Affect Portfolio Performance," *Journal of Investing,* Spring, 64–69.

Diltz, J. D., 1995, "The Private Cost of Socially Responsible Investing," *Applied Financial Economics,* 69–77.

Fama, E. F. and K. R. French, 1995, "Size and Book-to-Market Factors in Earnings and Returns," *Journal of Finance* 50, 131–155.

Fama, E. F. and K. R. French, 1992, "Cross-Sectional Variation in Expected Stock Returns," *Journal of Finance* 47, 427–465.

Guerard, J. B., Jr., forthcoming, "Is There a Cost to Being Socially Responsible in Investing: It Costs Nothing to be Good?" *Journal of Investing.*

Hamilton, S., H. J. Jo, and M. Statman, 1993, "Doing Well While Doing Good," *Financial Analysis Journal,* 62–66.

Kinder, P., S. D. Lydenberg, and A. L. Domini, 1993, *Making Money While Being Socially Responsible,* Harper-Business, New York.

Kurtz, L. and D. DiBartolomeo, forthcoming, "Socially Screened Portfolios: An Attribution Analysis of Relative Performance," *Journal of Investing.*

Luck, C. and N. Pilotte, 1993, "Domini Social Index Performance," *Journal of Investing,* 60–62.

Rothchild, J., 1996, "Why I Invest with Sinners," *Fortune.*

INTEGRATIVE INVESTING

Why Your Values Matter in the World of Money

THE GREENMONEY ON-LINE JOURNAL

Should you invest according to your values? Electronic magazine
The GreenMoney On-Line Journal *offers its guidance as to why your*
values matter in the world of money.

Whenever you make important decisions in your life, you act in accordance with your values and beliefs. Why would it be any different when making investment decisions?

Integrative Investing allows people to invest in a manner consistent with their values and beliefs concerning a variety of social and environmental issues. Another term used to describe this global movement is Socially Responsible Investing (SRI).

When you invest in a socially and environmentally responsible mutual fund, you are putting your money to work towards a better world and a more just society. You are voicing an opinion for positive social change, while helping to make it happen. You also know your money isn't going to finance businesses engaged in poor social and environmental practices. You are helping to create a sound and sustainable future. Investing for profit with principles.

The stock market moved up throughout 1995. Ten of the 41 socially responsible mutual funds returned more than 30%. The top fund was Citizens Trust Emerging Growth Fund with a total return of 40.7%. You can be ethical and make money.

Information on SRI is now available around the world, 24-hours a day. The Internet's World Wide Web is an exciting new medium for the exchange of information. We stepped into this arena during 1995 by launching The GreenMoney On-Line Journal. The website address is http://www.greenmoney.com.

As SRI continues to gain financial creditability and moves forward with conviction and commitment, it will increase its influence in the national and global conversation.

SCREENS

Investment screening integrates your values and your money. The complexity of our world is reflected in the following questions. The choices you make reflect your values and beliefs. You can screen in the positive and screen out the company or activities you don't want to support.

Do you want to avoid certain companies because of their products and corporate behavior? Do you want to be involved in shareholder activism using shareholder resolutions to change corporate behavior? What is the composition of a company's Board of Directors—do they represent a cross section of customers, community, employees, and shareholders? Is a company advertising in publications or on TV/Radio programs that you don't want to support? . . .

Approximately half of the largest 1,000 publicly traded U.S. companies meet most socially responsible mutual funds screening criteria. The Domini 400 Social Index contains 250 companies from the Standard & Poor's 500 (S&P 500). The new Citizens 300 Index contains 200 companies from the S&P 500.

Are there performance sacrifices when investing in socially and environmentally responsible ways? No. Consider these numbers: The Domini 400 Social Index (DSI) was launched in May 1990 by Kinder, Lydenberg and Domini (KLD) to track 400 companies that pass multiple social screens. From May 1990 through December 1995, the DSI returned 135.5% compared to 120.5% for the S&P 500. The DSI had its fifth anniversary last May. It demonstrated the long-term profitability of SRI, during the five-year period May 1, 1990–April 30, 1995. Total return for the DSI was 92.64% vs. 81.13% for the S&P 500. The annualized return for the DSI was 12.5% vs. 11.4% for the S&P 500. For more information call Karen Pratt of KLD at (617) 547–7479.

CASES IN VENTURE CAPITAL ETHICS

J. GREGORY DEES

Dees offers the following case studies as examples of the moral and ethical dilemmas facing entrepreneurs and venture capitalists.

The following examples are fictionalized representations of real situations. The names are made up and any similarity to existing individuals or firms is unintended. Each case is sketched with very limited background information. If you think something crucial is missing, fill it in with "what if" assumptions. If the missing information makes a difference to you, make note of how and why it makes a difference.

CASE 1—SKINFUSION, INC.

You are in the midst of due diligence concerning a major investment in SkinFusion, Inc., a company specializing in transdermal drug delivery systems. SkinFusion has an exciting new technology that company executives claim is lower cost, safer, and more precise than currently popular systems. This could be a big winner, if they are right. You have signed a term sheet, and, so far, you are pleased with what you are turning up on the due diligence. However, it is hard to find out what sort of competing technology is under development. In the midst of the due diligence, you receive a business plan from Patchaderm Pharmaceuticals, a direct competitor of SkinFusion with its own new technology. The plan came in unsolicited, but directed to your attention. The cover letter indicates that the CEO of Patchaderm read an article you wrote for a medical technology trade journal on methods of financing entrepreneurial ventures. He liked what he read and wants you to consider investing in his business.

1. Do you read the Patchaderm business plan? Do you pass it on to the associate helping with the due diligence? What is your rationale?
2. Do you respond to the CEO's letter? What do you say?
3. Would your behavior change if you were not so happy with what was turning up in the SkinFusion due diligence? Would it change if you had already closed the SkinFusion deal?
4. Assume that you are unable to resist a peek at the plan. After all, the SkinFusion investment could be a large and risky one. You are intrigued by what you read, but the plan just does not include enough information to decide who has the superior technology. The letter from Patchaderm's CEO invited you to come to the company. Do you accept Patchaderm's invitation? If so, what do you tell Patchaderm about your intentions in making the visit? How would you respond if Patchaderm's CEO asks you to sign a confidentiality agreement?

J. Gregory Dees, "Cases in Venture Capital Ethics." Reprinted by permission of the author.

5. Suppose that you visit Patchaderm and the issue of confidentiality is never discussed. Perhaps it just slipped their minds. After the visit, you are still convinced that SkinFusion is the best bet. However, you have gained valuable competitive information. After closing the deal, do you share any of this information with the SkinFusion management team? What would you share and how?

6. Suppose that after your visit you decide that Patchaderm would be a better investment than SkinFusion. Do you walk away from the SkinFusion deal? How do you explain this to SkinFusion management? If you invest in Patchaderm, do you share any of your knowledge about SkinFusion with Patchaderm management? Where do you draw the line?

CASE 2—PORTERWAVE, INC.

Your firm was a seed investor in PorterWave, Inc., putting up $100,000 of the initial $275,000 capitalization. The remainder was invested by the founder, her family and friends. The founder was Jane Porter, a brilliant engineer from Cal Tech who is pioneering the technology for portable, battery operated microwave ovens. After two years, she has produced a working prototype, and it is time for a major capital infusion. At least $5 million is needed to convert the prototype into a commercially viable design that might be sold or licensed to a major appliance manufacturer. Your firm is willing to invest more money, another $1 million, but you cannot be the lead investors in this next round. For a number of reasons, you simply do not have the funds available.

After a search for funding partners, Bluebird Ventures (BV) emerges as a strong potential lead. They would invest $3.2 million and bring in a third investor for the remaining $800,000. BV is a relatively new firm. You have not worked with any of its principals. They have a reputation for being smart and driving tough deals. You were not totally surprised when BV initially proposed a relatively low value for PorterWave stock. The PorterWave board (on which you sit) was disappointed with the offer, but, in the absence of any viable alternative, agreed to move forward with BV, into due diligence.

After taking an unusually long time to conclude the due diligence, BV announces that it must renegotiate the deal. Concerns about safety, competition, and time to market have led them to an even lower valuation, significantly lower. You are shocked. Their new assumptions seem far too pessimistic, but BV is adamant. This new deal would essentially wash-out the early investors. Even Jane Porter's share would be diluted to 5%. To add insult to injury, BV insists that Porter be put on a vesting schedule. She would have to earn her 5% by seeing the company through some key milestones. All this strikes you as grossly unfair. Your firm would never propose such a harsh deal. During your time on the board, you have developed a particularly close, friendly relationship with Porter and the other seed investors. For each of them, PorterWave was a significant personal investment. They trust you, as one of the second round investors, to see to it that they get a fair deal.

On the other hand, BV's new proposal, if accepted, would result in your firm gaining a larger share of PorterWave, more than enough to compensate for the dilution of your seed investment. PorterWave is running very low on cash, and you need to decide what to do about BV's new proposal.

1. Where are your primary loyalties and responsibilities in this situation?

2. If Porter comes to you (as a friend) asking for personal advice, what do you say? Do you confess that you think the deal is unfair?

3. Do you complain to BV about the new valuation? If so, how do you justify a better deal for seed investors and the founder?
4. Is there anything wrong with what BV did? If so, what? If you are not sure, what would you need to know to decide?

CASE 3—DESK BEAUTIFUL CORPORATION

Your firm is heavily invested in Desk Beautiful Corporation (DBC), a manufacturer and distributor of furniture systems for small businesses. These systems are designed to allow the offices to have a warm, home-style look. Electronic equipment can be easily hidden from view. The desks, shelves, and file cabinets are made of wood. Chairs and sofas are nicely upholstered in quality fabrics. DBC has been able, through efficient design, strategic procurement, and state-of-the-art production and distribution systems, to keep costs down. Its systems are priced to compete with the better-quality metal and laminated office systems. When DBC started up, it was alone in this niche, and it grew rapidly. However, in the last two years, three new competitors have entered the same niche. One of them is a division of a major office furniture manufacturer. As a result of the new competition, prices have been driven down further and margins have been squeezed. DBC is still the market leader and is profitable, but it has fallen slightly behind its original plan.

Six months ago, the CEO of DBC, Ralph Veneer, attended a seminar entitled "Beyond Compliance: Leading the Furniture Business Out of the Tropical Rain Forest." The seminar convinced Veneer that DBC was contributing to global environmental problems by purchasing timber harvested from tropical rain forests. At the last board meeting, Veneer gave a powerful multimedia presentation about the disastrous destruction of rain forests and its potential impact on the global environment and on indigenous people living in the forests. The DBC management team then presented a proposal for using less wood and switching to more environmentally friendly woods. Even with aggressive "green" marketing, the management team projected some continued loss of market share, increased costs, and a decline in profits as a result of this new strategy, at least in the near term. The impact could be as much as a twenty percent loss in the value of the firm, and it might mean a delay of a couple of years in the public offering that would provide your exit.

Veneer argued that DBC, as a profitable industry leader, should set a positive example. His conscience will not let him continue with the old practices. You were personally moved by his presentation. You have also become more deeply concerned about environmental issues in recent years. However, the other venture capitalists on the board are opposed to a change in policy. Your vote could well be the swing vote.

1. How do you vote on DBC's new "green" strategy? Why?
2. Do you consult anyone on this? Do you listen to your own conscience?
3. If the strategy is passed by the board, do you write down the investment in statements to your limited investors? How do you explain the write-down?
4. Does your decision about this strategy depend at all on who your limited partners are and what they might want? Does it depend on the view of the principals in your firm?
5. What would you do if Veneer simply implemented the strategy without bringing it to the board? Would this be grounds for firing him?
6. Would your views change if DBC was wildly profitable and far ahead of plan?

TOPIC STUDY: ETHICS AND INSIDER TRADING

THE INSIDE STORY OF AN INSIDE TRADER

Dennis B. Levine

In his letter granting permission to reprint the following article, Levine stated that, in writing the article, "it was my sincere desire that other young people could learn from my mistakes and not succumb to the pressures of the work place in advancing their careers." Levine, a partner to Ivan Boesky, was arrested for insider trading, setting off a barrage of arrests, including his partner, Ivan Boesky, and Michael Milkin. Levine traded on the stocks of soon-to-be-announced merger targets using mainly offshore bank accounts. His Nabisco trades reaped him a $2.7 million profit. In this article, Levine tells his personal story.

Waking early in my Park Avenue apartment on May 12, 1986, I read the morning papers, checked on the European securities markets, and ate breakfast with my wife, Laurie, then six weeks pregnant, and my son, Adam, who was 4. By 8 A.M. I was in downtown Manhattan, meeting with my staff at Drexel Burnham Lambert. At 33, I was a leading merger specialist and a partner in one of the most powerful investment banks on Wall Street. Among the many appointments on my calendar that day were meetings with two CEOs, including Revlon's Ronald Perelman, to discuss multibillion-dollar takeovers. I was a happy man.

In midafternoon two strangers, one tall and one short, came looking for me at Drexel. They didn't identify themselves, but the receptionist said they weren't dressed like clients. For ten months, I knew, the Securities and Exchange Commission had been investigating the Bahamian subsidiary of Bank Leu, the Swiss bank that had executed insider stock trades for me since 1980. That very morning I had spoken on the phone with one of the bank's employees, who reassured me that everything was under control. Still, I knew something was wrong, and I fled. While the authorities searched for me, I drove around New York in my BMW, making anxious calls on the car phone to my wife, my father, my boss. Before leaving the car, I hired a legal team headed by superstar lawyer Arthur Liman, who went on to serve as chief Senate counsel in the Iran-contra investigation and is now representing Michael Milken.

By the time I had hired Liman, my darkest secret was being broadcast by TV stations across the country. Early in the evening, I drove alone to the U.S. Attorney's office in lower Manhattan, expecting only to be served with a subpoena. The federal officers read me my rights instead. At the nearby Metropolitan Correctional Center, they locked me up with a bunch of drug dealers in a cell whose odor I won't soon forget. It was like an out-of-body experience. As I ate cornflakes at the prison cafeteria the next morning, I watched the story of my arrest on a TV wake-up show. My carefully orchestrated career, years of planning and sacrifice, thousands of hours of work that had lifted me from Bayside, Queens, to the pinnacle of Wall Street—all reduced to nothing. Just like that.

I have had four years to reflect on the events leading up to my arrest. Part of that time— 15 months and two days—I spent in Lewisburg federal prison camp in Pennsylvania. Getting your comeuppance is painful, and I have tried to take it on the chin. Unfortunately, my family also had to endure the trauma of humiliation, disgrace, and loss of privacy—and they did nothing to deserve it.

I will regret my mistakes forever. I blame only myself for my actions and accept full responsibility for what I have done. No one led me down the garden path. I've gained an abiding respect for the fairness of our system of justice: For the hard work and creativity I brought to my investment banking career, I was well rewarded. When I broke the law, I was punished. The system works.

People always ask, *Why would somebody who's making over $1 million a year start trading on inside information?* That's the wrong question. Here's what I thought at the time, misguided as I was: When I started trading on nonpublic information in 1978, I wasn't making a million. I was a 25-year-old trainee at Citibank with a $19,000 annual salary. I was wet behind the ears, impatient, burning with ambition. In those days people didn't think about insider trading the way they do now: You'd call it "a hot stock tip." The first U.S. criminal prosecution for insider trading wasn't until around that time, and it was not highly publicized. In the early years I regarded the practice as just a way to make some fast money. Of course I soon realized what I was doing was wrong, but I rationalized it as harmless. I told myself that the frequent run-ups in target-company stock prices before merger announcements proved others were doing it too.

Eventually insider trading became an addiction for me. It was just so easy. In seven years I built $39,750 into $11.5 million, and all it took was a 20-second phone call to my offshore bank a couple of times a month—maybe 200 calls total. My account was growing at 125% a year, compounded. Believe me, I felt a rush when I would check the price of one of my stocks on the office Quotron and learn I'd just made several hundred thousand dollars. I was confident that the elaborate veils of secrecy I had created—plus overseas bank-privacy laws—would protect me.

And Wall Street was crazy in those days. These were the 1980s, remember, the decade of excess, greed, and materialism. I became a go-go guy, consumed by the high-pressure, ultracompetitive world of investment banking. I was helping my clients make tens and even hundreds of millions of dollars. I served as the lead banker of Perelman's nearly $2 billion takeover of Revlon, four months of work that enabled Drexel to earn $60 million in fees. The daily exposure to such deals, the pursuit of larger and larger transactions, and the numbing effect of 60- to 100-hour work-weeks helped erode my values and distort my judgment. In this unbelievable world of billions and billions of dollars, the millions I made by trading on nonpublic information seemed almost insignificant.

At the root of my compulsive trading was an inability to set limits. Perhaps it's worth noting that my legitimate success stemmed from the same root. My ambition was so strong it went beyond rationality, and I gradually lost sight of what constitutes ethical behavior. At each new level of success I set higher goals, imprisoning myself in a cycle from which I saw no escape. When I became a senior vice president, I wanted to be a managing director, and when I became a managing director, I wanted to be a client. If I was making $100,000 a year, I thought, *I can make $200,000.* And if I made $1 million, *I can make $3 million.* And so it went. . . .

It was at Citibank that I met Robert Wilkis. A fit, balding junior officer a few years older than I, Bob struck me as terribly urbane when he introduced himself at a meeting for new employees. He was a Harvard grad with a Stanford MBA who spoke five languages. Bob shared my love of the stock market, and we became close friends. We would meet at the fourth-floor stock-quote terminal, where he monitored his personal portfolio while I tracked the latest M&A deals.

As a lending officer in the world corporate group, Bob had routine access to sensitive information about mergers Citibank might finance. Early in 1978 he told me he had identified a major U.S. company—let's call it ChemCorp—as a takeover target. He said he had bought its shares and recommended I do the same. I did: Borrowing on margin, I purchased $4,000 of ChemCorp stock. The merger never materialized and I sold the stock for about what I paid for it. To this day I'm not sure the transaction was illegal; Bob never told me he had inside information about ChemCorp. But it was well over a year before I dared make another such trade. . . .

During the year [I worked in Paris for Smith Barney], Bob Wilkis and I kept in touch by telephone, and in the spring of 1979 he visited Paris on business. Bob had also moved into investment banking by then, as an associate in international finance at Blyth Eastman Dillon. We talked at length about trading on the inside information we came across at work. By nature, investment banking requires that even junior people encounter nonpublic information as they work on prospective deals; both Bob and I learned of transactions long before they were announced.

When Bob was in Paris we decided to open accounts at Swiss banks. I borrowed as much as I could from my Ready Credit account and my family, telling them only that I had found some promising investment opportunities. With the $39,750 I raised, I opened a numbered account at Pictet & Cie in Geneva; Bob's was at Crédit Suisse. I didn't really begin buying stocks until Smith Barney moved me back to its New York office a few months later. I went to great lengths to avoid creating a paper trail for investigators to follow. Accustomed to confidential arrangements, Pictet's bankers suggested I use the code name Milky Way. *When you call,* they said, *why don't you just say it's Mr. Way?* They sent me no bank statements. I called in my trades from public phones—collect. (The bank extracted a service charge of about $20 per call.)

Bob and I tried to avoid linking our trading activities or creating noticeable patterns. That way, if one of us was found out, the other would be safe. We agreed to pool our information but to avoid any financial relationship. According to our pact, we would keep our trading secret, never share our stock tips with anyone else, and never trade in the U.S. Bob came up with the code name Alan Darby, which each of us used when calling the other at work.

The procedure was simple. In the normal course of business Bob might learn that Blyth—or his next employer, Lazard Frères—was representing one company in a prospective takeover of another. Let's call the target Flounder Corp. Bob would phone me at work, identifying himself as Darby if anyone other than I answered. We would set up a meeting, often a quick lunch of pizza or Chinese food. Between bites, he would tell me the inside dope on Flounder. We would also chat about work, family, movies—we were friends, remember—then say goodbye.

Before buying any shares, I would do enough research on Flounder to assure myself that its stock was worth buying at current prices even if the takeover never materialized. (Inside information is not always a sure thing: I lost as much as $250,000 on some trades.) If Flounder's fundamentals looked good enough, I would find a moment to step out to a pay phone and call my bank with a buy order. Once the public got wind of the takeover and bid up the stock, I would telephone again with a sell order. It was that simple. As often as not, of course, I'd provide information and Bob would trade.

My initial uneasiness gradually ebbed—there were no inquiries, and all of a sudden the balance in my account was over $125,000. . . .

My relationship with Ivan Boesky began innocently enough. Having learned to listen to the market's tom-toms as part of my legitimate career, I developed a network of sources that eventually included the man considered America's boldest and most influential stock speculator. Like the CIA, Ivan seemed to have sources everywhere: His intelligence was extremely valuable. And he was an important Drexel client. . . .

Ivan's attentions were flattering. He invited me to lunch at "21." He would telephone me at home, at work, even when I was on business trips or vacations, seeking information about deals. My home phone would ring well before 6 A.M.; Laurie would answer and hand me the receiver, saying, *It's Ivan,* rolling her eyes. He had such a insatiable desire for information that he would call me up to a dozen times a day. With Bob's knowledge, I began giving him tips in exchange for access to the vast store of market information in Ivan's head.

I wasn't telling Ivan anything very specific—it was more a matter of suggesting that, say, his investment in XYZ Corp. seemed worth holding on to. I never told him my oblique suggestions were based on nonpublic information, but over time he evidently learned their value. Then Ivan drastically changed the nature of our relationship by offering to pay for the information I was giving him, based on a percentage of his trading profits. He said something like, *You seem to have very, very good information. You should be compensated for it.*

Despite my own illicit activities, I was flabbergasted. I couldn't believe he would risk exposing himself so blatantly, by proposing something clearly illegal on its face. I already had a secret life, and it was not something I was anxious to expand: My safety depended on keeping the number of people who knew of my insider trading to a minimum. Besides, by then I had millions in my account at Bank Leu. I turned Ivan down and resisted his overtures for weeks.

I'm not quite sure why I finally accepted. Stupidity, I guess. And I don't know why Ivan engaged in illegal activities when he had a fortune estimated at over $200 million. I'm sure he derived much of his wealth from legitimate enterprise: He was skilled at arbitrage and obsessed with his work. He must have been driven by something beyond rational behavior. In any case, I never received a penny from him, though I was due $2.4 million under our formula when I was arrested.

When my scheme fell apart, it did so quickly. In the summer of 1985, Merrill Lynch received an anonymous letter accusing two of its brokers in Caracas, Venezuela, of insider trading; only one was subsequently charged. Unbeknownst to me, for years several Bank Leu executives had been making trades that mimicked mine, for their own accounts or for others'—apparently, the bank's policies condoned this. Disregarding my instructions to spread my orders among several brokers, they had funneled much of the business through Merrill Lynch. At least one trader there, in Caracas, apparently piggybacked on my trades too. Somebody blew the whistle, perhaps out of jealousy. Merrill Lynch, it seems, then informed the SEC, and just as my legitimate career was reaching its peak, the government began its ten-month investigation of Bank Leu. . . .

The day the government came looking for me, I was petrified about Laurie's reaction. Laurie is wonderful. Tutoring our daughter, Sarah, with flashcards or playing softball with Adam, she shows the patience of a grade school teacher, a career she gave up to raise our children. She is also assertive: She lets you know exactly what she thinks. Certain that she wouldn't approve and meaning to shield her from any legal consequences of my actions, I had never told her about my insider trading. It was a secret big enough to strain any marriage: Some spouses use drugs, others have extramarital affairs, I secretly traded stocks.

Laurie had no reason to suspect: We had always lived within my means. We stayed in a cramped one-bedroom apartment for almost three years after Adam was born, though I could have paid for almost any apartment in Manhattan with my offshore trading profits. . . .

The death blow came when Bob Wilkis asked to meet with me. To my amazement, he told me that he had tipped others, including a member of his family, and had been executing trades in the U.S. all along. That had created an easily detected trading pattern nearly identical to mine—more than enough to nail me. I knew I was finished and in the end my attorneys advised me that I had no choice but to settle with the government and tell the truth about everything and everybody involved in my case.

I pleaded guilty to four criminal charges related to my insider trading and settled civil charges with the SEC. Turning over cash and other assets, I made full restitution of my $11.5 million in trading profits. Everyone else involved in the case also entered guilty pleas and cooperated. Ivan Boesky turned himself in, pleading guilty to one criminal count and turning over $100 million. At that point I assumed the investigation was closed, but apparently Ivan's illicit activities extended far beyond his involvement with me. I had no inkling of his secret relationship with Marty Siegel, whose office was right next to mine at Drexel. The revelations of Ivan's paying Siegel off for inside information with suitcases of cash surprised me as much as anyone. So did Drexel's collapse and Michael Milken's settlement with the government. I don't think the firm's ethics were materially different from any other investment bank's.

On February 20, 1987, I pulled up to the federal courthouse in White Plains, New York, with my wife and lawyers. As our car approached I noticed dozens of reporters and camera crews standing outside. It reminded me of a lynch mob. Once inside, I learned that few experiences are more humbling than standing before a federal judge, publicly acknowledging guilt and being sentenced to jail. Less than four months after Sarah's birth, I began serving my sentence. Saying goodbye to your family is painful enough, but imagine having to explain to your 5-year-old son why his father is going to prison.

Although minimum-security prison camps have no walls, you are constantly reminded of your separation from family and society. I had no privacy, my moves were monitored, and my daily routine was controlled by others. I went from never having enough time to a place where everyone kills time. I mopped floors and mowed grass and spent hours just thinking. At first I could not come to grips with the turbulent changes in my life; I was burning with anger at myself. Eventually I decided to change my priorities and try to regain control over my life. I had entered prison grossly overweight, at 241 pounds. One outward sign of my new resolve: I lost 67 pounds in prison.

I got along all right with the other prisoners, many of them drug offenders with no convictions for violence; nobody bothered me. They loved TV shows like *Wiseguy* and *Miami Vice*—and the inmates always rooted for the crook. Having experienced prison, I'm saddened that most Americans apparently believe we can solve our drug problems by building more jails and locking more people up. From what I've seen, prisons don't solve social problems.

The other prisoners called me "Mr. Wall Street" and asked me for market advice. I always said no.

Money had little value, but there was a lively barter economy: If you were long on cigarettes, you could often buy a plate of linguini with clam sauce, heated in an aluminum pie tin over an electric iron. As one of the few nonsmokers in an institution that rationed cigarettes, I was a wealthy man. Laurie sent me a copy of *Bonfire of the Vanities,* Tom Wolfe's novel about a Wall Streeter who gets thrown in jail. I never felt quite like a Master of the Universe, but I saw parallels. . . .

I am rebuilding my life. I still feel the consequences of my mistakes and doubtless will forever. But I've been granted a precious second chance. This time around, I'm spending far more time at home with my family than ever before. I love the investment-banking business—it's in my blood—but as part of my settlement I agreed never to work for a securities firm again. I can still advise companies about raising money or doing deals, so I have started my own New York advisory firm, named Adasar Group after my children. My clients are smaller than they used to be, but much to my surprise, most people have treated my reentry into business with fairness and compassion. . . .

ETHICS, ECONOMICS, AND INSIDER TRADING

Ayn Rand Meets the Theory of the Firm

JONATHAN R. MACEY

Macey responds to Lawson's discussion of the moral basis of insider trading.

I. ETHICS VS. IDEOLOGY IN THE DEBATE AGAINST INSIDER TRADING

It is not difficult to confuse ethical judgments with ideological beliefs. Indeed, in close cases the distinction is quite subtle. At the extremes, however, the analysis is easy. Ethics has to do with the establishment of individual, moral standards of conduct. The goal of ethical theory is to arrive at clearly delineated moral standards from carefully constructed premises, which themselves are subject to justificatory critique.[1] Ideology, on the other hand, is merely a descriptive term for the prejudices of a particular class or group that are reflected in their doctrines and opinions. While ethical theory starts from the bottom and seeks to construct a set of principles from first premises, ideology starts at the top with its conclusions and proceeds downward to justify these results on sociological,[2] cultural,[3] psychological,[4] or epistemological[5] grounds. While ethical theory seeks to ground moral judgments on carefully constructed logical hypotheses, "[i]deology is an emotion-laden, myth-saturated, action-related system of beliefs and values about man and society, legitimacy and authority, acquired as a matter of routine and habitual reinforcement."[6]

Jonathan R. Macey, "Ethics, Economics, and Insider Trading: Ayn Rand Meets the Theory of the Firm." Reprinted by permission from *Harvard Journal of Law and Public Policy* (Summer 1988).

[1] D. LYONS, ETHICS AND THE RULE OF LAW 11–35 (1984).

[2] Karl Marx and Friedrich Engels were the initial proponents of this approach.

[3] Examples of the cultural, sometimes called "psychocultural," approaches to ideology are contained in the work of Clifford Geertz and Leon Dion:

Our hypothesis is that political ideology is a cultural and mental complex which mediates between the norms associated with given social attitudes and conduct and the norms which the political institutions and mechanisms tend to crystallize and propagate. In other terms, political ideology is a more or less integrated system of values and norms, rooted in society, which individuals and groups project on the political plane in order to promote the aspirations and ideals they have come to value in social life.

Dion, *Political Ideology as a Tool of Functional Analysis in Socio-Political Dynamics: An Hypothesis* v. 25 CANADIAN J. ECON. POL. SCI. 47, 49 (1959): *see also* Geertz, *Ideology as a Cultural System,* in IDEOLOGY AND DISCONTENT 47 (D. Apter ed. 1964) (examining the cultural elements embodied in ideology).

[4] Needless to say, the leading proponent of the psychological approach to ideology was Freud, who expounded the view that ideology is "essential to man's psychological well-being as well as to the continuity of culture," Rejai, *Ideology,* in 2 DICTIONARY: THE HISTORY OF IDEAS 552, 557 (1973).

[5] Etienne Bonnet de Condillac is "widely acknowledged as the founder of [the] school of ideology." *See id.* at 553.

[6] *Id.* at 558. *See also* R. GUESS, THE IDEA OF A CRITICAL THEORY 4–12 (1981).

Mr. Lawson fails to recognize that when commentators such as William Painter, Louis Loss, and Ralph Nader decry any and all forms of insider trading, they are not advancing any theory at all, much less an ethical theory. Rather, they are condemning insider trading on the basis that it is antithetical to a set of cultural norms that were acquired through routine and habitual reinforcement, and therefore are nothing more than ideologically-based belief systems. Professor Painter is particularly honest about the origins of his beliefs regarding insider trading. He scoffs at moral philosophy,[7] choosing instead to ground his arguments purely in emotional terms.[8] Indeed, in a triumph of anti-intellectual sophistry over reasoning and analysis, he defends arguments against insider trading on the grounds that they contain elements of "simplicity and immediacy which make up for their lack of theoretical respectability."![9]

Far from objecting to such anti-intellectualism, Mr. Lawson actually refers to such ramblings as "fair" questions with which all "legal scholarship must, at some point, come to grips."[10] Because the vast majority of Mr. Lawson's essay is a critique of the existing moral notions about insider trading, he ultimately ends up doing more to legitimize these empty ideas than to expand our understanding of insider trading.

Mr. Lawson thus appears to have exceedingly low standards for what constitutes ethical theory. It is therefore not surprising that he weaves his ideas rather confusingly throughout a discussion of the writings of others instead of expressing his own ideas about the ethics of insider trading in any systematic fashion.

Taken as a whole, what emerges from Mr. Lawson's effort is an analysis, albeit a highly inconclusive one, based on classical egoism, which he summarizes in a subsection titled "An Egoistic Interlude."[11] Egoism is the belief, which Mr. Lawson traces back to the classical Greek tradition of eudaimonism, that the individual's highest moral calling is to himself.[12] In essence, it seems, the egoist's moral calling in life is to "identify that human excellence that is distinctively his own—that is, his daimon—and the principles of conduct that allow him to develop that excellence and flourish as a person."[13] Unfortunately, of course, because "each person has unique potentialities that, in the particular circumstances

---

[7]But, after all, what is morality? Attempts to provide a "rational" foundation for moral judgments have a way of being unconvincing. The whole philosophy of ethical judgments has a pedantic quality which escapes the ordinary individual who merely stamps his or her foot and declares, inarticulately that "I don't care, it's just not right."

[8]Painter, *Book Review,* 35 GEO. WASH. L. REV. 146, 159 (1966). "Even if the content of moral statements be primarily emotive, which is doubtful, a satisfactory morality must be emotionally satisfying. . . ." *Id.*

[9]*Id.* at 159.

[10]Lawson, *The Ethics of Insider Trading,* v. 11, Harv. J. L. & Pub. Pol'y, 727, 775–83 (1988).

[11]*Id.* at 747. At one point Mr. Lawson includes a Lockean theory of insider trading, which I discuss in the following section. *See id.* at 763–69. Because Mr. Lawson believes that "something like a Lockean . . . approach flows from eudaimonism [classical egoism]," *id.* at 768, little is lost by not treating his Lockean arguments here.

[12]*Id.* at 748. Because of the highly individualistic nature of egoism, this belief system does not provide an acceptable basis for actually solving moral problems. The reason is that such problems characteristically involve conflicts of interest; the moral problem is to provide a fair solution. Imagine a judge deciding a case in a particular way on the ground that the outcome promotes her (the judge's) best interest! Egoism can be saved from irrelevancy only if it can be shown to require acts and decisions that involve a due concern for others. I am grateful to David Lyons for this point.

[13]*Id.* at 748.

in which he finds himself, ought to be actualized if he is to flourish as a person,"[14] it is not possible to construct any universally applicable principles of moral conduct. Thus, to mention but a few, Aristotle and Hegel are out, and Kant and Hume obviously are out also. Locke should be out too, but for some reason he is not.[15]

Mr. Lawson's idea is that most of the criticisms of insider trading are, in the final analysis, grounded on notions of altruism and are therefore unacceptable. Mr. Lawson finds it important to rehabilitate egoism because of the lack of good argument in favor of altruism.[16] This line of reasoning has two flaws that relate specifically to the insider trading debate.

First, as Mr. Lawson himself at times seems to recognize, there may not be a conflict between egoism and altruism.[17] Egoism at least pretends to concern itself with individual flourishing, not simply short-term with fulfillment at the expense of others. To say that someone is an egoist does not necessarily mean that he is not altruistic, particularly if altruism is the means through which he best can flourish. Indeed if one's "unique potentialities" are altruistic in nature, then the tenets of egoism and altruism would dictate the same conduct.

Second, and perhaps more importantly, it is not clear precisely what egoistic theory implies for insider trading besides a seemingly absurd result. If we take Mr. Lawson's suggestion seriously and look at the insider trading controversy by invoking an egoistic ethic, the analysis becomes virtually comic. Mr. Lawson appears to say that the egoist who finds himself in possession of material, non-public information about a particular firm must decide whether trading on the basis of that information is "self-fulfilling," that is, whether it "will allow him to develop . . . and flourish as a person.[18] Mr. Lawson defends this position against the straw-man argument that self-fulfillment is a better guide to human action than peer pressure. The more difficult question is whether self-fulfillment is a better guide to human action than one's own sense of individual duty and moral responsibility.

Frankly, the unrefined argument that acquiring money is good is not really worthy of discussion, because all sides—yes, even the egoists—agree that there is a significant difference between making money in some wealth-creating activity like investment or entrepreneurship and making money by stealing it.[19] The only moral (or economic) question worth asking is where insider trading lies along the continuum that runs from wealth creation to theft. Mr. Lawson does nothing to help us sort this out. Similarly, Mr. Lawson explains that refraining from insider trading might be a good idea if one has agreed not to engage in insider trading prior to disclosure, or if failure to disclose prior to trading would "seriously damage someone of great [objective] importance to him."[20] But these are precisely the situations that those of us who have been engaged in the study of insider trading have been study-

---

[14]*Id.* at 749.

[15]*See infra* note 27 (discussing application of Locke's work to insider trading).

[16]Lawson, *supra* note 10, at 747.

[17]*Id.* at 751–52.

[18]*See id.* at 748.

[19]*See id.* at 762 (The statement that "Theft is wrong" is "as close to an uncontroversial moral proposition as one is going to get")

[20]*Id.* at 752.

ing. What constitutes an "agreement" not to engage in insider trading? Is such an argument an implicit part of every manager's employment agreement? And if it isn't, why not?

The freedom given to corporate officers and directors as a manifestation of the separation of ownership and management in the large, publicly held corporation, makes contractarian analysis of insider trading issues very difficult.[21] Reasonable people, who agree on a wide range of corporate law matters, divide on the seemingly intractable issue of how to allocate the privilege to trade on material, non-public information.

As Mr. Lawson himself appears to suggest at various points in his article,[22] "[t]he moral inquiry with respect to insider stock trading thus centers on where the network of contracts between the firm and its shareholders, suppliers, lawyers, accountants, investment bankers, printers, and so on, places the right to trade on the information."[23] This is a point that has been made both implicitly and explicitly by many, including myself.[24] But it is not at all obvious what this inquiry has to do with egoism—or with altruism for that matter.[25]

To take a very simple example of the difficulty of determining whether a particular corporate act is consistent with ethical norms, suppose we observe a Harvard law student leaving Langdell Hall late one snowy evening. Shrouded beneath his parka is an electric typewriter that belongs to the law school. Is the student doing anything wrong in removing this typewriter? The answer depends on whether someone with legitimate authority (that is, the owner of the typewriter or his agent) has given the student permission to take the machine. The analysis is the same for traders who use inside information. In the first step of the analysis we invoke Locke to determine who has legitimate ownership rights over the relevant information. If it is the person trading in the information, there is no ethical problem whatsoever. We are simply observing a person making proper use of his assets. So, for example, there is no ethical issue when a tender offeror purchases stock in a target company before disclosing his plans to the target's shareholders. The tender offeror, as the creator of the news that there will be a tender offer, is the rightful owner, according to a Lockean analysis, of this information.[26] The problem arises when the person trading on the information is not its rightful owner. In such a case, we must first determine whether the trader has the actual or implied authority of the owner to use the information before we can know whether or not his actions are ethically justified. Thus, as is explored more fully below, the dichotomy between efficiency principles and the ethical norms implied by natural rights analysis is a false one. . . .

---

[21]Frank Easterbrook has been particularly alert to this problem. *See* Easterbrook, *Insider Trading as an Agency Problem,* in PRINCIPALS AND AGENTS: THE STRUCTURE OF BUSINESS 81–98 (Pratt & Zeckhauser eds. 1985).

[22]*See, e.g.,* Lawson, *supra* note 10, at 767–73.

[23]*Id.* at 766.

[24]*See* Haddock & Macey, *A Coasian Model of Insider Trading,* 80 Nw. U.L. REV. 1449 (1986).

[25]Mr. Lawson tells us that the contraction approach to insider trading finds is intellectual roots in Locke. *See* Lawson, *supra* note 10, at 769. Having said this, he then asserts that "something like a Lockean approach flows from eudaimonism [classical egoism]." But he declines to tell us how or why this connection is made.

[26]Macey, *supra* note 24, at 28 n.98 ("because a corporation that makes a tender offer expends great resources to do so, information that a target company is an appropriate target may be said to exist in a 'state of nature,' to use Locke's analysis").

WHERE SHOULD THE LINE BE DRAWN ON INSIDER TRADING ETHICS?

Yulong MaHuey-Lian Sun

The author of the following study contends that previous studies on insider trading ethics have failed to provide convincing arguments and consistent results. In particular, the arguments against insider trading are based primarily on moral and philosophical grounds and lack empirical rigor. This study intends to establish and examine the relationship between the ethical issue and economic issue of insider trading. It is argued that the ethics of insider trading is in essence an economic rather than a moral issue. It is so far not clear to what extent insider trading may increase or decrease shareholders wealth. Until then, the author argues that care must be taken to avoid over-regulating insider trading. Are you convinced?

1. INTRODUCTION

Is insider trading unethical? Is insider trading illegal? The answers depend on how we define insider trading and how we interpret the issue. Although the ethical issue in finance has received increasing attention from academic researchers, government agencies and business communities, it is still neither well researched nor understood. The growing importance of ethics in finance has undoubtedly been recognized by people from all disciplines. Even among academic researchers, however, there is still no consensus on what kinds of conduct should be regarded as unethical.

Opponents of insider trading seem simply to believe that insider trading is inherently immoral. For example, Werhane (1989) argues that insider trading, both in its present illegal form and as a legalized market mechanism, undermines the efficient and proper functioning of a free market. Proponents, on the other hand, assert that insider trading is a viable and efficient economic means and can be used to serve the best interests of shareholders and the economy at large. Manne (1966), for example, contends that insider trading provides a powerful incentive for creativity and is the only appropriate way to compensate entrepreneurial activity. More recently, Martin and Peterson (1991) have raised the question

"Where Should the Line Be Drawn on Insider Trading Ethics?" by Yulong MaHuey-Lian Sun, *Journal of Business Ethics* 17, no. 1 (January 1998), p. 67. Reprinted with permission of Kluwer Academic Publishing.

of whether the prohibition of insider trading is itself unethical. They argue that insiders who are also shareholders have the same rights as ordinary shareholders to trade based on their information and judgment. Thus, expropriating value from insiders by prohibiting insider trading is both senseless and immoral.

The conflict between these positions is due to the confusion over the definition of insider trading and over the interpretation of the economic impact of insider trading on firm value and social welfare. The purpose of this paper is to clarify these confusions by analyzing the nature of insider trading and by associating the ethical issue of insider trading with economic outcomes. We argue that insider trading is not necessarily unethical or illegal. If and only if such trading results in economic losses for the shareholders, should it be considered so. Therefore, we must question the present tendency toward over-regulating or prohibiting insider trading.

The rest of the paper is organized as follows: Section 2 analyzes the nature and rationale of insider trading and describes the legal issue of insider trading. Section 3 examines some of the major ethical arguments against insider trading and presents our argument that the ethical issue of insider trading ultimately boils down to an economic issue. Section 4 reviews the empirical and theoretical literature on the economic aspects of insider trading. . . .

2. THE NATURE OF INSIDER TRADING AND GOVERNMENT REGULATIONS

To examine the ethical aspect of insider trading, we must first understand the nature of insider trading. Confusion about and misinterpretation of this term, aggravated by unfriendly coverage in the media, has contributed to the insider trading controversy. To better understand the nature of insider trading, we must address three questions. First, who are the insiders? Second, what is illegal insider trading? Third, if ethics, as defined by Dobson (1993), is concerned with the motivations of human behavior, then what are the motives or rationale for insider trading?

Insiders, by the Securities and Exchange Commission's (SEC's) definition, are chairmen, directors, officers, etc., and principal shareholders with 10 percent or more of their own firm's common stock. These people are believed to have the opportunity to get access to their firm's private information. Corporate insiders, in particular, those who have managerial positions in the firm, are assumed to have superior information about the firm's future prospects, unavailable to the investing public and the current shareholders. It is easy to imagine that managers, who are supposed to serve the best interests of shareholders, may take advantage of this fiduciary relationship to act in their own self-interest through trading activities. However, insiders may trade on their own firm's stock for a number of reasons; it is important to understand that insider trading is not all based on private information. For this reason, not all insider trading is illegal or unethical.

Previous research has identified the following reasons for insider trading. (1) Portfolio diversification and liquidity adjustment. Firm managers often acquire stock through a plan or an exercise of options. They may later sell it to diversify their portfolios. Managers may also sell their stock due to financial need. This is why insiders have normally made more sales than purchases of their firm's stock. (2) Corporate control. Managers purchase their firm's stock to increase their share of total stockholding and enhance their voting power in the firm. (3) Sentimental reasons. For instance, two of Titan Corporation's insiders sold all of their shares in the firm shortly after they departed Titan. (4) Insider trading based on private information. This falls into two subcategories. First, insiders may purchase the firm's stock because they genuinely believe the stock is a good investment. Second, insiders may trade prior to announcements that will generate abnormal returns for themselves.

There is no cause for ethical concern in the first three categories. Even in the fourth category, only insider trading with prior knowledge of forthcoming announcements is obviously motivated by insiders' desire for exclusively personal gain. Since the public cannot observe the motives behind insider trading, they may react to the average level of insider trading as though it were evidence of the abuse of private information. However, this should not be the reason for considering all insider trading unethical or for completely outlawing it. As many have argued, the manager's ownership of a firm's stock may motivate him to improve firm performance and therefore increase firm value. Furthermore, the manager should have the same rights as other shareholders to trade his stock, as long as such trades are not motivated by private information. Precisely because of this, only insider trading motivated by nonpublic, material information is prohibited by the SEC's regulations.

The U.S. government regulations on insider trading can be traced back to 1934. To deal with fraud and manipulation in the securities markets, the SEC promulgated the Securities and Exchange Act of 1934, in which strict disclosure measures are employed to regulate insider trading. The SEC's concern with insider trading stems in part from the belief that insiders should not exploit their special positions for personal gains through short-term trading. In the act, Section 16(a) requires insiders to report transactions in their holdings to the SEC within 10 days of the end of the month in which the transaction takes place. In addition, Rule 10b-5 of the same act prohibits insider trading that is based on non-public, material information. In 1968, the so-called Williams Act Amendments were adopted to regulate insider trading on tender offer information. Rule 14e-3 under this declares that if a tender offer has commenced, trading while in possession of material nonpublic information acquired, directly or indirectly, from an insider is fraud, regardless of how or for what reason a person received it.

In 1984, a more stringent piece of legislation was passed to deter illegal insider trading. The Insider Trading Sanctions Act of 1984 broadens the SEC's authority to seek legal measures and increases the SEC's right to impose more penalties on illegal insider trading. In addition, after the Dennis Levine and Ivan Boesky cases, Congress passed the Insider Trading and Securities Fraud Enforcement Act of 1988 to boost both civil and criminal penalties and to extend these penalties to trading in derivative instruments.

It should be emphasized here that the SEC's prohibition of insider trading on private information is based on the belief that such trading results in economic losses for the shareholders, which in turn erodes the investing public's confidence in the market. Nevertheless, the question of whether insider trading actually increases or decreases a firm's value is not clearly understood and is still heavily debated among academic researchers. The current insider trading literature has not been able to provide the government and the public with conclusive results.

3. THEORETICAL ARGUMENTS OF INSIDER TRADING ETHICS

Although insider trading has been studied extensively, there is only limited research on the issue of insider trading ethics, and less empirical analysis. An analysis of some of the major arguments against insider trading may help shed some light on this ethical issue.

To judge whether insider trading is ethical or not, it is necessary to first define what ethics is. In a recent study, Dobson (1993) notes the importance of ethics in finance and attempts to clarify the issue. He argues that whether one is ethical or not cannot be determined by observing one's actions, but only by observing one's motivation for the actions. He contends that an individual who acts in a trustworthy manner is not an ethical individual if his action supports an underlying objective of material gain. One weakness in this definition is that motivation is not observable. The only way to "observe" motivation is to deduce it from action. Using this notion of ethics, it becomes difficult to reach a definite conclusion on the ethics of insider trading. Furthermore, if an individual truly believes that his actions are the most effective means to bring material gains for other people, can we call his actions unethical simply because he benefits as well? In essence, using motivation alone without evidence of action is probably too strong to be applicable, while using material gains alone without indicating the adverse effect on others is not sufficient to reach any conclusion on ethics either.

Poitras (1994) analyzes the relationship between ethics and the principle of shareholder wealth maximization, pointing out that pursuing shareholder wealth maximization does not necessarily result in socially responsible behavior. Nevertheless, few have challenged the claim that the maximization of shareholder wealth is itself a basic good principle generally used in finance. If we assume that a firm equates interests of its shareholders with those of society, then the firm's objective of maximizing shareholder wealth should not be questioned on the ethical grounds. Given this assumption, it seems logical to conclude that insider trading is unethical only if such trading leads to a wealth reduction for shareholders. On the other hand, if insider trading increases economic wealth of shareholders, few people would consider it unethical.

Critics of insider trading, however, reject the idea of relying on economic efficiency as an ethical principle. Moore (1990) denies the importance of economic value in determining the ethics of insider trading. While she admits that there are serious deficiencies in the current arguments against insider trading from the standpoint of fairness and information rights, she nonetheless believes that insider trading is unethical and should be prohibited because it erodes the fiduciary relationship that lies at the heart of the business organization and of American society. We must note, however, that the true foundation underneath the fiduciary relationship is essentially economic. If insider trading would, without a doubt, lead to an increase in shareholder wealth, such action would not be opposed by shareholders. This is, after all, what shareholders hire the manager for. Furthermore, if the increase in firm value leads to an increase in social wealth, on what grounds would society condemn that action? In this situation, the fiduciary relationship remains unharmed. Moore's belief that insider trading erodes the fiduciary relationship is based on the implicit assumption that insider trading will benefit insiders at the expense of ordinary shareholders. Thus, the real issue of insider trading ethics remains an economic one, whatever people willingly or unwillingly admit, whatever they explicitly or implicitly assume.

In another paper, Werhane (1989) asserts that insider trading cannot be justified from either an economic or a moral point of view. She argues that insider trading, whether it is legal or illegal, affects negatively the ideal of laissez-faire in any market, from both moral and economic perspectives. Werhane casts the moral issue in terms of fairness, arguing that insider trading is like playing a game with two different sets of rules for different players. In other words, she claims that insiders play a game with outsiders where insiders know all the rules and outsiders know only some of the rules. It is not clear, however, what kinds of rules the author is referring to. In the trading game between the insiders and the outsiders, the rules seem to be clearly stated before the start of the game. One may make a rule, for example, that insiders cannot trade on private information. But it should be emphasized that the existence of rules does not mean there will be no violations. As in any other game, however, the violator of the rules will be penalized. This is precisely the case with insider trading. Illegal insider trading is penalized through civil and criminal charges. If, on the other hand, insider trading is not regulated, then the game becomes one played between informed and uninformed players. Even in this situation, though, the rules of game are still known to all players. The difference is that the insiders are better armed players than the outsiders. The question is then whether we should allow the better equipped players to enter the game. One difficulty with mandating fairness is that even the opponents of insider trading cannot agree on what the term really means. For example, Moore (1990) contends that fairness is only an issue when one party has a legal obligation to disclose information to another. She writes: Suppose I am touring Vermont and come across an antique blanket chest in the barn of a farmer, a chest I know will bring $2,500 back in the city. I offer to buy it for $75, and the farmer agrees. If he had known how much I could get for it back home, he probably would have asked a higher price—but I failed to disclose this information. I have profited from an informational advantage. Have I been unethical? My suspicion is that most people would say I have not. While knowing how much I could sell the chest for in the city is in the interest of the farmer, I am not morally obligated to reveal it. I am not morally obligated to tell those who deal with me everything that it would be in their interest to know.

However, by Dobson's (1993) definition of ethics, such behavior is clearly unethical in that it is motivated by the desire for exclusively personal material gain. Furthermore, if the key to ethical behavior is the fulfillment of one's duties, then certain insider trading activities now held to be illegal might still be judged ethical. For example, Meulbroek (1992) conducted an empirical analysis of illegal insider trading and reported that few of the defendants in the illegal insider trading cases are corporate insiders who have the duty to report their transactions to the SEC. The SEC investigates not only corporate insiders, but anyone who obtains material, nonpublic information from a corporate insider or from an issuer, or who steals such information from another source. Clearly, we do not exempt people from prosecution simply because they do not have a direct obligation to a firm's shareholders.

The discussion has so far emphasized two points. First, the current arguments against insider trading ethics lack substance and consistency. Second, although most opponents of insider trading have failed to admit or to realize it, economic interest is the bottom line of the controversy over the ethical issue of insider trading. Consequently, the next section focuses on the economic aspect of insider trading.

4. REVIEW OF LITERATURE ON THE ECONOMIC ASPECT OF INSIDER TRADING

The economic impact of insider trading on shareholder wealth has been examined from both empirical and theoretical perspectives. Most empirical studies investigate how the market actually reacts to insider trading transactions, while theoretical studies analyze the issue of whether insider trading will help increase or decrease firm value.

Few would dispute that insider trading in the absence of government regulation would signal valuable information to the market, causing stock price to change accordingly. Given the existence of legal restrictions on illegal insider trading, will the market still react to insider trading in any significant way? There is a large amount of insider trading literature trying to answer this question by examining the insiders' trading profits. The empirical evidence on insider trading profitability indicates that insider trading does generate significant abnormal returns. For example, Seyhun (1986) reports that insiders earn about 3 percent abnormal returns over 300 days following the insider trading days, although most of those occur during the first 100 days after trading. Also, Lin and Howe (1990) study the profitability of insider trade in the over-the-counter (OTC) market and find significant abnormal returns over different event periods after intensive insider trading. These studies present empirical evidence indicating that insider trading does have a wealth effect on the firm's shareholders.

More compelling studies have focused on insider trading prior to significant corporate announcements. The argument is that any abnormal insider trading activities around the announcements are indications of corporate insiders' trading on private information. Karpoff and Lee (1991), for example, examine insider trading behavior before new issue announcements and find that managers show more net sales or their firm's stock prior to the announcements. Investigating insider trading and stock repurchases, Lee et al. (1992) also find significant abnormal insider buying and selling activities prior to the announcements. In another study, Pettit et al. (1995) report that the abnormal insider trading prior to stock repurchase announcements is caused mainly by abnormal selling activities.

These empirical studies provide some evidence that insiders can strategically control the timing of their transactions using nonpublic information. However, the fact that insiders may refrain from selling (buying) stock prior to favorable (unfavorable) announcements does not constitute illegal behavior; current laws can not force insiders to sell or buy stock. Furthermore, one can question the empirical evidence on statistical grounds. For example, is insider trading measured so that it captures the information contents of the trading? Can a rise in insider trading be attributed to other confounding news rather than one specific piece of information? Is the empirical testing method used appropriate?

On the theoretical side, numerous studies have examined the effects of insider trading on firm value and socioeconomic welfare without conclusive results. For example, Carlton and Fischel (1983) argue that insider trading may increase firm value, while Manove (1989) and Ausubel (1990) show that insider trading may actually decrease firm value. Leland (1992), however, suggests that the social desirability of insider trading depends on the nature of the production function. That is, the choice of the parameters in the production function may increase or decrease firm value. In a recent theoretical paper by Khanna et al. (1994), the model shows that society's preference of insider trading is not identical to that of the entrepreneurs/insiders, although these preferences do overlap. Therefore, they argue, there may be disagreements between firms and society about the conditions under which insider trading restrictions should be imposed. On the other hand, John and Mishra (1990) and John and Lang (1991) have both argued that strategic uses of insider trading in conjunction with corporate announcements may increase firm value. Both models show that the conjunction of insider trading and corporate announcement may be the least expensive way for a firm to convey its information to the public.

This inconclusive theoretical research demonstrates the difficulties in studying the economic effects of insider trading on firm value. The key issue facing researchers is to identify the benefits and costs of insider trading. The ultimate solution to the problem depends on the relative magnitude of these two values.

***

REFERENCES

Ausubel, L.: 1990, "Insider Trading in a Rational Expectations Economy", *The American Economic Review* 80, 1022–1041.

Carlton, D. and D. Fischel: 1983, "The Regulation of Insider Trading", *Stanford Law Review* 35, 322–376.

Dobson, J.: 1993, "The Role of Ethics in Finance", *Financial Analysis Journal* (November–December), 57–61.

John, K. and B. Mishra: 1990, "Information Content of Insider Trading around Corporate Announcements: The Case of Capital Expenditures", *Journal of Finance* 45, 835–855.

John, K. and L. H. Lang: 1991, "Insider Trading around Dividend Announcements: Theory and Evidence", *Journal of Finance* 45, 1361–1390.

Karpoff, J. and D. Lee: 1991, "Insider Trading before New Issue Announcements", *Financial Management* 20, 18–26.

Khanna, N., S. L. Slezak and M. Bradley: 1994, "Insider Trading, Outsider Search, and Resource Allocation: Why Firms and Society May Disagree on Insider Trading Restrictions", *The Review of Financial Studies* 7, 575–608.

Lee, D. S., W. H. Mikkelson and M. M. Partch: 1992, "Managers' Trading around Stock Repurchases", *Journal of Finance* 47, 1947–1961.

Leland, H.: 1992, "Insider Trading: Should It Be Prohibited", *Journal of Political Economy* 100, 859–887.

Lin, J. C. and J. S. Howe: 1990, "Insider Trading in the OTC Market", *Journal of Finance* 45, 1273–1284.

Manne, H. G.: 1966, *Insider Trading and the Stock Market* (Free Press, New York).

Manove, M.: 1989, "The Harm from Insider Trading and Informed Speculation", *Quarterly Journal of Economics* 104, 823–846.

Martin, D. W. and J. H. Peterson: 1991, "Insider Trading Revisited", *Journal of Business Ethics* 10, 57–61.

Meulbroek, L. K.: 1992, "An Empirical Analysis of Illegal Insider Trading", *Journal of Finance* 47, 1661–1670.

Moore, J.: 1990, "What Is Really Unethical about Insider Trading?" *Journal of Business Ethics* 9, 171–182.

Pettit, R., Y. Ma and J. He: 1995, "Do Corporate Insiders Circumvent Insider Trading Regulations: The Case of Stock Repurchases", Working Paper, University of Houston.

Poitras, G.: 1994, "Shareholder Wealth Maximization, Business Ethics and Social Responsibility", *Journal of Business Ethics* 13, 125–134.

Seyhun, H. N.: 1986, "Insider Profits, Costs of Trading, and Market Efficiency", *Journal of Financial Economics* 16, 189–212.

Werhane, P. H.: 1989, "The Ethics of Insider Trading", *Journal of Business Ethics* 8, 841–845.

TOPIC STUDY: ETHICS IN ACCOUNTANCY

I NEED EVERYBODY TO HELP OUT IN THE SHIPPING DEPARTMENT TODAY

DILBERT COMIC STRIP

Dilbert

"I Need Everybody to Help Out in the Shipping Department Today," Dilbert Comic Strip (2/2/96) by Scott Adams. Reprinted with permission from United Media.

EARNINGS
HOCUS-POCUS
How Companies Come Up
with the Numbers They Want
NANETTE BYRNES, RICHARD MELCHER, AND DEBRA SPARKS

> *Some students have contended that there are no ethical challenges in accounting because there are so many rules. There are therefore no gray areas: breaking the rules would clearly constitute legal violations. The authors of the following article would certainly beg to differ. How can the rules better protect against violations such as those described in the article? How can consumers and investors ensure that they obtain correct information?*

When America Online's management put together its quarterly financials early this summer, it was with some measure of pride, says new Chief Financial Officer J. Michael Kelly. Indeed, the results were remarkable. AOL would be posting a 900% rise in operating profits, to $57 million. At 23¢ per share, earnings would handily beat Wall Street's estimate of 19¢.

The excitement didn't last long. Soon, the Securities & Exchange Commission's officials began peppering the company with inquiries. Their beef, according to AOL: the company's plans to use a controversial accounting technique to instantly write off much of the value of two companies it had just purchased. By taking a charge for "in-process R&D" under way at the companies, AOL figured it could write off fully $20 million of the $29 million it was paying for NetChannel, an Internet television company, and a "substantial portion" of the $287 million it would pay for Mirabilis, a developer of real-time chat software.

The SEC appears to have found the size of the charges troubling, however, and by Aug. 4, the date of AOL's fourth-quarter earnings release, the issue hadn't been resolved. So Kelly did something rarely seen in Corporate America: He announced quarterly results that didn't go to the bottom line.

There was simply no way to calculate net income without the SEC's blessing on the charges. "We had such phenomenal operating results," says Kelly. "To hold that back for an unfinished accounting matter didn't seem appropriate." Investors didn't take the matter so lightly. In two days, they dumped 23 million shares, sending the stock down 5%.

AOL ought to have known better. After all, it's not the first time the company's accounting practices have been questioned. In 1996, after dubious investors challenged its policy of writing off marketing expenses over two years, AOL restated its numbers in a move that erased all its previous profits overnight. But a company that once might have been dismissed as a rogue is now just one face in a troubled crowd. Across Corporate America,

---

"Earnings Hocus-Pocus: How Companies Come Up with the Numbers They Want," by Nanette Byrnes, Richard Meicher and Debra Sparks, *BusinessWeek* (October 5, 1998), p. 134.

a wave of concern is rising about the quality of corporate earnings—and the tactics companies are using to calculate them.

Headlines this summer have been dominated by spectacular cases involving allegations of outright accounting lies: Cendant Corp. accused some former executives of fraudulently inflating income before charges by $500 million over three years, in large part by booking fictitious revenues. Livent Inc. allegedly kept two sets of books to mask extravagant expenses.

But forget about fraud for now. Regulators and investors are starting to focus on a far broader problem: companies bolstering their performance by using every legal accounting game in the book. They appear to be exploiting opportunities to jazz up their earnings like never before—all without stepping outside the loose confines of generally accepted accounting principles (GAAP).

That has led to a slew of spectacular collapses of companies caught playing fast and loose with their numbers. Investors in such onetime highfliers as Green Tree Financial, Waste Management, and Sunbeam have seen years of seemingly solid earnings vanish overnight. The culprit: overly rosy or misleading information about sales or expenses sometimes buried deep within their financial statements.

"Big Bath"   And that's only one part of the problem. SEC officials are also worried about the abuse of huge, virtually unrestricted "big-bath" write-offs. Indeed, write-offs such as Motorola's recent $1.98 billion restructuring charge have become all too common. Even that is small change compared with the multibillion-dollar charges taken by high-tech acquirers such as Compaq Computer Corp. and WorldCom Inc. to write off "in-process" research when they close a deal. Meanwhile, others have taken so many "extraordinary" charges year in and year out that the only thing truly out of the ordinary is a year without write-offs.

Of course, companies have always taken write-offs and restructuring charges. But nervous regulators and investors fear that such huge multiyear write-offs are increasingly distorting corporate earnings—so much so, in fact, that some question whether the underlying meaning of profit numbers and their value as a true reflection of corporate performance is getting trampled.

To understand why, remember what the earnings number is supposed to represent: an accurate snapshot of how well a company's operations performed in a given year. And one of the basic principles of accounting is that both revenues and costs should be matched to the year in which they occur. Otherwise, managers have too much leeway to massage the numbers, and "annual" performance becomes meaningless.

But the aim of many of today's giant write-offs is to front-load expenses. Charge off three years of expenses all at once, and by definition future earnings will be better. It's akin to making three years of mortgage payments at once, then claiming your income has grown.

Fueling the trend is the fact that stock traders tend to ignore big "one-time" charges, focusing instead on prospects. So even if the total dollars spent are the same, companies have a far greater incentive to take one large charge rather than stretch expenses out as money is actually spent. Indeed, the market's reaction encourages executives to make charges as big as possible. And that's got investors and the SEC worried that companies are burying all sorts of normal operating expenses into their restructuring charges. "Somebody

---

Accounting Tricks of the Trade

IN-PROCESS R&D CHARGES   Taken by the buyer at the time of an acquisition, these charges represent the estimated value of R&D at the purchased company. Because it is still "in process," the research is not yet commercially viable. Since it may prove worthless, it can all be written off. But by separating the expenses from revenues that might be gained in the future from the R&D, future earnings can get a big jump.

POOLING   A method of accounting for mergers and acquisitions that eliminates goodwill charges. All assets and liabilities of the companies are combined at book value, so there's no goodwill to depreciate. That boosts earnings, one reason use of pooling has exploded.

RESTRUCTURING RESERVE   Created by combining several years of expected future expenses and writing them all off at once as an "extraordinary" one-time charge. This jacks up future earnings.

REVENUE RECOGNITION   How quickly or slowly revenue is booked. It is especially important in industries such as software, where service contracts and upgrades can stretch revenue out for years. Booking revenues too early provides fertile ground for inflating sales and earnings.

---

woke up to the fact that if you take something as a restructuring charge, investors will forgive you immediately," says Robert S. Miller, the nonexecutive chairman brought in to clean up Waste Management. "We've almost lost the notion of what are earnings and what are one-time charges."

Why are so many questions about the quality of earnings arising now? For one, there's a mismatch between today's deal-oriented, high-tech economy and a decades-old accounting system in which only "real" assets such as bricks and mortar can be easily valued. Throw in an eight-year bull market in which earnings growth came to be the only measure many investors looked at, and add the pressure those market forces have created on managers to make the numbers look as good as possible. If anyone had set out to invent a system in which the means, motives, and methods to encourage companies to stretch earnings all came together perfectly, they couldn't have done a better job.

But with the economy slowing and Wall Street jittery, concerns are growing that companies desperate to keep up earnings and stock prices will practice even more aggressive accounting. Warns J. Michael Cook, chairman and CEO of Deloitte & Touche: "As economic pressures get tougher over the next 3 to 12 months, I worry whether the system will measure up."

More Disclosure?   He's not the only one. On Sept. 28, SEC chief Arthur Levitt will give a speech at New York University outlining plans to improve the accuracy of earnings. "We have become concerned that the quality of financial reporting is eroding," Levitt says. In recent weeks, the SEC's new chief accountant, Lynn Turner, has met with officials of Big Five accounting firms, Wall Street analysts, and CFOs to discuss concerns. "If the basic accounting foundation ever loses credibility with investors," Turner says, "then the whole [investing] process would fall apart."

Earnings: Now You See 'Em, Now You Don't

All-time record write-offs have wiped out a huge chunk of reported earnings. Though things aren't as bad as the early '90s, there is a key difference. The earlier write-offs came amid recession; more recently, write-offs soared despite a booming economy.

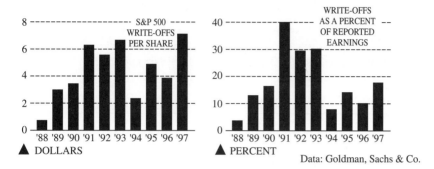

Data: Goldman, Sachs & Co.

The SEC won't say what steps it plans, but it may require more disclosure about restructuring reserves and the valuation of R&D write-offs. It's also concerned about how companies account for mergers. Talks on mergers and restructuring charges are also under way at the Financial Accounting Standards Board (FASB), an industry body chartered by the SEC that created and updates GAAP. But any FASB-driven changes could take years to iron out.

Of course, not every accounting charge reflects management efforts to fool investors. In many cases, the charges reflect real operating problems. Some experts argue, too, that in some ways the earnings picture is actually clearer today. Gabrielle Napolitano, an accounting analyst and portfolio strategist at Goldman, Sachs & Co., points out that low inflation has improved accounting for inventory and depreciation expenses.

Still, what's troubling is that massive charge-offs have been wiping out earnings at a time when the economy is booming. According to earnings-watcher First Call Corp., the number of companies taking restructuring charges jumped from 96 in 1995 to 230 last year. And despite a then seven-year-old expansion, companies in the Standard & Poor's 500-stock index wrote off $7.04 a share in earnings in 1997, topping the previous high of $6.61 in 1993, when Corporate America was struggling to dig out from the lingering effect of a recession. Fueled by merger-related charges, the S&P companies wrote off fully 17.7% of their earnings last year—more than triple the 5.6% Napolitano predicted at the year's start.

That's why the manner in which companies handle big write-offs is far from an arcane accounting debate. They can significantly alter the earnings picture investors see. Consider the case of Lucent Technologies Inc. As part of the process of Lucent's spin-off from AT&T in a 1996 public offering, the company took a big-bath charge in which it set up a $2.8 billion reserve to cover restructuring costs. To come up with that figure, the company in late 1995 estimated how much the restructuring would cost over several years. Lucent's reserve was to cover severance for 20,000 employees and the cost of exiting businesses such as AT&T's Phone Center Stores.

So far, so good—and there's where the first benefit comes in. By writing off several years worth of costs all at once rather than taking them each year as the money is spent, Lucent eliminated future costs from its books. It's a common practice—and one that automatically improves earnings down the line.

The gains didn't end there. As it turned out, Lucent put aside far more than was needed to cover the restructuring expenses—and the excess reserves have since helped the company smooth out what might otherwise have been much choppier earnings. One reason for the excess: The booming economy helped lower Lucent's costs as former employees quickly found new work. So Lucent converted some of its restructuring reserve back into income. Over three years, it took $382 million from reserves and added it back to pretax income. Thus, even as the reserve cut expenses, Lucent's income got a big boost, too.

ONE-TIME CHARGE OR ONGOING EXPENSE?

On July 20, McDonald's announced a $350 million restructuring charge, which included $190 million to install new cooking equipment. Shouldn't upgrading kitchens be a normal operating expense in the restaurant business? The SEC appears to think so. After it questioned the charge, McDonald's reversed it and lowered its special charge to $160 million. Booking the costs as it actually spends the money will cut an estimated $25 million to $35 million from earnings each quarter through 1999.

Lucent has also benefited from an accounting technique that's becoming wildly popular among high-tech companies—while drawing increased scrutiny from the SEC. As Lucent bought companies over the past two years, it wrote off $2.3 billion of in-process research and development. That figure—Lucent's estimate of the future value of R&D at the companies it bought—has allowed Lucent to avoid $2.3 billion in "goodwill." That's an accounting term for the premium paid for a business or asset above the value recorded on its books, which would normally have to be written off as an expense over many years.

Now, it's worth emphasizing that everything Lucent has done has been found to be in accordance with GAAP by its auditors, PricewaterhouseCoopers. The SEC has not challenged one of these moves. The company's filings and press releases clearly disclose exactly what it is doing. Indeed, every decision was made under the "letter and intent of the law," says controller James S. Lusk. "I don't believe in accounting cocaine." And Wall Street certainly likes the results: Lucent's shares have outperformed the S&P by 255% since its IPO.

But the question remains: What if Lucent hadn't taken a one-time charge but spread restructuring costs over the years it took to clean up? And what if the R&D had been written off over 10 years, a typical period?

The answer, according to Jack T. Ciesielski, a well-known accounting expert and money manager, is that Lucent's books would have reflected a much less smooth but possibly more accurate picture of management's ability to drive growth. Using the numbers Lucent reported in its SEC filings, Ciesielski first eliminated the effects of the restructuring reserve. Instead, he treated the expenses as normal costs in the years they occurred. Then, he eliminated the income created by the reserve reversals and calculated what goodwill would have been without the R&D write-offs. Along the way, he assumed all acquisitions came at the start of the year, and he used the corporate tax rate Lucent paid each year.

How do his figures compare with Lucent's operating income—net profits excluding special charges—the number that investors most closely watch? He calculates that in 1996, Lucent would have lost $49 million rather than its $1.05 billion operating earnings gain. Earnings last year, he figures, would have been a modest $1.11 billion, well below Lucent's $1.51 billion. And for the first three quarters of fiscal 1998, Lucent would have made $1.51 billion, $229 million less than the $1.74 billion it reported. "The reason managers love these [moves] is that they buy them time," says Ciesielski, publisher of *The Analyst's Accounting Observer.* "You wouldn't have a stock trading at the multiple Lucent is if they hadn't had this time to work all this out."

Lucent declined to comment on Ciesielski's analysis, saying through a spokesman: "To speculate or hypothesize about 'what if' scenarios when we adhered to strict accounting standards is simply not meaningful or productive."

So how can there be such disagreement over how to crunch the numbers? One culprit is an accounting system that many find obtuse and out of touch with an economy that is increasingly driven by technology and deal-making. The gray areas in GAAP are plentiful, and its terminology can be ill-defined. What constitutes a legitimate "one-time" charge, and how does it differ from the normal operating costs of doing business every quarter? GAAP offers few clues. Some vital intangible assets, such as the brainpower of a team of microchip designers, aren't measured at all. Other intangibles, such as patents, are valued by appraisal—a type of educated guess that is far from foolproof. Concludes Lawrence Revsine, a prominent accounting professor at Northwestern's J. L. Kellogg Graduate School of Management: "Accounting stinks."

One of the best illustrations of the mismatch between yesterday's accounting system and today's economy is seen in the exploding use of those R&D write-offs. Virtually unknown a decade ago, they have soared since IBM successfully used the technique to write off much of the cost of its 1995 acquisition of software maker Lotus Development. Today, such charges can reach billions of dollars.

To see why they're so popular, check out the payoff in WorldCom's $37 billion purchase of MCI Communications Corp. WorldCom estimates that MCI has R&D worth $6 billion to $7 billion under way but not yet ready for commercial application. Since World-Com may never see any benefit from that R&D—conceivably, it could all come to naught—accounting rules allow WorldCom to write it all off at once.

Does that mean MCI was really only worth $31 billion? Not necessarily. The real significance of that number lies elsewhere. Normally, any premium paid over "book value" would be called goodwill, which WorldCom would have to depreciate. Since that would cut into expenses for years, acquirers generally want to keep goodwill to a minimum.

Now here's where things get good. Since every dollar WorldCom can assign to in-process R&D is one less it has to call goodwill, it has every incentive to make the charge as big as possible. And acquirers have enormous leeway in valuing R&D. That's what really has the SEC worked up. It fears that companies are overstating these charges. Moreover, as with all front-loaded charges, writing off all R&D costs today will likely give future earnings a boost. When WorldCom actually turns some of that R&D into salable products, its earnings will look far juicier than they would have otherwise.

Gary Brandt, WorldCom's chief of investor relations, defends the treatment. But he concedes that if the charge were considered goodwill, WorldCom earnings would be cut by a minimum of $100 million a year, or 5¢ per 1.9 billion shares outstanding. If the SEC doesn't challenge the charge and it isn't reduced by WorldCom, it will be the largest in-process R&D write-off ever.

But the potential to inflate research costs isn't the SEC's only worry concerning write-offs. Some of these charges can also provide cover for ongoing operating costs that should be booked as they occur. McDonald's Corp. got its hand slapped for just such a move in August. The hamburger vendor elected to take all at once a $190 million charge for the cost of ditching old grills and ovens and installing new ones. But the SEC disagreed that these charges were a one-time extraordinary cost. After all, if upgrading kitchen equipment isn't a normal cost of doing business for a restaurant chain, what is?

Hooked   After discussions with the SEC, McDonald's decided to take the expenses as they are incurred. The company says it was not attempting to boost earnings by taking the one-time charge. Still, the shift will chop $25 million to $35 million a quarter from earnings through late 1999, estimates Merrill Lynch & Co. analyst Peter Oakes.

If companies get away with them, big charges can become addictive. Kellogg, AT&T, and General Motors have all taken a remarkable number of restructuring write-offs this decade—leading critics to question how "extraordinary" they are. For a clear picture of the benefits a company can derive from repeated write-offs, look no further than Eastman Kodak Co. Since 1991, Kodak has taken six extraordinary write-offs totaling $4.5 billion. That's more than all of its net profits for the past nine years.

Kodak has been in a major transition period, exiting five major business lines as sales have dropped 25% since the write-offs began. Still, critics point out that Kodak managed to report operating earnings throughout that period—but the repeated need for such extraordinary charges implies that those operating figures may have been of little value. "Charges after charges after charges—that says Kodak overreported earnings," says David W. Tice, publisher of *Behind the Numbers* and manager of the Prudent Bear Fund, which invests in undervalued stocks. Kodak declined to comment.

Meanwhile, the SEC is also taking a close look at another corporate addiction: merger mania. Some $1.2 trillion worth of deals have been announced already this year—greater than in all of 1997—and as many as one-third would not have been done without the in-process R&D charge or a technique known as pooling-of-interest accounting, says Stephen S. Smith, a managing director at investment bank Broadview Associates. Pooling lets companies combine their assets at book value, eliminating goodwill. Miller estimates that when USA Waste Services Inc. and Waste Management used pooling to combine in March in a $16 billion deal, they added $3 billion to $4 billion to earnings over the next several decades.

It isn't supposed to be easy to qualify for a pooling; companies must meet 12 tough criteria. Still, the incentive is so strong that pooling deals jumped from just 11 in 1990 to 364 so far this year, according to Securities Data Co. That's a problem, critics say, because the result can be to hide the premium one company is paying for another. "The real concern is that the acquiring company overpaid," says Bear, Stearns & Co. accounting analyst Pat Mc-Connell. "If they overpaid and management was stupid, that's important."

If many of the problems stem from ambiguities in GAAP, however, only so much blame can go to the system. After all, accounting's rules have been loose for years. What's pushing more managers through the loopholes today is the rise of momentum investing. For many on Wall Street, the only number that counts is the quarterly growth of earnings per share. One measure of the intensified interest: For years, First Call compiled daily lists during weeks when companies issue earnings, of which companies made, missed, or beat analysts' estimates. Now, First Call updates those lists two or three times a day. It even puts out lists during what's now called "pre-announcement season."

Meanwhile, many ignore the fundamentals behind the numbers. "There aren't enough skeptical investors," says the manager of a $4 billion mutual fund. "When investors punish companies for missing their quarterly earnings, it sends a message that they don't care how they get there."

Killing Field   That shift in market psychology has vastly increased the pressure for managers to meet earnings projections. And those that don't make the numbers generally get killed. "The penalties for missing your earnings are intense," says T.J. Rodgers, president and CEO of Cypress Semiconductor Corp. "If you miss one or two quarters, you can see your net worth and market cap cut in half. . . . It's harder to retain people if their stock options aren't worth anything. . . . Lots of CEOs have succumbed to that pressure." Indeed, the resulting pain is intensely personal, since more than half of CEO pay comes from stock options.

That market pressure can lead to disastrous accounting tricks such as those at Sunbeam, Waste Management, and Cendant. New management at the latter two have since conceded that the desire to meet Wall Street expectations seems to have been a huge driver of the problems, and analysts think it played a big role in Sunbeam's downfall as well.

The good times have also served to take investors' eyes off the ball. During the eight-year-long bull market, many took a "don't ask, don't tell" approach. As long as earnings were up, why look too closely at how management pulled it off? But those days are over. "There's a phenomenon in up markets that most analysts don't pay too much attention to accounting," says Gerald I. White of New York investment firm Grace & White Inc. "In bad markets, these problems come home to roost, and that's when people pay attention."

Those are exactly the sorts of issues that the stock market is starting to sort out. One result is that investors may put companies under more pressure to show that they have a solid foundation under their earnings. But the SEC seems more concerned there will be a rush in the other direction, toward more accounting smoke and mirrors. And some investment pros are arguing for a return to more fundamentals-driven stock picking. White argues that the current trend confirms his view that searching out companies with conservative accounting is best. Other investors are turning to other measures of corporate performance, such as Economic Value Added—net operating profit after taxes in excess of the cost of capital. That tool is used at Goldman Sachs and Credit Suisse First Boston.

The argument for those numbers is that they are harder to manipulate. But they are still not foolproof. Any company intent on jazzing up the numbers is probably going to figure out a way to obscure its true performance. "Increasingly, this culture is one of getting away with what you can," says investor Gary L. Pilgrim, founder of Pilgrim Baxter & Associates. "What we need is more integrity"—integrity in managers and integrity in their numbers.

WHERE ARE THE
ACCOUNTANTS?

RICHARD MELCHER

*Given the authors' concerns in the previous article, how can one not
blame the auditors? Why do these flagrant misrepresentations get
past those specifically charged with fact-finding? Melcher explains
that, contrary to the belief of some consumers and others, the rules
are not so clear and auditors are often not the ones to blame.*

It read like a primer on how to cook the books. In letters to the board of directors of Aviation Distributors Inc. and the Securities & Exchange Commission a year ago, the company's auditors, Arthur Andersen, wrote of sweeping irregularities. The allegations included falsified shipping documents and purchase orders—problems so great that Andersen could no longer attest to the accuracy of three earlier years of Aviation Distributors' financial reports.

Andersen resigned from the account. The move set in motion a quick chain of events, from the delisting of the $39 million company from the NASDAQ Small-Cap market (it's now traded over the counter) to the resignation of President and CEO Osamah S. Bakhit.

It all seems so straightforward—a perfect example of the role accountants are supposed to play in keeping the financial system honest. The problem is, it doesn't seem to happen as often as it should. As one apparently prosperous company after another saw earnings crumble in the wake of an accounting scandal over the past year, the auditors—at least in their public statements—often acted as surprised as investors to see years of previously reported profits go up in smoke. None of the major firms has emerged unscathed.

To take just one of the headline screamers, how did auditor Andersen miss the red flags at Sunbeam Corp. last year, when inventories began piling up and accounts receivables soared? Chief Executive Albert Dunlap had never been exactly reticent about his desire to do all he could to keep his high-octane stock levitating. So shouldn't someone have noticed when the company reported surging sales of heating blankets in the summer and barbecue grills in the late fall?

Yet at a board meeting on June 9, a partner at Andersen assured Sunbeam directors that the 1997 numbers complied with standard accounting procedures. Four days later, the scheme unraveling, Dunlap was fired. Sunbeam later acknowledged it was booking sales before the goods were actually delivered to stores. Today, the SEC is investigating Sunbeam's accounting. The company is expected to restate results for part of this year, 1997, and perhaps 1996. Andersen says it doesn't comment on clients.

Unfortunately, auditors seem to have allowed more and more of their clients to undercut the trustworthiness of their reported numbers with aggressive, albeit often legal, accounting for everything from restructuring or acquisition write-offs to the way sales are booked.

"Where Are the Accountants?" by Richard Melcher, *BusinessWeek* (October 5, 1998), p. 144.

"Within the Rules"   Certainly, no one would argue that auditors face an easy task. And give them their due: Auditing firms are resigning more accounts than ever, according to *Public Accounting Report* newsletter. And much of the problem stems from the fact that those generally accepted accounting principles give management wide latitude in how it puts together the books.

Consider what auditors suggest is an altogether typical set of circumstances leading to aggressive accounting. Executives face missed earnings expectations or a tight bank-lending covenant, and their bonuses hang in the balance. Suddenly, environmental or other legal liabilities are minimized, or inventory depreciation gets stretched out, or a big push is made to drum up end-of-quarter sales.

If the company's competitors pursue similar practices, executives are prone to ask auditors to follow the leader. "Everybody's doing it" becomes the rule—or the excuse—as lowest-common-denominator accounting takes hold. Rather than pushing their clients to uphold higher standards, accountants sometimes acquiesce in a race in which those most willing to stretch the rules define the industry standard. The bottom line: Too often, auditors "opine on what is acceptable, not what is appropriate," says Katherine A. Schipper, accounting professor at the University of Chicago Graduate School of Business.

Sure, there is a raft of industry requirements to detect fraud. But auditors sometimes have resisted some past efforts to toughen standards. An industry panel recommended four years ago that accounting firms not just verify that numbers meet GAAP requirements but that they go a step further and flag a company when its disclosures and estimates are aggressive. But the idea has been only "minimally" embraced by companies and auditors, says Donald J. Kirk, executive-in-residence at Columbia University and former chairman of the Financial Accounting Standards Board, who led the panel.

Foot in the Door   Those tendencies clearly have the Securities & Exchange Commission worried—and there are indications that the agency is determined to force changes. Spurred by the recent bookkeeping disasters, the SEC is sending a message that it expects more from the Big Five auditing firms—Andersen, Ernst & Young, Deloitte & Touche, PricewaterhouseCoopers, and KPMG Peat Marwick. In recent meetings, regulators have warned partners that as the economy slows, corporations will be under even more pressure to stretch rules to meet their earnings numbers. The fear is management will "build more optimism into financial reporting, and they want us to make sure we are appropriately tough," says Deloitte Chairman and CEO J. Michael Cook.

But the SEC's concerns go much deeper than that. Top agency officials, as well as some corporate directors and investors, worry that the explosion of nonauditing services at the Big Five, such as general consulting and merger advisory work, might create an incentive to go easy on auditing clients. Nonauditing services now make up more than 50% of revenues at the Big Five, according to *Public Accounting Report.* As the SEC's top accountant, Lynn Turner, puts it: "When an audit partner at a major firm is faced with a tough decision, can the partner make that decision based solely on his or her judgment about what is best for investors, without worrying about the impact on career or compensation?"

A year ago, the SEC signaled its concern by pushing for the formation of the Independent Standards Board. Made up of auditors and outsiders, the ISB plans to issue guidelines and rulings to help the industry police the conflicts created by its nonauditing business. Senior partners readily admit that auditing is intensely price-competitive and often serves as a wedge to get in the door to sell other products. But they deny that standards have suffered and say firms have safeguards to protect auditors' autonomy. Says Gregory A. Jonas, Andersen's managing director for financial statement assurance: "It's important that it's understood that those who stand up to pressure are rewarded as much as those who bring in new clients."

Another concern for regulators is the coziness that can develop between auditors and their clients. For reasons of career diversification and pay, many auditors switch over to the corporate finance staffs of their old clients. Corporate books end up being audited by the executives' former partners. Robert S. Miller, who was brought in to clean up a mess at Waste Management Inc., believes that may have been one factor behind the alleged accounting irregularities that led the company to restate six years of earnings downward by $1.75 billion. Many finance executives had come from Andersen, he says, creating "too much of a close relationship between senior auditors and senior managers."

The Big Five try to head off those problems by rotating a partner off an account every seven years and having a second partner, not involved in the audit, sign off on each account. But auditors will need to do more if they hope to regain investors' confidence. Corporate boards could go a long way toward helping by making sure audit committees consist of truly independent businesspeople. Critics suggest having companies disclose how much of an audit firm's fees are for nonauditing work. "Let the public know whether the audit is the dog or the tail," urges accounting analyst Abraham J. Briloff.

There are signs that the increased scrutiny—plus fear of lawsuits—is pushing the Big Five to step up their vigilance. Andersen will soon institute a scale for spotting fraud or over-aggressive accounting—for example, comparing market earnings expectations with management's ability to meet them. Already, the firm is encouraging auditors who spot oddities such as unsupported journal entries to dig for deeper problems. "You find out these things are like cockroaches: If you see one you're reasonably sure there are others," says Jonas.

But as long as corporate managers continue to look for ways to stretch the numbers, more problems are inevitable. "Investors have to understand that the safety net a clean-audit opinion provides can have big loopholes," warns Lawrence Revsine, an accounting professor at Northwestern University. Still, investors should expect better—from auditors and from the managers and board members who employ them.

Fixing the System

REGULATORS   Tighten accounting principles to limit wide range of management discretion. Determine whether auditors' expansion into consulting and advisory services leads to conflicts—and if so, restrict it.

AUDITORS   Pass judgment not just on whether numbers meet accepted principles but also whether management is stretching dangerously. Make sure auditors who just say no to clients are rewarded as well as those who bring in new business.

AUDIT COMMITTEES   Stay independent of management. Meet regularly and alone with outside auditors to seek straight answers on internal controls and management integrity.

THE ETHICAL TEMPERATURE AT ARCTICVIEW

GRANT RUSSELL

The following two case studies address some of the more difficult personal issues accountants might face. With both cases, it is important to place yourself in the position of the protagonist and to consider what you would do in similar circumstances.

"I don't know what to do, John."

Mary Benninger, in obvious discomfort, was discussing her employment situation with John Chu, an old friend from university. Both had graduated in the class of 1985 from Mackenzie King University and had then proceeded to complete their CMA's [Certified Management Accountants], graduating in 1987. John had been promoted quickly and now held the position of controller for Ace Seating Company, a division of a large multi-national auto supplier. Mary, on the other hand, had removed herself from full-time employment to raise her children and had only recently taken up her current position.

"I thought this was an ideal position: controller/office manager of a small growing company, full of new ideas, flexible on working hours, and Bob and I can really use the cash now, since he has been unable to work since his illness. But the situation sure turned sour quickly, and I really don't know who to talk to. In fact, I'm not sure that I should be talking to you!"

"Don't worry about that," John replied reassuringly. "You know that you can trust me—after all, I never did tell Bob about your adventure in Mabel MacKay Residence!"

Mary laughed. "That's okay, because I did . . . and I told him it was all your fault! But this situation is well beyond anything I think I can handle."

"I joined the company about six months ago. The company is a small, privately-held manufacturer that makes specialty chemicals in small quantities for testing labs, other manufacturing firms, etc. Most of our production and sales are so small that none of the big chemical companies wanted to enter the market. Henson Chemical grew rapidly and had increasing sales up to 2 years ago, when Dusque, the big integrated chemical company, set up a small subsidiary to do exactly what we are doing. I guess we shouldn't have been so successful! Dusque's sub must be losing money like crazy, since we've taken a real hit in sales and profits. Our business is down 30%, and the new plant that we built in Brampton 3 years ago is operating at 50% of capacity.

"I gather we were never very good at cost control and internal controls were virtually non-existent. When we were growing so quickly, sales were more important than costs. When things got tough, they dismissed my predecessor and hired me. They told me that I could have free rein to implement what I thought was necessary. Wow, is it necessary! The senior staff really don't know the difference between personal and corporate assets. I've got some really tough problems just in terms of separating personal and corporate expenses. Our sales and marketing expenses are double what I think they should be. But I think I can get this under control.

"The really big problem is our Northern Development grant. When business fell off, Brian Henson, our president, attended a seminar on how to get government grants. He discovered that a matching program was available for firms to establish northern manufacturing facilities. So Brian, and Herb Ottely, our VP Manufacturing, submitted a proposal to manufacture chemicals in Arcticview, where the mines have been playing out. The proposal had been prepared by a consultant for another unsuccessful grant application previously, and Brian and Herb simply updated it, changing the location of operations from Brampton to Arcticview. Arcticview is a really remote village, with 2,500 people and 5,000 caribou! The government must have been really desperate for anyone to locate there since they accepted the proposal very quickly, and both levels of government have provided matching funds of $750,000 for our new plant there, a total of $1,500,000 of government money. They have also guaranteed a bank loan for us of $750,000. We used the loan proceeds as our contribution."

"Well, that sounds great, Mary. What's the problem?"

"The problem is that after the funds were provided, we rented a temporary facility in Arcticview, and we hired a few staff there to maintain the building. However, we told the Ministry of Northern Development that the new equipment needed to be tested and the manufacturing process needed to be developed further. So the equipment was delivered to our Brampton facility. The equipment is currently being used to manufacture a new line of chemicals for us, one that will allow us to regain much of the market share we had lost to Dusque. The problem is that the grant requires us to use the funds in Arcticview."

John's reply was quick: "But will anybody check on how the funds are really being used?"

"That's what I'm worried about, John. At the present time, one of my tasks is to ensure that optimistic reports are sent about how development work is coming. In the short run, I can handle this, since there is a real need to shake down this new equipment. The supplier of the equipment had suggested 2 months, but the company has already been "testing" the equipment for 6 months in Brampton and are hoping that they can "test" the equipment for a full year."

"Well, after the year, they'll simply move the equipment up to Arcticview, and your problems will be over?" John responded.

"No, that's when my problems will really start. You see, there is absolutely no way that they can turn a profit up in Arcticview. We have to transport all the raw materials up there, and then ship the finished product back here. Even though it is new technology we are using, Dusques will be able very quickly to beat us on delivery costs."

"I see. Then you'll have to shut down operations and return the funds?"

Mary's reply was terse. "We can't. If we shut down operations here, we don't have enough funds to repay the loan and the resale value of the equipment is very low. Besides, we would be operating below breakeven on the balance of our operations."

"Wow! Major problems. What do they plan to do then?"

"Well, the equipment is actually relatively small and quite portable since only small quantities of the chemicals are produced in each batch. Brian plans to ship the equipment to Arcticview for a startup phase, and move workers temporarily from the Brampton plant, while the government publicity pictures are being taken. After a discreet period of time, they'll return the equipment to Brampton, and bring the workers back down. They'll continue to "produce" chemicals in Arcticview with a few local workers. However, the real operations will be here in Brampton. The grant contract states that the company is obligated to produce in Arcticview for only 3 years; they figure that if they can last for 2 years past the testing period, they will be able to keep the equipment and keep the company viable."

"But surely some government audits are necessary, Mary. What will they do then?"

"Believe it or not, John, the only audited statements the government requires is our financial statements from our external auditors. Brian figures that the auditors aren't particularly concerned about where we manufacture, since the financial statements don't show that detail anyway. As long as we can document all the equipment, inventory and labor, we'll probably be okay with the auditors. Brian and Herb have to complete an annual written report on how the grant is being used, but all I have to contribute is a brief statement on the "testing and setup" part, and, yes, provide the financials. I'm hoping that I won't have to even see their finished report! One of the things I can do is bill as much of our supplies as possible to the Arcticview plant and minimize the amount billed through the Brampton plant. Some of our labor costs in the Brampton plant will be billed through Arcticview as well. They'll serve as consultants to the Brampton operation, but be based in Arcticview. Because the equipment is portable, and the auditors really don't know the technical aspects of our business, we'll ship some equipment north for the audit, along with staff, to give the impression of a high level of activity.

"Brian and Herb tell me not to worry, that everybody does this for tax reasons, but I'm really confused on this point. The financial statements will be perfectly accurate and consistent with previous years, so I don't think anyone could nail me for my ethics here."

Mary continued, "Brian figures that nobody really could operate a manufacturing facility in Arcticview since both suppliers and markets are too far away. Training costs up there alone would blow our grant budgets. I agree with him that the government just wants to wave the flag a little bit for votes, and they must know or at least suspect what we are going to do. Besides, we are giving a few local people employment as custodians and also managing to keep Henson Chemical afloat during this tough time. Both Brian and Herb are upset that Dusque's subsidiary got a major government supply contract away from us, and are arguing that this government grant merely put us back on a level playing field.

"I've talked to both Brian and Herb about trying to get more government money to underwrite our transportation costs, but they are concerned about drawing attention to our situation. The grant also prohibits us from selling the equipment and using the funds for operating expenses.

"John, I'm really bewildered here. I signed a labor *contract* and it states that I can't talk to anyone. I've violated it already, talking to you, but I can't talk to anyone else. I signed a very restrictive employment contract (see box). Besides, I think that talking to the government would violate my professional code of ethics. Bob and I need the money to survive, and Henson has 60 employees that need their jobs. I'm having difficulty sleeping, but Bob keeps telling me to simply ignore the issue and do what I'm told. In all other aspects, this is a great job. Brian is wonderful to work for. If we can pull this off, he'll cut me in for equity participation. If I quit, I'll be a long time getting another job, and you'd better believe that Brian would not be helpful in getting me placed."

THE CONTRACT SIGNED BY MARY BENNINGER

The Employee expressly covenants and agrees that he/she will not at any time during or after the termination of his employment with the Company:

(A) reveal, divulge or make known to any person, firm or corporation, the contents of any formula, chemical compound, product or other substance owned or developed by the Company or the method, process or manner of manufacturing, compounding or preparing any of such formulae, compounds, products or substances or sell, exchange or give away, or otherwise dispose of any formula, compound, product or substance now or hereafter owned by the Company whether the same shall or may have been originated, discovered or invented by the Employee or otherwise;

(B) reveal, divulge or make known to any person, firm or corporation any secret or confidential information whatsoever, in connection with the company or its business, or anything connected therewith, or the name or any other information pertaining to its customers or suppliers;

(C) solicit, interfere with or endeavour to entice away from the Company any customer or supplier or any other person, firm or Corporation having dealings with the Company, or interfere with or entice away any other officer or employee of the Company.

THE ETHICAL DILEMMA AT NORTHLAKE

GRANT RUSSELL

Our story opens with an irate Jim McIntosh confronting his manager of corporate report-ing: "I thought we had an understanding on this issue, Frank. Tina tells me that you are threatening to go public with your stupid statements about the report. For Pete's sake, Frank, wake up and smell the coffee! You're about to damage all the important things in your life: your career, your friendships, and your company!"

Frank sat quietly in the overstuffed sofa in his V.P.'s expansive office. He thought that the pale green report lying on the desk looked innocent enough but it certainly had provided the basis for some serious turmoil. Jim stood by his desk trembling with rage. His face was bright red and mottled with anger. Frank had often seen Jim upset, but never in a temper such as this.

"I'm sorry, Jim," Frank replied softly, "I know how much this means to you, but I don't think that I have a choice in this matter. I can't sit idle while you and that twit from finan-cial analysis allow this report to go forward. You both know that these numbers have no foundation in fact."

The report, entitled, "Endangered Species: The Pulp and Paper Industry in the Upper Peninsula," laid out the industry's response to the new government proposals to put efflu-ent controls on the discharge of waste water from pulp and paper mills in environmentally sensitive regions of the province. One section of the report detailed the financial conse-quences of the emission controls as determined by each of the five pulp and paper compa-nies operating in the region. Amalgamated Forest Products had taken the industry lead in developing the report, and the company president, Jean Letourneau, was scheduled to tes-tify before a legislative sub-committee next week, giving the industry perspective on the proposed legislation.

Amalgamated had three major mills, located in some of the more remote locations in the province. The firm had been facing difficult financial times due to the recession, and this had caused substantial hardship in the three small communities where the mills were located. Corporate offices were located in Northlake, a town of approximately 10,000 people.

The section of the report dealing with the dollar impact to Amalgamated Forest Prod-ucts of installing the emission control equipment had been prepared by Tina Pacquette. Tina, a long-term employee of the firm, had risen through the accounting department to be-come the manager of financial analysis. While Tina and Frank were at equal levels in the organizational structure, their working relationship had not been particularly cordial. In Frank's opinion, Tina's work was barely adequate, but then, no one asked for his opinion.

"Well, Frank, your pig-headedness has really caused a problem for all of us! Wait here! I'll get Jean Letourneau, and we'll see what he thinks about your efforts!" Jim exited the office and slammed the door.

As he waited in the silence of his boss's beautifully decorated office, Frank looked back over his 10 years with Amalgamated Forest Products. Just like his father before him, Frank started with the firm after completing high school and his first job was as a yard man calling out damaged logs before processing. That's when Frank severely damaged his right leg on the job. He had been celebrating the birth of his son the night before and he was unable to manoeuvre his footing with the dexterity required. Surgery saved the leg and he was extremely grateful that the company had brought him inside to the accounting office. An accounting clerk's salary was low compared to being a yard helper, but in a short time his natural talent for analysis brought him to the attention of the vice-president, finance. Within two years, Jim McIntosh had arranged for him to go to university, complete his CMA designation after graduation, and then return to Amalgamated. The financial support provided by the firm had been adequate but not lavish by any means, and Jim had done well in his studies. He was the gold medalist for his province on the CMA examinations, and he had returned to Northlake in triumph. With three young children and a proud wife, Frank had been appointed to a new position in corporate reporting. After a year of having Jim as his mentor, he rose to the position of manager of corporate reporting.

The office door opened abruptly and Jim entered with the company president. Jean Letourneau was a distinguished man of approximately 60 years of age. He had a long history with Amalgamated and a solid reputation in the pulp and paper industry.

"What's the problem, Frank?" Jean's voice broke into the silence. "Jim tells me that you have a few concerns about the report that we're submitting to the legislative committee."

"Well, Mr. Letourneau, I think we—the company—have some major problems here. The report indicates that we'll have severe financial problems if we're forced into building a lagoon for waste water treatment. In fact, the report says we are likely to be pushed into bankruptcy if the legislation is passed. But we all know these estimates of costs are highly inflated. There's no way that our operating costs would be raised by 30 percent. I could see our operating costs rising by only 8–10 percent. That's what the internal report Tina wrote a year ago predicts and there's really been no significant change. Moreover, you have to testify before the legislative committee as to the truthfulness of this report—and there's not a shred of truth in it. The other cost estimates are all high, and the prediction of our product demand is based upon a further deepening of the recession. For our internal purposes, we have been using an estimated increase of 10 percent in demand."

"Slow down, son," Letourneau's calm voice broke in, "we have to use different figures for different purposes. When we report to our shareholders, we give them numbers that are substantially altered from the internal documents, right? In this case, we have to make those dunderheads in the government see what all this regulation is doing to us. Besides, they know we're going to use the most effective numbers to justify our position."

"But this isn't simply a matter of different figures," Frank sputtered. "These numbers have been totally fabricated. And they don't take into account the damage that we're doing to the Wanawashee River. The same stuff we're dumping was cleaned up by our competition years ago. The aboriginal community downstream is still drinking this garbage. We're going to be subject to a huge lawsuit if they ever trace it to us. Then, where will we be? I've got to worry about my professional obligations as well. If this blows up, you could go to jail, and I could get my designation revoked."

"We'll cross that bridge when we come to it," Jim McIntosh interjected. "You've got to remember what's at stake here. Northlake's totally dependent on the mill for its economic survival. As the mill goes, so goes the town. It's your buddies you'd be threatening to put out of work, Frank. This legislation may not bankrupt us, but it will certainly put a squeeze on profits. If profits are gone, no more reinvestment by Chicago. Head office is putting lots of pressure on us to improve the bottom line since the takeover last year. They're talking about cutting all of that new production line equipment we requested."

"The bottom line is this, Frank," Letourneau spoke softly. "You're an important part of our team—we've invested a lot in you. Jim was talking about working you into a new role: V.P.-controller. We'd hate to let you go because of this small issue. However, we need to have everybody working on the same goal. Besides, Jim tells me this isn't even your responsibility. If you hadn't picked up the copy of the report on Tina's desk, we wouldn't have even involved you. Now take the rest of the day off, go home to Cheryl and the kids, and take out that new speed boat of yours. Think the problem through, and I'm sure you'll see the long-term benefit of what we're doing. This pollution problem is a 'Northern problem' that we can resolve here, not in some fancy legislature in the south. Besides, we've had the problem for as far back as I can remember. So a few extra years certainly won't hurt."

Chapter 11

ETHICAL IMPLICATIONS OF TECHNOLOGY

From mainframe through personal computer to internet, the electronic computer has transferred information and human communication in unanticipated ways that are giving birth to what has been variously termed cyberspace, virtual reality or hyperreality. To live in this new milieu, however, requires not virtual but real ethics, grounded in practical and public reflection on the new technolife world.

—CARL MITCHAM

We must adjust to changing times and still hold to unchanging principles.

—President
Jimmy Carter

You say you want a revolution? Well, you know, we all want to change the world.

—John Lennon and
Paul McCartney

Things do not change; we change.

—Henry David Thoreau

With the advent of new technology, new ethical issues emerge. That is because we consider the advances of the technology before we consider the implications. While most firms provide internet access and e-mail for their employees, more than 70 percent of major U.S. firms monitor their employees' work, Internet usage and e-mail, double the number that did so in 1997.[1] Do you think about everyone who might see the e-mails you send? How do you know that your boss will not forward your disparaging remarks about a colleague directly to that colleague? It can be done with the touch of a key. Are there different issues that are raised by that concern as opposed to those that arose with a traditional written letter? When we mistakenly believe that no one is watching, we may engage in activities that we would otherwise refrain from doing. For instance, you may believe that hitting the "delete" key does actually delete an e-mail message. However, it does not always delete that message from the server, so it might have a negative impact in a lawsuit or be retrievable by your supervisor.

More than 80 percent of mid- to large-sized firms in the United States have Internet access policies, but there remains a problem. More than 60 percent of these companies have disciplined employees for violations of these policies, with the leading violations being access to pornography, online chat forums, gaming, investing or shopping at work.[2]

The above concern raises but one potential dilemma in connection with new technology. In order to address some of the issues that are presented by computers specifically, the Computer Ethics Institute has created "The Ten Commandments of Computer Ethics." The commandments include the following:

3. Thou shalt not snoop around in other people's computer files.
9. Thou shalt think about the social consequences of the program you are writing or the system you are designing.
10. Thou shalt always use a computer in ways that insure consideration and respect for your fellow humans.

Unfortunately, many of the ethical issues that arise in the area of managing information are not readily visible. When we don't completely understand the technology, we might

---

[1] American Management Association, "American Companies Increase Use of Electronic Monitoring," *http://www.amanet.org/research/press.htm.*
[2] Vasant Raval, "Ethical Behavior in the Knowledge Economy," *Information Strategy* 16, no. 3 (Spring 2000), p. 45.

not understand the ethical implications of our decisions. Can your employer read your e-mail? Your first response might be, "No, it doesn't have my secret password." However, experts tell us that any system is penetrable. Employers have been known to randomly read e-mails in order to ensure that the system is being used for business purposes. Is this ethical? Does it matter if there is a company policy that systems must only be used for business purposes, or that the employees are given notice that their e-mail will be read? These ethical issues may be compounded by the fact that there exists a knowledge gap between people who *do* understand the technology, and others who are unable to protect themselves precisely because they do *not* understand. You might not expect to be fired for sending out an e-mail; but if you thought about it a bit, you might have known what to expect.

Technology allows for access that was never before possible. Under previous circumstances, one could usually tell if someone had steamed open a letter over a teapot. However, today, you usually cannot discover if someone reads the e-mail you sent yesterday to your best friend. Access can take place unintentionally, as well. In doing a routine background check, a supervisor may unintentionally uncover information of an extremely personal nature that may bear absolutely no relevance to one's work performance. This occurs because the information, though previously unavailable or too burdensome to uncover, is now freely available from a variety of sources.

Moreover, because technology allows us to work from almost anywhere on this planet, we are seldom out of the boundaries of our workplace. For instance, just because you're going to your sister's wedding, this doesn't mean that your supervisor can't reach you. Here is the tough question: should your supervisor try to reach you just because she has the ability? Our total accessibility creates conflicts that we never before had to wrestle with. This accessibility therefore blurs the lines between our personal and professional lives.

Another challenge posed by the new technology accessible in the workplace is the facelessness that results from its use. If we have to face someone as we make our decisions, we are more likely to care about the impact of that decision on that person. Conversely, when we don't get to know someone because we don't have to see that person in order to do our business, we often don't take into account the impact of our decisions on that person. They become merely a name at the other end of an e-mail correspondence, rather than another human being. Given the ease and informality of electronic communications, we often "say" (write, e-mail, etc.) things to each other that we would never say to someone's face, precisely because we don't have to consider the impact of what we're saying. We are more careless with our communications because they are easier to conduct—just hit a button and it's sent.

The answer is simply that one needs to be mindful of how these communications might be used if they fell into someone else's hands! By using an appropriate combination of interpersonal contacts, we ensure that our accountability rests intact.

The law offers little protection or guidance in this area, especially given how new these issues really are. The Constitutional protections against unreasonable searches and seizures (through the Fourth Amendment) apply only to public sector employees and, to date, there has been no precedent in connection with Fourth Amendment protection of e-mail transmissions. State constitutions, such as California's, may provide protection against invasions of privacy but, again, there has been no precedent in this area. Exceptions in the Electronic Communications Privacy Act of 1986 leave e-mail privacy without protection and the proposed Privacy for Consumers and Workers Act has been subject to congressional debate barring its passage since 1991.

All that an employee may be left with is state common law protection against intrusion into seclusion; this protection guards against invasions into areas where the individual has a reasonable expectation of privacy or invasions that would be highly offensive to a reasonable person[3] Since the "reasonableness" of one's expectation of privacy regarding e-mail has yet to be determined, even this general protection offers little guidance.

Of course, these issues are not limited to the United States. The Global Business Privacy Project has identified seven major developments of importance to businesses in connection with cyberethics:

- The European Union (EU) Privacy Directive.

- The commencement of an international privacy standards process.

- New national and global information flows.

- Information superhighway initiatives.

- Model business principles for global businesses.

- New information technology applications.

- New global interest in fashioning consumer date protection laws.[4]

In particular, the EU Privacy Directive might present challenging issues for American businesses. It states that personal data may not be transferred to a non-EU state or organization unless that entity can guarantee protection of the data equivalent to the protections guaranteed by the EU directive in EU countries. The United States does not currently protect personal information to the same extent as the European Union and therefore firms who do business in the United States might be in violation of the directive if they transmit personal information from an EU country to their counterparts in the United States.

The Department of Commerce spent much of 2000 in high-level negotiations with the EU in order to define a "safe harbor" for American businesses who engage in data transfer. However, at press time of this text, the EU had not yet accepted the proposals by the Department of Commerce, claiming that the protections remained too vague. For the most up-to-date information on this topic, visit the Department of Commerce E-Commerce website.[5]

Electronic Performance Monitoring   As introduced above, technology invades and affects the employment relationship through employee electronic performance monitoring. Considerable controversy surrounds the issue of whether it is ethical for an employer to monitor the actions of employees through electronic surveillance. This type of monitoring may take the form of recording telephone calls of customer service representatives, electronically counting the number of keystrokes a word processor makes during the day, installing video cameras in the workplace, and so on. While the employer may argue that it has the right to monitor in order to adequately and accurately appraise its employees and maintain quality levels, employees argue that the monitoring causes undue stress and pressure, and is too invasive.

---

[3]Restatement (2d) of Torts 652B (1977).

[4]Global Business Privacy Project, *http://www.pandab.org/global.html*

[5]*http://www.ita.doc.gov/td/ecom/menu.html*

Where should the line be drawn? Most of us would agree that installing video cameras in the washrooms of the workplace may be going a bit too far to prevent theft; knowing where to draw the line before that might be more difficult. As long as technology exists to allow for privacy invasions, should the employer have the right to use it? What constitutes humane or inhumane use of this technology?

Consider whether invasive monitoring could be made ethical or humane. It has been suggested that due notice given to employees that they will be monitored, plus the opportunity to avoid monitoring in certain situations, would solve the ethical problems. For instance, if an employer chooses to monitor random phone calls made by its customer service representatives, it could so notify the workers that certain calls may be monitored and these calls would be signified by a beep on the line during the monitoring. In addition, if a worker is making a personal call, they may use a nonmonitored phone in order to avoid a wrongful invasion of her or his privacy.

However, this may not solve all of the concerns about monitoring. Suppose you are the employer and you want to make sure that your service representatives handle calls in a patient, tolerant, and affable manner. By telling the worker which calls you are monitoring, your employees may be sure to be on their best behavior during those calls. Random, anonymous monitoring may better resolve your concerns (but not those of the worker). A recent study found that electronic performance monitoring has undesirable impacts on monitored workers, such as a lower perception of the fairness of the evaluation, health problems, and increased stress.[6]

Additional Issues for Consideration   At the end of this chapter, you will find several articles that raise challenging issues that are only now coming to the forefront of public interest. First, DeGroat's article asks the reader to consider the digital divide between the haves (those who have access to technology and the information contained therein) and the have-nots (those who, for financial, geographic, or other practical reasons do not have access to technology). DeGroat asks us to consider who should bear the responsibility of providing access and what is the impact on non-profit organizations. Finally, Stavraka's article raises the issue of genetically modified foods which urges the reader to ask whether one should take advantage of **all** new technologies or are there some that are best left unused.

---

[6]Stephen Hawk, "The Effects of Computerized Performance Monitoring: An Ethical Perspective," *Journal of Business Ethics* 13 (1994), pp. 949–57.

A FUTURE FOR TECHNOLOGY AND ETHICS

AMANDA MUJICA, EDWARD PETRY, AND DIANNE VICKERY

Technology will impact everyone reading this text and most people in the universe; but have we truly considered the ethical impact of technology on our lives or merely embraced it as a result of its convenience? The authors of the following research report on the results from a widespread study on the impact of technology on workplace ethics.

Gadgets, bytes and e-stuff—they're the promise of the future. Right? Well, while cell phones, fax machines, beepers and computers make us work faster, a recent study found they are changing the way we work with one another, contributing to the pressure we're feeling and increasing the risk of unethical and illegal business practices. These were the main conclusions from a national study conducted in 1998 by the Ethics Officer Association (EOA) and the Society of Financial Service Professionals (SFSP).

The study, "Technology and Ethics in the Workplace: The Ethical Impact of New Technologies on Workers," was conducted with underwriting support from The Guardian Life Insurance Company of America and State Farm Insurance Companies and sought to measure whether or not the presence of new technologies in the workplace increased the risk of unethical and illegal business practices.

There were eight major objectives of the study. They were to:

1. Determine whether or not the presence and advance of new technologies in the workplace increases the risk of unethical and illegal business practices.
2. Determine what behaviors resulting from the use of new technologies workers believe to be unethical.
3. Determine the percentage of respondents who have committed unethical acts related to new technologies during 1997.
4. Ascertain what organizations can do to address pressure, fears and unethical and illegal behavior in this area.

"A Future for Technology and Ethics," by Amanda Mujica, Edward Petry and Dianne Vickery, *Business & Society Review* 104, no. 3 (1999), p. 279.

5. Measure the level of pressure that exists as a consequence of technologies in the work-place.
6. Measure the fears about the future that are a consequence of the presence and advancement of technology in the work environment.
7. Measure the comfort and/or anxiety level with new technologies.
8. Measure the usage level, usage patterns and the variety of goals for using new technologies in the work environment.

The survey was conducted via mail by International Communication Research (ICR) from February 23, 1998, through March 17, 1998. A total of 4,000 surveys were sent to a cross-section of American workers. Those receiving it represented household income levels and occupation categories that corresponded with the working population nationwide. The overall response rate was 24%, which is more than twice the typical response rate for this type of survey. The results presented in the final report were based on a total of 726 respondents, or 18% of the total (approximately 6% of the surveys were returned incomplete or otherwise unuseable). The margin for error was ± 3.5%.

TYPES OF TECHNOLOGIES WORKERS ARE USING

The study first asked a number of questions to gauge the types of technologies workers were using (Table 1). Two-thirds of the employees (61%) used at least five types of technology on the job. As one might expect, two of the most popular pieces of equipment were the desktop computer and the fax machine.

Also used by a majority of employees were message collecting and sending devices/systems, such as e-mail, answering machines and voice-mail.

When on-the-job usage patterns were analyzed by age group, the most significant difference occurred, when we looked at Internet usage. The overall percentage of those using the Internet was 42%. It dropped sharply to only 17% of those more than 60 years of age. By age group, the highest percentage of e-mail users were those between the ages of 55 and 59: 70%; compared to 58% overall.

TABLE 1

New Technologies Used On the Job			
Desktop computer	85%	Beeper/pager	32%
Fax machine	72%	Intranet/network	21%
E-mail	58%	Laptop computer	18%
Answering machine	57%	Palm computer	8%
Voicemail	52%	Video conferencing	8%
Cellular phone	44%	Personal electronic organizer	8%
Internet	42%	Robotics	1%
CD-Rom	38%		

Base = Total New Technology Users

Examining internet usage more closely, we found that while job-related internet use was reported by 42% of employees, Internet use for any purpose was reported by 64% of the respondents. When asked if they felt they were addicted to the Internet, only 2% said "yes." The response rate did not vary by gender or age. It was higher for those with a post-graduate education (4%). However, when asked if others they work with are addicted to the Internet, 50% said "yes." Sixty-five percent of those who work in large organizations (over 25,000 employees) said others they work with are addicted. By industry, this figure was highest in telecommunications (59%) and lowest in insurance (24%).

The study found that new technology primarily assists employees in improving their job performance, especially by increasing their productivity during work hours (66%) (Table 2). In addition, a majority of employees used technology to improve their on-the-job communications and personal job skills. A significant number (47%) reported they use new technologies as a time saver, to improve time management or to balance various responsibilities. Few said they use new technologies to develop a competitive edge, perhaps because they have come to view technology as a given that everyone has access to, thereby reducing its importance for competition. The least often stated goal for using new technology on the job was to increase productivity during commuting time (13%). However, the response was considerably higher among those in the 35–39 age group (24%), those who work part-time in the office and part-time on the road (24%) and those with household incomes more than $100,000 (25%).

Though 66% overall said they use new technologies to increase productivity during normal working hours, this percentage was highest among those 35–39 years old (80%) and it consistently increased with household income (52% with household incomes less than $25,000 and 76% for those with household incomes more than $100,000).

As one might expect, those 30–34 years of age were much more likely to say that they used new technology to help balance work and family responsibilities (53% versus 35% overall). Of the men surveyed, 37% say they use new technology to help balance work and family responsibilities compared to 33% of the women.

TABLE 2

Benefits of New Technology

Increased productivity during normal work hours	66%	Helped balance work and family needs	35%
Expanded job-related knowledge	54%	Expanded professional network	28%
Improved communications with co-workers	51%	Relieved job stress	26%
Developed job skills	50%	Developed competitive edge	18%
Improved time management	47%	Increased productivity during commuting time	13%
Improved communications with clients/customers	42%		

From these initial study questions we knew *what* technologies workers were using; we now wanted to look more closely at how these new resources were affecting workers and how they were utilizing technologies at work. With the remainder of the survey questions, we asked a number of questions and found three key, overarching themes: 1. Workers felt pressure from new technologies—"get work done faster, more efficiently"; 2. They also felt comfortable with new technologies—over 50% used e-mails, faxes, computers, answering machines and the Internet on a regular basis; and 3. The combination of pressure and comfort level with new technologies could be one of the factors that led 45% of all respondents to engage in unethical actions related to new technologies.

Let's take a closer look at each of these.

WORKERS FEEL PRESSURE FROM NEW TECHNOLOGIES

Workers were presented with 14 different sources related to new technologies that may or may not contribute to pressure. These sources included workplace factors such as increased productivity expectations, inadequate manuals, inadequate support and/or training, frustration with co-workers who didn't keep up with new technologies; as well as factors that extended beyond the workplace such as a blurring of the distinction between work and private time, and a fear of "big-brother"; and other factors that were at least in part self-imposed, including less tolerance for errors and the loss of person-to-person contact.

On average, employees named seven of the 14 factors as sources of pressure on the job. Thirteen of the 14 factors were listed by more than one-third of all employees.

Of the 14 factors, fear of being displaced (29%) was mentioned least often as a factor that exists on the job today as a consequence of new technologies. However, this factor was cited more often by: women (34%), those with some college/technical school (36%), those in the telecommunications industry (42%), and those with household incomes of less than $25,000 (49%).

The survey found that two-thirds (61%) of all respondents were using at least five types of new technology on the job and that these new office tools were causing them to feel pressure. When asked why new technologies were causing pressure, the most common responses were: increased productivity expectations, 81%; continual need to change/update the technology, 80%; increased frustration with co-workers who are not up-to-date, 61%; less tolerance for errors, 60%; inadequate manuals and/or training, 60%; and fear of losing data, 51%.

In all responses pertaining to pressure, women felt more pressure than men. The largest gender difference was "lack of understanding terminology or lingo": 70% women versus 51% men. Women also felt unfairly disadvantaged for being less familiar with the latest technology than men (39% versus 29%).

To analyze the sources of pressure further, respondents were asked to look at each of the factors they said existed in their work environment and assess whether those factors contributed to the pressure they were personally experiencing on the job or in the workplace. Analyzed in this way, when present in the workplace, the leading factor contributing to pressure on the job was inadequate manuals/training.

Women were more likely to experience a high degree of pressure from increased productivity expectations (74% vs. 61% for men). Similarly, there were significant gender differences in a number of other categories including pressure to keep up with continual changes in technology (71% women vs. 61% men), pressure due to less tolerance for errors (67% vs. 58%), and fear of losing data (66% vs. 55%).

A minority, but a still significant number of employees, felt unfairly disadvantaged because they were less familiar with the latest technologies. Overall, 33% felt unfairly disadvantaged. Women felt more disadvantaged than men (39% vs. 29%). There was no significant variation by age, but there was a clear correlation with education; the lower the education level the more likely the respondent was to feel unfairly disadvantaged. Among job titles/positions, business owners were the most likely to feel unfairly disadvantaged (46%), executives/senior managers were the least (23%). By industry, those in building/construction were the highest (44%), while manufacturing was the lowest (28%).

In 1997, the EOA and the SFSP conducted a national research study entitled the "Sources and Consequences of Workplace Pressure." Consistent with some of the findings in this study, it too pointed to a high degree of pressure on the average American worker. (See Petry et al., 1)

WORKERS ARE BECOMING MORE COMFORTABLE WITH NEW TECHNOLOGIES

When asked whether new technologies were crucial to their on-the-job success a large majority of respondents agreed. Eighty-seven percent agreed that "developing new technology and its capabilities is critically important to the success of my company or business." These findings did not vary by gender or age. In addition, 92% agreed with the statement that the use of latest technologies is a great improvement and advances business: only a small minority believed that new technologies created more problems than they solved.

Employees were not ill-at-ease with new technologies (Table 3). Only 1% said they are very uncomfortable/fearful of new technologies on the job.

Most respondents were comfortable with technology at work: 66% replied they are comfortable/at ease with new technologies on the job. Comfort level does decrease by age starting at a high of approximately 70% for those under 40 and decreasing steadily. While the comfort level decreases, even those more than 60 years of age report a 53% comfort level. These findings did not differ by gender.

And, employees have been getting more and more comfortable with technology over time. Within the one to five years of the study date, employees felt more comfortable with new technologies at work; 56% were more comfortable in 1998 than they were five years before; and 37% said they were more comfortable in 1998 than in 1997. Fifty-eight percent reported the same comfort level in 1998 as they had in 1997.

When asked whether they were interested in learning about the latest technologies, again, a large majority agreed. Ninety-six percent said that they are more or equally willing to learn new technologies today than they were five years ago. However, though comfort levels had increased over the last five years from the survey date, employees also thought they would fall behind in the years to come and were somewhat anxious about the future. Almost half (48%) said they were more comfortable in 1998 about the future than they expect to feel in 1999, and a majority (56%) expected to be less comfortable about the future five years from 1998.

TABLE 3

Are You More, Equally or Less Willing to Learn the Latest Technology Than You Were Five Years Ago?

More	62%
Equally	34%
Less	4%

How Comfortable Are You With Using New Technology and Equipment in the Workplace?

5-very comfortable	32%
4	34%
3	26%
2	7%
1-very uncomfortable	1%

Current Level of Comfort Compared to 5 Years ago

More comfortable	56%
Same	26%
Less	18%

Current Level of Comfort Compared to 1 Year Ago

More comfortable	37%
Same	58%
Less	5%

Current Level of Comfort Compared to What You Expect 1 Year from Now

More comfortable	48%
Same	48%
Less	4%

Current Level of Comfort Compared to What You Expect 5 Years from Now

More comfortable	56%
Same	35%
Less	9%

WORKERS ENGAGED IN UNETHICAL ACTIVITIES

The study found that nearly half (45%) of American workers engaged in a high-tech unethical act last year (Table 4).

Over one-quarter (27%) engaged in one or more of the following acts:

- Copied the company's software for home use

- Used office equipment to network/search for another job

- Made multiple copies of software for office use

- Accessed private computer files without permission

TABLE 4

Engaged in Unethical Action in Past Year

Created a potentially dangerous situation by using new technology while driving	19%
Wrongly blamed an error you made on a technological glitch	14%
Copied the company's software for home use	13%
Used office equipment to shop on the Internet for personal reasons	13%
Used office equipment to network/search for another job	11%
Made multiple copies of software for office use	11%
Accessed private computer files without permission	6%
Used new technologies to unnecessarily intrude	6%
on co-worker's privacy (such as paging during dinner)	
Listened to a private cellular phone conversation	5%
Visited pornographic websites using office equipment	5%
Sabotaged systems/data of former employer	4%
Sabotaged systems/data of current co-worker or employer	4%

- Listened to a private cellular phone conversation

- Visited pornographic websites using office equipment

- Sabotaged systems/data of former employer

- Sabotaged systems/data of current co-worker or employer

For the most part actions that were considered the most unethical—such as sabotaging systems or data, accessing private files without permission, and listening to private cellular phone calls—were committed the least often (Table 5). However, though the percentages are low for these actions the potential serious consequences coupled with the extremely high percentage who believed these actions to be highly unethical, makes even these relatively low percentages significant.

Among other significant findings: an equal percentage of men and women (5%) reported visiting a pornographic website using office equipment. The highest percentage in this category were those 50–54 years old (8%), business owners (11%) and those working "at home businesses" (12%).

Twenty-eight percent of workers between the ages 30–34 and 24% of those with postgraduate degrees admitted to copying the company's software for home use (compared to 13% overall).

We also presented workers with 16 actions related to technology in the workplace and asked them to indicate the extent to which they believed the action was unethical. Of the 16 actions, a majority felt strongly that 12 of the 16 were unethical.

However, the majority of respondents did not believe the following actions were unethical: play computer games on office equipment during work hours (51%), use office equipment to help your children/spouse do school work (63%), use company e-mail for personal reasons (66%) and use office equipment for personal reasons (71%).

TABLE 5

Actions Related to Technology Considered Unethical	
Sabotage systems/data of current co-worker or employer	96%
Sabotage systems/data of former employer	96%
Access private computer files without permission	93%
Listen to a private cellular phone conversation	92%
Visit pornographic websites using office equipment	87%
Use new technologies to unnecessarily intrude on co-workers' privacy (such as paging during dinner)	70%
Copy the company's software for home use	65%
Create a potentially dangerous situation by using new technology while driving	67%
Use office equipment to network/search for another job	66%
Wrongly blame an error you made on a technological glitch	61%
Make multiple copies of software for office use	59%
Use office equipment to shop on the Internet for personal reasons	54%

While only 29% overall consider the use of office equipment for personal reasons to be unethical, 60% of those over 60 years of age felt that it was.

Clearly, new technologies have changed the way we do our jobs and the way we work with one another. In terms of productivity and speed of communications, these changes have undoubtedly been positive. But what have been the costs? Have new technologies increased our level of anxiety? Have person-to-person relationships suffered? Do the benefits of new technologies require us to sacrifice our privacy and increase the risk of unethical and illegal behavior in the workplace?

SO WHAT DOES THE FUTURE HOLD?

When asked to look toward the 21st century, respondents saw a number of very serious problems facing our society related to new technology. They were:

- Increased availability of offensive/dangerous material on the Internet   76%

- Invasion of privacy by the government   76%

- Invasion of privacy by businesses   75%

- Loss of person-to-person contact   65%

- The accumulation of personal data in computer databases   64%

- The displacement of workers by technology   60%

- Monopolies in the software or information industries   60%

- Government efforts to limit freedom of speech on the Internet   50%

"When developing solutions, organizations need to be sure that the tactics they employ aren't as unethical as the actions they are designed to discourage," explains EOA Executive

Director Edward Petry. The survey found that American workers are *not* in favor of solutions that have a "Big Brother" overtone or those that may be perceived as invading privacy. They do not want government involved, nor do they want management to monitor or look into their e-mails and files.

For solutions, survey respondents overwhelmingly were in favor of more passive corporate solutions that center on empowering employees to change behavior. These solutions included: create personal use of company resources guidelines, 88%; create policies on personal use of technology, 87%; encourage employees to police themselves, 84%; install Internet blocking software, 83%; and start corporate training sessions on ethics, 81%.

"One of the survey objectives was to ascertain what organizations can do to address unethical corporate behavior," states Edward Miller, president of the SFSP. "We also recognized that corporations may need help in implementing the solutions workers wanted. We hope that managers will turn to the American Society and the EOA. The issues raised in the study are exactly the kind of complex, system-wide problems that bring managers to our meetings and programs."

An increasing number of organizations, large and small, are creating internal programs and policies to help employees make ethical business decisions related to new technologies. As an indication of the increasing interest in this area, nearly all of the member companies of the EOA have policies and guidelines related to the use of new technologies.

At conferences and other meetings, members of both the EOA and the SFSP have voiced their belief that new technologies in the workplace are a significant factor in increasing the risk of unethical and illegal business practices and the issue has been in the forefront of communications and educational planning.

New technologies have made a huge impact on corporations large and small. Today, to run a business with no laptop, no fax machine, and no salesman with a cell phone is practically unheard of. But organizations must ensure that along with these new tools they also provide guidelines, support and direction for their appropriate usage. The promises of new technologies abound but so too do the ethical issues they raise. With technology here to stay, it's high time for all organizations to take a close look at the ways employees are using these tools and create both the technological and ethical workplace of the future.

NOTES

1. Edward S. Petry, Amanda E. Mujica, and Dianne M. Vickery, "Sources and Consequences of Workplace Pressure: Increasing the Risk of Unethical and Illegal Business Practices," *Business and Society Review* 99, 25–30.

TECHNOLOGY AND ETHICS
Privacy in the Workplace
Laura P. Hartman

Privacy in the workplace is one of the more troubling personal and professional issues of our time. This excerpt outlines the status of privacy in the workplace from a technological as well as a legal perspective. What was once considered as an inalienable right has now been reassessed as our society and the business world have grown ever more complex. Traditional ethical analysis offers some guidance on how to evaluate the balance between a worker's right to privacy and an employer's need for information with which to manage the workplace. But guidance is not the same as resolution: as concerns workplace privacy rights, there are many more questions than answers.

***

A. Ethical Issues Unique to Information Technology

It appears to me that in ethics the difficulties are mainly due to the attempt to answer questions without first discovering precisely what question it is which you desire to answer.

—George Edward Moore

Information technology provides us with a host of ethical challenges. New technology poses new implications for the balance of power in the workplace. We now have in-home offices, allowing for greater invasions. Moreover, the line between personal and professional lives has become blurred, as workers conduct personal business in the office and professional business at home. The office usually provides faster, cheaper and easier access to the Internet, while some work must be done at home in order to be completed according to our modern, technologically enhanced pace.

Faculty members, for instance, do not go home and become people other than faculty members. We often conduct work at home such as grading, class preparation and so on. Similarly, our profession affords us a great deal of autonomy in terms of how we spend our days. We do not punch a clock or hand in a time sheet. All of my students have my home

---

number. My professional and personal lives are awfully blurred. (Sometimes, I wish they were not so blurred!)

Technology allows employers to ask more of each employee because now we are capable of greater production; we have greater abilities due to technology. We don't seem to know when our workday is over. I used to be a lawyer, and the understanding in that profession was, if you can work more hours, you do. This is because you will then be viewed as the preferred colleague. You will be the one who is going to get the plum assignments because you work so darn hard.

Other issues are raised by enhanced technology. For instance, should the technological ability to find something out make it relevant? With new employment-testing technology, you can find out all sorts of personal information. Through genetic testing, hair follicle testing, drug testing, your employer can find out anything it wants to know about you. Similarly, here, should the employer find out the information simply because it can?

In addition, new technology allows for a more faceless communication. If you have to fire someone, it is significantly easier to fire that person by e-mail than to walk into her or his office. In the latter case, you see the individual—desperate, perhaps disappointed, frustrated with the fact that you've worked them so hard and now you're terminating them. It's a lot easier to be nasty when you don't have to look your stakeholders in the face.

Finally, there is research showing that the excessive exertion of power and authority may lead to what they call a "semi-schizoid response," including insecurity, "disruption of biographical continuity," feelings of being overwhelmed and powerless, and doubts about worthiness. The implication is that, if someone questions you too much or takes away too much of your power, the ultimate cost may be your emotional security. Somewhat prophetically, Lawrence Lessig writes in his new bestseller, *Code,* "We have been as welcoming and joyous about the Net (and other technologies) as the earthlings were of the aliens in *Independence Day.* But at some point, we too will come to see a potential threat . . . and its extraordinary power for control."

B. Ethical Issues in the Privacy Arena

Specifically in connection with privacy, ethical issues arise with gathering information, assessing its accuracy, correcting it and disclosing it, as well as issues related to the substance of the information itself. Simply knowing that someone has personal information about you can feel invasive or violating. For that amorphous reason, privacy is a slightly difficult concept to define. Ethan Catch says it is "the ability to control what others can come to know about you." Why do we care that someone knows our personal information? We can imagine items of personal data that we simply do not want others knowing, whether or not they would actually do something with that information. We do not like people knowing things about us. It comes down to one's ability to be autonomous in controlling one's personal information.

Do you, personally, care about the information others know about you? Would you care if your boss knew of all your off-work activities? Consider Milton Hershey. Milton Hershey would tour Hershey, Pennsylvania, making note of workers' lawns that were not kept up, or homes that were not maintained. He would even hire private detectives to find out who was throwing trash in Hershey Park. Another business owner, Henry Ford, used to condition wages on workers' good behavior outside the factory. He had 150 inspectors in his "sociological department" to keep tabs on workers' hygiene habits and housekeeping.

Only recently did OSHA retract a statement that the occupational safety and health standards apply equally to workplaces and personal homes, when you work as a telecommuter. Can you imagine if you had to maintain the same standards of safety in your home that your employer must maintain at the traditional workplace?

C. Status of New Technology with Regard to Workplace Privacy

A multitude of basic and inexpensive computer monitoring products allows managers to track web use, to observe downloaded files, to filter sites, to restrict your access to certain sites, and to know how much time you have spent on various sites. These include products such as WebSense, Net Access Manager, WebTrack and Internet Watchdog.

One particular firm, SpyShop.com, claims to service one-third of the Fortune 500 firms. This firm sells items such as a truth-telling device that links to a telephone. You are told that you can interview a job candidate on the phone and the device identifies those who lie. Another firm, Omnitracks, sells a satellite that fastens to the top or inside of a truck. The product allows trucking firms to locate trucks at all times. If a driver veers off the highway to get flowers for her or his partner on Valentine's Day, the firm will know what happened.

SpyZone.com sells an executive investigator kit that includes the truth phone I mentioned earlier, as well as a pocket recording pen. Other outlets sell pinhole lens camera pens, microphones that fit in your pocket. The motto of one firm is "In God we trust. All others we monitor." That firm offers a beeper buster: a computer program that monitors calls placed to beepers within a certain vicinity. A screen on your computer will show you all the numbers so that you can determine whether the individual is being distracted during working hours.

D. Competing Interests

The predominant question that I have sought to answer by my recent research is whether a balance is possible between the employer's interest in managing the workplace and the employees' interest in privacy. Do employees even have a right to privacy? If one believes the answer is "no," then the entire issue becomes moot. If the employee does have some, even limited, right to privacy, one must seek to find a balance of interest. While we will return to the consideration of "rights" as we apply ethical theories, below, it is helpful to identify the proposed rights in dispute.

The employer has a right to manage the workplace. More specifically, employers want to manage the workplace so that they can place workers in the appropriate positions. They want to ensure compliance with affirmative action and administer workplace benefits. They want to ensure effective or productive performance. They need to know what their workers are doing in their workplace. The employer's perspective is as follows: "I am paying them to be there working. If they are not working, I should know that and either pay them less, or hire different workers." It seems like a relatively understandable concern.

Employees, on the other hand, want to be treated as free, equal, capable and rational individuals who have the ability to make their own decisions about the way their lives will unfold. They are interested in aiding their own personal development and valued performance (the lack of privacy may prevent "flow"); in conducting *some* personal business at the office; in being free from monitoring for performance reasons (wary of increased stress/pressure from monitoring); in being free from monitoring for privacy reasons; and in being able to review and to correct misinformation in data collected.

Consider the issue of personal work conducted at the office. I get to work some days at 7:00 A.M. and don't leave until 7:00 P.M. Last I heard, many doctors' offices are not open before or after 7:00 in the morning or night. So when is one supposed to call and make an appointment, much less ever go to an appointment, if one is punching the clock with those hours? The employer has to understand that workers must be able to call the doctor and make an appointment. Workers need to be able to conduct *involuntary* personal matters at the office. Now, one might not need to e-mail their mother or chat on the phone with friends. Should workers still have the right to conduct that *voluntary* personal business? Perhaps the resolution lies in the precise definition of voluntary or involuntary business.

III. THE LAW, NEW TECHNOLOGY AND WORKPLACE PRIVACY

As dictated by the ethical decision-making process, one must obtain all the unbiased facts before responding to an ethical dilemma. Where new technology impacts the dilemma, the "facts" may be all the more difficult to ascertain, since we are not yet completely equipped to obtain the necessary information. For example, some scholars contend that nearly everyone who has a computer (estimated to be about 80 percent of the U.S. workforce) is subject to some form of information collection, no matter how much we protect ourselves. Another source reports that more than 30 million workers were subject to workplace monitoring last year, up from only 8 million in 1991. We are not yet at a point where we can even determine whether this information is realistic.

We are relatively certain about the ways in which information is collected. As of 1999, two-thirds of mid- to large-size firms conduct some form of monitoring, whether it is computer-based monitoring, video monitoring, monitoring of personal investments, or maybe simply monitoring key card access to the building or parking garage (up from 30 percent in 1993). Our style of working, even of communicating, has created greater possibilities for monitoring. In connection with e-mail, for instance, more than 90 million American workers now send more than 2.8 billion e-mail messages per day, an average of 190 e-mails per day, per worker. We might not be too concerned about some forms of monitoring, while other forms might feel particularly invasive.

A. Federal Legislation

More than 100 bills on privacy protection have been introduced in Congress, but only one has been approved, on the collection of personal information from kids over the Internet. Also, the White House right now is only supporting privacy protections related to medical information privacy because they believe that this type of uncertainty will dissolve as firms and employees become more comfortable with the medium.

B. Constitutional Protections

The Fourth Amendment to the U.S. Constitution protects the "right of the people to be secure in their persons, houses, papers and effects, against unreasonable searches and seizures." This protection implies a reasonable expectation of privacy against intrusions *by the State, only.* As this provision of the Constitution does not apply to actions by private sector employers, their employees must rely instead on state-by-state laws and the common law made and accepted in the courts. Similar limitation exists in connection with the First Amendment's protection of personal autonomy and the Fifth Amendment's protection against self-incrimination—each of these only protects the individual from invasions by the State. Currently, there is proposed employment-related privacy legislation in several states that would apply to private sector employers, but those states fall in the distinct minority.

What the courts will generally consider in cases involving both the Fourth Amendment and common law privacy protections is 1) whether the employer has a legitimate business interest in obtaining the information, and 2) whether the employee has a reasonable expectation of privacy. Several examples of common law actions by the courts are illustrative of the courts' attempts at creating this balance. Perhaps more significant are the settlements reached by firms concerned about the *prospect* of a judge's decision.

C. Case Law

In one recent case, two McDonalds restaurant employees used voice-mail to transmit love messages during an affair. They believed that these messages were private since the firm told them that only they had the access codes. The franchise owner monitored the voice-mail messages and later played messages for the wife of one of the workers. The lovers sued for invasion of privacy. They settled for several million dollars, so we do not yet have any judge's decision in a situation like this.

In another case that never made it to the courts, the Minnesota Attorney General sued several banks for revealing personal information about clients to marketers in exchange for more than $4 million in fees. One bank eventually agreed to pay attorney fees plus $2.5 million to Habitat for Humanity.

While the law has not yet settled in connection with monitoring or the privacy of obtained information—hence the settlements—monitoring does seem justified by several cases where e-mail was later used as evidence to encourage a settlement. Within the past several years, several large firms, including R. R. Donnelly, Morgan Stanley, and Citicorp, have found that cases often hinged on e-mail transmissions that people originally thought were deleted. In one case, this included an e-mail containing 165 racial, ethnic and sexual jokes sent to the entire firm. In another, the e-mail included sexual jokes about why beer is better than women. Had the firms enforced stringent policies about the use of e-mail and monitored to enforce these policies, perhaps these e-mails would never have been sent.

A few short months ago, the *New York Times* also found itself facing some problems. They fired 24 employees at a Virginia payroll processing center for sending "inappropriate and offensive e-mail in violation of corporate policy." The public sector is not immune from similar challenges: The U.S. Navy reported that it had disciplined more than 500 employees at a supply depot for sending sexually explicit e-mail. It happens all the time, and it's continuing to happen. You would think that people would actually learn.

In cases where the courts have been able to address the issue, it seemed at first that *notice* of monitoring might emerge as the critical factor. Perhaps persuaded by early case law, of the 67 percent of mid- to large-size firms that monitor, 84 percent notify their employees of this activity. Notice might range from a one-line comment in the middle of an employee manual that someone receives on the first day of work, to a dialogue box reminding you that e-mail may be monitored that pops up each time you hit the "send" button to transmit an e-mail.

In an early case addressing this topic, the court in *K-mart v. Trotti* held that the search of an employee's company-owned locker was not appropriate because the workers were told to use their own personal lock. The basis for the decision was that the employees were left with the legitimate, reasonable expectation of privacy because it was their own lock. On the other hand, an employer's search of employee lunch buckets was held reasonable by another court only two years earlier.

In a later 1990 case, *Shoars v. Epson,* Epson won a suit filed by an employee who complained about e-mail monitoring. In that case, the court distinguished the practice of intercepting an e-mail transmission from storing and reading e-mail transmissions once they had been sent, holding that the latter was acceptable. In a 1992 action, Northern Telecom settled a claim brought by employees who were allegedly secretly monitored for more than 13 years. In this case, Telecom agreed to pay $50,000 to individual plaintiffs and $125,000 for attorneys' fees.

Similarly, an employee-plaintiff in a 1995 federal action won a case against his employer, where the employer had monitored the worker's telephone for a period of 24 hours to determine whether the worker was planning a robbery. The court held that the company had gone too far and had insufficient evidence to support its claims.

One might therefore conclude that, if an employer adequately notifies workers that it will conduct monitoring, it has effectively destroyed any reasonable expectation of privacy on the part of the workers. It would now be unreasonable to expect privacy since one is told not to expect it. However, in a case where the alternative extreme was true, where a firm notified workers that it would not monitor, the court did not follow congruent logic. It did not find a reasonable expectation of privacy based on a firm's pledge not to read e-mail.

In that case, *Smyth v. Pillsbury,* Smyth sued the firm after a manager read his e-mail. At the time, Pillsbury had a policy saying that it would not read e-mail. One might presume that this policy should have created this reasonable expectation of privacy. But instead, this was the first federal decision to hold that a private sector, at-will employee has no right of privacy in the content of one's e-mail when one sends it over the employer's computer system. The court held, "We do not find a reasonable expectation of privacy in the contents of e-mail communications voluntarily made by an employee to his supervisor over the company e-mail system, notwithstanding any assurances that such communications would not be intercepted by management."

IV. THE LIMITATIONS OF THE LEGAL SYSTEM: A CALL FOR ETHICS

The law offers little, if any, guidance in this area in connection with workplace monitoring, and technology as a whole. In fact, the development of our moral systems has not been able to keep pace with technological and medical developments, leaving us prey individually and societally to a host of dangers. And does this not represent our current situation in terms of technological advances?

It never occurred to most workers that some of this information was available or that they could be monitored in various ways. When employers' access to personal information is not apparent, employees do not adequately protect themselves against it. Failure to completely understand the new technology may prevent people from completely understanding their exposure or potential vulnerability.

In his State of the Union address, former President Clinton said, "Technology has to be carefully directed to assure that its reach does not compromise societal values. We have to safeguard our citizens' privacy." The primary ethical issue for analysis is whether the employee's fundamental right to privacy outweighs the employer's right to administer the workplace according to its desires. If not, is there a way to satisfy both parties? As law does not yet provide the answers, we turn to ethics for guidance.

The strongest, most persuasive and most consistent guidance in this area is based on a theory called Integrative Social Contracts Theory (ISCT), promulgated by Tom Donaldson and Tom Dunfee, both faculty in Wharton's ethics program. ISCT seeks to differentiate between those values that are fundamental across culture and theory ("hypernorms") and those values that are culturally specific, determined within moral "free space," and which are not hypernorms. In identifying values as hypernorms, Donaldson and Dunfee propose that one look to the convergence of religious, cultural and philosophical beliefs around certain core principles. Included as examples of hypernorms are freedom of speech, the right to personal freedom, the right to physical movement, and informed consent. In fact, individual privacy is at the core of many of these basic, minimal rights and is, arguably, a necessary prerequisite to many of them.

Specifically, ISCT seeks evidence of the widespread recognition of ethical principles that support a hypernorm conclusion, such as:

1. Widespread consensus that the principle is universal;
2. Component of well-known industry standards;
3. Supported by prominent nongovernmental organizations such as the International Labor Organization or Transparency International;
4. Supported by regional government organizations such as the European Union, the Organization for Economic Cooperation and Development, or the Organization of American States;
5. Consistently referred to as a global ethical standard by international media;
6. Known to be consistent with precepts of major religions;
7. Supported by global business organizations such as the International Chamber of Commerce or the Caux Roundtable;
8. Known to be consistent with precepts of major philosophies;
9. Generally supported by a relevant international community of professionals, e.g., accountants or environmental engineers;
10. Known to be consistent with findings concerning universal human values;
11. Supported by the laws of many different countries.

With regard to privacy, a key finding of a recent survey of the status of privacy in 50 countries around the world included the following conclusion:

> *Privacy is a fundamental human right recognized in all major international treaties and agreements on human rights. Nearly every country in the world recognizes privacy as a fun-*

damental human right in their constitution, either explicitly or implicitly. Most recently drafted constitutions include specific rights to access and control one's personal information.

Accordingly, it would appear that the value of privacy to civilized society is as great as the value of the various hypernorms to civilized existence. Ultimately, the failure to protect privacy may lead to an inability to protect personal freedom and autonomy.

The application of ISCT, however, has limitations. ISCT does not quantify critical *boundaries* for rights. If employees have a right to privacy based on a hypernorm, how far does it extend and what should happen in a conflict? Doesn't the employer have certain hypernorm-based rights that might be infringed by the protection of the employees' privacy right? To quantify the boundaries of the universal rights, one must therefore look beyond ISCT to a more fairness-based methodology.

Ethicist John Rawls's theory of distributive economic justice provides fairness-based guidance for quantifying the boundary levels of fundamental rights. Distributive justice is a teleological approach to ethical decision-making that defines ethical acts as those that lead to an equitable distribution of goods and services. To determine a fair method for distributing goods and services, Rawls suggests that one consider how we would distribute goods and services if we were under a "veil of ignorance" that prevented us from knowing our status in society (i.e., our intelligence, wealth, appearance). He asks that we consider what rules we would impose on this society if we had no idea whether we would be princes or paupers. Without knowing what role we might play in our society, would we devise a system of constant employee monitoring or complete privacy in all professional and personal endeavors? Rawls contends that those engaged in the exercise would build a cooperative system that was sensitive to the interests of all stakeholders. The reason Rawls believes that such a standard would emerge is that the members of the exercise do not know whether they would be among the employer population or employee population. Actions consistent with a system devised under a veil of ignorance are deemed ethical because of the inherent fairness of the system.

Rawls's theory of distributive justice does not provide guidance for identifying the categories of fundamental rights. What Rawls does provide is a method for establishing distribution rules that avoid market transgressions of the boundaries of ethical actions.

Conjoining ISCT and Rawlsian methods enables the identification of basic human rights and boundaries, and provides for a reasonable balance between economic and ethical consequences of privacy protection for both employees and employers. ISCT establishes the underlying or foundational hypernorms within a society, while distributive justice offers guidance on the extent of those hypernorms and the means by which to implement them.

Scholars are not in complete agreement as to whether a right to privacy is a hypernorm, though most would agree that some form of personal autonomy must be protected. As mentioned above, evidence of a hypernorm such as freedom from slavery unequivocally supports this conclusion—personal autonomy serves as a cornerstone of this protection. On the other hand, the quantification of one's right to privacy, in particular workplace privacy, is better identified using a Rawlsian analysis. A proposal for such a fairness-based balance follows.

The Implementation of an Ethical Resolution   Assuming for the purposes of this argument that privacy is a hypernorm, but one that may be limited by the employer's congruent right to managerial autonomy, how should the matter be resolved? I suggest a fairness-based decision based on two values: integrity and accountability.

Integrity, meaning consistency in values, would require that the decision-maker define her or his values, as well as create a prioritization of those values. This effort is often accomplished by a firm's mission statement or statement of values. Then, when faced with a dilemma or conflict between two or more of these values, the decision-maker will have internal as well as external guidance regarding the direction her or his decision should take. Second, no matter which direction is taken, the decision-maker must be accountable to anyone who is impacted by this decision. That would require a consideration of the impact of alternatives on each stakeholder; a balancing of that impact with the personal values addressed in the first step; and actions that represent the accountability to the stakeholders impacted by the decision.

Applying this process to a firm's response to monitoring and its impact on employee privacy, the firm may obtain guidance from its mission statement or alternative statement of values. Does monitoring satisfy or further the mission or values of the firm? Assuming that monitoring satisfies or furthers the values of the firm (since a negative relationship here would end the discussion and resolve the dilemma), the employer must impose monitoring in a manner that is accountable to those affected by the decision to monitor.

To be accountable to the impacted employees, the employer must respect their privacy rights and their right to make informed decisions about their actions. Accordingly, this model would require that the employer should give adequate notice of the intent to monitor, including the form of monitoring, its frequency, and the purpose of the monitoring. In addition, to balance the employer's interests with those of the workforce, the employer should offer a means by which the employee can control the monitoring in order to create personal boundaries. In other words, if the employer is randomly monitoring telephone calls, there should be a notification device such as a beep whenever monitoring is taking place, or the employee should have the ability to block any monitoring during personal calls. This latter option would address an oft-cited challenge to notification: If employees have notice of monitoring, there is no possibility of random performance checks. However, if employees can merely block personal calls, they remain unaware of which business-related calls are being monitored.

If It Feels Wrong, It Probably Is   Ethicist Gary Marks suggests that we look to a number of questions about monitoring, and he proposes that if you answer "yes" to these questions, your monitoring is more likely to be unethical.

- Does the collection of the data involve physical or psychological harm?

- Does the technique cross a personal boundary without permission?

- Could the collection produce invalid results?

- Are you being more intrusive than necessary?

- Is the data subject prohibited from appealing or changing the information recorded?

- Are there negative effects on those beyond the data subject?

- Is the link between the information collected and the goal sought unclear?

- Is the data being used in such a way as to cause a disadvantage to the subject?

As a manager, you are not without guidance on these issues. Kevin Conlon, district counsel for the Communication Workers of America, suggests additional guidelines that may be considered in formulating an accountable process for employee monitoring:

- There should be no monitoring in highly private areas, such as restrooms;

- Monitoring should be limited to the workplace;

- Employees should have full access to any information gathered through monitoring;

- Continuous monitoring should be banned;

- All forms of secret monitoring should be banned;

- Advance notice should be given;

- Only information relevant to the job should be collected;

- Monitoring should result in the attainment of some business interest.

Moreover, in its bargaining demands for last year, the Union of the United Auto Workers demanded concessions with regard to monitoring, including:

- Monitoring only under mutual prior agreement;

- No secret monitoring: advance notice required of how, when, and for what purpose employees will be monitored;

- Employees should have access to information gathered through monitoring;

- Strict limitations regarding disclosure of information gained through monitoring;

- Prohibition of discrimination by employers based on off-work activities.

***

From the employees' perspective, this type of resolution would respect their personal autonomy by providing for personal space, by giving notice of where that space ends, by giving them access to and the right to change or correct the information gathered, and by providing for monitoring that is directed toward the personal development of the employee and not merely toward catching wrongdoers.

From the employer's perspective, this balance offers a way to effectively but ethically supervise the work done by their employees. It protects the misuse of resources, while also allowing employers to better evaluate their workers and to encourage their workers to be more effective. I contend that any program that fails to satisfy these basic elements has the potential not only for ethical lapses, but also for serious economic problems.

Vice President and current presidential candidate Al Gore, who of course is an appropriate person to quote since he "invented" the Internet, claims that "new technology must not reopen the oldest threats to our basic rights: liberty and privacy. But government should not simply block or regulate all that electronic progress. If we are to move at a full speed ahead into the information age, government must do more to protect your rights—in a way that empowers you more, not less. We need an electronic bill of rights for this electronic age."

VI. CONCLUDING THOUGHTS

Before I conclude my remarks, I ask that you consider the following questions not only with regard to information technology and the impact that that technology has on your particular workplace, but also with regard to the ethical issues that arise in other areas of your work. Consider what you might be willing to quit over. What would be so damaging, so intrusive, so much of a violation of your personal space that you would simply quit right then and there? What could be so bad?

Second—and perhaps it seems extreme in this particular circumstance—what would you be willing to give your life for? You may not believe right now that information technology is going to present life-and-death ethical dilemmas. And yet when we consider the ultimate usage of some of that technology, it really does have a life-and-death impact. If you knew that it would have a fatal, negative impact, would you quit if your firm or client failed to ameliorate it? Monitoring probably does not fall within this range, but you can imagine situations where technology does allow such an extreme unethical and certainly illegal act.

The reason I want to conclude with this query is because this is really the purpose of the lecture. The world is a better place because you have thought about these questions now, rather than when you are first faced with these challenges in the workplace.

IN CYBERSPACE, EVERYONE CAN HEAR YOU SCREAM

Daniel S. Levine

Levine describes circumstances between Smith Barney and one of its ex-employees, Michael Lissack. The interaction became more extreme as a result of Lissack's use of a website to distribute information about his employment situation. It is interesting to note that Lissack has now removed the information referred to in this article from the Web.

Smith Barney, Inc., the New York investment banking firm, isn't too happy that Michael Lissack has set up a website.

Lissack, a whistleblower who gave up a 13-year career at Smith Barney, where he rose to become a managing director in the investment bank's public finance department, now continues his crusade against his former employer and others in the industry he says are cheating the public out of millions of dollars.

Earlier this month, attorneys for the investment firm sent letters to Lissack and his attorneys, accusing Lissack of infringing on the trademarks of Smith Barney and its parent Travelers Group, Inc.

Among other things, his website Municipal Bond Scandals features The Smith Barney Page, which includes a drawing of a pickpocket at work next to text that reads, "Making money the 'old fashioned way,' " a play on the company's slogan.

The case is another example of the equalizing effects of the Internet that allows a whistleblower to be heard as loudly as the multibillion dollar target of his alarm and the difficulties people have when they try to stifle free expression on the medium.

Even though Lissack responded to the first letter by taking down a Smith Barney logo from his site to avoid another legal battle, the letters persisted. Lissack said he believes Smith Barney's big concern is that as they push forward to make a big splash on the Internet, Web search engines will carry people interested in Smith Barney to his page.

In fact, that is a concern that Smith Barney's attorneys at Orrick, Herrington & Sutcliffe make clear in their letters. They want all references to Smith Barney struck from his pages. They accused him of repeatedly using the firm's name to cause search engines to find his page "as one of the most relevant on the subject of the 'Smith Barney.' "

Ironically, in their efforts to silence Lissack, they've merely spread references to the controversy throughout the Web and Usenet, expanding the chances that a search engine will point someone interested in Smith Barney to Lissack.

Lissack said he will not remove the Smith Barney references from his pages. He doesn't believe he is violating the company's trademark. Smith Barney intends to pursue further actions according to a representative quoted in The Bond Buyer.

Smith Barney is currently involved in a New York Stock Exchange arbitration case in which Lissack alleges the firm wrongfully discharged him for his whistleblowing and also defamed him. He is seeking $75 million in damages. Smith Barney filed a $15 million counterclaim charging that Lissack has tried to damage their business by spreading false and derogatory information.

He began supplying information to the FBI anonymously in Dec. 1993, 14 months before going public and being fired. He said he waited until then because he wanted to get as much of his deferred compensation as possible.

"Most of the people who blow the whistle are not in a financial position where they would still do it if they understood the consequences," said Lissack. "I, on the other hand, am still very comfortable."

That's not to say his whistleblowing experiences have been a lot of fun. During the ordeal and since, Lissack survived a suicide attempt, a divorce, the loss of his job as well as many friends.

On February 1, 1995, he informed his employer that he did not plan to remain silent when called before a grand jury. He was fired days later.

In a piece in the *New York Times,* Lissack shed light on what is known as "yield burning," a practice of charging excessive markups on government securities that are sold to municipalities. It has been estimated that in the early 1990s, Wall Street firms made an extra $1 billion from this practice.

Unlike refinancing a mortgage where a homeowner can retire high interest debt with new, lower-interest debt, because of the way deals are structured, municipalities usually have to wait at least 10 years before they can pay off bondholders. If interest rates fall, municipalities will refinance their debt and purchase Treasury securities with the proceeds and hold them in an escrow account until the higher interest bonds can be retired.

Under law, though, they are prohibited from profiting on those escrow accounts. So, Lissack said, the investment firms decided to capture that profit for themselves by marking up the Treasury securities and then getting opinions from friendly competitors that the securities were being sold at fair market price.

Lissack said his whistleblowing has been involved in more than one dozen civil and criminal investigations by the U.S. Securities and Exchange Commission, Internal Revenue Service and the U.S. Department of Justice. Smith Barney has previously denied any wrongdoing.

Though Smith Barney maintains a prominent place on his website, Lissack said he is trying to show the range of illegal and unethical activity investment firms perpetuate in the municipal bond market and to offer a source of broad and alternative coverage to the limited news people usually get about public finance.

One unexpected consequence of his website is that it has become a direct line for whistleblowers to pass on information about other Municipal Bond Scandals to authorities, while protecting their anonymity.

"The part I hadn't given any thought to is that I've created a safety net for people," he said. "They look at the page and get stuff to me to pass on."

ELEMENTS OF
A SUCCESSFUL
E-MAIL POLICY

GERARD PANARO

In an effort to avoid both ethical challenges and legal liability, more than two-thirds of medium- to large-sized firms in the United States have designed and implemented policies that address e-mail and other computer resource usage. Often the policy includes no more than notice to the workforce that e-mail or other use might be monitored. Mr. Panaro suggests additional elements that comprise a legally sufficient, defensible workplace e-mail policy.

1. **Written policy.** First, of course, any policy should be in writing. It should make clear to employees that the security of their e-mail is not guaranteed and that e-mail may not be protected by privacy law. The policy should state that employees should have no expectation of privacy in the workplace. Office equipment is the property of the company and for office use; employees' use of equipment is subject to monitoring, may be accessed with or without notice, disclosed to others, and used to evaluate, reward and/or discipline employees. The policy should state that messages on the system are considered to be company records.

It may be a good idea to explain to employees how e-mail works, so they understand better why it may not be as private or confidential as they assume. Any explanations should be accurate, however. Suppose, for example, that the IT department tells employees if they delete a message on the same day it is sent or received, before it is backed up overnight, it is gone forever and irretrievable; or suppose, in response to an employee's query, who wants to recover a message s/he has inadvertently deleted, IT says it cannot be recovered. Such statements could be evidence of an expectation of privacy: an employee says s/he thought it was OK to send and receive pornographic, racial or sexual jokes so long as they were immediately deleted.

It is also recommended that if the employer uses software that enables managers to know which employees may be using the internet, and which sites they may be visiting, that this information be disclosed up front to affected employees, and they be warned to make sure their internet use is for legitimate business only.

2. **Passwords don't guarantee privacy.** Second, a written e-mail policy will also warn that giving employees passwords, varying levels of message protection and other security measures does not necessarily create any right to privacy or guarantee no access. Make sure employees aren't misled. In fact, consideration should be given to insisting that

employees give all codes, passwords and other security information to someone in the company, in case of emergency.

3. **Reasons justifying access.** Third, it is important that the policy set forth the legitimate business reasons why e-mail may be monitored and accessed. Every possible justification listed below may not apply to every employer, but legitimate business reasons typically include the following:

- Assess performance

- Reduce personal communications

- Improve the work product

- Protect against theft, fraud, computer crime

- Remain competitive

- Search for violations in disclosing trade secrets

- Obtain information in a business emergency or the absence of the employee

- Retrieve lost messages

- Help employees effectively use the e-mail system

- Determine whether employee gossip hurts workplace morale

- Promote efficiency

- Provide a workplace that is free of unlawful discrimination (e.g., sexual, racial, other forms of illegal harassment)

- Insure that system is being used properly (e.g., no illegal gambling, no receipt, transmission or trafficking in obscenity, pornography, pedophilia)

- Investigate complaints of improper use (customers, other employees)

4. **Employee usage guidelines.** Fourth, the policy should establish employee usage guidelines, such as whether or not the system may be used for nonbusiness (personal) exchanges, and if so, when and to what extent. For example, the company may be willing to allow its employees to use e-mail for personal reasons outside of normal working hours, or if the employee is willing to pay for his or her usage. It is recommended that at least some personal use of e-mail almost has to be allowed, for at least three very practical reasons: employees can't completely control e-mail sent to them from other sources; employees are going to make personal use of the system anyway; policing and disciplining employees for personal use will be almost impossible, will divert the company from its primary business, and could backfire in the sense that it becomes so intrusive it triggers legal challenge.

5. **Violators subject to discipline.** Fifth, state in the policy that employees who violate it will be subject to discipline. There are a couple of guidelines to keep in mind here: if the company has an employment at will policy, then make sure this component of the e-mail policy is consistent with that policy; if the company follows a progressive discipline policy or dismisses only for cause, then the e-mail discipline policy should likewise be con-

sistent. The level of discipline will obviously be proportionate to the circumstances, such as nature of the violation, frequency, prior violations, etc.

6. **Dispute resolution procedure.** Sixth, consider providing in the policy a mechanism for addressing complaints. The company has be careful here, however, to strike the right balance: on the one hand, it will want to afford employees "basic due process"; but on the other, it does not want such an elaborate system of complaints, hearings, appeals, reviews, etc., as to make the process interminable.

7. **Managerial discretion.** Seventh, spell out when managers can search for or interfere with e-mail. This will be a crucial element of the policy, because if the company limits the circumstances under which it can access employees' e-mail, then it risks liability if it should ever exceed its own self-imposed limits. A long list of such occasions has already been given. Certainly, the company will want to reserve the right to go into e-mail in case of emergency, and emergency does not only refer to physical threats, such as fire or bomb scares. An emergency can be a customer or client screaming for something right away, and the person who would normally deal with the situation is out.

The company will also want the right to access employees' e-mail when it is investigating unlawful discrimination or harassment, based on sex, race, disability or any other protected category. In fact, in view of the recent Supreme Court decisions heightening employers' liability for harassment in the workplace, and cases that have been decided in light of the Court's opinions, this business justification becomes all the more compelling.[1]

A third obvious time when the employer may want the right to monitor is when the employee's performance, evaluation and/or appraisal are in issue. Whatever the criteria decided upon, the important point is to spell them out and be sure the company adheres to them.

---

[1]In 1998, the U.S. Supreme Court decided two cases that significantly raised the stakes for employers in sexual harassment suits (and, indeed, for claims of harassment under any other protected category, such as race, age, disability, religion, etc.), Burlington Industries, Inc. v. Ellerth, 118 S.Ct. 2257, and Faragher v. City of Boca Raton, 118 S.Ct. 2275. These are the major holdings of the two decisions on when an employer is liable for sexual harassment:

- As a threshold matter, to state a claim for unlawful sexual harassment under Title VII, the federal anti-discrimination statute, a victim must be able to show that the conduct complained of was sufficiently severe and pervasive (this will be discussed further below).
- Title VII is not a "general civility code." Discourtesy, rudeness, insensitivity, simple teasing, offhand comments, isolated incidents (unless extremely serious) will not amount to unlawful sexual harassment.
- In the case of sexual harassment by a co-employee, the employer is going to be liable only if it was negligent: that is, it knew or should have known the sexual harassment was going on, and did nothing to stop it.
- In the case of sexual harassment by a supervisor that results in an actual adverse job action against the victim, the employer will always be liable, regardless of how careful it was. An employer has no defense to such "quid pro quo" harassment by a supervisor.
- In the case of sexual harassment by a supervisor that does not result in an adverse job action against the victim ("hostile environment" sexual harassment), the employer will still be subject to suit. However, it may have a defense to the claim.
- The defense consists of two elements:
  - The employer acted promptly to prevent and correct sexual harassment and
  - The employee failed to take advantage of any preventive or corrective opportunities provided by the employer (e.g., failed to complain or use the sexual harassment policy).

8.   **Access by third parties.** Eighth, the policy should address the issue of third-party access. For example, a company may want to have a policy of being able to regulate the sources of e-mail and to delete or block transmissions to employees from sources not approved. It may also wish to forbid employees from accessing or subscribing to certain sites, even if the employee is willing to pay the cost.

9.   **Signed acknowledgement of having received policy.** Ninth, it is probably a good idea to have employees sign an acknowledgement or receipt form for the e-mail policy. If the policy is incorporated in an employee handbook, a receipt for the handbook is enough; if the policy is free-standing, it may have its own receipt form.

Practical Advice for Implementing the Policy   Writing a policy on e-mail in the workplace is only the beginning. An indispensable element to its success will be how the policy is implemented. In this respect, the following steps are recommended.

Perhaps the single most practical advice to give on implementing an e-mail policy is this: when monitoring does become necessary, *use the least intrusive means possible.* The simplest rule to follow may be that ordinarily, the company will not monitor employees' e-mail traffic unless and until a complaint is received or there is a rational basis or articulable suspicion that the system is being misused. An employee, for example, may complain that s/he is receiving annoying or harassing e-mail from another; an employee may complain that s/he is receiving objectionable e-mail from an anonymous source; an enforcement agency (whether the EEOC investigating a charge, a litigant or law enforcement) may request the company's cooperation in accessing employees' e-mail. A manager may notice that one of his or her subordinates seems to be spending an inordinate amount of time on e-mail, a customer may call to complain that its e-mails have not been answered, or a manager may notice a fall-off in productivity. But whatever the source or reason, the basic rule will be: We will not monitor any employee's e-mail unless a complaint has arisen or we have a reasonable suspicion that something is amiss.

A second way to make monitoring as unintrusive as possible, of course, is to limit those who have authority to monitor (to order monitoring), those to whom information is disseminated, and/or the nature, quantity and detail of information that is monitored or disclosed. For example, the company may give the right to monitor only to the IT department, only to HR, to security or to corporate counsel. The company might even contract out the job to an independent security or investigative firm.

A third technique is to avoid any intrusion into, or dissemination of, the actual contents of e-mail, but to monitor simply "transactional" or frequency information. To determine that an employee is abusing e-mail, as an illustration, it may only be necessary to document that whereas the average employee sends or receives only a dozen e-mails a day, this employee is sending or receiving more than a hundred. It would not even be necessary to go into contents; the numbers alone would raise suspicions or prove the point.

In implementing a policy on e-mail, especially if the policy is new, take multiple steps to make sure employees are aware of the policy and have received a copy. Some suggestions are to make the policy a part of the application process, include it with a letter offering a job, print free-standing copies of the policy and hand these out separately, even if the policy is already contained in the employee handbook; make employees sign a paper acknowledging receipt. Periodically review the policy, in light of experience, new developments, new cases, changes in technology or the business.

Summary and Conclusion   The law clearly recognizes and protects an employer's right to monitor employees' e-mail (and other office communications). Indeed, the authors of law review articles and op-ed pieces in newspapers and magazines decry the lack of protection for employees' privacy interests in the workplace. Employees have no automatic privacy rights in the workplace. The key to protecting itself is for the company to have a written policy on electronic communications in the workplace, make sure employees are aware of it, and to be judicious in its implementation of the policy in terms of making monitoring as little intrusive as possible.

THE ETHICAL AND LEGAL QUANDARY OF E-MAIL PRIVACY

Janice C. Sipior and Burke T. Ward

Most of us have never considered some of these issues, much less decided how we feel about them or know how our employer might feel about them. Sipior and Ward address some of these ethical issues and discuss how they might be resolved.

How private are employees' e-mail messages? The answer is unclear. This lack of clarity means that protection of employee e-mail will be at the forefront of legal controversy for at least the rest of the decade.

Privacy protection is not a new issue, and employee privacy encompasses a spectrum of issues, including:

- Drug testing;

- Searches of employees and their work areas;

- Psychological testing;

- Telephone, computer, and electronic monitoring; and

- Other types of employee surveillance.

The controversial nature of these areas demands that employers and employees, as well as those with whom they interact—consultants, information service support personnel, suppliers, and customers—be aware of, and responsive to, expectations of and concerns about privacy. Users and organizations naive about ethical conduct and the legal parameters concerning e-mail privacy are vulnerable to harm caused by intrusions. This article examines the potentially conflicting expectations of employers and employees regarding the ethical and legal aspects of privacy invasions in e-mail communications. It also examines the U.S. legal system to determine the applicability of federal and state constitutional law, state common law, and federal and state statutory sources in protecting e-mail privacy.

E-MAIL AND ETHICS

Organizations have an obligation to their employees, business partners, customers, and society, as well as to themselves, to act ethically. However, ethical behavior is often difficult to achieve. A primary concern is actual or potential harm to individuals and groups. What is ethical and what is unethical? Answers are not straightforward. Societal standards of "good," "right," and "moral" help guide our behavior, but do not provide definitive answers for all situations. The political debate on individual and workplace privacy highlights the lack of consensus of opinion with respect to ethics and privacy. Legislatures and courts are being asked to resolve the ethical and legal questions raised by drug testing, physical searches of persons and places, electronic surveillance, and other privacy issues. This article seeks to raise awareness of the ethical issues of e-mail privacy by identifying the vulnerabilities plaguing e-mail and the privacy expectations of employers and employees regarding their use of e-mail.

The increasing number of computer users, applications, and system interconnections, along with the increasing complexity of overall technological capabilities, means a greater chance for e-mail privacy to be compromised. E-mail privacy invasions are characterized along two dimensions: sources of invasion and types of invasion. E-mail communications are at risk for interception from sources both internal and external to the organization. Internal sources are people employed by the organization, including executives, managers, and co-workers. External sources are people with whom the organization interacts, through formal and informal relationships. Formal relationships can link service providers, consultants, suppliers, and customers. Interaction may also occur in the absence of formal relationships—with competitors, corporate spies, and hackers.

An invasion may be authorized or unauthorized—that is, it may be condoned by an internal authority, such as a manager, an external authority, such as a law-enforcement agency, or may be a totally unauthorized privacy violation. These combinations are organized into four cells. This article focuses on internally authorized interception of e-mail messages.

EMPLOYERS' VIEW OF E-MAIL PRIVACY

E-mail monitoring in organizations may be viewed by employers as a necessity, as well as a right. As owners of the resources, employers may assume the right to monitor e-mail. Such monitoring may or may not be ethically acceptable or legally permissible. But the reasons offered by employers for doing so may appear ethical and legal, including prevention of personal use or abuse of company resources, the prevention or investigation of corporate espionage or theft, cooperation with law-enforcement officials in investigations, the resolution of technical problems, or other special circumstances.

A grayer area is when internal e-mail monitoring is used to track worker performance. In this case, it is not just suspected individuals whose e-mail is read. Hardworking employees might use e-mail to help make a sale or to meet work deadlines; if not for their record of correspondence, their productivity and accomplishments may otherwise go unnoticed.

For publicly traded companies, an employer must ensure that employees abide by Securities and Exchange Commission rules. A company that fails to monitor performance by examining e-mail messages sent to external destinations might be failing to protect trade secrets and proprietary information.

To achieve the positive results in these examples, all messages sent and received by employees would be subject to scrutiny. Some may regard this as an unethical disregard of employee privacy. Information an employee intends to keep private and confidential may be examined. However, an employer could argue that since the e-mail system is owned by the employer and is to be used for the employer's purposes, the employee should not expect communications to be private. The employer would conclude that e-mail monitoring is not unethical because employees have no reasonable expectation of privacy with respect to the employer's e-mail system. Conversely, some may argue that monitoring is indeed an unethical invasion of an individual's privacy in light of the potential for negative consequences.

Monitoring can be a double-edged sword for those being monitored. Productive and exceptional employees, as well as employees who are unproductive, could be readily identified throughout the organization.

EMPLOYEES' VIEW OF E-MAIL PRIVACY

From the employees' perspective, the content—even the existence—of e-mail messages may be regarded as confidential, private correspondence between sender and receiver(s). This perception seems reasonable, given that e-mail is accessed as a facility in users' computer accounts, to which access is password-controlled, providing a sense of confidentiality. Further, most people are familiar with the privacy protection of the U.S. mail and may assume it applies to e-mail as well. Thus, users can mistakenly and reasonably assume that e-mail messages are free from interception.

Electronic surveillance for the purpose of improving job performance, product quality, and productivity takes many forms. For example, e-mail messages are usually sent and received in directly readable, unencrypted alphanumeric form, intended for immediate reading. Employee computer screens may be viewed or messages may be intercepted without employee knowledge or consent. E-mail messages are thus exposed to employer scrutiny. At Epson America, Inc., an e-mail system administrator, Alana Shoars, claimed to have been terminated in 1991 for protesting the routine practice of intercepting and printing employees' MCI e-mail. In her case, *Shoars v. Epson America, Inc.,* she claimed Epson's invasion of privacy and her termination violated California law [16]. In another 1991 case, *Bourke v. Nissan Motor Corp.,* two software specialists contended they were forced to quit after a supervisor read their personal e-mail correspondence, which included sexual statements [3]. They also claimed invasion of privacy and wrongful termination in violation of California law.

In both cases, the companies' right to manage their e-mail systems was legally recognized. But because both were tried in lower-level California state courts and have not yet worked their way through the appellate process, they are of minimal value as precedents. The question remains: Were the companies' actions ethical?

Many users expect that when they press the delete key on their computers, an e-mail message is actually deleted. However, user deletions are often archived on tape and stored for years. For example, a former employee of Borland International Inc. found, to his dismay, that deleted messages can be retrieved from the archives [14]. The employee was suspected of using a Borland-supplied MCI e-mail account to divulge trade secrets to his future employer—and Borland rival—Symantec Corp. Borland asked MCI Communications Corp. to retrieve the former employee's deleted messages. This alleged intrusion was viewed as a property right by Borland. Since Borland paid for the e-mail service, the employee's account became Borland's property upon his departure. The result: pending criminal investigations of both the sender and recipient, as well as a civil suit, *Borland v. Symantec.*

Perhaps the most infamous example of retrieval of deleted messages occurred in 1987–89 during Congress's Iran-Contra investigations. Deleted IBM PROFS e-mail correspondences between Oliver North and John Poindexter were retrieved from White House backup tapes. In testimony before the Senate, North said, "We all sincerely believed that when we sent a PROFS message to another party and punched the button 'delete' that it was gone forever. Wow, were we wrong." [9].

Regardless of the type or characteristics of e-mail system used, the question remains: what privacy protection, if any, does an employee have in e-mail communications? Such communications are usually made on the employer's premises, with the employer's equipment, on the employer's time, and at the employer's cost—to further the employer's objectives. With such a substantial employer investment, do employees have a legitimate expectation of e-mail privacy?

Despite employers' significant proprietary interests, employees do have expectations of privacy [10]. Given the potentially differing perceptions of employers and employees regarding e-mail privacy and the potential problems that can result from privacy intrusions, employees and employers both need to understand the privacy protection provided by the U.S. legal system. Although ethics and law are not identical, they do come in close contact. Law is often the vehicle for formally implementing ethics into social guidelines and procedures. . . .

ELECTRONIC COMMUNICATIONS PRIVACY ACT

In an influential 1985 study, the Congressional Office of Technological Assessment (OTA) found approximately 50% of the U.S. population believed computers threaten privacy rights and supported further action to protect these rights [10]. This study inspired Congress to enact the Electronic Communications Privacy Act (ECPA) of 1986 [19]. As a society, Americans generally value privacy. However, if a societal value, such as personal privacy, is not legally protected, is it a right? By implication, the American people seem to assume they are already endowed with this right. With respect to e-mail, the OTA stated "the existing protections are weak, ambiguous, or nonexistent" [10]. This lack of protection is significant because e-mail is vulnerable to interception, as identified by the OTA, at five specific stages:

- At the sender's terminal or electronic file;

- While being transmitted;

- When accessing the recipient's mailbox;

- When the communication is printed in hard copy; and

- When retained in the files of the e-mail service.

Relying on the 1985 study, the OTA concluded internal company e-mail systems were not covered by federal statute [10]. Congress used the ECPA to amend existing federal wiretap protection law to include most electronic communications. Its purpose was to extend privacy protections against wiretapping to new forms of electronic communications, including e-mail, cellular telephones, and data transmission, from improper interception.

Broadly, the ECPA prohibits interception of wire, oral, and electronic communications, as well as disclosure or use of such intercepted communications. The statute's broad definition of electronic communication includes e-mail. Further, in Title II, the EPA, subject to significant exceptions, prohibits access to and disclosure of stored electronic communications.

Two Exceptions

Whether coverage extends to monitoring the e-mail of private-sector employers is unclear because of two exceptions in the ECPA that were part of earlier federal wiretap protection law:

Business Use or Business Extension   This exception is the basis for most of the cases brought under the ECPA [5]. To be an effective defense against employee claims of e-mail privacy invasion, employers must demonstrate that a business use was the reason for the interception and that monitoring was conducted within the ordinary course of business [22]. In a 1983 case [22], brought under the prior federal wiretap protection law, an employer notified an employee that telephone sales calls were being monitored. This notification was interpreted to mean that the specific interception was in the ordinary course of business. The business purpose ended when it became apparent the telephone communication was personal. This exception, which can be applied to telephone communications, would seem to apply to e-mail. If an employer wants to ensure its e-mail system is used solely for work-related purposes, routine monitoring of the content of e-mail messages might be included under this exception.

Prior Consent   This exception may permit telephone and e-mail monitoring. Under it, employers may be able to protect themselves against the risk of liability by notifying employees their e-mail may be examined. Such consent may be expressed or implied but is limited to the scope of the consent. In the aforementioned 1983 case, the consent was only to the monitoring of business calls. The court refused to extend this consent to all telephone calls.

The issue of whether the ECPA protects the privacy of e-mail is unclear and is currently under debate in the courts. A review of relevant legal research seems to conclude that the ECPA does not afford significant privacy protection to employee e-mail communications [5, 6]. . . .

CONCLUSIONS

Various courts and legislative bodies have sought to balance employees' expectations of personal privacy with employers' proprietary and access interests. From a managerial perspective, e-mail—an increasingly important organizational resource touted as contributing to worker productivity—must be used in an ethical and legal manner. Since clear guidance is not provided by our legal system, organizations must formulate their own internal e-mail privacy policies. Lacking a formal policy, employee expectations of privacy may differ from their employers' perspectives. Even with a formal policy, this balance is not easily achieved because of the dynamic nature of information technology capabilities. The rapid pace of technological advances forces the legal system to resolve conflicts for which there is no precedent.

REFERENCES

1. Baumhart, J. T. The employer's right to read employee e-mail: Protecting property or personal prying? *The Labor Lawyer 8,* 4 (Fall 1992), 923–948.
2. Bloustein, E. J. Privacy as an aspect of human dignity: An Answer to Dean Prosser. *39 NYU Law Review, 962* 1001 (1964).
3. *Bourke v. Nissan Motor Corp.,* No. YC 003979 (Super. Ct. Cal. filed Jan. 4, 1991).
4. *Ettore v. Philco Television Broadcasting Co.,* 229 F. 2d 481 (3d Cir. 1956).
5. Griffin, J. J. The monitoring of electronic mail in the private sector workplace: An electronic assault on employee privacy rights. *Software Law Journal IV* (1991), 493–527.
6. Addressing the new hazards of the high technology workplace. *Harvard Law Review,* 104, 8 (June 1991), 1898–1916.
7. Heredia, H. F. Is there privacy in the workplace?: Guaranteeing a broader privacy right for workers under California law. *Southwestern University Law Review,* 22 1 (1992), 307–335.
8. *Luck v. Southern Pacific Transportation Co.,* 267 Cal. Rptr. 618 (Ct. App. 1990), cert. denied, 111 S. Ct. 344 (1990).
9. National Public Radio news broadcasts (1992).
10. Office of Technology Assessment (OTA), Federal Government Information Technology: Electronic Surveillance and Civil Liberties (1985).
11. *O'Connor v. Ortega,* 480 U.S. 709 (1987).
12. Privacy for Consumers and Workers Act, S. 984, H.R. 1900, (1993).
13. Restatement (Second) of Torts 652B (1977).
14. Shieh, J. and Ballard, R. E-mail privacy. *Educom Review* (March/April 1994), 59–62.
15. *Shoars v. Epson America, Inc.* No. SWC 112749 (Cal. Sup. Ct. filed July 30, 1990).
16. *Shoars v. Epson America, Inc.* No. BC 007036 (Cal. Sup. Ct. filed March 12, 1991).
17. *Skinner v. Railway Labor Executives Association,* 489 U.S. 602 (1989).
18. *Soroka v. Dayton Hudson Corp.,* 7 Cal. App. 4th 203, review granted, 4 Cal. Rptr. 2d 180 (1992).
19. 18 USC 2510–2521, 2701–1711 (1988).
20. *Vernars v. Young,* 539 F. 2d 966 (3d Cir., 1976).
21. Warren, S. D. and Brandeis, L. D. The right of privacy. *Harvard Law Review* (December 1890), 193–220.
22. *Watkins v. L. M. Berry & Co.,* 704 F. 2d 577 (11th Cir. 1983).
23. *Wilkinson v. Times Mirror Corp.,* 215 Cal. App. 3rd 1034 (Cal. App. 1 Dist. 1989).

ELECTRONIC MAIL AND PANOPTIC POWER IN THE WORKPLACE

Richard A. Spinello

In this paper, the author rejects the common viewpoint that monitoring employee e-mail is morally acceptable. Instead he contends that an individual has a prima facie *right to the confidentiality of his or her e-mail communications. Obviously this right must be carefully balanced with the corporation's information requirements and its "need to know." One way to achieve this balance is to insist that corporations seek only relevant knowledge about their workers using ordinary means of inquiry. E-mail monitoring, however, is an extraordinary method of acquiring information. Like other extraordinary methods, this type of surveillance is intrusive and offensive.*

ELECTRONIC MAIL AND PANOPTIC POWER IN THE WORKPLACE

1. Introduction

***

Many of the companies that have embraced a formal e-mail policy seem to believe that this goes a long way to legitimizing the archiving and random inspection of e-mail messages. There is a general sentiment in the business community that as long as employees are informed of this policy it is morally permissible to inspect their e-mail.

In this paper we reject this common but misguided viewpoint. Rather, we contend that an individual has a *prima facie* right to some level of confidentiality of his or her e-mail communications that at least includes protection from systematic monitoring.

***

Our underlying assumption throughout this presentation is that a strong presumption must be given to privacy rights in the workplace. Failure to do so is a manifestation of disre-

---

spect for the dignity and intrinsic worth of human beings that derives from their capacity for rational self-determination which is severely curtailed when the cloak of privacy is removed.

***

5. Privacy in the Workplace

. . . If we admit that all human beings have a basic right to privacy, does this right extend to the workplace? Indeed do employees have *any* rights in the workplace, or must they abandon their civil liberties when they cross the corporate threshold? This normative question is a highly controversial one which cannot be fully treated in this discussion. A convincing case for workplace rights has been made by many philosophers such as Werhane (1985). Suffice it to say that without any rights in their respective workplaces, human beings would be extremely vulnerable. They would find the work environment to be an oppressive and hostile place, and in the long run this would surely undermine important economic goals such as efficiency and productivity.

Kant sums up the essence of an individual's moral obligation to others as *respect,* which entails treating the other as an end and not merely as a means. If corporations as moral agents aspire to live up to this obligation they must respect the basic human rights of their workers, though the scope and nature of those rights in the work environment can certainly be debated.

If there are workplace rights, privacy must surely be one of them, given its great importance as noted above. There are several cogent arguments supporting workplace privacy rights, but we will focus on one line of reasoning which seems especially pertinent and tenable. The argument centers on each person's fundamental right to autonomy, to make choices freely and direct one's activities. As we argued above, privacy is a critical prerequisite for the exercise of one's autonomy. Without privacy, autonomy will be consistently threatened and enervated. Moreover, autonomy is a basic aspect of one's humanity according to moral common sense and most philosophical traditions. The Kantian conception of personhood, for example, links the moral worth of persons to "the supreme value of their rational capacities for normative self-determination" (Doppelt, 1988, p. 278). All normal persons have an innate capacity to determine and pursue their own conception of the "good life" and to respect that same capacity in others.

Kantian self-determination is protected in our society by the civil liberties guaranteed by our Constitution, and this protection should not be discarded in a corporate environment. Managers do not have some sort of moral immunity simply because they are interfering with the autonomy of *their* employees. Respect for the autonomy of others is a moral imperative that cannot be arbitrarily jettisoned or overridden for the sake of economic expediency. As Werhane (1985, p. 103) has argued, disrespecting the right to autonomy in the workplace "is equivalent to disrespecting employees as persons." And since privacy is a necessary condition of autonomous behavior, it follows that workers must have some sort of privacy rights.

Of course, this does not imply that employees have complete freedom in the workplace environment, since they are accountable to their employers for fulfilling the normal demands of their jobs. Autonomy and privacy must be circumscribed appropriately and circumspectly to help meet those demands. It does mean, however, that unless there is a *legitimate "need to know"* employers should not be gathering information about their employees that needlessly erodes their privacy and thereby threatens their basic autonomy.

The vast majority of employers would probably agree with all this, at least from a theoretical point of view. They do not deny that their workers are entitled to *some* level of privacy protection. Most employers, for example, do recognize that they should not spy on their workers at home or pry too deeply into the irrelevant details of their personal lives. Their tendency, however, is to acknowledge a narrow right to privacy, while civil libertarians would argue for a more robust right. There is also disagreement over the propriety of methods used to collect information about employees. Some corporations have employed questionable methods such as polygraph tests, psychological testing, and covert surveillance cameras to acquire data about their workers.

Given these disagreements, how do we achieve a reasonable balance between worker's privacy rights and the corporation's need for information? There seem to be at least two important guidelines that can help us to delineate the appropriate privacy zone for employees. First, employers should only gather *relevant* information about their employees. For prospective employees this will undoubtedly include job history and other important background information, while for employees already on the job it will include data related to job performance or the furtherance of corporate objectives. For instance if a bank manager is evaluating the performance of a commercial loan officer he or she must be able to assess the quality of loans that have been made, the efforts expended by the loan officer to open new accounts, expense reports associated with these activities, and so forth. Second, according to Velasquez (1992, p. 400), an employer should only utilize *ordinary* and common methods of acquiring information, that is, "the supervisory activities that are normally used to oversee employees' work." Employers should not routinely use extraordinary data collection methods which include the deployment of hidden surveillance devices, secret cameras, wiretaps, polygraph testing, and so forth. Like Velasquez, DesJardins (1985, p. 226) argues that extraordinary means of data collection such as "blanket surveillance of all employees" are illegitimate because they are so intrusive and potentially harmful. Hence they should not be adopted "unless the circumstances themselves are extraordinary" (Velasquez, 1992, p. 400). For instance, suspicion that trade secrets were being pilfered would certainly justify the use of extraordinary measures to ensure their protection. In some cases certain extraordinary methods may also be necessary for quality control purposes. For instance, if monitoring is the only way to really determine whether customers are being serviced appropriately over the phone or through the medium of e-mail, one could make a case that an exception should be made provided of course that employees are fully informed of this policy and the reasons for it.

Beyond any doubt, monitoring and reading electronic mail in a systematic fashion is a form of surveillance and hence falls under the classification of extraordinary data collection methods. Clarke (1988, p. 499) defines surveillance as the "systematic investigation or monitoring of the actions or communications of one or more persons." When an employer decides to print out and scrutinize every e-mail message as in the Epson case or to routinely read an employee's incoming and outgoing electronic mail on a regular basis, we are most definitely talking about a modified version of surveillance, since the employer is engaged in systematically monitoring the communications of its employees.

6. Problems with E-Mail Surveillance

Even if one concedes that monitoring e-mail is a form of surveillance and is an extraordinary means of inquiry into employee activities, it may not be immediately apparent that *this* type of surveillance is really impertinent or harmful. It is instructive to consider, therefore, precisely how the extraordinary data collection method of e-mail monitoring is an intrusive invasion of one's privacy.

Clearly, when one's electronic mail messages are randomly inspected, one's privacy is violated since confidentiality (or secrecy) and anonymity are lost. Recall that these are two key elements of Gavison's definition of privacy. The information in the message is no longer confidential since it is read by a third party (a systems administrator or a manager) and the names of the sender and receiver are exposed so both lose their anonymity (Doss, 1995).

But in what ways could this be officious and harmful? To begin with, many interactions in the workplace intersperse business and personal information; this often happens inadvertently when workers allude to certain aspects of their personal lives as they conduct business. It seems untenable and unrealistic to demand that workers refrain from doing this at all times. Also, employees who regularly work from 9 AM to 5 PM (and in many cases for much longer hours) often have no choice but to conduct some personal business affairs from their offices.

As a result, those companies which routinely inspect e-mail will sometimes become privy to an employee's business affairs or to sensitive details about an employee's personal life. For example, if Manager X inspects e-mail correspondence between Joe and Marie he may discover things about Joe's personal life that could affect Joe's relationship with Manager X, including Joe's future in the firm. Perhaps in the midst of an exchange of electronic messages Joe has confided in Marie a few details about his personal affairs, since they explain why he has been tardy in completing an assignment at work. Joe's autonomy has then become potentially impaired since his future plans and aspirations in the firm may be unduly interfered with in certain ways by Manager X who has become privy to this personal information without Joe's knowledge or consent.

Further the loss of *anonymity* could be consequential in some situations. For example, the correspondence between Joe and Marie might be perfectly innocuous and professional, but Marie's manager might draw an unwarranted inference from the frequency of those communications or it may be referenced out of context. This too might affect her future position in this company.

In addition, even if the communication between Joe and Marie is strictly business-related it may still contain sensitive corporate information meant only for specific individuals within the organization. Perhaps in a matrix-like organizational structure, Joe reports to Manager Y as well as Manager X and the communication with Marie involves information that pertains to Manager Y's domain but is of no concern to Manager X. If Manager X routinely inspects Joe's e-mail he is apt to gain access to this information which he shouldn't have. Here again Joe's autonomy could be compromised since Manager X may interfere directly or indirectly in Joe's activities involving Manager Y.

These fictional but realistic scenarios demonstrate why e-mail surveillance is so intrusive: exposing a person's communications (such as e-mail) for others to see clearly magnifies the risk of an extrinsic loss of freedom. Under usual circumstances therefore normal workplace communications should not be subject to these blanket surveillance techniques which are equivalent to a classic "fishing expedition." This prohibition on employers to refrain from this type of monitoring implies a moral, *prima facie* right to e-mail privacy. By safeguarding e-mail privacy a corporation preserves and protects an employee's autonomy or power of normative self-determination which is in jeopardy when privacy rights are infringed upon.

In summary then our basic argument supporting a right to e-mail privacy is as follows:

(1) In order to balance employee privacy rights with the information needs of corporations, employers should acquire *relevant* information by *ordinary* and customary means.

(2) Blanket surveillance techniques are a prime example of extraordinary means of inquiry which should not be employed unless there are tenable reasons because they are so obtrusive and harmful.

(3) Monitoring employee e-mail is a form of such blanket surveillance.

(4) Therefore unless there is a just cause or a genuine business necessity employers should be prohibited from using this extraordinary means of inquiry, and this implies that the employee has a *prima facie* right to some level of e-mail privacy, which at a minimum includes a right not to be subjected to the systematic monitoring of his or her e-mail communications.

***

8. Summary

In this paper we have sought to present a plausible case for a *prima facie* right to e-mail privacy. We have assumed that there should be civil liberties in the workplace and that privacy must be among them because of its significance and its role as a condition for the exercise of personal autonomy. We fully recognize that such privacy rights must be carefully balanced with the corporation's information needs and its own property rights. As a means of achieving this precarious balance we have followed the lead of many business ethicians and proposed that the employer should only gather relevant information using ordinary means of inquiry. This precludes arbitrary blanket e-mail surveillance.

Throughout this analysis our ultimate point of reference is a conception of humanity that is well grounded in the philosophical tradition but is particularly explicit in Kant's moral philosophy. We have been at pains to insist here that privacy is indispensable for the exercise of freedom, and philosophers like Kant have demonstrated that freedom is intimately connected with our dignity as human beings. All human beings have a special dignity or intrinsic worth because they are free rational agents capable of making decisions, setting goals, pursuing projects, and guiding their ethical conduct. This capacity for rational self-determination is one basis for the respect that is due to all persons.

It follows then that the suspension or attenuation of privacy rights cannot be done arbitrarily or for insubstantial reasons, since to do so is to devalue at least indirectly the intrinsic worth of human beings. The workplace as panopticon, as a place where privacy and autonomy are routinely and even casually restricted, is an affront to basic human dignity. Instead we claim that there must be a strong presumption in favor of privacy rights in the workplace. The burden of proof is on the organization to make the case that a particular situation warrants the use of extraordinary methods of inquiry such as e-mail surveillance. If there is no just cause, if a case cannot be made that would satisfy a reasonable, objective person, then there is no justification for using these extreme methods, and the employee's *prima facie* right to e-mail privacy must be safeguarded.

REFERENCES

Clark, R: 1988, "Information Technology and Dataveillance," *Communications of the ACM* 31 (5), 498–512.

DesJardins, J.: 1985, *Contemporary Issues in Business Ethics* (Wadsworth, Belmont, California).

Doppelt, G.: 1988, "Beyond Liberalism and Communitarianism: Towards a Critical Theory of Social Justice," *Philosophy and Social Criticism* 14, 271–292.

Doss, E. and M. Loui: 1995, "Ethics and the Privacy of Electronic Mail, *The Information Society* 11, 223–235.

Ewing, D.: 1982, *Do It My Way or You're Fired* (John Wiley & Son, New York).

Foucault, M.: 1979, *Discipline and Punish: The Birth of the Prison* (Vintage Books, New York).

Fromm, E.: 1968, *The Revolution of Hope: Toward A Humanized Technology* (Bantam Books, New York).

Gavison, R.: 1984, "Privacy and the Limits of the Law," *The Yale Law Journal* 89, 421–471.

Gould, C.: 1989, *The Information Web: Ethical and Social Implications of Computers* (Westview Press, Boulder, CO).

Reiman, J.: 1995, "Driving to the Panopticon: A Philosophical Exploration of the Risks to Privacy Posed by the Highway Technology of the Future," *Santa Clara Computer and High Technology Law Journal* 11 (1), 27–44.

Samuels, P.: 1996, "Who's Reading Your E-Mail? Maybe the Boss," *The New York Times,* May 12, F11.

Shaw, W. and V. Barry: 1989, *Moral Issues in Business* (Wadsworth Publishing Company, Belmont, CA).

Tuerkheirmer, F.: 1993, "The Underpinnings of Privacy Protection," *Communications of the ACM* 36 (8), 69–73.

Velasquez, M.: 1992, *Business Ethics: Concepts and Cases* (3rd ed.) (Prentice Hall, Inc., Englewood Cliffs, NJ).

Wasserstrom, R.: 1984, "Privacy: Some Arguments and Assumptions," in *Philosophical Dimensions of Privacy* (Cambridge University Press, New York), pp. 309–328.

Werhane, P.: 1985, *Persons, Rights, and Corporations* (Prentice Hall, Inc., Englewood Cliffs, NJ).

COMPLIANCE PROGRAMS, E-MAIL AND THE INTERNET

JEFFREY M. KAPLAN

Many ethics officers, in-house counsel, human resource staff and others are now being asked to assemble e-mail/Internet policies and procedures. However, because of the sudden way in which these issues have emerged, there are few published sources on establishing standards and systems to prevent and detect wrongful workplace use of these new technologies. Consider the following guidance from attorney Jeffrey Kaplan.

DEVELOPING STANDARDS

The first step in creating or enhancing a policy is determining whether to allow any personal use of e-mail or Internet in the workplace. Given the impracticality of a total ban (as well as the resentment that such an effort might engender) the trend here—exemplified by Bell South Corporation, which moved away from a "zero tolerance" policy—seems to be to allow a reasonable amount of such use.

The second step is to develop a catalog of prohibited or restricted conduct. Among the areas a company may wish to include in such a list are:

- Circulation of material with derogatory racial, religious or gender comments, or with sexual content or offensive language;

- Transmission of threatening, reckless, or maliciously false communications;

- Any activity constituting or promoting a criminal offense, potentially giving rise to civil liability, or otherwise violating any laws, regulations, applicable rules or company policy;

- Transmission of copyrighted documents that are not authorized for reproduction, or, without permission, of trade secrets or any other confidential information belonging to the company;

- Use in furtherance of the business activity of any other entity or to conduct a job search;

- Use that results in additional billing or direct cost to the company;

- Use without approval to solicit funds; distribute chain letters, literature or gifts; sell merchandise or services; collect signatures, conduct membership drives, etc.;

- Sending external broadcast messages;

- Use of other individuals' account names or passwords, or accessing resources to which employees have not been given access;

- Transmission of political statements not sanctioned by the company.

INTERNET CHATROOMS

Another area to consider—but which is in few, if any, policies at present—concerns participation in Internet chatroom discussions relating to one's employer. Employees should be warned of the possibility of insider trading, stock manipulation, and other securities law issues arising from inappropriate chatroom activities.

Finally, a policy should speak to the unique nature of e-mail. For example, one might note, as does Boeing Co., that because the source of an e-mail is clearly identifiable, care "must be taken to ensure such communications must not adversely affect the company or its public image or that of its customers, partners, associates, or suppliers." Similarly, one might remind employees that e-mail messages remain part of company records long after they have been supposedly deleted, a lesson which was learned most famously in the *Microsoft* antitrust case.

COMMUNICATING COMPANY STANDARDS

As important as developing or enhancing e-mail and Internet use standards is effectively *communicating* those standards to the workforce. Among the possibilities here (in addition to including the policy in one's code of conduct) are:

- Issuing an e-mail from top management to announce or reinforce the policy;

- Having the policy appear periodically on employees' computer screens when they log on;

- Continuously posting the policy on a company's intranet site;

- Requiring employees to acknowledge on the computer that they have read and agree to abide by the policy. (Any employee who failed to so acknowledge would presumably lose access to e-mail and the Internet.)

A company should also include discussion of these issues in its in-person training. Face-to-face communications may offer the best opportunity to make certain employees understand the dangers of misuse in this area and exactly what the company expects of them.

In addition, offensive or obscene e-mails are often received from outside a company rather than generated within it. Thus, an e-mail/Internet compliance program should provide means for "returning" inappropriate e-mails received from third parties (similar to policies requiring employees to return large gifts from vendors). For example, the policy could include sample language which, in a polite but firm manner, could be used by employees to respond to the receipt of any inappropriate e-mail from a third party by stating that company policy prohibits the receipt of such.

ENFORCEMENT

The final element of an e-mail/Internet ethics compliance program is enforcement. There are several steps a company can take to effectively enforce its policies in this area.

First, it is important to inform employees that they should have no expectation of privacy in workplace computer communications and that the company reserves the right to monitor such communications. (According to a study by the American Management Association, 27 percent of large U.S. firms checked employee e-mail in 1999—up from 15 percent in 1997.)

The fact that a company reserves the *right* to do this, however, does not mean that it should exercise its power in an unfettered way. That is, while many companies do conduct random checks of employees' computers, others are beginning to require some appropriate basis before taking such measures. The components of this type of procedure might include:

• An objective—but not overly legalistic—standard for authorizing such checks;

• A procedure for assuring that such a basis exists in individual cases—e.g., review by designated personnel in the Law and/or HR and/or Security departments.

Beyond monitoring through manual checking, some companies now use technologies that *automatically* monitor e-mail and Internet uses. For example, Mail Sweeper—a product of Content Technologies, Inc.—permits companies to examine outgoing messages for prohibited content.

COMPLIANCE AS A DEFENSE

The principle purpose of an e-mail/Internet use policy is, of course, to prevent and detect inappropriate behavior. However, as with other compliance fields, a good policy here can also serve as the basis—at least in some instances—of a defense to a lawsuit.

In this regard, a policy should underscore the need to report any violations by other employees. Doing so should help to minimize the likelihood of offensive e-mail and Internet usage contributing to the development of a "hostile workplace environment," and thus minimize harassment-related liability. Indeed, earlier this year, MCI Worldcom Inc. successfully defended itself against a lawsuit (*Daniels v. Worldcom*) charging racial harassment over its e-mail system, in part, due to its having an effective e-mail use policy. (The court's dismissal was also based upon the company's proactive and swift response to the plaintiffs' complaints.)

CONCLUSION

While companies need to have and enforce e-mail and Internet policies, there is also a real danger in instituting onerous standards, intrusive monitoring and unfair, policelike investigations. A heavy-handed approach in this area—which, regardless of what a policy says, seems to implicate *some* legitimate privacy interests—may well demoralize and alienate employees. As with all fields of compliance and ethics, care must be taken that the cure not be worse than the disease.

NON-PROFITS STILL
LACK TECHNOLOGY

T. J. DeGroat

*The "digital divide" separating the haves and the have-nots of tech-
nology is a term that is usually used in connection with the inequality of access to technology between income classes, national origins,
or races. In the context of this article, it represents the imbalance in
access to technology of for-profit firms and non-profit entities. Since
non-profits serve a significant role in our socioeconomic environment, this disparity has far-reaching implications.*

While most corporations are racing to keep up with the perpetual changes of technology,
many smaller community-outreach organizations are barely out of the starting block.

The Digital Divide may be decreasing, but still there is a desperate need for additional
computers and education in non-profit organizations and in low-income communities, said
Laurie Schoeman, who works at the Catholic Charities' Office of the Homeless and Hungry.

"A lot of churches and community organizations don't have the money to purchase top-
of-the-line computers to allow them access to the Internet," Schoeman said. "There's a
whole community of providers and advocates out there but if you can't access them you're
isolated."

Lack of education is a serious problem, Schoeman said. Many volunteers at small
churches in New York City are older people who didn't grow up with the Internet. Many
younger members of the community are computer illiterate because their schools couldn't
offer adequate services, she said.

"It just seems to me that the technology revolution hasn't hit everyone," Schoeman
said. "For every office that has 10 or 12 computers there are churches that have absolutely
no access."

Schoeman's New York-based organization has taken steps to attract computer donations. She has contacted computer manufacturers and searched for computer recycling programs but hasn't found much help, she said.

The group is looking for computers that have CD-Rom drives and can download at high
speeds. The technology is used for government programs, such as food-stamp eligibility
screening and to build small community hubs so people can develop computer skills,
Schoeman said.

"This is basically an indication of what low-income communities lack. It's part of a
quilt of challenges," she said.

GENETICALLY MODIFIED FOODS

Controversy Underscores Link between Consumer Perception and Corporate Reputation

CAROL STAVRAKA

> *Up to this point, much of our consideration of ethics in technology has focused on computer-based technology. Consider the other ways in which technology infiltrates our lives. The following article discusses the consumer naivete surrounding questions of biotechnology and the implications for consumer decision making.*

Consumer concern over genetically modified (GM) foods, particularly soy products, has spread from Europe and taken hold in the United States. Once hailed by manufacturers and farmers alike as a scientific breakthrough in which manipulated plant genes yielded more abundant, less expensive and more nutritional foods, the love affair with genetic modification is over. Instead, its unknown impact on people, animals and the environment is being harshly criticized by activists, consumers and even farmers, who were originally the biggest proponents of this technology.

Companies that manufacture these products, including DuPont, Monsanto Company, Novartis AG and Archer Daniels Midland Company (ADM), are at the center of a controversy that could have devastating effects on the industry. In December, farmers filed a class action suit against Monsanto charging insufficient testing and conspiracy to control the world's corn and soybean markets. Meanwhile, advocacy groups and the public have also taken an active role in the controversy—demanding further testing and regulatory measures requiring that GM foods be labeled to allow for consumer choice. The main fear is that GM foods have not been sufficiently tested to ensure that there are no harmful or deadly effects on people, animals or the environment.

Part of the public backlash may be due to the industry's failure to inform customers and address their concerns. Monsanto, for example, originally focused its educational programs on farmers rather than customers. "When Monsanto was originally talking with stock analysts about introducing genetically engineered products, the company thought Europe could be problematic, but believed that the U.S. would be okay," says Lloyd Kurtz, vice president of quantitative research at Harris Brettal Sullivan and Smith, a money management firm in San Francisco.

How has failure to communicate with consumers and their strong opposition to genetic modification impacted the bottom line. Just last week, when a proposed merger was announced between Monsanto and Pharmacia & Upjohn Inc. to create one of the largest pharmaceutical and biotechnology companies in the world, the $23.3 billion deal received a cool reception on Wall Street, with both stocks falling. Kurtz attributes this reaction to several factors: "Pharmacia is a drug company that does not have a lot of experience in agribusiness—a business in which the current climate is poor," he says, pointing to the decreasing value of soybean futures, currently priced at approximately half of their 10-year high. Consumers also play a role, he says. "Many view agribusiness as suspect already and it is incredibly unpopular with consumers." Monsanto, he says, primarily lost value due to previous Wall Street rumors indicating that Novartis would purchase Monsanto at a premium.

To better meet consumer needs and improve corporate reputation, some companies are addressing this growing concern. In August, ADM released a statement to its suppliers, advocating separation of genetically modified and non-modified crops. "We want to alert you to a change we are experiencing in consumer demand," the statement reads, "While ADM remains supportive of the science and safety of the biotech development and traditional plant breeding methods to improve crops and benefit customers, ADM's processing business is driven by the consumer's desire to have choices . . . we must supply products that our customers will purchase."

Kurtz believes that anticipating consumer needs is critical to maintaining a good reputation—and shareholder value. "Anytime the management of a company is talking to investment bankers more than their customers, there's a problem," he says. "Companies that have the best results are famously close to their customers."

Indeed, as consumers become more aware of business practices, the increasing importance of communicating with stakeholders is apparent. "Unfortunately, for some companies, consumer perceptions don't seem to matter until something happens," Kurtz says. "That's a critical mistake. Companies that are neglecting their consumers have problems that are building over time. When consumers finally get angry and have an alternative to go to, that's exactly what they will do," he concludes.

***

SUPERMARKETS TAKE ACTION AGAINST GENETICALLY MODIFIED FOODS FOLLOWING CONSUMER CONCERN

As opposition to genetically modified foods builds in the U.S., several leading grocery retailers are taking dramatic steps to eliminate these products from their shelves. Whole Foods Market Inc., the nation's largest natural food chain, recently pledged to eliminate GM products from its inventory at its 100 plus stores. Another leading natural supermarket chain, Wild Oats Markets, Inc., has made a similar commitment.

The potential hazards of genetically engineered foods have been debated for some time, with many expressing concerns over possible harmful effects of these products on people, animals and the environment. With little testing completed so far and no FDA-required labeling, many consumers, activists and farmers fear that unknown dangers may exist.

Wild Oats Markets has promised to use only natural (non-GM) foods for its private label products and dietary supplements. Whole Foods Market has also committed to eliminating GM products by mid-summer.

Margaret Wittenberg, vice president of governmental and public affairs for Whole Foods Markets who made this pledge during a National Public Radio broadcast, admits this is a challenge, especially since up to 60 percent of processed foods contain GM products. "Without labeling it's very hard to know," she said in the interview. "We have been working on this [goal] since last spring in answer to our consumers who have vehemently been telling us that they want to have the option to buy foods that do not contain genetically altered ingredients," she said. The company is developing its own auditing process in which the origin of all products will be traced back to the seed and verified with testing.

Organic labels are another way that retailers hope to identify natural products. The National Organic Standards Board, established by the Department of Agriculture to set organic certification standards, is working to design national requirements for organic growing, processing and labeling. Currently 17 states enforce organic standards with 11 operating their own certification programs and the remainder using private certifiers. Whole Foods Market and Wild Oats Markets, both of which advocate FDA labeling, testing and the public's right to know, are working with consumers to help promote these issues and support Citizens for Health, a non-profit organization that works to advance consumer access to natural health options. Other corporate supporters include General Nutrition Centers (GNC), Vegetarian Times Magazine, Twin Laboratories Inc. and Tree of Life Inc.

Part Three

ETHICS IN THE NATURAL AND GLOBAL ENVIRONMENTS

Chapter 12

ETHICS AND THE EARTH'S ENVIRONMENT

Those who would take over the earth
And shape it to their will
Never, I notice, succeed.
The earth is like a vessel so sacred
That at the mere approach of the profane
It is marred
And when they reach out their fingers it is gone.

—LAO TZU, *TAO TE CHING*, CHAP. 29

When I was studying law at a law school considered to be rather capitalistically oriented, my law and economics professors would usually point to the environment as the one area where the free market might not provide the *best* result. That's because each one of us, individually, is not so affected by one piece of trash or one scintilla of pollution in the air. To the contrary, if we balance our personal interests, it is often in our self-interest to pollute, rather than to clean up. On the other hand (and we have all heard this argument at one time or another), if we *all* polluted, even a small amount, the world would be a very dirty place in which we would not like to live. And that may be where we stand today.

I conduct a short, little experiment in my ethics class where I spill a bit of water on the floor from a soda can. The students can't believe that I am doing this and ignoring it. Then I ask them to go in the hallway just after classes have started and to observe similar behavior by the students. I don't set this up beforehand but, invariably, they *do* see this type of behavior in the hallway. Why does this happen? Do people think that others will pick up after them? Strolling across campus or in your office, do you *always* stop to pick up waste off of the floor? Why do you do this or why do you refrain from doing this?

From the moment a firm begins to produce, service, manufacture, or create, the operations of that firm impact the environment. Imagine the small decisions made by a company: Does it pack its glassware in plastic bubbles or corrugated wrapping? Does it publish a catalogue once a month or once a year? Is that catalogue published on paper or only through the internet? Does it meet with the community before choosing a disposal system? Each of these decisions will have an impact on our physical world, and it is critical to understand the law as it relates to the environment, as well as to be aware of the ethics of each decision.

And our decisions affect not only those around us, but others around the world. In 1991, Saddam Hussein soiled the Persian Gulf with the largest oil spill in history. Exxon has spent an estimated $3.5 billion in trying to clean up after the 1989 tragedy of the Exxon Valdez oil spill in Alaska. A considerable expanse of the former Soviet Union will remain uninhabitable for years as a result of the 1986 Chernobyl nuclear power plant accident.

Although the earth is a natural recycler of wastes—a very effective garbage dump—its ability to successfully neutralize the cumulative refuse of modern society is finite. Some concerns about pollution are centuries old, but the upsurge in population and increased industrialization and urbanization in the last 100 years have concentrated ever-increasing amounts of waste matter in small areas and put much greater pressure on the assimilative capabilities of the planet. Further, an improved understanding of the effects of various waste materials on the environment has generated widespread interest and awareness of pollution problems on the parts of both the general public as well as business decision makers.

But Who's to Pay?   Both of these stakeholders are understandably concerned, however, about who will pay for the costs of environmental awareness. As history has shown us, left alone, many firms are quite willing to pollute the environment. The additional damage to the environment caused by the acts of one firm may not be severe. Therefore, that one firm may not be persuaded to take action to prevent this damage. The cost of this damage seems outweighed by the cost to ensure that the environment is *not* harmed. In those cases where the acts of one firm do not have an extreme impact on the environment, but the same acts by a number of firms *would* have an extreme impact, it is arguable that the government must step in to regulate those acts. The government believes that it has no choice but to regulate the operations of businesses in order to maintain a clean and healthy environment.

For example, without regulation, a firm may consider that dumping its garbage into a canal is no big deal. In fact, perhaps the slight amount of garbage that this firm dumps *is* no big deal. However, if every firm were allowed to dump this amount, the canal would become excessively and irreversibly polluted. This situation may warrant government intervention. Or consider the possibility that we may all prefer less-costly, though more polluting cars. In this scenario, are the rights of future generations protected? They probably would have preferred that we were more careful so that their air would be cleaner.

Pollution, in this discussion, would be categorized by economists as an "externality." Wilfred Beckerman describes the economic analysis as follows:

[T]he costs of pollution are not always borne fully, if at all, by the polluter. . . . Naturally, he has no incentive to economize in the use [of the environment] in the same way that he has for other factors of production that carry a cost, such as labor or capital. . . . This defect of the price mechanism needs to be corrected by governmental action in order to eliminate excessive pollution.[1]

Business certainly is not the sole contributor to environmental pollution. Individual citizens are primarily responsible for particulate matter discharged by wood-burning stoves, indoor pollution from cigarette smoking, and air pollution caused by our national one-worker-per-car commuting habits. Most forms of pollution, however, probably do have some business connection—whether direct or indirect.

Are there solutions for these problems which are acceptable to all stakeholders concerned? Most people want a cleaner environment, yet the free market apparently is not of sufficient strength to guide the economy in that direction. The problem is not a failure in pricing system theory, but rather that the pricing system works to perfection, albeit in the wrong directions. This inconvenience can be traced to what economists call the externality, free good, or commons problem. Simply stated, producers have used the environment as a free garbage dump. In effect, producers can pollute a river and pass the costs (in the form of dirty water, dead fish, disease, and so forth) onto society as a whole. If a good can be obtained at no cost, an economist or a businessperson would be inclined to use as much of the free good as possible, and producers have done just that. There is no pricing incentive to minimize pollution if pollution has no direct cost to the company; in fact, the incentive is to maximize pollution. In this instance, the welfare of individuals acting in their own private interests does not coincide with the general good.

Collective Good   Another way in which an economist might examine the problem is as a collective good. If the citizens want a clean environment, the market would presumably reflect that desire by paying nonpolluting companies higher prices for their goods. Unfortunately, the

---

[1]Wilfred Beckerman, "Public Utilities Fortnightly," cited in Robert Solomon, *The New World of Business* (Maryland: Rowan & Littlefield, 1994), p. 319.

benefits of clean air and water are not restricted to those paying for them through higher prices, because equal benefits are bestowed on those persons still trading (at lower prices) with polluting companies. Thus a clean environment benefits everyone equally, regardless of each individual's contribution toward it. A rational utility-maximizing strategy for each person, then, is to patronize cheaper, polluting firms to the exclusion of the more expensive nonpolluters, despite the desire of society for a clean environment. Therefore industries have no incentive not to pollute. Externalities and collective goods are instances of market failure.

And What of the Law?   Obviously, international environmental problems cannot be cured merely by passing a new regulation in this country. Increasingly, the nations of the world are reaching understandings about cleansing the globe. In June 1992, environmental concerns drew together in Rio de Janeiro, Brazil, the largest gathering of heads of state in history. That remarkable assemblage for the Earth Summit testifies to the increasing global recognition of environmental problems and their critical role in international economic development and trade. Consider also the 1990 revision to the Montreal Protocol, a global environmental accord: "Driven by disturbing new evidence of a widening hole in the Earth's ozone layer, representatives of 53 nations agreed . . . to ban major ozone-destroying chemicals by the year 2000."

Similarly, in 1994, 64 nations added teeth to the 1990 Basel Convention (curbing transnational toxic waste shipment) by agreeing to immediately stop dumping toxic waste in developing countries. The United States, feeling, among other things, that certain materials such as scrap metal could properly be sent abroad for recycling if the receiving governments agree, has not ratified the Basel Convention.

Our steady, even spectacular, strides forward in environmental protection legislation have not dispelled the view, particularly among economists and businesspeople, that legislation is sometimes not the best remedy for environmental problems. To them, pollution control is not so much a matter of law as of economics. They believe that with proper incentives, the market will, in many instances, prove superior to legislation in preventing and correcting environmental problems. For example, twenty years ago, 164 pounds of metal were required to create 1,000 soda cans. In 1995, manufacturers have discovered better, more efficient uses of resources and now use only 35 pounds of metal for the same number of cans. In fact, The Heartland Institute, a conservative think tank based in Chicago, reports that air quality was improving as fast or faster before the Clean Air Act as it has since that time.

The general idea of economic efficiency and proper incentives is also well illustrated by New York City's efforts to deal with its daily production of 385 tons of sludge, which cannot legally be dumped into the ocean and which overwhelms local landfill capacity. Bio Gro Systems of Annapolis, Maryland, ships 100 tons of sludge daily by rail from New York City to Colorado and Arizona, where farmers are now on waiting lists to have the potent fertilizers spread on their land. The city pays Bio Gro but the sludge is free to farmers, whose reliance on chemical fertilizers has now been reduced.

Cost-Benefit   From the free market point of view, environmental legislation very often imposes unacceptable costs. *Fortune* asked, "How much is America overpaying for environmental regulations?" In 1990, our total bill for federal air and water legislation was estimated to be $320 billion, of which $79 billion came in direct costs while the balance was the result of reduced job growth, reduced capital formation, and lower savings. According to economists Michael Hazilla and Raymond Kopp, those costs resulted in a 5.8 percent reduction in the gross national product. Some of these costs appear to be excessive. For example, Brookings fellow Robert Crandall has calculated that solid and toxic waste cleanup regulations cost $5 billion to $9 billion annually. If that money saves half of the 1,100 additional annual cancers that the EPA attributes to the waste, the cost per cancer case prevented would be $10 million to $18 million.

Firms may reap results in other ways, as well. The market may support the efforts of environmentally conscious companies precisely *because* they're environmentally conscious. Consider the progress of Patagonia, Inc., the outerwear manufacturer whose sales increased by 20 percent in its last fiscal year. "Its founders and sole owners, Yvon Chouinard and his wife, Malinda, are determined to create a business that is successful in ways far different from what any business school will teach young prodigies." Patagonia has a list of five-year environmental goals (dating to 1994) which include the elimination of all solid waste sent to landfills from domestic facilities and the inclusion of environmental costs in accounting and production systems and decisions. Chouinard justifies his approach in the article included in this chapter and as follows:

> *I'm a pessimist about the fate of civilization. Ever since I can remember we've been losing on the environmental front, and all indicators say we are still losing now. Gains we make are wiped out by development or population growth. So, I'm pessimistic and I feel responsible to do all that I can. I figure the best tool I have to help the environment is this company.*

So, in helping the environment, Chouinard has been able to post earnings unmatched by many other firms!

One possible solution to remedy our environmental balance sheet and return us to a true free market would be to leave the risks of unintended (as well as intended) pollution to the insurance industry. A company could simply insure itself against claims of pollution and injured parties would sue the offending firm through its insurance company for restitution. In this way, firms who are more likely to suffer claims would have high insurance premiums, thus encouraging them to reduce their polluting behavior. Firms that did not have a history of polluting would have lower insurance premiums, thus awarding them a benefit for protecting the environment. The government could require a bond from companies that continue to engage in environmentally risky activities, similar to workers' compensation statutes. The end goals of accountability and responsibility would therefore be served.

A Balance?   Of course, unbridled faith in the free market is not likely to be in our long-term best interests. Chile's experience under General Augusto Pinochet from 1973 to 1990 illustrates the risk. Pinochet put his faith in the free market. With privatization and deregulation, he brought Chile the most vibrant economy in South America. However, many argue that Pinochet was also a dictator who failed to respect the individual basic human rights and property rights of his citizens. In addition, now that Pinochet is gone, the environmental price of unregulated growth is becoming apparent. Forests, streams, and valleys have been plundered. The result, as described in *Time* magazine, is most apparent in the smog-enshrouded capital, Santiago:

> *A thick layer of contaminants settles almost daily over the city, trapped by cold air and mountains on all sides. The causes of the filth: haphazard development and an out-of-control bus system that Pinochet began deregulating in 1975. Two thirds of the smog's harmful elements come from the 11,000 privately owned buses that spew diesel fumes through the city. The government bought out 2,600 of the worst offenders. But pollution still reached lethal levels for two days in July, forcing the government to shut schools and factories and to warn parents to keep their children indoors.*

The readings that follow present a variety of perspectives on the issue of responsibility and accountability for the environment and the corporate response. Should firms be held to a higher, similar, or lower standard than individuals? What tools might or should a firm use to assist it in its decision-making process? Assuming *no* government regulation, if you were beginning a firm today, how would you handle its environmental responsibility?

Children's book author Dr. Seuss offers his concern for a world without individual or government protection of the environment in his story of the Lorax. In his story, The Once-lers have come to the land of the Truffula trees, known for their bright colored tufts. The Once-lers cut down a Truffula trees to knit thneeds, a fine something that all people need.

> "Mister" he said with a sawdusty sneeze,
> "I am the Lorax. I speak for the trees.
> I speak for the trees, for the trees have no tongues,
> And I'm asking you, sire, at the top of my lungs"—
> He was very upset as he shouted and puffed—
> *"What's that THING you've made out of my Trufulla tuft?"*

After the world is turned upside down and the environment is ruined with thneed production, the manufacturer laments:

> Now all that was left 'neath the bad-smelling sky
> was my big empty factory . . .
> the Lorax . . .
> and I.
>
> The Lorax said nothing. Just gave me a glance . . .
> just gave me a sad, sad backward glance . . .
> as he lifted himself by the seat of his pants.
> And I'll never forget the grim look on his face
> when he heisted himself and took leave of this place,
> through a hole in the smog, without leaving a trace.
>
> And all that the Lorax left here in this mess
> was a small pile of rocks, with one word . . .
> "UNLESS."
> Whatever *that* meant, well, I just couldn't guess.

The word was explained to the manufacturer/narrator by the Once-ler who tells the reader:

> "UNLESS someone like you
> cares a whole awful lot,
> nothing is going to get better.
> It's not.

Take heed, Dr. Seuss seems to be telling us all, or be wary of what darkness may fall.

SHORT HYPOTHETICAL CASE

a. After being unemployed for several months, you've just started driving for a local transport company. The company transports and treats chemical waste. Disposal costs have doubled in the past year, putting a squeeze on your firm's profits. You pull in late one evening with a truckload of chemical waste. The supervisor is the only one at the plant. He tells you to drain the truck into a pipe at the back of the lot rather than into the normal holding tank. The tank is already full, he says. You find out later that the pipe dumps waste directly into a nearby creek. What do you do?

Hypotheticals were written by Catherine Haselden and are included in her manuscript, "The Ethics Game."

TOPIC STUDY: PUBLIC RELATIONS AND CORPORATE ENVIRONMENTALISM

SUSTAINABLE PR

David Shenk

Shenk discusses the notion that the environment can be marketed as a "distinct bottom-line advantage," as opposed to the concept that environmental awareness might really be such a business advantage. Are we simply slaves to marketing programs in connection with the environment because we know so little about the actual impact of businesses on our physical world?

The flighty excess of the Reagan years has given way to an era of stolid pragmatism, and public relations experts—the high priests of the Information Age—are bravely navigating the transition for us. Take the environment. "Gone is the idealistic 'Save the Whales' mentality of the 1980s, a period when companies had money to burn" on conservation, explains *O'Dwyer's PR Services Report.* "Environmental communications has come of age in the lean '90s. . . . Successful PR people will be those who can blend the cold-hearted reality of 1990s economics with the 1970s touching though somewhat naive concern for Mother Earth."

That fanciful '80s notion of "sustainable development" simply does not gibe with quarterly earnings pressure, so PR professionals have come up with a viable alternative which they proudly call "Sustainable PR." "The challenge," reads a Hill & Knowlton ad touting their in-house *Green Team,* "is to make the environment a distinct bottom-line advantage."

Here's how it works. In the '70s, Rockwell International might have foolishly assumed that it would eventually have to *clean up* its 166 separate hazardous waste sites in Rocky Flats, Colorado (including the infamous "Hillside 881," reportedly the most toxic site in the country).

Touching, but very naive. In the '90s, the company opts instead for a more economical demonstration of its deep commitment to the environment: an advertisement coupling the Rockwell logo to an Ansel Adams's photographic celebration of the earth in all its pristine and rugged glory. ("I saw that and went 'Achh!'" one Rockwell employee admits. "It seems kind of contradictory—but that's just my editorial opinion.")

The numbers show that Americans want sustainable *something.* Seventy-eight percent of consumers have demonstrated a willingness to switch to products perceived as

---

environmentally-sensitive, and in recent years the Green product market has skyrocketed to an annual $121.5 billion. With that kind of money at stake, the last thing we want to be is *naive.* The old unsophisticated us may have assumed that adopting a pro-environmental posture in the workplace would require a significant investment—modernized production facilities, recycled paper products, etc.; the new, more cunning us knows that a deep green corporate hue can be as simple as a fresh coat of paint. Does the name *Exxon Valdez* now rub you the wrong way? Exxon's green consultants thought it might, so they've changed it to the more huggable *SeaRiver Mediterranean.* Same single-hulled oil tanker; new, swarthy mien. Look for it off a rocky coast near you.

Does auto exhaust get you down? General Motors and Chrysler would like to try to assuage your guilt when you buy your next Jeep or Geo by planting a tree in your name. Here's hoping this gesture fires your ecological drive: you'd have to plant another 733 trees on your own to make up for the actual amount of CO_2 emitted during your average ten-year car life. *Achh!* (But that's just our editorial opinion.)

Luscious images of green rolling hills, sparkling rivers, copper canyons—why would anyone want to interfere with a good-hearted effort to bring a little nature back into the hectic consumer lifestyle? It turns out that the Federal Trade Commission is a real curmudgeon when it comes to marketing regular old GE lightbulbs as "energy-efficient." They ordered the company to cease the false claim. Also, no more will you find the upbeat three-arrow recycling logo on White Castle hamburger boxes, or the "chlorine-free" claim on Mr. Coffee filters. Technically speaking, neither one is. And since Ciba-Geigy's *Basus Flea & Tick Spray* actually does sort of contain some ozone-offending chemicals, the company had to drop the warm and sunny "ozone friendly" label. [From the *Ethics, Inc.* archive: In the '70s, Ciba-Geigy pushed the toxic envelope by testing herbicides on human subjects in Egypt and India.]

With the FTC meddling about, the eco image business isn't the sandbox it was in the mid-'80s. "PR pros are less giddy about the growth prospects for environmental PR than they were a few years back," laments an *O'Dwyer's* editorial. But don't count savvy companies out. They may not be interested in actual ecology ("no matter how idealistic a company sounds," reports *O'Dwyer's,* "it puts the bottom line ahead of cleaning up its mess. . . . Does the cost of sick days and hospitalizations due to exposure from the dirt outweigh a payroll?"), but with all these communications professionals about, there's more than one way to maintain a green glow while you thin a forest.

Purchase some credibility outright, for instance. As *O'Dwyer's* details: "Cash-rich companies, PR people say, are funding hard-up environmentalists groups in the belief the imprimatur of activists will go a long way in improving their reputation among environmentally aware consumers." Known as "cause-related marketing," this is Sustainable PR's marketing cousin. "It's a trade," explains Jim Andrews, editorial director of International Events Group, a specialist in the field. "You give money and you use the non-profit's logo, and you are acknowledged as more than a small line on the cause's annual report. You're almost . . . using *the cause* as a form of media."

Or try your hand at that *SeaRiver* name game. Meet the National Wetlands Coalition, a group of such renowned nature bunnies as Amoco, Arco, Chevron, Conoco, Exxon, Mobil, Shell and Texaco. As the name intimates, these are companies with a genuine interest in Wetlands conservation: *they want to stop it.* During the Bush administration, these faux-ecologists managed to redefine the national definition of wetlands, reducing the amount of land under federal protection by 50%.

The Environmental Conservation Organization (ECO) is another such group with an ironic *nom de green*. Like you and me, this group of real estate developers is disgusted by erosion and pollution. "Efforts to save the environment," its literature proclaims, "should not *erode* fundamental constitutional rights nor *pollute* our free-enterprise economy." Call your congressman now to help conserve the delicate Hardhat ecosystem.

There are many others—the Evergreen Foundation (a timber consortium), the Information Council for the Environment (coal, mining and public utilities), Oregonians for Food and Shelter (pesticide manufacturers), the Sea Lion Defense Fund (the Alaska fishing industry, fighting to *diminish* the Sea Lion's food sources), and a sentimental favorite, the U.S. Council for Energy Awareness (the nuclear power industry).

And, of course, Citizens For the Environment, a "grassroots environmental group that promotes market-based methods for protecting our environment." CFE has no citizen members, per se, unless you count corporate citizens like Amoco, Boeing, Chevron, Coors, GE, GM, Georgia-Pacific, and so on. This group also lobbies against environmental regulations, using the argument that big industry always has been and always will be the most pro-environmental force around.

Let's be open minded about this—maybe they have a point. Perhaps Dupont Chairman Edgar Woolard signaled an abrupt corporate turnaround with his shocking 1990 pronouncement that "we subscribe to the concept of sustainable development as outlined in the report of the World Commission on Environment and Development prepared under the leadership of former Prime Minister Bruntland of Norway." That same year, Dupont released their famous "Applause" commercial with penguins, sea otters, dolphins and gulls all clapping, flapping and squawking joyously to Beethoven's ever-mirthful "Ode to Joy," while a narrator informs us that Dupont has just placed orders for several double-hulled oil tankers. "Dupont. Better things for better living."

Then again, maybe not. Dupont's announcement is touching, but shareholders should be assured that the nation's number one polluter hasn't forgotten how to be cold-hearted in the lean '90s. They still dump chemicals into rivers and oceans, pump ash into the sky and inject toxic waste into underground geologic formations like no other American corporation. Around the time that Woolard announced his new enthusiasm for ecobusiness, he also unequivocally termed his company's 1.6 million pounds of pollution *per day* "safe."

Achh. Seems kind of contradictory. But that's just an editorial opinion.

GARNET HILL
HONORED FOR
RECYCLING EFFORTS

GARNET HILL

Every time I get a package from a mail-order company, I also receive a small blurb about how their packaging or marketing is environmentally correct. Would this claim encourage you to purchase more from this particular mail order catalog or to feel better about your environmentalism? Perhaps, or perhaps not. But there must be some incentive for firms to publish this material. Perhaps it is for public awareness, so that we (as consumers) become more aware of our impact on our physical world. To that perceived end, Garnet Hill catalog includes the following material in their shipments.

WE THOUGHT YOU WOULD BE INTERESTED

"Garnet Hill of Franconia has been presented with an Environmental Excellence Award for its recycling and waste reduction efforts by WasteCap of New Hampshire. Garnet Hill is a direct mail company specializing in products made from natural fibers. It recycles 64 tons of cardboard and over 4 tons of office paper per year.

"Sponsored by the New Hampshire Business and Industry association, WasteCap of New Hampshire assists companies with solid waste reduction and recycling efforts. Participating companies have significantly reduced purchasing, handling and disposal costs associated with solid waste" (*The Courier,* Littleton, 10/95).

Garnet Hill takes recycling seriously. As one of only four businesses in the state to receive this award, we are proud of our achievement. In addition to the efforts recognized above, we utilize recycled materials in all of our packaging. Our order form and all of our stationery is also printed on recycled stock. We have never used plastic 'peanuts' or plastic packing tape and recently eliminated the use of clear plastic tape over our shipping labels.

We are aware of the environmental challenges that face our industry and are doing whatever we can to reduce the amount of solid waste generated by our day-to-day operations. You can help us in this effort. If you are receiving more than one catalog with the same cover or would like to be removed from our mailing list please let us know. Call (800) 622-6216 and we will be happy to help you help us reduce waste.

Thanks for your patronage. We look forward to serving you again soon.

P.S. Please remember that our shipping boxes can be recycled. They also make great storage containers! The plastic bags containing the merchandise can also be reused in many different ways. They make great ice bags and can be used to store all sorts of household "stuff."

Garnet Hill, "Garnet Hill Honored for Recycling Efforts," Package Insert. Reprinted by permission of Garnet Hill.

DOES Q = E?
The Quality Equation
PATAGONIA, INC.

In its spring 1991, catalog, Patagonia explained, "Everything we make pollutes." In the essay the apparel and outdoor equipment manufacturer pointed out that the production of clothing has a negative impact on the environment: "synthetic fibers start as petroleum, for example, and a natural fiber, cotton, uses more pesticides and fertilizers than any other crop in the world." They also announced, however, that they had started a comprehensive Environmental Review Process of all of the methods and materials used in their clothing. They promised to continue to seek those materials and processes that lessened the environmental impact. In the essay that follows, Patagonia explains the philosophy behind its decisions.

Patagonia has an emerald green reputation. Is it deserved? The company has a strong history of employee activism, donates millions to grassroots environmental organizations, led the way in the use of recycled fibers in clothing and most recently, rejected cotton grown with synthetic chemical pesticides. Yet we can't claim the label "environmentally friendly business." If those who praise us assume that our production processes are always low-impact, that we always use the most environmentally sensitive materials available, that environmentalism reigns over other issues, they are wrong.

The fact remains: the clothing industry is dirty, and the production of our clothing takes a significant toll on the earth. No Patagonia products are genuinely sustainable. Producing synthetic fabrics, using industrial dyes, applying waterproof coatings, transporting raw materials and finished goods—these steps always involve an ecological price, always have an impact. There remains a direct connection between the manufacture of our clothing and the cascade of woes affecting the natural world.

We're not blind to that connection. We're aware of an immediate environmental crisis. But we also have a commitment to making the best quality products we possibly can. So we've deliberately chosen a dual focus: We will reduce our impact on the earth—but we will also continue making the best outdoor gear available. Sounds simple. But that challenge involves countless trade-offs that our customers should understand.

We've researched water-based coatings for our gear, rather than solvent-based coatings, and the concept is terrific: fewer volatile organic compounds are released and fewer toxins are used for the coating compounds. But these coatings are not yet durable enough to meet our rigorous performance standards. And so, while we keep researching water-based alternatives, we still use solvent-based coatings.

We're attempting to produce garments with every component made of the same fiber. A jacket made entirely of polyester, for example, would be much easier to recycle. But Delrin zippers and nylon snaps—which we now use—are much stronger than polyester ones. Switching to today's polyester parts could compromise strength, making the garments less reliable for a Denali ascent or a trip down the Rogue. And so, while we keep working on it, many of our products are made of a combination of fibers and materials.

We've made significant and lasting advances by using recycled plastic soda bottles in our PCR® Synchilla® fleece. But elsewhere in our line we still use virgin polyester. We're trying to make Capilene® from PCR, but the yarn is not yet available in a size small enough to make the quality fabrics we expect. We're close, but holding to our performance standards means that, in the short-term, we continue to rely on polyester made from virgin crude oil.

We're trying to base our decisions on the notion that quality and environmental protection should be one and the same: $Q = E$. Patagonia's definition of quality must encompass quality of life on earth. And our environmental innovations must meet the Patagonia customer's demand for quality. If we miss the mark on quality, environmental innovations can lose their appeal in the marketplace. For example, if we use a low impact dye that leaves the customer with a faded shirt nine months later, we show that $Q = E$. Our hope is that merging environmental standards and high quality standards will give our customers greater confidence when they bring environmental values to the marketplace. They will know that a "green" purchase can be a sound, practical investment.

We believe this dual focus has led to lasting changes. We've shown leadership with PCR Synchilla; we've stuck with our quality standards and have a product that cuts waste and substantially reduces our reliance on crude oil, a polluting, nonrenewable resource. We've made an even bigger step with our switch to 100% organic cotton. The conventional cotton economy relies on intensive use of synthetic pesticides that destroy biodiversity and contaminate ground water. Organic cotton makes a superb quality product with a substantial reduction in impact. We've begun to avoid harmful dyes, while still holding to color and colorfast standards. And we've long believed that making a great quality product is, in itself, an environmental statement: If the product has a long and useful life, our desires to consume more, to extract more resources from the earth, are kept in check.

But what of the short-term, what of the trade-offs? How, you may ask, can a company that obviously cares about the health of our planet and its inhabitants really say that environmental improvements should be weighed on a scale with product quality? How can we reject a low-impact dye because it fails to meet our standards for colorfastness, and continue to use a higher impact dye that ultimately damages rivers, streams or groundwater? Can we really say that fabric breathability is so important that we reject a process that might reduce our impact on the earth?

***

CHOOSING ORGANIC

Twenty years ago, I changed my eating habits after I read how much harm cattle grazing inflicts on the earth. That was an easy choice for me—especially when I realized I did not need a steady diet of red meat to sustain my health.

As a company, we face a similar choice. In the course of our ongoing environmental assessment, we discovered that the most damaging fiber used to make our clothing may actually be conventionally grown, 100% "pure" cotton. That's because the process of growing conventional cotton involves the heavy use of chemicals that toxify the soil, air and ground water. And since many of these chemicals were originally formulated as nerve gases for warfare, it is no surprise that where spraying occurs, health problems follow, including higher rates of cancer and birth defects in humans and wildlife. These are outrageous costs to pay for the battle against bugs. And it's a battle we'll never win: while the bugs adapt to the chemicals, the rest of us sustain the long-term damage.

Meanwhile, in our own backyard, a handful of farmers have been growing cotton without chemicals for years. Their yields are just as high, or nearly as high, as those of their "conventional" counterparts and the quality of their fibers is equal or sometimes better. The environmental difference? Of all the potential fibers for clothing, organically-grown cotton may be the least damaging and the most sustainable.

Knowing how destructive conventionally-grown cotton is, and that there's a viable alternative, Patagonia has to choose organic. Now that we know, it would be unconscionable for us to do anything less. That is why, as of this spring, we no longer use conventional cotton in any part of the line.

To change to organic cotton has its price. Organic farming is labor-intensive, and so it is more costly. And after the cotton leaves the field, nearly every step in production—ginning, spinning, and knitting or weaving—incurs added costs for our relatively small runs.

These higher costs also create new risks for our business. We've had to drop some products that no longer make economic sense to produce. And we have to be prepared for a loss in revenue should higher prices translate to fewer sales. We undertake another risk, too: we can't go back. To do so would violate our basic principles: to make a quality product and to reduce our environmental harms. Making clothes out of conventional cotton is something our company can no longer afford to do.

Cotton sportswear makes up a small part of our product line. As we look ahead, we see immense challenges in making our other products in ways less harmful to the landscape. Those challenges prove that our organic cotton project is a single step in a very long process—but an important step nonetheless.

We are betting that we have enough loyal customers who will make the same choice we have made here at Patagonia: to pay more now for organics rather than the hidden environmental costs later. It's a simple, personal choice, of course, to act on what we learn. We've all made such choices: to give up or cut down on red meat, to pay more for an energy-efficient appliance, or forgo a purchase entirely because it's not needed.

If these choices are simple and individual, their ripple effects are profound. The market is laserlike in its response to changes in what people want. Together we can create a significant business base for the organic cotton movement. We should. Organic farmers are returning to the only model we have for sustainable commerce, one that gives back to the planet as much as it takes out. Their success will be a quiet revolution in modern life. Let's follow their lead.

TOPIC STUDY: CORPORATE ENVIRONMENTAL RESPONSIBILITY

BUSINESS AND ENVIRONMENTAL ETHICS

W. MICHAEL HOFFMAN

Hoffman highlights the various influences in the relationship between business and its environment. He cites a claim by philosopher Norman Bowie that businesses have no obligation to their environment above and beyond that required by law, then disagrees and offers support for his own perspective.

. . . Concern over the environment is not new. Warnings came out of the 1960s in the form of burning rivers, dying lakes, and oil-fouled oceans. Radioactivity was found in our food, DDT in mother's milk, lead and mercury in our water. Every breath of air in the North American hemisphere was reported as contaminated. Some said these were truly warnings from Planet Earth of eco-catastrophe, unless we could find limits to our growth and changes in our lifestyle.

Over the past few years Planet Earth began to speak to us even more loudly than before, and we began to listen more than before. The message was ominous, somewhat akin to God warning Noah. It spoke through droughts, heat waves, and forest fires, raising fears of global warming due to the buildup of carbon dioxide and other gases in the atmosphere. It warned us by raw sewage and medical wastes washing up on our beaches, and by devastating oil spills—one despoiling Prince William Sound and its wildlife to such an extent that it made us weep. It spoke to us through increased skin cancers and discoveries of holes in the ozone layer caused by our use of chlorofluorocarbons. It drove its message home through the rapid and dangerous cutting and burning of our primitive forests at the rate of one football field a second, leaving us even more vulnerable to greenhouse gases like carbon dioxide and eliminating scores of irreplaceable species daily. It rained down on us in the form of acid, defoliating our forests and poisoning our lakes and streams. Its warnings were found on barges roaming the seas for places to dump tons of toxic incinerator ash. And its message exploded in our faces at Chernobyl and Bhopal, reminding us of past warnings at Three Mile Island and Love Canal. . . .

W. Michael Hoffman, "Business and Environmental Ethics." Reprinted by permission of the author.

I

In a 1989 keynote address before the "Business, Ethics and the Environment" conference at the Center for Business Ethics, Norman Bowie offered some answers to the first two questions.

> *Business does not have an obligation to protect the environment over and above what is required by law; however, it does have a moral obligation to avoid intervening in the political arena in order to defeat or weaken environmental legislation.*[1]

I disagree with Bowie on both counts.

Bowie's first point is very Friedmanesque.[2] The social responsibility of business is to produce goods and services and to make profit for its shareholders, while playing within the rules of the market game. These rules, including those to protect the environment, are set by the government and the courts. To do more than is required by these rules is, according to this position, unfair to business. In order to perform its proper function, every business must respond to the market and operate in the same arena as its competitors. As Bowie puts this:

> *An injunction to assist in solving societal problems [including depletion of natural resources and pollution] makes impossible demands on a corporation because, at the practical level, it ignores the impact that such activities have on profit.*[3]

If, as Bowie claims, consumers are not willing to respond to the cost and use of environmentally friendly products and actions, then it is not the responsibility of business to respond or correct such market failure.

Bowie's second point is a radical departure from this classical position in contending that business should not lobby against the government's process to set environmental regulations. To quote Bowie:

> *Far too many corporations try to have their cake and eat it too. They argue that it is the job of government to correct for market failure and then they use their influence and money to defeat or water down regulations designed to conserve and protect the environment.*[4]

Bowie only recommends this abstinence of corporate lobbying in the case of environmental regulations. He is particularly concerned that politicians, ever mindful of their reelection status, are already reluctant to pass environmental legislation which has huge immediate costs and in most cases very long-term benefits. This makes the obligations of business to refrain from opposing such legislation a justified special case.

I can understand why Bowie argues these points. He seems to be responding to two extreme approaches, both of which are inappropriate. Let me illustrate these extremes by the following two stories.

At the Center's First National Conference on Business Ethics, Harvard Business School Professor George Cabot Lodge told of a friend who owned a paper company on the banks of a New England stream. On the first Earth Day in 1970, his friend was converted to the cause of environmental protection. He became determined to stop his company's pollution of the stream, and marched off to put his new-found religion into action. Later, Lodge learned his friend went broke, so he went to investigate. Radiating a kind of ethical purity, the friend told Lodge that he spent millions to stop the pollution and thus could no longer compete with other firms that did not follow his example. So the company went under, 500 people lost their jobs, and the stream remained polluted.

When Lodge asked why his friend hadn't sought help from the state or federal government for stricter standards for everyone, the man replied that was not the American way, that government should not interfere with business activity, and that private enterprise could do the job alone. In fact, he felt it was the social responsibility of business to solve environmental problems, so he was proud that he had set an example for others to follow.

The second story portrays another extreme. A few years ago "Sixty Minutes" interviewed a manager of a chemical company that was discharging effluent into a river in up-state New York. At the time, the dumping was legal, though a bill to prevent it was pending in Congress. The manager remarked that he hoped the bill would pass, and that he certainly would support it as a responsible citizen. However, he also said he approved of his company's efforts to defeat the bill and of the firm's policy of dumping wastes in the meantime. After all, isn't the proper role of business to make as much profit as possible within the bounds of law? Making the laws—setting the rules of the game—is the role of government, not business. While wearing his business hat the manager had a job to do, even if it meant doing something that he strongly opposed as a private citizen.

Both stories reveal incorrect answers to the questions posed earlier, the proof of which is found in the fact that neither the New England stream nor the New York river was made any cleaner. Bowie's points are intended to block these two extremes. But to avoid these extremes, as Bowie does, misses the real managerial and ethical failure of the stories. Although the paper company owner and the chemical company manager had radically different views of the ethical responsibilities of business, both saw business and government performing separate roles, and neither felt that business ought to cooperate with government to solve environmental problems.[5]

If the business ethics movement has led us anywhere in the past fifteen years, it is to the position that business has an ethical responsibility to become a more active partner in dealing with social concerns. Business must creatively find ways to become a part of solutions, rather than being a part of problems. Corporations can and must develop a conscience, as Ken Goodpaster and others have argued—and this includes an environmental conscience.[6] Corporations should not isolate themselves from participation in solving our environmental problems, leaving it up to others to find the answers and to tell them what not to do.

Corporations have special knowledge, expertise, and resources which are invaluable in dealing with the environmental crisis. Society needs the ethical vision and cooperation of all its players to solve its most urgent problems, especially one that involves the very survival of the planet itself. Business must work with government to find appropriate solutions. It should lobby for good environmental legislation and lobby against bad legislation, rather than isolating itself from the legislative process as Bowie suggests. It should not be ethically quixotic and try to go it alone, as our paper company owner tried to do, nor should it be ethically inauthentic and fight against what it believes to be environmentally sound policy, as our chemical company manager tried to do. Instead business must develop and demonstrate moral leadership.

There are examples of corporations demonstrating such leadership, even when this has been a risk to their self-interest. In the area of environmental moral leadership one might cite DuPont's discontinuing its Freon products, a $750-million-a-year business, because of their possible negative effects on the ozone layer, and Procter & Gamble's manufacture of concentrated fabric softener and detergents which require less packaging. But some might argue, as Bowie does, that the real burden for environmental change lies with consumers, not with corporations. If we as consumers are willing to accept the harm done to the environment by favoring environmentally unfriendly products, corporations have no moral obligation to change so long as they obey environmental law. This is even more the case, so the argument goes, if corporations must take risks or sacrifice profits to do so. . . .

Even Bowie admits that perhaps business has a responsibility to educate the public and promote environmentally responsible behavior. But I am suggesting that corporate moral leadership goes far beyond public educational campaigns. It requires moral vision, commitment, and courage, and involves risk and sacrifice. I think business is capable of such a challenge. Some are even engaging in such a challenge. Certainly the business ethics movement should do nothing short of encouraging such leadership. I feel morality demands such leadership.

II

If business has an ethical responsibility to the environment which goes beyond obeying environmental law, what criterion should be used to guide and justify such action? Many corporations are making environmentally friendly decisions where they see there are profits to be made by doing so. They are wrapping themselves in green where they see a green bottom line as a consequence. . . .

The frequent strategy of the new environmentalists is to get business to help solve environmental problems by finding profitable or virtually costless ways for them to participate. They feel that compromise, not confrontation, is the only way to save the earth. By using the tools of the free enterprise system, they are in search of win-win solutions, believing that such solutions are necessary to take us beyond what we have so far been able to achieve.

I am not opposed to these efforts; in most cases I think they should be encouraged. There is certainly nothing wrong with making money while protecting the environment, just as there is nothing wrong with feeling good about doing one's duty. But if business is adopting or being encouraged to adopt the view that good environmentalism is good business, then I think this poses a danger for the environmental ethics movement—a danger which has an analogy in the business ethics movement.

As we all know, the position that good ethics is good business is being used more and more by corporate executives to justify the building of ethics into their companies and by business ethics consultants to gain new clients. . . .

Is the rationale that good ethics is good business a proper one for business ethics? I think not. One thing that the study of ethics has taught us over the past 2,500 years is that being ethical may on occasion require that we place the interests of others ahead of or at least on par with our own interests. And this implies that the ethical thing to do, the morally right thing to do, may not be in our own self-interest. What happens when the right thing is not the best thing for the business?

Although in most cases good ethics may be good business, it should not be advanced as the only or even the main reason for doing business ethically. When the crunch comes, when ethics conflicts with the firm's interests, any ethics program that has not already faced up to this possibility is doomed to fail because it will undercut the rationale of the program itself. We should promote business ethics, not because good ethics is good business, but because we are morally required to adopt the moral point of view in all our dealings—and business is no exception. In business, as in all other human endeavors, we must be prepared to pay the costs of ethical behavior.

There is a similar danger in the environmental movement with corporations choosing or being wooed to be environmentally friendly on the grounds that it will be in their self-interest. There is the risk of participating in the movement for the wrong reasons. But what does it matter if business cooperates for reasons other than the right reasons, as long as it cooperates? It matters if business believes or is led to believe that it only has a duty to be environmentally conscientious in those cases where such actions either require no sacrifice or actually make a profit. And I am afraid this is exactly what is happening. . . .

I am not saying we should abandon attempts to entice corporations into being ethical, both environmentally and in other ways, by pointing out and providing opportunities where good ethics is good business. And there are many places where such attempts fit well in both the business and environmental ethics movements. But we must be careful not to cast this as the proper guideline for business's ethical responsibility. Because when it is discovered that many ethical actions are not necessarily good for business, at least in the short run, then the rationale based on self-interest will come up morally short, and both ethical movements will be seen as deceptive and shallow.

III

What is the proper rationale for responsible business action toward the environment? A minimalist principle is to refrain from causing or prevent the causing of unwarranted harm, because failure to do so would violate certain moral rights not to be harmed. There is, of course, much debate over what harms are indeed unwarranted due to conflict of rights and questions about whether some harms are offset by certain benefits. . . .

Some naturalistic environmentalists only include other sentient animals in the framework of being deserving of moral consideration; others include all things which are alive or which are an integral part of an ecosystem. This latter view is sometimes called a biocentric environmental ethic as opposed to the homocentric view which sees all moral claims in terms of human beings and their interests. Some characterize these two views as deep *versus* shallow ecology.

The literature on these two positions is vast and the debate is ongoing. The conflict between them goes to the heart of environmental ethics and is crucial to our making of environmental policy and to our perception of moral duties to the environment, including business's. I strongly favor the biocentric view. And although this is not the place to try to adequately argue for it, let me unfurl its banner for just a moment.

A version of R. Routley's "last man" example[7] might go something like this: Suppose you were the last surviving human being and were soon to die from nuclear poisoning, as all other human and sentient animals have died before you. Suppose also that it is within your power to destroy all remaining life, or to make it simpler, the last tree which could continue to flourish and propagate if left alone. Furthermore you will not suffer if you do not destroy it. Would you do anything wrong by cutting it down? The deeper ecological view would say yes because you would be destroying something that has value in and of itself, thus making the world a poorer place.

It might be argued that the only reason we may find the tree valuable is because human beings generally find trees of value either practically or aesthetically, rather than the atoms or molecules they might turn into if changed from their present form. The issue is whether the tree has value only in its relation to human beings or whether it has a value deserving of moral consideration inherent in itself in its present form. The biocentric position holds that when we find something wrong with destroying the tree, as we should, we do so because we are responding to an intrinsic value in the natural object, not to a value we give to it. This is a view which argues against a humanistic environmental ethic and which urges us to channel our moral obligations accordingly.

Why should one believe that nonhuman living things or natural objects forming integral parts of ecosystems have intrinsic value? . . . I suspect Arne Naess gives as good an answer as can be given.

> *Faced with the ever returning question of "Why?" we have to stop somewhere. Here is a place where we well might stop. We shall admit that the value in itself is something shown in intuition. We attribute intrinsic value to ourselves and our nearest, and the validity of further identification can be contested, and is contested by many. The negation may, however, also be attacked through a series of "whys?" Ultimately, we are in the same human predicament of having to start somewhere, at least for the moment. We must stop somewhere and treat where we then stand as a foundation.*[8]

In the final analysis, environmental biocentrism is adopted or not depending on whether it is seen to provide a deeper, richer, and more ethically compelling view of the nature of things.

If this deeper ecological position is correct, then it ought to be reflected in the environmental movement. Unfortunately, for the most part, I do not think this is being done, and there is a price to be paid for not doing so. . . .

Furthermore, there are many cases where what is in human interest is not in the interest of other natural things. Examples range from killing leopards for stylish coats to destroying a forest to build a golf course. I am not convinced that homocentric arguments, even those based on long-term human interests, have much force in protecting the interests of such natural things. Attempts to make these interests coincide might be made, but the point is that from a homocentric point of view the leopard and the forest have no morally relevant interests to consider. It is simply fortuitous if nonhuman natural interests coincide with human interests, and are thereby valued and protected. Let us take an example from the work of Christopher Stone. Suppose a stream has been polluted by a business. From a homocentric point of view, which serves as the basis for our legal system, we can only correct the problem through finding some harm done to human beings who use the stream. Reparation for such harm might involve cessation of the pollution and restoration of the stream, but it is also possible that the business might settle with the people by paying them for their damages and continue to pollute the stream. Homocentrism provides no way for the stream to be made whole again unless it is in the interests of human beings to do so. In short it is possible for human beings to sell out the stream.[9] . . .

At the heart of the business ethics movement is its reaction to the mistaken belief that business only has responsibilities to a narrow set of its stakeholders, namely its stockholders. Crucial to the environmental ethics movement is its reaction to the mistaken belief that only human beings and human interests are deserving of our moral consideration. I suspect that the beginnings of both movements can be traced to these respective moral insights.

NOTES

1. Norman Bowie, "Morality, Money, and Motor Cars," *Business, Ethics, and the Environment: The Public Policy Debate,* eds., W. Michael Hoffman, Robert Frederick, and Edward S. Petry, Jr. (New York: Quorum Books, 1990), p. 89.
2. See Milton Friedman, "The Social Responsibility of Business Is to Increase Its Profits," *The New York Times Magazine* (September 13, 1970).
3. Bowie, p. 91.
4. Bowie, p. 94.
5. Robert Frederick, Assistant Director of the Center for Business Ethics, and I have developed and written these points together. Frederick has also provided me with invaluable assistance on other points in this paper.
6. Kenneth E. Goodpaster, "Can a Corporation Have an Environmental Conscience?" *The Corporation, Ethics, and the Environment,* eds., W. Michael Hoffman, Robert Frederick, and Edward S. Petry, Jr. (New York: Quorum Books, 1990).
7. Richard Routley and Val Routley, "Human Chauvinism and Environmental Ethics," *Environmental Philosophy,* Monograph Series, No. 2, eds., Don Mannison, Michael McRobbie, and Richard Routley (Australian National University, 1980), pp. 121ff.
8. Arne Naess, "Identification as a Source of Deep Ecological Attitudes," *Deep Ecology,* ed., Michael Tobias (San Marcos, CA: Avant Books, 1988), p. 266.
9. Christopher D. Stone, "Should Trees Have Standing?—Toward Legal Rights for Natural Objects," in *People, Penguins, and Plastic Trees,* pp. 86–87.

FORESTS OF THE NORTH COAST

The Owls, the Trees, and the Conflicts

LISA NEWTON AND CATHERINE DILLINGHAM

You may already be familiar with the basic facts of the next case. It addresses the battle between the logging community of the Pacific Northwest and the animal rights advocates who seek to protect the spotted owl population in that same area. Apparently, the two populations can not co-exist. As you read the case, do any alternatives come to mind for resolving this situation? The authors ask whether this case is, as the media contended, basically a class conflict between the blue-collar loggers and the elite, white-collar professional class that typifies the environmental movement.

The media have characterized the struggle between the loggers and the environmentalists as essentially a class conflict: the working-class lumbermen against the elite professional class that typifies the environmental movement. How does the United States generally handle white-collar versus blue-collar conflicts? Will the lessons learned elsewhere in that type of conflict help us here?

BACKGROUND: THE TRAGEDY OF TREES

"Save a Life, Kill a Tree?" is an article written by Sallie Tisdale; it describes the most recent "trees vs. people" ammunition, the anticancer drug taxol that is found in the bark of the Pacific Yew of the Northwest old-growth forests. "Save a Logger—Eat a Spotted Owl" is a bumper sticker commonly seen throughout this area. A grocery store in northern California recently displayed boxes of Spotted Owl Helper (a takeoff on Hamburger Helper). A recurring theme in this controversy is that something (usually a tree, but sometimes an owl) has to be killed in order to save something of human value; this gives the whole topic an overtone of tragedy. In tragedy, victory is impossible, and reconciliation comes at terrible cost. Simply because the issue will not yield to politically conscious pragmatism (the peculiarly American version of reason), it invites complications from the political and economic left and right and sanctions violence in defense of endangered values. Our first job, then, is to sort out the complications, so that the intersecting ethical dilemmas can be treated independently. Let us consider the issues:

1. *The owl.* The northern spotted owl is threatened with extinction by logging operations in the Northwest Forest. The owl is protected to some extent by the Endangered Species Act . . . , but the issues involved go beyond the law. Why might we have a moral obligation to save an endangered species? On the other hand, why should we care about insignificant faraway birds, anyway? What good is *biodiversity?* And what should we be willing to do to maintain it?

2. *The trees and the business practices that threaten them.* Ted Gup describes the owl as "a fine bird, yes, but . . . never really the root cause of this great conflict." It is the trees themselves—great groves of Sequoia and other cone-bearing trees, some of them more than 2,000 years old, spontaneously likened to the great cathedrals of Europe by many who have seen them—it is the trees that really fire the imagination. Do we have an obligation to preserve these trees, just as a singular treasure for the world?

   We live with a free-enterprise system that generally serves us well. Do we have an obligation either to protect businesses that operate in environmentally sensitive ways, or to require that all businesses do so? The case of Pacific Lumber Company shows a company that preserved environmental values pitted against hostile financial initiatives that were good for the shareholders but bad for the trees. Does the fiduciary duty of the company extend to the environment? Should the trees have a vote at the annual meeting? Do we have an obligation to protect the workers—the loggers, and their peculiarly specialized way of life?

3. *The varied roles of the government.* . . . What is the role of the government in protecting owls, trees, business, and ourselves? What do we want the government's role to be? What should government be empowered to do? at what cost?

All these questions turn on one indisputable fact: the Pacific Northwest Rainforests, ecosystems unlike any others in the world, have been logged for a century to the point of threatened extinction, not only of the species housed there but of the forests themselves. These forests are managed and regulated by an incredible mix of national bureaucracies; the actions of these agencies affect the livelihoods of millions of people and the economies of three states. The loggers and lumber companies are in conflict with the environmentalists; both parties are in conflict with the regulators; the politicians are on all sides of the conflict, depending on their constituencies; and everything ends up in court, where the "lawsuits, motions, and appeals . . . [seem to] have increased faster than the owl population."

THE OWL AND ITS TREES

The currents of the Pacific Ocean provide abundant warmth and moisture to the Northwest Coast of the United States. Through millions of years of evolution, these conditions have allowed the appearance, probably 6,000 years ago, of what we now call "old-growth forests." These are forests with some thousand-year-old stands, forests with trees that are 300 feet tall and ten feet in diameter, trees that are at least twice as massive as those found in tropical rainforests, trees that each contain enough lumber to build two houses. These forests extend from the Alaskan panhandle (Sitka Spruce) south through Washington and Oregon (Douglas Fir, Western Hemlock) to northern California (Redwoods, Ponderosa Pine). . . .

The owl is one of those species that requires unique stable conditions to survive: It appears to be totally dependent upon old-growth forest, and hunts there exclusively. To house the owl, the trees must be dense, and some proportion of them must be over 200 years old. Thus, the future of the northern spotted owl is linked with that of the old-growth forest, and the owl is therefore considered an *indicator* species—that is, a species whose condition will indicate the condition of the entire ecosystem (similar to the canary in the coal mine). Not only does the owl require old growth, it requires a lot of it. Studies have shown that, in northern California, each pair ranged among 1,900 acres of old growth; in Oregon, six pairs averaged 2,264 acres as their range; and six pairs studied in Washington had an average range of 3,800 acres.

ENDANGERMENT AND OBLIGATIONS

The northern spotted owl, then, is clearly endangered. To save it, we must save large numbers of the oldest trees. Given that 90 percent of the forest has been cut down already, virtually all the remaining old growth, whether in private or public hands, must be preserved. Should we do this for the sake of the owl?

Do we have an obligation to preserve endangered species? For starters, what does "preservation" mean in this context? If only the genetic material is in question, we can preserve the spotted owl by capturing a sufficient number of breeding pairs (say, 20), putting them in a climate-controlled zoo, and allowing them to produce baby owls to their hearts' content—and we can do this without gumming up the logging operations. (If no zoos have room for owls right now, we could freeze owl eggs indefinitely and regenerate the species any time it is convenient to do so.) Or does preservation of a wild species always mean preservation in the wild, living as the species has evolved to live, naturally? If this is preservation, then what cost are we expected to absorb to preserve the habitat? Granted that the owl is worth something to us (we would not wish it extinguished, other things being equal), but what is it worth when it affects these other things: jobs, regional economies, and the evolved lifestyle of the North Coast loggers?

The preservation of a species contributes to the biodiversity of the area—this means, literally, the number and variety of species that are living there. For any ecosystem, we assume that the species have evolved as members of a niche and that the destruction of one species, leaving its niche open and its role unfilled, will have an unfavorable impact on the others. For the sake of *all* species, then, we should preserve *each* species. We cannot predict just which of these species will suddenly prove to be dramatically useful to humans—by, say, providing a cure for cancer. . . . This argument was used, but only hypothetically, until the discovery of taxol, a drug that has recently shown better than expected results in treating ovarian and breast cancer; taxol originates in the bark (and perhaps the needles) of the Pacific Yew, which is indigenous to the old growth. The U.S. Forest Service used to consider the Yew a weed, to be removed from a clear-cut and burned; now, of course, there is pressure from many fronts to harvest these trees for the cancer drug. Would we have ever found out about this use for yew trees if the old groves had all been gone? For the sake of the human species, then, we should protect *any* species, no matter how humble, no matter what measures (within the obvious limits of reason) are required to preserve the conditions that species need to live.

ACTING TO PRESERVE THE SPECIES

Persuaded by such considerations, Congress passed the Endangered Species Act (ESA) in 1973. According to this bill, the National Marine Fishery Service (Department of Commerce) and the Fish and Wildlife Service (Department of the Interior) are empowered to list marine and land species, respectively, as either threatened or endangered; then, these species can no longer be hunted, collected, injured, or killed. The bill also prohibits any federal agency from carrying out or funding any activity that could threaten or endanger said species *or their habitats.* (This latter provision has caused the most controversy with regard to logging in the old-growth forests, but also other projects, such as dams, highways, and other development receiving federal funding.) Therefore, both the Bureau of Land Management (Department of the Interior) and the Forest Service (Department of Agriculture) must consult with the Fish and Wildlife Service before undertaking any action that might threaten a species such as the owl.

This bill is typical of environmental legislation on several counts: (1) It is informed by the best science available, so it is enlightened, far-reaching, and probably the world's most stringent species-protection legislation. To be in noncompliance with the ESA is a criminal act; both civil and criminal penalties are called for, including imprisonment. (2) This bill is also among those most pitifully funded. Until 1988, the yearly funding amounted to about the cost of 12 Army bulldozers. The 1988 amendments doubled the budget, but legislative environmentalists consider that the bill has nowhere near the support it needs to preserve marine and terrestrial species worldwide. (3) Three cabinet-level departments must work harmoniously together for the act to be implemented.

Implementation presents other problems. According to the 1982 amendment of the act, the economic implications of the protection of a species *may not* be considered in determining its status, whether or not it is endangered; that decision must be based "solely on the basis of the best scientific and commercial data." Economic factors *may* be considered after the listing, during the required preparation of a recovery plan for the listed species. (In practice, because of the complexities involved, few plans have been prepared.) The act also calls for a determination of the species' "critical habitat" but allows a year to elapse after the listing for the determination and acknowledges that, because of complications, the habitat might be indeterminable.

When determining the critical habitat, the Fish and Wildlife Service *must* include economic considerations. On two occasions, court-ordered reconsiderations on the basis of economic impact have impelled the FWS to reduce the acreage required to preserve the owl. Additionally, those who feel that their economic interests are damaged by species protection may appeal to the Endangered Species Committee (the "God Squad"). The bureaucratic hurdles to overcome on the way to actual protection of the owl seem daunting even to the most hardened Washington veterans; nevertheless, it *is* legal protection and, as such, the strongest statement that we can make, as a nation, about the value of our most threatened creatures.

THE TALLEST TREES ON EARTH

. . . Unfortunately for those who hope for the survival of these trees, they are the most commercially valuable trees in the United States. The extent of the original forest and of the remaining acreage is very debatable and probably depends on one's definition of "old growth," which is generally described as the largest old trees, living and dead, standing and fallen, within a multilayered canopy. Estimates of the extent of the original forest range from 20 to 70 million acres (depending on what is considered a large tree); some 70 to 95 percent of this forest has been logged over the last century, and the rate of logging has increased dramatically over the last few decades. Estimates are complicated, too, by the fragmentation of the forest by clear-cutting, leaving some stands isolated in a barren landscape.

From the corporate viewpoint, logging just makes good business sense. The woods, as a popular song would have it, are just trees, and the trees are just wood. Humans have always cut and processed timber for lumber—for houses, boats, fences, furniture—virtually since our beginnings on this planet, and the redwoods are eminently suitable for such harvest. The lumber from redwoods is beautiful, durable, light, strong, has good nail-holding capacity, and is insect- and fire-resistant. Each tree yields an average of 12 or 13 thousand board feet—enough to build two houses. The harvest is very profitable but strictly limited. Once those old-growth trees are logged, there will be no more: The trees will be gone forever. The second growth does not share the characteristics of the old growth in its resistance to insects, disease, fire, and decay, nor is it as dense and massive, of course. We might suppose that the twentieth-century remnants of a 2,000-year-old forest were composed of the best survivors of all attacks: The less-resistant trees will have succumbed centuries ago. The old growth is then an irreplaceable asset: It could be argued that it will become more valuable every year into the indefinite future and that it therefore demands careful husbanding and conservative forestry practices. Wise management would seem to require very sparing cuts of the old growth while encouraging plantations of new trees to satisfy demands for ordinary lumber.

TREES, THE ENVIRONMENT, AND THE LAW

Aristotle and Adam Smith both proved, in very different ways, that private property (specifically, land and all resources for production) was better off, more likely to be taken care of, than public property. We accept as established fact that a private owner is the best caretaker of property. The centrality of the right to private property in John Locke's writing depends on that presumption, as do our standard defenses of the American business system.

Is this presumption now generally false? Pacific Lumber's redwoods are clearly not safe in Hurwitz's hands. Do we have a legal right, then, to take the land away from him? We know that, under the doctrine of eminent domain, we can seize the redwoods for a new national park—but can we seize all that land just to continue a more conservative logging operation? What are the business imperatives of a company that logs redwoods? Is it a sufficient discharge of our obligations to replace 2,000-year-old groves with young growth that can be harvested in 40 to 80 years?

Another environmental effect of the logging, presently unmeasurable, is its contribution to global warming. The old growth is a veritable storehouse of carbon, a fact of increasingly intense interest, for carbon dioxide is the most important of the "greenhouse gases" credited with causing the projected global warming. While these trees are alive, they absorb huge amounts of carbon dioxide from the atmosphere in the photosynthetic process.

Nature's recycling laws require, of course, that the same amount of gas be returned to the atmosphere, through the trees' respiration and eventual decay, but that happens, as we have noted, over a period of hundreds of years.

When the trees are felled, the photosynthetic carbon dioxide absorption stops and, compounding the crime, when the resulting debris is burned, the stored carbon is abruptly added to the atmosphere as carbon dioxide. The timber industry has claimed that, by cutting old growth and planting young trees with a faster photosynthetic rate, they are actually ameliorating the threat of global warming. To be sure, a rapidly growing tree absorbs more carbon dioxide than a mature tree of the same size, but a small seedling does not approach the chemical activity of the enormous trees in the Northwest Forest, trees that are many times as massive as those found anywhere else in the world. The Northwest old growth "stores more carbon . . . than any other biome—twice as much per unit of area as tropical rainforests."

Incidentally, the claim of the timber companies—that their little plantings are really much better at taking carbon from the air than the mature redwoods—is typical of the self-serving half-truths that tend to harden attitudes in these controversies. This claim, with just enough scientific fact to make it respectable yet clearly in the service of company interests, enrages environmentalists and encourages public cynicism. Should the timber companies be held responsible for global warming—an unintended but predictable, consequence of their operations?

CREATIVE ALTERNATIVES

The strongest indication that the Forest Service and its allied agencies in the federal government might not be the true villains, however, lies in the work they do when the law asks them to think creatively about these forests and their future. Pursuant to the 1960 Multiple Use Sustained Yield Act . . . , the Forest Service, the Bureau of Land Management, and the U.S. Fish and Wildlife Service were asked to describe ways that the owl might be saved and the trees might be put to work for the nation without being cut down. The agencies did a fine job: The combined report of the Forest Service and the BLM, "Actions the Administration May Wish to Consider in Implementing a Conservation Strategy for the Northern Spotted Owl" (May 1, 1990), recommends a drastic cutback in the harvesting of old-growth trees by forbidding export of raw logs, then recommends and describes extensive educational and retraining programs for the loggers who are put out of work by the ban. Technical assistance would make logging and milling more efficient (avoiding the extensive waste entailed by present practices); recreational facilities would make the forests better-known and better-used and create political pressure to conserve the trees. Even more impressive is the FWS report, "Economic Analysis of Designation of Critical Habitat for the Northern Spotted Owl" (August 1991). Going beyond the multiple-use scenario, the report specifically addresses "non-use values," the value to the nation just to have the forests *there:* "Estimates of recreation user demand, benefits of scenic beauty, and benefits of water quality represent only a partial estimate of society's total value for the spotted owl and its associated habitat. The public also is willing to pay for the option of recreation use in the future, the knowledge that the natural ecosystem exists and is protected, and the satisfaction from its bequest to future generations. . . . The average willingness to pay higher taxes and wood product prices reported in a referendum contingent valuation format was $190 per year. The lower limit of the 98 percent confidence range was $117 per household."

These reports place the federal government's environmental services in a new and much better light. Bureaucrats in general, and federal bureaucrats in particular, have been harshly criticized for their role (or lack of same) in the protection of the forests. But these reports on alternate usage of the forests suggest, though, that the idealists who once joined government service to protect the nation's environmental heritage might still be around, waiting only for public opinion to catch up to them. A new agenda for the environment will require a trained corps of experts in science and policy to articulate a national environmental ethic and to frame the plans for implementation. In developing their reports, the Forest Service, the BLM, and the FWS have made an auspicious start.

SUMMARY

The heart of the problem, from an environmental point of view, is the old-growth forest. From the loggers' point of view, the problem is jobs. The owl, the financier, and the government agencies are all bit players in an agonizing twentieth-century drama of loss and conflict. We need not search for villains. Once we all thought that the forests were unlimited. The timber industry's managers watched the old growth disappear before their eyes and did not realize that it could not be restored—that once gone, it would be gone forever; but they were no more ignorant than their regulators, their customers, or their fellow citizens. The environmental movement is not the sole prerogative of Eastern elitists, as the loggers suspect, nor is the timber industry composed of a series of tintypes of Charles Hurwitz, as the environmentalists are convinced.

Protecting the forests will require the abolition of a way of life that has been honored and valued in the immediate past. What, exactly, are we prepared to do to compensate and redirect the people who are stranded by systematic and extensive preservation? On the other hand, are we prepared to spare ourselves that difficult decision by allowing the forests to be destroyed? Once the trees are gone, the industry will die, and the workers will be unemployed anyway, but then it will be *their* problem, not ours. How much are we willing to lose in order to avoid the pain of making this decision now—before it is too late? Our history suggests that we are willing to lose quite a bit.

The most disturbing aspect of our political response to these dilemmas, though, is the hypocrisy of the United States urging Brazil and other Third World countries to halt the cutting of their tropical rainforests to prevent the worsening of global warming, while we cut our forests about twice as fast. To quote an official with the Oregon Natural Resources Council, "It's interesting that we're telling Third World countries, 'don't cut your forests' [while] . . . we're wiping out our fish runs, we're wiping out our biotic diversity, we're sending species to extinction . . . we're not a Third World country. We're not so poor that we have to destroy our ancient forests. And we're not so rich that we can afford to."

ENVIRONMENT

HARVEY S. JAMES

Harvey James posted the following message to a business ethics list-server. James applies property rights and market analysis to a theory of corporate environmental ethics.

From:	JAMES, HARVEY
To:	Multiple recipients of list BETS-L <BETS-L@LISTSER. . .
Date	9/18/96 8:28A.M.
Subject:	Environment

Environmental consciousness is important to business only when it is in the interest of business to be conscious of the environment. So, John Trebnik is correct when he says the answer is simply grounded in economic theory. The important question is when is it in the interest of business to be environmental-friendly.

If a business knows that its customers want strong environmental policies, a business will follow, or lose sales, which is not profit maximizing. For instance, a clothing retailer that sells "outdoor" clothing will not want a reputation for trashing the environment—it's not good for business.

If a business uses "natural" resources for production purposes, then it will want to ensure that the resources are in as good a quality as possible in order to [keep] resource costs low. This also tends to lead to profit maximization. For instance, a logging firm will plant seedlings in order to replenish forest growth in lands the firm owns in order to provide logging opportunities in the future.

The interesting question has to do with when a firm will NOT want to be environmentally conscious. This occurs primarily when the property rights over resources are not clearly defined and enforced. For instance, a factory may dump waste by-products in the local lake because it does not own the lake and the lake owners do not enforce their right to clean lake waters. Hence, discussions of the environmental policies of firms should, in my opinion, be centered around property rights. The rest is, well, academic.

—Harvey S. James, Jr., Ph.D.

"Be right, and then be easy to live with, if possible, but in that order."

Harvey S. James, "Environment," E-mail posted to BETS-L, Listsever, September 18, 1996. Reprinted by permission of the author.

Chapter 13

ETHICS IN GLOBAL BUSINESS

List of Fashion Trendsetters	U.S. DEPARTMENT OF LABOR
"Help End Sweatshop Conditions for American Workers"	ROBERT B. REICH
"A Presidential Dilemma: America Go Global or America Stay Home?"	IAN SPAULDING, LORI MCDONOUGH AND LAWRENCE PONEMON

American businesses face a challenge of global competition which is greater than any time in the history of our country.

—ALEXANDER TROTMAN, CEO, FORD MOTOR COMPANY

When in Rome, do as the Romans. How many times have you heard this phrase? The essence of the rule is that one's actions will be judged according to the norms of the environment in which it takes place. This is not always the case; in many circumstances, we believe that our way is the right way and that alternatives are not acceptable. Consider the decision of Levi Strauss management to take their manufacturing business out of China in protest of China's history of human rights abuses. While it might have been acceptable in the Chinese culture, or at least tolerated, Levi Strauss did not want to be a part of it.

Similarly, there was uproar in mid 1996 when it was discovered that a clothing line sponsored by Kathie Lee Gifford was manufactured under conditions in other countries that appalled many Americans. Chicago Bulls basketball player Michael Jordan was forced to defend his role as spokesperson for Nike shoes when similar conditions were found in foreign Nike plants. (See discussion of The Gap's operations in El Salvador in this section.)

On the other hand, the "When in Rome" justification has been used to ethically exculpate American firms who do business in other countries and who have offered what we would consider to be bribes in order to get certain jobs done. Consider what you would do if the only way to obtain a certain permit or contract is to offer a bribe and that "everyone does it."[1] In addition, a firm may contend that if it does not act in ways similar to firms native to that country, it may lose business or be unable to do business there. Does that make it acceptable? Americans generally believe that bribery is wrong or unethical because it allows certain parties to obtain a privilege not afforded to others. On the other hand, while most Americans don't believe it is wrong or unethical to eat meat; individuals in other countries believe that eating meat is wrong and unethical. In the United States, men are limited to one wife. In other countries, that is considered unthinkable and humiliating. Who is right in each of these conflicts? Who should answer that question?

---

[1] Consider Transparency International's annual Bribe Payers and Corruption Perceptions Indexes. In 1999, TI found that Sweden scored 8.3 on a scale of 0–10 and South Korea scored a 3.4 (where 10 represented a perceived negligible level of bribery and 0 represented a perceived very high level of bribery). In terms of corruption, Denmark scored the highest with a 10 on a scale of 10–0, and Cameroon scored 1.5 (where business people, risk analysts, and the general public were asked about their perceptions of the degree of corruption and 10 represented highly clean while 0 represented highly corrupt. *http://www.transparency.de/documents/cpi/index.htm*

Are there any objective "rights" and "wrongs?" Is there anything that we would all agree is ethically wrong in the world or ethically right? Western and Eastern concepts of right and wrong may not be that far off. In a recent *Harvard Business Review* article, Wharton professor Thomas Donaldson demonstrates how Western and non-Western values may have a great deal in common. For instance, Donaldson links the Western values of individual liberty and human rights to the Japanese value of *kyosei* (living and working together for the common good) and the Muslim value of *Zakat* (the duty to give alms to the poor).[2]

Donaldson and colleague Thomas Dunfee suggest in their "integrative social contracts theory" that one can differentiate between those values which are fundamental across culture and theory ("hypernorms")[3] and those values which are determined within moral "free space" and are not hypernorms. Donaldson and Dunfee propose that one look to the convergence of religious, cultural, and philosophical beliefs around certain core principles as a clue to the identification of hypernorms. Donaldson and Dunfee include as examples of hypernorms freedom of speech, the right to personal freedom, the right to physical movement, and informed consent. As you consider these far-reaching rights, do you believe that all reasonable thinkers would agree as to their predominance and worthiness of protection? And should the majority truly rule here, as ISCT dictates through its reliance on a "convergence" of opinions?

In line with Donaldson's and Dunfee's effort to propose a means by which to apply ethical standards across borders, several proposed codes of conduct are presented in this section, including the U.S. Model Business Principles and the Caux Round Table Principles. Consider the similarities and differences between the proposed models of business behavior. If there are differences, do these difference in themselves evidence the fact that there is no general agreement regarding business conduct? If you were to create a model code of conduct for a global firm, would it resemble any of these codes?

Firms often complain that adhering to these codes of conduct is costly, imposing higher costs on them than those imposed on firms in other countries. Therefore, adherence to the codes places them at a competitive disadvantage in comparison to firms in less-regulated countries. Economists have called international labor standards "institutional intervention in competitive markets that impairs the workings of the invisible hand."[4] Free market economists believe that standards reduce efficiency, thereby increasing the cost of labor, lowering the employment of those affected, and benefitting higher cost competitors.[5] On the other hand, standards may be the only way to address a market failure—that is, the market fails to consider the nonfinancial conditions of employment and the nonfinancial impact of these conditions.

---

[2]Thomas Donaldson, "Values in Tension: Ethics Away from Home," *Harvard Business Review* (September/October 1996), pp. 48–62, 53.

[3]Thomas Donaldson and Thomas Dunfee, "Toward a Unified Conception of Business Ethics: Integrative Social Contracts Theory," *Academy of Management Review* 19 (1994), pp. 252, 264 (defining hypernorms as those principles that would limit moral free space, analogizing hypernorms to "hypergoods," "goods sufficiently fundamental as to serve as a source of evaluation and criticism of community-generated norms [within moral free space]").

[4]Richard B. Freeman, "A Hard-Headed Look at Labor Standards," *International Labor Standards and Global Economic Integration: Proceedings of a Symposium* (July 1994), p. 26.

[5]Ibid.

Harvard economist Richard Freeman asks whether there is any difference in the actual tee-shirt produced by individuals under differing conditions. In other words, is there any difference between a tee-shirt manufactured by political prisoners in a labor camp or sexually harassed women in a free trade zone in Central America, and a tee-shirt manufactured by workers under normal, acceptable conditions? If the price is the same, perhaps you will prefer the one made under ethical conditions. Perhaps you might even pay a slight premium for that shirt. However, the market evidences that, where the price of the latter is higher, the demand for decent labor standards declines. Fewer and fewer people are willing to pay a premium as the difference in price becomes greater. Freeman argues, therefore, that the market demand will sufficiently, efficiently, and satisfactorily determine labor conditions for manufactured goods.[6]

Beyond compliance to a central code of business behavior, firms must be sensitive to cultural differences in those countries in which they do business. Campbell Soup has learned that paying attention to cultural differences may mean the difference between reaping a profit and bearing a loss. In many countries, Campbell's discovered that other brands' dry soups were highly preferred to Campbell's canned, condensed soups. On the other hand, Campbell's duck-gizzard soup has high sales in Hong Kong and its Godiva Chocolate line sells well in Japan.[7] While answering the soup flavor needs of a country may seem to be trivial in light of other ethical-cultural conflicts, Campbell's was originally viewed as insincere and unresponsive by its foreign consumers—not too trivial to Campbell's.

Challenges to this cultural sensitivity are strong, however; and similar criticism can be leveled against Donaldson and Dunfee's formulation. How many cultures have to agree on a norm in order for it to rise to the level of a hypernorm? If one culture's standards seriously violate a norm that is generally accepted by many other cultures, are you comfortable saying that the minority is wrong and the majority is right? Moreover, ethicist Richard Nielsen questions whether ISCT is a realistic conception when there is a lack of freedom of voice in some communities.[8] Freedom of voice typically does not exist when there are significant power differences among segments of the relevant community, as would be the case with dictatorial governments and high-unemployment communities without effective labor unions. Though most societies have due processes in form, the substance of due process is often lacking. Other ethicists contend that the basic requirements of norm establishment do not exist in so many cultures that ISCT proves to be unreliable.

So how is one to determine right from wrong in the global arena? Perhaps that is the most significant question in this text. As discussed in the introduction to the first chapter, right and wrong depends, of course, on the standards by which you are judging the act or decision. As the national boundaries within our world market become increasingly blurred, so too do the cultural differences. One may question whether this, in itself, is a beneficial result. In the end, one may be merely left with the differences between each human on the earth and the variances in their personal value structures. Perhaps as we all become more and more familiar with varying value perspectives, we might be more likely to better understand and, hopefully, to accept these differences as valuable rather than threatening.

---

[6]Ibid, p. 27.

[7]Joseph Weber, "What's Not Cookin' at Campbell's," *Business Week* (September 23, 1996), p. 40.

[8]Richard P. Nielsen, "Do Internal Due Process Systems Permit Adequate Political and Moral Space for Ethics Voice, Praxis, and Community?" *Journal of Business Ethics,* 24, no. 1 (March 2000), p. 1.

TOPIC STUDY: ETHICAL PRINCIPLES GOVERNING GLOBAL BUSINESS

MODEL BUSINESS PRINCIPLES
U.S. DEPARTMENT OF COMMERCE

In an effort to codify the expectations of the American market, the U.S. Department of Commerce (DOC) issued its Model Business Principles in 1995 as guidelines for business conduct in the United States and abroad. While the principles comprise a voluntary code of conduct, the DOC hopes that they will encourage appropriate behavior.

Recognizing the positive role of U.S. business in upholding and promoting adherence to universal standards of human rights, the Administration encourages all businesses to adopt and implement voluntary codes of conduct for doing business around the world that cover at least the following areas:

1. Provision of a safe and healthy workplace.
2. Fair employment practices, including avoidance of child and forced labor and avoidance of discrimination based on race, gender, national origin or religious beliefs; and respect for the right of association and the right to organize and bargain collectively.
3. Responsible environmental protection and environmental practices.
4. Compliance with U.S. and local laws promoting good business practices, including laws prohibiting illicit payments and ensuring fair competition.
5. Maintenance, through leadership at all levels, of a corporate culture that respects free expression consistent with legitimate business concerns, and does not condone political coercion in the workplace; that encourages good corporate citizenship and makes a positive contribution to the communities in which the company operates; and where ethical conduct is recognized, valued and exemplified by all employees.

In adopting voluntary codes of conduct that reflect these principles, U.S. companies should serve as models, encouraging similar behavior by their partners, suppliers, and subcontractors.

Adoption of codes of conduct reflecting these principles is voluntary. Companies are encouraged to develop their own codes of conduct appropriate to their particular circumstances. Many companies already apply statements or codes that incorporate these princi-

---

U.S. Dept. of Commerce, U.S. Model Business Principles. (1995)

ples. Companies should find appropriate means to inform their shareholders and the public of actions undertaken in connection with these principles. Nothing in the principles is intended to require a company to act in violation of host country or U.S. law. This statement of principles is not intended for legislation.

MODEL BUSINESS PRINCIPLES: PROCEDURES

When President Clinton announced his decision to renew China's MFN status last year, he also announced a commitment to work with the business community to develop a voluntary statement of business principles relating to corporate conduct abroad. The President made clear that U.S. business can and does play a positive and important role promoting the openness of societies, respect for individual rights, the promotion of free markets and prosperity, environmental protection and the setting of high standards for business practices generally.

The Administration today is offering an update on our efforts to follow-through on the President's commitment to promote the Model Business Principles and best practices among U.S. companies. The Principles already have gained the support of some U.S. companies. A process is ongoing to elicit additional support for these Principles and to continue to examine issues related to them.

The elements of this process are as follows:

1. Voluntary Statement of Business Principles. The Administration, in extensive consultations with business and labor leaders and members of the Non-Governmental Organization (NGO) community, developed these model principles, which were reported widely in the press earlier this spring. This model statement is to be used by companies as a reference point in framing their own codes of conduct. It is based on a wide variety of similar sets of principles U.S. companies and business organizations already have put into global practice. The Administration encourages all businesses everywhere to support the model principles. (Copies of the model statement are available by calling the U.S. Department of Commerce Trade Information Center, 1-800-USA-TRADE.)

2. Efforts by U.S. Business. As part of the ongoing effort, U.S. businesses will engage in the following activities:

    (a) Conferences on Best Practices Issues. In conjunction with Business for Social Responsibility, a non-profit business organization dedicated to promoting laudable corporate practices, and/or other appropriate organizations, the Administration will work to encourage conferences concerning issues relating to the practices contained in the Model Business Principles. Such conferences can provide a forum for information-sharing on new approaches for the evolving global context in which best practices are implemented. (For further information on Business for Social Responsibility, contact Bob Dunn, President, (415) 865-2500.)

    (b) Best Practices Information Clearinghouse and Support Services. One or more non-profits will work with the U.S. business community to develop a clearinghouse of information regarding business practices globally. The clearinghouse will establish a library of codes of conduct adopted by U.S. and international companies and organizations, to be catalogued and made available to companies seeking to develop their own codes. The clearinghouse would be available to provide advice to companies seeking to develop or improve their codes, advice based on the accumulated experience of other companies. Business for Social Responsibility (described above) is highly respected and is one resource that businesses and NGO's alike can turn to for information on best business practices.

3. Efforts by the U.S. Government. The U.S. Government also will undertake a number of activities to generate support for the Model Business Principles:

   (a) Promote Multilateral Adoption of Best Practices. The Administration has begun and will continue its effort to seek multilateral support for the Model Business Principles. Senior U.S. Government officials already have met with U.S. company officials and U.S. organizations operating abroad as well as with foreign corporate officials to seek support for the Principles. For example, the American Chambers of Commerce in the Asia Pacific recently adopted a resolution by which their members agreed to work with their local counterparts in the countries in which they operate to seek development of similar best practices among their members. The United States also will present the Model Business Principles at the Organization for Economic Cooperation and Development (OECD) and the International Labor Organization (ILO) as part of these organizations' ongoing behavior. Therefore, on an annual basis, the Administration will offer a series of awards to companies for specific activities that reflect best practices in the areas covered by the Model Business Principles. The awards will be granted pursuant to applications by interested companies. NGOs and private citizens will be encouraged to call attention to activities they believe are worthy of consideration. (For further information on the Best Practices Awards Program, contact Melinda Yee, U.S. Department of Commerce, (202) 482-1051.)

   (b) Presidential-Business Discussions. The President's Export Council (PEC), a high-level advisory group of Chief Executive Officers, provides a forum for the President to meet regularly with U.S. business leaders to discuss issues relating to U.S. industries' exports and operations abroad.

For further general information about the Model Business Principles, please contact Jill Schuker, U.S. Commerce Department, (202) 482-5151, or David Ruth, U.S. Department of State, (202) 647-1625.

THE CAUX PRINCIPLES
THE CAUX ROUND TABLE

The Caux Round Table consisted of a group of international executives based in Caux, Switzerland. The group shared a belief that business organizations can be a powerful force for positive change in the quality of life for the world. The executives developed their principles based on the Minnesota principles created by the Minnesota Center for Corporate Responsibility in 1992. The Caux Principles are based in the conviction that we can all live together and act for the common good.

The Caux Principles are rooted in two basic ethical ideals: kyosei and human dignity. The Japanese concept of kyosei means living and working together for the common good—enabling cooperation and mutual prosperity to coexist with healthy and fair competition. Human dignity relates to the sacredness or value of each person as an end, not simply as the means to the fulfillment of other's purposes or even majority prescription. The general principles in section 2 clarify the spirit of kyosei and human dignity while the specific stakeholder principles in section 3 are concerned with their practical application. After reading the Principles, can you think of any issues that are not addressed?

SECTION 1. PREAMBLE

The mobility of employment, capital, produce, and technology is making business increasingly global in its transactions and its effects.

Laws and market forces are necessary but insufficient guides for conduct.

Responsibility for the politics and actions of business and respect for the dignity and interests of its stakeholders are fundamental.

Shared values, including a commitment to shared prosperity, are as important for a global community as for communities of smaller scale.

For these reasons, and because business can be a powerful agent of positive social change we offer the following principles as a foundation for dialogue and action by business leaders in search of business responsibility. In so doing we affirm the necessity for moral values in business decision making; without them, stable business relationships and a sustainable world community are impossible.

The Caux Round Table, *Caux Principles.* Reprinted with permission from *Business Ethics,* 52 S. 10th St., Suite 110, Minneapolis, MN 55403.

SECTION 2. GENERAL PRINCIPLES

Principle 1. The Responsibilities of Businesses:
Beyond Shareholders Toward Stakeholders

The value of a business to society is the wealth and employment it creates and the marketable products and practices it provides to consumers at a reasonable price commensurate with quality. To create such a value, a business must maintain its own economic health and viability, but survival is not a sufficient goal.

Businesses have a role to play in improving the lives of all their customers, employees, and shareholders by sharing with them the wealth they have created. Suppliers and competitors as well should expect businesses to honor their obligations in a spirit of honesty and fairness. As responsible citizens of the local, national, regional, and global communities in which they operate, businesses share a part in shaping the future of those communities.

Principle 2. The Economic and Social Impact of Businesses:
Toward Innovation, Justice and World Community

Businesses established in foreign countries to develop, produce or sell should also contribute to the social advancement of those countries by creating productive employment and helping to raise the purchasing power of their citizens. Businesses also should contribute to human rights, education, welfare, and vitalization of the countries in which they operate. Businesses should contribute to economic and social development not only in the countries in which they operate, but also in the world community at large, through effective and prudent use of resources, free and fair competition and emphasis upon innovation in technology, production methods, marketing and communications.

Principle 3. Business Behavior: Beyond the Letter
of the Law Toward a Spirit of Trust

While accepting the legitimacy of trade secrets, businesses should recognize that sincerity, keeping of promises and transparency contribute not only to their own credibility and stability but also to the smoothness and efficiency of business transactions, particularly on the international level.

Principle 4. Respect for the Rules

To avoid trade frictions and to promote freer trade, equal conditions for competition, and fair and equitable treatment for all participants, businesses should respect international and domestic rules. In addition, they should recognize that some behavior although legal, may still have adverse consequences.

Principle 5. Support for Multilateral Trade

Businesses should support the multilateral trade systems of the GATT/World Trade Organization and similar international agreements. They should cooperate in efforts to promote the progressive and judicious liberalization of trade, and to relax those domestic measures that unreasonably hinder global commerce, while giving due respect to national policy objectives.

Principle 6. Respect for the Environment

A business should protect and, where possible, improve the environment and promote sustainable development.

Principle 7. Avoidance of Illicit Operations

A business should not participate in or condone bribery, money laundering, or other corrupt practices: indeed, it should seek cooperation with others to eliminate them. It should not trade in arms or other materials used for terrorist activities, drug traffic or other organized crime.

SECTION 3. STAKEHOLDER PRINCIPLES

Customers

We believe in treating all customers with dignity irrespective of whether they purchase our products and services directly from us or otherwise acquire them in the market. We therefore have a responsibility to: provide our customers with the highest quality products and services consistent with their requirements; treat our customers fairly in all aspects of our business transactions including a high level of service and remedies for their dissatisfaction; make every effort to ensure that the health and safety of our customers, as well as the quality of their environment, will be sustained or enhanced by our products and services; assure respect for human dignity in products offered, marketing, and advertising; and respect the integrity of the culture of our customers.

Employees

We believe in the dignity of every employee and in taking employee interests seriously. We therefore have a responsibility to: provide jobs and compensation that improve workers' living conditions; provide working conditions that respect each employee's health and dignity; be honest in communications with employees and open in sharing information, limited only by legal and competitive restraints; listen to and, where possible, act on employee suggestions, ideas, requests, and complaints; engage in good faith negotiations when conflict arises; avoid discriminatory practices and guarantee equal treatment and opportunity in areas such as gender, age, race, and religion; promote in the business itself the employment of differently abled people in places of work where they can be genuinely useful; protect employees from avoidable injury and illness in the workplace; encourage and assist employees in developing relevant and transferable skills and knowledge; and be sensitive to serious unemployment problems frequently associated with business decisions and work with governments, employee groups, other agencies and each other in addressing these dislocations.

Owners/Investors

We believe in honoring the trust our investors place in us. We therefore have a responsibility to: apply professional and diligent management in order to secure a fair and competitive return on our owners' investment; disclose relevant information to owners/investors subject only to legal requirements and competitive constraints; conserve, protect, and increase the owners/investors' assets; and respect owners/investors' requests, suggestions, complaints, and formal resolutions.

Suppliers

Our relationship with suppliers and subcontractors must be based on mutual respect. We therefore have a responsibility to: seek fairness and truthfulness in all of our activities, including pricing, licensing, and rights to sell; ensure that our business activities are free from coercion and unnecessary litigation; foster long-term stability in the supplier relationship in return for value, quality competitiveness, and reliability; share information with suppliers and integrate them into our planning processes; pay suppliers on time and in accordance with agreed terms of trade; seek, encourage, and prefer suppliers and subcontractors whose employment practices respect human dignity.

Competitors

We believe that fair economic competition is one of the basic requirements for increasing the wealth of nations and, ultimately for making possible the just distribution of goods and services. We therefore have a responsibility to: foster open markets for trade and investment; promote competitive behavior that is socially and environmentally beneficial and demonstrates mutual respect among competitors; refrain from either seeking or participating in questionable payments or favors to secure competitive advantages; respect both tangible and intellectual property rights; and refuse to acquire commercial information by dishonest or unethical means, such as industrial espionage.

Communities

We believe that as global corporate citizens, we can contribute to such forces of reform and human rights as are at work in the communities which we are open to. We therefore have a responsibility in those communities to: respect human rights and democratic institutions, and promote them wherever practicable; recognize government's legitimate obligation to the society at large and support public policies and practices that promote human development through harmonious relations between business and other segments of society; collaborate with those forces in the community dedicated to raising standards of health, education, workplace safety and economic well-being; promote and stimulate sustainable development and play a leading role in preserving and enhancing the physical environment and conserving the earth's resources; support peace, security, diversity and social integration; respect the integrity of local cultures; and be a good corporate citizen through charitable donations, educational and cultural contributions and employee participation in community and civic affairs.

INTERNATIONAL ETHICS STANDARDS FOR BUSINESS

NAFTA, Caux Principles, and U.S. Corporate Codes of Ethics

PATRICIA CARLSON AND MARK BLODGETT

The authors compare the content of 31 corporate codes of ethics with the Caux Principles. Each of the codes is examined for representative words and phrases taken from the international code. The authors find that there remain areas of inadequate coverage in the corporate codes. The authors then discuss the three major ethical issues of NAFTA, comparing them to the Caux Principle.

NAFTA

This multilateral agreement was executed on January 1, 1994. Some of the main provisions of this unparalleled agreement deal with the elimination of tariff and non-tariff barriers and the facilitation of multinational corporate business operations. Also central to the agreement is a strong position on environmental protection (*San Diego Law Review,* 1994) and intellectual property. The agreement states that each party is to implement the provisions of the agreement so that "there will be a progressive elimination of all tariffs on goods qualifying as North American." It also calls for protection of the environment and intellectual property rights (Litka and Blodgett, 1995, p. 242). NAFTA's ample employment protections are of particular importance since Mexico does not enforce the liberal labor guarantees of its constitution that otherwise bear many similarities to U.S. and Canadian labor laws (Benton, 1993).

NAFTA's provisions deal with some of the most timely issues within the global environment. Do these issues reflect the concerns of businesses as players in a global ethical context? One indication of multinational concern is found in the Caux Round Table Principles of Business Ethics.

CAUX PRINCIPLES

Simultaneous with the implementation of the multilateral agreement (NAFTA) among the U.S., Canada and Mexico to promote free trade by eliminating tariff and non-tariff barriers was the creation of the Caux Principles. Considered to be the first international code of ethics for business, the Caux Round Table Principles originated from a meeting of international business leaders in Caux, Switzerland. These business leaders represented the U.S., Europe and Japan. The Principles are based on an original set of principles known as the Minnesota Principles, developed by the Minnesota Center for Corporate Responsibility (MCCR) affiliated with the University of St. Thomas in the Twin Cities, Minnesota.

The Japanese influence is particularly notable since their concept of *kyosei,* "living and working together for the common good" (*Nation's Business,* 1996, p. 12), is one of two ethical concepts permeating the Caux Principles. The other concept is "human dignity," defined by the code as the "sacredness or value of each person as an end, not simply as a means to the fulfillment of other's purposes or even majority prescription." (*SBE Newsletter,* 1995, p. 14).

The Caux Principles promote action to further these two main concepts of fairness and respect for others by promoting free trade, environmental and cultural integrity, and the prevention of actions that fall in the category of foreign corrupt practices as defined by U.S. law (bribery, money laundering, etc.). Among the principles that expand upon the concepts of fairness and respect for others are the following General Principles in Section 2 of the Caux Round Table Principles for Business:[1]

Principle 2. The economic and social impact of business

Principle 4. Respect for the rules

Principle 5. Support for multilateral trade

Principle 6. Respect for the environment

Principle 7. Avoidance of illicit operations

These principles are further explained as Stakeholder Principles of the Caux Round Table Principles for Business under the following topics: Customers, Employees, Owners/Investors, Suppliers, Competitors, and Communities. The purpose of this project was to examine codes of ethics from major corporations to determine whether they include the provisions of the Caux Principles. The following sections show the analysis of the data from the corporate codes of ethics and discuss the implications of the findings for responsible corporations acting in the international arena.

METHODOLOGY

The project was carried out in a large northeastern city during the months of February and March, 1994. Codes of ethics were solicited from businesses represented in the area, as evidenced by their presence in the yellow pages. The businesses were chosen based on two criteria: size and industry. Since larger businesses were considered most likely to have formal codes of ethics, the sample was limited to businesses with national prominence (national chains) or those easily recognizable as locally prominent. The industries selected

---

[1]The authors did not test the more general Caux Principles 1 or 3 in this project, since more extensive resources would be required. The authors investigated Caux Principle 3 in a previous project.

were: retail (fast food, grocery stores, department stores), financial services, utilities and health services.

Each business was contacted to determine the name of the person to whom a follow-up letter should be addressed. Once the name of the person was known, a letter soliciting the company code of ethics was sent by the researchers. A follow-up phone call to those businesses who had not responded within a 2 month time period resulted in a response rate of 84%; 37 letters were sent, 31 codes were received.

Each corporate code of ethics was read by one of the researchers, and references to important concepts were noted. The researchers each read a subset of the other researcher's codes so that the coding would be uniform.

Salient concepts were decided upon before the coding process by combining principles mentioned in NAFTA with those from the Caux Principles. NAFTA is essentially an international trade agreement, which addresses the main issues of multinational trade, environmental protection, intellectual property, and employment, among others. The Caux Principles contain a broad statement of ethical principles encompassing and enlarging upon these NAFTA provisions. The final coding scheme consisted of five all-encompassing concepts from the Caux Principles (see Table 1).

DATA

The typical composition of the codes of ethics includes three parts: (1) a cover letter, (2) a general statement at the beginning of the code, (3) a list of compliance situations in which ethical dilemmas may arise. A cover letter was included with 62% of the codes of ethics. The cover letter is always from the Chairman of the Board and/or the Chief Executive Officer (CEO). The letter contains broad general statements about the importance of the code of ethics, and, in many cases, it is this document that instructs the employee about correct behavior when a situation is not specifically mentioned in the code of ethics. It is interesting to note that fully 38% of the companies attached so little importance to the code of ethics that no cover letter from upper management was included.

TABLE 1

Data Collection Coding Table

Caux Principle	Name of Principle	Evidence in Corporate Code of Ethics
Principle 2	The economic and social impact of business	Importance of ethnicity, employee culture, equal opportunity, equal conditions
Principle 4	Respect for the rules	Intellectual property, copyright, trade marks
Principle 5	Support for multilateral trade	Trade, relationship with suppliers, free trade
Principle 6	Respect for the environment	Improve or promote sustainable development, prevent waste, environmental protection
Principle 7	Avoidance of illicit operations	Corrupt practices, bribes, arms, other corrupt practices

The general statement that prefaces the formal code of ethics usually consists of from two to six short paragraphs that include information about the importance of the code, who is held to obey the code, and it often contains information about the person who should be contacted when situations not covered in the code of ethics arise.

The final and longest part of the code of ethics (consisting of from 5 to 10 pages) is a list of compliance situations which could present an ethical dilemma to employees. The lists that are most helpful to employees are those that, in addition to listing the situations in formal terms, also give examples of actual situations (the examples are adapted to the particular industry). Some companies have only the lists without explanation or examples of situations. All of these sections were searched for references to the international ethics principles from the Caux Principles.

Each of the codes of ethics was examined for evidence of the five coding categories from Table 1. The data collected is shown in Table 2.

ANALYSIS

The primary objective of the study consisted in determining whether corporate codes of ethics contain any references that show an awareness of international ethical issues. This type of concern would be manifested by statements alluding to any of the General Principles of the Caux Round Table Principles for Business as shown in Table 1 above. The data collection resulted in the [Table 2] data set.

From the frequencies reported in the data set . . . the areas of major concern in corporate codes of ethics are evident. All of the codes of ethics contained references to illicit operations such as bribery and corrupt practices. Fully half of the codes of ethics contained references to the economic and social impact of business such as equal opportunity for all employees, the importance of ethnicity, and equal conditions of work. Nearly one third of the companies were concerned about multilateral trade and relationships with suppliers. However, a majority of the companies did not mention intellectual property, copyright, and trademarks; only four companies included statements about respect for the environment.

When the information from Table 2 is considered, several concerns of business become apparent:

TABLE 2

Data Set

	The Economic and Social Impact of Business	Respect for the Rules	Support for Multilateral Trade	Respect for the Environment	Avoidance of Illicit Operations
Number of Codes of Ethics	15	8	11	4	31

1. Businesses are very aware of the importance of instructing employees about one of the concepts—avoiding corrupt practices.
2. Businesses seem fairly aware of the importance of instructing employees about proper actions concerning two other concepts. The economic and social impact of business and support for multilateral trade are mentioned by at least one third of the codes of ethics.
3. Businesses are, however, for the most part, not instructing employees about actions regarding two important concepts—respect for the rules (illustrated by respect for intellectual property, copyrights, etc.) and respect for the environment—which are mentioned in only a few of the codes.

Organizations are apparently doing a good job of informing employees about only one out of the five principles, and they are doing an "OK" job for two more principles. What impact could the resulting lack of information have on employee actions in a domestic or an international setting? The importance of this question is discussed in the following section.

CONCLUSIONS AND RECOMMENDATIONS

The data show that employees are not informed about corporate preferences for action at least 50% of the time for four of the principles tested. In this scenario, corporations run the risk that employees will not know how to respond when faced with certain situations. This might lead to two undesirable results:

1. Employees might not act when action should be undertaken.
2. Employees might act in an inappropriate manner.

How important is correct action? From a societal point of view, the Caux Principles tell us that correct action is important and NAFTA tells us that correct action is important. Making incorrect choices concerning employment, trade, intellectual property or environmental protection will lead us to undesirable consequences such as child labor, unfair trade practices, pirating of copyrights, and environmental pollution. These actions have undesirable consequences at a societal level.

How important is correct action at an organizational level? In today's society organizations are expected to be responsible citizens at home. In our global economy organizations must also be responsible citizens abroad. This responsibility is enforced by laws and sanctions which organizations must respect or suffer the consequences in legal action.

Universal adoption of ethical standards such as the Caux Principles will enhance corporate codes of ethics as well as international treaties. From a practical point of view, when these ethical standards are translated into behavior, our global environment will be more desirable and organizations will be required to spend less time preparing for and carrying out litigation.

As members of the "local, national, and global communities in which they operate, businesses share a part in shaping the future" (*Society for Business Ethics Newsletter,* 1995). When corporations are actively promoting kyosei (living and working together for the common good) and human dignity (sacredness or value of each person) the result is a world society where employees, intellectual property, and the environment are respected, trade is enhanced, and business profits.

BIBLIOGRAPHY

1. Benton, Janine, "Extraterritorial Application of the ADA," *George Mason Independent Law Review,* vol. 2, no. 1, 1993, pp. 218–19.
2. Litka, M., and M. Blodgett, *International Dimensions of the Legal Environment of Business,* 3rd ed., South-Western College Publishing, Cincinnati, Ohio, 1995.
3. *Nation's Business,* vol. 84, no. 4, April, 1996.
4. *San Diego Law Review,* vol. 31, no. 4, Fall, 1994, pp. 1025–1055.
5. *Society for Business Ethics (SBE) Newsletter,* "Caux Roundtable Principles for Business," vol. 6, no. 1, May, 1995.

YOU HEARTLESS
AIR PIRATES!

GARRY TRUDEAU

DOONESBURY

by Garry Trudeau

DOONESBURY © 1972 G. B. Trudeau. Reprinted with permission of *Universal Press Syndicate*. All rights reserved.

TOPIC STUDY:
MULTICULTURAL PERSPECTIVE

FUNDAMENTAL INTERNATIONAL RIGHTS

THOMAS DONALDSON

Donaldson identifies some of the items that should appear on a list of fundamental international rights. Donaldson defines a fundamental international right as satisfying three conditions: the right must protect something of great importance, the right must be subject to substantial and recurrent threats, and the duties associated with the right must be limited in light of fairness and affordability.

. . . Though probably not complete, the following list contains items that appear to satisfy the three conditions and hence to qualify as fundamental international rights:

1. The right to freedom of physical movement
2. The right to ownership of property
3. The right to freedom from torture
4. The right to a fair trial
5. The right to nondiscriminatory treatment (freedom from discrimination on the basis of such characteristics as race or sex)
6. The right to physical security
7. The right to freedom of speech and association
8. The right to minimal education
9. The right to political participation
10. The right to subsistence

This is a minimal list. Some will wish to add entries such as the right to employment, to social security, or to a certain standard of living (say, as might be prescribed by Rawls' well-known "difference" principle). Disputes also may arise about the wording or overlapping features of some rights: for example, is not the right to freedom from torture included in the right to physical security, at least when the latter is properly interpreted? We shall not

Thomas Donaldson, *Fundamental International Rights*. Reprinted by permission of Oxford University Press, Inc.

attempt to resolve such controversies here. Rather, the list as presented aims to suggest, albeit incompletely, a description of a *minimal* set of rights and to serve as a beginning consensus for evaluating international conduct. If I am correct, many would wish to add entries, but few would wish to subtract them.

The list has been generated by application of the three conditions and the compatibility proviso. Each reader may decide whether the ten entries fulfill these conditions; in doing so, however, remember that in constructing the list one looks for *only* those rights that can be honored in some form by *all* international moral agents, including nation-states, corporations, and individuals. Hence, to consider only the issue of affordability, each candidate for a right must be tested for "affordability" by way of the lowest common denominator—by way, for example, of the poorest nation-state. If, even after receiving its fair share of charitable aid from wealthier nations, that state cannot "afford" kidney dialysis for all citizens who need it, then the right to receive dialysis from one's nation-state will not be a fundamental international right, although dialysis may constitute a bona fide right for those living within a specific nation-state, such as Japan.

Even though the hope for a definitive interpretation of the list of rights is an illusion, we can add specificity by clarifying the correlative duties entailed for different kinds of international actors. Because by definition the list contains items that all three major classes of international actors must respect, the next task is to spell out the correlative duties that fall upon our targeted group of international actors, namely, multinational corporations.

This task requires putting the "fairness-affordability" condition to a second, and different, use. This condition was first used as one of the three criteria generating the original list of fundamental rights. There it demanded satisfaction of a fairness-affordability threshold for each potential respecter of a right. For example, if the burdens imposed by a given right are not fair (in relation to other bona fide obligations and burdens) or affordable for nation-states, individuals, and corporations, then presumably the prospective right would not qualify as a fundamental international right.*

In its second use, the "fairness-affordability" condition goes beyond the judgment *that* a certain fairness-affordability threshold has been crossed to the determination of *what* the proper duties are for multinational corporations in relation to a given right. In its second use, in other words, the condition's notions of fairness and affordability are invoked to help determine *which* obligations properly fall upon corporations, in contrast to individuals and nation-states. The condition can help determine the correlative duties that attach to multinational corporations in their honoring of fundamental international rights.

---

*It is worth noting that fundamental international rights are not the only type of rights. In addition there are legal rights and nation-specific moral rights. For example, the right to sue for damages under the doctrine of strict liability (where compensation can be demanded even without demonstrating negligence) is a legal right in the United States, although it would not qualify as a fundamental international right and is not a legal right in some other nation-states. Similarly, the right to certain forms of technologically advanced medical care such as CAT scanning for cancerous tumors may be a nation-specific moral right in highly industrialized countries (even when it is not guaranteed as a legal right) but could not qualify at this point in history as a fundamental international right.

SAMPLE APPLICATIONS

Discrimination

The obligation to protect a person from deprivation of the right to freedom from discrimination properly falls upon corporations as well as governments insofar as everyday corporate activities directly affect compliance with that right. Because employees and prospective employees possess the moral right not to be discriminated against on the basis of race, sex, caste, class, or family affiliation, it follows that multinational corporations have an obligation not only to refrain from discrimination, but in some instances to protect the right to nondiscriminatory treatment by establishing appropriate procedures. This may require, for example, offering notice to prospective employees about the company's policy of nondiscriminatory hiring, or educating lower-level managers about the need to reward or penalize on the basis of performance rather than irrelevant criteria.

Physical Security

The right to physical security similarly entails duties of protection. If a Japanese multinational corporation operating in Nigeria hires shop workers to run metal lathes in an assembly factory, but fails to provide them with protective goggles, then the corporation has failed to honor the workers' moral right to physical security (no matter what the local law might decree). Injuries from such a failure would be the moral responsibility of the Japanese multinational despite the fact that the company could not be said to have inflicted the injuries directly.

Free Speech and Association

In the same vein, the duty to protect from deprivation the right of free speech and association finds application in the ongoing corporate obligation not to bar the creation of labor unions. Corporations are not obliged on the basis of human rights to encourage or welcome labor unions; indeed they may oppose them using all morally acceptable means at their disposal. But neither are they morally permitted to destroy them or prevent their emergence through coercive tactics; for to do so would violate their workers' international right to association. The corporation's duty to protect from deprivation the right to association, in turn, includes refraining from lobbying host governments for restrictions that would violate the right in question, and perhaps even to protesting host government measures in countering the well-documented tendency of multinationals to mask immoral practices in the rhetoric of "tolerance" and "cultural relativity." According to this algorithm, no multinational manager can naively suggest that asbestos standards in Chile are permissible because they are accepted there. Nor can a manager infer that the standards are acceptable on the grounds that the Chilean economy is, relative to the multinational's home country, underdeveloped. A surprising amount of moral blindness occurs not because people's fundamental moral views are confused, but because their cognitive application of those views to novel situations is misguided.

What guarantees that multinationals possess the knowledge or objectivity to apply the algorithm fairly? As Richard Barnet quips, "On the fifty-sixth floor of a Manhattan skyscraper, the level of self-protective ignorance about what the company may be doing in Colombia or Mexico is high." Can Exxon or Johns Manville be trusted to have a sufficiently sophisticated sense of "fundamental rights," or to weigh dispassionately the hypothetical attitudes of their fellow citizens under conditions of "relevantly similar economic development"? My answer to this is "perhaps not," at least given the present character of the decision-making procedures in most global corporations. But this only serves to underscore the need for more sophisticated, and more ethically sensitive, decision-making techniques in multinationals. And I would add that from a theoretical perspective the problem is a contingent and practical one. It is no more a theoretical flaw of the proposed algorithm that it may be misunderstood or misapplied by a given multinational, than it is of Rawls's theory of justice that it may be conveniently misunderstood by a trickle-down Libertarian.

What would need to change in order for multinationals to make use of the algorithm? Most of all, multinationals would need to enhance the sophistication of their decision making. They would need to alter established patterns of information flow and collection to accommodate moral information. They would need to introduce alongside analyses of the bottom line, analyses of historical tendencies, health, rights, and demography. And they might even find it necessary to introduce a new class of employee to provide expertise in these areas. However unlikely such changes are, I believe they are within the realm of possibility. Multinationals, the organizations capable of colonizing our international future, are no doubt also capable of applying—at a minimum—the same moral principles abroad that they accept at home.

BUSINESS ETHICS IN THE MIDDLE EAST

DOVE IZRAELI

To provide some basis for a multicultural perspective, the following items identify some of the key issues in business ethics facing other countries. Israeli details ethical issues facing businesses in the Middle East, while Guoxi discusses the ethical environment of business in mainland China.

INTRODUCTION

The idea of preparing a report on Business Ethics in the Middle East was initiated by the organizers of [the first] World Congress [of Business, Economics, and Ethics]. When the program chairperson, Dr. George Enderle, approached me to prepare the report, I immediately agreed to do so with the thought that gathering the material would provide me an opportunity to cooperate with Palestinians and scholars from other Middle Eastern countries working in the same field. I also welcomed the invitation because it focused on the interface of my three fields of specialization: Middle East Studies, Business (marketing and management), and Business Ethics. It also related to the peace process, which for me, like for many Israelis, is a life's dream coming true. Although I knew very little about the field of Business Ethics in other countries of the Middle East, I assumed that in this age of modern technology and internet, the search for information would be fairly straightforward and that my major task would be to plow through the material, analyze and evaluate it, discuss the main ideas with Arab scholars and others acquainted with the issues and report my findings for further discussion and research.

To my dismay, despite considerable effort on my part, the material gathering stage revealed very few research articles and despite my requests for information and contacts over the internet and netscape, I received few relevant responses. The purpose of this report, therefore, is to report on what I did find from secondary sources and personal interviews and suggest an agenda for future development. I wish to put special emphasis on the new challenges and opportunities generated by the peace process in the Middle East.

1. The Concept of Business Ethics in the Middle East

There is no commonly used term in either Arabic or Hebrew for the concept of Business Ethics. This suggests that the very concept is still unfamiliar for most people and approximate equivalents have to be constructed.

Dove Izraeli, *Business Ethics in the Middle East*. Reprinted by permission of the author.

2. Stereotypes about Business Ethics in the Middle East

There are many negative stereotypes of the level of Business Ethics in the Middle East. People from different countries whom I interviewed about their opinions and thoughts on the subject of Business Ethics in the region often responded with a chuckle or smile, a knowing wink and a derogatory wave of the hand. This was followed by a short explanation that these concepts are a contradiction in terms: business does not go with ethics and that Western norms of Business Ethics did not apply in the Middle East. Sometimes this would be followed by stories of their personal experiences of unethical behavior in business or of stories reported in the newspaper of business ethical misdeeds. Many referred to the practice of bakshish, translatable as tip or bribe, as an example of widespread corruption.

The responses I received were clearly stereotypical and influenced by prejudice and ignorance. But the Middle East is not unique in this respect. The media of all countries have reports of business scandals and I have found that in most countries people tend to consider that ethics and business are contradictory terms—an oxymoron. Such cynical and unfounded beliefs, however, are in themselves problematic in that they undermine the trust so important in business and economic development.

3. Business Ethics in the Academia

Apart from in Israel which I will return to, to the best of my knowledge Business Ethics is not institutionalized in the Academia in the Middle East. I was told by my interviews and my own search supported this finding that Business Ethics courses are not taught, very little research is being conducted, there are not any specific publications on the issues, nor any regular training on Business Ethics.

In Israel there is at least one elective Business Ethics course taught in all the business schools but in none is it compulsory. There is an Israeli text and reader on Business Ethics and a modest publication that appears at irregular intervals. In 1995 the Israeli Network for Social Responsibility established the Academic Forum for Ethics and Social Responsibility—a national network of academics from a variety of disciplines concerned with ethical issues in their respective fields. . . . The network held a founding conference in 1995 and provides an arena for stimulating interest in the teaching and research of ethics in different disciplines, including business and academic exchanges.

An Israeli initiative in cooperation with the Academia is the International Jerusalem Conference on Ethics in the Public Service, the third of which took place in Jerusalem in 1995 with participants from the Palestinian Authority. Unfortunately, repeated attempts to involve participants from other countries in the Middle East have not been successful to date. Hopefully with the progress of the peace process there will be more readiness on the part of other countries to participate.

An initiative outside the Middle East provides an interesting example of the way the Academia in countries with more developed Business Ethics programs may provide an impetus for the development of interest in the subject in the Middle East. I refer to the *Middle East Business Review*—a new journal out of the University of London whose first issue is announced in Netscape as scheduled to be published in Spring 1996. Although Business Ethics was not included in the subject areas to be covered, I expect that the review potentially provides a locale for publishing in this area as well. I would like to add that Israel unfortunately was not listed among the 14 Geographical areas of the Middle East to be included.

4. Business Ethics in the Private Sector

I found no Business Ethics initiatives in the private sector. None of the local companies have ethical codes although there are some beginnings among firms involved in multinational business. There are no business initiatives against corruption even though, with the growth of business, white collar crime is on the increase in all countries. With few exceptions, there are also no business initiatives in the training of employees or managers on Business Ethics.

5. Corruption

5.1 Government against Corruption   Most governments in the Middle East have agencies whose specific purpose is to combat corruption among government officials. For example: the Central Audit Agency and Administrative Control Agency in Egypt, the State Comptroller and Ombudsman and special police units to combat white collar crime in Israel. These agencies which focus on corruption in government administration have indirect relations to Business Ethics in so far as business is sometimes involved as culprits in the use of corruption for promoting its interests.

5.2 Comparative Measures of Corruption   The Berlin-based Transparency International Organization and Gottingen University recently published the results of an international poll, conducted in 54 countries using its Corruption Perception index. The 54 countries were rated on corruption defined as the misuse of public power for private benefits. These misuses include bribing public officials, taking kickbacks in public procurement or embezzling public funds. The index score was based on 10 international surveys of businessmen and reflects their impressions and perceptions and not necessarily the reality of the level of corruption of the country. The 54 countries were ranked according to their corruption index score from 1 (most corrupt) to 54 (least corrupt). The scores ranged from 0 (highest level of corruption) to 10 (lowest level). The scores and rank order for the five countries of the Middle East included in the survey are listed below:

Country	Score	Rank
Kuwait	2.58	8
Egypt	2.86	14
Turkey	3.54	22
Jordan	4.89	25
Israel	7.71	41

SOURCE: Yediot Ahronot 4.6.96 pp. 10–11 (Hebrew daily)

6. Business Ethics and the Ecology Movement

One of the interesting recent developments in the Middle East is the cross national cooperation in the field of ecology and the establishment of a roof organization for the ecology/environmental organizations in Egypt, Jordan, Israel and Palestine. The business community is in many cases represented in the organizations both in the participating countries and in EcoPeace, the roof organization.

The disastrous ecological consequences of the Gulf War was an important conscious-ness raising experience concerning the importance of guarding the environment and cata-lyst for a variety of initiatives. The Peace process was the catalyst for the establishment of EcoPeace. In March 1995, EcoPeace, a Middle Eastern Environmental NGO Forum began intensive activity serving as a linking organization among the ecological organizations in Egypt, Jordan, Israel and Palestine around issues which require cooperation across borders. EcoPeace provides an interesting model for the possibilities of cross national cooperation in this region. The first major project of EcoPeace is associated with the development of sustainable tourism for the Dead Sea area. EcoPeace has already held a number of confer-ences in those countries, with the purpose of gathering information, preparing development programs and putting pressure on government and business to give greater priority to eco-logical considerations. Its projects initiated in 1995 include: a Gulf of Aqaba Task Force, Development Projects Inventory and Review, Regional Experts Inventory, a Regional En-vironment Journal, a Capacity Building Program and a Regional Environmental Emergency Fund.

7. Cultural Issues in Business Ethics

Business Ethics are culture specific and what is considered normative in one culture may be considered unethical in another. In Arab countries favoritism, nepotism and personal connections have a significant impact on managers' decisions (for a review of research see Atiyyah, 1992). This is usually explained in terms of cultural factors such as strong kinship ties and obligations that expect individuals to give preference to family. David Weir (1993) suggests that there is a distinguishable Arab managerial paradigm built on the notion of "trading" and that emphasizes kinship and networked market orientation. In Israel political patronage is fairly widespread. The close ties between the various elites including economic and political elites also result in favoritism.

The subordinate position of women in the workforce and in business organizations is another cultural issue where normative standards of equality prevalent in most industrial-ized countries are not accepted in many Arab countries. Atiyyah (1992) notes that only 15% of Arab women in Arab countries above the age of 15 are actually in employment. The pro-portion of Arab women employed in Israel is not very much higher.

8. Looking to the Future

In conclusion I would like to consider some of the trends that I believe will impact on de-velopments in Business Ethics in the coming decade and some of the developments that are needed in a global economy.

8.1 The Globalisation of Business   The entry of multinational corporations which have developed codes of ethics and training programs in business ethics may further influence such developments through the implementation of similar policies in their Middle East sub-sidiaries.

There is the beginning of interests in the globalisation of business in the Middle East. The first conference on the Globalisation of Arab Business, being organized from the UK, will be held in Kuwait in September 1966. An awareness of and commitment to business ethics is especially important in international business where institutionalized safeguards are less established and transactions are between people from different cultures. The success of globalisation is dependent on the establishment of a universe of meaning and of discourse on normative patterns of behavior.

8.2 The Need for Incorporating the Stakeholder Concept   Business people in the Middle East have a very narrow and limited conception of who the stakeholders are in their organizations. It is usually limited to the stockholders. The need to establish a wider view of stakeholders as including workers, suppliers, consumers and the public at large as a necessary condition for the development of Business Ethics in the Middle East.

8.3 The Need for Understanding the Philosophical and Normative Underpinning of Business Ethical Behavior in the Middle East   Most concepts and courses on Business Ethics were developed in western Christian dominated countries. This leads to ethnocentric perspectives about ethical standards. There is a need to examine in what ways and to what extent the normative ideas about business behavior in the various cultures of the Middle East are similar to or different from those of the West.

8.4 The Peace Process   The peace process in the Middle East is still in embryo and years of hostility are not erased with the signing of treaties. Common business interests can be an important leverage for increasing trust and mutual understanding and the strengthening of business ethics would be an important catalyst in this process.

REFERENCES

1. Al-Alfy, Hassan. "Acquired Expertise in Adopting Practical Measures to Combat Bribing Government Officials." Unpublished paper presented at the 9th International Congress for Crime Prevention and Treatment of Offenders, Cairo, Egypt, May 4, 1995.
2. Atiyyah, Hamid S. "Research Note: Research in Arab Countries, Published in Arabic." *Organization Studies* 13:1 pp. 105–110. 1992.
3. Izraeli, Dove. "Business Ethics in Israel," in E. Freeman and P. Verhane (eds.) *Business Ethics Dictionary and Encyclopedia.* Cambridge, MA: Blackwell, 1996.
4. Weir, David. "Management in the Arab World." Paper presented at the first Arab Management Conference, Bradford University, Bradford, U.K., July 6–8, 1993, pp. 604–623.

MAJOR ISSUES OF BUSINESS ETHICS IN MAINLAND CHINA

GAO GUOXI

The author discusses the emergence of business ethics as an area of study in China and offers his prescription for further study and action.

By now the major issues that need more attention in the business ethics field in mainland China are the following: The academic discipline of business ethics requires the approval and support of entrepreneurs and enterprises; Equal treatment of technical and human aspects in management; The relationship between justice and efficiency in business organizations; Benefits and social obligation of business; The Corporate Identity System and its relationship between image creation and management practice; The scope of power of top management and its constraints; The ethical rationality of autonomous corporate management and macro-economic policy by the government.

The emergence of business ethics in mainland China represents a great challenge to this old and fresh continent and brings vital strength to the fields of ethical theories and business practices. While business ethics is still at its beginning, there are four major tasks for both scholars and entrepreneurs:

First, the in-depth investigation of the moral status and level of business activities in mainland China in order to adequately grasp the ethical problems involved in those activities. In the course of the reform and opening process the practices of life provide a particularly suitable atmosphere for the development of business ethics. With the help of surveys, personal interviews, and other techniques the actual situation is to be described and analyzed in objective and scientific terms. . . .

Second, the introduction of recent achievements in the field business ethics from outside China. It is of great importance to business education and practice under the conditions of the contemporary market economy. Nowadays academics as well as entrepreneurs are increasingly aware of this urgent need. They are realizing that theory and practice of business ethics in western countries are not only suitable to those countries, but also offer many experiences and insights to market economies in general. Hence an important project of the Centre of Applied Ethics is to introduce western business ethics to readers in China. Accordingly, various western approaches to business ethics were compared and published in the widely-known journal "Social Sciences Abroad."

Third, on the basis of a thorough understanding of the actual situation in China and the contribution from business ethics outside China, a kind of prolegomena of business ethics is to be developed that can operate effectively in the Chinese situation.[1]

Fourth, according to the normative and practical orientation of business ethics, cooperation between business practitioners and academics is crucial in order to develop operational guidelines for business practice which integrate both "good ethics" and "good business." This objective of business ethics is of paramount importance, yet very difficult to achieve because the successful integration depends not only on theoretical clarification and reasoning but also on the competence of and support of business people. . . .

Business ethics in mainland China is a new challenge to both academics and entrepreneurs which involves the following major issues:

1. Business ethics requires the approval and support of entrepreneurs and enterprises

Frankly speaking, without the support of business, business ethics remains a merely academic undertaking and cannot achieve its important tasks. As the investigation of the Centre for Applied Ethics on "Ethical Perceptions of Business People in East China" reveals, the enterprises which recognize the importance of business ethics are at a low percentage. Only a few companies realize that they should pay attention to the moral dimension of management. Some enterprises use business ethics as a tool for marketing or window-dressing. Therefore, it is important to develop rules and regulations on the basis of the appropriate roles and essential personal characteristics of business people. These guidelines should be neither purely external obligations nor arbitrary.

To implement business ethics in mainland China today, one has to pay more attention to the discipline of business codes of conduct. These operating rules and guidelines should be set up and enforced by established institutions and associations. However, the prevailing view in China is that, at present, the development of the economy be the most urgent objective. So most factories and districts strive for beneficial economic results. In contrast, ethics in business is not considered urgent to them.

This situation represents a great challenge for business ethics. To sensitize and educate business people is a very difficult task because many people in developing countries believe that the first and most important thing is to develop the economy while they lose sight of other essential things. The economy overrides everything at the first stage of development in a market economy. This prejudice strongly influences many people, including governors, entrepreneurs, and workers.

2. Equal treatment of technical and human aspects in management

Nowadays in China the two aspects of management and corporate life—technical and human resources—are not handled in a balanced way. In fact, technical considerations prevail in most enterprises which seek to increase their "utility." Certainly, there are also some companies which are sensitive to ethical issues and aspire for higher ethical standards; they anticipate the future of business in China.

3. The relationship between justice and efficiency in business organizations

Employees in enterprises are most concerned about the problem of distributive justice which has a direct impact on their activities in the workplace and their opinion about their organizations in the society. The criterion to measure the ethical level of the enterprise is to what extent the organization of labor is rational.

Along with the reform of the system of labor arrangements, many problems have arisen. For example, when a certain unit (such as a corporation, a workshop, or a group)

plans to reorganize its labor force, who should stay and who should be laid off? How should this question be dealt with by the social security system that is now in the process of radical transformation: by the old or the new system? If priority of employment is given to young workers, efficiency may be improved; however, the financial resources of the units were created by the older workers who have not reached the age of retirement yet and who would lose their investments. So the dilemma seems unavoidable: Either we seek justice and reduce efficiency or we choose efficiency and abandon justice. Moreover, the way of handling the layoff issue will certainly affect the motivations and activities of the employees. In short, the principle of justice in enterprises needs to be investigated seriously: what do equal opportunity and just distribution according to work mean? Does the principle of justice in enterprises include only these two aspects? Furthermore, a host of difficulties remains when tackling with the implementation of more just and more efficient organizations.

4. Benefits and social obligations of business

Business is the most important institution nowadays to provide the livelihood of people. In different forms of business organizations human beings spend a great deal of their time, do their work, and earn their living. However, business could not exist without the support of society that is necessary for the existence and development of business. Because business organizations exist in, and benefit from, society, they also have social obligations and should give something back to the society. This, however, does not just emerge spontaneously. Thus business ethics as a conscious endeavor is needed to advocate, promote, apply, and cultivate a balanced relationship between business and society. Committed entrepreneurs with their foresight, sagacity and unique mission play a critical role in this process which aims beyond the narrow benefits of business.

In contrast, enterprises may solely strive for accumulation of wealth and self-development and limit their responsibilities to maximizing their profits (and minimizing their losses) while denying any responsibility to society. They only seek their own interests and do not bring themselves into the whole social system. Therefore, the relationship between maximizing corporate profits and corporate social responsibility is a very important problem. For sure, enterprises should seek profits, but they should achieve it in an ethical way.

In ancient China the benefits produced by business (profit) were called "Li" while morality was called "Yi." Under normal conditions of the market economy both benefits and morality are the roots of the enterprise's existence and development. Only with this balanced view [does] the far-reaching importance of business ethics becomes understandable. The market economy is a kind of productive system in which the production for oneself is intrinsically interwoven with the production for others. Only through the production "for-others" can one produce "for oneself." This mutually dependent "metabolism of commodities" was characterized by Karl Marx as a relationship in which "individuals exist for others, but the others also exist for them." So the question arises as to what is the difference between the cooperation of enterprises in society and the selfish pursuit of corporate interest. How can the former be promoted and the latter be prevented? . . .

5. The ethical rationality of autonomous corporate management and macro-economic policy by the government

The aim of the macro-economic policy of the government is to determine the model of adjusting and controlling the markets according to economic and social criteria so that the enterprises are led by the markets. Although the role of government for macro adjustment and control by legislation and policies is indispensable, the market economy and government control cannot function without the moral support of the people and their adjusting values to the new situation. Only if the whole economy, the legislation, the governmental policies, and the conduct of enterprises are based on a common morality and value-orientation, the processes of adjusting and controlling the market economy can be realized in a conscientious, effective, and forceful way. Therefore, common criteria for value-orientation and codes of conduct are needed.

In spite of laws and regulations, the market economy leaves broad free space to the economic actors, which, in turn, involves ethical responsibility. To the extent one can make free choices, one bears ethical responsibility accordingly. While the market economy in the West has developed as a contract economy over a long period of time, the situation in China differs considerably. The contract economy in the West has been based on a developing civil society in which the contractual economic relationship among citizens is of far-reaching importance. By contrast, before the reform and opening in mainland China, social life was predominantly political. Over thousands of years the political social life has become a strong and pervasive tradition that covered all aspects and levels of social life while civil society did not flourish at all.

Against this historical backdrop, the support by the government to launch and foster the process of contractual relations is necessary. At the same time, however, the very idea of the contract economy requires to reduce as far as possible the control and interference of government. Hence, it demands a great amount of care to deal with the relationship between the government that tends to interfere and business that claims more autonomy.

What is necessary is that each market participant aims at striking a balance between both: to have the courage to resist the unreasonable interference of government, and, at the same time, to respect the reasonable authority of government. The enterprise as "social person" and market participant unavoidably faces the question of social morality that cannot be answered by the rules of the market and the laws of the state exhaustively. The rules of the market are but one kind of norms which need longstanding practice to become an internally accepted moral order. The laws basically contain minimal requirements. So a wide field of human behavior remains that is influenced and guided by norms of morality and habits.

Admittedly, there are many and great difficulties to develop business ethics in China. However, the society seems to expect that China will move towards a relatively comprehensive understanding and practice of business ethics.

ENDNOTE

1. In line with this, the Centre for Applied Ethics is preparing a series of books on applied ethics, including business ethics. It will not only analyze the situation of applied ethics in China, but also introduce the recent initiatives and achievements in the field of applied ethics abroad. However, the work is still at the first and second level mentioned above and is far from covering a comprehensive view on applied ethics in China.

ETHICS OF HOPE VERSUS ETHICS OF DISILLUSIONMENT

Tadeux Borkowski

Polish Professor Borkowski asked his students at the Jagiellonian University in Krakow to draft brief case studies highlighting specific instances of ethical breaches or dilemmas. Their perceptions and descriptions follow.

MARIUSZ ZAWADZKI

In 1988 the modern tannery started its work in Kracow. Due to industry restructuring starting in 1990 the financial situation got worse and worse each year. This situation was a result of breaking contracts with the eastern market which was the main buyer of the Kracow tannery products. In this difficult time the enterprise was transformed into a company belonging to the State treasury. After four years Jan Nowak became the main technology manager. He was an employee respected by the worker and managers, with long experience. Under his management, due to the introduction of many innovative reforms in manufacturing and sales the firm became profitable. One year after Jan Nowak became a technological manager, there was a failure of the main silo. The damage was due to faulty construction and was not a result of Nowak's neglect. In this silo there was stored acids necessary for technological treatment of leather. The damage to the silo involved a breakage in the middle of its acid-resistant surface. The acids being under pressure caused a quick corrosion of the outside of the container. The board of directors under Jan Nowak's chairmanship had two options:

The first was to replace the silo with a new one.

The second option was to lower the level of the acid to a point below the location of the damage, but in this case redundant acids had to be put into a river, due to a lack of a suitable container.

The first of the options would result in at least a three-month standstill, which in practice meant a collapse of the firm and sacking of all employees.

The second option would result in two-week standstill and biological contamination of a nearby river and ground waters within an area of several kilometres.

The question was: Should the management and the main technologist decide to deprive all employees of financial means and cause a collapse of the enterprise now that the firm

---

had become profitable and started to prosper in the free market economy? Or, perhaps should they contaminate the river and ground waters which would be used by local inhabitants, in this case preventing the firm from bankruptcy and giving work to 600 people. The manager knew that fines for environment contamination were relatively low and could be spread over time, and the firm had no time to spare. What should Jan Nowak do?

The solution to this problem occurred by chance. The fire brigade unit located in the same street got for testing some equipment for chemical life-saving which included a container for storing acids. This container was made available for the period required to repair the silo.

PIOTR KISIEL

I met a problem of unethical behaviour working in one of the shops in Kracow last year. It concerns many small shops, firms, and restaurants. For employers the main problem is the social security system not reformed for years. The owners do not want to employ workers permanently or in the column 'payment' put down a much lower amount. This happens because an employer must pay a tax of as much as 48% of the employee's pay. So, if a worker earned 1000 zloty, for example, then the cost of his/her employment would be about 1500 zloty, which would be a much higher sum. We must remember that as a rule in a small firm there is more than one employee. This can amount to astronomical sums which the firm's owner must pay for old age pensioners.

It seems that in the present government coalition there is not enough courage for radical changes in the whole system of social security. If the rates were lowered, the illegal employment would be diminished, because most of the owners would decide to reveal the real salaries of the employees. Then payments into the social security budget would certainly increase and the problem of old age pensioners would be solved.

On the other hand, very often it is in the interest of employees, young people, drop-outs to work illegally. They are registered in the employment office as unemployed, and in spite of that they work. They receive double income. We must remember that unemployment benefits are paid from our taxes and with the higher unemployment rate the government will not lower taxes. One of the elementary principles of economy says that taxes 'kill' entrepreneurship and too high taxes increase black market.

This problem is difficult to solve, but the act allowing clerks to examine citizens' bank accounts will only increase it.

MAGDALENA KUBICKA

In a shop selling household goods "Domar," a new shop assistant, was employed for a probation period. Apart from her, two other girls, Beata and Agnieszka, worked there as well. Work went on well. The new shop assistant got involved in the work very quickly, and the two girls helped her, because they had worked there for a few years. One day after work, when the owner counted the money, it turned out that a large sum of money was missing. Neither of the girls admitted to having taken the money. The whole affair ended with a warning and withholding the amount out of their salaries.

A few days later Beata noticed that it was her friend who was stealing the money. Next time when it turned out that the money was missing, the owner started to suspect the new shop assistant. Her explanations did not convince him and he decided to sack her. His suspicions seemed to be true because earlier such situations did not take place. Only Beata knew he was mistaken, and she had a great dilemma. She didn't know what to do. Should she tell the truth and lose a friend, or should she say nothing and in this way allow the innocent girl to be sacked?

TOPIC STUDY:
VALUES IN CONFLICT—
U.S. STANDARDS VS. OTHERS?

LEVI STRAUSS & CO.
AND CHINA

TIMOTHY PERKINS, COLLEEN O'CONNELL, CARIN OROSCO,
MARK RICKEY, AND MATTHEW SCOBLE

What should a firm do about human rights violations in a country where it is doing business? Levi Strauss & Co. has been continually praised for its response to human rights violations in China. Consider whether its choice would have been the same (or whether it would have had the same flexibility in its decision making) if it was merely a start-up firm rather than a well-entrenched success story.

PART A

The market that is the People's Republic of China consists of more than one billion consumers and offers low production costs, but its human rights violations have long been condemned by international bodies. In 1993, Levi Strauss & Co. (LS&Co.) faced one of its more difficult decisions in a long corporate history. Would it continue to conduct business in this enormously promising market or honor its relatively high ethical standards and withdraw?

Levi Strauss: History and Ethical Stance

Founded in the United States in 1873, LS&Co. enjoyed consistent domestic growth for generations and began overseas operations during the 1940s. The company became the world's largest clothing manufacturer in 1977 and achieved $2 billion in sales by the end of the decade. Having offered stock to the public during the 1970s to raise needed capital, management decided fourteen years later to reprivatize in a $2 billion leveraged buyout, the largest such transaction to date. Management's reasons included its heightened ability to "focus attention on long-term interests [and] . . . to ensure that the company continues to respect and implement its important values and traditions."[1] By 1993, LS&Co. produced merchandise in 24 countries and sold in 60.

    LS&Co. has been a leader among U.S.-based corporations in recognizing the importance of business ethics and community relationships. Two 1987 documents developed by

---

management summarize the unique values operating at LS&Co. The Mission Statement . . . affirms the importance of ethics and social responsibility, while the Aspirations Statement . . . lists the values intended to guide both individual and corporate decisions.

CEO Robert Haas frequently explains the importance of the Aspirations Statement as a way employees can realize the company Mission Statement and otherwise address factors that did not receive adequate consideration in the past. Efforts to take the values seriously have led to specific changes in human resources policies and practices. For instance, LS&Co. extends liberal domestic partner benefits, offers flexible-work programs, and has established child-care voucher programs. A series of classes for senior managers focuses on the Aspirations Statement. The company has also earned a reputation as an industry leader in facing controversial social issues. It was one of the first companies to establish programs to support AIDS victims.

In 1990, the company closed a Docker's plant in San Antonio, Texas, transferring production to private contractors in Latin America where wages were more competitive. LS&Co. provided a generous severance package for the laid-off workers that included 90-day notice of the plant closing and extended medical insurance benefits. LS&Co. also contributed $100,000 to local support agencies and $340,000 to the city for extra services to the laid-off workers.[2] Despite these efforts, the company received serious criticism for relocating the plant.

Ethical Standards for International Business

In early 1992, LS&Co. established a set of global sourcing guidelines to help ensure that its worldwide contractors' standards mesh with the company values. A group of 10 employees from different areas of the company spent nine months developing the guidelines. The group used an ethical decision-making model that ranked and prioritized all stakeholders to help design the guidelines. The model examines the consequences of each action and suggests a decision based on a balance between ethics and profits.

The ensuing guidelines, "Business Partner Terms of Engagement," . . . cover environmental requirements, ethical standards, worker health and safety, legal requirements, employment practices, and community betterment. Contractors must: provide safe and healthy work conditions, pay employees no less than prevailing local wages, allow LS&Co. inspectors to visit unannounced, limit foreign laborers' work weeks to a maximum of 60 hours, and preclude the use of child and prison labor.[3]

In addition, the company established "Guidelines for Country Selection." . . . These guidelines cover issues beyond the control of one particular business partner. Challenges such as brand image, worker health and safety, human rights, legal requirements, and political or social stability are considered on a national basis. The company will not source in countries failing to meet these guidelines.

The question would soon be raised: Does China meet these guidelines?

Human Rights and Labor Practices in China

China is ranked among the world's gravest violators of human rights, although Chinese officials do not regard their actions as such. The U.S. State Department says that China's human rights record falls "far short of internationally accepted norms."[4] Two more-egregious violations include arbitrary arrest and detention (with torture that sometimes results in death). Despite laws prohibiting arbitrary arrest and providing limits on detention, a commonly referenced clause states that family notification and timely charging are not required if such actions would "hinder the investigation."[5] Judicial verdicts are believed by many observers to be predetermined.

Chinese prison conditions are deplorable, and a long-standing practice holds that all prisoners, including political, must work. Chinese officials say that the fruits of prison-labor are used primarily within the prison system or for domestic sale.

Personal privacy is severely limited in China. Telephone conversations are monitored, mail is often opened and examined, and people and premises are frequently subjected to search without the necessary warrants. China has also engaged in forced family planning, with monitoring of a woman's pregnancy occurring at her place of employment.[6] Official rights to free speech and assembly are extremely restricted, as the world witnessed during the Tiananmen Square massacre in 1989.

Regarding labor conditions, China's leaders have refused to ratify the 10 guidelines prohibiting use of forced labor for commercial purposes established by the International Labor Organization Convention. Although China has regulations prohibiting the employment of children who have not completed nine compulsory years of education, child labor is widespread, especially in rural areas. Surveys show a recent increase in the dropout rate among southern Chinese lower-secondary schools, presumably because the booming local economy lures 12- to 16-year-olds away. At the time of LS&Co.'s deliberations regarding China, no minimum wage existed and safety conditions were found to be "very poor."

LS&Co. in China

This combination of government practices and labor conditions increased pressure within LS&Co. to rethink its decision to operate in China. Nineteen ninety-two operations in the country generated some 10 percent of the company's total Asian contracting and 2 percent of worldwide contracting. Its Chinese operations produced approximately one million pants and shirts in 1993 and operated directly or indirectly through some 30 Chinese contractors. Over one-half the goods produced in China were shipped to Hong Kong to be refined for sale in other countries. These contracts were estimated to be worth $40 million.

LS&Co. is only one of thousands of foreign firms operating in China. The other companies, especially prominent *Fortune 500* companies with factories or manufacturing contracts in China, are cognizant of the human rights and labor conditions. Most of these companies lobbied President Clinton to renew China's Most Favored Nation (MFN) trading status, arguing that the continuing presence of U.S. companies would have a positive influence on reform. According to this viewpoint, investments made by companies such as LS&Co. could transform working conditions and thereby accelerate movement toward the social, economic, and political standards favored by the United States and other western countries.

Should Levi Strauss Stay or Leave?

In assessing the objectionable conditions in China, LS&Co. management felt it could not improve the situation because the violations were well beyond what could be remedied strictly through company communication and cooperation with contractors. At issue were practices that had to be addressed on a larger, national scale.

Leaving the country would expose LS&Co. to the high opportunity cost of forgoing business in a large emerging market. Some managers and employees felt the company would be supporting a repressive regime if it remained in China, while others argued that LS&Co. is a profit-making business enterprise, not a human rights agency. This latter group saw as positive management's acknowledged responsibility to society, but it felt the company also needed to consider its responsibilities to shareholders and employees. Some employees argued that staying in China would enable LS&Co. to improve conditions for Chinese citizens. But other stakeholders countered that remaining in China would violate the company's own guidelines about where it would and would not conduct business.

Important issues that complicated the decision include: the possibility that China might not accept LS&Co. back if the company left until conditions improved. If the company ceased production in China, it might be difficult for it to sell product there due to high tariffs imposed on imported apparel. But, some voices argued, continuing to manufacture in China would have a damaging impact on Levi's reputation, possibly putting at risk its valuable brand image.

PART B

To address the many issues regarding LS&Co.'s continued operations in China, the company organized a China Policy Group (CPG). Composed of 12 employees who together devoted approximately 2,000 hours to reviewing the China situation, the CPG consulted human rights activists, scholars, and executives in its attempt to fully address the critical issues.

The group examined all the issues highlighted in Part A and found itself divided on the question. In March 1993, the CPG delivered a report to LS&Co.'s Executive Management Committee. On April 27, after a half-day of deliberation, this most-senior management group remained undecided over what to do.

Robert Haas Acts

Confronted by the indecision of the Executive Management Committee, LS&Co.'s CEO and Chairman, Robert Haas, ended the stalemate by recommending the company forgo direct investment in China and end existing contracts over a period of three years due to "pervasive violations of basic human rights."[7] He maintained that the company had more to gain by remaining true to its ideals than by continuing to produce in China.

Reactions to the Decision

LS&Co. did not publicly announce its decision, but the news hit the airwaves with a speed and volume that surprised all involved. John Onoda, LS&Co.'s vice president of corporate communications, explained: "We never intended to get in the spotlight. . . . It was leaked and got out in 20 minutes."

Many people were highly skeptical of the company's stated intentions. Some asserted it was only a public relations ploy engineered to make the company look good. "I don't see broad support of it," claimed Richard Brecher, director of business services at the U.S.-China Business Council. "[It] would be regarded much more seriously if Levi's had made direct investment in China."

In one respect, Brecher is right. The company did not directly invest in China; it produced its merchandise through Chinese contractors. In fact, on the sales side, LS&Co. jeans continue to sell in China through Jardine Marketing Services. Moving production contracts to other countries in Asia raised costs between four and ten percent, depending on which location was chosen. LS&Co. recognized this cost and considers it the price it must pay to uphold its integrity and protect its corporate and brand images.

Vice President Bob Dunn explained, "There's the matter of protecting our brand identity. Increasingly, consumers are sensitive to goods being made under conditions that are not consistent with U.S. values and fairness."[8] Linda Butler, director of corporate communications for LS&Co., iterated this sentiment when she affirmed that it was "better for us to honor our company's values."[9] Some even believe that the decision may ultimately prove profitable to the company. As one person claimed, "In many ways, it strengthens the brand. . . . This is a brand that thinks for itself, and these are values which people who buy the brand want for themselves. They're a badge product for youth who want to say 'I'm different.' "[10]

Impact in China

China's leadership showed no interest in the company's decision. One Chinese foreign ministry official was quoted, "At present there are tens of thousands of foreign companies investing in China. If one or two want to withdraw, please do."[11] Coincidentally, the LS&Co. decision-making process occurred as the United States considered extending China's MFN status. U.S. Trade Representative Mickey Kantor voiced his support for LS&Co. by stating, "As far as what Levi Strauss has done, we can only applaud it; we encourage American companies to be the leader in protecting worker rights and worker safety and human rights wherever they operate."[12]

More recently President Clinton renewed China's MFN trading status without requiring steps to improve human rights.[13] Clinton explained, "I believe the question . . . is not whether we continue to support human rights in China, but how we can best support human rights in China and advance our other very significant issues and interests. I believe we can do it by engaging the Chinese."[14]

The position of the Clinton administration is that the United States should continue trading with China and hope that economic involvement will contribute to improvement in the conditions of Chinese citizens. As one might surmise from the case, LS&Co. takes a different position.

ENDNOTES

1. *San Francisco Chronicle,* July 16, 1985, p. 51.
2. *The 100 Best Companies to Work for in America,* p. 502.
3. *Across the Board,* May 1994, p. 12.
4. *Far Eastern Economic Review,* April 14, 1994, p. 60.
5. *U.S. News & World Report,* August 2, 1993, p. 49.
6. Levi Strauss & Co. executive John Onoda, interview, February 1, 1995.
7. The CPG defined "pervasive human rights violations" as meaning when "the greater majority of the population are denied virtually all human rights. Most human rights violations are severe. Government has taken few or no actions to improve human rights climate and positive change is unlikely or, at best, uncertain."

8. *Wall Street Journal,* May 5, 1994, p. A18.
9. *Far Eastern Economic Review,* April 14, 1994, p. 60.
10. *Wall Street Journal,* May 5, 1994, p. A18.
11. *Far Eastern Economic Review,* April 14, 1994, p. 60.
12. *The New Republic,* June 14, 1993, p. 8.
13. *U.S. Department of State Dispatch,* May 30, 1994, p. 345.
14. *Across the Board,* May 1994, p. 12.

THE DENIM REVOLUTION

Levi Strauss & Co. Adopts a Code of Conduct

DEBORAH LEIPZIGER

Leipziger details the efforts of Levi Strauss & Co. to create and implement its global sourcing guidelines.

Let me introduce you to Shilpi, a thirteen-year-old girl from Bangladesh. Shilpi is part of a unique agreement with Levi Strauss & Co.: the clothing manufacturer pays for her to go to school! How did such an agreement come about?

When Levi Strauss & Co. discovered that its contractors in Bangladesh were employing children like Shilpi, senior management realized that it would need to be compassionate toward the children and their families, while maintaining their Global Sourcing Guidelines. Having recently adopted guidelines that prohibit child labor worldwide, by its own facilities and by suppliers, Levi Strauss & Co. considered the issue to be clear-cut. But then an interesting fact came to light. Some of these children were the sole wage-earners in their families. If fired, their families would very likely starve and the children would resort to begging and prostitution.

Levi Strauss & Co. was challenged to balance its commitment to ethical work standards with its effect for these families. The company made a courageous decision: pay for the children to go to school until their 14th birthday, and then give them the opportunity to come back and work at the factory. The company even paid for tuition, books, and uniforms.

After conducting a study of 800 transnational corporations, CEP [Council on Economic Priorities] and New Consumer have selected Levi Strauss & Co. as one of 20 corporations promoting ethical practices in developing countries. Interviews with senior management have been conducted at Levi Strauss & Co. headquarters and, in the near future, will be conducted with contractors in Costa Rica and Guatemala. CEP's Transnational Corporations Project is writing a case study on Levi Strauss & Co. and its code for contractors, known as the Global Sourcing Guidelines.

Global Sourcing Guidelines

While many transnational companies seek low-wage havens where occupational safety and environmental standards are not enforced, Levi Strauss & Co. will produce clothing only where strict safety and environmental standards are upheld and where employees are treated ethically. Under its Global Sourcing Guidelines, Levi Strauss & Co. requires that its contractors abide by the following criteria:

• Child labor is prohibited;

• Prison labor is prohibited;

• The work environment must be safe and healthy;

• Water effluence must be limited to certain prescribed levels;

• Employees cannot work more than sixty hours a week and must be allowed one day off in seven;

• Business partners must comply with legal business requirements.

After conducting audits of all of its 700 contractors' facilities, Levi Strauss & Co. concluded that 5 percent of them had to be dropped. Twenty-five percent needed to make improvements and the rest were in compliance.

Levi Strauss & Co. recognizes that there are certain factors that contractors cannot control, including human rights violations. Thus, Levi Strauss & Co. is the only company to have adopted Country Selection Guidelines, which include the following country selection criteria: impact on brand image, adoption of health and safety requirements, commitment to human rights and legal requirements, and the level of political or social stability.

Since the adoption of the guidelines, Levi Strauss & Co. is phasing out sourcing from China and has already left Myanmar (Burma) due to pervasive human rights abuses.

Implementing the Global Sourcing Guidelines

Levi Strauss & Co. has a long-established reputation for contracting from the best factories in each country where it operates. But management realized that this was not enough; a factory can be the best in all of Bangladesh and still not meet the Levi Strauss & Co. standards. Once Levi Strauss & Co. decided that a code of conduct was necessary for its factories, the real challenge became one of implementation: how to audit over 700 contractors and their subcontractors in over 60 countries. The company had not even been aware that some contractors had many subcontractors.

Many questions still needed to be resolved. For example: How clean should a factory be? How much improvement is warranted? While it was decided that audits should be standardized, there was a commitment to take local social and cultural customs into account. For example, in some cultures, toilet seats are not used, so if no toilet seats were found in a factory in this culture, no changes were necessary. However, if a factory in a country with a tradition of providing toilet seats failed to do so, seats would be required. A similar situation occurs with air conditioning—it would not be required if there were adequate ventilation. There is a base standard, but social and cultural factors are applied. Despite these differences, Levi Strauss & Co. still seeks to balance U.S. values with cultural differences in developing countries.

Audits were first conducted in Asia, where most of the company's contractors in developing countries are situated. Levi Strauss & Co. had already formulated the Sourcing Guidelines when a scandal broke over a large clothing supplier in Saipan, a U.S. territory

---

LEVI STRAUSS & CO. GUIDELINES FOR
COUNTRY SELECTION

The following country selection criteria address issues which we believe are beyond the ability of the individual business partner to control.

1. Brand Image

We will not initiate or renew contractual relationships in countries where sourcing would have an adverse effect on our global brand image.

2. Health & Safety

We will not initiate or renew contractual relationships in locations where there is evidence that Company employees or representatives would be exposed to unreasonable risk.

3. Human Rights

We should not initiate or renew contractual relationships in countries where there are pervasive violations of basic human rights.

4. Legal Requirements

We will not initiate or renew contractual relationships in countries where the legal environment creates unreasonable risk to our trademarks or to other important commercial interests or seriously impedes our ability to implement these guidelines.

5. Political or Social Stability

We will not initiate or renew contractual relationships in countries where political or social turmoil unreasonably threatens our commercial interests.

---

in Asia with a minimum wage far lower than that in the U.S. A large manufacturer that made clothes for Levi Strauss & Co. was found to be in violation of various U.S. laws. Because it had clear guidelines, Levi Strauss & Co. was able to withdraw immediately, while other companies took months deliberating alternatives.

While praise for the Global Sourcing Guidelines is widespread, there is some criticism. According to a labor analyst, Levi Strauss & Co. should provide a "living wage" for its workers in developing countries. A "living wage" would ensure that families could purchase an adequate level of food, clothing, and shelter. According to Dave Samson of Levi Strauss & Co., the company pays wages in the top third of the clothing sector in every country where it operates.

Results

After one year of conducting audits, 5 percent of the contractors were dropped. Many others made improvements, some with help from Levi Strauss & Co. For example, in the Dominican Republic, there are no building codes to ensure that factories are fireproof. Levi Strauss & Co. located an expert who assisted the contractor in fireproofing his factory. Another factory had only one exit for hundreds of employees. Levi Strauss & Co. required that the owner build another door. Contractors were required to clean toilets, insulate wires, and eliminate exposure to toxic chemicals.

For Levi Strauss & Co., the costs of implementing the Global Sourcing Guidelines have been significant. These include: the cost of excluding contractors that are not in compliance, the increased cost of goods, staff time for audits, penalties for cancellations, financial incentives for contractors to upgrade the facilities, training and travel, and staff resources for human rights reviews.

By applying guidelines for country selection, Levi Strauss & Co. has forgone the world's largest market: China. The company may also have limited access to countries in the future, because of pervasive human rights abuses.

"We believe companies have an obligation to see that workers are treated with respect and provided with a safe and healthy work environment regardless of where they reside in the world," says Bob Dunn, Vice President for Corporate Communications.

Says Dunn, "we also feel that it is important to put your stake in the ground on issues that you stand for such as human rights. We also understand that there is a cost involved in choosing to operate in an ethical way. We did not implement the Global Sourcing Guidelines for marketing gain, but rather because it was consistent with our corporate values." . . .

RE-EDUCATION
THROUGH LABOR

DAVID SHENK

> *Do you think it is just a Western concept to protect employees from torturous conditions? Shenk satirizes the concern that American firms are imposing their "Western" standards on other countries when they seek to improve working conditions. Should we instead stay out of other countries' business? Keep our standards to ourselves and simply accept that which occurs elsewhere as culturally defined? Does Shenk go too far?*

One is nibbling on one's morning scone, sipping one's latte and skimming the *Journal* when one notices that financial news has uncomfortably veered away from housing slowdowns and rocky pharmaceutical stocks. "To have Western standards," declares Chrysler Chairman Robert J. Eaton. "That's absolutely ridiculous." One's hands begin to shake. Multicultural creep on the Dow?

Oh, *phew,* nothing like that. Eaton is just pulling the proverbial rug out from under a Chinese employee, Gao Feng, who was arrested on suspicion of being a Christian and then, upon his release, fired for missing work without a reasonable explanation. "We can't assume [Gao] is 100% right and the government is 100% wrong," explains Eaton, demonstrating his American verve for due process and the democratic way. "We're a minority shareholder in a [joint-venture] company. We can't dictate."

Eaton is gearing up for his late-summer trip to China with twenty-three other top corporate executives and Commerce Secretary Ron Brown. It's the glorious consummation of the recent Clinton directive to de-link human rights policy from trade policy. After years of a forced interest in China's human rights policy, American business is now free to stop worrying about the prisoners of conscience and "re-education through labor." Clinton has decided to let business be business.

But somehow there are still all these pesky media distractions. First the truant Christian is demanding his job back, *loudly,* and then comes an all-too-credible report that Chrysler's joint venture company, Beijing Jeep, has been quietly—but not quietly enough—contracting out work to Beijing Autoworks Industrial Corporation, a known prison labor outfit. "What is a labor camp?" says Franc Krebs, president of Beijing Jeep, in response to the charge. "I've never been able to find one myself." After the allegations are specifically articulated—*Oh, THAT labor camp*—Krebs adopts Eaton's I'm-no-authoritarian rap. "We have kind of a distant relationship with BAIC," he says. "I don't go into his shop and tell him how to run it."

To go into another man's shop and demand a halt to the use of electric whips and "punishment beds"? To insist on protection from 180-degree flames and bandages for open baton wounds? How *Western;* how absolutely ridiculous.

"We're businessmen and we're playing our role," insists Hewlett-Packard's Jim Whittaker. "Certain issues are really government-to-government issues, and are being dealt with, some more successfully than others. It's the federal government that should be reflecting the human rights policies. I don't believe U.S. business should be a message carrier or an arm of the federal government."

For strict non-partisan, however, with only a vague sense of the human rights climate in China ("there have been ups and downs; things seem to be improving, and then things are not improving and so on"), Whittaker is terrifically eloquent on the plight of the Chinese *leadership.* "The Premier was over in Europe," he says. "He canceled a number of meetings because of protesters, and I guess he got a little upset, and he challenged publicly all European leaders. He said, 'I'll gladly exchange you my job. I'm trying to run a 1.2 billion-person economy and we want to grow, but we don't want to be unstable. It's a real challenge.' "

Instability is the hobgoblin of all great institutions, which perhaps explains the palpable empathy for the Chinese government emanating from American corporations. "China is striving to become a full and respected member of the international community of nations," declared a consortium of nine multinationals (AT&T, Boeing, Chrysler, Digital, Kodak, GE, Honeywell, Motorola, TRW) in a letter sent last spring to the White House. The U.S. Association of Importers of Textiles and Apparel similarly told Congress, "We have seen dramatic progress in China, both in its economy and in its human rights environment." The National Retail Federation's Robert Hall trumpeted its analysis that "the new engagement policy is clearly working."

Don't assume that these people are actual fools. Sounding dumb may just be their *strategy.* "Human rights begin with the basics," reads a Washington State Business Coalition press release, "including basic foods like those exported from Washington to China. 'Imagine if 1.2 billion Chinese each had an apple a day,' said Tom Mathison, president of Stemilt Growers."

Yes, of course. It *must* be a tactic. They must be concocting this prattle for a reason. Otherwise, why would they say such things when anyone is able to read Amnesty International's blunt analysis that "there has been no fundamental change in the government's human rights policy" in the past five years; that with as many as 40,000 executions last year, China was once again the gold medalist in rolling heads; that many of those not killed on the spot are held indefinitely without being charged or tried, without legal representation, and are frequently treated to lengthy beatings, electric shock, psychiatric torture, excruciating labor and solitary confinement in cells about the size of a first class airline seat.

". . . Feng Haiguang was subjected to two more beatings, where police electric whips and electric batons were used," recounts one prisoner in a letter smuggled to Amnesty. "Five political prisoners were locked up in [tiny] punishment cells, and each ordered to deliver at least 10,000 bricks per day."

The reason is, *it pays not to know.* Eaton et al. could easily keep up to speed on detailed reports of abuse, such as ". . . this caused Jiang's toe-nails to split, reducing his toes to bloody stumps"; but in this case the ignorance is profitable. "They have chosen not to be fully knowledgeable," says a senior Congressional staffer familiar with the issue, "because if they were fully knowledgeable, they might not be willing to do some of things that they're doing. Someone comes up and says, 'Did you know that the person who's producing these textiles is doing prison labor?' They say, 'No, we didn't know that. How could we know that? We're not responsible for all of our little production subsidiaries.' "

Meanwhile, back in Washington, the corporate interest in government-to-government dealings is quite active. "I've never seen the kind of intensive corporate presence on Capitol Hill that we saw this past spring, leading up to the MFN decision," says Mike Jendrzejczyk, Washington director of Human Rights Watch. "Congressional offices were being deluged by CEOs, presidents of banks, you name it."

"The pressure up here was incredible," confirms the Congressional staffer. "It was just amazing, really. There's money on the line—that's what this is all about."

A lot of money. *A lot.*

"We estimate that in ten years our cumulative sales to China will reach $158 billion assuming normalized relations," the nine CEO coalition wrote to Clinton, pressing for a "long term solution to the China MFN and human rights conundrum." Other lobbyists explained that early in the next century China is likely to become the world's biggest market.

Those sorts of dollar figures naturally make a person a little giddy; one might forget for a moment about international standards of decency and one might say a few things that, to western ears, seem absolutely ridiculous. "Low and middle income American families," warned Macy's chairman Myron E. Ullman III last spring, "will face higher prices and shortages of many familiar items" if Clinton insists on drawing a line in the sand on behalf of the persecuted Chinese democrats and intellectuals. What items of critical importance was he speaking of? National Retail Federation's Robert Hall later clarified that they foresaw "a heavy burden on American consumers" due to tariffs on footwear, toys and men's trousers.

Ridiculous, but it worked. American access to slave-labor slacks remains unimpeded, for the first time in years a President has had to have the courage to stand up and guarantee business that such vital access to cheap labor will not be sacrificed in the name of rigid Western standards of free speech, press, religion and so on (ad nauseam). With this key victory in hand, American business is pressing for more. "Now they're trying to get OPIC [Overseas Private Investment Corporation] guarantees to go into China," says the senior Congressional staffer. "Why the American taxpayer should have to underwrite these business risks is beyond me."

Now, imagine not 1.2 billion apple eaters per day, but *5 billion.* Imagine the whole world, de-linked. "If we can trade with China and other countries in Asia where there are human rights problems," says Irwin Jay Robinson, president of the Vietnam American Chamber of Commerce and an important leader in the new incorporated version of multicultural creep, "there is no reason to single out Vietnam." Lobbyists representing foreign ventures in Indonesia, India, and other non-western countries agree: Human rights begins with the basics. Let's be reasonable, and not too western.

TEE-SHIRTS AND TEARS
Third World Suppliers to First World Markets

LAURA B. PINCUS

It is important to note that these conditions do not exist only in foreign markets. U.S. Secretary of Labor Robert Reich made the following remarks in a keynote address at a conference on international labor standards:

> *I have had occasion over the past year to study a country in which many workers who have tried to organize themselves have been fired for their activities. It is a country in which there are sweat shops of the worst Third World variety. In fact, there are sweat shops in which young children are working.*
>
> *It is a country in which many workers are still exposed to hazards that kill and maim them. In this country just a week ago today, I had occasion to visit a plant to serve papers on a plant manager and a company—a very, very large company—where one worker was killed recently. Other workers had been maimed, suffering lost fingers and mangled arms, and yet the company still, still, refused to change its ways and come into compliance.*
>
> *The country I'm talking about is, obviously, the United States. I issue a warning to all of us—a warning to all Americans dealing with the issue of international labor standards. We must guard against too much self-righteous indignation.* (Robert B. Reich, "Keynote Address," International Labor Standards and Global Economic Integration: Proceedings of A Symposium, July 1994, p. 1)

The hottest places in hell are reserved for those who, in a period of moral crisis, maintain their neutrality.

—DANTE

Recent media attention has heightened our awareness of labor conditions in third world countries. While Americans otherwise may have been able to write off substandard labor conditions as another case of cultural variations, these recent cases garnered domestic interest as a result of the parties involved. Their names are about as American as Apple Pie.

The Gap. Kathie Lee Gifford. Even Michael Jordan. These are the contractors, the investors, the spokespeople who represent "sweatshops" where, allegedly, young girls are allowed only two restroom visits per day and, allegedly, the days sometimes consist of twenty-one straight hours of work.

LABOR CONDITIONS IN THE UNITED STATES

America's garment industry today grosses $45 billion per year and employs more than one million workers.[1] Uproar began in the Fall of 1995 when Secretary of Labor Robert Reich announced the names of several large retailers who may have been involved in an El Monte, California, sweatshop operation. Notwithstanding the fact that the retailers are not liable for the conditions if they have no knowledge of them, the companies involved in this situation agreed to adopt a statement of principles which would require their suppliers to adhere to U.S. federal labor laws.[2]

Reich followed this announcement with an appearance on the *"Phil Donahue Show"* where he discussed a situation at another plant that employed Thai workers at less than $1.00 per hour and kept its workers behind a barbed wire fence. Retailers respond that it is difficult, if not impossible, to police their suppliers and subcontractors, who may total more than 20,000 in some cases. And the pressures of the situation are only becoming worse. The apparel industry, which has borne the brunt of Reich's focus, is highly competitive, and extremely labor-intensive. Competition from companies in other countries that do not impose similar labor condition requirements is fierce. Consequently, one is not surprised to learn that a 1994 Labor Department spot check of garment operations in California found that 93 percent had health and safety violations.[3]

Manufacturers may have a bit more to be concerned about than retailers. Reich has recently involved a little-used provision in the Fair Labor Standards Act that holds manufacturers liable for the wrongful acts of their suppliers and that allows for the confiscation of goods produced by sweatshop operations.

Reich has now appealed to the retailers and manufacturers alike to conduct their own random spot checks. "We need to enlist retailers as adjunct policemen. At a time when business says to government, 'Get off our back. We can do it ourselves,' we're giving them the opportunity," Reich notes.[4] In June 1995, Reich established a consortium to police working conditions made up of manufacturers. The group, called Compliance Alliance, will police contractors conducting regular audits and will identify firms that pay less than minimum wage or otherwise violate the provisions of the Fair Labor Standards Act.[5] . . .

The Clinton Administration's voluntary Model Business Principles, published in May 1995, are relevant to this discussion. The principles encourage all businesses to adopt and implement voluntary codes of conduct for doing business around the world and suggest appropriate code coverage. . . .

AMERICAN ATTENTION DRIFTS
TOWARD OTHER COUNTRIES

Neil Kearney, general secretary of the International Textile, Garment and Leather Worker's Federation, describes the garment workplace as follows:

The reality today is that most of the 30 million jobs in the fashion industry around the world are low paid, often based in export processing zones where worker rights are usually suppressed. Wages are frequently below the subsistence level and falling in real terms. . . .

Management by terror is the norm in many countries. Workers are routinely shoved, beaten, kicked, even when pregnant. Attempts to unionize are met with the utmost brutality, sometimes with murder.[6]

Once the American public considered its own conditions, it looked to other countries to see how labor was treated there. Following Reich's slap on the hand to American manufacturers, media attention turned toward the conditions in Third World countries and toward American responsibility for or involvement in those conditions. In 1970, there were 7,000 multinational companies in the world. Today, there are more than 35,000.[7] The topic of conditions in those multinationals was destined for afternoon talk shows once it was announced that television personality Kathie Lee Gifford endorsed a line of clothing that had been made for Wal-Mart in Honduran sweatshops. These operations employed underage and pregnant women for more than 20-hour days at $.31 per hour. The conditions were extremely hot and no worker was allowed to speak during the entire day.

The situation was brought to the attention of the press by Charles Kernaghan, director of the National Laboi Committee, based in New York City. Kernaghan informed Gifford, and the press, of the conditions in the plant and asked her to respond. Gifford's immediate response was to immediately break off her relationship with the company.[8] Unfortunately, this is not what is always best for the exploited workers. Instead, Kernaghan impressed upon her the need to remain involved and to use her position and reputation to encourage a change in the conditions at the plants.

These arguments may remind the reader of those waged several years ago regarding divestment from South Africa. Proponents of investment argued that the only way to effect change would be to remain actively involved in the operations of the South African business community. Others argued that no ethical company should pour money into a country where apartheid conditions were allowed to exist. The same arguments can and have been made about conducting business in Third World countries, and Gifford found herself right in the middle of them.

THE EL SALVADORAN LABOR ENVIRONMENT

El Salvador is a country that has been ravaged by internal conflicts culminating in a civil war that lasted for many years. In 1992, with the advent of peace, the country sought to rebuild what it had lost during wartime and is now considered one of the fastest growing economies in Latin America.[9] The objective of the El Salvadorans involved in the rebuilding process was to help the poor to overcome the conditions of poverty, dependence, and oppression that they had experienced during the conflict. While the objectives of private investors may be different, all seem to share a common interest in social stability and development. Economist Louis Emmerij notes that the leading cause of social unrest is "the lack of sufficient and renumerative employment opportunities, bad living conditions and the lack of perspective and hope."[10]

In developing countries like El Salvador, long-term strategies for improving a poor household's ability to generate disposable income on a sustained basis must consider if households have the skills, education, and know-how to allow them to operate in the market. These strategies include support for training and education, access to markets, and access to technology and credit. A large part of the labor problem in the *maquiladores* is the lack of agreement between the workers and management as to the minimum level of productivity expected per day, the level of compensation for a worker who achieves that level, and who should assume the burden of training in order to increase productivity.

Yet, low wages are the prime magnet for multinational firms coming to El Salvador. In 1990, a glossy full-colored advertisement appeared in a major American apparel trade magazine showing a woman at a sewing machine and proclaiming, "Rosa Martinez produces apparel for U.S. markets on her sewing machine in El Salvador. *You* can hire her for 57 cents an hour." One year later, the same ad announced that Rosa's salary had gone down— "*You* can hire her for 33 cents an hour."[11] It appears that the publicists felt that Rosa's salary originally looked too high in the eyes of the market players.

Critical to understanding these conflicts is an understanding of the Salvadoran culture itself. Salvadoran workers are not exempt from the consequences of their history. When they enter the workplace, they expect to be exploited and do not trust management. In addition, as a result of the repressive conditions in El Salvador during the war, the society suffers from a general lack of candor and a tendency on the part of individuals to protect themselves by not telling the truth.[12] But this quality is different from the deception that occurs in American business dealings. In this situation, it serves as a means of self-protection in a culture that offers little else. Moreover, the government does not protect individual and business interests, thereby allowing cartels to develop, flourish, and continue.

The author of this case had the opportunity to travel to El Salvador in 1996 in order to observe a class in financial administration at an El Salvadoran university. During the course of a quiz in the class, the professor had reason to leave the classroom for a moment. Upon his return, he found that the students were now collaborating on the answers to the quiz. During the discussion that later ensued regarding the students' actions, the students articulated a need to help each other to succeed. They felt that they should bind together in order to help them all to move forward. If this meant helping a colleague who did not have time to study because he had to work to support his family, in addition to attending school, that seemed acceptable, if not necessary and ethical.[13]

During that same course, the graduate students (most, if not all, of whom worked full-time in professional positions) were asked to identify the principal barriers to trust in Salvadoran business relationships, and the means by which those barriers could be broken down. Students responded as follows (translated from Spanish):

> One barrier is that the big businesses are formed at the level of families and friends that form a close nucleus, prohibiting others from entering.

> The government does not enact laws to guarantee business interests and growth without the intervention of stronger, "bully" businesses.

> There is a failure of information—only certain people have access to the most important, business-related information. There is no requirement that business share information, even at a level that would mimic the American SEC requirements.

Create legal mechanisms that sanction companies violating the rules. These sanctions *do not* exist. Companies use illicit means to take advantage of their competitors and employing the same means is the only way to compete.

The period since the war has seen an increase in vandalism at an individual and corporate level, making it difficult to carry on a business.[14]

Consider the expectation of conflict in this scenario recounted by Fr. David Blanchard, Pastor of the Our Lady of Lourdes Church in Calle Real Epiphany Cooperative Association:

> *In February of 1994, the cooperative had a serious labor conflict. The women became quite adept at sewing lab coats. But in February 1994, when the only contract available was for sewing hospital bathrobes, a serious labor conflict arose. Unfortunately, the women who were elected by their peers to negotiate with the contractor made some serious errors in judgment when they calculated the time required to sew this item.*
>
> *At the time, some women were earning 80 colones daily (twice the minimum wage). Most were making 50 colones. Only a few apprentices were making less than the minimum wage.*
>
> *With the transition to sewing bathrobes, production, and therefore income, was cut in half. Six of the highest wage earners subsequently staged a sit-down strike at their machines, claiming that they were being oppressed.*
>
> *Father Blanchard asked, "Who negotiated your contract?"*
>
> *"Our representatives," they said.*
>
> *"Who elected your representatives?"*
>
> *"We did."*
>
> *"Who will suffer if this work is not completed?"*
>
> *"We will."*
>
> *These women had entered this project with no prior skills. They had received high-quality and expensive technical, legal and social training. They were all self-employed, but when their wages plunged, they felt oppressed, frustrated and angry, and ended up leaving the cooperative. . . . Some of these women will continue to suffer in poverty. It is certain that they are victims. But they are the victims of hundreds of years of oppression and not of the immediate circumstances sewing hospital bathrobes. They responded to the problems created by the lack of education and their lack of abilities by generating conflict.[15]*

Blanchard remarks that Salvadoran industrialists and managers are even more strident in generating conflict in the workplace. For instance, consider the case of the Mandarin factory and many other similar plants throughout El Salvador.

THE MANDARIN PLANT AND ITS LABOR CONDITIONS

The San Salvador Mandarin International plant was established in order to assemble goods to be shipped to the United States under contract with major U.S. retailers such as The Gap and Eddie Bauer. The plant was built in the San Marcos Free Trade Zone, a zone owned by the former Salvadoran Army Colonel Mario Guerrero and created with money from the Bush Administration's U.S. Agency for International Development (USAID). David Wang, the Taiwanese owner of the plant, subsequently hired Guerrero as its personnel manager. In addition, the company also hired ex-military, plain-clothed armed guards as security for the plant.[16] Factories in El Salvador, as in the United States, need protection for workers, for personal property, and for real property.

While personnel managers are not security guards, such appointments have become commonplace with Salvadoran industrialists precisely because they expect conflict in the workplace. However, in many situations, their personnel managers generate the conditions of conflict and attempt to control the conflict through the same methods employed during wartime.[17] For example, Colonel Guerrero himself told the workers at one point, "I have no problem, but perhaps you do; either the union will behave, leave, or people will die."[18]

While The Gap was one of the first companies to have a code of conduct for overseas suppliers (along with Reebok), this strategy might not be effective in the El Salvadoran business environment. Charles Kernaghan, director of the National Labor Committee in Support of Democracy and Human Rights in El Salvador (NLC), believed that a preexisting code of conduct was practically useless and stated the following in an interview with *Business Ethics* magazine in June 1996:

> *Consider the history of El Salvador's military, which specialized in the killing of nuns and priests and trade unionists. It is laughable to think that these same people will carry out a company's code of conduct. And there were no legal avenues to challenge any violation because the ministry of labor there is so ill-funded and ill-trained. So you can't depend on the laws. And the women were afraid to speak out.[19]*

After a bitter union-management struggle regarding working conditions and the termination of 100 union workers, the union and management reached an agreement. Unfortunately, the Mandarin did not abide by this agreement.

As North Americans became more and more aware of the working conditions in El Salvador, they began to take action against the retailers. On August 16, 1995, more than one hundred workers from UNITE (Union of Needles Trades and Industrial & Textile Employees) demonstrated in front of a Gap outlet store in downtown Toronto in protest of the working conditions at Gap suppliers. At the same time, thousands of miles South of Toronto, Guerrero claimed that "the working conditions here are good for us and good for the Salvadoran workers, but bad for those seeking to keep jobs in the United States. . . . [Without the jobs in the maquilas,] young women would have few other work options apart from prostitution or crime."[20] The story becomes further blurred, however, when Guerrero's comments are compared with an earlier statement by Mandarin owner David Wang in connection with the wages paid to Mandarin workers: "If you really ask me, this is not fair."[21]

"Workers wages make up less than 1% of the retail cost of GAP shirts. Is it any wonder that the company made $310 million in 1994, and paid its CEO Donald Fisher $2 million plus stock options?[22]

From Gap Sourcing Principles & Guidelines: "Workers are free to join associations of their own choosing. Factories must not interfere with workers who wish to lawfully and peacefully associate, organize or bargain collectively. The decision whether or not to do so should be made solely by the workers.[23]

Based on claims of a violation of its sourcing principles and in an effort to ameliorate the situation, The Gap decided to discontinue its relationship with the Mandarin (following in the footsteps of other previous Mandarin contractors such as Eddie Bauer, Liz Claiborne,

J. Crew, and Casual Corner); however, this action prompted strong cries of concern from labor activists. Contrary to the intentions of The Gap, this resolution was viewed as irresponsible and lacking in accountability.[24] Those concerned with the rights of workers in El Salvador contested The Gap's decision, claiming that this would be the worst possible solution to the problems in a country where 60 percent of the labor force is unemployed.[25] As a result of other pullouts, the Mandarin has had to cut its work force from 1,300 to 300, and 32 other maquilas have already shut down.[26] "Instead of acting responsibly and seeing that conditions are improved at Mandarin, the Gap is trying to wash its hands and to shift production to other maquilas in other countries with equally bad conditions."[27]

The Gap's original perspective is not without its supporters. Joan Spero, business executive and Secretary of State for Economic Affairs explains: "A world community that respects democracy and human rights will provide a more hospitable climate for American trade and commerce. . . . Repression fosters instability in the long run and puts investment at greater risk of expropriation and loss."[28] Consider as well the following comments of John Duerden, former president of Reebok:

> *As a public company, we have an ethical responsibility to build value for Reebok's share-holders—but not at all possible costs. What we seek is harmony between the profit-maxi-mizing demands of our free-market system and the legitimate needs of our shareholders, and the needs and aspirations of the larger world community in which we are all citizens.*[29]

"A VICTORY FOR ALL OF US WHO ARE DETERMINED TO ELIMINATE SWEATSHOPS AT HOME AND ABROAD."[30]

The situation took a drastic turn in December 1995 when Reverend Paul Smith called a meeting between The Gap's senior vice president for sourcing, Stan Raggio, Gap sourcing guidelines director, Dottie Hatcher, Gap consultant James Lukaszewski, Reverend David Dyson of the Interfaith Center for Social Responsibility, and Charles Kernaghan (NLC). The Gap was feeling pressure from all sides. On the one hand, labor, religious, consumer, solidarity, children's, and women's groups were arguing for dramatic changes in working conditions. On the other hand, the National Retailers' Federation contested the complaints and encouraged The Gap to ignore the demonstrations.

The Gap responded to the consumers, issuing a letter stating that it is "committed to ensuring fair and honest treatment of the people who make [its] garments in over 40 countries worldwide,"[31] and, in the words of the NLC, "took a major step forward in accepting direct responsibility for how and under what conditions the products it sells are made."[32] As a result of the meeting, The Gap agreed to implement an independent monitoring system in El Salvador, using the Human Rights Ombudsperson in El Salvador to monitor factories' compliance with its labor guidelines, as long as the Mandarin agreed to rehire the fired union activists.

The NLC and others saw this decision by The Gap as a benchmark against which all other multinational retailers will be measured. Says Kernaghan, "The message is clear: if you make it, you are responsible."[33] Not everyone agrees with Kernaghan's assessment. Larry Martin of the American Apparel Manufacturer's Association believes otherwise: "They've [labor] given us a black eye that most of us don't deserve. Most of us monitor contractors we use here and offshore."[34] One might understand Martin's concerns for the rest of American retailers when one considers the comments of U.S. Labor Secretary Robert Reich: "This raises the question for other big retailers who haven't moved in this direction—why not?"[35]

Most recently, the Salvadoran minister of labor established a government commission to review conditions in the free trade zone and indicated that foreigners would no longer be permitted to monitor the implementation of work codes in El Salvador.[36] This begs the question of why The Gap doesn't simply allow the El Salvadoran government to monitor the work conditions of the plant? Father Blanchard offers the following response:

> *We must consider what are the global consequences for disbanding this effort after less than one month in existence.*
>
> *For example, recently we have learned that the Commerce Department of the United States has informed the international fishing industry that it will not allow the importation of shrimp that are caught with nets that also snare turtles. All fishermen who use nets, and who wish to sell their produce in the United States, must use turtle-free nets. What is more, the industry must allow independent monitoring by outside agencies.*
>
> *Salvadoran law permits the use of turtle-snaring nets. The United States has no authority to control the Salvadoran shrimp industry (one of the largest sources of external revenue for the Government of El Salvador). It has complete authority to determine the conditions under which shrimp may be imported into the United States.*
>
> *The question remains: why not simply rely on the government of El Salvador to supervise compliance, especially given the importance of the shrimping industry in this country.*
>
> *The answer lies in norms for the modernization of government and general guidelines for development being promulgated by the World Bank, the InterAmerican Development Bank and other loaning agencies. Governments that contribute to international loaning agencies insist on down-scaling government and allowing compliance to be monitored by the private sector in alliance with independent monitoring groups. In this scheme, Congress passes the law defining the kinds of nets that are required in the shrimp industry; people concerned about the welfare of turtles contribute to organizations like the International Wildlife Fund to guarantee that these laws are enforced; organizations like the International Wildlife Fund in turn collaborate with the fishing industry to guarantee that the norms are followed. When all is said and done, if nobody cares about the welfare of turtles, the laws are not passed and compliance never takes place.*
>
> *What is good for turtles is also good for human beings.*[37]

ENDNOTES

1. Department of Labor, "No Sweat Initiative: Fact Sheet," http://www.dol.gov/dol/esa/public/forum/ fact.htm.
2. Susan Chandler, "Look Who's Sweating Now," *Business Week,* October 16, 1995, pp. 96, 98. (In March, 1996, 72 Thai workers at the El Monte sweatshop were awarded more than $1 million in back wages in connection with the scandal. George White, "Sweatshop Workers to Receive $1 Million," *L.A. Times,* March 8, 1996, p. B1.)
3. Ibid., p. 98. The study also found that 73 percent of the garment makers had improper payroll records, 68 percent did not pay appropriate overtime wages, and 51 percent paid less than the minimum wage.
4. Ibid, pp. 96, 98. Self-inspection may also be necessitated by the drop in the number of inspectors assigned by the Labor Department to investigate wage and hour law violations. Since 1989, that number has fallen from almost 1,000 to less than 800. Also see Andrea Adelson, "Look Who's Minding the Shop," *New York Times,* May 4, 1996, p. 17.
5. Stuart Silverstein, "Self-Regulatory Group to Police Clothes Makers' Work Conditions," *L.A. Times,* June 20, 1995, p. D1.

6.   http://www.dol/gov/dol/opa/public.forum/kearney.txt.

7.   Douglass Cassel, "Human Rights Violations: What's a Poor Multinational to Do?" Remarks before the Chicago Council on Foreign Relations, February 7, 1996, p. 10.

8.   "Gifford Counters Sweatshop Charges," May 2, 1996, p. 40 (Reuters).

9.   Michael McGuire, "Lost in the Junkyard of Abandoned U.S. Policy," *Chicago Tribune,* April 7, 1996, sec. 2, pp. 1, 4.

10. Louis Emmerij, *Social Tensions and Social Reform: Toward Balanced Economic, Financial and Social Policies in Latin America* (Washington, DC: Social Agenda Policy Group, Inter-American Development Bank, 1995), p. 7, *cited in* letter from Fr. David Blanchard, pastor, O.L. Lourdes in Calle Real Epiphany Cooperative Association, to Aaron Cramer, Director, Business and Human Rights Program, Business for Social Responsibility, February 6, 1996, p. 2.

11. Bob Herbert, "Sweatshop Beneficiaries," *New York Times,* July 24, 1995, p. A13.

12. Blanchard letter, p. 8, citing research by Fr. Ignacio Martin-Baro, a social psychologist and one of the six Jesuit priests slain in November 1989 at the University of Central America in El Salvador. The war has additional effects on the people of El Salvador, even if they were not alive at the time of the recent conflicts. For example, one American student recorded in his journal, "9/3/95: One of the little children handed me an old bullet that he must have found. I imagine there must be many bullets out there in the field. I just wanted the day to be over, for me and for this little boy." Student manuscript in possession of the author.

13. First-hand experience of the author, February 1996.

14. Student manuscripts in possession of the author (June 1996).

15. Blanchard letter, p. 5.

16. Terry Kelly, "The GAP: Brutality Behind the Facade," part of *World History Archives,* located at http://neal.ctstateu.edu/history/world.history/archives/canada/canada002.html, p. 1 (1995).

17. Blanchard letter, p. 6.

18. Kelly, "The GAP," p. 2.

19. Mary Scott, "Going After The Gap," *Business Ethics,* May/June 1996, p. 20.

20. Letta Taylor, "Salvadoran Clothing Factory Accused of Worker Abuse," *Roanoke Times and World News* (December 31, 1995) p. D4.

21. Bob Herbert, "Not a Living Wage," *New York Times,* October 9, 1995, p. A17.

22. Kelly, "The GAP," p. 2.

23. Gap, Inc., *Code of Vendor Conduct,* sec. VIII, 1996. See also Christian Task Force on Central America, "Urgent Action El Salvador," http://www/grannyg.bc.ca/CTFCA/act1295a.html (November 29, 1995) p. 1.

24. Letta Taylor, "Salvadoran Clothing Factory Accused of Worker Abuse," *Roanoke Times and World News,* December 31, 1995, p. D4; Joanna Ramey, "Worker Rights Groups Slam Gap for Ending El Salvador Contract," *Women's Wear Daily,* November 30, 1995.

25. Letta Taylor, "Salvadoran Clothing Factory," p. D4.

26. Ibid.

27. Christian Task Force on Central America (CTFCA), "Urgent Action El Salvador," http://www/grannyg. bc.ca/CTFCA/act1295a.html, Nov. 29, 1995, p. 2.

28. Quoted by Douglass Cassel, "Human Rights Violations: What's a Poor Multinational To Do?" remarks before the Chicago Council on Foreign Relations, Feb. 7, 1996, p. 9.

29. Quoted by Cassel, "Human Rights Violations," p. 9.

30. Words of Jay Mazur, UNITE President, in National Labor Committee, "Gap Victory," http://www.alfea.it/co-ordns/work/industria/gap-victory.html, Feb. 1996.

31. CTFCA, "Urgent Action El Salvador."

32. National Labor Committee, "Gap Agrees to Independent Monitoring Setting New Standard for the Entire Industry," http://www.alfea.it/coordns/work/industria/gap.agrees.html.

33. Quoted in Industrial Workers of the World, "Unions Win Victory in Gap Battle," *The Industrial Worker,* http://fletcher.iww.org/~iw/feb/stories/gap.html, February, 1995. See also Mary Scott, "Going After The Gap," *Business Ethics,* May/June 1996, pp. 18–20 ("What the Gap has done is historic. It will be a good pilot project to see if third party monitoring works," said Conrad McKerron, social research director of Progressive Asset Management).

34. Quoted in Paula Green, "The Gap Signs Accord on Conduct Code with U.S. Labor Group," *The News-Times,* http://www.newstimes.com/archives/dec2295/bzf.htm, 12/22/95, p. 2.

35. Quoted in United Auto Workers, "The Gap Agrees to Improve Conditions in Overseas Plants," *Frontlines,* http://www.uaw.org/solidarity/9601/frontlinesjan96.html, January 1996, p. 1.

36. Memo from Fr. David Blanchard to Mark Annerm Coordinator, Independent Monitoring Team, April 19, 1996, p. 4.

37. Ibid., pp. 5–6.

PHOTOS OF LABORERS

International Labour Office

In reading the material contained in this chapter it is easy to forget that real individuals, real working adults and children, are impacted by these fundamental international labor standards. Who did you picture as you read the previous excerpt? Do you see individuals that look very much like you or different from you? Consider the individuals photographed by International Labour Organization representatives in the following photographs.

A young street musician begging in Warsaw, Poland

Photograph by J. Maillard. Courtesy of the International Labour Office.

Textile weaving workshop in Jordan

Women workers in textile industry in Asunción, Paraguay

Young brick carriers in Madagascar

LIST OF FASHION TRENDSETTERS

U.S. DEPARTMENT OF LABOR

The retailers listed below have all pledged to help eradicate sweatshops in America and to try to ensure that their shelves are stocked with only "No Sweat" garments.

Abercrombie and Fitch	Dana Buchman
Lands End	Nordstrom
Baby Superstore	Elisabeth
Lane Bryant	Old Navy Clothing Store
Banana Republic	Express
Lerner New York	Patagonia
Bath & Body Works	Galyans Trading
Levi Strauss and Company	Penhaligon's
Bergner's	GapKids
Limited Too	Structure
Boston Stores	Gerber Childrenswear
Liz Claiborne Inc.	Superior Surgical Mfg.
Brylane	Guess Inc.
Mast Industries	The Limited
Cacique	Henri Bendel
NFL Properties	The Gap
Carson Pirie Scott	Jessica McClintock
Nicole Miller	Victoria's Secret Catalogue and Stores

This list is based on the voluntary efforts of the listed companies. They have agreed to: demonstrate a commitment to labor laws; cooperate with law enforcement agencies when violations of the law are found; and monitor working conditions, for example by

---

List of Fair Labor Fashion Trendsetters from Dept. of Labor, Released Dec. 5, 1995, in "GAP Stores Added to Fair Labor Fashion Trendsetter List," 12/02/95, http://gatekeeper.dol.gov/dol/opa/public/media/press/opa/opa95528. htm.

contracting with suppliers who monitor contractors or by conducting site visits of suppliers. (Companies not on this list also may follow these practices.)

The Trendsetters List is still open. Any company interested in joining the list may contact the U.S. Department of Labor at: Trendsetters, 200 Constitution Ave., NW, Washington, DC 20210. The Trendsetters List is not a "Where To Shop" list. A company's inclusion on the list does not constitute an endorsement by the U.S. Department of Labor.

**Help End
Sweatshop Conditions
for American Workers**
Robert B. Reich, Secretary
U.S. Department of Labor

Help End Sweatshop Conditions for American Workers.

Sweatshops still exist for many garment workers in America—sweatshops where workers earn less than 70 cents an hour and live in slavery-like conditions.

As Secretary of Labor, I am committed to ending this shameful practice. Even though many retailers and manufacturers have agreed to help eradicate sweatshops, it's going to take more.

Consumers like you can make a difference. You can exercise your right as a consumer to avoid buying sweatshop-made clothing. Please carry this card with you as a guide to "No Sweat" shopping.

Thank you for your support.

Robert B. Reich, Secretary
U.S. Department of Labor

"Help End Sweatshop Conditions for American Workers," Robert Reich Poster, http://www.dol.gov/dol/esa/public/nosweat/card.htm.

Three Clues for Consumers That Your Clothing is

NO SWEAT.

 You can ask your retailers questions about where and how the garments are made. Garment workers are required to be paid at least the minimum wage and overtime.

 You can ask your retailers whether they independently monitor garment manufacturers to avoid buying from sweatshops. Many retailers have voluntarily agreed to conduct site visits of suppliers to monitor working conditions.

 You can ask your retailers whether they support "No Sweat" clothing. Commitments from retailers to avoid buying sweatshop-made clothing can go a long way toward eradicating sweatshops in America.

A PRESIDENTIAL DILEMMA

America Go Global or America Stay Home?

IAN SPAULDING, LORI McDONOUGH, AND LAWRENCE PONEMON

The "Presidential Dilemma" demonstrates the difficulty of weighing personal beliefs against professional and global obligations. KPMG Peat Marwick presents this dilemma through its website in an innovative manner through which one can judge her or his personal solution against other website visitors. After choosing one of the four options to President Smith, the site takes you to a choice page that asks you your motivation for the choice, then explains how similar your choice was to that of others. In choosing your option and motive, would you have assumed that you were in the majority or minority, and were you correct in your assumption?

INTRODUCTION

Increasingly in the business world, U.S. companies pursuing a worldwide presence have to pay close attention to the ramifications of the global market—political, economic, and cultural.

Additionally, in a global context, executives sometimes have to choose between their personal beliefs and generally-held societal beliefs that they have a professional obligation to uphold.

The following hypothetical dilemma of an imaginary president in an election year has been chosen not just for its relevance to today's political realities, but because it pertains to these current business issues.

PRESIDENTIAL DILEMMA—BACKGROUND

Sam Smith is President of the United States. He is a moderate member of a conservative political party. In his youth, he observed people in poverty and the suffering it caused. As a result, Smith has resolved to use whatever power he acquired in his political career to help alleviate that suffering. At the same time, he sincerely believes that no Americans, rich or poor, can benefit without a safe and secure country, so Smith has always advocated a strong military defense.

The President is increasingly being viewed as "too soft" by the more conservative members of his party. His first term in office is nearing an end and he wants desperately to

---

Ian Spaulding, Lori McDonough, and Lawrence Ponemon, all of KPMG Peat Marwick.LLP, "A Presidential Dilemma: America Go Global or America Stay Home?" from http://www.us.kpmg.com/ethics/november96/story2.html

be re-elected. However, a more conservative challenger is gathering increasing support as a possible rival for the nomination.

Abroad, a powerful dictator, Malaan, has emerged in South Asia. Malaan has nuclear weapons and has begun an aggressive policy towards mainland China, even claiming that part of the Chinese empire rightfully belongs to his country. The angry Chinese have responded with their own aggressive rhetoric. This situation has made the U.S. military as well as the senior leaders of Smith's party very nervous.

At home, Smith is presiding over a recessionary economy. A surge in corporate downsizing has put unemployment statistics in double digits, and white-collar workers from the upper- and middle-classes are competing for minimum-wage jobs traditionally held by those from other groups. As a result, poverty levels are escalating out of control with heavy demands being placed on social services, i.e., food stamps, shelters, etc. Smith's opposing party is taking an isolationist, "America First" stance, claiming that the top priority of the nation is to deal with the economic emergency. This party strongly opposes any substantial increase in military aid, at least until the economy recovers.

SITUATION

The Pentagon is demanding a massive increase in military aid (though short of sending in ground troops) to contain the threat posed by Malaan. If Smith supports the Pentagon, his opposing party has vowed to fight the measure on the floor of the Senate, possibly leading to a humiliating defeat for Smith. Meanwhile, civil rights groups are protesting outside the White House, demanding more domestic aid. Finally, advocates of fiscal responsibility from both parties are protesting any increases in funding that might prevent a balanced budget.

If he could act solely in accordance with his personal values, Smith would fully fund both the military and domestic initiatives—but he knows that there is not nearly enough money to pursue that option.

ETHICS COMMENTARY

In business, as in government, the single most important factor about resources is that they are limited. This fact necessarily restricts the options of the most powerful executives, be they CEOs or presidents. And the fact of limited options means that ethical choices, no matter how painful, are sometimes necessary.

President Smith's dilemma is actually four separate dilemmas, all of them relevant to the ethics of business management:

- the problem of how to expand one's global presence at the least possible expense to one's domestic stakeholders

- the problem of reconciling one's personal beliefs with commonly-held societal beliefs that one has a professional obligation to uphold

- the problem of fiscal restraint versus fiscal risk, and of achieving an ideal balance between the two

- the problem of reconciling ideals to the practical compromises required to exercise and retain power

PRESIDENT SMITH'S OPTIONS

Imagine that you are President Sam Smith. The following options are possible actions you might pursue to deal with the situation described previously. Please click on the option you would choose. An analysis of the possible motives of that option will then appear. Select the button that most corresponds with your motive for choosing that option. The results of all the choices will be tabulated and a discussion of the results will appear in a future ethics page.

Option I   As President, you give the Pentagon all the money it demands to deal with Malaan, then go on television to get the nation's support behind this expensive defense initiative.

Option II   As President, you refuse the Pentagon's demand, choosing instead to back a multi-billion-dollar law providing aid to lower-income people hurt by the recession.

Option III   As President, you refuse to support either initiative; instead, you go on television calling for fiscal austerity to achieve a balanced budget to secure America's future.

Option IV   As President, you compromise, agreeing to provide the extra military spending, but for an amount considerably lower than requested, while at the same time agreeing to some government help to the poor at a level substantially below what your administration's critics are demanding.

YOUR ETHICAL DECISION AS PRESIDENT

You Chose Option I—You Comply with the Pentagon's Request for Funds

How this dilemma was answered by others in this survey:

Option I   17% chose Option I

As a motive, the choices were:

Motive 1.   In supporting the Pentagon, you place a higher value on your belief in a strong defense than on your belief in aiding the poor.

Motive 2.   In supporting the Pentagon, you decide to defer your dream of helping the poor in order to consolidate your position within your party, ensuring renomination.

You Chose Motive 1—In Supporting the Pentagon, You Place a Higher Value on Your Belief in a Strong Defense Than on Your Belief in Aiding the Poor

How this dilemma was answered by others in this survey:

Motive 1.   12% chose Option I AND Motive 1

Motive 2.   5% chose Option I AND Motive 2

YOUR ETHICAL DECISION AS PRESIDENT

You Chose Option II—You Refuse the Pentagon's Request for Funds, Giving Money to the Poor Instead

How this dilemma was answered by others in this survey:

Option II   **11% chose Option II**

As a motive, the choices were:

> **Motive 1.** In opposing the Pentagon, you place a higher value on your belief in helping the poor than on your belief in a strong defense.

> **Motive 2.** In opposing the Pentagon, you decide to appeal to large numbers of the electorate in their time of need, defying the right wing of your party.

You Chose Motive 1—In Opposing the Pentagon, You Place a Higher Value on Your Belief in Helping the Poor Than on Your Belief in a Strong Defense

How this dilemma was answered by others in this survey:

Motive 1.   **8% chose Option II AND Motive 1**

Motive 2.   **2% chose Option II AND Motive 2**

YOUR ETHICAL DECISION AS PRESIDENT

You Chose Option III—You Refuse the Pentagon's Request for Funds and Also Refuse Any Additional Aid to the Poor, in Order to Help Balance the Budget

How this dilemma was answered by others in this survey:

Option III   **13% chose Option III**

As a motive, the choices were:

> **Motive 1.** In opposing both the Pentagon and social welfare groups, you are placing the value of the nation's future fiscal health above your personal values, however strongly felt.

> **Motive 2.** In opposing both the Pentagon and social welfare groups, you are trying to buy time hoping that either the economic or the geopolitical crisis will blow over, making a final decision easier.

You Chose Motive 1—In Opposing Both the Pentagon and Social Welfare Groups, You Are Placing the Value of the Nation's Future Fiscal Health above Your Personal Values, However Strongly Felt

How this dilemma was answered by others in this survey:

Motive 1.   **10% chose Option III AND Motive 1**

Motive 2.   **2% chose Option III AND Motive 2**

YOUR ETHICAL DECISION AS PRESIDENT

You Chose Option IV—You Work Out a Compromise by Which You Give Something to the Pentagon and Something to the Poor

How this dilemma was answered by others in this survey:

Option IV   **56% chose Option IV**

As a motive, the choices were:

Motive 1.   In choosing not to choose between two of your most deeply-held values, you satisfy your own conscience.

Motive 2.   In giving a little to both sides, you place the abstract value of compromise above the complete satisfaction of your personal values.

Motive 3.   In not totally denying the needs of social interest groups, you hope to win over at least some liberal voters while retaining the loyalty of your party's right wing—and are willing to risk the possibility that no one will be happy.

You Chose Motive 1—In Choosing Not to Choose between Two of Your Most Deeply-held Values, You Satisfy Your Own Conscience.

Motive 1.   **8% chose Option IV AND Motive 1**

Motive 2.   **36% chose Option IV AND Motive 2**

Motive 3.   **9% chose Option IV AND Motive 3**

CONCLUSION

The following are some of the general conclusions that may be drawn from this dilemma:

- In business, we often have to choose between personal values and professional obligations.

- In a globally-oriented organization, a balance must be struck between the cost of international expansion and the price of maintaining the core domestic business.

- The desires and needs of the most crucial stakeholders in the organization (stockholders, managers, staff) have to be taken as seriously as the actions of one's current or potential competitors.

- An American organization operating abroad cannot expect to think or act in a vacuum; rather, it must understand the political, societal and business culture of the countries in which it does business.